THE

ALL ENGLAND

LAW REPORTS

1996

Volume 2

Editor
CAROLINE VANDRIDGE-AMES LLM

London
BUTTERWORTHS

UNITED KINGDOM	Butterworths a Division of Reed Elsevier (UK) Ltd, Halsbury House, 35 Chancery Lane, **London** WC2A 1EL and 4 Hill Street, **Edinburgh** EH2 3JZ
AUSTRALIA	Butterworths, **Sydney, Melbourne, Brisbane, Adelaide, Perth, Canberra** and **Hobart**
CANADA	Butterworths Canada Ltd, **Toronto** and **Vancouver**
IRELAND	Butterworth (Ireland) Ltd, **Dublin**
MALAYSIA	Malayan Law Journal Sdn Bhd, **Kuala Lumpur**
NEW ZEALAND	Butterworths of New Zealand Ltd, **Wellington** and **Auckland**
SINGAPORE	Reed Elsevier (Singapore) Pte Ltd, **Singapore**
SOUTH AFRICA	Butterworths Publishers (Pty) Ltd, **Durban**
USA	Michie, **Charlottesville**, Virginia

ISBN for the complete set of volumes: 0 406 85159 X
for this volume: 0 406 065020

Printed and bound in Great Britain by William Clowes Ltd, Beccles and London

House of Lords

The Lord High Chancellor of Great Britain: Lord Mackay of Clashfern

Lords of Appeal in Ordinary

Lord Keith of Kinkel
Lord Goff of Chieveley
Lord Jauncey of Tullichettle
Lord Browne-Wilkinson
Lord Mustill
Lord Slynn of Hadley
Lord Woolf
    (appointed Master of the Rolls
    4 June 1996)

Lord Lloyd of Berwick
Lord Nolan
Lord Nicholls of Birkenhead
Lord Steyn
Lord Hoffmann

Court of Appeal

The Lord High Chancellor of Great Britain

The Lord Chief Justice of England:

Lord Taylor of Gosforth (retired 3 June 1996)

Lord Bingham of Cornhill (appointed 4 June 1996)
(President of the Criminal Division)

The Master of the Rolls:

Sir Thomas Henry Bingham (appointed Lord Chief Justice 4 June 1996)

Lord Woolf (appointed 4 June 1996)
(President of the Civil Division)

The President of the Family Division: Sir Stephen Brown

The Vice-Chancellor: Sir Richard Rashleigh Folliott Scott

Lords Justices of Appeal

Sir Brian Thomas Neill
Sir Martin Charles Nourse
Sir Thomas Patrick Russell
Dame Ann Elizabeth Oldfield Butler-Sloss
Sir Murray Stuart-Smith
Sir Christopher Stephen Thomas Jonathan
    Thayer Staughton
Sir Anthony James Denys McCowan
Sir Alexander Roy Asplan Beldam
Sir Andrew Peter Leggatt
Sir Paul Joseph Morrow Kennedy
Sir David Cozens-Hardy Hirst
Sir Simon Denis Brown
Sir Anthony Howell Meurig Evans
Sir Christopher Dudley Roger Rose
Sir John Douglas Waite
Sir John Ormond Roch
Sir Peter Leslie Gibson
Sir John Stewart Hobhouse
Sir Denis Robert Maurice Henry
Sir Mark Oliver Saville

Sir Peter Julian Millett
Sir Swinton Barclay Thomas
Sir Robert Andrew Morritt
Sir Philip Howard Otton
Sir Robin Ernest Auld
    (Senior Presiding Judge for England and
    Wales)
Sir Malcolm Thomas Pill
Sir William Aldous
Sir Alan Hylton Ward
Sir Michael Hutchison
Sir Konrad Hermann Theodor Schiemann
Sir Nicholas Addison Phillips
Sir Mathew Alexander Thorpe
Sir Mark Howard Potter
    (appointed 5 June 1996)
Sir Henry Brooke
    (appointed 5 June 1996)
Sir Igor Judge
    (appointed 5 June 1996)

High Court of Justice

The Lord High Chancellor of Great Britain
The Lord Chief Justice of England
The President of the Family Division
The Vice-Chancellor
The Senior Presiding Judge for England and Wales
The puisne judges of the High Court

Chancery Division

The Lord High Chancellor of Great Britain
The Vice-Chancellor

Sir Jeremiah LeRoy Harman
Sir John Leonard Knox
Sir Donald Keith Rattee
Sir John Frank Mummery
Sir Francis Mursell Ferris
Sir John Murray Chadwick
Sir Jonathan Frederic Parker
   (Vice-Chancellor of the County Palatine
   of Lancaster)
Sir John Edmund Fredric Lindsay

Dame Mary Howarth Arden
Sir Edward Christopher Evans-Lombe
Sir Robin Raphael Hayim Jacob
Sir William Anthony Blackburne
Sir Gavin Anthony Lightman
Sir Robert Walker
Sir Robert John Anderson Carnwath
Sir Colin Percy Farquharson Rimer
Sir Hugh Ian Lang Laddie

Queen's Bench Division

The Lord Chief Justice of England

Sir Ronald Gough Waterhouse
   (retired 15 April 1996)
Sir Christopher James Saunders French
Sir Iain Charles Robert McCullough
Sir Oliver Bury Popplewell
Sir William Alan Macpherson of Cluny
   (retired 15 April 1996)
Sir Richard Howard Tucker
Sir Patrick Neville Garland
Sir Michael John Turner
Sir John Downes Alliott
Sir Harry Henry Ognall
Sir John Arthur Dalziel Owen
Sir Francis Humphrey Potts
Sir Richard George Rougier
Sir Ian Alexander Kennedy
Sir Stuart Neill McKinnon
Sir Mark Howard Potter
   (appointed Lord Justice of Appeal
   5 June 1996)
Sir Henry Brooke
   (appointed Lord Justice of Appeal
   5 June 1996)

Sir Thomas Scott Gillespie Baker
Sir Igor Judge
   (appointed Lord Justice of Appeal
   5 June 1996)
Sir Edwin Frank Jowitt
Sir Douglas Dunlop Brown
   (transferred from Family Division
   4 June 1996)
Sir Michael Morland
Sir Mark Waller
Sir Roger John Buckley
Sir Anthony Brian Hidden
Sir John Michael Wright
Sir Charles Barrie Knight Mantell
Sir John Christopher Calthorpe Blofeld
Sir Peter John Cresswell
Sir Anthony Tristram Kenneth May
Sir John Grant McKenzie Laws
Dame Ann Marian Ebsworth
Sir Simon Lane Tuckey
Sir David Nicholas Ramsay Latham
Sir Christopher John Holland
Sir John William Kay

[continued on next page]

Queen's Bench Division *(continued)*

Sir Richard Herbert Curtis
Sir Stephen John Sedley
Dame Janet Hilary Smith
Sir Anthony David Colman
Sir Anthony Peter Clarke
Sir John Anthony Dyson
Sir Thayne Forbes
Sir Michael Alexander Geddes Sachs
Sir Stephen George Mitchell
Sir Rodger Bell
Sir Michael Guy Vicat Harrison
Sir Bernard Anthony Rix
Dame Anne Heather Steel
Sir William Marcus Gage
Sir Jonathan Hugh Mance
Sir Andrew Centlivres Longmore
Sir Thomas Richard Atkin Morison
Sir Richard Joseph Buxton
Sir David Wolfe Keene

Sir Andrew David Collins
Sir Maurice Ralph Kay
Sir Frank Brian Smedley
Sir Anthony Hooper
Sir Alexander Neil Logie Butterfield
Sir George Michael Newman
Sir David Anthony Poole
Sir Martin James Moore-Bick
Sir Julian Hugh Gordon Langley
Sir Roger John Laugharne Thomas
Sir Robert Franklyn Nelson
   (appointed 16 April 1996)
Sir Roger Grenfell Toulson
   (appointed 17 April 1996)
Sir Michael John Astill
   (appointed 6 June 1996)
Sir Alan George Moses
   (appointed 13 June 1996)

Family Division

The President of the Family Division

Sir Anthony Barnard Hollis
Sir Edward Stephen Cazalet
Sir Robert Lionel Johnson
Sir Douglas Dunlop Brown
   (transferred to Queen's Bench Division
   4 June 1996)
Dame Joyanne Winifred Bracewell
Sir Michael Bryan Connell
Sir Jan Peter Singer

Sir Nicholas Allan Roy Wilson
Sir Nicholas Peter Rathbone Wall
Sir Andrew Tristram Hammett Kirkwood
Sir Christopher Stuart-White
Dame Brenda Marjorie Hale
Sir Hugh Peter Derwyn Bennett
Sir Edward James Holman
Dame Mary Claire Hogg
Sir Christopher John Sumner
   (appointed 13 June 1996)

CITATION

These reports are cited thus:

[1996] 2 All ER

REFERENCES

These reports contain references to the following major works of legal reference described in the manner indicated below.

Halsbury's Laws of England

The reference 26 *Halsbury's Laws* (4th edn) para 577 refers to paragraph 577 on page 296 of volume 26 of the fourth edition of *Halsbury's Laws of England*.

The reference 7(1) *Halsbury's Laws* (4th edn reissue) para 267 refers to paragraph 267 on page 200 of reissue volume 7(1) of the fourth edition of *Halsbury's Laws of England*.

Halsbury's Statutes of England and Wales

The reference 40 *Halsbury's Statutes* (4th edn) 734 refers to page 734 of volume 40 of the fourth edition of *Halsbury's Statutes of England and Wales*.

The reference 19 *Halsbury's Statutes* (4th edn) (1994 reissue) 497 refers to page 497 of the 1994 reissue of volume 19 of the fourth edition of *Halsbury's Statutes of England and Wales*.

The Digest

(formerly The English and Empire Digest)

The reference 37(2) *Digest* (Reissue) 424, *2594* refers to case number 2594 on page 424 of the reissue of green band volume 37(2) of *The Digest*.

The reference 27(1) *Digest* (2nd reissue) 330, *2849* refers to case number 2849 on page 330 of the second reissue of green band volume 27(1) of *The Digest*.

Halsbury's Statutory Instruments

The reference 17 *Halsbury's Statutory Instruments* 305 refers to page 305 of volume 17 of the grey volumes series of *Halsbury's Statutory Instruments*.

The reference 14 *Halsbury's Statutory Instruments* (1994 reissue) 201 refers to page 201 of the 1994 reissue of volume 14 of the grey volumes series of *Halsbury's Statutory Instruments*.

Cases reported in volume 2

	Page
A-G's Reference (No 3 of 1994) [CA]	10
Ahmed v Government of the Kingdom of Saudi Arabia [CA]	248
Aldington (Lord), Count Tolstoy-Miloslavsky v [CA]	556
Alexander (Jonathan) Ltd v Proctor [CA] ..	334
Alltime Securities Ltd, Doorbar v [CA] ..	948
Arab Republic of Egypt v Gamal-Eldin [EAT]	237
Bank of Credit and Commerce International SA, Re (No 8) [CA]	121
Bank of England, Three Rivers DC v (No 2) [QBD]	363
Barber v Staffordshire CC [CA]	748
Bate v Chief Adjudication Officer [HL] ..	790
Biggs v Somerset CC [CA]	734
Birse Construction Ltd v Haiste Ltd (Watson and ors, third parties) [CA]	1
Blaker, Oyston v [CA]	106
Bowerman & Partners (a firm), Mortgage Express Ltd v [CA]	836
Bristol and West Building Society v May May & Merrimans (a firm) [Ch D]	801
British Pregnancy Advisory Service, Goodwill v [CA]	161
Butte Mining plc, Ernst & Young (a firm) v [Ch D]	623
Campbell (a bankrupt), Re [Ch D]	537
Central Criminal Court, ex p Guney, R v [HL]	705
Chief Adjudication Officer, Bate v [HL] ..	790
Chief Constable of the Devon and Cornwall Constabulary, ex p Hay, R v [QBD] . ..	711
Chief Constable of the Devon and Cornwall Constabulary, ex p Police Complaints Authority, R v [QBD]	711
Christou, R v [HL]	927
Citi-March Ltd v Neptune Orient Lines Ltd [QBD]	545
Colmer (Inspector of Taxes), Imperial Chemical Industries plc v [HL]	23
Company, Re a (No 006798 of 1995) [Ch D]	417
Cook, ex p, R v Criminal Injuries Compensation Board [CA]	144
Corbett v Newey [CA]	914
Criminal Injuries Compensation Board, R v, ex p Cook [CA]	144
Debtor, Re a (No 2021 of 1995), ex p IRC v The debtor [Ch D]	345
Debtor, Re a (No 2022 of 1995), ex p IRC v The debtor [Ch D]	345
Debtor, Re a (No 340 of 1992), ex p the debtor v First National Commercial Bank plc [CA]	211
Desert Sun Loan Corp v Hill [CA]	847
Dhak v Insurance Co of North America (UK) Ltd [CA]	609

	Page
Diamond, Parr v (McGrigor Donald (a firm), third party) [Ch D]	774
Diamond, Possfund Custodian Trustee Ltd v (McGrigor Donald (a firm), third party) [Ch D]	774
Doorbar v Alltime Securities Ltd [CA]. ..	948
DTC (CNC) Ltd v Gary Sargeant & Co (a firm) [Ch D]	369
Ermakov, ex p, R v Westminster City Council [CA]	302
Ernst & Young (a firm) v Butte Mining plc [Ch D]	623
First National Commercial Bank plc, A debtor v (No 340 of 1992), ex p, Re the debtor [CA]	211
Fitzgerald v Williams [CA]..	171
Foster v Spencer [Ch D]	672
G (a minor) (social worker: disclosure), Re [CA]	65
Gahan v Szerelmey (UK) Ltd [CA]	291
Gamal-Eldin, Arab Republic of Egypt v [EAT]	237
Glasgow City Council, Kleinwort Benson Ltd v [CA]	257
Glengate-KG Properties Ltd v Norwich Union Fire Insurance Society Ltd [CA]	487
Goodwill v British Pregnancy Advisory Service [CA]	161
Government of the Kingdom of Saudi Arabia, Ahmed v [CA]	248
Gulf Petroleum International Ltd, Regia Autonoma de Electricitate Renel v [QBD]	319
Guney, ex p, R v Central Criminal Court [HL]	705
H and ors (restraint order: realisable property), Re [CA]	391
Haiste Ltd, Birse Construction Ltd v (Watson and ors, third parties) [CA] ..	1
Halifax Mortgage Services Ltd (formerly BNP Mortgages Ltd) v Stepsky [CA]	277
Hay, ex p, R v Chief Constable of the Devon and Cornwall Constabulary [QBD]	711
Haywood, Westminster City Council v [QBD]	467
Henry Smith's Charity (trustees of), Mainwaring v [CA]..	220
Hill, Desert Sun Loan Corp v [CA]	847
Imperial Chemical Industries plc v Colmer (Inspector of Taxes) [HL]	23
Insurance Co of North America (UK) Ltd, Dhak v [CA]	609
IRC, ex p, Re a debtor (No 2021 of 1995) v The debtor [Ch D]	345
IRC, ex p, Re a debtor (No 2022 of 1995) v The debtor [Ch D]	345
Islington London BC, Westdeutsche Landesbank Girozentrale v [HL]	961
Ismail v Richards Butler (a firm) [QBD] ..	506
John v MGN Ltd [CA]	35
Kershaw v Whelan [QBD]..	404

	Page
Kleinwort Benson Ltd v Glasgow City Council [CA]	257
L (a minor) (police investigation: privilege), Re [HL]	78
Linskills (a firm), Smith v [CA]	353
Long v Tower Hamlets London BC [Ch D] ..	683
Luc Thiet Thuan v R [PC]	1033
Mainwaring v Trustees of Henry Smith's Charity [CA]	220
May May & Merrimans (a firm), Bristol and West Building Society v [Ch D] ..	801
MGN Ltd, John v [CA]	35
Miller v Stapleton [QBD]	449
Ministry of Defence, Mulcahy v [CA]	758
Morris v Murjani [CA]	384
Mortgage Express Ltd v Bowerman & Partners (a firm) [CA]	836
Mulcahy v Ministry of Defence [CA]	758
Murjani, Morris v [CA]	384
Nelson v Rye [Ch D]	186
Neptune Orient Lines Ltd, Citi-March Ltd v [QBD]	545
Newey, Corbett v [CA]	914
Norwich Union Fire Insurance Society Ltd, Glengate-KG Properties Ltd v [CA].. ..	487
O'Regan v Williams [CA]	171
Official Receiver, Penrose v [Ch D]	96
Onibiyo, ex p, R v Secretary of State for the Home Dept [CA]	901
Oyston v Blaker [CA]	106
Parole Board, ex p Watson, R v [CA]	641
Parr v Diamond (McGrigor Donald (a firm), third party) [Ch D]	774
Penny v Penny [CA]	329
Penrose v Official Receiver [Ch D]	96
Plasplugs Ltd, Turner v [CA]	939
Police Complaints Authority, ex p, R v Chief Constable of the Devon and Cornwall Constabulary [QBD]	711
Polly Peck International plc (in administration), Re [Ch D]	433
Possfund Custodian Trustee Ltd v Diamond (McGrigor Donald (a firm), third party) [Ch D]	774
Practice Direction (admiralty: caveat by fax) [QBD]	210
Proctor, Jonathan Alexander Ltd v [CA] ..	334
R v Central Criminal Court, ex p Guney [HL]	705
R v Chief Constable of the Devon and Cornwall Constabulary, ex p Hay [QBD] ..	711
R v Chief Constable of the Devon and Cornwall Constabulary, ex p Police Complaints Authority [QBD]	711
R v Christou [HL]	927
R v Criminal Injuries Compensation Board, ex p Cook [CA]	144
R v Parole Board, ex p Watson [CA]	641
R v Secretary of State for the Home Dept, ex p Onibiyo [CA]	901
R v Thornton (No 2) [CA]	1023
R v Westminster City Council, ex p Ermakov [CA]	302
R, Luc Thiet Thuan v [PC]	1033
Regia Autonoma de Electricitate Renel v Gulf Petroleum International Ltd [QBD] ..	319
Richards Butler (a firm), Ismail v [QBD] ..	506
Romain v Scuba TV Ltd [CA]	377
Rye, Nelson v [Ch D]	186
S (a minor) v Special Educational Needs Tribunal [CA]	286
Sargeant (Gary) & Co (a firm), DTC (CNC) Ltd v [Ch D]	369
Schuppan (a bankrupt), Re [Ch D]	664
Scuba TV Ltd, Romain v [CA]	377
Secretary of State for the Home Dept, ex p Onibiyo, R v [CA]	901
Secretary of State for the Home Dept, T v [HL]	865
Sheffield Forgemasters Ltd, Wraith v [QBD]	527
Sheppard & Cooper Ltd v TSB Bank plc [Ch D]	654
Smith v Linskills (a firm) [CA]	353
Somerset CC, Biggs v [CA]	734
Special Educational Needs Tribunal, S (a minor) v [CA]	286
Spencer, Foster v [Ch D]	672
Staffordshire CC, Barber v [CA]	748
Stapleton, Miller v [QBD]	449
Stepsky, Halifax Mortgage Services Ltd (formerly BNP Mortgages Ltd) v [CA] ..	277
Szerelmey (UK) Ltd, Gahan v [CA]	291
T v Secretary of State for the Home Dept [HL]	865
TBP Industries Ltd, Thomas Witter Ltd v [Ch D]	573
Thornton, R v (No 2) [CA]	1023
Three Rivers DC v Bank of England (No 2) [QBD]	363
Tolstoy-Miloslavsky (Count) v Lord Aldington [CA]..	556
Tower Hamlets London BC, Long v [Ch D]..	683
TSB Bank plc, Sheppard & Cooper Ltd v [Ch D]	654
Turner v Plasplugs Ltd [CA]	939
Watson, ex p, R v Parole Board [CA]	641
Westdeutsche Landesbank Girozentrale v Islington London BC [HL]	961
Westminster City Council v Haywood [QBD]	467
Westminster City Council, ex p Ermakov, R v [CA]	302
Whelan, Kershaw v [QBD]	404
Williams, Fitzgerald v [CA]	171
Williams, O'Regan v [CA]	171
Witter (Thomas) Ltd v TBP Industries Ltd [Ch D]	573
Wraith v Sheffield Forgemasters Ltd [QBD]	527

Digest of cases reported in volume 2

ACCOUNTANT – Lien – Unpaid fees – Accountant exercising lien over books and papers of client – Whether books and papers 'accounting records'

DTC (CNC) Ltd v Gary Sargeant & Co (a firm) .. .. **Michael Crystal QC**   369

ACTION – Dismissal – Abuse of process of court – Civil action in negligence seeking to impugn earlier criminal conviction – Sustainability of claim

Smith v Linskills (a firm) .. .. **CA**   353

ADMIRALTY – Practice – Caveat against release – Praecipe for caveat against release by fax – Procedure for use

Practice Direction .. .. **QBD**   210

ARBITRATION – Costs – Security for costs – Arbitration commenced in England by agreement between parties ordinarily resident out of jurisdiction – Jurisdiction of English court to order security for costs

Regia Autonoma de Electricitate Renel v Gulf Petroleum International Ltd .. .. **Rix J**   319

BANKRUPTCY – Property available for distribution – Subsequent financial award to bankrupt – Whether award a future or contingent interest in 'property'

Re Campbell (a bankrupt) .. .. **Knox J**   537

COMPANY – Bank advancing funds to company – Loan secured by charges over third party deposits – Bank becoming insolvent – Whether deposits should be set off against company's debt

Re Bank of Credit and Commerce International SA (No 8) .. .. **CA**   121

—— Corporate personality – Lifting corporate veil – Holding and subsidiary companies

Re Polly Peck International plc (in administration) .. .. **Robert Walker J**   433

——Corporate personality – Lifting corporate veil – Whether company assets to be treated as shareholders' realisable assets

Re H and ors (restraint order: realisable property) .. .. **CA**   391

——Debenture – Demand made under debenture – Whether creditor allowing sufficient time to pass before appointing receivers

Sheppard & Cooper Ltd v TSB Bank plc .. .. **Blackburne J**   654

——Prohibited name – Director requiring leave – Test to be applied

Penrose v Official Receiver .. .. **Chadwick J**   96

——Winding up – Proof and ranking of claims – Rule against double proof

Re Polly Peck International plc (in administration) .. .. **Robert Walker J**   433

COMPENSATION – Criminal injuries – Rejection of claim – Relevance of applicant's good character – Sufficiency of reasons

R v Criminal Injuries Compensation Board, ex p Cook .. .. **CA**   144

CONFLICT OF LAWS – Foreign judgment – Enforcement – Issue estoppel – Whether decision of foreign court on procedural matter giving rise to issue estoppel

Desert Sun Loan Corp v Hill .. .. **CA**   847

——Jurisdiction – Claims in restitution against Scottish defendant – Whether English court having jurisdiction

Kleinwort Benson Ltd v Glasgow City Council .. .. **CA**   257

CONSTITUTIONAL LAW – Foreign sovereign state – Immunity from suit – Actions for unfair dismissal – Entitlement to immunity

Arab Republic of Egypt v Gamal-Eldin .. .. **EAT** 237

——Foreign sovereign state – Immunity from suit – Contract of employment – Entitlement to immunity in action for unfair dismissal

Ahmed v Government of the Kingdom of Saudi Arabia. .. .. **CA** 248

CONTRACT – Failure of consideration – Recovery of money paid under void interest rate swap agreement – Entitlement to compound interest – Date for payment of interest

Westdeutsche Landesbank Girozentrale v Islington London BC .. .. **HL** 961

——Restitution – Interest rate swap agreement – Whether restitutionary claim based on unjust enrichment a claim 'relating to a contract'

Kleinwort Benson Ltd v Glasgow City Council .. .. **CA** 257

——Restitution – Recovery of money paid under void interest rate swap agreement – Entitlement to compound interest

Westdeutsche Landesbank Girozentrale v Islington London BC .. .. **HL** 961

CONTRIBUTION – Third party proceedings – Claim 'in respect of the same damage' – Whether 'same damage' meaning damage suffered by same person

Birse Construction Ltd v Haiste Ltd (Watson and ors, third parties) .. .. **CA** 1

COSTS – Security for costs – Plaintiffs resident in Ireland – Rule empowering court to order security for costs against plaintiff ordinarily resident out of jurisdiction – Whether rule contrary to EC Treaty prohibition against discrimination on grounds of nationality

Fitzgerald v Williams, O'Regan v Williams .. .. **CA** 171

—— Taxation – Solicitor – Level of fees allowable – Whether costs 'reasonably incurred'

Wraith v Sheffield Forgemasters Ltd .. .. **Potter J** 527

COUNTY COURT – Costs – Jurisdiction – Litigant in person – Whether company without legal representation a 'litigant in person'

Jonathan Alexander Ltd v Proctor .. .. **CA** 334

CRIMINAL LAW – Bail – Recognisance – Forfeiture – Effect of defendant's arraignment – Whether surety's liability continuing after arraignment

R v Central Criminal Court, ex p Guney .. .. **HL** 705

——Murder – Intent – Transferred malice – Unlawful injury to child in utero – Whether victim required to be person in being at time of act causing death – Requisite intent

A-G's Reference (No 3 of 1994) .. .. **CA** 10

——Murder – Provocation – Characteristics of accused

Luc Thiet Thuan v R .. .. **PC** 1033

—— Murder – Provocation – Characteristics of accused – Battered wife syndrome

R v Thornton (No 2) .. .. **CA** 1023

——Murder – Provocation – Reasonable man

Luc Thiet Thuan v R .. .. **PC** 1033

——Murder – Provocation – Series of acts provoking loss of self-control

Luc Thiet Thuan v R .. .. **PC** 1033

——Separate trials – Separate counts – Admissibilty of evidence – Sexual abuse of children – Severance of indictment – Matters to be considered

R v Christou .. .. **HL** 927

DISCOVERY – Legal professional privilege – Implied waiver – Extent

    Kershaw v Whelan .. .. **Ebsworth J**   **404**

DIVORCE – Costs – Security for wife's costs – Whether court having jurisdiction to order security for costs after judgment

    Penny v Penny .. .. **CA**   **329**

EDUCATION – Local education authority – Statutory duty to provide special education – Appeal – Whether child proper party to appeal

    S (a minor) v Special Educational Needs Tribunal .. .. **CA**   **286**

EMPLOYMENT – Discrimination against a woman – Unfair dismissal and redundancy payments – Time limit for making claim – Whether extension of time warranted where claimant under mistake as to legal rights

    Biggs v Somerset CC .. .. **CA**   **734**

EQUITY – Laches – Availability of defence – Factors relevant to exercise of court's discretion

    Nelson v Rye .. .. **Laddie J**   **186**

ESTOPPEL – Issue estoppel – Dismissal of application on applicant's withdrawal – Whether applicant estopped from raising same issue in second action

    Barber v Staffordshire CC .. .. **CA**   **748**

EXECUTION – Writ of fi fa – Sheriff failing to gain access to debtor's premises – Sheriff returning writ as unsatisfied – Whether execution properly returned as unsatisfied

    Re a debtor (No 340 of 1992), ex p the debtor v First National Commercial Bank plc .. **CA**   **211**

FAMILY PROCEEDINGS – Confidential information in care proceedings – Disclosure – Legal professional privilege – Whether court entitled to disclose information to police

    Re L (a minor) (police investigation: privilege) .. .. **HL**   **78**

——Confidential information in care proceedings – Disclosure – Whether social worker entitled to disclose information from parents to police

    Re G (a minor) (social worker: disclosure) .. .. **CA**   **65**

HOUSING – Homeless person – Housing authority finding intentional homelessness – Whether deficient reasons in notification curable by affidavit evidence in course of proceedings

    R v Westminster City Council, ex p Ermakov .. .. **CA**   **302**

IMMIGRATION – Leave to enter – Refugee – Asylum – Whether a fresh 'claim for asylum' made

    R v Secretary of State for the Home Dept, ex p Onibiyo .. .. **CA**   **901**

——Leave to enter – Refugee – Asylum – Whether applicant involved in 'serious non-political crime'

    T v Secretary of State for the Home Dept .. .. **HL**   **865**

INCOME TAX – Company – Group relief – Entitlement – Consortium – Whether group relief available only where holding company's subsidiaries resident in the United Kingdom

    Imperial Chemical Industries plc v Colmer (Inspector of Taxes) .. .. **HL**   **23**

INDUSTRIAL TRIBUNAL – Procedure – Decision – Res judicata – Principles applicable where tribunal dismissed application without hearing evidence or argument

    Barber v Staffordshire CC .. .. **CA**   **748**

INJUNCTION – Interlocutory – Injunction restraining bankrupt from leaving jurisdiction – Whether pre-existing cause of action required

    Morris v Murjani .. .. **CA**   **384**

INSOLVENCY – Petition – Conditions for presentation – Whether defect in execution curable as procedural irregularity

    Re a debtor (No 340 of 1992), ex p the debtor v First National Commercial Bank plc .. **CA**   **211**

INSOLVENCY – Voluntary arrangement – Approval by creditors – Arrangement in respect of future rent – Whether creditor bound

    Doorbar v Alltime Securities Ltd .. .. **CA** 948

——Voluntary arrangement – Creditors' meeting – Proxies sent by fax – Validity

    Re a debtor (No 2021 of 1995), ex p IRC v The debtor, Re a debtor (No 2022 of 1995), ex p IRC v The debtor .. .. **Laddie J** 345

INSURANCE – Accident insurance – Perils insured against – Whether death resulting from deliberate drinking to excess caused by accidental means

    Dhak v Insurance Co of North America .. .. **CA** 609

——All risks insurance – Consequential loss policy – Construction of material damage proviso

    Glengate-KG Properties Ltd v Norwich Union Fire Insurance Society Ltd .. .. .. **CA** 487

LANDLORD AND TENANT – Lease – Statutory requirements – Whether letter confirming tenancy to commence on future date operating as a lease 'taking effect in possession'

    Long v Tower Hamlets London BC .. .. **James Munby QC** 683

——Leasehold enfranchisement – Tenants' rights of first refusal – Relevant disposal – Point at which notices conferring rights of first refusal required to be served

    Mainwaring v Trustees of Henry Smith's Charity .. .. **CA** 220

LEGAL AID – Assisted person's liability to pay costs – Limited certificate – Liability for costs for steps taken beyond scope of certificate

    Turner v Plasplugs Ltd .. .. **CA** 939

LIBEL AND SLANDER – Damages – Direction to jury – Matters to which trial judge may refer

    John v MGN Ltd .. .. **CA** 35

——Exemplary or punitive damages – Principles on which exemplary damages awarded – Test of recklessness

    John v MGN Ltd .. .. **CA** 35

LIMITATION OF ACTION – Extension of time limit – Exercise of discretion – Grant of leave ex parte – Legality

    Oyston v Blaker .. .. **CA** 106

——Land – Action against guarantor for recovery of arrears of rent – Whether six-year limitation period applying

    Romain v Scuba TV Ltd .. .. **CA** 377

——Land – Adverse possession – Period of adverse possession – Whether letter confirming grant of tenancy a lease in writing

    Long v Tower Hamlets London BC .. .. **James Munby QC** 683

——Trust property – Breach of fiduciary duty to account – Applicable limitation period

    Nelson v Rye .. .. **Laddie J** 186

MISREPRESENTATION – Fraudulent misrepresentation – Availability of damages where representation inducing contract made without dishonesty

    Thomas Witter Ltd v TBP Industries Ltd .. .. **Jacob J** 573

——Negligent misrepresentation – Award of damages where rescission for innocent misrepresentation inducing contract no longer a viable remedy

    Thomas Witter Ltd v TBP Industries Ltd .. .. **Jacob J** 573

NEGLIGENCE – Duty to take care – Serviceman – Whether soldier owing duty of care to fellow servicemen when engaging enemy during hostilities

    Mulcahy v Ministry of Defence .. .. **CA** 758

NEGLIGENCE – Information or advice – Knowledge third party might rely on information – Extent of duty of care in respect of woman made pregnant following reversal of vasectomy operation

    Goodwill v British Pregnancy Advisory Service .. .. **CA**   161

——Information or advice – Reliance – Share prospectus – Whether persons issuing prospectus owing duty of care to purchasers of after-market shares

    Possfund Custodian Trustee Ltd v Diamond (McGrigor Donald (a firm), third party), Parr v Diamond (McGrigor Donald (a firm), third party) . .. . **Lightman J**   774

PENSION – Pension scheme – Maladministration – Jurisdiction of pensions ombudsman – Legality of remedy

    Westminster City Council v Haywood .. .. **Robert Walker J**   467

——Pension scheme – Maladministration – Jurisdiction of pensions ombudsman to order compensation for distress and inconvenience

    Miller v Stapleton .. .. **Carnwath J**   449

POLICE – Discipline – Disciplinary proceedings – Judicial review – Whether officer facing disciplinary process can avoid adjudication by retiring

    R v Chief Constable of the Devon and Cornwall Constabulary, ex p Hay, R v Chief Constable of the Devon and Cornwall Constabulary, ex p Police Complaints Authority .. .. **Sedley J**   711

PRACTICE – Discontinuance of action – Discontinuance by plaintiffs – Whether defendant's counterclaim surviving discontinuance

    Ernst & Young (a firm) v Butte Mining plc .. .. **Robert Walker J**   623

——Dismissal of action for want of prosecution – Inordinate delay without excuse – Prejudice to defendant – Whether court required to set off value to defendant of having in hand money ultimately payable in damages

    Gahan v Szerelmey (UK) Ltd .. .. **CA**   291

——Service out of the jurisdiction – Service of English proceedings out of jurisdiction in breach of exclusive foreign jurisdiction clause – Whether English jurisdiction should be maintained

    Citi-March Ltd v Neptune Orient Lines Ltd .. .. **Colman J**   545

PRISON – Release on licence – Refusal to release on licence – Statutory review by Parole Board – Whether correct test applied

    R v Parole Board, ex p Watson .. .. **CA**   641

SOCIAL SECURITY – Income support – Severe disability premium – Entitlement – Effect of subsequent decision on earlier decision excluding entitlement

    Bate v Chief Adjudication Officer .. .. **HL**   790

SOLICITOR – Duty – Breach of duty – Solicitor acting for both purchaser and mortgagee in conveyancing transaction – Failure to communicate information to mortgagee – Liability to mortgagee

    Mortgage Express Ltd v Bowerman & Partners (a firm) .. .. **CA**   836

——Duty – Breach of trust – Mortgage transaction – Solicitor acting for both borrower and society – Payment away in breach of instructions – Factors to be considered

    Bristol and West Building Society v May May & Merrimans (a firm) .. .. **Chadwick J**   801

——Duty – Conflict of interest – Solicitor acting for lender and borrowers – Whether knowledge of borrower's misrepresentation coming to solicitors as solicitors for lender

    Halifax Mortgage Services Ltd (formerly BNP Mortgages Ltd) v Stepsky .. .. .. **CA**   277

——Duty – Conflict of interest – Whether retention of petitioning creditor's solicitors by bankrupt's trustee creating conflict of interest

    Re Schuppan (a bankrupt) .. .. **Robert Walker J**   664

SOLICITOR – Lien – Retaining lien – Jurisdicton of court to grant relief in equity

    Ismail v Richards Butler (a firm) ..   ..   **Moore-Bick J**   **506**

——Lien – Retaining lien – Solicitor ending retainer – Whether court entitled to make client's right to papers conditional on provision of security

    Ismail v Richards Butler (a firm) ..   ..   **Moore-Bick J**   **506**

——Payment of costs by solicitor personally – Costs incurred unreasonably or improperly – Jurisdiction to order solicitor to pay wasted costs

    Count Tolstoy-Miloslavsky v Lord Aldington   ..   ..   **CA**   **556**

——Payment of costs by solicitor personally – Costs incurred unreasonably or improperly – Winding up petition struck out as abuse of process of court – Whether order for wasted costs appropriate

    Re a Company (No 006798 of 1995)   ..   ..   **Chadwick J**   **417**

STATUTE – Construction – Reference to proceedings in Parliament as an aid to construction

    Three Rivers DC v Bank of England (No 2) ..   ..   **Clarke J**   **363**

TRUST AND TRUSTEE – Remuneration of trustee – Circumstances in which court will exercise jurisdiction to award remuneration

    Foster v Spencer   ..   ..   **Judge Paul Baker QC**   **672**

WILL – Condition – Conditional bequest – Will intended to take effect on completion of inter vivos gifts – Admissibility of extrinsic evidence

    Corbett v Newey   ..   ..   **CA**   **914**

——Construction – Intention of testator – Signed but undated will – Will intended to take effect on completion of inter vivos gifts – Validity

    Corbett v Newey   ..   ..   **CA**   **914**

House of Lords petitions

This list, which covers the period 14 March to 11 June 1996, sets out all cases which have formed the subject of a report in the All England Law Reports in which an Appeal Committee of the House of Lords has, subsequent to the publication of that report, refused leave to appeal. Where the result of a petition for leave to appeal was known prior to the publication of the relevant report a note of that result appears at the end of the report.

Mainwaring v Trustees of Henry Smith's Charity [1996] 2 All ER 220, CA. Leave to appeal refused 20 May 1996 (Lord Keith of Kinkel, Lord Mustill and Lord Nicholls of Birkenhead)

R v Ministry of Defence, ex p Smith [1996] 1 All ER 257, CA. Leave to appeal refused 19 March 1996 (Lord Keith of Kinkel, Lord Slynn of Hadley and Lord Hoffmann)

R v South Worcestershire Magistrates, ex p Lilley [1995] 4 All ER 186, DC. Leave to appeal refused 19 March 1996 (Lord Keith of Kinkel, Lord Slynn of Hadley and Lord Hoffmann)

Birse Construction Ltd v Haiste Ltd (Watson and others, third parties)

COURT OF APPEAL, CIVIL DIVISION

NOURSE, ROCH LJJ AND SIR JOHN MAY

1, 2 NOVEMBER, 5 DECEMBER 1995

Contribution – Third party proceedings – Claim 'in respect of the same damage' – Defective construction of reservoir for water authority – Defendant's liability to plaintiff construction company in respect of engineering consultancy – Third party's liability to water authority in respect of issue of certificates – Whether third party liable in respect of 'same damage' as defendant – Whether 'same damage' meaning damage suffered by same person – Civil Liability (Contribution) Act 1978, s 1(1).

A water authority awarded a contract for the design and construction of a reinforced concrete storage reservoir and associated building and engineering works to the plaintiff construction company, B Ltd, and appointed its own employee, N, as the construction engineer responsible for issuing the necessary certificates. B Ltd retained the defendant company, H Ltd, as consulting engineers for the project. On completion, the reservoir proved to be defective, and a settlement was reached between B Ltd and the water authority under which it was agreed that B Ltd would, at its own expense, construct a new reservoir and associated works. In due course B Ltd commenced proceedings against H Ltd, claiming damages for the ensuing loss and damage which it had suffered. H Ltd subsequently served a third party notice on N, claiming a contribution from him as a person liable in respect of the 'same damage' suffered by B Ltd pursuant to s 2[a] of the Civil Liability (Contribution) Act 1978, by reason of his alleged breach of contract and negligence. Thereafter, N issued a summons in the action under RSC Ord 14A to determine the question whether his liability to the water authority could be in respect of the 'same damage' as the liability of H Ltd to B Ltd for the purposes of s 1(1)[b] of the 1978 Act, contending that it could not since the damage suffered had to be that of the same person. The judge disagreed, holding that the Act provided a remedy regardless of the nature of the respective causes of action as well as of the identity of the person liable in respect of the same damage, that on a proper construction of the Act the 'same damage' referred to in s 1(1) did not necessarily mean damage suffered by the same person, and that to hold otherwise would require the words 'to that person' to be inserted after the word 'liable' and before the words 'in respect of the same damage' in s 1(1). The judge accordingly answered the question posed in the affirmative. N appealed. Before the hearing of the appeal additional allegations were raised by way of unopposed amendments to the third party notice to the effect that N was also liable to B Ltd for breach of duty of care and negligent misstatement.

---

a   Section 2, so far as material, is set out at p 4 *f* to *j*, post
b   Section 1, so far as material, is set out at p 4 *c d*, post

Held – (1) The 1978 Act was concerned with the relatively simple sharing of
existing liability and as such there was no reason to construe s 1(1) of the Act
otherwise than directly and simply as it stood. The simple direct reading of s 1(1)
was that any person who was liable in respect of any damage suffered by another
could recover a contribution from any other person liable in respect of the same
damage and, as a matter of construction, the 'same damage' could only refer to
the damage just referred to, which was damage suffered by the same person. The
true meaning of the section was clear and did not need the insertion of any
additional wording to give it that effect (see p 6 *g* to p 7 *e*, p 8 *e g h* and p 9 *c* to *e*,
post).

(2) In the circumstances, the loss suffered by the water authority was in not
having a completed properly working reservoir at the time that they expected,
whereas the loss sustained by B Ltd was in having to construct a second reservoir
as a result of their compromise with the water authority. The damages which H
Ltd might have to pay B Ltd or for which N might be liable to the water authority
for their respective breaches of contract or negligence, or for both, were
accordingly not in respect of damage suffered by the same person and did not
amount to the 'same damage' within s 1(1) of the Act. The question before the
judge should therefore have been answered in the negative. However, the fresh
allegations on the amended third party notice raised questions of fact and law
which were not so ill-founded in law that they should be struck out in limine and
on that basis the appeal would be allowed, but only in so far as it related to the
order made by the judge on the summons before him (see p 8 *c d j* and p 9 *e*, post).

Notes

For recovery of contribution, see 45 *Halsbury's Laws* (4th edn) para 1237, and for
cases on the subject, see 46 *Digest* (Reissue) 263, *2176–2177.*

For meaning of 'damage' and 'damages', see 12 *Halsbury's Laws* (4th edn) paras
1102–1103.

For the Civil Liability (Contribution) Act 1978, ss 1,2, see 13 *Halsbury's Statutes*
(4th edn) (1991 reissue) 578, 580.

Appeal

By notice dated 19 April 1995 the second third party, Eric Donald Newton,
appealed with leave from the judgment of Judge Newman QC given on 30 March
1995 in the Queen's Bench Division of the High Court, whereby he answered the
question in Mr Newton's summons issued on 7 September 1994 under RSC Ord
14A, in an action for damages arising under a contract for the construction of a
reinforced concrete storage reservoir brought by the plaintiff, Birse Construction
Ltd (Birse), against the defendant, Haiste Ltd, by deciding that any liability of Mr
Newton to Anglian Water Authority (which had appointed him as the engineer
for the purposes of the contract) was a liability 'in respect of the same damage' as
any liability of Haiste to Birse within the meaning of s 1(1) of the Civil Liability
(Contribution) Act 1978. On 23 June 1995 Judge Bowsher QC gave Haiste leave
to amend their third party notice against Mr Newton to add allegations (i) that Mr
Newton was in breach of his common law duty of care to Birse and (ii) that Birse
had relied to its detriment on a negligent misstatement made by Mr Newton.
The first third party, John Watson, Derek George Bradford and Michael Joseph
Takla (trading as Derek Bradford Associates (a firm)) took no part in the appeal.
The facts are set out in the judgment of Sir John May.

a *Richard Gray QC* (instructed by *Fenwick Elliott*) for Mr Newton.
   Robert Akenhead QC and *Adrian Williamson* (instructed by *Alastair Thomson &*
   Partners) for Haiste.

Cur adv vult

b 5 December 1995. The following judgments were delivered.

SIR JOHN MAY (giving the first judgment at the invitation of Nourse LJ). The
parties to this litigation comprise the plaintiff, Birse Construction Ltd (Birse), a
building and civil engineering contractor, who in February 1988 was awarded a
contract after tender by Anglian Water Authority (Anglian) for the design and
c construction of a reinforced concrete storage reservoir and associated building
and engineering works at Sutterton in Lincolnshire (the Sutterton reservoir
project). The defendant company, Haiste Ltd, are a firm of consulting engineers
and were retained by Birse to act as its consulting engineers in the preparation of
the tender for and the design of the reservoir project. The second third party, Mr
d Eric Donald Newton, was employed by Anglian and appointed by it as the
'engineer' for the purpose of the contract with Birse and as the 'construction
engineer' for the purpose of s 7 of the Reservoirs Act 1975 to issue all necessary
certificates. Birse thereafter purported to construct and complete the reservoir,
but it proved to be defective. In the result Anglian made a claim against Birse in
respect of the defective reservoir and its consequential losses. This claim was
e settled by an agreement between Anglian and Birse under which, inter alia, it was
agreed that the original reservoir as constructed could not be adequately repaired
or replaced and that Birse should at its own expense construct a new reservoir
and associated works.
    In due course, by a writ issued on 11 October 1993, Birse sued Haiste for
f damages for the loss and damage which it had suffered in the circumstances I
have outlined. A statement of claim was served by Birse on Haiste on 28
February 1994. On 6 June 1994 Haiste served a third party notice on Mr Newton
claiming contribution from him pursuant to s 2 of the Civil Liability
(Contribution) Act 1978 on the ground that he was a person liable in respect of
the same damage as Haiste to Birse, by reason of Mr Newton's alleged breach of
g contract and negligence.
    On 7 September 1994 Mr Newton issued a summons in the action under RSC
Ord 14A, which provides machinery for the determination summarily of a
question of law or construction arising in the course of litigation which would or
might finally determine the liability of Mr Newton to Haiste in the third party
h proceedings to which I have referred. To this end the summons asked, inter alia,
for the determination of this question:

'Can any liability of the Second Third Party to Anglian Water Authority be
a liability "in respect of the same damage" as any liability of the Defendant
to the Plaintiff within the meaning of that term in the Civil Liability
j (Contribution) Act 1978?'

    The summons originally asked two further questions, but before it came to be
heard it was conceded that in the light of the affidavit evidence filed these were
not suitable for determination under Ord 14A, as issues of fact to be tried were
raised. It was agreed, however, that the first question was suitable for
determination as this could, in one event, finally dispose of the litigation.

The summons came before Judge Newman QC hearing official referees'
business on 25 November 1994. After taking time to consider his judgment, the
latter handed this down on 30 March 1995. The judge answered the one question
in the affirmative. After argument he then gave Mr Newton leave to appeal, after
ordering him to pay Haiste's costs of the Ord 14A application in any event.
Notice of appeal was given on 19 April 1995 and we heard submissions therein on
1 and 2 November 1995.

The appeal raises a novel point under s 1(1) of the 1978 Act upon which neither
party has so far been able to find any authority. The material provisions of the
Act are as follows:

> '**1.**—(1) Subject to the following provisions of this section, any person
> liable in respect of any damage suffered by another person may recover
> contribution from any other person liable in respect of the same damage
> (whether jointly with him or otherwise).
>
> (2) A person shall be entitled to recover contribution by virtue of
> subsection (1) above notwithstanding that he has ceased to be liable in
> respect of the damage in question since the time when the damage occurred,
> provided that he was so liable immediately before he made or was ordered
> or agreed to make the payment in respect of which the contribution is sought
> ...
>
> (4) A person who has made or agreed to make any payment in bona fide
> settlement or compromise of any claim made against him in respect of any
> damage (including a payment into court which has been accepted) shall be
> entitled to recover contribution in accordance with this section without
> regard to whether or not he himself is or ever was liable in respect of the
> damage, provided, however, that he would have been liable assuming that
> the factual basis of the claim against him could be established ...
>
> **2.**—(1) Subject to subsection (3) below, in any proceedings for contribu-
> tion under section 1 above the amount of the contribution recoverable from
> any person shall be such as may be found by the court to be just and equitable
> having regard to the extent of that person's responsibility for the damage in
> question ...
>
> (3) Where the amount of the damages which have or might have been
> awarded in respect of the damage in question in any action brought in
> England and Wales by or on behalf of the person who suffered it against the
> person from whom the contribution is sought was or would have been
> subject to—(a) any limit imposed by or under any enactment or by any
> agreement made before the damage occurred; (b) any reduction by virtue
> of section 1 of the Law Reform (Contributory Negligence) Act 1945 or
> section 5 of the Fatal Accidents Act 1976; or (c) any corresponding limit or
> reduction under the law of a country outside England and Wales; the person
> from whom the contribution is sought shall not by virtue of any contribution
> awarded under section 1 above be required to pay in respect of the damage
> a greater amount than the amount of those damages as so limited or reduced
> ...
>
> **6.**—(1) A person is liable in respect of any damage for the purposes of this
> Act if the person who suffered it (or anyone representing his estate or
> dependants) is entitled to recover compensation from him in respect of that
> damage (whatever the legal basis of his liability, whether tort, breach of
> contract, breach of trust or otherwise) ...'

a The argument on behalf of Haiste before the judge, which he accepted, contended that the 'damage' with which this litigation is concerned was in substance the defective condition of the reservoir and the need to replace it. Although one can draw a distinction, as does the notice of appeal before us, between the damage suffered by Anglian, which at most could be the loss of the benefit and use of the new reservoir which they had contracted with Birse to

b design and construct, and/or with Mr Newton to oversee, on the one hand, and that suffered by Birse, which was the cost to it of rebuilding the reservoir, the ancillary losses which went with that necessary requirement and were not too remote and such matters as were referred to under the term of the settlement agreement between Birse and Anglian on the other hand, nevertheless each is properly to be considered as having been 'in respect of' the underlying 'damage'

c to which I have referred. The phrase 'in respect of' is a broad one, the argument stresses.

The judge went on to hold that, as a matter of construction, the 1978 Act provided a remedy regardless of the causes of action giving rise to the liability. Regardless, that is, of the nature of the respective causes of action as well as of the

d identity of the person liable in respect of the same damage. In other words, on a proper construction of the Act, the 'same damage' referred to in s 1(1) did not necessarily mean damage suffered by the same person. In his judgment below the judge said:

'To hold otherwise would require the words "to that person" to be inserted
e after the word "liable" and before the words "in respect of the same damage" in s 1(1) of the 1978 Act. Those words are not there, and if they were, they would be contrary to the patent intention of the Act, namely to make provision for contribution between persons liable for the same damage.'

With respect to the judge, it might be said that the last sentence in that passage
f from his judgment tended to beg the question in issue. Nevertheless, it is apparent from the respective arguments and from his judgment that, in his view, for the purposes of s 1(1) of the Act the relevant 'damage' could be the same even though not suffered by the same person.

Bearing in mind Haiste's contention that the nature of the two potential causes of action which might give rise to an entitlement to contribution can be
g disregarded, and to overcome a serious obstacle to Haiste's general argument, namely the difficulty of showing that Mr Newton was or would have been liable to Birse so as to come within s 1 of the 1978 Act, it was contended on behalf of Haiste that had Anglian sued Birse as a defendant, Birse could have issued contribution proceedings against Mr Newton under the 1978 Act and against

h Haiste in contract. Thus, given the wide construction to be given to the phrase 'the same damage', both Mr Newton and Haiste would be liable in respect of that same damage within the meaning of s 1(1).

Once one had reached this position, the argument continues that Birse could then establish a liability against Mr Newton by deploying against him s 1(1) of the
j Act. As we have seen, s 6(1) of the Act provides that contribution is recoverable from a person whatever the legal basis upon which the person who suffered the original damage can recover compensation for it from the putative contributor. Thus there can be no objection in law to deploying s 1(1) twice to justify a right to contribution which could not otherwise be brought within s 1(1).

In support of his appeal before us and his submission that the judge has erred in law in answering the question posed by the relevant summons in the

affirmative, counsel for Mr Newton submitted that the problem in this case was
a matter of construction of s 1(1). He contended that on its proper construction   *a*
the section meant that the person being given a right to recover contribution
must be liable to another person, who can only be the plaintiff in the material
litigation or someone with whom the person seeking compensation has reached
a bona fide settlement or compromise (see s 1(4)), and that the person seeking
contribution must be liable to the other person in respect of some damage   *b*
suffered by that other person. Given such a scenario, the person seeking
contribution will acquire a right to it in respect of his own liability from another
person (ie the contributor) if he can prove that the latter in turn is liable 'in
respect of the same damage'. As a matter of construction, and read within its own
sentence in s 1(1), 'the same damage' can only be the damage just referred to,
namely the damage suffered by the other person; that is the plaintiff or person   *c*
with whom settlement has been reached. Such a construction is, it is contended,
reinforced by the words in brackets—'whether jointly with him or otherwise'—
at the end of the subsection.

Mr Newton also pointed to the practical problems to which the judge's
decision gives rise. By s 2(1) the amount of contribution recoverable from any   *d*
person is such as shall be found by the court to be just and equitable having regard
to that person's responsibility for the damage in question. If it is only the
compensation due to a plaintiff which is in question, then all the circumstances
surrounding the claim are already in issue anyway, and apportionment between
two persons liable to the plaintiff can be fairly made. But if the judge's decision
below was correct, then the picture becomes confused and well-nigh impossible   *e*
to resolve. In the instant case the trial judge would have to assess Mr Newton's
degree of responsibility for Anglian's losses when Anglian is not a party and was
in fact Mr Newton's employer. Such losses may or may not be the same as the
losses Birse claims from Haiste. Then the judge would have to consider the
extent of Haiste's responsibility for the Birse losses. Against this background the   *f*
judge would have to decide what is the just and equitable contribution which Mr
Newton should make to the Birse losses only because of Mr Newton's liability to
Anglian.

It is common ground that the issues in this case are ones of construction. I
remind myself, first, that the statute which has to be construed is concerned with
contribution, that is the help that the law requires one party to give to another to   *g*
satisfy their common obligations to a third person. The 1978 Act is, in my
opinion, concerned with the relatively simple sharing of existing liability. I would
be surprised if against this background the Act created potentially complicated
and some might say tortuous legal relationships. With respect to the judge and
to the arguments put before us by counsel for Haiste, I think that the former was   *h*
wrong to hold that the answer to the question raised in the summons should be
in the affirmative.

I see no reason to construe s 1(1) of the Act otherwise than directly and simply
as it stands. Any person who is liable (see s 6(1)) in respect of any damage suffered
by another may recover contribution, partial help, from another person liable in   *j*
respect of the same damage. The simple direct reading of the subsection must in
my opinion lead one to conclude, first, that 'the same damage' can only refer to
the damage spoken of some dozen or so words earlier in the subsection. Further,
the simple approach necessarily involves that the statutory draftsman intended
that 'the same damage' should be damage suffered by the *same* person. I do not
think that the loss suffered by Anglian in not having a completed properly

a working reservoir at the time that they expected, the loss sustained by Birse in having to construct a second reservoir as a result of their compromise with Anglian, or the damages which Haiste may have to pay Birse, or for which Mr Newton may be liable to Anglian for their respective breaches of contract or negligence or for both, are 'the same damage' within s 1(1) of the Act, even though each may have been brought about because the first reservoir was badly

b constructed by Birse. A substantial part of the argument on behalf of Haiste on the appeal was based on the general contention that the damage founding the liability of all the parties in this case was, in substance, the defective condition of the reservoir and the need to replace it. Speaking loosely this is no doubt correct. In my opinion, however, the proper construction of s 1(1) of the 1978 Act and its correct application to the facts of the instant case requires a more precise analysis.

c   In rejecting the construction of s 1(1) which I prefer, as I have said, the judge expressed the view that such a construction would require the words 'to that person' to be inserted after the word 'liable' and before the words 'in respect of the same damage'. Such words were not there and, if they were, they would be contrary to the patent intention of the Act. I respectfully disagree. I agree that

d the presence of such additional words in s 1(1) would be wholly consistent with what I consider to be its true construction: their absence, however, does not lead me to conclude that my opinion as to the proper construction is wrong. The true meaning of s 1(1) is in my view quite clear even without those additional words.

In my opinion, therefore, the judge below was wrong to hold that the answer to the material question was Yes. I think that it should have been in the negative.

e

However, I should just mention that the 1978 Act was enacted following and clearly to give at least partial effect to a Law Commission report ordered to be printed on 9 March 1977 entitled *Law of Contract—Report on Contribution* (Law Com No 79). The report itself contained a proposed draft Bill to give effect to the Commission's proposals. The 1978 Act as subsequently enacted by Parliament

f followed the suggested draft Bill in substantial measure, although the final Act differed from the Bill in a number of particulars. Our attention was drawn to the report of the Law Commission by counsel for Mr Newton, in support of his argument that the 1978 Act did no more than widen the scope of the Law Reform (Married Women and Tortfeasors) Act 1935 so that a defendant could claim

g contribution from another who was liable to a plaintiff for breach of contract, breach of trust or other breach of duty, not merely as a joint tortfeasor.

Counsel for Haiste submitted that there were such differences between the draft Bill in the report and the 1978 Act, as ultimately enacted, as to preclude us from relying on the report for any assistance on the question of construction raised by this appeal.

h

I do not think that there is any ambiguity within the 1978 Act which might entitle me to look at the report. In my opinion, the proper construction of s 1(1) and associated provisions within the Act is clear and one needs no assistance in determining this from the Law Commission's report. However, if I were minded or entitled to take the report into account on this appeal, I would conclude that

j it supports the view on construction which I have expressed. It seems clear that the recommendation of the Law Commission was merely to widen the scope of the 1935 Act to the extent I have mentioned.

Were this all, then in my opinion this appeal should be allowed with the consequence that the third party proceedings by Haiste against Mr Newton should be dismissed.

However, at a late stage, namely on 23 June 1995, the court gave leave to
amend the third party notice. This was after the judgment and order now under a
appeal. The application for leave to amend was not opposed. In brief the
amendments add, first, allegations that Mr Newton owed a duty of care at
common law to Birse, that he was in breach of that duty and that such breach
caused or contributed to the deficiencies in the design and/or construction of the
reservoir and to its failure. The amendments secondly add an allegation that Mr b
Newton was guilty of a negligent misstatement upon which Birse relied to its
detriment.

Each of these fresh allegations raise difficult questions of fact and law. Whilst
I think that the allegations will be difficult to make out at trial, I cannot say that
they are so ill-founded in law that they should be struck out in limine.
c

In these circumstances I think that this appeal succeeds in part, that is in
relation to the order made by the judge on the summons before him. However,
for the reasons which I have just given, I do not think that we can prevent Haiste
from continuing its third party proceedings against Mr Newton on the amended
third party notice. For my part I should like to hear argument from counsel on
the precise terms of the order we should make on this appeal. d

ROCH LJ. I agree. A person liable for damage suffered by another may recover
contribution from any other person liable in respect of the same damage under
s 1(1) of the Civil Liability (Contribution) Act 1978, subject to the following
provisions of the section. The liability of the person claiming contribution, e
Haiste Ltd, and the liability of the person from whom contribution is claimed, Mr
Newton, does not have to be joint (s 1(1)), nor does the legal basis of the liability
of Haiste have to be the same as the basis of the liability of Mr Newton (s 6(1)).

The word 'damage' in the phrase 'the same damage' in s 1(1) does not mean
'damages'. This is demonstrated by other sections of the Act, for example s 2(3). f
By s 6(1) 'damage' is the harm suffered by 'another person', to use the phrase in
s 1(1), for which that person is entitled to recover compensation; it is not the
compensation which is recoverable, although in cases of purely financial loss it
may be commensurate with it.

For there to be an entitlement to claim contribution, the damage for which the
person who claims contribution and the person from whom contribution is g
claimed has to be the same damage, that is to say the sufferer must be the same
person or some person representing his estate or dependants. This is because the
person who is entitled to recover compensation for the damage has to be the
person who suffered the damage. I disagree with Judge Newman QC that this
interpretation of the Act requires the addition to s 1(1) of the Act of words that h
are not there. In my view, this is the correct construction to be placed on s 1(1)
when the Act is construed as a whole.

The damage suffered by Anglian Water Authority in this case was the physical
defects in the reservoir. The damage suffered by Birse Construction Ltd was the
financial loss of having to construct a second reservoir for Anglian. Anglian and j
Birse did not suffer the same damage. Consequently, I too would answer the
question raised in the summons in the negative.

NOURSE LJ. This appeal raises a short question of construction on s 1(1) of the
Civil Liability (Contribution) Act 1978:

a   'Subject to the following provisions of this section, any person liable in respect of any damage suffered by another person may recover contribution from any other person liable in respect of the same damage (whether jointly with him or otherwise).'

If due regard is paid to the wording of that provision, the question is also a simple one, in my judgment.

b   The first requirement is that there should be a person, A, who is liable in respect of damage suffered by another person, B. The second requirement is that there should be a third person, C, who is liable in respect of the same damage (whether jointly with A or otherwise). If those two requirements are satisfied, A may recover contribution from C.

c   The question is what is meant by the words 'the same damage'. The only synonym for 'same' being 'identical', the words, in their natural and ordinary sense, can only mean 'the damage suffered by that other person', ie B. No verbal addition or subtraction is necessary in order to arrive at this interpretation. The meaning of the words, as they stand, is plain. Their effect is simply to extend as against others the right to contribution which was formerly conferred against
d   joint tortfeasors only by s 6 of the Law Reform (Married Women and Tort-feasors) Act 1935. That is the significance of the words 'whether jointly with him or otherwise'.

For these reasons, which do little more than repeat the essential reasoning of Sir John May and Roch LJ, I agree that Judge Newman QC's construction of s 1(1)
e   was incorrect, and that the question raised in the summons ought to have been answered in the negative. However, since unopposed leave to amend the third party notice has now been given, I agree with Sir John May that we cannot prevent Haiste Ltd from continuing those proceedings against Mr Newton, and that we should hear argument from counsel as to the precise terms of the order to be made by this court.
f
Appeal allowed. Leave to appeal to House of Lords refused.

L I Zysman Esq   Barrister.

Attorney General's Reference (No 3 of 1994) *a*

COURT OF APPEAL, CRIMINAL DIVISION
LORD TAYLOR OF GOSFORTH CJ, KAY AND STEEL JJ
13, 14, 24 NOVEMBER 1995

b

Criminal law – Murder – Child in utero – Accused inflicting knife injury on pregnant woman – Child born grossly premature with knife wound – Child later dying from lung condition unconnected with wound – Accused charged with child's murder – Judge directing acquittal on grounds that conviction not possible in law – Whether injury to foetus constituting unlawful injury – Whether victim required to be person in being at time of act causing death – Requisite intent – Whether fact that child's death caused as a consequence of injury to mother precluding liability for murder or manslaughter – Criminal Justice Act 1972, s 36. *c*

In May 1990 the respondent stabbed his girlfriend, who was to his knowledge pregnant with his child. No injury to the foetus was detected and the respondent *d* pleaded guilty to a charge of wounding his girlfriend with intent to cause her grievous bodily harm. In June 1990 the respondent's girlfriend gave birth to a grossly premature daughter who was considered to have only a 50% chance of survival. At the time of the birth it was clear that, contrary to earlier belief, the knife had penetrated the foetus. The child died 120 days later from a lung *e* condition unconnected with the knife wound and the respondent was thereafter charged with her murder. At trial, the judge directed an acquittal on the ground that no conviction for either murder or manslaughter was possible in law. Under s 36(1) of the Criminal Justice Act 1972 the Attorney General subsequently referred to the Court of Appeal the questions (i) whether, subject to proof of requisite intent, the crimes of murder or manslaughter could be committed *f* where unlawful injury was deliberately inflicted to a child in utero or to a mother carrying a child in utero where the child was subsequently born alive, existed independently of the mother and then died, the injuries in utero either having caused or made a substantial contribution to the death, and (ii) whether the fact that the child's death was caused solely as a consequence of injury to the mother rather than as a consequence of direct injury to the foetus could remove any *g* liability for murder or manslaughter in those circumstances.

Held – (1) Murder or manslaughter could be committed where unlawful injury was deliberately inflicted either to a child in utero or to a mother carrying a child in utero in circumstances where the child was subsequently born alive, enjoyed *h* an existence independent of its mother and thereafter died, and where the injuries inflicted while in utero caused or contributed substantially to the death. Injury to the foetus was just as unlawful as any assault upon any other part of the mother, since before birth the foetus was treated as part of the mother until it had a separate existence of its own, and there was no requirement that the person who *j* died should be a person in being at the time the act causing the death was perpetrated (see p 17 *e*, p 20 *j* to 21 *a* and p 22 *c d*, post).

(2) The requisite intent to be proved in a case of murder in those circumstances was an intention to kill or cause really serious bodily injury to the mother, since the foetus before birth was regarded as an integral part of the mother, and there was no reason to prevent the operation of the concept of

a transferred malice, provided the jury was satisfied that the death was caused by the act of the accused. No difference in approach was required in relation to manslaughter, with appropriate modifications for the level of intent. Accordingly, the fact that the death of the child was caused solely as a consequence of injury to the mother rather than injury to the foetus did not negative any liability for murder and manslaughter, provided that the jury were satisfied as to

b causation (see p 18 *d*, p 19 *a*, p 20 *f* to p 21 *a* and p 22 *e*, post); *R v Mitchell* [1983] 2 All ER 427 applied.

Notes

For unlawful killing of a person, see 11(1) *Halsbury's Laws* (4th edn reissue) para 427.

c

Cases referred to in judgment

McCluskey v HM Advocate [1989] RTR 182, HC of Just.

R v Kwok Chak Ming (No 1) [1963] HKLR 226, HK HC; *rvsd on other grounds* [1963] HKLR 349, HK CA.

d *R v Latimer* (1886) 17 QBD 359, [1886–90] All ER Rep 386.

R v Mitchell [1983] 2 All ER 427, [1983] QB 741, [1983] 2 WLR 938, CA.

R v Senior (1832) 1 Mood CC 346, 168 ER 1298.

R v West (1848) 2 Car & Kir 784, 175 ER 329.

e ### Cases also cited or referred to in skeleton arguments

Burton v Islington Health Authority, de Martell v Merton and Sutton Health Authority [1992] 3 All ER 833, [1993] QB 204, CA.

R v Cheshire [1991] 3 All ER 670, [1991] 1 WLR 844, CA.

R v Crutchley (1837) 7 C & P 814, 173 ER 355.

f *R v Enoch* (1833) 5 C & P 539, 172 ER 1089.

R v Pagett (1983) 76 Cr App R 279, CA.

R v Sellis (1837) 7 C & P 850, 173 ER 370.

R v Shephard [1919] 2 KB 125, [1918–19] All ER Rep 374, CCA.

g ### Reference

The Attorney General referred to the court under s 36(1) of the Criminal Justice Act 1972 the following questions for consideration: (i) whether, subject to proof by the prosecution of the requisite intent in either case, the crimes of murder or manslaughter can be committed where unlawful injury is deliberately inflicted (a)

h to a child in utero or (b) to a mother carrying a child in utero, where the child is subsequently born alive, enjoys an existence independent of the mother, thereafter dies and the injuries inflicted while in utero either caused or made a substantial contribution to the death, and (ii) whether the fact that the death of the child is caused solely as a consequence of injury to the mother rather than as

j a consequence of direct injury to the foetus can negative any liability for murder or manslaughter in the circumstances set out in (i). The issues arose out of a prosecution of the respondent for murder, in which Holland J sitting in the Crown Court at Leeds on 6 July 1993 directed the jury to acquit on the grounds that even if the facts and inferences suggested by the Crown were established, they could not in law result in a conviction for either murder or manslaughter. The facts are set out in the opinion of the court.

Robert Smith QC and David Calvert-Smith (instructed by the Crown Prosecution
   Service) for the Attorney General.

a

Simon Hawkesworth QC and Andrew Lees (assigned by the Registrar of Criminal
   Appeals) for the respondent.

Cur adv vult

b

24 November 1995. The following opinion of the court was delivered.

LORD TAYLOR OF GOSFORTH CJ. This case comes before the court on a
reference by Her Majesty's Attorney General under s 36 of the Criminal Justice
Act 1972.

The respondent was charged with murder and was acquitted by direction of   c
the trial judge. In consequence of the judge's ruling the Attorney General has
referred a point of law for the opinion of this court. The point of law is
formulated as follows:

> '1   Subject to proof by the Prosecution of the requisite intent in either   d
> case: whether the crimes of murder or manslaughter can be committed
> where unlawful injury is deliberately inflicted: (i) to a child in utero (ii) to a
> mother carrying a child in utero where the child is subsequently born alive,
> enjoys an existence independent of the mother, thereafter dies and the
> injuries inflicted while in utero either caused or made a substantial
> contribution to the death. 2   Whether the fact that the death of the child is   e
> caused solely as a consequence of injury to the mother rather than as a
> consequence of direct injury to the foetus can negative any liability for
> murder or manslaughter in the circumstances set out in question 1.'

The facts   f

The facts that led to the charge of murder were that on 26 May 1990 the
respondent stabbed his girlfriend, who was to his knowledge pregnant with his
child. The stab wounds included one to the left lower abdomen which penetrated the uterus and the abdomen of the foetus.

The judge summarised the extent of the evidence as to the stage of pregnancy   g
at the time in this way:

> 'The contemporaneous belief was that the period of gestation to that date
> had been 22 weeks. Subsequent events suggested the period might have
> been nearer 24 weeks. If the period were 22 weeks, [the child] could not then   h
> be born so as to survive. If the period were 24 weeks, [the child] could have
> been born with a remote chance of survival put by Dr Dear at 10%. At all
> events the pregnancy had been so far uneventful and her then chance of
> proceeding to full term labour was good with interim premature labour
> assessed as a 1 in 1,000 risk.'

j

Following the stabbing the girlfriend was admitted to hospital. Surgery was
performed and a cut to the wall of the uterus was found. The belief then, which
later proved to be mistaken, was that there had been no injury to the foetus itself.
Accordingly the doctor limited his intervention to sewing up the wall and
prescribing a course of the drug indomethacin to prevent the onset of premature
labour.

The girlfriend made a good recovery and was discharged from hospital. However, on 11 June, without any further trauma, she suddenly went into labour and gave birth to a daughter. The size of the child at birth suggested that the period of gestation was more likely to be 26 weeks rather than the 24 weeks which had been believed to be the case. In any event the child was grossly premature, although she was then considered to have a 50% chance of survival. At the time of birth it was clear that the knife had, contrary to the earlier belief, penetrated the foetus and had cut through the left side of the abdomen.

The child survived for 120 days, receiving intensive neonatal care which the judge described as 'of an exemplary nature'. Such care included a number of surgical operations.

The judge summarised the evidence as to death in the following way:

'The cause of death was a lung condition, broncho-pulmonary dysplasia, which arose in the consistent failure of her lungs to function naturally and from the complications that inevitably arise from sustained reliance upon a ventilator, all such in turn arising from the premature birth. In essence, she was one of the 50% who statistically do not survive premature birth at 24–26 weeks. The injuries to her inflicted by the knife were repaired under general anaesthetic and made no direct contribution to her death, save through such strains arising from operative procedures as compounded the problems arising from immaturity.'

The respondent was charged with wounding his girlfriend with intent to cause her grievous bodily harm. Before the death of the child, he admitted that charge and was sentenced to four years' imprisonment, although at the subsequent murder trial the conviction was not adduced before the jury. After the death of the child, the respondent was charged with murder of the child and it is the trial of that charge that results in this reference.

At the conclusion of the prosecution case, submissions were made on behalf of the respondent: (1) that the evidence tendered to prove the vital causal link between the wounding and the death was insufficient for the case to be left to the jury; and in the alternative (2) that as a matter of law, even if the causal link could be established, the facts could not give rise to a conviction for either murder or manslaughter.

The judge ruled that there was evidence upon which a reasonable jury could conclude that the causal connection had been established, although, as he observed, whether they would in the light of already conflicting evidence on the subject was outside his concern. This reference is not in any way concerned with that ruling. He then decided that even if the facts and inferences suggested by the Crown were established, they could not in law result in a conviction for either murder or manslaughter and accordingly he directed the acquittal of the respondent.

The principles suggested on behalf of the Attorney General

The arguments that were advanced in the court below and before us were presented on behalf of the Crown by Robert Smith QC and on behalf of the respondent by Simon Hawkesworth QC and we record at once our indebtedness to each of them for the considerable assistance that they have provided by the quality and clarity of the submissions that they have made.

At the outset of his submissions Mr Smith set out four principles that he hoped to persuade the court were right, as follows. Where a child is born alive and

subsequently dies from injuries sustained by the child or the mother while the
child is in utero: (1) if an accused has inflicted a deliberate and unlawful injury to
a child in utero intending so to do, he has committed an offence of manslaughter
or murder depending upon what intent is proved and subject to proof of
causation, ie that the deliberate and unlawful act caused the death; (2) if the
accused's intent to inflict injury is to the mother alone and not to the foetus, the
offence of manslaughter or murder, subject to the same qualifications, is made
out by the doctrine of transferred malice; (3) the fact that the foetus is not a
person in being at the time of the unlawful act which is proved to have caused
death is no impediment to a successful prosecution for murder or manslaughter,
provided the child is subsequently born alive and achieves an existence independent of the mother; and (4) the fact that the mens rea of murder is not directed to
a person in being but to a child in the womb is not an impediment to a successful
prosecution. It is sufficient that the mens rea is directed to a child capable of
becoming a person in being or to the mother when she is carrying a child capable
of becoming a person in being.

We turn, therefore, to consider the law in the light of Mr Smith's propositions.

The position at common law

We have been referred to considerable learning on the position at common
law and to the limited number of authorities that cast light upon that position.
We can, however, deal with the matter relatively shortly because the effect of the
Homicide Act 1957 upon the mens rea for murder so alters the position that, save
perhaps in one area, the pre-1957 law is of limited relevance to the issue upon
which our opinion is sought.

Coke in his *Institutes of the Laws of England* (3 Co Inst (1680) 50) says:

'If a woman be quick with childe, and by a potion or otherwise killeth it in
her wombe; or if a man beat her, whereby the child dieth in her body, and
she is delivered of a dead childe, this is great misprision, and no murder ...'

We are in no doubt that his conclusion that such a killing is not murder still
represents an accurate statement of the law. Such facts may now give rise to the
statutory offence of child destruction created by the Infant Life (Preservation) Act
1929 or an abortion offence contrary to s 58 of the Offences against the Person
Act 1861, but they cannot constitute murder or manslaughter.

Coke continued:

'... but if the childe be born alive, and dieth of the potion, battery, or other
cause, this is murder: for in law it is accounted a reasonable creature, *in rerum
natura*, when it is born alive.'

Coke referred to a decision in 1327 (1 YB Edw III 23) in a case where a defendant
had beaten a woman who was pregnant with twins. As a result one was stillborn,
and the other died two days after its baptism. When the matter came before the
court Scrope J declined to treat it as felony. Coke's view was that this decision
was 'never holden for the law' which we understand to mean was never adopted
by the other judges as the law.

The contrary view was put forward in *Hale's Pleas of the Crown* (1 Hale PC
(1778) 433):

'If a woman be quick or great with child, if she take, or another give her
any potion to make an abortion, or if a man strike her, whereby the child

a   within her is kild, it is not murder nor manslaughter by the law of *England*, because it is not yet *in rerum natura*, tho it be a great crime, and by the judicial law of *Moses* was punishable with death, nor can it legally be known, whether it were kild or not ... So it is, if after such child were born alive, and baptised, and after die of the stroke given to the mother, this is not homicide.'

b   Commentators have sought to explain Hale's view by reference to his assertion 'nor can it legally be known, whether it were kild or not' which may have been true on the state of medical knowledge as it stood at the date when Hale wrote, but which can no longer be said to represent the position today. However, as Mr Hawkesworth argues, to attribute Hale's view solely to the impossibility of proof

c   of causation is to ignore the words 'because it is not yet *in rerum natura*'.

Hawkins, East and Blackstone all favoured the view of Coke rather than that of Hale.

Two reports of nineteenth century cases are relied upon by the Crown. The headnote in *R v Senior* (1832) 1 Mood CC 346, 168 ER 1298 reads:

d   'Giving a child, whilst in the act of being born, a mortal wound in the head, as soon as the head appears, and before the child has breathed, will, if the child is afterwards born alive, and dies thereof, and there is malice, be murder.'

The trial was in fact on a charge of manslaughter and the resulting conviction was

e   considered by all the judges except two at a subsequent meeting and they unanimously held that the conviction was right.

In *R v West* (1848) 2 Car & Kir 784, 175 ER 329 the headnote reads:

          'If a person, intending to procure abortion, does an act which causes a child to be born so much earlier than the natural time, that it is born in a state

f   much less capable of living, and afterwards dies, in consequence of its exposure to the external world, the person who, by this misconduct, so brings the child into the world, and puts it thereby in a situation in which it cannot live, is guilty of murder, and the mere existence of a possibility that something might have been done to prevent the death, would not render it

g   less murder.'

More detailed examination of the old law is unnecessary because it has to be borne in mind that until 1957 the felony-murder rule applied so that where, in the course of committing a felony, a death was caused, murder was established without the need to prove any further intention.

h

The position since 1957

Section 1 of the 1957 Act abolished the felony-murder rule so as to make the required mens rea no different if a killing was in the course or furtherance of a felony from a killing in any other circumstances. The law is now clearly settled

j   that a person can only be guilty of murder if, at the time, he either intends to kill or cause really serious bodily injury.

These changes mean that considerations arise now in relation to a charge of murder in circumstances such as those raised in the reference which would not have arisen before the 1957 Act and hence the pre-1957 authorities, even if conclusive before that date, can no longer determine the issues we are invited to consider.

We have found it helpful to start from a consideration of those matters that
need to be proved by the prosecution on a charge of murder and to consider
whether any of those elements require any specific provision to cater for the
unusual circumstances of a case such as this.

The classic definition of murder at common law was given by Coke (3 Co Inst
47):

> 'Murder is when a man of sound memory, and of the age of discretion,
> unlawfully killeth within any county of the realm any reasonable creature *in
> rerum natura* under the king's peace, with malice fore-thought, either
> expressed by the party, or implied by law, so as the party wounded, or hurt,
> &c die of the wound, or hurt, &c within a year and a day after the same.'

Leaving aside such matters as provocation and diminished responsibility,
which have no bearing upon the issues presently under consideration, the
prosecution must prove the following elements: (1) that the defendant did an act;
(2) that the act was deliberate and not accidental; (3) that the act was unlawful; (4)
that the act was a substantial cause of a death; (5) that the death was of a person
in being; (6) that death resulted within a year and a day; and (7) that at the time
of doing the act the defendant intended either to kill or to cause really serious
bodily injury to the victim or, subject to the extent of the doctrine of transferred
malice, to some other person.

Elements 1 to 6 represent the actus reus of murder and if any is absent the actus
reus will not be established. Element 7 is the mens rea of murder for which the
old expression, malice aforethought, was used.

The actus reus of murder

Clearly in a case such as that being considered the first and second elements are
simply a matter of evidence and present no particular problem of law. The third
element of unlawfulness does require further discussion in the light of a
submission made by Mr Hawkesworth that to cause injury to a foetus is not in
itself unlawful. He argues that since the foetus has no separate existence, causing
an injury to it is not unlawful unless it comes within the scope of one of the
statutory offences such as child destruction or abortion. We reject that
submission. In law the foetus is treated as a part of the mother until it has a
separate existence of its own. Thus to cause injury to the foetus is just as unlawful
as any assault upon any other part of the mother.

Mr Hawkesworth cautioned us that conclusions adverse to the respondent's
submissions might render a doctor who carried out a lawful abortion liable to
conviction if the foetus was born alive as a result of a lawful abortion and then
died thereafter. His reasoning was that the Abortion Act 1967, as subsequently
amended only provides that a registered medical practitioner shall not be guilty
of an offence under the law 'relating to abortion' and says nothing about not
being liable on a charge of murder.

In our judgment, Mr Hawkesworth's concerns in this regard are misplaced. A
doctor who carries out an abortion in accordance with the 1967 Act is not acting
unlawfully and hence, were such a doctor to be charged with murder, the charge
would fail because the element that the act must be unlawful could not be made
out. Just as a doctor who causes death in a bona fide surgical operation is not
guilty because he does nothing unlawful, so would a doctor carrying out a lawful
abortion be similarly protected. In the course of argument, the situation of a
foetus being born alive consequent upon a lawful abortion and subsequently

a being neglected or killed was touched upon, but such questions have no relevance to the issues which are raised by this reference and we make clear that we have given no consideration to them.

The fourth element to be established on a charge of murder is that the act was a substantial cause of death. This was the element that Hale doubted could ever be established, but clearly on medical evidence today a jury might properly be so

b satisfied. In the instant case there was a submission that the evidence was inadequate for a jury to reach a conclusion to that effect. The judge ruled against that submission and although the matter has not been argued before us he was, in so far as we can judge, right so to do.

The fifth element is that the death must be of a person in being. In its simplest

c form this means that to cause the death of a foetus in the womb cannot be murder. However, the situation under consideration raises the question whether the child needs to be in being at the time when the act causing death is done by the defendant. Clearly, when the respondent stabbed his girlfriend the child was not a person in being. It is at this point of the argument and for this purpose alone that Mr Smith places reliance upon the pre-1957 common law in support of his

d third principle, namely that the fact that the foetus is not a person in being at the time of the unlawful act which is proved to have caused death is no impediment to a successful prosecution for murder or manslaughter provided the child is subsequently born alive and achieves an existence independent of the mother. He argues that in this respect the 1957 Act did not change the law and that if the cases of *Senior* (1832) 1 Mood CC 346, 168 ER 1298 and *West* (1848) 2 Car & Kir

e 784, 175 ER 329 correctly represented the law, the law in this respect remains unaltered.

We have concluded that there is no requirement that the person who dies needs to be a person in being at the time that the act causing death is perpetrated. That, we are satisfied, was the position at common law and to hold otherwise

f would produce anomalies of an unacceptable kind. For example, a defendant who poisoned the water of a pregnant woman intending her to drink it and be killed, would not be guilty of murder if the woman gave birth to a child and then made up a bottle for the baby using the poisoned water which killed the child. On the other hand, if at the time of the poison being added, the child had already

g been born, and the mother for whom it was intended used the poisoned water in precisely the same way with the same consequences, it would amount to murder.

The sixth element, that death must result within a year and a day, provided an arbitrary time limit, which no doubt was introduced as a safeguard at a time when proof of causation was far from easy. Consideration of the desirability of

h retaining such a provision is currently the subject of debate but it has no relevance to our considerations.

The mens rea of murder

Thus we turn to the mental element of the crime of murder. It is argued on

j behalf of the Attorney General that the Crown can succeed in one of two ways. If the jury are satisfied that the defendant at the time when he did the act intended to kill or cause really serious bodily injury to the foetus, then it is said that this will suffice provided 'the intention is directed to a child capable of becoming a person in being' at a later date. In the alternative it is argued that an intention to kill or cause really serious bodily injury to the mother will suffice by reason of the doctrine of transferred malice.

In Smith and Hogan *Criminal Law* (7th edn, 1992) p 329, the authors' view of the position is stated as follows:

> 'In modern law, however, a person who intends to kill or cause serious injury to an unborn child does not have the *mens rea* for murder—he does not intend to kill or cause serious injury to a person in being—and should not be liable to conviction of that offence. If the child is born alive and dies of the injury inflicted with that intent he might be guilty of manslaughter if there was an obvious and serious risk ... that this might occur. If D's intention was to cause the death or serious injury to the mother he would, by 'transferred malice', be guilty of murder of the child who was born alive and died of the injury so inflicted.'

In so far as that passage, by implication if not expressly, rejects the concept of an intention directed towards a child capable of becoming a person in being, we agree. The concept is a wholly new one that it is sought to introduce and we do not see it as either necessary or desirable to add this gloss to the law.

That is not to say that we think if an intention is directed towards the foetus a charge of murder must fail. In the eyes of the law the foetus is taken to be a part of the mother until it has an existence independent of the mother. Thus an intention to cause serious bodily injury to the foetus is an intention to cause serious bodily injury to a part of the mother just as an intention to injure her arm or her leg would be so viewed. Thus consideration of whether a charge of murder can arise where the focus of the defendant's intention is exclusively the foetus falls to be considered under the head of transferred malice, as is the case where the intention is focused exclusively or partially upon the mother herself.

Transferred malice

It is, therefore, necessary to consider the concept of transferred malice in order to answer the questions posed in this reference. At its simplest the concept is that if a defendant intends to kill or cause really serious bodily injury to A but instead kills B, he is as guilty of the murder of B as if the object of his intentions had been B rather than A.

Mr Hawkesworth mounts his principal challenge to Mr Smith's contentions in this regard. He raises three arguments. (1) In applying the doctrine of transferred malice there is plainly a distinction to be drawn between transferring the malice of an offence of stabbing the mother, where the actus reus is the infliction of a stab wound, and the offence of murder here alleged, which is causing the death of the child by bringing about its birth at such a premature stage that it could not survive. The actus reus of the two crimes does not coincide, so that malice cannot be transferred. (2) All such cases proceed upon the assumption that at the time of the assault or blow aimed at A there is *at the same time* another person in being, B, namely the person who is the unintended victim. Since at the time of the stabbing the foetus was not a person in being, it *could not* be the subject of an offence contrary to s 18 of the 1861 Act. (3) In terms of causation the birth and eventual death of the baby was so far removed from the event of stabbing that malice cannot be transferred.

It is perhaps convenient to deal first with the second of those contentions, that malice cannot be transferred to a person who is not in being at the time of the act causing death. It is important to observe that malice cannot in any event be transferred until such time as the act affects the victim. For example, if a defendant sends a box of poisoned chocolates to A but B eats them and dies, it can a only be at the moment when B places a chocolate in his mouth that any question of transfer of malice can arise. That time would in such circumstances of necessity be significantly after the act done by the sender.

We can see no reason to hold that malice can only be transferred where the person to whom it is transferred was in existence at the time of the act causing death. It is perhaps pertinent to observe that a sufficient intention may be b directed at no individual but rather there may be an indiscriminate intention which will suffice. Thus a defendant who introduces poison into baby food on a supermarket shelf with an intention to kill some wholly unidentified child is clearly guilty of murder if a child later dies from eating the poisoned food. It would be a remarkable state of affairs if such a person was only guilty of murder if the child had already been born at the date when the poison was introduced to c the food. If in such cases of general malice there is no requirement that the child should already have been born, it is not easy to see why there should be a distinction drawn when malice is instead transferred from an intended victim to an unintended one. The example given earlier of poisoned water intended for the pregnant woman but used to make a bottle for the child demonstrates the possible unsatisfactory conclusions that would arise from such a rule.

d In support of his first and third contentions, Mr Hawkesworth has directed our attention to passages in Professor Glanville Williams Criminal Law—The General Part (2nd edn, 1961) pp 125–127, 132–134. The author contends (pp 125, 132–133):

e   'Although the decided cases do not show it, there can be no doubt that an unexpected difference of mode will be regarded as severing the chain of causation if it is sufficiently far removed from the intended mode ... There is another way in which it seems that the rule may be circumscribed. Hitherto it has been applied only in gross cases, and although there are no clear authorities on the bounds to be set to it, the rule should be confined to f cases where it appears to conform to the plain man's view of justice, and so should be limited to cases where the consequence was brought about by negligence in relation to the actual victim.'

To illustrate the second proposition Professor Williams says:

g   'Thus suppose that D shoots at O intending to kill him; the shot misses O and kills P, who, unknown to D was behind a curtain at the time. If P's presence could not possibly have been foreseen by D, it may be thought to be going too far to convict him of the murder of P.'

We, for our part, do not find Professor Williams' exoneration of D in respect of h murder to be self-evidently 'the plain man's view of justice' in the example he poses.

Professor Williams, as appears from the quoted passages, found no authority in support of either of his propositions. The only authority to which he makes reference in respect of the second proposition is R v Latimer (1886) 17 QBD 359, j [1886–90] All ER Rep 386, which he acknowledges to be against his contention.

In R v Mitchell [1983] 2 All ER 427, [1983] QB 741, decided after the date of Professor Williams' quoted work, this court considered a conviction for manslaughter arising where a defendant in the course of a quarrel in a queue hit another man, causing him to fall against an elderly woman who suffered a broken leg, an injury from which it appeared she was recovering until she suffered a pulmonary embolism which caused her death. No qualification of the sort

contended for was introduced in that case. The headnote of the case records the
decision of the court as follows:

> 'Held, dismissing the appeal, that to constitute the offence of manslaughter
> it was not necessary to establish that the unlawful and dangerous act was
> aimed at, or involved a direct attack or impact upon, the person who died;
> and that, accordingly, although the appellant had aimed no blow and had no
> physical contact with the woman who died, she was injured as a direct and
> immediate result of his act and died thereafter, and it was open to the jury to
> conclude that her death was caused by the appellant's act.' (See [1983] QB
> 741.)

Mr Hawkesworth has highlighted the words 'direct and immediate result' but the
context in which those words were used by Staughton J in giving the judgment
of the court was as follows ([1983] 2 All ER 427 at 432, [1983] QB 741 at 748):

> 'Although there was no direct contact between Mitchell and Mrs Crafts,
> she was injured as a direct and immediate result of his act. Thereafter her
> death occurred. The only question was one of causation: whether her death
> was caused by Mitchell's act. It was open to the jury to conclude that it was
> so caused; and they evidently reached that conclusion.'

We do not understand that the court was intending thereby to make the
'immediate' causing of injury a requirement of a conviction in such circumstances. In that particular case it was the fact that the injury was caused
immediately and the relevance of that fact was that the court did not have to
consider any questions of causation that might have arisen in different
circumstances.

Although not directly to the point, we find the approach of suggesting that
such matters go to causation of assistance. It is clear from *Mitchell*'s case that it is
unnecessary for the precise mechanism of death to be foreseen in manslaughter
and we are satisfied that the same is true for murder. We do not think it is right
or necessary to reintroduce any question of causation at the stage when mens rea
falls to be considered. Provided that the jury are satisfied that the death was
caused by the defendant's act, then we see no reason why the concept of
transferred malice should not operate.

Obviously, if the mode of death is utterly remote, there may be circumstances
in which this could be regarded as severing the chain of causation, but in the
instant case we cannot see that it should matter whether the child dies after birth
as a result of a stab wound suffered by the foetus before birth or as a result of
premature birth induced by the stabbing.

Equally, we can see no justification for the proposed qualification that some
degree of negligence towards the intended victim is required. Thus we can see
no reason to conclude that the doctrine of transferred malice is excluded in a
situation such as falls to be considered in the reference.

Manslaughter

The focus of our attention so far has been on the law relating to a charge of
murder. The reference also raises questions relating to a charge of manslaughter.
In the light of our conclusions relating to murder, we cannot see that any
different approach is required and none has been suggested to us in argument.
Clearly, the intention required for manslaughter will be less than that required to

a   establish murder but, with appropriate adjustment, we can see no reason to reach a different conclusion.

Recent authorities in other jurisdictions

We have been referred to two decisions in other jurisdictions where similar questions to those before us have arisen and it is helpful to consider them in the

b   light of our conclusions. In a Hong Kong case, *R v Kwok Chak Ming (No 1)* [1963] HKLR 226, the court was dealing with similar facts to those in this case, save that the cause of death was the stabbing of the foetus before it was born and not the inducing of premature birth. Jennings J, after reviewing much the same material as that placed before us, concluded that where a child is born alive but dies from an injury received before it is born, it could be murder and that accordingly there

c   was in that case a case to go before the jury. The Hong Kong Court of Appeal upheld that ruling saying ([1963] HKLR 349 at 354–355):

'In our view, when a baby is born alive but subsequently dies as a result of injury inflicted on it whilst in its mother's womb, the person inflicting those injuries may, when the other ingredients of murder or manslaughter are

d   present, be convicted of such a crime in respect of that child. It is, in our view, immaterial that, in such circumstances, the malice aforethought may have been directed against the mother rather than the child. The principle that where A, intending to kill or seriously injure B, unintentionally but, in pursuit of that purpose, kills C may be indicted for the murder of C, applies,

e   we think, with equal force even where C was only an embryo, or foetus at the time when the malice was manifested and the injury inflicted but is subsequently born alive and dies of the injury.'

It follows from what we have said that in that case we would have reached the same conclusion. The only way in which we would have departed from the

f   ruling of Jennings J was when he said in the course of his judgment (at 233):

'Since, however, it would be most unlikely in an ordinary case of stabbing for a person other than the one at whom the stab was directed to be grievously hurt by that stab, unless that person was pregnant, I would direct the jury that before it would be safe to convict the accused of the murder of

g   this child they would first have to be sure that the accused knew or ought to have known that the mother was pregnant at the time of the stabbing.'

This would be to introduce into the concept of transferred malice the requirement of negligence towards the actual victim which we have rejected.

The other decision is a Scottish case, *McCluskey v HM Advocate* [1989] RTR 182.

h   The case concerned a charge of causing death by reckless driving pursuant to s 1 of the Road Traffic Act 1972 (as amended), which provided: 'A person who causes the death of another person by the driving of a motor vehicle on a road recklessly … shall be guilty of an offence.'

The appellant had been convicted of causing the death of a child who had been

j   in utero at the time of an accident caused by the driving of the appellant but who had been born alive prematurely by caesarian section in consequence of the accident only to die from the injuries sustained in the accident whilst in utero. The High Court of Justiciary ruled that in such circumstances a conviction for the statutory offence was proper. There was nothing in the common law of either Scotland or England that required that culpable homicide in Scotland or manslaughter in England should be confined to the death of a person who was alive at the time when the injuries causing death were inflicted. Hence there was *a* no potential anomaly relating to this form of culpable homicide that might otherwise have required that 'the death of another person' must relate only to the death of a person alive at the time of the act of reckless driving. Whilst we recognise that our decision is more far-reaching than that conclusion, the two are at least consistent in their approach.

b

Conclusions

Our conclusions differ from those reached by the judge and it follows that we would have ruled that there was a case to go to the jury. That said, it should perhaps be recorded that on the state of the medical evidence, even before the defence raised any evidence of its own, it is far from clear that a jury was likely to be satisfied on the issue of causation. However, on our conclusions as to the law *c* the matter was one for the jury and not the judge.

It follows from the above that in our opinion the two questions posed in the reference should be answered in the following way. (1) Yes. Murder or manslaughter can be committed where unlawful injury is deliberately inflicted either to a child in utero or to a mother carrying a child in utero in the *d* circumstances postulated in the question. The requisite intent to be proved in the case of murder is an intention to kill or cause really serious bodily injury to the mother, the foetus before birth being viewed as an integral part of the mother. Such intention is appropriately modified in the case of manslaughter. (2) No. The fact that the death of the child is caused solely in consequence of injury to the mother rather than as a consequence of injury to the foetus does not negative any *e* liability for murder and manslaughter provided that the jury are satisfied that causation is proved.

Opinion accordingly. Leave to refer questions to the House of Lords granted.

N P Metcalfe Esq   Barrister.   *f*

a   # Imperial Chemical Industries plc v Colmer
     # (Inspector of Taxes)

HOUSE OF LORDS

b   LORD KEITH OF KINKEL, LORD BROWNE-WILKINSON, LORD MUSTILL, LORD NOLAN AND
     LORD NICHOLLS OF BIRKENHEAD

     30, 31 OCTOBER, 1 NOVEMBER 1995, 14 MARCH 1996

c   *Income tax – Company – Group relief – Entitlement – Consortium – Holding company
     – Business of company consisting mainly in holding of shares or securities of trading
     companies which were its 90% subsidiaries and which were not resident in United
     Kingdom – Whether 'holding company' for purposes of group relief – Whether group
     relief available only where holding company's 90% subsidiaries are resident in United
     Kingdom – Income and Corporation Taxes Act 1970, s 258(2)(5)(7).*

d
     The taxpayer company (ICI) owned 49% of the shares in a consortium which
     owned all the shares in a holding company (CAHH) which, in turn, held 100% of
     the shares in all but one of its 23 subsidiary trading companies. Both ICI and
     CAHH were incorporated in the United Kingdom, as were four of CAHH's
e   subsidiaries. A further six of CAHH's subsidiaries were resident in other member
     states of the European Union and the remaining 13 were resident outside the
     European Union. One of the UK subsidiaries made substantial trading losses in
     the years 1985, 1986 and 1987, which it surrendered to ICI, thereby allowing ICI
     to claim 'consortium relief', ie group relief, by reference to its 49% share in the
     consortium, under s 258(2)[a] of the Income and Corporation Taxes Act 1970,
f   which provided for tax relief on trading losses to be surrendered by a trading
     company owned by a consortium and claimed by another member of the
     consortium. The claim was rejected by the Revenue on the ground that CAHH
     was not a 'holding company' within s 258(5)(b) because its business did not
     consist wholly or mainly in the holding of shares or securities of trading
     companies, since under s 258(7) references in s 258 and the following sections to
g   'a company' were to be read as applying only to 'bodies corporate resident in the
     United Kingdom' with the result that CAHH was outside the ambit of s 258(5)(b)
     because of its non-resident subsidiaries. An appeal by ICI was dismissed by a
     special commissioner, but on a further appeal by ICI that decision was reversed
     by the judge on the grounds that the opening words of sub-s (7) identified those
h   companies which could benefit from the section rather than operating as a
     definition of 'company' wherever it appeared in the section. An appeal by the
     Crown was dismissed by the Court of Appeal, which held that the provisions of
     sub-ss (5)(b) and (7) represented two independent requirements which had to be
     satisfied in order to qualify for the relief and that sub-s (7) was not to be read into
j   the definition of 'holding company' in sub-s (5)(b). The Crown appealed to the
     House of Lords. ICI sought to support the Court of Appeal's decision on the
     ground that the Crown's construction conflicted not only with the provisions of
     the 1970 Act read alone but also with those provisions as construed in accordance

     ───
     a   Section 258(2), so far as material, is set out at p 26 *j* to p 27 *c*, post

with arts 52[b] and 58[c] of the EC Treaty, which enshrined the right to freedom of establishment for companies.

Held – When s 258 of the 1970 Act was considered alone, without reference to Community law, the opening words of sub-s (7) and their broad requirement that they should apply 'in this and the following sections' had to be read into all of the subsections of s 258, with the result that 'company' in the definition of 'holding company' in sub-s (5)(b) meant a company resident in the United Kingdom. It followed that so far as consortium relief was concerned, all members of the consortium had to be United Kingdom resident companies and the business of the holding company had to consist at least mainly in the holding of shares in United Kingdom resident trading subsidiaries. Since CAHH's business did not consist wholly or mainly in the holding of shares or securities of subsidiary companies resident in the United Kingdom, it was not a holding company within s 258(5)(b) and would not be entitled to consortium group relief. However, the 1970 Act had to be construed in a manner which avoided conflict with Community law, if such a construction was possible. In the instant case the applicability of arts 52 and 58 of the EC Treaty was not so obvious as to leave no scope for any reasonable doubt and, there being two possible constructions of the provisions of the 1970 Act, the applicability of arts 52 and 58 of the EC Treaty would be referred to the Court of Justice of the European Communities for consideration (see p 25 d to g, p 32 j to p 33 f, and p 34 e to g j, post).

Davies Jenkins & Co Ltd v Davies (Inspector of Taxes) [1967] 1 All ER 913 distinguished.

Notes

For group relief for consortia, see 23 *Halsbury's Laws* (4th edn reissue) para 942.

In relation to tax for companies' accounting periods ending after 5 April 1988, s 258 of the Income and Corporation Taxes Act 1970 was replaced by ss 402 and 413(2) to (6) of the Income and Corporation Taxes Act 1988. For ss 402 and 413 of the 1988 Act, see 44 *Halsbury's Statutes* (4th edn) (1993 reissue) 537, 553.

Cases referred to in opinions

CILFIT (Srl) and Lanificio di Gavardo SpA v Ministry of Health Case 283/81 [1982] ECR 3415.

Davies Jenkins & Co Ltd v Davies (Inspector of Taxes) [1967] 1 All ER 913, [1968] AC 1097, [1967] 2 WLR 1139, HL.

EC Commission v France Case 167/73 [1974] ECR 359.

F P H Finance Trust Ltd v IRC [1944] 1 All ER 653, [1944] AC 285, HL.

Mangin v IRC [1971] 1 All ER 179, [1971] AC 739, [1971] 2 WLR 39, PC.

---

b   Article 52, so far as material, provides: '... restrictions on the freedom of establishment of nationals of a Member State in the territory of another Member State shall be abolished by progressive stages ... Freedom of establishment shall include the right ... to set up and manage undertakings, in particular companies or firms within the meaning of the second paragraph of Article 58, under the conditions laid down for its own nationals by the law of the country where such establishment is effected ...'

c   Article 58, so far as material, provides: '... "Companies or firms" means companies or firms constituted under civil or commercial law, including co-operative societies, and other legal persons governed by public or private law, save for those which are non-profit-making.'

Appeal

a The Crown appealed from a decision of the Court of Appeal (Dillon, Stuart-Smith and Evans LJJ) ([1993] 4 All ER 705) of 15 July 1993 dismissing its appeal from a decision of Millett J ([1992] STC 51) of 5 December 1991 allowing an appeal by Imperial Chemical Industries plc (ICI) by way of a case stated by the Commissioner for the Special Purposes of the Income Tax Acts in respect of his

b decision given on 31 January 1990 that Coopers Animal Health (Holdings) Ltd, a company owned by ICI and another company, both of which were members of a consortium, was not a 'holding company' within s 258(5) of the Income and Corporation Taxes Act 1970 for the purposes of ICI's claim to group relief. The facts are set out in the opinion of Lord Nolan.

c *Alan Moses QC* and *Rabinder Singh* (instructed by the *Solicitor of Inland Revenue*) for the Crown.
   Peter Whiteman QC and *Christopher Vajda* (instructed by *Hammond Suddards*, Bradford) for ICI.

d Their Lordships took time for consideration.

14 March 1995. The following opinions were delivered.

LORD KEITH OF KINKEL. My Lords, for the reasons given in the speech to be delivered by my noble and learned friend Lord Nolan, which I have read in draft
e and with which I agree, I would make a reference to the Court of Justice of the European Communities under art 177 of the EC Treaty. The parties are invited to submit their proposals as to the precise form which the reference should take.

LORD BROWNE-WILKINSON. My Lords, I have read the speech of my noble
f and learned friend Lord Nolan, with which I agree. For the reasons which he gives, I, too, would refer the matter to the Court of Justice of the European Communities under art 177 of the EC Treaty.

LORD MUSTILL. My Lords, I have had the advantage of reading in draft the speech of my noble and learned friend Lord Nolan, with which I agree. For the
g reasons which he gives, I too would refer the matter to the Court of Justice of the European Communities under art 177 of the EC Treaty.

LORD NOLAN. My Lords, the facts of this case are straightforward and are not in dispute. They are as follows.
h Coopers Animal Health (Holdings) Ltd (CAHH) was incorporated on 17 May 1984. From that date its issued shares were owned beneficially as to 51% by the Wellcome Foundation Ltd and 49% by the respondent taxpayer, Imperial Chemical Industries plc (ICI).

CAHH carried on no business save that of holding shares in subsidiary
j companies trading in many parts of the world. Those subsidiaries were 23 in number. Four of them were resident in the United Kingdom, six resident in other member states of the European Union and the remaining 13 resident outside the European Union.

One of the four United Kingdom resident companies was Coopers Animal Health Ltd (CAH), which incurred substantial trading losses in carrying on its United Kingdom trade in each of its three accounting periods ending on 31

August 1985, 30 August 1986 and 29 August 1987. CAHH, ICI and the Wellcome
Foundation were, like CAH, all resident in the United Kingdom at all material   *a*
times. The question at issue is whether ICI is entitled to claim tax relief in respect
of the trading losses of CAH during those periods. The precise claim by ICI is that
it is entitled to set 49% of the losses for those periods (the proportion
corresponding to its shareholding in CAHH) against its chargeable profits for its
accounting periods ending on 31 December 1984, 1985, 1986 and 1987.   *b*

The relief which ICI seeks is that conferred by ss 258 to 264 of the Income and
Corporation Taxes Act 1970. (These provisions have been replaced by similar
provisions in the Income and Corporation Taxes Act 1988.) It is common ground
that the claim by ICI must succeed if CAHH is a holding company as defined by
s 258(5)(b), which reads:

  c

> '... "holding company" means a company the business of which consists
> wholly or mainly in the holding of shares or securities of companies which
> are its 90 per cent. subsidiaries, and which are trading companies ...'

The Crown contends that CAHH does not fall within this definition because of
the opening words of s 258(7), which read: *d*

> 'References in this and the following sections of this Chapter to a company
> apply only to bodies corporate resident in the United Kingdom ...'

The Crown submits that, as a result of these words, any reference to a
company or to companies in the relevant sections must be read as applying only   *e*
to a company or companies resident in the United Kingdom. On that basis,
although CAHH itself is a company resident in the United Kingdom, it does not
fall within the terms of sub-s (5)(b) because 19 of its 23 subsidiaries are resident
outside the United Kingdom. Therefore, it is submitted, the business of CAHH
cannot be said to consist wholly or mainly in the holding of shares or securities of
United Kingdom resident companies. This submission was upheld by the Special   *f*
Commissioner, Mr D C Potter QC ([1992] STC 51 at 52–56), but was rejected by
Millett J ([1992] STC 51) and by the Court of Appeal ([1993] 4 All ER 705).

The Crown now appeals to your Lordships' House. In its response, ICI
submits that the contentions of the Crown are in conflict not only with the
provisions of the 1970 Act read by themselves, but also with those provisions
when construed in accordance with Community law.   *g*

No reliance had been placed by ICI upon Community law in the proceedings
hitherto. I propose to approach the matter by first considering the opposing
arguments in the light of the relevant provisions of the 1970 Act when read by
themselves, as did the courts below, and then turning to the implications, if any,
of Community law.   *h*

Like all questions of construction, the question in the present case has to be
answered by reference to the relevant statutory provisions as a whole. The full
terms of s 258 (as amended by s 40(1) and (2) of the Finance Act 1981 and s 46(2)
of the Finance Act 1984) are:

> '(1) Relief for trading losses and other amounts eligible for relief from   *j*
> corporation tax may in accordance with the following provisions of this
> Chapter be surrendered by a company (called "the surrendering company")
> which is a member of a group of companies and, on the making of a claim by
> another company (called "the claimant company") which is a member of the
> same group, may be allowed to the claimant company by way of a relief from
> corporation tax called "group relief".

a

(2) Group relief shall also be available in accordance with the said provisions in the case of a surrendering company and a claimant company where either of them is a member of a consortium and the other is—(a) a trading company which is owned by the consortium and which is not a 75 per cent. subsidiary of any company; or (b) a trading company—(i) which is a 90 per cent. subsidiary of a holding company which is owned by the

b

consortium; and (ii) which is not a 75 per cent. subsidiary of a company other than the holding company; or ... (c) a holding company which is owned by the consortium and which is not a 75 per cent. subsidiary of any company: Provided that a claim shall not be made by virtue of this subsection if the share in the consortium of the member in the relevant accounting period of the surrendering company (or, where that company is a trading company

c

falling within paragraph (b) above, its holding company) is nil or if a profit on a sale of the share capital of the other company or its holding company which the member owns would be treated as a trading receipt of that member.

(3) Subject to the following sections of this Chapter, two or more claimant companies may make claims relating to the same surrendering company, and to the same accounting period of that surrendering company.

d

(4) A payment for group relief—(a) shall not be taken into account in computing profits or losses of either company for corporation tax purposes, and (b) shall not for any of the purposes of the Corporation Tax Acts be regarded as a distribution or a charge on income, and in this subsection "payment for group relief" means a payment made by the claimant company to the surrendering company in pursuance of an agreement between them

e

as respects an amount surrendered by way of group relief, being a payment not exceeding that amount.

(5) For the purpose of this section and the following sections of this Chapter—(a) two companies shall be deemed to be members of a group of companies if one is the 75 per cent. subsidiary of the other or both are 75 per

f

cent. subsidiaries of a third company, (b) "holding company" means a company the business of which consists wholly or mainly in the holding of shares or securities of companies which are its 90 per cent. subsidiaries, and which are trading companies, (c) "trading company" means a company whose business consists wholly or mainly of the carrying on of a trade or

g

trades.

(6) In applying for the said purposes the definition of "75 per cent. subsidiary" in section 532 of this Act any share capital of a registered industrial and provident society shall be treated as ordinary share capital.

(7) References in this and the following sections of this Chapter to a

h

company apply only to bodies corporate resident in the United Kingdom; and in determining for the purposes of this and the following sections of this Chapter whether one company is a 75 per cent. subsidiary of another, the other company shall be treated as not being the owner—(a) of any share capital which it owns directly in a body corporate if a profit on a sale of the shares would be treated as a trading receipt of its trade, or (b) of any share

j

capital which it owns indirectly, and which is owned directly by a body corporate for which a profit on the sale of the shares would be a trading receipt, or (c) of any share capital which it owns directly or indirectly in a body corporate not resident in the United Kingdom.

(8) For the purposes of this and the following sections of this Chapter, a company is owned by a consortium if three-quarters or more of the ordinary share capital of the company is beneficially owned between them by

companies of which none beneficially owns less than one-twentieth of that capital, and those companies are called the members of the consortium.'

Section 259(1), so far as relevant, reads as follows:

'If in any accounting period the surrendering company has incurred a loss, computed as for the purposes of subsection (2) of section 177 of this Act, in carrying on a trade, the amount of the loss may be set off for the purposes of corporation tax against the total profits of the claimant company for its corresponding accounting period ...'

Subsections (2), (3) and (6) extend the relief to cases where the surrendering company is entitled to capital allowances, or has incurred expenses of management or charges on income (such as interest payments) in excess of its income. Subsection (8), dealing with members of a consortium, provides (as substituted by s 40(3) and (7) of the 1981 Act):

'In applying any of the preceding subsections in the case of a claim made by virtue of section 258(2) above—(a) where the claimant company is a member of a consortium only a fraction of the loss referred to in subsection (1) above, or of the excess referred to in subsection (2), (3) or (6) above, as the case may be, may be set off under the subsection in question; (b) where the surrendering company is a member of a consortium that loss or excess shall not be set off under the subsection in question against more than a fraction of the total profits of the claimant company; and that fraction shall be equal to that member's share in the consortium in the accounting period referred to in section 258(2) above ...'

Thus it will be seen that, in the terms of s 258(8), CAHH is owned by a consortium consisting of ICI and the Wellcome Foundation. ICI is therefore entitled, by virtue of s 258(2) and s 259(1) and (8)(a), to relief in respect of its 49% share in the consortium for the trading losses suffered by CAH provided, and provided always, that CAHH is a holding company within the meaning of s 258(5)(b). And this, as I have said, depends upon whether s 258(7) requires the word 'companies' at the end of sub-s (5)(b) to be read as meaning 'bodies corporate resident in the United Kingdom'.

Was this the purpose that Parliament intended to achieve by the words used? The evident purpose of s 258(1) was to enable a parent company and its 75% subsidiaries to be treated as a single entity for tax purposes, merging the profits and the losses of individual members of the group in order to arrive at the taxable profit (if any). It is to be noted that in the case of what might be called ordinary group relief under s 258(1) the relief which may be claimed is not limited to the extent of the equity participation: a claim for 100% of the loss may be made under s 259(1) even if the equity participation is no more than 75%. Thus, to take the simple case where company A holds 75% and company B holds 25% of the shares in company C, company A can claim group relief in respect of the whole of company C's losses, irrespective of the 25% holding of company B, and irrespective, for that matter, of whether company B is resident or non-resident in the United Kingdom.

The extension of the concept of group relief to a consortium of companies under s 258(2) was presumably intended to encourage and facilitate the ad hoc merger of a number of different corporate interests in a single common enterprise. Under the terms of s 258(2) and (8) the relief depends upon the members of the consortium owning between them at least 75% of the shares in a company (which I shall call the 'consortium company') with none of them owning less than 5% of those shares. In this instance, however, the relief available is limited by s 259(8) by reference to the share in the consortium owned by the surrendering or claimant company. That is why ICI's claim in the present case is limited to 49% of the losses of CAH. But even so, the amount of the loss in respect of which relief is claimed could in certain cases be greater than the consortium member's share. Thus in the present case—and subject always to CAHH qualifying as a holding company within the meaning of s 258(5)(b)—ICI could still have made a claim in respect of 49% of the whole of the losses of CAH even if CAH had been owned as to only 90% by CAHH (see s 258(2)(b)(i)). Once again, the interest, and for that matter the residence, of the minority shareholder or shareholders would be ignored.

Thus both ordinary group relief under s 258(1) and consortium group relief under s 285(2) produce the result that the claimant and surrendering company may merge their profits and losses for United Kingdom tax purposes at least to the extent of the equity participation, direct or indirect, of the one in the other and sometimes to a somewhat greater extent. But this can only be done if they are both resident in the United Kingdom, because the opening words of s 258(7) make it plain that ss 258 and 259 only apply to such bodies. This has the effect of ruling out a claim by a body corporate which, although trading in the United Kingdom and therefore liable to United Kingdom tax, is not a United Kingdom resident.

Do the opening words of sub-s (7) have any wider effect? The Crown contends that, on their plain meaning, they have the effect of qualifying every reference to a company, or companies, in s 258 and the following sections. It follows that this qualification applies to the companies which are to be deemed to be members of a group under sub-s (5)(a), to each of the companies which form a consortium within the meaning of sub-ss (2) and (8), and to the holding company and the 90% subsidiary trading companies in the holding of whose shares its business wholly or mainly consists as described in sub-s (5)(b).

Millett J rejected the argument for the Crown because in his view it wrongly treated the opening words of sub-s (7) as definitive. He said ([1992] STC 51 at 58):

'In my judgment the Crown's submission confuses the meaning of the statutory language with its application. Statutes are not academic exercises in linguistics. They have external application, affecting real people and actual situations. If Parliament wishes to limit the scope of a statute so as to exclude a given situation from its application, it can do so in either of two ways. It can employ suitably restricted words in the operative provisions so that the particular situation does not come within them; or it can employ words apt to include the situation but direct that they should none the less not apply to it. In the opening words of sub-s (7) Parliament has adopted the latter technique. In my judgment, the opening words of sub-s (7) cut down the operation of s 258 to cases where the surrendering company and the claimant company are bodies corporate resident in the United Kingdom.'

In other words, Millett J treated the opening words of sub-s (7) as identifying the companies which could take advantage of the section, rather than as a definition of the word 'company' whenever it appeared in the section. In the Court of Appeal Dillon and Evans LJJ, with both of whom Stuart-Smith LJ agreed, reached the same conclusion though on slightly different grounds. Both were strongly influenced by the views expressed in your Lordships' House in *Davies Jenkins & Co Ltd v Davies (Inspector of Taxes)* [1967] 1 All ER 913, [1968] AC 1097, a

case decided under s 20 of the Finance Act 1953. Subsection (9) of that section
provided that for the purposes of the section 'company' included any body   *a*
corporate, but that references to a company should be taken to apply only to a
company resident in the United Kingdom and carrying on a trade wholly or partly
in the United Kingdom. Subsection (10) provided, again 'for the purposes of this
section', that a company making a subvention payment to another should be
treated as the other's associated company if, but only if, at all times between the   *b*
beginning of the payee company's accounting period in respect of which the
payment was made and the making of the payment one of them was a subsidiary
of the other or both were subsidiaries of a third company. The question that
arose was whether the requirement in sub-s (9) that references to a 'company'
should be taken to apply only to a trading company had to be read into sub-s (10),
with the result that for the section to apply both the payer and the payee   *c*
company had to continue to be trading companies up to the time when the
subvention payment was actually made, a condition which the payee company in
that case failed to satisfy.

The majority of their Lordships took the view that sub-ss (9) and (10) set forth
two qualifications, both of which had to be satisfied but which were independent   *d*
of each other. It followed that the provisions of sub-s (9) should not be read into
sub-s (10).

Adopting the same approach to the provisions of s 258(5)(b) and the opening
words of sub-s (7) in the present case, Dillon and Evans LJJ concluded that they
represented independent qualifications, and that the latter should not be read into
the former (see [1993] 4 All ER 705 at 711–712, 714).   *e*

I confess that I for my part cannot derive the same assistance from the views
expressed in the *Davies* case. It certainly provides an illustration, in a context not
very far removed from that of the present case, of the proposition that two
qualifying clauses in the same section need not necessarily be read together even
though both are introduced by the words 'for the purposes of this section'. The   *f*
question remains whether the language of the relevant provisions in the present
case allows or requires that result to be reached.

In argument before us, each of the parties pointed to the surprising and
apparently inexplicable results which would follow from the construction
advocated by the other. The strongest points made by Mr Moses QC for the
Crown in this connection appeared to me to be these.   *g*

First, he said, the taxpayer company's construction made nonsense of the
ordinary group relief provisions of s 258(1). For if one ignored the opening words
of sub-s (7) in determining whether the claimant and the surrendering company
were members of a group of companies within the meaning of sub-s (5)(a), then
it would follow that two resident subsidiaries of a non-resident parent company   *h*
could qualify as members of a group; but if the shares of the non-resident parent
were held by a United Kingdom resident company the provisions of sub-s (7)(c)
would exclude that company from the group relationship. This, submitted Mr
Moses, was a result which Parliament could hardly have intended to achieve. Put
positively, his submission was that the opening words of sub-s (7) could not
sensibly be confined to the surrendering company and the claimant company   *j*
referred to in sub-s (1) but must also govern the question whether the two
companies were members of a group of companies within the meaning of the
subsection. They must therefore be read into sub-s (5)(a) no less than sub-s (1).

Secondly, turning to the case of consortium relief under sub-s (2), Mr Moses
submitted that ICI's argument could not be reconciled with the apparent
legislative purpose. If ICI were right, the opening words of sub-s (7) applied to

a the claimant company and the surrendering company, and possibly to the holding company, but not to the other members of the consortium. From that it would follow that a United Kingdom resident member of the consortium could claim relief even if it only held 5% of the shares in the consortium company and the rest were held by non-resident companies. But that would make nonsense of the requirement, in sub-s (8), that the other members should be companies.

b There could be no reason why they should not be individuals or partnerships. Further, there would be no sense in the requirement that 75% of the ordinary shares in the consortium company should be owned by the members of the consortium. But if the Crown were right, consortium relief was confined to the case where at least 75% of the consortium company was held by a consortium which consisted entirely of United Kingdom resident bodies corporate, and

c which could thus be equated to a single composite United Kingdom resident company. This, submitted Mr Moses, was an intelligible concept in itself, and was in line with the concept of 75% ownership by a United Kingdom resident company which, in the Crown's submission, formed the basis of ordinary group relief. I notice, incidentally, though Mr Moses placed no reliance upon it, that the

d group income provisions which form part of the same chapter as the group relief provisions (Ch I of Pt XI of the 1970 Act), and which also deal with consortia, require all consortium members to be resident in the United Kingdom (see s 256(6)(c)).

The contrary view is summarised in the following passage from the judgment of Dillon LJ (at 711–712):

e

'This scheme is clearly designed to be applied only to companies which are resident in the United Kingdom. It is the intention to exclude companies not so resident, no doubt because they are subject to foreign and not United Kingdom tax law. But I do not see that that makes it necessary that the

f subsidiaries that a holding company has to have to qualify as a holding company under sub-s (5) must be wholly or mainly resident in the United Kingdom. The trading subsidiary which is the surrendering company under sub-s (2) must be resident in the United Kingdom and so must the claimant company and the holding company itself, because the effect on sub-s (2) of the opening words in sub-s (7) so requires. But where other subsidiaries of

g the holding company, in no way involved in the surrender of losses and claim for relief, are resident seems to be a matter of indifference. Indeed the use of the words "wholly or mainly" in the definition of "holding company" in sub-s (5) would seem to indicate that even on the Crown's argument relief would not be lost if the holding company had a minority of subsidiaries

h which were not resident in the United Kingdom. I cannot see why it should be relevant and make a difference in the result, if a majority and not a minority, of the holding company's subsidiaries are resident outside the United Kingdom; none of the subsidiaries not resident in the United Kingdom will be surrendering tax losses or making claims to consortium

j relief. In my judgment the definition of "holding company" in sub-s (5) and the opening words in sub-s (7) requiring companies to be resident in the United Kingdom are independent "qualifications" just as the requirements of sub-ss (9) and (10) in the section in the *Davies'* case were independent qualifications. That being so, since to require all or the majority of 90% subsidiaries of a holding company to be resident in the United Kingdom seems to be an irrational restriction in the scheme, I would hold that, in the context, the opening words of sub-s (7) are satisfied by being applied to the

surrendering company, the claimant company and the holding company
under sub-s (2) and do not have to be infused (as Lord Morris put it in the
Davies case [1967] 1 All ER 913 at 921, [1968] AC 1097 at 1119) into the
definition in sub-s (5).'

Evans LJ put the point succinctly in the earlier part of his judgment, before he
considered the effect of the *Davies* case, in these terms (at 715):

'We were told that statutory provisions corresponding with s 258(1) and
(2) introduced first the concept of group relief and then of consortium relief,
within the limits provided for. The question which naturally arises is: who
may take advantage of these provisions? Put another way: to whom do the
provisions apply? In my judgment, that is the question to which sub-s (7)
gives the answer. The section applies only to United Kingdom resident
companies. "References ... to a company" are to United Kingdom resident
companies only. In the result, therefore, sub-s (7) is concerned with the
application of the section and it may be said to provide a definition of
"company" which applies to the companies claiming and surrendering the
tax relief and perhaps the holding company also. But it does not follow that
it also defines "companies" where that word appears in the definition of
"holding company", and in my judgment it does not.'

The force of these considerations is much enhanced, to my mind, when one
comes to consider the practical difficulties to which the Crown's construction of
s 258(5)(b) may give rise. In the present case it appears to have been accepted by
ICI from the outset that if the Crown were right in saying that account could only
be taken under sub-s (5)(b) of 90% subsidiaries resident in the United Kingdom
then CAHH was disqualified simply on the basis of a head count. That is to say,
since 19 of its 23 subsidiaries were non-resident, its business could not be said to
consist 'wholly or mainly' in the holding of shares in United Kingdom resident
companies. But what if the numbers had been more evenly balanced? What if
there were, say, eight resident and eight non-resident subsidiaries? Mr Moses
acknowledged that mere numbers could not be decisive and that other factors,
such as turnover, might have to be taken into account. But there remains the
difficulty that turnover will fluctuate from one period to another. As Mr
Whiteman QC submitted on behalf of ICI, it would be highly unsatisfactory if
sub-s (5)(b) produced the result that the company in question could be a holding
company one year, but not the next, 'popping in and out of inland revenue
pigeon holes as trade was bad or good', to adopt the memorable phrase used by
Lord Atkin in *FPH Finance Trust Ltd v IRC* [1944] 1 All ER 653 at 661, [1944] AC 285
at 306.

I was at first inclined to think that this consideration must be regarded as
determining this issue in favour of ICI. For, as Lord Donovan said in *Mangin v
IRC* [1971] 1 All ER 179 at 182, [1971] AC 739 at 746:

'... the object of the construction of a statute being to ascertain the will of
the legislature, it may be presumed that neither injustice nor absurdity was
intended. If therefore a literal interpretation would produce such a result,
and the language admits of an interpretation which would avoid it, then such
an interpretation may be adopted.'

On reflection, however, I have concluded that whatever the difficulties may
be of applying sub-s (5)(b) in particular cases on the basis of the Crown's
construction, the result cannot be characterised as either unjust or absurd. The

a task of deciding whether the business of a particular company consists wholly or mainly in the holding of shares in 90% United Kingdom resident trading subsidiaries is not to my mind inherently so difficult as to be beyond the wit of appeal commissioners. The question should, of course, like that in *FPH Finance*, be answered by reference to all the factors, considered over a reasonable period of time.

b   Further, I am not satisfied that the language of the 1970 Act permits the construction for which ICI contends. That construction can only be upheld by confining the scope of the opening words of sub-s (7) to sub-ss (1) and (2) of s 258, a limitation which is very hard to reconcile with the broad requirement that they should apply 'in this and the following sections of this Chapter'. To confine their application to sub-ss (1) and (2) seems to me to be impermissibly selective, and

c unnatural. The provisions of sub-ss (1) and (2) seem to me inevitably to incorporate those of sub-ss (5) and (8). The former cannot be understood without reference to the latter and from this it must follow, to my mind, that the opening words of sub-s (7) should be read into all of them. The consequential proposition, so far as consortium relief is concerned, that all members of the consortium must

d be United Kingdom resident companies, appears to me, for the reasons given by Mr Moses, to be less surprising than the proposition that a 5% participation by a United Kingdom resident company was intended to suffice as a qualification. The proposition that the business of the holding company must consist at least mainly in the holding of shares in United Kingdom resident subsidiaries is also one which I find difficult to describe as surprising, let alone absurd or unjust. The fact that

e relief may be obtained despite some limited non-resident participation in the corporate structure is in no way inconsistent with the principle that the United Kingdom resident element should predominate throughout that structure. And the final requirement in sub-s (5)(b) that the subsidiaries should be trading companies again suggests that only United Kingdom resident subsidiaries were

f intended to be included. For if they were non-resident it would be irrelevant whether they were trading or not. Accordingly, apart from considerations of Community law, I would hold that the Crown's construction should be upheld.

It remains to consider whether this construction conflicts with the obligations of the United Kingdom under Community law. The argument that it does so is put forward in reliance upon arts 52 and 58 of the EC Treaty, which are directed

g against restrictions on the freedom of establishment of nationals (including companies) of one member state in the territory of another.

The argument may be illustrated in the context of the present case by assuming that CAHH had been formed with two 90% United Kingdom resident trading subsidiaries. At that stage it would clearly be a holding company within the

h meaning of sub-s (5)(b) and consortium relief would be available. If, however, it formed three further trading subsidiaries resident respectively in France, Germany and Italy, then on the basis of the Crown's construction it would cease to be a holding company and ICI and Wellcome could no longer claim consortium relief. (This example assumes that the 'wholly or mainly' test depends merely on the number of resident and non-resident subsidiaries, which

j is an over-simplification for the reasons which I have given, but which will serve for the purposes of illustration.) It is submitted that this represents the imposition of a discriminatory tax regime upon ICI and Wellcome—and, for that matter, upon CAHH—and thus a restriction upon their freedom of establishment.

In reply, Mr Moses submitted firstly that the point did not arise, because although a majority of subsidiaries of CAHH were non-resident, only a minority of them were resident in the European Union. The issue raised by ICI was therefore hypothetical, and should not be addressed unless and until it arose in *a* practice.

More generally, Mr Moses submitted that the difference in treatment which was shown in the example put forward by ICI was simply a difference in the treatment of United Kingdom resident companies under United Kingdom tax law. It resulted from the establishment of non-resident subsidiaries, but it was wholly immaterial for this purpose whether the subsidiaries were resident in the *b* European Union or elsewhere. Accordingly, no question of Community law arose.

On behalf of ICI, Mr Whiteman and Mr Vajda submitted that the point must be addressed in order to determine the scope and validity of s 258(5)(b), irrespective of the factual position in the present case. It must be addressed because if the construction placed by the Crown on s 258 (5)(b) were correct then *c* it would follow that, in the submission of ICI, the United Kingdom was in breach of its obligations under Community law. Reliance was placed in this connection on the approach adopted by the Court of Justice of the European Communities in *EC Commission v France* Case 167/73 [1974] ECR 359. It was unnecessary, continued counsel, to refer the matter to the Court of Justice under art 177 of the *d* EC Treaty because, in the words used by the court in *Srl CILFIT and Lanificio di Gavardo SpA v Ministry of Health* Case 283/81 [1982] ECR 3415 at 3431 (para 21), the answer was 'so obvious as to leave no scope for any reasonable doubt'. In other words, the doctrine of *acte clair* applied. But if there were any doubt about the matter, a reference fell to be made.

For my part, I am quite unable to accept that ICI is entitled to invoke the *e* doctrine of *acte clair*. On the contrary, I have considerable sympathy with the submissions of Mr Moses on both of the points which he raises. I feel compelled, however, to accept that the conditions which require us to refer the matter to the Court of Justice are satisfied. For in the first place there can be no doubt of our obligation to construe the 1970 Act in a manner which avoids conflict with *f* Community law, if such a construction is possible. Secondly, the judgments in the courts below have the effect, if only incidentally, of avoiding any risk of such a conflict; and they plainly constitute a possible view of the law, albeit one which, with some hesitation, I have felt unable to accept. And finally, the applicability of arts 52 and 58 in the circumstances of the present case seems to be to be undeniably a matter for the consideration of the Court of Justice. *g*

At the close of argument counsel for ICI put before us a draft of the questions which might form the subject of a reference, but the draft was not discussed in any detail. I would propose accordingly, subject to your Lordships' views, that the parties be invited to discuss and, if possible, agree upon the precise form of the questions, and to present a draft or drafts to your Lordships for consideration *h* at a further hearing. The question of costs might conveniently form the subject of submissions at the same time.

LORD NICHOLLS OF BIRKENHEAD. My Lords, for the reasons set out in the speech of my noble and learned friend Lord Nolan, with which I agree, I too *j* would make a reference to the Court of Justice of the European Communities.

Order accordingly.

Susan J Murphy   Barrister.

John v MGN Ltd

a

COURT OF APPEAL, CIVIL DIVISION
SIR THOMAS BINGHAM MR, NEILL AND HIRST LJJ
14–16, 20, 21 NOVEMBER, 12 DECEMBER 1995

b

Libel and slander – Damages – Direction to jury – Matters to which trial judge may refer in summing up – Whether permissible to refer to previous awards of Court of Appeal on appeal from excessive jury awards – Whether permissible to refer to previous jury awards in defamation actions or to awards made in personal injury actions –
c *Whether judge and counsel entitled to indicate to jury appropriate level of award – Whether award excessive.*

Libel and slander – Exemplary or punitive damages – Principles on which exemplary damages awarded – Insufficiency of compensatory damages – Test of recklessness – Newspaper libelling well-known singer – Whether publisher having no genuine belief in
d *truth of words published, suspecting words were untrue and deliberately refraining from checking – Whether award of compensatory damages adequately reflecting gravity of defendant's conduct – Whether exemplary damages award excessive.*

In December 1992 a national newspaper published an article about the plaintiff, a well-known singer and musician. A photograph of the plaintiff appeared on the
e front page together with the words 'World exclusive' and 'Elton's "diet of death"'. The article itself, located inside, alleged that the plaintiff was on a bizarre diet which involved him chewing food then spitting it out without swallowing, and that he had been observed at a party in Los Angeles spitting chewed food into a napkin. The article quoted the opinions of certain medical practitioners who
f regarded such behaviour as a form of bulimia, a potentially fatal eating disorder. The plaintiff commenced a libel action against the publishers of the newspaper and before trial amended the statement of claim to seek exemplary damages, on the basis, inter alia, that they had made no effort to verify the accuracy of the story by ascertaining whether the plaintiff had attended the party in question. At the trial the judge ruled that there was sufficient evidence of recklessness by the
g defendants to refer to the jury in relation to exemplary damages. The jury awarded damages of £350,000 to the plaintiff, comprising £75,000 compensatory damages and £275,000 exemplary damages. The defendants appealed on the grounds, inter alia, that: (i) the judge had misdirected the jury on the way they should approach the question whether they should award exemplary damages
h and that there was insufficient evidence of recklessness to leave the issue to the jury; and (ii) the sums awarded under both headings were grossly excessive.

Held – (1) When assessing compensatory damages in a defamation case a jury could in future properly be referred by way of comparison to the conventional
j compensation scales in personal injury cases as well as to previous libel awards made or approved by the Court of Appeal, and there was no reason why the judge, in his directions, or counsel should not indicate to the jury the level of award which they considered appropriate. Those changes of practice would not undermine but rather buttress the constitutional role of the libel jury by rendering their proceedings more rational and so more acceptable to public opinion. In the instant case, the directions to the jury were sufficient within the

existing guidelines to give them the assistance they required, but the size of the *a* award itself was excessive, because, although the article was false, offensive and distressing, it had not attacked the plaintiff's personal integrity or damaged his reputation as an artist. The court would accordingly substitute a figure of £25,000 (see p 51 *d* to *f*, p 52 *a* to *c*, p 54 *a* to *e*, p 55 *d* to *g* and p 59 *j* to p 60 *d*, post); *Cassell & Co Ltd v Broome* [1972] 1 All ER 801, *Sutcliffe v Pressdram Ltd* [1990] 1 All ER 269 and *Rantzen v Mirror Group Newspapers (1986) Ltd* [1993] 4 All ER 975 considered. *b*

(2) Where exemplary damages were claimed, the judge should give additional guidance to the jury to make it clear that before such damages could be awarded they had to be satisfied that the publisher had no genuine belief in the truth of what he published, but suspected that the words were untrue and deliberately refrained from taking obvious steps which, if taken, would have turned suspicion into certainty. It was only where the conditions for making an exemplary award *c* were satisfied, and only when the sum awarded to the plaintiff as compensatory damages was not in itself sufficient to punish the defendant and deter him and others from acting similarly that an award of exemplary damages should be added to an award of compensatory damages. On the facts, the defendants' total failure to check the story clearly constituted recklessness, with the result that the *d* judge had been right to refer the issue to the jury. Further, an award of exemplary damages was appropriate, since the award of compensatory damages was not sufficient adequately to reflect the gravity of the defendants' conduct, punish the newspaper and deter it and others from acting similarly. In the circumstances, however, the award of £275,000 was excessive and would be substituted with an award of £50,000, which was enough to ensure that justice was done to both sides *e* and would fully secure the public interest (see p 57 *j* to p 58 *f*, p 60 *j* to p 61 *a h* to p 62 *b h* and p 64 *e* to *h*, post); *Cassell & Co Ltd v Broome* [1972] 1 All ER 801 applied; *Riches v News Group Newspapers Ltd* [1985] 2 All ER 845 considered.

Notes   *f*
For the basis of an award of damages for libel and slander generally, see 28 *Halsbury's Laws* (4th edn) para 235, and for exemplary damagess, see ibid para 243.

Cases referred to in judgment
A-G v Guardian Newspapers Ltd (No 2) [1988] 3 All ER 545, [1990] 1 AC 109, [1988] *g*
    3 WLR 776, HL.
Carson v John Fairfax & Sons Ltd (1993) 178 CLR 44, Aust HC.
Cassell & Co Ltd v Broome [1972] 1 All ER 801, [1972] AC 1027, [1972] 2 WLR 645,
    HL.
Coyne v Citizen Finance Ltd (1991) 172 CLR 211, Aust HC.   *h*
Derbyshire CC v Times Newspapers Ltd [1993] 1 All ER 1011, [1993] AC 534, [1993] 2
    WLR 449, HL.
Derry v Peek (1889) 14 App Cas 337, [1886–90] All ER Rep 1, HL.
Gorman v Mudd [1992] CA Transcript 1076.
Houston v Smith [1993] CA Transcript 1544.   *j*
McCarey v Associated Newspapers Ltd (No 2) [1964] 3 All ER 947, [1965] 2 QB 86,
    [1965] 2 WLR 45, CA.
Manson v Associated Newspapers Ltd [1965] 2 All ER 954, [1965] 1 WLR 1038.
Praed v Graham (1889) 24 QBD 53, CA.
Rantzen v Mirror Group Newspapers (1986) Ltd [1993] 4 All ER 975, [1994] QB 670,
    [1993] 3 WLR 953, CA.

a Riches v News Group Newspapers Ltd [1985] 2 All ER 845, [1986] QB 256, [1985] 3
   WLR 432, CA.
   Rookes v Barnard [1964] 1 All ER 367, [1964] AC 1129, [1964] 2 WLR 269, HL.
   Sutcliffe v Pressdram Ltd [1990] 1 All ER 269, [1991] 1 QB 153, [1990] 2 WLR 271,
   CA.
   Tolstoy Miloslavsky v UK (1995) 20 EHRR 442, ECt HR.
b Uren v John Fairfax & Sons Pty Ltd (1966) 117 CLR 118, Aust HC.
   Walker v Shehan [1995] CA Transcript 1092.
   Ward v James [1965] 1 All ER 563, [1966] 1 QB 273, [1965] 2 WLR 455, CA.

Cases also cited or referred to in skeleton arguments

   AB v South West Water Services Ltd [1992] 4 All ER 574, [1993] QB 507, CA.
c Abbassy v Comr of Police of the Metropolis [1990] 1 All ER 193, [1990] 1 WLR 385, CA.
   Baden v Société Générale pour Favoriser le Développement du Commerce et de l'Industrie
   en France SA [1992] 4 All ER 161, [1993] 1 WLR 509.
   Black v North British Rly Co 1908 SC 444, Ct of Sess.
   Blackshaw v Lord [1983] 2 All ER 311, [1984] QB 1, CA.
d Bray v Ford [1896] AC 44, [1895–9] All ER Rep 1009, HL.
   Broadway Approvals Ltd v Odhams Press Ltd (No 2) [1965] 2 All ER 523, [1965] 1 WLR
   805, CA.
   Coloca v BP Australia Ltd (1992) 2 VR 441, Vict SC.
   Day v Woodworth (1850) 13 How 363, US SC.
   Donselaar v Donselaar [1982] 1 NZLR 97, NZ CA.
e Egger v Viscount Chelmsford [1964] 3 All ER 406, [1965] 1 QB 248, CA.
   Fielding v Variety Inc [1967] 2 All ER 497, [1967] 2 QB 841, CA.
   Hague v Deputy Governor of Parkhurst Prison, Weldon v Home Office [1991] 3 All ER
   733, [1992] 1 AC 58, HL.
   Hayward v Thompson [1981] 3 All ER 450, [1982] QB 47, CA.
f Heatons Transport (St Helens) Ltd v Transport and General Workers Union [1972] 3 All
   ER 101, [1973] AC 15, HL.
   Hennessy v Wright (No 2) [1888] 24 QBD 445, CA.
   Hill v Church of Scientology of Toronto (1994) 114 DLR (4th) 1, Ont CA.
   Horrocks v Lowe [1974] 1 All ER 662, [1975] AC 135, HL.
   Kiam v Neill [1994] EMLR 1, CA.
g Lamb v Cotogno (1987) 164 CLR 1, Aust HC.
   Lloyd v Grace Smith & Co [1912] AC 716, [1911–13] All ER Rep 51, HL.
   Maxwell v Pressdram (No 2) (1986) Times, 22 November; CA.
   Meridian Global Funds Management Asia Ltd v Securities Commission [1995] 3 All ER
   918, [1995] 2 AC 500, PC.
h Moore v News of the World Ltd [1972] 1 All ER 915, [1972] 1 QB 441, CA.
   Moussell Bros Ltd v London and North-Western Rly Co [1917] 2 KB 836, [1916–17] All
   ER Rep 1101, DC.
   New York Times Co v Sullivan (1964) 376 US 254, US SC.
   R v Adomako [1994] 3 All ER 79, [1994] 3 WLR 288, HL.
j R v Caldwell [1981] 1 All ER 961, [1982] AC 341, HL.
   R v Chief Metropolitan Stipendiary Magistrate, ex p Choudhury [1991] 1 All ER 306,
   [1991] 1 QB 429, DC.
   R v Cunningham [1957] 2 All ER 412, [1957] 2 QB 396, CCA.
   R v P & O European Ferries (Dover) Ltd (1990) 93 Cr App R 72.
   R v Savage [1991] 2 All ER 220, [1992] 1 AC 699, CA; affd R v Savage, R v Parmenter
   [1991] 4 All ER 698, [1992] 1 AC 699, HL.

Racz v Home Office [1994] 1 All ER 97, [1994] 2 AC 45, HL.

Ready Mixed Concrete (South East) Ltd v Minister of Pensions and National Insurance [1968] 1 All ER 433, [1968] 2 QB 497.

Robitaille v Vancouver Hockey Club (1981) 114 DLR (3d) 228, BC CA.

Rowland-Jones v City and Westminster Financial plc [1992] CA Transcript 639.

Royal Brunei Airlines Sdn Bhd v Tan [1995] 3 All ER 97, [1995] 2 AC 378, PC.

Seaboard Offshore Ltd v Secretary of State for Transport [1994] 2 All ER 99, [1994] 1 WLR 541, HL.

Sunday Times v UK (No 1) [1979] 2 EHRR 245, ECt HR.

Sunday Times v UK (No 2) (1991) 14 EHRR 229, ECt HR.

Taylor v Beere [1982] 1 NZLR 81, NZ CA.

Tesco Stores Ltd v Brent London BC [1993] 2 All ER 718, [1993] 1 WLR 1037, DC.

Tesco Supermarkets Ltd v Nattrass [1971] 2 All ER 127, [1972] AC 153, HL.

Times Newspapers Ltd v UK (5 March 1990, unreported), ECt HR.

Vane v Yiannopoullos [1964] 3 All ER 820, [1965] AC 486, HL.

Vorvis v Insurance Corp of British Columbia (1989) 58 DLR (4th) 193, Can SC.

W v Meah [1986] 1 All ER 935.

Wilkes v Wood (1763) Lofft 1, 98 ER 489.

Winter v News Scotland Ltd 1991 SLT 828, Ct of Sess.

XL Petroleum v Caltex Oil (1985) 155 CLR 448, Aust HC.

Appeal

By notice dated 1 December 1993 the defendant, MGN Ltd (the newspaper), appealed from the order of Drake J made on 4 November 1993 in the Queen's Bench Division of the High Court whereby he ordered on the verdict of the jury at the trial of a libel action brought by the plaintiff, Elton Hercules John, against the newspaper, that the plaintiff be awarded a total sum in damages of £350,000, being made up of an award of compensatory damages of £75,000 and exemplary damages of £275,000. The facts are set out in the judgment of the court.

Charles Gray QC and *Heather Rogers* (instructed by *Martin Cruddace*) for the newspaper.

Desmond Browne QC and *David Parsons* (instructed by *Frere Cholmeley Bischoff*) for the plaintiff.

Cur adv vult

12 December 1995. The following judgment of the court was delivered.

SIR THOMAS BINGHAM MR. This judgment is divided into three parts as follows. Part 1: the facts and the history of the action. Part 2: the principles of law relating to damages in defamation. Part 3: our conclusions on the summing up and the awards of damages.

PART 1 THE FACTS AND THE HISTORY OF THE ACTION

Neither the appellant, MGN Ltd (the newspaper), nor the respondent, Mr Elton John (the plaintiff), needs any introduction in this appeal which arises from a libel action brought by the latter in respect of an article published in the Sunday Mirror on 27 December 1992. At the conclusion of the trial before Drake J and a jury, the jury awarded the plaintiff £350,000 damages, comprising £75,000 compensatory damages and £275,000 exemplary damages, and judgment was entered accordingly.

a The issues in the present appeal concentrate entirely upon this award of
damages and its constituent parts. In a nutshell, the newspaper contends that as
a matter of principle there is no scope in law for awarding exemplary damages,
either generally or in the particular circumstances of the present case, so that the
question of exemplary damages should never have been left to the jury at all.
Alternatively it submits that the judge misdirected the jury both on exemplary
b and compensatory damages; and that in any event the sums awarded under both
headings were grossly excessive.

The argument before us has raised fundamental questions about jury awards
of compensatory and exemplary damages, both generally and with reference to
the facts of this case. We have thought it necessary and desirable to address these
questions in this judgment.

c

The article

In the top left-hand corner of the front page of the newspaper there appeared
in large letters, accompanied by a photograph of the plaintiff, the words in capital
letters 'World exclusive' and 'Elton's "diet of death"'. The reader was then
d invited to see pp 4 and 5, where the article appeared under a large headline
reading 'Secret of slim Elton's spitting image' and, in smaller letters, 'Doctors
warn his "don't swallow" diet is a killer'. Below this headline appeared the byline
'EXCLUSIVE from Tony Brenna in Los Angeles and Paul Scott in London'.

The text was in the following terms:

e
'ROCK superstar Elton John is hooked on a bizarre new diet which doctors
have warned could kill him. Millionaire Elton's weight has plummeted since
he started eating food then spitting it out without swallowing. The star, who
suffered from the eating disorder bulimia, has told friends in America: "I am
on the 'Don't swallow and get thin diet' and I can tell you it works. I have
f got the best of both worlds. I get the flavour without becoming a blimp."
But medical experts in Britain called on once-chubby Elton to give up the diet
fad before it makes him seriously ill. One said: "This is not a diet, it is another
form of bulimia, and that can kill people." Victims of the slimming disease
binge on food then force themselves to vomit. ELTON, 45, revealed his latest
craze at a Christmas party thrown by his manager, John Reid, at his
g Hollywood mansion. Guests at the glitzy bash, attended by stars including
L.A. Law heart-throb Corbin Bernsen, watched as Elton chewed party
snacks, then disposed of them in his napkin. He told revellers: "I love food.
I love to eat, but what's the point of swallowing it? You can't taste it as it goes
down your throat." The 5ft 6in star, who has been treated for drug, alcohol,
h and food addictions, boasted that his weight is almost down to 10 stone,
adding: "I have finally got all my addictions under control." But one
partygoer, who watched Elton spitting chewed shrimp and crab into his
napkin, said that the star looked tired and old. "He was wearing a black
turtle-neck jumper and a blazer that hung on him loosely. He didn't look
j well," she said. "He said he was no longer a bulimic, but he often enjoyed
eating without actually swallowing." The star joined Overeaters Anonymous when friends persuaded him to seek help about his constant bingeing.
He checked into a Chicago clinic on rock pal Rod Stewart's advice after
ordering Chinese food and steak from a hotel's room service three times in
one afternoon. Last year he confessed he gorged himself on food then made
himself sick for six years during "periods of intense distress". Elton, who had

jetted into Los Angeles from London, was hugged on his arrival by old pal
and manager, John Reid. John told him: "You're too thin. You mustn't a
overdo this dieting thing, Elton. You look as though you need a good meal."
Professor Hubert Lacey, who specialises in eating disorders at St George's
Hospital medical school in London, warned: "It is dangerous because the
people who do this are abusing food. It is likely to increase the problem for
the bulimic, because by spitting out they are starving themselves. Three or b
four hours later they could binge and then vomit." Paulette Maisner, who
runs the Maisner Centre for Eating Disorders in Brighton, added: "Chewing
food and not swallowing is one form of bulimia. It will cause all sorts of
psychiatric problems and will almost certainly lead to bingeing later. People
die from bulimia, although it is not recognised as a cause of death. They
usually die of heart attacks or kidney failure because they become c
dehydrated." A spokesman for Elton said: "I don't know anything about
this." But actress Darla Campbell, who chatted to Elton at the party, said:
"He told me, 'There was a time when I ballooned up to 12 stone 2lb and
those were the unhappiest days of my life. I couldn't look in the mirror.'"
Now the star says he is in great shape thanks to his support groups, including d
Alcoholics Anonymous and Overeaters Anonymous. "But I was still amazed
to see him spitting chewed shrimp into napkins" said Darla. "Some people
turned away politely when he did it, but Elton didn't seem embarrassed.'"

To the left of the article at the top there appeared a photograph of a somewhat
obese Mr John with the caption 'Fat and up—Elton John looking chubby but e
cheery'. On the opposite side appeared another photograph of a much slimmer
Mr John over the caption 'Slim down—rock superstar Elton seems thinner, but
so much more glum'.

The copy on which the article was based had been sent by Mr Brenna to the
deputy news editor four days earlier on 23 December. This copy was followed
shortly after by a memorandum of the same date, in response to an inquiry by the f
news editor, describing the alleged sources of Mr Brenna's material, viz Lisa
Stanley and Darla Campbell, who were uninvited guests at the party given by Mr
John Reid in Los Angeles, and who alleged that they had observed Mr John's
eating habits at the party and had spoken to him. It will be necessary in due
course to refer to these two documents and to a number of others in order to g
examine in more detail the provenance of the article as presented by the
newspaper. It is also the case for the newspaper, disputed by the plaintiff, that on
23 and 24 December a number of unsuccessful attempts were made by Mr Scott,
the co-author of the article, to contact various professional employees of Mr John
in order to check the story. h

What is undisputed is that on Christmas Eve Mr Scott telephoned Mr Frank
Presland, a partner in Messrs Frere Cholmeley Bischoff, the plaintiff's solicitors,
and a conversation ensued in which Mr Scott endeavoured to obtain Mr Reid's
telephone number in Los Angeles, as recorded by Mr Presland in his
contemporaneous attendance note as follows:
                                                                          j
'FILE: Elton John / Sunday Mirror
DATE: 24 December 1992
REF: FGP/WPS
Returning Mr Paul Scott's telephone call. Mr Scott told me he was from
the Sunday Mirror and they were thinking about running a story about Elton
John but had been unable to contact anybody at John Reid's office. The

a story, which he said was based upon "usual reliable sources" in Los Angeles was that Elton John had an eating disorder and had been recently observed chewing food and spitting it out rather then swallowing it. Mr Scott said it was obviously very bizarre behaviour. I said first of all that I did not know where Mr Reid was at present, but that it seemed unlikely that his allegation was true, but no doubt he would be very careful. He said that his source was

b "very reliable", and I said that I successfully sue many papers who had first of all told me that. I wished him a Merry Christmas.'

The correspondence

The letter before action on 29 December complained that the article was based

c on a completely invented story and was plainly libellous of the plaintiff, and sought, inter alia, a full and unqualified apology.

The editor replied that they were investigating the matter, and that their sources remained adamant that the plaintiff attended the party and made the remarks attributed to him, and that they would be interested to know where he said he was at the relevant time.

d The writ was issued on 6 January 1993. There then followed an interval of over two months, which culminated in a letter from the editor dated 11 March 1993 upon which the newspaper places great reliance, so that it is appropriate to quote it in full, together with the proposed apology:

e 'We have completed exhaustive enquiries into the matters raised in your letter of 29 December 1992. We would ask you to accept our apologies for the delay in letting you have our substantive response. As you will understand, our enquiries have entailed reverting to sources in California and this has meant that they have taken somewhat longer than we expected. We hope that Mr John will accept that this is, in fact, an indication that the

f Sunday Mirror has treated his complaint seriously and with great concern. Our report was written in good faith relying on sources who attended the party referred to in it. Indeed, the article came from an experienced freelance journalist in Los Angeles whose information is normally very reliable. Even after rigorous and extensive cross-examination by representatives of the Sunday Mirror, these sources still remain convinced in their own minds that

g the person they saw behaving in the manner described in the article was Elton John. We are therefore happy that our sources were seeking to tell us what they genuinely believed to be the truth. Be that as it may, the Sunday Mirror accepts Mr John's word. In the light of his assurance that he did not attend the party (and, of course, did not behave in the manner described), the

h only possible explanation is that our sources must have made a mistake. In those circumstances, we accept that the allegations published about Mr John should not have been made. We trust Mr John will accept that all at the Sunday Mirror sincerely regret that he should have been hurt and embarrassed by the story: please accept our unreserved apologies on his

j behalf. I would like to publish an appropriate apology and retraction at the earliest opportunity and I now attach a draft which we have prepared on which I would appreciate your comments. Further, we would be happy to participate in an agreed Statement in Open Court—we assume this is why you were instructed to issue proceedings in any event. Perhaps you would like to let us have a draft Statement for us to consider. We are keen to bring this matter to an amicable and honourable conclusion as soon as possible.

Notwithstanding the observation in your letter of 29 December, we feel sure
that Mr John will share our view that this is not, in fact, a case where "very
substantial damages" would be appropriate. Nonetheless, as a mark of our
sincerity and that of our proposed apology and in order that Mr John should
be spared the considerable inconvenience of attending Court to secure a sum
of damages to vindicate his reputation, we propose that, in return for your
client discontinuing his action: 1. We pay the sum of [figure omitted] to any
cause or charity which Mr John may care to nominate, and look forward to
hearing from him in this regard. 2. We publish an apology in an agreed
form. 3. We join in, if your client so wishes, a Statement in Open Court.
4. We meet your client's reasonable indemnity costs. We trust our offer will
be accepted in the conciliatory spirit in which it is made, and we look forward
to hearing from you at your earliest convenience.'

The proposed apology was in fact not enclosed with the letter of 11 March, but
was sent the next day by the newspaper's solicitor. It was in these terms:

'*Elton John—Apology* On 27 December 1992 the Sunday Mirror published
an article headlined "Elton's 'diet of death'". This was based on a freelance
report of his purported attendance at a party given by his manager John Reid
in Hollywood. Although it was published in good faith we are informed by
Mr John, and we fully accept, that he did not attend the party and accordingly
our comments about his dietary habits were without foundation. We
apologise unreservedly to Mr John for the distress caused by the article and
we propose to make an appropriate donation to a charity of his choice.'

This was rejected by Mr John's solicitors who particularly objected to what they
described as 'the mistaken identity theory' propounded by the editor, and sought
a fuller explanation as to the origins and background of the article as a
precondition for consideration by the plaintiff of the newspaper's proposals.

Meantime the statement of claim had been delivered on 19 January 1993, and
this was followed by the defence which denied that the words were defamatory,
a posture which was maintained by the newspaper throughout.

Further correspondence continued in the ensuing months. On 12 August 1993
Mr Presland wrote to the newspaper's solicitor:

'If your Editor is prepared to admit that the article was a wholly invented
piece of fiction which was irresponsibly published, then we may be able to
make some progress.'

This suggestion was rejected by the newspaper on 23 August. The letter in
reply contained this passage:

'The headline, in itself, would be accurate if it referred to his self-confessed
seventeen years of drug and dietary abuse which, if it had gone unchecked,
[would] have brought his life to a premature close. Your client freely admits
to the possession and use of illegal drugs and must be extremely fortunate
not ever to have been prosecuted for such use.'

The correspondence continued throughout the rest of the summer and early
autumn of 1993, with the plaintiff maintaining his demands, and the newspaper
repeating its offer to publish an agreed apology, an impasse which was never
resolved.

The introduction of the claim for exemplary damages

a   The original statement of claim did not claim exemplary damages, but by an amendment made with leave on 22 September 1993 such a claim was added, particularised as follows:

> *b*   '(1) The Plaintiff did not even attend the Christmas party hosted by Mr. John Reid at his house in Hollywood, which is referred to in the words complained of. (2) Due to his familiar appearance and status as a celebrity, the Plaintiff would be distinctly identifiable to persons attending social events in Hollywood. Contrary to the Defendant's contention in correspondence, there can in the premises be no question of the persons who are professed by the Defendant to be the source of the account of the
> *c*   Plaintiff's presence at the said party (that is to say, other party-goers) having simply made a mistaken identification of the Plaintiff. A prudent and easy way of verifying the accuracy and reliability of the account of the Plaintiff's presence at the said party would in the aforesaid circumstances have been to contact either the Plaintiff or Mr. Reid (or a member of the latter's staff) to enquire whether the Plaintiff had been present at the said party.
> *d*   (3) Notwithstanding the matters aforesaid, at no time prior to the publication of the said words did the Defendant or anyone on its behalf contact (either adequately or at all) either the Plaintiff or Mr. Reid (or a member of the latter's staff) to enquire whether the Plaintiff had been present at the said party. (4) In the premises the Defendant published the
> *e*   said words recklessly, not caring whether they were true or false. (5) The Defendant further chose to give the maximum publicity to the said words by promoting them in sensationalist terms on the front page of the Sunday Mirror in the manner set out under Paragraph 3 hereof. (6) The Defendant thereby employed the said words to attract members of the public to purchase the Sunday Mirror and it is to be inferred in the premises that the
> *f*   Defendant published the said words on the calculated basis that it was likely to gain more financially from such publication than it would have to pay to the Plaintiff if he sued and continued the proceedings to judgment.'

This amendment was resisted by the newspaper, whose appeal was dismissed by the Court of Appeal (Neill, Beldam and Henry LJJ) on 19 October 1993.

g

The eve of the trial

During the week before the trial began there was a last-minute flurry of activity. On 25 October 1993 the newspaper served a supplemental list of documents itemised below. On 26 October the newspaper's solicitors disclosed
h   the Sunday Mirror's sales figures each week from October 1992 to March 1993, which fluctuated between about 2·4m and 2·9m, with the issue presently in question standing at the bottom of the scale. On 27 October 1993 the plaintiff disclosed Mr Presland's attendance note.

The supplementary list comprised the following documents as far as relevant:
j   (i) Mr Brenna's original draft article; (ii) some shorthand notes of Mr Scott with the telephone numbers of the offices of persons employed professionally by the plaintiff; (iii) a tape of conversations between Mr Scott and two doctors, on or about 23 December 1992; (iv) the memorandum from Mr Brenna dated about 23 December referred to above; (v) an account dated 7 January 1993 of an interview between Mr Brenna and the two informants at the party, of which a tape was supplied to the plaintiff's solicitors on 1 November.

The list also referred to two documents which had been 'lost or destroyed', viz:
(a) an original draft article prepared by Mr Brenna and destroyed on his computer *a*
by adverse weather on 20 December 1992; (b) a tape of a prepublication interview
(together with transcript) with the two sources by Mr Brenna.

The provenance of the article

These documents, which vividly illustrate the provenance of the article, are *b*
relied on by both sides from their respective viewpoints on the issue of exemplary
damages.

The draft article by Mr Brenna was in the following terms:

'Rock star Elton John's weight has plunged and his clothes are hanging off *c*
him thanks to a bizarre new habit of eating food then spitting it out.
Attending a Hollywood Christmas party given for him by his manager, John
Reid, Elton was eating party snacks, then disposing of them in a napkin. "I
love food, I love to eat, but what's the point of swallowing it, you can't taste
it as it goes down your throat," Elton explained to puzzled guests. "I'm on
the great don't swallow the food and get thin diet, I can tell you it works." *d*
Elton, 45 and 5ft 6ins tall, who has been treated for drug, alcohol and food
addictions, said his weight had dropped to just over 10 stone—"and I've
finally got all my addictions under control." But according to a TV reporter
[name omitted] who watched Elton depositing chewed shrimp and crab in
his napkin, he looked tired and old. "He was wearing a black turtle neck and *e*
a blazer that hung on him loosely, he didn't look well", says Lisa. "He said
that he was no longer a bulimic, bingeing on food then rushing to the
bathroom to vomit it up, but he often enjoyed eating without actually
swallowing." Elton, who had just arrived from London, was hugged on
arrival by old pal John Reid, who commented: "Oh, God, you look
wonderful, but you're too thin. You mustn't overdo this dieting thing, *f*
Elton. It's not good for you, you look as though you need a good meal." But
that suggestion didn't please Elton according to actress [name omitted], who
chatted with him. "Elton told me, 'there was a time when I ballooned up to
170 pounds—and those were the unhappiest days of my life ... I couldn't
look in a mirror.'" Now Elton says he's in great shape, thanks to his various *g*
support groups: Alcoholics Anonymous and Overeaters Anonymous. "But I
was still amazed to see him spitting chewed shrimp into napkins," says [name
omitted]. "Some people turned away politely when he did it, but Elton
didn't seem in the least bit embarrassed. He smiled and said: 'I got the best
of both worlds, darling, I get the flavour without becoming a blimp.'"
h

Mr Brenna's contemporaneous memorandum, which began 'Tony Brenna, LA—
memo att news desk' stated as follows:

'With reference to Elton John bizarre eating habits story. Lisa Stanley
attended the Christmas party given by Elton's manager, George [sic] Reid, *j*
personally with two of her friends and spoke to Elton John for more than half
an hour. During that time he took a shrimp out of his mouth and put them
in a napkin. This action was also witnessed by Lisa's fellow guest Darla
Campbell, also at the party and quoted in the story. Both women know they
are on the record. Stanley is now working as a television reporter for the
American programme Hard Copy and has always been an entirely reliable

a source as far as I am concerned. I have her comments about the party on tape and in writing. Regards.'

The transcripts of the conversation with the two doctors contained discussions in general terms of the serious dangers of a regime of dieting as described in the article, but with no reference to the plaintiff personally.

b It will be remembered that it was stated in the newspaper's supplemental list of documents dated 25 October 1993 that the tape of the prepublication interview between Mr Brenna and his two sources (together with the transcript of the tape) had been lost or destroyed. A transcript was available, however, of the telephone conversations which Mr Brenna had with his two sources on 7 January 1993, and of the report which Mr Brenna sent to London on the same day.

c According to this transcript, in her conversation with Mr Brenna on 7 January Lisa Stanley described how she and Darla Campbell and another girl had lost their way en route to a different party, and, having followed some other cars, eventually arrived uninvited at Mr Reid's house at about 10.30 pm to 11 pm when the party was 'just winding down'. They soon realised they had come to the wrong party, but introduced themselves nonetheless and were welcomed by *d* Mr Reid. They then went into the kitchen and saw a man 'who ... looks exactly like Elton John', and who was referred to by the other people as Elton: '... he looked tired ... and he had a cocktail glass in one hand and coke in another and he was eating shrimps and he was chewing the shrimps and spitting them back out on a napkin'. What she said then happened she described as follows:

e   'So basically Darla started laughing and saying, my God what's he doing— why swallow it darling, you cannot taste it anyway, so when it goes down you cannot taste it anyway. So he and Darla start laughing and we said oh what a great way to lose weight, and he said "precisely". So then he said, I'm clean, I'm sober ... I want to stay healthy, I don't want to overload—I *f*   remember what else he said, I don't want to overload my body with too much.'

When asked by Mr Brenna how she knew he was Elton John she replied:

g   'I mean they were calling him Elton John, well they weren't calling him Elton John, they were calling him Elton ... Just the people in the kitchen. OK, actually one guy kept coming up to him saying sir, would you like another coke?'

Mr Brenna then asked Lisa Stanley whether she would have known Elton John. She replied:

h   'I had never seen him ... that was my first time in person. Come on, I was born and raised in this town, in my life I have seen him in concert about a dozen times. I am not from the Boondocks. I mean he did look thinner than the normal Elton John, and he does have those hair things.'

j Darla Campbell gave a similar description, and said she had no doubt it was Elton John, and that people were calling him Elton.

The trial

The trial began on 1 November 1993, and during his opening Mr Carman QC made it plain to the jury that, on the basis of this recently disclosed material, he was going to allege as part of his case on exemplary damages that parts of the article were pure invention by Mr Brenna and/or the newspaper's editorial staff, and that the newspaper was legally responsible for the former's recklessness.

On 1 November the plaintiff himself gave evidence, followed by Mr Presland, Mr Reid, and a number of representatives of the firm to whom, it was alleged, Mr Scott tried to speak just before Christmas.

The kernel of Mr John's evidence, concerning the effect the article had upon him, was well summarised by the judge in his summing up as follows:

'You bear in mind, you remember, the plaintiff's case on this that he had had terrible problems in his life with his addiction to drugs, alcohol and his eating problems. He had determined to give them up and he had worked very hard indeed, and for a year he had done nothing and cured himself of these addictions which, he realised, had made his life terrible. He had attended a hospital in Chicago. He had attended frequent meetings at Alcoholics Anonymous, Narcotics Anonymous, Overeaters or Bulimia Anonymous. He told you he had been to something like 1,350 meetings in order to have himself completely cured. He had cured himself. He had gone on the David Frost show in order to publicise the fact he was a cured man and, at the same time, he said he hoped to help others who had similar problems. Because of that he told you it was particularly distressful for him when this article was published. He told you of the circumstances in which the article came to his attention. He was at his home in Atlanta in America when his mother who had got the newspaper in England telephoned him. "She read the article out in full at my request", he said. "I was incensed, absolutely outraged. The most satisfactory thing I have done in my life is to admit my problems, the drugs and food and face up to it, and this article seemed to say I had problems", in other words, that he had failed to cure himself. Do take that into account in assessing the appropriate damages to award him as compensation for distress.'

Mr Reid described the party, and stated that the two girls had been asked to leave after three-quarters of an hour because they were drunk.

The other representatives testified that their respective offices were open during normal office hours on 23 and 24 December, and that they had no record of any call from Mr Scott. There was then a submission by Lord Williams QC on behalf of the newspaper that exemplary damages should not be left to the jury. One aspect of this submission related directly to the expanded case on exemplary damages, it being Lord Williams' contention that the newspaper was not vicariously responsible for Mr Brenna's recklessness if established. This submission was rejected by the judge, who held that there was evidence fit for the jury to consider: (a) as to the newspaper's own recklessness; and (b) as to the recklessness of Mr Brenna, whom the judge held to have taken part in the publication and for whom in any event the newspaper was vicariously responsible. The newspaper called no evidence.

The summing up and verdict

There were three issues for the jury to consider: (a) whether the words were defamatory; (b) if so, compensatory damages; and (c) exemplary damages. It is unnecessary to say any more about the first issue.

During the course of his summing up the judge considered the issue of compensatory and exemplary damages quite separately. We shall have to consider later the judge's directions on both compensatory and exemplary a   damages because one of the matters raised in the notice of appeal is that these directions were erroneous.

After a retirement of four hours, the jury returned with a unanimous verdict for the plaintiff on liability, and after a further hour's retirement returned with their award of damages by a ten to two majority.

b   *The grounds of appeal*

These may be summarised as follows.   (1) That the judge should have withdrawn the question of exemplary damages from the jury at the close of the plaintiff's case.   (2) That the judge misdirected the jury on the way they should approach the question whether they should award exemplary damages.   (3) That furthermore the sum awarded by the jury for exemplary damages was excessive
c   in that no jury properly directed could have arrived at it as an appropriate sum. (4) That the judge misdirected the jury on the question of compensatory damages.   (5) That, furthermore, the sum awarded for compensatory damages was excessive and unreasonable and incompatible with the award of the Court of Appeal in *Rantzen v Mirror Group Newspapers (1986) Ltd* [1993] 4 All ER 975, [1994]
d   QB 670.   (6) That in any event the awards of both compensatory and exemplary damages were so high as to amount to a restriction or penalty upon the defendant's freedom of expression, and therefore contrary to art 10 of the Convention for the Protection of Human Rights and Fundamental Freedoms (Rome, 4 November 1950; TS 71 (1953); Cmd 8969). Before we come to consider these grounds of appeal, however, it is first necessary to examine in some detail
e   the principles of law relating to damages in defamation and the present guidance given to juries in actions for libel and slander.

PART 2 THE PRINCIPLES OF LAW RELATING TO DAMAGES IN DEFAMATION

Introduction

f   It is standard practice for plaintiffs in defamation actions to claim damages and also an injunction against repetition of the publication complained of. If the action is compromised, the defendant ordinarily undertakes not to repeat the publication.   If the action goes to trial and the plaintiff wins and recovers damages, the defendant ordinarily undertakes not to repeat the publication, and if he is unwilling to give that undertaking an injunction restraining him from
g   further publication will usually be granted. But it is the award of damages, not the grant of an injunction (in lieu of an undertaking), which is the primary remedy which the law provides on proof of this tort, both because, save in exceptional cases, the grant of an injunction in practice follows and is dependent on success in recovering damages, and also because an injunction, while giving
h   the plaintiff protection against repetition in future, gives him no redress for what has happened in the past. It is to an award of damages that a plaintiff must look for redress, and the principles governing awards of damages are accordingly of fundamental importance in ensuring that justice is done to plaintiffs and defendants and that account is taken of such public interests as may be involved.

j   *Compensatory damages*

The successful plaintiff in a defamation action is entitled to recover, as general compensatory damages, such sum as will compensate him for the wrong he has suffered.   That sum must compensate him for the damage to his reputation; vindicate his good name; and take account of the distress, hurt and humiliation which the defamatory publication has caused.   In assessing the appropriate

damages for injury to reputation the most important factor is the gravity of the
libel; the more closely it touches the plaintiff's personal integrity, professional
reputation, honour, courage, loyalty and the core attributes of his personality, the
more serious it is likely to be. The extent of publication is also very relevant: a
libel published to millions has a greater potential to cause damage than a libel
published to a handful of people. A successful plaintiff may properly look to an
award of damages to vindicate his reputation: but the significance of this is much
greater in a case where the defendant asserts the truth of the libel and refuses any
retraction or apology than in a case where the defendant acknowledges the falsity
of what was published and publicly expresses regret that the libellous publication
took place. It is well established that compensatory damages may and should
compensate for additional injury caused to the plaintiff's feelings by the
defendant's conduct of the action, as when he persists in an unfounded assertion
that the publication was true, or refuses to apologise, or cross-examines the
plaintiff in a wounding or insulting way. Although the plaintiff has been referred
to as 'he', all this of course applies to women just as much as men.

There could never be any precise, arithmetical formula to govern the
assessment of general damages in defamation, but if such cases were routinely
tried by judges sitting alone there would no doubt emerge a more or less
coherent framework of awards which would, while recognising the particular
features of particular cases, ensure that broadly comparable cases led to broadly
comparable awards. This is what has happened in the field of personal injuries
since these ceased to be the subject of trial by jury and became, in practice, the
exclusive preserve of judges. There may be even greater factual diversity in
defamation than in personal injury cases, but this is something of which the
framework would take account.

The survival of jury trial in defamation actions has inhibited a similar
development in this field. Respect for the constitutional role of the jury in such
actions, and judicial reluctance to intrude into the area of decision-making
reserved to the jury, have traditionally led judges presiding over defamation trials
with juries to confine their jury directions to a statement of general principles,
eschewing any specific guidance on the appropriate level of general damages in
the particular case. While some distinguished judges (e g Diplock LJ in *McCarey v
Associated Newspapers Ltd (No 2)* [1964] 3 All ER 947 at 960, [1965] 2 QB 86 at 109)
have considered that juries should be informed in broad terms of the
conventional level of awards for personal injuries, not by way of analogy but as a
check on the reasonableness of an award which the jury are considering, this has
not been an authoritative view (see *Cassell & Co Ltd v Broome* [1972] 1 All ER 801
at 824, [1972] AC 1027 at 1071). Even in the rare case when a personal injury
claim was to be tried by a jury it was thought inappropriate that a jury should be
informed of the conventional level of awards (*Ward v James* [1965] 1 All ER 563 at
575–576, [1966] 1 QB 273 at 302), a striking departure from the modern practice
when judges are sitting alone.

Whatever the theoretical attractions of this approach, its practical disadvantages have become ever more manifest. A series of jury awards in sums wildly
disproportionate to any damage conceivably suffered by the plaintiff has given
rise to serious and justified criticism of the procedures leading to such awards.
This has not been the fault of the juries. Judges, as they were bound to do,
confined themselves to broad directions of general principle, coupled with
injunctions to the jury to be reasonable. But they gave no guidance on what
might be thought reasonable or unreasonable, and it is not altogether surprising

a that juries lacked an instinctive sense of where to pitch their awards. They were in the position of sheep loosed on an unfenced common, with no shepherd.

While the Court of Appeal reaffirmed the fundamental soundness of the traditional approach in *Sutcliffe v Pressdram Ltd* [1990] 1 All ER 269, [1991] 1 QB 153, the court did in that case recommend trial judges to draw the attention of juries to the purchasing power of the award they were minded to make, and of

b the income it would produce (see [1990] 1 All ER 269 at 283–284, 289, 293, [1991] 1 QB 153 at 178–179, 185–186, 190). This was thereafter done, and juries were reminded of the cost of buying a motor car, or a holiday, or a house. But judges were still constrained by authority from steering the jury towards any particular level of award.

Following the enactment of s 8(2) of the Courts and Legal Services Act 1990

c and the introduction of RSC Ord 59, r 11(4) in its present form, the Court of Appeal was for the first time empowered, on allowing an appeal against a jury's award of damages, to substitute for the sum awarded by the jury such sum as might appear to the court to be proper. This power was exercised in *Gorman v Mudd* [1992] CA Transcript 1076. In that case the plaintiff was a member of

d Parliament who sued one of her constituents for a libel contained in a mock press release. There was publication to 91 people only, but these were prominent, influential, local and knowledgeable members of the constituency party. The defendant advanced and persisted in pleas of justification and qualified privilege. The plaintiff alleged malice. There was a two-week trial, during which the plaintiff was the subject of insulting and distressing questions. The jury rejected

e the defence of justification and found that the defendant had been actuated by personal spite. They awarded compensatory damages of £150,000. The Court of Appeal held this award to be so grossly and seriously excessive and extravagant as to merit a new trial, but exercised its power to substitute an award and concluded that nothing in excess of £50,000 could be justified. Rose LJ observed:

f
> 'It was not even open to the judge, for example, to invite the jury to consider whether an award in one, two, three, four, five or six figures might be appropriate. This being the law, the inevitable consequence is that it is something of a lottery what sum a jury will award in an action for defamation ...'

g
In *Rantzen v Mirror Group Newspapers (1986) Ltd* [1993] 4 All ER 975, [1994] QB 670 the newspaper appealed against a jury's award of £250,000, contending that the size of the award was wholly disproportionate to the damage done to the plaintiff's reputation. The court concluded that at that time it would not be right to allow reference to be made to awards by juries in previous cases. But it took

h the view that awards made by the Court of Appeal stood on a different footing: over a period of time awards made by the Court of Appeal would provide a corpus to which reference could be made in subsequent cases (see [1993] 4 All ER 975 at 995, [1994] QB 670 at 694). With reference to the argument advanced for the newspaper that judges should be free to remind juries of conventional levels of awards of general damages for pain and suffering and loss of amenity in

j personal injury cases, the court reviewed previous authority and said ([1993] 4 All ER 975 at 997, [1994] QB 670 at 695):

> 'We see the force of the criticism of the present practice whereby a plaintiff in an action for libel may recover a much larger sum by way of damages for an injury to his reputation, which may prove transient in its effect, than the damages awarded for pain and suffering to the victim of an industrial

accident who has lost an eye or the use of one or more of his limbs. We have
come to the conclusion, however, that there is no satisfactory way in which
the conventional awards in actions for damages for personal injuries can be
used to provide guidance for an award in an action for defamation. Despite
[counsel for the defendant's] submissions to the contrary, it seems to us that
damages for defamation are intended at least in part as a vindication of the
plaintiff to the public. This element of the damages was recognised by
Windeyer J in *Uren v John Fairfax & Sons Pty Ltd* (1966) 117 CLR 118 at 150
and by Lord Hailsham LC in *Cassell & Co Ltd v Broome* [1972] 1 All ER 801 at
824, [1972] AC 1027 at 1071. We therefore feel bound to reject the proposal
that the jury should be referred to awards made in actions involving serious
personal injuries. It is to be hoped that in the course of time a series of
decisions of the Court of Appeal will establish some standards as to what are,
in the terms of s 8 of the 1990 Act, "proper" awards. In the meantime the
jury should be invited to consider the purchasing power of any award which
they may make. In addition they should be asked to ensure that any award
they make is proportionate to the damage which the plaintiff has suffered
and is a sum which it is necessary to award him to provide adequate
compensation and to re-establish his reputation.'

The parties in *Houston v Smith* [1993] CA Transcript 1544 were general medical
practitioners, formerly partners. The male plaintiff claimed damages for slander
against the female defendant, who had accused him of sexually harassing her and
members of her staff. The accusation was originally made before a small
audience in the practice waiting room, but was later repeated and a defence of
justification (albeit on a limited basis) was advanced and persisted in. The jury
awarded compensatory damages of £150,000. The Court of Appeal held that sum
to be excessive and substituted an award of £50,000. Hirst LJ said:

'I should add that this amount is, in my judgment, at the very top of the
range for a slander of this kind, and is only appropriate because of the very
grave and exceptional aggravating factors to which I have already referred.
Had the slander remained within the confines of the waiting room and, still
more, if the defendant had promptly apologised, the appropriate sum would
have been a very small fraction of £50,000.'

Neill and Beldam LJJ agreed.

For the newspaper in the present case Mr Gray QC repeats the argument
which he advanced, and which was rejected, in *Rantzen* on the permissibility of
referring to levels of awards in personal injury cases. He recognises the difficulty
of seeking to persuade the court now to accept an argument which it so recently
rejected, but contends that a number of factors justify reconsideration of that
ruling and a different result.

First, Mr Gray points out that the corpus of experience which the court in
Rantzen envisaged as a source of guidance has in practice scarcely developed, with
the result that juries still receive little assistance from that source.

Secondly, Mr Gray points to the continuance of what appear to be grossly
excessive awards. He instances the award of £750,000 to Mr Graham Souness,
settled (after the newspaper appealed) for £100,000; and the award of £1.5m to the
plaintiffs in *Walker v Shehan* [1995] CA Transcript 1092, again settled on appeal.

Thirdly, he draws attention to the changing views of a majority in the High
Court of Australia. In *Coyne v Citizen Finance Ltd* (1991) 172 CLR 211 a minority
favoured permitting reference to personal injury awards in directing libel juries.

In *Carson v John Fairfax & Sons Ltd* (1993) 178 CLR 44 the balance of opinion had
swung. It was now a majority, led by Mason CJ, who favoured permitting such
reference.

Fourthly, Mr Gray relies on art 10 of the European Convention on Human
Rights, coinciding (as this article has been authoritatively held to do: see *A-G v
Guardian Newspapers Ltd (No 2)* [1988] 3 All ER 545 at 580–582, 597, 615, 627, 652,
660, [1990] 1 AC 109 at 156–159, 178, 203, 218, 273, 283 and *Derbyshire CC v Times
Newspapers Ltd* [1993] 1 All ER 1011 at 1020, [1993] AC 534 at 550) with the
provisions of the English common law. This was an argument also advanced in
Rantzen, but since then the European Court of Human Rights has decided *Tolstoy
Miloslavsky v UK* (1995) 20 EHRR 442. In that case an award was made of £1·5m
compensatory damages, and the court held that the size of the award, in
conjunction with the lack of adequate and effective safeguards at the relevant
time (before *Rantzen*) against a disproportionately large award, amounted to a
violation of the defendant's rights under art 10 of the convention.

We are persuaded by Mr Gray's argument that this subject deserves
reconsideration, despite the short period since the *Rantzen* ruling was given. Any
legal process should yield a successful plaintiff appropriate compensation, that is,
compensation which is neither too much nor too little. That is so whether the
award is made by judge or jury. No other result can be accepted as just. But there
is continuing evidence of libel awards in sums which appear so large as to bear no
relation to the ordinary values of life. This is most obviously unjust to
defendants. But it serves no public purpose to encourage plaintiffs to regard a
successful libel action, risky though the process undoubtedly is, as a road to
untaxed riches. Nor is it healthy if any legal process fails to command the respect
of lawyer and layman alike, as is regrettably true of the assessment of damages by
libel juries. We are persuaded by the arguments we have heard that the subject
should be reconsidered. This is not a field in which we are bound by previous
authority (*Sutcliffe v Pressdram Ltd* [1990] 1 All ER 269 at 283, [1991] 1 QB 153 at
178) but it is necessary for us to review the arguments which have found favour
in the past.

In considering the criticisms of the present lack of guidance which is given to
juries on the issue of compensatory damages we have examined four possible
changes in the present practice: (a) reference to awards by other juries in
comparable actions for defamation; (b) reference to awards approved by the
Court of Appeal or substituted by the Court of Appeal in accordance with Ord 59,
r 11(4); (c) reference to the scale of damages awarded in actions for personal
injuries; and (d) submissions by counsel as to the appropriate award, coupled
with some guidance by the judge as to the appropriate bracket.

Other awards in actions for defamation

We wholly agree with the ruling in *Rantzen* that juries should not at present be
reminded of previous libel awards by juries. Those awards will have been made
in the absence of specific guidance by the judge and may themselves be very
unreliable markers.

The position may change in the future if the additional guidance which we
propose later in this judgment is given and proves to be successful. As was
pointed out in the course of argument, however, comparison with other awards
is very difficult because the circumstances of each libel are almost bound to be
unique. Furthermore, the corpus of such awards will be likely to become
unwieldy and time would be expended on the respective parties pointing to
features which were either similar or dissimilar in the other cases.

Awards approved or substituted by the Court of Appeal.

We agree with the ruling in *Rantzen* that reference may be made to awards approved or made by the Court of Appeal. As and when a framework of awards is established this will provide a valuable pointer to the appropriate level of award in the particular case. But it is plain that such a framework will not be established quickly: it is now five years since s 8(2) of the 1990 Act and Ord 59, r 11(4) came into force, and there is no case other than *Gorman*, *Rantzen* and *Houston* in which the court has itself fixed the appropriate level of award.

It is true that awards in this category are subject to the same objection that time can be spent by the parties on pointing to similarities and differences. But, if used with discretion, awards which have been subjected to scrutiny in the Court of Appeal should be able to provide *some* guidance to a jury called upon to fix an award in a later case.

Reference to damages in actions for personal injuries

In *Cassell & Co Ltd v Broome* [1972] 1 All ER 801 at 824, [1972] AC 1027 at 1071 Lord Hailsham LC gave his reason for rejecting comparison with awards of damages for personal injuries. He said:

'In actions of defamation and in any other actions where damages for loss of reputation are involved, the principle of restitutio in integrum has necessarily an even more highly subjective element. Such actions involve a money award which may put the plaintiff in a purely financial sense in a much stronger position than he was before the wrong. Not merely can he recover the estimated sum of his past and future losses, but, in case the libel, driven underground, emerges from its lurking place at some future date, he must be able to point to a sum awarded by a jury sufficient to convince a bystander of the baselessness of the charge. As Windeyer J well said in *Uren v John Fairfax & Sons Pty Ltd* (1967) 117 CLR 118 at 150: "It seems to me that, properly speaking, a man defamed does not get compensation *for* his damaged reputation. He gets damages *because* he was injured in his reputation, that is simply because he was publicly defamed. For this reason, compensation by damages operates in two ways—as a vindication of the plaintiff to the public, and as consolation to him for a wrong done. Compensation is here a solatium rather than a monetary recompense for harm measurable in money." This is why it is not necessarily fair to compare awards of damages in this field with damages for personal injuries. Quite obviously, the award must include factors for injury to the feelings, the anxiety and uncertainty undergone in the litigation, the absence of apology, or the reaffirmation of the truth of the matters complained of, or the malice of the defendant. The bad conduct of the plaintiff himself may also enter into the matter, where he has provoked the libel, or where perhaps he has libelled the defendant in reply. What is awarded is thus a figure which cannot be arrived at by any purely objective computation. This is what is meant when the damages in defamation are described as being "at large". In a sense, too, these damages are of their nature punitive or exemplary in the loose sense in which the terms were used before 1964, because they inflict an added burden on the defendant proportionate to his conduct, just as they can be reduced if the defendant has behaved well—as for instance by a handsome apology— or the plaintiff badly, as for instance by provoking the defendant, or defaming him in return. In all such cases it must be appropriate to say with Lord Esher MR in *Praed v Graham*, (1889) 24 QBD 53 at 55: "... in actions of a libel … the jury in assessing damages are entitled to look at the whole conduct of the defendant [I would personally add 'and of the plaintiff'] from the time the libel was published down to the time they give their verdict. They may consider what his conduct has been before action, after action, and in court during the trial."' (Windeyer J's emphasis.)

b This reasoning would weigh strongly against any attempt to equiparate damages for personal injuries and damages for defamation. It would not weigh so heavily, if at all, against reference to conventional levels of award for personal injuries as a check on the reasonableness of a proposed award of damages for defamation.

The reasons given by the Court of Appeal in *Sutcliffe v Pressdram* [1990] 1 All ER 269, [1991] 1 QB 153 for rejecting any analogy between defamation and personal c injury damages were twofold. The first was that the measure of damages is or may be different in the two cases, essentially because defamation damages have to reflect any aggravation caused to the plaintiff by the defendant's subsequent conduct, or any mitigation, and by the need to vindicate the plaintiff's good name (see [1990] 1 All ER 269 at 281, [1991] 1 QB 153 at 175). The second was that d Parliament has provided for different modes of trial in the two classes of case.

The first reason given for rejecting reference to personal injury awards was essentially that deployed by Lord Hailsham LC in *Cassell & Co Ltd v Broome*. We would make the same comment as we have made above. On the second reason we would make three observations. First, we simply do not know whether Parliament gave any thought to the assessment of damages by juries when e enacting s 69 of the Supreme Court Act 1981. Secondly, the making of grossly excessive awards by libel juries was not in 1981 the source of concern which it has since become. Thirdly, it is not suggested that juries should not assess damages in defamation actions, only that they should receive guidance when doing so.

In the passage from the judgment of the court in *Rantzen* which is quoted f above, the Court of Appeal essentially adopted the approach of Lord Hailsham LC in *Cassell & Co Ltd v Broome* in concluding that there was no satisfactory way in which conventional awards in actions for damages for personal injuries could be used to provide guidance for an award in an action for defamation. Much depends, as we now think, on what is meant by guidance: it is one thing to say (and we agree) that there can be no precise equiparation between a serious libel g and (say) serious brain damage; but it is another to point out to a jury considering the award of damages for a serious libel that the maximum conventional award for pain and suffering and loss of amenity to a plaintiff suffering from very severe brain damage is about £125,000 and that this is something of which the jury may take account.

h It is of interest that in the present case Drake J, who has much recent experience in this field, expressed some criticism of the existing rules. He observed:

'… counsel made submissions on the extent to which it is proper to address j the jury in speeches or in the summing up on the quantum of damages. I need only say that although I think the law is in need of change, I shall have regard to the guidelines given by the Court of Appeal in *Rantzen v Mirror Group Newspapers (1986) Ltd* [1993] 4 All ER 975, [1994] QB 670. I shall therefore not make any comparison with awards in personal injury cases. I shall invite the jury to consider the purchasing power of any award they make.'

It has often, and rightly, been said that there can be no precise correlation between a personal injury and a sum of money. The same is true, perhaps even more true, of injury to reputation. There is force in the argument that to permit reference in libel cases to conventional levels of award in personal injury cases is simply to admit yet another incommensurable into the field of consideration. There is also weight in the argument, often heard, that conventional levels of award in personal injury cases are too low and therefore provide an uncertain guide. But these awards would not be relied on as any exact guide, and of course there can be no precise correlation between loss of a limb, or of sight, or quadriplegia, and damage to reputation. But if these personal injuries respectively command conventional awards of, at most, about £52,000, £90,000 and £125,000 for pain and suffering and loss of amenity (of course excluding claims based on loss of earnings, the cost of care and other specific financial claims), juries may properly be asked to consider whether the injury to his reputation of which the plaintiff complains should fairly justify any greater compensation. The conventional compensatory scales in personal injury cases must be taken to represent fair compensation in such cases unless and until those scales are amended by the courts or by Parliament. It is in our view offensive to public opinion, and rightly so, that a defamation plaintiff should recover damages for injury to reputation greater, perhaps by a significant factor, than if that same plaintiff had been rendered a helpless cripple or an insensate vegetable. The time has in our view come when judges, and counsel, should be free to draw the attention of juries to these comparisons.

Reference to an appropriate award and an appropriate bracket

It has been the invariable practice in the past that neither counsel nor the judge may make any suggestion to the jury as what would be an appropriate award. This practice was in line with the practice followed in actions for personal injuries when such actions were tried with a jury. In *Ward v James* [1965] 1 All ER 563 at 576, [1966] 1 QB 273 at 302 the Court of Appeal gave reasons as to why no figures should be mentioned. It was said:

'If the judge can mention figures to the jury, then counsel must be able to mention figures to them. Once that happened, we get into the same trouble again. Each counsel would, in duty bound, pitch the figures as high or as low as he dared. Then the judge would give his views on the rival figures. The proceedings would be in danger of developing into an auction.'

In *Sutcliffe v Pressdram* [1990] 1 All ER 269 at 292, [1991] 1 QB 153 at 190 Russell LJ gave his reasons for rejecting the argument that counsel or the judge might be allowed to refer to figures. He approved the following passage in the summing up by Michael Davies J in that case:

'"Well, supposing I were to suggest a figure to you or a bracket. Supposing I were to say: 'If she succeeds, what about giving her between so much and so much.' Well, there are two possibilities. One is that you would say I was quite wrong and you would either give much more than I suggested or much less. Well now, can you imagine what would happen then? The party that did not like it, the plaintiff if you have given much less, or the defendant if you have given much more than I suggested, would be off to the Court of Appeal saying: 'Well, look at that jury, they were quite unreasonable. Here was this experienced judge suggesting a figure to them and they ignored it.' You can see readily how that would happen. Supposing you did give the a figure, or very close to the figure, that I suggested to you, well then, you would have been wasting your time here on damages, you would simply be acting as a rubber stamp for me ... So we look to you, as representatives of the public, applying the principles I have indicated, if you come to damages, to come to that figure.'

b We have come to the conclusion, however, that the reasons which have been given for prohibiting any reference to figures are unconvincing. Indeed, far from developing into an auction (and we do not see how it could), the process of mentioning figures would, in our view, induce a mood of realism on both sides.

In personal injury actions it is now commonplace for the advocates on both sides to address the judge in some detail on the quantum of the appropriate award. Any apprehension that the judge might receive a coded message as to the c amount of any payment into court has not to our knowledge been realised. The judge is not in any way bound by the bracket suggested, but he finds it helpful as a check on his own provisional assessment. We can for our part see no reason why the parties' respective counsel in a libel action should not indicate to the jury the level of award which they respectively contend to be appropriate, nor why d the judge in directing the jury should not give a similar indication. The plaintiff will not wish the jury to think that his main object is to make money rather than clear his name. The defendant will not wish to add insult to injury by underrating the seriousness of the libel. So we think the figures suggested by responsible counsel are likely to reflect the upper and lower bounds of a realistic bracket. The e jury must, of course, make up their own mind and must be directed to do so. They will not be bound by the submission of counsel or the indication of the judge. If the jury make an award outside the upper or lower bounds of any bracket indicated and such award is the subject of appeal, real weight must be given to the possibility that their judgment is to be preferred to that of the judge.

The modest but important changes of practice described above would not in f our view undermine the enduring constitutional position of the libel jury. Historically, the significance of the libel jury has lain not in their role of assessing damages, but in their role of deciding whether the publication complained of is a libel or no. The changes which we favour will, in our opinion, buttress the constitutional role of the libel jury by rendering their proceedings more rational g and so more acceptable to public opinion.

Exemplary damages

A summary of the existing English law on exemplary damages in actions for defamation, accepted by the Court of Appeal in *Riches v News Group Newspapers Ltd* [1985] 2 All ER 845 at 850, [1986] QB 256 at 269 as concise, correct and h comprehensive, appears in *Duncan and Neill on Defamation* (2nd edn, 1983) para 18.27. The passage remains a correct summary of the relevant law. So far as relevant to this case, and omitting footnotes and references, the passage reads:

'(a) Exemplary damages can only be awarded if the plaintiff proves that the defendant when he made the publication knew that he was committing j a tort or was reckless whether his action was tortious or not, and decided to publish because the prospects of material advantage outweighed the prospects of material loss. "What is necessary is that the tortious act must be done with guilty knowledge for the motive that the chances of economic advantage outweigh the chances of economic, or perhaps physical, penalty". (b) The mere fact that a libel is committed in the course of a business carried on for profit, for example the business of a newspaper publisher, is not by itself sufficient to justify an award of exemplary damages. (c) If the case is one where exemplary damages *can* be awarded the court or jury should consider whether the sum which it proposes to award by way of compensatory damages is sufficient not only for the purpose of compensating the plaintiff but also for the purpose of punishing the defendant. It is only if the sum proposed by way of compensatory damages (which may include an element of aggravated damages) is insufficient that the court or jury should add to it enough "to bring it up to a sum sufficient as punishment". (d) The sum awarded as damages should be a single sum which will include, where appropriate, any elements of aggravated or exemplary damages ... (f) A jury should be warned of the danger of an excessive award. (g) The means of the parties, though irrelevant to the issue of compensatory damages, can be taken into account in awarding exemplary damages ...'

This summary of the law was not challenged in argument before us, and it was not seriously argued that we could rule (even if we wished) that exemplary damages are not recoverable in defamation if the conditions required by authority for making such an award are established to the proper satisfaction of a jury. We were, however, reminded by the newspaper that in English law the award of exemplary damages is regarded as exceptional and in some ways anomalous. Authority, it was said, does not encourage any broadening of the categories of case in which such awards may be made nor any relaxation of the conditions for making them. Since art 10 of the European Convention on Human Rights requires any restriction on freedom of expression to be prescribed by law and necessary in a democratic society for the protection of reputation, it was argued that the conditions for making an exemplary award should be closely scrutinised and rigorously applied. Our attention was accordingly drawn to certain aspects of the conditions established by authority.

First, the state of mind of the defendant publisher. Little difficulty arises in the straightforward but relatively rare case in which it can be shown that the defendant actually knew that he was committing a tort when he published. The alternative state of mind—recklessness—is not so easy.

In *Derry v Peek* (1889) 14 App Cas 337, [1886–90] All ER Rep 1 Lord Herschell classically defined the state of mind necessary to establish deceit. He made clear that proof of fraud is essential and continued (14 App Cas 337 at 374, [1886–90] All ER Rep 1 at 22):

> 'Secondly, fraud is proved when it is shown that a false representation has been made (1) knowingly, or (2) without belief in its truth, or (3) recklessly, careless whether it be true or false. Although I have treated the second and third as distinct cases, I think the third is but an instance of the second, for one who makes a statement under such circumstances can have no real belief in the truth of what he states. To prevent a false statement being fraudulent, there must, I think, always be an honest belief in its truth.'

Important for present purposes is Lord Herschell's assimilation of recklessness and carelessness whether a statement is true or false, with lack of honest belief in its truth. He was at pains to distinguish these states of mind, which were sufficient to ground a claim in deceit, from the making of a false statement through lack of care and the making of a false representation honestly believed though on insufficient grounds, which were not (see eg 14 App Cas 337 at 375, [1886–90] All ER Rep 1 at 22).

a It would seem that Lord Devlin was thinking in a similar way, when he spoke in *Rookes v Barnard* [1964] 1 All ER 367 at 410, [1964] AC 1129 at 1227 of 'a cynical disregard for a plaintiff's rights'. Such, plainly, was the approach of Widgery J in *Manson v Associated Newspapers Ltd* [1965] 2 All ER 954 at 957, [1965] 1 WLR 1038 at 1040, where he ruled that exemplary damages may be awarded—

b 'in a case in which a newspaper quite deliberately publishes a statement which it either knows to be false or which it publishes recklessly, careless whether it be true or false ...'

He defined the question for him as whether he could, on the material available, tell the jury that they could consider exemplary damages if, having considered the material before them, they were driven to the inference that the article in c question had been published by the defendants 'conscious of the fact that it had no solid foundation'. In directing the jury he equated recklessness with not really believing a statement to be true at all. He instructed the jury that they had to be satisfied that the defendant had acted in a wicked and callous fashion (see [1965] 2 All ER 954 at 957, 958, [1965] 1 WLR 1038 at 1041, 1043).

d In *Cassell & Co Ltd v Broome* [1972] 1 All ER 801 at 831, [1972] AC 1027 at 1079 Lord Hailsham LC required 'knowledge that what is proposed to be done is against the law or a reckless disregard whether what is proposed to be done is illegal or legal'. Lord Reid spoke of 'contumelious disregard of another's rights' (see [1972] 1 All ER 801 at 838, [1972] AC 1027 at 1088). Lord Morris referred to a defendant wilfully or knowingly or recklessly peddling untruths and Viscount e Dilhorne approved that formula (see [1972] 1 All ER 801 at 843, 849, [1972] AC 1027 at 1094, 1101). Lord Diplock regarded this category as consisting of cases where 'an act known to be tortious was committed' and added:

f 'To bring a case within this category it must be proved that the defendant, at the time that he committed the tortious act, knew that it was unlawful or suspecting it to be unlawful deliberately refrained from taking obvious steps which, if taken, would have turned suspicion into certainty.' (See [1972] 1 All ER 801 at 872, 874, [1972] AC 1027 at 1129, 1130.)

Lord Kilbrandon referred to a publisher knowing or not caring whether his material is libellous and to a publisher knowing or having reason to believe that g publication would subject him to compensatory damages (see [1972] 1 All ER 801 at 876, [1972] AC 1027 at 1133).

Where actual knowledge of unlawfulness is not in issue, a jury direction based on reference to 'reckless, not caring whether the publication be true or false' is sanctioned by long usage and is not incorrect. The crucial ingredient of this state h of mind is, however, a lack of honest or genuine belief in the truth of what is published. That is what makes the publisher's conduct so reprehensible (or 'wicked') as to be deserving of punishment. Carelessness alone, however extreme, is not enough unless it properly justifies an inference that the publisher had no honest belief in the truth of what he published.

j It seems to us therefore that the phrase 'not caring whether the publication be true or false', though an accurate formulation of the test of recklessness, is capable of leading to confusion because the words 'not caring' may be equated in the jury's minds with 'mere carelessness'. We therefore consider that where exemplary damages are claimed the jury should in future receive some additional guidance to make it clear that before such damages can be awarded the jury must be satisfied that the publisher had no genuine belief in the truth of what he published. The publisher must have suspected that the words were untrue and have deliberately refrained from taking obvious steps which, if taken, would have turned suspicion into certainty.

Secondly, the publisher must have acted in the hope or expectation of material gain. It is well established that a publisher need not be shown to have made any precise or arithmetical calculation. But his unlawful conduct must have been motivated by mercenary considerations: the belief that he would be better off financially if he violated the plaintiff's rights than if he did not. Mere publication of a newspaper for profit is not enough.

We do not accept, as was argued, that in seeking to establish that the conditions for awarding exemplary damages have been met the plaintiff must satisfy the criminal, rather than the civil, standard of proof. But a jury should in our judgment be told that as the charge is grave, so should the proof be clear. An inference of reprehensible conduct and cynical calculation of mercenary advantage should not be lightly drawn. In *Manson* [1965] 2 All ER 954 at 959, [1965] 1 WLR 1038 at 1044 Widgery J directed the jury that they could draw inferences from proved facts if those inferences were 'quite inescapable', and he repeatedly directed that they should not draw an inference adverse to the publisher unless they were sure that it was the only inference to be drawn (see [1965] 2 All ER 954 at 959, 960, [1965] 1 WLR 1038 at 1045).

It is plain on the authorities that it is only where the conditions for making an exemplary award are satisfied, and only when the sum awarded to the plaintiff as compensatory damages is not itself sufficient to punish the defendant, show that tort does not pay and deter others from acting similarly, that an award of exemplary damages should be added to the award of compensatory damages. Since the jury will not know, when making their decision, what costs order will be made, it would seem that no account can be taken of the costs burden which the unsuccessful defendant will have to bear, although this could in itself have a punitive and deterrent effect. It is clear that the means of the defendant are relevant to the assessment of damages. Also relevant are his degree of fault and the amount of any profit he may be shown actually to have made from his unlawful conduct.

The authorities give judges no help in directing juries on the quantum of exemplary damages. Since, however, such damages are analogous to a criminal penalty, and although paid to the plaintiff play no part in compensating him, principle requires that an award of exemplary damages should never exceed the minimum sum necessary to meet the public purpose underlying such damages, that of punishing the defendant, showing that tort does not pay and deterring others. The same result is achieved by the application of art 10. Freedom of speech should not be restricted by awards of exemplary damages save to the extent shown to be strictly necessary for the protection of reputations.

The European Convention on Human Rights

The European Convention on Human Rights is not a free-standing source of law in the United Kingdom. But there is, as already pointed out, no conflict or discrepancy between art 10 and the common law. We regard art 10 as reinforcing and buttressing the conclusions we have reached and set out above. We reach those conclusions independently of the convention, however, and would reach them even if the convention did not exist.

PART 3 OUR CONCLUSIONS ON THE SUMMING UP AND THE AWARDS OF DAMAGES

We can now return to the facts of the case and consider the criticisms of the judge's summing up and of the awards of damages. We shall consider first the *a* summing up on compensatory damages and the award which was made under this heading.

Compensatory damages

We have already set out at the end of Part 1 of the judgment a summary of the alleged misdirections by the judge on the question of compensatory damages. It *b* is therefore necessary to make some further reference to the summing up.

The judge directed the jury that they should have regard to the extent of the publication, to the prominence of the publication and the words used. An article in a national newspaper will reach a much greater readership than one in a local newspaper. It was also necessary to take account of the position of the article in the newspaper. An article on the front page is more prominent than one in the *c* middle of the paper or 'tucked behind the greyhound results'.

The judge told the jury to consider the upset, hurt and distress caused to the plaintiff, and that in addition they should compensate him for the damage they thought had been caused to his character and reputation. He told them to have regard to how well known the plaintiff was.

d The judge then reminded the jury of the plaintiff's evidence as to the effect the article had on him. We have already set out this passage in the summing up.

A little later the judge added this warning:

> 'Against that, do treat matters in proportion, this upset and distress point. It is undoubtedly a form of very real hurt and distress to anyone to have their *e* character defamed. In other words, it is certainly to be hoped that by the successful results of a libel action the matter will have been publicised and put right in the minds of most of the readers who read the original article ... Bear in mind, therefore, in making any monetary award by compensation that it should be reasonable.'

f The judge then reminded the jury that the newspaper had not said that the article was true, though unfortunately he misquoted the letter of 11 March 1993 and gave the jury the impression it was the newspaper rather than the sources who remained convinced of the truth of the article. However, the jury had copies of the letter and would have been able to read it for themselves.

The judge then referred to the apology which had been offered and pointed *g* out that though the apology had not been agreed on behalf of the plaintiff, it was always open to the newspaper to publish its own form of apology at any time. Finally, he directed the jury to bear in mind the value of the money which they were dealing with. He said:

> 'When you have arrived provisionally at the figure, check again against the *h* value. What would you buy with your figure? What is it worth? Is it worth a compensatory holiday to forget the distress and hurt? If so, is it a weekend in Brighton or a long cruise? Would it purchase a motor car? If so, a fairly old car or a banger or a Rolls Royce or something like that?'

j He also invited the jury to consider the income which their award might provide if interest were paid at 10%.

We have considered the criticisms which were made in the grounds of appeal of this part of the summing up. We have come to the conclusion, however, that though there is some force in these criticisms it is impossible to say that they amount to misdirections which caused injustice. As was pointed out in the course of the argument, this was not a long case and the jury had heard all the evidence in the recent past. We consider that the summing up on compensatory

damages was sufficient within the existing guidelines to give the jury the help *a*
they needed.

We turn therefore to consider the size of the compensatory award, which was
£75,000.

We take account of the prominence given to this article in the Sunday Mirror
and of the distress and hurt which the plaintiff described in his evidence. It is also
relevant to note that though an apology was offered it was never published. This *b*
was not a trivial libel. The plaintiff had striven hard to overcome his previous
disabilities and, because he was a man with an international reputation, probably
every reader of the newspaper knew to whom the article referred.

Nevertheless, we have no doubt that the award of £75,000 was excessive.
Though the article was false, offensive and distressing it did not attack his
personal integrity or damage his reputation as an artist. We would substitute the *c*
figure of £25,000.

We turn therefore to the summing up in relation to exemplary damages and
the award of £275,000.

Exemplary damages   *d*

Under this heading it is necessary to consider a number of issues as follows.
(1) Was there sufficient evidence fit to be left to the jury that the newspaper
published the article recklessly, not caring whether it was true or false, having
regard to its state of mind and that of any relevant agent on 27 December? This
involves consideration in particular of whether there was a duty to check, and if *e*
so, what was Mr Brenna's position and role vis-à-vis the newspaper, and what if
any checks were carried out by Mr Brenna and/or the newspaper. (2) Was there
sufficient evidence fit to be left to the jury that the newspaper made the requisite
calculation? (3) Was the judge's direction under both these heads adequate?
(4) Was the 'if but only if' test satisfied? (5) Was the amount awarded manifestly
excessive?   *f*

Recklessness

It was apparent from the terms of Mr Brenna's draft article that he himself had
not been present at Mr Reid's party, and that the information contained in it was
derived from elsewhere, though at that stage only Darla Campbell was *g*
mentioned as the source.

Mr Brenna's memorandum followed shortly after on the same day, and
confirmed both that there were two sources for the story (Lisa Stanley and Darla
Campbell), and that Mr Brenna believed that the former was a reliable source.
But it made no suggestion that Mr Brenna had gone behind his two sources or *h*
made any other inquiries or cross checks in Los Angeles. Mr Scott himself, as he
stated to Mr Presland, regarded the story as 'bizarre'; and it was the newspaper's
case, based on the telephone numbers written on Mr Scott's notes, that he had in
fact checked or had attempted to check with a number of persons employed
professionally by the plaintiff in London, thus suggesting that he himself thought
it necessary to check. The one undoubted check which Mr Scott made, when he *j*
spoke to Mr Presland, gave him a clear warning that it seemed unlikely that the
allegation was true, and advised him to be very careful.

In all these circumstances it seems to us almost beyond argument that it was
necessary to check the veracity of the story, for which purpose the obvious
reference point was Mr Reid himself or, if he was unavailable, members of his
staff, all of whom would of course know the plaintiff, and be able to confirm or

a deny in answer to the most simple inquiry whether or not the plaintiff had in fact been present at the party, and if so, how he had behaved.

Mr Browne QC's case that, in failing to check, the newspaper was reckless, was based on two alternative propositions: first that the newspaper constituted Mr Brenna as its agent for checking, and that he was reckless in failing to make this very simple inquiry on its behalf; alternatively, if Mr Brenna was not its agent for

b checking, the newspaper itself was reckless in failing to check the story at the Los Angeles end, or indeed in London, apart from asking Mr Presland, who gave it no confirmation.

We deal first with Mr Brenna. It is common ground that his memorandum was furnished in response to an inquiry from the news editor, though there is no evidence as to the form of that inquiry. Mr Browne submitted that we should

c infer that it took the form of an instruction to check, and he bases this submission on the footing that Mr Brenna was the obvious person to be entrusted by the newspaper with checking, since he was the author of the article, lived in Los Angeles, was regarded by the newspaper as reliable, and (as his messages on 23 December show) had direct access into the newspaper computer system. Mr

d Browne also submitted that it is significant that in Mr Brenna's account dated 7 January 1993 he referred to the two women as being willing to testify 'on *our* behalf' (our emphasis).

In our judgment this evidence is not sufficient to support this inference. The news editor's request could just as well have been for a confirmation as to the reliability of the two sources and no more. The form in which Mr Brenna's

e account is couched, as Mr Gray rightly pointed out, tends to corroborate this interpretation, since if Mr Brenna had been asked to check it out on a wider basis, he would surely have made some reference to this.

What then is the position of Mr Scott himself and the newspaper executives in London? There is no suggestion that they checked direct with Mr Reid or his staff

f in Los Angeles. What is suggested by Mr Gray is that they checked with those representatives of the plaintiff whose telephone numbers appear on Mr Scott's hand-written note. Mr Gray invited us to draw the inference simply and solely from the writing down of those numbers that the calls were in fact made. In our judgment no such inference can be drawn in the absence of direct evidence from Mr Scott, since those entries denote no more than that the telephone numbers

g were in fact obtained by him; furthermore the representatives who gave evidence denied that there had been any such contact, and with no direct evidence to the contrary, it seems almost beyond doubt that the jury must have accepted their evidence. We would only add that even if there had been evidence of inquiries in London, we question whether they would have been any adequate substitute

h for the inquiry direct to Mr Reid or his staff in Los Angeles.

It follows, as Mr Browne submitted, that there is no evidence whatsoever of any inquiry of any kind being made or even attempted by Mr Scott or the other executives of the newspaper either in this country or in California, apart from that addressed by Mr Scott to Mr Presland, with the result already noted.

j Mr Gray's submission is that, even on this basis, there was room for no more than an inference of negligence or even gross negligence, which would fall short of recklessness. It was not, of course, for the judge to decide this point, but rather to rule whether the evidence was capable of supporting a conclusion of recklessness, it being for the jury to decide (as they plainly did) whether the case in recklessness was in fact made out.

It seems to us that the evidence did meet this test for a number of reasons. First, the newspaper itself, for the reasons already noted, regarded such an inquiry as requisite; secondly, the inquiry was extremely simple, involving no more than a telephone call to Mr Reid's home or office in Los Angeles, which the newspaper could easily have instructed Mr Brenna to make; thirdly, there was no urgency about the article, which was not news which would lose all interest if it was deferred a week or more to the next or subsequent issue of the Sunday Mirror; fourthly, it was an obviously damaging story about an extremely well-known public figure. In such circumstances the total failure to check was in our judgment so crass as to be capable of constituting recklessness.

We therefore conclude that there was evidence of recklessness fit to be left to the jury, and that the judge was right so to rule.

Calculation

Perhaps the most helpful authority on the practical application of the requirements under this heading is to found in *Riches v News Group Newspapers Ltd*. There it was held by the Court of Appeal (Stephenson, Parker LJJ and Park J) that there was evidence fit to be left to the jury on calculation, viz: (i) the article itself with its eye-catching headline, its 'exclusive' caption, and its position on the front page of an edition distributed nation-wide, which was described by Stephenson LJ as the factor on which the plaintiffs 'rested their case'; (ii) the fact that the jury were entitled to disbelieve the evidence of the editor that the motive for publication was public-spirited (see [1985] 2 All ER 845 at 852, 866–867, [1986] QB 256 at 272, 292 per Stephenson LJ and Park J).

The present case is almost a precise counterpart of the *Riches* case so far as the first heading is concerned. Mr Gray, however, submitted that this, taken by itself, is not enough and that more positive evidence is needed, though he does not of course go so far as to suggest that an actual pen-and-paper calculation must be shown. We would not be prepared to accept this submission, having regard to the great prominence of the presentation here, which (as in *Riches*) was the factor on which Mr John rested his own case, and which goes well beyond mere reliance on the bare fact that the newspaper is conducted for profit. But the matter does not end there, since in our judgment it was plainly open to the jury to infer from the letter dated 23 August quoted above that the newspaper reckoned that, having regard to the plaintiff's 'self-confessed seventeen years of drug and dietary abuse and his possession of drugs' for which he was 'extremely fortunate not ever to have been prosecuted', the plaintiff was very unlikely to sue. Mr Gray contended that no such inference could be drawn since, as he submitted, the plaintiff is a regular litigator in libel actions, but there was no evidence before the jury that he had any such disposition.

For these reasons we have come to the conclusion that there was sufficient evidence fit to go to the jury on calculation.

The summing up

The major criticisms advanced by Mr Gray are that the summing up was inadequate both in relation to recklessness and in relation to calculation. The question here is not whether the summing up was beyond criticism, but whether it meets the test of adequacy, in the sense that it drew to the jury's attention the relevant issues.

So far as recklessness is concerned, the nub of Mr Gray's criticisms is that a fuller direction was needed along the lines of that given by Widgery J in *Manson's* case. Here the judge directed the jury not once but several times that the plaintiff had to show on the evidence that the defendants deliberately committed the

a publication either knowing it was untrue or being reckless and not caring whether it was true or false.

For the reasons already explained, we consider this direction was sufficient, though we feel sure that in future a fuller direction will be given on the lines we have recommended.

So far as calculation is concerned, there is no criticism of the judge's direction

b as to the need for the plaintiff to prove a calculation, which was closely in line with that of Widgery J in *Manson's* case. The criticism here is that he failed to give the jury any adequate direction as to the way in which they should approach the question, and that he should have told them that the mere fact that the defendant published the newspaper for profit did not necessarily mean that it carried out any such calculation.

c We do not think this criticism is justified. The judge made it crystal clear that the calculation had to be deliberate, and he described it in a manner which seems to us amply sufficient:

> d 'Punitive damages can arise where the defendant deliberately commits the publication either knowing it is untrue or not caring whether it is true or false, and does so because he thinks he will pocket by it; he made the calculation: "Well, it will help the circulation of our newspaper. He may sue. He may not. If he does not so much the better. If he does we will try to settle and get out as quickly as we can. If we cannot do that and it goes to court we still think that the total cost to us, adding everything, damages ... and the
> e legal costs, all the lot, will still make it worth the gain for us to publish it. So we will go ahead."'

The other less fundamental criticisms are as follows.

(1) That he failed to direct them how they should determine whether or not the case was exceptional. We do not think he had any obligation to do so, and in

f any event he made it quite clear more than once that, even if the two main criteria were satisfied, the jury still had to consider whether in this case an award of exemplary damages was necessary. He closed his summing up with these words:

> g 'Punitive damages are only rarely awarded. They are generally not encouraged by the court, but they are there for you to award and it is your decision very much whether you think this case is one of those rare cases which does so qualify and, if so, what should be done about it.'

(2) That he should have focused the jury's mind on the facts and matters

h pleaded in the amended statement of claim. In the upshot this is exactly what the judge did. If, contrary to our view expressed above, Mr Brenna's conduct and state of mind had been relevant, then this would have been a valid criticism, as also would have been the criticism that he failed to give the jury any direction on vicarious liability.

j (3) That he failed to give the jury any adequate direction in this context as to the relevant facts, in particular those relied upon by the newspaper that the story was plausible, that Mr Brenna was regarded as a reliable source, and that the two informants did actually attend the party. All these matters were fully canvassed in his summary of the facts to the jury, and we do not think it was necessary for him to elaborate them again in the specific context of exemplary damages.

(4) That the judge misdirected the jury in telling them that the newspaper was a very large company with great means. Here it is not disputed that this could be

a relevant consideration, but it is said that there was no evidence of its means. The precise direction on this point was as follows:

> 'In a case of punishment, of punitive damages, you can bear in mind the means of the defendant because punishment clearly is affected by the means of the party paying. If you make an award which might badly hurt the ordinary man in the street it might be laughable to a large company with very great means. As the purpose of your award of damages is to punish for bad conduct and deter others, you should properly have in mind the means of the party who you are punishing. But having said that, I add again, do not because you may think the Mirror Group are very wealthy, go over the top on that account. Bear in mind always that you are to make an award which is reasonable.'

We do not think that this direction can be faulted in the case of a national newspaper with a circulation running into millions, whether or not, as Mr Gray submitted, this operation may not have been profitable during the era following Mr Robert Maxwell's death, of which there was no evidence.

'If but only if'

It is noteworthy that there is no criticism of the judge's direction on this point, which was clear and specific.

We must nonetheless decide ourselves whether that test is satisfied, bearing in mind the quantum of our award on compensatory damages.

The question is whether the sum which we have awarded for compensatory damages is sufficient to punish the newspaper and deter it and others. In our judgment it is not, since we do not think that this sum adequately reflects the gravity of the newspaper's conduct, or that it would deter it or other national newspapers of a similar character from such conduct in future. An award of exemplary damages is therefore, in our judgment, necessary to meet these two requirements.

The amount awarded

The jury awarded exemplary damages of £275,000, making a grand total of £350,000. Mr Browne supports that figure as reasonable, but in our judgment Mr Gray is right in his submission that this sum is manifestly excessive, and goes well beyond the minimum sum needed to meet the two relevant requirements. We think that those requirements will be fully met by an award of £50,000 exemplary damages, making a grand total of damages under both headings of £75,000, which will ensure that justice is done to both sides, and will also fully secure the public interest involved.

Appeal allowed in part. Leave to appeal to the House of Lords refused.

L I Zysman Esq   Barrister.

Re G (a minor) (social worker: disclosure)

COURT OF APPEAL, CIVIL DIVISION
BUTLER-SLOSS, AULD LJJ AND SIR ROGER PARKER
17 JULY, 25 OCTOBER 1995

Family proceedings – Confidential information in care proceedings – Disclosure to police of confidential information sought by local authority in care proceedings – Parents prepared to make admissions to social worker in care proceedings regarding injuries to child – Criminal proceedings pending against father – Whether social worker entitled to disclose information from parents to police without leave of court – Children Act 1989, s 98 – Family Proceedings Rules 1991, r 4.23.

The local authority instituted care proceedings in respect of a child, M, who had suffered a number of serious injuries which appeared to be non-accidental. M's parents were arrested and the father was committed for trial. At the trial the prosecution offered no evidence and the judge directed that the indictment remain on file. When a further child was born to the parents, the local authority obtained an interim care order in respect of him. The child's guardian ad litem prepared a report for the final determination of his future, which highlighted the risk of returning him to his parents without much fuller information about M's injuries. The parents indicated a willingness to discuss the circumstances of those injuries, but were concerned that they might be exposed to criminal proceedings if they made damaging admissions. The local authority, supported by the police who had been given leave to intervene, applied to the court for a ruling that they were entitled to disclose to the police any information obtained from the parents about the injuries to M. The judge upheld the argument of the parents and the guardian ad litem that, by virtue of r 4.23[a] of the Family Proceedings Rules 1991, the local authority was not so entitled, since any admissions were documents in family proceedings and could not be disclosed without leave of the court. The local authority appealed.

Held – (Auld LJ dissenting) The ambit of r 4.23 of the 1991 rules was limited to documents held by the court in the court file and consequently a social worker was at liberty to inform the police of any statement or admission, relevant to joint inter-agency investigations, which were made to him by a parent for use in care proceedings without first obtaining the leave of the court. A broader interpretation of the rule would bring within its ambit information at a stage when it was not intended to be covered and would be contrary to wider considerations of the best interests of the child. The different positions of social worker and guardian ad litem might create a certain anomaly, in that the same statement given to different people might be subject to different rules of confidentiality, but that might be a necessary consequence of their different statutory roles. It followed on the facts that any admissions which the parents made to a social worker regarding the circumstances of the injuries to M could be disclosed by the local authority to the police without obtaining the leave of the court. The appeal would accordingly be allowed (see p 73 b to j and p 77 c d, post); *Oxfordshire CC v P* [1995] 2 All ER 225 and *Cleveland CC v F* [1995] 2 All ER 236 considered.

---

a   Rule 4.23, so far as material, is set out at p 69 *d* e, post

Per Butler-Sloss LJ and Sir Roger Parker. The protection from
self-incrimination afforded by s 98[b] of the Children Act 1989 cannot be extended
to cover admissions made in advance of care proceedings to a social worker (see
p 73 *j* to p 74 *a c* to *f* and p 77 *e f*, post).

Notes

For disclosure of documents relating to wardship proceedings, see 5(2) *Halsbury's
Laws* (4th edn reissue) para 762, and for cases on the subject, see 28(3) *Digest* (2nd
reissue) 309–311, *2899–2908*.

For the Children Act 1989, s 98, see 6 *Halsbury's Statutes* (4th edn) (1992 reissue)
518.

For the Family Proceedings Rules 1991, r 4.23, see 12 *Halsbury's Statutory
Instruments* (1995 reissue) 93.

Editor's note For a subsequent House of Lords decision on whether legal
professional privilege against self-incrimination applies when leave is sought to
disclose to the police a medical report obtained by the mother regarding her care
of a child, see [1996] 2 All ER 78.

Cases referred to in judgments

Cleveland CC v F [1995] 2 All ER 236, [1995] 1 WLR 785.

D v National Society for the Prevention of Cruelty to Children [1977] 1 All ER 589,
[1978] AC 171, [1977] 2 WLR 201, HL; *rvsg* [1976] 2 All ER 993, [1978] AC 171,
[1976] 3 WLR 124, CA.

D (minors) (wardship: disclosure), Re [1994] 1 FLR 346, CA.

F (minors) (wardship: police investigation), Re [1989] Fam 18, [1988] 3 WLR 818, CA.

F (a minor) (publication of information), Re [1977] 1 All ER 114, [1977] Fam 58, [1976]
3 WLR 813, CA.

K and ors (minors) (disclosure of privileged material), Re [1994] 3 All ER 230, sub nom
Kent CC v K [1994] 1 WLR 912.

Oxfordshire CC v M [1994] 2 All ER 269, [1994] Fam 151, [1994] 2 WLR 393, CA.

Oxfordshire CC v P [1995] 2 All ER 225, [1995] 1 FLR 552.

R v Hampshire CC, ex p K [1990] 2 All ER 129, [1990] 2 QB 71, [1990] 2 WLR 649,
DC.

S and ors (minors) (wardship: police investigation), Re [1987] 3 All ER 1076, [1987]
Fam 199, [1987] 3 WLR 847.

Cases also cited or referred to in skeleton arguments

C (expert evidence: disclosure: practice), Re [1995] 1 FLR 204.

L (police investigation: privilege), Re [1995] 1 FLR 999, CA; *affd* [1996] 2 All ER 78,
HL.

Appeal

By notice dated 13 June 1995 the local authority appealed with leave from the
order of Judge Elystan Morgan in the Warrington County Court made on 22 May
1995, whereby he declared, on the local authority's application for a ruling, that
it was not entitled to disclose to the police (who had been given leave to
intervene) information received from either parent of a child relating to serious
injuries previously sustained by their older child, M. The child's guardian ad

---

b　　Section 98 is set out at p 74 *b c*, post

a litem took part in the proceedings. The facts are set out in the judgment of Butler-Sloss LJ.

Margaret de Haas (instructed by *Gerry Budd*, Chester) for the local authority.
Alex Stansby (instructed by *Michael Seward & Co*, Warrington) for the parents.
Paula Fallows (instructed by *Rowlands*, Stockport) for the guardian ad litem.
b *Peter Moss* (instructed by *Graham D Gordon*, Chester) for the police.

At the conclusion of the argument the court announced that the appeal would be allowed for reasons to be given later.

c 25 October 1995. The following judgments were delivered.

BUTLER-SLOSS LJ. The issues which arise in this appeal stem from the tension between the criminal and civil jurisdictions in cases of child abuse.

On 31 December 1992 a baby, M, aged six months, was taken by his mother to hospital and was found to have a number of serious injuries which appeared to *d* be non-accidental. The parents gave unsatisfactory accounts of the injuries and blamed each other. They were arrested and the father committed for trial. At the trial the prosecution offered no evidence and the judge directed that the indictment remain on the file. The local authority instituted care proceedings and the child is now living with the paternal grandparents.

e On 26 January 1995 J was born to the same parents and, in view of the injuries to M, the local authority obtained an interim care order on 2 February 1995. The main hearing as to J's future is to be in November. In an interim report the guardian ad litem of J has pointed to the risk of returning J to his parents without much fuller information about M's injuries. Any effective assessment of the parents as future carers by social workers is impeded by the lack of information *f* and the inability to evaluate the degree of risk to J of such a return.

The parents have indicated a willingness to discuss in fuller detail, and presumably with more candour, the circumstances of those injuries. They are, however, anxious not to expose themselves to criminal proceedings if they make damaging admissions. The issue came before Judge Elystan Morgan at Warrington County Court on 22 May 1995 whether the local authority would be *g* entitled, without leave of the court, to disclose to the Cheshire Police any information obtained from the parents about the injuries to M. The local authority, supported by the police, who were given leave to intervene, sought a ruling that they might give that information to the police. The parents and the guardian ad litem argued that the local authority was precluded from giving that *h* information without leave of the court, in accordance with the provisions of r 4.23 of the Family Proceedings Rules 1991, SI 1991/1247. The judge ruled that the local authority would not be entitled to relay any information received from the parents about M's injuries to the police. The local authority, supported by the police, appealed against that ruling to this court. Since there was some urgency *j* for a decision to be made in view of the pending care proceedings, we allowed the appeal, set aside the judge's declaration and substituted a declaration that the social worker is at liberty to inform the police of any statements or admissions made to him by the parents without leave of the court. We now give our reasons for that decision.

Before considering the decisions which touch on this issue, it is useful, in my view, to look at the context in which the police are involved in these cases of

injury to and abuse of children. They have, it seems to me, two functions in
particular, the investigation of crime and the protection of children, which
include statutory responsibilities, such as by s 46 of the Children Act 1989
(removal and accommodation of children by police in cases of emergency). In
their increasingly important role of child protection they fully participate all over
the country in inter-disciplinary arrangements recommended in the booklet
published in 1991 jointly by the Home Office, the Department of Health, the
Department of Education and Science and the Welsh Office, *Working Together
under the Children Act 1989*. In the introduction at para 1.9 it deals with Area Child
Protection Committees:

> 'The protection of children requires a close working relationship between
> social services departments, the police service, medical practitioners,
> community health workers, schools, voluntary agencies and others.
> Co-operation at the individual case level needs to be supported by joint
> agency and management policies for child protection.'

Consultation between the police and social services departments is set out in
paras 4.16 and 4.17. In para 4.17 it says:

> 'Difficulties will be encountered in joint inter-agency investigations but
> these can be minimised by the selection of specialist staff who undergo
> appropriate inter-agency training. However, it is essential that methods of
> joint working are established between the two agencies over and above the
> joint interviewing of child victims. There should be agreed procedures for
> the joint inter-agency investigation process which ensure that there is
> adequate planning and full consultation at all stages of any investigation.'

The *Working Together* booklet does not have any legal status but, with the
lessons of *Cleveland CC v F* [1995] 2 All ER 236, [1995] 1 WLR 785 in mind, the
emphasis upon co-operation, joint investigation and full consultation at all stages
of any investigation are crucial to the success of the government guidelines.
Those guidelines have been adapted for local use throughout England and Wales.
In Cheshire they are to be found in the red manual provided to us, *Cheshire Child
Protection Committee Manual of Procedures* (1993). It is published on behalf of the
Child Protection Committee. Paragraph 4.3 sets out that 'social services and
police should jointly investigate cases of sexual abuse and other forms of serious
abuse where there may be both criminal offences and child protection issues to
consider'. The police regularly attend child protection case conferences.

The consequence of the inter-disciplinary investigation is that there has to be
free exchange of information between social workers and police officers together
engaged in an investigation. At the stage of the commencement of the
investigation it will not be known in the majority of cases whether there will be
proceedings instituted by the local authority in respect of the children, and
perhaps even less certain whether there will be a criminal prosecution. The
information obtained by social workers in the course of their duties is, however,
confidential and covered by the umbrella of public interest immunity. It cannot
therefore 'be freely and widely published outside the proceedings' as was
suggested in relation to information provided to a guardian ad litem by Ward J in
Oxfordshire CC v P [1995] 2 All ER 225, [1995] 1 FLR 552. It can, however, be
disclosed to fellow members of the child protection team engaged in the
investigation of the possible abuse of the child concerned.

a   There is a long line of authority that Social Service Departments' case records and files are not produced on an application for discovery and are exempt from disclosure in court proceedings unless a judge rules to the contrary: see eg *D v National Society for the Prevention of Cruelty to Children* [1977] 1 All ER 589, [1978] AC 171 and *R v Hampshire CC, ex p K* [1990] 2 All ER 129, [1990] 2 QB 71. A summary of the relevant information contained in those case records is usually

b   provided in statements prepared by social workers for court proceedings and those documents *are* covered by r 4.23.

There are two stages for the local authority in a child protection investigation, the gathering of the information and the decision whether to take proceedings. In some cases protective measures have to be taken either immediately or during the progress of the investigation by an application for an emergency protection

c   order or interim care order. Once the application under Pt IV or Pt V of the 1989 Act for a care order, supervision order, or emergency protection order has been made, documents will be prepared for the court proceedings. Rule 4.23 provides:

d   '*Confidentiality of documents* (1) Notwithstanding any rule of court to the contrary, no document, other than a record of an order, held by the court and relating to proceedings to which this Part applies shall be disclosed, other than to ... [parties, legal advisers, etc] without leave of the judge or district judge.'

That rule precludes the disclosure of documents, held by the court and relating

e   to family proceedings, to anyone other than those named in the rule without the leave of the court. The narrow view is that documents created for the purpose of court proceedings do not attract control under r 4.23 until actually filed with the court. The alternative view is to include identifiable documents destined for the court within the control of the court. The rule follows the long-established practice of confidentiality of children proceedings, stemming from the practice in

f   wardship cases. This practice was considered by this court in *Re D (minors) (wardship: disclosure)* [1994] 1 FLR 346, where the father and grandfather of three children were charged with offences of indecency against them in criminal proceedings. They sought disclosure of documents in wardship proceedings in which the mother had alleged sexual abuse of one of the children. The Court of

g   Appeal gave leave to disclose some of the documents to the criminal trial and Sir Stephen Brown P said (at 350–351):

h   'The question of disclosing wardship documents for the purpose of the investigation of possible criminal offences has been the subject of consideration by the courts on a number of occasions. The principle is quite clear, and that is that the judge hearing an application for leave to disclose such documents must in the exercise of his discretion conduct a balancing exercise—that is to say, he has to balance the importance of confidentiality in wardship proceedings and the frankness which it engenders in those who give evidence to the wardship court against the public interest in seeing that

j   the ends of justice are properly served. In relation to criminal proceedings it is clear that the wardship court should not, as it were, seek to erect a barrier which would prejudice the operation of another branch of the judicature. There have been a number of cases where the discretion of the judge has been exercised to give leave to disclose to the Crown Prosecution Service matters which are part of the wardship file. Similar considerations will apply to defendants because it is in the interests of justice that a defendant in a criminal trial should have available all the relevant and necessary material for the proper conduct of his or her defence.'

In *Oxfordshire CC v M* [1994] 2 All ER 269 at 278, [1994] Fam 151 at 160, where this court required the disclosure of psychiatrists' reports to the court and to the other parties, Sir Stephen Brown P, in his judgment, said that children cases fall into a special category where the duty of the court is to investigate and where 'the court is bound to undertake all necessary steps to arrive at an appropriate result in the paramount interests of the welfare of the child'. He drew an analogy between wardship and the 1989 Act with which I respectfully agree. The underlying purpose of the practice both in wardship and in proceedings under the 1989 Act is to safeguard the welfare of the child and to encourage frankness in giving evidence and providing information to assist the court in determining the child's best interests. The confidentiality attaches to the documents in the custody of the court and covers the information contained within those documents. The problem of immunity from prosecution for those who give information which may incriminate them may be solved, in part at least, by the provisions of s 98 of the 1989 Act which offers protection from prosecution to those giving evidence in proceedings under Part IV or Pt V (e g care or emergency protection applications).

The extent of control over documents in wardship cases has never been defined but a distinction has been drawn between documents which were or were not before the court. In *Re D (minors) (wardship: disclosure)* [1994] 1 FLR 346 leave was given to disclose case notes and video recordings. The court held that the application regarding other documents was misconceived, since they had not been adduced in evidence in the wardship proceedings and had never been in the custody or control of the court. Booth J in *Re K and ors (minors) (disclosure of privileged material)* [1994] 3 All ER 230, [1994] 1 WLR 912 applied the principles in *Oxfordshire CC v M* and *Re D* to a Children Act application for disclosure under r 4.23. She held in an earlier decision *Re S and ors (minors) (wardship: police investigation)* [1987] 3 All ER 1076, [1987] Fam 199 that the court had no jurisdiction to order disclosure of local authority case records, since they did not relate to matters which were placed in evidence before the court. In *Re F (a minor) (publication of information)* [1977] 1 All ER 114, [1977] Fam 58 this court held that reports of the social worker and the Official Solicitor were clearly part of the proceedings. In *Re F (minors) (wardship: police investigation)* [1989] Fam 18 this court held that the court in wardship proceedings had an unfettered discretion whether to release information and decided that the documents produced to the court, including affidavits and documents, and other relevant information held by the local authority should be made available to the Crown Prosecution Service.

I turn now to two recent decisions of the Family Division, *Oxfordshire CC v P* [1995] 2 All ER 225, [1995] 1 FLR 552 and *Cleveland CC v F* [1995] 2 All ER 236, [1995] 1 WLR 785. In *Oxfordshire CC v P* a local authority initiated care proceedings in respect of a young baby who had suffered serious non-accidental injury. The mother confessed to the guardian ad litem that she had injured the child. The guardian informed the social worker, who passed on the information to the police. The Crown Prosecution Service wished to rely upon the confession to prove criminal charges against the mother, and obtained a witness statement from the guardian. The mother applied to have the guardian removed from the care proceedings. The main questions before Ward J were whether the guardian a was at liberty to disclose the mother's admissions to the social worker, whether the social worker was at liberty to disclose to the police, and whether the guardian should make a witness statement without leave of the court hearing the care proceedings. The judge terminated the guardianship and held that the privilege of confidentiality was a matter for the court and the guardian should not have acted without obtaining the leave of the court.

b I agree with the judge's decision to remove the guardian and, without having heard detailed argument, I would be disposed to agree with his view of the guardian's status. The judge, in a part of his judgment which was clearly obiter, referred to the importance of co-operation between social workers and the police and of the free exchange of information, but suggested that, strictly speaking, the local authority needed to obtain the leave of the court to tell the police if the c information has been obtained as a direct result of the pending proceedings. He then laid down some proposed guidelines in the hope of achieving an agreement as to the use of the information exchanged. He also expressed the view that s 98 of the 1989 Act was wide enough to protect the maker of an admission to the guardian or social worker.

d In *Cleveland CC v F* a local authority instituted care proceedings in respect of five children after the death of a baby sister. The mother did not make a statement because she was nervous of the consequences to herself and to the father. She applied to the court for a direction that any oral or written statement she made either to the guardian or to a social worker would be confidential to the care proceedings, a situation very similar to the present appeal. Hale J followed Ward e J in *Oxfordshire CC v P* and held that any incriminating statements which the mother might make to the guardian or a social worker were adequately protected from disclosure by s 98 and r 4.23. It would be a matter for the judge weighing the conflicting factors to decide whether to give leave for the information, if admissible, to be disclosed. She declined to make a declaration. She also sup-f ported the proposed guidelines suggested by Ward J. In the light of arguments advanced to us, those proposed guidelines are possibly misleading since they do not represent the current state of the law.

In so far as Ward J and Hale J appear to equate the position of the social worker with that of the guardian, I do not agree with them. The guardian is appointed by s 41 of the 1989 Act and his powers and duties are laid down by s 42, which g gives him a right of access to local authority records. When those proceedings are completed his function is ended (see the 1991 rules, and the Guardians ad Litem and Reporting Officers (Panels) Regulations 1991, SI 1991/2051). The guardian has no function outside the proceedings to which he has been appointed. It may be that disclosure of all documents emanating from or h information given to the guardian would be subject to the leave of the court. I would not wish to express a view, in the absence of argument, as to the scope of the guardian's duty to the court and whether it excludes the duty to inform the police of admissions of criminal offences, without obtaining leave of the civil court.

j A social worker's duties towards children in his area are far wider and are by no means confined to court proceedings. In many cases the children with whom he is concerned may never appear before a court. As I have already set out earlier in this judgment, some documents created by the Social Services Department will be covered by r 4.23, but many will not. The problem raised by this appeal would occur if an oral statement is made to a social worker for the purpose of care proceedings. A written statement by a parent, for instance, made for the purpose

of proceedings, whether handed to the social worker, guardian or to the court
direct, may be covered by r 4.23. Oral admissions made to a social worker which   *a*
he records in writing and places in the social work file do not, at that stage in my
view, come within the ambit of r 4.23. I recognise the perhaps rather fine
distinction of information in oral form provided to the social worker, not within
the rule, whereas the same or substantially the same information reduced to
writing by the social worker and filed with the court is within the rule. A   *b*
distinction has frequently to be made between documents created for court
proceedings and those which come into existence in the normal course of a social
worker's duties and it may be difficult to be sure on occasions which are which.
If the ambit of r 4.23 is limited to documents actually filed with the court, the
position is much more easily ascertainable. The present hypothetical case is clear
cut. The purpose of the proposed admissions in this appeal is to have an impact   *c*
on the outcome of the care proceedings which are imminent and the admissions
are designed both for the court and for consideration by the social workers.

The effect, however, of r 4.23 as interpreted by the judge, goes far wider and
the distinction which I draw, although it might seem to be artificial, is of the
utmost importance in the investigation of child abuse. All the information   *d*
garnered by the social workers is confidential and covered by public interest
immunity. All the information is subject to controls and cannot in any event be
disclosed to those not engaged in the investigation process. The Department of
Health has issued circular LAC (88) 17, giving guidance on confidentiality of
personal information held by local authorities; at 6-791, para 28, guidance is given   *e*
on disclosure by them to the police of personal information under certain
conditions. Some of the information is in the custody of and controlled by the
court and requires the leave of the court. The other information on the child
concerned is not and cannot be controlled by the court (see Sir Stephen Brown P
in *Re D (minors) (wardship: disclosure)* [1994] 1 FLR 346). Is r 4.23 to apply so that
the door is shut, during the course of the investigation, or even at its beginning,   *f*
on other members of the investigating team, so that they may not be given
relevant information, which would be or might be crucial to the child protection
team for the protection of the child and investigation of the facts relevant to long
term arrangements for the child, as well as wider considerations of public
interest? I can foresee a situation in which a child is taken to hospital with serious
injuries which appear to be non-accidental injury by one or both parents. An   *g*
emergency protection order is made and the child protection team, including
social workers and police, start their investigation. The mother is seen by the
social worker the same day and admits that she or her husband injured the child.
On the judge's interpretation, since there is an emergency protection order, if, as
it would be said, the admissions related to the emergency protection proceedings,   *h*
the social worker would have to apply to the judge for leave to tell other
members of the children protection team, such as the police officer, jointly
investigating the alleged non-accidental injury, what the mother had told him.
The joint investigation would be ineffective without a court order and each
discipline would go its own way, potentially reproducing the unsatisfactory   *j*
arrangements widely in place pre-Cleveland. The child protection case conference, made up as it is of members of various disciplines, not only social
workers, and which advises the Social Services Department on the steps to be
taken in the best interests of the child, would not be given the crucial information
about the admissions without application to the court. This would render
ineffective the deliberations of the case conference. Presumably, where proceed-

a ings were pending, the social worker could not even tell the paediatrician treating a child with an unexplained illness, in a possible Munchausen's syndrome by proxy case, that the mother had admitted that the cause of the illness was a drug administered by the mother. This carries the control of the court over the documents provided to it to excessive lengths and, if right, would drive a coach and horses through the carefully constructed joint arrangements for investigation *b* into child abuse, and might even put the child's welfare at risk.

I would, on balance, and in the absence of argument, give the more restrictive interpretation to r 4.23 and limit it to documents held by the court in the court file. I doubt that it extends to documents created for the purpose of the proceedings even if intended to be filed with the court, since they may not, in fact, become part of the court file. It is important that the rule should not be widely *c* and loosely interpreted so as to bring within its ambit information at a stage when I am sure it was not intended to be covered, and which would be contrary to wider considerations of the best interests of the child. The different positions of social worker and guardian may create a certain anomaly, in that the same statement given to different people may be subject to different rules of *d* confidentiality, but that may be a necessary consequence of their different statutory roles.

In my view, for the reasons which I have given, Ward J, in *Oxfordshire CC v P*, and Hale J, in *Cleveland CC v F*, were in error in considering that r 4.23 extended to oral statements made by a parent to a social worker. I can see no bar to exchange of information at any stage, save when caught by r 4.23, between those *e* engaged in the investigation of, protection from and prevention of child abuse. The exchange of information would cover those working together in inter-agency co-operation, in particular the police and the social worker, including the paediatrician or other mental health involvement where appropriate and would extend to reporting to the much larger group comprising the child *f* protection case conference.

The judge in the present case followed the decisions in *Oxfordshire CC v P* and *Cleveland CC v F* and applied them to the present hypothetical facts. His extension of the ambit of r 4.23 to cover any statement or admission made by one or both of the parents to a social worker went beyond its proper boundaries, and in my *g* view his declaration cannot stand. The question of leave under r 4.23 does not arise. A social worker, in my judgment, may and indeed ought to inform the police if admissions are made to him by the parents in this case which are relevant to the joint investigation.

I have had the opportunity of reading Auld LJ's judgment in draft and for the *h* reasons I have given I respectfully disagree with his conclusions on the ambit of r 4.23.

The decision of this court as to the scope of r 4.23 is sufficient to dispose of the appeal, but we have also heard some argument as to the scope of s 98 of the 1989 Act. Since both Ward J and Hale J have expressed opinions about s 98, I feel we *j* should make some limited observations about it. I do so with some hesitation, and conscious that any comments will be obiter and that the subject requires more careful consideration on another occasion.

The consequences of an admission and whether it may attract immunity will depend on the circumstances and in particular whether it falls within the scope of s 98. This section within the 1989 Act is designed to give protection from self-incrimination to those who are obliged to give evidence in public law child

cases and to make full and frank disclosure of matters relevant to the welfare of
the child.

Section 98 states:

'Self-Incrimination (1) In any proceedings in which a court is hearing an
application for an order under part IV or V, no person shall be excused
from—(a) giving evidence on any matter; or (b) answering any question put
to him in the course of his giving evidence, on the ground that doing so
might incriminate him or his spouse of an offence.

(2) A statement or admission made in such proceedings shall not be
admissible in evidence against the person making it or his spouse in
proceedings for an offence other than perjury.'

Ward J considered that the scope of s 98 extended to protecting admissions
made in advance of care proceedings to a social worker, and was supported in
that wide interpretation of the section by Hale J. Booth J in *Re K and ors (minors)
(disclosure of privileged material)* [1994] 3 All ER 230 at 235, [1994] 1 WLR 912 at
916, albeit in a somewhat different context, took a narrower view, and said that
the section provided protection to a witness who was required to give evidence
in relation to a child when such evidence could incriminate him or his spouse.

Section 98(2) refers to 'A statement or admission made in such proceedings',
which clearly refers back to s 98(1) which covers 'any proceedings in which a
court is hearing an application ...' I would doubt that sub-s (2) could be extended
as far as Ward J and Hale J have suggested or that it would cover the situations
postulated in *Oxfordshire CC v P* or *Cleveland CC v F*. That preliminary view is not
inconsistent with *Re F (a minor) (publication of information)* [1977] 1 All ER 114,
[1977] Fam 58, which dealt with documents in wardship proceedings which
would today be covered by r 4.23 and not by s 98. My preliminary view is not
intended to and cannot bind any criminal court in its duty to interpret s 98.

AULD LJ. The question before the court is whether any oral or written
statement that may be made by a parent to a social worker for use in care
proceedings, but not, or not yet, committed to a document held by the court,
may be disclosed to the police without leave of the court. The judge held that it
would require leave.

Any such statement, if it is to be of any use in care proceedings is likely to
become evidence in the case, whether in the form of a social worker's report of
what the parent has said or in the parent's own written statement. In either form
it seems to me that as soon as it reaches the court file it would be protected from
disclosure by r 4.23 as a 'document ... held by the court and relating to [the]
proceedings'. But what about disclosure of such a document before it becomes
part of the court file, or disclosure before or after that event of a document
containing information provided for the purpose of the care proceedings, e g
notes of interview and the like, on which the document is based?

In *Oxfordshire CC v P* [1995] 2 All ER 225 at 230, 1 FLR 552 at 556 Ward J, as he
then was, said, as to a guardian ad litem's report, that information obtained for its
preparation and on which it was based should have the same confidentiality as
the report itself. He added:

'It would be absurd to hold that information coming to the guardian ad
litem's knowledge could be freely and widely published outside the

a   proceeding before it had been reduced to writing and made a document in the proceedings.'

In *Cleveland CC v F* [1995] 2 All ER 236, [1995] 1 WLR 785 Hale J adopted the same approach in relation to a potential statement by a parent to a guardian or social worker made for the purpose of and in the course of care proceedings.

b   In my view, the important matter is not the person to whom the statement is made—guardian, social worker, or other—but the purpose for which it is made: the care proceedings. The approach of both Ward and Hale JJ are clear applications of that principle; they are of a piece with the approach of the court in wardship cases; and they accord with common sense.

c   As to wardship, similar issues arose in the interpretation of the words in s 12 of the Administration of Justice Act 1960 which made it a contempt of court to publish 'information relating to proceedings before any court sitting in private' in, inter alia, wardship proceedings. In *Re S and ors (minors) (wardship: police investigation)* [1987] 3 All ER 1076 at 1081, [1987] Fam 199 at 205, Booth J held that the formula included statements prepared by a person 'for the purposes of such d   proceedings', but not case records held by a social services department of a local authority not prepared for that purpose. In *Re F (minors) (wardship: police investigation)* [1989] Fam 18, the Court of Appeal upheld an order of Booth J in a wardship case in which she had exercised her discretion to permit what would otherwise have amounted to contempt under s 12 of the 1960 Act by ordering the e   local authority to disclose to the police a transcript of her judgment and also 'all the documents and information in their possession relating to the wards of court and these wardship proceedings' (see [1989] Fam 18 at 23). Whilst it is true that r 4.23, in its formula 'document ... held by the court', is expressed more tightly than that in s 12 of the 1960 Act ('information relating to proceedings'), the concerns and aims of care proceedings in this respect are much the same as they f   were in wardship. (See *Oxfordshire CC v M* [1994] 2 All ER 269 at 277–278, [1994] Fam 151 at 160 per Sir Stephen Brown P.)

As to common sense, I share Ward J's view that it would be absurd if a document or the preparatory material for it, created for the purpose of use in care proceedings, could be freely disclosed to third parties before the document is g   lodged with the court, and only become confidential thereafter. Here, the whole purpose of the proposed statements of the parents is that they should be put before the court in some documentary form in these care proceedings. There is no sense in allowing them to be freely disclosable when made, and delaying the protection of confidentiality until they take the form of, or are incorporated in, h   documents lodged with the court.

Accordingly, I respectfully differ from the views of Butler-Sloss LJ and Sir Roger Parker, and would uphold the judge's ruling that any statement made by either parent in and for the purpose of the care proceedings cannot be disclosed to the police without the leave of the court.

j   A civil court considering in a care or protection case whether to order disclosure of material, whether pursuant to r 4.23 or where it is protected by public interest immunity, should no doubt have regard to, inter alia, the probable consequence of disclosure in any subsequent criminal proceedings. However, it is not for this court to rule on the question of admissibility of such material in criminal proceedings. As Ward J indicated in *Oxfordshire CC v P* [1995] 2 All ER 225 at 231–232, 1 FLR 552 at 558, the question under s 98(2) of the 1989 Act

whether 'a statement or admission' is inadmissible because it was made 'in' care
or protection 'proceedings' is, in each case, for the criminal court.   *a*

Nevertheless, if the civil court is to exercise its discretion properly, it is
desirable that its general understanding of the interpretation of s 98(2) should be
the same as that of the criminal courts when they come to apply it. Ward J had
that in mind in *Oxfordshire CC v P* [1995] 2 All ER 225 at 232, [1995] 1 FLR 552 at
558 when, in relation to the sought disclosure from the mother, he said: *b*

> 'In order that this mother might gain in confidence and so unburden her
> heart, I agreed to express my view as to the meaning of s 98 ... leaving it to
> the criminal court to make of this opinion what it will.'

I approach the question in the same way. It seems to me that the words in s 98(2)
'a statement or admission made in such proceedings' do not mean only   *c*
statements or admissions made in oral evidence. The subject matter of
admissibility for decision by the criminal court under s 98(2) is wider than that of
the civil court in determining compellability to give evidence under s 98(1).
Section 98(1) is concerned with the giving of evidence in care or protection
proceedings under Pts IV and V of the Act; s 98(2) is concerned with the quite   *d*
separate matter of criminal proceedings and refers, not to evidence in the care or
protection proceedings, but to a statement or admission made in them.

I do not consider that the words in s 98(1) 'in any proceedings in which a court
is hearing ...' indicates that the words in s 98(2) '[a] statement or admission made
in such proceedings' means only a statement or admission made in the hearing of   *e*
them, that is, in the course of giving evidence. The reason for the difference is
plain. Much evidence in care proceedings is not given orally. A person is not
normally compellable to make a statement outside the witness box. He needs no
legal excuse of the sort provided by s 98(1) not to do so. Therefore, there was no
need to make any wider provision in s 98(1). However, it is obviously desirable,
if the cooperation of a parent or other person is to be obtained, that he or she   *f*
should enjoy the same immunity in any subsequent criminal proceedings in
respect of statements or admissions made for use at the hearing of care
proceedings as for those made orally in evidence at the hearing itself. I have
already remarked that s 98(2), unlike s 98(1), does not refer to 'evidence' in the
care proceedings, but simply to 'a statement or admission made in' them.
Accordingly, I agree with the approach of Ward and Hale JJ respectively in   *g*
Oxfordshire CC v P [1995] 2 All ER 225 at 232–234, [1995] 1 FLR 552 at 558–560, and
Cleveland CC v F [1995] 2 All ER 236 at 239, [1995] 1 WLR 785 at 788 that written
statements or oral statements made to and recorded by persons such as a social
worker or the guardian ad litem, for the purpose of care proceedings, are capable
of being ruled inadmissible under s 98(2).   *h*

I do not consider that s 48(2) of the 1989 Act, which expressly declares as
inadmissible in criminal proceedings statements or admissions of a person made
in compliance with an emergency protection order requiring him or her to give
information outside the witness box as to the whereabouts of a child, indicates a
narrower construction of s 98(2). First, a statement or admission made pursuant   *j*
to such an order is not made, in the words of s 98(1), 'in ... proceedings in which
a court is hearing an application for an order'; the order has been made, and the
statement or admission is made as a result of it. It would not be covered whether
a wide or narrow interpretation of s 98(2) is taken. Secondly, s 48, unlike the
more general provisions as to care and protection in Pts IV and V of the 1989 Act,
specifically imposes an obligation on a person to give information outside the

a witness box. In such circumstances, it was clearly necessary to spell out the corresponding protection in any criminal proceedings that might follow.

I add that, even where a statement or admission may not be protected by s 98(2), it is possible that the circumstances in which it was made may cause the court to exclude it under ss 76 or 78 of the Police and Criminal Evidence Act 1984.

b **SIR ROGER PARKER.** I have had the opportunity to read in draft both the foregoing judgments. I agree with the judgment of Butler-Sloss LJ. I respectfully differ from that of Auld LJ both with regard to r 4.23 and with regard to s 98(2) of the Children Act 1989.

My reasons for allowing the appeal can be very shortly stated. The wording of r 4.23 of the Family Proceedings Rules 1991, SI 1991/1247, appears to me to be
c plain. Leave to disclose is only required in respect of *documents* and only in respect of documents *held by the court*. The rule thus follows established wardship practice as can be seen from the judgments of this court in *Re D (minors) (wardship: disclosure)* [1994] 1 FLR 346. I can see neither need nor justification for extending the scope of the clear words so as to require leave for the disclosure of
d information imparted to a social worker and recorded in case notes or a report which for one reason or another has never reached the court. To do so would, in my view, not be construction but a complete rewriting of the rule and thus legislation, which is neither the function nor within the powers of the court.

As to the scope of s 98(2) of the 1989 Act, it will normally fall for decision if and when objection is taken in a criminal trial to the admission of some evidence, on
e the ground that it falls within the sub-section. It will then be considered and decided in the light of real facts. I therefore wish to add nothing to the observations on that matter contained in the judgment of Butler-Sloss LJ, save that the width afforded to it by Auld LJ appears to me to involve reading sub-s (1) as if it did not include the words 'in which a court is hearing an application for an
f order.' However desirable it may be thought to be that this should be done, and I do not think it is, it is surely for Parliament and not the courts to do it.

Appeal allowed.

Paul Magrath Esq   Barrister.

Re L (a minor) (police investigation: privilege) *a*

HOUSE OF LORDS

LORD JAUNCEY OF TULLICHETTLE, LORD MUSTILL, LORD LLOYD OF BERWICK, LORD
NICHOLLS OF BIRKENHEAD AND LORD STEYN

5–7, 11 DECEMBER 1995, 21 MARCH 1996
b

*Family proceedings – Confidential information in care proceedings – Disclosure to
police – Medical report concerning welfare of child – Privilege – Legal professional
privilege – Privilege against self-incrimination – Report prepared on mother's
instructions containing material adverse to mother's interests – Whether court should
order disclosure of report to police.* *c*

A young child whose parents were both drug addicts was admitted to hospital
and placed in intensive care after ingesting a quantity of methadone. The
mother's explanation was that the child had accidentally swallowed the
methadone while her attention was distracted, but the police suspected that she *d*
had deliberately administered the methadone to the child to pacify her when she
had toothache. However, the police at that stage decided not to press charges.
The local authority applied for a care order under Pt IV of the Children Act 1989
and in the course of those proceedings the district judge, in accordance with the
general practice then prevailing in the Family Division, made an order giving the
parents leave to disclose the court papers to a medical expert for the purpose of *e*
preparing a report on the frequency of the child's consumption of methadone
subject to the report being filed in court and disclosed to all parties. Thereafter
the mother commissioned a report by a consultant pathologist. His report, which
was filed in court pursuant to the district judge's order, substantially contradicted
the mother's account of how the child had ingested the methadone. The police *f*
became aware of the existence of the report and wished to obtain a copy for the
purpose of investigating whether the mother had committed a criminal offence
by deliberately administering methadone to the child. They therefore applied to
the court for leave to be provided with copies of medical reports in respect of the
child. The judge held that she had jurisdiction to order disclosure of the
pathologist's report to non-parties and exercised her discretion by ordering *g*
disclosure to the police. The mother appealed, contending that the judge had no
jurisdiction to order disclosure of the report to the police because it was protected
by legal professional privilege and its disclosure would infringe her privilege
against self-incrimination and, further, that the judge had exercised her discretion
wrongly. The Court of Appeal rejected those arguments and dismissed the *h*
appeal. The mother appealed to the House of Lords.

Held (Lord Mustill and Lord Nicholls of Birkenhead dissenting) – The appeal
would be dismissed for the following reasons—
  (1) There was a clear distinction between the privilege attaching to *j*
communications between solicitor and client and that attaching to reports by
third parties prepared on the instructions of a client for the purposes of litigation.
The privilege attaching to the solicitor-client relationship was absolute and
attached to all communications whether related to litigation or not, but the
privilege attaching to reports by third parties prepared for a client attached only
to documents or other written communications prepared with a view to

a litigation and, moreover, there was no property in the opinion of an expert witness, who could be subpoenaed to give evidence by the other side and could not refuse to answer questions as to his factual findings and opinion. Care proceedings under Pt IV of the 1989 Act were non-adversarial and investigative proceedings in which the judge was concerned to make a decision which was in the best interests of the child in question. Accordingly, not only was the notion

b of a fair trial between opposing parties of far less importance in care proceedings than in normal adversarial actions, but care proceedings were so far removed from normal actions that litigation privilege had no place in relation to reports obtained by a party thereto which could not have been prepared without the leave of the court to disclose documents already filed or to examine the child (see p 83 *d* to *f*, p 84 *j* to p 85 *c e* to p 86 *a*, p 88 *f g* and p 95 *b*, post); dictum of Lord

c Denning MR in *Harmony Shipping Co SA v Davis* [1979] 3 All ER 177 at 182, of Lord Scarman in *Re E (S A) (a minor) (wardship)* [1984] 1 All ER 289 at 290 and of Sir Stephen Brown P in *Oxfordshire CC v M* [1994] 2 All ER 269 at 278, 279 applied; *R v Derby Magistrates' Court, ex p B* [1995] 4 All ER 526 distinguished.

(2) At the time when the mother applied for the order the district judge had

d no reason to suppose that the report which was sought might incriminate her and therefore there was no reason not to make the order or to prevent disclosure of the report to all parties on the grounds of self-incrimination. Furthermore, since the mother voluntarily initiated the process, did not appeal the order when it was made and had filed it with the court without seeking a variation of the order, notwithstanding that the unfavourable nature of the report had by then become

e apparent, she was to be taken to have waived any claim which she might have had to privilege against self-incrimination (see p 87 *c* to *f*, p 88 *f g* and p 95 *b*, post).

(3) In exercising her discretion by ordering disclosure of the pathologist's report to the police, the judge had carefully considered the interests of the child on the one hand and the public interest in the due administration of justice on the

f other hand and had concluded that the best interests of the child would be served by disclosure and consequently there were no grounds for interfering with her decision. In reaching her decision that the best interests of the child would be served by disclosure, the judge was entirely justified and it could not possibly be said that she had acted in error (see p 87 *j* to p 88 *a c* to *g* and p 95 *b*, post).

g **Notes**

For legal professional privilege in general, see 13 *Halsbury's Laws* (4th edn) paras 71–85, and for cases on the subject, see 18 *Digest* (2nd reissue) 154–163, *1379–1428*.

For the Children Act 1989, Pt IV, see 6 *Halsbury's Statutes* (4th edn) (1992 reissue) 431.

h

Cases referred to in opinions

A (minors: disclosure of material), Re [1991] 2 FLR 473.

Barking and Dagenham London BC v O [1993] 4 All ER 59, [1993] Fam 295, [1993] 3 WLR 493.

j *Causton v Mann Egerton (Johnsons) Ltd* [1974] 1 All ER 453, [1974] 1 WLR 162, CA.

D H (a minor) (child abuse), Re [1994] 1 FLR 679.

E (S A) (a minor) (wardship), Re [1984] 1 All ER 289, [1984] 1 WLR 156, HL.

Harmony Shipping Co SA v Davis [1979] 3 All ER 177, [1979] 1 WLR 1380, CA.

Livesey (formerly Jenkins) v Jenkins [1985] 1 All ER 106, [1985] AC 424, [1985] 2 WLR 47, HL.

Official Solicitor v K [1963] 3 All ER 191, sub nom *Re K (infants)* [1965] AC 201,
[1963] 3 WLR 408, HL.　　　　　　　　　　　　　　　　　　　　　　　　　　　　　*a*
Oxfordshire CC v M [1994] 2 All ER 269, [1994] Fam 151, [1994] 2 WLR 393, CA.
Oxfordshire CC v P [1995] 2 All ER 225, [1995] Fam 161, [1995] 2 WLR 543.
R (a minor) (disclosure of privileged material), Re [1993] 4 All ER 702, sub nom *Essex
CC v R* [1994] Fam 167, [1994] 2 WLR 407.
R v Derby Magistrates' Court, ex p B [1995] 4 All ER 526, [1995] 3 WLR 681, HL.　　*b*
Ramsbotham v Senior (1869) LR 8 Eq 575.
Rank Film Distributors Ltd v Video Information Centre [1980] 2 All ER 273, [1982] AC
380, [1980] 3 WLR 487, CA; *affd* [1981] 2 All ER 76, [1982] AC 380, [1981] 2
WLR 668, HL.
Saxton (decd), Re, Johnson v Saxton [1962] 3 All ER 92, [1962] 1 WLR 968, CA.
Scott v Scott [1913] AC 417, [1911–13] All ER Rep 1, HL.　　　　　　　　　　　　*c*
Thain (an infant), Re, Thain v Thain [1926] Ch 676, [1926] All ER Rep 384, CA.
Waugh v British Railways Board [1979] 2 All ER 1169, [1980] AC 521, [1979] 3 WLR
150, HL.
Worrall v Reich [1955] 1 All ER 363, [1955] 1 QB 296, [1955] 2 WLR 338, CA.

d

Appeal

The mother of a child, L, appealed with leave granted by the Appeal Committee
from the decision of the Court of Appeal (Sir Thomas Bingham MR, Swinton
Thomas and Morritt LJJ) ([1995] 1 FLR 999) delivered on 14 March 1995
dismissing the mother's appeal from the order made by Bracewell J on 1 July 1994
ordering that a report relating to L prepared by Dr M W France, on the mother's　*e*
instructions, for the purpose of care proceedings initiated by the Manchester City
Council be disclosed to the Greater Manchester Police Authority. The facts are
set out in the opinion of Lord Jauncey of Tullichettle.

Lindsay Kushner QC and *Lesley Newton* (instructed by *Green & Co*, Manchester) for　*f*
the mother.
David M Harris QC and *Yvonne Coppel* (instructed by *Patrick Mulvenna*, Salford) for
the police authority.
David M Harris QC and *Anthony Hayden* (instructed by *Susan Orrell*, Manchester)
for the council.
Ernest Ryder (instructed by *Cliffords*, Alderley Edge) for the guardian ad litem.　　*g*

Their Lordships took time for consideration.

21 March 1996. The following opinions were delivered.
　　　　　　　　　　　　　　　　　　　　　　　　　　　　　　　　　　　　　h

LORD JAUNCEY OF TULLICHETTLE. My Lords, this appeal by a mother
involves consideration of the extent to which privilege, both legal professional
and against self-incrimination, is applicable in care proceedings under Pt IV of the
Children Act 1989.

On 16 January 1993 L, a child of two drug addicts, became seriously ill after　*j*
ingesting a quantity of methadone. Fortunately she recovered rapidly in hospital.
The mother's explanation was that the child's taking of the substance was at a
certain time and was accidental. Shortly thereafter Manchester City Council
obtained an emergency protection order in the Manchester City Magistrates'
Court and on 29 January 1993 interim care orders were granted and thereafter
renewed until 27 July 1994.

a   On 6 May 1993, on the application of both parents of L, who were by now no
longer cohabiting, a district judge made the following order:

'... the parents shall have leave to disclose to a medical expert the court
papers for the purpose of a report regarding the frequency of the
consumption of methadone by [L]. The identity of such expert is to be
b   disclosed to all parties. The report is to be filed by 27/5/93 ...'

The effect of this order was that the report when filed would be available for
inspection and copying by any party to the proceedings and the guardian ad litem
(r 10.20(1) of the Family Proceedings Rules 1991, SI 1991/1247). This order was
not appealed by either parent.
c
The mother's solicitors duly instructed a consultant chemical pathologist, Dr
France, who reported on 10 August 1993. This report, which was prepared
entirely on the basis of the hospital case notes already filed, concluded that there
was no evidence for habituation to methadone, but that the mother's account of
the time at which an accidental ingestion had taken place was not at all likely and
d   that the probable time of ingestion was very much later. The effect of this
conclusion was to cast serious doubts on the mother's account of accidental
ingestion. The report was filed by the mother's solicitors without any attempt to
vary the terms of the district judge's order.

Thereafter the police, while attending a case conference, came to hear of Dr
e   France's report and made application to be joined as a party to the proceedings
under r 4.2(a) of the 1991 rules and to be provided with copies of medical reports
on L for the purposes of investigating criminal offences. After sundry procedure
during the course of which she held that it was unnecessary to join the police
authority as a party, Bracewell J on 1 July 1994 pronounced an order authorising
disclosure of Dr France's report to the police authority. It was not disputed that
f   she had jurisdiction to order disclosure of filed documents but the mother argued
that the court had no jurisdiction to order disclosure to persons who were not
parties to the proceedings and that in any event the merits of the application
required that the court's discretion be exercised in favour of refusing disclosure.
Bracewell J held that she had jurisdiction to order disclosure to non-parties and
g   that conducting the appropriate balancing exercise her discretion should be
exercised in favour of disclosure.

The mother appealed and while accepting that in general the court had
jurisdiction to order disclosure to non-parties she maintained that it had no
jurisdiction to order disclosure of this report to the police authority because (i) it
h   was protected by legal professional privilege, and (ii) its disclosure would infringe
her privilege against self-incrimination. She further argued that the judge had
exercised her discretion wrongly. The Court of Appeal ([1995] 1 FLR 999)
rejected these arguments and dismissed the appeal. The mother now appeals to
this House.

j   Miss Kushner QC for the mother accepted that the order of 6 May 1993 was no
longer open to challenge but she maintained that the district judge had erred in
making it because legal professional privilege would necessarily attach to the
report. The absolute nature of such privilege should have been given effect to by
Bracewell J, as should the privilege against self-incrimination. It followed that in
failing to give proper effect to these two privileges the judge had exercised her
discretion erroneously.

Three questions fall to be considered by this House, namely legal professional
privilege, the privilege against self-incrimination, and the exercise by Bracewell J
of her discretion to order disclosure to the police authority.   *a*

Legal professional privilege

The order of the district judge was in the form of one approved by the Court
of Appeal in *Oxfordshire CC v M* [1994] 2 All ER 269, [1994] Fam 151 after an   *b*
unsuccessful challenge thereto by parents. Sir Stephen Brown P, after pointing
out that proceedings under the 1989 Act were not adversarial, stated that
children's cases 'fall into a special category where the court is bound to undertake
all necessary steps to arrive at an appropriate result in the paramount interests of
the welfare of the child' (see [1994] 2 All ER 269 at 278, [1994] Fam 151 at 161).
The reference to 'paramount interest' was a reference to s 1(1) of the 1989 Act,   *c*
which is in, inter alia, the following terms:

> 'When a court determines any question with respect to—(a) the
> upbringing of a child ... the child's welfare shall be the court's paramount
> consideration.'   *d*

Sir Stephen Brown P concluded his judgment in the following passage ([1994] 2
All ER 269 at 279, [1994] Fam 151 at 162):

> 'Children's cases are to be regarded as being in a special category. In these
> circumstances, the court has power to override legal professional privilege in   *e*
> relation to expert's reports when it gives leave to parties to obtain them.'

Their Lordships were informed that since the *Oxfordshire* case orders in that form
have regularly been made by judges in the Family Division.

Miss Kushner submitted that Dr France's report was the subject of legal
professional privilege, that such privilege was absolute (*R v Derby Magistrates'*   *f*
Court, ex p B [1995] 4 All ER 526, [1995] 3 WLR 681) and that it could be
overridden neither in the public interest nor in furtherance of the paramountcy
of the child's interests. The *Oxfordshire* case was wrongly decided.

In *R v Derby Magistrates' Court, ex p B* [1995] 4 All ER 526, [1995] 3 WLR 681 the
issue before this House was whether a witness summons could properly be issued   *g*
to compel production by a prosecution witness in committal proceedings of
proofs of evidence and attendance notes giving factual instructions to his solicitor
in earlier criminal proceedings arising out of the same event in which he had been
acquitted. Lord Taylor of Gosforth CJ, after analysis of earlier authorities, stated
([1995] 4 All ER 526 at 540–541, [1995] 3 WLR 681 at 695):
                                                                                  h

> 'The principle which runs through all these cases, and the many other cases
> which were cited, is that a man must be able to consult his lawyer in
> confidence, since otherwise he might hold back half the truth. The client
> must be sure that what he tells his lawyer in confidence will never be
> revealed without his consent. Legal professional privilege is thus much   *j*
> more than an ordinary rule of evidence, limited in its application to the facts
> of a particular case. It is a fundamental condition on which the
> administration of justice as a whole rests.'

The concluding paragraph of his speech contained the following passage,
([1995] 4 All ER 526 at 542, [1995] 3 WLR 681 at 696–697):

a
'But it is not for the sake of the appellant alone that the privilege must be upheld. It is in the wider interests of all those hereafter who might otherwise be deterred from telling the whole truth to their solicitors. For this reason I am of the opinion that no exception should be allowed to the absolute nature of legal professional privilege, once established.'

b
All the other members of the Appellate Committee were in agreement with these views.

It is clear from the reasoning of Lord Taylor CJ and of the other members of the committee that the reference to legal professional privilege was in the context of the relationship between solicitor and client. Indeed, there was no occasion to consider whether and in what other circumstances absolute legal professional

c
privilege might apply. Notwithstanding this, Miss Kushner maintained that the absolute nature of the privilege attaching to the solicitor-client relationship extended equally to all other forms of legal professional privilege.

My Lords, I reject this contention. There is, as Mr Harris QC for the city council and the police authority pointed out, a clear distinction between the

d
privilege attaching to communications between solicitor and client and that attaching to reports by third parties prepared on the instructions of a client for the purposes of litigation. In the former case the privilege attaches to all communications whether related to litigation or not, but in the latter case it attaches only to documents or other written communications prepared with a view to litigation (see *Waugh v British Railways Board* [1979] 2 All ER 1169 at 1174, 1178

e
and 1183, [1980] AC 521 at 533, 537 and 544). There is this further distinction that whereas a solicitor could not without his client's consent be compelled to express an opinion on the factual or legal merits of the case, a third party who has provided a report to a client can be subpoenaed to give evidence by the other side and cannot decline to answer questions as to his factual findings and opinion

f
thereon. There is no property in the opinion of an expert witness (see *Harmony Shipping Co SA v Davis* [1979] 3 All ER 177 at 182, [1979] 1 WLR 1380 at 1386 per Lord Denning MR)

Litigation privilege, as it has been called, is an essential component of adversarial procedure. In *Worrall v Reich* [1955] 1 All ER 363, [1955] 1 QB 296 it was held that one party to a litigation could not be compelled to produce to the

g
other party a medical report obtained for the purposes of the action. This case was followed in *Re Saxton (decd), Johnson v Saxton* [1962] 3 All ER 92 at 95, [1962] 1 WLR 968 at 972 in relation to the report of a handwriting expert, where Lord Denning MR said:

h
'In short, it is one of our notions of a fair trial that, except by agreement, one side is not entitled to see the proofs of the other side's witnesses.'

In *Causton v Mann Egerton (Johnsons) Ltd* [1974] 1 All ER 453 at 460, [1974] 1 WLR 162 at 170, which concerned the disclosure of medical reports in a personal injury action, Roskill LJ said:

j
'I am clearly of the view that this court has no power to order production of privileged documents ... so long as we have an adversary system, a party is entitled not to produce documents which are properly protected by privilege if it is not to his advantage to produce them, and even though their production might assist his adversary ...'

Finally, in *Waugh v British Railways Board* [1979] 2 All ER 1169 at 1176, [1980]
AC 521 at 536 Lord Simon of Glaisdale said:

> 'This system of adversary forensic procedure with legal professional advice
> and representation demands that communications between lawyer and
> client should be confidential, since the lawyer is for the purpose of litigation
> merely the client's alter ego. So too material which is to go into the lawyer's
> (ie the client's) brief or file for litigation. This is the basis for the privilege
> against disclosure of material collected by or on behalf of a client for the use
> of his lawyer in pending or anticipated litigation ...'

Lord Denning MR, Roskill LJ and Lord Simon of Glaisdale all emphasised the
important part which litigation privilege plays in a fair trial under the adversarial
system. This raises the question of whether proceedings under Pt IV of the 1989
Act are essentially adversarial in their nature. If they are, litigation privilege must
continue to play its normal part. If they are not, different considerations may
apply.

In *Official Solicitor v K* [1963] 3 All ER 191, [1965] AC 201, which concerned
disclosure of a guardian ad litem's report in wardship proceedings, Lord Evershed
pointed out that the purpose of the judicial inquiry was to make a decision about
the future upbringing of the infant, whereby the infant was in a special position
distinct from that of other parties (see [1963] 3 All ER 191 at 196, [1965] AC 201 at
218). Lord Devlin ([1963] 3 All ER 191 at 210, [1965] AC 201 at 240) quoted with
approval the following dictum of the trial judge, Ungoed-Thomas J:

> 'The jurisdiction regarding wards of court which is now exercised by the
> Chancery Division is an ancient jurisdiction deriving from the prerogative of
> the Crown as parens patriae. It is not based on the rights of parents, and its
> primary concern is not to ensure their rights but to ensure the welfare of the
> children ...'

He later stated ([1963] 3 All ER 191 at 210, [1965] AC 201 at 241):

> 'Where the judge is not sitting purely or even primarily as an arbiter but is
> charged with the paramount duty of protecting the interests of one outside
> the conflict, a rule that is designed for just arbitrament cannot in all
> circumstances prevail.'

Lord Scarman, in *Re E (S A) (a minor) (wardship)* [1984] 1 All ER 289 at 290,
[1984] 1 WLR 156 at 158–159, pointed out that a court in wardship proceedings
was not exercising an adversarial jurisdiction and that—

> 'Its duty is not limited to the dispute between the parties: on the contrary,
> its duty is to act in the way best suited in its judgment to serve the true
> interest and welfare of the ward. In exercising wardship jurisdiction, the
> court is a true family court. Its paramount concern is the welfare of its ward.
> It will, therefore, sometimes be the duty of the court to look beyond the
> submissions of the parties in its endeavour to do what it judges to be
> necessary.'

Since the judgment in *Official Solicitor v K* there have been numerous
pronouncements by judges of the Family Division stressing that proceedings in
wardship are non-adversarial. It is not necessary to refer to these and I simply
refer back to the passages which I have already quoted from the judgment of Sir
Stephen Brown P in *Oxfordshire CC v M* [1994] 2 All ER 269, [1994] Fam 151. In

these passages Sir Stephen Brown P was, as I understand him, equating the
a position in 1989 Act proceedings to wardship proceedings. The above dictum
would appear to provide firm support for the proposition that proceedings under
Pt IV of the 1989 Act are, like wardship proceedings, essentially non-adversarial
in their nature.

However, Miss Kushner argued that such statutory proceedings were not to be
b equiparated to wardship proceedings. This submission goes too far. It is, of
course, true that once a care order under Pt IV of the 1989 Act has been made it
is the local authority and not the court which has the direct responsibility for the
child, but until such an order has been made the role of the court under the 1989
Act does not differ significantly from its role in wardship proceedings. In reaching
a decision in either case the primary consideration was and is the welfare of the
c child.

I agree with Sir Stephen Brown P that care proceedings are essentially
non-adversarial. Having reached that conclusion, and also that litigation
privilege is essentially a creature of adversarial proceedings, it follows that the
matter is at large for this House to determine what if any role it has to play in care
d proceedings.

Before Dr France could report it was necessary to obtain the leave of the
district judge under r 4.23 of the 1991 rules to disclose to him the court papers.
His report appears to have been based entirely on the hospital case notes and
there is no suggestion that he had any communication with the mother.
Accordingly, all the material to which he had access was material which was
e already available to the other parties. To that extent the position is similar to that
in *Re Saxton (decd), Johnson v Saxton* [1962] 3 All ER 92, [1962] 1 WLR 968.
However in these proceedings, which are primarily non-adversarial and investigative as opposed to adversarial, the notion of a fair trial between opposing parties
assumes far less importance. In the latter case the judge must decide the case in
f favour of one or other party upon such evidence as they choose to adduce,
however much he might wish for further evidence on any point. In the former
case the judge is concerned to make a decision which is in the best interest of the
child in question and may make orders which are sought by no party to the
proceedings: ss 10(1)(b), 31(5), 34(5) of the 1989 Act. Furthermore, the court has
wide powers under r 4.11(9), (10) of the 1991 rules to require the guardian ad
g litem to obtain expert reports and other assistance. Thus the court is seeking to
reach a decision which will be in the best interests of someone who is not a direct
party and is granted investigative powers to achieve that end. In these
circumstances I consider that care proceedings under Pt IV of the 1989 Act are so
far removed from normal actions that litigation privilege has no place in relation
h to reports obtained by a party thereto which could not have been prepared
without the leave of the court to disclose documents already filed or to examine
the child. In reaching this conclusion I attach considerable importance to the
following dictum of Sir Stephen Brown P in *Oxfordshire CC v M* [1994] 2 All ER 269
at 278, [1994] Fam 151 at 161:

j   'If a party, having obtained the leave of the court, were to be able to
conceal, or withhold from the court, matters which were of importance and
were relevant to the future of the child, there would be a risk that the welfare
of the child would not be promoted as the Children Act 1989 requires.'

I would add that if litigation privilege were to apply to Dr France's report it could
have the effect of subordinating the welfare of the child to the interests of the

mother in preserving its confidentiality. This would appear to frustrate the
primary object of the 1989 Act.

I differ from Sir Stephen Brown P, with his great experience of proceedings
under the 1989 Act, only in as much as he concluded that in the foregoing
circumstances the court had power to *override* the privilege. The *Oxfordshire* case
was, however, argued on the assumption that the privilege existed but could be
overridden. This case was also argued on the same assumption in the Court of
Appeal, but Sir Thomas Bingham MR expressed doubt as to whether the
assumption was rightly made. His doubts were in my view well founded. The
better view is that litigation privilege never arose in the first place rather than that
the court has power to override it. It is excluded by necessary implication from
the terms and overall purpose of the 1989 Act. This does not of course affect
privilege arising between solicitor and client.

The form of the order in the *Oxfordshire* case has been used on many occasions
by judges in the Family Division. It is a sensible and competent order and I see
no grounds for interfering with a practice which experienced judges have found
to work well.

I would only add that the mother did not suggest that the order of 6 May 1993
was at fault in requiring her to disclose the identity of the expert to all parties. In
that situation the guardian ad litem could have requested the court to subpoena
Dr France under r 4.11(9)(c) of the 1991 rules and the latter could not have
refused to express his opinion on the matters submitted to him.

Voluntary disclosure

Mr Harris also argued that there was a duty on a party to care proceedings to
make voluntary disclosure of all matters likely to be material to the welfare of the
child. In support of this proposition he relied on three cases, namely *Re R (a
minor) (disclosure of privileged material)* [1993] 4 All ER 702, [1994] Fam 167, *Re D H
(a minor) (child abuse)* [1994] 1 FLR 679 and *Oxfordshire CC v P* [1995] 2 All ER 225,
[1995] Fam 161. In *Re R (a minor) (disclosure of privileged material)* [1993] 4 All ER
702 at 704–705, [1994] Fam 167 at 168–169 Thorpe J, after referring to legal
professional privilege as a creature of case law, continued:

'For my part, I would wish to see case law go yet further and to make it
plain that the legal representatives in possession of such material relevant to
determination but contrary to the interests of their client, not only are
unable to resist disclosure by reliance on legal professional privilege, but
have a positive duty to disclose to the other parties and to the court.'

In *Re D H (a minor) (child abuse)* [1994] 1 FLR 679 at 704 Wall J expressed the
opinion that the welfare principle enshrined in s 1 of the 1989 Act necessarily
imported the duty described by Thorpe J in *Re R (a minor) (disclosure of privileged
material)* and that the practice in family proceedings should follow Thorpe J's
judgment in that case. Finally in *Oxfordshire CC v P* [1995] 2 All ER 225 at 230,
[1995] Fam 161 at 166 Ward J said:

'In all cases where the welfare of children is the court's paramount
consideration, there is a duty on all parties to make full and frank disclosure
of all matters material to welfare whether those matters are favourable to or
adverse to their own particular case.'

Ward J ([1995] 2 All ER 225 at 231, [1995] Fam 161 at 167) pointed out that in
ancillary relief proceedings there is already a duty of full and frank disclosure: see

a *Livesey (formerly Jenkins) v Jenkins* [1985] 1 All ER 106 at 113, [1985] AC 424 at 436–437 per Lord Brandon of Oakbrook.

In view of the conclusions which I have reached on the matter of legal professional privilege, I do not find it necessary to come to a decision on this point. It may well be that this further development of the practice in cases where the welfare of children is involved is to be welcomed. But I prefer to wait until *b* the point arises directly for decision before determining whether such a duty exists and, if so, what is its scope.

Privilege against self-incrimination

Where a court is asked to make an order for disclosure, compliance with which is likely to involve the danger of self-incrimination by the defendant, an order *c* producing such a result should not be made: see *Rank Film Distributors Ltd v Video Information Centre* [1980] 2 All ER 273 at 286, 288, [1982] AC 380 at 416, 419 per Bridge and Templeman LJJ. This, however, was not such a case. When the mother applied for the order of 6 May 1993, the district judge had no reason to suppose that the report which was sought might incriminate the person who was *d* seeking it. In that situation he cannot be criticised for requiring disclosure of the report to all parties. It was only when the report became available that its possible incriminating effect became known and it was at that stage when the mother was first in a position to advance her claim to privilege by seeking a variation of that part of the order which required the report to be filed. In the event she filed the report without taking any steps to assert a claim for privilege. *e* Thus the mother voluntarily initiated the process, did not appeal the order when it was made and obtempered it without seeking a variation, notwithstanding that the unfavourable nature of the report had by then become apparent. In these circumstances she must be taken to have waived any claim which she may have had to privilege against self-incrimination consequent upon the order of the *f* district judge. In reaching this conclusion I should emphasise that although I have assumed that the mother may have had a claim to privilege in respect of the report I have not found it necessary to decide whether in law she would have had one but for her waiver. Any such claim would on any view have been of limited value, since Dr France, if subpoenaed as a witness, would have been bound to answer questions as to the opinion which he had formed after perusing the *g* hospital case notes and the mother would have been bound to answer questions as to the opinion expressed by Dr France in his report: see s 98 (1) of the 1989 Act.

Exercise of discretion by Bracewell J

The mother accepted that by reason of r 4.23 of the 1991 rules Bracewell J had *h* the power to order disclosure of Dr France's report to the police authority. However, she maintained that in exercising that power the judge had exercised her discretion erroneously. Her first attack on the judge's exercise of her discretion proceeded upon the basis that the district judge's order was improperly made. For the reasons which I have already given, this ground of attack fails. Her *j* second attack assumed the correctness of the district judge's order but proceeded on the basis that in balancing the competing public interests the provenance of the report and its self-incriminating nature should have outweighed other public interests. The mother also made a number of detailed criticisms of the judgment. The second attack also fails. Bracewell J carefully considered the interests of the child, on the one hand, and the public interest in the due administration of justice, on the other, while accepting that the report was privileged—an acceptance

which in the event did not require to have been made and was therefore
unnecessarily favourable to the mother.   In reaching her conclusion she said *a*
([1995] 1 FLR 999 at 1008):

> 'Weighing up the competing interests in the balancing operation, I am
> satisfied that the document should be disclosed. The guardian has carefully
> assessed the issues and supports disclosure on the basis that an informed
> decision by the police, which may result in prosecution or a decision not to *b*
> prosecute and/or in conviction or acquittal, is very significant in terms of the
> planning for the children's future as to the level of contact, if any, with the
> children and the degree of supervision in that the allegation of administering
> life threatening poison has serious implications for them and other children.'

My Lords, I can see no ground for interfering with Bracewell J's decision. In *c*
the Court of Appeal Sir Thomas Bingham MR, after a careful review of a number
of cases involving orders for disclosure of wardship documents, concluded that
the judge's exercise of her discretion was not plainly wrong and that her decision
was reasonable. I entirely agree with him and find it unnecessary to rehearse the
various cases to which he referred. I would only add that the judge took the view, *d*
which was entirely justified, that the best interests of L would be served by
disclosure. It could not possibly be said that in reaching such a decision she had
acted in error.   Indeed, in proceedings of this nature it would be most
unsatisfactory if the court, having information that the mother might have
committed a serious offence against the children whose welfare it was seeking to
protect, should be disabled from disclosing such information to the appropriate *e*
investigating authority.   Bracewell J's exercise of her discretion was in all the
circumstances entirely proper.

For all these reasons I would dismiss the appeal.

LORD MUSTILL. My Lords, I have had the advantage of reading in draft the *f*
speech prepared by my noble and learned friend Lord Nicholls of Birkenhead.
For the reasons which he gives, I would allow this appeal.

LORD LLOYD OF BERWICK. My Lords, I have had the advantage of reading
in draft the speech prepared by my noble and learned friend Lord Jauncey of
Tullichettle. For the reasons he gives, I would dismiss the appeal. *g*

LORD NICHOLLS OF BIRKENHEAD. My Lords, I would allow this appeal.
The parties' submissions traversed much ground, and I shall state my reasons as
succinctly as I may.

h

Legal professional privilege
   I do not believe the Children Act 1989 was intended to abrogate legal
professional privilege in family proceedings, or that it has done so.   Legal
professional privilege is deeply embedded in English law. This was confirmed
recently by your Lordships' House in *R v Derby Magistrates' Court, ex p B* [1995] 4 *j*
All ER 526, [1995] 3 WLR 681. The privilege against non-disclosure prevails even
where the privileged material might assist the defence of a person charged with
murder.
   Clear words, therefore, or a compelling context are needed before Parliament
can be taken to have intended that the privilege should be ousted in favour of
another interest. The 1989 Act contains neither. There is no express abrogation

a of the privilege. Nor do the provisions in the 1989 Act, designed to promote the welfare of children, carry with them an implication that in future parents who become involved in court proceedings are not to have the normal freedom to consult lawyers and potential witnesses, and to do so confidentially.

The 1989 Act represents a comprehensive and far reaching reform of child law. It integrates within one statute provisions regulating public and private rights and b responsibilities in respect of children. Central to the role of the court is the 'paramountcy' principle, set out in s 1. Whenever a court determines a question with respect to the upbringing of a child or the administration of a child's property, the child's welfare shall be the court's paramount consideration.

The application of this principle requires a judge to apply a particular test when deciding an issue regarding a child's upbringing. But it goes much further than c this. In practice the application of the paramountcy principle requires a judge, in the fashionable jargon, to be pro-active and not merely reactive. It means that in family proceedings as defined in the 1989 Act, the court is not concerned simply to decide an issue between the parties and to do so on the basis of the evidence the parties have chosen to present. The court is concerned to protect the child d and promote the child's welfare. The court is not confined to the issues, or the evidence, the parties have brought forward. Nor is it confined to the alternative courses proposed by the parties: see Re E (S A) (a minor) (wardship) [1984] 1 All ER 289, [1984] 1 WLR 156. During the proceedings the court may at any time, of its own motion, take steps which it considers necessary or desirable to protect the child or promote the child's welfare. The judge may call for more evidence or for e assistance from further parties or instigate applications for appropriate orders. The 1989 Act itself contains some specific examples of this: see, for instance, ss 10(1)(b), 31(5), 34(5) and 37(1). Rule 4.11(10) of the Family Proceedings Rules 1991, SI 1191/1247, imposes on the child's guardian ad litem a duty to provide the court with such assistance as the court may require. All this is well known.

f The special role of judges in family proceedings is of great importance. The role has attracted a variety of descriptions: parental, administrative, quasi-administrative, investigative, inquisitorial. These descriptions are contrasted with the adversarial nature of ordinary civil and criminal proceedings. These descriptions, and this contrast, do not in themselves provide an answer to the question raised by this appeal. Attaching the bewitching label of inquisitorial to g family proceedings says nothing about whether legal professional privilege should or should not be available to a person who is a party to the proceedings.

I can dispose of one point straightaway. The expression adversarial carries with it a connotation of confrontation and conflict. Ideally, these characteristics have no place in family proceedings. In family proceedings all parties should be h working together to assist the court in finding the answer which will best promote the welfare of the child. In practice matters are not so simple. A father who is alleged to have sexually abused his stepdaughter is concerned to protect his own reputation as well as his family life. He can hardly be blamed if he regards the proceedings as no less confrontational and adversarial than other civil j proceedings. This feature throws little light, if any, on the present question.

At bottom, the answer to the present question turns on what are the requirements of procedural fairness in the conduct of family proceedings. In this context the contrast between inquisitorial and adversarial needs handling with care, for at least two reasons. First, the contrast suggests that proceedings are either wholly adversarial or wholly inquisitorial. They partake wholly of the one character or wholly of the other. This is not always so. Proceedings may possess

some adversarial features and some inquisitorial features. Family proceedings *a*
are an example.

Secondly, and more importantly, the contrast can all too easily divert attention
from the crucial question. Fairness is a universal requirement in the conduct of
all forms of proceedings, inquisitorial as much as adversarial, although the
requirements of fairness vary widely from one type of proceedings to another.
The requirements of fairness depend upon matters such as the nature of the *b*
proceedings, the subject matter being considered, the rules governing the
conduct of the proceedings, the parties involved, the composition of the tribunal,
and the consequences of the decision. The distinction between the adversarial
and inquisitorial nature of the proceedings is no more than one of these elements,
although sometimes a very important element. The crucial question is not
whether, and to what extent, the proceedings are inquisitorial rather than *c*
adversarial. The question to be addressed is what is required if the proceedings
are to be conducted fairly.

Family proceedings are court proceedings. The court has to make decisions
affecting, often profoundly, the whole future of a child and his or her family.
Whenever necessary, the court makes findings on disputes of fact. It goes *d*
without saying that the parties to such proceedings are entitled to have a fair
hearing. Whatever fairness does or does not require in other contexts, in this
context a fair hearing includes at least the right to present one's case and to call
evidence.

Under English law an established ingredient of this right is legal professional *e*
privilege. Parties preparing for a court hearing may obtain legal advice in
confidence. A party cannot be required to disclose communications between
himself and his lawyer, or communications between the lawyer and third parties
which come into existence for the purpose of obtaining legal advice in connection
with the proceedings. A proof of evidence obtained from a potential witness of
fact is not disclosable. Nor is a report obtained from a potential witness of expert *f*
opinion. A party may be required to produce a witness statement or expert's
report in advance as a pre-condition to the admission of that evidence at the
hearing, but he is not required to disclose proofs of witnesses whose evidence he
does not intend to adduce at the hearing. The public interest in a party being able
to obtain informed legal advice in confidence prevails over the public interest in *g*
all relevant material being available to courts when deciding cases.

I can see no reason why parties to family proceedings should not be as much
entitled to a fair hearing having these features and safeguards as are parties to
other court proceedings. Indeed, it must be doubtful whether a parent who is
denied the opportunity to obtain legal advice in confidence is accorded the fair *h*
hearing to which he is entitled under art 6(1), read in conjunction with art 8, of
the European Convention for the Protection of Human Rights and Fundamental
Freedoms (Rome, 4 November 1950; TS 71 (1953); Cmd 8969).

Parents and other parties should be entitled to such a hearing notwithstanding
the special role of judges in family proceedings. If this is not to be, Parliament *j*
should say so expressly. Legal professional privilege is part of the established
framework within which judges discharge their special role in family
proceedings. The privilege against self-incrimination is another, important part
of the framework. The 1989 Act has supplied further pieces of the framework,
such as the threshold conditions which must be satisfied before a care order can
be made. The judges' special role is to be discharged within this framework, not

a outside it. The paramountcy principle must not be permitted to become a loose cannon, destroying all else around it.

Litigation privilege

Legal professional privilege is sometimes classified under two sub-headings: legal advice privilege and litigation privilege. The former, covering com-
b munications between a client and his legal adviser, is available whether or not proceedings are in existence or contemplated. The latter embraces a wider class of communications, such as those between the legal adviser and potential witnesses. These are privileged only when proceedings are in existence or contemplated. In the course of the submissions reliance was sought to be placed on this distinction. It was suggested that the 1989 Act has impliedly abrogated
c litigation privilege, while leaving legal advice privilege untouched.

I cannot accept this. The two sub-headings are integral parts of a single privilege. In the context of court proceedings, the purpose of legal advice privilege would be frustrated if the legal adviser could not approach potential witnesses in confidence before advising the client. This is as much true in family
d proceedings as any other.

This remains as true after the passing of the 1989 Act as before. The public interest reflected in the paramountcy principle does not self-evidently outweigh the public interest reflected in litigation privilege. The 1989 Act is not to be taken to have changed the balance. The paramountcy principle and litigation privilege
e are capable of co-existing without difficulty in the future, as they have in the past.

The authorities

The paramountcy principle, it should be remembered, is not a new concept. This was the principle acted upon by the Court of Chancery when exercising its
f jurisdiction over wards of court. In 1925 the principle was embodied in statute: in s 1 of the Guardianship of Infants Act 1925, subsequently re-enacted in s 1 of the Guardianship of Minors Act 1971 (see *Re Thain (an infant), Thain v Taylor* [1926] Ch 676 at 686, 691, [1926] All ER Rep 384 at 385, 387).

I am not aware of any case before *Re A (minors: disclosure of material)* [1991] 2 FLR 473 in which it has ever been suggested that legal professional privilege is not
g as much available in wardship cases, or in proceedings under the Guardianship of Infants Act 1925 or the Guardianship of Minors Act 1971, as in any other court proceedings. The power of the court to order a solicitor to disclose the whereabouts of a ward of court is not an example to the contrary. This is an application, in the wardship context, of the principle that a solicitor has no greater
h privilege than the client: see *Ramsbotham v Senior* (1869) LR 8 Eq 575 at 578 per Malins V-C.

The authorities do establish that all procedural rules are subject to one general exception, or limitation, which is particularly relevant in family proceedings. Procedural rules exist in order to further the object sought to be attained by the
j proceedings. They are aids to an end, not an end in themselves. Procedural rules must not be permitted to thwart the very purpose the proceedings are intended to achieve. Lord Devlin analysed this, with his customary cogency, in *Official Solicitor v K* [1963] 3 All ER 191 at 208–210, [1965] AC 201 at 237–241. Thus, where a hearing in public would endanger or defeat the objective of the proceedings, the court may sit in private, as happens in children cases and confidential information cases: see *Scott v Scott* [1913] AC 417, [1911–13] All ER Rep 1. The court has power

to act on undisclosed evidence in children cases where disclosure would involve
a real possibility of significant harm to the child: see *Official Solicitor v K*.

That is not the effect of legal professional privilege in the present situation.
The privilege is not in danger of thwarting the objective of family proceedings, or
the application of the paramountcy principle.

Let me explain why this is so. The context in which this question arises in the
present case, as in all the recent cases, is experts' reports. Courts need as much
information and assistance as possible. If an expert's report is obtained, the judge
wishes to know what the report says. But this does not reveal a problem whose
solution requires abrogating or overriding legal professional privilege, in whole
or in part. There is no *need* for this radical departure from established principle.
Parties are not able to suppress the evidence of an available expert. The views of
the expert, if desired, can always be made available within the existing legal
framework. In the time honoured aphorism, there is no property in a witness.
The fact that an expert or other potential witness has already been approached by
one party, and given a statement to that party, does not excuse him from giving
evidence at the hearing at the behest of another party. If necessary his attendance
can be compelled by service of a subpoena. He cannot be required to disclose the
contents of communications between himself and the first party's legal adviser.
But his evidence on the issue before the court, which is all that is material, can be
compelled.

With all respect to Johnson J, his obiter observations in 1991 in *Re A* (*minors:
disclosure of material*) [1991] 2 FLR 473 set the family courts on an erroneous path.
The judge's actual remarks in that case cannot stand with the subsequent decision
of this House in *R v Derby Magistrates' Court, ex p B* [1995] 4 All ER 526, [1995] 3
WLR 681. Johnson J did not hold that legal professional privilege had been
impliedly abrogated. He held that the court has power, in appropriate cases, to
override legal professional privilege attaching to an expert's report. He said the
power should be exercised rarely, with a balance struck between a number of
considerations. This approach, of the court conducting a balancing exercise on a
case by case basis, was firmly rejected by your Lordships' House in *R v Derby
Magistrates' Court, ex p B*. Once the privilege has attached to a document, the
privilege prevails.

The observations in *Re A* (*minors: disclosure of material*) [1991] 2 FLR 473 have
subsequently been used as the foundation for further developments. *Re A* was a
wardship case. In *Re R* (*a minor*) (*disclosure of privileged material*) [1993] 4 All ER
702, [1994] Fam 167 Thorpe J adopted the same approach to proceedings under
the 1989 Act, despite the restraining decision meanwhile of Douglas Brown J in
Barking and Dagenham London BC v O [1993] 4 All ER 59, [1993] Fam 295.

A further step was taken by the Court of Appeal in *Oxfordshire CC v M* [1994] 2
All ER 269, [1994] Fam 151. In that case the basis of the judgment of my noble
and learned friend Lord Steyn, then Steyn LJ, was that the 1989 Act has impliedly
abrogated the privilege, at least so far as experts' reports are concerned. The
precise extent of the implied abrogation was not spelled out, but I am unable to
discern any sound distinction between experts, who are potential witnesses of
expert opinion, and other potential witnesses. The statements of witnesses of fact
may be as relevant and important to an issue the court has to decide as the
statements of experts. Logically, both classes of statements are privileged, or
neither. And if the statements themselves are not privileged, nor are the letters
from the solicitor to which they are a response and with which they must be read.

a   Logically, there is no stopping place short of the abrogation of all litigation privilege. For the reasons I have given, I cannot agree with this.

Matters have now gone still further. In *Re R (a minor) (disclosure of privileged material)* [1993] 4 All ER 702 at 704–705, [1994] Fam 167 at 168–169, having referred to the court's ability to override legal professional privilege, Thorpe J said:

b
'For my part, I would wish to see case law go yet further and to make it plain that the legal representatives in possession of ... material relevant to determination [of the welfare issue] but contrary to the interests of their client, not only are unable to resist disclosure by reliance on legal professional privilege, but have a positive duty to disclose to the other parties
c   and to the court.'

A similar approach has since been adopted by Wall J in *Re D H (a minor) (child abuse)* [1994] 1 FLR 679 at 703 and Ward J in *Oxfordshire CC v P* [1995] 2 All ER 225 at 234–235, [1995] Fam 161 at 166–167. It follows from what I have already said that I part company with these observations. They are too sweeping. Indeed, I
d   have grave doubts whether there is such a duty.

Rule 4.23 and Oxfordshire CC v M

If, contrary to my view, the 1989 Act has impliedly abrogated legal professional privilege so far as experts are concerned, then the court's power to impose a
e   disclosure condition when giving leave under r 4.23 of the 1991 rules does not arise as a question. In the absence of the privilege, an expert's report and the letter of instructions will automatically be disclosable in every case. They will no longer be privileged from production. This will be so even when the expert has compiled his report without reference to any document on the court file and, hence, without leave being needed under r 4.23.
f
If, however, I am correct in believing the 1989 Act has not had this effect, the question which next arises is whether a disclosure condition can properly be imposed by the court when giving leave under r 4.23 or under the equivalent rule applicable in magistrates' courts. The starting point here is the purpose for which the rule has imposed a regime of confidentiality. The purpose, I apprehend, is to
g   protect the child from the risk of the adverse consequences to him or her which might follow from wider circulation of the evidence and other documents on the court file. That is the purpose for which the confidentiality exists. It cannot be right to use restrictions imposed for this purpose as the means to achieve another and unrelated purpose, namely that the person seeking an expert's advice must
h   disclose the advice received in any event. The rule ought not to be used as a means of preventing a party from obtaining advice in confidence from an expert. The need for leave, and the power to impose conditions when granting leave, ought not to be used as an oblique means of achieving an altogether different objective which could not be achieved directly. On this I agree with Steyn LJ's statement in *Oxfordshire CC v M* [1994] 2 All ER 269 at 280, [1994] Fam 151 at 163:
j
' ... if it be the case legal professional privilege attaches to experts' reports in care proceedings, it seems to me to follow that it would be wrong to exercise the power to attach conditions in order to destroy the privilege. If the privilege applies, it must be respected.'

It follows that I do not agree with Kennedy LJ's reasoning in that case.

Sir Stephen Brown P based his conclusion on the view that the court has power *a* to override legal professional privilege. He followed the same approach as Thorpe J in *Re R (a minor) (disclosure of privileged material)* [1993] 4 All ER 702, [1994] Fam 167. As already seen, this approach has since been overtaken by the decision in *R v Derby Magistrates' Court, ex p B* [1995] 4 All ER 526, [1995] 3 WLR 681.

b

Case management

I noted earlier that an expert can be compelled to give evidence on an issue in the proceedings, even if he has already made a privileged report to a party who decides not to put that report in evidence. I must now address an argument that, this being so, imposing a disclosure condition is no more than sound and sensible *c* case management. When the court imposes the condition it is doing no more than achieve, by a convenient and expeditious route, a result the court could in any event achieve: production of the expert's evidence on an issue in the proceedings.

If this were the only effect of a disclosure condition, I would agree with the submission. In practice, however, a disclosure condition would be bound to have *d* an inhibiting effect on communications between the solicitor and the expert. An expert's report usually has to be read in conjunction with the letter of instructions. The solicitor would always be looking over his shoulder, conscious he is writing an 'open' and not a privileged letter. The expert would need to confine himself strictly to the issue on which his advice is compellable, and not *e* range more widely, because his report also would be open and not privileged. These would be significant inroads into the freedom and frankness of confidential communication which the privilege exists to secure. For this reason a disclosure condition goes beyond the convenient ordering of evidence.

This mischief is not cured by giving a party leave to return to the court and *f* apply for the disclosure condition to be lifted after the report has been prepared. There could be no certainty that the condition would be lifted. So at the earlier stage, when the report is being obtained, the inhibitions on freedom of communication would still be present.

Your Lordships were told by Miss Kushner that the present practice is a cause of considerable anxiety to parents. I would expect this to be so. There are bound *g* to be problems when confidentiality is removed from communications a party needs to make in preparing properly for a hearing. I do not think the present practice can be regarded as satisfactory.

Discretion and other issues *h*

For these reasons I consider *Oxfordshire CC v M* [1994] 2 All ER 269, [1994] Fam 151 was wrongly decided and that the disclosure condition should not have been imposed in the present case. Had the condition not been imposed, Dr France's report would not have been on the court file. Accordingly the court's discretion to permit disclosure of filed documents ought not to have been, and ought not to *j* be, exercised in favour of any wider dissemination of the report. Bracewell J was bound by the decision in *Oxfordshire CC v M* [1994] 2 All ER 269, [1994] Fam 151. So was the Court of Appeal. Perforce they decided the case on the footing that the disclosure condition had been properly imposed. Altogether different considerations apply once it is seen that the condition should never have been there in the first place.

a   This conclusion suffices to dispose of the appeal. I prefer to express no view on the difficult points raised concerning the meaning and scope of s 98 of the 1989 Act. The interpretation of this section is better considered in the context of a live issue.

b   **LORD STEYN.** My Lords, I have had the advantage of reading in draft the speech prepared by my noble and learned friend Lord Jauncey of Tullichettle. For the reasons which he gives I would dismiss this appeal.

Appeal dismissed.

Celia Fox   Barrister.

Penrose and another v Official Receiver   *a*

CHANCERY DIVISION

CHADWICK J

9, 13, 18 OCTOBER 1995

b

Company – Prohibited name – Director – Former director of old company requiring leave to be director of new company having prohibited name – Principles on which leave may be granted – Old company wound up because unable to pay debts – Certain assets and liabilities transferred to new company with similar name – Directors of old company applying to be permitted to be directors of new company – Whether test of fitness to act as directors applying – Insolvency Act 1986, s 216(2)(3).   *c*

The applicants, a husband and wife, were sole directors of a company running coffee houses. The company ceased to trade on 12 September 1994 and on 26 June 1995 it was ordered to be wound up by the court on the ground that it was unable to pay its debts. The Official Receiver's report into the collapse of the   *d* company accepted the first applicant's assessment that it was attributable to the withdrawal of bank overdraft facilities, rapid expansion, lack of capital, inexperienced management and inadequate controls aggravated by declining turnover due to a downturn in trade. On the date the company ceased to trade certain of the company's assets and liabilities were transferred to a new company which had a name so similar to that of the old company that it was a 'prohibited   *e* name' within s 216(2)ᵃ of the Insolvency Act 1986. Section 216(3) therefore required the applicants, as former directors of the old company, to obtain the leave of the court to be directors of the new company. The district judge dismissed their application on the grounds that, while there was no suggestion of dishonesty or deviousness on their part, either in the new company or the old,   *f* they were inexperienced and the new company, as the old company had been, was undercapitalised and would therefore expose creditors to an unacceptable risk. The applicants appealed to the High Court against the refusal of leave, contending that by applying, albeit indirectly, a test of fitness to act as directors, which was only appropriate to an application under the Company Directors Disqualification Act 1986, the district judge had applied the wrong test.   *g*

Held – It was wrong in principle to treat an applicant who sought leave under s 216 of the Insolvency Act to be a director of a company with a prohibited name as if he were a person who had been disqualified under the Disqualification Act unless there was evidence which showed that he ought to be disqualified for one   *h* or more of the reasons pertinent under that Act. In particular, it was wrong to treat him, without evidence of misconduct, as if he were unfit to be a company director, since the disqualification imposed by s 216 of the Insolvency Act was not imposed for any of the reasons to be found in the Disqualification Act, ie because he had been convicted of an offence, found guilty of fraud, held to be in persistent   *j* breach of the company legislation or had been found to be unfit to be a director of a company. The disqualification imposed by s 216 of the Insolvency Act was imposed simply because the applicant wished to continue trading through a limited company with a prohibited name. Accordingly, in deciding whether to

---

a   Section 216, so far as material, is set out at p 98 *d* to *j*, post

a give leave under s 216(3) of the Insolvency Act, it was wrong in principle for the court to approach the matter in the way that it would approach an application for leave under s 17 of the Disqualification Act. The fact that the applicant intended to continue to trade through a company with a prohibited name did not entitle the court, without more, to impose restrictions on him as if he were a person who had been disqualified for some form of misconduct. It followed that the district

b judge had applied the wrong test and since there was no risk to the creditors of the old company and no more than the normal risk to the creditors of the new company and no other grounds to justify the refusal of leave, leave would be granted to the applicants to be directors of the new company (see p 103 *c* to *h* and p 104 *f* to *j*, post).

Per curiam. On an application for leave under s 216(3) of the Insolvency Act it

c would not be right for the court, in the absence of any factors leading to the conclusion that the applicants were unfit to be concerned in the management of the company, to refuse leave in the absence of undertakings as to the capital of the new company (see p 105 *f*, post); dictum of Morritt J in *Re Bonus Breaks Ltd* [1991] BCC 546 at 548–549 doubted.

d
Notes

For restriction on reuse of company names, see 7(2) *Halsbury's Laws* (4th edn reissue) paras 1912–1918.

For the Insolvency Act 1986, s 216, see 4 *Halsbury's Statutes* (4th edn) (1987

e reissue) 870.

For the Company Directors Disqualification Act 1986, s 17, see 8 *Halsbury's Statutes* (4th edn) (1991 reissue) 795.

Case referred to in judgment

f *Bonus Breaks Ltd, Re* [1991] BCC 546.

Cases also cited or referred to in skeleton arguments

Atlantic Computer Systems plc, Re [1992] 1 All ER 476, [1992] Ch 505, CA.

Secretary of State for Trade and Industry v Langridge [1991] 3 All ER 591, [1991] Ch 402, CA; *rvsg sub nom Re Cedac Ltd* [1990] BCC 555.

g
Appeal

By notice dated 20 September 1995 the applicants, Timothy James Alan Penrose and Ruth Finch Penrose, appealed from the order of District Judge Sankey, sitting in the Birmingham County Court, made on 13 September 1995, whereby he

h dismissed their application for a review of his order of 2 August 1995 dismissing their application for leave, under s 216(3) of the Insolvency Act 1986, to be directors of a new company by the name of Hudsons Coffee Houses (Holdings) Ltd (trading as Hudsons), which bore a name that was the same as or closely similar to that of a company which had gone into insolvent liquidation and of

j which they had been directors. The Secretary of State for Trade and Industry was the respondent to the appeal. The facts are set out in the judgment.

Michael Fay (instructed by *Irwin Mitchell*, Birmingham) for the applicants.

Sandra Bristoll (instructed by the *Treasury Solicitor*) for the Secretary of State.

Cur adv vult

18 October 1995. The following judgment was delivered.

CHADWICK J. This is an appeal from an order made on 13 September 1995 by District Judge Sankey sitting in the Birmingham County Court. The district judge dismissed an application by Timothy James Alan Penrose and Ruth Finch Penrose for leave, pursuant to s 216(3) of the Insolvency Act 1986, to be directors of a company known as Hudsons Coffee Houses (Holdings) Ltd.

The appeal raises a question of some general importance on which there is little or no reported authority directly in point: namely what principles should guide the court in the exercise of its discretion to grant leave to those who, having been directors of a company which has gone into insolvent liquidation, wish to continue trading through a new company which bears a name which is the same as, or closely similar to, that of the company which has failed.

Section 216 of the Insolvency Act 1986 is in these terms, so far as material:

'(1) This section applies to a person where a company ("the liquidating company") has gone into insolvent liquidation on or after the appointed day and he was a director or shadow director of the company at any time in the period of 12 months ending with the day before it went into liquidation.

(2) For the purposes of this section, a name is a prohibited name in relation to such a person if—(a) it is a name by which the liquidating company was known at any time in that period of 12 months, or (b) it is a name which is so similar to a name falling within paragraph (a) as to suggest an association with that company.

(3) Except with leave of the court or in such circumstances as may be prescribed, a person to whom this section applies shall not at any time in the period of 5 years beginning with the day on which the liquidating company went into liquidation—(a) be a director of any other company that is known by a prohibited name, or (b) in any way, whether directly or indirectly, be concerned or take part in the promotion, formation or management of any such company, or (c) in any way, whether directly or indirectly, be concerned or take part in the carrying on of a business carried on (otherwise than by a company) under a prohibited name.

(4) If a person acts in contravention of this section, he is liable to imprisonment or a fine, or both.

(5) In subsection (3) "the court" means any court having jurisdiction to wind up companies; and on an application for leave under that subsection, the Secretary of State or the official receiver may appear and call the attention of the court to any matters which seem to him to be relevant ...

(7) For the purposes of this section a company goes into insolvent liquidation if it goes into liquidation at a time when its assets are insufficient for the payment of its debts and other liabilities and the expenses of the winding up ...'

The circumstances in which leave is not required in a case to which the section applies are prescribed by rr 4.228, 4.229 and 4.230 of the Insolvency Rules 1986, SI 1986/1925. Those rules are in these terms:

'4.228. *First excepted case.*—(1) Where a company ("the successor company") acquires the whole, or substantially the whole, of the business of an insolvent company, under arrangements made by an insolvency practitioner acting as its liquidator, administrator or administrative receiver, or as a   supervisor of a voluntary arrangement under Part I of the Act, the successor company may for the purposes of section 216 give notice under this Rule to the insolvent company's creditors.

(2) To be effective, the notice must be given within 28 days from the completion of the arrangements, to all creditors of the insolvent company of whose addresses the successor company is aware in that period; and it must

b   specify—(a) the name and registered number of the insolvent company and the circumstances in which its business has been acquired by the successor company, (b) the name which the successor company has assumed, or proposes to assume, for the purpose of carrying on the business, if that name is or will be a prohibited name under section 216, and (c) any change of name which it has made, or proposes to make, for that purpose under section 28 of

c   the Companies Act.

(3) The notice may name a person to whom section 216 may apply as having been a director or shadow director of the insolvent company, and give particulars as to the nature and duration of that directorship, with a view to his being a director of the successor company or being otherwise

d   associated with its management.

(4) If the successor company has effectively given notice under this Rule to the insolvent company's creditors, a person who is so named in the notice may act in relation to the successor company in any of the ways mentioned in section 216(3), notwithstanding that he has not the leave of the court under that section.'

e
Rule 4.229 is in the form in which it was introduced with effect from 11 January 1988 by para 82 of Sch 1 to the Insolvency (Amendment) Rules 1987, SI 1987/ 1919:

'4.229. *Second excepted case.*—(1) Where a person to whom section 216

f   applies as having been a director or shadow director of the liquidating company applies for leave of the court under that section not later than 7 days from the date on which the company went into liquidation, he may, during the period specified in paragraph (2) below, act in any of the ways mentioned in section 216(3), notwithstanding that he has not the leave of the court under that section.

g
(2) The period referred to in paragraph (1) begins with the day on which the company goes into liquidation and ends either on the day falling six weeks after that date or on the day on which the court disposes of the application for leave under section 216, whichever of those days occurs first.

h   Rule 4.230 provides:

Third excepted case.—The court's leave under section 216(3) is not required where the company there referred to, though known by a prohibited name within the meaning of the section—(a) has been known by that name for the whole of the period of 12 months ending with the day before the liquidating

j   company went into liquidation, and (b) has not at any time in those 12 months been dormant within the meaning of section 252(5) of the Companies Act.'

Rule 4.227 empowers the court, when considering an application for leave under s 216 of the Act, to call on the liquidator, or any former liquidator, of the liquidating company for a report of the circumstances in which that company

became insolvent, and the extent (if any) of the applicant's apparent responsibility
for its doing so.   *a*

The applicants had been directors of Hudsons Coffee Houses Ltd at the date of
its liquidation on 26 June 1995. That company (to which I shall refer, for
convenience, as 'the old company') was ordered to be wound up by the court on
the ground that it was unable to pay its debts.

There is no doubt that the liquidation of the old company is an insolvent   *b*
liquidation for the purposes of s 216 of the 1986 Act. The application for leave
under s 216(3) of the Act was made on 3 July 1995. Again, there is no doubt that
the name Hudsons Coffee Houses (Holdings) Ltd (to which I shall refer as 'the
new company') is a prohibited name for the purposes of s 216(2).

The application when made was not supported by any affidavit as to the
circumstances which might lead the court to grant the leave sought. On 4 July   *c*
1995, apparently of his own motion, the district judge ordered the liquidator to
make a report to the court pursuant to r 4.227. That report was made on 21 July
1995 by the Official Receiver, who had become liquidator of the old company by
virtue of his office on the making of the order for winding up. At or about the
same time the first applicant, Mr Timothy Penrose, filed an affidavit in support of *d*
the application.

The report of the Official Receiver showed that the old company had been
incorporated on 4 June 1990 with an issued and paid up capital of £2. Mr Timothy
Penrose had been a director since 20 August 1990. Mrs Ruth Penrose was the
secretary of the company from that date and became a director on 6 April 1992.

The old company commenced trading in November 1990 with the aid of bank   *e*
facilities. Initially it traded only from City Plaza, Cannon Street, Birmingham. Its
business was that of a coffee house. In August 1992 the company expanded with
additional bank facilities. It opened additional premises in Northampton,
Coventry and Harrogate. Between December 1992 and December 1993—as
appears from the Official Receiver's report—Mr and Mrs Penrose injected some *f*
£60,000 into the business by way of a loan; and a third party investor introduced
a further £35,000. By the end of 1993 it was becoming apparent that the
expansion had been ill-advised. The Harrogate, Coventry and Northampton
branches were each making losses. The old company ceased to trade on 12
September 1994.

The directors took advice from a licensed insolvency practitioner. By a written *g*
agreement of 12 September 1994 the assets of the old company—and, in
particular, the lease and other assets at the Birmingham branch—were purchased
by the new company for some £36,000. That was done pursuant to a valuation
carried out by independent professional valuers in Birmingham. In addition to
the sale price specified in the agreement, liabilities of the old company totalling *h*
some £16,653 were assumed by the new company and employees previously
employed by the old company transferred to the new company.

The Official Receiver's report concludes with this comment on the cause of
failure:

'Timothy Penrose attributes the failure of the company to the withdrawal *j*
of bank overdraft facilities, rapid expansion, lack of capital, inexperienced
management and inadequate controls aggravated by declining turnover due
to a downturn in trade in the shopping developments. The official receiver's
enquiries are continuing, but the information at present to hand shows no
reason to disagree with the reasons given for the company's failure.'

a   The application for leave came before District Judge Sankey on 2 August 1995. The applicants appeared in the person of Mr Timothy Penrose. The district judge dismissed the application. No note of his reasons for doing so has been put before me.

Following an abortive attempt to appeal the order of 2 August 1995 to a circuit judge, the matter was referred back to District Judge Sankey. It came before him
b   by way of an application, under r 7.47(1) of the Insolvency Rules 1986, to review his order of 2 August. Further evidence was filed by Mr Archibald Gilmore, a chartered accountant and the auditor of the new company. District Judge Sankey heard the application on 13 September 1995. On that occasion the applicants were represented by counsel. The district judge declined to vary his order of 2 August 1995 and dismissed the application for review. It is from that order of 13
c   September 1995 that the appellants appeal to this court.

It is common ground that an appeal of this nature is a true appeal. I ought not to interfere with the district judge's order unless satisfied that he applied a wrong principle, or that he took into account matters which he should not have taken into account or failed to take into account matters which he should have taken
d   into account, or that in some other way his decision was plainly wrong. It is not open to me to substitute my own discretion for that of the district judge unless satisfied that he was wrong in principle.

The district judge gave reasons for his decision on 13 September 1995. It is convenient to refer to three paragraphs in his judgment. He said:

e   'The insolvency of the old company flowed from inexperience of the applicants, who were the sole directors of both the old and the new companies, which led them to expand too rapidly and to over-trade with inadequate capital and management controls. It ultimately resulted in a deficiency of over £200,000, having only made a profit in one period in its short history. The new company has the same inadequate level of capital
f   and seems to be trading solely on bank borrowing. The share capital is still only two £1 shares and the balance sheets show a deficit of £29,000, though Mr Gilmore explains that on insolvency an alteration of the treatment of some items would alter that to a modest surplus of £10,000 ...

There is no suggestion of dishonesty or deviousness on [the part of the applicants] either in the new company or the old, though that is not to say
g   that they could not be held to be unfit to act as directors based on their conduct of the old company ...

Were the present applicants accompanied on the board by a person experienced in the affairs of limited liability companies and with capital sufficient to trade without wholly relying on borrowing, I would be more
h   sympathetic to the application. I say that without any reflection on the integrity of the applicants, but enthusiastic faith in a business can lead to disastrous situations in limited liability companies.'

It is clear from his judgment that the district judge did not take the view that
j   trading under the name of the new company was going to cause any risk or detriment to the creditors of the old company. He did not take the view that the use of the new company's name was going to lead to expropriation out of the assets of the old company of goodwill or trade connection which could have been realised for the benefit of its creditors. He accepted that the applicants had paid 'over the odds' for the assets which they had taken over, and that they had caused the new company to make payments to the creditors of the old company in

respect of debts which those creditors would not otherwise have been able to recover.

It is also clear that the district judge did not base his judgment on any view that future creditors of the new company would be misled by the fact that it would be trading under the control of the applicant with a name similar to the name of the old company. His view was, in short, that the proposed trading through the medium of an undercapitalised company exposed the creditors of that company to an unacceptable risk. As he said, that was a risk which could have been minimised or reduced by the presence on the board of the new company of a person experienced in the affairs of limited liability companies. In practice that is not an option which the new company could afford.

The question, therefore, which I have to consider is whether it is appropriate, when considering an application for leave under s 216 of the 1986 Act, to take into account the risk that the new company will fail by reason of the lack of experience of its directors and the undercapitalisation of the company.

In my view it is necessary when considering that question, to keep in mind the provisions of the Company Directors Disqualification Act 1986. The Disqualification Act was enacted as part of the corpus of insolvency legislation of which the 1986 Act itself forms the principal statute. That legislation came into force, together, on 29 December 1986.

Sections 2, 3, 4, 5 and 6 of the Disqualification Act prescribe circumstances in which the court may—or, in the case of s 6, must—make a disqualification order against a person who has been a director of a company.

Section 2 of the Disqualification Act empowers the court to make a disqualification order against a person who has been convicted of an indictable offence in connection with the formation or management of a company. Section 3 enables the court to make such an order where a person has been persistently in default in relation to the keeping or filing of accounts and returns. Section 4 applies in cases where the person against whom the order is to be made has been guilty of an offence of fraud; and s 5 applies in cases of summary conviction.

Section 6(1) is in these terms:

> 'Duty of court to disqualify unfit directors of insolvent companies.—(1) The court shall make a disqualification order against a person in any case where, on an application under this section, it is satisfied—(a) that he is or has been a director of a company which has at any time become insolvent (whether while he was a director or subsequently), and (b) that his conduct as a director of that company (either taken alone or taken together with his conduct as a director of any other company or companies) makes him unfit to be concerned in the management of a company.'

Subsection (2) describes the circumstances in which a company is taken to have become insolvent. The test in para (a) of that subsection is identical to that in s 216(7) of the 1986 Act. Subsection (3) identifies 'the court' in terms which are the same as those in s 216(5) of the 1986 Act.

Section 7 of the Disqualification Act empowers the Secretary of State to apply for an order under s 6 if it appears to him that it is expedient in the public interest that a disqualification order should be made against any person. The application can be made by the Official Receiver in the case where the company is being wound up by the court.

Section 9 of the Disqualification Act requires the court, when determining whether a person's conduct as a director makes him unfit to be concerned in the *a* management of a company, to have regard to matters in Sch 1 to the Act. Those matters include misfeasance, breach of fiduciary duty, the extent of his responsibility for entering into avoidable transactions, failure to keep accounts and other matters of that nature.

Where a disqualification order has been made under the Disqualification Act the person disqualified may apply for leave to be a director of a company or to be *b* concerned in its management, notwithstanding the order—see ss 1(1) and 17(1) of that Act. Section 17(2) provides that on the hearing of an application for leave made by a person against whom a disqualification order has been made on the application of the Secretary of State, the Official Receiver or the liquidator, the Secretary of State, Official Receiver or liquidator shall appear and call the attention of the court to any matters which seem to him to be relevant—compare *c* s 216(5) of the 1986 Act.

The position, therefore, is that where the court has been satisfied that a person's conduct in relation to the affairs of an insolvent company makes him unfit to be concerned in the management of a company, the court must disqualify him; but may, none the less, give him leave to continue as a director in respect of *d* a particular company. In deciding whether or not to give that leave, the court must have regard to—and, in practice, is likely to attach considerable weight to— any report made by the Secretary of State or Official Receiver under s 17(2) of the Disqualification Act.

The disqualification imposed by s 216 of the 1986 Act is not imposed for any of the reasons to be found in ss 2 to 6 of the Disqualification Act. It is not imposed *e* because the applicant has been convicted of any offence, found guilty of any fraud, in persistent breach of any provision in company's legislation or found to be unfit to be a director of a company. It is imposed simply because the applicant wishes to continue trading through a limited company with a prohibited name.

In those circumstances, it seems to me wrong in principle to treat an applicant *f* who seeks leave under s 216 of the 1986 Act to be a director of a company with a prohibited name as if he were a person who had been disqualified for any of the reasons under the Disqualification Act unless there is evidence which shows that he ought to be disqualified for one or more of those reasons. In particular, it is wrong to treat him, without evidence of misconduct, as if he were unfit to be a company director.

g Accordingly, in deciding whether to give leave under s 216(3) of the 1986 Act, it seems to me wrong in principle to approach the matter in the way that a court would approach an application for leave under s 17 of the Disqualification Act. The fact that the applicant intends to continue to trade through a company with a prohibited name does not, in my view, entitle the court, without more, to *h* impose restrictions upon him as if he were a person who had been disqualified for some form of misconduct.

There will be cases in which the report of the Secretary of State or the Official Receiver made under s 216(5) of the 1986 Act discloses circumstances which would have led the court to disqualify the director under s 6 of the *j* Disqualification Act. In such cases it would be wrong to give leave under s 216 of the 1986 Act only to make a disqualification order under s 6 of the Disqualification Act on a subsequent application. In such cases leave under s 216 of the 1986 Act should not be granted save in accordance with the principles that would be applied on an application under s 17 of the Disqualification Act. But, unless the court is satisfied on the material which is before it on the application under s 216 of the 1986 Act that the applicant is a person whose conduct in

relation to that liquidating company makes him unfit to be concerned in the
management of a company, it should exercise its discretion under s 216(3) with   *a*
regard only to the purposes for which s 216 was enacted and not on the more
general basis that the public requires some protection from this applicant's
activities as a company director.

The purposes for which s 216 was enacted can be gleaned—in part at least—
from the excepted cases under the rules. Rule 4.228 permits a director of an   *b*
insolvent company to act as director of a new company with a prohibited name
provided that the business of the insolvent company has been acquired under
arrangements made by an insolvency practitioner and notice has been given to
the creditors of the insolvent company.

That rule identifies, and meets, two elements of mischief. First, the danger that
the business of the old insolvent company has been acquired at an undervalue—   *c*
or is otherwise to be expropriated—to the detriment of its creditors; and
secondly, the danger that creditors of the old company may be misled into the
belief that there has been no change in corporate vehicle. The 'phoenix' must be
disclosed as such.

The third excepted case in r 4.230 shows that the mischief is not thought to   *d*
exist in a case where the company having a prohibited name has been established
and trading under that name for a period of not less than 12 months before the
liquidating company went into liquidation. The former director of the
liquidating company can join, or can remain a member of, the board of such a
company without restriction. That must be because the mischief is not perceived
to exist when the company having a prohibited name is not a 'phoenix'.   *e*

In each of those excepted cases the director of the insolvent company can trade
under the new name notwithstanding that the new company may be as
undercapitalised as the old; and notwithstanding that his lack of management
skills may persist. If he is to be disqualified in those cases it must be because his
conduct merits a disqualification order under the Disqualification Act.   *f*

In the present case the district judge approached the matter on the basis that
he was entitled to refuse leave because he thought that the applicants were
inexperienced and the new company undercapitalised. Although he was right to
observe, as he did, that incompetence short of dishonesty could be a ground for
a disqualification order under s 6 of the Disqualification Act, he did not find, and
on the material before him could not have found, that their conduct in relation   *g*
to the old company had, in fact, made them unfit to act as directors.

In those circumstances I am satisfied that the district judge erred in principle.
Accordingly, I am free to substitute my discretion for his. In the light of the facts
disclosed in the Official Receiver's report and in the affidavit of Mr Gilmore, I am
satisfied that there is no risk to the creditors of the old company; and no risk to   *h*
the creditors of the new company beyond that which is permitted under the law
relating to the incorporation of limited liability companies—that is to say, no risk
beyond that which the legislature, in permitting those who are inexperienced to
trade through companies which are undercapitalised, must be taken to have
regarded as acceptable. Accordingly, it would not be right to refuse leave on   *j*
those grounds. There being no other grounds to justify refusal, I propose to grant
leave under s 216(3) of the 1986 Act.

I have been taken to the decision of Morritt J in *Re Bonus Breaks Ltd* [1991] BCC
546. So far as I am aware, that is the only reported case on an application under
s 216 of the 1986 Act. The position in that case—as it appears from the report—
was that there was no evidence that the old company had failed as a result of any

dishonesty by the directors. But the liquidator had reported that the old company
a had become insolvent for some time before it ceased trading. Morritt J was
offered a number of undertakings as to the capital and solvency of the new
company. He said (at 548–549):

b
'The one point that concerned me was the fact that the share capital of
£50,000 is plainly crucial to the attainment of the figures given in the
cash-flow forecast because without the paid-up share capital, there would
have to be bank borrowing which would be expensive. On further enquiry,
it appeared that the shares were redeemable only at the option of the
company within one and three years after its incorporation. Even then, it
seemed to me to be undesirable that the capital base should be capable of
c being removed at the option of the applicant and Mr Leader alone.
Accordingly, I enquired and was informed that an undertaking would be
given, that the company would not redeem any redeemable shares nor
purchase its own shares out of distributable profits for a period of two years
from today, unless, effectively, that was approved by a third director who
was not himself connected with either of the other two. That seems to me
d to be satisfactory. It would ensure, as it seems to me, that the capital base of
the company was maintained, and whilst the capital base is maintained in the
ownership of Mr Leader, it will give rise to the retention of his management
skills as well. There is no reason to think that the skills of the applicant, in
the artistic and promotion field in which she has been primarily concerned,
e would not be perfectly well directed within such a corporate structure. It
seems to me that this in the circumstances, is therefore an application I can
approve on the giving of that undertaking.'

Morritt J did not have to decide, as it appears from that passage, whether he
would have given leave if the undertakings had not been offered; although there
f is a clear indication that he might not have done so. It should be clear from my
judgment on the application before me that, in the absence of any factors leading
to the conclusion that the applicants were unfit to be concerned in the
management of the company, I would not share the view—if, indeed, that were
the view of Morritt J—that leave could be refused in the absence of undertakings
g as to the capital of the new company.

Order accordingly.

Celia Fox   Barrister.

Oyston v Blaker and others

a

COURT OF APPEAL, CIVIL DIVISION

BUTLER-SLOSS, HENRY AND PILL LJJ

14, 15 JUNE, 1 NOVEMBER 1995

b

Limitation of action – Extension of time limit – Discretion – Exercise of discretion – Defamation action – Facts relevant to plaintiff's cause of action not becoming known until after expiry of three-year limitation period – Plaintiff applying for leave to issue writ after expiry of statutory period – Master granting leave ex parte – Whether grant of leave ex parte an irregularity – Whether judge having discretion to refuse leave – Limitation Act 1980, ss 4A, 32A – RSC Ord 2, r 1(2), Ord 32, r 9.

c

On an application for leave under s 32A[a] of the Limitation Act 1980 to extend the three-year limitation period for defamation actions prescribed by s 4A[b] of the Act, a judge has a wide discretion to do what is just in all the circumstances, subject only to the court's overriding duty to exercise that discretion in a manner *d* consistent with the legislative purpose of the section. Moreover, it is an irregularity for a plaintiff to seek and obtain such leave ex parte, since RSC Ord 32, r 9(3)[c], which requires such application to be made by originating summons heard on notice, is clear and mandatory in form. Any leave wrongly obtained ex parte is liable to be set aside under Ord 2, r 1(2)[d], and in exercising his discretion *e* under that rule, a judge may, in addition to considering the question of prejudice, properly have regard to the gravity of the irregularity, the staleness of the claim, the strength of the case, the conduct of the parties and their advisers, any question of abuse of process, and any delay and the reasons therefor, in deciding whether the order granting leave should be set aside (see p 114 *e*, p 115 *a c*, p 116 *b* to *g* and p 119 *f* to p 120 *b*, post).   *f*

Notes

For the Limitation Act 1980, ss 4A, 32A, see 24 *Halsbury's Statutes* (4th edn) (1989 reissue) 653, 685.

g

Cases referred to in judgments

Aiden Shipping Co Ltd v Interbulk Ltd, The Vimeira [1986] 2 All ER 409, [1986] AC 965, [1986] 2 WLR 1051, HL.

G v G [1985] 2 All ER 225, [1985] 1 WLR 647, HL.

Metroinvest Anstalt v Commercial Union Assurance Co plc [1985] 2 All ER 318, [1985] *h* 1 WLR 513, CA.

R v Crown Court at Southwark, ex p Customs and Excise Comrs [1989] 3 All ER 673, [1990] 1 QB 650, [1989] 1 WLR 1054, DC.

---

a   Section 32A, so far as material, is set out at p 109 *d*, post

b   Section 4A, so far as material, provides: '... no such action [for libel or slander] shall be brought *j* after the expiration of three years from the date on which the cause of action accrued.'

c   Rule 9(3), so far as material, is set out at p 109 *f*, post

d   Rule 1(2) provides: '... the Court may, on the ground that there has been [a failure to comply with the requirements of the rules] ... set aside either wholly or in part the proceedings in which the failure occurred, any step taken in those proceedings or any document, judgment or order therein ...'

a Riddick v Thames Board Mills Ltd [1977] 3 All ER 677, [1977] QB 881, [1977] 3 WLR 63.

Sybron Corp v Barclays Bank plc [1985] Ch 299, [1984] 3 WLR 1055.

Cases also cited or referred to in skeleton arguments

Behbehani v Salem [1989] 2 All ER 143, [1989] 1 WLR 723, CA.

b Bank Mellat v Nikpour [1985] Com LR 158.

Bartlett v Barclays Bank Trust Co Ltd [1980] 1 All ER 139, [1980] Ch 515, CA.

Bibby Bulk Carriers Ltd v Cansulex Ltd, The Cambridgeshire [1988] 2 All ER 820, [1989] QB 155.

Black-Clawson International Ltd v Papierwerke Waldhof-Aschaffenburg AG [1975] 1 All ER 810, [1975] AC 591, HL.

c Camera Care Ltd v Victor Hasselblad AB [1986] 1 FTLR 348, CA.

Cepheus Shipping Corp v Guardian Royal Exchange Assurance plc (Note) [1995] 1 Lloyd's Rep 647.

Crest Homes plc v Marks [1987] 2 All ER 1074, [1987] AC 829, HL.

Disney v Plummer (note) [1991] FSR 165, CA.

d Electric Furnace Co v Selas Corp of America [1987] RPC 23, CA.

Fothergill v Monarch Airlines Ltd [1980] 2 All ER 696, [1981] AC 251, HL.

Frisby v Theodore Goddard [1984] CA Transcript 84.

Golden Ocean Assurance Ltd v Martin, The Goldean Mariner [1990] 2 Lloyd's Rep 215, CA.

e Hadmor Productions Ltd v Hamilton [1982] 1 All ER 1042, [1983] 1 AC 191, HL.

Hagen, The [1908] P 189, [1908–10] All ER Rep 21, CA.

Harkness v Bell's Asbestos and Engineering Ltd [1966] 3 All ER 843, [1967] 2 QB 729, CA.

Harrods (Buenos Aires) Ltd, Re (No 2) [1991] 4 All ER 348, [1992] Ch 72, CA.

Heaven v Road and Rail Wagons Ltd [1965] 2 All ER 409, [1965] 2 QB 355.

f Leal v Dunlop Bio-Processes International Ltd [1984] 2 All ER 207, [1984] 1 WLR 874, CA.

Lloyds Bowmaker Ltd v Britannia Arrows Holdings plc (Lavens, third party) [1988] 3 All ER 178, [1988] 1 WLR 1337, CA.

Marie Claire Album SA v Hartstone Hosiery Ltd [1993] FSR 692.

g Probe Data Systems Ltd, Re (No 3), Secretary of State for Trade and Industry v Desai [1992] BCLC 405, CA.

R v Kensington Income Tax Comrs, ex p Princess Edmond de Polignac [1917] 1 KB 486, DC and CA.

Singh v Observer Ltd (Note) [1989] 3 All ER 777, CA.

h Stewart Chartering Ltd v C & O Managements SA, The Venus Destiny [1980] 1 All ER 718, [1980] 1 WLR 460.

Thermax Ltd v Schott Industrial Glass Ltd [1981] FSR 289.

Ward v Lewis [1955] 1 All ER 55, [1955] 1 WLR 9, CA.

Appeal

j By notice dated 3 November 1993 the plaintiff, Owen Oyston, appealed with leave from the order of Ognall J dated 25 August 1993, whereby he set aside the order of Master Rose dated 18 September 1992 granting the plaintiff leave ex parte under s 32A of the Limitation Act 1980 to issue and serve on the defendants, Sir Peter Blaker, Robert Atkins and Bill Harrison, a writ alleging libel, slander and conspiracy, and struck out the plaintiff's claim in conspiracy as

an abuse of process of the court. The defendants cross-appealed. Before the
hearing the plaintiff abandoned his appeal against the striking out order. The *a*
facts are set out in the judgment of Henry LJ.

Anthony Scrivener QC and *Manuel Barca* (instructed by *Peter Carter-Ruck &
Partners*) for the plaintiff.
Desmond Browne QC and *Alexandra Marzec* (instructed by *Biddle & Co*) for the first *b*
defendant.
Timothy Sisley (instructed by *Goldkorn Davies Mathias*) for the second defendant.
Michael Briggs QC and *Harry Boggis-Rolfe* (instructed by *Philip Conn & Co*,
Manchester) for the third defendant.

Cur adv vult *c*

1 November 1995. The following judgments were delivered.

HENRY LJ (delivering the first judgment at the invitation of Butler-Sloss LJ).

1. *Introduction*   *d*
    The plaintiff is a well-known businessman, who alleges that he has been, inter
alia, defamed by a man called Michael Murrin, who is not a party to these
proceedings. In these proceedings he sues the three defendants, who are
respectively a former Conservative member of Parliament, a present Conservative member of Parliament, and a businessman, all with interests in public affairs
and/or business in Lancashire. He alleges that they authorised Murrin to *e*
publish the defamatory matter that he complains of, and that they conspired
with Murrin to injure and defame him. All numerical references are to the
numbered paragraphs and subparagraphs.

2. *The need for leave to bring these proceedings*   *f*
    2.1 The plaintiff needed the leave of the court before he could bring the
defamation proceedings. This was because without leave those proceedings
were statute-barred under s 4A of the Limitation Act 1980. He initially got that
leave from the master. When the matter went to the judge, Ognall J, he set aside
that order and refused leave. His refusal is now appealed to us.   *g*
    2.2 Section 4A reduced the Limitation Act period for proceedings such as
these from six years to three years, in line with the recommendation of the
Report of the Committee on Defamation (Cmnd 5909 (1975) chairman Sir Neville
Faulks). In so recommending the committee recognised the desirability of both:
(i) speedy vindication of plaintiffs' character; and (ii) defendants not having the *h*
anxiety, expense and inconvenience of a defamation action hanging over them
for an unnecessarily long period.
    2.3 This philosophy was taken further by the Neill Committee in the *Supreme
Court of Judicature Procedure Committee Report on Practice and Procedure in
Defamation* (1991), where a reduction of the three-year period to 12 months with
a discretion to 'disapply' the time limit was advocated (see ch 8 of the report). *j*
And those suggestions have been carried forward into the draft Bill now out for
consultation.
    2.4 The first formal step the plaintiff took to initiate such proceedings was
when he applied for the necessary leave in mid-September 1992, at which time
more than three years had elapsed since his causes of action had accrued (ie since

a the date of publication) in all but one of the 32 allegations of slander and libel he was to make. That exception was, we were told, included by mistake.

2.5 The writ also was founded in conspiracy for which no leave was required. But the judge was to strike out that claim in conspiracy as being an abuse of the process of the court. No appeal is pursued against that strike out.

2.6 The Faulks Committee had recognised the possibility of the plaintiff not *b* discovering the facts relevant to his cause of action in defamation until after the three-year period had expired. To guard against such an injustice, they recommended that the court should have power in the exercise of its discretion to give leave to bring a statute-barred action provided proceedings were instituted within 12 months of acquiring the relevant knowledge. This is enacted in s 32A of the 1980 Act.

c Both the heading and the sidenote to that section read: 'Discretionary extension of time limit for actions for libel or slander'. The section itself reads:

> 'Where a person to whom a cause of action for libel or slander has accrued has not brought such an action within the period of three years mentioned in section 4A of this Act ... because all or any of the facts relevant to that *d* cause of action did not become known to him until after the expiration of that period, such an action—(a) may be brought by him at any time before the expiration of one year from the earliest date on which he knew all the facts relevant to that cause of action; but (b) shall not be so brought without the leave of the High Court.'

e For convenience, I will refer to the facts defined in para (a) as 'the qualifying facts'.

2.7 The rules provide that application for leave is to be made inter partes. RSC Ord 32, r 9(3) provides: 'An originating summons by which an application for leave under ... the said section 32A is made shall be in Form No. 10 in *f* Appendix A.' Form 10 is expressed to be the 'expedited form' of originating summons. It requires a summons heard on notice. A blank is left in for the length of that notice, but a suggested 14 days is given for time for acknowledgment of service. In requiring leave to be given on notice to the potential defendant, thereby giving him a right to be heard, the rules follow the recommendation of the Faulks Committee.

g 2.8 But here, in circumstances which require examination, the master gave leave ex parte. Ognall J found that the master should not have dealt with this matter ex parte, saying '[Order 32, r 9(3)] makes it plain that no proceedings in which Form 10 must be used give the court jurisdiction to grant leave ex parte'. That conclusion followed from a concession by Mr Scrivener QC for the plaintiff *h* that the grant of leave was an irregularity. Mr Scrivener now seeks to withdraw that concession. If he was wrong in law to make it, he should be permitted to withdraw it.

2.9 Section 32A is central to the appeal before us, and it will be necessary to consider it in detail after the facts have been summarised.

j

3. The facts

3.1 The plaintiff complains that throughout the 1980s there was a defamatory whispering campaign against him. It seems that Murrin had investigated his activities and made serious allegations against him, first published to the media in June 1988, in a matter known as the Preston Docks statement. The plaintiff promptly obtained an injunction against Murrin, restraining further publication of that statement.

3.2 Subsequent to these events the Sunday Times, in consecutive articles on 17 and 24 September 1989, questioned certain joint ventures and share dealings involving the plaintiff, one Bookbinder (then the leader of the Derbyshire County Council) and that county council. The plaintiff issued proceedings against the Sunday Times, which proceedings were eventually settled, the paper paying him a considerable sum by way of damages and costs. The first Sunday Times article disclosed that the first and second defendants had funded Murrin to inquire into the plaintiff's links with local politicians. Both defendants were quoted by the Sunday Times as saying that these investigations had produced no evidence of wrongdoing. The plaintiff already had had suspicions that there were people behind the activities of Murrin. Murrin was to tell him that the first defendant had discouraged him from publishing the Preston Docks statement.

3.3 In the course of 1990 and 1991, before the Sunday Times action was disposed of, there were various meetings between Murrin and the plaintiff, the plaintiff's employees and his solicitors, the well-known firm of Messrs Peter Carter-Ruck & Partners. Early on in these meetings it emerged that Murrin often recorded phone calls. The plaintiff wished to obtain transcripts of those phone calls for use in the Sunday Times action. Murrin was not initially disposed to disclose those tapes. He needed, in the plaintiff's phrase, 'pushing'. Finally, on 10 January 1991 the plaintiff issued a subpoena requiring Murrin to produce the tapes. Certain of those tapes were delivered in the course of that year, and finally on 23/24 September 1991 all of the tapes were delivered. The Sunday Times action was settled very soon thereafter, the statement in open court being 7 October 1991. The material in those tapes is in large measure the basis of this action against the defendants. They contain the qualifying facts. This action, however, may be likened to Hamlet without the Prince, because while the action is based on what Murrin had said of the plaintiff in the telephone conversations he was taping, Murrin has not been made a party to the action. He, for good reason or bad (but probably not for no reason), was sued separately. It is a feature of this case that nothing is straightforward. It is clear from the tapes that Murrin was making serious allegations. The pleaded link with the defendants is that it is alleged that they 'authorised' the publications, as part of 'a calculated plan to injure the plaintiff by manipulating the media'. Each side accuses the other of such manipulation. Mr Scrivener QC opened the appeal to us on the basis that Murrin had 'changed sides'.

3.4 The relevance of the subpoena is this: the case in slander is founded on the tapes. The tapes were delivered by Murrin nine months after a subpoena was in place directing him to produce them in the Sunday Times action. No leave has at any time been given by the court allowing documents produced under the compulsion of the subpoena in that action to be used in this action. Therefore, if the judge, at the leave stage or at trial, were to find that the tapes had been produced under compulsion of the subpoena, then the action should be stayed as an abuse of process (see *Riddick v Thames Board Mills Ltd* [1977] 3 All ER 677, [1977] QB 881 and *Sybron Corp v Barclays Bank plc* [1985] Ch 299).

3.5 On the issue as to whether Murrin produced the tapes voluntarily, the judge was faced with a conflict of evidence on the affidavits. He found that, faced with that conflict, he could not be satisfied that Murrin handed over the tapes under the compulsive process of the subpoena. That conclusion is

a
challenged by way of a counter-notice, both in regard to the conclusion reached, and the manner in which it was reached, it being argued that the burden of proof should have been put on the plaintiff to show that the extant subpoena had not been a factor in the delivery of the tapes. But first it is necessary to consider the appeal proper.

3.6 It is common ground between the parties that the latest date for
b
commencement of defamation proceedings based on the contents of the tapes under the extended period given by s 32A of the 1980 Act would have been 12 months from the delivery those tapes on 23/24 September 1991. Once he had the tapes, the plaintiff had all the material he needed for his defamation proceedings. But it seems that he was in no hurry to bring those proceedings. The transcription of the tapes was completed by 11 November, but his solicitors
c
were not instructed in this matter until May 1992, though he was in touch with them about other matters in the interim. Having been so instructed, Peter Carter-Ruck & Partners took no formal steps to bring the proceedings until mid-September 1992, eight days before the final limitation period expired. Meanwhile the plaintiff talked to the media about his account of the campaign against him, and selected passages from the tapes were leaked by some source
d
to them.

3.7 In the event, on 15 September 1992, the plaintiff's solicitors went to the practice master with a writ and a draft affidavit. They pointed out to him that the limitation period expired in eight days time, and that the rules required that they sought leave by originating summons on notice to the prospective
e
defendants, the form allowing 14 days for acknowledgment of service. They asked the master's help as to how to deal with this self-inflicted problem and invited him to approve their intention to proceed ex parte. The master considered matters overnight and said on 16 September that he would hear the application ex parte. This he did on 18 September, and after a 10 to 15 minute
f
hearing, of which there is no note or other contemporaneous record, he granted leave. He had before him a draft writ making eight claims. On the face of them, four did not require the leave of the court: claims 6, 7 and 8, relating to conspiracy, and claim 4 to a slander published 'around 16 October 1990' (we were told that the latter claim was included 'by mistake').

3.8 The master gave no reasons for granting leave. We do not know why this
g
was, nor why he gave leave. The likelihood is that he regarded the application as straightforward. As the conspiracy claim did not need leave, he might have thought the leave requirement academic. But it is difficult to see how he could have regarded it as straightforward had he been told: first, of the existence of the subpoena covering the tapes and the fact that the court's consent to their use had
h
not been obtained; second, of the vulnerability of the claim for conspiracy (which I will consider next); and third, in relation to that part of the claim relating to the Preston Docks statement, that the plaintiff's 'knowledge' that the first and second defendants were behind the Preston Docks statement owed nothing to the tapes, but was complete after the Sunday Times publication in
j
September 1989.

4. The vulnerability of the conspiracy claim

4.1 Before the judge it was successfully contended that the pleading in conspiracy was a device to circumvent the limitation period in defamation. The judge found that the conspiracy claim was simply the defamation claim under a

different hat, with no direct pecuniary loss flowing from it, and so rightly struck
it out. But the mischief of the claim was that if the same issues as arose in
defamation could be litigated without leave in conspiracy, then the grant of
leave in defamation would appear academic. Various efforts were made before
the judge to validate the conspiracy claim by amendment, but he was to find
those efforts—

> 'a transparent and specious attempt to circumvent the clear prohibition
> on running conspiracy in tandem with defamation proceedings, and an
> attempt made necessary by the problems (whether of limitation or
> otherwise) seen to confront the plaintiff in his claim in libel and slander.'

4.2 As I have said, the conspiracy claim was struck out as an abuse of process
by the judge, and the appeal against that decision was abandoned.

5. The judge's findings

5.1 Such findings were the circumstances in which the master granted leave,
and the matter came before Ognall J.

His central preliminary finding was that for the master to have proceeded ex
parte was an irregularity within the meaning of Ord 2, r 1. Such irregularities
are not nullities: the decision was voidable, but not void. But if the master's
decision were set aside under Ord 2, r 1, then the plaintiff's claim would
inevitably fail, as there is no jurisdiction in the court to extend either of the
limitation periods contained in s 4A and s 32A. So the umbrella discretion that
the judge had to exercise was under Ord 2, r 1, the background against which he
had to exercise it was that the consequence of any validation would be to
deprive the defendants of a potential limitation defence, and the context in
which the discretion had to be exercised was that of s 32A.

5.2 His specific findings were as follows: (i) that in the face of the conflicting
affidavits, he could not find that Murrin handed over the tapes under the
compulsive process of the subpoena (paras 3.4–3.5); (ii) that the conspiracy claim
should be struck out as an abuse of process (paras 4.1–4.2); (iii) that it was a
breach of the rules and an irregularity to proceed ex parte (paras 7.10–7.14); (iv)
that leave should not have been given in relation to the Preston Docks
statement, as he had come by the relevant knowledge against all defendants at
the very latest by June 1991 (paras 3.1–3.2, 9.6); and (v) that the master's order
should be set aside on the basis that 'the nature and extent of the concealment
before the master amounted to a manipulation of his discretion' which so
seriously affected his grant of leave that the court should set it aside. This
decision was taken having regard to all the surrounding circumstances, and in
particular: (a) the non-disclosure to the master of the plaintiff's knowledge
before June 1991 of the salient facts relating to the Preston Docks statement
(including the failure to sue earlier) and the evidence relating to the exoneration
of the first defendant in relation thereto (paras 3.1–3.2, 9.6); (b) non-disclosure
to the master of the subpoena (paras 3.4–3.5, 9.3); (c) the failure to sue Murrin in
these proceedings, and the absence of satisfactory explanation for that (paras 3.3,
9.4–9.5); (d) the ten-month period of delay from completion of transcription of
the tapes to application to the master, the use made by the plaintiff of that
period, and the failure to disclose these matters, and also the failure to bring
proceedings earlier than the last minute (paras 3.6, 7.12, 9.7); (e) non-disclosure
of when the plaintiff came by those individual tapes delivered earlier than the

a whole archive, and the failure to sue on them (para 3.3); (f) the mischief of including on the writ the conspiracy claim and the slander of '16th October 1990' without disclosing the legal vulnerability of the former, or correcting the mistake that the latter is said to be (paras 3.7, 4.1–4.2); (g) the prejudice to the defendants in being improperly prevented from seeking to defeat the claim before the master at an inter partes hearing (paras 9.9–9.12).

b   5.3 Accordingly, he set aside the leave given by the master.

5.4 The plaintiff now appeals against the judge's decision, but has now abandoned his appeal in so far as it relates to the conspiracy claim, which therefore stands struck out. The defendants for their part have issued a cross-notice that the judge was wrong to find no abuse by reason of use of material obtained by subpoena.

c

6. The issues raised by the plaintiff on this appeal.

As there is no power under s 32A to extend the limitation period beyond 12 months from the date of acquiring the qualifying knowledge, it follows that to succeed the plaintiff must persuade us to restore the leave given by the master.
d This involves the following issues. (i) Was it an irregularity to proceed ex parte? (para 7). This issue raises two sub-issues: (a) was there a judicial discretion under s 32A? (paras 7.2–7.5); (b) what was the extent of that discretion? (see para 7.6–7.9). (ii) Was the plaintiffs in breach of the duty of full and frank disclosure required of those applying ex parte? (para 8). (iii) Was the judge acting within his discretion in his striking out of the leave given by the master? (para 9).

e

7. Was it an irregularity to proceed ex parte?

7.1 I deal first with the decision to proceed ex parte, and the judge's treatment of it. This is to some extent dependent on the proper construction of s 32A, first, as to whether there was here a discretion and, second, as to the extent of that
f discretion.

7.2 Was there here a s 32A discretion to refuse leave? It is suggested that once the judge found: (i) that the qualifying facts were only known to the plaintiff after the three-year limitation period had expired; and (ii) that he had brought the proceedings within 12 months of having acquired that knowledge, all
g conditions of s 32A were satisfied, and the judge was bound to grant leave.

7.3 This follows from a bold submission by Mr Scrivener that the judge's task under s 32A does not involve the exercise of any judicial discretion but is simply one of determining whether he is satisfied that the factual requirements of the section are met, namely whether the qualifying facts only became known to him
h within the last 12 months. If that were the case, then the application under s 32A (so far as it related to any material gleaned only from the tapes) would be a foregone conclusion: given the need for particularity in slander pleadings, the relevant facts could only become known on delivery of the tapes, and that was just within 12 months. If that were right, then the duty of disclosure which must be accepted by any litigant who moves ex parte is also drastically reduced, as
j before any examination of whether there has been a failure to disclose relevant material, the court must identify the extent of the judicial function which is the yardstick for relevance.

7.4 The judge rejected this submission on the basis of the clear words of para (b) of the section: if the court is satisfied of the qualifying facts under para (a), then: 'Such an action—(a) may be brought ... but (b) shall not be brought without the leave of the High Court.' The antithesis between 'may' and 'but', and the presence of para (b) are in my judgment only explicable by the fact that the grant of leave is discretionary, that is to say that the applicant must satisfy the judge both of the factual requirements of the section and that it is a proper case for the exercise of his discretion.

7.5 In those circumstances, while I do not find it necessary to rely as an aid to construction on the fact that both the heading and sidenote to the section (both of which are part of the Act) speak of a 'discretionary extension of time limit', I take the view that I would be able to consider the significance of the use there of the word 'discretionary' *provided* I properly take into account that the function of such headings 'is merely to serve as a brief and therefore necessarily inaccurate guide to the material to which it is attached' (see Bennion *Statutory Interpretation* (2nd edn, 1992) pp 510–512). Making all such allowance, those headings can be nothing but support for my interpretation, were such support necessary.

7.6 *The extent of the s 32A discretion*   Mr Scrivener's next submission is to challenge the width of the discretion. The judge, having correctly found that the court had a discretion, defined it in wide terms 'a wide discretion to do what appears just in all the circumstances', the classic broad judicial discretion. Mr Scrivener contends that the discretion must be restricted to simply considering whether the qualifying facts have been made out: that is to say he seeks to arrive at his original position (as stated in para 7.2) by another argument.

7.7 The words of the section impose no express limit on the exercise of the discretion. It simply says that leave is required. Mr Scrivener's formulation invites us to imply a limitation on that jurisdiction not provided for in the statute. To do so would be wrong in principle. Where a statute entrusts the court with a discretion expressed in wide terms, then, in the words of Lord Goff in *Aiden Shipping Co Ltd v Interbulk Ltd* [1986] 2 All ER 409 at 413, [1986] AC 965 at 975:

'Such a provision is consistent with a policy under which jurisdiction to exercise the relevant discretionary power is expressed in wide terms, thus ensuring that the court has, so far as possible, freedom of action, leaving it to the rule-making authority to control the exercise of discretion (if it thinks it right to do so) by the making of rules of court, and to the appellate courts to establish principles on which the discretionary power may, within the framework of the statute and the applicable rules of court, be exercised. Such a policy appears to me, I must confess, to be entirely sensible. It comes therefore as something of a surprise to discover that it has been suggested that any limitation should be held to be *implied* into the statutory provision which confers the relevant jurisdiction.' (Lord Goff's emphasis.)

And he was to say later ([1986] 2 All ER 409 at 416–417, [1986] AC 965 at 981):

'Courts of first instance are, I believe, well capable of exercising their discretion under the statute in accordance with reason and justice ... If any problem arises, the Court of Appeal can lay down principles for the guidance of judges of first instance; or the Supreme Court Rule Committee can propose amendments to the Rules of the Supreme Court for the purpose of controlling the exercise of the statutory power vested in judges subject to rules of court.'

a 7.8 Therefore the judge was right in his broad definition of his discretionary jurisdiction: to do what was just in all the circumstances. It is subject only to the court's overriding duty to exercise any discretionary power vested in it by an enactment in a manner consistent with the legislative purpose of the enactment.

7.9 That purpose was first to reduce the limitation period in defamation actions (for reasons already given), but second to allow plaintiffs who did not *b* discover the facts on which their action depended within the limitation period a short time after discovery to bring that action but only with the leave of the judge on the lines set out above.

7.10 *Should s 32A leave have been given ex parte?* The judge found that it was an irregularity that leave to bring proceedings should have been sought and *c* obtained ex parte. Mr Scrivener now contends (para 2.8) that it was no irregularity so to proceed. I do not agree. RSC Ord 32, r 9(3) is clear and it is mandatory in form. Mr Scrivener makes the point that nothing in the statute itself requires a hearing on notice. That point does not significantly advance his submission. As the first citation above from Lord Goff's speech shows, the legislature left the principles upon which the discretion should be exercised to *d* the Rules Committee. And they, in accordance with the recommendation of the Faulks Committee, *required* the application to be made on notice. The reason is clear—that where the plaintiff requires the court's discretion to revive a cause of action that would otherwise be time-barred, the potential defendant must be heard. That requirement now forms an important part of the statutory scheme. *e* The facts of this case clearly show the wisdom of that requirement.

7.11 Mr Scrivener submits that the 'inherent jurisdiction' of the court empowers it to permit this application to be made ex parte. It is clear that the court has an inherent jurisdiction where, for instance, there is a procedural gap in the rules. But there was no such gap here.

f 7.12 Here the plaintiff's specialist libel solicitors went to the practice master on 15 September (with eight days of the limitation period to run) with an express request to be heard ex parte, when the 'necessity' (if there was one) to proceed ex parte lay entirely at the door of them and/or their client. As the judge observed, they were sailing very close to the wind. They did not attempt to explain the delay, indeed, their stance is that delay is irrelevant. I disagree, for *g* reasons to be given.

7.13 In my judgment there was simply no need to proceed ex parte. The master should have set up a short-notice inter partes hearing before the judge. There was ample time for that, and this application should have gone straight to the judge. If at that hearing it then appeared that the matter could not be *h* concluded before the limitation period expired, then the judge could doubtless have preserved the position by granting leave to issue the writ as a holding exercise, without regard to the merits, on the plaintiff's undertaking to discontinue the action and pay the defendants' costs if the court found, after having considered the merits, that leave should not be given (for jurisdiction to *j* impose such a condition, see *R v Crown Court at Southwark, ex p Customs and Excise Comrs* [1989] 3 All ER 673 at 679, [1990] 1 QB 650 at 655 (counsel's submissions) and 661).

7.14 I have no hesitation in finding that it was an irregularity to proceed ex parte. And in the circumstances it was a serious one. It was the plaintiff's actions and inactions which deprived the defendants of their legal right to a hearing

before this writ was issued against them. So the judge had jurisdiction to set the
order granting leave aside, in the exercise of his discretion under Ord 2, r 1(2).   *a*

8. *Was the plaintiff in breach of the duty of disclosure imposed on those applying
ex parte?*
    8.1 The ordinary requirements of full and frank disclosure imposed on a
litigant applying ex parte applied here. The judge was right to hold that a breach   *b*
of that duty was a factor he could properly take into account in the exercise of
his discretion.
    8.2 The elements of non-disclosure complained of are to be found in paras 3.8
and 5.2 at (v)(a) to (f) above and are further dealt with in para 9 below. In my
judgment those are significant failures to disclose which would also give the   *c*
judge jurisdiction, in the exercise of his discretion, to set the order granting leave
aside.
    8.3 In so finding, I unhesitatingly reject the plaintiff's submission that once
the ex parte application is found to be based on an irregularity, and so liable to
be set aside under Ord 2, r 1(2), then any breach of the obligations of disclosure   *d*
becomes irrelevant. This court has held that the discretion under that rule has
been framed so as to give the judge the widest possible power in order to do
justice: see *Metroinvest Anstalt v Commercial Union Assurance Co plc* [1985] 2 All ER
318, [1985] 1 WLR 513. Thus in a proper case the judge, as well as considering
the question of prejudice, can have regard to the gravity of the irregularity, the
staleness of the claim, the strength of the case, the conduct of the parties and   *e*
their advisers, any question of abuse of process, and any delay and the reasons
for it. Limits should not be imposed on the discretion. Here, the judge regarded
the non-disclosure as a serious and substantial irregularity 'seriously infecting'
the proceedings. If he was rightly exercising his discretion in so finding, Ord 2,
r 1(2) entitled him to set aside the irregular proceedings.   *f*

9. *Was the judge acting within his discretion in his strike-out of the leave given
by the master?*
    9.1 I come then to the judge's exercise of his discretion to set aside the leave
wrongly obtained ex parte. He was right to proceed to consider the matter   *g*
under Ord 2, r 1(2). The words of that rule make it clear that the master's grant
of leave is to be treated as an irregularity, and not a nullity. Therefore it stands
until set aside. I examine it on that basis.
    9.2 It is said that the manner in which the judge exercised his discretion is
flawed because he took into account irrelevant matters in reaching his decision.   *h*
Specifically identified are: (i) the non-disclosure of the subpoena (para 9.3
below); (ii) no explanation being given for Murrin not being joined in these
proceedings (para 9.4 and 9.5 below); (iii) the inclusion of the claim in libel in
relation to the Preston Docks statement in the writ (para 9.6 below); and (iv) the
question of delay, and the failure adequately to explain it.
    9.3 The existence of the Murrin subpoena was not disclosed. The abuse of   *j*
process point turned on the fact that the tapes were delivered some months after
(and, it was contended, as a result of) the subpoena. Though the judge felt
unable to make that finding on a conflict of affidavits, it was clearly a real live
issue. The plaintiff did not disclose to the defendants the fact of the subpoena;
the defendants discovered it independently. Nor did the plaintiff disclose his

a solicitor's letter of 17 September 1991 to Murrin, which he relied on before the judge to justify the use of the tapes, undertaking to use them for 'no other purpose than ... [the plaintiff's] litigation against the Sunday Times and any other litigation that may arise to which the tape recordings have relevance'. As the judge pointed out, the existence of the subpoena would have been more likely to emerge if Murrin was a party to the proceedings. It was clearly a matter

b to be disclosed in any ex parte application. As the judge said, it went to the root of the slander allegations and the fact that it was not disclosed went to the question of conduct of the party seeking the discretion of the court, because if the defendant's point as to the subpoena were made out, the action would be an abuse of process. The judge had to consider whether the nature of the irregularity 'seriously infected' the proceedings by manipulating the master's

c discretion by getting a foot in the door by concealing the subpoena. He was to reach that decision as a result of an accumulation of matters. This was certainly a matter that a judge exercising the wide discretion under Ord 2, r 1(2) was entitled to take into account in reaching that decision.

9.4 The judge commented on the fact that there had been no satisfactory

d explanation of the failure to join Murrin in the action, making the obvious point that had he been joined, the subpoena point would have almost certainly emerged. The defendants also contended that the reason he was in a separate action was so that a settlement could be reached with him contingent upon his giving sufficient assistance to the plaintiff, the contention on the evidence being that Murrin was to be paid in cash or in kind for assisting the plaintiff. The judge

e was to say:

> 'It is nowhere satisfactorily explained why Murrin was sued separately, and it is another feature of the plaintiff's conduct which does not help [his] cause.'

f In the context of this case he was entitled to consider, and did not have to disregard, this obvious peculiarity in the proceedings.

9.5 Before us it was contended that the reason for suing Murrin separately was that he had already been sued in respect of the Preston Docks statement. I am not impressed by that explanation, particularly as that statement is pleaded

g as part of the conspiracy claim against him. I would echo the judge's finding.

9.6 The Preston Docks statement was a libel published by Murrin on 10 June 1988. The plaintiff deposed that the Sunday Times article (17 September 1988) gave him the names of the first and second defendants as those whom he believed had conspired with Murrin to injure him. He became aware of the third defendant's part at some time in 1990. The judge considered the evidence,

h and concluded that leave should not have been given under s 32A to issue proceedings relating to the contents of that statement. Additionally, the master should have been told that the evidence available to the plaintiff was to the effect that the first defendant had been against publication, and was thus exonerated. No explanation was advanced as to why no earlier action had been taken on that

j statement. No further comment was made by the judge in relation to that matter. He said that he was taking it into account in the exercise of his discretion, and in my judgment he was entitled to do so.

9.7 *Delay*   The judge's finding here was that no sufficient explanation was given as to why the plaintiff made his application at the late date he did, nor why he had not disclosed that it was not until seven or eight months after receipt of

the tapes that he instructed solicitors, six months after transcription and writing
to his member of Parliament complaining of 'nefarious proceedings'. The
plaintiff's stance is that as that is an irrelevant factor, so there was no need for
such disclosure. I do not agree. The essence of a genuine complaint in libel is
prompt action, particularly in those who need leave from the court because their
cause of action is by definition a stale one. The submission was made that the
delay was deliberate so as to enable the plaintiff to air his grievances to the media
in a way he would not have been able to had proceedings been pending. The
judge made no findings as to that, but did find that the facts relating to the delay
and an adequate explanation for it should have been put before the master. That
too was a matter he was entitled to take into account. The purpose of a libel
action is to clear the plaintiff's name. Here the plaintiff positively asserted that
his principal objective was to get an injunction. That stated objective does not
fit well with what followed. And the submission that delays within the 12 month
period are irrelevant is simply wrong in law.

9.8 Accordingly, I am satisfied that the judge did not take into account
irrelevant matters in arriving at his conclusion.

9.9 I turn next to the question of prejudice occasioned by the irregularity.
First, it is said that there was no prejudice. Second, it is contended that the judge
should not have found that the defendants were prejudiced by the fact that, as
the judge found: 'They were improperly prevented from seeking to defeat the
claim at the earliest opportunity.'

9.10 That they were so prevented is undoubtedly right. The defendants lost
the chance that the law affords them to defeat this claim before the master. Had
they done that, then they would have had the benefit of a solid limitation
defence. And much additional and unnecessary delay has been caused by
proceeding ex parte. That is in my judgment clearly capable of amounting to
prejudice.

9.11 And to look at the matter from the opposite point of view, where leave
is irregularly granted, there is some prejudice in writs being issued and served
(and publicised) on defendants who have been deprived, by the irregularity, of
the opportunity the law had sought to secure to them to prevent that.

9.12 The weight to be given to that prejudice was a matter for the judge. He
was entitled to come to the finding he did in relation to it. Accordingly, I for my
part find nothing to criticise in the judge's approach to the exercise of his wide
discretion.

9.13 The next question is whether on the facts as known and as found by the
judge, and on inferences legitimately to be drawn, he could in the exercise of
that discretion properly find that the plaintiff's conduct in this curiously framed
action for defamation in relation to matters now nearly seven years old was such
as to amount to an attempt to 'manipulate' the master's discretion which so
'seriously infected' these proceedings that the irregular leave granted should be
set aside. Parliament entrusted the exercise of that discretion to the judge. This
court may only interfere if the judge erred in law or reached a conclusion in the
exercise of his discretion 'outside the generous ambit within which a reasonable
disagreement is possible' (see G v G [1985] 2 All ER 225, [1985] 1 WLR 647, HL).
In my judgment neither of those justifications for review apply here. The judge
was entitled to make the findings he did on the material before him. He directed
himself correctly as to the law. He did not take into account irrelevant matters.

a And in the exercise of his discretion he reached a conclusion which he was entitled to reach.

9.14 I have taken into account the matters complained of in para 23 of the plaintiff's skeleton argument. I am not persuaded of the criticism in (a) or (b). The judge was entitled to make the criticism he did in (c), (d) and (e). Nothing in there in any way affects the judgment I have made.

b 9.15 Since writing this judgment, I have read the draft judgment of Pill LJ, and am in agreement with it.

9.16 For those reasons, I would dismiss this appeal. In the circumstances, I do not find it necessary to go on to consider the respondents' notices.

c **PILL LJ.** By order dated 18 September 1992, Master Rose granted leave to the appellant to issue and serve on the respondents a writ alleging libel, slander and conspiracy and a writ was issued three days later. Upon application by the respondents, Ognall J on 25 August 1993 ordered that so much of the appellant's writ as was pleaded in conspiracy be struck out and that the order giving leave to serve the writ be set aside. The appellant seeks, except with respect to

d conspiracy, to have the master's order restored.

Henry LJ has set out in his judgment the contents and effect of s 32A of the Limitation Act 1980. Because over a year has now elapsed since the date on which the appellant knew the relevant facts, any action by him can be defeated by limitation unless the master's order is restored. If the master's order is restored, the claim based on the 21 September 1992 writ can be pursued.

e I agree with Henry LJ's conclusion that a general discretion is conferred on the court by s 32A(b) of the Act, though I find it surprising, having regard to other similar statutory provisions and to the presence of the requirement for leave before issue of the writ, that the statute did not provide more detailed guidance as to the exercise of the discretion. I note the different approach followed in the

f draft Bill issued by the Lord Chancellor's Department for purposes of consultation in July 1995.

I also agree with Henry LJ and with Ognall J that it was an irregularity for the appellant to proceed ex parte in his application based on s 32A. The court has power under RSC Ord 2, r 1(2) to set aside the proceedings.

g Henry LJ has set out in detail the circumstances in which the application for leave was made to the master ex parte. I agree with his conclusion that the learned judge was entitled to exercise his power to set aside the master's order under Ord 2, r 1(2) as he did. For the reasons given by Henry LJ, I too consider that the manner and the circumstances in which the ex parte application was made so seriously infect the proceedings that the leave granted should be set

h aside.

The exercise of discretion under Ord 2, r 1(2) was in the context of leave granted pursuant to s 32A. The generality of the discretion under that section and the consequences of its exercise in a manner adverse to a plaintiff should be borne in mind when exercising Ord 2 powers and I do so in reaching my

j conclusion.

The relevant discretion in this case however is that conferred by Ord 2, r 1(2). I do not consider this an appropriate occasion to seek to establish, in the manner contemplated by Lord Goff in *Aiden Shipping Co Ltd v Interbulk Ltd, The Vimeira* [1986] 2 All ER 409, [1986] AC 965, principles upon which the s 32A discretion should be exercised save to say that the promptness with which the plaintiff acts

once he knows of the facts relevant to the cause of action is in my judgment a
relevant consideration.

Applications under s 32A should in my judgment normally be referred
promptly to a judge because of the possibility of appeals and the need to have
the issue authoritatively determined within the one-year period laid down by
the section.

BUTLER-SLOSS LJ. I also agree.

Appeal dismissed. Leave to appeal to the House of Lords refused.

*14 March 1996. The Appeal Committee of the House of Lords (Lord Jauncey of
Tullichettle, Lord Slynn of Hadley and Lord Hoffmann) refused leave to appeal.*

Paul Magrath Esq   Barrister.

a Re Bank of Credit and Commerce International SA (No 8)

COURT OF APPEAL, CIVIL DIVISION

b   ROSE, SAVILLE AND MILLETT LJJ

13–16 NOVEMBER, 20 DECEMBER 1995

Company – Compulsory winding up – Debtor – Mutual credits, debts and dealings between company and debtor – Set-off – Bank advancing funds to company –
c *Repayment of loan secured by charges over third party deposits – Bank becoming insolvent – Whether deposits should be set off against company's debt – Whether liquidators of bank entitled to claim total debt from company leaving depositors to prove in liquidation for deposits – Insolvency Rules 1986, r 4.90.*

d   A bank arranged to lend money to a borrower company, the principal debtor. The repayment of the loan was secured by a purported charge granted to the bank by a third party over funds which he had deposited with the bank. The bank subsequently went into liquidation before that loan (and other loans supported by the same type of security) had been repaid. The liquidators brought test cases in respect of two groups of borrowers, seeking directions from the court as to
e whether they should attempt to recover the full amount of each outstanding loan from the principal debtor, leaving the depositor to prove in the liquidation for the deposits purportedly charged to the bank, or only so much of the loan as exceeded the amount of the deposits. In both cases, the letters of lien / charge (the security documents) entitled the bank to satisfy the debts due from the principal
f debtors out of the deposits, and neither contained any express guarantee on the part of the depositor or any personal covenant, whether as surety or principal debtor, to repay the indebtedness of the principal debtor. The judge held that the liquidators were not required to give credit for the amount of the deposits before claiming from the principal debtors and were entitled to recover the whole of the debt, leaving the depositors to prove in the liquidation. The principal debtors
g (who were the respondents to the liquidators' applications for directions) appealed, contending inter alia that, in the light of r 4.90[a] of the Insolvency Rules 1986, which required set-off in circumstances where there were liabilities resulting from mutual dealings (including mutual credits / debts) between an insolvent company and any creditor of the company such that the sums due from
h one party could be set off against the sums due from the other before a claim could be made in the liquidation, the security documents were effective to make the debts due from the principal debtor out of the deposits also debts 'due from' the depositors as a result of the 'mutual dealings' with the bank within the meaning of r 4.90. Consequently, they contended that the amount of the
j deposits could be set off against the amounts owed by the principal debtors. The issue arose whether, in the absence of any personal guarantee or other obligation on the part of the depositors to pay the principal debts, there was at the date of the winding-up order any sum due from the depositor to the bank within the meaning of r 4.90.

---

a   Rule 4.90, so far as material, is set out at p 127 *b c*, post

Held – The appeals would be dismissed for the following reasons—

(1) The right of set-off under r 4.90 of the 1986 rules was mandatory, automatic and immediate on liquidation taking place, but only where the requirement of mutuality was satisfied, and it could not be triggered by an agreement for set-off in the absence of such mutuality. On the facts, while the depositors, by means of the security documents, had expressly authorised the bank to set off the debts due to them against the debts due from the principal debtors, that agreement did not give rise to any mutual obligations between the bank and the depositors, since it did not oblige the bank to set off, nor did it confer any right of set-off on the depositors or the principal debtors. In any event, since the security documents did not constitute a charge properly so-called, the agreement to set-off was ineffective once the bank was in liquidation. It followed that the principal debtors could not succeed under r 4.90 (see p 127 *d e* and p 142 *j* to p 143 *d g*, post); *National Westminster Bank Ltd v Halesowen Presswork and Assemblies Ltd* [1972] 1 All ER 641 and *Stein v Blake* [1995] 2 All ER 961 applied; *MS Fashions Ltd v Bank of Credit and Commerce International SA (in liq) (No 2)*, *High Street Services Ltd v Bank of Credit and Commerce International SA (in liq)*, *Impexbond Ltd v Bank of Credit and Commerce International SA (in liq)* [1993] 3 All ER 769 distinguished.

(2) The judge had correctly dismissed the principal debtors' claim to be discharged from their liability for the principal debts because the bank was no longer able to repay the deposits at face value, because: (i) the bank had not disposed to or improperly made away with the deposits; they were still available to the depositors, and the fact that they were no longer worth face value was irrelevant since a secured creditor had no duty to maintain the value of the security; and (ii) the loss of the securities would in any event only discharge the debtor who had provided them (see p 140 *h* to p 134 *a c* and p 142 *g*, post).

Per curiam. A charge-back, such as that created when a depositor purports to charge deposits made to a bank by way of security, does not create and vest in the chargee a proprietary interest in the debt which he owes to the chargor and is not, therefore, a charge properly so-called within the meaning of s 395 of the Companies Act 1985. Consequently, the legal effect of a charge-back is purely contractual and takes effect according to its tenor (see p 133 *j* to p 134 *a c*, post); *Re Charge Card Services Ltd* [1988] 3 All ER 702 approved.

Decision of Rattee J [1994] 3 All ER 565 affirmed.

Notes

For mutual creditors and set-off, see 3(2) *Halsbury's Laws* (4th edn reissue) paras 535–537, and for cases on the subject, see 5(1) *Digest* (2nd reissue) 359–361, 10751–10761.

For the Insolvency Rules 1986, r 4.90, see 3 *Halsbury's Statutory Instruments* (1995 reissue) 346.

Cases referred to in judgment

Blagden, Ex p (1815) 19 Ves 465, 34 ER 589, LC.

British Eagle International Airlines Ltd v Cie Nationale Air France [1975] 2 All ER 390, [1975] 1 WLR 758, HL.

Broad v Commissioner of Stamp Duties (1980) 2 NSWLR 40, NSW SC.

Charge Card Services Ltd, Re [1986] 3 All ER 289, [1987] Ch 150, [1986] 3 WLR 697; *affd* [1988] 3 All ER 702, [1989] Ch 497, [1988] 3 WLR 723, CA.

a Ellis & Co's Trustee v Dixon-Johnson [1925] AC 489, [1925] All ER Rep 715, HL; affg [1924] 2 Ch 451, CA.

Esanda Finance Corp Ltd v Jackson [1993] 11 ACLC 138, S Aust SC; rvsg [1992] 10 ACLC 1251.

Graham v Russell (1816) 5 M & S 498, 105 ER 1133, Ex Ch.

Hanson, Ex p (1806) 12 Ves 346, 33 ER 131, LC.

b Jones v Mossop (1844) 3 Hare 568, 67 ER 506, V-C.

Kitchen's Trustee v Madders [1949] 2 All ER 1079, [1950] Ch 134, CA.

Mackay, Ex p, ex p Brown, re Jeavons (1873) LR 8 Ch App 643, 42 LJ Bcy 68, LJJ.

Mersey Steel and Iron Co Ltd v Naylor Benzon & Co (1884) 9 App Cas 434, [1881–5] All ER Rep 365, HL.

Middleton v Pollock, ex p Knight and Raymond (1875) LR 20 Eq 515.

c MS Fashions Ltd v Bank of Credit and Commerce International SA (in liq) (No 2), High Street Services Ltd v Bank of Credit and Commerce International SA (in liq), Impexbond Ltd v Bank of Credit and Commerce International SA (in liq) [1993] 3 All ER 769, [1993] Ch 425, [1993] 3 WLR 220, Ch D and CA.

National Westminster Bank Ltd v Halesowen Presswork and Assemblies Ltd [1970] 3 All

d ER 473, [1971] 1 QB 1, [1970] 3 WLR 625, CA; rvsd [1972] 1 All ER 641, [1972] AC 785, [1972] 2 WLR 455, HL.

Stein v Blake [1995] 2 All ER 961, [1996] 1 AC 243, [1995] 2 WLR 710, HL.

Stephens, Ex p (1805) 11 Ves 24, 32 ER 996, LC.

Vulliamy v Noble (1817) 3 Mer 593, [1814–23] All ER Rep 597, 36 ER 228, LC.

Webb v Smith (1885) 30 Ch D 192, CA.

e Welsh Development Agency v Export Finance Co Ltd [1992] BCLC 148, CA.

Cases also cited or referred to in skeleton arguments

Barclays Bank Ltd v Quistclose Investments Ltd [1968] 3 All ER 651, [1970] AC 567, HL.

f Carter, Re, Carter v Carter (1885) 55 LJ Ch 230.

Century Steel and Boiler Ltd, Re (1981) 36 NBR (2d) 490, NB CA.

China and South Sea Bank Ltd v Tan [1989] 3 All ER 839, [1990] 1 AC 536, PC.

Clarkson v Smith & Goldberg (1925) 58 OLR 241, Ont SC.

Crowther v Elgood (1887) 34 Ch D 691, CA.

Cuckmere Brick Co Ltd v Mutual Finance Ltd [1971] 2 All ER 633, [1971] Ch 949, CA.

g Curwen v Milburn (1889) 42 Ch D 424, CA.

Debtor, Re a (No 627 of 1936) [1937] 1 All ER 1, [1937] Ch 156, CA.

General Exchange Bank, Re, Re Lewis (1871) LR 6 Ch App 818.

Gossett v Merchants and Planters Bank (1962) 235 Ark 655, 361 SW (2d) 537, Ark SC.

Hague v Dandeson (1848) 2 Exch 742, 154 ER 689.

h Hirachand Punamchand v Temple [1911] 2 KB 330, CA.

James, Ex p, re Condon (1874) LR 9 Ch App 609, [1874–80] All ER Rep 388, CA.

Jeffery's Policy, Re (1872) 20 WR 857.

Mayer v Murray (1878) 8 Ch D 424.

Metall und Rohstoff AG v Donaldson Lufkin & Jenrette Inc [1989] 3 All ER 14, [1990]

j 1 QB 391, CA.

Moore v Darton (1851) 4 De G & Sm 517, [1843–60] All ER Rep 814, 64 ER 938, V-C.

Moschi v Lep Air Services Ltd [1972] 2 All ER 393, [1972] 2 WLR 1175, HL.

Neste Oy v Lloyds Bank plc [1983] 2 Lloyd's Rep 658.

Palmer v Hendrie (1859) 27 Beav 349, 54 ER 136.

Paterson v Murphy (1868) 38 LJ Ch 46.

Robinson v Rutter (1855) 4 E & B 954, 119 ER 355.

Sass, Re, ex p National Provincial Bank of England Ltd [1896] 2 QB 12.
Standard Chartered Bank Ltd v Walker [1982] 3 All ER 938, [1982] 1 WLR 1410, CA.
Swire v Redman (1876) 1 QBD 536, [1874–80] All ER Rep 1255, DC.
Ulster Bank Ltd v Lambe [1966] NI 161, NI QBD.
United Dominions Trust Ltd v Kirkwood [1966] 1 All ER 968, [1966] 2 QB 431, CA.
Williams v Price (1824) 1 Sim & St 581, 57 ER 229.

Appeal

In two test cases the appellants, (1) Rayners Enterprises Inc (Rayners), a principal debtor, and Mohamed Jessa, a depositor who purported to charge deposits with the bank to secure loans to Rayners, and (2) a group of principal debtors, the Solai Group (comprising Agrichemicals Ltd, Bishopswood Estates Ltd, Eurofert Ltd, Solai Holdings Ltd, Solai Services Ltd and Tradeworth Ltd) and Société Générale de Gestion et Services SA (SGGS), a depositor who purported to charge deposits with the bank to secure loans to the Solai Group, appealed from the decision of Rattee J ([1994] 3 All ER 565) on 9 March 1994, whereby he held in favour of the respondent liquidators of the Bank of Credit and Commerce International SA, Christopher Morris, John Parry Richards, Stephen John Akers and Nicholas Roger Lyle, on their application for directions, that they were not required to give credit for the amount of the deposits made by the depositors before claiming to recover the amount of the indebtedness of the principal debtors. The facts are set out in the judgment of the court.

John McDonnell QC (instructed by *Haring Ross Gagrat & Gardi*) for Rayners and Mr Jessa.
Christopher Carr QC and *Michael Todd* (instructed by *Charles Russell*) for the Solai Group and SGGS.
Robin Dicker (instructed by *Lovell White Durrant*) for the liquidators.

Cur adv vult

20 December 1995. The following judgment of the court was delivered.

ROSE LJ. These appeals arise in two test cases in which the liquidators of Bank of Credit and Commerce International SA (the bank) seek the directions of the court in the following circumstances. In a large number of cases the bank lent money to a customer (the principal debtor). A third party (the depositor) deposited money with the bank and purported to charge the deposit to the bank with repayment of the loan. The charge was by way of non-recourse collateral security; the bank did not obtain a personal covenant or guarantee of repayment from the depositor. Before the loan was repaid the bank went into liquidation. The liquidators seek directions whether they should attempt to recover the whole of the outstanding loan from the principal debtor and leave the depositor to prove in the liquidation of the bank for the amount of the deposit after the loan has been fully repaid; or whether they should set off the amount of the outstanding loan against the deposit and claim from the principal debtor only so much, if any, of the loan as exceeds the amount of the deposit. Rattee J held that the liquidators are not required to give credit for the amount of the deposit before claiming to recover the amount of the indebtedness of the principal debtor; and the principal debtors, who were the respondents to the liquidators' applications, now appeal from his decision.

a The appellants, who were the respondents to the liquidators' applications, fall into two groups. In the first group, the principal debtor is a Panamanian company, Rayners Enterprises Inc (Rayners), and the depositor is a Mr Jessa. Mr Jessa, who is understood to be the beneficial owner of Rayners and who is not resident or domiciled in the United Kingdom, began to deposit money with the Luxembourg branch of the bank in the 1970s. From 1987 onwards Rayners

b invested in property in England with money borrowed from the London branch of the bank against the security of letters of charge/lien over Mr Jessa's sterling deposits in Luxembourg. Each of the letters contained a limit of the sum for which the deposit in question was security. The total balance in the deposit accounts on the date of the bank's liquidation was £3,430,953; the total sum secured by the deposits was £1,381,011. The amount of Rayners' indebtedness to

c the bank on 30 September 1993 (which is after the date of liquidation) converted into dollars is said to be $US3,513,258, that is to say substantially in excess of the face value of the bank's security. The debt is presently due and payable. The bank holds charges over land belonging to Rayners as other security for the debt.

In the second group, the principal debtors are a group of companies called the

d Solai Group and the depositor is Société Générale de Gestion et Services SA (SGGS). The Solai Group were customers of the Wembley branch of the bank. In 1990 they obtained new facilities from the bank. These were contained in a facility letter in which the bank set out the terms on which it was prepared to grant facilities to companies within the Solai Group. These facilities included a loan facility not exceeding £6m and sterling and dollar overdraft facilities not

e exceeding £3m and $8m respectively. The facility letter required security both real and personal, including security in the form of cash deposits to be placed with the bank. In order to provide this security SGGS, a Panamanian company which is said to be owned and controlled by the same family as the Solai Group, placed two deposits with the Luxembourg branch of the bank. One was a deposit of

f £3,037,741; the other of $8,018,000. SGGS executed a letter of lien/charge by which it constituted the deposits security for all the outstanding debts of the Solai Group up to a limit of $20m. The deposits were thus security for both the overdraft facilities and the term loan. The term loan has, however, since been repaid, and the face value of the deposits now broadly corresponds with the amount owing from the Solai Group to the bank. The overdrafts were repayable

g on demand, and demand was made by the provisional liquidators of the bank following their appointment.

The facility letter also required security in the form of a guarantee from a first class bank. In fact the bank accepted two letters of guarantee, one in respect of the dollar deposit and one in respect of the sterling deposit, given by its

h Luxembourg branch to its Wembley branch. Both branches were part of the same corporate entity. Following their appointment and the default of the Solai Group in making repayment of the principal debt, the provisional liquidators demanded payment of the amounts due from the Luxembourg branch under its guarantees. No payment was received. The legal consequences, if any, of these

j curious transactions have been the subject of argument before us.

The letters of lien/charge in the two cases are in similar terms. Neither contains any express guarantee on the part of the depositor or any personal covenant, whether as surety or principal debtor, to repay the indebtedness of the principal debtor. In this respect the present case is to be distinguished from the three cases which were considered by Hoffmann LJ sitting at first instance in *MS Fashions Ltd v Bank of Credit and Commerce International SA (in liq) (No 2), High Street*

Services Ltd v Bank of Credit and Commerce International SA (in liq), Impexbond Ltd v Bank of Credit and Commerce International SA (in liq) [1993] 3 All ER 769, [1993] Ch 425. Those proceedings concerned loans made by the bank to three different companies, viz MS Fashions Ltd, High Street Services Ltd and Impexbond Ltd, secured by a letter of lien/charge over money deposited with the bank by a depositor and by the personal guarantee of the depositor. Hoffmann LJ held that the effect of the automatic operation of set-off in bankruptcy was to extinguish the liability of the depositor under his guarantee; that this amounted to payment of the guaranteed debt; and that accordingly it extinguished the liability of the principal debtor to the bank. There was no appeal in relation to the loans made to MS Fashions, where the liquidators had demanded repayment from the depositor under his guarantee. The liquidators appealed in relation to the other two companies, where no demand had been made, but the Court of Appeal ([1993] 3 All ER 769, [1993] Ch 425) upheld the decision of Hoffmann LJ that the effect of the security documentation, which constituted the depositor a principal debtor, was to dispense with the need for a prior demand.

The question in the present case is whether the absence of any personal obligation on the part of the depositor to pay the principal debt is a material distinction which compels a different result. If it is, then, it is submitted, the result is a paradox; an insolvent creditor is in a better position if he has not obtained a personal guarantee than if he has.

The arguments on these appeals have been elaborate and far-ranging, but in the end we believe that the problem is susceptible of a simple solution. Before dealing with the appellants' arguments it is necessary to summarise the terms of the letters of lien/charge; to set out the terms of r 4.90 of the Insolvency Rules 1986, SI 1986/1925, which provides for mutual dealings and set-off in companies liquidation, and to say something about the legislative history and effect of the rule.

The letters of lien/charge

The terms of the letters of lien/charge are set out in full in the judgment below and it is not necessary to reproduce them here (see [1994] 3 All ER 565 at 570–571). They purported (i) to create in favour of the bank a lien or charge on the balances maintained by the depositor with the bank for all the outstanding liabilities of the principal debtor to the bank; (ii) to give the bank power to withdraw any of the sums standing to the credit of the depositor with the bank and utilise them in the reduction or discharge of the liabilities of the principal debtor without prior reference to the depositor; (iii) to prohibit the depositor from 'encumbering, assigning or dealing with' the deposits in any way; and (iv) to allow the bank to refuse to release the deposit to the depositor unless or until the entire outstanding liabilities of the principal debtor whether actual or contingent have been repaid in full and the bank is under no obligation to provide or make available banking facilities to the principal debtor.

Two observations may be made. First, the letters purport to operate by way of charge. A power for the grantee to apply property of the grantor in or towards the discharge of the liabilities, whether of the grantor or a third party, which power the grantee may or may not choose to exercise, is the standard language of a charge. Secondly, each of the charges is expressed to operate to secure the outstanding liabilities of the principal debtor, not of the depositor. Each of them is a classic example of a collateral security.

a Although the deposits were made with the Luxembourg branch of the bank the parties have agreed that the issues on the present application should be determined on the footing that the relevant law is, or is the same as, English law. They reserve their right to argue hereafter that that is not the case.

Rule 4.90

b Rule 4.90 is in the following terms:

'*Mutual credit and set-off* (1) This Rule applies where, before the company goes into liquidation there have been mutual credits, mutual debts or other mutual dealings between the company and any creditor of the company proving or claiming to prove for a debt in the liquidation. (2) An account
c shall be taken of what is due from each party to the other in respect of the mutual dealings, and the sums due from one party shall be set off against the sums from the other ... (4) Only the balance (if any) of the account is provable in the liquidation. Alternatively (as the case may be) the amount shall be paid to the liquidator as part of the assets.'

d The essential question in the present case is whether, in the absence of a personal guarantee or other obligation on his part to pay the amount of the principal debt, there was at the date of winding up order any sum due from the depositor to the bank within the meaning of r 4.90.

The operation of the rule is mandatory, automatic and immediate on the bankruptcy or liquidation taking place (see *National Westminster Bank Ltd v*
e *Halesowen Presswork and Assemblies Ltd* [1972] 1 All ER 641, [1972] AC 785 and *Stein v Blake* [1995] 2 All ER 961, [1996] 1 AC 243).

The right to set off mutual debts and credits was recognised at an early date by the courts administering bankruptcy, and was first given a statutory basis by the Act 4 & 5 Anne c 17 (to prevent frauds frequently committed by bankrupts
f (1705)), s 11. The set-off sections of the 1825 and 1849 Acts (s 50 of the Bankruptcy Act 1825 and s 171 of the Bankruptcy Law Consolidation Act 1849) referred to the set-off of provable debts and contained no reference to mutual dealings. Until the Bankruptcy Act 1869 contingent debts and liabilities, as well as claims to unliquidated damages, were incapable of proof and, therefore, of set-off. Section 31 of the 1869 Act provided that, with certain exceptions not
g material for present purposes:

'... all debts and liabilities, present or future, certain or contingent, to which the bankrupt is subject at the date of the order of adjudication, or to which he may become subject during the continuance of the bankruptcy by reason of any obligation incurred previously to the date of the order of
h adjudication, shall be deemed to be debts provable in bankruptcy ...'

It also defined the word 'liability' as including—

'any obligation or possibility of an obligation to pay money or money's worth on the breach of any express or implied covenant, contract, agreement, or undertaking, whether such breach does or does not occur, or
j is or is not likely to occur or capable of occurring before the close of the bankruptcy ...'

The effect of the 1869 Act was that contingent liabilities, in the sense of contingent obligations to pay money or money's worth, and claims for unliquidated damages for breach of contract became for the first time admissible

to proof. At the same time the set-off section of the 1869 Act (s 39) added a   *a*
reference to mutual dealings and omitted all reference to provable debts.

The definition of provable debts remained virtually unchanged in succeeding
Bankruptcy Acts until the enactment of the Insolvency Act 1986, when it was
expanded to include unliquidated damages in tort. Provable debts, now known
as bankruptcy debts (s 324), are still limited to liabilities to pay money or money's
worth (s 382 (1), (4)). The wording of s 39 of the 1869 Act was reproduced by s 38   *b*
of the Bankruptcy Act of 1883 and s 31 of the Bankruptcy Act 1914; these sections
applied to companies' winding up as well as bankruptcy. No relevant changes to
insolvency set-off were recommended by the Insolvency Law Review Committee; its principal recommendation, that the operation of the set-off should no
longer be mandatory, was not implemented (see *Insolvency Law and Practice:
Report of the Review Committee* (Cmnd 8558 (1982), chairman Sir Kenneth Cork)).   *c*
Section 31 of the 1914 Act was recast in simpler and more modern form by r 4.90
of the 1986 rules, but this was clearly not intended to alter its substantive scope
or effect.

It has been said many times that the right of set-off in bankruptcy is a rule as to
debts and liabilities provable. It was on this basis that s 39 of the 1869 Act and its   *d*
successors were made applicable in companies' winding up (see *Mersey Steel and
Iron Co Ltd v Naylor Benzon & Co* (1884) 9 App Cas 434 at 437–438, [1881–5] All ER
Rep 365 at 367). In *Re Charge Card Services Ltd* [1986] 3 All ER 289, [1987] Ch 150,
following an extensive review of the authorities, Millett J held that any claim
which is admissible to proof is capable of set-off if the other requirements of   *e*
set-off are satisfied. The converse is equally true: a claim is not capable of set-off
unless it is admissible to proof. This is plain from the terms of r 4.90 itself, which
applies only where a creditor proves or claims to prove in the liquidation. To
qualify for set-off, therefore, the creditor's claim must be capable of proof. In
Kitchen's Trustee v Madders [1949] 2 All ER 1079, [1950] Ch 134 set-off was refused
because (after the date of the bankruptcy) the creditor had undertaken not to   *f*
prove. Cohen LJ said ([1949] 2 All ER 1079 at 1084, [1950] Ch 134 at 143):

> 'I think that when the defendants undertook not to prove this debt they
> were in effect agreeing that the debt should not be treated as a provable debt,
> *and if it were not a provable debt it clearly could not be the subject of set-off under
> s. 31.*' (My emphasis.)   *g*

This is true of both sides of the account. The right to set off a particular claim
depends on the nature and character of the claim itself and not upon the side of
the account on which it is to be placed (see *Graham v Russell* (1816) 5 M & S 498
at 501, 105 ER 1133 at 1134).   *h*

Insolvency is concerned with the distribution of the debtor's uncharged assets
among his unsecured creditors. Trust property and security stand outside the
scheme of distribution and the scope of insolvency set-off. Set-off ought not to
prejudice the right of a secured creditor to enforce his securities in any order he
chooses and at a time of his choice.   *j*

Although guarantees are merely personal securities they are governed by a
similar principle; to allow the principal debtor to compel the creditor to look to
the surety rather than his own personal liability (or vice versa) would invert the
ordinary order of priorities between the creditor (the senior creditor), the surety
(the junior creditor) and the principal debtor. Disregard of this principle is
capable not only of seriously prejudicing the creditor, whether solvent or

a insolvent, but, as some of the illustrations given by counsel for the liquidators demonstrate, could easily give rise to problems to which there is no solution.

Mutuality

    The object of set-off in bankruptcy is to avoid the perceived injustice to a man who has had mutual dealings with an insolvent of having to pay in full what he *b* owes to the insolvent while having to rest content with a dividend on what the insolvent owes him. At the same time the effect of the set-off is to prefer one creditor over the general body of creditors, and accordingly it is confined within narrow limits. The principal limiting requirement is that of mutuality. If there is no mutuality there is no set-off. If A and B have mutual dealings with each other as a result of which A owes B £x and B owes A £y and either of them becomes *c* insolvent, then the two debts not only may but must be set off and only the balance proved or claimed as the case may be. But if A owes B £x and B owes C £y and any of them becomes insolvent the two debts cannot be set off even if there is an express agreement by the three of them that B may set them off; such an agreement is contrary to the scheme of distribution on insolvency and cannot *d* prevail over the rules which require pari passu distribution (see *British Eagle International Airlines Ltd v Cie Nationale Air France* [1975] 2 All ER 390, [1975] 1 WLR 758).

    The requirement of mutuality is, therefore, central to bankruptcy set-off. It has always been rigorously enforced. Prior to *MS Fashions Ltd* [1993] 3 All ER 769, [1993] Ch 425, in the absence of special circumstances, the benefit of the set-off *e* was never made available to a third party in the position of the appellants who have no claims of their own capable of being set off. It is not the function of insolvency set-off to confer a benefit on a debtor of the insolvent who has not been a party to the mutual dealing, nor to afford a preference to a creditor who has no liability to the insolvent or whose liability is only secondary and is capable *f* of being satisfied by the party primarily liable. Provided that no claim is made against him, there is no injustice to such a creditor in requiring him to prove for his debt.

The legal nature of a charge-back

    When money is deposited in a bank the property in the money itself passes to *g* the bank. In place of his money the depositor obtains a chose in action consisting of a debt due to him from the bank. The relationship between the depositor and the bank is that of creditor and debtor. If the depositor purports to charge the deposit to the bank by way of security he is purporting to create a charge in favour of his debtor over the debt which is due from his debtor to himself. In *Re* *h* *Charge Card Services Ltd* [1986] 3 All ER 289 at 308–309, [1987] Ch 150 at 175–176 Millett J held that such a charge (a 'charge-back') does not create a charge in the strict sense of the word, although he was careful to say that it does not follow that it is incapable of creating an effective security.

    The appellants found an elaborate argument on that decision. They submit *j* that the grant of a charge-back necessarily imports an agreement by the depositor that the amount secured by the charge-back is to be treated as an amount due from himself to the bank so that it can be made the subject of set-off against what is due to him from the bank. If a charge-back is incapable of constituting a charge, they submit, then this is the only mechanism by which a collateral security for the indebtedness of a third party can be validly created in favour of the bank. All the depositor can do is give the bank a right of set-off which will be effective in the event of his own insolvency; and it will be effective in this event only if it falls *a* within what is permitted by r 4.90. That rule only permits what is due from the bank to the depositor to be set off against what is due to the bank from the depositor, and not what is due from a third party. It follows, it is said, that a collateral charge-back to secure a debt due from a third party must either be wholly ineffective or it must be construed as implying a promise on the part of the depositor to pay the debt of the third party or at least as resulting in the third *b* party's liability being treated as a debt due from the depositor.

As will appear, we do not accept this. It follows that the legal nature of a charge-back, and in particular the question whether it does or does not constitute a charge properly so called, is not determinative of these appeals. Apart from the possible existence of a requirement to register and the consequences of a failure to do so, it has no relevance except in the event of the insolvency of the party *c* granting the charge-back; and even in that event it has no practical significance. It is, therefore, not strictly necessary to decide whether the decision of Millett J in *Re Charge Card Services Ltd* was correct. Since, however, the point has been fully argued and raises a matter which is thought by the commercial community to be of great importance, it is desirable that this court should express a view upon it. *d* We have carefully reconsidered the question, and we are particularly grateful for the detailed and comprehensive skeleton argument of counsel for the liquidators in which the arguments and authorities both judicial and academic which support the contrary view to that expressed by Millett J are fully marshalled.

The question in *Re Charge Card Services Ltd* was whether a charge-back on book *e* debts was required to be registered under s 95 of the Companies Act 1948. Millett J held, in favour of the chargee (the financier), that it was not. A contrary decision would have threatened to put many ordinary commercial transactions at risk. Margin deposits, for example, placed with a stockbroker or commodity dealer by a corporate customer would be registrable. Despite this, the decision caused consternation among members of the banking community, who tended to *f* overlook the fact that the decision was favourable to them.

Millett J held that a charge-back did not take effect as a charge stricto sensu because it failed to create and vest in the chargee a proprietary interest in the property charged. It therefore lacked an essential element in a charge properly so called. The judge based this conclusion on his view that a man cannot have a *g* proprietary interest in a debt or other obligation which he owes another. Such an interest was, in the judge's words, 'conceptually impossible'.

This statement of what many would consider to be obvious proved to be highly controversial. It has received mixed reviews by academic writers. The principal critic has been Philip Wood (see 'Three problems of set-off: contin- *h* gencies, build-ups and charge-backs' (1987) 8 Co Law 265; 'Charge Card revisited' (1988) IFL Rev Feb p 26 and *English and International Set-Off* (1989) paras 5-134 to 5-181). Dr Fidelis Oditah has written to much the same effect (see 'Financing trade credit' (1992) JBL 541). Dr Derham takes a middle view (*Set-Off in Insolvencies* (1987) pp 301–305). He agrees that an assignment by way of security by the creditor to the debtor is not possible, since this would result in the debtor *j* becoming his own creditor. But he considers that this should not be a problem where no assignment is involved.

A notable supporter of the decision in *Re Charge Card Services Ltd* is Professor Goode. In *Legal Problems of Credit and Security* (2nd edn, 1988) p 125 he has written:

a   'The essential point is that a debt is a species of property only in the relations between the creditor and a third party who takes an assignment of the debt. As between debtor and creditor a debt is purely an obligation. The creditor does not *own* the debt, he is owed it.'

The creditor does, of course, own the debt in the sense that he can assign it to a third party. The discovery in comparatively modern times that the right to

b   receive payment of a debt is a saleable commodity has been of enormous commercial and economic importance; it hugely expanded the opportunities for obtaining credit by permitting the recycling of receivables and their use as security for financing: see Oditah, *Legal Aspects of Receivables Financing* (1991) pp 1–2. The question is not whether the *creditor* can own and assign the right to

c   receive payment of a debt to a third party, but whether it can be sold or made available by way of security *to the debtor* and yet kept alive. The difficulty that needs to be faced is that *the debtor* cannot be made to own the debt which he owes and which he is incapable of assigning. This is not merely a matter of semantics. The distinction between property and obligation lies at the heart of our juris-prudence.

d   Professor Everett has also supported the decision in *Re Charge Card Services Ltd*: see her article 'Security over bank deposits' (1988) 16 ABLR 351. She commented that the foundation for the decision was 'laid many years ago'.

The decision was certainly not original. It was preceded by a decision at first instance in Australia, *Broad v Commissioner of Stamp Duties* (1980) 2 NSWLR 40, in

e   which Lees J held (at 46): 'there can be no mortgage or charge in favour of oneself of one's own indebtedness to another' and followed and applied earlier observa-tions to the same effect which had been made in England at the highest level.

In *National Westminster Bank Ltd v Halesowen Presswork and Assemblies Ltd* [1970] 3 All ER 473 at 487, [1971] 1 QB 1 at 46 Buckley LJ said:

f   'No man can have a lien on his own property, and consequently no lien can have arisen affecting that money or that credit ... I cannot myself understand how it could be said with any kind of accuracy that the bank had a lien on its own indebtedness to the [company].'

That passage was subsequently approved in the House of Lords by Viscount

g   Dilhorne and Lord Cross of Chelsea (see [1972] 1 All ER 641 at 646, 653, [1972] AC 785 at 802, 810). Lord Cross said in terms: 'I agree with Lord Denning MR and Buckley LJ that a debtor cannot sensibly be said to have a lien on his own indebtedness to his creditor.' It is true that these comments were made in relation to a lien rather than a charge, and that a lien, unlike a charge, can only

h   attach to tangible property. But the word 'lien' rather than 'charge' is traditionally used in a banking context (witness the so-called banker's lien), and the reason why it was said that a bank could not be said to have a lien on the credit balance in its customer's account was clearly based on the relationship between the parties and not on the nature of the security.

j   The decision has also had a mixed reception from the judiciary. It was followed by the Supreme Court of South Australia in *Esanda Finance Corp Ltd v Jackson* [1993] 11 ACLC 138 (King CJ, Cox and Matheson JJ), reversing Zelling AJ ([1992] 10 ACLC 1251). It was doubted by Dillon LJ in *Welsh Development Agency v Export Finance Co Ltd* [1992] BCLC 148 at 166–167. Dillon LJ's observations were clearly obiter, but we have naturally given them close attention to see whether they should lead us to take a different view from that taken by Millett J.

Dillon LJ began by saying that he saw no basis for the conclusion in the
judgment itself. This is disappointing, not only in itself, but because it means that
he deprived himself of an opportunity to deal with the reasoning on which,
rightly or wrongly, the judge had based his conclusion. He contented himself by
saying that he saw no reason why the transactions in *Ex p Mackay, ex p Brown, re
Jeavons* (1873) LR 8 Ch App 643, 42 LJ Bcy 68 and *Webb v Smith* (1885) 30 Ch D 192,
neither of which was cited in *Re Charge Card Services Ltd*, should not be valid in
law (see [1992] BCLC 148 at 166–167). Since Millett J did not question the legal
validity of a charge-back there seems to be little force in this objection. He
disposed of the observations in *National Westminster Bank Ltd v Halesowen Presswork and Assemblies Ltd* as being directed to a different situation, which is
undoubtedly true if he meant (as we think he did) different from the situation in
the case before him, but which is not true if he meant different from the situation
in *Re Charge Card Services Ltd* (or the present case).

Counsel for the liquidators, like others who have criticised the reasoning in *Re
Charge Card Services Ltd*, place great reliance upon the decision of the Divisional
Court in Bankruptcy in *Ex p Mackay*. In that case a bankrupt had assigned certain
patents in consideration of the payment of royalties, and had agreed that the
assignees should be entitled to repay themselves an advance which they had
made to him by retaining one-half of the royalties which would otherwise be paid
to him. The question for decision was not whether that transaction was valid or
enforceable in the bankruptcy, but whether the court had jurisdiction to order a
sale of a moiety of the future royalties under r 78 of the Bankruptcy Rules 1870.
The assignees obtained an order for sale from the registrar, but the trustee in
bankruptcy appealed on the ground that the royalties were from their nature
unsaleable.

Rule 78 provided for an application for sale to be made by any person claiming
to be a mortgagee of *or to have security over* any part of the bankrupt's estate or
effects. The questions for determination, therefore, were (i) whether the
assignees could be said to have a security within the meaning of that expression
in r 78 over the royalties which they were entitled to retain; and (ii) whether the
right to receive such royalties could be said to be property of the bankrupt.

Counsel for the trustee submitted (LR 8 Ch App 643 at 646):

'... there was no mortgage of the royalty or security upon it. There is
nothing which can be sold under the 78th rule of the *Bankruptcy Rules*, 1870.
A man cannot have a charge on a debt which is due from himself.'

Mellish LJ interrupted (42 LJ Bcy 68 at 69): 'Why cannot a man have a charge on
a debt due from himself as well as on a debt due from any other?' The reports do
not indicate what reply was received to this question. In his judgment upholding
the order for sale James LJ merely said (LR 8 Ch App 643 at 647): 'It appears to me
... that there is a good charge upon one moiety of the royalties, because they are
part of the property and effects of the bankrupt.' Mellish LJ agreed, but his
judgment, like the remainder of the judgment of James LJ, was exclusively
concerned with a different question which only affected the other moiety of the
royalties.

In our opinion the question which Mellish LJ asked in the course of argument
was not answered and did not need to be answered. The question was not
whether the assignees had a proprietary interest in their obligation to pay
royalties to the bankrupt, but whether the court had power to order the sale to a
third party of the bankrupt's right to receive them. The order for sale was upheld

a   because the assignees' right of retainer was a security within the meaning of that expression in the rules; and because the bankrupt's right to receive the royalties was part of the property and effects of the bankrupt. Neither proposition conflicts with anything in *Re Charge Card Services Ltd*. Millett J did not suggest that a charge-back did not constitute security; he went out of his way to indicate the opposite. Although James LJ used the word 'charge' (which did not appear in

b   r 78) he clearly used it in the wider sense of 'mortgage or security' (the expression actually found in the rule). It was not necessary to the decision to inquire whether the security in question constituted a charge properly so called. We might add that, even if the word 'charge' had been used in the rules, it is doubtful that the answer should have been any different. Given the statutory context, viz the sale to a third party of the right of the chargor to receive the royalties, the rule

c   probably required to be given a wide ambit.

     Webb v Smith (1885) 30 Ch D 192 is of no assistance on the present question. It is merely an example of an auctioneer's lien on the proceeds of sale for his costs of the sale. There is, of course, no inconsistency between the existence of an auctioneer's particular lien, which is well established, and the decision in *Re*

d   *Charge Card Services Ltd*. An auctioneer holds the property for sale until sale and the proceeds of sale when received by him in a fiduciary capacity as agent for the vendor. The subject matter of his lien is, therefore, not the debt which he owes his client, but the money itself. That money is trust money. If the auctioneer pays it into a bank account, he holds the chose in action, ie the debt due from the bank to himself, in trust to discharge his own lien and subject thereto in trust for

e   his client. There is no charge-back. If the auctioneer becomes insolvent, there is no question of any set-off. Subject to the lien, the money in the account does not form part of the insolvent estate.

     Other criticisms of the reasoning in *Re Charge Card Services Ltd* seem to us to carry little weight. It is said that Millett J attached too much importance to the

f   fact that the debtor cannot sue himself; an unenforceable debt is still a debt even if it is unenforceable by action, for example if it has become statute-barred. That is true, but there is something distinctly odd about a chose in action which could never have been the subject even of an unsuccessful action. The concept of a debt which one owes to oneself must, we think, inhabit the same territory as a covenant with oneself and the grant of a lease to oneself.

g   Then it is said that the fact that the debtor cannot sue himself does not matter: he does not need to do so. That is precisely the point which Millett J made when he said ([1986] 3 All ER 289 at 309, [1987] Ch 150 at 176):

h   'The debtor cannot, and does not need to, resort to the creditor's claim against him in order to obtain the benefit of the security; his own liability to the creditor is automatically discharged or reduced.'

     It is said that some legal mechanism must be involved. That is true; the mechanism is that of set-off. This process can be variously described, but a

j   debtor's right to appropriate a debt which he owes to his creditor and apply it in reduction or discharge of a debt which is owed to himself whether by the creditor or a third party is in our opinion accurately described as a right of set-off.

     After much fuller citation of authority than was available to Millett J and after a prolonged consideration of the arguments to the contrary, we would affirm his decision that a charge-back does not create and vest in the chargee a proprietary interest in the debt which he owes to the chargor; and that it is not, therefore, a

charge properly so called within the meaning of s 395 of the Companies Act 1985 *a*
(which replaced s 95 of the 1948 Act).

Charge-backs are a commonplace. Charges over bank deposits in favour of the
bank and charges of policies of life assurance in favour of the insurer (which have
always been held to operate by way of set-off) are everyday examples. It is
important that such routine financing arrangements should not be put at risk. If
the reasoning in *Re Charge Card Services Ltd* led to the conclusion that charge- *b*
backs were invalid or ineffective to give security in the event of the chargor's
insolvency, then that reasoning would be suspect; and if it could not be faulted
then we would be willing to sacrifice doctrinal purity on the altar of commercial
necessity. But we are satisfied that neither conclusion would be justified.

The legal effect of a charge-back: insolvency of the chargor   *c*

Since a charge-back is incapable of vesting a proprietary interest in the chargee,
its effect is purely contractual. It takes effect according to its tenor. The terms of
the letters of charge/lien in the present case expressly prohibit the depositor from
dealing with the deposit or from withdrawing it while the principal debt is unpaid
and gives the bank power to set off the amount of the deposit against the principal *d*
debt. We should expect these consequences to follow from the use of the word
'charge' itself, even if they were not expressly spelled out in the document
creating the charge-back.

These provisions fetter the depositor's use of the deposit while the principal
debt remains unpaid. In his hands the deposit—his chose in action—is a flawed
asset. If he becomes insolvent, the asset forms part of the insolvent estate, but it *e*
remains a flawed asset subject to the same contractual restrictions as before. If
the charge-back secures a pre-existing obligation of the depositor, as in *Re Charge
Card Services Ltd*, the bank is entitled, and may be bound, to set off the amount of
the deposit against it under r 4.90. The same result will follow if the charge-back
is supported by a personal covenant or guarantee of the depositor.   *f*

If the charge-back is a non-recourse collateral security which secures the debt
of a third party, the bank will be unable to set off the amount of the deposit
against the debt owing to it from the third party. But this will be of little if any
practical significance. The bank has the money; the depositor's trustee or
liquidator cannot obtain payment while the debt of the third party is outstanding.
But it will be his duty to get in the deposit as one of the assets of the estate. It will *g*
almost invariably be in the interests of the general body of creditors for him to
permit the bank to recoup itself out of the deposit, take delivery of any other
securities which the bank holds for the principal debt, and seek to recover from
the principal debtor.

h

The legal effect of a charge-back: insolvency of the chargee

In the present case it is the bank which has become insolvent. That is an event
which was obviously not within the contemplation of the parties to the letters of
lien/charge. We accept the submission of counsel for the appellants that the
prohibition on the depositor assigning or dealing with the deposit in any way was *j*
not intended to prohibit him from applying the deposit in payment of the
principal debt, that being the very purpose for which the deposit was made in the
first place. But while the bank could not object to the depositor using the deposit
in this way while the bank was solvent (whether the depositor was solvent or
not), the liquidation of the bank put an end to the depositor's ability to do so.
When a bank honours its customer's cheque in favour of a third party and debits

a the customer's account, it is treated as repaying part of its debt to its customer and as paying his money to the third party. A bank is not obliged to comply with its customer's instructions as to the application of money standing to the credit of his account unless he is entitled to withdraw the money. Once the bank is in liquidation, however, the customer's right to withdraw the money is enforceable only by set-off or proof in the liquidation; and if set-off is not available the right
b of proof is unlikely to yield sufficient for the customer's purpose.

Is there a personal obligation?

The fact that a charge-back does not vest a proprietary interest in the chargee does not warrant the implication of a personal obligation to pay on the part of the chargor. The charge takes effect according to its tenor and as such has substantial
c legal effect. It is not necessary to import a personal undertaking to pay on the part of the chargor in order to give the charge-back legal effect. Nor is the use of the word 'charge' sufficient for this purpose. How can it be, given the common use of the charge to create non-recourse collateral security? If the mere use of the word 'charge' imported a personal obligation on the part of the chargor, s 28(1)(a)
d of the Land Registration Act 1925 would be otiose.

The 'tenable view'

In the *MS Fashions Ltd* case [1993] 3 All ER 769, [1993] Ch 425 the letters of lien / charge contained a provision that the liability of the depositor should be that of a principal debtor. This was construed at first instance not only as dispensing with
e any need for the bank to serve a demand upon the depositor but as creating a personal obligation on the depositor to pay the principal debt. Hoffmann LJ said ([1993] 3 All ER 769 at 774, [1993] Ch 425 at 431):

> *f* 'Mr Thomas [counsel for the defendant] also said that the reference to liability being as that of principal debtor in the ... letters of charge was odd because the letters did not expressly create any liability. They merely constituted a charge over the deposit in favour of BCCI. On the other hand, I think it is a tenable view that such charges over deposits can be analysed as the creation of a liability on the part of the chargor for the company's debt, not exceeding the amount of the deposit, which can be set off against BCCI's
> *g* liability to repay the deposit. It seems to me that the reference to the liability of the depositor ... should, as a matter of construction, be taken as having this effect.'

If this means that the mere creation of a charge over a fund of money creates a
h personal obligation on the part of the chargor to pay the secured debt out of the charged fund, then we disagree with it. A charge over land or other property makes the charged property itself answerable for the debt. It does not make the chargor personally answerable. If the chargor disposes of the equity of redemption, he clearly cannot be said to have any outstanding obligation to the chargee. It makes no difference that the subject matter of the charge is a
j non-assignable deposit of money. The chargee's remedies lie against the deposit; he has no personal claim in debt against the chargor.

If, however, Hoffmann LJ was intending to say no more than that the result of the charge-back could be regarded as exposing the depositor to the liability of having his deposit applied in discharge or reduction of the principal debt, then of course we agree with him. But this is to use the word 'liability' in the sense of 'risk', not in the sense of 'obligation'. Such a risk is not a 'liability' within the

meaning of s 382 of the 1986 Act and is neither admissible to proof as a
bankruptcy debt nor capable of set-off.

Counsel for the appellants sought to base an argument to the contrary on a
passage in the speech of Lord Cross in *British Eagle International Airlines Ltd v Cie
Nationale Air France* [1975] 2 All ER 390 at 409, [1975] 1 WLR 758 at 778. In that
passage, however, Lord Cross was dealing with the ordinary meaning of the
word 'debt', and considered that it included a right to receive settlement of a
pre-existing monetary obligation exclusively through the medium of a clearing
system. That is of no assistance on the present question.

In the Court of Appeal in *MS Fashions Ltd* [1993] 3 All ER 769 at 785, [1993] Ch
425 at 447 Dillon LJ construed the reference to the depositor's liabilities as
meaning the liabilities of the principal debtors which were charged on his
deposits, and relied on other provisions in the letters of lien/charge which
included those liabilities within the definition of the depositor's indebtedness. No
such provisions are to be found in the letters of lien/charge in the present case.

The surety's right to pay off the principal debt

One of the rights which a surety has is to pay off the debt, take over any
securities held by the creditor, and proceed himself against the principal debtor.
The appellants submit that it makes no difference that the creditor is insolvent,
and that there is no reason in principle why the surety should not pay off the
creditor by appropriating the indebtedness of the creditor to him. We have
already explained why the insolvency of the creditor makes all the difference. It
is because the surety can only direct the application of the debt which is owed to
him if he can obtain payment; once the creditor is insolvent he can only obtain
payment by proof or set-off; proof will not yield sufficient for the purpose; and
set-off is only available if r 4.90 permits it.

A number of different submissions based on the surety's right to pay off the
principal debt were made during the course of argument, some of them
bordering on the absurd. Thus it was submitted that a surety has a right to be
indemnified by the principal debtor; that on satisfaction of the indemnity the
principal debtor is subrogated to the rights of the surety; and that the principal
debtor can then set off any liability which is owed by the creditor against the
principal debt. This can be dismissed out of hand. A surety has no right to be
indemnified by the principal debtor until he has paid the whole of the principal
debt. Until then his only right is to require the principal debtor to pay the debt
and exonerate him from liability. If the surety pays the debt he is entitled to be
subrogated to the creditor's rights against the debtor. If the principal debtor pays
the debt there is no question of his being subrogated to the surety's rights against
the creditor. Once the principal debt is paid, whether by the principal debtor or
the surety, there is nothing against which the debt due from the creditor can be
set off.

The appellants submit that there exists a non-statutory equitable right of set-off
in bankruptcy which is wider than the statutory right, and rely on *Ex p Stephens*
(1805) 11 Ves 24, 32 ER 996 and *Jones v Mossop* (1844) 3 Hare 568, 67 ER 506 in
support of this proposition, as well as in support of other submissions founded
upon the surety's right to pay off the principal debt. *Ex p Stephens* is a difficult case
which bears a superficial resemblance to the facts of the present case, and was
among the authorities relied on by Hoffmann LJ in *MS Fashions Ltd*. It merits
re-examination.

Ex p Stephens

In this case Miss Stephens instructed her bankers to sell her exchequer annuities which were of a value in excess of £3,000 and invest the proceeds in navy annuities in her name. They informed her that they had carried out her instructions. Miss Stephens' brother James Stephens afterwards borrowed £1,000 from the same bankers on the security of a joint and several promissory note of himself and Miss Stephens. The bankers later became bankrupt, and it was discovered that they had sold the exchequer annuities but had not purchased the navy annuities. The assignees under the commission in bankruptcy brought an action at law against James Stephens alone on the promissory note. Miss Stephens and her brother then brought proceedings in equity for orders that Miss Stephens might set off what was due on the note against what was due to her from the bankrupts; that she might prove for the residue; that the assignees might be restrained from suing on the note; and that the note might be delivered up.

The petitioners conceded that there was no set-off, the action being brought against James Stephens only, who had no cross-claim against the bankrupts. Lord Eldon LC upheld the petition and granted the relief sought. He began by accepting that Miss Stephens had a right of set-off. From the moment the proceeds of the sale of the stock came into the hands of the bankrupts 'they were debtors to her for that sum'. But she was ignorant of her right of set-off. She signed the note as surety for her brother under the supposition that she had stock standing in her name; she was not aware that she was a creditor of those to whom she gave the note. Lord Eldon LC continued (11 Ves 24 at 26, 32 ER 996 at 997):

'The question upon the petition is treated as a question of set-off. But *it is not here raised as a question of set-off in the strict and technical sense.* The question upon the whole is, whether the Chancellor, exercising the jurisdiction in bankruptcy, viz. both a legal and equitable jurisdiction, *can interpose against an action, brought by the assignees, not against Miss Stephens, but against her brother, upon his note, as a several promisory* [sic] *note; who, not being a creditor upon them, clearly could not set off any debt joint or several in that action.'* (My emphasis.)

The question, therefore, which Lord Eldon LC was addressing was *not* whether Miss Stephens had a right of set-off—she plainly had—but whether she had an equity to prevent the assignees from bringing an action at law against her brother on the promissory note. Lord Eldon LC clearly recognised that her brother had no defence to such a claim; for if he had, the intervention of equity would not be required. The entire judgment is predicated on the premise that the brother could not avail himself of the right of set-off which was available to Miss Stephens.

In the next passage of his judgment Lord Eldon LC disposed of the contention for which it has been relied on by the appellants before us (11 Ves 24 at 27, 32 ER 996 at 997):

'It is true, where the Court does not find a natural equity, going beyond the statute the construction of the law is the same in equity as at law ... But that does not affect the general doctrine upon natural equity. So, as to mutual debt and credit, equity must make the same construction as the law ...'

The question, therefore, was whether the circumstances of the case raised an equity in Miss Stephens to prevent the assignees from avoiding the set-off by bringing proceedings against the brother alone, a course which they would be entitled to take if there were no equity to prevent it.

Lord Eldon LC found such an equity. He said:

> 'But in this case my ground is, that the contract was entered into by Miss Stephens in ignorance; and, if not, I should make the same construction; for *if they had her money in their hands*, as she was upon the face of the instrument a surety, *it was against conscience to do any act as against her, which should prevent her having what was no more than the proper use of her own money* ... and it was competent to her, if she had made the discovery immediately after the transaction on account of her brother, to have desired, that so much of the debt should be cancelled, and the difference paid; and to have said, she had a demand against her brother for the sum of £1,000, as paid to his use; also upon the statute of mutual debts and credits; *and they shall not be permitted to say, she shall not, if she chooses, pay the debt; when the consequence is, that she loses her money, and they can call upon him.* If she had this equity before the bankruptcy, so she had it afterwards; and therefore she has a clear right to say, they shall hold *£1,000 of her money in discharge of the note*; and shall deliver up the note. The consequence is, they are prevented from suing upon the note by the clear demand of justice she has against them ...' (My emphasis.)

As Jessel MR later pointed out in *Middleton v Pollock, ex p Knight and Raymond* (1875) LR 20 Eq 515 at 519–520, there were two grounds for the decision, both based on the fraud of the bankers. The first ground was that Miss Stephens had been induced to become surety for her brother by the fraudulent concealment of the creditors; this would entitle the court to set aside the note, presumably against both parties to it. It is, however, the second ground which is of interest. Here Lord Eldon LC's reasoning is tolerably plain. The relationship between the bankers and Miss Stephens was that of trustee and beneficiary. They held the proceeds of sale of her exchequer annuities on trust to invest them in navy annuities in her name. Had they done so, as they told her they had, she would have been the legal and beneficial owner of the stock and would have suffered no loss by the bankruptcy. Pending the purchase, the proceeds of sale were 'her money in their hands'. Had they invested them in stock in their own names the stock would have been trust assets and would not have formed part of the insolvent estate. Had they told her that they had not purchased any stock but held the money in her account, she could have applied it in payment of her liability on the note. Their failure to tell her what they had done denied her that opportunity, and consequently they 'could not be permitted to say' that she had not used the money to pay the debt, when the result of their saying so would cause her loss and expose her brother to an action at law.

This is a classic example of the way equity operates. At law, Miss Stephens had a right of set-off but her brother had none. He was outside the ambit of the mutual dealings and could not avail himself of her right of set-off. She was discharged but he was not. But if the bankers had performed the fiduciary obligations which they owed to Miss Stephens, she could have paid the debt. If she had done so, the assignees would have had no claim against her brother. Since their bankruptcy had deprived her of the opportunity of paying the note, they could not deny that she had done so, and must submit to an order that they held £1,000 of her money upon trust to discharge the note.

It is clear that the fraud was central to the decision. Even without it Miss Stephens would have had a right of set-off and would have been discharged from liability on the note; but she would have been discharged by set-off, not payment. The case proceeds on the basis that a joint and several debtor could set off a debt owed to him by his creditor, but the creditor could normally avoid the set-off by a proceeding against the other joint and several debtor who had no debt due to him which he could set off. Since it is obvious that actual payment by the surety discharges the principal debtor, who is then exposed to a claim by the surety, it follows that neither of these consequences was thought to follow from the operation of the statutory set-off provisions on the bankruptcy of the creditor. This can only be on the basis that, in a three-party situation, discharge by set-off b is not to be equated with discharge by payment so as to avoid the need for mutuality. Lord Eldon LC held that, where the creditor fraudulently concealed the existence of his own indebtedness and thereby deprived the surety of the opportunity to pay the debt, equity would not allow him to treat the debt as unpaid as against the principal debtor.

In *Ex p Blagden* (1815) 19 Ves 465 at 467, 34 ER 589 at 590 Lord Eldon LC said c that but for the fraud he would have doubted much whether the decision in *Ex p Stephens* was right; and in a supplementary note to *Ex p Stephens* the case is described as turning expressly upon fraud (see 2 Ves 243, 34 ER 1077). The case has been consistently so explained in later cases: see *Ex p Hanson* (1806) 12 Ves 346, 33 ER 131, *Vulliamy v Noble* (1817) 3 Mer 593 at 621, [1814–23] All ER Rep 597 d at 604, *Jones v Mossop* (1844) 3 Hare 568 at 573, 67 ER 506 at 509 and *Middleton v Pollock* (1875) LR 20 Eq 515 at 520–521. *Ex p Hanson* was the converse of *Ex p Stephens*, in that it was the principal debtor who had the right of set-off and the assignees of the bankrupt creditor were proceeding against the surety. They were not allowed to do so. There was of course no need for any special equity in this case. The discharge of the principal debtor necessarily discharged the surety. e But the discharge of the surety did not necessarily discharge the principal debtor; he was not discharged unless the surety was discharged by actual payment. *Ex p Stephens* was explained as turning on the fraud.

In *Middleton v Pollock* 20 Eq 515 at 520–521 Jessel MR accepted that Miss Stephens had an indisputable right of set-off. The bankers were severally liable f to her for £3,000 and she was severally liable to them for £1,000. Jessel MR explained that she could not be deprived of her right by the fraud which had prevented her from asserting it before the bankruptcy. Like Hoffmann LJ in *MS Fashions* [1993] 3 All ER 769 at 780, [1993] Ch 425 at 438, we find that explanation puzzling. He said:

g   '... I cannot follow why it mattered that Miss Stephens had not asserted a right of set-off before the bankruptcy and therefore needed only be relieved, on the ground of fraud, against that omission. I can only think that the consequences of the mandatory principle ... were not as fully appreciated in 1875 as they are today.'

h We do not think that Lord Eldon LC did dispute Miss Stephens' right of set-off or consider that it mattered *to her* that she had not asserted it before the bankruptcy. Whether this is so or not, however, is immaterial; it is now settled that the set-off operates automatically upon the date of bankruptcy, and that the hindsight principle enables debts to be treated as owing or not on that date with j the benefit of hindsight (see *Stein v Blake* [1995] 2 All ER 961, [1996] 1 AC 243). What is clear, however, is that Lord Eldon LC recognised that this was not sufficient to discharge *her brother*; only actual payment by Miss Stephens would do that. Hence his order, not that Miss Stephens was discharged by set-off (which was never in dispute) but that the assignees held £1,000 of her money in trust to discharge the note.

It is for future consideration whether this can stand with the mandatory nature of insolvency set-off, but we do not see why not. It is obvious that the creditor cannot both setoff against the surety *and* recover from the principal debtor. The question is which remedy the creditor should pursue. The mandatory nature of set-off does not dictate an answer; for if the creditor recovers from the principal debtor there is nothing due from the surety to be set off. The retroactivity principle under which the liquidation and distribution of the assets of the insolvent are treated as notionally taking place simultaneously on the date of the bankruptcy would seem to provide the solution. If the recovery of the debt from the principal debtor during the liquidation is also to be treated as notionally taking place at the date of bankruptcy, then it must be treated as taking place at the same time as the set-off, or at any rate not afterwards. If so, it cannot provide a defence to the principal debtor. The only question is whether the principal debtor is discharged by the set-off simultaneously available to the surety, or whether the creditor can recover from the principal debtor and, having recovered, submit to a proof from the surety without any discount on the basis that, with hindsight, it has appeared that nothing was due from the surety at the date of bankruptcy. The mischief against which bankruptcy set-off is directed would indicate that the correct approach is in the latter sense.

Whatever be the true position, however, it is clear that *Ex p Stephens* provides no assistance to the present appellants. The case is no authority for the existence of any equitable right of set-off in bankruptcy wider than the statutory right. The equity which Lord Eldon LC enforced was a different equity altogether. Unlike Miss Stephens, the depositors are not personally indebted to the bank, and have no right of set-off and no equity to compel the bank to resort to the security which they provided in exoneration of the appellants.

Nor can the appellants derive any assistance from *Jones v Mossop* (1844) 3 Hare 568, 67 ER 506. The party whose set-off was there being asserted was an insolvent debtor but not a bankrupt, and bankruptcy set-off was not available in such a case. But there were cross-claims which would have been subject to ordinary non-bankruptcy set-off before the insolvency, and the only question was whether that right of set-off was extinguished by the insolvency. Wigram V-C held that it was not. The case cannot help parties who have no rights of set-off outside the bankruptcy and who cannot bring themselves within the requirements of bankruptcy set-off.

Loss of the security

It is a settled rule of equity that if a secured creditor sues for his debt he is under an obligation to deliver the security to the debtor on receiving payment of the debt; and that, if he has in the meantime lost or improperly made away with the security, he cannot have judgment for the debt (see *Ellis & Co's Trustee v Dixon-Johnson* [1925] AC 489, [1925] All ER Rep 715). In that case the creditor had improperly sold the securities, and was unable to maintain the action without first repurchasing them.

In the present case the judge dismissed the appellants' claim to be discharged from their liability for the principal debts because the bank is no longer able to repay the deposits at face value. In my judgment he was right to do so, for two reasons.

In the first place, the bank has not disposed of or improperly made away with the deposits. They are still available to the depositors. The true complaint is not that the bank has made away with the deposits or cannot restore them to the depositors, for their claims continue to exist and they may still prove for them; but that the deposits are no longer worth face value. But a secured creditor is under no duty to maintain the value of the security; his only duty is not to lose or

a injure it. Diminution in value of the security cannot be equated with loss of or injury to the security for the purpose of the rule under discussion, and in our opinion it does not matter that the diminution in value is the result of the creditor's own insolvency. In the present case the bank was liable to repay the deposits. Its liability to do so arose by virtue of the deposits, not of the letters of lien/charge, which in fact limited its liability to repay the deposits. The
b depositors can enforce the bank's liability to repay the deposits by proof or set-off. As secured creditor the bank has no separate liability to the depositors not to become insolvent so that it cannot repay the deposits in full. If the depositors could prove both for the return of their deposits and for the loss due to the bank's failure to repay them in full, they would be proving twice for the same debt.

In the second place, the loss of the securities discharges the debtor who
c provided them. If they are provided by the principal debtor, their loss discharges the principal debtor and must necessarily discharge the surety as well. If they are provided by the surety, however, their loss may discharge him, but we can see no basis on which it should occasion the discharge of the principal debtor.

The appellants seek to overcome this second difficulty by submitting that the
d bank was under a direct obligation to the appellants to preserve the security provided by the depositors. The argument, if we have understood it correctly, is that the depositors have a claim against the appellants for the loss which they have sustained by the insolvency of the bank; that the bank is liable to indemnify the appellants against this claim; and that the appellants can set off their right to indemnity against the principal debt. In our opinion the argument breaks down
e at every stage. The depositors have no claim against the appellants in respect of the loss which they sustain by the insolvency of the bank; there is no evidence that the appellants guaranteed the solvency of the bank, and they cannot be assumed to have done so. If they did, there is no evidence that the bank asked them to do so, and in the absence of such a request the bank is not liable to
f indemnify them. If it is so liable, there is a double proof; and given the nature of the primary relationship between the parties in which the depositors are sureties we would expect them to be preferred to the principal debtors.

Purpose trusts

The appellants submit that the deposits were paid to the bank on trust to be
g applied for a particular purpose, viz the discharge of the principal debt, and are accordingly now held by the liquidators on trust to use them for the same purpose. Accordingly, it is submitted, the depositors can now require the liquidators either to apply the funds for the stipulated purpose or to return them in specie to the depositors.

h The submission is misconceived. The moneys, when deposited, became the property of the bank at law and in equity. The choses in action, that is to say the debts owed by the bank to the depositors, were the property of the depositors both at law and in equity, and became the subject of the charge-backs. These *allowed* the bank to apply them in discharge or reduction of principal debts; they
j did not *compel* the bank to do so. Subject thereto, the choses in action belong beneficially to the depositors, and are enforceable by proof.

Marshalling

Rayners submit that they (or more accurately the depositor) can compel the bank to have resort to the deposits by invoking the equitable doctrine of marshalling. The bank, they point out, has two securities for the debt, viz the English mortgages and the Luxembourg deposits. If the bank takes the deposits in satisfaction of the principal debt, this will leave the mortgages available to *a* compensate the depositor. The doctrine of marshalling, they submit, prevents a creditor who has the means of satisfying his debt out of several funds from prejudicing another creditor whose security comprises only one of the funds.

The submission is completely misconceived. The doctrine of marshalling applies where there are two creditors of the same debtor, each owed a different debt, one creditor (A) having two or more securities for the debt due to him and *b* the other (B) having only one. B has the right to have the two securities marshalled so that both he and A are paid so far as possible. Thus if a debtor has two estates (Blackacre and Whiteacre) and mortgages both to A and afterwards mortgages Whiteacre only to B, B can have the two mortgages marshalled so that Blackacre can be made available to him if A chooses to enforce his security against *c* Whiteacre.

For the doctrine to apply there must be two debts owed by the same debtor to two different creditors. It has no application in a case such as the present, where there is only one debt, even though there are two debtors liable in respect of it. The surety's right to be indemnified by the principal debtor, which arises only after the surety has paid the debt in full, makes him a creditor of the principal *d* debtor in respect of the same debt as that for which the principal debtor was formerly liable to the creditor.

But in any case the doctrine would not help Rayners (or, more accurately, the depositor). It is never allowed to delay or defeat the creditor with several securities in the collection of his debt and the enforcement of his securities. He is allowed to realise his securities as he pleases. The doctrine goes no further than *e* this: that if the creditor (A) with several securities (Blackacre and Whiteacre) chooses to resort to the only security (Whiteacre) which is available to another creditor (B), as he is entitled to do, B may have resort to Blackacre. In the present case, therefore, the doctrine, even if applicable, would not enable the depositor to compel the bank to have resort to the deposits; it would merely allow him *f* recourse to the deposits if the bank resorted to the mortgages.

The liquidators' demand

Following their appointment by the English court as provisional liquidators of the bank the liquidators made a demand on the Luxembourg branch for payment of the principal debts owing by the Solai Group. It is not clear why they did this. *g* 'Payment' by one branch to another branch of the same legal entity is meaningless. But it may have been thought administratively necessary in order to establish the debts as assets of the English liquidation rather than of some apprehended future insolvency proceedings in Luxembourg. The Solai Group submit that the letters of demand constituted an appropriation of the *h* Luxembourg deposits to the debts. But there is no evidence of this. The letters themselves do not purport to appropriate the deposits to the debts. Such appropriation requires appropriate entries to be made in the bank's books. There is no evidence that any such entries have been made, and the liquidators have deposed to the fact that they have made no such appropriation. *j*

Conclusion

In our judgment the problem in the present case is susceptible of a simple solution. The appellants were indebted to the bank. Their controlling shareholders deposited moneys with the bank. If the case had stopped there, there could have been no question of set-off in the bank's insolvency. The bank could not have set off the debts which it owed to the depositors against the debts which a their companies owed to the bank. The requirement of mutuality would have been absent. Even if all parties agreed that the bank should set off the amounts in question, it could not have done so after the bankruptcy. In the absence of the necessary mutuality, the set-off would have contravened the statutory scheme of distribution in insolvency. Once insolvency supervenes, r 4.90 requires set-off in the situations in which it is applicable and public policy forbids it where it is not.

b By the letters of lien/charge the depositors have agreed with the bank that it may apply the amounts standing to the credit of their deposit accounts in discharge or reduction of the indebtedness of the appellants. That is an express agreement that the bank may set off the debts due to the depositors against the debts due from the appellants, and as such it is ineffective once the bank is in liquidation. But in any case the letters of lien/charge only *authorise* the bank to

c set off the debts due to the depositors against the debts due from the appellants, they do not *oblige* the bank to do so; and they confer no rights of set-off on the depositors or the appellants. The appellants must, therefore, succeed under r 4.90 or not at all. Despite all the sophisticated arguments of counsel for the appellants, they have been unable to persuade us that the mandatory set-off

d under r 4.90 is triggered by an agreement for set-off where the requirement of mutuality is absent, or that the fact that the agreements for set-off were comprised in charge-backs supplied the missing element of mutuality.

We recognise that this conclusion gives rise to the paradox which we have mentioned, unless the decision in *MS Fashions* is restricted to its own facts, the depositor in that case being treated as a principal debtor and not a surety. But the

e conclusion is inevitable if serious prejudice to the general body of creditors is to be avoided. We do not consider the conclusion to be unjust. It appears to be so only because the sureties are the controlling shareholders of the principal debtors and so have a common interest in dictating how the creditor shall enforce its security. As we have stated earlier, however, it is not the function of insolvency

f set-off to prefer a creditor who is not indebted to the insolvent estate, or whose liability is secondary only and capable of being discharged by the party primarily liable. There is no injustice in requiring a creditor against whom no claim is made to prove for the debt which is due to him. If it is thought unacceptable that the outcome should depend on whether collateral security is given to secure the debt of the principal debtor or a secondary obligation of the surety, then it is the

g decision in *MS Fashions* which requires reconsideration.

We dismiss the appeals.

Appeals dismissed. Leave to appeal to the House of Lords refused.

h *8 March 1996. The Appeal Committee of the House of Lords gave leave to appeal.*

L I Zysman Esq   Barrister.

R v Criminal Injuries Compensation Board, ex parte Cook

a

COURT OF APPEAL, CIVIL DIVISION

BELDAM, HOBHOUSE AND ALDOUS LJJ   *b*

28 NOVEMBER, 18 DECEMBER 1995

Compensation – Criminal injuries – Reduction of award or rejection of claim – Character and way of life of victim – Victim murdered while unlawfully at large while serving prison sentence – Board refusing compensation to victim's wife because of *c* *victim's criminal convictions – Whether board took into account wife's good character – Whether board gave adequate reasons for rejecting application – Whether wife entitled to oral hearing – Criminal Injuries Compensation Scheme 1990, paras 6(c), 24.*

In 1990 the applicant's husband was murdered when he was unlawfully at large   *d* while serving a prison sentence for armed robbery. The applicant applied to the Criminal Injuries Compensation Board for compensation for his murder pursuant to the Criminal Injuries Compensation Scheme 1990, but her application was rejected by a single member of the board on the ground that paras 6(c) and 15 of the scheme required the board to have regard to the character of the deceased as shown by his criminal convictions and that, accordingly, it was   *e* inappropriate that an award be made from public funds in respect of his death. The applicant subsequently sought an oral hearing under para 24 of the scheme but that too was refused by the board. Thereafter the applicant sought judicial review of both decisions. Her application was refused, and on appeal she contended (i) that the board had failed to take into account her good character   *f* and circumstances, or alternatively if it had, that it had failed to give any indication in its reasons that it had done so and (ii) that the board had wrongly refused her application for an oral hearing, since the substantive application had raised a point of principle and it was far from evident that the initial denial of compensation was correct.

g

Held – The appeal would be dismissed for the following reasons—

(1) The board, in giving reasons for a decision refusing compensation, was only required to give sufficient detail to enable the applicant to know what conclusion had been reached on the principal issue or issues; it was not required to deal with every material consideration to which the board had had regard. If   *h* the reasons given were sufficient, they could not be reviewed in judicial review proceedings unless the board had misconstrued its mandate or the decision was unreasonable. In the instant case, the board's decision that no award out of public funds was appropriate in view of the bad character of the deceased gave adequate reasons; it did not refer to the character of the applicant because there was no   *j* need to do so; she was of good character and therefore that factor did not indicate refusal of an award. It followed that the judge had correctly concluded that there was nothing to suggest that the single member had failed to exercise his discretion correctly or that his decision was unreasonable (see p 150 *c* to *g*, p 152 *a* to *e*, p 153 *a b j*, p 156 *e* to *h*, p 157 *a d*, p 158 *d* and p 159 *d h* to p 160 *d*, post); *Re Poyser and Mills' Arbitration* [1963] 1 All ER 612 and *Bolton Metropolitan DC v*

a *Secretary of State for the Environment* [1995] JPL 1043 applied; *R v Criminal Injuries Compensation Board, ex p Gambles* [1994] PIQR 314 overruled.

(2) An applicant for compensation under the scheme would only be entitled to an oral hearing under para 24 if no award was made or if there was a reduced award and there was a dispute as to the facts or conclusions on which the initial or reconsidered decision was based, or if it appeared that the decision might have

b been wrong in law or principle. Since there was no dispute as to the material facts nor the conclusion on which the decision was based, and the application for an oral hearing raised nothing new, it was open to the board to conclude that the initial decision was right in law and principle. It followed that their decision that an oral hearing would serve no useful purpose was correct and, moreover, not open to challenge in proceedings for judicial review (see p 153 *h* to p 154 *c* and

c p 160 *d*, post).

Notes

For the Criminal Injuries Compensation Scheme in general and claims for compensation, see 11(2) *Halsbury's Laws* (4th edn reissue) paras 1499, 1509, and

d for cases on the subject, see 15(2) *Digest* (2nd reissue) 588–594, *24299–24321*.

Cases referred to in judgments

Associated Provincial Picture Houses Ltd v Wednesbury Corp [1947] 2 All ER 680, [1948] 1 KB 223, CA.

e *Bolton Metropolitan DC v Secretary of State for the Environment* [1995] JPL 1043, HL.
Lane v Holloway [1967] 3 All ER 129, [1968] 1 QB 379, [1967] 3 WLR 1003, CA.
Poyser and Mills' Arbitration, Re [1963] 1 All ER 612, [1964] 2 QB 467, [1963] 2 WLR 1309.
R v Criminal Injuries Compensation Board, ex p Aston [1994] COD 500.
R v Criminal Injuries Compensation Board, ex p Gambles [1994] PIQR P314.

f *R v Criminal Injuries Compensation Board, ex p Hopper* (7 July 1995, unreported), QBD.
R v Criminal Injuries Compensation Board, ex p Jobson (4 May 1995, unreported); *affd* [1995] CA Transcript 1503.
R v Criminal Injuries Compensation Board, ex p Thompstone, R v Criminal Injuries

g *Compensation Board, ex p Crowe* [1984] 3 All ER 572, [1984] 1 WLR 1234, CA.
Union of Construction, Allied Trades and Technicians v Brain [1981] ICR 542, CA.

Cases also cited or referred to in skeleton arguments

R v Civil Service Appeal Board, ex p Cunningham [1991] 4 All ER 310, CA.

h *R v Criminal Injuries Compensation Board, ex p Thomas* [1995] PIQR 99.
R v Lancashire CC, ex p Huddleston [1986] 2 All ER 941, CA.

Appeal

By notice dated 10 November 1994 the applicant, Renee Florence Cook, appealed

j with leave from the order of Potts J made on 12 October 1994, whereby he refused her application for judicial review of (i) the decision of Michael Lewer QC, sitting as a single member of the Criminal Injuries Compensation Board, dated 23 March 1992 refusing her application for compensation for the murder of her husband, and (ii) the subsequent refusal by the board on 4 September 1992 of her application for an oral hearing. The facts are set out in the judgment of Aldous LJ.

Alan Newman QC and *Adrian Jack* (instructed by *Needleman Knowles*) for the   *a*
applicant.
Michael Kent (instructed by the *Treasury Solicitor*) for the board.

Cur adv vult

18 December 1995. The following judgments were delivered.   *b*

ALDOUS LJ (giving the first judgment at the invitation of Beldam LJ). With
leave, the applicant, Mrs Renee Cook, appeals from the order of Potts J in which
he rejected her challenge by way of judicial review of two decisions of the
Criminal Injuries Compensation Board. In those decisions the board refused her
compensation for the murder of her husband and, subsequently, an oral hearing.   *c*

Mrs Cook married her husband in 1958 and has three grown-up children. Her
husband, whom I will call the deceased, worked when he was not in prison as a
tailor. He had a number of convictions but the relevant one is his conviction on
31 July 1981 for armed robbery for which he was given 16 years' imprisonment.

By November 1990 the deceased was finishing his sentence and was due to be   *d*
paroled in December. He had been given a job as a cleaner in the prison hostel
which is outside the Maidstone Prison walls and he had a certain amount of
freedom. He was allowed an hour's exercise every day which could be taken
anywhere in Maidstone within a seven-mile radius of the centre of the town. On
Monday, 19 November 1990 he was picked up in Maidstone by a long-time
girlfriend called Linda Calvey and driven by her to an address in London.   *e*
Technically he was unlawfully at large. Calvey and Cook arrived at the address
at about 12.30 pm and went into the house. Opposite the house was a park and
unbeknown to the deceased, one Daniel Reece, a serving prisoner on home leave,
was waiting for him. Calvey had arranged for him to kill Cook for a fee alleged
to be £10,000. Reece crossed the road, kicked in the front door of the house and   *f*
ran to the kitchen. He was armed with a sawn-off shotgun with which he shot
Cook in the elbow. Reece then lost his nerve and Calvey took the gun, ordered
Cook to his knees, and shot him once in the head killing him instantly. On 12
November 1991 Reece and Calvey were convicted of murder and sentenced to
life imprisonment.

It is not in dispute that Mrs Cook was not party to the deceased's criminal   *g*
activities. She said in her affidavit that she was looking forward to moving to the
country when her husband came out of prison and that work as a tailor had been
lined up for him.

On 15 May 1991 Mrs Cook sought compensation under the Criminal Injuries
Compensation Scheme 1990 for her husband's murder. Her application was   *h*
considered by Mr Lewer QC and his decision was communicated to the applicant
in a letter dated 23 March 1992. That letter stated:

> 'This application has been considered by Mr Michael Lewer QC, a Member
> of the Board, who has disallowed it with the following observations:
> "Paragraphs 6(c) and 15 of the Scheme require me to have regard to the   *j*
> character of the deceased as shown by his criminal convictions. At the time
> of his tragic death the deceased was still serving a prison sentence for serious
> crime, and I regret to have to tell the applicant that because of that it would
> be inappropriate that an award should be made from public funds in respect
> of his death."'

a After receiving that letter the applicant did not appeal, but applied for an oral hearing. Her application stated:

'1. I am the Applicant and I do not have any previous criminal convictions. I was entirely ignorant of my husband, the deceased's criminal activities and I was entitled to look to him for my financial support following his imminent release from prison when he had been offered a job as a [tailor] at a wage of
b £170 per week. 2. There is no rule of common law which would have the effect of disallowing my claim in the manner of the Board's decision; matters of public policy and the doctrine of contributory negligence have no application to the claim. 3. It is wholly inequitable in all the circumstances that the application should be disallowed for the reasons given or at all and I have a
c good and substantial claim not only for general damages and bereavement but also for loss of financial support.'

The application was refused. The reasons for refusal were given in writing after the application for judicial review had been made. After reciting the basic facts, the document stated:

d '8. This Board considered all the documents in the case including document 15, which details the circumstances in which the deceased met his death, and document 16, which gives particulars of his criminal convictions. We also considered document 9 which gives the applicant's reasons for not accepting the decision of the Single Member from which it was clear that the
e contents of documents 15 and 16 were not in dispute. 9. Under Paragraph 6(c) of the Scheme the Board is bound to have regard to the criminal convictions of the deceased in deciding whether an award of compensation to the applicant should be withheld or reduced. In this case the deceased was still serving a sentence of 16 years imprisonment for armed robbery at the time of his death and we therefore concluded that an oral hearing would
f serve no useful purpose, as it would make no difference to the Single Member's decision, which was not wrong in law or principle, and in that it was bound to fail. The application for a hearing was therefore refused.'

The applicant sought judicial review both of the decision to refuse compensation and of the decision to refuse her an oral hearing. Potts J refused
g the order sought.

Before considering the submissions made in this court, and the judgment of the judge, it is necessary to set out the relevant provisions of the 1990 scheme, which are exhibited to the applicant's affidavit of 27 November 1992.

Paragraph 4 of the scheme is concerned with its scope. It is in this form:
h

'4. The Board will entertain applications for ex gratia payments of compensation in any case where the applicant or, in the case of an application by a spouse or dependant (see paragraphs 15 and 16 below), the deceased, sustained in Great Britain ... personal injury directly attributable—
j (a) to a crime of violence (including arson or poisoning) ...'

Paragraphs 6, 15, 22 and 24 provide:

'6. The Board may withhold or reduce compensation if they consider that ... (c) having regard to the conduct of the applicant before, during or after the events giving rise to the claim or to his character as shown by his criminal convictions or unlawful conduct—and, in applications under paragraphs 15 and 16 below, to the conduct or character as shown by the criminal *a* convictions or unlawful conduct, of the deceased and of the applicant—it is inappropriate that a full award, or any award at all, be granted ...

15. Where the victim has died in consequence of the injury, no compensation other than funeral expenses will be payable for the benefit of his estate, but the Board will be able to entertain applications from any person who is a dependant of the victim within the meaning of section 1(3) of the *b* Fatal Accidents Act 1976 or who is a relative of the victim within the meaning of Schedule 1 to the Damages (Scotland) Act 1976. Compensation will be payable in accordance with the other provisions of this scheme to any such dependant or relative ...

22. Every application will be made to the Board in writing as soon as possible after the event on a form obtainable from the Board's offices. The *c* initial decision on an application will be taken by a single member of the Board, or by any member of the Board's staff to whom the Board has given authority to determine applications on the Board's behalf. Where an award is made the applicant will be given a breakdown of the assessment of compensation, except where the Board considers this inappropriate, and *d* where an award is refused or reduced, reasons for the decision will be given. If the applicant is not satisfied with the decision he may apply for an oral hearing which, if granted, will be held before at least two members of the Board excluding any member who made the original decision ...

24. An applicant will be entitled to an oral hearing only if ... (c) no award *e* or a reduced award was made and there is a dispute as to the material facts or conclusions upon which the initial or reconsidered decision was based or it appears that the decision may have been wrong in law or principle. An application for a hearing which appears likely to fail the foregoing criteria may be reviewed by not less than two members of the Board other than any member who made the initial or reconsidered decision. If it is considered on *f* review that if any facts or conclusions which are disputed were resolved in the applicant's favour it would have made no difference to the initial or reconsidered decision, or that for any other reason an oral hearing would serve no useful purpose, the application for a hearing will be refused. A decision to refuse an application for a hearing will be final.'

g

Before the judge, three submissions were made on behalf of the applicant. First, that para 6(c) only allowed the board to withhold compensation in applications under paras 15 and 16, as was this application, where 'the conduct or character as shown by the criminal convictions or unlawful conduct, of the deceased and of the applicant' so indicated. In view of the word 'and' between *h* the words 'the deceased' and 'the applicant' there was a requirement that both the deceased and the applicant must be of a bad character. As the applicant had no convictions and had not taken part in any unlawful conduct, para 6(c) could not apply. Therefore, it was said, the decision of the board refusing compensation under that paragraph was founded upon a wrong interpretation of the paragraph. *j*

The judge held:

'Paragraph 6 confers a discretion on the board to withhold or reduce compensation. Paragraph 6(c) lists those matters to which regard must be had in the exercise of that discretion. The fact that the board is enjoined to consider one element in the list, for example, "the conduct or character" of

a
an applicant by virtue of para 15, does not, in my judgment, exclude consideration of "the conduct or character" of the deceased upon whom she founds her claim. This, even when her conduct or character are beyond reproach. I therefore reject Mr Jack's first submission. His "construction point" fails.'

b
The applicant now accepts that that conclusion reached by the judge was correct.
The second matter argued before the judge was that the board failed to take account of the good character of Mrs Cook. Alternatively, if it did, then it failed to give an adequate indication that it had and also failed to indicate that it had considered ordering reduced compensation. The judge held:

c
'... it is suggested that when he came to disallow the application, the single member wrongly failed to take into account the good character and circumstances of the applicant, and failed to give any indication that he had considered ordering reduced compensation as opposed to no compensation at all. I am unable to accept this submission. In my judgment, the observations of Mr Lewer, cited at the beginning of this judgment, are

d
perfectly clear. They show that he had regard to the criminal convictions of Mr Cook. In the circumstances that arose, and having regard to the way the observations are couched, I am satisfied that it was unnecessary for Mr Lewer to say that he had given thought to the making of a reduced award and decided against it. In my judgment, it is clear that Mr Lewer, in

e
concluding as he did, took into account the fact that at the time of his death the deceased man was still serving a prison sentence for serious crime and concluded that that fact, together with the criminal record of the deceased, was enough to make any award inappropriate, whatever the character of the applicant. This is no reason to think that Mr Lewer failed to exercise his discretion correctly. I am quite unable to say that that decision was

f
Wednesbury unreasonable (see Associated Provincial Picture Houses Ltd v Wednesbury Corp [1947] 2 All ER 680, [1948] 1 KB 223).'

Before this court those submissions were repeated. Mr Newman QC, who appeared for Mrs Cook, drew our attention to the judgment of Donaldson MR in R v Criminal Injuries Compensation Board, ex p Thompstone, R v Criminal Injuries

g
Compensation Board, ex p Crowe [1984] 3 All ER 572, [1984] 1 WLR 1234. Even though the wording of the para 6(c) that was considered by Donaldson MR in that case was different to that in the 1990 scheme, Mr Newman was right in his submission that the judgment made it plain that the word 'or' in the first part of para 6(c) should be read disjunctively. From that it followed that compensation

h
may be refused if the applicant is of bad character, even though his bad character did not give rise to the injury. Further, I believe that the wording of the second part of para 6(c) makes it clear, even if it is not explicit from Ex p Thompstone, that the board may take into account the bad character of the deceased and the bad character of the applicant or absence of bad character of the applicant. That I

j
believe was not in dispute between the parties in this case.
The attack upon the board's decision was not that it was one which no reasonable body could have reached. It was conceded that the convictions of the deceased were such that the board could have decided to refuse compensation. The complaint was that the board had not arrived at its decision in an appropriate way. In particular it had not taken account of the good character of Mrs Cook and had not weighed that against the bad character of the deceased to arrive at a

decision as to what compensation, if any, should be awarded. Thus the attack of the applicant was against the reasons given and the reasoning applied.

Paragraph 22 of the scheme requires the single member to give reasons for his decision if an award is refused or reduced; but there is nothing in the language of that paragraph which requires him to deal specifically with every material consideration. In *Bolton Metropolitan DC v Secretary of State for the Environment* [1995] JPL 1043 the House of Lords had to consider the adequacy of reasons given by the Secretary of State for his decision in a planning matter. The duty to give those reasons arose from r 17(1) of the Town and Country Planning (Inquiries Procedure) Rules 1988, SI 1988/944. Those rules required the Secretary of State to 'notify his decision ... and his reasons for it, in writing to all persons entitled to appear at the inquiry who did appear' (r 17(1)).

That duty does not seem to me to differ in principle from the duty upon the single member imposed by para 22 of the 1990 scheme. That being so, the observations of Lord Lloyd in the *Bolton Metropolitan DC* case are apposite. From his speech, a speech with which the rest of their Lordships agreed, I believe it is clear that the board's reasons should contain sufficient detail to enable the reader to know what conclusion has been reached on the principal important issue or issues, but it is not a requirement that they should deal with every material consideration to which it has had regard. If the reasons given are sufficient, they cannot be reviewed in judicial review proceedings unless the board misconstrued its mandate or the decision is *Wednesbury* unreasonable (see *Ex p Thompstone* [1984] 3 All ER 572 at 576, [1984] 1 WLR 1234 at 1238).

In the present case there was one main issue, namely whether the applicant was entitled to an award under the scheme in the light of the bad character of the deceased and the good character of the applicant. If the board had decided she was entitled to an award, it had to go on to decide whether it should be a full compensatory award or a reduced one. The decision of the board was that no award out of public funds was appropriate because of the character of the deceased. The reasons given were in my view adequate. They did not refer to the character of the applicant and there was no need to do so. She was of good character and therefore that did not indicate refusal of an award. In the view of the board the character of the deceased was sufficient to lead the board to the decision it reached. No doubt her character was considered by the board as were all the relevant facts that were before it.

Mr Newman also submitted that the reasons given by the single member showed an error in the board's mandate. Relying upon the judgment of Sedley J in *R v Criminal Injuries Compensation Board, ex p Gambles* [1994] PIQR P314, he submitted that the reasons given showed that the board failed to proceed in the three stages which were necessary, namely to ask itself: (a) does the character of the deceased and the applicant make a full award inappropriate? (b) If so, to what extent does their conduct impact on the appropriateness of an award? (c) What award, if any, should the applicant consequently receive?

In that case, Mr Gambles was injured in a fight outside a public house. The decision of the single member of the board was: 'The applicant provoked and was willing to participate in a fight. The application was rejected under paragraph 6(c) of the Scheme' (see [1994] PIQR P314 at P315).

At the request of Mr Gambles, his application was reconsidered by the full board. They came to the same conclusion as the single member. The last paragraph of their decision encapsulated their reasons for their refusal to make an award (at P316):

a
'13. After submissions we retired. Having had an opportunity of hearing evidence from the applicant we formed the view that we believed that the statement made to the police was an accurate account of what occurred. Our findings of that statement are that the applicant was, for whatever reason, ready to fight and that unhappily, as often happens, he then received much more serious injuries than might have been expected. We considered

b
the appropriateness of a reduced award but as we found that he had evinced a willingness to engage in violence which culminated in the assault upon him, we disallowed his application completely under paragraph 6(c).'

Counsel for Mr Gambles submitted that the finding of the board was flawed because it omitted an essential matter to which the board's reasoning had to be

c
directed under the scheme, namely the question why the applicant's willingness to fight should result in a nil award rather than a reduced award. Sedley J said (at P318):

d
'In my judgment the facts found by the Board are capable of sustaining the whole spectrum of possible decisions, from a nil award to a complete award, although the latter may well be frankly unlikely. This, precisely, is the broad discretion for which Mr Kent [counsel for the board] contends. Given the fact that the assault on the applicant, who was not armed, was made with a beer glass at a point at which the applicant had approached the aggressor but

e
not, on the evidence, assaulted him, I am not disposed to accept Mr Kent's submission that the case is one in which only a nil or much reduced award is feasible. All the possible levels of award lie within the range of decision compatible with the finding that the applicant was ready to fight in the material circumstances. Accepting as I do the submission that it is more nearly a moral judgment than a causative link that is postulated by paragraph

f
6, it is still for the Board to establish a rational and proportionate nexus between the conduct of the applicant before and during (and in other cases after) the events, and in other cases his character too, before these can reduce or extinguish the award to which he would otherwise be entitled. Common law cases like Lane v Holloway [1967] 3 All ER 129, [1968] 1 QB 379 do, I think, assist as illustrations, though no more, of what common sense and equity

g
may yield in this context. The Board in such a case as this has therefore to proceed in three stages: A. Does the applicant's conduct make a full award inappropriate? B. If so, to what extent does the applicant's conduct impact on the appropriateness of an award? C. What award if any should the applicant consequently receive? I accept Mr Drabble's [counsel for the

h
applicant] submission that the Board's reasoning goes from A to C, omitting B entirely. In this situation, and even though the reasons have been volunteered at the Court's invitation rather than having been required by law, it is not right for the Court to supply the want by assuming the existence of the very thing that reasons are there to demonstrate, namely that the

j
conclusion has been reached by an appropriate process of reasoning from the facts. I am acutely conscious of the distinction and experience of the three members of the Board, as indeed of the single member who preceded them; but just as they have their task, I have mine, and the conclusion I have come to is that there is a defect in the reasoning of the Board such that its decision cannot stand.'

I believe that the reasoning and the conclusion reached by Sedley J in *Ex p Gambles* is wrong. A decision that no award was appropriate out of public funds is equivalent to deciding that the award should be nil. The question that the board had to ask was the equivalent of the third question suggested by the judge—should the applicant receive an award and, if so, what amount? It is only if the board comes to the conclusion that the applicant should recover an award that it need go on to decide whether it should be a full award or some other figure. Further, in my view the reasons given by the board were adequate. It is not incumbent upon the board, as suggested by Sedley J, to demonstrate in their reasons that the conclusion has been reached by an appropriate process of reasoning from the facts. The reasons must be adequate and comply with the principles to which I have referred earlier in this judgment.

I also cannot agree that—

'it is still for the Board to establish a rational and proportionate nexus between the conduct of the applicant before and during (and in other cases after) the events, and in other cases his character too, before these can reduce or extinguish the award to which he would otherwise be entitled.' (See [1994] PIQR P314 at P318.)

I am not sure what it is that the judge thought should have a nexus with the conduct and character of the applicant. Even so, I am clear that the board does not have to establish anything. Their duty is to consider the material circumstances and to arrive at a decision as to whether there should be an award out of public funds and if so, what. That requires judgment not a complicated step-by-step approach.

Ex p Gambles was considered in *R v Criminal Injuries Compensation Board, ex p Hopper* (7 July 1995, unreported). That was an application for judicial review where a claim had been made for compensation which had been refused by the board under para 6(c) of the scheme. The conclusion of the board was:

'The applicant's character and way of life as evidenced by the list of convictions and cautions makes it inappropriate that he should receive an award of compensation from public funds.'

Buxton J held, rightly in my view, that the reasons given by the board were adequate and proper. He rightly distinguished *Ex p Gambles*. He cited this passage from the judgment of Donaldson MR in *Ex p Thompstone* [1984] 3 All ER 572 at 576, [1984] 1 WLR 1234 at 1239:

'In each case, although different categories of circumstances can be taken into account, the issue is the same. Is the applicant an appropriate recipient of an ex gratia compensatory payment made at public expense?'

The judge went on:

'I would respectfully adopt that ... as a brief summary of the implications of para 6(c). I say, as Donaldson MR said, that the question is whether the applicant is an appropriate recipient of an ex gratia payment, judged in the light of his previous convictions. That formulation excludes, in my view, an obligation on the part of the board to engage in the balancing exercise for which Mr Lederman [counsel for the applicant] contends. It reinforces that the board's approach in this case was correct and was entirely in accordance with the duty placed upon them under para 6(c).'

a   I agree.

I have found nothing which suggests that the single member misconstrued the board's mandate. He concluded that an award was not appropriate out of public funds because of the bad character of the deceased. He knew of the character of the applicant. His reasons were adequate in that they stated in an intelligible fashion the reason why he had concluded that such an award was not *b* appropriate. There was no need for him to go on and set out in any greater detail the reasoning which he adopted to arrive at that conclusion. I therefore believe that the judge was right to conclude that there was nothing to suggest that Mr Lewer failed to exercise his discretion correctly and that it was not possible to say that his decision was *Wednesbury* unreasonable.

The applicant also submitted before the judge that the board was wrong not to *c* allow an oral hearing pursuant to para 24 of the scheme. The judge rejected that complaint. He said:

> '... there is no material before me to suggest that what is stated in para 7 of the board's written reasons, namely that Mr Crowley QC and Miss Cotton QC followed the procedure provided by para 24 of the scheme, is anything
> *d* other than correct. It is not disputed that the board then considered all the documents in the case, para 6(c) of the scheme, and the terms of Mr Lewer's disallowance of compensation. The board concluded that an oral hearing would serve no useful purpose because "it would make no difference to the single member's decision which was not wrong in law or principle". The
> *e* board was of the view that, if this matter went to an oral hearing, it was bound to fail, and declined to order an oral hearing accordingly. In my view this reasoning cannot be faulted. There are no grounds for saying that the board exercised its discretion wrongly in refusing an oral hearing. The decision in question was one that the board was entitled to take, and this ground fails also.'
f

Before us it was submitted on behalf of the applicant that para 24 of the scheme provided a low threshold for the granting of an oral hearing and that an oral hearing should be granted if the original determination may have been wrong. Thus, in this case, where the applicant's application to the board raised a point of principle and it was far from self-evident that the decision was right, an oral *g* hearing should have been granted.

I am not sure what was meant by a low threshold, but there can be no doubt as to the meaning of para 24 of the scheme. The board has a discretion whether to appoint an oral hearing. Paragraph 24 makes it clear that the applicant will only be entitled to a hearing if no award was made or there is a reduced award *h* and there is a dispute as to the facts or conclusions upon which the initial or reconsidered decision was based, or if it appears that decision may have been wrong in law or principle. There was no dispute in this case as to the material facts nor the conclusion upon which the decision was based. The application for an oral hearing raised nothing new. Thus it was quite open to members of the *j* board to conclude that the decision was right in law and in principle. I therefore conclude that their decision that an oral hearing would serve no useful purpose, because it would make no difference to the single member's decision which was not wrong in law or principle, was right and in any case is not open to attack in proceedings for judicial review.

In my view the conclusion reached by Potts J was correct and this appeal should be dismissed.

HOBHOUSE LJ. On this appeal from the judgment of Potts J refusing the motion of Mrs Cook for the judicial review of two decisions of the Criminal Injuries Compensation Board, two points have been argued. About the second I do not wish to add anything to what has already been said by Aldous LJ. I agree with him that the board properly refused Mrs Cook an oral hearing under para 24 of the scheme. The board was entitled to take the view that there was no dispute as to the material facts or conclusions upon which the decision of the single member was based and that it did not appear that his decision might have been wrong in law or principle. They were entitled to take the view that her application for a hearing appeared likely to fail those criteria and that an oral hearing would serve no useful purpose. Their decision to refuse an application was final. They have given clear and sufficient reasons for their decision.

It is the other part of the case about which I wish to add something to what has already been said by Aldous LJ. Mrs Cook sought an order from the court quashing the decision of the single member refusing her application for compensation under paras 4 and 15 of the scheme. As is clear from the decision letter dated 23 March 1992, the single member refused her application applying para 6(c) of the scheme. He gave his reasons:

> 'Paragraphs 6(c) and 15 of the Scheme require me to have regard to the character of the deceased as shown by his criminal convictions. At the time of his tragic death the deceased was still serving a prison sentence for serious crime, and I regret to have to tell the applicant that because of that it would be inappropriate that an award should be made from public funds in respect of his death.'

It is clear from these reasons that the single member was deciding that the board should withhold compensation on the ground that it considered that, having regard to the character of Mr Cook as shown by his criminal convictions, it was inappropriate that any award be granted. The submission of Mr Newman QC, who appeared in this court for Mrs Cook, was put in two ways. First, it was said that it should be inferred from these reasons that the single member 'wholly disregarded the blameless character of' Mrs Cook and had therefore failed to take into account a relevant consideration. Secondly, he submitted that it was also to be inferred that he had not considered whether some reduced compensation would have been not inappropriate and solely considered whether or not compensation should be wholly withheld. It was accordingly submitted that we should conclude that the single member had not applied the appropriate criteria and had not exercised the judgment (or discretion) required by para 6.

These submissions each relate to inferences which it was said should be drawn from the reasons of the single member and therefore had to be made in the context of the actual circumstances under which Mrs Cook was making her application for compensation and the grounds upon which it was based and take into account the adequacy of the reasons given by the single member for his actual decision. Under para 22, 'where an award is refused or reduced, reasons for the decision will be given' by the single member. The submissions of counsel for Mrs Cook to this court were rather different from those to Potts J; before us particular reliance was placed upon the judgment of Sedley J in *R v Criminal Injuries Compensation Board, ex p Gambles* [1994] PIQR 314, to which I will have to return.

The factual context

a   Mr Cook had a serious criminal record. He had been sentenced to terms of imprisonment on no fewer than four occasions. The first of these was in 1956. In 1975 he was convicted by a jury on two counts of robbery for which he was sentenced by the trial judge to 14 years' imprisonment. However, in June 1977 the Court of Appeal quashed those convictions. We have not been told anything b about the facts which led to his being charged with those offences or to the quashing of the convictions. Mr Newman frankly accepted that the offences of which he was convicted in July 1981 were of such gravity as to make any examination of his earlier involvements with the criminal courts academic. In 1981 he was convicted of an offence of armed robbery for which he received a sentence of 16 years' imprisonment and an offence of possessing a firearm with c intent to endanger life for which he was sentenced to three years' imprisonment concurrent. He must clearly have been very seriously involved in a major incident of violent criminal conduct.

At the time of his death in November 1990, Mr Cook was serving his sentence at Maidstone prison. He was nearing the time when he would become eligible d for parole and as a result it appears (to quote from a document signed by Det Insp George of the Metropolitan Police, which Mrs Cook had submitted to the board in support of her application)—

'he had a certain amount of freedom in that he was allowed an hours exercise per day and this could be taken anywhere in Maidstone within a e   seven mile radius of the centre of the town. Any previous exercise time he had not used up could be saved and used at any given time.'

This lax regime gave him opportunities to meet up with his 'long-time girl friend' Linda Calvey and go up to London with her. In doing so he was breaching the f terms on which he was outside the prison and he was unlawfully at large. On Monday, 19 November he went up to London with her again and was there killed by her after Daniel Reece, a serving prisoner on home leave from prison in Weymouth and recruited by Linda Calvey to kill him, had failed to do so. The motive for the murder of Mr Cook was never clearly established but Mrs Cook in para 9 of her affidavit sworn on 27 November 1992 gives some indication of the g circumstances. She says:

'Calvey, it transpired at the trial, had extensive criminal connections. She had married her husband in 1970 when he was actually serving a sentence for robbery. Her husband was shot dead by police 8 years later in the course of a foiled robbery of a supermarket. In 1986 she herself was sentenced to 5 h   years for conspiracy to rob.'

It is therefore an inevitable inference that Mr Cook's death had something to do with his association with known criminals.

Mrs Cook described her own position in the document in which she asked for j an oral hearing. The document supporting her original application is not extant. It is accepted that it contained a similar statement and was seen by the single member. She said:

'I am the applicant and I do not have any previous criminal convictions. I was entirely ignorant of my husband, the deceased's criminal activities and I was entitled to look to him for my financial support following his imminent release from prison when he had been offered a job as a [tailor] at a wage of *a* £170 per week.'

The decision

It is on these facts that counsel submits that Mrs Cook was entitled to expect that, notwithstanding her husband's appalling criminal record, she would be *b* awarded at the least some reduced compensation in respect of the criminal killing of her husband. However, he accepts, clearly correctly, that it was not irrational for the single member (and the board) to conclude that no award should be made to Mrs Cook, notwithstanding her good character and lack of involvement in her husband's criminal activities. The circumstances under which her husband met his death and his own criminal record were sufficient to justify the board in *c* concluding, in accordance with para 6 of the scheme, that it was inappropriate to make any award to her in respect of his death.

It follows that this case does not come into that category of cases where the decision requires some special justification. To use an analogy, if a court makes an order for costs which follow the event, that order requires no special *d* justification and no special reasons need be given; if, on the other hand, some special order for costs is made which does not follow the event, the court needs to give reasons which justify such an order, otherwise it may be inferred that the decision was irrational or arrived at on some wrong basis. What reasons have to cover depends upon the application which is being made and the character of the decision. *e*

Thus the reasons for the decision of the single member (and, when relevant, the board) must be such as not to disclose a decision which is irrational or arrived at on the wrong basis. The decision of the single member to refuse to make any award to Mrs Cook was not on its face irrational. The reasons therefore did not need to rebut a prima facie inference of irrationality. As regards the making of *f* the decision on the right basis, the facts were not in dispute. The case was one which necessitated the board exercising its discretion under para 6. The reasons of the single member, short though they were, made it clear that the application was being refused under para 6(c) and that it was the character of Mr Cook as shown by his criminal convictions which led the single member to conclude that it would be inappropriate that an award should be made from public funds in *g* respect of his death. The reasons do not justify any inference that any wrong principle was applied; the only justified inference is that the single member was applying para 6 in accordance with its terms.

The reasons confirm that the single member had regard to the relevant paragraph of the scheme and arrived at his decision on a ground which was *h* provided for by the scheme. Therefore Mrs Cook's attack upon his reasons cannot be sustained. She has shown no basis for the inferences which she alleges nor for an intervention by a court by way of judicial review.

Ex p Gambles   *j*

The appellant submitted that a more exacting approach was required and that the court should say that the reasons were inadequate and/or the decision flawed because the reasons of the single member did not refer expressly to the good character of Mrs Cook and did not expressly explain why some partial award should not have been made. This submission was founded upon what was said by Sedley J in *R v Criminal Injuries Compensation Board, ex p Gambles* [1994] PIQR a 314. Aldous LJ has already set out how that case came before the Divisional Court and has summarised the relevant parts of the judgment of Sedley J. Like Aldous LJ, I have difficulty in accepting the correctness of that decision but, in any event, I consider that the statements of law in the relevant part of the judgment should not be approved by this court. Since hearing this appeal, I have inquired to what extent *Ex p Gambles* has been referred to in subsequent cases. As far as I can be ascertained, three other judges of the Divisional Court have had occasion to consider *Ex p Gambles*. In two cases it has been distinguished: *R v Criminal Injuries Compensation Board, ex p Aston* [1994] COD 500 and *R v Criminal Injuries Compensation Board, ex p Hopper* (7 July 1995, unreported). In *R v Criminal Injuries Compensation Board, ex p Jobson* (4 May 1995, unreported), a case under para 6(a), Dyson J adopted the three questions posed by Sedley J and adapted them to the case before him; however, he did not consider that this disclosed any invalidity of the decision of the board, and he instead decided the case before him on the ground that the board had failed to give adequate reasons and remitted the application to the board. It appears that *Ex p Gambles* has not been referred to in any judgment of this court.

d In my judgment, *Ex p Gambles* seeks improperly to extend the scope of judicial review from an assessment of the propriety of the decision to an evaluation of its merits. Sedley J states that 'the facts found by the Board are capable of sustaining the whole spectrum of possible decisions, from a nil award to a complete award, although the latter may well be frankly unlikely', thus recognising that any one of those decisions would not be irrational (see [1994] PIQR P314 at P318). He then continued:

> 'Accepting as I do the submission that it is more nearly a moral judgment than a causative link that is postulated by paragraph 6, it is still for the Board to establish a rational and proportionate nexus between the conduct of the applicant before and during (and in other cases after) the events, and in other cases his character too, before these can reduce or extinguish the award to which he would otherwise be entitled ... The Board in such a case as this has therefore to proceed in three stages: A. Does the applicant's conduct make a full award inappropriate? B. If so, to what extent does the applicant's conduct impact on the appropriateness of an award? C. What award if any should the applicant consequently receive? I accept Mr Drabble's [counsel for the applicant] submission that the Board's reasoning goes from A to C, omitting B entirely. In this situation, and even though the reasons have been volunteered at the Court's invitation rather than having been required by law, it is not right for the Court to supply the want by assuming the existence of the very thing that reasons are there to demonstrate, namely that the conclusion has been reached by an appropriate process of reasoning from the facts.'

It is apparent from these quotations that the decision of the board in *Ex p Gambles* was not on its face irrational, nor did it seek to found upon some consideration which should have been excluded. There was no basis for a complaint that the applicant had been deprived of a fair procedure by reason of some absence of reasons. Sedley J formulated a principle which, like Aldous LJ, I find lacking in clarity, and then prescribed by reference to that principle a series of steps which he says must be expressly spelt out in the reasons if a decision is to be allowed to stand. What Sedley J was doing was, in truth, not identifying any defect in the decision but criticising the clarity and the completeness of the thought processes as set out in the reasons. He also would apparently impose *a* upon the decision-maker, the board, a burden of establishing, by reference solely to what is expressly stated in the reasons, rationality and proportionality when the decision itself raises no question of irrationality or disproportion.

Such considerations may be relevant to an appeal but do not suffice for setting aside by way of judicial review a decision which is not prima facie irrational or improper. Where the decision itself gives rise to an inference of irrationality or *b* impropriety, the reasons have to be sufficient to rebut that inference. In such a case the approach of Sedley J would be appropriate. But that was not the situation in *Ex p Gambles*. The decision whether it is appropriate that an award be granted is for the board, not the court. Unless the reasons had justified the conclusion that the decision was actually irrational or had justified the inference that the decision has been arrived at on an improper basis, the court was not at *c* liberty to quash the decision. Judicial review is concerned with the propriety and validity of the decision, not with the quality of the articulation of the reasons. The judgment in *Ex p Gambles*, if accepted as a statement of the law, would inevitably lead to the quashing of decisions which were not invalid or improper and were not flawed by any procedural irregularity. *d*

Further, in my judgment, *Ex p Gambles* is inconsistent with the decision of the Court of Appeal in *R v Criminal Injuries Compensation Board, ex p Thompstone, R v Criminal Injuries Compensation Board, ex p Crowe* [1984] 3 All ER 572, [1984] 1 WLR 1234. Those cases also concerned para 6(c) of the scheme. The claims arose out of fights in which the two applicants had been involved. Both the applicants had *e* numerous previous convictions but the incidents in which they were assaulted were unconnected with the circumstances of their convictions. Each had been refused compensation by the board. They applied for judicial review on the ground that the board ought to have had regard to the fact that their injuries did not arise in any way from the conduct disclosed by their criminal convictions; their applications were dismissed. The judgment of Donaldson MR ([1984] 3 All *f* ER 572 at 575, [1984] 1 WLR 1234 at 1238), with which the other members of the Court of Appeal agreed, referred to the conclusion of the board—

'The Board therefore retired to consider the case. When they returned they said that, having regard to the applicant's character and way of life as disclosed by his convictions, it was not appropriate that he should receive *g* any award at all from public funds',

and the appellants' submissions that the board should have stated some basis on which it had concluded that the criminal conduct was relevant to the refusal to award compensation. They submitted that the approach of the board left it 'free *h* to reach capricious decisions ... because the paragraph as construed by the board is incapable of judicial application'. Donaldson MR continued ([1984] 3 All ER 572 at 576, [1984] 1 WLR 1234 at 1238–1239):

'I am quite unable to accept the submissions. The scheme does not give rise to any right to compensation. It contemplates only that in some cases, *j* more closely defined by the terms of the scheme, the public purse should be opened to make ex gratia compensatory payments. The scheme is discretionary and the discretion is that of the board. It follows that the board's decisions can be reviewed if it misconstrues its mandate or, on *Wednesbury* principles, must be deemed to have done so since its decision is one which no reasonable body could have reached on the facts if it had correctly

a
construed its mandate: see *Associated Provincial Picture Houses Ltd v Wednesbury Corp* [1947] 2 All ER 680, [1948] 1 KB 223 ... The public servant who before or after the event embezzles public funds might well not be thought to be an appropriate recipient of public bounty, although that would depend on the circumstances and be a matter to be considered by the board. The second [category] is "the character, conduct and way of life" of the
b
applicant, where it is much less likely that this will have any ascertainable bearing on the occurrence of the injury, but again may be such that the applicant would not be thought to be an appropriate recipient of public bounty. In each case, although different categories of circumstances can be taken into account, the issue is the same. Is the applicant an appropriate recipient of an ex gratia compensatory payment made at the public expense?
c
As with all discretionary decisions, there will be cases where the answer is clear one way or the other and cases which are on the borderline and in which different people might reach different decisions. The Crown has left the decision to the board and the court can and should only intervene if the board has misconstrued its mandate or its decision is plainly wrong. Neither
d
can in my judgment be said in the present appeals.'

In my judgment, *Ex p Gambles* should not be regarded as good law. If the challenge to the decision of the Criminal Injuries Compensation Board cannot be made good applying the criteria stated in the judgment of Donaldson MR, judicial review must be refused. The character of the scheme and of the decisions of the
e
board which implement it is as stated by Donaldson MR. Unless it can be shown that the board has disregarded the terms of the scheme, the decision of the board must stand.

The requirement for reasons
f
Aldous LJ has referred to the fact that the single member is required to give reasons for his decision. Under the scheme only the single member was under an express duty to give reasons; and he only has to give reasons if he is refusing an award or is making a reduced award. This is because there is a right of appeal from the single member to the board under paras 22 to 27. If the applicant is to form a view about whether to be satisfied with the single member's decision or
g
to appeal, the applicant must be able to understand why the decision has gone against him. In order to prepare his appeal and apply for an oral hearing under paras 23 and 24, and to make out his case under para 25, the applicant must be aware of the single member's reasons so that he knows which to accept and which to challenge and on what basis to argue that an award, or greater award, should have been made in his favour.
h
The classic statement of the standard of reasons required is to be found in *Re Poyser and Mills' Arbitration* [1963] 1 All ER 612 at 616, [1964] 2 QB 467 at 477–478 per Megaw J:

j
'The whole purpose ... was to enable persons whose property or interests were being affected by some administrative decision or some statutory arbitration to know, if the decision was against them, what the reasons for it were. Up to then, a person's property and other interests might be gravely affected by a decision of some official, the decision might have been perfectly right, but the person against whom it was made was left with the real grievance that he was not told why the decision had been made ... proper, adequate, reasons must be given; the reasons that are set out ... must be

reasons which not only will be intelligible, but also can reasonably be said to deal with the substantial points that have been raised ...' *a*

As Donaldson MR said in *Union of Construction, Allied Trades and Technicians v Brain* [1981] ICR 542 at 551, the reasons must 'tell the parties in broad terms why they lose or, as the case may be, win'. In every case the adequacy of the reasons must depend upon the nature of the proceedings, the character of the decision-making body and the issues which have been raised before it, particularly if they include issues of fact. *b*

In the present case the reasons of the single member were on any view brief but no separate ground of application for judicial review has been based upon this. They were adequate for their purpose. They made clear the basis of the decision. They enabled Mrs Cook to understand why she had been unsuccessful *c* and to prosecute her appeal. Speaking for myself, I would prefer in future to see rather fuller reasons in cases such as this; it is usually a better practice to make explicit what is otherwise only implicit. However, they sufficed for the purpose for which they were required.

d

Conclusion
I agree that this appeal fails and must be dismissed.

BELDAM LJ. I agree.

Appeal dismissed. Leave to appeal to the House of Lords refused. *e*

L I Zysman Esq   Barrister.

a # Goodwill v British Pregnancy Advisory Service

COURT OF APPEAL, CIVIL DIVISION

PETER GIBSON AND THORPE LJJ

14 DECEMBER 1995, 17 JANUARY 1996

b

Negligence – Information or advice – Knowledge third party might rely on information – Vasectomy operation – Vasectomy not permanent – Liability to woman made pregnant – Man advised after vasectomy that he would not need to use contraception in future – Plaintiff having sexual relationship with man three years later and becoming pregnant – Whether person performing vasectomy operation could have known advice
c *to man would be communicated to and acted on by plaintiff – Whether person performing vasectomy operation owing duty of care to plaintiff.*

In 1985 M, who later had sexual intercourse with the plaintiff, underwent a vasectomy operation arranged by the defendant pregnancy advisory service. The
d defendants advised M that the operation had been successful and that he would not need to use contraception in future. In 1988, the plaintiff commenced a sexual relationship with M. Having been told by him that he had had a vasectomy and of its purported success and permanency, and having consulted her own doctor, who assured her that the chances of her becoming pregnant by M were minute, the plaintiff did not use any form of contraception in their
e relationship and nor did M. In 1989 the plaintiff became pregnant by M and later gave birth to a daughter. She brought an action against the defendants, claiming damages for the expenses of the birth, the cost of bringing up her daughter and loss of income arising from her reduced working hours. The county court judge dismissed an application by the defendants to strike out the action on the grounds
f that it disclosed no reasonable cause of action and was frivolous, vexatious or an abuse of the process of the court. The defendants appealed. The plaintiff contended that, although the case did not fall within an established category of negligence, the plaintiff should, by applying the incremental approach to negligence, be afforded a remedy in tort by analogy with established categories.

g **Held** – For a plaintiff to have a sustainable case in negligence against a defendant in respect of a financial loss arising from reliance on advice given by the defendant, the plaintiff had to show, inter alia, (i) that the defendant knew, either actually or inferentially, that the advice communicated by him was likely to be acted upon by the plaintiff, without independent inquiry, for a purpose, whether
h particularly specified or generally described, which was made known, either actually or inferentially, to the defendant at the time when the advice was given, and (ii) that it had been so acted upon by the plaintiff to his detriment. On the facts, the defendants could not have known that their advice to M would be communicated to the plaintiff and relied upon by her as a warranty of M's
j permanent infertility, and they could not know that if communicated to the plaintiff it was likely to be acted upon by her without independent inquiry, since they could know nothing about the likely course of action of M's future sexual partners. The plaintiff was not in a sufficient or any special relationship with the defendants such as to give rise to a duty of care and it could not properly be said of the defendants that they had voluntarily assumed responsibility to the plaintiff when giving advice to M. Furthermore, the plaintiff had consulted her own doctor, who had alerted her to the possibility (albeit very small) that, despite the

vasectomy, M could make her pregnant and she chose to take that risk. *a*
Accordingly, she could not claim that in ceasing to use any contraceptive method
she had been induced by and relied on M's bare assertion that he had had a
vasectomy and could not have any more children. It followed that she had no
reasonable cause of action and that her claim was frivolous or vexatious or an
abuse of process. The appeal would therefore be allowed and the action struck
out (see p 166 *e*, p 167 *h* to p 169 *g j* to p 170 *e*, post). *b*

Dictum of Lord Oliver in *Caparo Industries plc v Dickman* [1990] 1 All ER 568 at
589 applied.

Thake v Maurice [1986] 1 All ER 497 and *White v Jones* [1995] 1 All ER 691
distinguished.

Notes   *c*
For duty of care and economic loss, see 34 *Halsbury's Laws* (4th edn) para 53, and
for cases on the subject, see 36(1) *Digest* (2nd reissue) 307–315, 2439–2469.

Cases referred to in judgments
Anns v Merton London Borough [1977] 2 All ER 492, [1978] AC 728, [1977] 2 WLR
1024, HL.   *d*
Caparo Industries plc v Dickman [1990] 1 All ER 568, [1990] 2 AC 605, [1990] 2 WLR
358, HL.
Goymer v Lombard North Central Wheelease Ltd (1993) Times, 1 April, [1993] CA
Transcript 238.
Halliday v Shoesmith [1993] 1 WLR 1, CA.
Hedley Byrne & Co Ltd v Heller & Partners Ltd [1963] 2 All ER 575, [1964] AC 465, *e*
[1963] 3 WLR 101, HL.
*Henderson v Merrett Syndicates Ltd, Hallam-Eames v Merrett Syndicates Ltd, Hughes v
Merrett Syndicates Ltd, Arbuthnott v Feltrim Underwriting Agencies Ltd, Deeny v
Gooda Walker Ltd (in liq)* [1994] 3 All ER 506, [1995] 2 AC 145, [1994] 3 WLR
761, HL.   *f*
Holt v Payne Skillington (1995) Times, 22 December, [1995] CA Transcript 1631.
McNaughton (James) Papers Group Ltd v Hicks Anderson & Co (a firm) [1991] 1 All ER
134, [1991] 2 QB 113, [1991] 2 WLR 641, CA.
Thake v Maurice [1986] 1 All ER 497, [1986] QB 644, [1986] 2 WLR 337, CA.
White v Jones [1995] 1 All ER 691, [1995] 2 AC 207, [1995] 2 WLR 187, HL.   *g*

Case also cited or referred to in skeleton arguments
Lonrho plc v Tebbit [1991] 4 All ER 973; *affd* [1992] 4 All ER 280, CA.

Appeal   *h*
By notice dated 4 April 1995 the defendants, British Pregnancy Advisory Service,
appealed with leave from the order of Judge Paul Clark made in the Oxford
County Court on 27 March 1995 whereby he refused their application made
under CCR Ord 13, r 5 to strike out the claims of the plaintiff, Alison Caroline
Faith Goodwill, for damages for economic loss, on the grounds that the amended
particulars of claim disclosed no reasonable cause of action and that the pleadings *j*
were frivolous or vexatious or an abuse of the process of the court. The facts are
set out in the judgment of Peter Gibson LJ.

Roger Stewart (instructed by *Reynolds Porter Chamberlain*) for the defendants.
Cherie Booth QC (instructed by *Linnells*, Oxford) for the plaintiff.

Cur adv vult

a 17 January 1996. The following judgments were delivered.

PETER GIBSON LJ. The law of negligence, and in particular that part relating to the recovery of damages for economic loss caused by negligent statements or advice, has undergone a number of shifts in direction. The attempt in *Anns v Merton London Borough* [1977] 2 All ER 492, [1978] AC 728 to lay down a principle
b of general applicability did not find favour for long. Instead, whilst certain key ingredients of the tort, such as foreseeability, proximity, assumption of responsibility and reliance have been identified, it has been held that the law should develop incrementally by reference to or analogy with established categories of situations where the law has recognised that a duty of care arises and a plaintiff
c may recover for his loss. The situation in the present case, it is accepted on behalf of the plaintiff, does not fall within an established category, but, it is suggested, it requires only a modest step from an established category and one which should on the favoured incremental approach now be taken to afford the plaintiff a remedy in tort. That is challenged by the defendants who say that it requires a
d giant and impermissible leap from an established category and that not even arguably was any duty of care owed by these defendants to this plaintiff in the circumstances of this case.

This is an appeal by the defendants, British Pregnancy Advisory Service, from the order of Judge Paul Clark in the Oxford County Court on 27 March 1995. He
e refused to strike out the claims of the plaintiff, Mrs Goodwill. The application to strike out had been made under CCR Ord 13, r 5 on grounds which can be divided into two. One was that the amended particulars of claim disclosed no reasonable cause of action. The other was that those pleadings were frivolous or vexatious or an abuse of the process of the court. I take the essence of the second ground to be that the plaintiff's claims were manifestly unsustainable. The judge
f gave leave to appeal.

The facts alleged in the particulars of claim dated 30 March 1992 as further and better particularised on 28 August 1992 and as amended on 16 August 1993 can be summarised as follows. The defendants are a charity engaged in the arrangement and provision of sterilisation operations including vasectomies and
g associated counselling services. The defendants arranged for a vasectomy to be performed on a Mr MacKinlay on 28 November 1984. A little over three months later two semen samples were provided by Mr MacKinlay to the defendants. On 2 April 1985 the defendants informed him by letter that the tests on the samples had proved negative, that the vasectomy had been successful and that Mr
h MacKinlay no longer needed to use any other method of contraception. In March 1988 the plaintiff, Mrs Goodwill, then a 40-year-old teacher, commenced a sexual relationship with Mr MacKinlay. The plaintiff knew of his vasectomy and of its purported success and permanency in that in March 1988 he volunteered to her that he did not want to have any more children and that accordingly he had had
j a vasectomy and could not have any more children. Induced by and in reliance on that knowledge she ceased to use a contraceptive coil in May 1988 and no other method of contraception was used by him or her. Prior to January 1989 the vasectomy underwent spontaneous reversal, thereby causing him to regain his fertility. She became pregnant by him in or about January 1989. She learnt on 26 April 1989 that she was pregnant. It was then too late for an abortion. She gave birth to a daughter on 5 November 1989.

Proceedings were commenced by the plaintiff against the defendants on 2 April 1992. The allegations of a duty of care, foreseeability and negligence were pleaded in this way:

'5. The Defendants well knew, or ought to have known, that the said MacKinlay and any existing or future sexual partner of the said MacKinlay would or would be likely to rely on the information contained in the said letter [of 2 April 1985] as warranting that the said MacKinlay had been rendered permanently infertile. In the premises, the Defendants owed a duty to the Plaintiff to take reasonable care to ensure that the matters stated in the said letter were true ... 9. In stating in the said letter of 2nd April 1985 that the said vasectomy operation had been successful and that the said MacKinlay no longer need use any other method of contraception, the Defendants acted negligently and in breach of the duty of care which they owed to the Plaintiff.

PARTICULARS OF CLAIM   The Defendants were negligent in that they: a) failed to warn the said MacKinlay whether adequately or at all as to the possibility of late spontaneous reversal of the vasectomy at a time when such possibility was or ought to have been well known to them; b) failed to warn the said MacKinlay adequately or at all of the possible impregnation of a sexual partner in consequence of such late spontaneous reversal; c) failed to advise the said MacKinlay adequately or at all as to the necessity of further contraceptive protection to eliminate as far as practicable the possibility of impregnation of an existing or future sexual partner.'

The plaintiff claimed that she had suffered loss and damage consisting of the expenses at her daughter's birth, the cost of bringing her daughter up and the loss of income due to the reduction of her working hours. At 30 March 1992 the accrued damages were estimated at nearly £11,500 and further damages were alleged to be accruing at a little over £10,000 pa. There is thus no claim other than for financial loss.

A defence was served on 29 July 1992. The defendants served a third party notice on Mr MacKinlay, to which he served a defence on 12 April 1993. On 24 June 1994 the case was set down for trial. Witness statements were exchanged in December 1994, the plaintiff supplying a proof of evidence which she had signed on 10 October 1989. On 25 January 1995 the defendants applied to strike out, but the judge on 27 March dismissed the application.

The judge first considered the application to strike out on the ground of no reasonable cause of action, correctly confining his attention to the pleaded facts. He could not find that it was clear beyond doubt that the plaintiff had no reasonable cause of action, and he expressed himself as 'satisfied that the case, whatever its potential weaknesses, is fit for judicial decision under this heading'.

The judge then turned to the application to strike out on the grounds that the claims were frivolous or vexatious or an abuse of the process of the court. For this he looked at the other evidence outside the amended particulars of claim, including the plaintiff's proof of evidence. From the further evidence the following matters were revealed.

(1) At the time of the vasectomy and of the letter of 2 April 1985 Mr MacKinlay was married and both he and his wife received counselling from the defendants.

(2) The plaintiff at that time was also married and had one son but was divorced in March 1988.

a   (3) In March 1988 the plaintiff met Mr MacKinlay and commenced a sexual relationship with him a month later.

(4) In May 1988 the plaintiff consulted her own general practitioner about removing her contraceptive coil; she discussed with the GP the fact that Mr MacKinlay had told her that he had had a vasectomy and the GP said something like 'it was only a one in a million chance of getting pregnant' and she was assured
b   that there was only a minute chance of becoming pregnant.

(5) On 4 April 1989 the plaintiff went to see her GP, thinking that there was a minute chance that she might be pregnant, but discounted such thoughts because Mr MacKinlay had had the vasectomy. She was told that she might be suffering from an ovarian cyst.

c   (6) The plaintiff underwent a scan and was told on 26 April that she was 14 weeks pregnant.

(7) When the plaintiff discovered she was pregnant, she was pleased; she had hoped to have another baby and had been disappointed when, at the time her relationship with Mr MacKinlay developed, she realised that he had had a vasectomy and she could not have had children by him. But her feelings were
d   greatly affected by the knowledge that she was a single person. Mr MacKinlay was married and living with his wife and family and the chances were that if she decided to go ahead and have the baby she would have to do so as a single parent. She was also upset that she had lost the chance of a termination because by the time the pregnancy was diagnosed it was too late.

e   (8) The plaintiff spent a couple of weeks in a great state of turmoil and anxiety before deciding to go ahead with the pregnancy. Although it might have been still possible to terminate the pregnancy, the implications were much more serious because the foetus was so well developed and because of her belief that life was sacred. She also knew in her heart of hearts that she could not abort the life that she had previously thought was an omen of death.

f   The judge said that in the light of the evidence to which I have referred in para (4) above the question of the causal link between the defendants' statement to Mr MacKinlay and the plaintiff's pregnancy might be a difficult area in her case but he did not find that her pleadings should be struck out on the grounds that they were frivolous or vexatious or an abuse of process.

g   Further, he said that in any case the application was made very late and referred to the observations of this court in *Halliday v Shoesmith* [1993] 1 WLR 1 at 5, where Beldam LJ (with whom Stocker LJ agreed) said:

'It seems to me that where a party to litigation delays making an application of this kind until the opposite party has incurred all the costs of
h   preparing for trial and has indicated that he is himself intending to exercise his right to proceed to trial, he has conducted himself in a way which has induced the opposite party to incur costs and expense and, if his contentions be right, has unwarrantably increased the potential liability of the opposite party to pay his costs. It seems to me that such an application should, in the
j   ordinary way, be made at the earliest opportunity and that a court should not embark on hearing such an application at the eleventh hour, save in the most exceptional case and on receiving a valid explanation for the lateness of the application.'

The judge said that this was about the eleventh hour and he did not find it to be an exceptional case. Accordingly he dismissed the application.

To deal with the last point first, the county court (like the High Court: see RSC Ord 18, r 19(1)) is expressly empowered under CCR Ord 13, r 5 to strike out 'at any stage of the proceedings'. Of course litigants should be encouraged, if they are minded to make an application to strike out, to do so earlier rather than later. But if the trial will be long and expensive and the claims are hopeless, it defies common sense to refuse to allow the saving of the time and expense of the trial simply in order to punish the applicant party for failing to strike out earlier. Similar views were expressed by this court in *Goymer v Lombard North Central Wheelease Ltd* (1993) Times, 1 April, [1993] CA Transcript 238, Leggatt LJ saying 'the court will not nowadays feel precluded from exercising its power on the ground that trial is imminent or that issue has been joined on the pleadings'. *Halliday v Shoesmith* was a case where the application to strike out had not been made until the trial. In the present case, although the case has been set down for trial, the substantial costs of a trial lasting two to three days would be saved if the application to strike out succeeded. The application to strike out was made shortly after the exchange of witness statements and the defendants particularly rely on the plaintiff's proof of evidence which they then saw for the first time. Miss Booth QC for the plaintiff sensibly accepted that the real question in this case is whether the grounds for the application to strike out were made out. If so, the lateness of the application could not be determinative.

Miss Booth, in supporting the conclusions of the judge, reminded the court that the power to strike out should only be exercised in plain and obvious cases, and submitted that a case which raises complex issues of law and fact is not suitable for resolution on an application to strike out. She further submitted that these considerations are all the stronger in an area of developing law. I do not dissent from those propositions, but, on careful consideration of all the circumstances, I am left in no doubt but that the judge was wrong on each of the two grounds on which the application to strike out was made. I shall discuss each in turn.

No reasonable cause of action

Miss Booth put her case on duty of care in this way. A, a doctor, voluntarily agrees to provide a service for B, which includes performing an operation and giving informed advice about the possible consequences of that operation. The purpose of that operation is to render B permanently sterile. It is reasonably foreseeable and accepted that the doctor owes a duty of care to that person's current partner. It is further foreseeable in today's society that the patient may have sexual relations with another partner. It is therefore merely an incremental extension of the law to extend to that partner the duty owed by A to B when A provides the service for B.

In support of that submission Miss Booth referred to the familiar remarks of Lord Morris in *Hedley Byrne & Co Ltd v Heller & Partners Ltd* [1963] 2 All ER 575 at 594, [1964] AC 465 at 502–503:

'My lords, I consider that it follows and that it should now be regarded as settled that if someone possessed of a special skill undertakes, quite irrespective of contract, to apply that skill for the assistance of another person who relies on such skill, a duty of care will arise. The fact that the service is to be given by means of, or by the instrumentality of, words can make no difference. Furthermore, if, in a sphere in which a person is so placed that others could reasonably rely on his judgment or his skill or on his a   ability to make careful inquiry, a person takes it on himself to give information or advice to, or allows his information or advice to be passed on to, another person who, as he knows or should know, will place reliance on it, then a duty of care will arise.'

b   In *Henderson v Merrett Syndicates Ltd, Hallam-Eames v Merrett Syndicates Ltd, Hughes v Merrett Syndicates Ltd, Arbuthnott v Feltrim Underwriting Agencies Ltd, Deeny v Gooda Walker Ltd (in liq)* [1994] 3 All ER 506 at 518–519, [1995] 2 AC 145 at 178 Lord Goff referred to that passage and to certain others from the speech of Lord Devlin in *Hedley Byrne* as stating the governing principles.

Miss Booth also relied on *White v Jones* [1995] 1 All ER 691, [1995] 2 AC 207 as providing an example of an analogous situation in which a duty of care has been
c   recognised. In that case a solicitor who was instructed to prepare a will but delayed in carrying out his instructions was held to owe a duty of care to the intended beneficiaries. She submitted that a woman who had a sexual relationship with Mr MacKinlay is in an analogous position to the intended beneficiaries under the will, because just as the solicitor was employed to confer
d   a benefit (in the form of bequests) on a particular class of people (the beneficiaries), so the doctor is employed to confer a benefit (not getting pregnant) on a particular class of people (women who have sexual relationships with Mr MacKinlay). I admire the ingenuity of the suggested analogy, but I have to say that I am wholly unpersuaded that the analogy is real.

It must be recognised that *White v Jones* belonged to an unusual class of cases.
e   A remedy in tort was fashioned to overcome the rank injustice that the only persons who might have a valid claim (the testator and his estate) had suffered no loss and the only persons who had suffered a loss (the disappointed beneficiaries) had no claim. I do not see any comparable injustice in the present case. On the contrary, it might be said that to give a remedy to the plaintiff against the
f   defendants in the circumstances of the present case would not be fair, just or reasonable. The doctor who performs a vasectomy on a man on his instructions cannot realistically be described as employed to confer a benefit on the man's sexual partners in the form of avoiding pregnancy. Still less can he be so described when he is giving advice on tests after the operation. The doctor is concerned only with the man, his patient, and possibly that man's wife or partner if the
g   doctor intends her to receive and she receives advice from the doctor in relation to the vasectomy and the subsequent tests. Whether the avoidance of pregnancy is a benefit or a disadvantage to a sexual partner of the man will depend on her circumstances. If the existence of that partner is known to the doctor and the doctor is aware that she wishes not to become pregnant by the man and the
h   vasectomy is carried out to meet her wish as well as the man's wish, it may be said that the doctor is employed to confer that benefit on her. But that is not this case. In any event, in this case no complaint is made of the vasectomy: it is only the advice following the vasectomy that the doctor gave the man that is the subject of complaint. I cannot accept that the present is a *White v Jones* type of
j   case at all.

Miss Booth also drew our attention to *Thake v Maurice* [1986] 1 All ER 497, [1986] QB 644, which is the case closest to the present one on its facts. That was a successful action in contract and in tort by a husband and wife whom the defendant surgeon had failed to warn of the slight risk that the husband's vasectomy might not leave him permanently sterile. But in that case advice on the husband's vasectomy was given directly to him and his wife, and both signed

forms consenting to the vasectomy. There could be no doubt therefore but that
a duty of care was owed by the surgeon to the wife when the surgeon advised the
husband and the wife that they might reasonably take no further contraceptive
precautions.

In my judgment, for the plaintiff to have a sustainable case in negligence
against the defendants in respect of a financial loss arising from reliance on advice
given by the defendants, it must appear that arguably the governing principles
laid down in the *Hedley Byrne* case [1963] 2 All ER 575, [1964] AC 465 are satisfied.
The words of Lord Oliver in *Caparo Industries plc v Dickman* [1990] 1 All ER 568 at
589, [1990] 2 AC 605 at 638 have been taken by this court to be a clear statement
of the guidance to be obtained from *Hedley Byrne* on the proximity or relationship
which must exist between the giver of the advice and the person who acts on it if
there is to be a cause of action in negligence (see *James McNaughton Papers Group
Ltd v Hicks Anderson & Co (a firm)* [1991] 1 All ER 134 at 143, [1991] 2 QB 113 at
124 and *Holt v Payne Skillington* (1995) Times, 22 December). Lord Oliver said:

> 'What can be deduced from the *Hedley Byrne* case, therefore, is that the
> necessary relationship between the maker of a statement or giver of advice
> (the adviser) and the recipient who acts in reliance on it (the advisee) may
> typically be held to exist where (1) the advice is required for a purpose,
> whether particularly specified or generally described, which is made known,
> either actually or inferentially, to the adviser at the time when the advice is
> given, (2) the adviser knows, either actually or inferentially, that his advice
> will be communicated to the advisee, either specifically or as a member of an
> ascertainable class, in order that it should be used by the advisee for that
> purpose, (3) it is known, either actually or inferentially, that the advice so
> communicated is likely to be acted on by the advisee for that purpose
> without independent inquiry and (4) it is so acted on by the advisee to his
> detriment. That is not, of course, to suggest that these conditions are either
> conclusive or exclusive, but merely that the actual decision in the case does
> not warrant any broader propositions.'

Of these conditions, I need only fasten on (3), although I am extremely dubious
on the plaintiff's pleadings as to the satisfaction of conditions (2) and (4). How
the defendants knew or should have known that their advice would be
communicated to the plaintiff and relied upon by her as (according to the
pleadings) a warranty of permanent infertility when she did not meet, or
commence a sexual relationship with, Mr MacKinlay until three years later, it is
not apparent. It is not pleaded that the advice was in a form showing that the
defendants expected or intended its communication to Mr MacKinlay's sexual
partners, nor is it pleaded that Mr MacKinlay alerted the defendants that he
would be passing on the advice to his sexual partners. However, no particulars
were sought of the factual allegation of knowledge in this respect and, confined
as we are under this head to the pleadings, I would not decide the case on this
ground. I am equally doubtful that the pleadings make the allegation that the
plaintiff acted upon the advice without independent inquiry, when the pleading
merely alleges that the plaintiff was induced by and relied on knowledge obtained
from the statement of Mr MacKinlay that he had had a vasectomy and could not
have any more children and does not link Mr MacKinlay's words with the advice
in the letter of 2 April 1985. But in any event I do not see how condition (3) is
satisfied. It is not alleged nor could it reasonably be alleged that the defendants
knew that their advice when communicated to the plaintiff was likely to be acted

a upon by her without independent inquiry. The defendants could know nothing about the likely course of action of future sexual partners of Mr MacKinlay.

In my judgment on the plaintiff's pleadings the defendants were not in a sufficient or any special relationship with the plaintiff such as gives rise to a duty of care. I cannot see that it can properly be said of the defendants that they voluntarily assumed responsibility to the plaintiff when giving advice to Mr

b MacKinlay. At that time they had no knowledge of her, she was not an existing sexual partner of Mr MacKinlay but was merely, like any other woman in the world, a potential future sexual partner of his, that is to say a member of an indeterminately large class of females who might have sexual relations with Mr MacKinlay during his lifetime. I find it impossible to believe that the policy of the law is or should be to treat so tenuous a relationship between the adviser and the

c advisee as giving rise to a duty of care, and there is no analogous situation recognised as giving rise to that duty.

Frivolous or vexatious or an abuse of process

The insubstantial nature of the plaintiff's case is even more apparent if matters

d outside the pleaded case are taken into consideration. There is nothing in the plaintiff's own evidence or elsewhere to support the allegation that the defendants knew that their advice to Mr MacKinlay would be communicated to the plaintiff in order that it should be used by her, still less that they knew that it would be relied on by her as a warranty of permanent infertility. But it is condition (4) of Lord Oliver's conditions that is, in my view, plainly not satisfied.

e It is beyond belief that in ceasing to use any contraceptive method this mature educated woman was induced by and relied on Mr MacKinlay's bare assertion to her that he had had a vasectomy and could not have any more children, given that she only removed her contraceptive coil after taking advice from her GP on that and on the fact that Mr MacKinlay had told her that he had had a vasectomy.

f What the GP told her in any event alerted her to the possibility, albeit very small, that despite the vasectomy Mr MacKinlay would make her pregnant. She took that risk. I would add that when she discovered the pregnancy, contrary to the pleading, it is plain that at 14 weeks' pregnancy it was certainly not too late to have an abortion, but that she chose not to, albeit for understandable reasons.

Miss Booth sought to rely on Mr MacKinlay's defence to the third party notice.

g But this, to my mind, further reinforces the view that the plaintiff's case is manifestly unsustainable. It is apparent from it that when advice on the vasectomy was given to Mr MacKinlay and his wife, they were advised to read the documents on male sterilisation which were provided by the defendants and in which a warning about failure following two clear samples was given. The

h letter of 2 April 1985, by which, it will be recalled, the defendants informed Mr MacKinlay that tests on the two samples had proved negative, must therefore be read subject to that warning.

For these reasons, which owe much to Mr Stewart's cogent arguments, I would allow the appeal and strike out the plaintiff's claim.

j

THORPE LJ. I agree that the defendant is entitled to succeed on the application of 25 January 1995 on both its grounds for the reasons given by Peter Gibson LJ.

Viewing the plaintiff's case as pleaded, it does not survive the application of the six tests suggested by Neill LJ in *James McNaughton Papers Group Ltd v Hicks Anderson & Co (a firm)* [1991] 1 All ER 134 at 144, [1991] 2 QB 113 at 125. In particular, to use the terminology of the third test, the plaintiff as advisee is not

entitled to look to the third party and through him to the adviser for guidance. *a*
Indeed, use of that terminology only serves to demonstrate how tenuous is the
relationship between the plaintiff and the defendant. The reality is that the
doctor advised Mr MacKinlay. They are in reality the adviser and the advisee.
The plaintiff is no nearer the doctor adviser than one who some three and half
years after the operation commenced a sexual relationship with his patient.
Equally, the class to which the plaintiff belongs is in my judgment potentially *b*
excessive in size and uncertain in character. Thirdly, the state of knowledge of
the adviser militates against the plaintiff. The doctor in the circumstances regards
himself as advising the patient and, if a married man, the patient's wife. It cannot
be said that he knows or ought to know that he also advises any future sexual
partners of his patient who chance to receive his advice at second hand.
Presented with such a set of facts a doctor is entitled to scorn the suggestion that *c*
he owes a duty of care to such a band so uncertain in nature and extent and over
such an indefinite future span. Finally, I consider that the plaintiff fails the test of
reliance. In reality a woman exploring the development of a sexual relationship
with a new partner takes much on trust before experience corroborates or
exposes his assurances. Her responsibility is to protect herself against unwanted *d*
conception and to take independent advice on whatever facts he presents. Thus
I conclude that on an analysis of the pleadings alone the plaintiff's claim discloses
no reasonable course of action.

I also conclude that a further analysis of the pleadings and the exchanged
witness statement entitles the defendant to succeed on the second ground. The *e*
plaintiff's statement is commendable for its candour, but it is fatal to her case in
that it establishes the following important facts. (1) In about April 1988 at the
commencement of the sexual relationship and when protected by a coil the
plaintiff sought independent medical advice. (2) Her doctor informed her that
there was an extremely remote chance of conception despite her partner's
vasectomy. Nevertheless she had the coil removed. (3) On 4 April 1989 she *f*
consulted her doctor thinking that she might be pregnant but accepted his advice
that she possibly had an ovarian cyst. (4) On 21 June when informed of her
pregnancy she was relieved and pleased. Subsequently she quailed at the
consequences but, although termination was still medically open, she could not
accept it psychologically and emotionally. Accordingly she elected to go on to *g*
give birth. Those facts simply demonstrate how far-fetched is this claim.

The lateness of the application is no bar to success. It was issued one month
after the delivery of the plaintiff's witness statement. Any prejudice to the
plaintiff can be compensated in costs.

h

Appeal allowed.

Paul Magrath Esq   Barrister.

a ## Fitzgerald and others v Williams and others
O'Regan and others v Williams and others

COURT OF APPEAL, CIVIL DIVISION

b SIR THOMAS BINGHAM MR, WAITE AND OTTON LJJ

4–7, 20 DECEMBER 1995

Costs – Security for costs – Plaintiff ordinarily resident out of the jurisdiction – Plaintiffs resident in Republic of Ireland – Plaintiffs bringing proceedings against defendants claiming damages for fraudulent misrepresentation and recovery of funds –

c *Interlocutory order requiring plaintiffs to give security for costs of first defendant – Whether court having jurisdiction to make order – Whether rule providing for security for costs amounting to discrimination on grounds of nationality – Whether rule contrary to Community prohibition against such discrimination – RSC Ord 23, r 1(1) – EC Treaty, arts 6, 220.*

d
The 87 plaintiffs in two consolidated actions claimed to have been victims of a fraud perpetrated by the first defendant, in which he had raised funds by selling subscriptions to various works of art which turned out to be worth a fraction of their represented value. Of the 87 plaintiffs, 81 were resident in the Republic of

e Ireland. In May 1994 the plaintiffs commenced proceedings in the High Court in Dublin, claiming damages for fraudulent misrepresentation and the recovery of sums allegedly belonging to them. Thereafter the plaintiffs applied to the English courts for and obtained a worldwide Mareva injunction. On the first defendant's application, the deputy judge discharged that injunction, and ordered the plaintiffs to give security for the first defendant's costs in the sum of £100,000

f pursuant to RSC Ord 23, r 1(1)[a], which empowered the court to make orders against plaintiffs ordinarily resident out of the jurisdiction which it could not make against plaintiffs ordinarily resident within it. The plaintiffs appealed. The question which arose, in relation to the Irish plaintiffs, was whether the court had jurisdiction to make an order for security against them or, if it had, whether it should refrain from exercising its discretion to make such an order on the basis (i)

g that they had rights under art 6[b] of the EC Treaty to be free from discrimination on the grounds of nationality and (ii) that arts 6 and 220 of the Treaty, read in conjunction with the Convention on Jurisdiction and the Enforcement of Judgments in Civil and Commercial Matters 1968 (set out in Sch 1 to the Civil Jurisdiction and Judgments Act 1982), precluded justification of any national rule

h of civil procedure which discriminated on grounds of nationality.

Held – While an English court had jurisdiction under RSC Ord 23, r 1(1) to order a plaintiff ordinarily resident out of the jurisdiction to give security for costs, it should never exercise its discretion under that rule to order security to be given

j by an individual plaintiff who was a national of and resident in another member state party to the 1968 convention in the absence of very cogent evidence of substantial difficulty in enforcing a judgment in that other member state, since such a plaintiff suing in England had a Community right pursuant to art 6 of the

---

a   Rule 1, so far as material, is set out at p 179 *j* to p 180 *a*, post

b   Article 6, so far as material, is set out at p 181 *j*, post

EC Treaty (which a national court had to protect) not to be the subject of
discrimination on grounds of nationality. The rule clearly fell within the scope of
arts 6 and 220^c of the Treaty provisions, which conferred rights directly
enforceable in member states following legislative implementation of the 1968
convention, and involved covert discrimination on grounds of nationality in that
different plaintiffs were treated differently, since most plaintiffs in England
ordinarily resident outside the jurisdiction would not be British. Further, the
discrimination could not be justified by any objective circumstances in relation to
those who were nationals of and resident in other member states party to the
convention, since there was evidence that enforcement of any judgment in
Ireland presented no difficulty. It followed that no order for security should have
been made against the Irish plaintiffs. Their appeal would accordingly be allowed
and the order for security made against them set aside (see p 182 *h* to p 183 *g j*, p
184 *b h* and p 185 *b* to *j*, post).

Mund & Fester v Hatrex Internationaal Transport Case C-398/92 [1994] ECR I-467
followed.

Berkeley Administration Inc v McClelland [1990] 1 All ER 958 not followed.

Notes
For court's power to order security for costs where the plaintiff is ordinarily
resident out of the jurisdiction, see 37 *Halsbury's Laws* (4th edn) para 299, and for
cases on the subject, see 37(2) *Digest* (Reissue) 430–433, 2634–2653.

For Community prohibition of discrimination based on nationality, see 51
Halsbury's Laws (4th edn) para 2.295.

For the Civil Jurisdiction and Judgments Act 1982, Sch 1, see 22 *Halsbury's
Statutes* (4th edn) (1995 reissue) 545.

Cases referred to in judgments
Bankers Trust Co v Shapira [1980] 3 All ER 353, [1980] 1 WLR 1274, CA.
Banque Belge pour L'Etranger v Hambrouck [1921] 1 KB 321, CA.
Berkeley Administration Inc v McClelland [1990] 1 All ER 958, [1990] 2 QB 407, [1990]
    2 WLR 1021, CA.
Corfu Navigation Co v Mobil Shipping Co Ltd, The Alpha [1991] 2 Lloyd's Rep 52, CA.
De Bry v Fitzgerald (1988) [1990] 1 All ER 560, [1990] 1 WLR 552, CA.
El Ajou v Dollar Land Holdings plc [1994] 2 All ER 685, CA.
Hubbard v Hamburger Case C-20/92 [1993] ECR I-3777.
Mund & Fester v Hatrex Internationaal Transport Case C-398/92 [1994] ECR I-467.
Porzelack KG v Porzelack (UK) Ltd [1987] 1 All ER 1074, [1987] 1 WLR 420.
R v IRC, ex p Commerzbank AG Case C-330/91 [1993] 4 All ER 37, [1994] QB 219,
    [1994] 2 WLR 128, ECJ.
R v Secretary of State for Transport, ex p Factortame Ltd Case C-221/89 [1991] 3 All
    ER 769, [1992] QB 680, [1992] 3 WLR 288, ECJ.
Slazengers Ltd v Seaspeed Ferries International Ltd, The Seaspeed Dora [1987] 3 All ER
    967, [1988] 1 WLR 221, CA.
Sundt Wrigley & Co Ltd v Wrigley [1993] CA Transcript 685.

---

c   Article 220, so far as material, provides: 'Member States shall ... enter into negotiations with each
     other with a view to securing for the benefit of their nationals: the protection of persons and the
     enjoyment and protection of rights under the same conditions as those accorded by each State to its
     own nationals ...'

Cases also cited or referred to in skeleton arguments

a   *Amministrazione delle Finanze dello Stato v Simmenthal SpA* Case 106/77 [1978] ECR 629.

Agip (Africa) Ltd v Jackson [1992] 4 All ER 451, [1991] Ch 547, CA.

Biggs v Somerset CC [1995] ICR 811, EAT.

Boussac Saint Frères SA v Gerstenmeier Case 22/80 [1980] ECR 3427.

b   *Brinks-MAT Ltd v Elcombe* [1988] 3 All ER 188, [1988] 1 WLR 1350, CA.

Cala Cristal SA v Emran Al-Borno (Mubarak Abdulaziz al Hassawi, third party) (1994) Times, 6 May.

Collins v Imtrat Handesgesellschaft mbH, Patricia Im- und Export Verwaltungs-gesellschaft mbH v EMI Electrola GmbH Cases C-92/92, C-326/92 [1993] 3 CMLR 773, ECJ.

c   *Costa v ENEL* Case 6/64 [1964] ECR 585.

Da Costa en Schaake NV v Nederlandse Belastingadministratie Joined cases 28, 29, 30/62 [1963] ECR 31.

Derby & Co Ltd v Weldon (No 1) [1989] 1 All ER 469, [1990] Ch 48, CA.

Dormeuil Frères SA v Nicolian International (Textiles) Ltd [1988] 3 All ER 197, [1980]
d   1 WLR 1362.

Equal Opportunities Commission v Secretary of State for Employment [1994] 1 All ER 910, [1995] 1 AC 1, HL.

Factortame v Secretary of State for Transport [1989] 2 All ER 692, [1990] 2 AC 85, HL.

Factortame v Secretary of State for Transport (No 2) [1991] 1 All ER 70, [1991] 1 AC 603, HL.

e   *Fietje, Criminal proceedings against* Case 27/80 [1980] ECR 3839.

Firma Molkerei-Zentrale Westfalen/Lippe GmbH v Hauptzollamt Paderborn Case 28/67 [1968] ECR 143.

Garland v British Rail Engineering Ltd Case 12/81 [1982] 2 All ER 402, [1983] 2 AC 751, ECJ and HL.

f   *Macarthys Ltd v Smith* Case 129/79 [1981] 1 All ER 111, [1981] QB 180, ECJ and CA.

Mercantile Group (Europe) AG v Aiyela [1994] 1 All ER 110, [1994] QB 366, CA.

Norwich Pharmacal Co v Customs and Excise Comrs [1973] 2 All ER 943, [1974] AC 133, HL.

NV Algemene Transport—en Expeditie Onderneming van Gend & Loos v Nederlandse
g   *administratie der belastingen* Case 26/62 [1963] ECR 1.

Oppenbaar Ministerie of the Netherlands v van Tiggele Case 82/77 [1978] ECR 25.

R v Secretary of State for Employment, ex p Seymour-Smith [1996] All ER (EC) 1, [1995] ICR 889, CA.

Shields v E Coomes (Holdings) Ltd [1979] 1 All ER 456, [1978] 1 WLR 1408, CA.

h   *Smith (W H) Do It All Ltd v Peterborough City Council, Payless DIY Ltd v Peterborough City Council* [1991] 4 All ER 193, [1991] 1 QB 304, DC.

Sotgiu v Deutsche Bundespost Case 152/73 [1974] ECR 153.

Tate Access Floors Inc v Boswell [1990] 3 All ER 303, [1991] Ch 512.

Thune v London Properties Ltd [1990] 1 All ER 972, [1990] 1 WLR 562, CA.

j   *United Norwest Co-operatives Ltd v Johnstone* [1994] CA Transcript 1482.

Wilson Vehicle Distributions Ltd v Colt Car Co Ltd [1984] BCLC 93.

Interlocutory appeals

By notice dated 9 August 1995 the plaintiffs, 81 of whom (including John Fitzgerald and Tom O'Regan) were Irish citizens resident in the Republic of Ireland, appealed from the order of Sir John Wood, sitting as a deputy judge of

the High Court in the Queen's Bench Division, made on 23 June 1995 requiring
them to provide security for the costs of the first defendant, Bryn Lloyd Williams,   *a*
in the sum of £100,000 within 14 days in respect of two actions (which were
subsequently consolidated) which they had brought against him and other
defendants, Doris Renate Williams, Art Investments Ltd, Saloschin
Establishment, Albert Mayer and Bank in Liechtenstein AG, claiming damages
for fraudulent misrepresentation and the recovery of sums allegedly belonging to   *b*
them. The plaintiffs also appealed from earlier orders of Sir John Wood made on
9 and 10 March 1995 discharging a Mareva injunction granted by Tuckey J on 13
September 1994 on the ground of non-disclosure, granting the first defendant
leave to draw on funds to which the plaintiffs had made a proprietary claim,
refusing to secure funds held by the sixth defendant for the fourth defendant and
as to the mode of trial. The facts are set out in the judgment of Sir Thomas   *c*
Bingham MR.

Peter Havey and *Andrew Fraser-Urquhart* (instructed by *Marrache & Co*) for the
    plaintiffs.
Andrew Macnab (instructed by the *Treasury Solicitor*) as amicus curiae.   *d*
The first defendant appeared in person.
The remaining defendants did not appear or were not represented.

Cur adv vult

e
20 December 1995. The following judgments were delivered.

SIR THOMAS BINGHAM MR. We have to resolve five main issues, all arising
out of interlocutory orders made by Sir John Wood sitting as a deputy judge of
the High Court in the Queen's Bench Division. Most of those issues (concerning   *f*
the discharge of a Mareva injunction on grounds of non-disclosure, leave given to
the first defendant to draw on funds to which the plaintiffs make a proprietary
claim, the securing of funds held by the sixth for the fourth defendant and the
mode of trial) turn very largely on the facts of the case and raise no question of
general legal importance. One of the issues (concerning the ordering of security
against plaintiffs ordinarily resident outside England and Wales but within a   *g*
member state of the European Union) raises a legal question of general
significance.

The facts
    There are (we are told) 87 plaintiffs in these two consolidated actions. All   *h*
except six of them are Irish citizens ordinarily resident in Ireland. Their common
link is that all claim to have been victims of a fraud perpetrated by the first
defendant, who alone is the respondent to the appeals and application before us.
In the first instance, these proceedings were issued against him alone; the other
defendants were added later.   *j*
    Of these additional defendants, the second defendant is the first defendant's
wife; the third defendant is an Irish company owned and controlled by the first
defendant and now in liquidation; the fourth defendant is a Liechtenstein
establishment owned or controlled by the first defendant and now in liquidation;
the fifth defendant, a Liechtenstein lawyer, was the trustee and is now the
liquidator of the fourth defendant; and the sixth defendant is a Liechtenstein bank

a   at which the fourth defendant had an account into which money emanating from the plaintiffs was paid.

Among the plaintiffs in the actions are two (Mr Willcox and Mr Murray) whose roles are rather different from all the other plaintiffs. They were agents working in Ireland for a life assurance company and had in that capacity acquired a clientele. During 1992 the first defendant invited Willcox and Murray to act as

b   selling agents of a limited edition of prints of original works of art. The distinctive feature of this scheme (described in the action as Scheme I) was that buyers, or investors as they were called, would have the right to sell their prints back to the third defendant after one year for a guaranteed profit of 14·3%. For reasons which are not at present clear, Scheme I was aborted.

It was followed by Scheme II, which related to works of art said to form part

c   of what was called the Saloschin Collection. The Saloschin Collection was said to include, among other works, original works by German expressionist artists, removed from that country shortly before the 1939–45 war. They had been collected by the father of a gentleman who lived in Oxfordshire under the name of George Saunders but who also bore the French title Vicomte Drevelle du

d   Frenes and the Brazilian title Marques von Saloschin. An exhibition of these German expressionist works had been touring a number of American colleges since 1991. They were said to have been valued at about £IR2m. The essence of Scheme II was the sale of complete sets of reproductions of these German expressionist works, the inducement being a profit of 100% obtainable on resale of the edition. A number of buyers agreed to buy sets of these prints, for which

e   they paid in advance.

Scheme II was followed by Scheme III. Scheme III related not to the German expressionist works which had been included in the travelling exhibition in the United States but to 26 original paintings by old masters which were part of the Saloschin Collection. These paintings were said to have been authenticated by

f   an expert art historian in London. The essence of the scheme was very simple. Willcox and Murray would buy the 26 old masters and 100 sets of the Scheme II prints from the fourth defendant for $US5·25m and would resell to Malaysian buyers for $US10·5m. Willcox and Murray were to raise the purchase price of $US5·25m by soliciting subscriptions from investors, who would receive payment of 180% of the sum subscribed when the onward sale to the Malaysians

g   was completed. The first defendant said that he had himself paid £851,948 to the fourth defendant as a deposit on the purchase price to secure the purchase of the works.

None of the Scheme II investors ever received any of the German expressionist reproductions. Some of them asked for their money back, which they received

h   with a profit of 100% added. The great majority asked that their Scheme II subscriptions should be treated as subscriptions to Scheme III; they were accordingly treated as Scheme III subscribers and credited with subscriptions of twice what they had subscribed under Scheme II, the addition representing their 100% profit.

j   Pursuant to Scheme III, Willcox and Murray made agreements to buy the old masters and the prints from the fourth defendant and resell them to Malaysian buyers at the prices mentioned. They also raised nearly £2m by way of original subscription and transferred subscription (including the notional profit which was credited to Scheme II subscribers).

Scheme III was never carried through. Doubts were raised about the authenticity of the German expressionist works touring the United States, which were impounded by the police. A professional valuation of the old masters showed them to be worth a very small fraction of their previous alleged valuation and cast doubt on their provenance.

The very greatly simplified narrative set out above represents the plaintiffs' version of events. It is not accepted by the first defendant, who claims to be a victim, not a perpetrator, of fraud. The court has not investigated the facts and cannot express any view, even a provisional view, on where the truth lies. But it has never been suggested that the plaintiffs' account does not disclose an arguable case of fraud.

On 11 and 16 May 1994 the writs in these actions were issued. Apart from Willcox and Murray, the plaintiffs are those who subscribed to Scheme III. Their complaint is that representations said to have been made by the first defendant to Willcox and Murray and passed on by them to these plaintiffs were fraudulent, and that they were in the result cheated out of the sums which they subscribed. They claim damages for fraudulent misrepresentation, and also equitable tracing remedies in relation to the sums which they subscribed. None of these plaintiffs makes any claim against Willcox and Murray. Instead, Willcox and Murray themselves seek relief as a result of the fraud of which they claim to have been the unwitting instrument.

On 18 May 1994 the High Court in Dublin, on the application of 55 plaintiffs (including Willcox and Murray) and on reading two affidavits of Murray, made an order freezing the proceeds of a forthcoming sale of the premises in Dublin occupied by the third defendant. After that order Murray on 2 June 1994 swore an affidavit in the Irish proceedings on which the narrative summary given above is based. On 3 July 1994 Mr Ensor, a Dublin solicitor acting for the first defendant, swore an affidavit in the Irish proceedings. There is an unresolved dispute whether this affidavit (the Ensor affidavit) was served on the plaintiffs' Irish solicitors. It was a short, two page, affidavit which made two points: first, that the Dublin premises occupied by the third defendant were owned not by the first defendant but by a pension fund; and secondly, that the first defendant would strenuously contest the allegations of wrongdoing made against him. On 11 July 1994 the High Court in Dublin continued its earlier order and in addition ordered the first defendant on affidavit to disclose his assets in Ireland and all documents relating to them. In response to this order the first defendant swore an affidavit on 5 August 1994 (the Irish discovery affidavit). In this affidavit the first defendant deposed, so far as relevant, (a) that his majority shareholding in the third defendant was held as bare trustee for Saunders, (b) that he had a 25% interest in the proceeds of the sale by Willcox and Murray of the Scheme III old masters and prints, and (c) that the premises referred to above were owned by a pension fund of which the first defendant was a trustee and a potential beneficiary but in which he held no personal beneficial interest.

On 13 September 1994 the plaintiffs in both these actions applied to Tuckey J for the grant of a worldwide Mareva injunction against the first defendant. The application was made ex parte and was supported by an affidavit of Willcox, who exhibited and verified both the proposed statements of claim in the actions and the Irish affidavit of Murray. The judge gave leave to amend the writs, ordered that the two actions be consolidated and granted the injunction sought. This injunction was continued by consent, subject to some variations, on 23 September 1994, pending a proposed application to discharge. The first and second defendants applied to discharge the Mareva injunction on 27 September 1994.

On 10 March 1995 Sir John Wood discharged the Mareva injunction granted
a by Tuckey J as against the first defendant on the ground that the plaintiffs had not
made proper disclosure when applying for the order, but he replaced that
injunction with a more limited order applying to certain of the first defendant's
assets. The assets so restrained did not include a house in Hertfordshire said to
have been bought with moneys emanating from the plaintiffs.

b
Issue (1): non-disclosure
In seeking ex parte relief an applicant must disclose to the judge any fact known
to him which might affect the judge's decision whether to grant relief or what
relief to grant. It is no answer for an applicant who falls down on his duty to show
that his breach of duty was committed in good faith and inadvertently, or to show
c that the relief would have been granted even had he complied with his duty. The
courts have traditionally insisted on strict compliance with this rule, as affording
essential protection to an absent defendant, and as applications for ex parte relief
have multiplied so the importance of complying with this duty has grown. The
law does not however *require* a judge to whom an application for discharge is
d made to grant that relief on proof that there was material which should have been
but had not been disclosed to the original judge. The later judge has then to
exercise his own judgment whether, in all the circumstances, the interests of
justice are best served by discharging, or maintaining, or varying the original
order. In making this judgment he will have regard to the importance of securing
compliance with the fundamental principle, but he will have regard also to the
e significance in the context of the particular case of the facts which had not been
disclosed when they should have been. Sir John Wood was reminded of
well-known authorities establishing these principles and made reference to them
in judgments given on 16 February and 7 March 1995. I do not think it necessary
to discuss these authorities since the principles are not in my view open to
f question.

The judge's main reason for discharging Tuckey J's order was that the plaintiffs
had failed when making their application to disclose the Ensor affidavit. This
failure, he held, had led Tuckey J to regard the plaintiffs' claim as open and shut,
a claim to which there was no defence. He should have known, and it might have
affected his mind had he known, that the plaintiffs' claim was to be strenuously
g resisted. The judge acquitted the plaintiffs' Irish solicitors (who were, it
appeared, responsible for a failure of communication with their English counter-
parts) of any impropriety; but he held that their innocent error justified discharge
of the order.

Giving, as I hope, appropriate weight to the assessment of the case made by
h this very experienced judge after a long hearing, I cannot share his view. The
plaintiffs' case deployed before Tuckey J presented, on its face (and that
qualification is very important), a formidable case of deliberate fraud by the first
defendant. Tuckey J may well have wondered whether the facts deposed to, if
true, permitted of any innocent explanation, but he was not told that the case was
j open and shut or that it would be undefended, and he would well know from
experience that the first defendant would in all probability challenge the plaintiffs'
version of the facts and resist the very large claim made against him. Had Tuckey
J been told of the first defendant's intention strenuously to resist the claim, it
would, in the absence of any particularised rebuttal, have affected his mind not at
all. This was not a ground of non-disclosure on which the first defendant initially
relied in seeking discharge; it emerged during the hearing as a result of the judge's

questions. In my view this non-disclosure afforded no adequate ground for *a* discharging the injunction in all the circumstances.

The judge also relied, but to a much lesser extent, on non-disclosure of the first defendant's Irish discovery affidavit. The plaintiffs accept in this court that this affidavit was material to the risk of dissipation, which was of course an issue which Tuckey J had to consider. In my view it was, at best, technically so, since in this affidavit the first defendant had in effect disclaimed beneficial ownership *b* of any asset in Ireland. He had thrown no light at all on where the money received from the plaintiffs had gone. Had this affidavit been drawn to the notice of Tuckey J, I do not see how it could have affected his mind, save perhaps by strengthening his suspicions.

As presented to Tuckey J, this was in my opinion an archetypal case calling for injunctive relief and would have been so even if the Ensor affidavit and the first *c* defendant's Irish discovery affidavit had been disclosed to him and even if the other factual points argued on the application for discharge and before this court had been raised before him. Justice to the plaintiffs required that assets held by the first defendant be preserved pending a decision on the merits, subject to such terms as justice to the first defendant required. In my view the judge was wrong *d* to discharge Tuckey J's order.

Issue (2): the plaintiffs' proprietary claim

This issue is the subject of an appeal and an application for leave to appeal.

The plaintiffs' point is in essence very simple. It is (1) that they have a legal and equitable proprietary claim to the funds advanced by them on the strength of *e* fraudulent misrepresentations made by the first defendant and his agents and to assets representing the proceeds of such funds; and (2) that any sums drawn by the first defendant with the leave of the court for living or legal or business expenses should in the first instance be drawn from funds frozen by the court in the exercise of its Mareva jurisdiction and not from funds which the court has *f* ordered to be preserved pending determination of a dispute as to the ownership of such funds.

I do not understand the legal arguability of stage (1) of this argument to be challenged if the plaintiffs make good the facts they assert. But since the first defendant appeared in person before us, counsel for the plaintiffs rehearsed the legal basis of his claim, referring us to Goff and Jones *The Law of Restitution* (4th *g* edn, 1993) p 75ff, *Banque Belge pour L'Etranger v Hambrouck* [1921] 1 KB 321, *Bankers Trust Co v Shapira* [1980] 3 All ER 353, [1980] 1 WLR 1274 and *El Ajou v Dollar Land Holdings plc* [1994] 2 All ER 685. I am left in no doubt but that the plaintiffs' claim, whether ultimately held to be right or wrong, is arguable.

Stage (2) of the argument follows. A defendant should not be entitled to draw *h* on a fund which may belong to a plaintiff until he shows that there is no fund of his own on which he can draw. Where he shows that he has no funds of his own on which he can draw, the court must make a difficult decision, as explained by this court in *Sundt Wrigley & Co Ltd v Wrigley* [1993] CA Transcript 685. But the plaintiffs may very well be right in contending that that stage has not yet been *j* reached in this case. The judge was, I think, wrong not to accept both limbs of the plaintiffs' argument at this interlocutory stage.

On this point I would grant leave to appeal and allow both appeals. The plaintiffs are in my view right to contend that unless and until the first defendant can establish on proper evidence that there are no funds or assets available to him to be utilised for payment of his legal fees and other legitimate expenses, other a than assets to which the plaintiffs maintain an arguable proprietary claim, he should not be allowed to draw on the latter type of assets.

The first defendant argued before us that he was being denied funds needed for the conduct of his defence. This may or may not be so. But the principles are clear. If the first defendant can make a case for the release of additional funds to him, he should make an appropriate application to the judge.

b
Issue (3): securing of funds held by the sixth defendant

The plaintiffs seek an order that the first defendant do instruct the fifth defendant irrevocably to instruct the sixth defendant to undertake to the plaintiffs, alternatively to the High Court of Justice in London, to hold all moneys standing to the credit of the fourth defendant's account with the sixth defendant

c to the order of the court. This order differs from the order sought from Sir John Wood, who dismissed the application made to him.

The plaintiffs rest their case on the propositions: (1) that they have an arguable proprietary claim to the fund held by the sixth defendant to the order of the fourth defendant; (2) that the sixth defendant will comply with the directions of

d the fifth defendant; (3) that the fifth defendant will comply with instructions of the first defendant; and (4) that justice demands the preservation of this fund pending resolution of the issues in this action.

For reasons already given, (1) is arguably correct. It would seem very likely that (2) is correct. The evidence suggests that (3) is correct. I would accept argument (4). There is in my judgment jurisdiction to make the order sought.

e I would allow the plaintiffs' appeal and make the order as asked.

Issue (4): mode of trial

On 23 June 1995 Sir John Wood ordered that this consolidated action be tried by a judge and jury. He held, quite correctly, that since the plaintiffs' charge against the first defendant was one of fraud the first defendant was entitled to an

f order for trial with a jury unless the court was of opinion that the trial required any prolonged examination of documents or accounts which could not conveniently be made with a jury. The judge was not, on the material before him, of that opinion, so his order followed.

The order made by the judge may well turn out to be correct, but I do not feel

g able at this stage to hold that it is. There has not as yet been anything approaching full discovery. It is unclear how much documentation will have to be considered. It is, however, possible that tracing the money subscribed by the plaintiffs may call for prolonged examination of documents and accounts, as may any issue relating to the provenance and history and authenticity of the Saloschin

h Collection. It is in my judgment premature to make any decision on the mode of trial.

I would allow the plaintiffs' appeal and make no order save that the mode of trial be determined hereafter on application duly made.

Issue (5): security for costs

j On 23 June 1995 Sir John Wood ordered that the plaintiffs give security for the first defendant's costs in the sum of £100,000 within 14 days. He made his order under RSC Ord 23, r 1(1), which (so far as relevant) provides:

'Where, on the application of a defendant to an action or other proceeding in the High Court, it appears to the Court—(a) that the plaintiff is ordinarily resident out of the jurisdiction ... then if, having regard to all the

circumstances of the case, the Court thinks it just to do so, it may order the *a*
plaintiff to give such security for the defendant's costs of the action or other
proceeding as it thinks just.'

This will hereafter be referred to as 'the rule'.

One of the plaintiffs in the action is ordinarily resident in England. She is not
on any showing liable to give security. Plainly the judge overlooked her special *b*
position. But it is not her position which lies at the heart of this appeal.

Of the remaining 86 plaintiffs, one is resident in New York, one in Canada,
three in the Isle of Man and 81 in the Republic of Ireland. The primary question
which now arises concerns these Irish plaintiffs. The question is whether they
have rights in Community law which this court must respect by holding that it
has no jurisdiction to make an order for security against them or, if it continues *c*
to have jurisdiction, by refraining from the exercise of its discretion to make an
order against them.

This is by no means the first time that the English courts have had occasion to
consider this question. But in view of its importance, and because the first
defendant was unrepresented, we asked the Attorney General to instruct an *d*
amicus. This he duly did and we are grateful for the assistance which Mr Andrew
Macnab has given.

In *Porzelack KG v Porzelack (UK) Ltd* [1987] 1 All ER 1074, [1987] 1 WLR 420 an
English company sued here by a German company sought an order for security
under the rule. By this time the Civil Jurisdiction and Judgments Act 1982, giving *e*
effect to the Brussels Convention on Jurisdiction and Enforcement of Judgments
in Civil and Commercial Matters (set out in Sch 1 to the 1982 Act), had been
brought into force. Under the convention a judgment in any contracting state
must be recognised in any other without any special procedure being required.
All member states of the Community are parties to the convention. Browne-
Wilkinson V-C did not understand the 1982 Act to deprive him of jurisdiction to *f*
make an order for security against a national of a member state ordinarily
resident in a member state other than the United Kingdom, nor did he regard the
convention as a conclusive factor against making an order in such a case. But he
regarded the ease of enforcement for which the convention provided as an
important matter of which full account should be taken in deciding whether to
order security or not, and on the facts he made no order. *g*

In *De Bry v Fitzgerald* (1988) [1990] 1 All ER 560, [1990] 1 WLR 552 the judge
ordered a plaintiff resident in France to give security under the rule. The plaintiff
appealed. His first two grounds were that the judge had wrongly failed to take
account of a source of funds available to the plaintiff within this jurisdiction and
that the judge had wrongly discounted the relative ease of enforcing judgments *h*
as between member states parties to the convention. All members of the court
upheld the second of these grounds; Lord Donaldson of Lymington MR upheld
the first also. That made it unnecessary for the court to consider a third ground,
that the rule contravened art 7 of the EEC Treaty (now art 6 of the EC Treaty)
because it discriminated against nationals of other member states. Lord *j*
Donaldson MR did however recommend urgent review of the rule: he had in
mind that it should be amended to reflect its rationale, that a defendant should be
entitled to security if there was reason to believe that in the event of his
succeeding and being awarded costs he would have real difficulty in enforcing
that order. Lord Donaldson MR envisaged that security could be ordered if
a plaintiff so arranged his affairs as to make enforcement very difficult or

a impossible. On this basis there would be no discrimination based on nationality or residence but a rule based on the need to administer justice effectively.

This decision was followed by *Berkeley Administration Inc v McClelland* [1990] 1 All ER 958, [1990] 2 QB 407, in which defendants sued here sought security under the rule against plaintiff companies ordinarily resident in other member states, parties to the convention. The plaintiffs objected, and the deputy judge at first

b instance accepted that art 7 of the Treaty precluded the making of such an order, which he would otherwise have made. The defendants' appeal was successful. Parker and Russell LJJ rested their judgments on the conclusion that since the rule related to residence and not nationality it did not discriminate, even covertly, on the grounds of nationality and so did not offend against art 7. Staughton LJ reached the same destination but by a different route. He held that a provision

c (such as the rule) directed at those not ordinarily resident here was tantamount in its practical effect to a provision directed at nationals of other countries or principally affected nationals of other countries. But he then considered whether the different treatment for which the rule provided was objectively justifiable and concluded that the conferment of a discretion was objectively justifiable. His

d preferred conclusion was that there was no discrimination under the rule since there was no different treatment which was not objectively justified.

We have been asked to reconsider this line of authority in the light of *Mund & Fester v Hatrex Internationaal Transport* Case C-398/92 [1994] ECR I-467. The facts of that case were these. Hatrex was an international carrier based in the Netherlands. It carried goods on behalf of a German principal, which were

e damaged in transit in Germany. The German principal assigned its rights to Mund. Mund applied to the Landesgericht in Hamburg for an order of seizure against the Hatrex lorry used for the transport, which was still in Germany. The application was made under para 917 of the German Code of Civil Procedure (the ZPO), which provided:

f '(1) An order for the seizure of assets shall be made when it is to be feared that enforcement of the judgment would otherwise be made impossible or substantially more difficult.

(2) The fact that judgment is to be enforced abroad shall be considered sufficient grounds for a seizure order.'

g Mund's application for a seizure order was dismissed because the Landesgericht held para 917(2) to be no longer applicable to the enforcement of judgments in states which were party to the convention. Mund accordingly appealed to the Hanseatisches Oberlandesgericht, which made a reference to the Court of Justice of the European Communities under art 177. The question was whether

h para 917(2), in authorising seizure even if enforcement was to take place in a country which was party to the convention, was contrary to the prohibition of discrimination laid down by art 7 of the Treaty. That article (now art 6 of the EC Treaty), so far as relevant, provides:

j 'Within the scope of application of this Treaty, and without prejudice to any special provisions contained therein, any discrimination on grounds of nationality shall be prohibited.'

The conclusion reached by the court was ([1994] ECR I-467 at 481–482):

'Article 7 of the EEC Treaty, read in conjunction with Article 220 of the Treaty and the Brussels Convention of 27 September 1968 on Jurisdiction

and the Enforcement of Judgments in Civil and Commercial Matters,
precludes a national provision of civil procedure which, in the case of a
judgment to be enforced within national territory, authorizes seizure only
on the ground that it is probable that enforcement will otherwise be made
impossible or substantially more difficult, but, in the case of a judgment to
be enforced in another Member State, authorizes seizure simply on the
ground that enforcement is to take place abroad.'

En route to that conclusion the Court of Justice considered certain preliminary
issues. First, it considered whether para 917(2) fell within the ambit of the Treaty.
It held, agreeing with Advocate General Tesauro, that it did (see [1994] ECR I-467
at 478 (para 12)). It then asked whether para 917(2) entailed a covert form of
discrimination. Again agreeing with the Advocate General, it concluded that it
did, because while a judgment to be enforced abroad might be against a German
national—

'the latter situation is rare, the great majority of enforcements abroad
being against persons who are not of German nationality or against legal
persons not established in the Federal Republic of Germany. It follows that
the national provision in question leads in fact to the same result as
discrimination based on nationality.' (See [1994] ECR I-467 at 479 (para 16).)

The court then considered whether para 917(2) could be justified by objective
circumstances, and once again agreed with the Advocate General. It accepted
that a presumption of difficulty in enforcing a judgment in a non-member
country was legitimate, but held that such a presumption was not justified where
enforcement was to take place in a member state party to the convention ([1994]
ECR I-467 at 480):

'20. Consequently, although the conditions for enforcing judgments and
the risks attached to the difficulties raised by enforcement are the same in all
the Member States, Paragraph 917(2) of the ZPO in essence considers those
risks and difficulties to be sure and certain solely because enforcement will
take place in the territory of a Member State other than Germany.
21. It follows that the national provision is not justified by objective
circumstances.'

In the light of *Mund* (see also *Hubbard v Hamburger* Case C-20/92 [1993] ECR
I-3777, which is entirely consistent with *Mund*) I can turn to consider the questions which arise in this case.
(i) Does the rule fall within the scope of the Treaty provisions?
The answer must be affirmative. It is true that para 917(2) relates to security
for a future judgment and the rule relates to security for further costs of litigation,
but I cannot think that this factual distinction could be held to support a
difference of principle between them. Both provisions look towards a future
judgment, for compensation in one case, for reimbursement of the costs of
litigation in the other. The same legal rule must in my view govern both.
(ii) Do arts 6 and 220 of the EC Treaty confer rights directly enforceable in
member states following legislative implementation of the convention?
Again the answer must be affirmative. *Mund* clearly proceeded on that basis.
(iii) Is the rule discriminatory?
The rule plainly empowers the court to make orders against plaintiffs
ordinarily resident out of the jurisdiction which it could not make against

a plaintiffs ordinarily resident within it. (The special position of plaintiffs ordinarily resident in Scotland and Northern Ireland does not call for consideration here.) It therefore involves discrimination in the sense used by the Court of Justice in *Mund*, in that different plaintiffs are treated differently.

(iv) Is that discrimination based on nationality?

b On its face, the discrimination for which the rule provides is based on ordinary residence, not nationality. A British national ordinarily resident abroad may be required to give security, a foreign national ordinarily resident within the jurisdiction may not. But there is a close analogy with *Mund*: just as most German judgments to be enforced outside Germany would not be against Germans, so most plaintiffs in England ordinarily resident outside the jurisdiction c would not be British. Just as para 917(2) was held to be covertly discriminatory on grounds of nationality, so must the same conclusion follow in relation to the rule.

(v) Is such discrimination on grounds of nationality justified by objective circumstances in relation to those who are nationals of and resident in other member states parties to the convention?

d Paragraph 917(2) gave effect to an irrebuttable presumption that a judgment would be impossible or substantially more difficult to enforce if it was to be enforced outside Germany. *Mund* is clear authority for the proposition that such a presumption is repugnant to the Treaty in so far as it applies where enforcement is to be in another member state party to the convention.

e The rule differs from para 917 in two important respects: first, it contains no explicit presumption that a judgment will be more difficult to enforce abroad; secondly, it does not impose an obligation on the court to make an order where the condition for making an order is satisfied but confers a discretion. Since, however, if the foregoing reasoning is correct, a plaintiff suing in England, who f is a national of and resident in another member state party to the convention, has a Community right which a national court must protect not to be the subject of discrimination on grounds of nationality, it is necessary to ask whether any modification of English law or practice is called for to protect that right. The answer compelled by *Mund* in my view is: the English court should never exercise its discretion under the rule to order security to be given by an individual plaintiff g who is a national of and resident in another member state party to the convention, at any rate in the absence of very cogent evidence of substantial difficulty in enforcing a judgment in that other member state.

It is unnecessary for purposes of this appeal to form any view whether the qualification just expressed is sound in Community law or not. The Court of h Justice may well have contemplated that there could never be significantly greater difficulty enforcing a judgment in one member state rather than another since it regarded the Community as 'a single entity', and it may be that enforcement action under the Treaty would be the appropriate response to any failure by a member state to give full practical effect to the convention. On the j other hand, there was no suggestion in *Mund* that there was any difficulty enforcing in the Netherlands, so the question did not arise. The question may have to be addressed when and as it arises, perhaps with the benefit of a reference to the Court of Justice. But the question does not arise in this case either. The evidence is not that enforcement in Ireland is difficult, but rather that it presents no difficulty. It follows, in my view, that no order for security should have been made against the Irish plaintiffs.

Nothing in this judgment bears on the case in which security is sought against   *a*
a foreign insolvent company, whether resident in a member state or not. Nor is
it suggested that the traditional practice of the English court requires any
modification where the plaintiff is ordinarily resident in a country which is not a
member of the Community.

The appeal of the Irish plaintiffs and of the single English plaintiff must be
allowed and the order for security made against them set aside. We have   *b*
considered whether the order should stand, or any varied order be made, against
the New York, Canadian and Manx plaintiffs who are, we are told, substantially
financing this litigation. I conclude that no order should be made against them.

(i) There are, it appears, sufficient assets held by the Irish plaintiffs. It might
not be easy for the first defendant to ascertain which of the Irish plaintiffs own
these assets, but that is a difficulty the first defendant would face even if all the   *c*
plaintiffs were ordinarily resident within the jurisdiction.

(ii) It would not be just to order the New York, Canadian and Manx plaintiffs
to give security for more than a proportionate share of the first defendant's costs.
But where there is sufficient security within the jurisdiction, and the assets of the
Irish plaintiffs must for present purposes be treated as if they were within the   *d*
jurisdiction, the court has discouraged orders against plaintiffs ordinarily resident
outside the jurisdiction on an aliquot basis (see *Slazengers Ltd v Seaspeed Ferries
International Ltd* [1987] 3 All ER 967, [1988] 1 WLR 221 and *Corfu Navigation Co v
Mobil Shipping Co Ltd, The Alpha* [1991] 2 Lloyd's Rep 52). I would accordingly set
aside the judge's order in its entirety.

The first defendant has complained that Tuckey J should have ordered the   *e*
plaintiffs to give security for their undertaking in damages. This point is not the
subject of an appeal by the first defendant (although it was relied on as another
reason why the Mareva injunction should not have been granted), and we have
no detailed particulars of the loss which the first defendant may have suffered or
may suffer as a result of the injunction made against him. But I have considerable   *f*
sympathy with the substance of this complaint. The case is one in which security
of this kind might well be thought appropriate. This is, however, a matter for
decision by the judge if and when application is made.

We would ask counsel for the plaintiffs to prepare an appropriate minute of
order.
                                                                                    g

WAITE LJ. I agree with the judgment of Sir Thomas Bingham MR and support
his conclusions for all the reasons that he gives. I do not wish to add anything.

OTTON LJ. I have had the advantage of reading in draft the judgment of Sir
Thomas Bingham MR with which I agree, and wish only to add a few   *h*
observations by way of emphasis.

On the question of non-disclosure, I am not satisfied that, had Tuckey J been
informed of the existence or contents of the affidavit of Mr Ensor, he would have
come to a different decision and refused to grant a Mareva injunction or in the
form that he did. Mr Ensor deposed merely that the first defendant would be   *j*
contesting the plaintiffs' claim for interlocutory relief in the Irish proceedings.
Even if this were a material fact (which I doubt), in my judgment, it was not of
sufficient substance or significance to justify withholding ex parte interlocutory
relief in the English proceedings.

As to the proprietary claim, I am similarly satisfied that the first defendant has
not yet established that there are no 'clean' assets available to him for the conduct

a of his defence and his legitimate expenses which would enable the court to release part of the proprietary funds for this purpose. Given that the plaintiffs have an arguable claim to the proprietary fund and that justice requires the fund to be preserved pending the outcome of the action (in my view) it follows that the plaintiffs are entitled to an order requiring the first defendant to instruct the fifth defendant, in turn, to instruct the sixth defendant to hold the moneys in the b fourth defendant's account in the terms sought.

Turning to the security of costs which concerns primarily the 81 plaintiffs resident in the Republic of Ireland, I have come to the conclusion that the reasoning of the majority of this court in *Berkeley Administration Inc v McClelland* [1990] 1 All ER 958, [1990] 2 QB 407 can no longer stand following the decision of the Court of Justice of the European Communities in *Mund & Fester v Hatrex* c *Internationaal Transport* Case C-398/92 [1994] ECR I-467. In essence, the majority view was that RSC Ord 23, r 1(1)(a) is not discriminatory on grounds of nationality because it is expressly based on residence which does not fall within the ambit of art 7 of the EEC Treaty (now art 6 of the EC Treaty). The article provides, so far as material:

d
'Within the scope of application of this Treaty, and without prejudice to any special provisions contained therein, any discrimination on the ground of nationality shall be prohibited.'

e This article was considered by the Court of Justice in *Mund*. The manner in which that court approached the issue has already been analysed by Sir Thomas Bingham MR. Although the provision in question was not based on residence, the reasoning in *Mund* establishes unequivocally, in my view, that a national provision dealing with enforcement of judgments which is founded on criteria which may affect nationals of European Union member states is capable of f amounting to covert discrimination on grounds of nationality for the purpose of art 7 and, I would add, by implication, the right to establishment under art 52 (see *R v Secretary of State for Transport, ex p Factortame Ltd* Case C-221/89 [1991] 3 All ER 769 at 814, [1992] QB 680 at 735–736 and *R v IRC, ex p Commerzbank AG* Case C-330/91 [1993] 4 All ER 37 at 56, [1994] QB 219 at 239).

g It follows that if a national provision operates to affect principally nationals from member states to their disadvantage in comparison with nationals of the legislating state (even if it may affect nationals of the legislating state) it will be held to be covert discrimination contrary to art 6 unless it can be objectively justified. In my view, Ord 23, r 1(1)(a) does so operate and there is no basis of fact in this case which would permit this court to hold that the provision can be h objectively justified and applied on the ground of difficulty of enforcement.

Thus the English court is bound to follow the Court of Justice jurisprudence: art 6 is directly applicable and Ord 23, r 1(1)(a), in so far as it confers jurisdiction to order security for costs against the Irish plaintiffs, must be disapplied.

j *Appeals allowed.*

L I Zysman Esq   Barrister.

Nelson v Rye and another

a

CHANCERY DIVISION

LADDIE J

24–27, 30–31 OCTOBER, 1, 21 NOVEMBER 1995

b

Limitation of action – Trust property – Breach of fiduciary duty to account – Plaintiff musician bringing action against business manager to account for income – Whether cause of action in contract or breach of fiduciary duty to recover property under constructive trust – Applicable limitation period – Limitation Act 1980, s 21(1)(b).

c

Equity – Laches – Defence – Availability – Plaintiff musician bringing action against business manager to account for income received over ten-year period – Plaintiff not having previously requested account or attended meetings to discuss financial position – Whether delay in commencing proceedings unreasonable – Whether delay prejudicial to defendant – Factors relevant to exercise of court's discretion.

d

Between 1980 and 1990 the plaintiff musician retained the defendant as his manager to administer and organise his business affairs pursuant to an oral agreement under which it was agreed that the defendant would receive 20% of the plaintiff's income and would account to him at regular intervals. In fact no account was ever requested or provided. In October 1990 the defendant terminated his business relationship with the plaintiff, and in December 1991 the plaintiff issued a writ against him, seeking, inter alia, an account of the moneys received by the defendant during the ten-year period in which he managed the plaintiff's affairs. Prior to the trial of the action, the plaintiff obtained summary orders for accounts. At the trial of the outstanding claims, the defendant raised two defences in respect of the duty to account for the period prior to December f 1985: (i) that the statutory limitation period for contractual causes of action applied to render the plaintiff's action relating to that period out of time and (ii) that, pursuant to the equitable doctrine of laches and acquiescence, the plaintiff's delay in commencing proceedings was unreasonable and prejudicial to the defendant so as to constitute a complete defence to that part of the action. In response, the plaintiff contended that his cause of action was not contractual but g rather for breach of fiduciary duty and accordingly outside the Limitation Act 1980, or alternatively for breach of trust, in which case no statutory limitation period applied by virtue of s 21(1)(b)[a] of the 1980 Act, which provided, inter alia, that no period of limitation prescribed by the Act applied to an action by a beneficiary of a trust to recover trust property from the trustee.

h

Held – (1) An action for breach of fiduciary duty simpliciter was outside the provisions of the 1980 Act and therefore not subject to a period of limitation; but where a breach of fiduciary duty gave rise to a constructive trust, s 21 of the 1980 Act applied to determine whether there was an applicable limitation period and j its duration. An action for breach of an express trust was, in like manner, subject to the limitation provisions of s 21, and in neither case was it possible to avoid any limitation period imposed by the Act by treating the case as one of breach of fiduciary duty. On the facts, there was no dispute that the defendant was under

---

a   Section 21, so far as material, is set out at p 195 *c*, post

a a fiduciary duty to the plaintiff to account annually; he did not do so and was therefore in breach of that duty, and while not every fiduciary relationship gave rise to a constructive trust, the one at issue had done so. The defendant had received the plaintiff's income, which was trust property; the balance left after all proper deductions was also trust property and the plaintiff's action was an action to recover that property. It followed that no limitation period applied, either b because the cause of action was outwith the 1980 Act, or because it fell squarely within s 21(1)(b) (see p 198 *g* to p 199 *d h j*, post); *A-G v Cocke* [1988] 2 All ER 391 applied.

(2) The equitable doctrine of laches and acquiescence was not technical or arbitrary and, as such, the court would determine the availability of the defences by considering the circumstances of the particular case, including the period of c delay, the extent to which the defendant's position had been prejudiced by the delay, and the extent to which the prejudice was caused by the actions of the plaintiff. In the circumstances, there had been an unreasonable delay in the commencement of the proceedings, largely due to the plaintiff's wilful refusal to involve himself in his financial affairs, with the result that it would be d unreasonable and unjust to allow the plaintiff to assert his right to an account against the defendant for the period prior to December 1985. It followed that the defences of laches and acquiescence were made out in respect of the plaintiff's claim for accounts for that period (see p 201 *c d*, p 203 *b* to *h* and p 204 *c* to *g*, post).

Notes

e For limitation of actions in respect of trust property in general, see 28 *Halsbury's Laws* (4th edn) paras 833–841, and for cases on the subject, see 32(2) *Digest* (2nd reissue) 408–418, *3094–3150*.

For the Limitation Act 1980, s 21, see 24 *Halsbury's Statutes* (4th edn) (1989 reissue) 671.

f

Cases referred to in judgment

A-G for Hong Kong v Reid [1994] 1 All ER 1, [1994] 1 AC 324, [1993] 3 WLR 1143, PC.

A-G v Cocke [1988] 2 All ER 391, [1988] Ch 414, [1988] 2 WLR 542.

AKCO Music and Records Inc v Music Collection International Ltd [1995] RPC 657.
g *Burdick v Garrick* (1870) LR 5 Ch App 233.

Erlanger v New Sombrero Phosphate Co (1878) 3 App Cas 1218, [1874–80] All ER Rep 271, HL.

Infabrics Ltd v Jaytex Ltd [1981] 1 All ER 1057, [1982] AC 1, [1981] 2 WLR 646, HL.

Lazard Bros & Co v Fairfield Properties Co (Mayfair) Ltd (1977) Times, 13 October.
h *Lindsay Petroleum Co v Hurd* (1874) LR 5 PC 221.

North American Land and Timber Co v Watkins [1904] 1 Ch 242.

Soar v Ashwell [1893] 2 QB 390, [1891–4] All ER Rep 991, CA.

Tito v Waddell (No 2), Tito v A-G [1977] 3 All ER 129, [1977] Ch 106, [1977] 2 WLR 496.
j *United Australia Ltd v Barclays Bank Ltd* [1940] 4 All ER 20, [1941] AC 1, HL.

Cases also cited or referred to in skeleton arguments

Archbold v Scully (1861) 9 HL Cas 360, 11 ER 769.
Brown v IRC [1964] 3 All ER 119, [1965] AC 244, HL.
Chan v Zachariah (1984) 154 CLR 178, Aust HC.

Dorling v Honnor Marine Ltd [1963] 2 All ER 495, [1964] Ch 560; *affd in part* [1964] *a*
    1 All ER 241, [1965] Ch 1, CA.
Godfrey v Lees [1995] EMLR 307.
Goldsworthy v Brickell [1987] 1 All ER 853, [1987] Ch 378, CA.
Guinness plc v Saunders [1990] 1 All ER 652, [1990] 2 AC 663, HL.
Healey v Healey [1915] 1 KB 938.
Henry v Hammond [1913] 2 KB 515, DC.   *b*
Howitt v Hall (1862) 6 LT 348.
International Factors Ltd v Rodriguez [1979] 1 All ER 17, [1979] QB 351, CA.
Jarvis (decd), Re, Edge v Jarvis [1958] 2 All ER 336, [1958] 1 WLR 815.
Life Association of Scotland v Siddal (1861) De G F & J 58, [1861–73] All ER Rep 892,
    45 ER 800, CA.   *c*
Mitchell v Ealing London BC [1978] 2 All ER 779, [1979] QB 1.
O'Sullivan v Management Agency and Music Ltd [1985] 3 All ER 351, [1985] QB 428,
    CA.
Stroud Architectural Systems Ltd v John Laing Construction Ltd [1994] 2 BCLC 276.
Tintin Exploration Syndicate Ltd v Sandys (1947) 177 LT 412.
Zang Tumb Tuum Records Ltd v Johnson [1993] EMLR 61, CA.   *d*

Action

By writ issued on 23 December 1991 the plaintiff, William Nelson, commenced
proceedings against the first and second defendants, Mark Rye and Cocteau
Records Ltd, seeking (i) an account of the moneys received by Mr Rye on behalf *e*
of Mr Nelson while acting as his business manager during the period August 1980
to October 1990, (ii) damages for infringement of the copyright in certain musical
compositions and (iii) delivery up of certain master recordings of Mr Nelson's
performances. Mr Rye counterclaimed for commission and expenses due and
owing from Mr Nelson. By order dated 19 May 1992 Master Dyson ordered an
account in respect of all moneys received by the defendants on behalf of Mr *f*
Nelson and by order dated 25 November 1993 he ordered a further and better
account. Cocteau Records was struck off the register in 1994 and took no part in
the action. The facts are set out in the judgment.

Robert Anderson (instructed by *Russells*) for Mr Nelson.   *g*
Robin Oppenheim (instructed by *John Byrne & Co*) for Mr Rye.

                                                        Cur adv vult

21 November 1995. The following judgment was delivered.
                                                                             h

LADDIE J. Mr William Nelson, the plaintiff in this action, is a popular musician.
From about 1972 to 1977 he was a member of a group called 'Be Pop Deluxe'.
From 1977 to 1980, he was a member of another group known as 'Bill Nelson's
Red Noise'. Since 1980 he has pursued his career as a solo musician. There are
two defendants named on the writ. The first, Mr Mark Rye, was Mr Nelson's *j*
manager from the second half of 1980 to late 1990. He was appointed pursuant
to an oral contract. The second defendant, Cocteau Records Ltd, was struck off
the register about a year ago. It is in fact the second company bearing that name.
The first (Cocteau 1) was incorporated on 27 November 1984 and was struck off
the register on 12 July 1988. The second defendant (Cocteau 2) was incorporated
on 17 November 1988.

a   From August 1980 onwards, Mr Rye ran Mr Nelson's affairs on the latter's behalf. The relationship between them gradually deteriorated in circumstances which I will touch upon later. On 2 October 1990 Mr Rye wrote to Mr Nelson terminating their business relationship. A month later, solicitors acting for Mr Nelson wrote to Mr Rye raising questions about the manner in which he had carried out his duties as a manager. The ensuing correspondence records a

b   widening of the gap between the parties. On 23 December 1991 the writ in this action was issued.

In these proceedings Mr Nelson seeks three types of relief. First he seeks an account of the moneys received by Mr Rye while acting as his manager. Secondly, he seeks relief in relation to alleged infringement of the copyright in certain musical compositions contained in an album called 'Simplex'. Thirdly, he

c   has sought delivery up by Mr Rye of certain master recordings of his performances which, at the date of the writ, were in Mr Rye's possession. There is also a counterclaim by Mr Rye for commission and expenses due and owing from Mr Nelson. It is not now in dispute that Mr Rye can raise these claims and I do not need to consider the counterclaim further.

d   It is convenient to mention here two other companies. As Mr Nelson said in his witness statement, during the oral discussions leading to the management contract, he and Mr Rye talked about setting up a new company to look after Mr Nelson's interests. That company was Happytronics Ltd. It was incorporated on 26 August 1980 a few days after the oral contract was made. Its function was to be the conduit through which all or substantially all of Mr Nelson's income and

e   business expenditure could be funnelled. Its two directors were Mr Nelson and Mr Rye. It was effectively the vehicle through which Mr Rye managed Mr Nelson's affairs until it was struck off the register on 30 March, 1993. The other company is Nelsongs Ltd. It was originally called Cant Eat Records. It changed its name to Nelsongs on 12 March 1982. Its purpose was to receive on Mr

f   Nelson's behalf his income from music publishing. It does not appear that there was any such income until the very end of 1984 at the earliest. It was struck off the register on 7 March 1989.

THE WITNESSES

g   In relation to many of the issues which have to be determined in this action, the primary source of evidence is the oral testimony of witnesses, relevant contemporaneous documents either never having existed or now no longer being traceable. Because of their importance, I think it is appropriate to consider at the outset the impact the witnesses made on me. Besides Mr Byrne, Mr Rye's solicitor, who gave purely formal evidence, three witnesses were called. Each of

h   them had served signed witness statements in advance. Mr Christopher Rowland Thomas is a chartered accountant. He was involved in doing accountancy work in relation to the affairs of Happytronics Ltd and the Cocteau 1 company for most of the period with which this dispute is concerned. He was called by the defence. He gave his evidence clearly and straightforwardly. I accept his evidence as being

j   truthful throughout. Mr Mark Rye also gave evidence. It was very apparent that he was hurt and disappointed that he had been sued by Mr Nelson. He explained how he had been a fan of Mr Nelson and even now respected his artistic talents. He felt that he had given his all to helping Mr Nelson, even to the extent of making significant financial sacrifices to keep Mr Nelson's head above water. Not surprisingly, he could not always recall with precision the details of what had happened 10 to 15 years ago. However, having observed him carefully in the

witness box, and having compared his version of events with such documents as
do still exist, I accept that all of his evidence, save possibly in relation to one minor
issue, was truthful. At one point Mr Nelson said that Mr Rye was telling 'fairy
stories' in relation to the issues in dispute and that '[Mr Rye] always told
deceptions and lies'. I reject those allegations. If Mr Nelson harboured those
feelings during the ten years of the relationship, he had no justification for doing
so.

The only witness called on behalf of the plaintiff was Mr Nelson himself. I
observed him carefully while he was in the witness box. I have compared his
evidence with the contemporaneous documents and, after the trial, I re-read his
witness statement and my note of his evidence in full. Like Mr Rye, it is
unsurprising that he could not recall with precision events of a decade or more
ago. However, in many areas he gave forthright evidence. I did not find him a
convincing witness. I have come to the conclusion that in a number of crucial
areas his evidence was either seriously unbalanced or simply not truthful. In
relation to those issues where the evidence of Mr Rye and Mr Nelson are in
conflict, I have no hesitation in accepting the evidence of Mr Rye.

ISSUES RELATING TO THE ACCOUNT

It is not in dispute that an account must be given. However, as mentioned
above, Mr Rye alleges that Mr Nelson owes him various sums and has raised a
counterclaim in respect of them. On 19 May 1992 Master Dyson ordered an
account in respect of all moneys received by the defendants on behalf of Mr
Nelson. Following objections on behalf of Mr Nelson to Mr Rye's compliance
with that order, on 25 November 1993 Master Dyson ordered a further and better
account. I was informed that Mr Nelson asserts that the account is still deficient,
but that even on the figures so far disclosed, Mr Rye owes him nearly £280,000.
On the other hand Mr Rye asserts that the accounts demonstrate that Mr Nelson
owes him just over £64,000.

I am not directly concerned with the account as such. However two areas of
dispute exist which may significantly affect not only the size of the amount found
due, but also who owes it to whom. First there is disagreement as to the precise
financial terms of the contract between Mr Nelson and Mr Rye. Secondly Mr Rye
raises various Limitation Act 1980 and laches defences.

The terms of the retainer

Originally, when performing with Be Bop Deluxe, Mr Nelson was managed by
a Mr Colin Mauston. That relationship was terminated in 1975. Litigation
ensued. In 1975 Be Bop Deluxe signed up with a new manager, Mr Mike Dolan
of Arnakata Management. Mr Nelson says that he began having money troubles
with Arnakata. In 1980 he was summoned to Mr Dolan's office and was told that
Arnakata was no longer willing to manage him. In fact Arnakata was having
serious financial problems and soon ceased trading. Apparently Mr Dolan
suggested that Mr Rye might be a suitable candidate to take over as Mr Nelson's
manager. In about August 1980, Mr Rye visited Mr Nelson's home in Yorkshire.
It is not in dispute that at some time during that meeting, whether while walking
in the garden or in the local village, it was agreed that Mr Rye would become the
new manager. It is also not in dispute that financial terms were discussed. Mr
Nelson said that it was agreed that Mr Rye would receive '20% of my income'.
He says that he understood 'income' to mean the money that was left, after all
expenses had been paid. On the other hand, Mr Rye says that he made it perfectly

a   clear that his terms were 20% of gross fees. He says that it was also agreed that
    in addition to these fees he would be entitled to reimbursement of all his
    expenses. Mr Nelson denies that.

        Both Mr Nelson and Mr Rye did their best to recall the words used by them in
    their meeting in Yorkshire some 15 years ago. However their recollections of
    matters more recent than then were understandably hazy and it is not
b   unreasonable that after all this time their recollections should have become
    moulded by what they now think they must then have agreed. Indeed, Mr
    Nelson was unable to challenge Mr Rye's assertion that he had used the words
    'gross income', all he could say was that he has now no recollection of that having
    been said.

        Since the parties did not reduce the results of their discussion to writing, the
c   court must do its best by looking at the surrounding circumstances, including
    such documents as still exist, to determine what was agreed.

The rate of commission

        As I have already indicated, Mr Nelson cannot recall precisely what was said at
d   the meeting. He simply understood that Mr Rye would charge a commission of
    20% 'on my income'. He said he could not challenge Mr Rye's recollection. Mr
    Rye says he has a good recollection of what was discussed. He said that he knew
    full well the difference between gross and net income and made it clear that he
    would only take on Mr Nelson if his commission was based on the former. In
    particular he says that it was apparent to him that if the commission was based on
e   net income and Mr Nelson's expenses matched or exceeded his income, then he,
    Mr Rye, would be working for nothing. Mr Nelson agreed that was a possibility
    but that it was a risk Mr Rye had chosen to take.

        In my view it is likely that this was an important consideration for Mr Rye at
    the time. When Mr Nelson parted company with Arnakata, he had just been
f   dropped by EMI, the recording company. Mr Rye said that he was aware that
    EMI were substantially unrecouped on advances they had made to Mr Nelson
    while he was under contract to them. In other words, he knew that there was a
    risk that Mr Nelson's net income might be very small or non-existent. It would
    not have made commercial sense for him to have taken on Mr Nelson for a
    commission based on net income. Mr Nelson says that he was not aware that
g   EMI was substantially unrecouped. I think that is unlikely. Furthermore Mr Rye
    had been associated with Mr Nelson before the management agreement was
    entered into. In 1979 Mr Nelson had his own record label, 'Cocteau' (the
    subsequent incorporation of Cocteau 1 was to protect the name used on the
    label), under which he put out his own records. Mr Nelson at that time was
h   managed by Arnakata Management. They employed Mr Rye to help put out a
    recording of Mr Nelson's music called *Do you dream in colour* late in that year. As
    Mr Nelson admits, that record 'died'. Therefore, at the time that Mr Rye and Mr
    Nelson were negotiating in August 1980, Mr Rye knew that Mr Nelson's last
    record had been a commercial failure. This reinforces my view that it would
    have made no commercial sense to Mr Rye to have accepted commission on net
j   income.

        In addition there are documents in existence which support Mr Rye's version
    of events. First, on 19 February 1981 Mr J Wyllie, a solicitor acting on behalf of
    Mr Rye, sent a telex to Mr Gentle, a solicitor acting on behalf of Mr Nelson. By
    that stage Mr Rye had formed Happytronics Ltd. The telex was in the following
    terms:

'Following our telephone conversation yesterday herewith proposed letter *a*
from the company providing Mark Rye's services to Happytronics Limited:
From ... Limited [Mr Rye had his own company into which his own income
was paid.] To Happytronics Limited:

Dear Sirs,

Mark Rye

This is to confirm the arrangement between us whereby we agree to make *b*
available to you the administrative and managerial services of Mark Rye on
a non exclusi[v]e basis to administer and organised [sic] your business
arrangements generally and in particular to enable you to comply with your
obligations to Bill Nelson in the letter from you to Bill Nelson of even date
herewith. In consideration of our agreeing to provide such services you *c*
agree to account to us for 20% of your gross income from the activities of Bill
Nelson whether as shareholder director or otherwise and you shall account
to us for the income payable to us promptly after receipt unless we agree
otherwise. Please sign the attached copy of this letter to indicate your
agreement to its terms ... Please let me know if you think this is satisfactory
and I will let you have copies typed for signature.' *d*

Although a letter in those terms does not appear to have been signed, the
financial terms there recorded do not appear to have been disputed. Mr Gentle
replied by letter dated 25 February 1981, in which he said as follows:

'I have now had a further discussion with Bill Nelson, and notwithstanding *e*
your telex of 19th February last, I really can find no justification for
proceeding on the basis as set out. It appears to me that Happytronics
Limited should be treated as Bill's production company. It seems to be
agreed that Mark should receive a 20% commission and I would suggest that
there is an agreement between Happytronics Limited and whatever limited
company which has the benefit of Mark's services ...' *f*

The letter went on to suggest other modifications to the proposals in the Wyllie
telex. However, the suggestion in that telex that the agreed terms were 20% of
gross income was not challenged. Under cross-examination, Mr Nelson accepted
that this correspondence was discussed between him and Mr Gentle at the time.
He did not suggest that Mr Gentle's reply was written other than under *g*
instructions from him. There would have been a very substantial difference
between the two bases for calculating Mr Rye's commission. In those
circumstances, had the oral agreement been for a percentage based on net
income, it is most unlikely that this feature of Mr Wyllie's telex would have
passed without correction. *h*

Furthermore, under cover of a letter dated 28 March 1983 Mr Rye sent Mr
Nelson a statement of income and expenditure for Happytronics for 1980 and
1981. The letter invited Mr Nelson to raise any queries he might have. The
statement shows that over the two-year period, expenditure exceeded income to
the tune of £25,792.95. However the statement also shows that in that period Mr *j*
Rye drew a commission of £9,000. Mr Nelson did not dispute having received
and read these figures. If his account of the financial terms agreed between him
and Mr Rye was correct, Mr Rye was not entitled to any commission at all. Mr
Nelson said that he did not notice the inclusion of the commission in these
figures. I do not accept that evidence. At the time that he changed management
to Mr Rye in 1980, Mr Nelson was owed some £48,000 by Arnakata. That money

a was never paid. Mr Nelson had mortgaged his house at the end of 1980 or beginning of 1981 to maintain his standard of living. I accept Mr Rye's evidence that throughout the ten years Mr Nelson demanded more and more money. I do not believe that he failed to notice the £9,000 commission paid to Mr Rye. It was one of the largest expenses on the statement of expenditure. If, as he now says, the commission was agreed to be on net income, I have little doubt he would

b have complained that Mr Rye's deduction of commission was not justified. He did not do so because, at the time, he knew that commission was due on gross income.

Mr Rye's expenses

As I have mentioned, Mr Rye also says that it was agreed that, in addition to
c his 20% commission, he was entitled to be reimbursed his expenses. Once again in the statement of income and expenditure sent under cover of the letter of 28 March 1983, sums can be identified as being expenses paid to Mr Rye.

Mr Rye explained what he meant by expenses. He said: 'I meant that if I went on tour to the US, my expenses would be met. If I hired a van, my costs would
d be met. I did not need to pay myself.' I am by no means convinced that these are really his personal expenses at all. If he hired a van for use by Mr Nelson or his support team, that would appear to me to be a legitimate business expense of Mr Nelson. Similarly, if Mr Nelson wanted his agent to attend him on tour, the cost of that also might well be a legitimate business expense of Mr Nelson. In any event, I accept Mr Rye's evidence that he believes he mentioned his personal
e expenses to Mr Nelson. I also accept that it is quite possible that Mr Rye mentioned expenses in the sense indicated above to Mr Nelson. If so, Mr Nelson would not and did not understand those expenses to be the personal expenses of Mr Rye. It is not proved that Mr Rye's requirement for his own personal expenses to be met was ever communicated properly to Mr Nelson and it follows
f that I find there was no agreement that these expenses be paid. It is notable that in the Wyllie/Gentle correspondence to which I have referred, there is no mention of personal expenses.

It was argued on behalf of Mr Rye that even if payment of expenses was not agreed, a term to that effect should be implied to give business efficacy to the agreement. I reject that argument. If Mr Rye was to obtain a 20% commission
g on gross income, there is no compelling reason to imply any such term. On the contrary, I think that there are just as good reasons of business efficacy why such a term should be excluded.

The period of accounting

h The third feature of the oral agreement in relation to which a dispute arose was the frequency with which Mr Rye had to account to Mr Nelson. It was not disputed that Mr Rye agreed to account regularly and also that the parties did not turn their minds to the question of how regular that should be. Mr Anderson, who appeared on behalf of Mr Nelson, suggested that quarterly or half-yearly
j accounting should be implied. Mr Oppenheim for Mr Rye suggested annual accounting.

The argument in favour of quarterly accounting was that VAT returns have to be produced each quarter and it was convenient and proper to use that opportunity to produce accounts for Mr Nelson. I was not clear on what basis Mr Anderson's alternative suggestion of six-monthly accounts was based, other than that it was less burdensome than quarterly accounts but not as unreasonably

relaxed as annual accounts. On the other hand Mr Oppenheim says that annual *a*
accounting makes sense, since all or most of Mr Nelson's income was to pass
through Happytronics and the filing of annual accounts would be necessary for
that.

Mr Oppenheim's argument is to be preferred. When the court implies a term
it must do so in the circumstances prevailing at the time the contract was entered
into. In this case those circumstances include the fact, as I hold it to be, that the *b*
parties had agreed that management of Mr Nelson's affairs would take place
substantially through the medium of a company. This is consistent with Mr
Nelson's witness statement in which he described the discussions with Mr Rye at
the end of 1980. He said '[Mr Rye] talked about setting up a new company to look
after my interests after the Arnakata debacle'. The company formed for that
purpose was Happytronics. An officious bystander would have assumed that *c*
annual accounting would be sufficient. Indeed, if the company was to be the
vehicle, it might well be thought that the company accounts would serve as the
management accounts. I think it most improbable that reasonable business
people in these circumstances would have suggested quarterly or even half-yearly
accounts. As long as Mr Nelson was receiving his 'wages' from the company, I *d*
do not think it would have been reasonable for him to be expected to review or
for Mr Rye to provide accounts twice, let alone four times a year.

DELAY, LACHES AND ACQUIESCENCE

On behalf of Mr Rye it is said that even though Mr Nelson is entitled to an
account, he is not entitled to an account in respect of the period before 24 *e*
December 1985. This is put two ways. First it is said that the claims here are
covered by the provisions of the Limitation Act 1980. In essence this is a claim
for an account arising out of an alleged breach of contract. The limitation period
is therefore six years. Mr Nelson denies that any limitation period applies to the
causes of action here. This issue raises points of some legal nicety. Secondly, it *f*
is said that even if Mr Nelson is right on this issue, Mr Rye can rely on s 36(2) of
the 1980 Act, which provides: 'Nothing in this Act shall affect any equitable
jurisdiction to refuse relief on the ground of acquiescence or otherwise.' It is said
that here the equitable jurisdiction should be invoked to prevent Mr Nelson from
now seeking an account in relation to the pre-1985 period. Mr Oppenheim is
prepared to accept that the defence will not run in respect of the accounts from *g*
24 December 1985 onwards.

Does a statutory limitation period apply?

The parties' arguments

Mr Anderson's argument is simple and falls into two parts. First, he says that *h*
the 1980 Act prescribes limitation periods for certain causes of action only.
Causes of action which are not expressly covered by the Act are not subject to a
period of limitation. Actions for breach of fiduciary duty are outwith the Act, so
no limitation period applies to them. In support of this he drew my attention to
Tito v Waddell (No 2), Tito v A-G [1977] 3 All ER 129 at 249–250, [1977] Ch 106 at
251 and to *A-G v Cocke* [1988] 2 All ER 391 at 395, [1988] Ch 414 at 421. In the latter *j*
Harman J said:

'I had cited to me by counsel for the second defendant most interesting
authorities under the 1939 Act. He particularly took me to Megarry V-C's
judgment in *Tito v Waddell (No 2), Tito v A-G* [1977] 3 All ER 129 at 248–250,
[1977] Ch 106 at 250–251, but, although that was on a somewhat different

a section to the present form of s 23 of the 1980 Act, Megarry V-C comes to a conclusion, which I think is the same as the conclusion I have come to, that a claim to an account simpliciter based on a fiduciary relationship and nothing more is not barred by any period of limitation. The observation in that case was obiter because he had held there was no fiduciary relationship arising.'

b
  , In the alternative Mr Anderson relied on the provisions of s 21(1) of the 1980 Act, which is in the following terms:

   'No period of limitation prescribed by this Act shall apply to an action by a beneficiary under a trust, being an action—(a) in respect of any fraud or
c fraudulent breach of trust to which the trustee was a party or privy; or (b) to recover from the trustee trust property or the proceeds of trust property in the possession of the trustee, or previously received by the trustee, or previously received by the trustee and converted to his use.'

d Mr Anderson relied particularly on para (b). He puts his argument in relation to this section in two ways. First, he said that where persons occupy a fiduciary position they are treated for the purpose of limitation as trustees, and time never runs in their favour. He relied on *McGee on Limitation Periods* (2nd edn, 1994) pp 247–248; *Burdick v Garrick* (1870) LR 5 Ch App 233; *North American Land and Timber Co v Watkins* [1904] 1 Ch 242 and *Soar v Ashwell* [1893] 2 QB 390, [1891–4]
e All ER Rep 991. Secondly, he said that Mr Rye would be treated as a constructive trustee of any moneys which he held or profit which he obtained by virtue of a breach of his fiduciary duties. Since s 38(1) of the 1980 Act provides that the terms 'trust' and 'trustee' have the same meaning as in the Trustee Act 1925, s 21(1)(b) applies as much to constructive trustees as to express ones.

f Mr Oppenheim approached the issue of limitation in an entirely different way. First, he drew my attention to s 23 of the 1980 Act, which provides:

   'An action for an account shall not be brought after the expiration of any time limit under this Act which is applicable to the claim which is the basis of the duty to account.'

g He argues that the basis of the duty to account in this action is the contract entered into between Mr Nelson and Mr Rye. Time therefore ran against Mr Nelson for the purposes of an account or other monetary claim from the date of breach of the relevant contractual obligation. The period of limitation for breach
h of contract is set at six years in accordance with s 5 of the 1980 Act. He says that s 21 has no application. He says that even if there was no time limit for a claim for breach of fiduciary duty or trust, that has no application here. Were this not so, s 21 would have the effect of circumventing and rendering nugatory the provisions of s 23. He says that it is not contended that the fiduciary duties arose from anything other than the contractual agreement between the parties. There
j was no fiduciary obligation which predated the agreement. He said that this was not inconsistent with *A-G v Cocke* because in that case Harman J was careful to qualify his views ([1988] 2 All ER 391 at 395, [1988] Ch 414 at 421):

   '... a claim to an account simpliciter based on a fiduciary relationship *and nothing more* is not barred by any period of limitation.' (My emphasis)

Furthermore, he says that Tito v Waddell (No 2) is not relevant because the a
problem under the Limitation Act 1939 addressed by Megarry V-C in that case
has now been resolved by s 23 of the 1980 Act.

The argument then proceeds as follows. First, he says it is no longer necessary
or helpful to look at old cases, such as Soar v Ashwell, to determine what the
limitation period is for actions for breach of fiduciary duty. Prior to s 68(17) of
the Trustee Act 1925, constructive trustees were treated differently to express b
trustees, and the old jurisprudence relating to limitation periods for breach of
fiduciary duty developed while that difference existed. He says that if a fiduciary
breaches his obligation and he holds as a trustee at all, he is treated as a
constructive trustee. He accepts that for the purpose of s 21(1)(b) of the 1980 Act,
the constructive trustee is treated in the same way as an express trustee as a result c
of the provisions of s 38(1). However, he says that the fact that Mr Rye received
moneys on behalf of, and stood in a fiduciary relationship to, Mr Nelson does not
necessarily make Mr Rye a constructive trustee of all the moneys so received. He
said that it is always a factual question, dependent upon the nature and content
of the fiduciary obligation, whether breach of the obligation gives rise to
proprietary remedies by way of constructive trust. In relation to this he relied on d
certain passages in Meagher, Gummow and Lehane Equity: Doctrines and Remedies
(2nd edn, 1984), in Bowstead on Agency (15th edn, 1985) and in an article written
by Sir Peter Millett 'Bribes and Secret Commissions' [1993] RLR 7. In particular,
Sir Peter said (at 23):

> 'When, then, is a fiduciary to be treated as held to be a trustee of money or e
> property which has been entrusted to him by or for the account of his
> principal? The question is a familiar one which commonly arises in cases of
> agency. An agent is a person who acts for another ... he may or may not be
> a trustee ... The position is not necessarily the same where money payments
> are concerned. An agent who receives money from or for his principal is not f
> necessarily a trustee, even though he is a fiduciary. At law, the relationship
> between the agent and his principal is that of debtor and creditor. In equity,
> however, the relationship of trustee and beneficiary may be superimposed ...
> In other cases the question whether an agent is a trustee depends on all the
> circumstances and in particular the intention of the parties, express or g
> inferred. There is no single test; the usual approach is to consider whether it
> is appropriate to superimpose a trust relationship onto the commercial
> relationship which exists between the parties; or whether it was
> contemplated that the agent should be free to treat the money as his own, in
> which case no trust relationship is created. It is fundamental to the existence
> of a trust that the trustee is bound to keep the trust property separate from h
> his own and apply it exclusively for the benefit of his beneficiary. A right of
> the agent to mix his principal's money with his own and use it as part of his
> cash-flow is inconsistent with the existence of a trust.'

Mr Oppenheim says that here there is no reason why a constructive trust should j
be imposed on top of the creditor/debtor relationship which exists between Mr
Rye and Mr Nelson. He pointed to a number of factors which supported that
conclusion. In particular he referred to the fact that there was no obligation on
Mr Rye to keep his commission money separate from Mr Nelson's and further
that Mr Rye invested his own money in the service company. He took out a
second mortgage on his own home to meet some of the service company's debts.

a   Finally, Mr Oppenheim says that even if there is a constructive trust in this case, on its true construction, s 21(1)(b) only comes into play if the plaintiff can demonstrate a prima facie case that there is identified property in specie held by Mr Rye which belongs to Mr Nelson. He says that Mr Nelson fails on that issue as well.

b   *Conclusions*

In resolving these arguments, I think it is helpful to bear in mind what the limitation defence is and how it relates to the defences of laches, acquiescence and delay. Outside the statutory provisions there are principles which provide that in some circumstances, normally associated with significant delay, it will be inequitable to allow a plaintiff to enforce his rights. The requirements and
c   limitations of this equitable doctrine will be considered later. For present purposes it is sufficient to note that whether the plaintiff is barred from relief is determined on the particular facts of the case. Account is taken of the actions and behaviour of the plaintiff and defendant and sometimes the impact on third parties. It is a flexible defence.

d   This is to be compared with limitation periods provided by statute, particularly the 1980 Act and its predecessors. The statutes have imposed essentially arbitrary time limits on certain defined causes of action. It does not matter in such cases whether the plaintiff is to blame for not keeping within the time limit, nor is it relevant that in some cases it will be thought unfair that the defendant is allowed off the hook. The defendant is entitled to play possum in the hope that the
e   plaintiff will make a mistake and fail to commence proceedings before the statutory time limit is breached. If the limitation period is exceeded then the defendant is entitled to call down the guillotine on the plaintiff's action unless a statutory exception exists, such as the extension of time provided by s 32 of the 1980 Act in cases where there is fraud or concealment.

f   Furthermore, the arbitrary time limits imposed by statute vary from cause of action to cause of action. For example, an action for breach of contract must be commenced within six years, an action upon a speciality must be commenced within twelve years and an action in respect of personal injuries must be commenced in many cases within three years. What then if one set of facts gives rise to two or more potential causes of action with different limitation periods?
g   For example, it may well be that the breakdown of a relationship which arises out of a contract gives rise to alternative causes of action for breach of contract, negligence and breach of trust. No doubt the injured party cannot use the alternatives so as to receive duplicate or triplicate relief (see *United Australia Ltd v Barclays Bank Ltd* [1940] 4 All ER 20, [1941] AC 1 and *A-G for Hong Kong v Reid*
h   [1994] 1 All ER 1, [1994] 1 AC 324), but that does not mean that he can not sue under all of the heads simultaneously. Each cause of action may have its own strengths and weaknesses so that, say, the plaintiff may succeed in his cause of action based in negligence but fail in his action for breach of contract, or vice versa. In particular, where a limitation period exists and can be invoked in
j   relation to one cause of action, it is nihil ad rem that no, or a different, limitation period applies to an alternative cause of action which has been or could have been pleaded by the plaintiff.

Historically, actions by beneficiaries against trustees for misappropriation of trust property have been excluded from the imposition of such arbitrary time limits. The courts and the legislature have treated trustees as bearing a special responsibility to the trust property and the beneficiary's interest in it. The

beneficiary's right to complain of breach of trust has been treated as persisting   *a*
indefinitely unless, of course, in all the circumstances it would be inequitable to
allow him to enforce his rights. There is nothing to which my attention has been
drawn which suggests that the 1980 Act effected a significant change in this area.

With these considerations in mind it is possible to address the arguments
advanced by the parties to this action.

In my view s 23 of the 1980 Act does not have the meaning for which Mr   *b*
Oppenheim contends. The section simply confirms that the limitation period
which applies to a particular cause of action applies equally to the relief by way of
account which flows from it. For example, in this case certain claims for
copyright infringement arise. Section 96(2) of the Copyright, Designs and Patents
Act 1988 entitles a copyright owner to seek relief by way of an account where   *c*
infringement is proved. The effect of s 21 of the 1980 Act is that the limitation
period for the account is the same as that for the claim for infringement. I do not
accept that s 21 has the effect of circumventing and rendering nugatory the
provisions of s 23. The former is concerned with whether or not there is a
limitation period for actions for breach of trust, whereas the latter is only
concerned with the limitation period to be applied to a form of relief which may   *d*
be ordered in favour of a successful plaintiff.

Since that is so, what limitation period, if any, applies to the cause of action in
this case? As I have indicated above, where a limitation period exists and can be
invoked in relation to one cause of action, it is nihil ad rem that no, or a different,
limitation period applies to an alternative cause of action which has been or could   *e*
have been pleaded by the plaintiff. If the cause of action here is one for breach of
fiduciary duty or breach of trust, it does not avail Mr Rye to argue that the
relationship arose out of a contract and that the relationship between him and Mr
Nelson can be treated as one between debtor and creditor. If Mr Nelson had
chosen to sue for breach of contract alone, then the limitation period for   *f*
contractual claims would have applied. He has not done so. If Mr Oppenheim's
argument on this was right, the provisions of s 21(1) would be virtually valueless
because in most cases of breach of trust the trustee would be able to argue that
he could have been sued for breach of contract.

I accept Mr Anderson's basic premise that the 1980 Act only imposes limitation
periods on those actions it specifically identifies. A cause of action for which the   *g*
1980 Act, or other legislation, makes no limitation provision is not subject to a
limitation period. Actions for breach of fiduciary duty are not expressly covered.
It follows that prima facie no limitation applies to them. However, if this was all,
s 21 would serve little purpose. As far as I can see, in all cases of breach of trust
covered by the section it would be possible to say that there had been a breach of   *h*
fiduciary duty. Although, as I have held, no limitation period applies to actions
for breach of fiduciary duty simpliciter and s 21(1) provides that no limitation
period applies in respect of many actions for breach of trust, some actions for
breach of trust are the subject of limitation periods—see s 21(3). If those are
treated as actions for breach of fiduciary duty, the limitation would be   *j*
sidestepped.

The fallacy, it appears to me, is to treat breach of fiduciary duty and breach of
trust as different causes of action. In a case where, because of the existence of a
fiduciary duty, a constructive trust comes into existence, breach of trust and
breach of fiduciary duty are the same cause of action. Similarly, where an express
trust has been created, breach of that trust and breach of fiduciary duty are also

a the same cause of action. It is therefore not possible to sidestep the limitation provisions of s 21(3) by referring to the action as one for breach of fiduciary duty.

Since I accept Mr Oppenheim's argument that not all breaches of fiduciary duty give rise to constructive trusts, the following propositions appear to follow. (1) An action for breach of fiduciary duty simpliciter is outside the provisions of the Limitation Act 1980 and therefore is not subject to a period of limitation. (See *b* *A-G v Cocke* [1988] 2 All ER 391, [1988] Ch 414.) (2) Where a breach of fiduciary duty gives rise to a constructive trust, the provisions of s 21 of the 1980 Act determine whether there is a limitation period, and its duration. (3) An action for breach of an express trust is, in like manner, subject to the limitation provisions of s 21. (4) In neither case (2) or (3) is it possible to avoid any limitation period imposed by the 1980 Act by treating the case as one of breach of fiduciary *c* duty.

There is no dispute between the parties that Mr Rye owed Mr Nelson a fiduciary duty. He was obliged to account to Mr Nelson annually. He did not. There has been a breach of that duty and, prima facie, no limitation period applies. Mr Oppenheim's arguments to the effect that the cause of action did not *d* fall within the ambit of s 21(1)(b) would only help Mr Rye if he had also succeeded in persuading me that the action should be treated as one for breach of contract rather than breach of fiduciary duty. Since he has failed to persuade me of that, no limitation period applies, either because the cause of action is outwith the 1980 Act or because it falls within s 21(1)(b) (it was not suggested that the action came *e* within s 21(3)). In the circumstances it is not necessary to determine under which head this action falls. Nevertheless, it is clear to me that this case does fall within s 21(1)(b). Although not all fiduciary relationships give rise to constructive trusts, this one did. As Sir Peter Millett said in 'Bribes and Secret Commissions' [1993] RLR 7 at 23:

f 'Every agent is a fiduciary; he may or may not be a trustee. Often he holds no money or property for his principal. If he receives goods from his principal, he may be a bailee only. Where, however, he receives property from a third party intended for his principal, his obligation will almost invariably be to transfer it in specie to his principal and, if so, he will be treated as holding it as trustee for his principal. He cannot assert a beneficial *g* title to property which was never intended to be his.'

In this case Mr Nelson left all of his financial affairs to Mr Rye. All of his various sources of income were to be handled by his manager. Mr Rye accepted that he was not free to treat Mr Nelson's income as his own. He never did. The fact, as *h* I find, that Mr Rye did not take out all the commission to which he was entitled and put his own funds in to keep Mr Nelson afloat, does not alter the nature of his interest in Mr Nelson's income. If it were otherwise, any agent in a fiduciary relationship to his principal could prevent a constructive trust from arising by failing to take his permissible deductions from the trust fund or by putting his *j* own money in, even if this was not sought by the beneficiary. Furthermore, I reject Mr Oppenheim's argument that s 21(1)(b) does not apply because the constructive trust contained no property in specie. The subsection requires that the action be one to recover from the trustee 'trust property or the proceeds of trust property in the possession of the trustee'. Mr Rye received Mr Nelson's income. That was trust property. The balance left after all proper deductions is also trust property. This is an action to recover that property.

It follows that no limitation period applies in this case. However, that does not
dispose of this part of the case. Mr Rye argues that it would be inequitable by   *a*
reason of laches, acquiescence and delay to allow Mr Nelson to maintain this
action at least in respect of the period before 24 December 1985.

The equitable defence

For Mr Nelson it was argued that to succeed on this issue, Mr Rye must show: *b*
(a) there was an express or implied representation by the plaintiff that he intended
not to compel performance in specie by the defendant of the obligation in
question; (b) that the plaintiff was aware, or ought to have been aware, of the
possibility that the defendant would act to his prejudice in reliance on the
representation; and (c) in consequence of that representation, it becomes unjust   *c*
to grant the equitable relief sought as the defendant has been prejudiced by
reliance on it (in the sense of being in a 'substantially worse position' than he
would otherwise have been). For these propositions Mr Anderson relied on *Spry
on Equitable Remedies* (4th edn, 1990) pp 236–238. In relation to laches, he said that
in order to raise a prima facie case, a defendant must establish two facts: (a) that
there has been unreasonable delay by the plaintiff; and (b) that there has been   *d*
consequent substantial prejudice or detriment to the defendant which justifies
the refusal of the equitable relief sought. He said that mere delay per se is not
sufficient. A defendant must show a causal link between the delay and the
prejudice/detriment (see *Lindsay Petroleum Co v Hurd* (1874) LR 5 PC 221 at 239–
240, *Lazard Bros & Co v Fairfield Properties Co (Mayfair) Ltd* (1977) Times, 13   *e*
October and *Spry on Equitable Remedies* (4th edn, 1990) pp 227–228). At least at
one stage in his argument, Mr Anderson suggested that the defendant needs to
prove that the prejudice was substantially caused by the delay.

It can be misleading to approach the equitable defences of laches and
acquiescence as if they consisted of a series of precisely defined hurdles over each
of which a litigant must struggle before the defence is made out. In *Lindsay*   *f*
Petroleum Co v Hurd (1874) LR 5 PC 221 at 239–240 the Privy Council stated:

> 'Now the doctrine of laches in Courts of Equity is not an arbitrary or a
> technical doctrine. Where it would be practically unjust to give a remedy,
> either because the party has, by his conduct, done that which might fairly be   *g*
> regarded as equivalent to a waiver of it, or where by his conduct and neglect
> he has, though perhaps not waiving that remedy, yet put the other party in
> a situation in which it would not be reasonable to place him if the remedy
> were afterwards to be asserted, in either of these cases, lapse of time and
> delay are most material. But in every case, if an argument against relief,   *h*
> which otherwise would be just, is founded upon mere delay, that delay of
> course not amounting to a bar by any statute of limitations, the validity of
> that defence must be tried upon principles substantially equitable. Two
> circumstances, always important in such cases, are, the length of the delay
> and the nature of the acts done during the interval, which might affect either
> party and cause a balance of justice or injustice in taking the one course or   *j*
> the other, so far as relates to the remedy.'

In *Erlanger v New Sombrero Phosphate Co* (1878) 3 App Cas 1218 at 1279–1280,
[1874–80] All ER Rep 271 at 286, after quoting this passage, Lord Blackburn went
on to say:

a
'I have looked in vain for any authority which gives a more distinct and definite rule than this; and I think, from the nature of the inquiry, it must always be a question of more or less, depending on the degree of diligence which might reasonably be required, and the degree of change which has occurred, whether the balance of justice or injustice is in favour of granting the remedy or withholding it. The determination of such a question must

b
largely depend on the turn of mind of those who have to decide, and must, therefore, be subject to uncertainty; but that, I think, is inherent in the nature of the inquiry.'

So here, these defences are not technical or arbitrary. The courts have indicated over the years some of the factors which must be taken into consideration in

c
deciding whether the defence runs. Those factors include the period of the delay, the extent to which the defendant's position has been prejudiced by the delay, and the extent to which that prejudice was caused by the actions of the plaintiff. I accept that mere delay alone will almost never suffice, but the court has to look at all the circumstances, including in particular those factors set out above, and then decide whether the balance of justice or injustice is in favour of granting the

d
remedy or withholding it. If substantial prejudice will be suffered by the defendant, it is not necessary for the defendant to prove that it was caused by the delay. On the other hand, the plaintiff's knowledge that the delay will cause such prejudice is a factor to be taken into account. With these considerations in mind, I turn to the facts.

e
It was not in dispute that no formal request for a written account was made during the ten years of the management agreement and that no account which would satisfy a lawyer was ever provided. Why was this so?

In the witness box, Mr Nelson sought to portray himself as naive in matters financial. He said that he had been badly treated by his manager. The flavour of his complaints can be gauged from the following passage in his witness

f
statement:

'I have been in the dark about the legal and financial position concerning my affairs for many many years. My previous management went into liquidation owing me money. I trusted Mark Rye absolutely. However, I have never had a real explanation from him of what has happened to my

g
income over the years.'

It would have been possible to discuss the accounts with Mr Thomas around the table. That could have been with or without Mr Rye present. There is no doubt from the documents that Mr Thomas suggested to Mr Nelson that they talk or

h
meet. On 14 April 1986 Mr Thomas sent a letter to Mr Nelson, to which was attached a compliment slip on which Mr Thomas had written the following:

'Bill, Thank you for the forms. They are all in order—I must write the attached letter as the company's auditor. Please telephone me if you require some further information.'

j
The letter to which the compliment slip was attached was in strong terms. It mentioned the fact that Mr Thomas' firm had not been paid and was reluctant to carry out further work. It also contained the following:

'As we have previously explained PAYE regulations have been breached by drawing money out of the company without accounting for the tax due. These amounts are not small and place a considerable burden on the company. You must be aware that the Inland Revenue will take all steps to recover the tax lost with interest and penalties, and prosecute the directors for the offences committed ... We understand that you hope to receive a substantial advance from CBS in the immediate future. We would advise you that you give serious consideration to allocating funds to deal with your outstanding financial affairs and tax liabilities without delay. We trust that these matters will be put right but should you wish to meet and discuss any aspects we are happy to do so.'

On 16 February 1987 Mr Thomas wrote to Mr Nelson again. He said:

> 'Please do try and get in touch with me next time you are in London as I do think it is important that we meet up so that I can explain things more fully and we can plan our way forward.'

Similarly, Mr Rye's evidence, which I accept, was that he tried to explain the financial position to Mr Nelson on numerous occasions, and he suggested Mr Nelson should go to see Mr Thomas if he had any problem with the figures. For example, on 17 October 1986 Mr Rye wrote to Mr Nelson as follows:

> 'Chris Thomas has finally sent me some draft accounts for Happytronics Ltd. I propose we have a meeting to look at them. When is your next London Lodge Meeting and we can make it at the same time?'

It is also clear that in fact two meetings with Mr Thomas (not one as suggested by Mr Nelson) were arranged, but were both cancelled by Mr Nelson.

Mr Nelson's oral evidence on these issues was contradictory or implausible. He said that he would ask for business meetings with Mr Thomas, but that Mr Rye would say he could not afford to go to accountants or bookkeepers. When it was put to him that he knew who Mr Thomas was and could have contacted him, his response was that he didn't meet Mr Thomas until the end of the relationship with Mr Rye, but not through lack of asking. He said that if a meeting had been arranged at a date which was convenient, he would have been prepared to meet. He said that he asked Mr Rye to set up meetings but they were not set up. He claimed that for ten years he had asked Mr Rye to set up meetings. However he also said that he did *not* ask for meetings with Mr Thomas because (a) Mr Thomas was a friend of Mr Rye, (b) Mr Thomas said that he didn't have enough information from Mr Rye (evidence which itself is difficult to reconcile with the Mr Nelson's accurate oral testimony that he never spoke to Mr Thomas throughout the ten years of the management agreement) and (c) Mr Rye had all the information so that he, Mr Nelson, was powerless to advance without it.

When challenged as to why he did nothing, since he was asking for and being refused accounts, Mr Nelson said:

> '[Mr Rye] had all my property. I didn't want to rock the boat. I thought he might do a runner. I thought that a real possibility.'

This picture of a man willing to listen to explanations and scared to challenge his manager for fear that he would run off with his property is difficult to reconcile with his evidence that he trusted Mr Rye absolutely (see the extract from his witness statement referred to above) and his oral testimony that he did nothing about demanding a proper account because he accepted Mr Rye's explanation that everything was in order. Mr Nelson agreed that he cancelled the one meeting with Mr Thomas which he remembered had been arranged because he a said that he was told about it at the last minute and had already checked out of his hotel and had a lot of luggage with him.

I think Mr Nelson got closer to the truth when he said :

'If he [Rye] asked me [to come to meetings] and I refused there could be many reasons. I was working non-stop. I had very little spare time.'

b In my view there was a wilful refusal by Mr Nelson to involve himself in his financial affairs. He deliberately ignored advice both from Mr Rye and Mr Thomas to get round the table to see how the figures worked out. I find as a fact that he declined to attend two meetings with Mr Rye and Mr Thomas for no good reason. He was happy to drive his Rolls Royce, live in a mansion and take far more out of Happytronics than could be justified on the basis of its receipts, but
c he did not want to know the details of how the sums added up—or failed to add up. He rejected all advice. He was not interested in the account as between him and Mr Rye. He knew or suspected that working out any of the figures would merely confirm that he was living beyond his means. This was something which he preferred to ignore. He would leave his manager and Mr Thomas to sort out
d the problems. His only concerns arose when Mr Rye sought to put a brake on his wages. I accept that then he would demand to know why he could not have more and, from time to time, asked to see the figures. But this was simply part and parcel of trying to place the blame for his financial problems on others and, in particular, Mr Rye. During the ten years of the relationship, Mr Nelson did not want an account and that was apparent to Mr Rye. He wanted to complain about
e lack of funds, but he was not interested in any explanation which would support Mr Rye's constant warning that he was living beyond his means. In particular he did not want to see it in black and white. Mr Thomas told Mr Rye that he wanted a meeting between the three of them so that he, Mr Thomas, could explain to Mr Nelson that he could not continue to draw 'vast amounts out of the company
f when it does not have the funds'. Even if Mr Nelson was not aware of the contents of this particular communication between Mr Thomas and Mr Rye, he was aware that this was the message he would be given if there was a meeting and it was not one he was prepared to listen to. He was quite content to convince himself that he was too busy to meet to discuss the problems. I have little doubt that had Mr Rye not terminated the relationship in 1990, Mr Nelson would have
g continued to refuse to look at any accounting material. As far as Mr Rye is concerned, I find that he wanted and tried to explain the accounts to Mr Nelson. It was in his interests to do so.

I have come to the conclusion that there was unreasonable delay in commencing these proceedings.

h I turn to consider whether Mr Rye has suffered prejudice as a result of that delay. Mr Oppenheim relied on two matters. First he says that documents relevant to the account which did exist in the past now no longer exist. Secondly he says that it is inevitable that matters more than six years ago will be poorly remembered. In other words, Mr Rye's ability to give evidence has been
j prejudice by the delay. I will consider each of these in turn, but before doing so I should mention one matter. Mr Nelson has raised before the master certain objections to the account given by Mr Rye. In particular, although Mr Nelson accepts that Mr Rye was entitled to deduct legitimate expenses, a very large number of expenses claimed have been challenged on the basis that vouchers do not exist to support them. Mr Nelson is therefore seeking to have excluded from the account some or all of these expenses. Mr Anderson confirmed before me

that Mr Nelson intends to continue to attack the account rendered on behalf of
Mr Rye on this basis.

As far as the vouchers are concerned, Mr Rye's evidence was that from time to
time, when he wanted space, he would clear out of storage and destroy old
documents. In particular invoices and receipts and the like would fall within the
category of documents eligible for disposal. He said that he would not
deliberately dispose of any vouchers less than six years old. This space-making
exercise was not regular nor was it consistent. The result is that very many, but
not all, vouchers which were more than six years old have gone. Under
cross-examination, Mr Rye said that as soon as he received the letter from Mr
Nelson's solicitors shortly after 21 December 1990 he stopped this deliberate
destruction practice, at least in relation to Mr Nelson's affairs. It is apparent that
Mr Rye's document retention practices within the six-year period are less than
perfect. Even comparatively recent documents can no longer be found.

I turn now to the second part of Mr Oppenheim's argument on prejudice,
namely that the passage of time will make it more difficult for his client to give
reliable evidence in relation to the first half of the 1980s. Whenever there is delay,
the party being sued can claim that the passage of time will make it more difficult
for him to present evidence in support of his case. Mr Rye is particularly anxious
that he will find it impossible to recall the minutiae of what expenses, including
many very small ones, were incurred on what date and for what purpose. The
court should bear in mind that a party may be inclined to understate his powers
of recall when it is in his interests to do so. Nevertheless I am satisfied that Mr
Rye's fears are justified. We are not here considering major events in Mr Rye's
life but the comparative trivia of the day-to-day movement of funds in a small
business. During the existence of his managerial relationship with Mr Nelson, Mr
Rye had every reason to believe that Mr Nelson was not in the slightest bit
interested in raking through the minutiae of what expenses were paid on his
behalf. Indeed, I accept Mr Rye's evidence that Mr Nelson made it clear to him
that his primary duty was to pass money to Mr Nelson and that if that involved
deferring or declining payment to others, so be it.

I have considered all of the above matters. In my view Mr Rye will suffer
substantial prejudice for both of the reasons advanced by Mr Oppenheim and this
is a case where it would be unreasonable and unjust to allow Mr Nelson to assert
his right to an account against Mr Rye in the period prior to 24 December 1985.
The defence of laches or acquiescence is made out. In his reply speech, Mr
Anderson suggested that because Mr Rye said that he did not throw away further
relevant documents once he had received Russells' letter of 26 November 1990,
the period of prejudice only extended up to six years before that date, that is to
say it was only documents earlier than that which might have been destroyed.
Therefore, he argued, if the defence runs it should only cover the period before
26 November 1984.

I do not accept that argument either. As I have already noted, Mr Rye had a
less than perfect document retention procedure. Even if the deliberate
destruction policy was suspended on receipt of the Russells letter, it is likely that
documents have been lost with the passage of time. It is likely that this will
include some documents dated between November 1984 and December 1985.
Their absence now is no less a prejudice to Mr Rye than the absence of earlier
documents. Furthermore, Mr Anderson's argument does not address the
significant prejudice which Mr Rye will suffer by reason of the difficulty of
recalling all the minutiae up to December 1985.

a   As I have said, it would be quite unjust to allow Mr Nelson now to seek an account prior to 24 December 1985. I should make it clear that I would have come to the same conclusion even had I been persuaded by Mr Anderson that the defendant must show a causal link between the delay and the prejudice/detriment of which he complains. If Mr Nelson had made it clear that he wanted a proper account earlier on in their relationship, I think it most likely that few, if
b   any, of the vouchers from those early days would have gone missing. It is unrealistic for Mr Nelson to demand that Mr Rye identify precisely which vouchers have been disposed of which would not have been otherwise. In my view, the detriment in these proceedings which I have indicated the defendant has suffered by reason of the plaintiff's failure to ask for an account earlier or
c   complain when it was not forthcoming, is largely due to that delay and the manner in which Mr Nelson treated Mr Rye's persistent attempts to make him sit down and look at the figures.

CONVERSION

d   The issues in relation to this claim are simple. It is not in dispute that until very shortly before the trial Mr Rye had in his possession a number of master or production tapes of recordings made by Mr Nelson. These are set out in schedule 2 to the statement of claim. It was also accepted before me that the return of those articles was demanded by Russells in a letter dated 29 November 1991. On
e   behalf of Mr Nelson I was asked to consider whether at that date he had a right to immediate possession. Mr Rye refused to return the recordings until a few days before the trial. The only relief which Mr Nelson now seeks is a declaration of his entitlement to the recordings and costs.

The position adopted on behalf of Mr Rye has changed since the defence was
f   originally served in March 1992. At first it was alleged that the recordings were retained pursuant to a collateral oral agreement in favour of Happytronics, Cocteau 1 or Cocteau 2. An attempt to amend this at the last moment to raise an inconsistent plea was only allowed on terms as to costs which Mr Rye was not prepared to accept. At the trial Mr Oppenheim's position was that it was open to him to challenge Mr Nelson's claim to be entitled to possession. I let him develop
g   that argument. Save in relation to the recording called 'Simplex', no questions of licence were advanced. As far as the latter is concerned, whether or not Mr Rye was entitled to retain possession is tied up with the issue of whether or not he had, or had the benefit of, a licence to make or authorise the making of Simplex records. That is at the heart of the copyright case. If at the date of Russells'
h   demand in November 1991, Mr Rye was entitled to retain that master tape for the purpose of making records, the case in conversion will fail. I will therefore consider the claim in conversion against all the recordings except for Simplex.

On the evidence it appears that the tapes were made by or on behalf of Mr
j   Nelson. In some cases the manufacture may have been paid for by one or other of his companies on his behalf. However, I also accept that in those cases he had a beneficial interest in them and that once a demand had been made for their return in Russells' letter he had an immediate right to possession. Once that demand had been made, Mr Rye should have returned the tapes. The cause of action has been made out for all the recordings save in relation to Simplex, which I will deal with separately.

COPYRIGHT   *a*

Once again, the issues relating to this claim are fairly straightforward. Mr Nelson alleges that he is the owner of the copyright in certain musical compositions contained in the Simplex album. It was not disputed that copyright subsists in those compositions as musical works under s 12 of the Copyright, Designs and Patents Act 1988. It was also not disputed that the ownership of that copyright vests in Mr Nelson. Compact discs (CDs) of the Simplex album have   *b* been made since the termination of the management agreement. Some have been made by a French company and supplied to Cocteau 2. It was also alleged that CDs were made by an American company called Enigma Entertainment Corp. In his reply speech Mr Anderson accepted that even if Enigma had made such CDs, that would have taken place out of the jurisdiction and can not amount   *c* to infringement. Furthermore it was not proved that Enigma had made any CDs at all. It is not in dispute that the CDs made for Cocteau 2 contain copies of the copyright works. Manufacture of those CDs without licence will constitute an infringement of Mr Nelson's copyright pursuant to the provisions of s 16 of the 1988 Act. Pursuant to ss 16 and 18 of the 1988 Act it is an infringement to put into circulation in the United Kingdom copies of the musical works which had not   *d* previously been put into circulation. The real issue on this part of the case is only one of licence.

It was in relation to the issues surrounding the manufacture of the Simplex CDs that I have difficulty in accepting all of Mr Rye's evidence. Initially he said that he arranged manufacture of copies of the album before he terminated the   *e* management agreement on 2 October 1990. He said that they already had been ordered before he sent out an offer for sale to members of Mr Nelson's fan club on 6 November 1990. The circular containing that offer stated that the album would be 'available on cassette only' and would cost £4·00. Subsequently a business in which Mr Nelson had an interest, Magpie Mail Order, offered the CDs   *f* for sale to the fans at £8·50. Mr Rye said that reference to 'cassettes' in the November offer was a clerical error and that only CDs had ever been contemplated. This version of events would have been consistent with his evidence that the CDs were ordered before October 1990. In my view, in relation to this, Mr Rye's evidence was not to be relied on. He knew very well the difference between a cassette and a CD. I do not accept that a clerical error was   *g* made. What he contemplated in November 1990 was the manufacture of cassettes. They were to be sold at the cheaper price of £4·00 rather than £8·50 which could have been demanded for the CD. In the end only CDs were made and they were only ordered after the circular dated 6 November 1990 and therefore after the end of the management agreement. During the trial,   *h* documents consistent with this were discovered by Mr Rye. He then accepted that manufacture did not occur until after the management agreement was terminated. On the balance of probabilities not only were the CDs made after that date, they were also ordered after that date.

However, that does not necessarily mean that Mr Rye is liable for infringement   *j* of copyright by manufacture. It was not asserted that he personally had manufactured the CDs, only that he had authorised the unlicensed manufacture. Therefore the question which has to be addressed is whether the manufacture of the CDs in late 1990 or early 1991 was unlicensed. A person can only be liable for authorising infringement if the primary actor could himself be guilty of infringement. As Hoffmann LJ put it in *AKCO Music and Records Inc v Music* a   *Collection International Ltd* [1995] RPC 657 at 660: 'authorising is a tort only if the act authorised is an act restricted by the copyright.'

In relation to this issue Mr Nelson said in his witness statement that he delivered the master recordings of the Simplex album to Mr Rye 'in about late 1988—early 1989 to be released on the Cocteau label'. He went on to explain that there was not enough money to permit production at that time and that Enigma,

b   to whom the album was offered, were not planning anything 'at the moment'. He went on to say: 'I therefore assumed that the recordings would be released as and when an opportunity arose.' Under cross-examination, Mr Nelson said that he 'needed Simplex to be released'.

When Russells wrote to Mr Rye on instructions to complain about the release of the album, the only objection was as to the price, namely £4·00, at which it was

c   thought it was to be released. Thus, in a letter of 21 December 1990 Russells wrote:

d   'As regards your comments on *Simplex* this is being released at a price of £4·00. That is not a full price release. Please immediately confirm by return that this will now be corrected and that the album *will be sold* at a full price and provide us with details of the number of copies that you have sold at £4·00.' (My emphasis)

Mr Nelson said under cross-examination that the correspondence from Russells put too much emphasis on price and that the main point he wanted conveyed was that the album should not be released at all. I reject that evidence. I think it is

e   clear that Mr Nelson wanted the album released under his Cocteau label. That is what he told his solicitors and that is what they told Mr Rye. Furthermore, Mr Nelson confirmed under cross-examination that if Cocteau was to make money it had to be able to release records. He said: 'I wanted Simplex released by Cocteau. I wanted it out on my own label'.

f   Mr Rye knew that was Mr Nelson's wish. In my view what happened to Simplex was what Mr Nelson intended. It was released under the Cocteau label. The Cocteau companies were set up for the purpose of running Mr Nelson's record business. There was no suggestion that on termination of the management agreement it was expected that Cocteau would stop putting out Mr Nelson's records. On the contrary, Mr Nelson expected his Cocteau company to

g   continue to trade. Cocteau 2 had a licence from Mr Nelson to manufacture and sell Simplex. It is clear that the order for the manufacture of the albums was placed by Cocteau 2. That manufacture could not have been an infringement. The fact that Mr Rye, in his position of director of the company, authorised it to proceed with licensed manufacture cannot be an infringement either.

h   I should add that Mr Nelson asserted that he did not know of the existence of Cocteau 2. The letter which Mr Rye sent terminating the management agreement contained the following:

j   'Income from your record sales controlled by Cocteau Records diminishes by the month whilst publishing income is now virtually non-existent ... I shall try and arrange for the company overdraft and liabilities to be paid from the stock I hold and then I shall arrange to have the company struck off or liquidated as advised with a final set of accounts then being prepared by the accountants.'

In para 20 of his witness statement, Mr Nelson says that he was not aware of the incorporation of *either* of the Cocteau companies. That evidence was clearly

false. He was appointed a director of Cocteau 1 and had signed the necessary
forms consenting to that which were filed at Companies House. In a letter dated
24 January 1990, Mr Nelson wrote to Mr Rye asking for 'details of the corporate
structure of Cocteau Records'. In their letter to Mr Rye of 26 November 1990
Russells stated:

> '... [Mr Nelson] understood that a company called Cocteau Records
> Limited was established in or around 1981/1982 to take care of his recording
> interests ...'

I have no doubt that Mr Nelson knew full well that a Cocteau company existed
in 1990 and that it organised the manufacture and release of his records. Whether
that company was Cocteau 1 or Cocteau 2 was a matter of indifference to Mr
Nelson. It was suggested that even if he knew of the existence of Cocteau 1, he
was not aware of Cocteau 2. It is true that the documents which Mr Nelson had
to sign to make him a director of Cocteau 2 were sent to him but not returned.
Mr Nelson says that he never received them and did not know about them. I
think that is unlikely. I have come to the conclusion that it is more likely that he
knew of the formation of Cocteau 2 and chose not to complete the forms sent to
him. The reason for this course of inaction is not hard to find. On 4 March 1986
Mr Nelson received a letter from Companies House in relation to the late filing
of accounts for Happytronics. It included the following:

> 'As a director of the company, you are personally responsible for the
> delivery of all accounts due since your appointment and for all outstanding
> annual returns, whenever due. If the outstanding documents are not
> received within 28 days, you may be prosecuted ... If found guilty you could
> be fined and possibly disqualified as a company director.'

That was reinforced by Mr Thomas' letter to him of 14 April 1986, which has
been referred to above. It also told Mr Nelson that, as a director of a defaulting
company, he might be prosecuted. The message clearly struck home because a
year later in a letter to Mr Thomas, Mr Nelson wrote:

> '... due to the pressing legal problems as a result of Companies House, I
> better not rock the boat too much at this stage as I'm implicated simply by
> being a director, despite having no control over the financial affairs of the
> company.'

Although he denied it when giving oral evidence, I think it is likely that Mr
Nelson chose not to sign the documents which would have made him a director
of Cocteau 2, so as to avoid being responsible for its affairs.

For the above reasons I hold that it is likely that Mr Nelson knew of the
existence of both Cocteau companies and was happy for whichever happened to
be in existence at the time to organise the release of his records.

This does not finally dispose of the question of copyright infringement. Under
the Copyright Act 1956 it was not an infringement of copyright to sell
reproductions of a copyright work unless they were unlicensed. An attempt to
treat such activities as a 'publication' of the copyright work and therefore an
infringement under s 2(5)(b) of the 1956 Act failed in *Infabrics Ltd v Jaytex Ltd*
[1981] 1 All ER 1057, [1982] AC 1. Under the combined effect of ss 16(1)(b), 16(2)
and 18(2) of the 1988 Act, it is now an act of primary infringement to issue copies
of a copyright work to the public without licence where those copies were not
previously in circulation. This category of infringement is not limited to the issue

a of copies the manufacture of which was unlicensed. It follows that it is now possible to infringe copyright by issuing authorised copies of a copyright work (for example made by or on behalf of the copyright owner) to the public, if the act of issuing itself has not been licensed. Mr Rye could still be held to infringe if he authorised the release of Simplex and that release was not authorised.

In the many cases this new category of infringement will not make a significant
b difference to the position of the parties. Even in the absence of an express licence to sell, it is likely that in many situations a licence to manufacture for the purpose of sale will carry such a licence with it by necessary implication. In the current case there clearly was a licence to whichever Cocteau company existed to issue copies of the Simplex album to the public, including the members of the Nelson fan club. Some 299 CDs out of a total of 995 manufactured were sold to fans. Mr
c Rye's involvement in that could not constitute authorising an infringing activity. Copies of the album were not only sold to members of the fan club. Cocteau Records 2 owed £3,000 to another company, See For Miles Records Ltd, in respect of storage charges. The balance of 696 CDs were sent to the latter company in lieu of the those charges. I hold that trading the albums to meet the
d commercial needs of Cocteau Records was contemplated and agreed to by Mr Nelson.

However, in his reply speech Mr Anderson raised a new point. He had elicited in cross-examination that See For Miles Records Ltd was a company in which Mr Rye had a significant interest. That interest had not been disclosed to Mr Nelson. Mr Anderson argued that in view of Mr Rye's fiduciary duty to Cocteau 2, it was
e not open to him to arrange for the latter company to supply records to See For Miles Records, effectively for his own benefit, and that that transaction was accordingly unlicensed. Even if he were correct on this point, there is nothing to suggest that the price achieved for these CDs, equivalent to £4·29 each, was not fair and it is likely that Mr Nelson has suffered no or very little as a result of the
f transaction. However, the argument is flawed. As indicated above, the sale or disposition by Cocteau 2 was licensed. Any sale or disposition by the company cannot be an infringement of Mr Nelson's rights. If complaint can be raised to the transaction with See For Miles Records it is not as an act of copyright infringement. It could only have been put forward as a breach of fiduciary duty as between Cocteau 2 and Mr Rye. It could not be a breach of fiduciary duty as
g between Mr Rye and Mr Nelson, because it has not been alleged that at the time of the transaction the former owed a fiduciary duty to the latter. In addition no such claim for breach of fiduciary duty was pleaded on behalf of Mr Nelson, nor was leave to amend sought. I therefore reject this argument also.

h *Judgment accordingly.*

Celia Fox   Barrister.

Practice Direction a

QUEEN'S BENCH DIVISION

Admiralty – Practice – Caveat against release – Praecipe for caveat against release by fax – Procedure for use – RSC Ord 75, r 14A. b

1. The purpose of the new RSC Ord 75, r 14A[a] is to avoid prejudice to claimants should a release of a vessel and/or cargo be sought after the court offices are closed to the public.

2. The designated fax number for the filing of a praecipe for caveat against release by fax is 0171-936 6056. c

3. It is essential that the designated fax number is used *and no other*, as that fax machine is manned 24 hours per day by court security staff. (Telephone number 0171-936 6000.)

4. Use of a fax number other than that designated will be ineffective for the purposes of the rule. d

5. The Admiralty and Commercial Registry will not accept a praecipe for caveat on the designated fax number or any other during the times the office is open to the public.

6. The praecipe for caveat should be transmitted with a note in the following form, for ease of identification by security staff:

'Caveat against release. Please find praecipe for caveat against release of e the ... (name of ship/identify cargo) ... for filing in the Admiralty and Commercial Registry.'

P M MILLER
15 January 1996   Admiralty Registrar. f

---

a   *Editor's note*: RSC Ord 75, r 14A was inserted by r 8 of the Rules of the Supreme Court (Amendment No 3) 1995, SI 1995/3316, and came into force on 15 January 1996.

Re a debtor (No 340 of 1992), ex parte the debtor v First National Commercial Bank plc and another

COURT OF APPEAL, CIVIL DIVISION

STUART-SMITH, WAITE AND MILLETT LJJ

28 FEBRUARY 1995

Execution – Writ of fi fa – Sheriff failing to gain access to debtor's premises – Sheriff returning writ as unsatisfied – Whether execution properly returned as unsatisfied – Whether defect curable as procedural irregularity – Insolvency Act 1986, s 268(1) – Insolvency Rules 1986, r 7.55.

Insolvency – Petition – Conditions for presentation – Proof of debtor's inability to pay – Summary judgment for amount of debt – Attempted execution of writ of fi fa – Sheriff failing to gain access to debtor's premises – Whether execution properly returned as unsatisfied – Whether defect curable as procedural irregularity – Insolvency Act 1986, s 268(1)(b) – Insolvency Rules 1986, r 7.55.

The appellant banks issued a writ against the respondent claiming £800,000 plus interest under two guarantees and obtained summary judgment for the sum of £910,071. The appellants delivered a writ of fieri facias to the sheriff, who twice visited the respondent's home but failed to obtain access; he subsequently indorsed the writ to the effect that despite attendance to levy on the goods and chattels of the respondent he had been unable to gain access to seize such goods and chattels and was therefore returning the writ as being unsatisfied. The appellants served a bankruptcy petition stating that the sheriff had 'made a return to the effect that the execution was unsatisfied as to the whole' of the debt. The respondent applied to the county court to strike out the petition on the ground that it was misconceived as none of the conditions set out in s 267[a] of the Insolvency Act 1986 had been fulfilled, namely that it had not been shown that there was a debt which the debtor appeared either to be unable to pay or had no reasonable prospect of being able to pay. The district judge held that the return, in merely asserting that on an unstated number of occasions, at unstated hours, and in unstated circumstances, the sheriff had failed to obtain access, did not comply with s 268(1)(b)[b] of the 1986 Act in that 'execution … in respect of the debt' had not been 'returned unsatisfied in whole or in part'. However, the district judge further held that the defect was a 'formal defect or irregularity' for the purposes of r 7.55 of the Insolvency Rules 1986 and did not invalidate the insolvency proceedings, since s 268 was merely a definition of inability to pay; the real test was whether the debtor was solvent and whether injustice would be done by a continuance of the petition. He also held that the petition should be allowed to proceed on the basis that the appellant would not be prejudiced. The respondent appealed. The judge, while affirming the district judge's decision that the sheriff's return did not comply with s 268(1)(b), held that the sheriff's failure to carry out the command in the writ could not be rectified as an irregularity

under r 7.55 of the 1986 rules, since that rule referred only to irregularities in the
proceedings, not in carrying out the conditions precedent to presentation of the
petition. The judge accordingly allowed the appeal and dismissed the petition.
The appellants appealed.

Held – (1) Where a petitioning creditor sought to prove the inability of an
individual to pay his debts by the return of an execution as unsatisfied in whole
or in part, s 268 of the 1986 Act required the court to inspect the return which the
sheriff had made to the writ of execution. Since the sheriff could not properly
make a return until after he had levied execution, the section therefore contemplated that execution should have taken place; a writ of execution should have
been issued to the sheriff, the sheriff should have executed it, and should have
indorsed a return on the writ stating the manner in which he had executed it. No
form of return existed to the effect that the sheriff had been unable to levy
execution. Unless a petitioning creditor could bring himself strictly within the
words of s 268(1)(b) by establishing that an execution had taken place but that it
was unsatisfied, and that that appeared from the return made by the sheriff, he
could not present a bankruptcy petition. If the sheriff was unable to obtain access
there was no execution, with the result that the sheriff's return in the instant case
was a false return (see p 215 *j* to p 216 *a e*, p 217 *b* to *d*, p 218 *f* and p 219 *b*, post);
Munk v Cass (1841) 9 Dowl 332 applied; *Re Douglas (Griggs) Engineering Ltd* [1962]
1 All ER 498 doubted.

(2) The appellants' failure as petitioning creditors to prove the respondent's
inability to pay his debts by the method provided by s 268(1)(b) of the 1986 Act
was not a formal defect, nor was it an irregularity of the kind to which r 7.55
related. In the absence of the necessary evidence to support the petition the court
was unable to treat the debtor as being unable to pay his debts within the
meaning of s 267 of the 1986 Act and accordingly had no ground upon which it
could make a bankruptcy order. The appeal would accordingly be dismissed (see
p 218 *g* to p 219 *b*, post).

Decision of Aldous J [1994] 3 All ER 269 affirmed.

Notes

For the execution of a writ of fi fa, see 17 *Halsbury's Laws* (4th edn) paras 427–435
and 462–499, and for cases on return to the writ, see 21(2) *Digest* (2nd reissue)
478–485, 2933–3010.

For bankruptcy petitions, see 3(2) *Halsbury's Laws* (4th edn reissue) paras 117–
126.

For the Insolvency Act 1986, ss 267, 268, see 4 *Halsbury's Statutes* (4th edn) (1987
reissue) 910, 911.

For the Insolvency Rules 1986, r 7.55, see 3 *Halsbury's Statutory Instruments*
(1995 reissue) 443.

Cases referred to in judgments

Douglas (Griggs) Engineering Ltd, Re [1962] 1 All ER 498, [1963] Ch 19, [1962] 2
　　WLR 893.
Flagstaff Silver Mining Co of Utah, Re (1875) LR 20 Eq 268.
Munk v Cass (1841) 9 Dowl 332.
Yate Collieries and Limeworks Co, Re [1883] WN 171.

a
Cases also cited or referred to in the skeleton arguments
Company, Re a [1974] 1 All ER 256, [1973] 1 WLR 1566.
Debtor, Re a (No 1 of 1987, Lancaster), ex p the debtor v Royal Bank of Scotland plc [1989] 2 All ER 46, [1989] 1 WLR 271, CA.
Debtor, Re a (No 190 of 1987) (1988) Times, 21 May.
King v Commercial Bank of Australia Ltd (1921) 29 CLR 141, Aust HC.
b   *Levi v Abbott* (1849) 4 Exch 588, 154 ER 1348.
Worsley, Re, ex p Gill (1957) 19 ABC 105, NSW SC.

Appeal

c
By notice dated 12 July 1993, the petitioning creditors, First National Commercial Bank plc and First National Bank plc, appealed from the decision of Aldous J ([1994] 3 All ER 269), who allowed an appeal by the debtor from the decision of District Judge Dinnock, sitting in Kingston-upon-Thames County Court on 3 February 1993, dismissing his application to strike out the bankruptcy petition. The facts are set out in the judgment of Millett LJ.

d
David Halpern (instructed by *Berwin Leighton*) for the appellants.
Simon Mortimore QC and *Hashim Reza* (instructed by *Wrights*) for the respondent.

e
MILLETT LJ (delivering the first judgment at the invitation of Stuart-Smith LJ). This is an appeal by the petitioning creditors, First National Commercial Bank plc and First National Bank plc, from a judgment of Aldous J ([1994] 3 All ER 269) given on 22 June 1993, when he allowed an appeal by the debtor from an order of District Judge Dinnock in the Kingston-upon-Thames County Court and dismissed the bankruptcy petition.

f
The bankruptcy petition arose out of guarantees which the debtor had given to the appellants in 1990 in respect of the debts of a company called Cambridge Trust plc, of which the debtor was a shareholder and director. The guarantees were for a total sum of £800,000 together with interest. The debtor appreciated that he would be unable to pay the sums due under the guarantees and proposed a voluntary arrangement with his creditors, but his proposals were rejected. The appellants demanded payment in October 1991. Their demand was not met.

g
They issued a writ on 5 May 1992 and obtained summary judgment from Master Gowers for £910,071 and costs on 27 October 1992. The debtor appealed to the judge, but his appeal was dismissed by Roger Kaye QC, sitting as a deputy judge of the High Court in the Chancery Division, on 18 December 1992. A further appeal by the debtor to this court was dismissed by us earlier today.

h
Meanwhile the appellants decided to bring bankruptcy proceedings. They were particularly anxious to obtain a bankruptcy order before 7 December 1992, because the debtor had transferred a half interest in the matrimonial home to his wife two years before that date. They had some six weeks after the judgment of Master Gowers in which to take the necessary steps to commence bankruptcy proceedings. They did not, however, serve a statutory demand, as they might have done. Instead, on 11 November 1992 they issued a writ of fieri facias. It was delivered to the sheriff on 3 December. The sheriff attended at the debtor's home on 10 and 14 December but he found no one at home and he was unable to gain access. The appellants' solicitors countermanded the execution on 15 December, and on 18 December 1992 the sheriff indorsed the writ as follows:

j

'I certify and return that despite attendances at [the address of the debtor] *to
levy on the goods and chattels of the within named* [debtor] *I have been unable to
gain access to seize such goods and chattels. I therefore return this writ as being
unsatisfied in whole.'*

The appellants served a bankruptcy petition on 7 January 1993. The petition
stated that the debtor was indebted in the sum of £910,071 and that the—

'Sheriff ... made a return ... to the effect that the execution was unsatisfied
... as to the whole ... and the above-mentioned debt represents the amount
by which the execution was returned unsatisfied.'

On 18 January 1993 the debtor applied to strike out the petition on the ground
that none of the preconditions for the service of a bankruptcy petition required
by s 267 of the Insolvency Act 1986 had been fulfilled. His application was
unsuccessful before the district judge but succeeded before the judge ([1994] 3 All
ER 260), and the appellants now appeal to us.

Under the former bankruptcy law a bankruptcy petition had to be founded on
an act of bankruptcy committed by the debtor. These were specified in s 1 of the
Bankruptcy Act 1914. The act of bankruptcy most commonly relied upon was
the failure of a debtor to comply with the requirements of a bankruptcy notice
served upon him by a judgment creditor: see s 1(1)(g) of the 1914 Act. Others,
which might have become relevant in the circumstances of the present case, were
para (e), '... suffering an execution upon his goods, under which the goods are
either sold or held by the sheriff for 21 days ...' and para (d), '... with intent to
defeat or delay his creditors ... departs from his dwelling-house, or otherwise
absents himself, or begins to keep house ...' The former required an actual
seizure of the debtor's goods by the sheriff to have taken place. If the judgment
debtor refused the sheriff entry, the court would treat him as having committed
an act of bankruptcy by 'keeping house'; and if the sheriff was unable to gain
access the court could infer that the debtor was absenting himself with intent to
defeat or delay his creditors. Either the debtor was keeping house or he was
deliberately absenting himself, in either case with intent to defeat or delay his
creditors, and in either case he would have committed an act of bankruptcy.

All that has been swept away by the 1986 Act. The very concept of the act of
bankruptcy has been abolished. Instead, s 267 of the 1986 Act provides, in sub-s
(2):

'Subject to the next three sections, a creditor's petition may be presented
to the court in respect of a debt or debts only if, at the time the petition is
presented ... (c) the debt, or each of the debts, is a debt which the debtor
appears either to be unable to pay or to have no reasonable prospect of being
able to pay ...'

Section 268 defines the circumstances in which a debtor can be regarded as
unable to pay his debts or as having no reasonable prospect of being able to pay
them. Subsection (1) deals with the case where the debtor appears to be unable
to pay a debt. It provides:

'For the purposes of section 267(2)(c), the debtor appears to be unable to
pay a debt if, but only if, the debt is payable immediately and either—(a)
[providing for the service of a statutory demand and the failure of the debtor
to comply with the demand or to have the statutory demand set aside] or (b)

a execution or other process issued in respect of the debt on a judgment or order of any court in favour of the petitioning creditor, or one or more of the appellants to whom the debt is owed, has been returned unsatisfied in whole or in part.'

Subsection (2) deals with the case where the debtor appears to have no reasonable prospect of being able to pay a debt, but it applies if, and only if, the
b debt is not immediately payable, so that it has no application in the circumstances of the present case.

Those provisions to some extent mirror the provisions which are applicable to the compulsory winding up of a company. Section 122 of the 1986 Act provides that a company may be wound up by the court, inter alia, if it is unable to pay its
c debts; and s 123 provides that a company is deemed to be unable to pay its debts in a number of different situations. Subsection (1)(a) provides for the service of a statutory demand. Paragraphs (b) and (e) provide:

'(b) if, in England and Wales, execution or other process issued on a judgment, decree or order of any court in favour of a creditor of the
d company is returned unsatisfied in whole or in part ... (e) if it is proved to the satisfaction of the court that the company is unable to pay its debts as they fall due.'

Accordingly, in assimilating the law of bankruptcy to the law of company winding up, the 1986 Act took two, but only two, of the methods provided in
e companies' winding up by which a creditor could establish that a company was unable to pay its debts, and it did not enact any provision corresponding to s 123(1)(e), which allows proof of the company's inability to pay its debts by any evidence which satisfies the court of the fact.

Provisions corresponding to s 123 of the 1986 Act were included in every
f Companies Act since 1862. Accordingly, authority on the circumstances in which execution may be treated as returned unsatisfied in whole or in part may be found in cases concerned with the winding up of companies. But, as I have said, there is one major difference. In the case of a company, its inability to pay its debts may be proved in any manner; an unsatisfied execution or the failure to comply with a statutory demand are only two of the methods by which it can be proved.
g Under the new code of personal bankruptcy introduced by the 1986 Act, however, the ability of an individual to pay his debts can be proved by only the two methods provided for by s 268; that is to say by the failure of the debtor to satisfy a statutory demand, or by the return of an execution as unsatisfied in whole or in part.

The first question which arises is whether in the present case the execution was
h returned unsatisfied. The form of a writ of fi fa can be found in *The Supreme Court Practice 1995* vol 2, p 26. It is, of course, like any other writ, a command of the Queen. It is addressed to the sheriff and requires him to seize goods, chattels and other property of the debtor in his county, and it is accompanied by a command that the sheriff should indorse on the writ *immediately after execution thereof* a
j statement of the manner in which the sheriff has executed it and send a copy of the statement to the creditor.

Section 268 of the 1986 Act requires the court to inspect the return which the sheriff has made to the writ of execution. But he cannot properly make a return until *after he has levied execution*. The section therefore contemplates that execution shall have taken place; that is to say that a writ of execution shall have

been issued to the sheriff, that the sheriff shall have executed it, and that he shall
have indorsed a return on the writ stating the manner in which he has executed it.

The manner in which a sheriff may indorse a return on a writ of execution has
been settled for centuries. There are three ordinary forms of return which are
applicable to the writ of fi fa. They are to be found in 17 *Halsbury's Laws* (4th edn)
para 497. They are: (i) fieri feci; (ii) nulla bona; and (iii) 'the goods and chattels
seized remain in my hands unsold for want of buyers'. The first is applicable
where the sheriff has seized and sold goods sufficient in value to satisfy the
amount to be levied. If the goods seized have realised insufficient to discharge
the whole sum due, the return of fieri feci can be combined with one of the other
two returns. The return of nulla bona is applicable where there are no goods of
the judgment debtor in the sheriff's bailiwick, the proceeds of which are available
to satisfy the writ. It is a good return if there are no goods at all, or if the proceeds
of the goods that have been sold have not proved sufficient to pay the costs of
levying execution. The third form of return, that 'the goods and chattels seized
remain in my hands unsold for want of buyers', may be used in appropriate cases
where no one has bid for the goods, or where no offer has been made of an
amount which reasonably approaches their value. There are other rare forms of
return in special cases, but none of them would be applicable in the circumstances
of the present case.

No form of return exists to the effect that the sheriff has been unable to levy
execution, and the form of the writ of fi fa indicates that this would not be a
proper return since the sheriff cannot make a return until he has executed the
writ. There is old authority to this effect in *Munk v Cass* (1841) 9 Dowl 332, which
contains the following passage:

'The substance of that return was, that the sheriff's officer ... had gone to
the premises of the defendant, and found them barricaded ... so as to be
inaccessible down to the time of making the return, by reason of which the
sheriff was unable to say whether ... the defendant, had any goods whereon
a levy might be made; that the sheriff could not find that [the defendant] had
any other residence wherein any property of which he was possessed could
be found.'

It was submitted that that was a sufficient excuse for the sheriff's failure to
execute the writ, and that the execution should be treated as unsatisfied.
Williams J stated in the course of argument that the sheriff did not say positively
either that there were goods or that there were no goods. Counsel pointed out
that the sheriff could not make any other return (at 333):

'He had no right to break open the outer door, in order to ascertain
whether there were goods on which he might levy ... and he could not
return nulla bona, because he would be liable, if there were any goods on
which a levy might be made, to an action for a false return.'

Williams J held that this was not a proper return. He said (at 333):

'No instance has been shewn to me in which it has been held, that the
sheriff can make such a return as this. No doubt he is in a situation of
difficulty. That, however, is not a case of novelty, as the sheriff is often
placed in positions of difficulty, out of which he must get as well as he can ...
He must either return that there are no goods to take, or he must take them.'

a   If s 268 of the 1986 Act were introducing a new ground by which a petitioning creditor could establish the debtor's inability to pay his debts, I for my part might have been willing to discard the old law on the subject of executions and to apply a liberal and purposive construction to the section. But it is not. The section is plainly derived from the Companies Acts, and the absence of any provision corresponding to s 123(1)(e) of the Companies Act 1985 shows that Parliament intended to confine the manner in which the petitioning creditor could establish

b   the debtor's insolvency within narrow limits. In my judgment, unless a petitioning creditor can bring himself strictly within the words of the relevant paragraph by establishing that an execution has taken place but that it is unsatisfied, and that this appears from the return made by the sheriff, then he cannot present a bankruptcy petition. If the sheriff is unable to obtain access, as

c   in the present case, or if the judgment debtor refuses entry, as in *Munk v Cass*, then in either case there is no execution. In my view the sheriff's return in the present case was a false return. Likewise, a return to the effect that the writ has not been executed (for example, because the judgment debtor had ceased to trade) would not be a proper return. Sheriffs sometimes return that the judgment debtor has

d   no assets at the address given. As at present advised, I am of the opinion that that is not a proper return. The sheriff must state that the judgment debtor either has assets, or that he has no assets within the bailiwick.

    The sheriff need not, of course, express himself in Latin, but the return should be short and concise and correspond as nearly as practicable to the old forms of return. He should not enter upon a lengthy explanation of the circumstances

e   which precluded him from levying execution.

    Before us counsel for the appellants has submitted that the authorities under the Companies Acts show that the court takes a liberal approach to the requirement in respect of unsatisfied executions in founding a winding up petition. But on examination the cases do not support the submission. The first

f   case which was cited to us was *Re Flagstaff Silver Mining Co of Utah* (1875) LR 20 Eq 268. The petition was presented by a judgment creditor who sought a winding-up order on the ground that the company was unable to pay its debts. The petitioner had not issued execution on the judgment, but this was because the company's solicitors had informed the petitioner that the company had no

g   property on which he could levy execution. After the petition was presented the company managed to pay the petitioner's debt, but it did not pay his costs and the petition therefore came on for hearing. The petitioner asked for the costs of the petition. Counsel for the company referred to s 80(2) of the Companies Act 1862, which was concerned with unsatisfied execution, and submitted that—

h   'a company cannot be deemed to be unable to pay its debts unless the judgment creditor petitioning has actually issued execution, and such execution has been returned unsatisfied in whole or in part.' (See LR 20 Eq 268.)

j That submission completely ignored the existence of sub-s (4) (which corresponded to s 123(1)(e) of the 1986 Act). Hall V-C gave judgment for the petitioner. He said (at 269):

      'Where the judgment creditor is told by the company that they have no assets on which he can levy, that is evidence of their inability to pay their debts, so as to relieve the judgment creditor from the necessity of actually *a* levying.'

In my judgment that was a case in which the court accepted the admission of no assets as evidence of inability to pay the debt which satisfied sub-s (4). It did not accept the admission as evidence of an unsatisfied execution, and could not sensibly have done so.

The second case is to the same effect. It is *Re Yate Collieries and Limeworks Co* *b* [1883] WN 171, where the circumstances were very similar. The petitioning creditor was a judgment creditor. The company's solicitors stated that all its property had been taken possession of by a mortgagee and that there was nothing on which the plaintiff could levy execution. Accordingly, the judgment creditor did not attempt to levy execution but presented a winding-up petition and relied *c* upon the solicitors' statement as evidence that the company was unable to pay its debts. North J held, on the authority of *Re Flagstaff Silver Mining Co of Utah*, that the evidence was sufficient. That, in my judgment, was another case on s 80(4) of the 1862 Act.

The third case is a more modern one: *Re Douglas (Griggs) Engineering Ltd* [1962] 1 All ER 498, [1963] Ch 19, where, in reply to the petitioning creditor's solicitors, *d* the company's solicitors wrote stating that there were no assets of the company either at the solicitor's office or at the company's place of business upon which execution could be levied in respect of a judgment debt. On a petition for the compulsory winding up of the company, Pennycuick J held that, having regard to the letter of the company's solicitors, the company must be deemed to be unable *e* to pay its debts within the meaning of s 223(b) of the Companies Act 1948. When I first read the headnote, I thought that that must be a misprint for s 223(d), but the judgment of Pennycuick J refers unmistakeably to para (b) (that is to say the unsatisfied execution paragraph). With all respect to Pennycuick J, I think on that occasion Homer must have nodded. It was a clear case in which, following the *Flagstaff Silver Mining* case, the court was entitled to rely on the admission of the *f* company's solicitor as evidence that it was unable to pay its debts. It should have been treated as a case under s 223 para (d) and not para (b). For my own part I do not see how it can possibly be said that an execution has been returned unsatisfied in whole or in part if no writ of execution has been issued at all.

Finally, counsel for the appellants submitted that we ought to exercise the *g* power in r 7.55 of the Insolvency Rules 1986, SI 1986/1925, to waive a formal defect or irregularity. That rule provides:

'No insolvency proceedings shall be invalidated by any formal defect or by any irregularity, unless the court before which objection is made considers that substantial injustice has been caused by the defect or irregularity, and *h* that the injustice cannot be remedied by any order of the court.'

In my judgment, reliance on that rule fails as soon as the nature of the defect in the present case is appreciated. It is the failure of the appellants to prove the debtor's inability to pay his debts by either of the only two methods provided for by the 1986 Act. That is not a formal defect, nor is it in my judgment an *j* irregularity of the kind to which r 7.55 relates. Since the appellants served no statutory demand, although they were in a position to do so, they must prove that they sought to levy execution on the debtor's goods and the execution was returned unsatisfied. They proved the former but not the latter. As a result, they failed to prove the facts necessary to support the petition. In the absence of the a necessary evidence, the court was unable to treat the debtor as being unable to pay his debts within the meaning of s 267 of the 1986 Act and accordingly had no ground upon which it could make a bankruptcy order.

For my part I would dismiss the appeal.

WAITE LJ. I agree.

b **STUART-SMITH LJ.** I also agree.

Appeal dismissed.

Paul Magrath Esq   Barrister

Mainwaring v Trustees of Henry Smith's Charity a

COURT OF APPEAL, CIVIL DIVISION

SIR THOMAS BINGHAM MR, SIMON BROWN AND HUTCHISON LJJ b

6, 7, 16 FEBRUARY 1996

Landlord and tenant – Leasehold enfranchisement – Tenants' rights of first refusal – Relevant disposal – Landlord contracting to sell premises subject to tenants' rights to purchase freehold, but without serving notices conferring rights of first refusal – c *Contract providing that service of statutory notices subject to satisfaction of condition precedent – Prospective purchaser serving notices inquiring whether tenants wished to exercise rights of first refusal – Tenant seeking service of notices by landlord – Whether 'relevant disposal' made – Whether landlord 'proposing' to make relevant disposal – Point at which notices conferring rights of first refusal required to be served – Landlord and Tenant Act 1987, ss 4, 5, 18.* d

The appellant, M, was a statutory tenant of premises in Kensington which constituted part of an estate owned by the respondent trustees. The premises fell within the scope of the Landlord and Tenant Act 1987, which provided by s 5^a that where the landlord proposed to make a 'relevant disposal' affecting the e premises, he should serve a notice on qualifying tenants affording them the right of first refusal, and by s 18^b granted a permissive right to prospective purchasers to inquire of tenants whether they had rights under any s 5 notice served by the landlord and to invite them to assert those rights. In July 1995 the trustees agreed to sell the estate to W, a charitable trust. The relevant contract provided, inter alia, (i) that the trustees had not served s 5 notices and that the property was sold f subject to and notwithstanding any rights the tenants had under the 1987 Act; (ii) that after the date of the sale agreement W would serve on specified tenants s 18 notices; and (iii) that if as a result of the tenants' responses the property was to be treated as one to which the Act applied, the completion date would be postponed and the trustees would serve s 5 notices on the qualifying tenants once the estate g management scheme application (which the trustees had made in 1984) had been finally determined. In accordance with the agreement, W served a s 18 notice on M, who, with a majority of the other qualifying tenants, responded by stating that they wished to avail themselves of the right of first refusal conferred by a s 5 notice, if served. Upon the trustees' refusal, pursuant to their contract with W, h to serve s 5 notices until after the estate management scheme application had been determined, the appellant applied to the county court for an order requiring the trustees to serve s 5 notices on her and the other qualifying tenants so as to enable them to pursue their rights under the Act. The application was refused, on the ground that the time for serving s 5 notices would not come until the outcome of the estate management scheme application. On M's appeal, the j issues arose whether (i) there had been a 'relevant disposal' within the meaning of s 4^c of the 1987 Act or, alternatively, (ii) the trustees 'proposed' to make a

---

a   Section 5, so far as material, is set out at p 223 *j* to p 224 *c*, post
b   Section 18, so far as material, is set out at p 224 *j* to p 225 *g*, post
c   Section 4, so far as material, is set out at p 232 *g*, post

a relevant disposal within the meaning of s 5 and (iii) if so, whether the trustees had failed to comply with their statutory duties by failing to serve notices under s 5.

Held – (1) A 'relevant disposal' within the meaning of s 4 of the 1987 Act referred to a completed conveyance and not an exchange of contracts for the sale of premises to which Pt I of the Act applied. That construction was supported by
b sub-s (2), which, by excluding as relevant disposals certain forms of final transfer, indicated that it was the final transfer and not the preliminary agreement which was intended to be treated as the relevant disposal. On the facts, moreover, it was clear that the contract as it stood was not specifically enforceable by the court so long as the condition as to the approval of the estate management scheme had
c not been fulfilled and the trustees had not complied with their statutory obligation to serve notices under s 5. It followed that no relevant disposal had taken place (see p 232 *h* and p 233 *b* to *f*, post).

(2) The expression 'proposes' in s 5 of the 1987 Act denoted a state of mind between mere consideration of a possible course of action, on the one hand, and
d a fixed and irrevocable determination to pursue that course of action, on the other, and it was necessarily implicit in the legislation that a proposal was none the less such even though the tenants of the affected premises were entitled to assert their right to buy. It could not be suggested that a party did not propose to do that which he had bound himself to do by contract, and the fact that a third
e party might succeed in defeating or frustrating his proposal did not mean that he ceased to propose, only that he might be unsuccessful in implementing his proposal. On the facts, it was clear that the trustees were 'proposing' to make a disposal for the purposes of s 5, since the parties had contractually adopted the s 18 procedure, which was only appropriate where disposal by a landlord was
f proposed, and W had itself stated in the s 18 notices it served that it was 'proposing' to take a disposal of the trustees' interest in the building (see p 233 *j* to p 234 *b d* to *g*, post).

(3) While there was no precise period within which a notice under s 5 of the 1987 Act was required to be served by a landlord who proposed to make a
g relevant disposal, the effect of s 5(2)(c) and (d) was to require the notice to be served a minimum of 4 months before the date of the relevant disposal, and s 18 plainly envisaged that a s 5 notice should have been served by the time a prospective purchaser became entitled to serve a notice under s 18. It followed that the trustees should have served s 5 notices on M and the other qualifying
h tenants of the premises at or within a few days of contracting with W and possibly even sooner, and that they were in breach of their statutory duty in failing to do so. The appeal would accordingly be allowed on that issue (see p 235 *h* to p 236 *b*, post).

j Per curiam. Although the use of the s 18 notice procedure in circumstances where the prospective purchaser, as a result of comprehensive disclosure by the original landlord, is in full possession of details of the terms on which the various tenants hold their interests and where it has contracted with the original landlord that no s 5 notice shall be served, is not expressly prohibited in the 1987 Act, it is highly artificial and far from what the draftsman of the Act can have intended (see p 235 *d* to *g*, post).

Notes

a

For notices conferring rights of first refusal, see 27(2) *Halsbury's Laws* (4th edn reissue) paras 1595–1600, and for notices served by prospective purchasers, see ibid para 1611.

For the Landlord and Tenant Act 1987, ss 4, 5, 18, see 23 *Halsbury's Statutes* (4th edn) (1989 reissue) 388, 389, 407.

b

Cases referred to in judgment

Belvedere Court Management Ltd v Frogmore Developments Ltd [1996] 1 All ER 312, CA.
Central Trust and Safe Deposit Co v Snider [1916] 1 AC 266, PC.
Cunliffe v Goodman [1950] 1 All ER 720, [1950] 2 KB 237, CA.
Magdalen and Lasher Charity, Hastings (Trustees) v Shelower (1968) 19 P & CR 389,   c
CA.
Wilkins v Horrowitz [1990] 2 EGLR 217.

Cases also cited or referred to in skeleton arguments

Alsop Wilkinson (a firm) v Neary [1995] 1 All ER 431.   d
Manchester Ship Canal Co v Manchester Racecourse Co [1901] 2 Ch 37, CA.
Pritchard v Briggs [1980] 1 All ER 294, [1980] Ch 338, [1979] 3 WLR 868, CA.
Richardson v Leathbond Ltd (31 October 1994, unreported), Cty Ct.
Tyson v Carlisle Estates Ltd [1990] 2 EGLR 229.
Wood Preservation Ltd v Prior (Inspector of Taxes) [1968] 2 All ER 849; *affd* [1969] 1
All ER 364, [1969] 1 WLR 1077, CA.   e

Appeal

By notice dated 5 December 1995 Zipporah Mainwaring (the applicant) appealed from the order of Judge Uziell-Hamilton sitting in the West London County Court on 20 November 1995 whereby, subject to undertakings on the part of the   f
respondents, the trustees of Henry Smith's Charity (the Smith trustees), she refused the applicant's originating application dated 19 September 1995 for inter alia an order that the Smith trustees issue to the applicant a notice pursuant to the terms of s 5 of the Landlord and Tenant Act 1987 in relation to the proposed disposal of the property known as 38–62 Yeoman's Row, London SW3 to Wellcome Trust Ltd as trustees of The Wellcome Trust. The Smith trustees   g
cross-appealed, seeking to vary the undertakings ordered by the judge. The facts are set out in the judgment of the court.

The applicant appeared in person.
David Neuberger QC and *Erica Foggin* (instructed by *Denton Hall*) for the Smith   h
trustees.

Cur adv vult

16 February 1996. The following judgment of the court was delivered.

j

SIR THOMAS BINGHAM MR. Henry Smith, a well-to-do salter, died in 1628, making in his will a number of charitable bequests. Among these were two bequests of £1,000, to be invested in land for the benefit of charitable causes. His trustees invested the money in 84 acres of land, which, happily for posterity, lay close to the village of Brompton, just to the west of what was then the built-up area of London. Over the centuries the tide of development flowed westwards, *a*   and on the land there was built what came to be known as the Kensington Estate of the Trustees of Henry Smith's Charity, now comprising some 58 acres of prime residential and commercial development. The value of the estate became very great, and large sums were over the years paid to charity as a result.

b   In July 1995 the trustees of Henry Smith's Charity (the Smith trustees) agreed to sell the Kensington Estate to Wellcome Trust Ltd as the trustees of The Wellcome Trust (Wellcome), another famous charity. Ms Zipporah Mainwaring (the applicant) is a tenant of the Smith trustees. She complains that the Smith trustees' omissions at the time of this agreement and since have violated her rights under the Landlord and Tenant Act 1987. Her complaint was rejected by Judge Uziell-Hamilton in the West London County Court on 20 November 1995. The applicant appeals to this court from that decision.

c

I

Sir Thomas Bingham MR touched on the genesis of the 1987 Act in section VI of his judgment in *Belvedere Court Management Ltd v Frogmore Developments Ltd* [1996] 1 All ER 312 at 325. The Act provides that if, in certain closely defined *d* situations, a landlord proposes to dispose of his interest in premises of a certain kind, the tenants living in those premises shall have a priority right to acquire that interest on the same terms as those on which the landlord is willing to dispose of the interest to another. The long title of the 1987 Act describes it as 'An Act to confer on tenants of flats rights with respect to the acquisition by them of their landlord's reversion ...'

e   Section 1 of the 1987 Act provides (in part):

'*Qualifying tenants to have rights of first refusal on disposals by landlord.*—(1) A landlord shall not make a relevant disposal affecting any premises to which at the time of the disposal this Part applies unless—(a) he has in accordance *f*   with section 5 previously served a notice under that section with respect to the disposal on the qualifying tenants of the flats contained in those premises (being a notice by virtue of which rights of first refusal are conferred on those tenants); and (b) the disposal is made in accordance with the requirements of sections 6 to 10.

(2) Subject to subsections (3) and (4), this Part applies to premises if—(a) *g*   they consist of the whole or part of a building; and (b) they contain two or more flats held by qualifying tenants; and (c) the number of flats held by such tenants exceeds 50 per cent. of the total number of flats contained in the premises ...'

h   The applicant lives as a statutory tenant in a flat at 40 Yeoman's Row, SW3, which is part of an unpretentious block built in the 1950s containing flats numbered 38–62 (even numbers) Yeoman's Row (the building). It is common ground in these proceedings that the building falls within the scope of the 1987 Act, that the Smith trustees are the applicant's landlord and that the applicant herself is a qualifying tenant within the meaning of the 1987 Act. The meaning *j*   of the expression 'relevant disposal' is governed by s 4 of the 1987 Act: the construction of that section is central to one of the issues in these proceedings, and the section is quoted in section III below.

Section 5 of the 1987 Act is important. It opens:

'*Requirement to serve notice concerning rights of first refusal.*—(1) Where, in the case of any premises to which this Part applies, the landlord proposes to make a relevant disposal affecting the premises, he shall serve a notice under *a* this section on the qualifying tenants of the flats contained in the premises.

(2) A notice under this section must—(a) contain particulars of the principal terms of the disposal proposed by the landlord, including in particular—(i) the property to which it relates and the estate or interest in that property proposed to be disposed of, and (ii) the consideration required by the landlord for making the disposal; (b) state that the notice constitutes *b* an offer by the landlord to dispose of the property on those terms which may be accepted by the requisite majority of qualifying tenants of the constituent flats; (c) specify a period within which that offer may be so accepted, being a period of not less than two months which is to begin with the date of service of the notice; and (d) specify a further period within which a person or persons may be nominated for the purposes of section 6, being a period of *c* not less than two months which is to begin with the end of the period specified under paragraph (c) ...'

Subsection (4) provides that where a landlord has not served a notice under the section on all of the qualifying tenants on whom it was required to be served by sub-s (1), he shall nevertheless be treated as having complied with that subsection *d* if he has served the notice on not fewer than 90% of the qualifying tenants on whom it was required to be served. It is a notable feature of the section that although it lays a clear mandatory duty on a landlord, there is apparently no sanction against a landlord who fails to comply: in practice, neglect of the statutory duty has been common and has given rise to considerable litigation. *e*

Section 6 governs the situation where the requisite majority of qualifying tenants inform the landlord that they wish to accept the offer contained in his notice and nominate someone to act on their behalf. In that event the landlord may not during a period of 12 months following acceptance dispose of his interest except to a person or persons nominated for the purposes of the section by the requisite majority of qualifying tenants of the constituent flats. Sections 7 and 8 *f* of the 1987 Act govern rejection of the landlord's offer, the making of a counter-offer by the tenants and the making of a fresh offer by the landlord. All offers and counter-offers are treated as if made subject to contract (s 20(2)).

Section 9 provides for the withdrawal of either party from the transaction. By sub-s (4) the landlord may indicate an intention no longer to proceed with the *g* disposal of his interest, and in that event he is not entitled to dispose of it (unless he embarks on the s 5 procedure all over again). The person nominated by the requisite majority of qualifying tenants to act on their behalf may similarly withdraw from the transaction and must do so if he becomes aware that the number of qualifying tenants of the constituent flats desiring to proceed with the *h* acquisition of the landlord's interest is less than the requisite majority of qualifying tenants of those flats (sub-s (3)). The landlord's offer lapses if the building in question ceases to be one to which the 1987 Act applies and the landlord gives the appropriate notice (s 10).

Sections 11 to 17 govern the rights of qualifying tenants against a purchaser from a landlord who has disposed of his interest to such purchaser without *j* fulfilling his obligations under ss 1 to 9. In such event, the qualifying tenants have rights (although lesser rights) against such purchaser or a subsequent purchaser.

Section 18 provides:

'*Notices served by prospective purchasers to ensure that rights of first refusal do not arise.*—(1) Where—(a) any disposal of an estate or interest in any premises *a* consisting of the whole or part of a building is proposed to be made by a landlord, and (b) it appears to the person who would be the transferee under that disposal ("the purchaser") that any such disposal would, or might, be a relevant disposal affecting premises to which this Part applies, the purchaser may serve notices under this subsection on the tenants of the flats contained in the premises referred to in paragraph (a) ("the flats affected").

b (2) Any notice under subsection (1) shall—(a) inform the person on whom it is served of the general nature of the principal terms of the proposed disposal, including in particular—(i) the property to which it would relate and the estate or interest in that property proposed to be disposed of by the landlord, and (ii) the consideration required by him for making the disposal; *c* (b) invite that person to serve a notice on the purchaser stating—(i) whether the landlord has served on him, or on any predecessor in title of his, a notice under section 5 with respect to the disposal, and (ii) if the landlord has not so served any such notice, whether he is aware of any reason why he is not entitled to be served with any such notice by the landlord, and (iii) if he is not so aware, whether he would wish to avail himself of the right of first refusal *d* conferred by any such notice if it were served; and (c) inform that person of the effect of the following provisions of this section.

(3) Where the purchaser has served notices under subsection (1) on at least 80 per cent. of the tenants of the flats affected and—(a) not more than 50 per cent. of the tenants on whom those notices have been served by the *e* purchaser have served notices on him in pursuance of subsection (2)(b) by the end of the period of 28 days beginning with the date on which the last of them was served by him with a notice under this section, or (b) more than 50 per cent. of the tenants on whom those notices have been served by the purchaser have served notices on him in pursuance of subsection (2)(b) but *f* the notices in each case indicate that the tenant serving it either—(i) does not regard himself as being entitled to be served by the landlord with a notice under section 5 with respect to the disposal, or (ii) would not wish to avail himself of the right of first refusal conferred by such a notice if it were served, the premises affected by the disposal shall, in relation to the disposal, be treated for the purposes of this Part as premises to which this Part does not *g* apply ...'

There are significant distinctions between this section and s 5.

It is, first of all, plain that whereas s 5 imposes a mandatory statutory duty on landlords, s 18 grants a permissive right to prospective purchasers. This *h* distinction is not hard to explain. Section 5 is directed to ensuring that the object of the 1987 Act, to give qualifying tenants an opportunity to purchase their landlord's reversion if he proposes to sell, is effectually achieved. By contrast, the primary object of s 18, as the heading of the section makes clear, is to enable a prospective purchaser to protect himself against the risk that he may buy the *j* landlord's interest only to find that the tenants assert their right to acquire that interest from him. Section 18 enables a prospective purchaser to protect himself against that risk by ascertaining whether the tenants have rights under the 1987 Act, and if they do calling upon them to assert those rights; if the tenants fail to assert those rights, they lose them and the prospective purchaser can proceed without the risk of losing the fruits of his purchase. This procedure has the incidental result of alerting a tenant, hitherto unaware of the impending purchase

and of his rights, to his rights under the 1987 Act, but that would not appear to be
the main object of the section.   *a*

The second important distinction concerns the provisions for service.
Whereas the landlord under s 5 must serve not less than 90% of the qualifying
tenants, the prospective purchaser under s 18 need only serve 80% of the tenants.
This distinction is again readily understandable. The landlord is in a position to
know who his tenants are, and whether or not they are qualifying. The   *b*
prospective purchaser, by contrast, may have little information about who the
tenants are and whether they are qualifying tenants or not. Since the prospective
purchaser must in a notice served under s 18(2)(b) invite the tenants whom he
serves to state whether the landlord has served on those tenants a notice under
s 5, it is to be inferred that the prospective purchaser is likely to be unaware   *c*
whether such a notice has been served or not. But where the original landlord
and the prospective purchaser are acting in concert, the possibility of abuse exists,
as the applicant showed by a hypothetical example. If a qualifying building had
20 tenants, of whom 11 were qualifying and 9 not, the original landlord and the
purchaser, with access to full information, could combine to serve the requisite
percentage of 80% of tenants under s 18 by serving the nine non-qualifying   *d*
tenants and seven qualifying tenants. The nine non-qualifying tenants would
either fail to respond, or respond correctly acknowledging no entitlement to
service of a s 5 notice. It would then be impossible for the qualifying tenants to
muster the requisite 50% majority of the tenants served. In this way, the rights
of the qualifying tenants (where the landlord had not himself served s 5 notices)
would be defeated. The applicant did not suggest that this hypothetical example   *e*
matched the facts of this case, which it plainly does not. The possibility of abuse
does, however, exist, and it appears that s 18 has been abused by unscrupulous
landlords.

The third obvious distinction between the two sections concerns the period
allowed to the tenants to respond to the notice served by the landlord and the *f*
prospective purchaser, a minimum of two months under s 5 and 28 days under
s 18. The distinction is again understandable. In responding to a s 5 notice, the
qualifying tenants have to make a decision whether they wish to buy on the terms
of the landlord's offer, which involves the making of a joint decision whether they
can between them raise the necessary purchase price. In a case such as the   *g*
present, the sum involved may be very considerable, and the raising of finance
may inevitably take some time. The tenants served under s 18 do not have, at
that stage, to carry out that task: they simply have to decide whether they are
qualifying tenants and whether they would wish to avail themselves of the right
of first refusal conferred by a s 5 notice if it were served. It is not surprising that *h*
the time allowed for a response to that notice is very much shorter. The
possibility does, however, exist that if a tenant is absent from his flat, whether on
holiday or for reasons of business or sickness, the s 18 notice may simply fail to
come to his attention in time for him to respond to it, and in such a situation the
benefit of the 1987 Act will be lost unless the landlord has observed, or observes,
his duty to serve a notice under s 5.   *j*

Reference should lastly be made to s 19 of the 1987 Act, which provides:

'*Enforcement of obligations under Part I.*

(1) The court may, on the application of any person interested, make an
order requiring any person who has made default in complying with any

a   duty imposed on him by any provision of this Part to make good the default within such time as is specified in the order.

(2) An application shall not be made under subsection (1) unless—(a) a notice has been previously served on the person in question requiring him to make good the default, and (b) more than 14 days have elapsed since the date of service of that notice without his having done so.

b   (3) The restriction imposed by section 1(1) may be enforced by an injunction granted by the court.'

II

On 12 October 1994 the Smith trustees applied to the leasehold valuation c   tribunal for approval of a proposed estate management scheme relating to parts of the Kensington Estate. This application was made under s 70(1) of Pt I, Ch IV of the Leasehold Reform, Housing and Urban Development Act 1993. In making this application the Smith trustees appreciated that their tenants could exercise rights of enfranchisement under the Leasehold Reform Act 1967, the 1987 Act d   and the 1993 Act. The object of the scheme, if approved, was to enable the Smith trustees to continue to exercise powers of management over parts of the Kensington Estate of which they had ceased to be freehold owners. At the time when this application was made, the Smith trustees were in communication with Wellcome, but it appears that no bargain had yet been made.

On 24 July 1995 the Smith trustees and Wellcome executed 144 contracts by e   which the Smith trustees were to sell the entirety of the Kensington Estate to Wellcome. One of these was a main contract and covered all the properties believed by the parties to be subject to no claims for enfranchisement under the 1987 Act. The remaining 143 contracts related to separate buildings in relation to which it was thought that the tenants might enjoy such rights. One of these f   contracts related to the building. By the contract the Smith trustees agreed to sell and Wellcome to buy this building for £1,057,255 on the conditions set out in the contract. In recognition of the difficulty of finalising a sale contract of this kind when the affairs of the estate were inevitably in a constant state of flux, the parties adopted a 'deadline date' of 2 June 1995. Clause 13 of the contract is material to the present proceedings and must be quoted so far as relevant:

g
'Service of Notices under the Act   13.1 The Vendor has not served any notices on the Tenants under the provisions of Section 5 of the Act and the Property is sold subject to and notwithstanding the rights (if any) which the Tenants may have by virtue of the provisions of the Act

13.2 The Purchaser will procure that the Purchaser's Solicitors will on the h   second Working Day following the date of this Agreement serve upon each of the Section 18 Tenants at the relevant address set out in the schedule headed "Blocks and tenants on Smith's Charity where Landlord & Tenant Act 1987 applies" supplied by the Vendor's Surveyors to the Purchaser's Solicitors dated 6th June 1995 as varied by written alterations notified to the j   Purchaser's Solicitors by the Vendor's Surveyors prior to the date hereof a Section 18 Notice PROVIDED THAT where any such address is within the Kensington Estate such service will be effected by personal delivery through the letterbox of the relevant flat or building containing the relevant flat (the person effecting such personal delivery making an affidavit of due service forthwith thereafter) and in all other cases such service will be effected by sending the Section 18 Notice by recorded delivery post

13.3 The Purchaser will procure that the Purchaser's Solicitors will supply
to the Vendor's Solicitors a copy of each Section 18 Notice and will further
supply to the Vendor's Solicitors a copy of any written reply which may be
received to any Section 18 Notice as soon as reasonably practicable after the
same has been received by the Purchaser's Solicitors

13.4 As soon as reasonably practicable after the expiry of a period of
twenty-nine days after the date of delivery or posting of the Section 18
Notices (or if all Section 18 Notices shall not be delivered or posted on the
same day then the date of delivery or posting of the last of them) the
Purchaser will procure that the Purchaser's Solicitors confirm to the
Vendor's Solicitors which Section 18 Tenants have given a written response
to their respective Section 18 Notice (if they have not already provided a
copy of the same to the Vendor's Solicitors)

13.5 If as a result of the Section 18 Tenants' responses as referred to in
Clause 13.4 the Property shall be treated for the purposes of the Act as
premises to which the Act does not apply completion of the sale and
purchase hereby agreed will take place in accordance with Clause 17 on the
Initial Completion Date

13.6 If as a result of the Section 18 Tenants' responses as referred to in
Clause 13.4 the Property shall be treated for the purposes of the Act as
premises to which the Act applies in accordance with the provisions of
Section 18(3) of the Act then the following provisions shall apply:—(a) The
Completion Date shall be postponed until the last Working Day of the
calendar month in which the date falls ("the Date") on which the Vendor
shall no longer be obliged to transfer the Property to the Tenants or their
nominee pursuant to the Act in accordance with Clause 13.6(d) or the last
Working Day of the calendar month following the calendar month in which
the Date falls if the result would otherwise require the Completion Date to
occur less than 6 Working Days after the Date; (b) The Vendor will procure
that the Vendor's Solicitors shall ... (ii) (if the Property is within the area of
the Estate Management Scheme Application) as soon as reasonably
practicable after the Estate Management Scheme Application has been
withdrawn dismissed or approved (with or without amendments) and the
provisions of Section 74(2) of the Leasehold Reform, Housing and Urban
Development Act 1993 have therefore ceased to apply in relation to the
Property; serve a notice under Section 5 of the Act upon each of the Tenants
who are "qualifying tenants" as defined in the Act and supply a copy of each
such notice and any response thereto to the Purchaser's Solicitors as soon as
reasonably practicable after the same has been served or received as the case
may be; (c) The Vendor will comply with all the requirements of Section 5
of the Act and as quickly as reasonably possible and will keep the Purchaser's
solicitors informed of progress thereon and supply copies of all relevant
correspondence notices or other relevant papers under the Act (d) If at any
time the Vendor ceases to be obliged under the provisions of the Act to
transfer the Property to the Tenants or their nominee then the Vendor will
procure that the Vendor's Solicitors will forthwith notify the Purchaser's
Solicitors PROVIDED THAT for the avoidance of doubt it is not the parties'
intention to serve the said notices prior to an appeal being lodged by the
Tenants against the approval of the Estate Management Scheme Application
where it is known or believed that such an appeal is to be lodged

a
13.7 Nothing in this Agreement contained shall prevent the Vendor from selling the Property to the Tenants or their nominee if the Vendor is obliged so to do pursuant to the Act and in such a case the Vendor's obligation to sell and the Purchaser's obligation to purchase the Property pursuant to this Agreement will become void and of no further force or effect simultaneously with completion of the sale of the Property to the Tenants or their nominee

b
as aforesaid and the Purchaser will forthwith after such completion remove any entries which it may have made in the Land Charges Register or any other register protecting its right to purchase the Property

13.8 In the event that on the 30th March 1997 completion of the sale of the Property (whether to the Purchaser or to the Tenants or their nominee) has not taken place then the following provisions shall apply:—(a) The Vendor

c
shall withdraw from any negotiations then continuing with the Tenants and/or their nominee; (b) The Vendor and the Purchaser shall endeavour to agree the open market value of the Property as at the 30th March 1997 such value being calculated on the same basis as the basis used to agree (on behalf of the Vendor and the Purchaser respectively) the Price as stated in the Information Sheet annexed hereto but if the parties are unable to agree such

d
open market value then the same shall be determined by an independent chartered surveyor experienced in the Central London residential market appointed by the President of the Royal Institution of Chartered Surveyors on the application of either of the parties and that surveyor shall act as an expert and shall afford to each of the parties the opportunity to make

e
representations to him on such value; (c) The said open market value agreed or determined as aforesaid shall be substituted for the Price for all purposes as between the Vendor and the Purchaser and as between the Vendor and the Tenants or their nominee; (d) If once the said open market value has been agreed or determined as aforesaid the Act applies to the Property the

f
Vendor shall forthwith serve a notice under Section 5 of the Act upon each of the "qualifying tenants" and the provisions of Clauses 13.6(a)–(d) and 13.7 shall apply; (e) If the Vendor is not obliged to serve notice(s) under Section 5 of the Act pursuant to Clause 13.8(d) then completion of the sale of the Property to the Purchaser will take place in accordance with the provisions of Clause 13.6(a) as though "the Date" therein referred to was the date on

g
which the said open market value as agreed or determined as aforesaid'

The expression 'Section 18 Tenants' was defined to mean those tenants whose names and addresses were included in the schedule referred to in cl 13.2.

h
The Smith trustees undertook that they would not after the date of this contract grant or enter into any agreement to grant a new lease, licence, tenancy or occupation of the building or take a surrender of or enter into an agreement to surrender any lease. Condition 3 of the Law Society's National Conditions, giving a right to rescind, was specifically excluded. A schedule to the contract prescribed the form of s 18 notice to be served by Wellcome.

j
On the same day, 24 July 1995, the chairman of the Smith trustees wrote to the applicant among other tenants and said:

'I am writing to let you know that my fellow Trustees and I have decided to accept an offer for the sale of the whole of the Kensington Estate (which includes your property), which has been made by the Wellcome Trust.'

On 25 July the chairman of the board of governors of Wellcome wrote to the *a*
applicant among other tenants and said:

> 'You should by now have received a letter from Smith's Charity explaining
> that they have contracted to sell the Kensington Estate to the Wellcome
> Trust.'

On 26 July 1995 estate agents acting for the Smith trustees and Wellcome wrote *b*
to the applicant and other tenants explaining why the Smith trustees had sold and
Wellcome bought the Kensington Estate. On 27 July 1995 solicitors acting for
Wellcome issued to the applicant, among others, a notice under s 18 of the 1987
Act. Signed on behalf of Wellcome the notice read:

> 'We are proposing to take a disposal of an interest in the property known *c*
> as 38–62 (even) Yeomans Row, London, SW3 2AL from The Trustees of
> Henry Smith's Charity at the price of £1,057,255 ...'

The notice contained an invitation to the applicant substantially in the terms
required by s 18(2)(b) of the 1987 Act.

On 2 August 1995 the applicant wrote to the Smith trustees complaining that *d*
a notice under s 5 had not been served and contending that this omission had not
been remedied by service of a notice by the prospective purchaser under s 18.
With her letter she enclosed a notice under s 19 of the 1987 Act requiring the
Smith trustees to serve on her and on the other qualifying tenants of the building
a notice under s 5 within seven days of the date of the notice. The Smith trustees *e*
promptly replied: they did not accept that the legal requirements of the 1987 Act
had not been observed, and pointed out that s 5 notices would be served on those
tenants whose responses to the s 18 notices required it.

A majority of the qualifying tenants in the building (including the applicant)
responded to the s 18 notices by stating that they would wish to avail themselves
of the right of first refusal conferred by a s 5 notice if it were served, which it had *f*
not been. On 6 September 1995 solicitors acting for the Smith trustees wrote a
letter in which they agreed that more than 50% of the qualifying tenants of the
building had served positive responses within the time limit, but they continued:

> 'The provisions of the Contract between our clients and Wellcome now
> require Section 5 notices to be served on the qualifying tenants of your *g*
> building. However, since your building falls within the area of the Estate
> Management Scheme application dated 12th October 1994, the Contract
> provides that Section 5 notices will not be served until after that application
> has been finally determined. We are hoping that the application will be
> heard before the Leasehold Valuation Tribunal in the latter half of October, *h*
> but we obviously do not know how long thereafter it will take before the
> application is finally determined. Accordingly, you and your fellow
> -qualifying tenants of the building will not be receiving Section 5 notices
> immediately, but please rest assured that no further steps will be taken with
> regard to the disposal of your building to Wellcome until after Section 5 *j*
> notices have been served and the necessary procedures complied with
> thereafter.'

On 15 September 1995 solicitors for the Smith trustees wrote to the leasehold
valuation tribunal asking that Wellcome should be joined with the Smith trustees
as an applicant for approval of the estate management scheme already submitted.
The original scheme has since been amended, and it is the subject of considerable

a opposition. There have been various adjournments of the hearing, which has not yet begun although we understand it is due to begin during this month. An aggrieved party has a right of appeal to the Lands Tribunal.

On 19 September 1995 the applicant issued her application in these proceedings. On 20 November 1995 Judge Uziell-Hamilton ruled against the applicant. Having studied the 1987 Act, the judge reluctantly concluded that the

b time had not yet passed by which s 5 notices had to be served. She concluded that that time would not come until the result of the application to the leasehold valuation tribunal was known. The judge was, however, concerned at the risk of prejudice to the applicant and other qualifying tenants if the hearing of that application was unduly delayed and accordingly invited undertakings to be given which would ensure the expeditious prosecution of that application.

c

III

The first issue argued before us was whether the 24 July 1995 contract between the Smith trustees and Wellcome for the sale of the building was a 'relevant disposal' within the meaning of the 1987 Act. The applicant (who argued her case

d in person with uncommon clarity, skill and good humour) submitted, perhaps surprisingly, that it was. Mr David Neuberger QC for the Smith trustees contended that it was not. The answer to this question must turn primarily on the construction of s 4 of the 1987 Act, which, as amended and so far as relevant, reads:

e   *'Relevant disposals.*—(1) In this Part references to a relevant disposal affecting any premises to which this Part applies are references to the disposal by the landlord of any estate or interest (whether legal or equitable) in any such premises, including the disposal of any such estate or interest in any common parts of any such premises but excluding—(a) the grant of any

f   tenancy under which the demised premises consist of a single flat (whether with or without any appurtenant premises); and (b) any of the disposals falling within subsection (2).

(1A) Where an estate or interest of the landlord has been mortgaged, the reference in subsection (1) above to the disposal of an estate or interest by the landlord includes a reference to its disposal by the mortgagee in exercise of a

g   power of sale or leasing, whether or not the disposal is made in the name of the landlord; and, in relation to such a proposed disposal by the mortgagee, any reference in the following provisions of this Part to the landlord shall be construed as a reference to the mortgagee.

(2) The disposals referred to in subsection (1)(b) are—(a) a disposal of—(i)

h   any interest of a beneficiary in settled land within the meaning of the Settled Land Act 1925, or ... (iii) any incorporeal hereditament; (aa) a disposal consisting of the creation of an estate or interest by way of security for a loan; (b) a disposal to a trustee in bankruptcy or to the liquidator of a company; (c) a disposal in pursuance of an order made under section 24 or 24A of the

j   Matrimonial Causes Act 1973 or section 2 of the Inheritance (Provision for Family and Dependants) Act 1975; (d) a disposal in pursuance of a compulsory purchase order or in pursuance of an agreement entered into in circumstances where, but for the agreement, such an order would have been made or (as the case may be) carried into effect; (e) a disposal by way of gift to a member of the landlord's family or to a charity; (f) a disposal by one charity to another of an estate or interest in land which prior to the disposal

is functional land of the first-mentioned charity and which is intended to be
functional land of the other charity once the disposal is made; (g) a disposal   a
consisting of the transfer of an estate or interest held on trust for any person
where the disposal is made in connection with the appointment of a new
trustee or in connection with the discharge of any trustee; (h) a disposal
consisting of a transfer by two or more persons who are members of the
same family either—(i) to fewer of their number, or (ii) to a different   b
combination of members of the family (but one that includes at least one of
the transferors); (i) a disposal in pursuance of—(i) any option or right of
pre-emption binding on the landlord (whether granted before or after the
commencement of this section), or (ii) any other obligation binding on him
and created before that commencement; (j) a disposal consisting of the
surrender of a tenancy in pursuance of any covenant, condition or   c
agreement contained in it; (k) a disposal to the Crown; and (l) where the
landlord is a body corporate, a disposal to an associated company.

(3) In this Part "disposal" means a disposal whether by the creation or the
transfer of an estate or interest and—(a) includes the surrender of a tenancy
and the grant of an option or right of pre-emption, but (b) excludes a disposal   d
under the terms of a will or under the law relating to intestacy; and
references in this Part to the transferee in connection with a disposal shall be
construed accordingly.

(4) In this section "appurtenant premises", in relation to any flat, means
any yard, garden, outhouse or appurtenance (not being a common part of   e
the building containing the flat) which belongs to, or is usually enjoyed with,
the flat ...'

It would be absurd if, in a transaction of this kind, there were two relevant
disposals, one on the exchange of contracts and another on completion, and
neither party contended for this construction. It is therefore necessary to choose   f
between these two events as the 'relevant disposal'.

In support of her contention that the exchange of contracts was the relevant
disposal for purposes of the 1987 Act, the applicant drew attention to the
reference in s 4(1) to 'any estate or interest (whether legal or equitable)' and relied
on the familiar principle that a purchaser of real property becomes the equitable
owner of the property upon exchange of contracts. This, she said, was reflected   g
in the ordinary rule which transfers the risk in the property to the purchaser on
exchange, so obliging such purchaser to insure the property in the absence of any
contrary provision. She relied by analogy on s 4(3) and sub-s (2)(i)(i), which made
it clear that it was not the exercise of an option or right of pre-emption which
constituted a relevant disposal under the 1987 Act but the grant of such an option   h
or right of pre-emption.

Mr Neuberger relied on *Wilkins v Horrowitz* [1990] 2 EGLR 217 as authority for
the proposition that it is the completed conveyance and not the exchange of
contracts which constitutes the relevant disposal under the 1987 Act. He adopted
the extensive reasoning which led the Yorkshire Leasehold Valuation Tribunal to   j
that conclusion. Prompted by the court, he pointed out that in sub-s (2)(d) the
draftsman had excluded as a relevant disposal not an agreement made to
anticipate a compulsory purchase order but a disposal made in pursuance of such
an agreement. He pointed out that on the applicant's construction it would not
have been necessary for the draftsman to exclude from the definition under
sub-s (2)(i)(ii) a disposal in pursuance of any other obligation binding on the

a landlord and created before the commencement of the section, since such a disposal would not have been a relevant disposal anyway. More generally, Mr Neuberger accepted that on exchange of contracts a purchaser of real property is ordinarily regarded as the equitable owner of the property in question. But that, he submitted, was on the assumption (usually sound) that such a contract is specifically enforceable (see Megarry and Wade *The Law of Real Property* (5th edn,

b 1984) p 602 and *Central Trust and Safe Deposit Co v Snider* [1916] 1 AC 266 at 272). Here, said Mr Neuberger, the court would not on any showing order specific performance of the contract at this stage, since if the requisite majority of tenants served positive responses to s 18 notices the contract was subject to a condition (the approval of the estate management scheme) which had not been fulfilled, and the court would not in any event order the parties to complete this contract

c so long as the Smith trustees had not complied with their statutory obligation to serve s 5 notices.

With any other Act we would think it extraordinary that doubt should exist on a point as fundamental as this. We have to say that we do not find the answer indicated with an acceptable degree of clarity in the language of the section itself

d or elsewhere in the 1987 Act. It would, however, appear that in sub-s (2) of the section the draftsman has been primarily (although not consistently) concerned to exclude as relevant disposals certain forms of final transfer, which may perhaps indicate that it was the final transfer and not the preliminary agreement which he intended to be treated as the relevant disposal. We agree with Mr Neuberger that

e the reasoning in *Wilkins v Horrowitz* is persuasive, and it has (as we understand) been treated as authoritative for the past five years. We would also accept Mr Neuberger's argument that an application by the prospective purchaser for specific performance of the sale contract in respect of this building would not as matters now stand succeed, for the reasons which he gives. On balance, therefore, we prefer Mr Neuberger's argument on this point and would hold that

f there has not been a relevant disposal of the building.

If, as the applicant contends, that conclusion is wrong and the exchange of contracts is the 'relevant disposal' under the 1987 Act, she would certainly have rights which she could pursue against Wellcome and it may be that the court could properly restrain completion until the Smith trustees had performed their

g duty under the 1987 Act to serve s 5 notices or even order the Smith trustees to perform their statutory duty to serve notices if they were in breach of duty in failing to do so. Having regard to the conclusion we have reached we do not think it necessary to explore these possibilities.

h
                                      IV

The second major issue argued on the appeal was whether, within the meaning of s 5, the Smith trustees have at any time in the past, or do now, 'propose' to make a relevant disposal affecting the premises.

j It is in our view clear that the expression 'proposes' describes a state of mind somewhere between mere consideration of a possible course of action at one extreme and a fixed and irrevocable determination to pursue that course of action at the other. As Lord Denning MR observed in *Trustees of the Magdalen and Lasher Charity, Hastings v Shelower* (1968) 19 P & CR 389 at 392, contrasting different expressions to be found in the Landlord and Tenant Act 1954:

'The word "proposes" is different from the word "intends". A man may   *a*
propose to do a thing without having formed a fixed and settled intention to
do it.'

A 'proposal' under the 1987 Act means that a project must have moved out of 'the
zone of contemplation ... into the valley of decision' (see *Cunliffe v Goodman*
[1950] 1 All ER 720 at 725, [1950] 2 KB 237 at 254 per Asquith LJ).   *b*

Mr Neuberger submitted that on the present facts the Smith trustees had never
at any stage 'proposed' to dispose of their interest in the building to Wellcome,
since they had at all times acknowledged and provided for the possibility that the
tenants might assert their rights to buy the interest of the Smith trustees
themselves. Alternatively, he argued that if the Smith trustees had at the time of
contract 'proposed' to transfer their interest to Wellcome, they had ceased so to   *c*
propose when the tenants made positive responses to the s 18 notices served by
Wellcome.

In our opinion both these arguments face insuperable difficulties. It is
necessarily implicit in the legislation that a proposal is none the less such because
the tenants may assert their right to buy. Furthermore, it flies in the face of   *d*
common sense to suggest that a party does not propose to do that which he binds
himself to do by contract. The fact that a third party may succeed in defeating or
frustrating his proposal does not mean that he ceases to propose, only that he
may be unsuccessful in implementing his proposal. If the requisite majority of
qualifying tenants had not made positive responses under s 18, the Smith trustees
would have been legally bound to sell their interest in the building to Wellcome.   *e*
If the tenants' purchase were to founder, perhaps because two of the qualifying
tenants died or moved out of their flats so that there was no longer the requisite
majority of qualifying tenants, or because the tenants were unable to raise the
necessary finance, the Smith trustees would remain bound to sell to Wellcome.
Cases could well arise in which it might be very doubtful whether a landlord's   *f*
plans had hardened sufficiently to be regarded as a proposal, but on the facts here
it is impossible to feel any doubt. The unreality of Mr Neuberger's argument is,
we think, underlined by the contractual adoption of the s 18 procedure, which is
(as s 18(1)(a) makes plain) only appropriate where a disposal by the landlord is
proposed, and Wellcome stated in the s 18 notices which they issued that they
were 'proposing' to take a disposal of the interest of the Smith trustees in the   *g*
building. We have no hesitation in rejecting the arguments of Mr Neuberger on
this issue.

V

Under the contractual scheme adopted by the Smith trustees and Wellcome,   *h*
s 5 notices were not to be served in the first instance by the Smith trustees but
were to be served (after final determination by the leasehold valuation tribunal
or the Lands Tribunal on appeal of the application for approval of the estate
management scheme) if the requisite majority of qualifying tenants in the
building made a positive response within the time limited to the s 18 notices to   *j*
be served by Wellcome. The applicant argued that that was not a sufficient
compliance with what the 1987 Act required: in her submission, it was the
statutory duty of the landlord to serve s 5 notices as soon as he proposed to make
a relevant disposal. Mr Neuberger took issue with that contention. He argued
that there was no provision in the 1987 Act governing the time at which the s 5
notices were to be served, provided that service preceded the making of the

a relevant disposal. It was open to the landlord, he argued, to delay service of s 5 notices as long as he wished provided that he served them before making a relevant disposal.

The applicant pointed out that delay after the exchange of contracts in serving s 5 notices could prove prejudicial to the tenants. Several of the qualifying tenants of the building were elderly, and their death or departure could deprive *b* the tenants of their rights under the 1987 Act altogether. Furthermore, on 24 July 1995 the tenants' interests were not the subject of an estate management scheme; if service of s 5 notices were delayed until an estate management scheme in some form had been approved (if it ever was), the value of the tenants' interests would be diminished since the development rights in the property would be controlled by Wellcome and not by the tenants themselves. These points are not without *c* force, but in our judgment the choice between the competing contentions on this point must be governed by the proper construction of the 1987 Act and not by consideration of how the proper construction may in practice affect either one party or the other.

While there is no express provision in the 1987 Act which prohibits the use of *d* the s 18 procedure in the manner for which the parties have provided by contract in this case, it seems to us obvious that this is not what the draftsman intended. The requirement that a prospective purchaser should only have to serve 80% of all the tenants in a building rather than 90% of the qualifying tenants makes no practical sense in a situation where the prospective purchaser, as a result of comprehensive disclosure by the original landlord, is in full possession of details *e* of the terms upon which the various tenants hold their interests. It makes even less sense for a prospective purchaser to inquire of tenants whether they have received a s 5 notice from their landlord when the prospective purchaser knows that the original landlord has contracted with him that no such notice shall be served. While, as pointed out above, the s 18 procedure may operate so as to *f* confer an incidental benefit on the tenant, the primary purpose of the section (as we have suggested) is to afford protection to the prospective purchaser, and the present situation is not one in which the prospective purchaser has any conceivable need for such protection. That the s 18 procedure is capable of abuse has been demonstrated above. We are quite sure that the Smith trustees, who have throughout acted on the most eminent advice, have not in any way *g* intended to abuse the rights of their tenants. We do, however, regard the use of s 18 in the present circumstances as highly artificial and a far cry from what the draftsman of the 1987 Act can have intended.

Since 'propose' is not an expression apt to denote an instant of time, and since the 1987 Act prescribes no time period for service of a s 5 notice, it cannot be held *h* that there is any precise period within which a s 5 notice must be served by a landlord who proposes to make a relevant disposal. We also agree with Mr Neuberger that 'where', the opening word of s 5(1), is a somewhat odd word for a draftsman to use: an expression such as 'as soon as', 'once', 'when' or 'if' might have been clearer. But the effect of s 5 (2)(c) and (d) is to require the notice to be *j* served a minimum of four months before the date of relevant disposal, and the natural reading of the section is in our view that a landlord must serve a s 5 notice on the qualifying tenants as soon as he proposes to make a relevant disposal to a third party (which of course involves settlement of the purchase price and the terms upon which the landlord proposes to sell). Section 18 plainly envisages that a s 5 notice should have been served by the time that a prospective purchaser may, if he wishes to protect himself, serve a notice under s 18.

On our reading of the 1987 Act, the Smith trustees should have served s 5
notices on the applicant and the other qualifying tenants of the building at or *a*
within a few days of the date of their contract with Wellcome and possibly even
sooner. We consider that they were in breach of their statutory duty in failing to
do so and remain in breach. We hold that such notices should now be served.
We would allow the applicant's appeal on this point.

We have not heard full argument on what s 5 notices, if served now, may or *b*
should contain. There may well be a difference between the parties on that
question. If there is, and it cannot be resolved, we would wish to hear argument
before making any final order.

These conclusions make it unnecessary for us to consider an argument raised
by the Smith trustees by a notice of cross-appeal concerning the undertakings
which they gave in the county court.   *c*

Appeal allowed.

L I Zysman Esq   Barrister.

Arab Republic of Egypt v Gamal-Eldin and another

EMPLOYMENT APPEAL TRIBUNAL

MUMMERY J, MR J D DALY AND MR J C RAMSAY

2 MARCH, 6 JUNE 1995

Constitutional law – Foreign sovereign state – Immunity from suit – Contract of employment – Foreign nationals employed as drivers at medical office of London embassy of foreign state – Action for unfair dismissal – Foreign state claiming immunity – Whether industrial tribunal having jurisdiction to hear complaints – Whether medical office maintained for 'commercial purposes' – State Immunity Act 1978, ss 2, 4, 16.

The applicants, Egyptian nationals resident in London, were employed under contracts of employment made in the United Kingdom as drivers at the medical office of the Egyptian Embassy. The medical office, which was physically separate from the embassy and had little day-to-day contact with it, was concerned with the procurement of medical services in the United Kingdom for Egyptian nationals which could not otherwise be obtained within the Egyptian health service. The applicants were employed to collect patients from the airports and drive them either to hospitals, or to hotels in order to await treatment. When they were dismissed from their employment the applicants brought claims for unfair dismissal to an industrial tribunal. No notice of appearance was served on behalf of the embassy, but the chief medical counsellor wrote two letters to the industrial tribunal, asserting that the applicants were Egyptian nationals subject only to Egyptian law. The industrial tribunal held preliminary hearings to determine the issue of jurisdiction to consider the claims, and found that the medical office was engaged in an area of commercial activity of a private law character, with the result that s 4[a] of the State Immunity Act 1978, which provided that a state was not immune in respect of proceedings relating to a contract of employment between the state and an individual where the contract was made in the United Kingdom, gave the tribunal jurisdiction, since s 4 could not be disapplied by s 16[b] where the employment was for an office, agency or establishment maintained by the state in the United Kingdom for commercial purposes. The Arab Republic of Egypt appealed, and provided affidavit evidence on the issues of state immunity and waiver of immunity. The applicants submitted that the appeal tribunal could not consider the affidavits since they constituted new evidence which had been available at the time of the hearing before the industrial tribunal but had not been put before it.

Held – The appeal would be allowed for the following reasons—

(1) If an industrial tribunal failed to give effect to an immunity in fact enjoyed by a foreign state as a result of not having all the relevant evidence at the hearing, it was the duty of the appeal tribunal to correct the error and give effect to the immunity, even if that meant departing from the rules which normally applied to

---

a   Section 4, so far as material, is set out at p 246 *g* to *j*, post

b   Section 16, so far as material, is set out at p 246 *a*, post

the admission of new evidence on appeal. It followed in the instant case that the
appeal tribunal was not precluded from admitting and considering the affidavit a
evidence from the Arab Republic of Egypt as to state immunity, waiver of
immunity and non-attendance at the earlier hearings (see p 242 j to p 243 c and
p 247 j, post).

(2) In the circumstances, the Arab Republic of Egypt had not irrevocably
submitted to the jurisdiction of the tribunal under s 2^c of the 1978 Act by taking b
steps in the proceedings, on the grounds that: (i) as the chief medical officer was
not the head of the diplomatic mission and was not a person who had entered the
contracts of employment, he had no deemed authority to submit to the
jurisdiction on behalf of his state; (ii) the sending of letters to the tribunal by the
chief medical officer did not amount to the entering of a notice of appearance;
and (iii) neither the sending of the letters nor their contents constituted a c
submission to the jurisdiction of the industrial tribunal within the meaning of
s 2(1) of the 1978 Act (see p 244 c to p 245 c and p 247 j, post).

(3) On the facts, the medical office was certified as part of the premises of the
mission of the Arab Republic of Egypt, and the two applicants, as employees in
the administrative and technical service of the mission, were members of the d
mission. It followed that, by virtue of s 16 of the 1978 Act, state immunity
remained in force. Moreover, even if the applicants had not been part of the staff
of the mission, the purposes and activities of the medical office, which acted
throughout as a representative of the Arab Republic of Egypt and its embassy,
were not 'commercial purposes' within the exception to immunity contained in
s 4(3) of the Act, but were within the sphere of governmental or sovereign e
activity. It followed that the industrial tribunal erred in law in deciding that the
Arab Republic of Egypt could not claim immunity in the proceedings, and there
was no jurisdiction in the industrial tribunal to hear the applications (see p 246 d
e and p 247 f to j, post).

f

Notes

For immunity of foreign states, see 18 *Halsbury's Laws* (4th edn) para 1548, and for
cases on the subject, see 1(1) *Digest* (2nd reissue) 69–81, 546–601.

For the State Immunity Act 1978, ss 2, 4, 16, see 10 *Halsbury's Statues* (4th edn)
(1995 reissue) 758, 760, 768.

g

Cases referred to in judgment

Hellyer Bros Ltd v McLeod [1987] 1 WLR 728, [1987] ICR 526, CA.
I Congreso del Partido [1981] 2 All ER 1064, [1983] 1 AC 244, [1981] 3 WLR 328, HL.
Kingston v British Railways Board [1984] ICR 781, CA.
Ladd v Marshall [1954] 3 All ER 745, [1954] 1 WLR 1489, CA. h
Littrell v United States of America (No 2) [1994] 4 All ER 203, [1995] 1 WLR 82, CA.
Sengupta v Republic of India [1983] ICR 221, EAT.
United Arab Emirates v Abdelghafar [1995] ICR 65, EAT.
Wileman v Minilec Engineering Ltd [1988] ICR 318, EAT.

j

Cases also cited or referred to in skeleton arguments

Barber v Thames Television plc [1991] ICR 253, EAT; *rvsd* [1992] ICR 661, CA.
House v Emerson Electric industrial Controls [1980] ICR 795, EAT.

---

c Section 2, so far as material, is set out at p 244 d, post

Kapur v Shields [1976] 1 All ER 873, [1976] ICR 26.

Lee Ting Sang v Chung Chi-Keung [1990] 2 AC 374, [1990] 2 WLR 1173, PC.

Khawaja v Secretary of State for the Home Dept [1983] 1 All ER 765, [1984] AC 74, HL.

Russell v Elmdon Freight Terminal Ltd [1989] ICR 629, EAT.

Interlocutory appeal

By notice dated 18 May 1994 (and later amended) the Arab Republic of Egypt appealed from the decision of the industrial tribunal sitting at London (North) on 10 March 1994, and notified to the appellant by letter dated 7 April 1994, that it had jurisdiction under s 4(2)(a) of the State Immunity Act 1978 to consider complaints made by the applicants, Nehad Gamal-Eldin and Mohammed Hassan El-Abiary, that they had been unfairly dismissed by the Office for Medical Affairs of the Embassy of the Arab Republic of Egypt in London and rejecting the appellant's plea of state immunity. The facts are set out in the judgment of the appeal tribunal.

Karen Walden-Smith (instructed by *Jansons*) for the Arab Republic of Egypt.
Peter Bibby (instructed by the *Free Representation Unit*) for the applicants.

Cur adv vult

6 June 1995. The following judgment of the appeal tribunal was delivered.

MUMMERY J. Mr Gamal-Eldin and Mr Mohammed El-Abiary are Egyptian nationals resident in London at the material time. Until they were dismissed on 15 January 1993 they were both employed under contracts made in the United Kingdom as drivers at the medical office of the Arab Republic of Egypt Embassy at 47 Longridge Road, London SW5. The preliminary question for decision is whether the industrial tribunal has jurisdiction to determine the claims for unfair dismissal made by both applicants in originating applications presented on 13 April 1993.

The industrial tribunal held at London (North) on 10 March 1994 decided that, having regard to s 4(2)(a) of the State Immunity Act 1978, it had jurisdiction to consider the complaints, and rejected the plea of state immunity. After it had been notified of the extended reasons for the decision on 7 April 1994, the Arab Republic of Egypt appealed against that decision by a notice of appeal served on 27 May 1994, subsequently amended with leave to take a point under s 16 of the 1978 Act, to the effect that the two applicants were members of the diplomatic mission.

The issues

The arguments advanced by Ms Walden-Smith for the Arab Republic of Egypt and Mr Bibby for the two applicants on the issue of state immunity raised the following questions on the interpretation and application of the 1978 Act. (1) Has the Arab Republic of Egypt submitted to the jurisdiction of the industrial tribunal? If not, (2) does the medical office form part of the mission of the Arab Republic of Egypt? If so, (3) were the two applicants members of the mission? If so, (4) is the medical mission maintained by the Arab Republic of Egypt in the United Kingdom for 'commercial purposes'?

Before we deal with those issues we must first decide a preliminary point taken by Mr Bibby on the jurisdiction of this tribunal to entertain this appeal.

The preliminary point on jurisdiction

Mr Bibby argued that this appeal does not raise any question of law. Therefore *a* the appeal tribunal has no jurisdiction to determine it. The appeal is an impermissible late attempt to introduce evidence available at the time of the hearing before the industrial tribunal, but not put before it. The purpose of introducing that evidence is to persuade this tribunal to do something which it has no power to do, that is to make new findings of fact contrary to facts correctly *b* found by the industrial tribunal on the evidence before it.

The correctness of that submission must be tested against the history of the proceedings, the provisions of the 1978 Act and the powers of this tribunal to admit evidence on appeal to challenge findings of fact made by the industrial tribunal.

c

The course of the proceedings

These proceedings took the following course.

(1) The originating applications presented on 13 April 1993 were served on the Arab Republic of Egypt under cover of letters via the Foreign and Commonwealth Office dated 5 May 1993. *d*

(2) At that time the medical counsellor at the mission was Dr El-Dieb. He was appointed on 8 April 1992 and remained in office until May 1994. He had previously dealt with another application for unfair dismissal brought against the Arab Republic of Egypt by a Mr Younnis. In that case an industrial tribunal had upheld a claim to state immunity without any attendance on behalf of the Arab *e* Republic of Egypt.

(3) No notice of appearance (IT3) was served. Dr El-Dieb wrote two letters to the industrial tribunal concerning the applications. The first letter, dated 28 June 1993, related to Mr El-Abiary's application. The second letter, dated 16 August 1993, related to Mr Gamal Eldin's application. It is not necessary at this stage to examine the contents of the letters. *f*

(4) The chairman of the industrial tribunal notified the Arab Republic of Egypt by a notice of 20 July 1993 that there would be a preliminary hearing to determine the issue of jurisdiction to consider the case. A hearing date was fixed for 4 October 1993. That hearing was adjourned until 10 March 1994. The Arab Republic of Egypt was not represented at either hearing. Mr Bibby represented *g* the applicants at both hearings. At the hearing on 10 March evidence was given by both applicants. A written statement from Mr Younnis, formerly employed by the Arab Republic of Egypt as an accountant, was also admitted.

(5) The industrial tribunal, in its extended reasons notified to the parties on 7 April 1994, made the following crucial findings of fact. Both applicants were *h* Egyptian nationals employed by the medical office as drivers. The medical office, which is physically separate from the embassy and had little day-to-day contact with it, is concerned with the provision of medical services in the following circumstances:

'The medical office was situated some four miles away from the embassy *j* and was managed by Dr M El-Dieb. It was an office agency or establishment maintained by the Egyptian state in the United Kingdom for commercial purposes. The office was concerned with the procurement of medical services in the United Kingdom to treat Egyptian nationals who generally travelled to London by air to become patients in London hospitals and to receive treatment which was not otherwise available within the Egyptian a health service. The applicants collected these patients from the airports and drove them either to hospitals where they were to receive their treatment or otherwise to hotels where they would await admission into hospital. They also translated for the patients at the hospitals. The office did not charge for this service. The medical office was responsible for transactions of a commercial or professional nature in that it procured and paid for the

b services provided and these transactions were those into which a state entered or engaged otherwise than in the exercise of sovereign authority.' (See para 2.)

(6) The tribunal concluded, in para 4 of the extended reasons, that—

c 'the medical office were engaged "within an area of activity trading or commercial, or otherwise of a private law character, in which the state had chosen to engage." We accordingly find that in the particular circumstances of these cases section 4 gives jurisdiction to a tribunal to consider the complaints of the applicants.'

d (7) The tribunal also concluded that the applicants were not part of the Arab Republic of Egypt's diplomatic mission within the meaning of the Vienna Convention on Diplomatic Relations (set out in Sch 1 to the Diplomatic Privileges Act 1964). There was no evidence that they were members of the mission, which they denied.

(8) Finally, the tribunal concluded that Dr El-Dieb, on behalf of the medical
e office, had in the two letters canvassed the merits of each case before raising the issue of immunity in November 1993 and had therefore taken steps in the proceedings.

(9) Following notification of the decision, the Arab Republic of Egypt requested a review, but that was refused, and there was no appeal against the
f refusal.

(10) An appeal was served on 27 May 1994, shortly after solicitors had been instructed. The grounds of the appeal were that the tribunal had erred in law in concluding that it had jurisdiction to consider the applicants' claims of unfair dismissal. The particular grounds canvassed in the notice of appeal were, first, that the tribunal's findings of fact did not justify the conclusion that the work
g formerly undertaken by the applicants in relation to their contracts of employment was work for an office agency or establishment maintained by the State of Egypt in the United Kingdom for commercial purposes (see s 4(2)(a) of the 1978 Act). Secondly, the tribunal erred in concluding that the Arab Republic of Egypt or its medical office were engaged in an area of activity, trading or commercial or
h otherwise, of a private law character. Rather it was in the sphere of governmental or sovereign activity. Thirdly, and finally, the tribunal erred in concluding from the correspondence before it that Dr El-Dieb had taken steps in the proceedings relating to the merits of the applications such that the Arab Republic of Egypt was precluded from raising the issue of immunity under the 1978 Act. The applicants
j took the point in their answers that the appeal tribunal had no jurisdiction because the grounds of appeal revealed no point of law.

(11) The appeal first came before this tribunal on 14 October 1994 when the Arab Republic of Egypt asked for an adjournment in circumstances described in the judgment given on that application. The adjournment was opposed, but granted on terms. Those terms included directions that the Arab Republic of Egypt file and serve affidavit evidence relevant to the questions of state

immunity, waiver of immunity and non-attendance at the earlier hearings. Affidavits were duly served on behalf of the Arab Republic of Egypt. The *a* affidavits were sworn by Dr El-Dieb, Mr Mahmoud Abdou and Mr David Burchnall. The affidavit by Mr Burchnall was relevant to the question whether the medical office form part of the Arab Republic of Egypt's mission. No evidence was served in response to those affidavits, though leave had been granted for that to be done. No notice was given of intention to cross-examine *b* the deponents of the affidavits.

The jurisdictional issue

Mr Bibby made the following submissions objecting to the jurisdiction of the appeal tribunal.

(1) The affidavit evidence filed on behalf of the Arab Republic of Egypt is *c* inadmissible, because it does not satisfy the requirements of *Ladd v Marshall* [1954] 3 All ER 745, [1954] 1 WLR 1489, which apply as much to appeals to the Employment Appeal Tribunal as to the appeals to the Court of Appeal (see *Kingston v British Railways Board* [1984] ICR 781 at 795–796 and *Wileman v Minilec Engineering Ltd* [1988] ICR 318). No attempt was made by Ms Walden-Smith to *d* show that the evidence could not have been obtained with reasonable diligence for use at the hearing. It was either available for use at the hearing or could have been obtained with reasonable diligence. This requirement of *Ladd v Marshall* is similar to the ground on which a review may be sought under r 11(1)(d) and (e) of Sch 1 to the Industrial Tribunal (Constitution and Rules of Procedure) Regulations 1993, SI 1993/2687. An application for a review was made, refused *e* and was not appealed. The appellant should not be in any better position on an appeal than it had been on its unsuccessful application for a review.

(2) No new point of law is taken on the appeal to which the evidence is directed. The fact that the new evidence goes to jurisdiction does not make it admissible in relation to an appeal on a point of law determined by the industrial *f* tribunal. It was decided in *Hellyer Bros Ltd v McLeod* [1987] 1 WLR 728 that it was not permissible to take a new point of law on appeal which required new evidence, unless there were special or exceptional circumstances.

(3) The facts relevant to jurisdiction have been determined by the tribunal. They cannot be reversed or redetermined by an appeal tribunal on appeal. There is no relevant distinction between facts which go to the jurisdiction and other *g* facts against which a party may wish to appeal, any more than there is a distinction between errors of law that go to the jurisdiction and errors of law that do not. It is within the jurisdiction of the industrial tribunal to find facts which go to the jurisdiction. As long as it has applied the law correctly to the facts found by it, there is no ground of appeal. On this aspect of the appeal Mr Bibby referred *h* us to decisions on public law which we do not find it necessary to examine for the purpose of deciding this appeal.

The essence of Mr Bibby's argument is that it is for the industrial tribunal to determine the facts on which a claim to immunity is based. The tribunal has done that. There is no scope for review of those findings of fact by the appeal tribunal. *j* The fact that the Arab Republic of Egypt is a sovereign state does not justify departure from established principles or practice.

Conclusion on the jurisdictional question

We agree with Ms Walden-Smith that the appeal tribunal is not precluded from admitting and considering the new evidence. No evidence was presented *a* to the tribunal by the Arab Republic of Egypt at either hearing as a result of a misunderstanding by Dr El-Dieb, the medical counsellor. He thought that in these matters (and his evidence was not challenged by cross-examination) it was unnecessary for anyone to attend the industrial tribunal on behalf of the Arab Republic of Egypt and, indeed, that it would not be correct for anyone to attend. This explanation has to be considered in the context of immunity cases to which

b special considerations apply. There is a discussion of those considerations, in particular the role of the court under s 1(2) of the 1978 Act, in the recent decision of this tribunal in *United Arab Emirates v Abdelghafar* [1995] ICR 65. Section 1(2) provides: 'A court shall give effect to the immunity conferred by this section even though the State does not appear in the proceedings in question.' If the industrial tribunal fails to give effect to an immunity in fact enjoyed by the Arab Republic

c of Egypt as a result of not having all the relevant evidence, it is, in our view, the duty of the appeal tribunal to correct this error and give effect to this immunity, even if that means departing from the rules which normally apply to the admission of new evidence on appeal.

In any event, so far as this tribunal is concerned, the admission of evidence has

d already been determined by the order made on 14 October when the case was adjourned with directions for affidavit evidence on each side. That order was not appealed.

When Ms Walden-Smith took this point, Mr Bibby asked us to review our earlier decision under r 33 of the Employment Appeal Tribunal Rules 1993, SI 1993/2854, or for leave to appeal against that decision out of time. He argued

e that those directions were only given by the tribunal on an application for an adjournment. In those circumstances the evidence filed pursuant to those directions should be treated only as 'de bene esse'. The directions did not pre-judge the question of admissibility. We have not been persuaded by Mr Bibby that we should grant a review, but we grant an extension of time for

f appealing against that decision to the date when the time for appealing against this decision expires.

Submission to the jurisdiction

Mr Bibby argued on behalf of the applicants that the industrial tribunal had found as a fact that the Arab Republic of Egypt had irrevocably submitted to the

g jurisdiction by taking steps in the proceedings. He referred to s 2(1) and (3)(b) of the 1978 Act, which provides:

'(1) A State is not immune as respects proceedings in respect of which it has submitted to the jurisdiction of the courts of the United Kingdom ...

h (3) A State is deemed to have submitted ... (b) subject to subsection (4) and (5) below, if it has intervened or taken any step in the proceedings.'

Subsection (4) provides that sub-s (3)(b) does not apply to intervention or any step taken for the purpose only of claiming immunity. Subsection (5) provides that sub-s (3)(b) does not apply—

j

'to any step taken by the State in ignorance of facts entitling it to immunity if those facts could not reasonably have been ascertained and immunity is claimed as soon as reasonably practicable.'

Mr Bibby also referred to art 3 of the European Convention on State Immunity and Additional Protocol (Basle, 16 May 1972; Misc No 31 (1972); Cmnd 5081):

'1. A contracting State cannot claim immunity from the jurisdiction of a court of another contracting State if, before claiming immunity, it takes any step in the proceedings relating to the merits.'

It was argued that the Arab Republic of Egypt had taken steps in these proceedings by entering notices of appearance which engaged in the case on the merits without making any express claim to immunity. The industrial tribunal properly treated the letters referred to above as notices of appearance. Section 2(5) of the 1978 Act could not be relied upon, as it was not raised in the notice of appeal. In any case, there were no facts of the kind referred to in that section.

We do not accept Mr Bibby's arguments on this point. We agree with Ms Walden-Smith that the tribunal erred in law in holding that there was a submission to the jurisdiction under s 2. Our reasons for this conclusion are as follows.

(1) It is provided in s 2(7):

'The head of a State's diplomatic mission in the United Kingdom, or the person for the time being performing his functions, shall be deemed to have authority to submit on behalf of the State in respect of any proceedings; and any person who has entered into a contract on behalf of and with the authority of a State shall be deemed to have authority to submit on its behalf in respect of proceedings arising out of the contract.'

The letters held by the industrial tribunal to be a notice of appearance and to constitute a submission to the jurisdiction were written by Dr El-Dieb. He was the director of the medical office at that time, but he did not occupy the position of the head of the diplomatic mission of the Arab Republic of Egypt in the United Kingdom. He is not, therefore, deemed to have authority to submit to the jurisdiction on behalf of his state. There was no evidence that he had express authority to submit to the jurisdiction. Nor was he the person who had entered into the contract of employment with either of the applicants. Mr Bibby sought to avoid the application of these provisions by arguing, first, that they only applied to a 'deemed submission' for the purposes of s 2(3) and that this was a case of an express submission on behalf of a state; secondly, that the 'person' who had entered into the contract of employment refers not to the individual who entered into the contract, but to the official persona by whom the contract had been entered into (ie the director of the medical office). In our view, neither contention is a correct construction of s 2(7) of the 1978 Act.

(2) We also agree with Ms Walden-Smith that the tribunal erred in law in holding that a step was taken in these proceedings by the entering of a notice of appearance. The position is that a letter was sent to the industrial tribunal by Dr El-Dieb on 28 June 1993 in respect of Mr El-Abiary's application. It was explained in the letter that Mr El-Abiary was an Egyptian national subject only to Egyptian law. A further letter was sent on 16 August 1994 in respect of Mr Gamal-Eldin clarifying that he was an Egyptian citizen. In the meantime, on 1 July 1993 the industrial tribunal wrote to the Arab Republic of Egypt seeking a notice of appearance in respect of both applications. The response on 2 July was to request that all correspondence be sent to the Foreign and Commonwealth Office. In these circumstances, it is our view that neither of the letters constitutes a notice of appearance within the meaning of the 1993 Regulations governing procedure in the industrial tribunals. Neither letter states an intention to resist the claims.

a   Therefore no step was taken in the proceedings within the meaning of s 2(4) of the 1978 Act.

(3) Finally, we are of the view that neither the sending of the letters nor the contents of them constituted a submission to the jurisdiction of the industrial tribunal within the meaning of s 2(1). Each letter seeks to explain what happened. The assertion of Egyptian nationality in relation to the applicants is *b*   more indicative of a claim to an immunity than of an intention to submit to the jurisdiction. Nothing in either letter states that there is an intention to resist the proceedings. The chairman's notice of a hearing on a preliminary issue of immunity is more consistent with the view that there was no submission to the jurisdiction than that there was one. In our view, neither letter evidences an intention to waive immunity or to submit to the jurisdiction nor could they be *c*   reasonably understood to be so.

The mission and the medical office

We heard argument concerning the status of the medical office: whether it formed part of the mission and whether the two applicants were members of the *d*   staff of the mission. We gave leave to Ms Walden-Smith to amend her notice of appeal to raise a point whether the two applicants were members of the staff of the mission. That point was raised in the affidavit evidence served in November 1994. We decided to grant leave to amend since the point was canvassed in the affidavits and there is no prejudice to the respondents in granting leave. They have not been taken by surprise.

e   Ms Walden-Smith submitted that the medical office forms part of the mission and that the two applicants were members of the mission. The evidence establishes that the medical office is one of several offices under the jurisdiction of the main embassy. It occupies a self-contained building at 47 Longridge Road, London SW5, three or four miles from the building occupied by the main *f*   Embassy at 26 South Street, London W1. The activities of the medical office come under the jurisdiction of the ambassador. He is ultimately responsible for its activities. As confirmed by a certificate from the Foreign and Commonwealth Office dated 6 October 1994, the medical office has been accepted as part of the premises of the Egyptian Embassy for the purposes of the Diplomatic and Consular Premises Act 1987. Such a certificate is granted only for the period for *g*   which the diplomatic premises of a state are used for the purposes of its mission. The functions of the medical office are consistent with the non-exhaustive list of functions set out in art 3 of the Vienna Convention ratified by the United Kingdom in 1964. Reliance was also placed on art 1 of that convention, which provides that the expression 'members of the mission' include, inter alia, *h*   'members of the administrative and technical staff'.

Against that background it is necessary to refer to ss 4 and 16 of the 1978 Act. It does not appear from the extended reasons that the industrial tribunal was asked to consider the provisions of s 16. Section 4 of the 1978 Act is concerned with contracts of employment, and provides in sub-s (1):

j   'A State is not immune as respects proceedings relating to a contract of employment between the State and an individual where the contract was made in the United Kingdom or work is to be wholly or partly performed there.'

Section 16 is concerned with excluded matters, and provides:

'This Part of this Act shall not affect any immunity or privilege conferred
by the Diplomatic Privileges Act 1964 or the Consular Relations Act 1968;
and ... (a) section 4 above does not apply to proceedings concerning the
employment of the members of a mission within the meaning of the
Convention scheduled to the said Act of 1964 or of the members of a
consular post within the meaning of the Convention scheduled to the said
Act of 1968 ...'

Article 1 of the Vienna Convention defines various expressions:

'... (b) the "members of the mission"' are the head of the mission and the
members of the staff of the mission; (c) the "members of the staff of the
mission" are the members of the diplomatic staff, of the administrative and
technical staff and of the service staff of the mission ... (f) the "members of
the administrative and technical staff" are the members of the staff of the
mission employed in the administrative and technical service of the mission
...'

In our view, on the facts set out above, the two applicants were members of
the staff of the mission employed in the administrative and technical service of
the mission. The fact that no certificate has been produced proving that they
were members of the mission does not affect the validity of that conclusion.
They were employed as drivers. Drivers form part of the administrative and
technical staff. As is clear from the decision in *Sengupta v Republic of India* [1983]
ICR 221 at 229 the immunity extends to members of staff of the mission carrying
out work of the mission 'in however humble a role'.

Commercial purposes
Even if the applicants were not part of the staff of the mission, immunity would
still, in our view, apply in this case on the true construction of s 4 of the 1978 Act.
Subsection (1) disapplies the immunity as respects proceedings relating to a
contract of employment between the state and an individual where the contract
was made in the United Kingdom or the work is to be wholly or partly performed
there. That is prima facie the case here. It is then provided, however, that the
section does *not* apply if—

'(a) at the time when the proceedings are brought the individual is a
national of the State concerned; or (b) at the time when the contract was
made the individual was neither a national of the United Kingdom nor
habitually resident there.' (See s 4(2).)

In this case both applicants are Egyptian nationals. That provision in sub-s (2) is,
however, subject to sub-s (3), which provides:

'Where the work is for an office, agency or establishment maintained by
the State in the United Kingdom for *commercial purposes,* subsection (2)(a)
and (b) above do not exclude the application of this section unless the
individual was, at the time when the contract was made, habitually resident
in that State.'

Neither applicant was habitually resident in Egypt at the relevant time. The
question arises whether the medical office was maintained by the Arab Republic
of Egypt in the United Kingdom 'for commercial purposes'. It is necessary to
refer to other provisions. Section 17(1), which applies for the interpretation of

a   Pt I of the 1978 Act, stipulates that 'commercial purposes' means 'purposes of such transactions or activities as are mentioned in s 3(3) above'. Section 3(3) states that 'commercial transaction' means:

b   '(a) any contract for the supply of goods or services; (b) any loan or other transaction for the provision of finance and any guarantee or indemnity in respect of any such transaction or of any other financial obligation; and (c) any other transaction or activity (whether of a commercial, industrial, financial, professional or other similar character) into which a State enters or in which it engages otherwise than in the exercise of sovereign authority ...'

It was argued by Mr Bibby that the medical office was conducting commercial transactions by making contracts for medical services and that their purchase and c   arrangement was not in the exercise of sovereign authority. Transactions were entered into otherwise than in the exercise of sovereign activity. He relied on the decision in *I Congreso del Partido* [1981] 2 All ER 1064, [1983] 1 AC 244 and the distinction between commercial activity and sovereign state activity.

As appears from the more recent decision of *Littrell v United States America (No d   2)* [1994] 4 All ER 203 at 211, 212–213, [1995] 1 WLR 82 at 89, 91, the proper approach to the question whether an activity is commercial or in exercise of sovereign authority, involves looking at all the circumstances in relation to the activities and their context and then consider all the factors together. No one factor is in itself determinative in characterising the activity as sovereign or non-sovereign. It is relevant to look at the nature of the activity, the identity of e   those who deal with it, and the place where it takes place in order to resolve this question.

On this part of the case we agree with Ms Walden-Smith. The purposes of the medical office were not 'commercial purposes' within the exception to immunity contained in s 4(3) of the 1978 Act. The purposes and activities of the medical f   office are described in detail in the affidavit evidence. They are within the sphere of governmental or sovereign activity. The medical office was used by the government of the Arab Republic of Egypt to provide guidance, advice and expert care to patients referred by the government of the Arab Republic of Egypt for medical treatment in the United Kingdom. The medical office acted throughout as a representative of the Arab Republic of Egypt and its embassy. g   The salaries of the medical office were paid by the government of the Arab Republic of Egypt and all payments to the medical office were made by the government of Egypt.

Conclusion

h   For all those reasons, we conclude that the industrial tribunal erred in law in deciding that the Arab Republic of Egypt could not claim immunity in these proceedings. We allow the appeal. There is no jurisdiction in the industrial tribunal to hear these applications.

j   *Order accordingly.*

K Mydeen Esq   Barrister.

Ahmed v Government of the Kingdom of Saudi Arabia

a

COURT OF APPEAL, CIVIL DIVISION

STUART-SMITH, PETER GIBSON AND HUTCHISON LJJ

6 JULY 1995

b

Constitutional law – Foreign sovereign state – Immunity from suit – Contract of employment – British appellant employed in London embassy of foreign state – Appellant given copy of letter from solicitors to embassy official advising on English law on protection of employment – Appellant subsequently claiming unfair dismissal – Foreign state claiming immunity – Whether appellant a 'member of the mission' – Whether solicitors' letter a 'written agreement' by foreign state to submit to jurisdiction – Diplomatic Privileges Act 1964, Sch 1, art 1 – State Immunity Act 1978, ss 4(1), 16(1)(a).

c

The appellant, a British national, was employed as a secretary in the Saudi Arabian Embassy in London from May 1988, initially without a written contract of employment. At a meeting attended by local staff and the military attaché in November 1990, the appellant was given a copy of a solicitors' letter of advice addressed to the military attaché, which stated that any staff member who was dismissed would have certain rights and protection under English law and, if *e* termination was for any reason deemed to be unfair, an industrial tribunal had power to award compensation. In March 1991 the appellant signed a contract of employment in Arabic with the Government of the Kingdom of Saudi Arabia, represented by the Saudi Arabian military attaché, which provided, inter alia, for termination on the cancellation of the post, or when the appellant's services were no longer needed, or on 'general interest grounds', in which case the appellant *f* had no right to be given reasons. A further clause provided for disputes to be resolved by a Saudi Arabian inspectorate whose decision would then become final. In February 1992 the appellant was dismissed without being given reasons and she brought a claim for unfair dismissal before an industrial tribunal. At a preliminary hearing to determine whether Saudi Arabia could claim state *g* immunity, the tribunal held that for the purposes of s 16(1)[a] of the State Immunity Act 1978 the appellant was a 'member of the mission' within the meaning of art 1[b] of the Vienna Convention on Diplomatic Relations (which had the force of law in the United Kingdom by virtue of s 2(1) of the Diplomatic Privileges Act 1964 and was set out in Sch 1 thereto) and therefore that her *h* contract of employment was not excluded from immunity by s 4(1)[c] of that Act, which provided that a state was not immune in respect of proceedings relating to a contract of employment made in the United Kingdom or where the work was wholly or partly to be performed there. However, the tribunal held that the solicitors' letter constituted a 'written agreement', by means of which Saudi Arabia had submitted to the jurisdiction for the purposes of s 2(2)[d] of the 1978 *j* Act. Saudi Arabia successfully appealed to the Employment Appeal Tribunal on

d

a   Section 16, so far as material, is set out at p 251 *c*, post
b   Article 1, so far as material, is set out at p 251 *d e*, post
c   Section 4(1) is set out at p 250 *j h*, post
d   Section 2, so far as material, is set out at p 253 *b* to *d*, post

a   the submission to jurisdiction issue and the appellant appealed to the Court of Appeal, contending principally that she was not a 'member of the mission' within the meaning of art 1.

Held – (1) On the plain meaning of s 16(1)(a) of the 1978 Act a foreign state enjoyed immunity in respect of proceedings concerning the employment of a

b   member of its embassy staff who was employed in the administrative and technical service of the embassy, since that person was clearly a 'member of the mission' within the meaning of art 1 of the convention, regardless of whether his appointment was notified to the Foreign and Commonwealth Office. Moreover, the meaning of art 1 could not be qualified to include those who were actually or notionally sent from abroad by the state, or linked to a test of nationality. It

c   followed that the appellant, as a member of the Embassy's technical and administrative staff, was a member of the mission as defined by art 1 (see p 251 *h* to p 252 *c f* to p 253 *a*, p 255 *j* and p 256 *a* to *c*, post).

(2) On the facts, it was clear that the solicitors' letter was not a 'written agreement' for the purposes of s 2(2) of the 1978 Act, since it was not a complete

d   agreement in writing between the parties and there was nothing on its face to show that it was intended by Saudi Arabia to be an offer to be accepted by the appellant by entering into a contract of employment. Further, the letter did not purport to be an agreement to submit to jurisdiction; it was no more than a letter containing the solicitors' opinion for the benefit of the military attaché to whom it was addressed and, in any event for there to have been a submission to the

e   jurisdiction it would have had to have been shown either that the head of the Saudi Arabian diplomatic mission had so submitted, or that the person entering into the alleged contract by the letter did so on behalf of and with the authority of Saudi Arabia, neither of which had been shown. It followed that the appeal would be dismissed (see p 254 *j* to p 255 *b h j* and p 256 *a* to *c*, post).

f   **Notes**

For immunity of foreign states, see 18 *Halsbury's Laws* (4th edn) para 1548, and for cases on the subject, see 1(1) *Digest* (2nd reissue) 69–81, 546–601.

For the Vienna Convention on Diplomatic Relations, see 18 *Halsbury's Laws* (4th edn) para 1560.

g   For the Diplomatic Privileges Act 1964, Sch 1, art 1, see 10 *Halsbury's Statutes* (4th edn) (1995 reissue) 680.

For the State Immunity Act 1978, ss 2, 4, 16, see ibid 758, 760, 768.

Cases referred to in judgments

h   *Kharaskhoma Exploring and Prospecting Syndicate, Re* [1897] 2 Ch 451, CA.

R v Secretary of State for the Home Dept, ex p Bagga [1991] 1 All ER 777, [1991] 1 QB 485, [1990] 3 WLR 1013, CA.

Secretary of State for Employment v Globe Elastic Thread Co Ltd [1979] 2 All ER 1077, [1980] AC 506, [1979] 3 WLR 143, HL.

j   *Sengupta v Republic of India* [1983] ICR 221, EAT.

Interlocutory appeal

By notice dated 15 February 1994 Mrs Golfidan Saleh Ahmed appealed from the decision of the Employment Appeal Tribunal (Knox J, Mr A Ferry and Mr J A Scouller) on 8 October 1993 dismissing her cross-appeal and allowing the appeal of the respondent employer, the Government of the Kingdom of Saudi Arabia,

from the decision of an industrial tribunal sitting at London (South) on 10 March
1993, whereby, on a preliminary hearing of Mrs Ahmed's complaint of unfair
dismissal, it held by a majority (the chairman dissenting) that it had jurisdiction
to hear the complaint. The facts are set out in the judgment of Peter Gibson LJ.

Mark Hoyle (instructed by *Carpenter & Co*, Wallington) for Mrs Ahmed.
Nigel Giffin (instructed by *Travers Smith Braithwaite*) for the Government of the
Kingdom of Saudi Arabia.

PETER GIBSON LJ (giving the first judgment at the invitation of Stuart-Smith
LJ). This is an appeal by Mrs Ahmed, the applicant to an industrial tribunal. She
is a British national but was employed as a secretary by the Saudi Arabian
Embassy in London from 8 May 1988 to February 1992 when she was dismissed.
No reasons have been given for her dismissal, despite repeated requests on her
behalf. She applied to an industrial tribunal, complaining of unfair dismissal
under the Employment Protection (Consolidation) Act 1978. At a preliminary
hearing to determine an objection to jurisdiction which was taken by the
respondent, the Government of the Kingdom of Saudi Arabia (Saudi Arabia), the
industrial tribunal by a majority (the chairman being in the minority) held that
they had jurisdiction to entertain Mrs Ahmed's application. But the Employment
Appeal Tribunal allowed the appeal of Saudi Arabia and held that the industrial
tribunal had no jurisdiction in this matter.

The issue of jurisdiction turns on whether state immunity applies in the
circumstances of the present case. It is Mrs Ahmed's submission that it does not
apply for either or both of two distinct reasons. One is that she was not a
'member of a mission' within the meaning of the Vienna Convention on
Diplomatic Relations (set out in Sch 1 to the Diplomatic Privileges Act 1964) and
accordingly by the combined effect of ss 4(1) and 16(1)(a) of the State Immunity
Act 1978 (the 1978 Act) Saudi Arabia cannot claim immunity in the proceedings
brought by Mrs Ahmed. The other is that Saudi Arabia has submitted to the
jurisdiction on the facts of this case. I shall discuss these in turn.

Member of a mission
The general rule as to state immunity is contained in s 1(1) of the 1978 Act:

> 'A State is immune from the jurisdiction of the courts of the United
> Kingdom except as provided in the following provisions of this Part of this
> Act.'

It is not in dispute that an industrial tribunal is a court for the purposes of the Act
(s 22(1)).
But by s 4(1), which is also in Pt I of the Act:

> 'A State is not immune as respects proceedings relating to a contract of
> employment between the State and an individual where the contract was
> made in the United Kingdom or the work is to be wholly or partly performed
> there.'

Then in sub-s (2) there are provisions disapplying that section in specific
circumstances, for example, if at the time when the proceedings are brought the
individual is a national of the state concerned or at the time when the contract
was made the individual was neither a national of the United Kingdom nor
habitually resident there. But that in turn is subject to a qualification in sub-s (3):

a

'Where the work is for an office, agency or establishment maintained by the State in the United Kingdom for commercial purposes, subsection (2)(a) and (b) above do not exclude the application of this section unless the individual was, at the time when the contract was made, habitually resident in that State.'

b

Had the Act stopped there, the case for Mrs Ahmed as to jurisdiction would be unanswerable. However, by s 16(1), which is also in Pt I of the Act, it is provided as follows (so far as material):

'This Part of this Act does not affect any immunity or privilege conferred by the Diplomatic Privileges Act 1964 ... and—(a) section 4 above does not apply to proceedings concerning the employment of the members of a mission within the meaning of the Convention scheduled to the said Act of 1964 ...'

c

Article 1 of the convention, so scheduled, provides a number of relevant definitions:

d

'... (b) the "members of the mission" are the head of the mission and the members of the staff of the mission; (c) the "members of the staff of the mission" are the members of the diplomatic staff, of the administrative and technical staff and of the service staff of the mission ... (f) the "members of the administrative and technical staff" are the members of the staff of the mission employed in the administrative and technical service of the mission ...'

e

However, the term 'the mission' is not defined.

As I understood him, it is not disputed by Mr Hoyle for Mrs Ahmed that as a secretary she was a member of the embassy's administrative and technical staff, being employed in the embassy's administrative and technical service. But it is submitted for her that she was not a member of the mission because the ordinary meaning of 'mission' is a body of persons sent to a foreign country to serve their home government, and Mrs Ahmed was not sent from Saudi Arabia but was a locally recruited British citizen, employed in a clerical capacity and without any diplomatic status. However, Mr Hoyle recognises from the convention itself, if nowhere else, that the members of the mission cannot be limited to those who enter the United Kingdom by reason of being sent from the state in question: they include those who are already in the United Kingdom and whose appointments are notified to the Foreign and Commonwealth Office (art 39). Mrs Ahmed's appointment was not so notified. More particularly, he said that the term 'members of a mission' means those who are actually or notionally sent from abroad by the state.

f

g

h

The industrial tribunal were unanimous in rejecting the argument based on membership of a mission, and in my judgment they were plainly right to do so. In my opinion the only question on this point is whether Mrs Ahmed is a member of a mission within the meaning of art 1, that question being relevant to whether Saudi Arabia is immune as respects proceedings relating to her contract of employment. It is a separate and irrelevant question whether she herself is entitled under art 39 to enjoy privileges and immunities. It has never been claimed that she was so entitled. There is nothing in s 16(1)(a) of the 1978 Act nor in art 1 of the convention that links membership of a mission with the tests laid down, for example, in art 39 as to the persons who are entitled to enjoy privileges

j

and immunities and as to the time when that enjoyment commences. As Knox J, *a* giving the judgment of the Employment Appeal Tribunal, said:

> 'Article 39 qualifies the extent to which immunities can be enjoyed … Article 1 on the other hand … is the definition section which is referred to in s 16(1)(a) of the [State Immunity Act 1978] and we see no basis upon which there should be any implication to cut down the plain meaning of the *b* paragraph in question.'

In my judgment, whether or not the appointment of a member of the mission is notified to the Foreign and Commonwealth Office, a person who falls within the definition of 'members of a mission' is a member of the mission for the purposes of s 16(1)(a). To my mind it is clear that by being a member of the *c* embassy staff employed in the administrative and technical service of the embassy, she was a member of the mission.

If authority were needed for the proposition that membership of a mission for the purposes of the convention is not dependent upon notification to the Foreign and Commonwealth Office, it is to be found in the decision of this court in *R v Secretary of State for the Home Dept, ex p Bagga* [1991] 1 All ER 777, [1991] 1 QB 485. *d*

Mr Hoyle submitted that it would be against the spirit and unnecessary for the letter of the 1964 Act and the 1978 Act if provisions enacted in the 1964 Act were held to prevent a person like Mrs Ahmed from enjoying rights under UK legislation as a British citizen working here under a contract entered into here.

His strongest argument, as it seemed to me, was based on the point that s 4 of *e* the 1978 Act has only very limited scope when read with s 16(1)(a) in the way that found favour with the industrial tribunal and the Employment Appeal Tribunal. That may well be so, and I have considerable sympathy with the argument that a locally employed person of British nationality should be able to enjoy the rights and protection afforded by the Employment Protection (Consolidation) Act 1978. But we are bound by the clear wording of the statute. Mr Hoyle's attempt *f* to introduce into the meaning of art 1, with its reference to the mission, words which qualify the meaning of that mission so as to include those who are actually or notionally sent from abroad by the state, seems to me not to provide any practicable test capable of sensible application. If a diplomat who has been recruited to be the head of the mission in this country is to be treated as notionally *g* sent from abroad, why stop there? Why should not anyone who falls within the definition of 'members of the mission' to be found in art 1 equally be deemed to be notionally sent from abroad? In my judgment there is simply no basis in art 1 for any qualification of the type for which Mr Hoyle contended.

Similarly, it seems to me quite hopeless to argue as he did that nationality *h* should provide a test of who is a member of a mission. That is not to be found in art 1. Further, as Browne-Wilkinson J said in *Sengupta v Republic of India* [1983] ICR 221 at 225:

> '… section 16(1)(a) operates to exclude jurisdiction over claims relating to the employment not only of diplomatic staff but also of lower grade *j* administrative, technical and domestic staff irrespective of their nationality.'

I respectfully agree.

Manfully though Mr Hoyle attempted to get this part of his argument on its feet, it seems to me quite impossible in view of the fact that s 16(1)(a) has directed that a state enjoys immunity in respect of proceedings concerning the a employment of the members of a mission within the meaning of the convention. I would therefore reject this ground of appeal.

Submission to the jurisdiction

The statutory provisions relevant to the question whether Saudi Arabia submitted to the jurisdiction are contained in s 2 of the 1978 Act:

b
'(1) A State is not immune as respects proceedings in respect of which it has submitted to the jurisdiction of the courts of the United Kingdom.

(2) A State may submit after the dispute giving rise to the proceedings has arisen or by a prior written agreement; but a provision in any agreement that it is to be governed by the law of the United Kingdom is not to be regarded

c as a submission …

(7) The head of a State's diplomatic mission in the United Kingdom, or the person for the time being performing his functions, shall be deemed to have authority to submit on behalf of the State in respect of any proceedings; and any person who has entered into a contract on behalf of and with the

d authority of a State shall be deemed to have authority to submit on its behalf in respect of proceedings arising out of the contract.'

The facts which were found by the industrial tribunal and are relevant to this question can be summarised as follows. Mrs Ahmed, who was employed in the Defence Office of the Saudi Arabian Embassy, initially received no written

e contract of employment. In November 1990 consideration was given to the provision of written contracts. The local staff were worried at the prospect. At or after a meeting attended by local staff and the military attaché and his assistant, Mrs Ahmed received a copy of a solicitors' letter dated 16 November 1990 and addressed to the military attaché. It was headed 'Termination of Staff Employ-

f ment' and the first three paragraphs read:

'As requested, I am writing to confirm the position under English law relating to the termination of Contracts of Employment. Staff members may have rights that are granted specifically by a Contract of Employment, or only those rights that are declared by Statute; I understand that the Embassy staff do not have Contracts of Employment. If the employment of a staff

g member is terminated, the statutory provisions will apply, which are now mainly contained in the Employment Protection (Consolidation) Act.'

In the final paragraph the solicitors wrote:

h 'If a termination of employment was for any reason deemed to be "unfair", an Industrial Tribunal has power to award compensation.'

At the top of the letter the military attaché had written a note in Arabic to his assistant: 'For your information. Do whatever you think.'

A solicitor in attendance at the meeting advised Mrs Ahmed that she had the

j same rights and protections as any English employee and that if her employment was terminated she could go to an industrial tribunal. In March 1991 she signed a contract of employment in Arabic. It was headed 'Contract of Employment for employees of Embassies and Attaché's Offices Abroad'. The parties were expressed to be Saudi Arabia, represented by the Saudi Arabian Defence Attaché, and Mrs Ahmed. Among the provisions were the following:

'19. The Contract is curtailed in the following cases ...   4. The
cancellation of the post or when the services of [Mrs Ahmed] are no longer *a*
needed ... 8. Dismissal on general interest grounds. (In this case [Mrs
Ahmed] does not have the right to be given reasons.)'

And cl 21 provides for disputes to be resolved by the General Inspectorate for
Civil Services in the Kingdom of Saudi Arabia whose decision would then *b*
become final.

Mrs Ahmed's contentions before the industrial tribunal were that the letter of
16 November 1990 constituted a submission to the jurisdiction; it was distributed
to the staff by the authority of the military attaché, delegated to his assistant; the
term 'written agreement' in s 2(2) of the 1978 Act did not necessarily mean a
binding contract; alternatively it amounted to a contract in the sense of a *c*
collateral contract; the intention of the letter was to make the staff believe that
they would be protected by English statute law. The two industrial members of
the industrial tribunal accepted those contentions, their reasons being as follows:

'In the absence of any statutory definition of "written agreement" they
consider that the solicitors' letter, in the circumstances in which it was *d*
written, amounts to a written agreement within the meaning of the [1978
Act]. They would add, in effect, that [Saudi Arabia] is estopped from denying
that it has submitted to the jurisdiction and that it would be unjust to deprive
[Mrs Ahmed] of her remedy in all the circumstances of the case.'

The point on estoppel was not one raised by Mrs Ahmed and was not *e*
supported by her before the Employment Appeal Tribunal, nor before us, no
doubt because it is clearly established that an industrial tribunal may not enlarge
its jurisdiction on the basis of an estoppel (see *Secretary of State for Employment v
Globe Elastic Thread Co Ltd* [1979] 2 All ER 1077, [1980] AC 506).

The main question raised before us, as it was before the industrial tribunal and *f*
the Employment Appeal Tribunal, was whether by a written agreement prior to
the dispute giving rise to the proceedings Saudi Arabia submitted to the
jurisdiction. The solicitors' letter of 16 November was said to be that written
agreement. Mr Hoyle said of that letter that it was 'part of the package of the
documents for the new written contract of [Mrs Ahmed]'. But it was received by *g*
her at or after the meeting in November 1990 whereas it was not until March 1991
that she entered into her contract of employment, and there is no reference in
that employment contract to that letter nor to the Employment Protection
(Consolidation) Act 1978, nor does it give her rights consistent with those
conferred by that Act. Mr Hoyle further said that the letter was 'by nature of an
offer accepted by the applicant when she went ahead and signed her contract of *h*
employment' and that it was 'a unilateral contract; the offer of rights to go to the
statutory tribunal, and enjoy contractual rights, was accepted by [Mrs Ahmed]
when she signed the [employment contract]'. I do not agree. The letter is no
more than a letter containing the opinion of the solicitors who wrote it for the
benefit of the military attaché to whom it is addressed, and, as Knox J pointed out, *j*
it was a very much less than complete statement of English law because it did not
refer to the 1978 Act. True it is that it was received by Mrs Ahmed, but it is not
clear by what means. There is nothing on the face of the document to show that
it was intended by Saudi Arabia as an offer to be accepted by entering into a
contract of employment, nor is there any finding that when Mrs Ahmed entered
into her contract of employment months later, she did so by way of such

a acceptance. The letter is simply not in the form of an offer at all. Nor do I understand how such a letter can be said to amount to a contractual statement by Saudi Arabia such as might form the basis of a collateral contract. The letter itself is plainly not a contract.

But the difficulties in Mr Hoyle's submission do not stop there. A written agreement must be an agreement in writing between two or more parties. It is
b quite impossible to say that the solicitors' letter, even with the writing on it by the military attaché, amounts to such an agreement between Saudi Arabia and Mrs Ahmed. Nor does it purport to be an agreement to submit to the jurisdiction. I repeat that it simply contains the solicitors' opinion.

Similar reasoning led the chairman of the industrial tribunal to hold that there
c was no written agreement within the meaning of s 2(2) of the 1978 Act. As he said: 'A written agreement to submit to the jurisdiction should be complete in itself and should not require oral evidence to explain it.'

So too Knox J found it impossible to construe the solicitors' letter as a prior written agreement to submit to the jurisdiction. He pointed out that neither the solicitors nor the military attaché who wrote the superscription were entering
d into an agreement with another party, and he continued:

'It is only when one adduces the oral evidence that Mrs Ahmed gave to the Industrial Tribunal that this document with its superscription can even be argued to enter the field of written agreement and it seems to us in principle
e that a document which needs to be supplemented by oral evidence in order to become part of an agreement between two parties is something which falls significantly short of itself being a prior written agreement.'

He referred to the statement of Lindley LJ in Re Kharaskhoma Exploring and Prospecting Syndicate [1897] 2 Ch 451 at 464 on what was meant by 'a contract in
f writing': 'a document which only discloses part of a contract is not a contract in writing.' Knox J said that that seemed to encapsulate the requirement that if there was to be an agreement in writing you must have the whole of the agreement in writing.

In his skeleton argument, Mr Hoyle had submitted that Lindley LJ's statement
g was irrelevant because the crucial phrase in that case was 'a contract duly made in writing', not 'a written agreement'. I am afraid that the suggested ground of distinction is too subtle for me, and the common sense of the statement is too obvious to need defending. In my judgment the chairman of the industrial tribunal and the Employment Appeal Tribunal were plainly correct on this point.

h For the sake of completeness I would add that on yet another point taken by the chairman of the industrial tribunal and by a respondent's notice before us Mrs Ahmed would fail, even if on all other points she had been right. For there to be a submission by Saudi Arabia to the jurisdiction it would have to be shown either that the head of the Saudi Arabian diplomatic mission by the solicitors' letter had
j so submitted or that the person entering into the alleged contract by the letter did so 'on behalf of and with the authority of' Saudi Arabia. That has not been shown.

For these reasons, despite the natural sympathy which I feel for Mrs Ahmed as an employee in this country unable to invoke the protection of Employment Protection (Consolidation) Act 1978, I have reached the clear conclusion that this appeal must be dismissed.

HUTCHISON LJ. I agree that this appeal must be dismissed for the reasons that
Peter Gibson LJ has given. In particular I agree with his construction of s 16(1)(a) a
of the State Immunity Act 1978. It is a curious fact that, so construed, s 16 appears
almost completely to emasculate s 4. I should, therefore, have been receptive to
any viable argument on construction which did not lead to this result. However,
I regret to say that I feel unable to accept the validity of any of the ingenious
submissions that have been advanced by Mr Hoyle as to why we should reach a b
different conclusion. Accordingly, with some regret, I agree that this appeal must
inevitably be dismissed.

STUART-SMITH LJ. I also agree that this appeal must be dismissed for the
reasons given by Peter Gibson and Hutchison LJJ.

c

Appeal dismissed.

Paul Magrath Esq   Barrister.

Kleinwort Benson Ltd v Glasgow City Council

COURT OF APPEAL, CIVIL DIVISION
LEGGATT, ROCH AND MILLETT LJJ
4, 5 DECEMBER 1995, 25 JANUARY 1996

Conflict of laws – Jurisdiction – Challenge to jurisdiction – Restitution – Bank entering into interest rate swap contracts with local authority – Agreements subsequently declared void ab initio – Bank bringing restitutionary claims in England against local authority domiciled in Scotland – Scottish authority challenging jurisdiction of English court – Whether English court having special jurisdiction over bank's claim – Whether claim 'relating to a contract' or 'relating to tort' – Civil Jurisdiction and Judgments Act 1982, Sch 4, art 5(1)(3).

Contract – Restitution – Interest rate swap agreement – Bank entering into interest rate swap agreements with local authority – Agreements ultra vires the local authority – Whether bank's claim for restitution based on unjust enrichment 'relating to a contract' – Civil Jurisdiction and Judgments Act 1982, Sch 4, art 5(1)(3).

In 1982 the defendant, a Scottish local authority, entered into a number of interest rate swap agreements with the plaintiff bank. Following the House of Lords ruling that such transactions were ultra vires the local authorities and void ab initio, the bank brought an action in England against the defendant, claiming restitution of the balance standing to the credit of the defendant under the transactions when they were aborted on the basis of unjust enrichment. The defendant however challenged the jurisdiction of the English court and applied for an order dismissing the action on the ground that it was domiciled in Scotland for the purposes of the Convention on Jurisdiction and the Enforcement of Judgments in Civil Matters 1968 (set out in Sch 1 to the Civil Jurisdiction and Judgments Act 1982) and should be sued in the courts of Scotland pursuant to s 16(1)[a] of and art 2[b] of Sch 4 to the 1982 Act, which made provision for the allocation of jurisdiction within the United Kingdom. The bank contended, inter alia, that the English court had jurisdiction under the special provisions embodied in art 5(1)[c] of Sch 4 to the Act, which provided (i) that a person domiciled in a part of the United Kingdom could be sued in another part in 'matters relating to a contract' in the courts for the 'place of performance of the obligation in question' (art 5(1)) and, 'in matters relating to tort', where the harmful event occurred (art 5(3)). The judge granted the defendant's application and struck out the bank's claim, holding that the agreements which had been declared void ab initio were not open to classification as 'matters relating to a contract' under art 5(1) so as to allow jurisdiction in the courts of the country of performance of the obligations arising from the transactions and that a claim for unjust enrichment did not fall within the terms of art 5(3). The bank appealed to the Court of Appeal, which

a   Section 16(1), so far as material, provides: 'The provisions set out in Schedule 4 ... shall have effect
     for determining, for each part of the United Kingdom, whether the courts of law of that part or any
     particular court of law in that part, have or has jurisdiction in the proceedings where—(a) the
     subject-matter of the proceedings is within the scope of the 1968 Convention as determined by
     Article 1 ... and (b) the defendant or defender is domiciled in the United Kingdom ...'
b   Article 2 , so far as material, is set out at p 267 h, post
c   Article 5, so far as material, is set out at p 262 h, post

stayed the proceedings and referred to the Court of Justice of the European
Communities for a preliminary ruling the question whether the claim was within   a
the scope of art 5(1) or 5(3) of Sch 4. The Court of Justice held that it did not have
jurisdiction to give a preliminary ruling because the convention did not apply to
the dispute and there was nothing in the 1982 Act (which made a clear distinction
between the convention and Sch 4) which required the application of Community law. The Court of Appeal therefore resumed hearing the appeal.   b

Held (Leggatt LJ dissenting) – A claim to recover money paid under a contract
which was a nullity because of the recipient's lack of capacity to enter into the
transaction was 'a matter relating to a contract' for the purposes of art 5(1) of the
1968 convention. Indeed, the correct approach in determining whether a claim
was to be regarded as falling within art 5(1) was to ask whether for the purposes   c
of the convention, which applied to a number of member states with different
national laws and systems of characterisation, the defendant should broadly be
regarded as being sued in a matter relating to a contract; it was wrong to ask
whether the claim would be characterised as contractual under domestic law. On
that basis, a 'contract' was a consensual arrangement intended to create legal   d
relations and to be legally enforceable and therefore included a void contract,
while the expression 'place of performance of the obligation in question' meant
'intended place of performance of the supposed obligation'. It followed that the
English court had jurisdiction, under the special jurisdiction conferred by art 5(1)
of the convention (as set out in Sch 4 to the 1982 Act) to entertain the claim of the
plaintiff bank against the defendant, which was domiciled in Scotland, for the   e
recovery of money paid out under the terms of the interest rate swap contracts,
which had subsequently been held to be void ab initio. The bank's appeal would
accordingly be allowed (see p 267 j to p 268 a e to p 269 a c to f h to p 270 b, p 271
g, p 273 c to p 274 e j, p 275 d to g and p 276 a to f, post).
    Martin Peters Bauunternehmung GmbH v Zuid Nederlandse Aannemers Vereniging   f
Case 34/82 [1983] ECR 987 considered.
    Decision of Hirst J [1994] 4 All ER 865 reversed.

Notes
For the jurisdiction of the courts with respect to the Convention on Jurisdiction
and Enforcement of Judgments in Civil and Commercial Matters 1968, see 8   g
Halsbury's Laws (4th edn) paras 768B–768F.
    For the Civil Jurisdiction and Judgments Act 1982, s 16, Sch 4, arts 2, 5, see 11
Halsbury's Statutes (4th edn) (1991 reissue) 1113, 1190.

Cases referred to in judgments   h
Arcado SPRL v Haviland SA Case 9/87 [1988] ECR 1539.
Effer SpA v Kantner Case 38/81 [1982] ECR 825.
Ets A de Bloos SPRL v Société en commandite par actions Bouyer Case 14/76 [1976]
    ECR 1497.
Hazell v Hammersmith and Fulham London BC [1991] 1 All ER 545, [1992] 2 AC 1,   j
    [1991] 2 WLR 372, HL.
Kalfelis v Bankhaus Schröder Münchmeyer Hengst & Co Case 189/87 [1988] ECR
    5565.
Martin Peters Bauunternehmung GmbH v Zuid Nederlandse Aannemers Vereniging
    Case 34/82 [1983] ECR 987.

a *Reichert v Dresdner Bank AG* Case C-261/90 [1992] ECR I-2149.

Westdeutsche Landesbank Girozentrale v Islington London BC, Kleinwort Benson Ltd v Sandwell BC [1994] 4 All ER 890; *affd in part* [1994] 4 All ER 890, [1994] 1 WLR 938, CA.

Cases also cited or referred to in skeleton arguments

b *Davenport v Corinthian Motor Policies at Lloyds* 1991 SLT 774, Ex Div.

Dumez France and Tracoba v Hessische Landesbank (Helaba) Case C-220/88 [1990] ECR I-49.

Engdiv Ltd v G Percy Trentham Ltd 1990 SLT 617, OH.

Gubisch Maschinenfabrik KG v Palumbo Case 144/86 [1987] ECR 4861.

c *Handelswekerij G J Bier BV v Mines de Potasse d'Alsace SA* Case 21/76 [1976] ECR 1735.

Handte & Cie GmbH v Traitements mécano-chimiques des surfaces (TMCS) Case C-26/91 [1992] ECR I-3967.

Industrie Tessili Italiana Como v Dunlop AG Case 12/76 [1976] ECR 1473.

d *Ivenel v Schwab* Case 133/81 [1982] ECR 1891.

Lipkin Gorman (a firm) v Karpnale Ltd [1992] 4 All ER 512, [1991] 2 AC 548, HL.

Netherlands State v Rüffer Case 814/79 [1980] ECR 3807.

Shearson Lehman Hutton Inc v Treuhand für Vermögensverwaltung und Beteiligungen (TVB) mbH Case C-89/91 [1993] ECR I-139.

e *Shevill v Presse Alliance SA* Case C-68/93 [1995] All ER (EC) 289, [1995] 2 WLR 499, ECJ.

Somafer SA v Saar-Ferngas AG Case 33/78 [1978] ECR 2183.

Strathaird Farms Ltd v GA Chattaway & Co 1993 SLT (Sh Ct) 36.

f **Appeal**

By notice dated 26 March 1992 the plaintiff, Kleinwort Benson Ltd, appealed with leave from the decision of Hirst J ([1994] 4 All ER 865, [1993] QB 429) on 27 February 1992 striking out its action against the defendant, Glasgow City Council, for restitution of the sum of £807,230 standing to the council's credit g under seven interest rate swap agreements which were null and void ab initio, on the ground that the court had no jurisdiction to hear the claim. On 18 May 1993 the Court of Appeal (Lloyd, Mann and Steyn LJJ) ([1994] 4 All ER 865, [1994] QB 404) stayed the proceedings and referred to the Court of Justice of the European Communities for a preliminary ruling the question whether the claim was a matter 'relating to a contract' within the meaning of art 5(1) of the Convention h on Jurisdiction and the Enforcement of Judgments in Civil and Commercial Matters 1968 (set out in Sch 1 to the Civil Jurisdiction and Judgment Acts 1982). On 28 March 1995 the Court of Justice ([1995] All ER (EC) 514, [1996] QB 57) held that it did not have jurisdiction to give a preliminary ruling on the question submitted to it. On 4 December 1995 the Court of Appeal resumed the hearing j of the appeal. The facts are set out in the judgment of Leggatt LJ.

Thomas Beazley and *Adrian Briggs* (instructed by *Clifford Chance*) for the bank.

Michael Burton QC and *Jonathan Tecks* (instructed by *Lewis Silkin*) for Glasgow.

Cur adv vult

25 January 1996. The following judgments were delivered.

a

LEGGATT LJ. This is the resumption of an appeal by Kleinwort Benson Ltd (Kleinwort) from the order of Hirst J ([1994] 4 All ER 865, [1993] QB 429) dated 27 February 1992 in favour of the City of Glasgow District Council (Glasgow) setting aside the writ and service of it on the ground that the court has no jurisdiction over Glasgow in respect of the subject matter of the claim. When this matter was last before this court on 18 May 1993 the facts and the outline of the dispute were stated in the judgment of the court by Lloyd LJ (see [1994] 4 All ER 865 at 882–883, [1993] QB 429 at 411–412). Since it is for present purposes undesirable to divagate from them, I shall substantially reproduce them without further acknowledgment.

b

In 1981 there came into existence a new type of financial transaction known as an interest rate swap contract. Such contracts are of many kinds. But in its simplest form it consists of an agreement between two parties whereby one pays to the other, over a period of months or years, sums calculated by reference to the difference between a fixed rate of interest and the current market rate of interest from time to time. The principal sum is purely notional and exists solely for the purpose of calculating the obligations of the parties to pay differences. The essential feature of the transaction is that it is a futures contract, the financial outcome of which depends on future movements in interest rates. From about 1982 interest rate swap contracts came to be used by a number of local authorities, of which Glasgow was one. In September 1982 Glasgow entered into seven transactions with Kleinwort. In *Hazell v Hammersmith and Fulham London BC* [1991] 1 All ER 545, [1992] 2 AC 1 the House of Lords held that all such transactions were void ab initio for lack of capacity to enter into them. There followed many claims in the Commercial Court, mostly by banks against local authorities. In the first such action Hobhouse J held in *Westdeutsche Landesbank Girozentrale v Islington London BC, Kleinwort Benson Ltd v Sandwell BC* [1994] 4 All ER 890 that the bank was entitled to recover from the local authority the balance standing to the credit of the local authority when the transactions were aborted by the decision of the House of Lords. That decision was upheld in this court ([1994] 4 All ER 890, [1994] 1 WLR 938), but judgment is still awaited in a further appeal to the House of Lords.

c

d

e

f

The writ in the present action was issued on 6 September 1991. It sought restitution of the sum of £807,230, then standing to the credit of Glasgow under the seven interest rate swap transactions to which I have referred.

g

It is a special feature of the action that the respondents are domiciled in Scotland. On 16 October 1991 they issued a summons by which they claimed a declaration that the English courts, and in particular the Commercial Court in London, have no jurisdiction to hear the claim. They say that the proper place to bring proceedings is in the courts of Scotland. Before us Mr Burton QC for Glasgow has acknowledged that the principal reason for reliance upon that argument is that the period of limitation which is or may be applicable is shorter in Scotland than in England. A reason for preferring the English courts (apart from the convenience of Kleinwort) might be that all the transactions are admittedly governed by English law.

h

j

The jurisdiction issue arose under the provisions of Sch 4 to the Civil Jurisdiction and Judgments Act 1982. Unless otherwise stated, references in this judgment to articles are to articles of Sch 4. That enacted in relation to countries of the United Kingdom provisions comparable with those in the Convention on *a* Jurisdiction and the Enforcement of Judgments in Civil and Commercial Matters 1968 (the Brussels Convention) (set out in Sch 1 to the 1982 Act) in relation to contracting states.

Founding on the principle of art 2 that a person should be sued in the courts of his own domicile, Glasgow asserted their rights to be sued in Scotland. Kleinwort maintained that the English courts had jurisdiction under the special provisions *b* embodied in art 5(1), which concerns matters relating to a contract; in art 5(3), which concerns matters relating to tort; in art 5(8), which concerns proceedings asserting rights over movable property; and in art 6(1), which concerns one of a number of defendants.

Hirst J found against Kleinwort on all points. Kleinwort appealed to the Court of Appeal, which ruled against them on the art 6(1) point. During the course of *c* the appeal Kleinwort abandoned the art 5(8) point. In relation to the remaining points under art 5(1) and (3) questions as to the scope and relationship of the parallel provisions of the Brussels Convention were referred to the Court of Justice of the European Communities for a preliminary ruling on 18 May 1993.

For purposes of this appeal what proves to be determinative is the answer to *d* the question whether national or European law should be applied to the construction of Sch 4. Because the convention does not apply to this dispute, nothing in the 1982 Act requires the application of European law. The distinction between the convention and Sch 4 is important. It is clearly drawn by the 1982 Act. Whereas by s 3(1) the meaning and effect of the convention are to be determined *in accordance with* the principles laid down by and any relevant *e* decisions of the Court of Justice, s 16(3) provides that in determining any question as to the meaning and effect of Sch 4 *regard shall be had* to any relevant principles and any relevant decisions of the Court of Justice (my emphasis). In the one case the principles and decisions apply; in the other regard is merely to be had to them. In my judgment, therefore, there can be no doubt that national law *f* (whether of England, Scotland or Northern Ireland) is to prevail.

That that is so appears clearly from the judgment of the Court of Justice in this case. In relation to its jurisdiction the court said ([1995] All ER (EC) 514 at 529–530, [1996] QB 57 at 82–83 (paras 14–22)):

g '14. It is common ground that the purpose of the interpretation which the court is asked to give of the convention provisions at issue is to enable the national court to decide on the application not of the convention but of the national law of the contracting state to which that court belongs.

15. Under those circumstances the question arises as to the jurisdiction of the court to give a preliminary ruling on the question submitted by the Court *h* of Appeal.

16. Far from containing a direct and unconditional renvoi to provisions of Community law so as to incorporate them into the domestic legal order, the 1982 Act takes the convention as a model only, and does not wholly reproduce the terms thereof.

j 17. Though certain provisions of the 1982 Act are taken almost word for word from the convention, others depart from the wording of the corresponding convention provision. That is true in particular of art 5(3).

18. Moreover, express provision is made in the 1982 Act for the authorities of the contracting state in question to adopt modifications "designed to produce divergence" between any provision of Sch 4 and a corresponding provision of the convention, as interpreted by the court.

19. Accordingly, the provisions of the convention which the court is asked to interpret cannot be regarded as having been rendered applicable as such, in cases outwith the scope of the convention, by the law of the contracting state concerned.

20. The 1982 Act does not require the courts of the contracting state to decide disputes before them by applying absolutely and unconditionally the interpretation of the convention provided to them by the court.

21. Indeed, in terms of the 1982 Act, when national courts apply provisions modelled on those of the convention, they are required only to have regard to the court's case law concerning the interpretation of the corresponding provisions of the convention. In contrast, when the convention applies to the dispute, s 3(1) of the 1982 Act provides: "Any question as to the meaning or effect of any provision of the Convention shall, if not referred to the European Court in accordance with the 1971 Protocol [the Protocol on the interpretation of the 1968 Convention by the European Court, set out in Sch 2 of the 1982 Act], be determined in accordance with the principles laid down by and any relevant decision of the European Court."

22. In a case such as that in the main proceedings, where the convention is not applicable, the court of the contracting state in question is therefore free to decide whether the interpretation given by the court is equally valid for the purposes of the application of the national law based on the convention.'

As the court acknowledged, the English court is free to decide whether the interpretation given by the Court of Justice is equally valid for the purposes of the application of English law based on the convention. In short, it is English law that is to be applied, not European law. It is true that regard is to be had to European law, with the result that English law will, where possible, be so interpreted as not to conflict with it, and in case of doubt about English law so as to correspond with it. But that does not entitle this court to reach a conclusion at variance with English law in the interests of applying its own view of an uncertain and disputed principle of European law. If Parliament had intended that jurisdictional disputes of this kind should be determined in accordance with European law, it would have so provided.

So far as material, art 5 reads:

'A person domiciled in a part of the United Kingdom may, in another part of the United Kingdom, be sued:

(1) in matters relating to a contract, in the courts for the place of performance of the obligation in question ...

(3) in matters relating to tort, delict or quasi-delict, in the courts for the place where the harmful event occurred or in the case of a threatened wrong is likely to occur ...'

Before this court, as before the Court of Justice, Kleinwort contend that, where proceedings are brought against a defendant for restitution in respect of money paid to that defendant by the plaintiff under a contract which is a nullity because one of the parties did not have capacity to enter into it, the defendant is being sued (a) 'in matters relating to a contract', or alternatively, (b) 'in matters relating to tort delict or quasi-delict' within the meaning respectively of paras (1) or (3) of art 5. If Kleinwort are correct that Glasgow are being so sued, it is common *a* ground that for purposes of art 5(1) and (3) England would be 'the place of performance of the obligation in question' or 'the place where the harmful event occurred'.

The judge held that, because the contracts were void, there were no contracts to which the claim could relate; and that it was not based on tort. He therefore declined jurisdiction under both provisions of art 5.

b   For Kleinwort, Mr Beazley submits that the relevant articles of Sch 4, as of the Brussels Convention, must be independently interpreted. So the rules about jurisdiction do not affect the classification of an action for the purpose of determining the applicable principles of liability. The jurisdictional concepts must be interpreted chiefly by reference to the system and objectives of the convention so as to ensure its efficacy.

c   Mr Beazley argued that restitutionary claims do not fall into a single category. The language, system and objectives of the Brussels Convention strongly suggest that the expression 'in matters relating to a contract' should include a claim for recovery of moneys paid under a contract which one party had no capacity to make. Those words do not confine the article to claims under a contract or to a contract that is valid. It may legitimately be said that the payments of which *d* recovery is sought in these proceedings were made under a contract, notwithstanding that it was subsequently declared to have been void. Mr Beazley submits that for purposes of an independent, as distinct from a national, interpretation, no distinction can properly be drawn between a contract which is void, and a contract which is or is to be avoided. There are many cases in which *e* claims under a contract are joined in the same action with alternative claims to recover money paid under it in the event that it is held to be a nullity. This approach does not conflict with other cases, properly understood, in which the Court of Justice has considered art 5(1). Mr Beazley relied particularly on art 10(1)(e) of the Convention on the Law applicable to Contractual Obligations 1980 *f* (the Rome Convention) (enacted into English law by the Contracts (Applicable Law) Act 1990, s 2 and Sch 1) as an example of the consequences of nullity being treated for purposes of European law as governed by the law applicable to a contract. He relied also on what he claimed as 'substantial academic support'.

Our attention has been drawn by each side to a plethora of extracts from learned writers and from the submissions to the Court of Justice of lawyers on *g* behalf of other member states, all said to favour its own cause. In my judgment it suffices to focus for present purposes on a few decisions of the Court of Justice for the principles involved and (so far as appropriate) to apply them in the light of the submissions of counsel appearing before us. They are entitled to derive inspiration rather than authority from other sources without the need for the *h* court to evaluate those other sources independently.

For Glasgow, Mr Burton submitted that restitution on the ground of unjust enrichment is a different cause of action from contract or tort. Thus, he started from an appraisal of those causes of action for purposes of English law. He did so upon the theoretical footing that the interpretation of Sch 4 is a matter for the *j* English court, by contrast with the corresponding provisions of the convention, which are for the Court of Justice.

Mr Burton argues that art 2 is the primary, fundamental and normal basis of jurisdiction, and is wholly appropriate for a claim in restitution. There is ample authority that the scope of the derogations from art 2 constituted by arts 5(1) and 5(3) is to be restrictively interpreted. Both are separate from restitution. Mr Burton submits that there is no justification for descrying a close connecting factor between the claim in restitution and any court other than the Scottish courts.

In this court it was Mr Burton's main argument that in present circumstances art 5(1) is both inappropriate and inapplicable. He submitted that the paragraph is intended to enforce contractual provisions, and that the word 'obligation' means one that is contractual or consensual, because it is concerned with enforcement of a contract in the place of performance. Following the judge, Mr Burton submitted that there is no contract, no contractual obligation, and no place of performance of such an obligation. It is therefore not helpful to ask where the contract would have been performed. Where, as here, there was no contract, the claim is not in contract or for the enforcement of a consensual obligation, but by operation of law by way of unjust enrichment.

An important case for present purposes is *Martin Peters Bauunternehmung GmbH v Zuid Nederlandse Aannemers Vereniging* Case 34/82 [1983] ECR 987. The dispute was between a German company (Peters) and a Dutch association, of which Peters was a member. It concerned the recovery of sums payable by Peters under an internal rule adopted by the association and binding on its members. The first question for the court was:

'Does Article 5(1) of the Convention apply to claims which are made by an association constituted under private law possessing legal personality against one of its members in a matter relating to obligations in regard to the payment of a sum of money and which have their basis in the relationship between the parties by virtue of membership, such relationship arising from the defendant party's joining the association as a member by virtue of a legal transaction entered into for that purpose?' (See [1983] ECR 987 at 1001 (para 6).)

The judgment began by referring to the fact that—

'Article 5 of the Convention makes provision in a number of cases for a special jurisdiction which the plaintiff may choose, in derogation from the general jurisdiction provided for in Article 2(1) of the Convention.' (See [1983] ECR 987 at 1001 (para 7).)

The court observed that the concept of matters relating to a contract 'should not be interpreted simply as referring to the national law of one or other of the States concerned', and emphasised that—

'the concept of matters relating to a contract should be regarded as an independent concept which for the purpose of the application of the Convention, must be interpreted by reference chiefly to the system and objectives of the Convention, in order to ensure that it is fully effective.' (See [1983] ECR 987 at 1002 (paras 9, 10).)

In that case it appeared to the court that—

'membership of an association creates between the members close links of the same kind as those which are created between the parties to a contract and that consequently the obligation to which the national court refers may be regarded as contractual for the purpose of the application of Article 5(1) of the Convention.' (See [1983] ECR 987 at 1002 (para 13).)

The court accordingly answered the first question by saying:

a   '... obligations in regard to the payment of a sum of money which have their basis in the relationship existing between an association and its members by virtue of membership are "matters relating to a contract" within the meaning of Article 5(1) ...' (See [1983] ECR 987 at 1003 (para 15).)

When this problem was sent to the Court of Justice, it sent it back on the ground that the interpretation of Sch 4 is a matter for this court. Since art 5 is concerned
b   with exceptions to the general rule created by art 2, the provisions of art 5 are to be construed restrictively for purposes of English as well as Community law. Most European jurisdictions, including England and Scotland, regard restitution as a separate cause of action from contract and tort. The *Peters* case shows that under Community law the court will assume jurisdiction even in a case where the
c   relationship between the parties is not contractual, but only akin to contract. But there still is a continuing consensual basis for the action. The point of conferring a special jurisdiction for contractual matters is that there may be expected to be a connection between the place of performance of the obligation in question and the courts for that place.

d   Here the cause of action arises only because there proved *not* to be any contractual relationship between the parties. They had, of course, contracted with each other in the belief that they were entering into an enforceable contract. The place where the contract was, or would have been, performed, if it had been enforceable, is quite irrelevant. Thus the quirk that the contracts provided for payment in London is happenstance and has nothing to do with the question
e   whether money thus paid should be repaid.

To accord to the English courts jurisdiction it would be necessary to construe the phrase 'matters relating to a contract' as meaning 'matters relating to a relationship which the parties erroneously believed to be contractual.' As S J Whittaker puts it in *Chitty on Contracts* (27th edn, 1994) vol 1, para 1-023):

f   'A void contract is strictly a contradiction in terms, because if an agreement is truly void it is not a contract; but the term is a useful one and well understood by lawyers. Properly speaking, a void contract should produce no legal effects whatsoever. Neither party should be able to sue the other on the contract ... If money has been paid, it should be recoverable by an action
g   in restitution, because the money was not due.'

Here there was a relationship between the parties which was akin to contract, but it was bereft of legal effect when transactions of that nature were adjudged by the House of Lords to be void.

Article 10(1) of the Rome Convention affords a paradigm of this dispute
h   because by sub-para (e) it expressly includes the consequences of nullity within the scope of the law of contracts. Both parties regard that provision as conclusive. Mr Beazley submits that it shows that most of the member states treat the consequences of nullity as within the scope of the law of contracts. Mr Burton, on the other hand, submits that the very fact that the paragraph was left out of
j   the article by the reservation of the United Kingdom demonstrates a determination within the United Kingdom to exclude the consequences of nullity from the scope of the law of contracts. It is true that this shows that the general approach under Community law is to regard the consequences of nullity as contractual in nature. But it equally demonstrates an intention for the purposes of national law to exclude the consequences of nullity from the contractual context. As the Lord Advocate (Lord Fraser of Carmyllie) remarked when

introducing the Bill for the Contracts (Applicable Law) Act 1990 in the House of Lords: 'Under both English and Scottish law, such questions [about the nullity of contracts] do not form part of the law of contract, but of the law of restitution or recompense' (see 513 HL Official Report (5th series) col 1259, 12 December 1989).

It is said that if the claim in restitution is regarded as 'a matter relating to a contract', the 'obligation' relied on is to repay, and if that occurs it will be in London. But in art 5(1) the phrase 'performance of the obligation in question' most naturally refers to the performance prescribed by the contract of relevant contractual obligations: in other words, the payment in London of money due under the supposed contract. That has nothing to do with the claim in restitution, which is concerned with the repayment of money received by Glasgow.

Mr Burton relies strongly on *Ets A de Bloos SPRL v Société commandite par actions Bouyer* Case 14/76 [1976] ECR 1497. In that case it was held that in a dispute about the consequence of breach by a grantor of a contract granting an exclusive concession, such as the dissolution of the contract, the 'obligation' to which art 5(1) refers is 'the contractual obligation forming the basis of the legal proceedings'. The court concluded ([1976] ECR 1497 at 1508 (para 14)):

'In a case where the plaintiff asserts the right to be paid damages or seeks a dissolution of the contract on the ground of the wrongful conduct of the other party, the obligation referred to in Article 5(1) is still that which arises under the contract and the non-performance of which is relied upon to support such claims.'

The submission seems to me artificial that the 'obligation' referred to is merely that which accords to the court special jurisdiction under art 5(1). The case is simply authority for the proposition that 'the obligation referred to in Article 5(1) is ... that which arises under the contract ...' It is not that which would have arisen if there had been a contract, nor that which arises from the fact that there was no contract.

Paying all permissible regard to the principles and decisions of the Court of Justice, in my judgment the judge rightly concluded that, once the contract between the parties has been held void, it can be seen that there never was a contract, and it is therefore impossible to regard a claim for unjust enrichment as a matter relating to a contract. The claim in restitution therefore falls outwith the scope of art 5(1).

Article 5(3)

Mr Beazley submits, in the alternative, that the claims in this action fall within art 5(3). The expression 'in matters relating to tort, delict or quasi-delict' (like the expression 'in matters relating to a contract') has an independent meaning under the Brussels Convention. Article 5(3) covers a wide diversity of kinds of liability, and, as held by the Court of Justice in *Kalfelis v Bankhaus Schröder Münchmeyer Hengst & Co* Case 189/87 [1988] ECR 5565 at 5585 (para 17), the article covers—

'*all* actions which seek to establish the liability of a defendant and which are not related to a "contract" within the meaning of Article 5(1).' (My emphasis.)

To the like effect, see also *Reichert v Dresdner Bank AG* Case C-261/90 [1992] ECR I-2149.

In *Kalfelis* [1988] ECR 5565 at 5584 (para 14) the second question posed was, as the court put it:

'... intended essentially to ascertain, first, whether the phrase "matters relating to tort, delict or quasi delict" used in Article 5(3) of the Convention must be given an independent meaning or be defined in accordance with the applicable national law and, secondly, in the case of an action based concurrently on tortious or delictual liability, breach of contract and unjust enrichment, whether the court having jurisdiction by virtue of Article 5(3) may adjudicate on the action in so far as it is not based on tort or delict.'

It was the first part of the question which the court was answering in the passage previously cited. But in answering the second part of the question the court, after observing that art 5 must be interpreted restrictively, stated unequivocally ([1988] ECR 5565 at 5586 (para 21)):

'... a court which has jurisdiction under Article 5(3) over an action in so far as it is based on tort or delict does not have jurisdiction over that action in so far as it is not so based.'

This action is based, not on tort or delict, but on unjust enrichment, and is accordingly not within art 5(3). In my judgment the judge came to the right conclusion on this point also.

It is 13 years now since the void transactions were entered into. So far this litigation has benefited only the lawyers. It had taken four hearings, including two in this court, to decide which court should determine the dispute. No doubt that is because Glasgow know that they will be likely to lose in this country, and hope that they might do better in Scotland. If no appeal is permitted to the House of Lords on the issue of jurisdiction, the time may not be far off when a court will determine whether Glasgow should part with the balance that happened to stand in their favour when it became apparent that their contracts with Kleinwort were void. Already the aggregate costs probably exceed the sum at issue. *Omnia Romae cum pretio.*

For the reasons I have given I would dismiss the appeal.

ROCH LJ. The question of which courts in the United Kingdom have jurisdiction to decide the issues which arise between the parties to this appeal is to be determined by the provisions set out in Sch 4 to the Civil Jurisdiction and Judgments Act 1982 (see s 16(1) of the Act).

The respondents say that this case is one where the Scottish courts, as the courts of the respondents' domicile, have exclusive jurisdiction under art 2 in section 1 of Sch 4, the respondents being the defendants in the action. Article 2 provides:

'Subject to the provisions of this Title, persons domiciled in a part of the United Kingdom shall ... be sued in the court of that part.'

Article 2 is reinforced by the terms of art 3, which provides:

'Persons domiciled in a part of the United Kingdom may be sued in the courts of another part of the United Kingdom only by virtue of the rules set out in Sections 2, 4, 5 and 6 of this Title.'

The appellant's submission is that this case is one where the Scottish courts and the English courts have concurrent jurisdiction because this is a case which falls

within the exceptions to the basic rule that the courts of a defendant's domicile
have exclusive jurisdiction, to be found in section 2 and art 5 of Sch 4. The
appellant relies on art 5(1) and (3).

The conclusion that I have reached is that the appellant is correct that this case
comes within the terms of art 5(1).

Article 5(1) provides:

   'A person domiciled in a part of the United Kingdom may, in another part
   of the United Kingdom, be sued: (1) in matters relating to a contract, in the
   courts for the place of performance of the obligation in question ...'

Whether this case comes within the terms of art 5(1), in my view turns upon the
meaning of the words 'a contract' and the words 'the obligation' in that article. If
the phrase 'a contract' is to be interpreted solely with reference to English law,
then I would have agreed that this case could not be 'a matter relating to a
contract', because under English law this contract was void ab initio; it was a
nullity; it never existed. Equally, if Mr Burton's submission that the words 'the
obligation' are properly to be construed as referring only to contractual obligations, that is to say obligations which English law would classify as contractual,
then this case does not fall with art 5(1).

Both questions therefore raise the same fundamental issue: is art 5(1) to be
interpreted by the application of the law of England and Wales or should a wider
interpretation be given to its terms?

Mr Beazley's first submission was that the interpretation of art 5 where it
appears in section 2 of Sch 4 to the Act must be the same as the interpretation of
that article where it appears in section 2 of Sch 1 to the Act. Were that not to be
so, then different answers might be given to questions of jurisdiction depending
on whether the defendants in the proposed action were domiciled in Scotland or
whether the defendants were domiciled in another member state of the
European Community, although the wording of the articles which the English
courts were applying to arrive at such answers were identical and were contained
in the same statute. Further, submitted Mr Beazley, such an approach would be
inconsistent with decisions of the Court of Justice in such cases as *Martin Peters
Bauunternehmung GmbH v Zuid Nederlandse Aannemers Vereniging* Case 34/82
[1983] ECR 987 and *Arcado SPRL v Haviland SA* Case 9/87 [1988] ECR 1539. In the
second of those cases the Court of Justice said ([1988] ECR 1539 at 1554 (paras 10
and 11)):

   '10 ... Having regard to the objective and the general scheme of the
   [Convention on Jurisdiction and the Enforcement of Judgments in Civil and
   Commercial Matters 1968], it is important that, in order to ensure as far as
   possible the equality and uniformity of the rights and obligations arising out
   of the Convention for the Contracting States and the persons concerned, that
   concept should not be interpreted simply as referring to the national law of
   one or other of the States concerned.
   11. Consequently, the concept of "matters relating to a contract" is to be
   regarded as an independent concept which, for the purpose of the application of the Convention, must be interpreted by reference principally to the
   system and the objectives of the Convention in order to ensure that it is fully
   effective.'

The Court of Justice there was in effect repeating its statement of the correct
approach to the interpretation of the Convention on Jurisdiction and the

a Enforcement of Judgments in Civil and Commercial Matters 1968 (set out in Sch 1 to the 1982 Act) (the Brussels Convention) made in the *Martin Peters* case. I accept Mr Beazley's first submission.

What then is the proper interpretation of art 5(1)? Mr Burton says that matters relating to a contract, even adopting a wider approach, cannot embrace the claims in the present case. This 'contract' was a nullity through a lack of capacity b in the respondents to enter into such a transaction. That would be the result in several other European systems of law; indeed in all those systems which the respondents' lawyers have been able to research. The claims are claims for repayment of moneys on the basis that the respondents have been unjustly enriched. If the respondents have the obligation to repay these moneys, such obligations are not contractual obligations nor are they matters 'relating to a c contract.'

If the words in art 5(1) 'a contract' include a contract void ab initio, then it cannot in my view be doubted that actions to recover moneys paid in the mistaken belief that there was a valid contract between the parties must be 'matters in relation to a contract.' In the *Martin Peters* case the Court of Justice d decided that the Dutch courts had jurisdiction over the defendants, a construction company domiciled in Germany, although there was no contract between the parties under Dutch law. The material paragraph of this part of the court's decision reads ([1983] ECR 987 at 1002 (para 13)):

e 'In that regard it appears that membership of an association creates between the members close links of the same kind as those which are created between the parties to a contract and that consequently the obligations to which the national court refers may be regarded as contractual for the purpose of the application of Article 5(1) of the Convention.'

That case is not an exact parallel to the present case because in that case the f national law did not classify the relationship between the association and the German construction company as one of contract; but it is similar in that in that case, as in this, under the national law there was no contract. In my view, the case is a guide to the proper approach to art 5(1).

Another indication is to be found in art 10(1) of the Convention on the Law applicable to Contractual Obligations 1980 (the Rome Convention) (enacted into g English law by the Contracts (Applicable Law) Act 1990, s 2 and Sch 1) dealing with the scope of the applicable law. That article provides:

'The Law applicable to a contract by virtue of Articles 3 to 6 and 12 of this Convention shall govern in particular ... (e) the consequences of nullity of h the contract.'

The importance of this article in my opinion is that it demonstrates that in European law the word 'contract' embraces a contract that is a nullity. In other words, that European law does not treat a void contract as a contract which does not have and has never had any existence. It is in the eyes of the European law a j contract, albeit a void contract.

In the present case, under English law there was no contract between the parties. The only reason for that was that our law has been found to be that such a transaction is beyond the capacity of a local authority. The transaction or arrangement was consensual. The appellant and the respondents entered into it freely, intending to be bound by its terms. That is why the payment of the sums which the appellant seeks to recover from the respondents were made by the appellant and accepted by the respondents. There was, in my judgment, a contract in the wider sense.

The word 'obligation' in art 5(1) is not confined to contractual obligations. Had that been the intention of the drafters of the convention or the parliamentary draftsmen, then the word 'contractual' would have qualified the word 'obligation'. In my opinion the absence of any qualification of the word 'obligation' throws light upon the meaning to be given to the words 'a contract'.

In reaching this view, I have not overlooked the decision of the European Court in *Ets A de Bloos SPRL v Société en commandite par actions Bouyer* Case 14/76 [1976] ECR 1497. In that case Bouyer, who are domiciled in France, granted de Bloos, who were domiciled in Belgium, the exclusive right to distribute Bouyer's products in Belgium, Luxembourg and Zaire. De Bloos complained of a unilateral breach of the contract without notice by Bouyer and sued Bouyer in Belgium for a declaration that under Belgium law the agreement should be dissolved on the ground of Bouyer's wrongful conduct and the payment of damages pursuant to Belgium law. The Belgian court only had jurisdiction if art 5(1) of the Brussels Convention applied. The contract contained several obligations, some of which were to be performed in different countries. Further, as a result of the outline contract granting an exclusive sales concession, successive sales had been concluded. The question submitted by the Court of Appeal at Mons to the Court of Justice was which of these various obligations were 'the obligation in question' referred to in art 5(1). The Court of Justice answered that question in their judgment, which reads ([1976] ECR 1497 at 1508–1509 (paras 10–16)):

'10. Because of this, Article 5(1) of the Convention cannot be interpreted as referring to any obligation whatsoever arising under the contract in question.

11. On the contrary, the word "obligation" in the article refers to the contractual obligation forming the basis of the legal proceedings.

12. This interpretation is, moreover, clearly confirmed by the Italian and German versions of the article.

13. It follows that for the purposes of determining the place of performance within the meaning of Article 5, quoted above, the obligation to be taken into account is that which corresponds to the contractual right on which the plaintiff's action is based.

14. In a case where the plaintiff asserts the right to be paid damages or seeks dissolution of the contract on the ground of the wrongful conduct of the other party, the obligation referred to in Article 5(1) is still that which arises under the contract and the non-performance of which is relied upon to support such claims.

15. For these reasons, the answer to the first question must be that, in disputes in which the grantee of an exclusive sales concession charges the grantor with having infringed the exclusive concession, the word "obligation" contained in Article 5(1) of the Convention of 27 September 1968 on jurisdiction and the enforcement of Judgments in Civil and Commercial Matters refers to the obligation forming the basis of the legal proceedings, namely the contractual obligation of the grantor which corresponds to the contractual right relied upon by the grantee in support of the application.

16. In disputes concerning the consequences of the infringement by the grantor of a contract conferring an exclusive concession such as the payment

a   of damages or the dissolution of the contract, the obligation to which reference must be made for the purposes of applying Article 5(1) of the Convention is that which the contract imposes on the grantor and the non-performance of which is relied upon by the grantee in support of the application for damages or for the dissolution of the contract.'

b   The wording of paras 11 and 15 is appropriate to the question referred to the court in that case, but I do not read the judgment of the court as confining 'the obligation in question' to obligations which are strictly called contractual obligations under the domestic law of the court considering the question of jurisdiction. Indeed there is ample authority that the question of jurisdiction is not to be determined by an application of national law.

c   The result is desirable because it would give concurrent jurisdiction to the courts of the country, the law of which will most probably govern the dispute between the parties. The law of the country where the defendant is domiciled may have little to do with the dispute. A defendant company may well carry on a substantial part, indeed a major part, of its business in a country or countries other than the country of its domicile. The *Martin Peters* case appears to be an example. In the present case, it would seem that if the matter were to be heard in Scotland, the Scottish courts would have to apply English law. The respondents seek to establish that the Scottish courts have exclusive jurisdiction because there are advantages for them to be derived from the procedural laws of Scotland, for example a shorter limitation period.

e   In its judgment in *Effer SpA v Kantner* Case 38/81 [1982] ECR 825 at 834 (para 6) the Court of Justice said:

f   'It is clear from the provisions of the Convention, and in particular from the preamble thereto, that its essential aim is to strengthen in the Community the legal protection of persons therein established. For that purpose the Convention provides a collection of rules which are designed *inter alia* to avoid the occurrence, in civil and commercial matters, of concurrent litigation in two or more Member States and which, in the interests of legal certainty and for the benefit of the parties, confer jurisdiction upon the national court territorially best qualified to determine

g   a dispute.'

In my judgment the interpretation of art 5(1) advanced by the appellant achieves the objective of conferring jurisdiction upon the national court territorially best qualified to determine the dispute in this case.

h   It would not follow from this decision, in my opinion, that all claims for restitution based on unjust enrichment would come within the terms of art 5(1), because in many such cases, the basis of the claim will be other than the existence of a void contract.

j   **MILLETT LJ.** The principal question in this appeal is whether a claim to recover money paid under a contract which is ultra vires the recipient is 'a matter relating to a contract' within art 5(1) of the Convention on Jurisdiction and the Enforcement of Judgments in Civil and Commercial Matters 1968 Matters (set out in Sch 1 to the 1982 Act). More generally, it is whether the word 'contract' in that article is capable of including a contract which is void because it is beyond the capacity of one of the parties.

Strictly speaking, the question arises under art 5(1) of section 2 of Sch 4 to the *a*
Civil Jurisdiction and Judgments Act 1982 and not art 5(1) of the convention, and
is a question of English domestic law not Community law. But this makes no
practical difference, save that an authoritative ruling of the Court of Justice of the
European Communities is not available. The first part of the 1982 Act
incorporates the convention into the law of the United Kingdom. Section 2(1)
provides that the convention has the force of law in the United Kingdom, and *b*
s 3(1) states that any question as to the meaning or effect of the convention is to
be determined 'in accordance with the principles laid down by and any relevant
decision of the European Court'. The second part of the Act establishes a scheme
for allocating jurisdiction within the United Kingdom between the courts of
England and Wales, Scotland and Northern Ireland. The scheme is contained in
Sch 4 to the Act and is closely modelled on the convention. Section 16(3) of the *c*
Act states that in determining any question as to the meaning or effect of any
provision contained in Sch 4 'regard shall be had to any relevant principles laid
down by the European Court ... and to any relevant decision of that court as to
the meaning or effect of [the 1968 Convention]'.

Articles 2 and 3 of Sch 4 replicate arts 2 and 3 of the convention. Article 2 *d*
provides that persons domiciled in a part of the United Kingdom shall be sued in
the courts of that part. Article 3 provides that persons domiciled in a part of the
United Kingdom may be sued in the courts of another part of the United
Kingdom only by virtue of the rules set out in sections 2, 4, 5 and 6 following.
Article 5 confers special jurisdiction in certain classes of case. Article 5(1) and (3)
provides: *e*

'A person domiciled in a part of the United Kingdom may, in another part
of the United Kingdom, be sued:
(1) in matters relating to a contract, in the courts for the place of
performance of the obligation in question ...
(3) in matters relating to tort, delict or quasi-delict, in the courts for the *f*
place where the harmful event occurred ...'

This reproduces the identical wording of the corresponding provisions of the
convention. It is to be observed that art 5 does not include any special provision
for restitutionary or quasi-contractual claims or claims based on unjust enrichment. *g*

Except where Sch 4 of the Act modifies the corresponding provisions of the
convention, therefore, Parliament must have intended to adopt the same criteria
for allocating jurisdiction between the courts of different parts of the United
Kingdom as those which are applied by the Court of Justice in allocating
jurisdiction between the courts of different member states. The difference in *h*
terminology adopted by ss 3(1) and 16 merely reflects the fact that in the one case
decisions of the Court of Justice are binding and in the other of persuasive
authority. In the one case we are to apply Community law; in the other case we
are to apply national law which, save as Parliament has directed otherwise, has
adopted the same criteria as Community law. The requirement that we are to *j*
have regard to decisions of the Court of Justice on the meaning and effect of the
convention would be meaningless unless we were to adopt the same principles
of construction as those of that court.

Three things follow. First, art 2 provides the general criterion for founding
jurisdiction; the defendant is to be sued in the courts of his domicile. Article 5
confers a special jurisdiction which derogates from the general rule, and must be

a construed restrictively (see *Martin Peters Bauunternehumung GmbH v Zuid Neder-landse Aannemers Vereniging* Case 34/82 [1983] ECR 987). Secondly, the various matters specified in art 5 are not necessarily exhaustive. If a claim cannot be brought within art 5, it can always be pursued in the courts of the defendant's domicile. Thirdly, the expression 'matters relating to a contract' must be given an independent or autonomous interpretation. The characterisation of causes of action for domestic law purposes is not determinative of their characterisation for

b jurisdictional purposes (see the *Martin Peters* case). A court may acquire jurisdiction under art 5(1) on the basis that the matter relates to a contract, and then decide the claim in accordance with its own domestic law which character-ises it as a delictual or other non-contractual claim.

c   In considering whether a claim is to be regarded as falling within art 5(1) (or art 5(3)), therefore, it is wrong to ask whether the claim would be characterised as contractual (or tortious) under domestic law. The correct approach is to ask whether, for the purposes of the convention, which applies to a number of member states with different national laws and systems of characterisation, the defendant should broadly be regarded as being sued 'in a matter relating to a

d contract' (or tort, delict or quasi-delict). The jurisdictional criteria must be interpreted by reference to the system and objectives of the convention in order to ensure that it is effective. Those objectives include legal certainty, consistency, the avoidance of parallel proceedings, and the avoidance of possibly conflicting decisions in different jurisdictions. The principal rationale for the special

e jurisdictions conferred by art 5 is that there should be, in certain clearly defined situations, 'a particularly close connecting factor between a dispute and the court which may be called upon to hear it, *with a view to the efficacious conduct of the proceedings*' (my emphasis) (see the *Martin Peters* case [1983] ECR 987 at 1002 (para 11)).

f   It is to be observed that jurisdiction is not allocated according to the remedy sought. Provided that the matter relates to a contract, the jurisdiction conferred by art 5(1) is available whether the plaintiff seeks to enforce the contract, either specifically or by way of damages for breach, or to escape from it and recover money paid under it. Some restitutionary claims, at least, fall within art 5(1). Further, jurisdiction is not allocated by reference to the cause of action. The

g words 'matters relating to a contract' are intentionally indefinite. They are designed to get away from technical classifications of causes of action in national laws, which may well differ. The expression 'matters relating to a contract' is not, in my opinion, to be equated with 'contractual causes of action' or 'the enforcement of contractual obligations' or even 'claims based on contract'.

h   There seems no doubt that, while national laws of contract differ, there is a general sense in which the word contract is understood by the signatories to the convention. English notions of consideration and privity must be discarded. But at its irreducible minimum a contract is a consensual arrangement intended to create legal relations and to be legally enforceable.

j   So I come at last to the central question: does the word 'contract' in art 5(1) include a void contract? The respondents say No. A void contract is a nullity. It is not a contract. It has no legal effect. It gives rise to no legal obligations. There is no place of performance. If one party claims to recover money paid pursuant to it, his claim is not a contractual claim. The action lies in restitution, not contract. The recipient's obligation to repay is not a contractual obligation. It does not arise from the void contract, which is incapable of generating any legal

rights and obligations. It arises solely by reason of the original payment and
because the recipient would be unjustly enriched if he were allowed to retain it.   *a*

These are powerful arguments, but I am not persuaded by them. They appear
to me to depend upon the kind of analysis which is employed by a national law
in the classification of causes of action for domestic purposes, rather than the very
broad and unanalytical approach which the convention requires. Even if every
member state treats a contract as a nullity if one of the parties lacks capacity, this   *b*
should not be treated as if it were a rule of natural law and of universal
application.

In the present case the parties purported to enter into a contract. They
assumed obligations to each other and intended them to be legally enforceable.
The payments were made and received on an agreed basis, and are explicable   *c*
only by reference to the supposed contract. When parties act pursuant to a such
a contract, the intended place of performance is no less relevant a connecting
factor because the contract is afterwards found to be void.

I can see no reason, as a matter of language, why the word 'contract' in art 5(1)
should not include 'void contract' and the expression 'place of performance of the
obligation in question' should not mean 'intended place of performance of the   *d*
supposed obligation'.   There is a real difference between the case where
negotiations have not led to a concluded contract, where there is no contract at
all, and the case where they have led to a contract, so that there is an agreement
in fact, but one of the parties lacks contractual capacity, so that there is no
contract in law.   *e*

Every legal system has to make provision for contracts which are defective for
one reason or another. They may lack the necessary legal formalities; they may
be contrary to public policy or illegal; they may be made by a party without
capacity or by an agent without authority; they may contain some unresolved
uncertainty or ambiguity, or be incomplete in some material particular; or the   *f*
consent of one of the parties may be vitiated by mistake or misrepresentation or
duress or some other factor. The consequences of these defects may differ. Some
may make the contract void; others may make it voidable; still others may make
it merely unenforceable. But these are merely useful shorthand methods of
describing the different legal consequences which follow from the defect in
question. A defect which renders a contract void in one jurisdiction may merely   *g*
make it voidable in another. A voidable contract which is avoided may be treated
as void ab initio in one jurisdiction and not in another.

In English law want of capacity, like mistake, sometimes makes a contract void
and sometimes makes it voidable. A contract entered into by a party acting ultra
vires is void; a contract entered into by a minor, or a person under the influence   *h*
of drink, or a person of unsound mind, is voidable. A contract which is properly
described as void is not necessarily a complete nullity. A contract which is
entered into by an agent without authority, for example, does not impose any
legal obligations upon the principal, but it may afterwards be ratified by him.

So it is best to lay aside these terms when considering the meaning of art 5(1)   *j*
of the convention. They merely tell us what the consequences of the defect are
in national law. That is not relevant to the allocation of jurisdiction under the
convention, which must be ascertained independently of the national laws of the
member states. The question, therefore, is not whether a contract which is 'void'
under national law is a contract for the purposes of art 5(1), but whether a
contract which is ultra vires one of the parties is such a contract.

a In the present case the parties, the European Commission, and the governments of various member states submitted written observations to the Court of Justice on the question which was referred to it. The Commission, the United Kingdom, France and Spain, as well as the appellant, submitted that the question should be answered in the affirmative, that is to say in favour of a ruling that the claim brought by the appellants was 'in a matter relating to a contract'. Only the *b* respondents and Germany submitted that the question should be answered in the negative. There is no authoritative ruling of the Court of Justice on the point. Academic opinion on the question is divided. Article 10(1)(e) of the Convention on the Law applicable to Contractual Obligations 1980 (the Rome Convention) (enacted into English law by the Contracts (Applicable Law) Act 1990, s 2 and Sch 1) refers the consequences of nullity of a contract to the applicable law, that is to *c* say the law chosen by the parties or the law with which the supposed contract has the closest connection. Despite the superficially unanswerable logic of the respondents' arguments, therefore, the opposite conclusion is plainly tenable.

Three considerations persuade me that it is also correct. First, in most cases the validity of the contract will be in issue. It would not be consistent with the *d* objectives of the convention if a court having jurisdiction to decide the validity of the contract did not also have jurisdiction to decide the consequences; or if it had jurisdiction to grant relief in one event and not in the other. It should not be necessary in order to found jurisdiction that the claimant should be compelled to allege the validity of the contract if its invalidity is not seriously disputed.

Secondly, it is often notoriously difficult to distinguish between contractual *e* and restitutionary causes of action. Claims in quantum meruit, for example, are usually thought of as contractual, and in most situations are clearly 'matters relating to a contract'. But there is a respectable case for classifying all such claims as restitutionary, and in some situations they clearly are. The remedy is available, for example, at least in English law, even where the party who received the *f* benefit of the services lacked contractual capacity. Jurisdiction under the convention should not depend upon such nice distinctions of the national laws.

Thirdly, if the claim is properly regarded as 'a matter relating to a contract', then the court having jurisdiction under art 5(1) is the court for the place where the supposed contractual obligation should have been performed, not the place where the unjust enrichment occurred and the restitutionary obligation arose. *g* This produces a scheme for the allocation of jurisdiction which is both coherent and satisfying. Suppose P agrees to buy goods from D, the goods to be delivered in London and payment to be made in Frankfort. P pays for the goods, but the goods are not delivered. P has a choice of remedies. He can sue D for damages for breach of contract, bringing the action in England, the place where the *h* obligation to deliver the goods should have been performed. Or he can treat the contract as discharged by breach and sue to recover the payment for a total failure of consideration. The nature of the remedy sought does not prevent the action from being tried in England, the place of performance of the contractual obligation, the breach of which has given rise to the relief claimed. Next, suppose *j* that after one consignment has been delivered, D refuses to deliver any more, and alleges want of contractual capacity. P may accept this or dispute it. If he accepts it, or it is established, he is entitled to recover the payment after giving credit for the value of the consignment delivered. It makes no sense to deprive the court in England of jurisdiction to try the action, England being the intended place of performance of the supposed obligation the failure to perform which has given rise to the relief sought. The factor which connects the dispute with England is the same whether D's contention that he lacked contractual capacity is right or wrong.

The respondents' arguments all proceed from three basic assumptions: (i) that all member states recognise the existence of three categories of civil action, contractual, delictual and restitutionary, with broadly the same lines of demarcation; (ii) that all restitutionary claims must be treated alike; and (iii) that they fall outside art 5(1) and (3). In my view the structure of the convention precludes that analysis. Its failure to provide specifically for restitutionary claims must, I think, be due to a recognition of the fact that they overlap with contractual and delictual claims and that the lines of demarcation are not identical in the various national laws. A claim to recover money paid under a valid contract where there has been a total failure of consideration, for example, is a restitutionary claim in a contractual context; restitutionary claims for wrongs are delictual or quasi-delictual; a claim by the victim of fraud to trace and recover his money would not be classified by English law as either contractual or delictual, but in civilian systems which deny the possibility of restitutionary proprietary claims it would probably be classified as delictual.

Accordingly, I reject the respondents' submission that all restitutionary claims necessarily fall outside art 5. For the reasons I have endeavoured to express, I accept the appellant's submission that a claim to recover money paid under a supposed contract which is rendered abortive by the recipient's want of contractual capacity is 'a matter relating to a contract' within art 5(1). I am not deterred by the need to read the word 'contract' in that article as meaning 'void contract' or the expression 'place of performance of the obligation in question' as 'intended place of performance of the supposed obligation'. I would leave it for future consideration whether the word 'contract' is capable of including 'anticipated contract', but I would not exclude it as a possibility. Many civilian systems require good faith in the negotiation of a proposed contract. Is a breach of such an obligation not 'a matter relating to a contract'? I pose the question, not to suggest an answer, but to indicate that the answer is not obvious.

This makes it unnecessary to decide whether the present claim falls within art 5(3), and I prefer to express no opinion on that question.

Roma locuta est, causa finita non est. I would allow the appeal.

Appeal allowed.

Mary Rose Plummer   Barrister.

a # Halifax Mortgage Services Ltd (formerly BNP Mortgages Ltd) v Stepsky and another

COURT OF APPEAL, CIVIL DIVISION

b
KENNEDY, MORRITT AND WARD LJJ

23 NOVEMBER 1995

Solicitor – Duty – Conflict of interest – Solicitors acting for both lender and borrowers on further mortgage of matrimonial home – Husband and wife informing lender that loan required for their joint benefit – Husband informing solicitors that purpose of loan
c *for his sole benefit – Solicitors subsequently being instructed also to act for lender – Whether lender fixed with constructive notice of husband's purpose – Whether knowledge coming to solicitors as solicitors for lender – Law of Property Act 1925, s 199.*

In 1990 the defendants, Mr and Mrs S, applied to the plaintiff building society for
d a loan by way of a further mortgage on their home. In their application they stated that the purpose of the loan was to purchase family shares in a business. However, when Mr S later instructed solicitors, he informed them that the true purpose of the loan was to pay off his own business debts. The same solicitors were subsequently appointed to act on behalf of the building society as the lender in the transaction, and they completed the building society's standard form report
e on title without making any qualification as to the intended use of the loan. Mr and Mrs S fell into arrears with their payment of the mortgage instalments and thereafter the building society obtained an order for possession of the property. The wife appealed against that order, contending that the building society had constructive notice of the fact that the loan was not going to be used for the joint
f benefit of the husband and the wife, and that her right as against her husband to have the mortgage set aside was therefore enforceable against it. The judge dismissed her appeal on the ground that, notwithstanding the relationship of principal and agent between the building society and the solicitor, the solicitors' knowledge of the true purpose of the loan could not be imputed to the building society. The wife appealed to the Court of Appeal. The issue arose whether
g s 199(1)[a] of the Law of Property Act 1925, which provided that a purchaser (which included a lender) could not be prejudicially affected by notice of any fact or thing unless it had come to the knowledge of his solicitor or other agent 'as such' in the same transaction, or would have come to the knowledge of his solicitor or other agent if they had made reasonable inquiries, applied in the
h circumstances.

Held – On the plain wording of s 199(1)(ii)(b) of the 1925 Act, knowledge possessed by solicitors who were acting for both a borrower and a lender in the same transaction could not be imputed to the lender unless that knowledge was
j received by the solicitors in the capacity of solicitors for the lender 'as such'. On the facts, the information as to the true purpose of the remortgage loan imparted by Mr S came to the knowledge of the solicitors while they were acting as the solicitors for Mr and Mrs S alone. That knowledge, once acquired, remained with the solicitors and could not be treated as coming to them again when they were

---

a   Section 199, so far as material, is set out at p 284 *d*, post

instructed on behalf of the lender, with the result that knowledge of the relevant
matters, facts or things did not come to the solicitors as solicitors for the lender a
'as such'. It followed that s 199 of the Act precluded the solicitors' knowledge of
the relevant matters or facts being imputed to the lender. The appeal would
accordingly be dismissed (see p 284 f to h and p 285 b c, post).

Decision of Edward Nugee QC [1995] 4 All ER 656 affirmed on other grounds.

b

Notes
For solicitors acting for opposing interests, see 44(1) *Halsbury's Laws* (4th edn
reissue) para 150, and for cases on the subject, see 44 *Digest* (Reissue) 126–127,
1227–1240.

For the Law of Property Act 1925, s 199, see 37 *Halsbury's Statutes* (4th edn) 323.

c

Cases referred to in judgments
Barclays Bank plc v O'Brien [1993] 4 All ER 417, [1994] 1 AC 180, [1993] 3 WLR 786,
    HL.
Cave v Cave (1880) 15 Ch D 639.
CIBC Mortgages plc v Pitt [1993] 4 All ER 433, [1994] 1 AC 200, [1993] 3 WLR 802, d
    HL.
El Ajou v Dollar Land Holdings plc [1994] 2 All ER 685, CA.
Payne (David) & Co Ltd, Re, Young v David Payne & Co Ltd [1904] 2 Ch 608, Ch D
    and CA.
Rolland v Hart (1871) LR 6 Ch App 678.
Wyllie v Pollen (1863) 3 De GJ & Sm 596, 46 ER 767. e

Appeal
By notice dated 11 August 1995 the second defendant, Penelope Stepsky,
appealed with leave of the Court of Appeal from the decision of Edward Nugee
QC ([1995] 4 All ER 656, [1996] Ch 1) sitting as a deputy judge of the High Court f
in the Chancery Division on 16 June 1995, whereby he dismissed Mrs Stepsky's
appeal from the order of Master Moncaster dated 12 July 1994 directing Mrs
Stepsky and her husband, Joseph Emanuel Stepsky (the first defendant), to deliver
up possession of the property known as 88 Osidge Lane, Southgate, London, to
the plaintiff, Halifax Mortgage Services Ltd (formerly BNP Mortgages Ltd). Mr
Stepsky took no part in the proceedings. The facts are set out in the judgment of g
Morritt LJ.

Martin Mann QC and *Amanda Harington* (instructed by *J J Goldstein & Co*) for the
    wife.
Romie Tager QC and *Hugh Jackson* (instructed by *Glenisters*, Ruislip) for the lender. h

MORRITT LJ (delivering the first judgment at the invitation of Kennedy LJ). On
19 July 1990 the plaintiff (the lender) advanced £128,215 to Mr and Mrs Stepsky
(the husband and the wife respectively) on the security of a first charge over their
home, 88 Osidge Lane, Southgate, London N14 5JG, of which they were j
registered in HM Land Registry as the joint proprietors. Of the moneys so
advanced, after paying the costs involved, £104,139 was paid to the Guardian
Building Society in redemption of their pre-existing first charge and the balance
of £23,200 was paid to the credit of the account of the husband. On 27 January
1992, default having occurred in making the repayments due under the legal
charge, the lender issued an originating summons seeking an order for possession

a of the property. On 12 July 1994 the master made the order sought in summary proceedings under RSC Ord 88.

On 9 October 1994 the wife made an affirmation in support of her appeal to the judge in which she affirmed:

> b '2. On or about mid 1990 I, together with my husband the First Defendant, applied for a mortgage with the Plaintiff. As far as I am aware the solicitors acting for lender and borrowers were Roiter Zucker. 3. My husband told me that the purpose of the loan was for home improvements and to purchase carpets for the home, as well as redeeming the original mortgage with Guardian Building Society, in the amount of approximately £85,000. When I signed the mortgage application form, I did not read it and
> c relied completely upon my husband, as I usually do and have always done. 4. I have now discovered that in reality the funds obtained from the Plaintiff were used to pay off my husband's various business debts. Indeed my husband instructed Roiter Zucker to pay Bank Leumi and other creditors, to whom he owed substantial sums without my knowledge. I am advised that as Roiter Zucker were acting for the lenders, their knowledge is imputed to
> d the Plaintiff. Accordingly the Plaintiff had constructive knowledge that I was a surety. In those circumstances I was not independently advised as to the true purpose of the loan, which was manifestly disadvantageous to me. Had I known of the true purpose of the application to the Plaintiff's [sic] I would not have agreed to execute the mortgage.'

e In a further affirmation made by her on 3 February 1995 she stated in relation to the execution of the charge:

> 'I attended the firm Roiter Zucker together with my husband and my brother in law and his wife who were also executing their Mortgage at the same time. I was not explained or advised as to the affect [sic] or
> f consequences of executing the Legal Charge. I was simply told to sign in the appropriate place, which I did. The whole episode lasted no longer than 3 or 4 minutes.'

The wife's appeal came before Edward Nugee QC sitting as an deputy judge of the High Court in the Chancery Division. In his judgment given on 16 June 1995
g ([1995] 4 All ER 656, [1996] Ch 1) he dismissed the wife's appeal on the ground that the knowledge of Messrs Roiter Zucker (the solicitors), then acting for the lender and for the husband and wife, as to the purpose of the loan was not to be imputed to the lender. Accordingly, he held that there was no reasonable probability of the wife having a defence to the lender's claim and affirmed the
h master's order for possession in favour of the lender. This is an appeal of the wife from that decision.

The details of the transaction can be seen clearly from the documents in the possession of the lender and those in the possession of the solicitors, of which copies were provided by them to the lender. Thus, on 7 May 1990 the husband
j and the wife completed a mortgage application form seeking a loan by way of remortgage of their home in the sum of £128,000. They stated that it was charged to the Guardian Building Society to secure a debt then amounting to £99,000. They indicated that they wished to instruct the solicitors to act on their behalf. Their personal details, as completed, revealed that for 28 years the husband had been employed by Ashley & Sons Ltd, a company carrying on the business of soft furnishers and decorators, in which he held 50% of the shares, and that the wife

was employed as a salesperson by a different company carrying on the business
of ladies fashions. The purpose of the remortgage further advance was stated to
be 'to buy family shares in business'. The form concluded with a declaration,
which each signatory was invited to read carefully before signing, that 'the
information given in this application is true and complete to the best of my
knowledge and belief'. At the end of the form both husband and wife signed and
dated it.

On 12 June 1990 the husband instructed the solicitors on the telephone. The
solicitors' attendance note of that conversation reads as follows:

'JS [Mr Stepsky] telephoned DF [Mr Franks of the solicitors]. He is
expecting an offer of re-mortgage through BMP [sic] and Scottish Life for
£128,000.00. His existing mortgage is with the Guardian Building Society for
£99,000.00. Of the difference of £29,000 approximately £20,000 to £22,000
will have to go to Bank Leumi and the balance to him which will be
re-invested into the Company out of which we will be able to recover our
costs on the outstanding company matters.'

Bank Leumi were bankers to Ashley & Sons Ltd.

On 13 June 1990 the lender made a written offer to the husband and wife of
loans in the aggregate sum of £128,000 on the terms set out in the offer. The
purpose of the loans was expressed to be 'Purchase of Shares', but the lender's
solicitors were 'to be advised'. The duplicate offers were, as requested therein,
duly countersigned, indicating their acceptance by both the husband and the
wife, and returned to the lender.

The documents supplied by the lender to the husband and wife included a
form entitled 'General Instructions to Solicitors' and another described as 'Report
on Title'. The former contained the following material provisions.

First, there was an introductory sentence:

'Neither the General Instructions to Solicitors set out herein or the form of
Report on Title detract from or limit the general responsibility of the
Solicitor instructed by the lender under general law as Solicitor for the
lender.'

Then, the following provisions applied:

'1. SOLICITOR'S CONDITIONS The Borrower named in the enclosed Offer of
Home Loan has today nominated your firm to act in this matter and you are
therefore requested to act on behalf of the lender in the investigation of title
to the Security Property and perfection of the lender's title to the security
required by the said Offer ...

4. TITLE ... Please report any matter which ought to be brought to the
attention of the Lender ...

12. OFFER Please ensure that all the details as shown on the Offer of Home
Loan are correct and report to the Lender any discrepancies ...'

The report on title required the solicitors to complete and sign it, containing their
confirmation that 'title is good and marketable and can properly be accepted as
security'. These documents were passed on by the husband to the solicitors on
19 June 1990.

After carrying out the normal conveyancing steps appropriate to a transaction
of this sort, on 12 July Mr Franks of the solicitors attended at the home of the

a husband and wife to obtain their signatures to the mortgage documents. His contemporary handwritten note records:

'12/7. DF attg Mr and Mrs Stepsky at their home. Went over mortgage terms/redemption arrangements/policies. Problem with Guardian. DF to consider this. JS to give details for payment of residue of mortgage advance—NOT to Banker—get snaffled—Wayne present and signed consent.
b Discussed business problems. Egd 1½ hrs.'

On 13 July the solicitors completed, without any relevant qualification, and returned to the lender the report on title. At about the same time the husband instructed the solicitors on the telephone to pay the balance of the mortgage advance into his account with Abbey National plc. Completion took place on 19
c July 1990. The advance was paid to the solicitors and they disbursed it in the payments to which I referred earlier. It is not disputed that the sum paid to the husband was used by him in payment of creditors of his business or otherwise for his own purposes and not in payment for home improvements or in the purchase of carpets.

d   In his judgment the judge commenced by recording certain matters which were common ground. The first was that, as the appeal was from a summary judgment given on affidavit evidence, the issue at that stage was whether there was a fair or reasonable probability of the wife having a real or bona fide defence. The second was that the defence asserted by the wife relied on principles established in *Barclays Bank plc v O'Brien* [1993] 4 All ER 417, [1994] 1 AC 180 and
e *CIBC Mortgages plc v Pitt* [1993] 4 All ER 433, [1994] 1 AC 200 which, so far as relevant, he correctly summarised as follows:

'(1) Where a wife has been induced to execute a mortgage of jointly owned property by her husband's undue influence, misrepresentation or some other legal wrong, she has a right as against him to have the mortgage
f set aside. (2) The wife's right to have the mortgage set aside is enforceable against a third party who had actual or constructive notice of the circumstances giving rise to her right or for whom the husband was acting as agent. (3) Where the mortgage transaction is on the face of it not to the wife's financial advantage and carries a substantial risk of the husband committing a legal or equitable wrong entitling the wife to set aside the
g transaction, as for example where it is apparent that the wife is acting as a surety for her husband, the creditor is put on inquiry and has constructive notice of the wife's rights unless he takes reasonable steps to ensure that her agreement to participate in the transaction was properly obtained. (4) Where there is no indication that the transaction is anything other than
h a normal advance to husband and wife for their joint benefit, the creditor is not put on inquiry and, if the husband is not acting as the creditor's agent and the creditor has no actual notice of the circumstances giving rise to the wife's rights, the creditor cannot be fixed with constructive notice of them.' (See [1995] 4 All ER 656 at 659, [1996] Ch 1 at 3–4.)
j
After setting out the facts, substantially as I have described them, the judge concluded, notwithstanding the submission to the contrary of counsel for the lender and his own considerable doubt as to the truthfulness of parts of the evidence of the wife, that as against her husband she had a fair and reasonable probability of a defence of misrepresentation inducing her to execute the mortgage, or of undue influence. He also concluded that the lender did not have

actual or constructive knowledge (otherwise than through the solicitors) that the
further advance was not to be applied for the joint benefit of the husband and the *a*
wife. There is no appeal against either of those conclusions.

The judge then considered the argument for the wife based on the knowledge
of the solicitors. This comprised three steps. The first was to the effect that the
solicitors knew that the further advance was going to be used to meet the debts
of the husband's company, and that this was not the purpose for which the *b*
husband and the wife had applied for the loan and was not a purpose which
benefited them jointly. Second, such knowledge was acquired by the solicitors in
the course of a transaction in which they acted in that capacity for the lender and
which they were under a duty to communicate to the lender. Third, such
knowledge must be imputed to the lender in accordance with the long-
established principles set out in 1(2) *Halsbury's Laws* (4th edn reissue) para 149 and *c*
Bowstead on Agency (15th edn, 1985) p 412.

The judge then considered *Wyllie v Pollen* (1863) 3 De GJ & Sm 596, 46 ER 767;
Rolland v Hart (1871) LR 6 Ch App 678 and *Cave v Cave* (1880) 15 Ch D 639 (all of
which preceded s 3 of the Bankruptcy Act 1882, the predecessor of s 199 of the
Law of Property Act 1925) and posed the issue between the parties in these terms: *d*

> 'The issue between the parties can thus be stated as follows: where a
> solicitor is acting for both a borrower and a lender in the same transaction,
> and he obtains from the borrower knowledge of some fact which it is his
> duty to the borrower not to disclose to the lender without the borrower's
> consent, and which it is his duty to the lender to communicate to him, is *e*
> knowledge of that fact to be imputed to the lender?' (See [1995] 4 All ER 656
> at 666, [1996] Ch 1 at 11.)

Having referred further to the submissions of counsel, he recorded:

> 'It is thus common ground between the parties that Roiter Zucker, by *f*
> continuing to act for both the defendants and the plaintiff after being told
> that the purpose of the remortgage was not to purchase shares for the benefit
> of both defendants, as the plaintiff had been led to believe, but to enable the
> debts of Mr Stepsky's business to be discharged, and by failing to inform the
> plaintiff of this material fact, were in breach of their duty to the plaintiff ...
> What is the consequence, however, as between the borrower and the lender *g*
> if the solicitor does not carry out his duty, which is either, with the
> borrower's consent, to inform the lender of the material fact, or to tell the
> lender that a conflict of interests has arisen and that he must cease to act for
> it? Is the solicitor's knowledge of the material fact to be imputed to the
> lender? A similar issue has arisen in two cases in the Court of Appeal in *h*
> which the question has arisen whether knowledge of a material fact is to be
> imputed to a company, where such knowledge was acquired by one of its
> directors in the course of acting for a third party with conflicting interests. In
> both cases it was held that the knowledge of the director could not be
> imputed to the company.' (See [1995] 4 All ER 656 at 667–668, [1996] Ch 1 *j*
> at 13–14.)

The two cases to which he referred are *Re David Payne & Co Ltd, Young v David
Payne & Co Ltd* [1904] 2 Ch 608 and *El Ajou v Dollar Land Holdings plc* [1994] 2 All
ER 685. The judge considered that neither could be distinguished, and continued
[1995] 4 All ER 656 at 671, [1996] Ch 1 at 17:

a
'In my judgment the principles stated in *Re David Payne & Co* and *El Ajou v Dollar Land Holdings plc* in relation to information communicated to a director are equally applicable in the case of other agents such as solicitors; but the circumstances in which they have to be applied may differ from case to case, and care is needed in analysing the position in each case and in applying the principles to it.'

b
The judge then sought to apply those principles to the facts of the case. In considering the passage in his judgment in which he did so and which I shall quote, it is necessary to bear in mind that the solicitors were not parties to the proceedings and had not given any affidavit or other evidence beyond the contents of their file. Though they had offered to provide a statement, they were c not asked by either party to do so. The judge's conclusion was as follows [1995] 4 All ER 656 at 671–672, [1996] Ch 1 at 17–18:

'When Roiter Zucker received their instructions from the plaintiff, they had already been told by Mr Stepsky that the true purpose of the loan was different from what the plaintiff believed it to be. Their prima facie duty to d the plaintiff was to communicate this information to the plaintiff. This duty, however, conflicted with their duty to the defendants not to inform the plaintiff without the defendants' consent. In the absence of such consent, their duty to communicate the information to the plaintiff was superseded by a duty to tell the plaintiff that they could no longer act for it because a conflict of interests had arisen. Roiter Zucker were at no time free to pass on e to the plaintiff the information which they had obtained as solicitors for the defendants ... they had no duty as solicitors for the plaintiff to receive such information, which had only come into their possession as solicitors for the defendants. In this situation it is in my judgment clear that, notwithstanding the relationship of principal and agent which came into existence between f the plaintiff and Roiter Zucker as a consequence of the plaintiff's instructions to Roiter Zucker to act for it, Roiter Zucker's knowledge of the true purpose of the loan cannot be imputed to the plaintiff. I do not consider that it would have made any difference if the plaintiff had been put on inquiry by the mortgage application form and come under a duty to investigate the purpose for which the loan was going to be applied or the manner in which Mrs g Stepsky was going to receive legal advice; or in other words if the case had been governed by the principles stated in *Barclays Bank plc v O'Brien*, rather than by those stated in *CIBC Mortgages plc v Pitt*. Even if the plaintiff had employed Roiter Zucker to discharge such duty, Roiter Zucker would still not have been free, except with the defendants' consent, to pass on to the h plaintiff the information which they had obtained from the defendants, their duty to the plaintiff would still have been to tell it that they could no longer . act for it because a conflict of interests had arisen, and their knowledge of the true purpose of the loan could still not, in my judgment, have been imputed to the plaintiff ... Roiter Zucker were committing a breach of their duty to j the plaintiff by failing to tell it that they could no longer act for it and by continuing to do so after the conflict of interests had arisen; but, unless their continuing to act for the plaintiff in breach of such duty can itself be characterised as a kind of fraud ... I do not think it is essential to find that they were committing a fraud on the plaintiff in order that their knowledge should not be imputed to it. I conclude therefore that the plaintiff did not have notice that any part of the loan was going to be applied for a purpose which was not for the joint benefit of the defendants, and that it was not therefore put on inquiry and cannot be fixed with constructive notice of the misrepresentation or undue influence on which Mrs Stepsky relies.'

On this appeal the wife contended in the written argument supplied to the court in advance of the hearing that the judge was wrong for basically two reasons. The first was that as between the lender and the solicitors there was a paramount duty owed by the latter to disclose the true purpose of the loan to the former. The second was that there was no conflict because the husband was contractually bound to inform the lender of the true purpose of the loan. In either event, so the argument ran, the knowledge of the solicitors was to be imputed to the lender.

Neither party's written argument made any reference to s 199 of the 1925 Act and it seems that that section was not drawn to the attention of the judge either. So far as relevant it provides:

'(1) A purchaser shall not be prejudicially affected by notice of ... (ii) any other instrument or matter or any fact or thing unless ... (b) in the same transaction with respect to which a question of notice to the purchaser arises, it has come to the knowledge of his counsel, as such, or of his solicitor or other agent, as such, or would have come to the knowledge of his solicitor or other agent, as such, if such inquiries and inspections had been made as ought reasonably to have been made by the solicitor or other agent.'

Counsel for the wife submitted that that section did not apply, as the knowledge came to the knowledge of the solicitors for the lender as such when they were instructed to act on behalf of the lender on 19 June 1990. In the case of the wife it was submitted that the solicitors were not instructed by her as 'agents to know'.

I do not accept either of these submissions. In my view the section has to be applied in accordance with its terms to the facts of this case. There is no doubt that the information as to the true purpose of the remortgage loan imparted by the husband came to the knowledge of the solicitors on 12 June 1990 as the solicitors for the husband and wife alone, for they were not instructed to act for the lender until 19 June at the earliest. That knowledge once acquired remained with the solicitors and cannot be treated as coming to them again when they were instructed on behalf of the lender. As counsel for the wife accepted, their knowledge cannot be treated as divided or as disposed of and reacquired in that way. The conclusion seems to me to be inescapable: namely, that knowledge of the relevant matters, facts or things did not come to the solicitors as the solicitors for the lender. Accordingly, it did not come to them 'as such'. It was not disputed that the lender is a purchaser within the definition contained in s 205 of the 1925 Act. Consequently s 199(1)(ii)(b) of that Act precludes the solicitors' knowledge of the relevant matters or facts being imputed to the lender.

Moreover, it seems to me that the wife faces a dilemma. If the section does not apply, so that the knowledge of the solicitors is to be imputed to the lender, it is difficult to see why, on the same basis, the same knowledge should not be imputed to the wife as well. I do not accept the suggestion that the solicitors were instructed on behalf of the wife in some lesser or ministerial capacity when compared with their position as the solicitors for either the lender or the husband. The wife was a joint owner of the property and jointly liable for the mortgage being redeemed and for that by which it was to be replaced. In those a circumstances it is at least arguable that she would have no claim to set aside the transaction as against the husband, so that there would be no equity of which the lender could have notice anyway. Even if she did have some such equity, from the lender's point of view she was being represented by the same solicitors, who might fairly be assumed by the lender to be performing their duty to all three clients. These latter points relating to the position of the wife were not fully

b argued and I mention them for completeness only.

In my judgment the wife's appeal fails because, on the plain wording of s 199(1)(ii)(b) of the 1925 Act, the knowledge possessed by the solicitors as to the use to which the surplus moneys available in consequence of the remortgage were to be applied is not, on the facts of this case, to be imputed to the lender. I would dismiss this appeal.

c

WARD LJ. I agree.

KENNEDY LJ. I also agree.

d *Appeal dismissed.*

Paul Magrath Esq   Barrister.

S (a minor) v Special Educational Needs Tribunal and another

COURT OF APPEAL, CIVIL DIVISION

LEGGATT, MILLETT LJJ AND SIR RALPH GIBSON

13 DECEMBER 1995

Education – Local education authority – Statutory duty to provide special education – Statement of special educational needs proposing ordinary maintained school for dyslexic child – Parent appealing to special educational needs tribunal – Child appealing to High Court – Whether child proper party to appeal – Whether court may give judgment on merits if child not proper party – Tribunals and Inquiries Act 1992, s 11(1).

A local education authority made an assessment of the special educational needs of a dyslexic child, S, in a statement made under the provisions of the Education Act 1993, proposing a particular ordinary maintained secondary school, rather than the residential independent special school contended for by the mother, as being appropriate to address S's specific learning difficulties. S's mother appealed to a special educational needs tribunal, which confirmed the authority's proposal. S, by his mother and next friend, appealed to the High Court. On the preliminary issue whether S was a proper party to make the appeal, the judge held that an appeal from a decision of the tribunal pursuant to s 11 of the Tribunals and Inquiries Act 1992[a] could only be made by a party to the proceedings, and in the statutory context of the 1993 Act the only parties were the parents of the child and the local education authority. S was therefore not entitled to make the appeal and the court had no jurisdiction to hear it. The judge offered S's counsel the opportunity of applying to add or substitute the mother as a party but that offer was declined and he proceeded to consider the merits and dismiss the appeal. S appealed to the Court of Appeal, both on the merits and on his standing to make the appeal, contending principally that while the parent was consistently identified in the 1993 Act and regulations made thereunder as the person bringing the appeal, that did not necessarily preclude a child from falling within the definition 'party to proceedings' for the purposes of s 11(1) of the 1992 Act.

Held – The term 'party', as normally understood and for the purposes of s 11(1) of the 1992 Act, meant a litigant, not a beneficiary of the litigation, and it was clear from the 1993 Act and the regulations made thereunder that the child was not contemplated as being a party to the proceedings in that or any other sense, save in so far as the child was the subject of the appeal. Since an appeal from a decision of the tribunal could only be made by a party to the proceedings, it followed that the child had no right of appeal. The conclusion reached by the judge that S was not a party entitled to make the appeal was therefore correct, even though he had erred in proceeding to hear the appeal. In the absence of any application by the mother to be added or substituted as appellant, the court had no jurisdiction to

---

a Section 11, so far as material, provides: '(1) ... if any party to proceedings before any tribunal ... is dissatisfied in point of law with a decision of the tribunal he may ... either appeal from the tribunal to the High Court or require the tribunal to state and sign a case for the opinion of the High Court ...'

a entertain the appeal. The appeal would accordingly be dismissed (see p 288 *h*, p 289 *f* to *j* and p 290 *a* to *c*, post).

Decision of Latham J [1996] 1 All ER 171 affirmed.

Notes

b For children with special educational needs and the extent of the local authority's duty, see 15 *Halsbury's Laws* (4th edn reissue) paras 126–132.

Cases cited or referred to in skeleton arguments

Crofton Investment Trust Ltd v Greater London Rent Assessment Committee [1967] 2 All ER 1103, [1967] 2 QB 955, DC.

c *Green v Minister of Housing and Local Government* [1966] 3 All ER 942, [1967] QB 606, DC.

L, Re [1994] ELR 16 CA.

Minister of National Revenue v Wrights' Canadian Ropes Ltd [1947] AC 109, PC.

Mountview Court Properties Ltd v Devlin (1970) 21 P & CR 689, DC.

Poyser and Mills' Arbitration, Re [1963] 1 All ER 612, [1964] 2 QB 467.

d *R v Hackney London BC, ex p T* [1991] COD 454.

R v Knightsbridge Crown Court, ex p Aspinall Curzon Ltd (1982) Times, 16 December.

R v Medical Appeal Tribunal, ex p Gilmore [1957] 1 All ER 796, [1957] 1 QB 574, CA.

R v Mid-Glamorgan CC, ex p Greig (1988) Independent, 1 June.

R v Nat Bell Liquors Ltd [1922] 2 AC 128, [1922] All ER Rep 335, PC.

e *R v Northumberland Compensation Appeal Tribunal, ex p Shaw* [1952] 1 All ER 122, [1952] 1 KB 338, CA.

R v Parole Board, ex p Gittens [1994] COD 351.

R v Preston Supplementary Benefits Appeal Tribunal, ex p Moore, R v Sheffield Supplementary Benefits Appeal Tribunal, ex p Shine [1975] 2 All ER 807, [1975] 1 WLR 624, CA.

f *R v Southampton Justices, ex p Green* [1975] 2 All ER 1073, [1976] QB 11, CA.

R v Surrey CC Education Committee, ex p H (1984) 83 LGR 219, CA.

William Hill Organisation Ltd v Gavas [1990] IRLR 488, CA.

Appeal

g By notice dated 18 August 1995 S, a dyslexic 13-year-old suing by his mother and next friend, appealed with leave from the decision of Latham J ([1996] 1 All ER 171, [1995] 1 WLR 1627) made on 25 July 1995, whereby he dismissed S's appeal from the decision of the first respondent, the Special Educational Needs Tribunal, made on 2 February 1995 dismissing his appeal from an amended statement of special educational needs made in respect of S under s 168 of the Education Act

h 1993 approving an ordinary maintained school proposed by the local education authority, Westminster City Council (the second respondent), as appropriate for S's secondary education. The facts are set out in the judgment of Leggatt LJ.

Philip Engelman (instructed by *Teacher Stern Selby*) for the appellant.

j *J Richard McManus* (instructed by the *Treasury Solicitor*) for the tribunal.

Tanya Callman (instructed by *Colin Wilson*) for the second respondent.

LEGGATT LJ. This is an appeal by leave of the judge from the judgment of Latham J ([1996] 1 All ER 171, [1995] 1 WLR 1627) given on 25 July 1995 whereby he dismissed the appeal to the High Court of a boy who is now nearly 13½ years old and has been referred to as 'S'. That appeal was against the decision of the

Special Educational Needs Tribunal (the tribunal) made on 2 February 1995. The
tribunal had dismissed the appellant's appeal against the provisions of an
amended statement of special educational needs dated 6 September 1995, in error
for 1994. The particular part of the statement objected to was the decision not to
amend the school specified in the statement.

The appeal to the judge was, as it happened, the first such appeal on a point of
law against the decision of a tribunal pursuant to the provisions of s 11(1) of the
Tribunals and Inquiries Act 1992.

The first point that was raised before the judge concerned his jurisdiction to
entertain the appeal observing that S himself, by his mother and next friend, was
the sole appellant. The judge held, in a careful and comprehensive passage from
his judgment, that the only right of appeal to the tribunal was that given by ss 169,
170 and 172 of the Education Act 1993.

Mr Engelman, who appears in this court for S as he did before the judge, has
taken us through those provisions and has shown us in addition the provisions of
s 173, which also make provision for a parent to appeal. It is not necessary to
consider in detail those statutory provisions. Suffice to refer by way of example
to s 169(2) which provides that the child's parent may appeal to the tribunal
against the decision, that is (for purposes of that section) a decision not to make
a statement.

To the like effect are regulations made under s 180 of the 1993 Act which
provide for the conduct of appeals as parties only by parents and the local
education authority. Once more Mr Engelman has shown us most of the salient
provisions of the Special Educational Needs Tribunal Regulations 1994, SI 1994/
1910. Each of those provisions refers to a parent as making the relevant appeal or
signing the appeal or delivering notice of appeal and like provisions. Perhaps
most telling of all in the present context is the definition in reg 2 of the term 'child'
in respect of which it is provided: 'In these Regulations, unless the context
otherwise requires ... "child" means the child in respect of whom the appeal is
brought ...'

Mr Engelman, in face of those provisions both of the statute and of the
regulations made under it, very properly acknowledges that the parent is
consistently identified as the person bringing the appeal. None the less, he is
emboldened to argue that that does not necessarily preclude a child from falling
within the definition of 'party to proceedings' for purposes of s 11 of the 1992 Act
when appeal is made to the High Court.

In aid of that submission, Mr Engelman contended both in writing in his
skeleton argument and orally before this court, first, that the child plainly is a
party to the proceedings in question. That appears to me to beg the question to
which the submission relates. The term 'party' as normally understood is a party
to litigation, playing a prescribed part. The child, as appears from the statute and
regulations made under it, is not contemplated as being a party to the
proceedings in that or any other sense, save insofar as the child is, of course, the
subject of the appeal.

Next Mr Engelman submits that there is no reason of construction or policy
which should preclude a child from being a party to the proceedings before the
tribunal. That is a negative submission which would not, even if it were valid,
take him far. But in my judgment it cannot be valid since there is no provision
made for a child to be a party to proceedings. Mr Engelman then submits that, if
his construction be correct that the child is to be regarded as a party to the
proceedings, that removes what he calls the 'dilemma' as to the definition of a

a child for purposes of s 156(5) of the 1993 Act which he says the judge declined to resolve.

What the judge said was as follows ([1996] 1 All ER 171 at 174, [1995] 1 WLR 1627 at 1630):

b 'It was pointed out in argument that a child for the purposes of the relevant part of the 1993 Act includes, pursuant to s 156(5), any person who has not attained the age of 19 years and is a registered pupil at a school. Theoretically, therefore, an adult affected by any of the relevant decisions would not be able to invoke the jurisdiction of the tribunal himself, but would only be able to do so through his parents. The words of the statute are however clear. The only person who can invoke the jurisdiction of the c tribunal is the parent.'

I consider that the judge in that passage came to the correct conclusion that, however anomalous it might appear, if the situation were to arise that an 18-year-old child was the subject of an appeal to the tribunal, that appeal could d only be brought by his or her parent since that is what the 1993 Act dictates. That there might be dispute between a child who had attained his majority and his parents is obviously possible, but that is a situation with which this court is not now concerned and with which the court would deal appropriately should it arise.

In writing, though not orally, Mr Engelman submits that the true analysis is e that the parent acts as the child's agent and there is no reason why the child cannot step into the shoes of the parent for the purposes of an appeal to the High Court. Mr Engelman also argues orally, though not in writing, that the court should incline to treat the child as an appellant, since the policy of the 1993 Act is to protect, and look after the interests of the child.

f In my judgment the judge came to a conclusion that was impeccable as well as inescapable. For purposes of s 11 of the 1992 Act, 'party' is to be treated as meaning a litigant, not a beneficiary of the litigation. But since the child has no right of appeal, it does not avail him to show that his parent was acting as his agent. In any event, the parent does not act in that capacity nor is the parent entitled to bring an appeal in that capacity or in his or her own right. In my g judgment, this court therefore has no jurisdiction to entertain this appeal.

Having determined that the mother was the right party, the judge offered the appellant's counsel the opportunity of applying to add or substitute the mother as a party. That opportunity was, however, deliberately declined. The judge nonetheless proceeded to hear the appeal on the ground that the matters raised h are important to the appellant, as of course they are, and that the appeal was the first of its kind to reach the High Court. No doubt he was prompted by the best of motives. As far as I am able to judge from the written submissions of counsel, not having heard counsel orally in relation to the other points set out in the notice of appeal, the judge came to the right conclusion on all the issues before him. Yet j in entertaining the appeal (apart from the jurisdictional point to which I have already referred) the judge, in my judgment, was wrong. No reason was proffered to the court for not seeking to add the mother as a party. It would have given jurisdiction to the court where otherwise, if my conclusion be accepted by my brethren, there was none. The most obvious inference is that the mother would not have been entitled to legal aid or have been entitled to it only on terms that were or would have been unacceptable to her. In any event, the effect of

deciding the merits was to cause the legal aid fund to incur the cost of so doing
which it otherwise would not have borne.

In this court the mother has not made any application to be added or
substituted as appellant. In my judgment, for the reasons I have indicated, we
have no jurisdiction to entertain the appeal. We should refuse to give judgment
on the merits of it, since such a judgment would be both obiter and hypothetical.
To do so would not only be contrary to principle, but would enable the appeal to
be conducted at the expense of the legal aid fund when the true appellant may not
be entitled to that benefit. I would dismiss the appeal.

MILLETT LJ. I agree.

SIR RALPH GIBSON. I also agree.

Appeal dismissed. Leave to appeal to the House of Lords refused.

L I Zysman Esq   Barrister.

a # Gahan v Szerelmey (UK) Ltd and another

COURT OF APPEAL, CIVIL DIVISION

NOURSE, HOBHOUSE LJJ AND SIR CHRISTOPHER SLADE

b 26 OCTOBER 1995

Practice – Dismissal of action for want of prosecution – Inordinate delay without excuse – Prejudice to defendant – Size of claim increased by delay – Whether financial prejudice due to delay sufficient to justify striking out – Whether defendant having to bring into account value to him of having in hand money, but for period of delay, payable as damages to plaintiff.

c

In September 1988 the plaintiff sustained serious injuries at work when the scaffolding on which he was standing gave way beneath him. He subsequently brought proceedings against his employers and the scaffolders claiming damages
d in respect of his injuries. The pleadings were closed and discovery was completed by July 1991 but although the action should have been set down by the end of December 1991, the plaintiff's solicitors took no further steps in the proceedings. In June and July 1994 the defendants issued summonses to strike out the action for want of prosecution. The master granted the defendants' applications and, on
e the plaintiff's appeal, the judge affirmed the master's order, finding that the plaintiff's delay was inordinate and inexcusable and that the difference in the quantum of the plaintiff's damages for loss of earnings as between that which would have been awarded at a trial in 1992 and that which would be awarded at a trial in 1995 (ie at least £12,000 to £15,000) would cause the defendants more than minimal financial prejudice. However, in establishing that prejudice, the
f judge held that the benefit enjoyed by the defendants in having the use of the money ultimately to be paid in damages was not to be taken into account by way of set-off. The plaintiff appealed.

Held – A defendant who sought to have an action against him struck out on the
g ground that the plaintiff's delay had caused him financial prejudice had to bring into account the value to him of having in hand the money which, but for the delay, he would have had to pay to the plaintiff by way of damages. Thus, to ascertain the true prejudice to the defendants there had to be set against the sum which would be awarded at the delayed trial (i) the fall in the spending power of
h money during the period of the delay and (ii) the interest and/or capital appreciation which the defendant or his insurers would have been able to earn in respect of that sum over the period of the delay. Once both sides of the calculation had been taken into account it would only be in a very limited category of cases that a defendant could establish serious prejudice by reason of the postponement of judgment. It followed that the judge was in error in refusing to
j take into account the monetary benefit to the defendants of having the money in hand and the court was accordingly free to exercise the discretion afresh. On the facts the defendants had not shown sufficient financial prejudice to justify striking out the case for want of prosecution. The plaintiff's appeal would accordingly be allowed, and his action allowed to proceed against both defendants (see p 294 *h* to p 295 *b f* to *h*, p 296 *e* to *j*, p 297 *b c*, p 299 *e* to p 300 *a d e* and p 301 *a*, post).

Hayes v Bowman [1989] 2 All ER 293 and dictum of Neill LJ in *Doyle v Robinson* [1994] PIQR P59 at P63 applied.   *a*

Notes
For dismissal of actions for want of prosecution, see 37 *Halsbury's Laws* (4th edn) paras 447–450, and for cases on the subject, see 37(3) *Digest* (Reissue) 67–78, 3293–3341.   *b*

Cases referred to in judgments
Birkett v James [1977] 2 All ER 801, [1978] AC 297, [1977] 3 WLR 38, HL.
Doyle v Robinson [1994] PIQR P59, CA.
Hayes v Bowman [1989] 2 All ER 293, [1989] 1 WLR 456, CA.
          c

Cases also cited or referred to in skeleton arguments
Birkett v Hayes [1982] 2 All ER 710, [1982] 1 WLR 816, CA.
Dexter v Courtaulds Ltd [1984] 1 All ER 70, [1984] 1 WLR 372, CA.
Hornagold v Fairclough Building Ltd [1993] PIQR P400, CA.
Read v Harries [1995] PIQR Q25.   *d*
Roebuck v Mungovin [1994] 1 All ER 568, [1994] 2 AC 224, HL.
Trill v Sacher [1993] 1 All ER 961, [1993] 1 WLR 1379, CA.
Wright v British Railways Board [1983] 2 All ER 698, [1983] 2 AC 773, HL.

Appeal   *e*
By notice dated 28 February 1995 the plaintiff, Dermitt Michael Gahan, appealed with leave granted by Simon Brown LJ on 24 February 1995 from the decision of Sir Peter Webster sitting as a judge of the High Court in the Queen's Bench Division on 1 December 1994 whereby he affirmed the order of Master Turner made on 10 August 1994 striking out for want of prosecution the plaintiff's claim in a personal injury action against the first and second defendants, Szerelmey *f* (UK) Ltd and Mattison Scaffolding and Cradle Contractors (a firm). The facts are set out in the judgment of Nourse LJ.

Peter Birts QC and *Adrian Jack* (instructed by *Ziadies & Co*) for the plaintiff.
Richard Methuen (instructed by *Mackrell Turner Garrett*) for the first defendant.   *g*
Simon King (instructed by *Vizards*) for the second defendants.

NOURSE LJ. On 1 December 1994 Sir Peter Webster, sitting as a judge of the High Court in the Queen's Bench Division, affirmed an order of Master Turner made on 10 August 1994 striking out the claim of the plaintiff, Mr Gahan, in a personal injury action for want of prosecution. The judge refused the plaintiff *h* leave to appeal to this court, but leave was granted by Simon Brown LJ on 24 February 1995. Shortly stated, the question at issue is whether a defendant who claims that the plaintiff's inordinate and inexcusable delay has given rise to financial prejudice to him of the kind identified in *Hayes v Bowman* [1989] 2 All ER 293, [1989] 1 WLR 456 and *Doyle v Robinson* [1994] PIQR P59, must bring into *j* account the value to him of having in hand the money which, but for the delay, he would have had to pay to the plaintiff by way of damages.

On 28 September 1988 the plaintiff, then aged 53, sustained serious injuries at work when the scaffolding boards on which he was standing gave way. His employer was the first defendant, Szerelmey (UK) Ltd; the second defendants a were the scaffolders, Mattison Scaffolding and Cradle Contractors (a firm). The plaintiff claims that there had been a history of defects with the scaffolding prior to the accident, including a report detailing serious concerns made only the day before it happened. He claims that his injuries were caused by the negligence of both defendants. He also claims that the first defendant owed him a non-delegable duty to ensure the safety of the working platform under the Con-

b struction (Working Places) Regulations 1966, SI 1966/94. In giving judgment, Master Turner said:

c '... it is not just a question of the scaffold being defective, but also of its being overloaded and of boards being moved. Both defendants blame each other. No one suggests realistically that the plaintiff was responsible: working on a scaffold is dangerous and accidents seldom lie at the plaintiff's foot.'

The writ in the action was issued on 1 September 1990. The pleadings were closed and discovery had been completed by July 1991. In March 1992 the first defendant served its replies to a request for particulars pursuant to an order

d obtained by the plaintiff. In early 1992 the plaintiff underwent an arthrodesis to fuse his ankle. Unfortunately the operation was unsuccessful in reducing the pain.

Up to that point the case had been handled by an assistant solicitor in the plaintiff's solicitors who had stopped working full time and eventually, in the summer of 1993, left the firm in order to get married. The file was then

e transferred to the senior partner. On 20 August 1993 the plaintiff served interrogatories on the first defendant, but those were ignored because no notice of intention to proceed had been served. At about that time the senior partner in the plaintiff's solicitors was diagnosed as suffering from cancer, which started deleteriously to affect his work. He died on 24 July 1994.

f The judgment of Sir Peter Webster was to the following effect. First, he held that the action should have been set down by the end of December 1991. Secondly, he held that the delay of two and a half years between then and June and July 1994, when the summonses to strike out were issued, was both inordinate and inexcusable. However, he was not satisfied that the defendants had established the likelihood of any evidential prejudice as arising from the

g delay. On the other hand, he held that the difference in the quantum of the plaintiff's damages for loss of earnings as between those which would have been awarded at a trial in 1992 and those which would be awarded at a trial in 1995 would cause the defendants more than minimal prejudice.

Having said that, in very round terms, it looked as if there would be a

h difference of at least something between £12,000 and £15,000 over and above the award of about £100,000 which would have been made had the trial taken place in 1992, the judge continued:

j 'Mr Jack asks me to offset against those differences the monetary benefit which he says the defendants will have enjoyed by having the use of the money ultimately to be paid in damages if an award is made for three years before that happens, and he makes a number of calculations about the value of the returns on investments which the defendants would obtain; but I refuse to take this suggested set-off into account. In the first place there is no common ground between counsel as to whether the returns should be taken, for this purpose, as gross or net figures; but more significantly I have

no evidence that the defendants would or should have been able to invest
that money at all. Of course, it may be inherently probable that an insurance
company will always be able to invest £100,000 if it has no immediate need
for it, but I am not prepared to assume for the purposes of this argument that
that is so or that I should make the assumption for this purpose that it would
be so. I have not been told of any case in which this set-off has been claimed
and approved and, as I have said, for those reasons I refuse to take it into
account.'

The judge concluded that it was likely that the defendants would suffer more
than minimal financial prejudice on account of the trial being delayed by between
two and a half and three years. With regard to the last sentence in the passage I
have read, we are informed by junior counsel for the plaintiff, who also appeared
before the judge below, that he was not referred to *Hayes v Bowman*. That was
certainly a case in which the set-off was claimed. It was also one in which, as I
think, it was approved.

The nature of the financial prejudice which is liable to be caused to the
defendant by delay in bringing a personal injuries action to trial was succinctly
stated by Leggatt LJ in *Doyle v Robinson* [1994] PIQR P59 at P64:

'Where a plaintiff sustains personal injuries and thereby incurs a loss of
earnings likely to last for the rest of his working life, the longer the time that
elapses between the date of the accident and the date of trial, the larger will
be the sum recoverable by way of damages for loss of earnings.'

That that is capable of being serious prejudice to the defendant within the
principles stated in *Birkett v James* [1977] 2 All ER 801, [1978] AC 297 was first
recognised by this court in *Hayes v Bowman*. It may arise in either or both of two
ways. First, as Leggatt LJ said in *Doyle v Robinson* [1994] PIQR P59 at P64:

'... because the multiplier used in assessing future loss of earnings will
decrease by less than the number of years of actual loss of earnings that
elapse between accident and trial.'

Secondly, because the assessment of the plaintiff's loss of earnings, being made as
at the date of trial, may, in times when percentage increases in wages regularly
outstrip increases in the rate of inflation, result in a real increase in the
multiplicand.

All this is now well established and, apart from an argument of Mr Birts QC to
which I will refer in due course, is not in dispute between the parties to this
appeal. What is in dispute is the judge's view that in assessing the extent of the
financial prejudice there must be left out of account the value to the defendant of
having in hand the money which, but for the delay, he would have had to pay to
the plaintiff by way of damages.

If the question is viewed as one of principle, it admits of only one answer. The
value to the defendant must be brought into account. If it is not, the prejudice
will be assessed by reference to a balance sheet consisting only of liabilities. True,
it may be difficult to value the assets, more difficult than to state the liabilities, but
that is no reason for leaving them out of account.

In *Hayes v Bowman* it was accepted by the experienced leading counsel who
appeared for the defendant that, in order to make a fair comparison, the
defendant must give credit for the use which he or his insurers would have had
of the money eventually awarded during the period of the delay (see [1989] 2 All

a ER 293 at 297, 300, [1989] 1 WLR 456 at 462, 465). Proceeding on that footing, Slade LJ said that if the true prejudice to the defendant or his insurers was to be ascertained, there had to be set against the sum which would be awarded at the delayed trial (a) the fall in the spending power of money during the period of the delay, and (b) the interest and/or capital appreciation which the defendant or his insurers would have been able to earn in respect of the sum which would have

b been awarded at a trial held timeously if they had retained it in their hands over the period of the delay (see [1989] 2 All ER 293 at 304, [1989] 1 WLR 456 at 469–470).

On this appeal Mr Methuen, for the first defendant, and Mr King, for the second defendants, have submitted that in Hayes v Bowman the point went by way of concession and, moreover, by a concession which was wrongly made. They

c have relied on Doyle v Robinson, in which there is hardly a trace of the point having been taken, and from that they argue that it must be a bad one. I am unable to agree. True, with hindsight it seems curious that the point is not referred to in the judgments. More than one explanation has been suggested, but the probable one appears to be that the point was not taken at first instance and could not

d therefore have been taken on appeal. It is to be noted that Doyle v Robinson, like Hayes v Bowman, was a case where this court emphasised that the question of serious prejudice was essentially one for the judge below. Whatever the explanation, I am in no doubt that the concession was correctly made in Hayes v Bowman. I am also of the opinion that Doyle v Robinson is no authority for the proposition that it was incorrectly made. The point was simply not considered.

e Further, as I read the judgments in Hayes v Bowman, all the members of this court in that case were of the view that the concession was correctly made.

Counsel for the defendants have advanced further arguments in support of the view that the value to the defendants of the money in hand should not be brought into account, principally on the ground that it involves complicated and

f speculative calculations which would unduly impede the expeditious hearing of these applications by Queen's Bench masters, district judges and judges in chambers. I will return to that point later. Apart from that, there is nothing of substance in any of the defendants' further arguments. It is for the defendant to show that the plaintiff's inordinate and inexcusable delay has given rise to serious prejudice to him or his insurers. If he alleges the kind of financial prejudice

g alleged here, he cannot do so by relying on a one-sided balance sheet. The assets must be computed as stated by Slade LJ in Hayes v Bowman. Any difficulties there may be in making the computation are not a justification for not making it. They may be a means of deterring defendants from relying on this kind of prejudice except in clear and obvious cases. That that would be so was, I think, the

h expectation of this court in Hayes v Bowman.

In Doyle v Robinson [1994] PIQR P59 at P63 Neill LJ referred to the primary argument of counsel for the plaintiff, which was that in order to strike out an action on this basis it was necessary for the defendant to put before the court detailed calculations, preferably backed by evidence, so that the judge could see

j precisely the losses and gains which the plaintiff would make as a result of the delay. Having expressed the view that it was unnecessary to approach the matter on that basis, Neill LJ said (at P63):

'It will all depend on the facts of the case. In some cases, such as this, the calculation of the extra sum to be paid is really very simple ... It seems to me that it is wrong to impose upon a defendant the burden of calling actuarial or

detailed evidence in every case. Sometimes it can be a matter of simple
calculation by counsel, or, if necessary, the figures can be included in an
affidavit. There is no need to burden a defendant with the costs, which
might be very substantial, of actuarial evidence in a simple case such as this.'

As a general statement I entirely and respectfully agree.

It is to be noted that in *Hayes v Bowman* the matter was dealt with on a
hypothetical basis. Immediately following the passage in Slade LJ's judgment to
which I have referred, he said that the attention of the court had been drawn to
no figures in respect of the fall in the spending power of money during the period
of delay (see [1989] 2 All ER 293 at 304, [1989] 1 WLR 456 at 470). However,
figures of that kind can readily be ascertained from specialised works on the
subject. Slade LJ went on to say that, in regard to the interest and/or capital
appreciation which the defendant or his insurers would have been able to earn in
respect of the lower sum, counsel for the defendant had invited the court to
assume that interest would have been earned at a maximum rate of 7.5% net
compound. In the ordinary run of cases, where the defendant is either insured,
or is a commercial concern which could be expected to put money in hand to the
same sort of use, calculations along those lines can readily be made without a lot
of fuss and trouble. It may be that in the case of an uninsured individual
defendant it will not be quite so simple. In such a case it may be necessary for him
to put in an affidavit dealing with his means. Whatever the position, and
however it is dealt with, I repeat that the defendant cannot rely on a one-sided
balance sheet.

That is what the defendants did in this case. The judge did not accept their
figures as they stood because he was not convinced, even taking into account the
plaintiff's age, that the difference in the multiplier would be as much as that
suggested. As Mr Methuen has pointed out, that was a point taken by the judge
in favour of the defendants. But he also took account of the calculations made by
counsel for the plaintiff as to the liabilities side of the balance sheet, and he
adjusted the figures accordingly. He refused to take into account the monetary
benefit to the defendants of having the money in hand. In that, for the reasons I
have given, I respectfully think that the judge was in error.

That means that we in this court must exercise the discretion afresh. It has not
been suggested on behalf of either defendant, on the basis of the material before
the judge and this court, that the necessary degree of financial prejudice has been
shown, on the footing, as I hold, that the value to the defendants of the money in
hand must be brought into account. In those circumstances I find myself in the
same position as Otton J at first instance in *Hayes v Bowman*. I read the passage
from his judgment quoted by Lloyd LJ ([1989] 2 All ER 293 at 300, [1989] 1 WLR
456 at 465):

"'It seems to me that taking the matter overall the defendant has not
established a sufficient degree of prejudice to justify exercising my discretion
to dismiss the case for want of prosecution.'"

In giving brief reasons for granting leave to appeal, on consideration of the
documents, Simon Brown LJ said:

'The court may wish to consider generally this suggested head of
prejudice. Is this sort of complicated financial evidence to be adduced (by

a   both sides) routinely in all striking out cases where no evidential prejudice can be established? It is a depressing thought.'

Perhaps in reliance on the first sentence in that passage Mr Birts, for the plaintiff, has sought to argue that it is still open to this court, on grounds of policy, to say that this kind of prejudice shall no longer be admissible in cases of this kind.
b   However, we have made it very clear during Mr Birts' argument that we regard ourselves as bound by the decisions in *Hayes v Bowman* and *Doyle v Robinson* on that point. Subject to that, I am in general sympathy with Simon Brown LJ's observations, which support the view that this kind of prejudice should only be capable of being relied on in clear and obvious cases.

For these reasons I would allow the appeal, so that the plaintiff's action can
c   proceed against both defendants.

HOBHOUSE LJ. I agree with the judgment of Nourse LJ, with his conclusion that this appeal should be allowed, and with the reasons that he has given for it.

The starting point of this topic is the judgment in *Birkett v James* [1977] 2 All ER
d   801, [1978] AC 297. A defendant who is applying to dismiss an action for want of prosecution has to satisfy the court that there has been inordinate and inexcusable delay on the part of the plaintiff which has caused prejudice to the defendant or has made a fair trial impossible. The prejudice to the defendant can come under any of a number of heads, as is demonstrated by the decided cases. *Hayes v Bowman* [1989] 2 All ER 293, [1989] 1 WLR 456 clearly shows that one of
e   those heads is financial prejudice. Croom-Johnson LJ said ([1989] 2 All ER 293 at 298, [1989] 1 WLR 456 at 463):

'The court is not construing a statute. It is using its discretion in the exercise of its inherent jurisdiction. The statement by Lord Diplock in *Birkett*
f   *v James* [1977] 2 All ER 801 at 805, [1978] AC 297 at 318 is that the action will be struck out if the delay gives rise to a substantial risk that it is not possible to have a fair trial of the issues in the action or is such as is likely to cause or to have caused serious prejudice to the defendant. It gives no hint as to what is meant by "prejudice". For my part, if "prejudice" is given its ordinary meaning of "detriment", I do not see why delay which has caused the claim
g   to grow in the course of three years by £16,637 has not caused prejudice to the defendant, and serious prejudice at that.'

Leggatt LJ in *Doyle v Robinson* [1994] PIQR P59 at P64 expressed himself in similar terms: 'So the increase in damages on account of their delayed assessment is itself capable of constituting serious prejudice to the defendants caused by the
h   delay.' The prejudice nevertheless has to be a real prejudice, not some notional prejudice which is arrived at on some artificial basis. The acceptance in this court by the respondents that, if both sides of the calculation are taken into account, they can no longer show serious financial prejudice, demonstrates that their argument cannot be sound. On the face of it, delay in having to meet a judgment
j   which will be entered against you is an advantage. Therefore, a defendant will on the face of it, other things being equal, benefit, not suffer prejudice, by reason of the postponement of the judgment day. It is only because of the special rules relating to the assessment of damages in personal injury actions that the point which arose in *Hayes v Bowman* can be used to support an argument by the defendant that he has suffered prejudice as a result of the delay.

But, because it is necessary to consider whether there is actual prejudice, it is necessary to look at the whole position. Thus, the court must take account of the fact that the defendant will have had the use of the money which is required in order to meet the judgment during the period of delay. Further, the effect of inflation may likewise benefit the defendant, because he will be paying a monetary judgment in depreciating currency. Both those factors were pointed out in the judgments of the Court of Appeal in *Hayes v Bowman*, and in particular by Slade LJ, where he said ([1989] 2 All ER 293 at 304, [1989] 1 WLR 456 at 469):

'Counsel for the defendant has convinced me that at least in the great majority of cases delay of the trial from year A to a later year B will result in the defendant having to pay an award of £x + y rather than £x, for the reasons which he gives. Nevertheless, I am not satisfied that this will necessarily leave the defendant out of pocket in terms of real money. Whether or not it does so, it seems to me, will depend largely on two factors, namely: (a) whether £x + y exceeds £x by an amount exceeding the rate of inflation operating during the period from year A to year B, and (b) the amount of interest which the defendant has been able to earn on the £x retained by him during that period.'

Therefore, it is necessary in all cases falling within this class to consider whether, on balance, the delay has caused significant prejudice to the defendant. It does not necessarily follow from the simple comparison of the two calculations of the damages that that will be the case. In *Hayes v Bowman* the Court of Appeal and, indeed, Otton J were not persuaded that there was significant prejudice to the defendant as a result of the delay.

The same position, as has been pointed out, pertains in the present case. Once the potential advantages to a defendant in a postponed judgment are taken into account, as well as the question of an increased monetary judgment, then it is possible, as is the case here, that there is no clear balance of advantage and disadvantage. Some of the figures which have been referred to demonstrate this type of consideration. To be required to pay 30% for putting off a liability for seven to eight years may be no disadvantage. In the present case, on the most adverse figures to the plaintiff, to put off a liability for three years against an increment of 15% likewise may not demonstrate any clear detriment.

The matters which have to be taken into account by the court are matters which are not arcane or esoteric. Inflation factors and rates of interest are commonly dealt with by the courts in the assessment of damages and the award of interest on damages, whether allowed on a summary judgment or after a trial. The court has access, if it does not already have the knowledge, to inflation tables and to interest rates, as is demonstrated, for example, by reference to *The Supreme Court Practice*, and both masters and district judges are familiar with the short-term interest rate and with the judgment rates. Therefore, the assessment of the balance of advantage or disadvantage, in terms which are sufficient for the purpose of determining an application to dismiss for want of prosecution, is well within the competence and the resources of those who are having to decide such applications.

I would respectfully adopt what was said by the Court of Appeal with regard to evidence in *Doyle v Robinson,* and quote from what was said by Beldam LJ:

'Nor would I accept the submission which was made that the court could not validly exercise its discretion unless there was put before it by the a defendant an accountant's or actuarial report dealing in detail with all the many unknown or uncertain factors which might influence the amount of the increased damages faced by the plaintiff. I agree, therefore, with [Neill LJ] that in many cases it will be possible for the judge, looking at the circumstances of the case as a whole, and looking at the length of the delay, to form an estimate of the degree of prejudice.' (See [1994] PIQR P59 at P64.)

b Beldam LJ was there referring, as had Neill LJ before him in a passage quoted by Nourse LJ, to the comparison between judgments which might be given at one day or another; but the same approach is appropriate to evaluating the value of money during a period of delay. There is no need to burden the court in the ordinary case with accountants' or actuarial evidence. Indeed, in my judgment it would clearly be inappropriate to do so. Therefore, the type of considerations
c which have been canvassed in the present case do not give rise to a need for specific evidence to be placed before the court.

That said, it must always be borne in mind that on any such application it is for the defendant to satisfy the court of the relevant matters. If there are special circumstances upon which the defendant relies, including, for example, special
d financial circumstances of his own, or something else which affects him in a way which would not normally be assumed to be the case, then the defendant has to put the appropriate evidence before the court. The concern quite rightly expressed by Simon Brown LJ when giving leave to appeal in this case is one which, in my judgment, in the vast majority of these cases should not in practice
e arise.

With the guidance that has been given by the Court of Appeal on this occasion, it should be clear to practitioners that it is only in a very limited category of cases that the point raised in *Hayes v Bowman* and *Doyle v Robinson* will give a justification for an assertion that the defendant has suffered prejudice. That is because, once both sides of the equation have been taken into account, it will not
f normally be the position that serious prejudice has been made out.

SIR CHRISTOPHER SLADE. I agree with both judgments. I add a few observations of my own, principally because I was a party to the decision of this court in *Hayes v Bowman* [1989] 2 All ER 293, [1989] 1 WLR 456.
g Notwithstanding the opening submissions of Mr Birts QC, that decision and that in *Doyle v Robinson* [1994] PIQR P59 are in my opinion clear authority for the proposition that, where there has been inordinate and inexcusable delay in prosecuting a claim for personal injuries, the potential increase in damages due to their delayed assessment may in some cases give rise to potential prejudice to the
h defendant sufficiently substantial to justify dismissal of the action for want of prosecution. To this extent those two authorities are in my opinion binding on this court.

The decision in *Doyle v Robinson* further shows that, in order to show substantial prejudice, it is not ordinarily necessary for the defendant to undertake the burden of putting before the court an accountant's or actuary's report dealing
j in detail with all the many unknown or uncertain factors which might influence the amount of the increased damages faced by the defendant. As Neill LJ said (at P63): 'Sometimes it can be a matter of simple calculation by counsel, or, if necessary, the figures can be included in an affidavit.' Nevertheless, in my judgment, whatever the form of the calculation relied on by the defendant for this purpose, it must be a realistic calculation of the potential additional overall

monetary loss. It cannot, in my view, be considered a realistic calculation if it has regard only to the debit side of the defendant's balance sheet, namely the *a* potential increase in damages, and wholly disregards the credit side, namely the benefit which he or his insurers must presumably have derived from the use of the amount of the increase over the period of the relevant delay.

As Mr Methuen has submitted, it appears from the report that the calculations placed before the court of first instance and the Court of Appeal in *Doyle v* *b* *Robinson* did not attribute any credit of this nature to the defendant, and that it was not argued in either court that any such attribution should be made. In the light of what had been said in *Hayes v Bowman*, I think this was perhaps a somewhat surprising omission. But if, as appears, the point was not raised in argument in either court, I do not see how the judge at first instance in that case can be criticised for failing to take it, or how the Court of Appeal could have *c* properly interfered with the exercise of his discretion on that account.

In the present case, the judge said that he had not been told of any case in which the set-off in question had been claimed and approved. From this I infer that he had not been referred to the decision in *Hayes v Bowman*. He had apparently no knowledge of that decision, save in so far as it had been referred to in *Doyle v* *d* *Robinson*. In my judgment, however, with all respect to him, he erred in principle in declining the invitation to take any suggested set-off of this nature into account. This court is accordingly free to exercise the discretion anew. For the reasons given by Nourse and Hobhouse LJJ, I think that, when the relevant set-off is taken into account, the defendants have failed to show that the relevant delay *e* has, on balance, caused them any substantial prejudice.

I would add two further comments in conclusion. First, in giving my judgment in *Hayes v Bowman* I suggested that pleas of this type would avail a defendant only where he was in a position to produce 'compelling evidence of substantial financial prejudice' (see [1989] 2 All ER 293 at 304, [1989] 1 WLR 456 at 470). Notwithstanding my use of the word 'evidence', I of course accept that, as *Doyle* *f* *v Robinson* shows, the relevant figures can properly be presented to the court not necessarily by way of formal evidence and, furthermore, can be presented with a fairly broad brush. Generally it will not be appropriate to invite the court to embark on a detailed analysis of a mass of detailed figures in cases such as this. Correspondingly, I do not think it will ordinarily be incumbent on defendants or *g* their insurers to adduce evidence as to the particular use which, owing to their individual circumstances, they would have been able to make of the sum eventually awarded during the period of the delay. I think that, ordinarily, it would suffice for their counsel to produce figures for the credit side of the account simply by reference to supposed prevailing rates of interest, as I believe was done in *Hayes v Bowman*. If this course is ordinarily adopted and the guidance *h* given in *Doyle v Robinson* is followed, this should at least go a long way to meeting the very pertinent anxieties of Simon Brown LJ to which reference has already been made. Secondly, the present case seems to me to illustrate that it may be only in rare personal injury cases that a defendant who is unable to satisfy the court as to evidential prejudice will be able to satisfy it on the figures that the *j* delay has caused him financial prejudice sufficient to justify the striking out of the claim for want of prosecution.

For my part, therefore, without intending any criticism whatsoever of counsel for the respective defendants in the present case, I think that, for the future, counsel instructed for defendants in this class of case should think it right to take *a* an alternative point relating to alleged financial prejudice by no means as a matter of course. As Nourse LJ has indicated, I anticipate that pleas of this nature should and will in the future be allowed only in plain and obvious cases.

I would concur in allowing this appeal, so that the action can proceed against both defendants.

b *Appeal allowed.*

L I Zysman Esq   Barrister.

R v Westminster City Council, ex parte Ermakov *a*

COURT OF APPEAL, CIVIL DIVISION
NOURSE, HUTCHISON AND THORPE LJJ
13, 14 NOVEMBER 1995

b

Housing – Homeless person – Duty of housing authority to provide accommodation – Person becoming homeless intentionally – Finding by authority of intentional homelessness – Authority notifying appellant of decision and of reasons – Applicant applying for judicial review of decision – Reasons notified to applicant not authority's true reasons – Authority submitting affidavit evidence stating true reasons – Judge admitting affidavit evidence and dismissing appeal – Whether deficient reasons in notification could be made good by affidavit evidence in course of proceedings – Housing Act 1985, s 64(4).

c

The applicant, a national of the Republic of Uzbekistan, and his family came to the United Kingdom from Greece and applied to the respondent council to be *d* housed on the ground that they were homeless. The applicant made a full statement, explaining that they had moved to Greece from Uzbekistan partly because of the political climate there and partly so that his wife could look after her sick father, but that the father's relations had persecuted and threatened the lives of him and his family. Pursuant to its statutory duty to ascertain whether the applicant had become homeless intentionally, the council wrote to persons in *e* Greece seeking corroboration of his account but received no reply. Thereafter, the council's principal homelessness officer, L, made the decision that the appellant had become homeless intentionally; and pursuant to the council's obligation under s 64(4)[a] of the Housing Act 1985, the applicant was notified of that decision and of the reasons for it, namely that the council was not satisfied *f* that the applicant had experienced harassment in Greece and that it was therefore reasonable that he and his family should continue to live there. The applicant applied for judicial review of the decision. For the purpose of the proceedings L swore an affidavit explaining that the true reasons for his decision were not those expressed in the decision letter but rather that he was satisfied that, notwithstanding the matters disclosed in the applicant's statement, it would have *g* been reasonable for him and his family to continue to occupy the accommodation he rented in Greece. At the hearing, the deputy judge permitted the council to rely on L's affidavit evidence to justify the legality of their decision and dismissed the application. The applicant appealed, contending that the deputy judge had erred in paying regard to the affidavit evidence, since wholly *h* deficient statutory reasons could not be made good by such evidence in the course of proceedings. The council contended that since the requirements of s 64 as to notification were purely procedural, notification of the wrong reasons was a purely technical error that should be allowed to be corrected by the affidavit of the decision-maker.

j

Held – (1) In the context of s 64 of the 1985 Act, it was unrealistic to seek to draw any significant distinction between the decision and the communication of the decision with reasons, or to treat the giving of reasons as purely procedural. Since

a　Section 64(4), so far as material, is set out at p 309 *c*, post *a* s 64 required that reasons should be given at the same time as the decision was communicated, it followed that if no reasons or wholly deficient reasons were given, an applicant for judicial review was prima facie entitled to have the decision quashed as unlawful, whether or not he could show that he had suffered any prejudice thereby (see p 315 *g h*, p 316 *h*, p 317 *d* to *g* and p 318 *a*, post); dictum of Schiemann J in *R v Tynedale DC, ex p Shield* (1987) 22 HLR 144 at 148–149

b approved.

(2) Although the court could and, in appropriate cases, would admit evidence to elucidate or, exceptionally, correct or add to the reasons given by a housing authority, it would be very cautious about doing so; the function of such evidence would generally be elucidation, not fundamental alteration, as for example where an error had been made in transcription or expression, or a word or words had

c been inadvertently omitted. However, in cases where the reasons stated in the decision letter had been shown to be manifestly flawed, it should only be in very exceptional cases that relief should be refused on the strength of reasons adduced in evidence after the commencement of proceedings, even where it was clear that on reconsideration by the authority the decision would be the same. It followed

d that efforts to secure a discretionary refusal of relief by introducing late evidence of true reasons significantly different from the stated reasons were unlikely to succeed (see p 315 *h* to p 316 *h*, p 317 *d* and p 318 *a*, post); dictum of Steyn LJ in *R v Croydon London Borough, ex p Graham* (1993) 26 HLR 286 at 292 applied; dictum of Rose J in *R v Northampton BC, ex p Carpenter* (1992) 25 HLR 349 at 356 approved.

(3) On the facts, the deputy judge had not approached the decision with those

e principles in mind and had not even considered refusing to determine the application on the basis of the substituted reasons. It followed that since the only reasons given for the decision were defective, in that they were not the true reasons, the appeal would be allowed, the deputy judge's decision set aside, the decision of the housing authority quashed and the case remitted to the council for

f reconsideration (see p 316 *j* to p 317 *b d* and p 318 *a*, post).

Notes

For nature of judicial review, see 1(1) *Halsbury's Laws* (4th edn reissue) para 60.

For accommodation for homeless persons, see 22 *Halsbury's Laws* (4th edn)

g paras 509–513, and for cases on intentional homelessness, see 26(2) *Digest* (2nd reissue) 486–506, 2590–2655.

For the Housing Act 1985, s 64, see 21 *Halsbury's Statutes* (4th edn) (1990 reissue) 103.

Cases referred to in judgments

h *Great Portland Estates plc v Westminster City Council* [1984] 3 All ER 744, [1985] AC 661, [1984] 3 WLR 1035, HL.

Hobbs v Sutton London Borough (1993) 26 HLR 132, CA.

Poyser and Mills' Arbitration, Re [1963] 1 All ER 612, [1964] 2 QB 467, [1963] 2 WLR 1309.

j *R v Croydon London Borough, ex p Graham* (1993) 26 HLR 286, CA.

R v Northampton BC, ex p Carpenter (1992) 25 HLR 349.

R v Swansea City Council, ex p John (1982) 9 HLR 55.

R v Tynedale DC, ex p Shield (1987) 22 HLR 144.

R v Westminster City Council, ex p Bishop (9 February 1993, unreported), QBD; *affd* (1993) 25 HLR 459, CA.

Save Britain's Heritage v Secretary of State for the Environment [1991] 2 All ER 10, sub
nom *Save Britain's Heritage v Number 1 Poultry Ltd* [1991] 1 WLR 153, HL.

Thornton v Kirklees Metropolitan BC [1979] 2 All ER 349, [1979] QB 626, [1979] 3
WLR 1, CA.

R v Westminster City Council, ex p Augustin (1993) 25 HLR 281, CA.

Cases also cited or referred to in skeleton arguments
Lally v Kensington and Chelsea Royal Borough (1980) Times, 27 March.
R v Brent London Borough, ex p McManus (1993) 25 HLR 643.
R v Director of Housing and Community Services, Thurrock BC, ex p Williams (1981) 1
HLR 128.
R v Gloucester City Council, ex p Miles (1985) 17 HLR 292, CA.
R v Gravesham BC, ex p Winchester (1986) 18 HLR 207.
R v Hillingdon London Borough, ex p H (1988) 20 HLR 554.
R v Islington London Borough, ex p Trail [1994] 2 FCR 1261.
R v Reigate and Banstead BC, ex p Paris (1984) 17 HLR 103.
R v Swansea City Council, ex p Hearn (1990) 23 HLR 372.
R v Tower Hamlets London Borough, ex p Monaf (1988) 20 HLR 529, CA.
R v Tower Hamlets London Borough, ex p Ojo (1991) 23 HLR 488.
R v West Dorset DC, ex p Phillips (1984) 17 HLR 336.
R v Woodspring DC, ex p Walters (1984) 16 HLR 73.

Appeal
By notice dated 27 September 1994 the applicant, Andrei Ermakov, appealed
from the decision of Sir Louis Blom-Cooper QC, sitting as a deputy judge of the
High Court in the Queen's Bench Division, on 7 September 1994 dismissing his
application for judicial review of the decision (notified by letter dated 18 January
1994) from the respondents, Westminster City Council, refusing him
accommodation on the ground that his homelessness was intentional for the
purposes of s 64 of the Housing Act 1985. The facts are set out in the judgment
of Hutchison LJ.

John Samuels QC and *Anthony Jerman* (instructed by *Moss Beachley & Mullem*) for
the applicant.
Clive Hugh Jones (instructed by *Colin Wilson*) for the respondents.

HUTCHISON LJ (delivering the first judgment at the invitation of Nourse LJ).
On 7 September 1994 Sir Louis Blom-Cooper QC, sitting as a deputy judge of the
High Court in the Queen's Bench Division, dismissed an application for judicial
review made by Mr Andrei Ermakov by which he sought to have quashed a
decision by Westminster City Council on 18 January 1994 that he and his family
were intentionally homeless. The main issue of law that arises for consideration
on this appeal is whether the judge erred in having regard to reasons for their
decision advanced by the council's principal homelessness officer, Mr Lodge, in
an affidavit, when those reasons were fundamentally different from the reasons
communicated to Mr Ermakov in the council's s 64 letter notifying him of their
decision and the reasons for it. The appeal is brought with the leave of the judge.

The applicant and his family arrived in the United Kingdom by air on 9 July
1993. They remained at the airport for some days but on 14 July applied to the
respondent council to be housed on the ground that they were homeless.
Pursuant to its duty under s 62 of the Housing Act 1985 the respondents

a embarked on inquiries to satisfy themselves whether he was homeless and in priority need—questions not difficult to answer—and whether he had become homeless intentionally, which was, as often happens, the crucial question.

Those inquiries were, of course, made more difficult by the fact that the applicant spoke little English and that the last home he had had was in Greece. The respondents' inquiries continued over some months and, in the course of b them, they addressed letters (which produced no response) to persons in Greece whom they thought might be able to corroborate parts of the applicant's account of why he and his family had left their last home.

However, there came a time, in November 1993, when the respondents asked the applicant to make a written statement in his own language recounting the circumstances in which he left Greece. The judge relied mainly on this statement c when summarising the facts, and I can do no better than rely in turn on his clear summary. The judge said:

'The applicant is a national of the Republic of Uzbekistan (formerly in the USSR). He married Ellada Rentas (a woman of mixed Russian and Greek d parentage) in 1982. Their first child, Ellinika, was born on 2 July 1987. They lived in Tashkent until April 1988, when they moved to Thessalonika in Greece. The move was made partly because of the political climate in Uzbekistan and partly because Mr Ermakov's father-in-law, a man called Kostas Rentas, a Greek national who had returned to Greece after many years' residence in Uzbekistan, had expressed the wish that his daughter e should come to care for him, following a diagnosis that he was suffering from prostate cancer. From the written statement of the applicant to the local authority in August 1993, the following facts emerge. The Ermakovs experienced extreme hostility from Mr Rentas' family, who took the view that the Ermakovs had come to Greece simply to benefit financially from Mr f Rentas and to acquire a share in his estate on his death. The applicant's brother-in-law, Nikas Rentas, threatened Mr Ermakov's life and demanded that the family leave the country. The applicant and the family persevered, however, living in various villages near Mr Ermakov's father-in-law, despite an increasing campaign of harassment from the Rentas family. The g applicant's wife obtained a Greek passport in 1991, she being a Greek national. The applicant recalls many and, he says, increasingly serious incidents as time progressed. He states that extreme pressure was brought to bear on one of his employers to sack him. This culminated in the applicant being assaulted at work, sustaining head injuries and being forced to leave his job. Repeated threats to the life of the applicant and those of his family were h made. He states that on more than one occasion someone tried to run him down in an unmarked car. By the time of the birth of the second daughter in February 1993 the family were in an anxious and distressed state. Mr Ermakov states that he genuinely feared that the death threats made to his wife could soon be carried out. The Ermakovs' last address in Greece was j [an address in Thessalonika]. They discovered that their landlady at that address had been threatened with violence unless she evicted them and was fearful for her own safety. The applicant then received information that Nikas Rentas had "taken out a contract on his life". In a state of fear they decided that they had to leave their accommodation and leave the community altogether. Wishing to leave the country, they considered a return to Uzbekistan, but, because of circumstances occurring there in 1993,

and the applicant, being a Christian, had experienced problems with the
military there and states he had been shot at, they decided not to go to
Uzbekistan. Instead they entered the United Kingdom on 9 July 1993, at
which time they presented themselves to Westminster City Council as
homeless persons.'

The translation of the statement became available to the respondents on 11
January 1994. On 18 January they notified the applicant and his wife of their
decision in a letter from Mr Kevin Humphreys, a homelessness officer. The
material part of that letter reads:

'I have to inform you that upon completion of our enquiries it is the
opinion of this authority;—1. That you are homeless, 2. that you are in
priority need, 3. but, that you are intentionally homeless for the following
reasons;—That you and your family had accommodation to occupy at [the
address in Thessalonika]. This Authority is not satisfied that you and your
family experienced harassment and therefore, it was reasonable for you and
your family to continue to remain in occupation at the above address. This
Authority will therefore not be providing you with alternative accommodation.'

This letter has to be considered in conjunction with the entry made by Mr
Humphreys on the history sheet on 14 January, which reads:

'Discussed case with BL [Mr Lodge]. Applicant's statement returned from
translator. There is no evidence to confirm applicant's story/claims of
harassment or intimidation. Therefore it was reasonable for him to remain
in residence in Greece—his statement and confirmed at personal interview
that he came to UK to make a better life for himself and family. Decision of
IH [intentional homelessness] made by BL.'

It was on the basis of the reasons given in the letter of 18 January for the finding
of intentional homelessness that the application for judicial review was made.
The original grounds were: (1) failure to make adequate inquiries by following
up the letters that had been sent to Greece addressed to the landlord of the
premises the family had occupied and to Mr Rentas, the wife's father;
(2) wrongfully assuming that the lack of response to the letters indicated that the
applicant's claims of harassment were untrue; (3) failing formally to interview
the applicant to test and give him a chance to respond to their concerns about the
veracity of his claims; and (4) failing properly to decide whether or not the
applicant did suffer from the harassment complained of.

It is, in the light of what I am about to say, unnecessary to say anything about
those grounds beyond stating that they persuaded Brooke J to grant leave on 11
May 1994, when he directed that the respondents' affidavits should be filed within
28 days. The notice of motion was dated 20 May. On 27 June Mr Lodge swore
the affidavit on which the main argument before the judge and on this appeal has
focused, and it was presumably served on the applicant's solicitors within a short
time thereafter. The hearing took place on 6 September and the judge gave
judgment on 7 September.

In his affidavit Mr Lodge says that he made the decision, basing himself on the
translation of the statement. He explains in some detail why he concluded that
the matters disclosed in the statement did not make the accommodation in which
the applicant had been living in Greece unreasonable to occupy—or, as it might

a more felicitously have been put, that, notwithstanding the matters disclosed in the statement, he was satisfied that it would have been reasonable for the applicant and his family to continue to occupy the accommodation in Greece. Some of his detailed reasoning would be material in the context of other grounds relied on by the applicant in this appeal but, for the purposes of considering this first and main ground, it is necessary to focus only on the following passage:

b   'I therefore reached the decision of intentional homelessness. I did not consider it necessary to interview Mr Ermakov having received the statement. The statement is detailed and there is no indication that Mr Ermakov may not have put forward the grounds for his application. Nor did I consider it necessary to make any further enquiries. Two letters sent to *c* Greece had not been answered and I relied upon Mr Ermakov's own statement. This was not a case where the Council received conflicting evidence and needed to decide which evidence to choose. It was a case where I was able to make a decision on the basis of a detailed statement. In this regard I took account of the fact that Mr Humphreys had informed me that although Mr Ermakov spoke English, it was preferable for him to put his *d* case in his own language. I have read Mr Humphreys' note for the 14th January 1994 entered by him after I had made the decision. Regretfully that note is an inaccurate record of the reasons for my decision. As his supervising officer I should have checked this part of the notes before the file was disclosed but did not do so.'

e   While it is not, in my view, entirely clear from those paragraphs whether Mr Lodge was in terms accepting the truth of the applicant's account rather than simply reaching his conclusions on an 'even if true' basis, it appears from observations made by the judge that the former was intended, and the hearing proceeded on that basis.

f   There was also an affidavit, sworn on 18 July, in which Mr Humphreys, referring to his having read Mr Lodge's affidavit, laconically accepted that his note of 14 January was inaccurate.

In the course of his arguments in this court Mr Jones, for the respondents, suggested in one way and another that the differences between the reasons given in the decision letter and those deposed to in the affidavit were not particularly *g* significant. I feel it right to state at the outset my view that they were of the greatest significance. The letter, as the judge rightly accepted, 'expressed disbelief in the applicant's story of his abandonment of his last settled accommodation in Greece', and said nothing at all on the question whether, if true, the applicant's account would have made it reasonable for him to leave. *h* The affidavit, on the other hand, accepted the truth of what was said but explained why, in the view of Mr Lodge, the events recounted did not justify the conclusion that it would not have been reasonable for him to continue to occupy the premises in Greece. It is difficult to imagine a starker contrast.

Before the judge, counsel for the applicant objected to the admission of the two *j* affidavits on two grounds. The first was that they were out of time and, while Mr John Samuels QC in his skeleton argument for this appeal has, as it were in passing, sought to revive this point, it seems to me unrealistic to do so; and anyway, assuming the affidavits were otherwise admissible, their admission despite their lateness was a matter for the judge's discretion.

The main ground of objection was the contention that these affidavits were not admissible or, if they were, ought not to have been admitted in the particular

circumstances of this case. The judge was referred to various authorities—Mr
Samuels has referred us to those and others—and he ruled that the evidence was
admissible and ought to be admitted. The judge's reasoning was as follows:

'If what is really challenged is the decision of the local authority for which
reasons must be given, it is the real reasons and not the form in which the
real reasons appear in the decision-letter that is vital. A failure to record
accurately the real reasons cannot shut out from this court's sight, on judicial
review, those real reasons. The decision-maker, who discloses his or her
reasons for the decision, must be allowed to say so, even if those reasons are
palpably inconsistent with the reasons stated formally in the decision-letter.
In this case Mr Lodge did not compose the decision-letter of 18 January 1994.
That was done by Mr Humphreys, his junior officer. Had Mr Lodge been
both the decision-maker and author of the letter, there might be a question
of which of the two versions was the real reason. It might be in that
hypothetical state of affairs that the court would draw an adverse inference
and conclude that the ex post facto affidavit evidence was designed to
remedy a fatal flaw in the reasoning process. With all respect to Steyn LJ's
dictum in *R v Croydon London Borough, ex p Graham* (1993) 26 HLR 286 at 292
[to which I shall come] I do not think there is any question of
discouragement or otherwise to local authorities to supplement material
gaps. What the local authority must do in judicial review proceedings is to
adduce the evidence of its real reasons for its decision. If they depart from
the reasons stated in the decision letter, that fact must be revealed for this
court to determine the reviewability of the reasoned decision ...
Accordingly, I admitted the affidavit evidence of Mr Kevin Humphreys and
Mr Brian Lodge, on the grounds of their testimony about the
decision-making process and about the reasons that Mr Lodge arrived at for
deciding as he did. I should add that I cannot conceive of any circumstances
when it would be right to exclude from judicial review proceedings evidence
of the real reasons for a decision made by a local authority, however much
they might be regarded as supplementary to, and even be an afterthought to
those reasons given to the homeless person at the time of the decision, if only
because the court should never be left in doubt about the real reason. If there
is any doubt about the real reason for a decision, then the applicant must
succeed; the decision would be unlawful. If there is any suspicion that the
deponent of the affidavit is deliberately changing the reasons, the court will
no doubt either cross-examine the deponent in this court or reject the
evidence.'

Characterising the dispute as one of admissibility is perhaps inappropriate.
The respondents' case was that they had wrongly stated a reason which was not
their true reason. Plainly it was incumbent on them to disclose this fact, by one
means or another: it is unthinkable that they should have sought to defend their
decision on a false basis. Some authorities might, perhaps, have simply written
indicating that they conceded that the claim for judicial review must succeed on
the ground that there had been a fundamental failure to comply with the
requirements of s 64 as to the provision of reasons.

However, since the authority chose to disclose the true reasons—and the fact
that the reasons given in the letter were not the true reasons—on affidavit and
wished to continue to contest the proceedings, it was in one sense inevitable that
the judge should admit the affidavits. The real question was not whether they

a   should be admitted, but whether the respondents should be permitted to rely on them and justify the legality of their decision on the basis of them.

There is a good deal of authority which touches on this question. Before considering the cases to which we have been referred, I propose to state briefly what appear to me to be some of the factors of special importance to its resolution in this particular case. They are the following factors.

b   (1) This is a case in which the obligation to give reasons and to give them at the time the decision is communicated is a statutory one. Section 64(4) of the 1985 Act, as material to the present context, provides:

c   'If the local housing authority notify the applicant ... (c) that they are satisfied that he became homeless ... intentionally ... they shall at the same time notify him of their reasons.'

(2) Nowhere in Pt III of the 1985 Act is there any express requirement that the authority shall take a decision on the questions into which s 62 obliges them to inquire. However, that section and s 64 plainly imply such a requirement. The terms of s 64, the marginal note to which reads 'Notification of decision and reasons', to my mind suggest that decision and notification of it are regarded as going very much hand in hand. Of course, it has to be accepted that a decision must always precede notification, for reasons which are obvious. For practical purposes, however, there is much to be said for the view that the decision and its communication to the applicant are contemporaneous.

e   (3) The affidavits of Mr Lodge and Mr Humphreys did not merely correct, amplify or explain the reasons given in the decision letter—they put forward entirely new reasons, completely at odds with those given in the letter. Moreover, they put forward those new reasons five or six months after the decision letter had been sent and, of course, only after judicial review proceedings had been launched.

It is well established that an obligation, whether statutory or otherwise, to give reasons for a decision is imposed so that the persons affected by the decision may know why they have won or lost and, in particular, may be able to judge whether the decision is valid and therefore unchallengeable, or invalid and therefore open to challenge. There are numerous authoritative statements to this effect: see e g

g   *Thornton v Kirklees Metropolitan BC* [1979] 2 All ER 349 at 354, [1979] QB 626 at 638 per Megaw LJ and *R v Croydon London Borough, ex p Graham* (1993) 26 HLR 286 at 291–292 (a case to which further reference will be made), where Sir Thomas Bingham MR said—

h   'I readily accept that these difficult decisions are decisions for the housing authority and certainly a pedantic exegesis of letters of this kind would be inappropriate. There is, nonetheless, an obligation under the [Housing Act 1985] to give reasons and that must impose on the council a duty to give reasons which are intelligible and which convey to the applicant the reasons why the application has been rejected in such a way that if they disclose an error of reasoning the applicant may take such steps as may be indicated.'

I should also refer, though Mr Samuels drew our attention to it in a slightly different context, to the classic statement of Lord Scarman in *Great Portland Estates plc v Westminster City Council* [1984] 3 All ER 744 at 752, [1985] AC 661 at 673:

'*Failure to give reasons.* When a statute requires a public body to give   *a*
reasons for a decision, the reasons given must be proper, adequate and
intelligible. In *Re Poyser and Mills's Arbitration* [1963] 1 All ER 612, [1964] 2
QB 467 Megaw J had to consider s 12 of the Tribunals and Inquiries Act 1958
which imposes a duty on a tribunal to which the Act applies or any minister
who makes a decision after the holding of a statutory inquiry to give reasons
for their decision, if requested. Megaw J commented ([1963] 1 All ER 612 at   *b*
616, [1964] 2 QB 467 at 478): "... Parliament having provided that reasons
shall be given, in my view that must clearly be read as meaning that proper,
adequate, reasons must be given; the reasons that are set out ... must be
reasons which not only will be intelligible, but also can reasonably be said to
deal with the substantial points that have been raised ..."'

c

Starting from this point of principle, Mr Samuels' argument, expressed in its
simplest form, is that it cannot be right to admit, for the purposes of its being
relied on in justification of the decision, such evidence as was admitted in this
case, since to do so nullifies the very objects and advantages underlying the
requirement to provide reasons. He concedes that there are authorities which   *d*
support the proposition that evidence may be admitted to amplify the reasons
given in the decision letter, but he seeks to distinguish them from the present
case, and argues that the weight of authority is against allowing wholly deficient
statutory reasons to be made good by affidavit evidence in the course of
proceedings. I must consider some of the authorities to which he drew our
attention.   *e*

R v Swansea City Council, ex p John (1982) 9 HLR 55, a case on which the judge
relied, concerned a decision of intentional homelessness where the decision letter
in effect gave no reasons at all, since it suggested that the applicant was
intentionally homeless merely because an order for possession had been made for
breach of tenancy conditions—an approach which the judge, Woolf J, said would   *f*
have been wrong. The relevant part of the judgment is as follows (at 63):

'[Counsel for the applicant] says the council, having put their case in that
way on notice to the applicant, are not entitled to refer to the true reasons,
which are the reasons set out in the affidavit of [the officer of the housing
department] which I have read and which are much fuller than the letter of   *g*
17 December. It is right that section 8 of the [Housing (Homeless Persons)
Act 1977] places an obligation upon the authority to give to the applicant the
reasons for their decision. However, it does not seem to me that that is
anything more than a procedural requirement. If a decision is properly
reached then the fact that proper reasons have not been given to an applicant   *h*
does not prevent the council from justifying their decision by reliance upon
the proper reason. Therefore, although I would have taken a different view
if the letter had set out the only reasons of the council on the basis I indicated
earlier in this judgment, on the true reasons of the council I find this
application fails.'

j

Despite the judge's acceptance that this was a case of amplification of reasons, it
does seem to me to be a case which lends support to the proposition that
fundamentally different reasons may be advanced at the hearing and may defeat
an application to quash the decision, the reasons for which in the statutory
notification are inadequate. It cannot, in my judgment, be treated on its facts as
a case of mere amplification and explanation.

a R v Westminster City Council, ex p Bishop (9 February 1993, unreported), a decision of Robert Carnwath QC sitting as a deputy judge of the High Court, was another authority on which the judge placed reliance. That again was a case involving a finding of intentional homelessness, in which the original decision and reasons dated 7 October 1991 were on reconsideration affirmed by a decision taken in February but not communicated to the applicant until July 1992. The

b point taken on reasons was that the July letter did not mention a reason to be found in the February memorandum evidencing the decision. The judge, who was referred to a number of authorities, said:

'In homeless persons cases the courts have, in practice, been prepared to accept evidence, at least to amplify the stated reasons. Generally I would

c adopt what was said by Woolf J ... in R v Swansea City Council, ex p John (1982) 9 HLR 55 ... In this case ... the reasons are clearly stated in the letter and they are generally consistent with the affidavit. The injunction point [that was the additional reason] was considered by the authority, and failure to mention that in the July letter does not, in my view, preclude the court from having regard to it. Accordingly, I do not think that this challenge can succeed on

d the simple ground that the reasons were inadequately stated.'

Ex p Bishop went to appeal, but this point was not considered.

Hobbs v Sutton London Borough (1993) 26 HLR 132 was a case upon which the judge in the present case placed particular reliance. In my view, however, Mr Samuels is right when he submits that it is of only limited significance, since a

e point was not taken on the propriety of admitting further material to supplement the decision letter which admittedly failed to comply with the requirements of s 64(4). All that can be said is that it is an example of a case in which the court did not demur when asked to look at affidavit evidence, to which no objection had been taken by the applicant.

f Mr Samuels referred us to a number of cases which he submitted were authority the other way. Not all of them, in my judgment, are helpful, but some must be referred to as they do provide support for the applicant's argument. The first of these is R v Croydon London Borough, ex p Graham (1993) 26 HLR 286, from which I have already cited a passage in the judgment of Sir Thomas Bingham MR. The headnote includes, in para (2), a statement of principle plainly based on that

g passage, and the following further statement (at 287):

'(3) The idea that material gaps in the reasons can always be supplemented *ex post facto* by affidavit or otherwise ought not to be encouraged.'

h This is obviously based on a passage in the judgment of Steyn LJ, cited to the judge and referred to by him in the present case, as follows (at 292):

'I agree with the reasons of Sir Thomas Bingham M.R. There is only one point on which I would add a few remarks. There was some debate about the obligation under section 64 of the Housing Act 1985 to give reasons. I

j readily accept that the reasons may be very brief and must be read in the context of the matter in question. But to my mind the statutory obligation necessarily imports a duty to furnish adequate reasons for the decision having regard to the issue, or issues, to which the decision relates. In my judgment the idea that material gaps in the reasons can always be supplemented *ex post facto* by affidavit or otherwise ought not to be encouraged. That in effect is what we have been asked to do on behalf of the

council. No doubt questions of the sufficiency of reasons usually involve a
judgment as to matters of degree. Nevertheless it seems to me that if the
reasons are insufficient to enable the court to consider the lawfulness of the
decision the obligation of furnishing reasons has been breached and in that
event the decision itself will be unlawful.'

It is not entirely clear to me from this passage whether Steyn LJ was saying that
reasons can never be supplemented or explained, or that caution should be
exercised in allowing that to happen: it depends on the sense in which one
understands 'always' and 'ought not to be encouraged'. Certainly the concluding
sentence tends to support the former construction. However, construing the
paragraph as a whole, I do not understand Steyn LJ to be saying that reasons can
never be supplemented in evidence. The judgment of Sir Thomas Bingham MR
does not provide further guidance on this point, and Hoffmann LJ, who
dissented, does not refer to this aspect of the case.

The judge in the present case characterised the passage in Steyn LJ's judgment
as an obiter dictum. It is, on the basis of the facts to be gleaned from the report,
not altogether easy to determine whether or not this is correct, and I do not
propose to take time discussing the point. What is undoubted is that Steyn LJ felt
impelled to express his views in the terms that he did, regarding them as material
and important in the context, and those views naturally command great respect.

This authority is generally consistent with a number of previous decisions at
first instance, to some of which I shall refer. However, even without the
assistance which they give, it is possible to state two propositions which the
judgments in *Ex p Graham* support. (1) If the reasons given are insufficient to
enable the court to consider the lawfulness of the decision, the decision itself will
be unlawful; and (2) the court should, at the very least, be circumspect about
allowing material gaps to be filled by affidavit evidence or otherwise.

Of the earlier cases cited by Mr Samuels it seems to me that two are particularly
relevant in the present context. The first is the decision of Schiemann J in *R v
Tynedale DC, ex p Shield* (1987) 22 HLR 144. That was a case where the authority's
decision letter of April 1989 asserted merely that it was under no duty to rehouse
the applicant, having fulfilled its obligation to him when it had rehoused him in
1979. At the judicial review hearing a lengthy affidavit from the senior housing
officer advanced reasons which, as the judge said, 'bore little or no relation to
what appears in the letter'. The judge recorded that he had been told that it was
accepted that the applicant was threatened with homelessness and had a priority
need: these matters had not been dealt with originally or in the affidavits. In the
course of a judgment upholding the applicant's challenge, the judge said (at 148–
149):

'Mr. Stoker, on behalf of the council, submits, first, that the letter of April
29, 1986, is not the decision but the notification of the decision. I have no
evidence from which I can discover who took the decision and when, but Mr
Stoker tells me that the decision was taken by the deponent Stephenson.
Secondly, Mr. Stoker submits that once the decision had been taken, this
could only be challenged for perversity or procedural irregularity in the
decision-making process. The failure to comply with section 64 is of no
relevance to the legality of the decision itself. Thirdly, he submits that the
decision is not one verging on absurdity, nor does it on its face betray an
error of law because, he says, there is no face that I can look at, the decision
having preceded in time the letter. In my judgment, I am entitled to treat the

a   letter of April 29, 1986, as the decision of the authority, just as the court will treat the decision letter of the Secretary of State on an appeal under section 36 of the Town and Country Planning Act 1971 as the decision of the Secretary of State. It is no doubt true in every case that the decision conceptually precedes the communication of that decision in letter form, but it is not permissible for the court, in my judgment, to go behind that letter b   and hear evidence as to what the real reasons were. This is consistent with the general procedure adopted by the courts in relation to administrative decisions in cases where the decision maker is obliged to give reasons for his decision. One of the purposes of requiring the decision maker to state his reasons is to give the recipient of the decision the opportunity of challenging it … I am prepared to accept that the court has jurisdiction not to quash the c   decision if satisfied that there would be no purpose in so doing, having regard to the totality of the evidence before the court. Nevertheless, where a decision letter is manifestly flawed, in general the court would be slow not to quash. In my judgment, in the present case it would be right to quash the decision and I shall do so.'

d   This is a helpful decision. I bear in mind that, in *Ex p Bishop*, the deputy judge, to whom it was cited, cautioned against treating the Town and Country Planning Act 1971 as too close an analogy, for reasons which he explained. Nonetheless, I am attracted by the obvious good sense of treating the decision letter as in practice synonymous with the decision (which seems to me to provide a practical e   answer to the analysis, favoured by Woolf J in *Ex p John*, that the failure to give reasons is merely a procedural defect, not affecting the validity of the decision itself). Moreover, this decision is very much in line with the interpretation of Steyn LJ's observations in *Ex p Graham*, which I have already suggested—that the court should be circumspect about admitting evidence to make good patent defects in the reasons stated in the decision letter.

f   Finally, on this point, there is the decision of Rose J in *R v Northampton BC, ex p Carpenter* (1992) 25 HLR 349. One of the issues arising for consideration was the adequacy of reasons for a finding of intentional homelessness, and the application for judicial review succeeded on the basis that the decision letter was manifestly defective in failing to address the reasons why the applicant had left the previous g   accommodation. In the course of his judgment Rose J recorded that the respondent had relied on Schiemann J's observations in *Ex p Shield* to the effect that, even where the reasons in the decision letter were inadequate, the court might refuse relief if satisfied on all the evidence that no useful purpose would be served by granting it, and he also mentioned the contrary submission for the h   applicant. The judge said, apropos those rival submissions (at 356):

'It may well be that there was material which, when analysed, balanced and considered, would have justified the housing authority in reaching the conclusion which they did. But I have no doubt at all that the letter of decision dated September 25 (paragraph 3) is manifestly defective in failing j   to address the reasons why the applicant had left Edinburgh and to express a decision about them. In my judgment it is not adequate for a local authority to give as a reason so general a phrase as "regard has been given to the general circumstances prevailing in relation to housing in the district of Edinburgh Council" even when coupled with the somewhat contentious phrase, "you chose to leave." If the balancing exercise which Mrs. Treacy [the housing officer] describes as carrying out on the information which was

available to her had been expressed in that letter as having been carried out,
the position would no doubt be different. I am wholly unpersuaded by   *a*
[counsel for the respondents] that the comment by Schiemann J. which I
have cited is, save in very exceptional circumstances, an appropriate
approach to a case of this kind. The whole purpose of section 64 is to enable
someone who is entitled to a decision to see what the reasons are for that
decision and to challenge those reasons if they are apparently inadequate.'   *b*

For the respondents, Mr Jones seeks to support the judge's decision essentially
on the grounds relied on by the judge. I begin by referring to para 7 of his concise
and helpful skeleton argument. Here he argues that, since the council were
bound to state their true reasons, there was no point in the matter being
reconsidered simply so that a correct s 64 notice could be served. The   *c*
requirements of s 64, he argues, are procedural—the decision is one thing, the
notification and reasons another. While the reasons should be intelligible, there
is no reason why they should not be corrected or supplemented. That this can be
done is apparent from the consistent practice of the courts, exemplified by the
cases on which the judge relied, of permitting the reasons to be supplemented—
he relies in particular on *Ex p John*. Any prejudice can be remedied by   *d*
adjournments, orders for cross-examination and costs.

Expanding his submissions in argument before us, Mr Jones made a number of
points. First, he invited us to distinguish the practical from what he described as
the technical position—the court should be deciding real, not technical, issues.
Had the judge not permitted the respondents to rely on the reasons disclosed in   *e*
the affidavit, and simply quashed the order and remitted the matter, this would
have been to allow a technicality to triumph. This was a case in which the details
of the decision had been accurately stated—all that had gone wrong was the
purely technical error of giving the wrong reasons. This could and should be
allowed to be corrected by the affidavit of the decision-maker, whose bona fides   *f*
were not challenged, and who had not written the decision letter.

Then Mr Jones, relying on *Save Britain's Heritage v Secretary of State for the
Environment* [1991] 2 All ER 10, [1991] 1 WLR 153, argued that no prejudice had
been caused, and that this authority in the field of planning law was applicable to
this case. He particularly relied on the speech of Lord Bridge (see [1991] 2 All ER
10 at 23–24, [1991] 1 WLR 153 at 167).   *g*

I cannot accept this argument. That case was one in which the reasons had
been fully and clearly stated by the inspector in his report, and the question was
whether the Secretary of State had adopted those reasons or not and whether, if
he had not, the applicants, a non-statutory conservationist group whose primary
purpose was to stimulate public awareness of what it perceived to be a threat to   *h*
the nation's architectural heritage, were entitled to complain as having been
prejudiced. The issues there were wholly different.

He also referred us to *R v Westminster City Council, ex p Augustin* (1993) 25 HLR
281, a homelessness decision in this court, in which the original decision letter
omitted to mention an important aspect of the reasons, and the court was   *j*
prepared to have regard to a subsequent letter which fully explained the
reasoning. That, however, was a case where the elaboration, as not infrequently
occurs, preceded the launching of proceedings for judicial review. That is a
wholly different case from the present.

Mr Jones also took us to a passage in Wade and Forsyth *Administrative Law* (7th
edn, 1994) pp 258–260, headed 'Failure to state reasons'. All I propose to say

a about that is that it certainly does not support Mr Jones's wide submission that failure to state reasons in cases such as this is a mere technicality.

In the end, as I understood it, Mr Jones was disposed to concede that, while there might be cases in which the court could and should treat inadequacy of reasons or incorrect reasons as being a ground for quashing the decision, it should, where the true reasons were tendered, allow them to be given and decide
b the substantial point in the light of the correction.

These submissions seem to me to disregard the authorities to which we have been referred. Moreover, underlying Mr Jones's approach was the notion that the quashing of the decision for lack of proper reasons was a mere formality, in that it left the authority, in a case such as the present, with no more than a sort of mechanical or formal function to perform: they would simply, tomorrow as it
c were, send a further letter in effect incorporating the reasoning contained in Mr Lodge's affidavit. I do not for a moment accept that that is the correct approach. What was sought by the applicant was not an order of mandamus requiring the authority to give reasons, but an order of certiorari quashing the decision coupled with mandamus directing them to reconsider the application. If such orders are
d granted, they necessarily involve proper reconsideration. Of course the authority are entitled, on that reconsideration, to take account of the information obtained by them in the course of their earlier inquiries; but reconsideration of the decision is not and cannot be a mere formality. In such a case the authority should invite the applicant to make any further representations that he wishes, and should take account of any made by or on his behalf and of any further information obtained
e by them or coming into their possession from some other source. The frequent practice of the courts when orders of this sort are quashed is not to make orders of mandamus directing reconsideration, because it is thought unnecessary to make such orders against responsible local authorities, who can be trusted to do without compulsion what an order would direct them to do. It does not need to
f be said that that practice in no way lessens the obligation that reconsideration entails.

In my judgment the weight of authority to which we have been referred favours the applicant, and I accept the general thrust of Mr Samuels' submissions. My conclusions in relation to this first and main ground of appeal are as follows.
g (1) It is unrealistic to seek to draw any significant distinction, in the context of s 64, between the decision and the communication of the decision with reasons, or to treat the giving of reasons as purely procedural. In reaching this conclusion I am influenced by the fact that the section in terms requires reasons to be given at the same time as the decision is communicated; by Schiemann J's observations in *Ex p Shield*; and by the many cases in which such decisions have been quashed
h for inadequacy of reasons.

(2) The court can and, in appropriate cases, should admit evidence to elucidate or, exceptionally, correct or add to the reasons; but should, consistently with Steyn LJ's observations in *Ex p Graham*, be very cautious about doing so. I have in mind cases where, for example, an error has been made in transcription or
j expression, or a word or words inadvertently omitted, or where the language used may be in some way lacking in clarity. These examples are not intended to be exhaustive, but rather to reflect my view that the function of such evidence should generally be elucidation not fundamental alteration, confirmation not contradiction. Certainly there seems to me to be no warrant for receiving and relying on as validating the decision evidence—as in this case—which indicates that the real reasons were wholly different from the stated reasons. It is not in my

view permissible to say, merely because the applicant does not feel able to
challenge the bona fides of the decision-maker's explanation as to the real
reasons, that the applicant is therefore not prejudiced and the evidence as to the
real reasons can be relied upon. This is because, first, I do not accept that it is
necessarily the case that in that situation he is not prejudiced; and, secondly,
because, in this class of case, I do not consider that it is necessary for the applicant
to show prejudice before he can obtain relief. Section 64 requires a decision and
at the same time reasons; and if no reasons (which is the reality of a case such as
the present) or wholly deficient reasons are given, he is prima facie entitled to
have the decision quashed as unlawful.

(3) There are, I consider, good policy reasons why this should be so. The cases
emphasise that the purpose of reasons is to inform the parties why they have won
or lost and enable them to assess whether they have any ground for challenging
an adverse decision. To permit wholesale amendment or reversal of the stated
reasons is inimical to this purpose. Moreover, not only does it encourage a sloppy
approach by the decision-maker, but it gives rise to potential practical difficulties.
In the present case it was not, but in many cases it might be, suggested that the
alleged true reasons were in fact second thoughts designed to remedy an
otherwise fatal error exposed by the judicial review proceedings. That would
lead to applications to cross-examine and possibly for further discovery, both of
which are, while permissible in judicial review proceedings, generally regarded as
inappropriate. Hearings would be made longer and more expensive.

(4) While it is true, as Schiemann J recognised in *Ex p Shield*, that judicial
review is a discretionary remedy and that relief may be refused in cases where,
even though the ground of challenge is made good, it is clear that on
reconsideration the decision would be the same, I agree with Rose J's comments
in *Ex p Carpenter* that, in cases where the reasons stated in the decision letter have
been shown to be manifestly flawed, it should only be in very exceptional cases
that relief should be refused on the strength of reasons adduced in evidence after
the commencement of proceedings.   Accordingly, efforts to secure a
discretionary refusal of relief by introducing evidence of true reasons significantly
different from the stated reasons are unlikely to succeed.

(5) Nothing I have said is intended to call in question the propriety of the kind
of exchanges, sometimes leading to further exposition of the authority's reasons
or even to an agreement on their part to reconsider the application, which
frequently follow the initial notification of rejection. These are in no way to be
discouraged, occurring, as they do, before, not after, the commencement of
proceedings. They will often make proceedings unnecessary. They are in my
judgment very different from what happened in this case.

I also wish to emphasise that all that I have said is with reference only to the
provisions of s 64 of the 1985 Act.

(6) The judge did not in my view approach the decision, which in the exercise
of his judgment he had to make, with the principles that I consider the authorities
establish in mind. Whereas he should have adopted an approach consistent with
that indicated in the judgment of Steyn LJ in *Ex p Graham*, what he did was to treat
the application as one which he could not even consider rejecting. This is
apparent from the passage in his judgment which I have already cited. I have little
doubt that had the judge approached the matter with the correct principles in
mind he would have concluded that this was not a case in which the respondents

a should be permitted to substitute wholly different reasons and, in reliance on those reasons, seek to justify their decision.

(7) On the first ground I consider that this appeal should succeed, the judge's decision should be set aside, the decision of the authority quashed, and the case remitted for reconsideration on the simple ground that, as the affidavit evidence of the respondents concedes, the only reasons given for the decision are defective,
b in that they are not the true reasons and are not relied on.

I end by saying that, without objection from the parties, we heard argument first on this first and main ground of appeal. In the light of the view that we took on that ground we did not hear argument on, and therefore say nothing about, the other two grounds of appeal relied on by the applicant, which were that the
c judge should have found that the authority had failed to make adequate inquiries as to whether the applicant was intentionally homeless, and that the respondents were not entitled, on the facts disclosed, to be satisfied that he was.

THORPE LJ. I agree.

d
NOURSE LJ. I also agree. Mr Jones has relied strongly on the view expressed by Woolf J in *R v Swansea City Council, ex p John* (1982) 9 HLR 55 at 63 that the obligation imposed on a local housing authority by s 64(4) of the Housing Act 1985 to notify the applicant of their reasons for being satisfied that he became homeless intentionally is nothing more than a procedural requirement; so that if
e a decision is properly reached, the fact that proper reasons have not been given does not prevent the authority from justifying their decision by subsequent reliance on the proper reasons. Accordingly, Mr Jones submits, while a failure properly to notify an applicant of their reasons would expose the authority to an order of mandamus directing them to do so, it can never, or perhaps virtually
f never, expose them to an order of certiorari quashing their decision that he became homeless intentionally. The reasons can always be corrected or supplemented later.

Like Hutchison LJ, I am quite unable to accept a submission in that extreme form. I am in no doubt that Parliament intended that in some circumstances a
g local housing authority's failure properly to notify an applicant of their reasons should invalidate their decision that he had become homeless intentionally. General principles which should guide the court's decision in a particular case have been stated by Hutchison LJ, with whose judgment I am in complete agreement.

h I wish only to add this. The true reason for the council's decision in this case was that although they accepted the applicant's account of the harassment he had experienced in Greece, nevertheless it could not be said that it was not reasonable for him and his family to continue to occupy the accommodation he rented there. However, in the decision letter of 18 January 1994 it was stated that the council were not satisfied that the applicant and his family experienced harassment; in
j other words, that they did not accept the applicant's account. As Hutchison LJ has pointed out, there is a stark contrast between the true reason and the reason stated. More particularly, the reason stated, having been based apparently on the applicant's credibility, a matter essentially for the council, was one which was inherently likely to discourage him from challenging the decision by way of proceedings for judicial review. The true reason, being one which gave rise to a

mixed question of fact and law, would not have had that effect or, at all events, would not have had it to the same extent.

For these reasons, as well as for those stated by Hutchison LJ, it is clear to me that the council's decision cannot stand. The appeal is allowed.

Appeal allowed. Leave to appeal to the House of Lords refused.

L I Zysman Esq   Barrister.

Regia Autonoma de Electricitate Renel v Gulf Petroleum International Ltd

QUEEN'S BENCH DIVISION (COMMERCIAL COURT)

RIX J

10 FEBRUARY 1995

Arbitration – Costs – Security for costs – Claimant ordinarily resident out of the jurisdiction – Arbitration commenced in England – Parties' sole connection with England being their agreement that arbitration should take place there – Whether court having jurisdiction to order security for costs – Whether security for costs should be ordered – Arbitration Act 1950, s 12.

In 1993 R, the electricity utility of Romania, entered a four-year contract for the supply of crude oil with G Ltd, a newly-formed company incorporated in the British Virgin Islands, but with its head office in Puerto Rico. The contract contained an arbitration clause which provided that English law should be used to interpret the agreement and to resolve all claims or disputes arising out of or in connection with the agreement; that any such claim or dispute not settled by negotiation should be determined by arbitration in London; and that any arbitration 'shall be conducted in accordance with the provisions of the English Arbitration Acts as amended from time to time'. In 1994 G Ltd purported to accept R's alleged repudiation of the contract and that led shortly thereafter to the commencement of arbitration proceedings. R applied pursuant to s 12 of the Arbitration Act 1950[a] for security for costs against G Ltd, on the grounds that it was a company ordinarily resident out of the jurisdiction and that there was reason to believe that it would be unable to pay R's costs if R were to be successful in defending the claim. In opposing the application, G Ltd contended principally that in a unique arbitration between two parties who had no connection whatsoever with England, but who had chosen London as a convenient place in which to conduct an arbitration, as a matter of general principle no order for security for costs should be made.

Held – (1) The question whether an arbitration was one in which an order for security for costs was appropriate was to be determined by the parties' intention derived from the arbitration agreement itself, in particular the kind of arbitral procedure which the parties had envisaged, and whether the making of an order for security for costs would be consistent with the nature of the agreement. In the circumstances, the invocation of English arbitration law was express and not merely consequential upon the choice of London as the arbitration forum, and while the instant case was not the normal maritime or commodity arbitration case found so commonly in London, it was nevertheless a case in which the parties had expressly embraced the arbitration law of England, including the power to order security for costs (see p 323 *j*, p 324 *g* to p 325 *g*, post); *Coppée Lavalin SA/NV v Ken-Ren Chemicals and Fertilizers Ltd (in liq), Voest-Alpine AG v Ken-Ren Chemicals and Fertilizers Ltd (in liq)* [1994] 2 All ER 449 considered.

---

a   Section 12, so far as material, provides in relation to arbitration proceedings: '... (6) The High Court shall have ... the same power of making orders in respect of—(a) security for costs ... as it has for the purpose of and in relation to an action or matter in the High Court ...'

(2) Although there was no evidence that G Ltd was insolvent, there was no guarantee that it would, unless supported by its associate companies, have sufficient assets against which to enforce an order for costs in the arbitration proceedings. Since the instant case was one where a respondent in an arbitration had asked for security for costs against a foreign claimant where that claimant was of uncertain means, the application for security had been made in reasonable time and there was nothing about the merits of the case to affect the exercise of the court's discretion one way or the other, an order for security for costs would be made in the sum of £200,000. The application would therefore be allowed (see p 326 *f*, p 327 *g* and p 328 *b c h*, post).

Notes

For power of the court to award security for costs in arbitration proceedings, see 2 *Halsbury's Laws* (4th edn reissue) para 677, and for cases on the subject, see 3(1) *Digest* (2nd reissue) 430–431, 3484–3486.

For the Arbitration Act 1950, s 12, see 2 *Halsbury's Statutes* (4th edn) (1992 reissue) 585.

Cases referred to in judgment

Bank Mellat v Helliniki Techniki SA [1983] 3 All ER 428, [1984] QB 291, [1983] 3 WLR 783, CA.

Coppée Lavalin SA/NV v Ken-Ren Chemicals and Fertilizers Ltd (in liq), Voest-Alpine AG v Ken-Ren Chemicals and Fertilizers Ltd (in liq) [1994] 2 All ER 449, [1995] 1 AC 38, [1994] 2 WLR 631, HL.

Flender Werft AG v Aegean Maritime Ltd [1990] 2 Lloyd's Rep 27.

K/S A/S Bani v Korea Shipbuilding and Engineering Corp [1987] 2 Lloyd's Rep 445, CA.

Porzelack KG v Porzelack (UK) Ltd [1987] 1 All ER 1074, [1987] 1 WLR 420.

Cases also cited or referred to in skeleton arguments

Aeronave SpA v Westland Charters Ltd [1971] 3 All ER 531, [1971] 1 WLR 1445, CA.

Behbehani v Salem [1989] 2 All ER 143, [1989] 1 WLR 723, CA.

Brink's-MAT Ltd v Elcombe [1988] 3 All ER 188, [1988] 1 WLR 1350, CA.

Crozat v Brogden [1894] 2 QB 30, [1891–4] All ER Rep 686, CA.

Janred (orse Jenred) Properties Ltd v Ente Nazionale Italiano per il Turismo [1986] 1 FTLR 14, CA.

Mayer Newman & Co Ltd v Al Ferro Commodities Corp SA, The John C Helmsing [1990] 2 Lloyd's Rep 290, CA.

National Bank of Sharjah v Dellborg (1992) Times, 24 December, [1992] CA Transcript 1050.

Parkinson (Sir Lindsay) & Co Ltd v Triplan Ltd [1973] 2 All ER 273, [1973] QB 609, CA.

Trident International Freight Services Ltd v Manchester Ship Canal Co [1990] BCLC 263, CA.

Summons

By summons dated 12 December 1994 the plaintiff, Regia Autonoma de Electricitate Renel (Renel), the state electricity authority of Romania, applied pursuant to s 12 of the Arbitration Act 1950 for an order that the defendant, Gulf Petroleum International Ltd (Gulf), a company incorporated in the British Virgin Islands, provide security for Renel's costs in defending a claim made by Gulf in *a* arbitration proceedings between the parties arising from a contract dated 24 February 1993, the agreed place of arbitration being London. The application was heard and the judgment was given in chambers. The case is reported by permission of Rix J. The facts are set out in the judgment.

Mark Pelling (instructed by *Paisner & Co*) for Renel.

b *Stanley Brodie QC* and *Joanna Pollard* (instructed by *Dibb Lupton Broomhead*) for Gulf.

RIX J. This is an application pursuant to s 12 of the Arbitration Act 1950 for security for costs in an arbitration which is taking place before Sir Patrick Neill QC as sole arbitrator here in London and due for hearing on 29 March 1995.

c The arbitration in question is between Gulf Petroleum International Ltd as claimants (whom I shall refer to as 'Gulf') and Regia Autonoma de Electricitate Renel as respondents (whom I shall refer to as 'Renel'). Gulf is a comparatively recently formed company incorporated in the British Virgin Islands, but apparently with its head office in Puerto Rico, which is part of a group of

d companies which, inter alia, operate some 270 petrol stations in Puerto Rico together with two oil refineries there. Renel are in effect the electricity utility of Romania. The arbitration in question arises out of a contract between those parties dated 24 February 1993 which in essence provided for the supply by Gulf to Renel of crude oil shipments to be paid for by the counter-supply by Renel to Gulf of refined petroleum products to the value of 70% of the crude oil shipments

e and otherwise by payments in Romanian lei and dollars. That contract was due to last for four years.

On 5 April 1994 Gulf purported to accept Renel's alleged repudiation of that contract and that led shortly thereafter to the commencement of the arbitration and to the service of points of claim in that arbitration on 24 June 1994. The

f pleadings, which were closed with service of points of reply on 30 September 1994, but have also gone through amendments and the service of subsequent further and better particulars, are quite lengthy and I will not attempt to summarise them in this judgment. It appears, however, that at any rate one essential point at issue in the arbitration is whether Gulf was entitled to accept Renel's failure to provide a cash deposit in Romanian lei of 175% of the sale price

g of the anticipated first shipment under the contract, as the failure of a condition precedent entitling Gulf to terminate the contract on the basis of Renel's repudiation of it.

Mr Stanley Brodie QC, who appeared on behalf of Gulf, submits that the essential issues in the arbitration are very simple and that upon examination they

h are clearly in Gulf's favour, so that he is entitled to say, as he submits, that there is such an apparent preponderance of merit in Gulf's favour that I should take that factor into account for the purpose of exercising my discretion in respect of this application for security for costs. However, in *Porzelack KG v Porzelack (UK) Ltd* [1987] 1 All ER 1074 at 1077, [1987] 1 WLR 420 at 423 Browne-Wilkinson V-C

j said:

'Undoubtedly, if it can clearly be demonstrated that the plaintiff is likely to succeed, in the sense that there is a very high probability of success, then that is a matter that can properly be weighed in the balance. Similarly, if it can be shown that there is a very high probability that the defendant will succeed, that is a matter that can be weighed. But for myself I deplore the attempt to

go into the merits of the case unless it can be clearly demonstrated one way
or another that there is a high degree of probability of success or failure.'

I take into account not only that well-known dictum, but also the fact that I am
concerned in this case not with a piece of litigation before the courts, but with an
arbitration which is before a separate and consensual tribunal. It is that tribunal
(Sir Patrick Neill QC) which bears the burden of the reference in that arbitration
and in whose sole jurisdiction the task of deciding the merits between the parties
lies. Unless, therefore, this were such a case as might have led Gulf to come
directly to this court in effect to say that there is no dispute between the parties,
then it seems to me that I would be trespassing on the arbitrator's jurisdiction to
attempt to decide the discretionary question of this application for security for
costs by reference to the merits in the arbitration.

Having looked briefly at the pleadings in the arbitration and at some essential
documents which Mr Brodie has brought to my attention, I will say nothing
further than that I put out of account for the purpose of this application any
question of the merits in the arbitration and I say nothing whatsoever about
them.

The next matter which I should mention, and which Mr Brodie has put at the
forefront of his submissions in opposition to Renel's application for security for
costs, is the comparatively recent decision in the House of Lords in *Coppée Lavalin
SA/NV v Ken-Ren Chemicals and Fertilizers Ltd (in liq), Voest-Alpine AG v Ken-Ren
Chemicals and Fertilizers Ltd (in liq)* [1994] 2 All ER 449, [1995] 1 AC 38.

Mr Brodie relies upon that decision for the submission that, in what he
describes as a unique or 'one-off' type of arbitration between two parties who
have no connection whatsoever with England, but who merely happen to have
chosen London as a convenient place in which to conduct an arbitration, as a
matter of general principle, for the reasons set out in particular in Lord Mustill's
and Lord Woolf's speeches in *Coppée Lavalin*, no order for security for costs
should be made in this case. He relies in particular on certain dicta in *Coppée
Lavalin* which he submits are free from and go beyond the factual position in that
case (which was that there the arbitration agreement provided for arbitration in
London in accordance with the Rules of Conciliation and Arbitration of the
International Chamber of Commerce (the ICC)). In particular, he refers me to
where Lord Mustill said ([1994] 2 All ER 449 at 468, [1995] AC 38 at 62–63):

> 'The first step must therefore be to identify, so far as is possible, the kind of
> arbitral procedure which the parties have envisaged. Mainly, this will be
> concerned with proceedings within the arbitration itself. Often the answer
> may be given directly by the incorporation of a set of standard arbitration
> rules. In other instances the combination of the choice of venue with the
> nature of the subject matter will yield an implied choice. For example, in the
> days before maritime arbitration became the subject of published
> contractual rules, the choice in a charterparty case of London arbitration
> coupled with a provision that the arbitrators were to be commercial men
> would be a very strong indication that the procedures were to take that
> informal shape which had been commonplace in the resolution of such
> disputes in London for many years. Similarly, in the small minority of cases
> where the assistance of the court is invoked because the procedures in a trade
> arbitration are said to have gone amiss, the parties by choosing London as a
> venue might fairly be said to have expected the court to follow the generally
> permissive approach to deviations from the procedural norm which the

a English courts have adopted in relation to such arbitrations for many decades.'

He also relies on a passage where Lord Mustill said ([1994] 2 All ER 449 at 470, [1995] 1 AC 38 at 65):

b 'But I believe that in any case which is out of the ordinary the court should pause and look carefully for considerations which point the other way; and, in particular, should have regard to the particular type of arbitration in the course of which the application is brought.'

He also relies on passages in Lord Woolf's speech such as where Lord Woolf refers to 'whether this is a sufficiently exceptional case to justify departing from
c what should be the normal approach to ordering security for costs in arbitrations of this nature', and then where he said:

'Unfortunately, however, the majority of arbitration agreements, particularly where they are of an international character of the type which is
d being considered here, do not make clear what are the parties' intentions with regard to exercise of the power of the High Court, contained in s 12(6)(a), to make an order for security of costs. In those circumstances, the court has no alternative but to exercise the power in a manner which it deems most closely accords with what would have been likely to have been agreed to be the appropriate approach by the parties if they had been
e required to deal with the question. This is of particular importance in relation to an order for security of costs since it is an order which is not normally an incident of litigation in the courts in this country and a type of order which is without a counterpart in many jurisdictions. It cannot therefore be readily assumed that the power to make such an order was a
f power which the parties intended should be exercised when they entered into the arbitration agreement. This is so even if, as here, the parties have by electing London as the seat of the arbitration made it clear that in general English legal procedure should apply to the conduct of the arbitration. When faced with an application for security in relation to such an arbitration, the general approach of the courts has to be to look at all the circumstances
g and to ask whether it is consistent with the nature of the arbitration agreement for an order for security for costs to be made.' (See [1994] 2 All ER 449 at 472, 473, [1995] 1 AC 38 at 66, 67–68.)

Mr Brodie in particular drew my attention to that sentence in the passage which I have just cited in which Lord Woolf contemplates that the mere election
h of London as the seat of arbitration, while making it clear that in general English legal procedure should apply to the conduct of the arbitration, is not in itself an answer to the question of whether the arbitration in question is one in which it is appropriate (save in exceptional circumstances) to order security for costs.

Before stating my conclusion upon Mr Brodie's reliance on such dicta in *Coppée*
j *Lavalin*, I should refer to the terms of the arbitration clause in question in this case, particularly as those dicta make it clear that it is the intention which is sought to be derived from the arbitration agreement itself which is critical to the correct approach of the court to the question of its powers and discretion. The arbitration agreement in this case is contained in cl 29 of the contract and that reads as follows :

'The proper law of the agreement is the law of England and English law shall be used for interpreting the Agreement and for resolving all claims or disputes arising out of or in connection with the Agreement (whether based in contract, in tort or on any other legal doctrine). Any such claim or dispute not settled by negotiation shall be determined by arbitration in London before a single arbitrator to be agreed by the parties or failing agreement upon the appointment of an arbitrator within 14 days of either party requesting arbitration[. T]he arbitrator shall be appointed by the President for the time being of the International Petroleum Exchange or if he should fail to make such appointment within 21 days of a request by either party to make such appointment, then by the High Court of Justice in London pursuant to the Arbitration Act 1950. The arbitration shall be conducted in accordance with the provisions of the English Arbitration Acts as amended from time to time and in the English language. Neither party shall make an application to the High Court of Justice for Leave to Appeal pursuant to Section 1 of the Arbitration Act 1979 against any final award made by the Arbitrator agreed upon or as appointed in accordance with the provisions hereof.'

It will be noted from the terms of that clause that this is not a comparatively simple arbitration agreement which refers to London merely as the seat of an arbitration, perhaps, as in *Coppée Lavalin* itself, pursuant to some international set of arbitration rules. It is a comprehensive acceptance of the relevance and importance of the substantive law of England and the arbitration law of England. It expressly provides that the arbitration shall be conducted in accordance with the provisions of the English Arbitration Acts as amended from time to time. It expressly provides for the President of the International Petroleum Exchange, which is based in London, to appoint an arbitrator in the absence of agreement, or if he should fail to make such an appointment then it is to be done by the High Court of Justice in London. Moreover, it is not entirely the case that the parties are unconnected with London. Gulf has a London office, sometimes referred to as its liaison office in London, and the address of that office is printed upon its stationery.

It seems to me that, although the contract in this case is not like those standard charterparty or commodity contracts which contain within themselves standard arbitration clauses providing for arbitration in London, nevertheless this is a contract concerning the supply of crude oil, a commodity concerning which arbitration in London frequently takes place, and in any event it seems to me that the arbitration agreement in this case is well described in the language which Bingham LJ used in *K/S A/S Bani v Korea Shipbuilding and Engineering Corp* [1987] 2 Lloyd's Rep 445 at 453, where he said, in relation to the contract in that case:

'(3) Although acknowledging that the incorporation of English law and the service provision distinguish this case from *Bank Mellat v Helliniki Techniki SA* ([1983] 3 All ER 428, [1984] QB 291), the learned Judge does not appear to have treated these features as being of any weight. In my view the *Bank Mellat* judgments do treat these as weighty considerations, going to show that the parties are not arbitrating here as a mere convenience or simply because it is a neutral forum, but because they intend to embrace the English legal system. (4) There is no real evidence to support the conclusion that the parties chose to come here for reasons of mere convenience. It is true that the builders' solicitor deposes to that effect, but he appears to be a   drawing an inference from the contract and I think the correct inference is the opposite one.'

Although those words were stated in respect of an arbitration agreement which in that case was referred to as providing for a type of maritime arbitration which has for many years and regularly been conducted in London, it seems to me that those words mutatis mutandis well describe the effect of the special
b   clause agreed in this case. It seems to me that these considerations fit well with what Lord Mustill had said in the *Coppée Lavalin* case [1994] 2 All ER 449 at 468, [1995] 1 AC 38 at 62, where he said: 'The first step must therefore be to identify, so far as is possible, the kind of arbitral procedure which the parties have envisaged.'

c   I would also draw attention to the importance in *Coppée Lavalin* of the context in which their Lordships' speeches were framed, namely the context of an arbitration clause which only invoked English arbitration law implicitly by reference to the choice of London as the forum of arbitration, but which expressly incorporated the ICC arbitration rules. In the present case, however, the invocation of English arbitration law is express and not merely consequential
d   upon the choice of London as forum. Moreover, it is important to note that Lord Mustill considered that the incorporation of the ICC rules in the *Coppée Lavalin* case was of particular importance for the context of that case ([1994] 2 All ER 449 at 469, [1995] 1 AC 38 at 63):

e   'More than this they have signified that although the arbitration must perforce be physically located somewhere, it is the invariable framework of the ICC rather than the diverse local laws and practices which is to form the context within which the dispute is resolved. I would go further, and assert that the choice of ICC arbitration is an indication that the parties are looking for a relationship with particular national courts which is less closely coupled
f   than would otherwise be the case.'

For these reasons I take account of the fact that this is not perhaps the normal maritime or commodity arbitration case which is found so commonly in London, but is nevertheless a case in which the parties have embraced the arbitral law of England in its full panoply.
g   The next question that I must consider is the question of Gulf's means or, as Mr Pelling on behalf of Renel would put it, its insolvency. In this case Renel rely for their application not only on RSC Ord 23, r 1 and the fact that Gulf is ordinarily resident out of the jurisdiction, which is not in dispute, but also on s 726(1) of the Companies Act 1985, under which it is necessary for the court's
h   jurisdiction that it appears by credible testimony that there is reason to believe that the company will be unable to pay the defendant's costs if successful in his defence.

There is in truth very little evidence before me concerning Gulf's means. It was only incorporated on 19 January 1993. Its first major contract, that with
j   Renel, ended in disarray without the shipment of any oil under it, and has led to this arbitration. A Dun & Bradstreet report procured by Renel on Gulf indicates that nothing, in effect, is known about it. It is without apparent assets and indeed, subject to one further matter, I do not think that that is in dispute. What Mr Brodie says is that it is supported by funds from the successful group of which it is a part and also (and this is the matter which I was indicating just a moment ago) that it has one other very important contract, namely, a very long-term contract

with the Bucharest municipal authority for the creation of a chain of petrol
stations in Bucharest.

That contract was entered into on 4 August 1994, shortly after a hearing before
Sir Patrick Neill in the arbitration in these proceedings on 19 July 1994 at which
the solicitor then temporarily representing Renel stated that Renel were minded
to apply for security for costs against Gulf. Mr Brodie relies upon that contract
and its timing to submit that it is good evidence of Gulf's bona fides and,
moreover, he relies upon the work being performed under that contract to
submit, on the basis of evidence before me in the affidavit of Michael Komissar,
that Gulf is building up assets within Romania which would be available to Renel
in the event of an order in Renel's favour for costs arising out of the arbitration.

The effect of the evidence of Mr Komissar is that Gulf, together with its
associated companies, has to date invested $US1m in the petrol station project in
Bucharest, and that by the end of 1995 some ten petrol stations will have been
built, at a cost of something in the region of $1m each, so that by that time a total
of some $10m will have been invested in the project.

In my judgment these submissions are to the point, and if I were confident that
the investment of which Mr Komissar speaks was one which had led, or would
by the end of the first half of 1995 have led, to a situation where Gulf in its own
name had net realisable assets in Romania upon which Renel could enforce an
order for costs, then I would accept that there was no need for Renel to have
additional security in this case. But on the evidence before me, which refers to
this investment being done by Gulf together with its associated companies and
which also gives me very little, if any, insight into the net asset position of Gulf in
Romania, I feel, in my judgment, that I cannot place any particular reliance upon
those matters.

I am therefore prepared to look upon Gulf as being a company which is not
insolvent (there is no evidence to that effect), which is in essence being supported
by its associate companies, which is an active company in good standing, but
which nevertheless may well not have, unless it is supported by its associate
companies, assets with which to meet an order for costs in the arbitration if it is
unsuccessful there.

The next matter which I must consider is Mr Brodie's submission that an order
for security for costs is inappropriate in this case because, at the hearing before Sir
Patrick Neill on 19 July 1994 when Renel's solicitor made mention of the prospect
of an application for security for costs, Sir Patrick, in response to a brief
submission by Mr Brodie that such an order for security for costs was
inappropriate in the present case, indicated that he agreed. It is submitted that I
should pay regard to that expression of opinion and decline to make an order
upon the present application. It is clear from what Mr Brodie has told me about
the context of his submissions on that occasion that Sir Patrick's comment had
nothing to do with the merits in the arbitration, indeed points of defence had not
yet been served on that occasion, but rather with Mr Brodie's submission along
the lines of that which he has made before me based on the *Coppée Lavalin* case,
that this was the kind of international arbitration between foreign parties with no
connection with England which meant that an order for security for costs should
in principle not be made.

However, as Mr Brodie has frankly accepted before me, on the material before
Sir Patrick Neill on that occasion all that he knew about the parties was that they
were both in a very large way of business. Against the background of the contract
in this case, providing as it did for four years' supply of large quantities of crude

a oil, I could well imagine that Sir Patrick considered that there was no question or need for any protection for Renel in terms of security for their costs.

I have of course the greatest respect for Sir Patrick's immense experience in international arbitration, but it seems to me that Mr Pelling is right in his submission that the question of security for costs is one for my decision, one that is not within the jurisdiction of an arbitrator, and is a matter which I must deal *b* with on the material and submissions before me today, which clearly go much further and wider than the brief submissions made to Sir Patrick on that occasion.

Mr Brodie next submitted that security for costs should not be ordered in this case because Renel had delayed in their application. The brief chronology relevant to that submission is as follows. The matter of security for costs was raised before the arbitrator at the hearing which I have mentioned on 19 July *c* 1994. At that time Renel had no London solicitors and it was known by all concerned that Mr Lionel Bloch, who appeared before Sir Patrick on that day, did so only as a matter of convenience and courtesy and because he can speak Romanian, and was immediately bowing out of the picture. It was contemplated, however, and indeed ordered by Sir Patrick, that London solicitors be appointed *d* and nominated to Gulf within two weeks. Renel failed to do that, and indeed failed to notify Gulf of the appointment of Messrs Paisner & Co as their London solicitors until 15 September 1994, the day on which their points of defence were served.

Nothing further was heard about security for costs until 18 October 1994 when Paisner & Co wrote to Gulf's Israeli lawyers requesting such security. The *e* matter was then debated in correspondence between the parties. By a letter of 31 October Gulf made it clear that its position was that Renel must go to court in order to obtain security. There was then a pause of a few weeks until 23 November 1994 when, by a letter of that date, Paisner & Co took up the matter again and asked if Gulf were willing to accept service of proceedings. Gulf made *f* it clear that it was not willing to do so and so on 7 December 1994 Renel initiated this application by seeking and obtaining leave ex parte to issue their originating summons and to serve it out of the jurisdiction upon Gulf.

On 12 December the summons was issued; on 21 December the affidavit in support of that application was served; on 6 January the summons was served on Gulf; on 8 February Gulf served its affidavit in response, and this hearing takes *g* place on 10 February.

In my judgment there has been no such delay in this case as to render it inequitable that Renel's application for security for costs should be dealt with on what is otherwise its merits. Although a certain amount of time has gone by since the question of security for costs was first raised, nevertheless this is an arbitration *h* which was only commenced in the middle of last year and which is on course for hearing at the end of March 1995. In that context and bearing in mind, as I do, certain difficulties which Renel's London solicitors may have had in obtaining instructions from their clients in Romania, and in any event, I think that the question of security has been brought on without any unreasonable delay. Nor *j* is it submitted that there is any particular prejudice caused to or suffered by Gulf as a consequence of the timetable which I have outlined. On the contrary, that timetable might have been significantly shortened if Gulf had been willing to forgo the need to obtain leave for service out of the jurisdiction and to effect that service upon it.

Moreover, the material before me as to the quantum of costs in question indicates that the real burden of the expense in preparation for the hearing of this arbitration is only taking place in the months immediately leading up to the hearing, the position being that as of 21 December 1994 on Renel's figures the costs expended amounted to some £47,000; on Gulf's figures that would be a figure of some £40,000; whereas on Renel's figures the estimated costs to the conclusion of the arbitration are a further £266,000 or, on Gulf's figures, a further £95,000 odd.

In these circumstances it seems to me that this is a not untypical case where a respondent in an arbitration or a defendant in litigation asks for security for costs against a foreign plaintiff or claimant where that plaintiff or claimant is of uncertain means, where the application for security has been made in reasonable time, where there is nothing about the merits of the case to affect the exercise of my discretion one way or the other, and in those circumstances, having considered carefully the full and helpful submissions made before me on both sides, it seems to me that I should make an order for security for costs in favour of Renel in this case.

So far as the quantum is concerned, there is a great difference between the parties' figures. A substantial measure of that difference is due to a difference of £75,000 in respect of the estimated costs of expert witnesses. It seems to me that taking a broad brush, as I have been invited to do, and bearing in mind that the basis upon which the £100,000 estimated as expert witness fees has not in my view been sufficiently established before me, I can say that the figure in respect of which I will make an order in this case is £200,000.

I should add that there is no question in this case of the application for security for costs being used to oppress Gulf or to stifle this claim. Mr Brodie has very fairly told me that if, contrary to his submissions on principle upon the details of the case, I were minded to make an order for security for costs, that order would be complied with and there would be no delay consequent upon the order to the progress of this arbitration.

Finally, I should mention Mr Brodie's submission that I should order counter-security from Renel in respect of the estimated arbitration fees of $85,000 on the basis of the approach to be found in cases such as *Flender Werft AG v Aegean Maritime Ltd* [1990] 2 Lloyd's Rep 27 and other cases mentioned in that report. This, however, is not a case such as can be found in those decisions where it is a matter of happenstance as to which of the parties became claimant and which respondent counterclaimant; nor is it a case in which Renel's counterclaim adds anything at all to its defence. In those circumstances I do not accede to Mr Brodie's submission that I should make such counter-security a term of the security for costs which I order.

In the result, therefore, I accede to this application in the sum of £200,000 and I will hear the parties as to the precise form in which I should make that order.

Order accordingly.

K Mydeen Esq   Barrister.

Penny v Penny

a

COURT OF APPEAL, CIVIL DIVISION

BUTLER-SLOSS AND HUTCHISON LJJ

b

2, 22 NOVEMBER 1995

Divorce – Costs – Security for wife's costs – Judgment in ancillary proceedings – Husband ordered to make periodical payments and pay costs of proceedings – Husband leaving England and removing assets from jurisdiction – Wife's solicitors applying for security for untaxed costs – Husband applying for downward variation of periodical payments – Whether court having jurisdiction to order security for costs after judgment.

c

d In divorce proceedings issued by the wife, the husband applied for ancillary relief. The order made on the ancillary application included the disposition of the former matrimonial home and division of the equity and required the husband to make periodical payments to the wife. The husband was ordered to pay the costs of the ancillary proceedings, and was subsequently ordered to pay the costs of his appeal. The former matrimonial home was sold, and the husband revealed his

e intention to move abroad. He removed virtually all of his assets out of the country and instructed his solicitors to apply to vary downwards the periodical payments order. The wife's solicitors took a number of steps to safeguard their client's wife's position over the untaxed costs, and in particular applied for security for those costs in the estimated sum of £11,500, on the grounds of the husband's imminent departure from England and the fear that he might not pay

f the costs. At the hearing of the wife's application, the husband was ordered to provide security for the costs potentially arising on taxation of the wife's bill of costs, and his application for variation of the order for periodical payments was stayed until such provision. The judge upheld that order on appeal, and the husband appealed to the Court of Appeal, contending principally that the judge

g had lacked jurisdiction to make the order.

Held – An application for security for costs which was directed exclusively to past costs ordered after judgment could not be made where there were no pending proceedings upon which a stay could be imposed and, equally, could not be made

h in respect of such costs using the sanction of a stay on future separate proceedings, since security for costs was not intended as a remedy for the enforcement of costs already incurred in respect of proceedings which had come to an end. On the facts, the husband's variation application, while dependent on the divorce petition for its existence, was nevertheless a separate proceeding and

j the judge therefore lacked jurisdiction to make the order. Moreover, even if the judge had jurisdiction, the order made was not reasonable or just in the circumstances, since (i) the bill of costs had not been taxed and the husband's obligation to pay the costs had not yet arisen, and (ii) there was no evidence before the court that the husband had failed or refused to honour his obligations or that he was not going to pay. The appeal would accordingly be allowed (see p 332 *g j* to p 333 *g j*, post).

Notes

For security for costs in general, see 37 *Halsbury's Laws* (4th edn) paras 298–305, and for cases on the subject, see 37(2) *Digest* (Reissue) 428–436, *2615–2673*.

Cases referred to in judgments

Brown v Haig [1905] 2 Ch 379.
Procon (GB) Ltd v Provincial Building Co Ltd [1984] 2 All ER 368, [1984] 1 WLR 557, CA.

Cases also cited or referred to in skeleton arguments

B (infants), Re (Note) [1965] 2 All ER 651, [1965] 1 WLR 946.
Parkinson (Sir Lindsay) & Co Ltd v Triplan Ltd [1973] 2 All ER 273, [1973] QB 609, QBD and CA.
Porzelack KG v Porzelack (UK) Ltd [1987] 1 All ER 1074, [1987] 1 WLR 420.
Taly NDC International NV v Terra Nova Insurance Co Ltd (Chandler Hargreaves Whittall & Co Ltd, third party) [1986] 1 All ER 69, [1985] 1 WLR 1359, CA.

Appeal

By notice dated 23 May 1995 the respondent husband, Robert Timothy Penny, appealed with leave from the order of Judge Cotton made in the York County Court on 26 April 1995, whereby he dismissed the husband's appeal from the decision of District Judge Elliot made on 16 March 1995 ordering that he provide security for the untaxed costs of the petitioner wife, Jane Anne Penny, incurred on an application for ancillary relief in divorce proceedings on which an order for periodical payments had been made on 21 December 1993, and that his application for variation of the order for periodical payments be stayed until such security was provided. The facts are set out in the judgment of Butler-Sloss LJ.

Patrick Hamlin (instructed by *Ashworth Tetlow & Co,* York) for the husband.
Simon Jack (instructed by *Denison Till,* York) for the wife.

Cur adv vult

22 November 1995. The following judgments were delivered.

BUTLER-SLOSS LJ. This is an appeal by a former husband from the order of Judge Cotton on 26 April 1995 in the York County Court dismissing an appeal from an order for security for costs made by District Judge Elliot on 16 March 1995.

The parties, who are now divorced but whom, for convenience, I shall call 'husband' and 'wife', were married on 21 September 1974. The wife issued a divorce petition on 20 January 1993 in which she claimed ancillary relief. She continued to live in the former matrimonial home and did not apply for any financial provision to be made to her. The husband issued an application for ancillary relief on 30 March 1993. A district judge heard the application and made an order on 21 December 1993 and the decree was made absolute on the following day. The order included the disposition of the former matrimonial home either by transfer to the husband or by sale and division of the equity. The wife was to receive a lump sum of £65,000. The husband was ordered to pay periodical payments to the wife and to pay the costs of the ancillary relief proceedings. The husband's appeal against the order was heard by a circuit judge on 5 May 1994 and the husband was ordered to pay the costs of the appeal. The

a parties were in dispute over the contents of the house which required the help of
their solicitors. The house was sold on 21 December 1994. On 14 February 1995
the wife and her solicitors heard for the first time that the husband was moving
to live and work in Indonesia. He removed virtually all his assets out of the
country. He instructed his solicitors to apply to vary downwards the order for
periodical payments and they informed the wife's solicitors of the proposed
b variation application. The husband left England for Indonesia on 3 March.

The wife's solicitors took four steps to safeguard the wife's position over the
untaxed costs. They wrote asking for reassurance that the costs would be paid
and did not receive that assurance. They prepared the bill, lodged it on 2 March
and received an early date for taxation. The solicitors also issued an application
for security for costs in the estimated sum of £11,500. The affidavit in support of
c the application for security for costs sworn by the solicitor on 3 March recited the
fact of the husband's imminent departure from England and the fear that he
might not pay the costs. The solicitor did not know that the variation application
had been issued on the same day and the affidavit did not refer to, or apply for,
security for costs in respect of the impending proceedings. The solicitors also
d issued an application for injunctive relief under s 37 and an interim order was
granted by the district judge on 23 March and discharged by the judge on 26 April,
in respect of which there is no appeal.

The application for security for costs was heard inter partes by the district
judge on 16 March, who was told that the variation application had been made.
He made an order as follows:
e

'IT IS ORDERED THAT (1) Unless and until the Respondent [husband] do pay
into Court or deposit with his Solicitors a sum of £11,500·00 to meet costs
potentially arising on taxation of the Petitioner's bill of costs in the divorce
proceedings. IT IS DIRECTED THAT the Respondent's application to vary the
existing periodical payments order in favour of the Petitioner be stayed.'
f

The husband appealed that order to Judge Cotton, who upheld the decision of
the district judge. He held that the wife came within the provisions of CCR Ord
13, r 8. He also held that under Ord 50, r 9 the district judge was entitled to make
the order for security for costs after judgment and also to put a stay upon the
separate application for variation of periodical payments.
g The first argument raised by Mr Hamlin for the husband depends upon a
construction of Ord 13, r 8, which states:

'(1) Where on the application of a defendant to an action or other
proceeding, it appears to the court that the plaintiff is ordinarily resident out
h of England and Wales, then if, having regard to all the circumstances of the
case, the court thinks it reasonable to do so, it may order the plaintiff to give
such security for the defendant's costs of the action or other proceeding as it
thinks just.

(2) The references in paragraph (1) to a plaintiff and a defendant shall be
construed as references to the person (however described on the record)
j who is in the position of plaintiff or defendant, as the case may be, in the
proceedings in question, including proceedings on a counterclaim.'

The judge also relied upon Ord 50, r 9, which I set out here for convenience:

'Where by or under any Act or rule any person is required or authorised to
give security for costs in relation to proceedings in a county court, then,

subject to any express provision, the security shall be given in such manner, at such time and on such terms, if any, as the court may direct.'

Mr Hamlin submitted that the wife did not come within the definition of a defendant within r 8 for the purpose of applying for security for costs for two reasons. First, she was the petitioner in the divorce proceedings upon which the ancillary relief was dependent and second, although the husband filed the notice of ancillary relief, she was in reality the plaintiff in those proceedings. I have no hesitation in rejecting both those propositions. Although she was petitioner to the main suit, the ancillary relief proceedings are separate from it and the rule recognises that parties may be within the same action both plaintiff and defendant. As to Mr Hamlin's second submission, the provisions of para (2) of r 8 do not in my judgment contemplate the sort of assessment that his argument envisages. They are there merely to ensure that a party, such as a counter-claiming defendant, cannot defeat an application on the narrow ground that he is described in the pleadings as defendant. I see no basis for saying, simply because the wife had an interest which was one of the objects of the ancillary relief proceedings brought by the husband to determine, that that makes her a plaintiff in those proceedings.

Mr Hamlin submitted under his next ground of appeal that the district judge had no jurisdiction to make the order. He argued that an order for security for costs could not be made after judgment in respect of costs incurred in those proceedings which had been concluded by the judgment. He further argued that the variation application was a separate proceeding and not amenable to a stay pending payment of costs in earlier different proceedings. His final submission was that, if there were jurisdiction to make the order, it was an improper exercise of the discretion of the district judge to make it.

Jurisdiction

The object of the rule is to deal with the situation in which there is likely to be difficulty in enforcing an order for costs against a plaintiff ordinarily resident abroad. It is a discretionary remedy which is similar to but more limited than RSC Ord 23, r 1. It is necessary to make a prompt application and delay is a relevant factor in the exercise of discretion. The sanction for non-payment of security for costs is a stay upon pending proceedings until it is paid.

I agree with Mr Hamlin that the purpose of security for costs sits uneasily with an order after judgment. CCR Ord 50, r 9, relied upon by the judge, does not provide the power as such but is directed to the exercise of discretion as to how to use it. In general, security for costs looks to protect costs to be incurred in the future and the effect of judgment is to complete the proceedings unless there are ends to be tied up, such as in *Brown v Haig* [1905] 2 Ch 379, where an order was made after judgment but in respect of future proceedings directed by the judgment, in that case the taking of an account before an official referee. Although in *Procon (GB) Ltd v Provincial Building Co Ltd* [1984] 2 All ER 368, [1984] 1 WLR 557 the order was not confined to future costs, but included costs already incurred in the action, the litigation was continuing. In my judgment, security of costs is not intended as a remedy for the enforcement of costs already incurred in respect of proceedings which have come to an end. One has only to formulate the contrary proposition to see how incongruous such an order would be. Mr Jack for the wife sought to meet this point by treating the husband's application to vary periodical proceedings as continuing proceedings analogous to *Brown v Haig*. Within the ambit of Ord 13, r 8, a variation application, although it depends a   upon the divorce petition for its existence and retains the same number, is, like the original ancillary relief application, a separate proceeding in which either party may be the applicant or respondent and in the position of plaintiff or defendant. If, for instance, an application to vary periodical payments were made many years later by an applicant living out of the jurisdiction, it would be extraordinary, on an application for security for costs, to order the costs of the original suit or the substantive ancillary relief hearing to be paid as part of that

b   security. A sum to cover the costs of the pending variation application, on the other hand, might properly be required, without which there would be a stay of the new proceedings. In respect of the costs of the former proceedings which the applicant had failed or refused to pay, the court would have the power to refuse to entertain a variation hearing since he was in breach of a court order. It is clear

c   that an application for security for costs, directed exclusively to past costs ordered after judgment, cannot be made where there are no pending proceedings upon which a stay can be imposed. Equally, such an application ought not to be made in respect of past costs after judgment, using the sanction of imposing a stay upon future separate proceedings.

d

Discretion

Even if the district judge had jurisdiction which, for the reasons I have set out above, I do not consider he had, this was not an order which he should have made. When the matter was before the district judge and the judge the bill had not been taxed and the husband's obligation to pay the costs had not yet arisen.

e   The bill was taxed in the sum of £10,004 on 25 April 1995 and the husband paid the costs on receiving the taxed bill. While it is true that this husband did not accept any order of the court without appealing it, that was his right. There was no evidence before the court that, upon exhausting his rights of appeal, he had failed or refused to honour his obligations. Despite the fears of the wife there was

f   nothing to show he was not going to pay. Further, the application for security for costs was, in the wife's solicitor's affidavit, based entirely upon the past costs and there was no application for, nor intention to apply for, security for the costs of the variation application. In the circumstances of this case the order of the district judge approved by the judge was not reasonable or just.

g   Had it been thought by the court, in this case, proper to protect the wife, the husband's lawyers could have been warned that he would have to pay the costs before the variation application was heard by the court. Although the wife's solicitors were understandably anxious to protect their client who was not in receipt of legal aid and would have to find the costs out of her own pocket if not paid by the husband, they employed the wrong strategy to achieve their ends and

h   both the district judge and the judge were in error in acceding to the application. Although the costs in question have been paid by the husband and there is no effective application before this court, costs have been incurred and in my view it was proper for this court to hear the appeal.

I would allow the appeal and set aside the orders of the district judge and of the

j   judge.

HUTCHISON LJ. I agree.

Appeal allowed.

Paul Magrath Esq   Barrister.

Jonathan Alexander Ltd v Proctor

a

COURT OF APPEAL, CIVIL DIVISION
HIRST, PETER GIBSON LJJ AND BUXTON J
19, 21 DECEMBER 1995

b

County court – Costs – Jurisdiction – Litigant in person – Director representing company at county court trial – Court awarding costs in favour of company – Whether company without legal representation entitled to recover costs – Whether company a 'litigant in person' – Litigants in Person (Costs and Expenses) Act 1975, s 1(1) – Supreme Court Act 1981, s 51 – CCR Ord 38, r 17.

c

The court has no jurisdiction under s 51[a] of the Supreme Court Act 1981 to award costs to a successful plaintiff company which has appeared and acted by its director at trial, since there are no provisions in the County Court Rules or in any other enactments which enable such costs to be paid to a company director or other company representative who has been granted a right of audience under *d* that section. Moreover, a company is not a litigant in person for the purposes of s 1[b] of the Litigants in Person (Costs and Expenses) Act 1975 and is therefore unable to recover costs under CCR Ord 38, r 17[c], since (i) the company, being incapable of appearing in person, must appear by a representative and (ii) in view of extensive authority it is highly improbable that the Act applies to a company *e* so represented in the absence of any indication that Parliament intended the term 'litigant in person' to so apply (see p 338 *d* to *j*, p 339 *j*, p 340 *d* to *j*, p 341 *b* to *f h* to p 342 *a e f*, p 343 *c* to *g* and p 344 *a b*, post).

Notes

For costs recoverable in county court proceedings by a party not employing a *f* solicitor, see 10 *Halsbury's Laws* (4th edn) paras 605–606.

For costs of litigants in person, see 37 *Halsbury's Laws* (4th edn) para 750.

For the Litigants in Person (Costs and Expenses) Act 1975, s 1, see 11 *Halsbury's Statutes* (4th edn) (1991 reissue) 896.

For the Supreme Court Act 1981, s 51, see ibid 1019.

g

Cases referred to in judgments

Arbuthnot Leasing International Ltd v Havelet Leasing Ltd [1991] 1 All ER 591, sub nom *ALI Finance Ltd v Havelet Leasing Ltd* [1992] 1 WLR 455.

Buckland v Watts [1969] 2 All ER 985, [1970] 1 QB 27, [1969] 3 WLR 92, CA.   *h*

Frinton and Walton UDC v Walton and District Sand and Mineral Co Ltd [1938] 1 All ER 649.

Hart v Aga Khan Foundation (UK) [1984] 1 All ER 239, [1984] 1 WLR 994; *affd* [1984] 2 All ER 439, [1984] 1 WLR 994, CA.

Kinnell (Charles P) & Co Ltd v Harding Wace & Co [1918] 1 KB 405, [1918–19] All ER Rep 594, CA.   *j*

---

a   Section 51, so far as material, is set out at p 336 *g* to *j*, post
b   Section 1, so far as material, is set out at p 337 *e*, post
c   Rule 17, so far as material, provides: '(1) Where ... costs of a litigant in person are ordered to be paid ... there may be allowed ... such costs as would have been allowed if the work ... had been done or made by a solicitor on his behalf ...'

a   *London Scottish Benefit Society v Chorley* (1884) 13 QBD 872, [1881–5] All ER Rep 1111, CA.

Meridian Global Funds Management Asia Ltd v Securities Commission [1995] 3 All ER 918, [1995] 2 AC 500, [1995] 3 WLR 413, PC.

Piper Double Glazing Ltd v DC Contracts (1992) Ltd [1994] 1 All ER 177, [1994] 1 WLR 777.

b   *Scriven v Jescott (Leeds) Ltd* (1908) 53 SJ 101.

Supply of Ready Mixed Concrete, Re (No 2), Director General of Fair Trading v Pioneer Concrete (UK) Ltd [1995] 1 All ER 135, [1995] 1 AC 456, [1994] 3 WLR 1249, HL.

Tesco Supermarkets Ltd v Nattrass [1971] 2 All ER 127, [1972] AC 153, [1971] 2 WLR 1166, HL.

c   *Tritonia Ltd v Equity and Law Life Assurance Society* [1943] 2 All ER 401, [1943] AC 584, HL.

Cases also cited or referred to in skeleton arguments

London CC and London Tramways Co, Re (1897) 13 TLR 254, DC.

d   *R v Stafford Stone and Eccleshall Magistrates' Court, ex p Robinson* [1988] 1 All ER 430, [1988] 1 WLR 369.

Appeal

By notice dated 30 June 1994 the plaintiff company, Jonathan Alexander Ltd, appealed with leave granted by Steyn LJ on 26 October 1994 from the order of e   Deputy Circuit Judge Hunter made on 3 June 1994 in the West London County Court, whereby he allowed the appeal of the defendant, Amanda Proctor, from the order for costs made against her by District Judge Trent on 7 April 1994, pursuant to an order of Judge Medawar QC made on 16 December 1993 giving judgment for the company with costs to be determined. The facts are set out in the judgment of Hirst LJ.

f

Allen Dyer (instructed by *Goodman Derrick*) for the company.
David Lord (instructed by *Payne Hicks Beach*) for the defendant.

Cur adv vult

g   21 December 1995. The following judgments were delivered.

HIRST LJ. This is an appeal brought with leave of the single judge by the appellants, Jonathan Alexander Ltd (the company), from the order of Deputy Circuit Judge Hunter, made on 3 June 1994 in the West London County Court, h   whereby he ordered that the appeal of the respondent, Amanda Proctor (the defendant), from the order for costs made against her by District Judge Trent on 7 April 1994, be allowed.

The company claimed against the respondent the sum of £1,702·63, being the balance of the cost of building work. To that claim, which was not disputed as to j   the unpaid balance, there was a defence and counterclaim, supported by an extensive Scott schedule, alleging that some of the work was not done properly and that some of the materials supplied were of poor quality. After a three-day trial the company succeeded, and the sum of no less than £14,300 counterclaimed was reduced to £1,672. Judge Medawar QC ordered that there be judgment for the company on the claim in the sum £30·63 (the counterclaim being dismissed), and that the company's costs in the action, to include the claim and the counterclaim, were to be taxed on scale 2 'with leave to the defendant to argue costs as a preliminary point before the District Judge'.

At the trial, the company had been represented by one of its directors with leave of the court, and the crucial question which Judge Medawar was in effect reserving to the district judge was whether, in the circumstances, it was in principle entitled to recover its costs. These total a sum of approximately £25,000, of which the lion's share is in respect of an hourly rate for the director's time, though they also include some £7,500 disbursed in respect of the fees of expert witnesses, on which we were not asked to make a separate ruling.

On 7 April 1994 the matter came before District Judge Trent. He dismissed the defendant's application for an order that the company was not entitled to its costs pursuant to Judge Medawar's order. However, District Judge Trent's decision was reversed on appeal on 3 June 1994 by Deputy Circuit Judge Hunter.

In his judgment, the judge relied on a passage in *The County Court Practice 1995* p 1595, which states under the heading 'Meaning of "costs"':

'In the present context the term "costs" is used to connote the cost of conducting litigation but—save in the case of a litigant in person—includes solely the remuneration of solicitors (and occasionally lay representatives in small claims matters), including repayment of disbursements (including counsel's fees) incurred in the course of litigation.'

The judge then identified the source of the court's power, cited below, to give leave for a director to appear on behalf of the company, but said that there was nothing to suggest that the exercise of this power 'endows the company with the status of a litigant in person', and that this was supported by a further note in *The County Court Practice 1995* p 1639, which states:

'A litigant in person is now entitled to recover costs: Litigants in Person (Costs and Expenses) Act 1975. There is no definition of a "litigant in person" in either the Act or the Rules, nor is there a reported case on the point. It is suggested that a company which is allowed to appear by a director or other officer is not entitled to costs as a litigant in person as the company itself cannot appear personally but only by an agent.'

On behalf of the appellant, Mr Dyer submitted that the correct starting point is s 51 of the Supreme Court Act 1981 (as substituted by s 4 of the Courts and Legal Services Act 1990), which provides so far as relevant as follows:

'(1) Subject to the provisions of this or any other enactment and to rules of court, the costs of and incidental to all proceedings in—(a) the civil division of the Court of Appeal; (b) the High Court; and (c) any county court, shall be in the discretion of the court.

(2) Without prejudice to any general power to make rules of court, such rules may make provision for regulating matters relating to the costs of those proceedings including, in particular, prescribing scales of costs to be paid to legal or other representatives.

(3) The court shall have full power to determine by whom and to what extent the costs are to be paid ...'

This, he submitted, gave the court the widest possible discretion, and he drew particular attention in the present context to the words 'legal *or other representatives*' at the end of s 51(2). This provision, he submitted, rendered inaccurate the notes quoted above from *The County Court Practice*, at all events *a*   since 1981. He suggested that the editors had not caught up with the present statutory position.

Mr Dyer pointed out that the power in the court to grant a right of audience on behalf of a company to a director is now based on s 27(2)(c) of the 1990 Act, which gives a right of audience before a court in relation to any proceedings to a person who 'has a right of audience granted by that court in relation to those *b*   proceedings'.

So far as the county court is concerned, however, this power extended back well over 100 years (see s 72 of the County Courts Act 1888, reproducing s 10 of the repealed County Courts Act 1852; see also *Charles P Kinnell & Co Ltd v Harding Wace & Co* [1918] 1 KB 405, [1918–19] All ER Rep 594).

c   In summary, he submitted that, the director having been granted a right of audience in this action as the company's representative, the trial judge had a completely unfettered discretion to award the company its costs pursuant to s 51 of the 1981 Act.

As a second string to his bow, Mr Dyer submitted that the company was a *d*   litigant in person within the scope of s 1(1) of the Litigants in Person (Costs and Expenses) Act 1975, which provides that, in proceedings inter alia in a county court:

> 'Where ... any costs of a litigant in person are ordered to paid by any other party to the proceedings ... there may, subject to rules of court, be allowed *e*   on the taxation or other determination of those costs sums in respect of any work done, and any expenses and losses incurred, by the litigants in or in connection with the proceedings to which the order relates.'

He submitted that the phrase 'in person' defines the status of the litigant, ie as *f*   being an unrepresented as opposed to a represented litigant; thus the term 'litigant in person' is as apposite to a company as it is to an individual, seeing that the company remains the litigant throughout, and seeing that the Act, which gives no definition of a litigant in person, draws no distinction between an individual and a corporate person.

On behalf of the defendant, Mr Lord made it clear that the court's power to *g*   grant a right of audience to the director was not disputed, and so not the issue presently before this court.

On the first issue raised by Mr Dyer, Mr Lord submitted that the crucial question was to determine the meaning of the term 'costs' in the relevant legislation and rules of court. Apart from two special exceptions referred to *h*   below, this term was, he submitted, restricted first to charges and disbursements incurred by solicitors, and secondly, since 1975, to sums in respect of any work done, and any expenses and losses incurred, by litigants in person.

The former was provided for by CCR Ord 38, r 3(1), which stipulated under the heading 'Costs to be regulated by scales' that: 'For the regulation of solicitors' *j*   charges and disbursements ... there shall be three scales of costs ...' The latter were provided for by Ord 38, r 17 under the heading 'Litigant in person', which, in effect, reproduces s 1 of the 1975 Act.

The two special exceptions are: (1) a fee or reward charged by a lay representative in small claims proceedings, as laid down in Ord 19, r 4(1), which provides—

'In this rule, "costs" means—(a) solicitors' charges, (b) sums allowed to a
litigant in person pursuant to Ord 38, rule 17, (c) a fee or reward charged by
a lay representative for acting on behalf of a party in the proceedings';

and (2) in the High Court, a case falling within RSC Ord 62, r 2(2), which provides
that Ord 62 shall have effect—

'with such modifications as may be necessary, where by virtue of any Act
the costs of any proceedings before an arbitrator ... are taxable in the High
Court.'

Thus, in *Piper Double Glazing Ltd v DC Contracts (1992) Ltd* [1994] 1 All ER 177,
[1994] 1 WLR 777 Potter J held that arbitration costs fall within the scope of this
rule, seeing that under s 18(1) of the Arbitration Act 1950, unless a contrary
intention is expressed therein, every arbitration agreement is deemed to include
a provision that the costs shall be in the discretion of the arbitrator, and that any
costs directed by an award to be paid shall, unless the award otherwise directs, be
taxable in the High Court. It follows, Mr Lord submitted, that the first note
quoted above from *The County Court Practice 1995* is accurate.

I now proceed to consider these rival arguments.

The lynchpin of Mr Dyer's argument is s 51 of the 1981 Act. It is, in my
judgment, of paramount importance to observe that in sub-s (1) the general
discretion is subject to the provisions of 'this or any other enactment and to rules
of court', and that sub-s (2) empowers (but does not require) the making of
provision in the rules prescribing inter alia 'scales of costs to be paid to legal or
other representatives'.

It follows that one must look to any other relevant enactments and to the
relevant rules of court in order to determine the extent of the courts' jurisdiction.
Only if and to the extent that such enactments or rules make provision in relation
to costs to be paid to a company director, or other company representative, who
has been granted a right of audience, can such a person fall within the scope of
the words 'other representatives' in s 51(2).

No such provisions appear in the rules, as Mr Lord rightly points out. Indeed,
the only rule relating to other representatives is CCR Ord 19, r 4(1)(c), quoted
above, dealing with lay representatives in small claims proceedings. The 1975
Act, of course, falls within the category of any other enactment in s 51(1). It
follows that, in my judgment, s 51 does not avail Mr Dyer.

This conclusion is reinforced by a further point made by Mr Lord, which is to
my mind valid, that, if Mr Dyer's argument were right, there would seem to be
no need for the special provision relating to arbitration costs as identified in the
Piper Double Glazing case, nor for Ord 19, r 4(1)(c).

It follows, in my judgment, that Mr Dyer can only succeed if he can bring his
case within the 1975 Act. Ingenious though Mr Dyer's submission was, I found
it very difficult to reconcile with the ordinary meaning, as I understand it, of the
description 'litigant in person', viz an unrepresented individual. To extend this
description to a company would require clear words, yet there is nothing in the
1975 Act which enlarges the ordinary meaning.

I would therefore, as a matter of first impression, reject the submission that a
company can constitute a litigant in person. This first impression is fully
confirmed by the reasons advanced by Peter Gibson LJ in the judgment which he
is about to deliver, with all of which I agree. I would therefore dismiss this appeal.

a I do so with great regret, since it seems to me that this case reveals a serious lacuna in the law, and results in a considerable injustice to the company, which properly incurred very substantial costs in defeating a grossly inflated counterclaim. This may be an appropriate topic for consideration by the Rules Committee, since it would seem that a quite simple amendment to the rules could bring company directors within the scope of 'other representatives' under *b* s 51(2) of the 1981 Act. The judge's judgment makes it clear that leave for such representation is regularly granted in the county court.

PETER GIBSON LJ. There are two issues in this appeal. One is whether the costs on scale 2 awarded to the successful plaintiff company, which appeared and acted by its director at the trial in the county court proceedings, included costs *c* incurred otherwise than in consequence of the employment of a solicitor. The other is whether the company, so acting and appearing, is a litigant in person for the purposes of the Litigants in Person (Costs and Expenses) Act 1975 and so able to recover costs pursuant to CCR Ord 38, r 17.

d (1) *Costs*

 The first issue turns on the meaning of the term 'costs'. On this issue Mr Dyer's argument for the company proceeded on the footing that the company was not a litigant in person. His submission was that under s 51 of the Supreme Court Act 1981 (now s 4(1) of the Courts and Legal Services Act 1990), which gave the court, including the county court, the widest discretion in relation to the costs of and *e* incidental to all proceedings, and enabled rules of court to be made prescribing scales to be paid to legal or other representatives, costs could not be limited to the costs of legal representatives, including their disbursements. He submitted that an unjustified fetter was placed on the court's discretion by the judge and by the passages in *The County Court Practice 1995* to which Hirst LJ has referred.

f The discretion conferred on the court was by s 51(1) subject to the provisions of the 1981 Act or any other enactment (no such provision is suggested apart from the 1975 Act) and to the rules of court.

 I turn first to the rules of court prescribing scales of costs to be paid to legal and other representatives.

 In the County Court Rules 1981 the relevant rule is Ord 38, r 3. It is apparent *g* from r 3(1) that the scales of costs are for the regulation of solicitors' charges and disbursements. True it is that following the 1975 Act Ord 38, r 3(3D) was introduced and that allows a litigant in person, in the circumstances there specified, to receive a gross sum. But apart from the special provisions in Ord 38, r 17, which relate to litigants in person, and to the equally inapplicable provision *h* in Ord 19, r 4 relating to costs in small claims cases (which specifically allow the costs of lay representatives of a party), there is nothing to suggest that the term 'costs' can refer to other costs such as those actually or notionally incurred by a party, who is not a solicitor, spending time on the litigation instead of earning money elsewhere.

j There is, therefore, no provision of the rules that would enable the plaintiff, who was not, and did not employ, a solicitor, to recover costs. That is consistent with the meaning traditionally attributed to 'costs'. In *London Scottish Benefit Society v Chorley* (1884) 13 QBD 872 at 876, [1881–5] All ER Rep 1111 at 1113 (a case in which it was held that a solicitor who was made a party to an action and defended it successfully, himself was entitled to the same costs as if he had employed a solicitor) Bowen LJ pointed out that costs are the creation of statute.

He went on to refer to the passage in 2 Co Inst 288, as affording a key to the true view of the law of costs:

> 'Here is express mention made but of the costs of his writ, but it extendeth to all the legal cost of the suit, but not to the costs and expenses of his travel and loss of time, and therefore "costages" cometh of the verb "conster," and that again of the verb "constare," for these "costages" must "constare" to the court to be legal costs and expenses.'

Bowen LJ continued (13 QBD 872 at 877, [1881–5] All ER Rep 1111 at 1113):

> 'What does Lord Coke mean by these words? His meaning seems to be that only legal costs which the Court can measure are to be allowed, and that such legal costs are to be treated as expenses necessarily arising from the litigation and necessarily caused by the course which it takes. Professional skill and labour are recognised and can be measured by the law; private expenditure of labour and trouble by a layman cannot be measured.'

These remarks were approved and applied by this court in *Buckland v Watts* [1969] 2 All ER 985, [1970] 1 QB 27.

The enactment of the 1975 Act was intended to enable the court to provide that a litigant in person, who would otherwise not obtain an award of costs for his work, could recover. As was said by Lloyd J in *Hart v Aga Khan Foundation (UK)* [1984] 1 All ER 239 at 241, [1984] 1 WLR 994 at 997:

> 'The whole object of an award for costs is to indemnify the successful party to a greater or lesser extent against costs which he has in fact incurred. He cannot recover costs which he has not incurred. To this general principle Parliament has provided a limited exception in the case of a litigant in person. Provided he has suffered pecuniary loss, he can recover for work which he has himself done up to two-thirds of what would have been allowed if that work had been done by a solicitor.'

As Lloyd J stated, prior to the 1975 Act, litigants in person were not allowed anything for their time and trouble, but only for their out-of-pocket expenses (see [1984] 1 All ER 239 at 240, 242, [1984] 1 WLR 994 at 996, 998). Although he was speaking in a High Court case, in my opinion, the same applies to the county court. If Mr Dyer were right, the 1975 Act operates to limit the discretion of the court to indemnify the litigant in person for his time and trouble. I cannot accept that. But for the 1975 Act the litigant in person could not recover 'costs' at all.

The construction of 'costs' which I favour is also in accord with the emphasis laid by Potter J in the arbitration case *Piper Double Glazing Ltd v DC Contracts (1992) Ltd* [1994] 1 All ER 177, [1994] 1 WLR 777 on the wording of RSC Ord 62, r 2(2) as to Ord 62 having effect 'with such modifications as may be necessary', which enabled him to allow the recovery of costs of non-qualified representatives.

Accordingly, there being no statutory provision or rule of court that assists the company, I am in no doubt but that Mr Dyer cannot succeed on the first issue.

(2) *Litigants in Person (Costs and Expenses) Act 1975*

A company is a persona ficta. As has been said of a company, 'it does not have a soul to be damned or a body to be kicked'. It is a consequence of the artificial nature of the company as a legal person that inevitably actions by it and decisions for it have to be taken by natural persons. The law of agency is at the root of company law (see Gower's *Principles of Modern Company Law* (5th edn, 1992) pp a 139, 164). The acts of the authorised agent, acting within the scope of his authority, are under the ordinary principles of agency the acts of the company. When a company authorises a director to act and appear for it in court proceedings, and the court allows the director to act and appear, the company acts and appears by the director. The company is the litigant.

b The crucial question is whether it can be said of the company so acting and appearing that it is a litigant in person for the purposes of the 1975 Act. Mr Dyer would answer that question in the affirmative. In agreement with Mr Lord, I would unhesitatingly answer that question in the negative. I do so for the following reasons.

c (i) A litigant in person in ordinary parlance is a party to litigation who represents himself by appearing in court himself. If someone other than himself represents him, then notwithstanding that that other person is his agent, that party is not a litigant in person. The statement which Hirst LJ has cited from *The County Court Practice 1995* p 1639 accords with how, in my opinion, the term 'litigant in person', in relation to a company, would generally be understood. The company appears by a representative, its director, and hence it is not a

d litigant in person.

(ii) It has repeatedly and authoritatively been stated that a company cannot appear in person (see Co Litt 66b, *Charles P Kinnell & Co Ltd v Harding Wace & Co* [1918] 1 KB 405 at 413, [1918–19] All ER Rep 594 at 598 per Swinfen Eady LJ, *Frinton and Walton UDC v Walton and District Sand and Mineral Co Ltd* [1938] 1 All ER 649 at 649 per Morton J and *Tritonia Ltd v Equity and Law Life Assurance Society*

e [1943] 2 All ER 401 at 402, [1943] AC 584 at 586 per Viscount Simon LC, with whom Lord Atkin, Lord Thankerton, Lord Macmillan and Lord Clauson agreed). It has also been said that a company is not in the same position as a litigant in person (see *Scriven v Jescott (Leeds) Ltd* (1908) 153 SJ 101 per Bray J). Against that background, it is to my mind highly improbable that without any indication that

f Parliament intended the term 'litigant in person' to apply to a company, the 1975 Act applied to a company represented by a director.

I would, therefore, dismiss this appeal. But I would like to add two further comments. The first is that, although we have been told that of the claimed costs of £25,000, £7,500 consists of experts' fees, we have not been asked to rule on whether such disbursements made by the company can be recovered under an

g award of costs. The second is that, like Hirst LJ, it does seem to me to be unjust that a successful party is prevented from recovering any costs if it is a company choosing to act by its own director, whereas an individual in such circumstances can recover under the 1975 Act. I, too, hope that this can be looked at by the rule-makers, particularly as it would appear from the judge's judgment that in the

h county court companies regularly act and appear by lay representatives.

BUXTON J. I agree with Hirst and Peter Gibson LJJ that the first basis on which the appellant company put its case must fail. Counsel for the company relied heavily on s 51(2) of the Supreme Court Act 1981. That subsection, however,

j does no more than create a rule-making power in respect of scales of costs to be paid to 'legal or other representatives'; the latter, by s 51(13), being 'any person exercising a right of audience or right to conduct litigation on his behalf'. It is argued that in this case the director, Mr Buchanan, was exercising a right of audience under s 27(2)(c) of the Courts and Legal Services Act 1990, as a person granted a right of audience by the court in relation to the proceedings in which he was permitted to represent the company. However, even granted that that is

so, s 51(2) of the 1981 Act does no more than create vires to make rules in relation
to the scales of costs, if any, to be paid to such a representative. It says nothing as
to whether or not any particular category of representative is entitled to costs, or
whether his client is entitled to have him feature on his bill of costs. It does not
displace in any particular case the rule that allowable costs are, and are limited to,
remuneration for the exercise of professional legal skill (see *Buckland v Watts*
[1969] 2 All ER 985 at 987, [1970] 1 QB 27 at 37 per Sir Gordon Willmer, applying
the judgment of Bowen LJ in *London Scottish Benefit Society v Chorley* (1884) 13
QBD 872 at 876, [1881–5] All ER Rep 1111 at 1113, a case already referred to by
Peter Gibson LJ). It was that rule that required the passing of the Litigants in
Person (Costs and Expenses) Act 1975 to make specific provision for the
remuneration of litigants in person. However, this part of the company's
argument does not rely on the 1975 Act, but on a general right to claim costs in
respect of a (legally) unqualified representative. No such right exists.

The alternative and less preferred way in which the company puts its case is
quite different. On this basis of claim, Mr Dyer says that Mr Buchanan, in arguing
the case, was not a representative of the company, but was the company itself. It
was the company that was in court. It was therefore a litigant in person and can
claim remuneration as such, though now subject, as on the first basis of claim it
would not have been, to the limits as to quantum prescribed by, in particular,
CCR Ord 38, r 17(4).

This way of putting the claim is attacked in two ways by the defendant. First,
it is said that it is not legally possible for the company to act 'in person', or directly
as itself at all. The company can only act by its agent; so Mr Buchanan could only
have been an agent for the company, and could not be the company in person.
Second, even if that is not right, the 1975 Act by its terms only applies to
individuals and not to companies.

I am satisfied, as are Hirst and Peter Gibson LJJ, that the second of these
arguments is correct, and therefore that this part of the appeal must also fail in
any event. I do, however, consider also the first argument deployed by the
defendant, because the view that I take of it is relevant also to the narrower
question of the construction of the 1975 Act. I address this issue with
considerable diffidence, not least because my approach to it differs somewhat
from that of Peter Gibson LJ.

I start with the issue of principle argued by the defendant. Although a
company can only act by an agent, because there is no such thing as 'the
company' as such, there are often situations where it is possible, and sometimes
necessary, to say that 'the company' has done something or has acted in a certain
way. That fact, and the legal grounds on which that conclusion is reached, are
described in the opinion of the Privy Council delivered by Lord Hoffmann in
Meridian Global Funds Management Asia Ltd v Securities Commission [1995] 3 All ER
918 at 923–924, [1995] 2 AC 500 at 506–507. It is true that in that case, as in the
cases which the court applied, namely *Tesco Supermarkets Ltd v Nattrass* [1971] 2
All ER 127, [1972] AC 153 and *Re Supply of Ready Mixed Concrete (No 2), Director
General of Fair Trading v Pioneer Concrete (UK) Ltd* [1995] 1 All ER 135, [1995] 1 AC
456, the Board was speaking of 'attribution' in the sense of culpability. I do not,
however, see that that can make a difference to the way in which the court should
approach the root question, 'Was the act of individual A in law the act of
company B?' Where, as in the present case, the managing director of the
company undertakes a specific task for the company, I do not find difficulty in
principle in contemplating that the rules governing the attribution of his acts to

a the company make his acts those of the company itself, and not merely those of an agent of the company. The case would be different if the company employed someone who, in the case of an individual litigant, would be regarded as an agent: most conspicuously a solicitor, or a lay claims consultant or other representative.

That, however, is as to principle. As I will explain later in this judgment, in this particular case the circumstances in which, and the rules under which, Mr
b Buchanan was permitted to act for the company, prevented his acts being attributed to the company as its own. The company thus fails on this point in the event, even though I cannot accept the defendant's argument in the broad and general terms that it was advanced.

Even, however, if I am wrong about that, and it was indeed the company that
c was conducting the case in the person of Mr Buchanan, the question remains of whether the company was a litigant 'in person' for the purposes of the 1975 Act. A series of cases, very conveniently summarised in the judgment of Scott J in *Arbuthnot Leasing International Ltd v Havelet Leasing Ltd* [1991] 1 All ER 591 at 595, [1992] 1 WLR 455 at 460, indicates that it was generally accepted before 1975 that
d the expression 'litigant in person' was applicable only to an individual. This, I should emphasise, is a different proposition from the rule that applies in the High Court that a company must be represented by solicitors and counsel. The proposition concerns not a rule of representation, but the meaning of the term 'in person'. Judges of high authority who assumed that that term could only apply to an individual include Morton J in *Frinton and Walton UDC v Walton and District*
e *Sand and Mineral Co Ltd* [1938] 1 All ER 649 at 649 and Viscount Simon LC in *Tritonia Ltd v Equity and Law Life Assurance Society* [1943] 2 All ER 401 at 402, [1943] AC 584 at 586. Given that usage, it was in my view incumbent on the draftsman of the 1975 Act to employ specific language if he sought to extend the provisions of that Act to limited companies. By adopting the expression 'in person' he did
f the reverse of that. And, quite apart from the language used in the Act, there is no reason to think that Parliament did intend to extend the relief granted by that Act beyond the case of individuals. Twenty years later, and with the experience of changing patterns of litigation and of representation, particularly in the county courts, it is possible that a different policy view would be taken if the issue was reconsidered. However, the extension of the provisions of the 1975 Act to limited
g companies would indeed be an extension of those provisions, and not an application of them.

There is a further reason why the 1975 Act cannot apply to limited companies in the absence of specific provisions to that effect. That the 1975 Act so applies only even starts to be arguable if the company itself can be said to be present in
h court. I have indicated how, in my view, it may be possible in general terms to approach that first hurdle. However, in the case before us an officer of the company can only act for the company with the leave of the court. That is clear from the provisions as to rights of audience already cited in this judgment, and from the long-standing practice in the county courts that is set out in the
j judgment of Swinfen Eady LJ in *Kinnell v Harding Wace & Co* [1918] 1 KB 405 at 413, [1918–19] All ER Rep 594 at 598. Mr Buchanan thus acted in court and could only have so acted with the leave of the judge. However, if (as the argument that the company was there in person demands) Mr Buchanan was the company, he would have been present as a litigant, and thus would have had a right to act and be present there whatever the judge's view of the matter. This consideration I think demonstrates that, even if it is theoretically possible to say that a company

itself appears in court, it is not possible to advance that proposition when the person said to be the company is in court not by right but only with leave.   *a*

Those considerations lead me to conclude that, against the background of the rules of the court as to representation, it is not in fact possible in this case to say that the company itself acted. This difficulty is a further reason for thinking that the terms of the 1975 Act cannot and do not apply to limited companies.

For those reasons, I would, like Hirst and Peter Gibson LJJ, dismiss the appeal.   *b*

Appeal dismissed. Leave to appeal to House of Lords refused.

Paul Magrath Esq   Barrister.

a # Re a debtor (No 2021 of 1995), ex parte Inland Revenue Commissioners v The debtor

Re a debtor (No 2022 of 1995), ex parte Inland Revenue Commissioners v The debtor

b

CHANCERY DIVISION

LADDIE J

17, 20 NOVEMBER 1995

c *Insolvency – Voluntary arrangement – Interim order – Creditors' meeting – Voting in respect of voluntary arrangements – Proxies sent by fax – Creditor transmitting to chairman's office by fax completed form of proxy – Chairman declining to act on faxed voting instructions – Whether faxed document a form of proxy 'signed by the principal' – Whether faxed proxy valid – Insolvency Rules 1986, r 8.2(3).*

d

On Friday, 9 June 1995 the Commissioners of Inland Revenue sent by first class post a completed form of proxy directing the chairman of the meeting of creditors, summoned pursuant to s 257 of the Insolvency Act 1986 and convened for the afternoon of Monday, 12 June, to cast their vote against the debtors' proposals for voluntary arrangements. The form arrived on Tuesday morning.
e On the morning of the creditors' meeting the commissioners transmitted to the chairman's office by fax the completed form of proxy. On receipt the chairman telephoned the commissioners to verify the contents of the fax. He was however unable to speak to the relevant officer prior to the meeting, with the result that he declined to act on the faxed voting instructions. The commissioners issued
f originating applications seeking reversal of the chairman's decision to refuse to admit their debt for voting purposes and revocation of the approvals of the debtors' arrangements. The district judge held that a faxed proxy was not 'signed' as required by the Insolvency Rules 1986, r 8.2(3), which provided that a 'form of proxy shall be signed by the principal, or by some person authorised by him' and that the original proxy had to be available at the meeting. The commissioners
g appealed.

Held – A proxy form was signed for the purposes of r 8.2(3) of the 1986 rules if it bore upon it some distinctive or personal marking which had been placed there by, or with the authority of, the creditor. When a creditor faxed a proxy form to
h the chairman of a creditors' meeting he transmitted the contents of the form and the signature applied to it. The receiving fax was instructed by the transmitting creditor to reproduce his signature on the proxy form which was itself being created at the receiving station. It followed that the received fax was a proxy form signed by the principal or by someone authorised by him. The appeal
j would therefore be allowed (see p 349 *f g* and p 351 *b d* to p 352 *e*, post).

Notes

For summoning of creditors' meeting and proxies, see 3(2) *Halsbury's Laws* (4th edn reissue) paras 91, 92, 266–275.

For the Insolvency Rules 1986, r 8.2, see 3 *Halsbury's Statutory Instruments* (1995 reissue) 444.

Cases referred to in judgment

Cranley Mansions Ltd, Re [1994] 1 WLR 1610.

Goodman v J Eban Ltd [1954] 1 All ER 763, [1954] 1 QB 550, [1954] 2 WLR 581, CA.

Jenkins v Gaisford, Re Jenkins (decd)'s goods (1863) 3 Sw & Tr 93, 164 ER 1208.

Phillipson, Re (13 September 1993, unreported), Cty Ct.

Sheehan, Re (25 May 1994, unreported), Cty Ct.

Cases also cited or referred to in skeleton arguments

Agip (Africa) Ltd v Jackson [1992] 4 All ER 385, [1990] Ch 265.

Bishopsgate Investment Management Ltd (in prov liq) v Maxwell, Cooper v Maxwell, Mirror Group Newspapers plc v Maxwell [1992] 2 All ER 856, [1993] Ch 1, CA.

Debtor, Re a (No 1 of 1987) [1989] 2 All ER 46, [1989] 1 WLR 271, CA.

Dorman Long & Co Ltd, Re [1934] Ch 635, [1933] All ER Rep 460.

English, Scottish and Australian Chartered Bank, Re [1893] 3 Ch 385, [1891–4] All ER Rep 775, CA.

Firstpost Homes Ltd v Johnson [1995] 4 All ER 355, [1995] 1 WLR 1567, CA.

Hastie & Jenkerson (a firm) v McMahon [1991] 1 All ER 255, [1990] 1 WLR 1575, CA.

Lazarus Estates Ltd v Beasley [1956] 1 All ER 341, [1956] 1 QB 702, CA.

London CC v Agricultural Food Products Ltd [1955] 2 All ER 229, [1955] 2 QB 218, CA.

Palmer (decd) (a debtor), Re [1994] 3 All ER 835, [1994] Ch 316, CA.

R v Cowper (1890) 24 QBD 533, CA.

Tennant v London CC (1957) 121 JP 379, CA.

Appeal

The Commissioners of Inland Revenue appealed from the decision of District Judge White sitting in the Exeter County Court dismissing the applications by the commissioners to revoke approval given at a creditors' meeting in relation to individual voluntary arrangements to be entered into pursuant to Pt VIII of the Insolvency Act 1986 under s 262(1)(b) of the Act and r 5.17 of the Insolvency Rules 1986, SI 1986/1925. The respondent to the appeal was the chairman of the meeting, William White. The debtors were represented but took no part in the proceedings. The facts are set out in the judgment.

Malcolm Davis-White (instructed by the *Solicitor of Inland Revenue*) for the commissioners.

Andreas Gledhill (instructed by *Wansbroughs Willey Hargrave*, Bristol) for the chairman.

Edward Counsell (instructed by *Michelmore Davies & Bellamy*, Sidmouth) for the debtors.

LADDIE J. This is an appeal from a decision of District Judge White whereby he dismissed the Inland Revenue's applications to revoke approval given at a creditors' meeting in relation to individual voluntary arrangements (IVAs) to be entered into pursuant to Pt VIII of the Insolvency Act 1986 under s 262(1)(b) of the Act, and r 5.17 of the Insolvency Rules 1986, SI 1986/1925.

The background facts are as follows. Mr White was chairman of the meeting on the afternoon of Monday, 12 June 1995, pursuant to s 257 of the Act, at which the debtors' creditors were due to vote on their proposals for voluntary arrangements. On Friday, 9 June the commissioners sent by first class post a completed form of proxy directing Mr White to cast their votes against the debtors' proposals. The form should have arrived in normal course of post in a good time for the Monday meeting. It is not in dispute that it actually arrived on the Tuesday morning. However, on the morning of the creditors' meeting the commissioners transmitted to Mr White's office by fax the completed form of proxy. On receipt Mr White apparently telephoned the Inland Revenue to attempt to verify the contents of the fax. Having been unable to speak to the relevant officer prior to the meeting, he declined to act on the faxed voting b instructions. In so doing he believed himself to be acting in accordance with guidance issued by the Department of Trade and Industry. On 7 July the commissioners issued the originating applications herein seeking reversal of Mr White's decision to refuse to admit their debt for voting purposes, revocation of the approvals of the debtors' arrangements, and an order for costs against Mr White.

c The sole issue before me is the validity of a faxed proxy in the context of creditors' meetings under the relevant insolvency rules. The questions this gives rise to can be conveniently stated as follows. (1) Should the faxed proxy of the Inland Revenue have been accepted? (2) If so, what consequences should now follow?

d The decision of the learned district judge was, first, that a faxed proxy was not 'signed' as required by the 1986 rules and particularly r 8.2(3). Secondly, that the original proxy had to be available at the meeting and a copy would not do. The applicant submits that the faxed proxy was signed within the meaning of the rules and, further or alternatively, that a copy of such a signed proxy available at the meeting meets the requirements of the 1986 rules.

e Before me Mr Davis-White appeared for the commissioners. Mr White was represented by Mr Gledhill. He made it clear to me that Mr White did not consider it appropriate for him to support or resist the relief sought by the commissioners against the debtors. That was also the stance he had adopted before the district judge. He said that he is, however, entitled on this appeal, as f at first instance, to protect his own interests and specifically to explain and justify to the court his decision to decline to act in accordance with the fax sent to him by the commissioners, to resist any application for costs against him, and to give the court such other assistance as it may require in disposing of these proceedings. In fact before me Mr Gledhill argued firmly in support of the district judge's judgment, and he was entitled so to do.

g The debtors were represented before me by Mr Counsell, but he took no part in these proceedings, his interest only being to address me on the question of relief in the event of the appeal being successful.

The parties agreed that there was virtually no direct authority on the point raised in this appeal. In *Re Cranley Mansions Ltd* [1994] 1 WLR 1610 Ferris J h referred to the arguments presented to him on the point, but came to the view that it was neither necessary nor wise for him to express a view given his conclusion on other matters. There have apparently been at least two decisions at county court level where faxed proxies have been ruled to be in order. The first was *Re Sheehan* (25 May 1994, unreported) a decision of Judge Griffiths in the j Swansea County Court. The second was *Re Phillipson* (13 September 1993, unreported) a decision of Judge Hunt in the Harrogate County Court. A brief note of these cases is set out in an article by Adam Goodison and John Briggs 'The validity of faxed proxies' (1994) 7 Insolvency Intelligence 57, reflected in the current edition of *Muir Hunter on Personal Insolvency* pp 7022/1, para 7–028, the commentary on r 5.14. The parties agreed that the matter must therefore be approached as one of principle and construction of the Act and rules.

First I deal with the scheme of the 1986 legislation. It is as follows. Sections
252 to 255 of the Act deal with interim orders, which in effect provide a breathing *a*
space for a debtor while his proposals for voluntary arrangement are under
consideration. Interim orders were made in this case. Once an interim order is
made, the nominee is to report to the court on the debtor's proposals (s 256) and
this also was done in this case. Where the nominee has recommended the
convening of a creditors' meeting, he shall convene the same as proposed in his *b*
report unless the court otherwise orders, and that is according to s 257 of the Act.
In this case the notice was dated 25 May 1995. The proposals are then put to a
meeting of creditors, who may, subject to certain limits, approve the same as
originally put forward, or with modifications (s 258). At such a meeting, the
resolution approving the proposal or modification must be passed by a majority
in excess of three-quarters in value of those creditors present in person or proxy *c*
and voting on the resolution. Those voting against must not include more than
half in value of the creditors. For these purposes a special definition of 'creditors'
is adopted.

If approved, the proposals as approved take effect as if made at the meeting and
by persons who had notice of the meeting and were entitled to vote as if he were *d*
a party to the arrangement (s 260). They can have the effect of restricting and
extinguishing in part the debts owed to the creditors. Certain persons, including
creditors, are given locus to apply to the court on the grounds that the
arrangements as approved unfairly prejudice the interests of a creditor or there
has been some material irregularity at the meeting. If the court upholds the
complaint, it can revoke or suspend approval and/or give a direction for a further *e*
meeting to reconsider the original proposal or consider any revised proposals (see
s 262).

Part 8 of the 1986 rules deals with the question of proxies which may be used
at creditors' meetings. It should be noted that those provisions apply not just to
creditors' meetings for IVAs but also to company voluntary arrangements, *f*
administration, administrative receivers, liquidations and bankruptcy. The
relevant rules are as follows:

> '8.1—(1) For the purposes of the Rules, a proxy is an authority given by a
> person ("the principal") to another person ("the proxy-holder") to attend a
> meeting and speak and vote as his representative ...   *g*
> 8.2 ... (2) No form of proxy shall be used at any meeting except that which
> is sent out with the notice summoning the meeting, or a substantially similar
> form.
> (3) A form of proxy shall be signed by the principal, or by some person
> authorised by him (either generally or with reference to a particular *h*
> meeting). If the form is signed by a person other than the principal, the
> nature of the person's authority shall be stated ...
> 8.4—(1) Subject as follows, proxies used for voting at any meeting shall be
> retained by the chairman of the meeting.
> (2) The chairman shall deliver the proxies, forthwith after the meeting, to
> the responsible insolvency practitioner (where that is someone other than *j*
> himself).'

Mr Gledhill submitted that it is necessarily implicit in r 8.4 that for the purposes
of the rules at least the presence of a signed proxy form is a prerequisite for
voting. This is consistent with r 8.5, which provides that creditors and others in
attendance have an entitlement to inspect proxies and associated documents at

a the meeting. It is not permissible for a proxy holder to be admitted to vote at a meeting subject to subsequent production of documentation he ought to have brought with him or previously lodged with the chairman. Creditors' meetings are the sovereign body of voluntary arrangements. Their outcome and the substance of debtor's proposal is often significantly moulded by individual creditors' perceptions at the meeting of whether or not their vote is capable of *b* being decisive. Amendment to the debtor's proposals may be tabled.

However, this does not resolve the question which I have to address, namely whether the faxed document received by Mr White was, in the words of r 8.2(3), a form of proxy 'signed by the principal'.

Mr Davis-White presented me with an illuminating history of the use of proxies by creditors under the Bankruptcy Act 1914, the Companies Act 1929 and *c* the Companies Act 1948. He said that the development of this legislation showed a progressive move away from strict formalities. No doubt this is so but I think it is necessary to look at the 1986 Act and rules as an entirely new code. The policy underlying this new code is that referred to in the report of the review committee on *Insolvency Law and Practice* (Cmnd 8558 (1982), chairman Sir *d* Kenneth Cork) para 917, where the following was said:

'We consider it unsatisfactory that creditors, whose experience would be invaluable to the liquidator or trustee, are discouraged from participating in the administration of an insolvent estate. We are in no doubt that the machinery should be such as to allow, and indeed encourage, those creditors *e* who have a genuine interest to involve themselves in all types of insolvent administration.'

However, that also is of no assistance in resolving the issue here. It is clear that compliance with some formality is required. In particular the formality of signing the proxy has not been removed even if the other formalities have.

f There being no direct authority on the point, I must approach this issue from first principles. Although the rules stipulate that the form of proxy must be signed, it was, I believe, common ground that 'signing' in the context could not be restricted to the narrow concept of marking a substrate manually by direct use of a pen or similar writing instrument. It was conceded that a proxy form could *g* be 'signed' by use (by the creditor or his agent) of a stamp. Similarly, if a form had a signature impressed on it by a printing machine in the way that share dividend cheques frequently are signed by company secretaries, the form can be said to be 'signed'.

This approach has been followed in other fields. Mr Davis-White drew my *h* attention to *Jenkins v Gaisford, Re Jenkins (decd)'s goods* (1863) 3 Sw & Tr 93, 164 ER 1208. That case concerned the validity of a codicil to a will. Section 9 of the Wills Act 1837 in force at the time of that decision required the will or any codicil to be signed at the end by the testator. Towards the end of his life the testator became infirm and had difficulty in writing or signing his name. He had an engraving of his signature made and this was used under his direction by his agent, Mr Atkins, *j* to sign documents, including the codicil in issue. In coming to the conclusion that the codicil was duly executed, the court said (3 Sw & Tr 93 at 96, 164 ER 1208 at 1209):

'It has been decided that a testator sufficiently signs by making his mark, and I think it was rightly contended that the word "signed" in that section must have the same meaning whether the signature is made by the testator himself, or by some other person in his presence or by his direction, and therefore a mark made by some other person under such circumstances must suffice. Now, whether the mark is made by a pen or by some other instrument cannot make any difference, neither can it in reason make a difference that a fac-simile of the whole name was impressed on the will instead of a mere mark or X. The mark made by the instrument or stamp used was intended to stand for and represent the signature of the testator. In the case where it was held that sealing was not signing, the seals were not affixed by way of signature.'

My attention was also drawn to *Goodman v J Eban Ltd* [1954] 1 All ER 763, [1954] 1 QB 550 in which the Court of Appeal had to consider whether a bill on the bottom of which a solicitor had placed a copy of his signature by use of a rubber stamp had been signed in accordance with the provisions of s 65 of the Solicitors Act 1932. By a majority (Denning LJ dissenting) the court held that it had. Evershed MR stated ([1954] 1 All ER 763 at 765, [1954] 1 QB 550 at 555):

'I confess that, if the matter were res integra I should be disposed to think, as a matter of common sense and of the ordinary use of language, that when Parliament required that the bill or letter should be "signed" by the solicitor, it was intended that the solicitor should personally "sign" the bill or letter in the ordinary way by writing his name (or, where appropriate, the name of his firm) in his own hand with a pen or pencil.'

However, Evershed MR then referred to a number of cases dealing with a variety of situations in which signing was required by statute, including *Jenkins v Gaisford*, and continued ([1954] 1 All ER 763 at 766, [1954] 1 QB 550 at 557):

'In my judgment, therefore, it must be taken as established that where an Act of Parliament requires that a document be "signed" by a person, prima facie the requirement of the Act is satisfied if the person himself places on the document an engraved representation of his signature by means of a rubber stamp. Indeed, if reference is made to the SHORTER OXFORD ENGLISH DICTIONARY ... it will be found that the primary meaning of the verb "to sign" is not confined to actual writing with a pen or pencil, but appears to have related to marking with the sign of the cross. The later meanings include: "(ii) To place some distinguishing mark upon (a thing or person) ... (iv) to attest or confirm by adding one's signature; to affix one's name to (a document, etc.).' It follows, I think, that the essential requirement of signing is the affixing, either by writing with a pen or pencil or by otherwise impressing on the document one's name or "signature" so as personally to authenticate the document. If this view be right, then, since the formula used in the Solicitors Act, 1932, does not differ from that in the Wills Act, 1837, s. 9, and the Statute of Frauds, s. 4, there seems no reason why a different requirement is imposed from that in the other cases—which is no more than the personal authentication of the individual "signing".'

Romer LJ also expressed some initial reservations but, having considered the function which a signature was to perform, agreed with the views of Evershed MR. In particular he cited with approval the following definition from *Stroud's Judicial Dictionary*:

'Signed; signature. (1) Speaking generally, a signature is the writing, or otherwise affixing, a person's name, or a mark to represent his name, by a himself or by his authority ... with the intention of authenticating a document as being that of, or as binding on, the person whose name or mark is so written or affixed.'

The concession made by Mr Gledhill as to signing by stamp or printing machine was, I believe, correct. Furthermore, it was not in dispute that the b stamp or printing machine could be operated by an agent (see in particular r 8.2(3)). The requirement of signing in r 8.2(3) is to provide some measure of authentication of the proxy form. Of course even if the rule were strictly limited to signature by direct manual marking of the form, the authentication is not perfect. Signatures are not difficult to forge. Furthermore, in the overwhelming majority of cases in which the chairman of a creditors' meeting receives a proxy c form, the form will bear a signature which he does not recognise and may well be illegible. Authenticity could only be enhanced if the creditor carrying suitable identification signed the form in person in the presence of the chairman. Even there the possibility of deception exists.

It seems to me that the function of the signature is to indicate, but not d necessarily prove, that the document has been considered personally by the creditor and is approved of by him. It may be said that a qualifying proxy form consists of two ingredients. First, it contains the information required to identify the creditor and his voting instructions and, secondly, the signature performing the function set out above. When the chairman receives a proxy form bearing what purports to be a signature, he is entitled to treat it as authentic unless there e are surrounding circumstances which indicate otherwise. Once it is accepted that the close physical linkage of hand, pen and paper is not necessary for the form to be signed, it is difficult to see why some forms of non-human agency for impressing the mark on the paper should be acceptable while others are not.

For example, it is possible to instruct a printing machine to print a signature by f electronic signal sent over a network or via a modem. Similarly, it is now possible with standard personal computer equipment and readily available popular word processing software to compose, say, a letter on a computer screen, incorporate within it the author's signature which has been scanned into the computer and is stored in electronic form, and to send the whole document including the signature by fax modem to a remote fax. The fax received at the remote station g may well be the only hard copy of the document. It seems to me that such a document has been 'signed' by the author.

With these considerations in mind, I have come to the conclusion that a proxy form is signed for the purposes of r 8.2(3) if it bears upon it some distinctive or personal marking which has been placed there by, or with the authority of, the h creditor. When a creditor faxes a proxy form to the chairman of a creditors' meeting he transmits two things at the same time, the contents of the form and the signature applied to it. The receiving fax is in effect instructed by the transmitting creditor to reproduce his signature on the proxy form which is itself being created at the receiving station. It follows that, in my view, the received j fax is a proxy form signed by the principal or by someone authorised by him. The view which I have reached appears to me to be consistent with the realities of modern technology. If it is legitimate to send by post a proxy form signed with a rubber stamp, why should it not be at least as authentic to send the form by fax?

The facts of the present case illustrates the point well. Here the proxy form was sent both by post and by fax. Such being the nature of postal delivery, the creditor could not be certain whether his proxy was received at all or on time. On

the other hand, when the fax is transmitted he knows that it has been received
because, first, he obtains an answerback code and, secondly, an activity report is
normally printed out. From the chairman's point of view, there is nothing about
a received fax which puts him in a worse position to detect forgeries than when
he receives through the post or by hand delivery a document signed by hand by
a person whose signature he has never seen before or one signed by stamping.
The reality is that fax transmission is likely to be a more reliable and certainly is a
more speedy method of communication than post. It would be a pity if r 8.3(3)
required creditors to convey their views to the chairman by the older, slower and
less reliable form of communication.

Finally, there are three matters I should mention. First, Mr Gledhill argued
that if the Inland Revenue was correct in its view, at least two signed proxy forms
would exist, namely one fed into the fax by the creditor and the one received by
the chairman of the meeting. He says that that is not possible because r 8.1(3)
stipulates that 'only one proxy may be given by a person for any one meeting'. I
do not accept this argument. What the rule is referring to is the 'proxy', referred
to in r 8.1(1)—ie the *authority* given by the creditor to the proxy holder. Only one
authority may be given for the meeting. The proxy form evidences or confirms
that authority. Whether there is more than one form is irrelevant.

Secondly, both counsel invited me to make clear, as I now do, that the views I
express as to whether a fax document bearing a fax signature is 'signed' has only
been considered in this case in relation to Pt 8 of the Insolvency Rules 1986.
Different considerations may apply to faxed documents in relation to other
legislation.

Thirdly, I have only been concerned here with an IVA. Part 8 of the rules
applies to proxies used in other creditors' meetings as well. Mr Davis-White
submitted that it was possible that r 8.2(3) might mean different things for
different proceedings. There is no need for me to express a view on that.

Appeal allowed.

Celia Fox   Barrister.

a

Smith v Linskills (a firm) and another

COURT OF APPEAL, CIVIL DIVISION

SIR THOMAS BINGHAM MR, PETER GIBSON AND SCHIEMANN LJJ

23, 24 JANUARY, 5 FEBRUARY 1996

Action – Dismissal – Abuse of process of court – Collateral attack on final decision of court of competent jurisdiction in previous proceedings – Plaintiff bringing civil action against former solicitors for damages for negligence in conduct of his defence – Whether civil action an abuse of process of court – Whether plaintiff having had full opportunity to put forward case – Whether new evidence entirely changing aspect of criminal case – Whether plaintiff's claim sustainable in law.

In 1984 the plaintiff was convicted of aggravated burglary and sentenced to seven years' imprisonment. The Court of Appeal refused leave to appeal. In 1990, having served his sentence, the plaintiff brought civil proceedings against the solicitors who had acted for him in relation to the trial, claiming damages for negligence in the preparation and conduct of his defence. On the solicitors' application the claim was struck out by the district judge as an abuse of the process of the court on the basis that it was contrary to public policy for a conviction in a criminal court to be impugned in a civil action by a person seeking to relitigate the same issue. The plaintiff appealed and the judge in chambers reversed that decision and ordered the trial of a preliminary issue, namely whether, if the solicitors had been negligent and the plaintiff had been convicted as a result of that negligence, the plaintiff's claim was sustainable in law and/or should be allowed to proceed. On the trial of that issue, the plaintiff submitted that there was fresh evidence which, but for the solicitors' negligence, could have been available at the trial. However, the judge held that the plaintiff's case was not sustainable and should not be allowed to proceed. The plaintiff appealed to the Court of Appeal, contending that, having served his sentence, he had no ulterior motive of seeking to impugn his conviction in bringing the proceedings, that the solicitors' negligence had prevented him from having a full opportunity of contesting the case in the Crown Court, and that the fresh evidence available justified making an exception to the rule of public policy that a collateral attack in civil proceedings on a decision of a criminal court of competent jurisdiction was an abuse of process.

Held – The basis of the rule of public policy that the use of a civil action to mount a collateral attack on a decision of a criminal court of competent jurisdiction was an abuse of process was the importance of finality in litigation, the impossibility in a coherent legal system of having two final but inconsistent decisions of courts of competent jurisdiction and the virtual impossibility of fairly retrying at a later date the issue which had been before the court on the earlier occasion. An ulterior motive on the part of the intending plaintiff was not a necessary ingredient for holding proceedings to be an abuse of process, although if an ulterior motive was shown to be present that provided a strong and additional ground for doing so. Since the plaintiff had had a full opportunity of contesting the case against him in the Crown Court and the fresh evidence did not satisfy the strict test of entirely changing the aspect of the case, his claim had rightly been

held to be an abuse of process. The appeal would therefore be dismissed (see p
358 *a* g to p 379 *d f g*, p 360 *b* to *d* and p 361 *g j* to p 362 *h*, post).

    Hunter v Chief Constable of West Midlands [1981] 3 All ER 727 and *Walpole v
Partridge & Wilson (a firm)* [1994] 1 All ER 385 applied.

    Decision of Potter J [1995] 3 All ER 226 affirmed.

Notes

For striking out pleadings for abuse of process, see 37 *Halsbury's Laws* (4th edn)
para 434.

Cases referred to in judgment

Bragg v Oceanus Mutual Underwriting Association (Bermuda) Ltd [1982] 2 Lloyd's Rep
    132, CA.
Hunter v Chief Constable of West Midlands [1981] 3 All ER 727, [1982] AC 529, [1981]
    3 WLR 906, HL; *affg* sub nom *McIlkenny v Chief Constable of West Midlands Police
    Force* [1980] 2 All ER 227, [1980] QB 283, [1980] 2 WLR 689, CA.
Ladd v Marshall [1954] 3 All ER 745, [1954] 1 WLR 1489, CA.
Phosphate Sewage Co Ltd v Molleson (1879) 4 App Cas 801, HL.
Reichel v Magrath (1889) 14 App Cas 665, HL.
Saffron v Federal Comr of Taxation (1991) 102 ALR 19, Aust Fed Ct.
Stephenson v Garnett [1898] 1 QB 677, CA.
Walpole v Partridge & Wilson (a firm) [1994] 1 All ER 385, [1994] QB 106, [1993] 3
    WLR 1093, CA.

Cases also cited or referred to in skeleton arguments

Ashmore v British Coal Corp [1990] 2 All ER 981, [1990] 2 QB 338, CA.
Chaplin v Hicks [1911] 2 KB 786, [1911–13] All ER Rep 224, CA.
Cullen v Eaton-Smith and Downey (a firm) [1993] CA Transcript 1636.
Hornal v Neuberger Products Ltd [1956] 3 All ER 970, [1957] 1 QB 247, CA
Kitchen v Royal Air Forces Association [1958] 2 All ER 241, [1958] 1 WLR 563, CA.
Rondel v Worsley [1967] 3 All ER 993, [1969] 1 AC 191, HL.
Saif Ali v Sydney Mitchell & Co (a firm) (P, third party) [1977] 3 All ER 744, [1980] AC
    198, CA.
Somasundaram v M Julius Melchior & Co (a firm) [1989] 1 All ER 129, [1988] 1 WLR
    1394, CA.
Spring v Guardian Assurance plc [1994] 3 All ER 129, [1995] 2 AC 296, HL.

Appeal

By notice dated 12 May 1994 the plaintiff, Christopher Daniel Smith, appealed
from the decision of Potter J ([1995] 3 All ER 226) on 18 April 1994 whereby he
determined, on the trial of a preliminary issue, that the plaintiff's action brought
by writ issued on 20 June 1990 seeking damages against the defendants, Messrs
Linskills (a firm of solicitors) and Julian Sorel Linskill (his former solicitor), on the
ground that they had been negligent in the conduct of his defence in previous
criminal proceedings which had resulted in his conviction, was not sustainable in
law and should not be allowed to proceed. The facts are set out in the judgment
of the court.

Andrew Nicol QC and *Gavin Millar* (instructed by *Strain Keville & Co*) for Mr Smith.
Guy Mansfield QC and *Andrew Sander* (instructed by *Weightman Rutherford*,
    Liverpool) for the defendant.

Cur adv vult

a

5 February 1996. The following judgment of the court was delivered.

SIR THOMAS BINGHAM MR. Mr Smith, the plaintiff in these proceedings,
appeals from a decision of Potter J ([1995] 3 All ER 226) given in Manchester on
b 18 April 1994. The judge determined a preliminary issue against Mr Smith in this
action brought by Mr Smith against his former solicitor. He held that Mr Smith
was seeking by the action to challenge the final decision of a criminal court which
he had had a full opportunity to resist and that Mr Smith was unable to bring this
claim within any of the exceptions to a general rule of public policy which
precludes the making of such a claim. He accordingly held the action to be an
c abuse of the process of the court and ruled that it should not proceed. Mr Smith
now seeks to challenge the judge's decision.

I

On the evening of 13 December 1983 a gang of four or five men, all but one of
d them masked, burst into the home of Mr and Mrs Bancroft in Prestatyn in North
Wales. They tied up members of the family and forced Mr Bancroft at knifepoint
to hand over the contents of a safe. The gang were disturbed by the arrival of a
visitor at the front door of the house and made their escape through the back. In
due course two men were arrested and charged with aggravated burglary. They
were tried in the Crown Court at Mold (Judge David QC and a jury) in July 1984.
e One of the defendants was a man named Hayes, who was said to be the
member of the gang who had not been masked and who was identified by Mr
Bancroft and his son. He was convicted and sentenced and is not involved in
these civil proceedings.

The other defendant was Mr Smith. He was not identified by sight or voice as
f a member of the gang. There were three main planks to the prosecution case
against him. One was the evidence of a Mr Broomhead, a man with an
unsavoury criminal record and a paid police informer, who testified that when he
and Mr Smith had earlier been fellow prisoners Mr Smith had confessed to the
commission of this crime. The second plank was an alleged association between
Mr Smith and Mr Hayes. It was established that they had known each other some
g years before when Mr Smith had been a prison officer and Mr Hayes had been a
prisoner serving a sentence, but the evidence of a continuing association between
them amounted at the trial to very little. The third plank of the prosecution case
was evidence that one of the members of the gang appeared to be aware of the
existence of a safe in Mr Bancroft's house, and also familiar with the layout of the
h house and with the possible means of exit at the back. This raised a possible
inference against Mr Smith, since he was the son-in-law of Mr and Mrs Bancroft,
and therefore was in a position to know of the safe (which virtually no one
outside the immediate family did), and also to be familiar with the geography of
the house. At the trial Mr Smith raised a defence of alibi, which was strongly
challenged by the prosecution; the prosecution accordingly relied on what was
j suggested to be an obviously false defence. Mr Smith was convicted and
sentenced to seven years' imprisonment. He applied for leave to appeal against
his conviction but this was refused by Hollis J on paper on 22 November 1984.
He renewed his application to the Court of Appeal (Criminal Division) but was
again refused leave on 11 July 1985. He served the appropriate part of his
sentence.

On 20 June 1990, after his release from prison, Mr Smith issued the writ in these
proceedings against the defendant, who had acted as his solicitor in the criminal
proceedings. His claim was for damages for negligence and breach of contract by
the defendant as his solicitor in the preparation of his defence to the criminal
charge. The essence of his complaint was that it was the defendant's negligence
which had led to his conviction and sentence. Paragraph 15 of his amended
statement of claim served on 9 January 1992 conveniently summarises the
particulars of negligence on which he relies:

> 'The defendant:—(i) failed to request an old-style committal; (ii) failed to
> visit the Plaintiff sufficiently to take instructions and prepare for trial; (iii)
> failed to provide the Plaintiff with copies of the depositions so as to obtain his
> instructions on them; (iv) failed to arrange an identification parade to see
> whether Mrs Bennett could identify him; (v) failed to take statements from
> three prisoner witnesses, Pawlicki, Johnson and Klein, despite repeated
> requests by the Plaintiff; (vi) failed to trace and take a statement from the
> landlady at the Copplehouse pub; (vii) failed to consult the Plaintiff, or check
> the evidence that could be given by potential alibi witness before settling the
> alibi notice; (viii) failed to take any timely or adequate statement from the
> Plaintiff's wife and sister-in-law; (ix) failed to follow an obvious and
> reasonable inquiry as to the key Prosecution witness' motive for giving
> evidence against the Plaintiff; (x) failed to take any steps to ensure that the
> case did not come on before the Defence was properly prepared, or to get the
> case vacated when it came on prematurely; (xi) failed to brief Counsel in a
> timely manner and to arrange a pre-trial conference with him before the day
> of the trial.'

The defendant applied to strike out the action as an abuse of the process of the
court and this order was made by District Judge Harris on 16 July 1991. Mr Smith
appealed and his appeal came before Steyn J in Liverpool on 6 November 1991.
He allowed the appeal and set aside the order of the district judge. But he ordered
the trial of a preliminary issue of law, namely:

> '... whether if the Defendant was negligent and the Plaintiff was convicted
> because of the said negligence the Plaintiff's case is sustainable in law and/
> or should be allowed to proceed ...'

It was this preliminary issue which came before Potter J. He ruled that Mr
Smith's case was not sustainable in law and should not be allowed to proceed. It
is the correctness of that decision which Mr Smith now challenges.

II

The leading modern authority on abuse of process in cases such as the present
is *Hunter v Chief Constable of West Midlands* [1981] 3 All ER 727, [1982] AC 529. At
the outset of his speech, with which the other members of the House agreed,
Lord Diplock said ([1981] 3 All ER 727 at 729, [1982] AC 529 at 536):

> 'My Lords, this is a case about abuse of the process of the High Court. It
> concerns the inherent power which any court of justice must possess to
> prevent misuse of its procedure in a way which, although not inconsistent
> with the literal application of its procedural rules, would nevertheless be
> manifestly unfair to a party to litigation before it, or would otherwise bring
> the administration of justice into disrepute among right-thinking people.

a The circumstances in which abuse of process can arise are very varied; those which give rise to the instant appeal must surely be unique. It would, in my view, be most unwise if this House were to use this occasion to say anything that might be taken as limiting to fixed categories the kinds of circumstances in which the court has a duty (I disavow the word discretion) to exercise this salutary power.'

b Later in his speech Lord Diplock laid down what has since been regarded as the governing rule on this subject ([1981] 3 All ER 727 at 733, [1982] AC 529 at 541):

'The abuse of process which the instant case exemplifies is the initiation of proceedings in a court of justice for the purpose of mounting a collateral attack on a final decision against the intending plaintiff which has been made *c* by another court of competent jurisdiction in previous proceedings in which the intending plaintiff had a full opportunity of contesting the decision in the court by which it was made.'

He continued ([1981] 3 All ER 727 at 733–734, [1982] AC 529 at 541–542):

d 'My Lords, collateral attack on a final decision of a court of competent jurisdiction may take a variety of forms. It is not surprising that no reported case is to be found in which the facts present a precise parallel with those of the instant case. But the principle applicable is, in my view, simply and clearly stated in those passages from the judgment of A L Smith LJ in *e* *Stephenson v Garnett* [1898] 1 QB 677 and the speech of Lord Halsbury LC in *Reichel v Magrath* (1889) 14 App Cas 665 which are cited by Goff LJ in his judgment in the instant case. I need only repeat an extract from the passage which he cited from the judgment of A L Smith LJ in *Stephenson v Garnett* [1898] 1 QB 677 at 680–681: "... the Court ought to be slow to strike out a statement of claim or defence, and to dismiss an action as frivolous and *f* vexatious, yet it ought to do so when, as here, it has been shewn that the identical question sought to be raised has been already decided by a competent court." The passage from Lord Halsbury LC's speech in *Reichel v Magrath* 14 App Cas 665 at 668 deserves repetition here in full: "... I think it would be a scandal to the administration of justice if, the same question having been disposed of by one case, the litigant were to be permitted by *g* changing the form of the proceedings to set up the same case again."'

III

Mr Smith certainly initiated the present proceedings. It is also clear that his *h* conviction in the Crown Court at Mold, upheld on appeal, amounted to a final decision by a court of competent jurisdiction in previous proceedings against him.

Mr Andrew Nicol QC, for Mr Smith, argues that the issue in the present proceedings is not the same issue as was decided in the Crown Court. To an *j* extent this is so. In the Crown Court the question was whether, applying the criminal standard of proof, Mr Smith was shown to have committed the crime with which he was charged. In the present proceedings the issue is whether his former solicitor handled his defence negligently. It is, however, plain that the thrust of his case in these proceedings is that if his criminal defence had been handled with proper care he would not, and should not, have been convicted. Thus the soundness or otherwise of his criminal conviction is an issue at the heart

of these proceedings. Were he to recover substantial damages, it could only be   *a*
on the basis that he should not have been convicted. Even if he were to establish
negligence, he could recover no more than nominal damages at best, if the court
were to conclude that even if his case had been handled with proper care he
would still have been convicted. It follows, in our judgment, that these
proceedings do involve a collateral attack upon the decision of the Crown Court.
We understand Lord Diplock, by 'collateral', to have meant an attack not made   *b*
in the proceedings which gave rise to the decision which it is sought to impugn;
not, in other words, an attack made by way of appeal in the earlier proceedings
themselves.

It was not, as we understand, the intention of the House in *Hunter* to lay down
an inflexible rule to be applied willy-nilly to all cases which might arguably be said
to fall within it. Lord Diplock was at pains to emphasise the need for flexibility   *c*
and the exercise of judgment. Ralph Gibson LJ was, in our opinion, correct when
he said in *Walpole v Partridge & Wilson (a firm)* [1994] 1 All ER 385 at 392, [1994]
QB 106 at 116:

> 'The decision of their Lordships in *Hunter's* case ([1981] 3 All ER 727, [1982]
> AC 529), however, was, in my judgment, not that the initiation of such   *d*
> proceedings is necessarily an abuse of process but that it may be. The
> question whether it is so clearly an abuse of process that the court must, or
> may, strike out the proceedings before trial must be answered having regard
> to the evidence before the court on the application to strike out. There are,
> in short, and at least, exceptions to the principle.'   *e*

It is none the less noteworthy that in *McIlkenny v Chief Constable of West Midlands
Police Force* [1980] 2 All ER 227 at 247, [1980] QB 283 at 333 Goff LJ, whose
judgment was unreservedly approved by the House of Lords, expressed the
opinion that relitigation of an issue which had previously been the subject of final
decision 'must prima facie be an abuse of the privilege of the court to allow the   *f*
matter to be litigated all over again'. In the present case Mr Nicol has, rightly in
our judgment, devoted his argument to seeking to show that certain ingredients
of Lord Diplock's rule are not present here.

IV

In his statement of principle already quoted, Lord Diplock referred to the need   *g*
for the intending plaintiff to have had a full opportunity of contesting the decision
against him in the first court. This was an echo of the judgment of Goff LJ in
McIlkenny [1980] 2 All ER 227 at 245, [1980] QB 283 at 330. In this case, Mr Nicol
argued, Mr Smith had not enjoyed a full opportunity to contest the decision in the
Crown Court, because the negligence of the defendant had prevented him   *h*
deploying the full case which he would wish to have deployed.

This argument is, in our judgment, founded on a misunderstanding of what
Lord Diplock meant. It is plain from his speech (see [1981] 3 All ER 727 at 734,
[1982] AC 529 at 542 and the authority relied on) that Lord Diplock was giving his
ruling with reference to both civil and criminal cases. It is evident in civil cases   *j*
particularly that a party may lack any opportunity to resist a hostile claim, as for
example where judgment is entered against him on the ground of procedural
default, or may lack a full opportunity, as when summary judgment is given
against him. We understand Lord Diplock to have been intending to preserve a
party's right to make a collateral attack on a decision made against him in such
circumstances. We cannot think that Lord Diplock would have regarded Mr

a Smith as lacking a full opportunity of contesting the Crown Court decision against him when he had had the benefit of a solicitor and counsel throughout the proceedings, had pleaded not guilty, had attended every day of the trial, had been able to give instructions to counsel on the cross-examination of prosecution witnesses, had given evidence himself, had called witnesses, had sought to establish an alibi, had had the benefit of submissions made to the jury on his

b behalf, had pursued an application for leave to appeal against his conviction, had settled grounds of appeal drawing attention to some at least of his complaints about the manner in which his case had been conducted by his solicitor, and had renewed his application for leave to appeal to the full court on the initial refusal of leave. Even if it be true that valid criticism can be made of the conduct of his defence, it seems to us quite impossible to hold that Mr Smith lacked a full

c opportunity to contest the charge. Were this the correct meaning of the rule, then the rule itself would be virtually meaningless, since it is hard to imagine a case in which a convicted defendant could not find some plausible ground upon which to criticise the preparation of the defence by his solicitor. We fully appreciate the great difficulty which faces any convicted defendant seeking to

d challenge his conviction on appeal on the grounds that his defence had been negligently conducted; this does not, however, lead to the conclusion that such a defendant lacked a full opportunity to contest the charge against him.

V

e It was argued for Mr Smith that these proceedings were not an abuse because it had not been found that his real purpose in bringing them was to attack his conviction. Since he has now served his sentence (unlike the intending plaintiff in *Hunter*) his only and genuine purpose is to recover damages for professional negligence. That, it is said, distinguishes the case from *Hunter*.

It is certainly true that in his speech in *Hunter* [1981] 3 All ER 727 at 733, [1982]

f AC 529 at 541 Lord Diplock attached considerable significance to the ulterior purpose which lay behind the proceedings brought by the intending plaintiff in that case. We have no doubt at all but that the existence of such an ulterior motive provides a strong and additional ground for holding proceedings to be an abuse. The question is whether such an ulterior motive is a necessary ingredient

g of abuse. In our judgment it is not. We consider that the law was accurately stated by Ralph Gibson LJ in *Walpole* [1994] 1 All ER 385 at 396, [1994] QB 106 at 120 when he said:

'I am unable to attach any decisive importance to the point about dominant purpose upon which [counsel for the plaintiffs] relied. In *Hunter's*

h case ([1981] 3 All ER 727, [1982] AC 529) the collateral attack upon the final decision of Bridge J on the voire dire was an abuse of the process because based upon no sufficient fresh evidence. The fact that the purpose of the plaintiffs was to provide themselves with an argument upon which to attack the true validity of their convictions supported the conclusion that those

j proceedings amounted to an abuse of process; but it seems clear to me that, if their purpose had been the apparently more acceptable aim of recovering damages for the injuries which they claimed were inflicted by the police, the proceedings would unquestionably have remained an abuse of process because it constituted a collateral attack upon a final decision which was manifestly unfair to the defendants and because it was such as to bring the administration of justice into disrepute. No doubt, when it is present, some

collateral purpose on the part of the plaintiff, other than the pursuit of his
remedy at law, will be relevant to the assessment of the case and to the *a*
exercise of the court's discretion for the purpose of deciding whether it is
shown so clearly to be an abuse of process that the proceedings should be
struck out. If, however, it is clearly shown that the plaintiff's claim is a
collateral attack upon a final Judgment within the principle stated and
applied in *Hunter's* case, then the simple purity of his purpose in seeking *b*
financial damages alone would not save his action.'

We agree. The rule with which we are here concerned rests on public policy.
The basis of that public policy, further considered below, is the undesirable effect
of relitigating issues such as this. We cannot see how those undesirable effects
are mitigated by the motive of the intending plaintiff to recover damages rather *c*
than simply to establish the unsoundness of the earlier decision. *Bragg v Oceanus
Mutual Underwriting Association (Bermuda) Ltd* [1982] 2 Lloyd's Rep 132 and *Saffron
v Federal Comr of Taxation* (1991) 102 ALR 19, relied on by Mr Smith, do not
persuade us to the contrary: in those cases the relevant proceedings were not, in
any event, initiated by the party accused of abuse.

d

VI

It is plain from *Hunter* [1981] 3 All ER 727 at 736, [1982] AC 529 at 545 that the
existence at the commencement of the civil action of 'fresh evidence' obtained
since the criminal trial may justify making an exception to the general rule of
public policy that the use of civil actions to initiate collateral attacks on final *e*
decisions against the intending plaintiff by criminal courts of competent
jurisdiction should be treated as an abuse of the process of the court. It is also
plain that the test to be met by such evidence is a strict one, stricter than the
ordinary Court of Appeal test for receiving new evidence (that the evidence
'would probably have an important influence on the result of the case, although *f*
it need not be decisive' (see *Ladd v Marshall* [1954] 3 All ER 745 at 748, [1954] 1
WLR 1489 at 1491)): the new evidence must be such as 'entirely changes the
aspect of the case' (see *Phosphate Sewage Co Ltd v Molleson* (1879) 4 App Cas 801 at
814 and *Hunter* [1981] 3 All ER 727 at 736, [1982] AC 529 at 545). Mr Nicol relied
on this exception to the general rule, putting his argument in two ways.

First, he relied on the formulation of the preliminary issue ordered by Steyn J *g*
to be tried. Since the issue required the court to assume that the defendant had
been negligent and that Mr Smith had been convicted because of such negligence,
it followed that the new evidence on which he now sought to rely would entirely
change the aspect of the case, since it made the difference (ex hypothesi) between
conviction and acquittal. *h*

This argument is in our opinion ingenious, but quite contrary to the intention
of Steyn J. He concluded that there were issues to be explored which could not
sensibly be decided on a striking-out application. There were 'important and
complex legal issues to be tried after a fuller examination of the facts'. He made
an order for discovery, and envisaged the calling of oral evidence. We infer that *j*
he did not intend the court which was to determine the preliminary issue to be
bound to accept the truth of all the facts pleaded. Before Potter J the fresh
evidence on which Mr Smith now seeks to rely was examined, and the present
argument was not advanced on his behalf. If the preliminary issue had been
intended to assume that Mr Smith's new evidence entirely changed the aspect of
the case, there would in truth have been no preliminary issue to determine. We

a   are satisfied that it is necessary to examine Mr Smith's fresh evidence as the judge did.

In his second and alternative argument Mr Nicol submitted that there was fresh evidence which satisfied the strict test laid down. The evidence in question falls under several heads.

(1) Evidence from a former prisoner, Pawlicki. He gave evidence at the
b   original trial. There is nothing to show that he could have given any additional evidence.

(2) Evidence from a former prisoner, Johnson. There is no statement from Johnson. It is unclear what additional evidence he could have given.

(3) Evidence from a former prisoner, possibly named Klein. He has not been traced, and there is no statement from him. Klein, it is suggested, could have
c   testified that Broomhead confided to him before Mr Smith's trial that he (Broomhead) would do everything in his power to make life difficult for Mr Smith because he was a former prison officer. Little significance can be attached to unsubstantiated double hearsay attributed to an untraced witness.

(4) Evidence from the landlady of the Copplehouse pub. She has not been
d   identified or traced. We do not know what evidence she could have given.

(5) Evidence from Mr Smith's wife and sister-in-law. We have no statement. We do not know what evidence either could have given.

(6) Evidence concerning Broomhead, the main prosecution witness against Mr Smith. It appears that in the years since Mr Smith's trial, Broomhead has been convicted on several occasions, receiving sentences which perhaps reflect
e   co-operation with the prosecuting authorities. It also appears that at a later trial, when he was again giving evidence of an alleged confession made by a defendant, he confessed to perjury and retracted his evidence. None of this evidence could have been adduced at Mr Smith's trial in the Crown Court, since the events had not occurred. As it was, Judge David directed the jury:

f   'He is a criminal, he has been [in] trouble, served terms of imprisonment, and for dishonesty ... He charged for his information. He is a paid informer. Paid informers are not always the most reliable people ... And all that I would have thought adds up to this so far as Broomhead is concerned, this is a witness whose evidence you should approach with great care.'

g   It is not clear what additional evidence could have been given at the trial (Klein perhaps apart) to discredit Broomhead.

There is in our judgment no fresh evidence which brings Mr Smith within measurable distance of satisfying the test laid down by authority.

h   VII

There can be no doubt that Lord Diplock's rule rests on considerations of public policy. Steyn J felt that this public policy could profitably be reviewed. He was plainly mindful of the cases since 1981 which have exposed the fallibility of the trial and appellate processes.

j   The main considerations of public policy which underlie the existing rule are, as we understand, threefold.

(1) The affront to any coherent system of justice which must necessarily arise if there subsist two final but inconsistent decisions of courts of competent jurisdiction. Such would, we think, be the case here if there were a subsisting Crown Court decision that Mr Smith was, beyond reasonable doubt, guilty of aggravated burglary and a subsisting civil court decision that if his defence had

been properly prepared he would and should have been acquitted. No reasonable observer could view this outcome with equanimity.

We cannot of course shut our eyes to the possibility that a criminal defendant may be wrongly convicted, perhaps because his defence was ineptly prepared or conducted. When that occurs, it represents an obvious and serious injustice. There are two possible solutions. One is to relax the present restraint on seeking to establish that injustice by civil action. The other is to ensure that, in appropriate cases, the conviction itself can be reviewed. It seems to us clear that it is this second solution which has, over the past century, been favoured: by giving a criminal defendant a right of appeal; by providing a relatively low standard for the admission of fresh evidence on appeal; by empowering the appellate court to order a new trial; by giving the Home Secretary power to refer a case back to the Court of Appeal; and by proposals to establish a new review body.

(2) The virtual impossibility of fairly retrying at a later date the issue which was before the court on the earlier occasion. The present case exemplifies the problem. It is over 12 years since the crime was committed. Recollections (of the participants and the lawyers involved) must have faded. Witnesses have disappeared. Transcripts have been lost or destroyed. Mr Hayes may, or may not, be available to testify. Evidence of events since the trial will be bound to intrude, as it already has. It is futile to suppose that the course of the Crown Court trial can be authentically recreated.

(3) The importance of finality in litigation. The present rule has been seen by some as a rule invented by judges to protect their professional brethren. It is, of course, true that no one welcomes a negligence claim against him. But the maxim interest reipublicae ut finis sit litium was not invented by English judges, and nothing (on one view) could better serve the personal interests of the legal profession than endless relitigation of the same issues. If, as suggested in Dickens' *Bleak House*: 'The one great principle of English law is, to make business for itself', there could be no better way of doing so. But the view has long been taken that a final decision should, save in special circumstances, be final.

These broad considerations of public policy remain compelling. Even if it were open to this court to vary the general rule propounded in *Hunter's* case, we would not feel justified in doing so.

VIII

In our judgment, Potter J came to the right conclusion for the right reasons. We would have thought it necessary to discuss some of these matters at greater length, had he not dealt with them so clearly in his judgment, to which we would pay an admiring tribute.

Appeal dismissed. Action to be struck out. Leave to appeal to the House of Lords refused.

L I Zysman Esq   Barrister.

a Three Rivers District Council and others v Bank of England (No 2)

QUEEN'S BENCH DIVISION (COMMERCIAL COURT)

CLARKE J

b 27 NOVEMBER 1995

Statute – Construction – Parliamentary materials – Speeches of ministers proposing Bills for second reading – Reference to proceedings in Parliament as an aid to construction – Whether court may look at parliamentary history of legislation as aid to
c *interpretation.*

Where the court is seeking to construe a statute purposively and consistently with any relevant European legislation, or the object of the legislation under consideration is to introduce into English law the provisions of an international
d convention or European directive, it is of particular importance to ascertain the true purpose of the statute, and in those circumstances the court may adopt a more flexible approach to the admissibility of parliamentary materials than that established for the construction of a particular provision of purely domestic legislation (see p 366 *d* to *f*, post).

Pepper (Inspector of Taxes) v Hart [1993] 1 All ER 42 and *Melluish (Inspector of*
e *Taxes) v BMI (No 3) Ltd* [1995] 4 All ER 453 considered.

Notes

For jurisdiction of court to consider enacting history of an Act as an aid to construction, see 44 *Halsbury's Laws* (4th edn reissue) paras 1419–1422, and for
f cases on the subject, see 45 *Digest* (Reissue) 315–316, *2720–2732.*

Cases referred to in judgment

Garland v British Rail Engineering Ltd Case 12/81 [1982] 2 All ER 402, [1983] 2 AC 751, [1982] 2 WLR 918, ECJ and HL.

Litster v Forth Dry Dock and Engineering Co Ltd [1989] 1 All ER 1134, [1990] 1 AC 546
g [1989] 2 WLR 634, HL.

Melluish (Inspector of Taxes) v BMI (No 3) Ltd [1995] 4 All ER 453, [1995] 3 WLR 630, HL.

Pepper (Inspector of Taxes) v Hart [1993] 1 All ER 42, [1993] AC 593, [1992] 3 WLR 1032, HL.

h *Pickstone v Freemans plc* [1988] 2 All ER 803, [1989] AC 66, [1988] 3 WLR 265, HL.

R v International Stock Exchange of the UK and the Republic of Ireland Ltd, ex p Else (1982) Ltd [1993] 1 All ER 420, [1993] QB 534, [1993] 2 WLR 70, CA.

Factortame Ltd v Secretary of State for Transport [1989] 2 All ER 692, [1990] 2 AC 85, [1989] 2 WLR 997, HL.

j *von Colson v Land Nordrhein-Westfalen* Case 14/83 [1984] ECR 1891.

Application

The plaintiffs, Three Rivers District Council and 6,018 others who had made deposits with the Bank of Credit and Commerce International SA (in liquidation) (BCCI), together with BCCI as non-claiming plaintiffs, applied for leave to refer to two speeches made by ministers in Parliament in the main action brought by the plaintiffs against the defendant, the Bank of England, for misfeasance in public office in the performance of the Bank's duty to supervise banking operations in the United Kingdom. The facts are set out in the judgment.

Sir Patrick Neill QC, David Vaughan QC, Dominic Dowley and *Robin Dicker* (instructed by *Lovell White Durrant*) for the plaintiffs.
Nicholas Stadlen QC, Paul Lasok QC, Mark Phillips, Bankim Thanki and *Rhodri Thompson* (instructed by *Freshfields*) for the Bank of England.

CLARKE J. This is an application by the plaintiffs for leave to refer to two speeches made by ministers in Parliament. The first is that made by the Minister of State at the Treasury on 23 November 1978, when he moved the second reading of the Bill which subsequently became the Banking Act 1979 and the second is that made by the Economic Secretary to the Treasury on 28 November 1986, when he moved the second reading of the Bill which became the Banking Act 1987.

The notice given in accordance with the relevant practice direction says that the plaintiffs intend to refer to those speeches in support of an argument that the Bank of England's contentions in its written submissions that the Banking Acts of 1979 and 1987 were not intended by Parliament to impose on the defendant an obligation to protect depositors and potential depositors from negligence, impropriety, dishonesty, etc on the part of credit institutions are wrong and that such plainly was the intention of Parliament in passing those Acts.

Mr Stadlen QC on behalf of the Bank of England submits that the plaintiffs are not entitled to rely upon the statements, in accordance with the strict criteria laid down in *Pepper (Inspector of Taxes) v Hart* [1993] 1 All ER 42, [1993] AC 593 and *Melluish (Inspector of Taxes) v BMI (No 3) Ltd* [1995] 4 All ER 453, [1995] 3 WLR 630. He submits that those cases are authority for the proposition that parliamentary materials (which are limited to clear statements by the minister or other promoters of the bill directed to the very point in question in the litigation) are admissible only where (1) the question in issue between the parties is the true construction of a provision in the relevant statute; (2) the provision is ambiguous or obscure or its literal meaning leads to an absurdity; or (3) the statements are directed to the specific statutory provision under consideration.

Subject to one point, I accept the submission that those cases are authority for those propositions in the case of ordinary domestic legislation. The one point is that in each case the House of Lords was considering a question of construction of a particular statutory provision. It was not considering the case where the court might be considering the purpose or object of a statute for some reason other than the construction of a particular statutory provision. Moreover, the House was considering a purely domestic statute. In my judgment, it does not necessarily follow that the principle applies so narrowly to a case where the purpose of the legislation is to introduce into English law the provisions of an international convention or of a European directive, even where the question is one of construction; a fortiori to a case where the question for decision is not one of construction.

Neither *Pepper v Hart* nor *Melluish v BMI* was considered such a case, since both cases were concerned with taxing statutes unconnected with the European Union. In my judgment, the authorities suggest that the court's approach to such cases may well be more flexible.

a   In *Pickstone v Freemans plc* [1988] 2 All ER 803, [1989] AC 66 the House of Lords permitted reference to be made to parliamentary materials in considering s 1(2)(c) of the Equal Pay Act 1970, which was introduced by the Equal Pay (Amendment) Regulations 1983, SI 1983/1794, in order to give effect to a decision of the Court of Justice of the European Communities. Lord Keith said ([1988] 2 All ER 803 at 807, [1989] AC 66 at 112):

b   'The draft regulations of 1983 were presented to Parliament as giving full effect to the decision in question. The draft regulations were not subject to the parliamentary process of consideration and amendment in committee, as a Bill would have been. In these circumstances and in the context of s 2 of the European Communities Act 1972 I consider it to be entirely legitimate
c   for the purpose of ascertaining the intention of Parliament to take into account the terms in which the draft was presented by the responsible minister and which formed the basis of its acceptance. The terms in which it was presented to the House of Commons are set out in the speech of my noble and learned friend Lord Templeman. Much the same was said before
d   the House of Lords. There was no suggestion that the exclusionary words in para (c) were intended to apply in any other situation than where the man selected by a woman complainant for comparison was one in relation to whose work para (a) or para (b) applied. It may be that, in order to confine the words in question to that situation, some necessary implication falls to be made into their literal meaning. The precise terms of that implication do not
e   seem to me to matter. It is sufficient to say that the words must be construed purposively in order to give effect to the manifest broad intention of the maker of the regulations and of Parliament.'

It is, as it seems to me, plain from Lord Keith's approach that the reason why the terms in which the draft regulations were presented to Parliament were
f   admissible was to ascertain the purpose of the provisions. That is because the words in such a statute are to be construed purposively.

In the same case Lord Oliver held that words must be implied into the section in order to achieve the purpose which he had gleaned from the minister's explanatory note to the regulations, which was not, of course, part of the
g   regulations themselves. He relied upon the following passage from the speech of Lord Diplock in *Garland v British Rail Engineering Ltd* Case 12/81 [1982] 2 All ER 402 at 415, [1983] 2 AC 751 at 771:

'My Lords, even if the obligation to observe the provisions of art 119 were
h   an obligation assumed by the United Kingdom under an ordinary international treaty or convention and there were no question of the treaty obligation being directly applicable as part of the law to be applied by the courts in this country without need for any further enactment, it is a principle of construction of United Kingdom statutes, now too well established to call for citation of authority, that the words of a statute passed
j   after the treaty has been signed and dealing with the subject matter of the international obligation of the United Kingdom, are to be construed, if they are reasonably capable of bearing such a meaning, as intended to carry out the obligation and not to be inconsistent with it. A fortiori is this the case where the treaty obligation arises under one of the Community treaties to which s 2 of the European Communities Act 1972 applies.'

Similarly, Lord Templeman said ([1988] 2 All ER 803 at 815, [1989] AC 66 at 123):

> 'In *von Colson and Kamann v Land Nordrhein-Westfalen* Case 14/83 [1984]
> ECR 1891 at 1909 (para 28), 1910–1911 (operative part of the judgment (para
> 3)) the European Court advised that in dealing with national legislation
> designed to give effect to a directive: "3 It is for the national court to
> interpret and apply the legislation adopted for the implementation of the
> directive in conformity with the requirements of Community law, in so far
> as it is given discretion to do so under national law."'

Similar considerations to those expressed in *Pickstone's* case appear in *Litster v Forth Dry Dock and Engineering Co Ltd* [1989] 1 All ER 1134, [1990] 1 AC 546.

It may be said that the approach to construction should be the same in both European and non-European cases because in *Pepper v Hart* Lord Browne-Wilkinson said that one of the reasons for the approach adopted in that case was that statutes should be construed purposively. There is obviously some force in that point but it does seem to me that, in the light of the principles discussed in the *Garland, Litster* and *Pickstone* cases, where the court is seeking to construe a statute purposively and consistently with any relevant European materials, including directives, it is of particular importance to ascertain the true purpose of the statute.

In these circumstances, I would expect the courts to adopt a somewhat more flexible approach than that laid down in *Pepper v Hart* and *Melluish v BMI*, which had no international or European element. In this connection I note that in *Pickstone v Freemans plc* Lord Templeman expressed the view that, at least in the context of unamended regulations, it was permissible to have regard both to the explanations of the government and to the criticisms voiced by members of Parliament.

It is not, however, at present necessary to determine in the instant case the question whether a more flexible approach can be adopted in an international or European context. Like *Pepper v Hart* and *Melluish v BMI*, both the *Pickstone* and *Litster* cases involved the question of construction of a statutory provision, or perhaps the question whether words should be implied into a statutory provision, which may amount to much the same thing.

Mr Stadlen submits that no question of construction of a particular provision of either statute arises in the instant case, at least at this stage. That may be so. In that connection I wait the further development of the plaintiffs' submissions, although I note from Sir Patrick Neill QC's submission that it is the plaintiffs' case that some implication may be required in the Banking Acts.

The plaintiffs say that, quite apart from any question of construction, it is relevant to note that one of the purposes of the 1979 Act was to comply with the United Kingdom's obligation under the Council Directive (EEC) 77/780 on the coordination of laws, regulations and administrative provisions relating to the taking up and pursuit of the business of credit institutions. They say that, in order to consider whether and to what extent that is so, reference should be made to the parliamentary materials. As Sir Patrick Neill put it, the court can look at the material to see what the object was.

It appears to me that the object or purpose of the statutes may be material to a number of aspects of the preliminary issues which I am at present considering. Mr Stadlen submits that the Bank of England owes no duty of care or statutory a   duty to the plaintiffs. Indeed, he submits that that is common ground. His submissions have ranged over a wide area of principle and policy.

It is at least relevant to those submissions that Parliament has enacted statutes, neither of which contains an express statutory duty, and one of which provides, in effect, that neither the Bank nor its servants or agents shall be liable for anything done or omitted to be done in the discharge, or purported discharge of b   its functions under that Act in the absence of bad faith. It is also part of the Bank of England's argument that there should be no extension of the tort of misfeasance in public office, which is what it says the plaintiffs' case involves.

It seems to me that in evaluating those submissions it is, or may be, relevant to consider the object and purpose of the Banking Acts 1979 and 1987. It also seems to me that the purpose and object of the statutes are, or may be, relevant to the c   issues between the parties arising out of the 1977 banking directive. Mr Lasok QC has made detailed submissions as to the meaning and effect of the terms of the directive and its recitals.

In that connection Sir Patrick Neill has drawn attention, without objection, to the original proposed draft directive, to the opinion of the Economic and Social d   Committee and to the subsequent amendments to the recitals in the directive. The relevance of such materials is recognised by the Court of Appeal in *R v International Stock Exchange of the UK and the Republic of Ireland Ltd, ex p Else (1982) Ltd* [1993] 1 All ER 420, [1993] QB 534, where the court itself asked to see them. It is not in dispute that, as Lord Browne-Wilkinson put it in *Pepper v Hart* [1993] 1 All ER 42 at 61, [1993] AC 593 at 630:
e

> 'This rule [the exclusionary rule] has now been relaxed so as to permit reports of commissioners, including Law Commissioners, and white papers to be looked at for the purpose solely of ascertaining the mischief which the statute is intended to cure but not for the purpose of discovering the f   meaning of the words used by Parliament to effect such cure ...'

He also said ([1993] 1 All ER 42 at 65, [1993] AC 593 at 635):

> 'As I have said, the court can now look at white papers and official reports for the purpose of finding the "mischief" sought to be corrected, although not at draft clauses or proposals for the remedying of such mischief. A g   ministerial statement made in Parliament is an equally authoritative source of such information; why should the courts be cut off from this source of information as to the mischief aimed at? In any event, the distinction between looking at reports to identify the mischief aimed at but not to find the intention of Parliament in enacting the legislation is highly artificial. h   Take the normal Law Commission report which analyses the problem and then annexes a draft Bill to remedy it. It is now permissible to look at the report to find the mischief and at the draft Bill to see that a provision in the draft was not included in the legislation enacted (see *Factortame Ltd v Secretary of State for Transport* [1989] 2 All ER 692, [1990] 2 AC 85). There can be no j   logical distinction between that case and looking at the draft Bill to see that the statute as enacted reproduced, often in the same words, the provision in the Law Commission's draft. Given the purposive approach to construction now adopted by the courts in order to give effect to the true intentions of the legislature, the fine distinctions between looking for the mischief and looking for the intention in using words to provide the remedy are technical and inappropriate. Clear and unambiguous statements made by ministers in

Parliament are as much the background to the enactment of legislation as white papers and parliamentary reports.'

Those statements were made in the course of the consideration by Lord Browne-Wilkinson of what materials could be looked at for the purposes of construction of a particular statutory provision. It seems to me, however, that if the objects of the statutes are relevant for any purpose, it would indeed be odd if the only documents which could not be looked at were the statements of the ministers promoting the Bill, when it is permissible to have regard to other materials, including proposals by the Commission, reports of the Economic and Social Committee, Law Commission Reports and white papers.

I recognise, of course, that ministerial statements are only part of the relevant materials. How much, if any, assistance they will be remains to be seen, but I decline to rule them inadmissible. I have already expressed the view that they are relevant, or potentially relevant, to some of the Bank of England's submissions, both those advanced by Mr Stadlen and those advanced by Mr Lasok. They also seem to me to be relevant or potentially relevant to the plaintiffs' submissions on the 1977 directive. Those submissions have not yet been developed, but as I understand them at present, the plaintiffs say, inter alia, that the 1977 directive conferred certain rights on the plaintiffs, and that it was the duty of the United Kingdom to implement the directive in order to ensure that the plaintiffs were able to exercise those rights in England. In particular, they say that it was the duty of the legislature and the executive and that it is the duty of the courts to discharge the duty imposed upon the United Kingdom in order to ensure that the plaintiffs have effective rights.

The correct legal analysis of the position thus depends, or may depend, in part at least, upon whether and to what extent Parliament enacted the provisions of the 1977 directive. A consideration of that question involves or may involve a consideration of the 1979 and 1987 Acts, which in turn involves a consideration of the object and purpose of the Acts. That in its turn involves, or potentially involves, a consideration not only of the European materials relevant to the directive, to which I have referred, but also of what the minister said.

I am not, of course, prejudging in any way whether any of the steps of the plaintiffs' argument should be accepted, but I accept Sir Patrick Neill's submission that I should look at the minister's statements, which I have not yet done. There is, in my judgment, nothing in *Pepper v Hart* or *Melluish v BMI* which prevents me from doing so, because they were considering a different and much narrower question, namely the question of construction of particular statutes.

I would only add that, although I have not yet heard argument as to what approach I should adopt to any particular white paper, I think it very likely that I shall adopt the same approach.

Order accordingly.

K Mydeen Esq   Barrister.

a DTC (CNC) Ltd v Gary Sargeant & Co (a firm)

CHANCERY DIVISION

MICHAEL CRYSTAL QC SITTING AS A DEPUTY JUDGE OF THE HIGH COURT

b 16, 19 JANUARY 1996

Accountant – Lien – Unpaid fees – Particular lien – Books and papers of client coming into possession of accountant during course of ordinary professional work – Whether accountant entitled to exercise lien over books and papers for unpaid fees – Whether books and papers 'accounting records' subject to statutory duties as to location and c *inspection – Companies Act 1985, ss 221, 222.*

In May 1993 the plaintiff company retained the defendant firm of chartered accountants and thereafter delivered to the defendant various documents relating to its business affairs. When the retainer was terminated in May 1995 the d plaintiff asked for the return of its documents. The defendant claimed that it was owed £4,715·49 in respect of unpaid professional fees and purported to assert a lien over certain categories of documents belonging to the plaintiff, including sales and purchase invoices, cheque books, paying-in books and bank statements, until the unpaid fees were discharged. Other documents, including lists of aged debtors and creditors and bank payments and receipts, were returned. e Thereafter the plaintiff commenced proceedings seeking an order that the defendant deliver up all accounting records still in its possession, on the basis that ss 221[a] and 222[b] of the Companies Act 1985 imposed a mandatory duty on the plaintiff to keep its accounting records at its registered office and open to public inspection. The defendant, while conceding that the relevant documents were f capable of being accounting records within the meaning of s 221 of the Act, nevertheless contended that the documentation which had been returned to the plaintiff contained full details of the information withheld, with the result that the withheld documents were no longer accounting records within the meaning of s 221.

g **Held** – An accountant could not exercise a lien over books or documents of a client company which were accounting records within the meaning of ss 221 and 222 of the 1985 Act and were required by statute to be kept at a particular place, or to be available for a particular purpose such as inspection. Further, once a document was created as an accounting record within s 221, it did not lose its h status as such, even though an accountant had collated the information contained in it and transposed that information in whole or in part onto some other document. On the facts, the documents sought to be returned would ordinarily be classed as accounting records within the meaning of s 221 of the Act, and accordingly the defendant could not lawfully maintain a claim to a lien over them. The plaintiff was therefore entitled to an order for delivery up (see p 373 j *d* to *g*, p 374 *h j*, p 375 *b* to *f* and p 376 *f* to *h*, post).

Re Capital Fire Insurance Association (1883) 24 Ch D 408 and *Re Firedart Ltd, Official Receiver v Fairall* [1994] 2 BCLC 340 applied.

---

a   Section 221, so far as material, is set out at p 373 *j* to p 374 *c*, post
b   Section 222, so far as material, is set out at p 374 *e* to *g*, post

Notes

For particular liens, see 28 *Halsbury's Laws* (4th edn) paras 534, 541, and for cases *a*
on the subject, see 32(2) *Digest* (2nd reissue) 38–39, *239–241* and 9(2) *Digest* (2nd
reissue) 305–307, *5458–5466*.
    For the Companies Act 1985, ss 221, 222, see 8 *Halsbury's Statutes* (4th edn)
(1991 reissue) 312, 313.

b

Cases referred to in judgment

Anglo-Maltese Hydraulic Dock Co Ltd, Re (1885) 54 LJ Ch 730.
Capital Fire Insurance Association, Re (1883) 24 Ch D 408, CA.
Firedart Ltd, Re, Official Receiver v Fairall [1994] 2 BCLC 340.
Woodworth v Conroy, Conroy v Woodworth [1976] 1 All ER 107, [1976] QB 884,
    [1976] 2 WLR 338, CA.   *c*

Case also cited or referred to in skeleton arguments

Chantrey Martin & Co v Martin [1953] 2 All ER 691, [1953] 2 QB 286, CA.

Motion   *d*

By notice dated 11 January 1995 the plaintiff, DTC (CNC) Ltd, sought an order
that the defendant firm of chartered accountants, Gary Sargeant & Co (the firm),
deliver up to the plaintiff all accounting record documents owned by the plaintiff
and held by the firm under a purported lien pending discharge of unpaid
professional fees. The facts are set out in the judgment.

e

John Machell (instructed by *Kingsford Stacey*, agents for *Dawbarns*, Wisbech) for the
    plaintiff.
Richard Handyside (instructed by *Clarkson Wright & Jakes*, Orpington) for the firm.

Cur adv vult
f

19 January 1996. The following judgment was delivered.

MICHAEL CRYSTAL QC.

Introduction
In May 1993 the plaintiff company, DTC (CNC) Ltd, retained the defendant firm *g*
of chartered accountants, Gary Sargeant & Co (the firm), to act as the plaintiff's
accountants. The plaintiff thereafter delivered to the firm documents dealing
with its business affairs. The firm's retainer was terminated in May 1995. The
plaintiff asked to have its documents returned. The firm claimed to be owed
£4,715·49 in respect of unpaid professional fees. In these circumstances it *h*
contends that it is entitled to assert a lien over certain categories of documents
belonging to the plaintiff, which are still in the firm's possession, until its unpaid
professional fees are discharged. The question which I have to decide is whether
the firm's claim to rely on such a lien is good in law.

j

The notice of motion
    The present proceedings were commenced by the plaintiff on 24 November
1995. A statement of claim has been served. By notice of motion dated 11
January 1996 the plaintiff seeks, so far as is material to this judgment, the
following relief. (1) An order that the firm do deliver up to the plaintiff: (a) the
plaintiff's statutory registers, (b) the plaintiff's statutory book of minutes, and (c)

a the plaintiff's company seal. (2) An order that the firm do deliver up to the plaintiff all accounting record documents owned by the plaintiff which are in the possession of the firm.

On 12 January 1996 the firm's solicitors wrote to the plaintiff's solicitors, so far as material, as follows:

b 'Our client is prepared to make available to you for collection those documents specified at paragraphs 1a and 1b of the Notice of Motion. Please let us have your client's proposed arrangements for collection. Our client is not in possession of your client's company seal, specified at paragraph 1c of the Notice of Motion and therefore our client is unable to produce this to your clients. All other accounting record documents formally held by our client, which your client was entitled to have returned, were collected by your client on 29 June 1995. Those items collected by your client were as set out in our letter to Leigh Williams of 27 June 1995. We have advised our client that he has a valid lien over the remainder of the documents held by him and which are referred to in your client's Notice of Motion. Our client has performed work in relation to those documents for which your client refuses to pay. There are therefore no further items your client is entitled to.'

c

d

The motion was argued on 16 January 1996. By that stage the documents referred to in paras 1(a) and (b) of the notice of motion had not in fact been collected. However, in the light of the offer to return these documents, there was no remaining dispute before me as to the right of the plaintiff to their return. Having regard to the claim by the firm's solicitors that the firm was not in possession of the plaintiff's company seal, Mr Machell, counsel for the plaintiff, accepted that he could not continue to seek its delivery up on this motion. Accordingly, no live issue arose on para 1 of the notice of motion.

e

The position in relation to para 2 of the notice of motion was different. On 27 June 1995 the firm's solicitors had written to the plaintiff's solicitors, so far as material, as follows.

f

g 'Our client has now reviewed the papers in his possession and has found records relating to the years ended 93 and 94. We have advised our client to release these papers to you. Please confirm when your client intends to collect these papers and we shall make arrangements with our client ... Our client is only bound to release to yours accounting records which will be released in addition to the above. These documents are: 1. aged debtors 31 March 1995 2. aged creditors 31 March 1995 3. listing of bank payments and receipts 4. sales day book and 5. purchase day book. Our client will not release management accounts and trial balance documents over which he has a good and proper lien.'

h

I should mention that the 1993 and 1994 records covered the periods up to 30 September 1994.

Paragraph 2 of the notice of motion refers to 'all accounting record documents owned by the Plaintiff'. Paragraph 4 of the statement of claim is more specific. It refers to the following categories:

j

'... a. sales invoices; b. purchase invoices; c. cheque books; d. paying-in books; e. bank statements; and f. other accounting record documents.'

Items (a) to (e) are at the heart of the dispute between the parties on this motion. Paragraph 7(e) of the statement of claim introduced two further specific categories of documents, 'periodic management accounts and trial balance documents'. Although there was some discussion about the categories pleaded in para 4(f) and in para 7(e) of the statement of claim, I did not understand Mr Machell in the end to contend that the court could deal with those categories on this motion. Therefore, it is with the categories identified in para 4(a) to (e) of the statement of claim, which I have set out above, that this judgment is principally concerned.

Mr Handyside, counsel for the firm, did not submit that there were any particular documents within any of the relevant categories which required specific individual treatment. Accordingly, I am able to approach the issue on a category or class basis rather than on an individual or contents basis.

The accountants' lien

It is well established that, in general terms, accountants in the course of doing their ordinary professional work may acquire the right to exercise a particular lien over any books of account, files and papers which their clients deliver to them (see the decision of the Court of Appeal in *Woodworth v Conroy, Conroy v Woodworth* [1976] 1 All ER 107, [1976] QB 884). However, the right to exercise such a lien is not enforceable in all circumstances. Section 246(2) of the Insolvency Act 1986 renders any lien unenforceable to the extent that its enforcement would deny possession of any books, papers or other records to an 'office-holder' (an administrator, liquidator or provisional liquidator of a company).

Furthermore, there is a line of authority in relation to solicitors which makes it clear that a solicitor is not able to exercise a lien over books or documents of a client company which are required by statute or by its articles of association to be kept at a particular place, or to be available for a specific purpose such as inspection. In *Re Capital Fire Insurance Association* (1883) 24 Ch D 408 the company's solicitor claimed a lien over its share register and minute book. Cotton LJ, with whom Bowen LJ agreed, stated the following principle (at 418–419):

'Two of these documents, viz., the register of shareholders and the minute book, stand in a peculiar position. Can the Appellant establish any lien upon them so as to prevent the official liquidator from having them in his possession for the purposes of the winding-up? In my opinion he cannot. No doubt a solicitor gets his lien without any special contract, but still his lien arises from contract, and he can claim no greater lien than the person who puts the documents into his hands is capable of creating. It is true that the directors of the company have a general power of dealing with the property of the company, but, so far as no express power is given to them, they have only such powers of mortgage and sale as are reasonably incident to the business they carry on, they must not deal with any property of the company in a way inconsistent with the objects and constitution of the company, and this decides the case as to these two books. The register of shareholders is a book which, under the Companies Act, 1862, s. 32, is to be kept at the office of the company for the purposes there mentioned, and that being so, in my opinion the directors have no power to deal with it in such a way as to interfere with these purposes. It is true that when a winding-up order has been made the purposes of a going company are at an end, but there arise on the making the order similar duties, which make it necessary that the register a should be in the hands of the liquidator. As regards the book containing the minutes of meetings the case is not so clear, but, having regard to the articles and constitution of the company, I am of opinion that the directors have no authority to deal with that book so as to deprive themselves of the full power of using it for the purposes of the company.'

b Re Capital Fire Insurance Association was followed by Kay J in Re Anglo-Maltese Hydraulic Dock Co Ltd (1885) 54 LJ Ch 730. He observed (at 731):

'... that such books as by the articles of the company or the Companies Acts ought to be kept at the registered office of the company, or to be dealt with in any special way, are books which ought not to be placed in the hands of the solicitor to the company, and are therefore books over which the
c solicitor can obtain no lien.'

There appears to me to be no relevant distinction to be made between the position of a solicitor and that of an accountant in this respect. In my judgment, therefore, the principle laid down by the Court of Appeal in Re Capital Fire Insurance Association applies equally to accountants and to solicitors.
d The Institute of Chartered Accountants of England and Wales produces a handbook for the guidance of its members (the ICAEW Handbook). The 1995 ICAEW Handbook was referred to in the course of argument. It includes a section on liens. Paragraph 18 of the relevant section is in these terms:

'An established line of authority exists in which the courts have held that
e no lien can exist over books or documents of a registered company which, either by statute or by the articles of association of the company, have to be available for public inspection or to be kept at the registered office or some other specified place or to be dealt with any in any special way. The main cases are Re Capital Fire Insurance Association ((1883) 24 Ch D 408) and Re
f Anglo-Maltese Hydraulic Dock Co Ltd ((1885) 54 LJ Ch 730). Although those cases concern solicitors' liens, the same principles apply in the case of accountants. Examples of documents which those cases held could not become the subject of a lien are the register of members and directors' minute books which the articles of association would almost certainly, expressly or impliedly, require to be kept available at all material times for
g the use of directors.'

This paragraph is in my view an accurate summary of the law on this point.
The decision in Re Capital Fire Insurance Association would have provided ample authority to justify an order in this case for the delivery up of the documents referred to in para 1(a) and (b) of the notice of motion if such an order had in fact
h been necessary. In the result, as I have already mentioned, there has been an offer of delivery up of the plaintiff's statutory registers and book of minutes.

Accounting records

Section 221 of the Companies Act 1985, as inserted by s 2 of the Companies Act
j 1989, imposes a duty on a company to keep accounting records. Subsections (1) to (3) of that section are in the following terms.

'(1) Every company shall keep accounting records which are sufficient to show and explain the company's transactions and are such as to—(a) disclose with reasonable accuracy, at any time, the financial position of the company at that time, and (b) enable the directors to ensure that any balance sheet and profit and loss account prepared under this Part complies with the requirements of this Act.

(2) The accounting records shall in particular contain—(a) entries from day to day of all sums of money received and expended by the company, and the matters in respect of which the receipt and expenditure takes place, and (b) a record of the assets and liabilities of the company.

(3) If the company's business involves dealing in goods the accounting records shall contain—(a) statements of stock held by the company at the end of each financial year of the company, (b) all statements of stocktakings from which any such statement of stock as is mentioned in paragraph (a) has been or is to be prepared, and (c) except in the case of goods sold by way of ordinary retail trade, statements of all goods sold and purchased, showing the goods and the buyers and sellers in sufficient detail to enable all these to be identified.'

Subsection (5) provides that where a company fails to comply with the section every officer of the company who is in default is guilty of an offence unless he shows that he acted honestly, and that in the circumstances in which the company's business was carried on the default was excusable.

Section 222 specifies where and for how long such accounting records are to be kept. Subsection (1) is in the following terms:

'(1) A company's accounting records shall be kept at its registered office or such other place as the directors think fit, and shall at all times be open to inspection by the company's officers.'

Subsection (4) creates a criminal offence to the like effect of that to be found in s 221(4). Subsections (5), so far as material, and (6) are in the following terms:

'(5) Accounting records which a company is required by section 221 to keep shall be preserved by it—(a) in the case of a private company, for three years from the date on which they are made, and (b) in the case of a public company, for six years from the date on which they are made ...

(6) An officer of a company is guilty of an offence, and liable to imprisonment or a fine or both, if he fails to take all reasonable steps for securing compliance by the company with subsection (5) or intentionally causes any default by the company under that subsection.'

These are important provisions of the 1985 Act. There is a criminal sanction if they are not complied with. The provisions impose mandatory duties on a company and its officers in connection with the keeping of accounting records, their preservation and their location, viz the company's registered office, or such other place as the directors think fit. The accounting records are at all times to be open to inspection by the company's officers. In these circumstances documents which are accounting records within the meaning of s 221 in my judgment fall squarely within the principle laid down by the Court of Appeal in *Re Capital Fire Insurance Association*.

The question which therefore arises is whether all or any of the categories of documents identified in para 4(a) to (e) of the statement of claim are 'accounting records' within the meaning of s 221. Mr Handyside, on behalf of the firm, conceded that each of the relevant classes of documents were capable of being accounting records within the meaning of s 221. This concession was inevitable.

a In my judgment, each of these classes of documents is not only capable of being, but ordinarily would be, accounting records within the meaning of s 221.

Mr Handyside's submission, however, was this. The aged debtors to 31 March 1995 documents and sales day book already returned to the plaintiff contain a summary of sales invoices. The aged creditors to 31 March 1995 documents and purchase day book already returned contain a summary of purchase invoices.
b The documents already returned listing bank payments and receipts include all the information contained in the plaintiff's cheque books, paying-in books and bank statements. Accordingly, Mr Handyside submits, the documentation already returned to the plaintiff contains full details of the information contained in the documentation which has been withheld by the firm. Therefore, he says, the withheld documents are no longer accounting records within the meaning of
c s 221.

In my judgment this submission is wrong. The fact that documents which are accounting records have been reviewed by an accountant, and summarised in other documents, does not mean that the source documents thereby cease to be accounting records within s 221. As Mr Machell observed, the logical conclusion
d of such an argument would be that once final accounts had been prepared all the source documentation would cease to be accounting records within s 221. This cannot be right. Furthermore, s 222(5)(a) provides that accounting records, which a company is required by s 221 to keep, shall be preserved by it, in the case of a private company, for three years from the date on which they are made. The source documents are, in my view, records which plainly fall within the
e preservation provisions of s 222(5). It would be extraordinary if, notwithstanding the fact that the source documents are required to be preserved by the 1985 Act as accounting records, they would have lost such a status for the purpose of determining whether an accountants' lien can attach to them.

In my judgment, once a document is created as an accounting document
f within s 221, it does not lose its status as such an accounting record because an accountant collates the information contained in or derived from it, and transposes such information in whole or in part onto some other document or documents.

Mr Machell referred to *Re Firedart Ltd, Official Receiver v Fairall* [1994] 2 BCLC
g 340. This was a directors disqualification case heard by Arden J. It was alleged, inter alia, that the director in question had failed to maintain accounting records as required by s 221. Arden J accepted the Official Receiver's complaint that it had not been possible to verify and explain all of the company's expenditure due to a lack of supporting vouchers and explanations (see [1994] 2 BCLC 340 at 345–346). Arden J concluded (at 346–347):
h

'Failure to make the relevant entries at all is obviously a breach of s 221. Failure to maintain documentary evidence sufficient to explain expenditure is equally a breach of the section.'

j Arden J's approach appears to me to be inconsistent with Mr Handyside's present submission.

Mr Handyside further submitted that a ruling in favour of the plaintiff would be inconsistent with the decision of the Court of Appeal in *Woodworth v Conroy* [1976] 1 All ER 107, [1976] QB 884. He relied on certain observations of Lawton LJ. The other members of the Court of Appeal agreed with Lawton LJ, who observed:

'I would adjudge that accountants in the course of doing their ordinary professional work of producing and auditing accounts, advising on financial problems and carrying on negotiations with the Inland Revenue in relation to both taxation and rating have at least a particular lien over any books of account, files and papers which their clients delivered to them and also over any documents which have come into their possession in the course of acting as their clients' agents in the course of their ordinary professional work.' (See [1976] 1 All ER 107 at 110, [1976] QB 884 at 890.)

In my judgment these observations do not cover, nor, with respect, were they intended to cover, the issue now before the court. Neither the reported arguments of counsel in that case, nor the judgments mention the point now at issue. The earlier decision of the Court of Appeal in *Re Capital Fire Insurance Association* was not cited. The then applicable statutory precursor of s 221 of the 1985 Act, s 147 of the Companies Act 1948 (subsequently replaced by s 12 of the Companies Act 1976), does not appear to have been referred to. The Court of Appeal in that case was not considering the ambit of exceptions to the right to exercise an accountants' lien. I accordingly reject Mr Handyside's further submission.

I have already referred to the *1995 ICAEW Handbook*. For completeness I should refer to para 19, which is in the following terms:

'Counsel advises that a lien will probably not be upheld in relation to the accounting records which a company must keep in order to comply with section 221 of the Companies Act 1985. Such records are documents which must by reason of that section be kept by the company, and which under section 222 must be kept at the registered office of the company or at such other place as the directors of the company think fit and must at all times be open to inspection by the officers of the company. It should be appreciated that "accounting records" within the meaning of section 221 covers a wide range of documents.'

In my judgment the potential ambit of 'accounting records' falling within the meaning of s 221 of the 1985 Act is very wide indeed.

Conclusion

I am satisfied that each of the categories of documents pleaded in para 4(a) to (e) of the statement of claim are 'accounting records' within the meaning of s 221. Accordingly, the firm cannot lawfully maintain a claim to a lien over them. The plaintiff is therefore entitled to an order from the court for their delivery up. I will discuss with counsel the precise form of such an order.

Order accordingly.

Celia Fox   Barrister.

a # Romain and another v Scuba TV Ltd and others

COURT OF APPEAL, CIVIL DIVISION
EVANS, WAITE LJJ AND SIR JOHN MAY
6, 10 NOVEMBER 1995

b *Limitation of action – Land – Action for recovery of arrears of rent – Action against guarantor of tenant's undertaking to pay rent – Lease and guarantee under seal – Whether action against guarantor being action to recover 'damages in respect of arrears of rent' – Whether six-year limitation period applying to action – Limitation Act 1980, s 19.*

c Section 19[a] of the Limitation Act 1980, which provides that no action shall be brought 'to recover arrears of rent, or damages in respect of arrears of rent, after the expiration of six years from the date on which the arrears became due', applies not only to actions against the lessee but also to actions against the d guarantor of the lessee's undertaking to pay the rent reserved by the lease, notwithstanding that both the lease and guarantee are under seal. The absence of any express reference to the surety in the section is not significant; indeed, the legal nature of the cause of action against the surety explains the reference to an action for damages, which otherwise would have no clear meaning (see p 381 *f* and p 383 *f*, post).

e **Notes**

For actions to recover rent, see 27(1) *Halsbury's Laws* (4th edn reissue) para 255, and for limitation of such actions, see ibid para 259.

For the Limitation Act 1980, s 19, see 24 *Halsbury's Statutes* (4th edn) (1989 f reissue) 669.

Cases referred to in judgments

Birkett v James [1977] 2 All ER 801, [1978] AC 297, [1977] 3 WLR 38, HL.
Brown's (J) Estate, Re, Brown v Brown [1893] 2 Ch 300.
Hawkins (decd), Re, Hawkins v Hawkins [1972] 3 All ER 386, [1972] Ch 714, [1972] g 3 WLR 265.
London and County (A & D) Ltd v Wilfred Sportsman Ltd (Greenwoods (Hosiers and Outfitters) Ltd, third party) [1970] 2 All ER 600, [1971] Ch 764, [1970] 3 WLR 418, CA.
Milverton Group Ltd v Warner World Ltd [1995] 2 EGLR 28, CA.
h *Moschi v Lep Air Services Ltd* [1972] 2 All ER 393, [1973] AC 331, [1972] 2 WLR 1175, HL.
President of India v La Pintada Cia Navegacion SA [1984] 2 All ER 773, [1985] AC 104, [1984] 3 WLR 10, HL.
Royton Industries Ltd v Lawrence [1994] 1 EGLR 110.
j *Swift (P & A) Investments (a firm) v Combined English Stores Group plc* [1988] 2 All ER 885, [1989] AC 632, [1988] 3 WLR 313, HL.

Cases also cited or referred to in skeleton arguments
Allied London Investments Ltd v Hambro Life Assurance Ltd [1984] 1 EGLR 16.

a Section 19 is set out at p 379 *a*, post

Barclays Bank plc v Miller (Frank, third party) [1990] 1 All ER 1040, [1990] 1 WLR 343, CA.

Bradford Old Bank Ltd v Sutcliffe [1918] 2 KB 833, CA.

Carter v White (1883) 25 Ch D 666, [1881–5] All ER Rep 921, CA.

Kumar v Dunning [1987] 2 All ER 801, [1989] QB 193, CA.

Appeal

By notice dated 30 December 1994 the third defendant, Steven Graham Brown, appealed with leave from the order of Simon Goldblatt QC, sitting as a deputy judge of the High Court in the Queen's Bench Division, dismissing his appeal from the decision of Master Eyre given on 19 October 1994, whereby he directed that an action brought by the plaintiffs, Philip Romain and Elizabeth Wolfson, against Scuba TV Ltd, Dennis Gordon Brown and the third defendant, claiming, inter alia, arrears of rent due under a lease dated 29 November 1982 of premises known as 640 Lea Bridge Road, Leyton, Essex and made between the plaintiffs and the first defendant, as lessee, and the second and third defendants, as guarantors, should not be struck out as against the third defendant for want of prosecution. The first and second defendants took no part in the proceedings. The facts are set out in the judgment of Evans LJ.

Guy Fetherstonhaugh (instructed by *Penningtons*, Basingstoke) for the defendant.

Leslie Michaelson (instructed by *Brown & Emery*, Watford) for the plaintiff.

Cur adv vult

10 November 1995. The following judgments were delivered.

EVANS LJ. The main issue in this appeal is whether the limitation period in a claim against the guarantor of a tenant's obligation to pay rent is twelve or six years, when both the guarantee and the lease are under seal. The guarantor is the third defendant in the action and the appellant in this court.

The question arises because the plaintiff landlords are liable to have a large part of their claim dismissed for want of prosecution; in other words, they or their representatives have been guilty of inordinate and inexcusable delay in the prosecution of the action. But if the limitation period is twelve years they could bring fresh proceedings if the present ones were dismissed, and it would be wrong to make the order in such circumstances (see *Birkett v James* [1977] 2 All ER 801, [1978] AC 297). On the other hand, if the limitation period is six years, most but not all of the claims were statute-barred when the application to dismiss the action for want of prosecution was made by the third defendant on 26 September 1994 and those claims, the defendant submits, should be dismissed accordingly. Master Eyre and the deputy judge, Simon Goldblatt QC, both held that the relevant period is twelve years. The third defendant's application therefore failed, and he now appeals.

A further issue is the date when the plaintiffs' cause or causes of action arose under the guarantee.

Section 8 of the Limitation Act 1980 provides that 'actions on a specialty' shall not be brought after the expiration of twelve years from the date on which the cause of action accrued (sub-s (1)) unless a shorter period is prescribed by any other provision of the Act (sub-s (2)). The defendant says that s 19 applies to a a claim against the guarantor of a tenant's obligation to pay rent. Section 19 reads as follows:

> '*Time limit for actions to recover rent.*—No action shall be brought, or distress made, to recover arrears of rent, or damages in respect of arrears of rent, after the expiration of six years from the date on which the arrears became due.'

b

THE LEASE

The lease of shop, offices and other premises at No 640 Lea Bridge Road, Leyton, Essex, was made under seal and dated 29 November 1982 for a period of 21 years. The second and third defendants were parties to it as joint guarantors
c of the first defendant, who was the lessee. Their undertaking is contained in cl 5:

> 'THE Guarantors ... hereby jointly and severally covenant with the Landlords that the Lessee will at all times during the continuance of this demise pay the rents hereby reserved and will also duly observe and perform the covenants on the part of the Lessee hereinbefore contained and that they
d will pay and make good to the Landlords on demand all losses damages costs and expenses thereby arising or sustained or incurred by the Landlords ...'

The last phrase 'thereby arising' etc does not make grammatical sense. We were told that words were omitted from the draft which make it clear that the reference intended is to a relevant default by the lessee. This does not affect the
e interpretation of the operative part of the clause, with which we are concerned.

DOES S 19 APPLY?

So the question is whether the claim against the guarantors under this clause following the lessee's failure to pay instalments of rent when they fell due is
f 'brought ... to recover arrears of rent, or damages in respect of arrears of rent' within s 19. If it is, then the relevant period is six years. If it is not, then because the action is brought 'on a specialty', s 8 applies and the period is twelve years.

The judge held that the claim is made under what may be called the second part of the undertaking by the guarantors: not for breach of their covenant that the lessee would pay the rents reserved by the lease, but under the words which
g follow: 'and that they will pay ... on demand all losses ... thereby arising [from default by the lessee].' He did not decide whether the first part gave rise to a separate cause of action but he said that if it did, it was difficult to avoid the conclusion that that was a claim for arrears of rent or for damages in respect of arrears of rent to which s 19 applied. But the claim for losses etc payable on
h demand was, he held, though not without hesitation, outside the section. He said that 'an action whose origin is a demand by the landlord in respect of the obligations of a surety in a lease under seal is not to be categorised as an action brought to recover damages in respect of arrears of rent'. He held, therefore, that the limitation period is twelve years, which had not expired, and that it would be
j inappropriate to strike out any part of the claim. The third defendant appeals.

The precise nature of the obligations of a surety, or guarantor, has been considered in a number of authorities, to which we were referred. The lessee's covenant to pay rent runs with the land—that is to say it may be enforced by a succeeding landlord even when the benefit of the covenant has not been assigned to him—and so does the surety's undertaking as regards that covenant also (see *P & A Swift Investments (a firm) v Combined English Stores Group plc* [1988] 2 All ER

885, [1989] AC 632, and compare *Royton Industries Ltd v Lawrence* [1994] 1 EGLR
110). Where a rent instalment is paid by the guarantor, at least in a case where
the guarantor expressly undertakes the same obligations as the lessee, then the
lessee's obligation is discharged also (see *Milverton Group v Warner World* [1995] 2
EGLR 28). But this does not lead, Mr Michaelson for the plaintiffs submits, to the
conclusion that the obligations of the guarantor and the lessee are one and the
same. He points to the judgment of the Court of Appeal in *London and County (A
& D) Ltd v Wilfred Sportsman Ltd (Greenwoods (Hosiers and Outfitters) Ltd, third
party)* [1970] 2 All ER 600 at 603, [1971] Ch 764 at 780 per Russell LJ: 'But in law
they were nothing but payments under the guarantee in satisfaction of the third
party's contractual obligation thereunder ...' and to the statement in the previous
edition of *Woodfall on Landlord and Tenant* (28th edn, 1978) para 7.085 (not in the
current edition) that 'Payment of arrears of rent by a guarantor of the lessee's rent
does not discharge the lessee' (cited in *Milverton Group* [1995] 2 EGLR 28 at 29 by
Glidewell LJ).

The court held in *Milverton Group* that that general statement was not justified
by the earlier authorities, and was too broad. Hoffmann LJ said that the facts in
London and County Ltd were unusual, because the erstwhile guarantor as well as
paying under the guarantee had acquired the reversion from the original landlord
and then claimed successfully to forfeit the lease for the tenant's failure to pay the
previous instalment of rent. The result could be justified 'on the basis that the
guarantor was entitled to be subrogated to the previous landlord's claim for the
rent and so, on acquiring the reversion, was entitled to exercise the right to forfeit
for non-payment' (see [1995] 2 EGLR 28 at 31). In *Re Hawkins (decd), Hawkins v
Hawkins* [1972] 3 All ER 386, [1972] Ch 714 Megarry J held that payments by a
guarantor in respect of interest due from the debtor retained their identity as
interest even though they were paid by force of the guarantee. Megarry J said
([1972] 3 All ER 386 at 398, [1972] Ch 714 at 728):

'What matters is the nature or quality of the thing paid and not the source
of the obligation to pay it. Rent is rent, a fine is a fine, a debt is a debt, and
interest is interest, whoever pays it.'

That was, however, a case where the guarantor was liable as primary obligor.

So Mr Michaelson submits that it was wrong to go so far as to describe the
obligations of guarantor and tenant as a 'single set', as Hoffmann LJ did in
Milverton Group, except possibly when the guarantor expressly undertakes the
same obligations as the tenant. This is because their obligations are separate and
distinct. The lessee undertakes to pay the rent, a liquidated sum, whilst the
guarantor undertakes that the lessee will perform that obligation, this being a
separate covenant which is broken if the lessee defaults and which renders the
guarantor liable in damages for the amount of the rent, but not for the rent itself.

This is the classic definition of the liability of a guarantor, as stated by Lord
Diplock in *Moschi v Lep Air Services Ltd* [1972] 2 All ER 393, [1973] AC 331, nor is
it disputed by Mr Fetherstonhaugh who appeared for the third defendant. So the
submission supports the landlords' contention that their claim against the
guarantors is not 'for arrears of rent', and therefore not within the first of the two
categories described in s 19. But it leads them into difficult terrain when the
second category is considered. Their claim admittedly is for damages; is it for
'damages in respect of arrears of rent', in which case also s 19 applies? The
question seems to compel an affirmative answer unless, as Mr Michaelson

a submits, the section is not concerned with claims against guarantors or other third parties, but only with claims against lessees.

This is, in my view, the central issue raised by this appeal. Apart from the literal meaning of the words, there are two formidable obstacles in the way of the landlords' contention. First, s 19 does not say that its operation is limited to lessees and others in like estate; it could easily have done so. Secondly, if its scope b is so limited, it is near impossible to give any realistic meaning to the phrase 'damages in respect of arrears of rent', particularly in the light of the House of Lords decision in *President of India v La Pintada Cia Navegacion SA* [1984] 2 All ER 773, [1985] AC 104 to the effect that no claim lies for general damages as opposed to interest when the breach of contract consists of the failure to pay a liquidated sum.

c On the other hand, the lineage of s 19 can be traced back through the Limitation Act 1939 (s 17, 'action ... to recover arrears of rent ... or damages in respect thereof') to the Real Property Limitation Act 1833 (s 42, 'no Arrears of Rent') and to the Limitation Act 1623, which refers to 'all actions of Debt for Arrears of Rent' (s 3). There is no express provision for the liability of a d guarantor, and it can fairly be said, in my view, that the statutes were concerned with the situation of the tenant, rather than of third parties, including sureties or guarantors.

The consequence, of course, if the tenant is protected by a six-year limit but the guarantor under seal is not, is that the latter remains liable 'in respect of' the same e obligations for the full period of twelve years, and for longer if no cause of action arises against him until the landlord demands payment from him.

I have come to the clear conclusion that s 19 applies the six-year time limit not only to actions against the lessee but also to actions against the guarantor of his undertaking to pay the rent reserved by the lease. In both cases, the action is f brought 'to recover arrears of rent, or damages in respect of arrears of rent' and the absence of any express reference to the surety is not, in my judgment, significant. The legal nature of the cause of action against the surety is entirely apt to explain the reference to an action for damages, which otherwise would have no clear meaning at all.

Equally, it is unnecessary in my judgment to consider further whether it is g appropriate to describe the obligations of the lessee and his surety as the same or forming 'a single set'. They are undoubtedly separate obligations, because they are owed by separate obligors, and their content cannot be for all purposes identical, if only because the liability of one is contingent upon default by the other. Nor is it necessary in the present case to consider the effect of words by h which the surety expressly undertakes the liabilities of the primary obligor. If such words existed here, it would be even clearer than it already is that the action against the surety falls within the scope of s 19, so that the six-year limit applies to the claim for, or rather in respect of, unpaid rent.

As for the authorities referred to above, it is wrong as a matter of law, in my j judgment, to attempt to deduce from them any general rule as to whether or not the guarantor's obligation is the same as that of the principal debtor or lessee. Payment of rent by the guarantor discharges the lessee (see *Milverton Group* [1995] 2 EGLR 28); but it does not enable the lessee to dispute a claim to forfeit the lease by the guarantor as assignee of the landlord's rights (see *London and County Ltd* [1970] 2 All ER 600, [1971] Ch 764). 'Rent is rent' but not necessarily for all purposes and between all the parties concerned. And as Lord Reid said in *Moschi*

v Lep Air Services Ltd [1972] 2 All ER 393 at 398, [1973] AC 331 at 344, the starting
point for any consideration of the liability of a guarantor is the guarantee itself:

> 'I would not proceed by saying this is a contract of guarantee and there is
> a general rule applicable to all guarantees. Parties are free to make any
> agreement they like and we must I think determine just what this agreement
> means.'

The issue was argued before us primarily as a matter of principle and upon the
basis that cl 5 imposed only one obligation on the third defendant as guarantor.
Mr Michaelson for the plaintiffs relied in the alternative on the judge's interpretation of the clause, whereby the relevant undertaking was to pay losses etc on
demand and the question whether the preceding words of guarantee gave rise to
a separate obligation was left open. Mr Fetherstonhaugh for the third defendant
did not expressly challenge this construction, but he made it clear that in his
submission the obligation was one of guarantee and the subsequent reference to
payment on demand was no more than 'procedural', amplifying the same
obligation. The same arguments are relevant to the second issue in the appeal,
which is whether the plaintiffs' cause of action arises when the rent becomes due
and the lessee's default occurs, or only when payment is demanded of the
guarantor.

The general rule that when the clause provides for a demand to be made then
the cause of action arises only when the demand is made is well established (see
Re J Brown's Estate, Brown v Brown [1893] 2 Ch 300). I do not see any reason for
departing from it in the present case. Similarly, the wording of cl 5 does not, in
my judgment, create two separate obligations, but only one. Each of the
guarantors undertook the obligations of a surety for the covenants of the lessee,
and as regards rent the possibly wider liability to pay the amount of losses etc, but
they stipulated for a demand to be made, as they were entitled to do.

CONCLUSION

Limitation

It follows that in my judgment the six-year limitation defence is available to the
third defendant against the claim in respect of arrears of rent, and that each
relevant cause of action arose only when payment was demanded under the
guarantee. The result, we were told, is that some but not all of these claims were
statute-barred at the relevant time (see below). The action should therefore be
permitted to proceed in respect of the remaining rent claims, together with other
claims, e g for dilapidations, to which the twelve-year limit under s 8(1) applies.

Dismissal for want of prosecution

We allowed an application at the hearing of the appeal for leave to file a
respondent's notice which contends that no part of the claim should be dismissed
because the action will continue in any event in respect of those claims for arrears
of rent which were demanded within the six-year period and other claims not
concerning rent. Moreover, the judge 'ought further to have held that the
defendants would suffer no serious prejudice if the entirety of the claim (as
opposed to part only) was allowed to proceed and further that it would be
possible in the circumstances to have a fair trial of the issues'.

The judge made the following finding which although contingent was a clear
exercise of his discretion:

a 'I add this, that if I had taken a different view of the application of s 19 of the Limitation Act 1980, I should then in the exercise of my discretion have struck out those parts of the plaintiffs' claim which relate to losses, damages, costs or expenses arising more than six years before the date of the relevant demand.' (The last phrase may be mistranscribed but the meaning is clear.)

b The plaintiffs' submission, therefore, is that because some claims will proceed to trial it is wrong to strike out others which, if they stood alone, would not be allowed to do so. I agree with Mr Fetherstonhaugh's reply that this is to stand the rule upon its head. If in relation to some claims the defendant has suffered prejudice, or a fair trial is not possible, then the fact that there are other claims which must go to trial, notwithstanding that the defendant is or may be under the *c* same disadvantages in seeking to defend them, does not provide any justification for not striking out the former when that is otherwise the correct thing to do.

A question arose in the course of argument as to the relevant date for determining whether claims should not be struck out on the ground that fresh proceedings are not or would not be time-barred, in accordance with *Birkett v James* [1977] 2 All ER 801, [1978] AC 297. It might become necessary to *d* distinguish between the date of the defendant's summons and the dates of the hearing before the master and the rehearing before the judge, to say nothing of any subsequent appeal, and it would also be relevant to consider whether or not the plaintiffs' solicitors had responded to the summons by issuing a protective writ (see *Birkett v James* itself). We understand, however, that these problems are *e* unlikely to arise in the present case, and the parties have agreed that we should not identify those claims which should be permitted to proceed.

For these reasons, I would allow this appeal and dismiss some at least of the rent claims and make an order or declaration in such terms as may be agreed.

WAITE LJ. I agree.
f
SIR JOHN MAY. I also agree.

Appeal allowed.

Paul Magrath Esq   Barrister.

Morris v Murjani

a

COURT OF APPEAL, CIVIL DIVISION

HIRST, PETER GIBSON LJJ AND BUXTON J

20 DECEMBER 1995

b

Injunction – Interlocutory – Injunction restraining appellant from leaving jurisdiction – Bankrupt – Trustee having suspicion of undisclosed assets – Trustee having power to enforce bankrupt's statutory duties – Trustee applying for bankrupt's committal for contempt of court and injunction restraining him from leaving jurisdiction until after hearing – Whether court having jurisdiction to grant injunction – Whether pre-existing cause of action required – Insolvency Act 1986, ss 333, 366.

c

The appellant was declared bankrupt in 1991 but had since continued to lead a luxurious lifestyle. The trustee in bankruptcy, believing that the appellant was concealing assets, commenced proceedings seeking his committal for contempt of court. He also applied ex parte for, inter alia, an injunction restraining the appellant from leaving the country pending the hearing of the application for committal. The injunction was granted over a limited period in order to secure the appellant's compliance with his duty under s 333[a] to supply to the trustee such information as he might require for the purposes of carrying out his statutory functions. Thereafter, the appellant applied to set aside the injunction on the ground that the court had no jurisdiction to make the order. The judge dismissed the appellant's application, holding that there had been jurisdiction to grant the injunction which he then continued on the basis that the obligation of the bankrupt under s 333 and the correlative right of the trustee to require the bankrupt to do those things which he could be required to do created a hybrid right for the trustee, in appropriate cases, to seek the protection of the court. The appellant appealed to the Court of Appeal, contending that the right to an interlocutory injunction was dependent on a pre-existing cause of action, and that his duty to provide information to the trustee did not give rise to a cause of action in the trustee.

d

e

f

g

Held – The requirement of a pre-existing cause of action as the basis of the jurisdiction to grant an interlocutory injunction was only binding in cases involving an ordinary dispute relating to the alleged violation of private rights. Such cases could be distinguished from those involving s 333 of the 1986 Act, which imposed a type of public duty on a bankrupt which was plainly designed to assist the trustee in bankruptcy in the performance of his statutory duties. In such a case, the trustee was able to enforce the bankrupt's duties under s 333 in a number of ways: he could institute contempt proceedings under s 333(4), or seek orders under s 366[b], in respect of which injunctive relief might be granted. Since the distinction between a duty to comply with an order on the bankrupt under s 366 and a duty imposed on him by statute under s 333, following the court's adjudication order, was a tenuous one, there was no reason why the court could

h

j

---

a   Section 333, so far as material, is set out at p 386 j, post

b   Section 366, so far as material, provides: 'At any time after a bankruptcy order has been made the court may … summon to appear before it … the bankrupt …'

a not grant an injunction in circumstances such as those in the instant case. The
   appeal would accordingly be dismissed (see p 388 g to p 389 fj to p 390 d, post).
   Siskina (cargo owners) v Distos Cia Naviera SA, The Siskina [1977] 3 All ER 803 and
   Mercedes-Benz AG v Leiduck [1995] 3 All ER 929 distinguished.
   Re Oriental Credit Ltd [1988] 1 All ER 892 considered.

b **Notes**

   For jurisdiction to grant relief by way of injunction, see 24 *Halsbury's Laws* (4th
   edn reissue) paras 810–816, and for cases on the subject, see 28(4) *Digest* (2nd
   reissue) 115–118, 4667–4683.

   For the Insolvency Act 1986, ss 333, 366, see 4 *Halsbury's Statutes* (4th edn)
c (1987 reissue) 967, 999.

   Cases referred to in judgments

   Chief Constable of Hampshire v A Ltd [1984] 2 All ER 385, [1985] QB 132, [1984] 2
      WLR 954, CA.
   Chief Constable of Kent v V [1982] 3 All ER 36, [1983] QB 34, [1982] 3 WLR 462, CA.
d *Mercedes-Benz AG v Leiduck* [1995] 3 All ER 929, [1996] 1 AC 284, [1995] 3 WLR
      718, PC.
   North London Rly Co v Great Northern Rly Co (1883) 11 QBD 30, CA.
   Oriental Credit Ltd, Re [1988] 1 All ER 892, [1988] Ch 204, [1988] 2 WLR 172.
   Siskina (cargo owners) v Distos Cia Naviera SA, The Siskina [1977] 3 All ER 803,
e   [1979] AC 210, [1977] 3 WLR 818, HL.

   Cases also cited or referred to in skeleton arguments

   A-G v Chaudry [1971] 3 All ER 938, [1971] 1 WLR 1614, CA.
   Associated Newspapers Group plc v Insert Media Ltd [1988] 2 All ER 420, [1988] 1
f   WLR 509.
   Bayer AG v Winter [1986] 1 All ER 733, [1986] 1 WLR 497, CA.
   Carroll, Re [1931] 1 KB 104, [1930] All ER Rep 189, CA.
   Chiltern DC v Keane [1985] 2 All ER 118, [1985] 1 WLR 619, CA.
   Cooper v Whittingham (1880) 15 Ch D 501.
g *Harmsworth v Harmsworth* [1987] 3 All ER 816, [1987] 1 WLR 1676, CA.
   House of Spring Gardens Ltd v Waite [1985] FSR 173, CA.
   *MacLaine Watson & Co Ltd v Dept of Trade and Industry, Re International Tin Council,
      MacLaine Watson & Co Ltd v International Tin Council, MacLaine Watson & Co
      Ltd v International Tin Council (No 2)* [1988] 3 All ER 257, [1989] 1 Ch 286, CA.
h *South Carolina Insurance Co v Assurantie Maatschappij 'de Zeven Provincien' NV, South
      Carolina Insurance Co v Al Ahlia Insurance Co* [1986] 3 All ER 487, [1987] AC 24,
      HL.

   Appeal

   By notice dated 19 December 1995 Mohan Bhagwandas Murjani appealed with
j leave from the order of Sir John Vinelott sitting as a judge of the High Court on
   18 December 1995, whereby he ordered the continuation of an interlocutory
   injunction granted by Rimer J on 1 December 1995 restraining the appellant from
   leaving the country pending the hearing of an application by the respondent
   trustee in bankruptcy, Christopher Morris, for the committal of the appellant for
   contempt of court. The facts are set out in the judgment of Peter Gibson LJ.

Matthew Collings (instructed by *Nabarro Nathanson*) for Mr Murjani.

Philip Marshall (instructed by *Dibb Lupton Broomhead*) for the trustee.

PETER GIBSON LJ (delivering the first judgment at the invitation of Hirst LJ). This is an appeal, brought with the leave of the judge, by Mr Murjani from the order of Sir John Vinelott sitting as a judge of the High Court. That order was made as recently as 18 December 1995 and I am grateful to counsel for the speed with which they have prepared this appeal, including their helpful skeleton arguments. The respondent to the appeal is Mr Christopher Morris, the trustee in bankruptcy of Mr Murjani.

The trustee commenced proceedings seeking the committal of Mr Murjani for contempt. He also applied ex parte to Rimer J for, amongst other orders, an injunction restraining Mr Murjani from leaving the jurisdiction pending the hearing of the contempt application and an order for delivery up of his passport. That injunction was granted by Rimer J over a limited period. On 18 December Sir John Vinelott heard two applications inter partes. One application by Mr Murjani was to set aside the injunction of Rimer J on the grounds that the court had no jurisdiction to make the order, and also that the order was made without disclosure of all relevant facts. The other application was by the trustee seeking a continuation of Rimer J's injunction. Sir John Vinelott dismissed Mr Murjani's application but acceded to the trustee's application, giving Mr Murjani liberty to apply for modifications of the injunction as well as a cross-undertaking in damages. In making that order, the judge held that there was jurisdiction for Rimer J to grant the injunction and he exercised his discretion to order the continuation of the injunction.

The appeal has been limited to the issue of jurisdiction. It is, therefore, unnecessary to state the background facts in any great detail. Mr Murjani is a member of a family which formerly had extensive trading interests in Hong Kong. In 1979–80 trusts were set up for the benefit of the Murjani family, Mr Murjani's own assets being included in the assets transferred to the trust. Since then Mr Murjani has resided partly in New York and partly in London. He was made bankrupt on 19 December 1991 with debts of about £12m but, nevertheless, he has maintained a luxurious lifestyle. The first trustee in bankruptcy who succeeded the Official Receiver reported in 1992 that he was not hopeful of making any realisations and that he was satisfied that the Murjani family trusts could not be attacked. The present trustee, Mr Morris, was appointed on 23 December 1993. He was not satisfied that Mr Murjani had made full disclosure. On the trustee's application the automatic discharge, which Mr Murjani would have obtained through lapse of time after his bankruptcy, was suspended.

In December 1995 the application to Rimer J was made. The basis of the injunction granted by Rimer J was that it was in aid of securing the compliance by Mr Murjani with his duties under s 333 of the Insolvency Act 1986. Section 333, which is entitled 'Duties of bankrupt in relation to trustee', provides:

'(1) The bankrupt shall—(a) give to the trustee such information as to his affairs, (b) attend on the trustee at such times, and (c) do all such other things, as the trustee may for the purposes of carrying out his functions under any of this Group of Parts reasonably require ...'

Those are general duties without prejudice to which other specific duties (such as that in s 312, obliging the bankrupt to deliver up to the trustee possession of any *a* property, books, papers or other records of which he has possession or control) are also laid on the bankrupt.

Sir John Vinelott, in holding that Rimer J had jurisdiction to grant the injunction, expressed his reasoning in this way:

> 'Section 333 of the Insolvency Act imposes a duty on the bankrupt and I cite "to give to the trustee such information as to his affairs ... attend on the *b* trustee at such times, and ... do all such other things as the trustee may ... require". There is no equivalent section in the field of corporate insolvency. The obligation of the bankrupt and correlative right of the trustee to require the bankrupt to do those things which he can be required by the trustee to do creates a hybrid right for the trustee in appropriate cases to seek the *c* protection of the court by, for example, seeking an injunction restraining the bankrupt from disposing of assets and where appropriate a mandatory injunction to give details of assets the title to which is vested in the trustee by virtue of the bankruptcy order. So, for example, if the bankrupt had valuable chattels in his possession, the trustee could in principle claim a mandatory injunction requiring the bankrupt to give full details of those chattels and *d* take steps to obtain possession of them. If that is right, then I can see no obstacle in principle to granting an injunction restraining the bankrupt from leaving the jurisdiction while the trustee pursues his request for information. This right to information might be lost if the bankrupt leaves. Section 333(4) provides that if the bankrupt without reasonable excuse fails to comply with *e* any obligation imposed by the section he is guilty of contempt of court and this is one way in which the trustee's power to obtain information can be enforced. But it is not exclusive, and does not exclude other steps as ancillary to the right to information to bring bankruptcy assets under his control. Contempt under s 333(4) is a civil contempt which is ancillary to a civil right. So also, in a case of great urgency, the trustee may ask the court to issue a *f* warrant for the arrest of the debtor. Under s 364 that power may be exercised if there are reasonable grounds to believe that there are books, papers and records which the bankrupt has concealed or destroyed or is about to conceal or destroy which the trustee has a right to obtain. In the instant case there are allegations that the bankrupt has concealed assets and *g* papers which the trustee wishes to obtain for the purpose of obtaining information to which he has a right under s 333. As Mr Marshall (appearing on behalf of the trustee) pointed out, it would be absurd in the present case that the trustee could obtain an order for arrest of the bankrupt but could not obtain a lesser order restraining him from leaving the jurisdiction. An application for the bankrupt's arrest might be followed by an application for *h* relief pending hearing of the motion for committal for conduct in respect of which the arrest was ordered. An injunction obtained could have precisely the same effect and purpose [in restraining the bankrupt] from leaving the jurisdiction.'

j Mr Collings, for Mr Murjani, submits that the judge erred in holding that there was jurisdiction to grant the injunction. He submits that the familiar statement by Lord Diplock in *Siskina (cargo owners) v Distos Cia Naviera SA, The Siskina* [1977] 3 All ER 803 at 824, [1979] AC 210 at 256 continues to be good law and that it governs the present case. Lord Diplock considered the condition in RSC Ord 11, r 1(1)(i) 'if in the action begun by the writ ... an injunction is sought ...' and continued:

'The words in sub-para (i) are terms of legal art. The sub-paragraph speaks of "the action" in which a particular kind of relief, "an injunction", is sought. This pre-supposes the existence of a cause of action on which to found "the action". A right to obtain an interlocutory injunction is not a cause of action. It cannot stand on its own. It is dependent upon there being a pre-existing cause of action against the defendant arising out of an invasion, actual or threatened, by him of a legal or equitable right of the plaintiff for the enforcement of which the defendant is amenable to the jurisdiction of the court. The right to obtain an interlocutory injunction is merely ancillary and incidental to the pre-existing cause of action. It is granted to preserve the status quo pending the ascertainment by the court of the rights of the parties and the grant to the plaintiff of the relief to which his cause of action entitles him, which may or may not include a final injunction.'

That case related to an ordinary dispute involving the alleged violation of private rights. Very recently the correctness of *The Siskina* has been confirmed by the Privy Council in *Mercedes-Benz AG v Leiduck* [1995] 3 All ER 929, [1996] 1 AC 284, another case involving an ordinary dispute relating to private rights. Mr Collings submits that an interlocutory injunction is always incidental to, and dependent upon, the enforcement of a substantial right such as gives rise to a cause of action and proceedings based upon that cause of action. Mr Collings accepted the examples given by the judge that the trustee could seek an injunction restraining the bankrupt from disposing of assets, an injunction to disclose assets, the title to which is vested in the trustee by virtue of the automatic vesting in the trustee of the bankrupt's estate under s 306 of the 1986 Act, an injunction requiring the bankrupt to give full details of chattels in his possession and an injunction allowing the trustee to obtain possession of the chattels. But he submits that the injunction in this case went impermissibly further. He relied in particular on the decision of Harman J in *Re Oriental Credit Ltd* [1988] 1 All ER 892, [1988] Ch 204. In that case Harman J said that a statutory duty under the Companies Act 1985 to co-operate with, and give information and produce material to, liquidators, did not create a cause of action in the liquidators. Mr Collings submitted that the present case was indistinguishable.

Attractively though Mr Collings presented these arguments, I am not persuaded by them. In my judgment, the present litigation is not, and is not like, the litigation affecting private rights of litigants, such as was the case in *The Siskina*. Whilst I accept that this court is bound by what Lord Diplock said in relation to the type of case in which Lord Diplock's remarks were made, and to which his remarks were directed, I protest against the application of the words even of so eminent a judge as Lord Diplock as though they were words in a statute of universal application.

I also accept that the wide discretion of s 37 of the Supreme Court Act 1981, giving the court power to grant an injunction in all cases in which it appears to the court to be just and convenient to do so, does not entitle the court to exercise its discretion unless there is some substantive right, the infringement of which is threatened. I respectfully agree with the remarks of Lord Mustill in the *Mercedes-Benz* case [1995] 3 All ER 929 at 942, [1996] 1 AC 284 at 303:

'But the action or other originating process in which the application for an injunction is embodied founds upon an assertion of substantive rights whose validity is a prerequisite of the proper grant of relief. The remedy is knitted together with the rights and the threatened infringement of them.'

a   Those remarks seem to be entirely apposite to the present circumstances.
    In the present case, it is not in dispute that s 333(1) of the 1986 Act has imposed a type of public duty on the bankrupt, though not one, in my view, such as would be enforceable only at the suit of the Attorney General. The duty is owed, as Mr Collings accepts, to the trustee, who is the person designated as being able to require the performance and determine the content of that duty and who can
b   enforce it. A trustee has the right, and in appropriate circumstances it may be said that he also has the duty, to enforce the statutory duty owed by the bankrupt. The bankrupt's estate has become vested in the trustee as a result of the adjudication order made by the court. The trustee must therefore collect the assets of the estate as speedily as possible, which may require the obtaining of information in order to trace the relevant assets. His ultimate object is to make
c   a distribution in accordance with the statutory scheme. The duties imposed on the bankrupt are all plainly designed to assist the trustee in the performance by him of his statutory functions.
    The trustee may enforce the bankrupt's duties under s 333 in a number of ways. He can in an appropriate case institute contempt proceedings under
d   s 333(4). He can seek orders under s 366. Mr Collings accepted that if an order under s 366 had been obtained, an injunction such as was granted in the present case would lie. To my mind, for the purposes of granting injunctive relief, the distinction between a duty to comply with an order on the bankrupt under s 366 and a duty imposed on him by statute under s 333, following the court's adjudication order, is a tenuous one. Like the judge, I can see no reason why the
e   court cannot grant an injunction in circumstances such as the present. It would be extraordinary if the trustee could obtain an order for the arrest of the bankrupt but could not obtain the less severe remedy restraining the bankrupt from leaving the jurisdiction.
    If one looks more widely at other circumstances in which injunctions have
f   been granted, it is apparent that the jurisdiction exercised by the court would not fit within Mr Collings' formulation. A chief constable has been granted an injunction by this court to prevent the dissipation of identifiable money in a bank account alleged to have been obtained by fraud: see *Chief Constable of Kent v V* [1982] 3 All ER 36, [1983] QB 34, explained in *Chief Constable of Hampshire v A Ltd* [1984] 2 All ER 385, [1985] QB 132 on the basis that the chief constable has a
g   general duty to recover stolen property and restore it to the true owner. That duty founds a sufficient interest to enable an injunction to be granted to the chief constable.
    In *Re Oriental Credit Ltd*, in which Harman J refused to discharge an injunction which he had granted restraining the applicant from leaving the jurisdiction, he
h   did not treat himself as limited to granting an injunction only in the circumstances suggested by *The Siskina*. He specifically said that, in his view, he had the power to grant the injunction although it was not in aid of a legal right or for the protection of an equitable interest. It was an order made in aid of and ancillary to an order under s 561 of the Companies Act 1985 (see [1988] 1 All ER
j   892 at 895, [1988] Ch 204 at 208). That litigation contained different provisions from the bankruptcy provisions of the 1986 Act. There was no section corresponding to s 333. If and in so far as any comments made by Harman J are inconsistent with the approach which I would favour, they are not binding on this court.
    For these reasons, which are essentially the same as those of the judge, I would hold that there was jurisdiction to grant an injunction in the present case. As the

judge's exercise of discretion is not challenged, it follows that I would dismiss this appeal.

a

BUXTON J. I agree that this appeal should be dismissed for the reasons Peter Gibson LJ has given. As he has demonstrated, the rights and position of the trustee under s 333 of the Insolvency Act 1986 amply fulfil the requirements for the issue of injunctive relief that were set out in the judgment of Cotton LJ in *North London Rly Co v Great Northern Rly Co* (1883) 11 QBD 30 at 39, a classic statement that has governed this question for over 100 years. That statement was relied on by Lord Diplock in *Siskina (cargo owners) v Distos Cia Naviera SA, The Siskina* [1977] 3 All ER 803 at 824, [1979] AC 210 at 256. As Peter Gibson LJ has further demonstrated, in *The Siskina* Lord Diplock spoke in terms of the availability of a right to proceed by writ in a private law sense because in that case that was the only basis of jurisdiction on which an application for an injunction could be founded. As Peter Gibson LJ has shown, the present case is entirely different and there is ample jurisdiction for the court to proceed by way of injunction.

b

c

d

HIRST LJ. I agree with both judgments and I also would dismiss this appeal.

Appeal dismissed.

Paul Magrath Esq   Barrister.

a   # Re H and others (restraint order: realisable property)

COURT OF APPEAL, CIVIL DIVISION
ROSE, ALDOUS LJJ AND SIR IAIN GLIDEWELL
b   13, 14, 16 FEBRUARY 1996

Company – Corporate personality – Lifting corporate veil – Shareholders – Realisable property – Shareholders being charged with evasion of customs and excise duty effected through company – Court appointing receiver to manage and sell shareholders'
c   *realisable property – Whether company assets to be treated as shareholders' realisable property – Criminal Justice Act 1988, s 77.*

The three defendants and the intervenor owned 100% of the issued share capital of two family companies. In August 1995 the Commissioners of Customs and Excise applied ex parte to the court for orders under s 77[a] of the
d   Criminal Justice Act 1988 to restrain them from dealing with their realisable property and to appoint a receiver to take possession of and manage that property, on the basis that through the companies and otherwise they had committed excise duty fraud in relation to alcoholic liquor in a sum estimated in excess of £100m. The orders were duly made and specifically referred to a
e   number of bank accounts, motor vehicles, properties and shares in a considerable number of companies, including the two family companies. Several days thereafter the three defendants were arrested and charged with excise duty evasion offences. The defendants subsequently applied by summons to amend the restraining order to prevent the receiver disposing of their assets without their agreement or the leave of the court and the
f   intervenor sought an injunction to the same effect. As a preliminary matter the judge rejected the defendants' challenge to the jurisdiction of the judge who had made the ex parte orders and then dismissed the applications. The defendants and the intervenor appealed, contending inter alia that the receiver could not treat the assets of the two family companies as the realisable property
g   of the defendants.

Held – Where a defendant had used the corporate structure as a device or façade to conceal his criminal activities, the court could lift the corporate veil and treat the assets of the company as the realisable property of the defendant
h   under the 1988 Act. On the facts, there was a prima facie case that the defendants controlled the two companies, that the companies had been used for the fraudulent evasion of excise duty on a large scale, that the defendants regarded the companies as carrying on a family business and that they had benefited from company cash in substantial amounts; and further no useful purpose would have been served by involving the companies in the criminal
j   proceedings. In all the circumstances it was therefore appropriate to lift the corporate veil and treat the stock in the companies' warehouses and the companies' motor vehicles as realisable property held by the defendants. It followed that the judge had correctly rejected the challenge to the court's

---

a   Section 77, so far as material, is set out at p 395 *f* to *h*, post

jurisdiction. The appeals would accordingly be dismissed, although the sale of
non-depreciating or non-surplus assets would be stayed pending an application
by the receiver for the court's directions (see p 401 *e* to p 402 *e g j* to p 403 *a*,
post).

    Re O (disclosure order) [1991] 1 All ER 330 distinguished.

    Adams v Cape Industries plc [1991] 1 All ER 929 considered.

Notes

For piercing the corporate veil, see 7(1) *Halsbury's Laws* (4th edn reissue) para
90.

    For the Criminal Justice Act 1988, s 77, see 12 *Halsbury's Statutes* (4th edn)
(1994 reissue) 1213.

Cases referred to in judgments

Adams v Cape Industries plc [1991] 1 All ER 929, [1990] Ch 433, [1990] 2 WLR 657,
    Ch D and CA.

Borland's Trustee v Steel Bros & Co Ltd [1901] 1 Ch 279.

Brydges v Brydges [1909] P 187, CA.

Company, Re a (1985) 1 BCC 99,421, CA.

Macaura v Northern Assurance Co Ltd [1925] AC 619, [1925] All ER Rep 51, HL.

*Merchandise Transport Ltd v British Transport Commission, Arnold Transport
    (Rochester) Ltd v British Transport Commission* [1961] 3 All ER 495, [1962] 2 QB
    173, [1961] 3 WLR 1358, CA.

O (disclosure order), Re [1991] 1 All ER 330, [1991] 2 QB 520, [1991] 2 WLR 475,
    CA.

P, Re (26 July 1994, unreported), QBD.

Salomon v Salomon & Co [1897] AC 22, [1895–9] All ER Rep 33, HL.

Cases also cited or referred to in skeleton arguments

Aiden Shipping Co Ltd v Interbulk Ltd, The Vimeira [1985] 3 All ER 641, [1986] 1
    AC 965, CA.

Allied Arab Bank Ltd v Hajjar [1987] 3 All ER 739, [1988] QB 787.

Anton Piller KG v Manufacturing Processes Ltd [1976] 1 All ER 779, [1976] Ch 55,
    CA.

Arab Monetary Fund v Hashim [1989] 3 All ER 466, [1984] 1 WLR 565.

Atlas Maritime Co SA v Avalon Maritime Ltd, The Coral Rose (No 3) [1991] 4 All ER
    783, [1991] 1 WLR 917, CA.

Behbehani v Salem [1989] 2 All ER 143, [1989] 1 WLR 723, CA.

Bekhor (A J) & Co Ltd v Bilton [1981] 2 All ER 565, [1981] QB 923, CA.

Bhimji v Chatwani (No 3) [1992] 4 All ER 912, [1992] 1 WLR 1158, CA.

Clayhope Properties Ltd v Evans [1986] 2 All ER 795, [1986] 1 WLR 1223, CA.

Columbia Pictures Industries Inc v Robinson [1986] 3 All ER 338, [1987] Ch 38.

Defendant, Re a (1987) Independent, 2 April.

Derby & Co Ltd v Weldon [1989] 1 All ER 469, [1990] Ch 48, CA.

Derby & Co Ltd v Weldon (No 3) [1989] 3 All ER 118, [1990] Ch 65.

DHN Food Distributors Ltd v Tower Hamlets London BC [1976] 3 All ER 462, [1976]
    1 WLR 852, CA.

J, Re [1992] CA Transcript 1295.

Jones v Lipman [1962] 1 All ER 442, [1962] 1 WLR 832.

K (restraint order), Re [1990] 2 All ER 562, [1990] 2 QB 298.

a *M (restraint order), Re* [1992] 1 All ER 537, [1992] QB 377.
Manchester and Milford Rly Co, Re, ex p Cambrian Rly Co (1880) 14 Ch D 645, CA.
Manor Electronics Ltd v Dickson [1988] RPC 618.
Moss Steamship Co Ltd v Whinney [1912] AC 254, [1911–13] All ER Rep 344, HL.
Parsons v Sovereign Bank of Canada [1913] AC 160, PC.
Paterson v Gas Light and Coke Co [1896] 2 Ch 476, CA.
b *Paulin, Re, Re Crossman* [1935] 1 KB 26, CA.
Peters, Re [1988] 3 All ER 46, [1988] QB 871, CA.
R v Dickens [1990] 2 All ER 626, [1990] 2 QB 102, CA.
Rank Film Distributors Ltd v Video Information Centre [1981] 2 All ER 76, [1982] AC 380, HL.
c *Sartoris's Estate, Re, Sartoris v Sartoris* [1892] 1 Ch 11, [1891–4] All ER Rep 193, Ch D and CA.
SCF Finance Co Ltd v Masri [1985] 2 All ER 747, [1985] 1 WLR 876, CA.
Slater v Comr of Police of the Metropolis (1996) Times, 23 January.
Smith, Stone and Knight Ltd v Birmingham Corp [1939] 4 All ER 116.
Thermax v Schott Industrial Glass Ltd [1981] FSR 289.
d *Third Chandris Shipping Corp v Unimarine SA, The Pythia, The Angelic Wings, The Genie* [1979] 2 All ER 972, [1979] QB 645, QBD and CA.
Tinsley v Milligan [1993] 3 All ER 65, [1994] 1 AC 340, HL.
US v Milwaukee Refrigerator Transit Co (1905) 142 Fed 247, Wis Cir Ct (ED).
Woolfson v Strathclyde Regional Council 1978 SLT 159, HL.

e
Interlocutory appeals

By amended notice dated 12 January 1996 the three defendants appealed, with leave granted by the Court of Appeal on 21 December 1995, from the order of Dyson J on 19 December 1995 dismissing their summons dated 15 December 1995 seeking, inter alia, variation of the order of Popplewell J made on 18 f August 1995, whereby, on an ex parte application by the Commissioners of Customs and Excise, he restrained the defendants (which at the time included the intervenor) from dealing with their realisable property and appointed a receiver in respect of that property. By notice dated 2 February 1996 the intervenor appealed (also with leave granted by the Court of Appeal on 21 g December 1995) from the order of Dyson J dismissing his summons dated 19 December 1995 seeking, inter alia, an injunction to restrain the receiver from selling certain companies' assets pending determination of an application by the intervenor to discharge or vary Popplewell J's order. The facts are set out in the judgment of Rose LJ.

h
John Higham QC and *Jonathan Crystal* (instructed by *Stringer Saul*) for the defendants.
Michael Hartman (instructed by *Bhardwaj Singh & Co*) for the intervenor.
Andrew Mitchell and *Alastair Walton* (instructed by *Denton Hall*) for the receiver.
Andrew Mitchell and *Kennedy Talbot* (instructed by the *Solicitor for Customs and Excise*) for the commissioners.

j

ROSE LJ. This is an appeal with the leave of the Court of Appeal from the judgment of Dyson J on 19 December 1995. The proceedings arise under the Criminal Justice Act 1988. The appellants are AH, SH and KH (the defendants). SSH intervenes (the intervenor).

On 18 August 1995 Popplewell J, on an ex parte application by HM Customs and Excise, made a number of orders, in particular restraining the defendants from dealing with their realisable property and appointing a receiver—

'to take possession of preserve collect get in sell receive and manage all the realisable property of the Defendant and including for the avoidance of doubt the management of the affairs of the companies named ... above ...'

The defendants at that time included the intervenor. The companies included HWB Ltd and HWL Ltd (the companies). The restraint order made against all the defendants specifically referred to seven bank accounts, a considerable number of motor vehicles, several properties, and shares in a considerable number of companies, including HWB Ltd and HWL Ltd. Paragraph 2 of the order was in these terms:

'The Defendant and any person having possession of realisable property of the Defendant do forthwith deliver up to the Receiver possession of all such realisable property, including but not limited to shares held by the Defendant [in a number of companies including HWL Ltd and HWB Ltd] ...'

Paragraph 4 was in these terms:

'The Receiver shall have the following powers without prejudice to any existing powers vested in her whether by statute or otherwise—(a) power to determine whether in the light of the circumstances of the trading position of any or all of the said companies there is any justification in allowing them to continue to trade and in the event that there be no such justification then the power to institute winding up proceedings in respect of the company or companies in question. In the event that a company or companies are viable then the power to continue to manage the business of the said company or companies if such management is consistent with the purpose of this Order namely to preserve the realisable property of the defendant herein ... (d) power to execute all such documents in the name of and on behalf of the Defendant as may be necessary to receive, preserve, manage and or sell the realisable property of the Defendant ... (i) power to sell any vehicle that is considered by the receiver to be an asset that is likely to significantly depreciate or is surplus to the proper administration of any of the businesses under her control or unnecessary for the defendant (should he be admitted to bail) to have the use of from day to day.'

The basis of the application to the judge and the order which he made was that the defendants, through the companies and otherwise, had carried out excise duty fraud in relation to alcoholic liquor in a sum then estimated as being in excess of £100m.

On 21 August 1995 the defendants were arrested and charged with excise duty evasion offences between January and August 1995. They own between them 75% of the issued share capital of both companies. The remaining 25% of the shares in the companies is owned by the intervenor, who has not been charged with any offence. He is on bail and is to be further interviewed in April. Although the documents before the court do not show this, it is apparently common ground that the order of Popplewell J in relation to the a intervenor was in part discharged by Sedley J on 25 August, although the restraint of the intervenor remained in force. On the same occasion Sedley J, and subsequently Hooper J and Collins J, varied the order of Popplewell J in respects which are, for present purposes, immaterial.

Matters then came before Dyson J on the hearing of three summonses. One, by the Customs and Excise to add a further company to the list of companies b referred to in the order, is of no present significance. A summons by the defendants sought amendment of para 4 of Popplewell J's order, so as to prevent the receiver from disposing of the companies' assets prior to 28 February 1996 or thereafter, save with the agreement of the defendants and the intervenor or the leave of the court. A summons by the intervenor sought an injunction to restrain the receiver from selling the two companies' assets c pending determination of an application to discharge or vary Popplewell J's order restraining the intervenor, and provision in relation to the intervenor's living and legal expenses was sought. The issue of discharge and variation was apparently dealt with by Dyson J on the same occasion. Furthermore, although the summonses of the defendants and the intervenor did not refer to d the matter, the jurisdiction of Popplewell J to make the order in the form in which he did was challenged before Dyson J by way of a preliminary point. The intervenor also sought orders for the realisation of his 25% shares and permission to run HWL Ltd, although these matters were not referred to in his summons. The judge rejected the challenge to jurisdiction and dismissed the applications of the defendants and the intervenor. Against that decision the e defendants and intervenor appeal to this court.

Before turning to the rival submissions, it is necessary to describe the legislative framework of Pt VI of the 1988 Act. Section 71 confers on Crown Courts and magistrates' courts the power to make confiscation orders, the amount of such orders being limited by sub-s (6) to the benefit from the offence f or the amount realisable, whichever is the less. Section 77(1) empowers the High Court to 'prohibit any person from dealing with any realisable property', that being a restraint order. Subsection (3) provides that a restraint order may apply '(a) to all realisable property held by a specified person, whether the property is described in the order or not'. Subsection (8) is in these terms:

g   'Where the High Court has made a restraint order, the court may at any time appoint a receiver—(a) to take possession of any realisable property, and (b) in accordance with the court's directions, to manage or otherwise deal with any property in respect of which he is appointed, subject to such exceptions and conditions as may be specified by the court; and may h   require any person having possession of property in respect of which a receiver is appointed under this section to give possession of it to the receiver.'

Section 74(1)(a) defines realisable property as 'any property held by the defendant'. Section 102(1) and (7) provides:

j   '(1) … "interest", in relation to property, includes right; "property" includes money and all other property, real or personal, heritable or moveable, including things in action and other intangible or incorporeal property …

(7) Property is held by any person if he holds any interest in it.'

Section 82 applies to the powers of a receiver. Subsections (2) and (4) provide:

> '(2) Subject to the following provisions of this section, the powers shall be exercised with a view to making available for satisfying the confiscation order or, as the case may be, any confiscation order that may be made in the defendant's case the value for the time being of realisable property held by any person by the realisation of such property ...
>
> (4) The powers shall be exercised with a view to allowing any person other than the defendant or the recipient of any such gift to retain or recover the value of any property held by him.'

For the defendants, Mr Higham QC's broad submission is that, although Popplewell J was entitled to treat the defendants' shares in the companies as realisable property within the Act, a receiver taking possession of the shares could only exercise the voting and other rights of a shareholder and could not manage the company, that being the responsibility of the company's directors. It was not open to the judge to short-circuit Companies Act procedures and purport to empower the receiver to dispose of the assets of the companies. Such assets are not realisable property of the defendants.

In support of that submission, he addressed three issues. First, he says the terms of the 1988 Act, in particular s 77(8), empower the court to appoint a receiver in relation only to realisable property of the defendants. The reference in s 77(8)(b) to 'any property' has to be read as a reference to realisable property because the purpose of restraint orders, to which the appointment of a receiver is ancillary, is to preserve the value of assets which may later be required to satisfy a confiscation order. The statutory definitions of 'realisable property' in s 74(1)(a) and 'property' in s 102(1) and (7) are confined to property in which the defendant holds an interest. Restraint orders are directed by s 77(1) to realisable property. The reference to property at the end of s 77(8) must be a reference back to realisable property in (a). There are similar references to property in other sections of the Act. As examples, see s 77(3)(a), which I have read, and ss 80(3)(a) and 88(1)(a), which it is unnecessary to read. Such a construction, submits Mr Higham, was adopted by May J in *Re P* (26 July 1994, unreported). Accordingly, he submits that Dyson J was wrong to accept that there is any power under s 77 to appoint a receiver for property which is not realisable.

Secondly, he submits that the companies' assets were not realisable property of the defendants. A company is a separate legal entity. Its assets belong to the company, not to its shareholders (see, for example, *Borland's Trustee v Steel Bros & Co Ltd* [1901] 1 Ch 279 at 288 per Farwell J and *Macaura v Northern Assurance Co Ltd* [1925] AC 619 at 626, 630 and 633, [1925] All ER Rep 51 at 54 and 55 per Lord Buckmaster, Lord Sumner and Lord Wrenbury). Accordingly, unless it is appropriate to pierce the corporate veil, a company's assets cannot be regarded as a defendant's realisable property. Such piercing was not considered by either Popplewell J or Dyson J, but is raised before this court in the respondents' notice. Mr Higham says the evidence before the court does not justify piercing. In particular, the evidence is insufficiently precise as to which companies are involved in criminal activities and to what extent. No charges have been brought against the companies or the intervenor. It was accepted that there were some legitimate parts to the business, because this was the reason for applying for a receiver. Control of the companies by the defendants *a* is inadequate to justify an allegation of criminal activity by the companies. He referred to *Adams v Cape Industries plc* [1991] 1 All ER 929, [1990] Ch 433. He accepts that if the companies were set up solely for the purpose of criminal activity, there would be little difficulty in piercing the corporate veil. But he does not accept that piercing is permissible if a business is set up or used for purposes which, to a significant or substantial extent, are illegitimate. A large *b* quantity of stock on which duty has not been paid was seized and remains with the Customs and Excise. Stock now sought to be sold off is not tainted with illegality.

Mr Higham's fall-back position, if he fails on his first two submissions, is that Dyson J should have directed the receiver not to sell assets of the companies other than perishables or those otherwise declining in value. The Act does not *c* provide for realisation until a confiscation order has been made after trial. The purpose of appointing a receiver was to preserve, not to sell off, assets, and the court's directions should have been sought prior to selling off as though on a closing-down. Dyson J was, says Mr Higham, in an impossible position, in that he was not asked to consider whether it was right to deprive the defendants of *d* their source of livelihood while the criminal proceedings remain unresolved. This court should therefore consider the matters afresh and order that there be no sale of non-perishables pending further directions of the court.

For the intervenor, Mr Hartman adopts, or at least does not dissent from, most of Mr Higham's submissions, save in two respects. First, unlike Mr *e* Higham, he contends that shares in the companies are not realisable assets, on the grounds, as I understand him, that they were acquired for value untainted by criminal activity and that, in the light of s 74(5)(a), there is no evidence as to their value at the time of their acquisition. In my judgment this argument is not well founded. Source of funding is relevant under the Act when assessing benefit after conviction, but neither source of funding nor value are relevant to *f* determination as to a defendant's realisable assets. Mr Hartman further submits that the Act provides no jurisdiction to appoint a receiver in relation to a company which is not a party to proceedings because s 37(1) of the Supreme Court Act 1981 requires a company to be made a party.

The second respect in which Mr Hartman differs from Mr Higham is in *g* submitting that the court can, on the material before it, here look behind the corporate veil to decide whether the companies are being used as a sham, so as to make it just and convenient to appoint a receiver. However, says Mr Hartman, the ability to look behind the corporate veil does not create jurisdiction, and an inquiry can only properly be conducted if the company is *h* a party to the proceedings. He relies on *Brydges v Brydges* [1909] P 187 at 191 per Farwell LJ. Mr Hartman stresses the terms of s 82(4). The powers of appointing a receiver must be exercised with a view to allowing the intervenor 'to retain or recover the value of any property held by him'. The judge, he says, had no proper regard to this. If the corporate veil is to be lifted, there should be a direction that 25% of the assets and profits be paid to the intervenor.
j There was no reason to appoint a receiver of the companies in this case. Dyson J failed properly to carry out the necessary balancing act in the light of the intervenor's affidavit, which raised credible issues contravening the basis on which Popplewell J had made his order. He was wrong to find that the companies' assets were the assets of the defendants and that the defendants controlled the companies. As the purpose of his order was to preserve the

legitimate part of the business, the intervenor was the proper person to
continue running the business and the restraint order against him should have
been discharged. Furthermore, the order does not protect the intervenor
against self-incrimination or provide for his legal expenses.

For the Customs and Excise and the receiver, Mr Mitchell makes
submissions in support of Dyson J's decision and the additional grounds in his
notice under RSC Ord 59, r 7(1). He submits that there are four possible routes
whereby jurisdiction is conferred to appoint a receiver to manage the
companies' assets. First, somewhat faintly, he contends that the definitions in
s 102 of 'interest' and 'property' are such as to confer jurisdiction to empower
a receiver not only to exercise all the shareholders' rights but also to ensure
that the value of the assets of the company is maintained. The bundle of rights
which a shareholder has is 'property' and include an interest in the company.
Such an 'interest' is also property by virtue of sub-s (7). By virtue of s 82(2) the
value of the shares has to be made available by the receiver and that value can
only be maintained if the receiver manages the company's affairs.

Secondly, he submits that s 77(8) is to be interpreted by reading the word
'and' at the end of (a) disjunctively, so that the subsection is to be understood
as conferring power to appoint a receiver both in relation to realisable property
under (a) and in relation to any property under (b). Section 82(4) shows that
Parliament envisaged circumstances in which a receiver could possess an
innocent third party's property. Accordingly, jurisdiction to appoint a receiver
to manage a company's underlying assets is conferred by s 77(8).

Thirdly, he says the judge was right to conclude that a court has an inherent
power to appoint a receiver to manage the companies' affairs. *Re O (disclosure
order)* [1991] 1 All ER 330, [1991] 2 QB 520 shows that the court has the inherent
power to make the 1988 Act work properly and the power to appoint a receiver
must include a power to make the receiver's work effective, that is, enabling
him to manage the companies' affairs. On the balance of convenience, the
judge was right to make such an order because there was prima facie evidence
of a large fraud and the defendants were, in the light of the evidence to which
in a moment I shall come, 'cash-rich and income-poor'.

Fourthly, the companies were nothing more than a sham, providing a façade
for the defendants' illegal activities. The court should therefore look behind
and lift the corporate veil.

His written skeleton relied on *Adams v Cape Industries plc* [1991] 1 All ER 929
at 1022, [1990] Ch 433 at 539, and in oral argument he referred to *Re a Company*
(1985) 1 BCC 99,421.

In support of this submission he relied on the evidence contained in the
defendants' own affidavits sworn the day after the hearing before Dyson J, an
affidavit sworn by their solicitor in September 1995 and an affidavit of Mr
Matthews of the Customs and Excise, which were both before the judge, and
an affidavit sworn by the receiver on 11 January 1996.

Mr Higham suggested it was unfair for this court to draw inferences from the
defendants' own affidavits, which they had had to swear in response to an
order for disclosure, which were not directed to the corporate veil question,
and which they had had no opportunity of explaining in oral evidence. I am
wholly unable to accept that submission. The information in those affidavits
was necessarily well known to the defendants and could not possibly be said to
take them by surprise. Indeed, it appears that had they complied with the

a court's order as to when those affidavits would be sworn, they would have been sworn long before 20 December. I see no possible unfairness in this court considering their content and drawing such inferences as may be appropriate from that content, both in itself and in conjunction with the other affidavit evidence to which I have referred.

b Each defendant has a wife and at least two dependent children. Each claims to have a gross monthly income of £2,312, yet their solicitor's affidavit claims that AH's monthly expenditure is £4,939; SH's, £11,731; and KH's, £8,441. That expenditure includes large sums by way of pension policy premiums and mortgage payments, which are wholly inconsistent with the incomes claimed. Furthermore, each defendant refers to, and seeks in the affidavit to explain, a very large sum of cash found in his house by the Customs and Excise. There c was £40,000 in a trunk kept by AH's wife, £16,000 of which is said to have been saved from his monthly salary and £21,000 of which allegedly belongs to HWB Ltd and was awaiting banking. There was £40,000 in SH's bedroom, said to be takings from HWB Ltd awaiting banking, and £12,500 in his wife's trunk. There was £76,000 in KH's bedroom, also said to await banking for HWB Ltd. d In addition, SH swears as follows:

> 'Following the raid by HM Customs & Excise in December 1994, stocks were sold but at that time, not all of these sales were paid for. In about June 1995, I received approximately £400,000 in respect of these earlier sales which I then sent to India ...'

e The implications of this passage, particularly as to the control and appropriation of company assets, are obvious.

The receiver's evidence as to the state of the companies' books is as follows. In relation to HWL Ltd:

f 'There was in existence a computer record purporting to be a stock list. However, this was out of date, indicating no sales in 1995. There were no computer records of purchases. A file was found of outstanding invoices, but these related mainly to running expenses rather than stock purchases. In respect of sales, there were handwritten daily cash sheets showing sums of cash received every day. However, these did not identify purchasers nor the nature of the stock sold. No stock movement schedules or ledger g were found, nor any other record [or] document relating to sales. A computer record of outstanding debts was discovered (to a total of over £4·4m, half of which were debts from associated companies) but no supporting invoices were located. No nominal ledgers, showing the current trading position of the company have been located. No staff or h payroll details and no fixed asset register were located. No management accounts were located.'

As to HWB Ltd:

j 'There was in existence a computer record purporting to be a stock list. However, no sales were indicated within the previous 12 months. There was a nominal ledger found indicating purchases for the year to September 1995 of £55m. However, there were no underlying records and the sales figures were not recorded at all on this document. In respect of sales, a sales book was found together with handwritten daily cash sheets showing sums of cash received every day. This showed sales of £32m in the calendar year to August 1995. This figure [was] contradicted by computer records showing sales of £23m. A record of outstanding debts was discovered (to a total of over £1·5m, most of which were debts from associated companies). No staff or payroll details and no fixed asset register were located. No management accounts were located.'

In relation to another related company:

'No stock valuation reports were found, nor any information in relation to purchases. As mail began to arrive and known creditors were identified it became impossible to identify creditors of £52,000. A sales book has been found indicating sales from March to August 1995 of £8·5m. A computer record showed the last day of trading to have enjoyed a turnover of £103,000. Historical information could not be extracted from the computer. Debtors were shown as £329,000 together with a list of debtors ... No nominal ledger or fixed asset register has been located.'

The affidavit of the receiver goes on to say, in respect of all the companies, that the majority of their stock is claimed by the Customs and Excise as liable to forfeiture as VAT and/or excise duty had not been paid. She reached the conclusion that there was insufficient financial information to decide that the companies could resume trading. She also considered the potential liabilities which would be incurred in the form of trading debts at a time when the ability to meet trading debts was uncertain. She was therefore in a position of holding substantial stocks in the companies and had to decide how to dispose of it, and she took advice in that respect.

The affidavit of Mr Matthews indicates the substantial number of interrelated companies of which the defendants or their relations were at one time or another directors. It suffices to say that all the defendants were directors of HW Ltd, which went into liquidation following the Customs and Excise raid in December 1994; that the defendants and the intervenor each, as I have said, hold 25% of the shares of HWB Ltd and HWL Ltd; that the directors of HWB Ltd are SH's wife and a relative of the defendants who lives in British Columbia; and that AH was a director of HWL Ltd from its incorporation in November 1994 until the following March. Observations and inquiries during 1995 have shown that the HW companies, including HWB Ltd and HWL Ltd, were apparently receiving huge quantities of spirits, wines and beers on which duty had not been paid. The defendants appear to have abused the administrative accompanying documents scheme, using forged Italian customs stamps. According to Mr Matthews, the defendants appear to be responsible for conducting such business at a level which involved a loss to Customs and Excise of at least £1m a week.

I should add that although, as I have said, the intervenor is the registered owner of 25% of the shares of the companies, it is the prosecution case that he does not hold those shares beneficially.

In the light of this evidence, submits Mr Mitchell, it is appropriate to lift the corporate veil and to treat the stock in the companies' warehouses and the motor vehicles as realisable property of the defendants. Popplewell J accordingly had jurisdiction to make the order which he did in relation to that stock, and Dyson J was right not to discharge or vary it.

In my judgment neither s 102(1) and (7) nor s 77(8), properly construed, confers on the court jurisdiction, for which Mr Mitchell contends, to appoint a a receiver of the companies' property. As to s 102, a statute's definition section is, in itself, an unlikely source of conferment of power and, broad though the definition of property is, that definition, neither alone nor in conjunction with other definitions in the section, is in my view able to sustain Mr Mitchell's argument. As to s 77(8), if Mr Mitchell's disjunctive construction of (a) and (b) were correct, (a) would be otiose, for 'any property' and 'manage or otherwise

b deal' in (b) respectively embrace 'realisable property' and taking possession in (a). Accordingly, and for the other reasons advanced by Mr Higham, s 77(8) cannot in my view be construed so as to confer jurisdiction.

With regard to inherent jurisdiction, on which Dyson J relied by analogy with *Re O (disclosure order)*, I am not persuaded that this analogy is sound. I accept, of course, as Lord Donaldson MR said ([1991] 1 All ER 330 at 334, [1991]

c 2 QB 520 at 528): '... the High Court must have been intended to have power to render effective a restraint order made under section 77 ...' In that case, the court's conclusion that there was jurisdiction to make an order for disclosure, so as to identify and ascertain the whereabouts and value of assets, merely provided teeth to render effective undoubted existing powers. In the present

d case, however, what is sought to be achieved by Mr Mitchell's reliance on the court's inherent power is, as it seems to me, the creation of a wholly new power, whereby the court can deal with the realisable property of another in the same way as the realisable property of the defendants. In my judgment *Re O* does not support such a conclusion.

I turn to the corporate veil. This involves two questions: first, whether in

e law it is permissible to pierce or lift the veil; secondly, whether, on the evidence before the court, this should be done in the present case.

As to the law, the general principle remains that which was enunciated in *Salomon v Salomon & Co* [1897] AC 22, [1895–9] All ER Rep 33, namely that a company duly formed and registered is a separate legal entity and must be

f treated like any other independent person with its own rights and liabilities distinct from those of its shareholders. But a succession of cases throughout the twentieth century show, as Danckwerts LJ said in *Merchandise Transport Ltd v British Transport Commission, Arnold Transport (Rochester) Ltd v British Transport Commission* [1961] 3 All ER 495 at 518, [1962] 2 QB 173 at 206–207:

g   '... where the character of a company, or the nature of the persons who control it, is a relevant feature the court will go behind the mere status of the company as a legal entity, and will consider who are the persons as shareholders or even as agents who direct and control the activities of a company which is incapable of doing anything without human assistance.'

h   In *Adams v Cape Industries plc* [1991] 1 All ER 929 at 1024, [1990] Ch 433 at 542 Slade LJ, giving the judgment of the Court of Appeal (of which Mustill and Ralph Gibson LJJ were the other members) cited this passage and added: 'The correctness of this statement has not been disputed.' The court also assumed to be correct the proposition that—

j   'the court will lift the corporate veil where a defendant by the device of a corporate structure attempts to evade (i) limitations imposed on his conduct by law ...' (See [1991] 1 All ER 929 at 1026, [1990] Ch 433 at 544.)

Clearly, as a matter of law, the corporate veil can be lifted in appropriate circumstances.

As to the evidence, it provides a prima facie case that the defendants control
these companies; that the companies have been used for fraud, in particular the
evasion of excise duty on a large scale; that the defendants regard the
companies as carrying on a family business, and that company cash has
benefited the defendants in substantial amounts. It is, I think, conceded by the
defendants and the intervenor (and, if not conceded, the contrary is
unarguable) that if the companies had been about to be charged with criminal
offences, Popplewell J could have appointed a receiver of the companies'
realisable property; and, indeed, all the companies' shareholders were
represented before Popplewell J. In my judgment, the Customs and Excise are
not to be criticised for not charging the companies. The more complex
commercial activities become, the more vital it is for prosecuting authorities to
be selective in whom and what they charge, so that issues can be presented in
as clear and short a form as possible. In the present case, it seems to me that
no useful purpose would have been served by introducing into criminal
proceedings the additional complexities as to the corporate mind and will
which charging the companies would have involved. Conversely, there could
have been justified criticism had the companies been charged merely as a
device for obtaining orders under the Act in relation to their assets.

In all the circumstances, I am entirely satisfied that it is appropriate to lift the
corporate veil in this case and to treat the stock in the companies' warehouses
and the motor vehicles as property held by the defendants. Accordingly,
Dyson J was correct to reject the challenge to the court's jurisdiction. I would
add that, in a case where the corporate veil cannot properly be lifted, it may be
open to a prosecutor to apply to the court under s 37 of the Supreme Court Act
1981 for the appointment of a receiver of the company.

There remains, in relation to the defendants and the intervenor, the question
of variation. Although I accept that Mr Mitchell's reason for including
sub-paras (a) and (i) in para 4 in the order which he sought was to avoid doubt
about, and to clarify, the receiver's powers, Popplewell J's inclusion of those
subparagraphs in the order made suggests, to my mind, that the judge intended
that the receiver should seek the court's directions as to winding up and the
sale of non-depreciating or non-surplus items. Such an intention on the judge's
part would be consonant with the general practice in relation to the court's
control of receivers. For my part, therefore, without varying the terms of
Popplewell J's order, I would order a stay on the sale of non-depreciating or
non-surplus goods pending an application by the receiver for the court's
directions.

The only remaining matter is the intervenor's application for variation of the
restraint against him to provide for legal expenses and against self-
incrimination. Although we are told these matters were raised before the
judge, they were, like jurisdiction, further novel points which had not been
raised in the summonses before him: indeed, his judgment contains no
reference to the self-incrimination point. The judge referred to the lack of
material evidence before him. I am unpersuaded that, in so far as the matters
were raised, he fell into any error. If the intervenor wishes to pursue these
matters, it seems to me that the proper course is for him to take out a summons
supported by affidavit evidence in the usual way.

Save to the extent of ordering the stay which I have indicated, I would
dismiss these appeals.

a **ALDOUS LJ.** I would also dismiss these appeals for the reasons given by Rose LJ.

SIR IAIN GLIDEWELL. I entirely agree.

Appeals dismissed. Leave to appeal to the House of Lords refused.

b
L I Zysman Esq   Barrister.

Kershaw v Whelan

a

QUEEN'S BENCH DIVISION AT LIVERPOOL

EBSWORTH J

25 SEPTEMBER, 12 OCTOBER 1995

b

Discovery – Legal professional privilege – Waiver – Implied waiver – Extent – Client bringing action against solicitor for breach of contract and negligence – Client alleging deliberate concealment of facts on which claim based – Solicitor seeking discovery of documents from earlier related proceedings – Whether documents relating to earlier proceedings covered by client's waiver of privilege.

c

On the death of the plaintiff's father intestate in April 1979 the sum of £44,377, being his entitlement from a company pension fund, became available for distribution subject to the absolute discretion of the trustees of the fund. The plaintiff, who suffered from major disabilities, was required by his father's widow *d* to leave the family home against his wishes and move into institutional accommodation. Before distributing the fund, the trustees consulted the defendant solicitor who was at the time acting for the widow. By a letter dated 20 June 1979 the defendant stated that the plaintiff's needs were being met through his placement in a home and partly as a result of that letter the trustees *e* applied £39,041 of the fund to the widow, dividing the remaining £5,336 equally between the plaintiff and his sister. The plaintiff thereafter issued abortive proceedings, through several different firms of solicitors, in both the Chancery and Queen's Bench Divisions relating to his father's estate. In March 1991 the plaintiff commenced proceedings against the defendant, claiming damages for negligence and breach of contract. He contended that the letter of 20 June 1979 *f* had been written in breach of a duty owed to him, on the basis that at that time the defendant had been acting for him as well as the widow. The defendant denied that he had been acting for the plaintiff or that he was in breach of duty and pleaded that the action was statute-barred because of the lapse of time. The plaintiff contended that the letter of 20 June 1979 had been deliberately concealed *g* from him and since he had not discovered and could not with due diligence have discovered the relevant facts on which his claim was based before April 1985, the limitation period ran from that date. The defendant applied for discovery of documents, including solicitor/client correspondence, arising from the previous proceedings in files of the plaintiff's former solicitors.

h

Held – A solicitor who was sued by a former client was entitled to discovery and inspection of privileged documents in the files of solicitors who had previously acted for the plaintiff in separate but related proceedings, since the plaintiff had, by bringing those proceedings, impliedly waived his privilege in relation to those documents. On the facts, the plaintiff had, by his plea of deliberate concealment *j* of the defendant's letter, waived his privilege in respect of solicitor/client documents related to that issue, and there was no logical basis for distinguishing . between documents from the plaintiff's former solicitors and those of his present solicitors where the various solicitors had essentially dealt with the same subject matter. It followed that the defendant was entitled to discovery and inspection

a of such documents as went to the knowledge of the letter of 20 June 1979 and an
order to that effect would be made accordingly (see p 414 g to p 416 b, post).
Lillicrap v Nalder & Son (a firm) [1993] 1 All ER 724 applied.

Notes

For legal professional privilege, see 13 *Halsbury's Laws* (4th edn) paras 71–84, and
b for cases on the subject, see 18 *Digest* (2nd reissue) 154–179, *1379–1596*.

Cases referred to in judgment

Balabel v Air-India [1988] 2 All ER 246, [1988] Ch 317, [1988] 2 WLR 1036, CA.
Calcraft v Guest [1898] 1 QB 759, [1895–9] All ER Rep 346, CA.
Hearn v Rhay (1975) 68 FRD 574, US District Ct (Wash ED).
c *Jones v G D Searle & Co Ltd* [1978] 3 All ER 654, [1979] 1 WLR 101, CA.
Lillicrap v Nalder & Son (a firm) [1993] 1 All ER 724, [1993] 1 WLR 94, CA.
Nederlandse Reassurantie Groep Holding NV v Bacon & Woodrow (a firm) [1995] 1 All
ER 976.

d **Summons**

By a summons issued on 28 July 1995 the defendant solicitor, Alan H Whelan,
applied inter alia for an order for the discovery and inspection of privileged
documents in the possession, custody or power of the plaintiff, Ian Kershaw, in
an action which the plaintiff had brought against him claiming damages for
e breach of duty of care, negligence and breach of fiduciary duty in relation to the
division of his father's estate. The district judge adjourned the matter without
hearing to allow a High Court judge to decide whether the summons should be
granted. The summons was heard in chambers but judgment was given by
Ebsworth J in open court in Liverpool. The facts are set out in the judgment.

f *Nicholas Davidson QC* (instructed by *Wansbroughs Willey Hargrave*, Leeds) for the
defendant.
Ian Leeming QC (instructed by *H F T Gough & Co*, Whitehaven) for the plaintiff.

Cur adv vult

g 12 October 1995. The following judgment was delivered.

EBSWORTH J. The summons before me falls into two parts, the first concerned
with discovery of documents, the second with the timetable laid down for the
conduct of the litigation.
h The terms of paras (1) and (2) of the summons are:

'(1) The plaintiff do within seven days serve a list of documents for the
purposes of the preliminary issue which lists the documents coming into
existence on or before 16 April 1985 which are or have been in his possession,
custody or power relating to the issues: (a) when he did discover the
j concealment alleged in the amended reply; (b) when any agent of his
discovered that concealment; (c) when he ought reasonably to have
discovered that concealment; (d) when any agent of his ought reasonably to
have discovered such concealment. (2) The plaintiff do within ten days
permit the defendant to inspect and take copies of: (a) the documents listed
pursuant to paragraph (1) of this order; (b) the documents described in

schedule 1, part 2, of the plaintiff's list of documents dated 8 December 1984 on or before 16 April 1985.'

The final application is also of relevance:

'If and to the extent that the court considers that schedule 1, part 2, of the plaintiff's list dated 8 December 1984 described documents with insufficient particularity to enable the court to determine whether to order production of the documents there referred to, the defendant will ask the court to order the plaintiff to serve a list enumerating such documents with sufficient particularity to enable the court to determine the issue.'

The summons has been carefully and helpfully argued by leading counsel on both sides with skeleton arguments amplified by oral submissions. It was originally listed before the district judge but adjourned by him without hearing argument as a matter more suited to the judge. Both sides agree the summons raises a matter of some public importance as a matter of principle which has not been the subject of previous direct judicial decision. I have for that reason agreed that judgment be given in open court. The summons raises one major substantive point relating to legal privilege: whether Mr Whelan, who is a solicitor and who is sued by (allegedly) a former client, is entitled to discovery and inspection of privileged documents in the files of solicitors previously acting for the plaintiff which relate to separate proceedings and which include notes of advice given by solicitors and opinions/advices of counsel.

I have for the purposes of the summons considered the pleadings, previous orders of the court of 12 March 1992 and 17 June 1994, together with the affidavits of Martin Parr, the solicitor with conduct of the proceedings for the defendant, and the exhibits thereto. From those documents and the skeleton arguments and chronology I have taken the background to this matter.

The proceedings were commenced by writ on 11 March 1991 as a claim for damages for breach of trust/breach of contract or negligence from 1979 to about March 1985 in the management or control of the payment of moneys due to the plaintiff following the death of his father. The essence of the plaintiff's claim is that following the death, intestate, of his father, Cyril, on 14 April 1979 he was entitled to share in the estate of the deceased together with his adopted sister and the deceased's widow. Under the laws of intestacy the bulk of the estate devolved on the widow. The late Cyril Kershaw had for many years been employed by Nestlés and was a member of their company pension fund. Upon his death there was available the sum of £44,377 subject to absolute discretion of the trustees of the fund as to the application of the moneys between different classes of beneficiaries. Letters of administration had been granted to the plaintiff and the widow on 24 January 1980; the defendant solicitors were by that time certainly acting for the widow. There is an issue on the pleadings as to whether they were acting for the plaintiff: he asserts they were: the defendant denies it. The defendant says that from July 1979 until January 1980 the plaintiff was represented by Messrs Michael Cain & Kerr. The plaintiff at the time of the death and at all times afterwards has suffered from major disabilities, being spastic and almost blind. After the death of Mr Kershaw the widow did not want the plaintiff to remain in the family home; he moved to other, institutional, accommodation which he disliked. He was at the time about 20.

The trustees of the pension fund consulted the defendant (then with the firm of Messrs Pattinson & Scott) before taking a decision upon the distribution of the a fund. He replied by letter dated 20 June 1979. As the result in part at least of that letter the trustees applied the moneys available as to £39,041 to the widow and £5,336 to the plaintiff and his sister in equal shares. The plaintiff contends that that division was inequitable and that it came about because the letter written by the defendant influenced the trustees in favour of the widow, in particular by stating that his, the plaintiff's, needs were met by his placement in a home.

b This action is based upon a claim that the plaintiff was not treated properly overall and that the letter of 20 June 1979 was written in breach of duty owed by Mr Whelan to him. The defence denies breach of duty in any form and at para 22 pleads the Limitation Act 1980 as to both tort and contract. In particular, the defence relies upon certain documents/letters passing between the plaintiff and his then solicitors, Messrs Mannheim & Otto, and the defendant in 1983 as to the c pension fund decision. The amended reply relies upon s 32(1)(b) of the 1980 Act and pleads that the plaintiff did not discover and could not with due diligence have discovered the relevant facts until 16 April 1985.

The plaintiff has engaged in other litigation relating to his late father's estate. d He commenced proceedings in the Chancery Division pursuant to the Inheritance (Provision for Family and Dependants) Act 1975 in 1983; there were further (consolidated) proceedings. In those proceedings the plaintiff was represented by Michael Cain & Kerr and from a date in 1982 by Mannheim & Otto, who periodically instructed counsel on his behalf. There were further proceedings commenced in the Queen's Bench Division in 1987 against this e defendant, the widow, the trustees of the pension fund and the defendant's former firm. Those proceedings were in similar form to these and were not served on this defendant. I do not know what happened to those proceedings but I understand the Chancery proceedings were dismissed for want of prosecution. The documentation now sought will have come into existence in/for the purposes of those actions. The writ of 27 July 1987 was issued by Messrs Addle- f shaw Sons & Latham, solicitors in Manchester.

The history of this action

The statement of claim was served on 26 September 1991. The defence was g served on 12 November 1991 and pleaded the 1980 Act in respect of negligence, later amended to extend that plea to contract and further to plead laches, acquiescence and delay in respect of any equitable claim.

On 18 November 1991 the defendant issued a summons to strike out. The reply was filed on 9 January 1992. On 29 January 1992 the district judge dismissed h the defendant's summons to strike out and for the trial of a preliminary issue on limitation. That matter was heard on appeal by Rose J on 12 March 1992. Rose J ordered a trial of the *then* limitation issues as a preliminary issue. At that stage no question of s 32 of the 1980 Act had arisen. The issue has not yet been tried more than three years on. 17 March 1994 was the first time the plaintiff raised the matter of s 32 of the 1980 Act. He now pleads at para 7 of the amended reply: 'As j to paragraph 22 of the defence, the plaintiff relies (so far as may be necessary) on section 32(1)(b) of the Limitation Act 1980.'

On 17 June 1994 the defendant served a rejoinder putting date of knowledge in issue, placing specific reliance on the earlier proceedings. On 27 September 1994 the defendant served his list of documents for the preliminary issue and on 8 December 1994 the plaintiff served his list.

The list

Schedule 1, part 1 runs to three sections. Section 1 deals with the solicitor files *a* and runs to 403 listed items in meticulous compliance with RSC Ord 24, r 5. The first sections set out papers of Michael Cain & Kerr from 17 July 1979 to 4 August 1982; the second those of Mannheim & Otto from 13 August 1982 to 4 March 1986; Messrs Vaudreys from 7 July 1986 to 5 December 1986; Addleshaw Sons & Latham from 21 July 1987 to 23 April 1988 and the present solicitors, Messrs *b* H F T Gough & Co, from 10 May 1991 and continuing.

The list further includes the court papers relating to the earlier proceedings, including affidavits sworn in those actions. Extensive general correspondence including that with Nestlés is disclosed.

Schedule 1, part 2 contains instructions to counsel, counsel's advices, correspondence with the Legal Aid Board, correspondence between the plaintiff/ *c* Mrs Marsden on his behalf and his solicitors, solicitors' notes and memoranda. Mrs Marsden acted as the next friend of the plaintiff's sister in the proceedings under the 1975 Act and is the deceased's sister. The plaintiff's solicitors by letter of 31 August 1995 confirmed that Sch 1, part 2 was intended to refer to the files of the plaintiff's previous solicitor, in particular Cain & Kerr and Mannheim & *d* Otto, as well as their own. It is clear from the detailed lists in Sch 1, part 1 that much of the content of those files *has* been listed by way of disclosure. The plaintiff objects to production of the solicitor/client correspondence and notes leading up to the disclosed letters, and the court paperwork in earlier proceedings. It is that issue I have to determine.

I am satisfied that the form in which the documents in part 2 are listed is in *e* proper compliance with Ord 24, r 5(2), subject to the issue of waiver of privilege. I am further satisfied that letters and other communications between the plaintiff and his various solicitors in connection with and in contemplation of the earlier inheritance proceedings are privileged. The test is whether the communication or other document is made confidentially for the purposes of legal advice; those *f* purposes have to be broadly construed.

This case is about whether privilege has been waived by the plea of deliberate concealment. The defendant does *not* seek to say that privilege has been waived in respect of *all* solicitor/client material, only with respect to such material as goes to the issue of deliberate concealment.

Mr Davidson QC argues that where a claim to privilege is disputed the *g* documents with respect to which privilege is claimed ought to be identified so that, assuming the description to be true, it can be seen whether or not the claim to privilege attaches to such documents. He seeks an order for a further list identifying any documents which go to the issue of deliberate concealment. Mr Leeming QC asserts that further definition of the documents is not necessary or *h* justified in a case where privilege ought not, as a matter of principle, to be waived.

The central document

The trustees of the pension fund contacted Pattinson & Scott on a date(s) prior *j* to 20 June 1979 in relation to the fund and the needs of the beneficiaries. On 20 June 1979 the defendant replied by letter. The distribution of the fund in the manner I have set out took place in September 1979. For the purposes of this summons one can accept that the trustees placed some reliance on the letter. The plaintiff claims that letter was deliberately concealed from him, that he did not discover the facts until 16 April 1985 and could not have done so and that *a* limitation starts to run then. The date of his knowledge or potential for knowledge is therefore the central matter of the case.

Documents already disclosed are of relevance. On 11 August 1983 Nestlés wrote to Messrs Gatey Heelis, solicitors (not acting for the plaintiff), which disclosed that in March 1983 they had been in correspondence with the plaintiff's then solicitor Mannheim & Otto. They further referred to the existence of the

b letter of 20 June 1979. That letter of 11 August 1983 was produced in an affidavit sworn by Mrs Marsden on 21 September 1984 and served upon the plaintiff's solicitor in the inheritance proceedings on 27 September 1984. The letter did not state the exact contents of the document of 20 June 1979, but needs to be seen in the context of earlier letters.

c On 7 July 1981 Michael Cain & Kerr received details of the distribution of the pension scheme pursuant to a request to the defendant's then firm.

On 18 January 1983 Mannheim & Otto on behalf of the plaintiff asked for details of the scheme, how the award was made and who made the decision. On 7 February 1983 Nestlés wrote to the plaintiff's then solicitor setting out the manner in which they had exercised their discretion. They made it clear that they

d did so on the basis of information supplied to them as to the respective needs of the beneficiaries. Mrs Marsden's affidavit and the letter from Gatey Heelis established the defendant's firm as the source of the information.

A question obviously arises as to whether or not Mannheim & Otto communicated that information to their client. The answer to it is obviously material

e to the question of knowledge.

On 6 February 1985 the defendant wrote to Mannheim & Otto and another firm of solicitors, Messrs Banks Kendall, in which they raised the issues arising from the letter of 20 June 1979 and asked whether allegations of 'influencing' Nestlés were being made. On 14 March 1985 the widow swore an affidavit in

f which the letter of June 1979 was produced again.

The defendant again says that there is an obvious inference that there would have been communication directly/indirectly with the plaintiff over these matters and that what was said to him would go to the issue of knowledge of the facts. If there are documents or notes or advices pertaining to these matters the defendant says that whilst privileged they should be subject to discovery. He also

g argues that because they do not wish to trawl through the solicitor/client communications generally (and accept they may not be entitled so to do) the contents of Sch 1, part 2 should be more specifically listed.

Privilege

h Legal professional privilege attaches to such communications as pass between solicitor and client which are brought into existence or occur in the course of the performance of the solicitor's professional duty or function as a solicitor retained to give professional advice. Its justification is that a client in prosecuting a claim or substantiating a defence should be able to place unrestricted confidence in the

j solicitor/professional agent in order that he may receive proper advice and assistance. The privilege is that of the client, not of the solicitor. It can only be waived by the client expressly or by implication. It is obvious that the bounds of 'implied waiver' must be carefully contained if it is not to undermine the substance of the privilege, but equally, as Taylor LJ observed, the scope of legal professional privilege must itself be kept within justifiable bounds (see *Balabel v Air-India* [1988] 2 All ER 246 at 255, [1988] Ch 317 at 332).

There is nothing in the documents before me to suggest that the advices etc to
which the defence seek access do not fall within the proper ambit of legal *a*
professional privilege, even though the actual litigation in the course of which
they were given has been concluded or has lapsed. The fact that documents were
brought into existence for the purposes of a particular action which has been
concluded was treated as immaterial in *Calcraft v Guest* [1898] 1 QB 759, [1895–9]
All ER Rep 346, the general rule being 'once privileged, always privileged'. This *b*
case therefore seems to me to be about *waiver* and indeed it is to the authorities
relating to that concept that counsel have invited my attention.

The authorities

Jones v G D Searle & Co Ltd [1978] 3 All ER 654, [1979] 1 WLR 101 was an action
for personal injuries which on its face was statute-barred. A limitation defence *c*
was pleaded and the plaintiff in reply relied upon s 2D of the Limitation Act 1939
(s 2D had been inserted into the statute by s 1 of the Limitation Act 1975); the
reply referred to counsel's opinion having been taken by the plaintiff. The
defendants served interrogatories by which they sought to ascertain whether
there had been other opinions (oral or written) from counsel and in particular *d*
whether the opinions had been favourable or unfavourable. The plaintiff
objected to the latter interrogatory on grounds of legal professional privilege.
This plea succeeded before the district registrar and the judge at first instance but
failed on appeal. It was held—

> 'allowing the appeal, that before the court could be satisfied, under section *e*
> 2D of the Act, that it was equitable to allow the plaintiff's action to proceed,
> it had to have regard to the matters referred to in subsection (3) including not
> only whether the plaintiff had received legal advice but also the "nature of
> any such advice"; that those words referred to the character of the advice in
> so far as it was relevant to the question whether the plaintiff had acted *f*
> promptly and reasonably after she had knowledge of the information which
> might give rise to a cause of action; and that, since it was relevant in the
> circumstances for the court to know whether the advice was favourable to
> the plaintiff's alleged cause of action, the defendants were entitled to an
> answer to their seventh interrogatory.' (See [1979] 1 WLR 101.)

g
Section 2D of the 1939 Act, and in particular sub-ss (1) and (3), is set out in the
judgment of Roskill LJ ([1978] 3 All ER 654 at 656, [1979] 1 WLR 101 at 103):

> 'Section 2D of the 1939 Act is the all important statutory provision for the
> purpose of this appeal and I will read part of that section: "(1) If it appears to
> the court that it would be equitable to allow an action to proceed having *h*
> regard to the degree to which—(a) the provisions of section 2A or 2B of this
> Act prejudice the plaintiff or any person whom he represents, and (b) any
> decision of the court under this subsection would prejudice the defendant or
> any person whom he represents, the court may direct that those provisions
> shall not apply to the action, or shall not apply to any specified cause of action *j*
> to which the action relates." I need not read sub-s (2); I go to sub-s (3): "In
> acting under this section the court shall have regard to all the circumstances
> of the case and in particular to—(a) the length of, and the reasons for, the
> delay on the part of the plaintiff ... (e) the extent to which the plaintiff acted
> promptly and reasonably once he knew whether or not the act or omission
> of the defendant, to which the injury was attributable, might be capable at

a   that time of giving rise to an action for damages; (f) the steps, if any, taken by the plaintiff to obtain medical, legal or other expert advice and the nature of any such advice he may have received."'

It was held that the interrogatory should be answered. Roskill LJ said ([1978] 3 All ER 654 at 657–658, [1979] 1 WLR 101 at 105–106):

b   'It seems to me that Parliament has said that, if a plaintiff seeks the benefit which s 2D confers so as to deprive a defendant of his entitlement to rely on a time limit to which he would otherwise undoubtedly be entitled, the plaintiff has to satisfy the court of certain matters. One is that the plaintiff has acted promptly and reasonably after obtaining the relevant information.

c   Plainly the obtaining of the relevant medical, legal or other expert advice will or may in certain cases bear upon the degree of expedition which a plaintiff has shown. Therefore it is right that a plaintiff should, when it is relevant, be required to state quite generally "the nature of the advice" he or she has received. What is relevant here is whether that advice was favourable or unfavourable to his or her case.'

d   Eveleigh LJ underlined that a critical factor in the decision was the wording of the section in relation to the 'nature of any such advice he may have received'. He said ([1978] 3 All ER 654 at 658, [1979] 1 WLR 101 at 106):

e   'I agree. I think that the court would be slow to take away a well established privilege from a plaintiff and certainly would require some positive indication that the legislature so intended. If counsel's argument had rested on the wording of s 2D(3)(e) in isolation, I think there would be strong reason to reject his submission on the basis that there was no sufficient positive indication that the principle was to be taken away.

f   However the wording of s 2D(3)(f) refers specifically to "the nature of any such advice he may have received". Thus the provision is that the court is under a duty to consider the nature of advice received by the plaintiff; and if the court is under a duty to consider the advice, it seems to me that the court must be in a position to demand evidence as to what the nature of the advice was.'

g   Roskill LJ went out of his way to state that it did not follow from the order to answer the interrogatory that the opinions would be liable to discovery or production (see [1978] 3 All ER 654 at 656, [1979] 1 WLR 101 at 104). The case does not therefore assist directly on the matter before me for two reasons: firstly

h   as to the actual wording of the statute, secondly because it does not cover discovery. The court gave no indication as to its view on that issue. The case is however of value as an illustration of an exception to the generally absolute nature of legal professional privilege.

Lillicrap v Nalder & Son (a firm) [1993] 1 All ER 724, [1993] 1 WLR 94 is more

j   directly in point. The plaintiff property developers sued their solicitors for failure to advise them on rights of way material to the title of a property which they purchased when the defendants were acting for them. The defence admitted negligence but denied the plaintiffs' claim that if they had been correctly advised they would not have purchased the property. The defendants had acted for the plaintiffs on a series of earlier matters of a similar nature and the plaintiffs had ignored their advice. They sought leave to amend to plead those earlier matters;

May J refused leave and ordered the defendants to deliver up all confidential
documents relating to those matters. On appeal it was held— a

> 'allowing the appeal, that where a client sued his solicitor he impliedly
> waived his claim to privilege and confidence in relation to all matters which
> were relevant to an issue in the proceedings; that the particulars in question
> were relevant to the issue of causation of loss and, therefore, the defendants
> were entitled to include those particulars in their defence; and that,
> accordingly, the judge's order would be set aside.' (See [1993] 1 WLR 94.)

The court gave full consideration to the extent of privilege and the circumstances
in which it is taken to be waived and was specifically concerned with the extent
to which a plaintiff suing his solicitor in respects of one discrete retainer waives
privilege not only in respect of that but in certain respect, of the earlier retainers.
Dillon LJ quoted extensively from the judgment of May J ([1993] 1 All ER 724 at
729, [1993] 1 WLR 94 at 99):

> '"I return to what I regard as the heart of the matter—waiver. A client who
> sues his solicitor invites the court to adjudicate the dispute and thereby, in
> my judgment, waives privilege and confidence to the extent that is necessary
> to enable the court to do so fully and fairly in accordance with the law,
> including the law of evidence. I suspect that at the fringes each case will
> depend on is own facts. Normally, the waiver will extend to facts and
> documents material to the cause of action upon which the plaintiff sues and
> to the defendant's proper defence to that cause of action. The bringing of a
> claim for negligence in relation to a particular retainer will normally be a
> waiver of privilege and confidence for facts and documents relating to that
> retainer, but not without more for those relating to other discrete retainers."
> I agree with that. The waiver can only extend to matters which are relevant
> to an issue in the proceedings and, privilege apart, admissible in evidence.
> There is no waiver for a roving search into anything else in which the
> solicitor or any other solicitor may have happened to have acted for the
> clients. But the waiver must go far enough not merely to entitle the plaintiff
> to establish his cause of action but to enable the defendant to establish a
> defence to the cause of action if he has one. Thus it would extend to matters
> under earlier retainers, as in the hypothetical example I have given, which
> established that the experience of the client was to the knowledge of the
> solicitor such that the solicitor was not in breach of duty as alleged.'

Both Mr Davidson and Mr Leeming, of course, accept the essentials of that
passage, but Mr Davidson places specific weight upon his words 'or any other
solicitor' as having application in this case. Mr Leeming argues that that goes too
far and was not necessary for the decision in *Lillicrap v Nalder & Son*. Russell LJ
dealt in succinct terms with the nature of privilege and waiver ([1993] 1 All ER
724 at 731, [1993] 1 WLR 94 at 101):

> 'The objection to this course is based upon the sacrosanct nature of the
> relationship between client and solicitor. I recognise of course that concept
> of legal professional privilege which is plainly in the public interest.
> However, in my judgment, once it is conceded that there is implied waiver
> of privilege when proceedings are instituted against a solicitor, I can see no
> warrant for the submission that the waiver is confined to the documents and
> communications between solicitor and client within the specific retainer

a forming the subject matter of the proceedings. The parameters of the retainer, to my mind, erect an artificial barrier. In my judgment, by bringing civil proceedings against his solicitor, a client impliedly waives privilege in respect of all matters which are relevant to the suit he pursues and, most particularly, where the disclosure of privileged matters is required to enable justice to be done. This is another way of expressing the view that May J
b expressed in his judgment in the passage to which Dillon LJ referred.'

Farquharson LJ underlined the importance of identifying the issue between the parties and the matters material to that issue. Once that is done then as a matter of fairness and justice waiver extends to documents and information, otherwise privileged, which are relevant to those issues and which it would be unfair to
c exclude (see [1993] 1 All ER 724 at 732, [1993] 1 WLR 94 at 102).

Nederlandse Reassurantie Groep Holding NV v Bacon & Woodrow (a firm) [1995] 1 All ER 976 is a decision of Colman J in which he considers the meaning of *Lillicrap v Nalder & Son*. The case arose from the provision of advice on business transactions to the plaintiff Dutch corporation by a team of legal and non-legal advisers. The plaintiffs sued the non-legal advisers in negligence; the defendant
d non-legal advisers sought disclosure of communications between the plaintiffs and the legal advisers. It was necessary for Colman J to decide whether the plaintiff by initiating proceedings against the non-legal advisers waived privilege in respect of communications for the legal co-advisers.

It was held (at 978):

e '(3) A client who sued his solicitor for negligence was presumed to have waived the privilege arising from the confidential relationship between them and was thus precluded from asserting that the solicitor had acted in breach of duty and, at the same time, seeking to enforce against that same solicitor a duty of confidence arising from their professional relationship in
f circumstances where such enforcement would deprive the solicitor of the means of defending the claim. Waiver of privilege did not however apply outside the solicitor-client relationship to cases where privilege prevented defendants gaining access to evidence that might assist in the defence, as where a defendant asserted that communications between a plaintiff and his solicitor were likely to be evidentially relevant to an issue and it would be
g unfair if he did not have access to them in order to assist his defence. Indeed, if the principle were of such general application it would involve a fundamental inroad into the scope of legal professional privilege. On the facts, it was clear that the documents in question were privileged by reason of the legal professional relationships between the plaintiff and [the legal
h advisers] and not between the plaintiff and the accountants, who of course were not legal advisers, and therefore there could be no question of any implied waiver of privilege in respect of the claim brought against the accountants.'

j Having set out passages from the judgments in *Lillicrap v Nalder & Son* Colman J went on (at 986):

'The true analysis of what the courts are doing in such cases of so-called implied waiver of privilege is, in my judgment, to prevent the unfairness which would arise if the plaintiff were entitled to exclude from the court's consideration evidence relevant to a defence by relying upon the privilege arising from the solicitor's duty of confidence. The client is thus precluded

from *both* asserting that the solicitor has acted in breach of duty and thereby
caused the client loss and, to make good that claim, opening up the *a*
confidential relationship between them and at the same time seeking to
enforce against the same solicitor a duty of confidence arising from their
professional relationship in circumstances where such enforcement would
deprive the solicitor of the means of defending the claim. It is fundamental
to this principle that the confidence which privilege would otherwise protect *b*
arises by reason of the same professional relationship between the parties to
the litigation. The underlying unfairness which the principle aims to avoid
arises because the claim is asserted and the professional relationship opened
for investigation against the very party whose duty of confidence is the basis
of the privilege. It is against the unfairness of both opening the relationship
by asserting the claim and seeking to enforce the duty of confidence owed by *c*
the defendant that the principle is directed.' (Colman J's emphasis.)

That passage clearly confines *Lillicrap v Nalder & Son* within fairly narrow bounds
and either does not take into account the passage in the judgment of Dillon LJ
where he refers to 'other solicitors', or discounts it. Colman J specifically rejects
the American approach in *Hearn v Rhay* (1975) 68 FRD 574, which held that *d*
waiver is to be implied as between solicitor and client where (1) the plaintiff has
filed suit against the solicitor and asserted privilege, (2) the plaintiff has put the
protected information in issue by making it relevant to the case, and (3) the
application of privilege would have denied the opposing party access to
information vital to his defence. Colman J concluded ([1995] 1 All ER 976 at 987): *e*

'But, as I have already explained, the foundation of the waiver is not merely
that the assertion of privilege leads to the inaccessibility of evidence relevant
to a defence. It is the inconsistency of the plaintiff on the one hand opening
the professional relationship to the inspection of the court and on the other
hand seeking to enforce confidentiality so as to exclude communications to *f*
which the professional relationship between the same parties has given rise.'

Again, it is not directly in point, albeit a helpful illustration of the application of
the principles relating to waiver of privilege.

In the light of the authorities, in a case where a plaintiff sues his solicitor and
seeks to rely upon a section of the 1980 Act to deprive a defendant of an otherwise *g*
unassailable defence one must establish what the Act requires the plaintiff to
show and in the light of that, what is relevant to that issue. Here the principal
issue is deliberate concealment and the plaintiff's date of knowledge of the letter
of 20 June and/or its purport; date of knowledge of course extends to the date
upon which the plaintiff could with reasonable diligence have discovered it. That *h*
issue will fall to be considered against a background of litigation relating to the
estate of the late Mr Kershaw pursuant to the inheritance proceedings. I am
unable to accept Mr Leeming's argument that those are 'wholly different'
proceedings. They are discrete, they took a different legal form and they
involved parties in addition to this plaintiff but they related to essentially the same *j*
subject matter. The distribution of the pension fund was an important element
in the inheritance proceedings although not a part of the estate and it would be
unreal to pretend one could put the two matters into watertight compartments.
The plaintiff was however represented by different solicitors in those proceedings
and different counsel. The defendants seek not only full discovery by list to
identify the advices/opinions given but also *discovery* of those documents. The

a authorities which I have set out are not directly in point and I must therefore consider their application to these facts against the important principle of legal privilege. *Jones v G D Searle & Co Ltd* [1978] 3 All ER 654, [1979] 1 WLR 101 does not greatly assist me. The provisions of s 2D of the 1939 Act directly refer to advices received and their existence and conclusions were obviously relevant to the question of whether the plaintiff could successfully invite the court to
b disapply the ordinary time limits. Section 32 does not contain such a reference. Further, *Jones v G D Searle & Co Ltd* does not deal with discovery; the latter does not automatically follow from waiver of privilege. *Nederlandse Reassurantie Groep Holding NV v Bacon & Woodrow* [1995] 1 All ER 976 was not concerned with an action brought against a solicitor and it does not appear to me that there could have been an implied waiver of legal professional privilege by the bringing of an
c action against accountants and other non-legal advisers. It is the passage in *Lillicrap v Nalder & Son* [1993] 1 All ER 724 at 729, [1993] 1 WLR 94 at 99 where Dillon LJ said 'There is no waiver for a roving search into anything else in which the solicitor or any other solicitor may have happened to have acted for the clients' which is critical to this case.

d
Conclusions

The solicitors' files of the plaintiff's former solicitors are in the hands of his present solicitor. In my judgment they are subject to the same rules of discovery as the file of his present solicitors, which means that letters and other
e communications between solicitor and client will be privileged, as will advices, opinions and file notes. I can see no logical basis for distinguishing between those files and those of the plaintiff's present solicitors where the various solicitors were dealing with essentially the same subject matter. The distribution of the pension fund clearly impinged upon the inheritance matters; that would be one of the reasons why solicitors were corresponding about it.
f
Having reached the conclusion that the earlier files and the earlier proceedings fall into the same category as the present file and the present proceedings, the question arises as to whether the plaintiff by suing the defendant has impliedly waived his undoubted privilege. Waiver is not lightly to be inferred; although privilege is an aspect of the law of evidence and not of constitutional rights, it is
g firmly established in our law for sound reasons of public policy. The wording of s 32 of the 1980 Act, unlike s 14, does not contain any references to legal or other advice but I adopt the passage in the judgment of Dillon LJ in *Lillicrap v Nalder & Son* which I have already quoted and conclude that the plea of deliberate concealment *has* had the effect of waiving privilege in respect of such documents
h as go to the issue. As Russell LJ said in *Lillicrap v Nalder & Son* [1993] 1 All ER 724 at 731, [1993] 1 WLR 94 at 101:

'... by bringing civil proceedings against his solicitor, a client impliedly waives privilege in respect of *all* matters which are relevant to the suit he
j pursues and, most particularly, where the disclosure of privileged matters is required to enable justice to be done.' (My emphasis.)

In *Lillicrap v Nalder & Son* the material was held in files of the same solicitors in respect of discrete transactions; I can see no difference in principle where his present solicitors hold files of the clients' earlier solicitors in relation to discrete but essentially related factual matters.

I do not consider the further listing of such documents is unduly burdensome: the period involved is restricted; it certainly ends with the date of knowledge claimed in the amended particulars.

I therefore order that the plaintiff do specifically identify by list such documents encompassed in Sch 1, part 2 of his list that go to knowledge of the letter of 20 June 1979 and further that the relevant parts of such documents be made available for inspection by the defendant within 28 days.

The second part of the summons is procedural and designed to progress the action. It is fundamentally important that this litigation makes progress; it has for whatever reason been going on far too long. I take the view that District Judge Galloway's extensive order of 17 June should stand altered only to the extent that is necessary to accommodate this order and the new date for the hearing of the preliminary issue. The costs should be determined at the hearing of the preliminary issue when it will be apparent whether this exercise served any purpose. If there *are* no documents as yet undisclosed relevant to knowledge it will not have done.

Order accordingly.

K Mydeen Esq   Barrister.

a   # Re a company (No 006798 of 1995)

CHANCERY DIVISION

CHADWICK J

b   11, 12, 15, 16 JANUARY 1996

Solicitor – Payment of costs by solicitor personally – Costs incurred unreasonably or improperly – Solicitor swearing affidavit in support of petition to wind up company as insolvent – Solicitor having no grounds for believing company to be insolvent – Solicitor knowing petition bound to fail if fought on merits – Whether solicitor acting improperly
c   *or unreasonably – Whether order for wasted costs appropriate – Supreme Court Act 1981, s 51(6).*

An engineering and contracting company engaged the petitioner as a sub-contractor in the redevelopment of a hospital site. On leaving the site the
d   petitioner submitted to the company a draft final account, having adjusted the sub-contract price to make a deduction for works which had not been done, but giving no credit for amounts paid by way of interim payments. In the ensuing discussions, the parties failed to reach agreement as to the sum due. The petitioner instructed its solicitors, without having made any statutory demand, to present a petition under the Insolvency Act 1986 for the company to be
e   wound up on the ground that a demand for payment had been made and that the company had failed to pay and was insolvent and unable to pay its debts. The petitioner's solicitor advised that the company appeared solvent on its balance sheet, and that if a substantial dispute could be shown the petition would risk being struck out, but nevertheless presented the petition and swore
f   an affidavit in support asserting on oath a belief that, on his perusal of the relevant documentation, the facts stated in the petition were to the best of his knowledge true. The judge struck out the application as an abuse of the process of the court, ordering the petitioner to pay the company's costs on an indemnity basis, and directed a further hearing to hear the company's application for a wasted costs order against the petitioner's solicitors under s 51(6)[a] of the
g   Supreme Court Act 1981.

Held – A solicitor who swore an affidavit in support of a winding-up petition, asserting on oath a belief that a company was insolvent on the ground that a debt was owing and the company was unable to pay its debts as they fell due, acted
h   improperly if he did not hold that belief; and he acted unreasonably if there were no grounds upon which a competent solicitor could have reached that view on the material available to him. Further, while it was not necessary for there to be a statutory demand, or even, in exceptional circumstances, any demand at all, the court would not easily be satisfied that a company was unable to pay its debts from the mere non-payment of a debt which had never been demanded of it. On
j   the facts, the circumstances of non-payment came nowhere near those required for an inference of an inability to pay, since the amount said to have been

---

a   Section 51(6), so far as material, provides: 'In any proceedings ... the court may ... order the legal or other representative concerned to meet, the whole of any wasted costs or such part of them as may be determined in accordance with rules of court.'

demanded was based on adjustments to the account which had been made by the petitioner unilaterally and of which the company had no knowledge; the *a* solicitor had sworn the affidavit in support of the winding-up petition in circumstances in which he knew or had to be taken to know that the petition was one which, if fought on its merits, would fail. It followed that the solicitor had acted unreasonably and would accordingly be ordered to pay the whole of the wasted costs incurred by the company pursuant to s 51(6) of the 1981 Act *b* (see p 429 *a* to *c*, p 430 *d* to *h* and p 431 *h* to p 432 *b*, post).

Ridehalgh v Horsefield [1994] 3 All ER 848 applied.

Notes

For the jurisdiction of the court to order costs against a legal representative personally, see 44(1) *Halsbury's Laws* (4th edn reissue) paras 167–174, and for *c* cases on solicitors' liability for costs in misconduct in contentious matters, see 44 *Digest* (Reissue) 430–435, 4668–4723.

For the Supreme Court Act 1981, s 51, see 11 *Halsbury's Statutes* (4th edn) (1991 reissue) 1019.

d

Cases referred to in judgment

Company, Re a (1950) 94 SJ 369.
Cornhill Insurance plc v Improvement Services Ltd [1986] 1 WLR 114.
Ridehalgh v Horsefield [1994] 3 All ER 848, [1994] Ch 205, [1994] 3 WLR 462, CA; rvsg sub nom *Re a Company (No 0022 of 1993)* [1993] BCC 726.
Taylors Industrial Flooring Ltd v M & H Plant Hire (Manchester) Ltd [1990] BCLC *e* 216, CA; rvsg [1990] BCC 44.

Cases also cited or referred to in skeleton arguments

Debtor, Re a (No 1 of 1987, Lancaster), ex p the debtor v Royal Bank of Scotland plc [1989] 2 All ER 46, [1989] 1 WLR 271, CA. *f*
Mine Exc Pty Ltd v Henderson Drilling Services Pty Ltd (in liq) (1989) 1 ACSR 118, W Aust SC.
Newman Air Charter Pty Ltd, Re (1991) 6 ACSR 435, W Aust SC.

Application

g

The company applied pursuant to s 51(6) of the Supreme Court Act 1981 for an order that Messrs Jeffrey Green Russell (JGR), solicitors to the petitioner, Seftacraft Ltd, pay the whole of the costs incurred by the company on the petitioner's application for the winding up of the company which was struck out as an abuse of process by Chadwick J on 28 November 1995, when the judge *h* ordered that the petitioner pay the company's costs of the petition and of the motion to strike it out and directed a further hearing of the matter to enable JGR to be heard on the application. The facts are set out in the judgment.

Claire Staddon (instructed by *Mills & Reeve*, Cambridge) for the company.
Robin Potts QC (instructed by *Jeffrey Green Russell*) for JGR. *j*

CHADWICK J. On 1 November 1995 Seftacraft Ltd (the petitioner) presented a petition under the Insolvency Act 1986 for the winding up of the applicant company. On 28 November 1995 I struck out that petition on the grounds that its presentation had been an abuse of the process of the court. I ordered that the a petitioner should pay the company's costs of the petition and of the motion to strike out, such costs to be taxed on the indemnity basis if not agreed. I directed a further hearing of that company's motion to enable the petitioner's solicitors, Messrs Jeffrey Green Russell, to be heard on the company's application for an order, pursuant to s 51(6) of the Supreme Court Act 1981, that that firm should pay the whole of the wasted costs incurred by the company. It is that application

b which is now before me.

Section 51 of the 1981 Act applies to all proceedings in the High Court. Subsection (6) empowers the court to order the legal or other representative concerned to meet the whole of any wasted costs, or such part of them as may be determined in accordance with *The Supreme Court Practice*. Wasted costs means, inter alia, any costs incurred by a party as a result of any improper,

c unreasonable, or negligent act on the part of any legal or other representative or any employee of such a representative.

Messrs Jeffrey Green Russell, to whom I shall refer for convenience as 'JGR', were the solicitors instructed by the petitioner at the time of the presentation of the petition. The affidavit verifying the petition was sworn by Mr Philip

d Graham Cohen, a partner in that firm. The company's application for a wasted costs order is founded upon JGR's participation in the presentation and verification of the petition.

The basis upon which the petitioner had sought an order for the winding of the company appears from paras 5, 6 and 7 of the petition:

e   '5. The company is indebted to your petitioner in the sum of £44,010·91 in respect of day work and contract labour services supplied at Ashford Hospital site between 21 September 1994 and 25 June 1995. 6. Your petitioner has made demand of the company for payment of this debt but the company has failed and neglected to pay or satisfy the same or any part

f   thereof. 7. The company is insolvent and unable to pay its debts.'

The petition was verified, in accordance with r 4.12(1) of the Insolvency Rules 1986, SI 1986/1925, by a short formal affidavit sworn by Mr Cohen. The relevant paragraphs in that affidavit are these:

g   '3. I have been concerned in the matters giving rise to the petition and have the requisite knowledge of the matters referred to in the petition from my perusal of the invoices, statements and other documentation relevant to this matter, the records of the company filed at Companies House and my client's instructions. 4. The statements in the petition now produced and

h   shown to me marked "A" are true to the best of my knowledge, information and belief.'

When the motion to strike out the petition came before me on 28 November 1995 there was no other evidence in support of the petition. The company did not appear at that hearing. Three affidavits had been filed on behalf of the

j company. The principal affidavits were those of Trevor Lambert-Gorwyn, a quantity surveyor employed by the company, and Mr Clive Alan Moore, the company's financial director. Mr Moore exhibited, inter alia, a copy of the company's audited financial statements for the year ended 31 December 1994. Mr Lambert-Gorwyn exhibited contractual documentation between the company and the petitioner.

On the basis of that material I formed the view which I expressed in the following passage of the judgment which I gave on that day:

'On the material before me it is impossible to understand how a petition could have been presented on the basis of an allegation that the petitioner had made demand for the sum of £44,010·91, or how it could be said that the company had failed or neglected to pay or satisfy a demand for that amount; nor is it possible to understand how it could be alleged that the company is insolvent and unable to pay its debts. Clearly, that allegation could not be based upon the company's balance sheet. Equally clearly the allegation could not be based upon a failure to pay debts as they became due. There is no material to support a contention that a debt of £44,010·91 has ever become due from the company to the petitioner. Prima facie, therefore, the presentation of the petition was a clear abuse of the process of the court. It was an attempt to bring pressure to bear upon this substantial contracting company by subjecting it to the consequences which flow from the presentation of a winding-up petition.'

Encouraged, perhaps, by those remarks, the company has pursued its application for a wasted costs order against JGR. RSC Ord 62, r 11(4) requires that no order shall be made under s 1(6) of the 1981 Act unless the court has given the legal representative concerned a reasonable opportunity to appear and show cause why an order should not be made. In giving directions that the motion should be restored before me for that purpose, I said:

'It will be apparent from this judgment that I have been unable to understand from the material before me how Mr Cohen could properly have sworn the affidavit which he did swear on 1 November 1995 in support of the petition. In those circumstances it seems to me appropriate that I should direct that JGR appear before me and show cause why I should not make the wasted costs order against that firm.'

In response to those directions JGR have appeared before me with leading counsel, Mr Potts QC. Mr Cohen has sworn three further affidavits to explain the circumstances in which the petition came to be presented and his first affidavit sworn. It is clear from Mr Cohen's further evidence that, whatever might have been the impression to be gained from paras 5 and 6 of the petition and from his first formal affidavit verifying that petition, he does not suggest that the petitioner ever made demand of the company for payment of the sum of £44,010·91. Nor does he suggest that the company ever acknowledged that it was indebted in a sum of that amount.

The amount of the alleged debt, £44,010·91, was derived from a schedule supplied to Mr Cohen by his client, the petitioner. Neither that schedule nor that figure were disclosed to the company at any time before the presentation of the petition on 1 November 1995. No information from which it could be deduced why the petitioner claimed payment in the amount of £44,010·91 was disclosed to the company at any time before Mr Cohen's second affidavit was sworn on 6 December 1995 in response to the application for a wasted costs order.

In order to understand the circumstances in which the petition was presented it is necessary to examine the contractual position between the company and the petitioner. The company is a substantial engineering and contracting company.

a During 1994 and 1995 it was engaged, under a sub-contract from Taylor Woodrow, in carrying out works in connection with the redevelopment of Ashford Hospital. The petitioner is a contractor specialising, inter alia, in the supply and installation of pipework. On 31 March 1994 the company invited the petitioner to tender for sub-contract work at the Ashford Hospital site. The petitioner submitted its tender on 29 July 1994. That tender was accepted by the
b company on 16 August 1994.

The sub-contract sum for works to be done by the petitioner was £125,851·09. The terms of the sub-contract are to be found; first, in the invitation to tender (which is described as a 'form of inquiry') and the conditions attached thereto; second, in the company's standard conditions of sub-contract, reference B26/91 (which were incorporated by the acceptance on 16 August 1994, which itself was
c countersigned by the petitioner); and, third, in a sub-contract addendum attached to that acceptance. The conditions of tender included the following.

'2. The subcontract entered into will be subject to the company's standard conditions of sub-contract, reference sub-con B26, and by virtue of these conditions it shall also be subject to the head form of contract between
d the employer and the main contractor except insofar as that shall be specifically varied between the main contractor and the employer ... 11. No variations to the works are to be carried out or alterations made to the specification unless instructed in writing by our subcontract instruction and/or subcontract variation order. To avoid delays in payment of any
e variation that may occur to your works during the contract period, you are required to note the following: (a) Invoices for payment of variations will not be paid without a copy of our written authorisation attached to the invoice. (b) Variations must be carried out on schedule of rates unless authorised by the employer to be executed on day work. Day work sheets must be signed by our engineer and submitted within seven days following
f the week ending when the work was executed. Day work sheets submitted after this period will not be dealt with until final account stage. (c) Where practical all variations are to be priced prior to the commencement of the work. (d) All variation orders and day work sheets must be uniquely numbered, legible and fully describe the work carried out.'

g The conditions of sub-contract in the form B26/91 included:

'11. Valuation of Variations 1. All authorised variations to the subcontract works shall be valued in the manner provided by this clause, and the value whereof shall be added to or deducted from the subcontract
h sum. 2. The value of all authorised variations shall be ascertained by measurement and by reference to the rates and prices specified in this subcontract for the like or analogous work, but if there are no such rates or prices, or if they are not applicable, then such value shall be a fair and reasonable valuation in all the circumstances ... 12. Payment of sub-
j contractor The subcontract price referred to in the form of subcontract acceptance shall be paid by the contractor for the subcontractor in the following manner: The contractor shall pay to the subcontractor the total value of the work executed by him in respect of which payment has been made to the contractor. All such payments to the subcontractor shall be subject to retentions throughout at such rates for such periods and for such purposes as under the provisions of the main contract. The employer is

entitled to make such retentions against the contractor so far as they relate
to the subcontract works.'   *a*

The sub-contract addendum attached to the acceptance of 16 August 1994
made further provision for variation works and payment:

> '3. Further to clause 11(b) of our conditions of tender variations will only
> be paid for on a day work basis if this has been agreed in writing prior to *b*
> commencement of the work. Subcontractors' record sheets or day work
> sheets presented for signature will be signed for record purposes only and
> will solely be to verify that the work has been executed. It will not in any
> way convey or confirm the company's agreement that the subcontractor is
> entitled to be paid for the work, or that the hours and materials recorded are *c*
> correct ... 6. Payment applications to be submitted monthly no later than
> the 20th day of each month. Each application must be supported with
> sufficient detail, breakdown and substantiation to enable a thorough check
> to be made of the amount being claimed ... 8. Payment terms and
> conditions to be in accordance with the company's conditions of
> sub-contract ref: B26/91, but to be made seven days after receipt of *d*
> payment by the company ... 10. Further to clause 11(c) of our conditions
> of tender, all variation costs are to be submitted together with full
> substantiation detailed measures and cost breakdowns within 14 days of
> being instructed.'

The manner in which the provisions in the sub-contract for payment of the *e*
sub-contractor were given effect in practice was described by Mr Lambert-
Gorwyn in his affidavit of 9 November 1995:

> 'Interim applications for payment. 11. Each month subcontractors
> would make an interim application for payment. Clause 6 of the addendum
> to the contract with [the petitioner] specified that this had to be submitted *f*
> by the 20th of each month as [the company] in turn submitted an interim
> application for payment to Taylor Woodrow on the 25th of each month ...
> 13. The interim application for payment would set out which works
> covered by [the petitioner's] contract had been undertaken that month, and
> also work which [the petitioner] considered to be variations to their
> contract. If an item was identified by the subcontractor as a variation it was *g*
> my role to thoroughly check the details of the application to see whether it
> was a true variation to the subcontract. If any of these alleged variations
> were variations to [the company's] contract, these would be forwarded to
> the client for their approval and subsequent payment. On receipt of such
> payments the subcontractor would be entitled to be paid at the appropriate *h*
> rate. 14. [The petitioner] made a number of applications for interim
> payments. After each application for payment I wrote to [the petitioner]
> and informed them how much I had certified as an interim advance. In the
> vast majority of cases I supplied [the petitioner] with a detailed breakdown
> of the methods I had employed to arrive at the figure certified as an interim *j*
> advance. I can confirm that [the petitioner] had been paid £147,412·02
> (exclusive of value added tax) by way of interim advances.'

There is exhibited to Mr Lambert-Gorwyn's affidavit a document in respect
of payment application No 4 made by the petitioner. This illustrates the process
which Mr Lambert-Gorwyn has described. It shows that, in relation to

a application No 4 (made in October 1994), each item of work, whether done as part of the contract works or as a variation to those works, has been given a value by the petitioner in its claim for interim payment and has been allowed a value by the company in making payment. The value allowed by the company is, in some cases, the same as that claimed by the petitioner, and in other cases less than that claimed.

b The petitioner left the Ashford Hospital site at the end of June 1995 without, it is said, having completed all the sub-contract works. On 9 August 1995 the petitioner submitted to the company a document described as a draft final account. The draft final account is made up of (i) a sum of £122,880·03 said to be in respect of 'the revised order value', and (ii) further sums, totalling £73,072·27, in respect of 28 separate items under the general heading 'day work

c schedule'. The revised order value of £122,880·03 represents an adjustment to the sub-contract price of £125,851·09, after deducting certain works which were not done. The day work schedule is a summary of the variations claimed in the interim payment applications with certain adjustments. Together the revised order value and the items in the day work schedule amount to £195,952·30. The

d draft final account gives no credit for the amount paid by way of interim payments.

The letter of 9 August 1995, under cover of which the petitioner sent to the company its draft final account, concludes with the following sentence: 'Would you please contact the writer to arrange a meeting for next week to discuss and agree the above.' The company responded to that letter by a fax dated 8

e September 1995. The response includes a summary of comments, over four pages, on each of the items in the draft final account. Mr Lambert-Gorwyn deposes that a meeting to discuss those items took place, and he exhibits a schedule showing the values which, as a result of that meeting, the company was prepared to agree in respect of the various items in the day work schedule. The

f amount of the revised order value (£122,880·03) was agreed.

Following the meeting, the total amount which the company was prepared to agree, as shown in Mr Lambert-Gorwyn's schedule (after including the whole of the revised order value of £122,880·03, but before deducting certain contra-claims which were being raised by the company as a result of the petitioner's premature departure from the site), was £143,478·33. That was, of course, less

g than the amount (£147,412·02) which, as Mr Lambert-Gorwyn had deposed, the company had already paid to the petitioner on account in response to the interim payment applications.

It appears clear from the documents to which I have referred that the

h petitioner's letter of 9 August 1995 with the draft final account, the company's response of 8 September 1995, and the subsequent meeting, were part of the normal process of agreeing a final account which may be expected to take place at the conclusion of a construction contract. There is nothing in those documents, or elsewhere in the correspondence, which suggests that the company was refusing to agree matters which it knew ought to have been

j agreed with intent to delay payment. Disagreement as to the amount, if any, to be paid for variations to the contract works is a common feature of construction contracts.

On 18 October 1995 the petitioner submitted a further claim for direct loss and expense under cl 13.1.3 of the standard form of contract JCT80 DOM/1 in an amount of £48,297·77. The petitioner's letter of that date concludes with the sentence: 'We would initially request that a substantial payment on account is discharged pending agreement of the final account and claim.' The reference in that sentence to the final account is a reference back to the account submitted on 9 August 1995. The petitioner, on 18 October 1995, was seeking interim payment on account pending agreement (a) of that final account, and (b) of the direct loss and expense claim. There is no suggestion in that letter that the petitioner then took the view that the company was acting in bad faith in refusing to agree outstanding items in the final account.

It was very shortly after that letter of 18 October 1995 that the petitioner consulted Mr Cohen. Mr Cohen has put in evidence an attendance note of a meeting with his client on 20 October 1995. That attendance note includes the following passages:

'PGC [Mr Cohen] attending Jo Cates and Mrs Scott in conference at these offices regarding [the company]. They have now finished the work in Ashford. [The company] have asked them to do work on another half million project elsewhere but they won't because [the company] won't pay them for the Ashford job. The difference between them is some £50,000. [The company] are using their usual tricks for non-payment. If you do not get a signed order for day work they won't pay it. If you do get a signed order they say that the engineer who signed it did not have authority or that it should have been included as part of the contractual works anyway, or they arbitrarily come round afterwards and revalue the work with a surveyor or deny that it was authorised etc ... We were having difficulty as they were trying to explain to me the reasons advanced by [the company] for not paying which reasons simply didn't hold water and which PGC therefore had difficulty in understanding. We resolved that it would be simpler if they were simply to formulate their claim as they didn't have a statement or anything with them, and PGC would then leave [the company's lawyers] to try to make sense of their stupid reasons for non-payment and at least the issues would then be clear. In order to facilitate the clearance of the issues PGC advised on the form of statement he wanted. The situation is that they haven't put in any invoices, architects' certificates etc. They submit applications which don't include VAT, [the company] then decide how much of the application they [feel] like paying (apparently a total of £151,000 has been paid) and add the VAT onto the bit that they feel like paying and send it back. As a result there is slippage all the way and the claim will have to be formulated on applications to which we will then have to add VAT. [Mrs Scott] will give me the details of the applications, application numbers, dates etc. a sub-total, and then take away what they have already paid ... I explained there were no easy solutions. The claim would go to the OR's department and they weren't likely to resolve the matter for a year or more during which they may become disheartened because instead of getting money from [the company] they would be paying out money to quantity surveyors and me. They said they understood this was a well-known tactic of [the company] to pay their sub-contractors nicely during the currency of the contract, but withhold the last payment (after they didn't need them any more), whereas it was the last payment which was the subbies' profit. [The company] had done this for a number of other subcontractors and many had been forced into liquidation as a result. He said that [the company] estimated their jobs in so a   ridiculously competitive a fashion that the only way in which they could hope not to make a loss is on the basis they would force those subcontractors into liquidation ... [Mr Cates] felt that [the company] were insolvent and using moneys due to subcontractors to prop up their cash flow. He said he couldn't hang around for a year to get paid by [the company] as he had to pay his labourers, and he knew they were just

b   stringing him along for as long as possible, and what legal weapons were there to force them to pay their debts. I said that if they were insolvent and there was no merit in their dispute then we could issue winding up proceedings. I advised him as to the grounds upon which such proceedings may be opposed in terms of the bona fide dispute upon substantial grounds. I said that we had litigated against [the company] before and they had

c   proved amenable to winding up petitions. But here the dispute appeared fairly well documented. I said if they could convince the court that the dispute was substantial then he was contemplating an extremely high risk strategy ... He asked how long the winding up route would take. I said that a petition issued today would have a return date around 6 December, but

d   one would expect it to be resolved before then. [Mr Cates] said he wanted to try his luck at the winding up route first. Although the dispute looked like a genuine dispute he said that [the company] knew in their heart of hearts that it was a try on although that might not be apparent to me, and that when faced with the petition they would concede. He asked if we could issue a petition. I said we could get one on its feet via a statutory

e   demand which would take 21 days. He said he couldn't wait 21 days. I said that on profit and loss account they were insolvent, although they appeared solvent on balance sheet, and we could issue a petition on the basis of [the profit and loss] account, but we would have to monitor it very carefully to make sure it didn't rebound on him. The balance sheet was supported by almost £64m of debtors, high in relation to turnover, and we did not know

f   how old they were, and whether they should have been provided for or prudently written off. Also the American parent company had just emerged from Chapter 11 bankruptcy in the States which was a good sign in one way, but a bad sign in the other. I said that if the petition was seriously challenged he should let it go and sue in the ordinary way ... The

g   subcontract includes standard terms which purport to incorporate the terms of the main contract also, which he is deemed to have accepted. He has no idea what is in the main contract, but appreciates he may be lumbered with its provisions.'

h   Mr Cohen elaborates on that attendance note in paras 2.28 and 2.29 of the affidavit which he swore on 6 December 1995. In para 2.29 he says:

'Accordingly, on my instructions the company had put the basis for a dispute in place. I did not believe it to be a real substantial or bona fide dispute. The amount due to [the petitioner] was £44,010·91 representing

j   the difference between [the petitioner's] valuation of £192,478·78 (as amended) and the company's valuation of £148,467·87. The calculation of that balance is at pp. 6 and 7 of PGC7 below. This calculation was supplied to me by [the petitioner] before presentation of the petition. As appears from exhibit TGL 4 of Mr. Lambert-Gorwyn's affidavit of 9 November 1995, [the petitioner] had submitted a draft valuation supported by detailed

documentation on 9 August 1995 for £195,952·30. On 18 October 1995 [the
petitioner] submitted a claim to the company for £48,297·77. The petition *a*
debt of £44,010·91 constitutes, as pp. 6 and 7 of PGC7 demonstrate, a
downward revision of the earlier calculation. [The petitioner] now value
the works at £192,478·78 as against a company's valuation of £148,467·87,
plus the entire £44,010·91 was comprehended within payment applications
previously made to the company by [the petitioner].' *b*

In so far as it might be understood from that passage that the petition debt of
£44,010·91 represented a downward revision of an earlier claim of £48,297·77,
the passage is clearly in error. The claim for £48,297·77 had nothing whatever
to do with the petition debt. That claim was a direct loss and expenses claim.
That petition debt is said to be in respect of day work and contract labour. *c*

Further explanation of the basis of the figure of £44,010·91 was put forward by
Mr Cohen in his fourth affidavit, sworn on 15 January 1996 during the course of
the hearing before me. He explains in that affidavit, and in the documents which
are exhibited to it, that the figure is reached by subtracting the amount which
the company had allowed as a value against the contract works and the day
works claimed in the interim payment applications (that is to say a total of *d*
£148,467·87) against the total amount that had been claimed by the petitioner
(that is to say £192,478·78). The amount claimed by the petitioner did, of course,
represent a reduction from the amount of £195,952·30 which had been included
in the draft final account sent on 9 August 1995. The revised or reduced figure
was never communicated to the company. *e*

It was on the basis of the exercise which I have described that Mr Cohen
swore, on 1 November 1995, that he had been concerned in the matters giving
rise to the petition and had the requisite knowledge of the matters referred in
the petition from his perusal of the invoices, statements and other documentation relevant to the matter, and his client's instructions. The matters of which
he was there professing to have knowledge were that the company was indebted *f*
to the petitioner in the sum of £44,010·91, and that the petitioner had made
demand of the company for payment of that debt.

A petition for the winding up of the company may be presented by a creditor
(see s 124 of the 1986 Act). The circumstances in which the company may be
wound up are described in s 122(1) of the 1986 Act. They include, at para (1)(f), *g*
the inability of the company to pay its debts. Accordingly, a creditors' petition
for a winding up will normally need to allege both that the petitioner is a creditor
of the company and that the company is unable to pay its debts. Section 123(1)
lists circumstances in which a company is deemed unable to pay its debts. Those
include, at para (a), neglect to pay a sum in respect of which the creditor has *h*
served on the company a statutory demand and, at para (e), 'if it is proved to the
satisfaction of the court that the company is unable to pay its debts as they fall
due'. Section 123(2) provides that 'a company is also deemed unable to pay its
debts if it is proved to the satisfaction of the court that the value of the
company's assets is less than the amount of its liabilities taking into account its
contingent and prospective liabilities'. The test under s 123(2) is often described *j*
as the test of 'balance sheet' solvency.

In his affidavit of 1 November 1995 Mr Cohen refers to knowledge obtained
from the records of the company filed at Companies House. In context that
must be a reference to the company's financial statements in respect of the year
ended 31 December 1994, which had been filed, and which, as Mr Cohen

a acknowledges in later evidence, he had seen. The information from those accounts, as it appears from the affidavit, formed at least part of the basis upon which, on 1 November 1995, Mr Cohen felt able to verify to the best of his knowledge, information and belief that the company was insolvent and unable to pay its debts.

b It appears from the attendance note of 20 October 1995, to which I have already referred, that Mr Cohen had advised the petitioner on that date that the company appeared solvent on its balance sheet. The balance sheet of the company as at 31 December 1994 discloses shareholders' funds in excess of £12m. That figure is arrived at after taking account of current assets of some £70m and deducting current liabilities (in the form of creditors whose debts fall due within one year) of £61m. The current assets include stock of £1m, debtors c of approximately £64m, and cash at bank and in hand of £5·3m.

As Mr Cohen points out in his later affidavits, it appears from the notes to the accounts that the cash at bank represents moneys lodged with the company's bankers against potential liabilities in respect of performance bonds. The £64m of debtors includes trade debtors of £20m, amounts recoverable on contracts of d £32m, and amounts owed by the parent and fellow subsidiary undertakings of some £9·5m. The directors' report contains the information that the company's ultimate holding company had just emerged from Chapter 11 administration in the United States with a net worth of $US81m, having successfully completed its financial reconstruction. In those circumstances Mr Potts did not feel able to e submit that any court would be persuaded from an examination of the 1994 accounts that the company could be regarded as insolvent on what I have described as a balance sheet basis; and, as I have said, Mr Cohen did not himself take that view in his attendance note of 20 October.

The accounts to 31 December 1994 disclose a loss for that year of £3·9m. But it also appears from those accounts that that loss is wholly attributable to what f are described as 'discontinued operations'. The loss on discontinued operations was £6,200,000, to set against a profit on continuing operations of £2,100,000. Accordingly, on the basis of the 1994 accounts and the directors' report, there was no reason to think that the company would not trade profitably during 1995.

I find myself unable to understand what was meant by the phrase in Mr g Cohen's attendance note that 'on profit and loss account [the company was] insolvent', and that the petition could be issued 'on the basis of [the profit and loss] account'. Mr Potts did not feel able to help me with an explanation based on the accounts. His submission was that Mr Cohen was entitled to take the view that the company was insolvent because it had failed to pay a debt which was due to the petitioner.

h There is no doubt that the terms of s 123(1)(e) of the 1986 Act enable the court to reach the conclusion that a company is unable to pay its debts as they fall due on any evidence which satisfies it of that fact. It is not necessary for there to be a statutory demand; nor, in exceptional circumstances, is it necessary for there to be a demand at all. But, as it appears to me, the statutory provision which j deems inability to pay debts on failure to meet a statutory demand suggests, at the least, that the court should be slow to reach the conclusion that a company is unable to pay its debts from the mere fact of non-payment of a debt which has never been demanded of it at all.

I was, of course, referred to the decisions in *Cornhill Insurance plc v Improvement Services Ltd* [1986] 1 WLR 114 and *Taylors Industrial Flooring Ltd v M & H Plant*

Hire (Manchester) Ltd [1990] BCLC 216. In *Cornhill Insurance* [1986] 1 WLR 114 at
118 Harman J explained that in circumstances where a company fails to pay a *a*
debt which is admittedly due, it will be no answer to a winding-up petition to
show that the company is solvent on a balance sheet basis. He adopted this
passage from the judgment of Vaisey J in *Re a company* (1950) 94 SJ 369: 'Rich
men and rich companies who did not pay their debts had only themselves to
blame if it were thought that they could not pay them.'   *b*

   Cornhill Insurance was a remarkable case on its facts. The allegation of
insolvency against the insurance company was founded on a failure to pay an
insurance claim in respect of two specific items of damage. The amount of those
items had been agreed at £1,154 in the course of a telephone conversation on 12
June 1985 between the solicitors for the claimants and the loss adjusters acting *c*
for the insurance company. They had also been the subject of a specific request
for payment by solicitors' letter on 14 June 1985. In those circumstances, when
the matter came before him on 22 July 1985, Harman J was not prepared to treat
the threat to present a winding-up petition as an abuse of the process of the
court; and, in particular, was not willing to restrain the presentation of that
threatened petition. The facts in *Cornhill Insurance* were very far removed from *d*
the facts now before me.

   In *Taylors Industrial Flooring Ltd v M & H Plant Hire (Manchester) Ltd* [1990]
BCLC 216 the petition was based upon invoices which had been delivered to the
company in an aggregate sum of £9,875. The company raised a dispute as to the
period of credit to be allowed for payment. There was no dispute that the *e*
invoices were payable; the dispute was whether they had become due for
payment under the terms of the contract at the time when the petition was
presented. Scott J took the view that, a reason for non-payment having been put
forward by the company, it would not be right to infer inability to pay from the
fact of non-payment. The reason put forward might not be a very good reason,
but in the absence of any evidence that it was not being put forward honestly, *f*
he was not prepared to infer that the company could not pay the debt. He said
([1990] BCC 44 at 46–47):

      'In my judgment, something more must be proved than simply that the
      company has not paid a debt. In some cases the circumstances surrounding *g*
      the non-payment may justify the inference that the debtor is unable to pay
      its debts as they fall due. A series of dishonoured cheques might justify that
      inference. But in the present case a reason for non-payment has been put
      forward.'

                                                                                    h
The Court of Appeal, in reversing the decision of Scott J, held that the reason put
forward was so untenable that it could not be regarded as a substantial ground
for disputing that the debts claimed in respect of the January and February
invoices were not due for payment. In effect the court held that the supposed
dispute was not bona fide. Dillon LJ explained the position ([1990] BCLC 216 at
220):   *j*

      'Therefore the position was that the company had not paid a debt as it fell
      due and had no substantial ground for opposing it. Therefore there was
      evidence of insolvency.'

a A feature of both the *Cornish Insurance* case and the *Taylors* case is that the company knew what it was being asked to pay and did not or could not, bona fide, dispute that the amount that it was being asked to pay was payable.

In the present case the amount said to have been demanded is an amount which was never communicated to the company and which the company could not have worked out for itself. The amount of £44,010·91 was based on certain
b adjustments to its draft final account which had been made by the petitioner unilaterally and of which the company had no knowledge. Further, the amount demanded cannot be reconciled with the amount which Mr Lambert-Gorwyn says that the company had paid by way of interim application. In my view, even if the claim in respect of day work resulting from variations were wholly substantiated, the circumstances of non-payment come nowhere near those
c which are required for support of an inference of inability to pay debts under s 123(1)(e) of the 1986 Act.

Mr Cohen relies on other matters in his affidavit of 6 December 1995. He recites a history of late payment by the company in other cases and of attempts by other suppliers to obtain payment. In my view no reliance can be placed on
d that history in deciding whether this company was unable to pay its debts on 1 November 1995. The facts upon which Mr Cohen relies are disputed by the company; but, accepting those facts at their face value, what they would show is that this is a company which—perhaps like other companies in the construction industry—chooses not to pay its debts until it is obliged to do so. The facts alleged demonstrate that, when obliged to pay by the threat or
e presentation of a winding-up petition, the company appears to have no difficulty in finding moneys sufficient to satisfy the creditor.

In those circumstances I have to decide, for the purpose of s 51(6) of the 1981 Act, whether in swearing the affidavit which he did swear on 1 November 1995, Mr Cohen acted improperly, unreasonably or negligently.

f Guidance as to the test to be applied for that purpose has been given by the Court of Appeal in its decision in *Ridehalgh v Horsefield* [1994] 3 All ER 848, [1994] Ch 205 and other appeals reported there. Sir Thomas Bingham MR explains the terms 'improper', 'unreasonable' and 'negligent' in the context of an application for a wasted costs order:

g   '"Improper" means what it has been understood to mean in this context for at least half a century. The adjective covers, but is not confined to, conduct which would ordinarily be held to justify disbarment, striking off, suspension from practice or other serious professional penalty. It covers any significant breach of a substantial duty imposed by a relevant code of
h   professional conduct. But it is not in our judgment limited to that. Conduct which would be regarded as improper according to the consensus of professional (including judicial) opinion can be fairly stigmatised as such whether or not it violates the letter of a professional code. "Unreasonable" also means what it has been understood to mean in this context for at least half a century. The expression aptly describes conduct which is vexatious,
j   designed to harass the other side rather than advance the resolution of the case, and it makes no difference that the conduct is the product of excessive zeal and not improper motive. But conduct cannot be described as unreasonable simply because it leads in the event to an unsuccessful result or because other more cautious legal representatives would have acted differently. The acid test is whether the conduct permits of a reasonable

explanation. If so, the course adopted may be regarded as optimistic and as reflecting on a practitioner's judgment, but it is not unreasonable. The term "negligent" was the most controversial of the three. It was argued that the 1990 Act, in this context as in others, used "negligent" as a term of art involving the well-known ingredients of duty, breach, causation and damage. Therefore, it was said, conduct cannot be regarded as negligent unless it involves an actionable breach of a legal representative's duty to his own client, to whom alone a duty is owed. We reject this approach. (1) As already noted, the predecessor of the present Ord 62, r 11 made reference to "reasonable competence". That expression does not invoke technical concepts of the law of negligence. It seems to us inconceivable that by changing the language Parliament intended to make it harder, rather than easier, for courts to make orders. (2) Since the applicant's right to a wasted costs order against a legal representative depends on showing that the latter is in breach of his duty to the court it makes no sense to superimpose a requirement under this head (but not in the case of impropriety or unreasonableness) that he is also in breach of his duty to his client.' (See [1994] 3 All ER 848 at 861–862, [1994] Ch 205 at 232–233.)

In my view this is not a case in which Mr Cohen can be said to have acted negligently. It is plain from his attendance note of 20 October 1995 that he knew just what he was doing. He knew that his client was embarking on a high-risk strategy; and that if a substantial dispute existed that strategy would result in the petition being struck out. He advised his client to that effect.

Nor, on the evidence which is before me, am I prepared to hold Mr Cohen guilty of impropriety. I have no doubt that a solicitor who swears an affidavit in which he verifies that a debt is owing, or that a company is insolvent, when he does not have any belief that those facts are true, will be guilty of conduct which would be regarded as improper within the test indicated by Sir Thomas Bingham MR. Mr Cohen has gone on oath to verify that he believed on 1 November 1995 that £44,010·91 was owing by the company to the petitioner; and that he believed that the company was insolvent. He has not been cross-examined on his affidavit. Whatever I may think of the grounds on which he says he based his belief, I cannot hold that he did not truly believe that which he says, on his oath, that he did believe.

The question, in my view, is whether his conduct was unreasonable; that is to say whether he swore an affidavit in support of this petition asserting facts which any competent solicitor must have appreciated could not be established on the evidence available; and that he swore that affidavit not for the purpose of obtaining a winding-up order, but for the purpose of bringing pressure to bear upon the company so that it would pay what was claimed rather than suffer the consequences of the advertisement of the petition.

In that context it is material to note that, when deciding the appeal in *Philex plc v Golban* (reported with *Ridehalgh v Horsefield* [1994] 3 All ER 848 at 878, [1994] Ch 205 at 250, to which I have referred), Sir Thomas Bingham MR said:

'We do not suggest that there could never be circumstances in which a solicitor who advised his client to make use of a threat of proceedings that would (if brought) amount to an abuse of the process might be found to have been guilty of improper or unreasonable conduct.' (See [1994] 3 All ER 848 at 882, [1994] Ch 205 at 254–255.)

a   The Court of Appeal differed from the conclusions reached by Knox J as to the facts in that case. (His decision is reported as *Re a company (No 0022 of 1993)* [1993] BCC 726.) But that does not, in my view, throw doubt upon that judge's conclusion that, if the facts supported a finding that the solicitor had been party to a course of action designed to achieve a collateral object, rather than to achieve the purpose for which the proceedings were ostensibly brought, that
b   conduct might properly be described as unreasonable.

It is a feature of the winding-up process that the presentation of a petition may have very serious consequences for the company against which it is presented whether or not, on the hearing of the petition, it is held the petitioner is entitled to a winding-up order. Those consequences arise by virtue of the provisions of
c   ss 127 and 129 of the 1986 Act. Section 129(2) provides that, in the absence of some prior resolution for voluntary winding up, if a winding-up order is eventually made, the winding up of a company is deemed to commence at the time of the presentation of the petition for winding up, and s 127 provides that where a winding-up order is eventually made any disposition of a company's property made after the commencement of a winding up is, unless the court
d   otherwise orders, void.

The effect is that a person dealing with the company after a petition has been presented is at risk that any disposition of the company's property effected in the course of that dealing will be held void if a winding-up order is eventually made. In practice, once a third party comes to know of the presentation of a petition,
e   it may very well refuse to have further dealings with the company until the petition has been disposed of. It is common for a company's banker to freeze its bank account once the bank learns of the presentation of a petition.

It is, perhaps, for that reason, amongst others, that a petition may not be advertised during a period of seven days from service on the company. A company upon whom a winding-up petition is served, or against whom a
f   petition is threatened, must pay the debt, or must incur the expense of an application to strike out or to restrain presentation of the petition. If the company allows the petition to be advertised then there is a serious danger that the damage that will be done to the company by the advertisement will far outweigh any commercial advantage in disputing a genuinely disputed debt.
g   Those facts lead to the opportunity for abuse. The presentation of the petition, or the threat to present the petition, imposes on the company a commercial pressure which is different in kind from the issue of a writ. It is, of course, that opportunity to exert commercial pressure which leads to the creditor's decision to present a petition rather than to take proceedings in the Official Referees' corridor.
h
I am satisfied that the matters to which I have referred were perfectly well known to Mr Cohen; that they formed part of the thinking disclosed in his attendance note of 20 October 1995; and that he allowed himself to be party to a course of action which was thought to be in his client's commercial interest in circumstances in which he knew, or must be taken to have known, that this was
j   a petition which, if fought on its merits, would fail. I do not hold that a solicitor who, on his client's express instructions, presents a petition in those circumstances must, necessarily, be said to have acted unreasonably or improperly. I do hold that a solicitor who, in swearing an affidavit in the short statutory form to support a winding-up petition, asserts on his oath a belief that a debt is owing and that the company is insolvent, acts improperly if he does not

have that belief; and acts unreasonably if there are no grounds upon which a competent solicitor could reach that view on the material available to him.

For the reasons which I have given I am satisfied that, in swearing the affidavit which he did swear on 1 November 1995, Mr Cohen acted unreasonably; and that accordingly it is open to me to make a wasted costs order against his firm under s 51(6) of the 1981 Act. On the facts of the present case, the unreasonable conduct which I have identified has led the company to incur wasted costs in relation to the petition, to its motion to strike out, and ancillary applications. I propose to order that the whole of those wasted costs be paid by JGR.

Order accordingly.

Celia Fox   Barrister.

a

Re Polly Peck International plc (in administration)

CHANCERY DIVISION (COMPANIES COURT)
b ROBERT WALKER J
22, 23, 24 NOVEMBER, 6 DECEMBER 1995

Company – Winding up – Proof and ranking of claims – Rule against double proof – Holding company using subsidiary to issue bonds and on-loan funds raised – Holding company and subsidiary both going into liquidation – Subsidiary and bondholders
c *lodging claims under holding company's scheme of arrangement in respect of bond funds – Whether claims in respect of the same debt – Whether rule against double proof precluding payment of dividend to subsidiary.*

Company – Corporate personality – Lifting corporate veil – Holding and subsidiary
d *companies – Whether subsidiary the agent or nominee of holding company – Whether subsidiary and holding company should be treated as one economic unit.*

Between 1987 and 1990 a holding company, PPI, set up a special purpose, wholly-owned subsidiary in the Cayman Islands in order to raise finance to develop the group's business activities by means of a number of bond issues. The
e subsidiary, PPIF, issued the bonds to a group of foreign banks which managed the issues and also acted as principal paying agents. PPIF's repayment obligations were guaranteed by PPI and all funds received by PPIF were on-loaned to PPI. Each bond issue included inter alia a provision for PPI to be substituted for PPIF as the principal obligor and was formally documented by a public bond issue
f agreement, a guarantee agreement and a prospectus. In practice, once PPIF had formally joined in a bond issue, its subsequent involvement was minimal; in particular, it had no current account at a bank and all payments of interest, fees and costs in connection with the bonds were made by PPI. In October 1990 PPI went into administration and in May 1995 a scheme of arrangement was approved, which included a provision prohibiting any creditor from proving more
g than once in respect of any scheme claim. In March 1995 PPIF itself was placed in creditors voluntary liquidation in the Cayman Islands and its liquidators thereafter submitted a notice of claim to the scheme supervisors of PPI, claiming £485m in respect of the sums on-loaned. The banks as bondholders also lodged claims amounting to £85m against PPI pursuant to the guarantees. After admitting the
h bulk of the banks' claims, the supervisors applied to the court seeking directions as to (i) whether PPIF was entitled to maintain a claim in the arrangement separate to those of the banks in respect of what was, in substance, the same debt, or alternatively (ii) whether the rule against double proof precluded PPIF from receiving a dividend in addition to that payable to the banks.

j

Held – In determining whether two claims were so closely connected as to be, in substance, claims in respect of the same debt, the court would look to the legal substance of the relevant transaction and not to the economic substance, if different. It was not open to the court to disregard the principle of separate corporate personality and to treat a closely-integrated group of companies as a single economic unit on the basis merely of perceived injustice, particularly where

the separate legal existence of those companies assumed greater importance once
they became insolvent. Having regard to the legal documents entered into on the
occasion of each bond issue, it was impossible to conclude that a relationship of
agency or nomineeship could be inferred between the companies, with the result
that the on-loan could not be eliminated as a significant part of the composite
transaction. Further, since PPIF was clearly more than a mere facade and there
was no legal basis on which the PPI group could be regarded as a single economic
unit, it followed that the claims were not, in substance, claims in respect of the
same debt and were not precluded by the rule against double proof. Both claims
would accordingly be admitted in full as scheme liabilities (see p 444 *d e j* to p 445
a j to p 446 *c j*, p 447 *g j* and p 448 *e* to *j*, post).

Notes
For provable debts and the rule against double proof to claims in respect of
guarantees, see 7(2) *Halsbury's Laws* (4th edn reissue) paras 1747, 1758.
    For piercing the corporate veil, see 7(1) *Halsbury's Laws* (4th edn reissue)
para 90.

Cases referred to in judgment
Adams v Cape Industries plc [1991] 1 All ER 929, [1990] Ch 433, [1990] 2 WLR 657,
    Ch D and CA.
AG Securities v Vaughan, Antoniades v Villiers [1988] 3 All ER 1058, [1990] 1 AC 417,
    [1988] 3 WLR 1205, HL.
Aslan v Murphy (Nos 1 and 2), Duke v Wynne [1989] 3 All ER 130, [1990] 1 WLR 766,
    CA.
Bank of Tokyo Ltd v Karoon [1986] 3 All ER 468, [1987] AC 45, [1986] 3 WLR 414,
    CA.
Barclays Bank Ltd v TOSG Trust Fund Ltd [1984] 1 All ER 628, [1984] AC 626, [1984]
    2 WLR 49, CA; *affd* [1984] 1 All ER 1060, [1984] AC 626, [1984] 2 WLR 650, HL.
Canada Rice Mills Ltd v R [1939] 3 All ER 991, PC.
Chow Yoong Hong v Choong Fah Rubber Manufactory Ltd [1961] 3 All ER 1163, [1962]
    AC 209, [1962] 2 WLR 43, PC.
Ellis v Emmanuel (1876) 1 Ex D 157, [1874–80] All ER Rep 1081, CA.
Firestone Tyre and Rubber Co Ltd v Lewellin (Inspector of Taxes) [1957] 1 All ER 561,
    [1957] 1 WLR 464, HL.
Ford & Carter Ltd v Midland Bank Ltd (1979) 129 NLJ 543, HL.
Furniss (Inspector of Taxes) v Dawson [1984] 1 All ER 530, [1984] AC 474, [1984] 2
    WLR 226, HL.
Gilford Motor Co Ltd v Horne [1933] Ch 935, [1933] All ER Rep 109, CA.
Helby v Matthews [1895] AC 471, [1895–9] All ER Rep 821, HL.
Hoey, Re, ex p Hoey (1918) 88 LJKB 273, DC.
IRC v Duke of Westminster [1936] AC 1, [1935] All ER Rep 259, HL.
Jones v Lipman [1962] 1 All ER 442, [1962] 1 WLR 832.
Liverpool, The (No 2) [1960] 3 All ER 307, [1963] P 64, [1960] 3 WLR 597, CA; *rvsg*
    [1960] 1 All ER 465, [1963] P 64 [1960] 2 WLR 541.
McEntire v Crossley Bros Ltd [1895] AC 457, [1895–9] All ER Rep 829, HL.
Melton, Re, Milk v Towers [1918] 1 Ch 37, [1916–17] All ER Rep 672, CA.
Meridian Global Funds Management Asia Ltd v Securities Commission [1995] 3 All ER
    918, [1995] 2 AC 500, [1995] 3 WLR 413, PC.
Moss, Re, ex p Hallet [1905] 2 KB 307, [1904–7] All ER Rep 713, DC.
Oriental Commercial Bank, Re, ex p European Bank (1871) LR 7 Ch App 99, LJJ.
Palette Shoes Pty Ltd v Krohn (1937) 58 CLR 1, Aust HC.

a *Prudential Assurance Co Ltd v Newman Industries Ltd (No 2)* [1982] 1 All ER 354, [1982] Ch 204, [1982] 2 WLR 31, CA.

Salomon v Salomon & Co Ltd, Salomon & Co Ltd v Salomon [1897] AC 22, [1895–9] All ER Rep 33, HL.

Sass, Re, ex p National Provincial Bank of England [1896] 2 QB 12.

Welsh Development Agency v Export Finance Co Ltd [1992] BCLC 148, CA.

b *Woolfson v Strathclyde Regional Council* 1978 SLT 159, 1978 SC 90, HL.

Cases also cited and referred to in skeleton arguments

British Eagle International Airlines Ltd v Cie Nationale Air France [1975] 2 All ER 390, [1975] 1 WLR 758, HL.

Company, Re a (No 002470 of 1988), ex p Nicholas [1991] BCLC 480, Ch D; sub nom
c *Nicholas v Soundcraft Electronics Ltd* [1993] BCLC 360, CA.

De Salaberry Realties Ltd v Minister of National Revenue (1974) 46 DLR (3d) 100, Can Fed Ct.

DHN Food Distributors Ltd v Tower Hamlets London Borough [1976] 3 All ER 462, [1976] 1 WLR 852, CA.

d *FG (Films) Ltd, Re* [1953] 1 All ER 615, [1953] 1 WLR 883.

Holdsworth (Harold) & Co (Wakefield) Ltd v Caddies [1955] 1 All ER 725, [1955] 1 WLR 352, HL.

Revlon Inc v Cripps & Lee Ltd [1980] FSR 85, Ch D and CA.

Scottish Co-op Wholesale Society Ltd v Meyer [1958] 3 All ER 66, [1959] AC 324, HL.

Smith Stone & Knight Ltd v Birmingham Corp [1939] 4 All ER 116.
e

Summons

f By summons dated 31 July 1995 Christopher John Barlow, Ian Douglas Barker Bond and Christopher Morris, the supervisors of a scheme of arrangement in respect of Polly Peck International plc (in administration) (PPI), sought directions under the scheme in relation to the notice of claim of the respondents, Polly Peck International Finance Ltd (PPIF) (a subsidiary of PPI, incorporated in the Cayman Islands) and the claims of Arab Banking Corporation-Daus & Co GmbH, appointed by the court on 1 August 1995 to represent a number of banks holding bonds issued by PPIF and guaranteed by PPI. On 5 September 1995 Mr Registrar Buckley ordered the hearing of a preliminary issue as to whether the respondent
g could maintain a separate claim in the arrangement from that of the bondholders, or whether the rule against double proof precluded it from receiving a dividend in addition to the dividend payable to the bondholders. The facts are set out in the judgment.

h *Leslie Kosmin QC* and *David Chivers* (instructed by *Cameron Markby Hewitt*) for the applicants.
Gabriel Moss QC (instructed by *Lovell White Durrant*) for the respondents.

Cur adv vult

j 6 December 1995. The following judgment was delivered.

ROBERT WALKER J.

Polly Peck: the scheme of arrangement

In the late 1980s Polly Peck International plc (PPI) was the holding company of a fast-growing group with a diversified range of interests. The group's core activities were agriculture and food production but they extended to electrical

consumer goods, textiles, pharmaceuticals, cosmetics and tourism. PPI had
subsidiaries in many countries including England, north Cyprus, Turkey, Hong
Kong, the United States, Switzerland and Liberia.

PPI ran into severe financial difficulties in 1990 and on 25 October 1990 it went
into administration. The purposes of the administration order made by Morritt J
were those specified in s 8(3)(a) and (d) of the Insolvency Act 1986, but it is now
clear that PPI is not going to be able to trade out of its difficulties. The purposes
of the administration have been extended to seeking approval of a scheme of
arrangement, and after a creditors' meeting on 26 April 1995 a scheme of
arrangement was approved on 11 May 1995 and took effect on 18 May.

The scheme provides (para 2) for the usual moratorium and (para 3) for the
collection and realisation of PPI's assets. Scheme claims were to be notified to the
scheme supervisors who could admit or reject them in whole or part, or refer
them to the court. Paragraph 7(i) provides that the supervisors are not to admit
any claim which would not be admissible in a liquidation if PPI had gone into
compulsory liquidation on the date when the scheme took effect.

Paragraph 9 of the scheme provides for the distribution of the scheme assets
(after provision for costs and preferential claims and subject to some special
provisions as to the so-called club banks) rateably between scheme creditors
whose claims have been admitted. Paragraph 9.9 is in these terms:

'No scheme creditor shall be entitled to receive an amount in the scheme
which exceeds the amount of his scheme claim nor to prove more than once
in respect of any scheme claim, and for the avoidance of doubt the rule
against double proof shall apply in respect of all distributions and reserves
made in the scheme.'

The scheme is therefore on familiar lines, providing for a sort of notional
liquidation in advance of any actual liquidation, with a view to saving costs.

The matter which I have to decide is a preliminary issue (ordered by Mr
Registrar Buckley on 5 September 1995) on a summons seeking directions under
the scheme. The issue is as to the application of the rule against double proof.
The circumstances in which the issue arises are connected with a subsidiary of
PPI, Polly Peck International Finance Ltd (PPIF), which was incorporated in the
Cayman Islands on 20 May 1987.

The bond issues

Between June 1987 and February 1990 there were no fewer than eight bond
issues which raised a total of SwF 665m and DM 100m—a total of over £400m at
current exchange rates—for the PPI group. Except for some points of difference
summarised below, all eight issues were arranged on the same general lines: they
comprised unsecured, unsubordinated fixed-rate bearer bonds issued by PPIF and
guaranteed by PPI. The lead manager for the Swiss franc issues was SG Warburg
Soditic SA (Warburg SA) and for the single DM issue, Arab Banking Corporation-
Daus & Co GmbH (ABC-Daus). ABC-Daus assumed the position of trustee for
the bondholders under the DM issue. Each of these lead managers also acted as
principal paying agent.

a   The eight bond issues were as follows.

	Amount	Payment date	Rate	Redemption
1	SwF 65m	7 July 1987	3%	1997
2	SwF 75m	13 Aug 1987	6%	1992
3	SwF 50m	19 Nov 1987	$6\frac{1}{4}\%$	1990
4	SwF 100m	7 April 1988	$5\frac{3}{4}\%$	1993
5	DM 100m	20 April 1988	6%	1993
6	SwF 125m	20 Sept 1989	$5\frac{5}{8}\%$	1994
7	SwF 100m	1 March 1989	$6\frac{1}{4}\%$	1996
8	SwF 200m	1 March 1990	$8\frac{3}{4}\%$	1997

In the event only SwF 150m was raised under the last issue.

e   There were two main differences between the issues. The first issue was convertible into ordinary shares of PPI (a right reflected in the interest rate) and the whole issue was in fact converted into PPI ordinary shares, or (as to a small balance) redeemed, before PPI crashed. The first issue is nevertheless significant because in other respects it set the pattern for later issues. The DM issue was established with ABC-Daus as a trustee—a feature not found in the SwF issues—and it did not in terms provide for PPI to be liable as a principal obligor (although

f   PPI's obligations as guarantor were stated in cl 3 of the guarantee agreement to be 'autonomous and independent'). It is however common ground that nothing turns on any difference between PPI's obligations under the SwF issues (which were governed by Swiss law) and its obligations under the DM issue (which was governed by German law).

g   The first issue was discussed at a meeting at 42 Berkeley Square, London W1 (then PPI's head office) on 5 May 1987. It was chaired by Mr David Fawcus, then PPI's finance director, and attended by representatives of Warburg SA, two firms of London solicitors, and Stoy Hayward (PPI's auditors) as well as by PPI personnel. It considered a board paper (prepared by Mr Wood, the group

h   treasurer) which proposed 'that the bonds be issued in the name of a new Cayman Islands subsidiary under the guarantee of [PPI]' in order to avoid onerous listing requirements in London, and achieve certain tax advantages. The board paper estimated the costs of the issue:

j   'In simple terms, front end costs are likely to be about £1.6m or just under 4% of total raised. Annual costs will be about 3·3% or 6·0%, inclusive of hedging expenses, for tranche A and B respectively.'

(The two tranches had different coupons and conversion terms.) The board paper assumes, but does not refer to the proceeds of the issue being lent on to PPI.

PPI, through its London solicitors, then took advice from Cayman attorneys as to the formation and use of a Cayman financial vehicle. The Cayman attorneys gave full written advice in a faxed letter dated 11 May 1987. Their advice included the following advice as to the on-loan from PPIF (as it was named on its incorporation) to PPI:

'It is usually the case that commercial paper issues and traditional forms of Eurocurrency financing can be structured so as not to constitute "banking business". However, some care needs to be paid to the manner in which funds are raised and are then on-lent to the parent or other companies within the relevant group. Thus, the on-lending arrangements should be evidenced by appropriate documentation (which can of course be relatively brief given the in-house nature of the transactions). In particular those on-lending arrangements should be structured so that the repayment of the loans is not simply on a demand basis. Other clients at this firm have not met any difficulty meeting these parameters. Cayman Islands' Companies Law follows English legal principles. Thus a company should only enter into transactions intended for its benefit and the directors must act in good faith in the interests of the company. As a result, the financing arrangements should be structured so as to produce a profit (albeit small) for the Cayman Islands' company. Generally-speaking this is achieved by the company charging a rate of interest when on-lending these funds which is higher than the rate it pays on the borrowed funds or by the company charging a fee.'

On 13 May 1987 there was a board meeting of PPI at 42 Berkeley Square attended by Mr Asil Nadir (the chairman and chief executive of PPI), Mr Ellis (a senior executive), Mr Fawcus (the finance director) and others. The board considered the paper on the convertible SwF issue and approved it, subject to approval by certain other interests. PPIF was then incorporated with Mr Moon (a Cayman attorney), Mr Nadir, Mr Ellis and Mr Fawcus as its directors. It had an authorised capital of SwF 1m, divided into shares of SwF 1; 25,000 of them were issued and credited as fully paid. PPIF has always been a wholly-owned subsidiary of PPI. Mr Moon resigned as a director at the first board meeting of PPIF held on 28 May 1987. Thereafter the board of PPIF consisted solely of individuals who were also PPI directors, meeting at 42 Berkeley Square. There was never any attempt to argue that PPIF's directing mind was outside the United Kingdom or that the company was non-resident for United Kingdom tax purposes (indeed, its residence in the United Kingdom was necessary for purposes of group relief).

There are some features common to all the bond issues which call for mention, because they were relied on by counsel in their submissions. Each of the bond issues stated in its prospectus that the proceeds of the issue were to be used for refinancing and development of the Polly Peck group's business activities. The form of words used varied to some extent (the exact words of each prospectus are quoted in para 16 of an affidavit sworn on 27 September 1995 by Mr David Kidd, a partner in the firm of solicitors acting for the scheme supervisors); but the general effect did not vary much.

Each of the Swiss bond issues also included in its conditions a provision for PPI or another non-Swiss subsidiary of PPI to be substituted for PPIF as the principal obligor, with the consent of Warburg SA, such consent not to be unreasonably withheld so long as the bondholders' interests were adequately protected (especially as regards tax). The DM bond issue contained a similar provision for substitution in a manner satisfactory to ABC-Daus.

The on-loan from PPIF to PPI

The Cayman attorneys' advice that the on-lending arrangements should be evidenced by appropriate (if brief) documentation was not carried through, so far

a   as the administrators' scrutiny of PPI's papers has revealed. In October 1987
London solicitors sent instructions to tax counsel to settle a draft loan agreement
for the on-loan from PPIF to PPI. That was after the second SwF issue had been
completed and when the third issue was about to be completed. After some
supplementary instructions had been sent and a consultation had been held in
January 1988, tax counsel settled the draft agreement on 29 February 1988 in a
b   form which recited an on-loan from PPIF to PPI of approximately SwF 135·15m,
the balance of SwF 4·85m (representing the costs of the first two SwF issues
totalling SwF 140m) being treated as an arrangement fee payable by PPI to PPIF.
The draft provided in advance for similar treatment of future costs of the first two
issues. (The lawyers were in fact being rather overtaken by events, because by the
time the draft was settled the third SwF issue had also been completed and the
c   fourth SwF issue, and the DM issue, must have been in the pipeline.) The draft
loan agreement provided for the on-loan to carry interest—

> 'payable half-yearly at the rate of ¼ per cent above the rate of interest
> payable by PPIF in respect of the corresponding tranche of the Bonds [viz the
> first two issues] or at such other rate or rates as shall from time to time be
d   > agreed between the parties.'

As I have said, no executed loan agreement between PPIF and PPI (either in the
above or in any other form) has been found and there is no evidence (either in the
form of board minutes or in any other form) that any such loan agreement ever
existed. The draft settled by tax counsel provides some evidence at least as to the
e   transaction having had the character of a loan.

In practice, once PPIF had formally joined in a bond issue, its involvement in
the subsequent management of the issue seems to have been minimal. It had no
current account at a bank (though the proceeds of each issue do seem to have
been held briefly to an account in PPIF's name at the lead manager's bank.) In
f   practice all payments of interest, fees and costs in connection with the bonds seem
to have been made by PPI, and the state of account between PPI and PPIF can be
determined only by internal accounting records kept at PPI's offices and from
PPIF's financial statements. There are financial statements of PPIF for the
accounting period to 31 December 1988, signed by Mr Nadir and Mr Fawcus and
audited by Stoy Hayward, which show PPIF as having a revenue reserve of SwF
g   696,000 at 31 December 1988. This appears to reflect the ¼% turn (provided for
in the draft loan agreement) on outstanding bonds to the amount of about SwF
435m; this was on the basis that PPI had borne initial costs of bond issues which
by then amounted to SwF 10m. PPI's practical responsibility for servicing the
bonds was also reflected in communications from the principal paying agents:
h   Warburgs SA sent demands for interest direct to PPI, and ABC-Daus sent them to
PPIF 'care of' PPI.

Another scrap of evidence is a letter that Mr Spencer of Stoy Hayward wrote to
Mr Fawcus on 29 September 1987. Mr Spencer referred to an election under the
Income and Corporation Taxes Act 1970, s 256 (group relief) which was
j   outstanding and advised that—

> 'if you are funding the interest payment from PPI it is important initially
> that this will be in the form of an interest-free advance which can be set off
> against the interest payment due and payable once we have formally received
> clearance from the Inland Revenue.'

Mr Fawcus wrote on the letter a manuscript note to Mr Wood:

'A lot of garbage. Just note that PPI should not pay interest to PPIF until tax status of PPI is cleared. Until then payments should take the form of an advance.'

So despite his initial comment Mr Fawcus seems to have understood and accepted the essential point of the advice.

Apart from its involvement in the bond issues PPIF was a party to two other group transactions. On 4 November 1987 it provided security to Banque Paribas (Suisse) SA for an advance of SwF 15m. On or about 19 October 1987 it joined with PPI in a joint and several guarantee to a Hong Kong group creditor, BSR International plc. Both these seem to have been short-term transactions which give rise to no continuing liability.

I have gone into these factual matters at what would be, in other circumstances, excessive detail because of the submission made to me by Mr Leslie Kosmin QC (who appears with Mr David Chivers for the supervisors) that PPIF was, in relation to the bond issues, a cipher, agent or nominee. That submission is controverted by Mr Gabriel Moss QC, who appears for both the respondents, PPIF and ABC-Daus. They have a common interest in resisting the conclusion that this is a case of double proof (if they fail in that their interests will diverge as to which claim should be rejected; but the order for a preliminary issue recognises that that second stage may not be reached).

Before making any finding on the secondary issues of fact (that is whether PPIF was a cipher, agent or nominee) I must summarise the claims that have been put in, and then turn to the questions of law that have been argued before me.

The notices of claim

PPIF was placed in creditors' voluntary liquidation in the Cayman Islands on 23 March 1995. It has two chartered accountants as joint liquidators, one practising in the Cayman Islands and one in London. On 24 May 1995 the London-based liquidator, Mr Beirne, submitted to the scheme supervisors a notice of claim (as at 15 May 1995) approximately as follows:

	SwF	DM	total (£)
principal	600m	100m	361m
interest	209m	32m	124m
total	809m	132m	485m

The claim for interest was based on the bond rates, plus ¼%, for periods starting in late 1989 or in 1990.

On 9 June 1995 ABC-Daus gave notice of a claim (as at 15 May 1995) for about £64·65m, about £44m of which represented principal (the rest was for interest, including £7m default interest under the German civil code, and £170,000 legal costs). It has been agreed that Warburg SA should act as agent for the Swiss bondholders, who have claims against both PPIF and PPI. The total claims against PPI so far notified by Warburg SA amount to about £421m.

When Mr Kidd swore his affidavit on 27 September 1995 the position was that the bulk of the ABC-Daus claim had been admitted by the scheme supervisors, *a* apart from the default interest, and the Warburg SA claim had been admitted almost in its entirety. Mr Moss tells me, no doubt correctly, that the default interest has since been admitted. Bondholders' admitted claims against PPI as guarantor are therefore of the order of £485m. PPIF's unadmitted claim is approximately the same size. Apart from these claims and the 'club bank' claims, there are other scheme claims against PPI amounting to a sum of the order of

b £1bn. The double proof point does therefore have a significant effect on the distribution of assets.

A dividend of 1·1p in the pound has already been paid under compromise arrangements approved by Mr Registrar Buckley on 19 October 1995. The scale of further dividends will, I understand, depend on the outcome of pending litigation.

c The issue which I have to decide is put this way in para 44 of Mr Kidd's affidavit.

'Having investigated PPIF's claim in the Scheme, the Supervisors have become concerned that, due to what appeared to them to be the lack of separate corporate personality on the part of PPIF, the Court might hold that

d the corporate veil should be lifted so preventing PPIF from maintaining a claim separate from the bondholders' claims against PPI. Alternatively, even if PPIF is entitled to a separate claim, such a claim might be held to arise out of what is, in substance, the same debt (being the debt to the bondholders), so that PPIF would be barred from receiving a dividend in addition to that payable to the bondholders by the rule against double proof. In these

e circumstances the Supervisors have decided, on the basis of legal advice that they should seek directions from the Court before paying any dividends to both the bondholders and PPIF.'

f *The rule against double proof*

The rule against double proof is a long-standing principle of the law of bankruptcy, and has applied in the winding up of companies since the Companies Act 1862 (see *Re Oriental Commercial Bank, ex p European Bank* (1871) LR 7 Ch App 99). It has often been described in terms of straightforward and obvious fairness, depending on substance, not form. Thus in that case Mellish LJ said (at 103–104):

g

'But the principle itself—that an insolvent estate, whether wound up in Chancery or in Bankruptcy, ought not to pay two dividends in respect of the same debt—appears to me to be a perfectly sound principle. If it were not so, a creditor could always manage, by getting his debtor to enter into several distinct contracts with different people for the same debt, to obtain higher

h dividends than the other creditors, and perhaps get his debt paid in full. I apprehend that is what the law does not allow; the true principle is, that there is only to be one dividend in respect of what is in substance the same debt, although there may be two separate contracts.'

j See also *Re Moss, ex p Hallet* [1905] 2 KB 307 at 312, [1904–7] All ER Rep 713 at 715, *Re Melton, Milk v Towers* [1918] 1 Ch 37 at 60, [1916–17] All ER Rep 672 at 682–683, *Re Hoey, ex p Hoey* (1918) 88 LJKB 273 at 274, *The Liverpool (No 2)* [1960] 3 All ER 307 at 313, [1963] P 64 at 84 and *Barclays Bank Ltd v TOSG Trust Fund Ltd* [1984] 1 All ER 628 at 636 and 653–654, [1984] AC 626 at 636 and 659–660 per Oliver and Slade LJJ respectively. In the last case Kerr LJ said ([1984] 1 All ER 628 at 645, [1984] AC 626 at 649):

'The rule against double proof is highly technical in some facets of its application, but ultimately it is based on what the court regards as justice *a* between all the creditors.'

It appears that the most technical facet which Kerr LJ had in mind was the distinction (discussed in the judgment of Oliver LJ ([1984] 1 All ER 628 at 641–642, [1984] AC 626 at 643–644), between the guarantee of a part of a debt, and the *b* guarantee of the whole debt subject to a limitation on the guarantor's liability. I will call this the *Ellis v Emmanuel* distinction (see *Ellis v Emmanuel* (1876) 1 Ex D 157, [1874–80] All ER Rep 1081; also, *Re Sass, ex p National Provincial Bank of England* [1896] 2 QB 12). In *Barclays Bank Ltd v TOSG Trust Fund* the Court of Appeal had the difficult task of applying the *Ellis v Emmanuel* distinction, by analogy, to unusual and complicated facts (on which the House of Lords then took a different *c* view, so that no question of double proof arose).

Much the commonest situation in which the rule against double proof applies is that of suretyship. Indeed it has been said that it applies only in a situation which actually is, or is analogous to, that of suretyship (the latter category includes the old cases on negotiable instruments considered in *Re Oriental Commercial Bank, ex* *d* *p European Bank*). It is therefore convenient to set out some very elementary rules as to suretyship, shorn of complications arising from the provision of security or from the *Ellis v Emmanuel* distinction. In what follows, C is the principal creditor, D the principal debtor, and S the surety (and all are companies).

(1) So long as any money remains due under the guaranteed loan, C can proceed against either D or (after any requisite notice) S. *e*

(2) If D and S are both wound up, C can prove in both liquidations and hope to receive a dividend in both, subject to not recovering in all more than 100p in the pound.

(3) S's liquidator can prove in D's liquidation (under an express or implied right of indemnity) only if S has paid C in full (so that C drops out of the matter and S *f* stands in its place).

(4) As a corollary of (3) above, S's liquidator cannot prove in D's liquidation in any way that is in competition with C; though S has a contingent claim against D (in the event of C being paid off by S), S may not make that claim if it has not in fact paid off C. *g*

The situation in (2) above is what insolvency practitioners call a 'double-dip', which is permissible; the situation in (4) above is the simplest case of what would be double proof, which is not permissible.

So far as the basis of the rule needs (or indeed allows of) further explanation it is that the surety's contingent claim is not regarded as an independent, *h* free-standing debt, but only as a reflection of the 'real' debt—that in respect of the money which the principal creditor had loaned to the principal debtor. Similarly in the cases analogous to a suretyship situation: in *Re Hoey* the only true debt, in substance, was to the mortgagee, Mr O'Brien, and Dr Hoey's covenant with his wife (when he conveyed the mortgaged property to her) to pay off the mortgage *j* was merely a reflection of his existing liability to Mr O'Brien, and of his aspiration that he (Dr Hoey) would bear it, in exoneration of the mortgaged property. Similarly in *The Liverpool (No 2)* (the most distant analogy for application of the rule, since it was an admiralty case) the Court of Appeal concluded that the only true liability, in substance, was that arising from the negligent navigation of the tanker, and that the claim against the owners of the beached coaster (which the Mersey Docks and Harbour Board had under its statutory powers) was in a substance a partial reflection of the primary liability—in short, part of the same debt.

In *Barclays Bank Ltd v TOSG Trust Fund Ltd* (where the Court of Appeal were also ready to extend the suretyship analogy some way, though on a view of the facts which the House of Lords held to be mistaken) Oliver LJ said in a passage which I have referred to but not yet set out ([1984] 1 All ER 628 at 636, [1984] AC 626 at
b 636), that it was a fallacy to argue—

c 'that, because overlapping liabilities result from separate and independent contracts with the debtor, that, by itself, is determinative of whether the rule can apply. The test is in my judgment a much broader one which transcends a close jurisprudential analysis of the persons by and to whom the duties are owed. It is simply whether the two competing claims are, in *substance*, claims for payment of the same debt twice over.' (Oliver LJ's emphasis.)

'Substance', corporate personality and the corporate veil

d Mr Kosmin relied strongly on this passage in contending that the bond issues by PPIF (guaranteed by PPI) and PPIF's on-lending to PPI were so closely connected as to result in the bondholders' claim against PPI as guarantor and PPIF's claim against PPI as principal creditor being 'in substance, claims for payment of the same debt twice over'. Mr Kosmin developed his argument in various ways which naturally involved some overlap; but I hope I can fairly summarise the way
e he put his case as follows: (1) that on a correct view of the facts, PPIF was in effecting the bond issues (a) an agent or nominee for PPI or alternatively (b) a cipher or facade for PPI; (2) that even if PPIF acted as an independent principal, the on-lending within the Polly Peck group was still so much a part of the same composite transaction as not to rank, in substance, as a separate debt. Mr Kosmin
f accepted that there is no authority illustrating the application of the rule against double proof in this sort of situation (that is, indebtedness within a group of companies) but called in aid the words of Kerr LJ in *Barclays Bank Ltd v TOSG Trust Fund Ltd* [1984] 1 All ER 628 at 647–648, [1984] AC 626 at 652:

g '... sometimes, in new situations, the court has to find a just solution which stems simply from the nature of the transaction, the relationship between the parties and their presumed common intention.'

Mr Moss for his part says, rightly, that this sort of transaction of guaranteed borrowing and on-lending by a special-purpose financial vehicle is a common-
h place occurrence in capital markets (this point is borne out by the letter from the Cayman attorneys, which seems to be giving fairly standard advice in a fairly standard situation). Mr Moss goes on to submit that the double proof point, if sound, would introduce a new and alarming element of uncertainty into capital markets. I think this argument in terrorem may be a bit overstated, since investors in unsecured bonds issued in this way must be relying on the credit
j rating of the guarantor, and not on some calculation of the chances of a 'double-dip' against the guarantor and the financial subsidiary in the event of default. Nevertheless, the point raised is a novel point of some commercial importance.

Before I examine more closely the different ways in which Mr Kosmin puts his case it may be helpful to make some preliminary points. First, as to substance. In *Welsh Development Agency v Export Finance Co Ltd* [1992] BCLC 148 at 185

Staughton LJ said (in the context of deciding whether a commercial document
effected a sale or a charge):

> 'The problem is not made any easier by the variety of language that has
> been used: substance, truth, reality, genuine are good words; disguise, cloak,
> mask, colourable device, label, form, artificial, sham, stratagem and pretence
> are "bad names", to adopt the phrase quoted by Dixon J in *Palette Shoes Pty Ltd
> v Krohn* (1937) 58 CLR 1 at 28. It is necessary to discover, if one can, the ideas
> which these words are intended to convey. One can start from the position
> that statute law in this country, when it enacts rules to be applied to particular
> transactions, is in general referring to the legal nature of a transaction and not
> to its economic effect. The leading authority on this point, albeit in a case
> from Malaya, is the advice of Lord Devlin in *Chow Yoong Hong v Choong Fah
> Rubber Manufactory Ltd* [1961] 3 All ER 1163 at 1167, [1962] AC 209 at 216:
> "There are many ways of raising cash besides borrowing ... If in form it is not
> a loan, it is not to the point to say that its object was to raise money for one
> of them or that the parties could have produced the same result more
> conveniently by borrowing and lending money."'

Those were statutory contexts (registration of charges and regulation of money-
lending) but I think they also support the general proposition that when the law
is looking for the substance of a matter, it is normally looking for its legal
substance, not its economic substance (if different). As Robert Goff LJ put it in
Bank of Tokyo Ltd v Karoon [1986] 3 All ER 468 at 486, [1987] AC 45 at 64, we are
concerned not with economics but with law.

Second, the House of Lords affirmation in *Salomon v Salomon & Co Ltd, Salomon
& Co Ltd v Salomon* [1897] AC 22, [1895–9] All ER Rep 33 of the separate legal
personality of even a 'one-man' company does not of course mean that registered
companies have all the characteristics of, and no characteristics not shared by,
natural persons. One aspect of this has recently been explained by Lord
Hoffmann in giving the opinion of the Privy Council in *Meridian Global Funds
Management Asia Ltd v Securities Commission* [1995] 3 All ER 918, [1995] 2 AC 500.
Another aspect is that whereas natural persons do not (since the abolition of
slavery and the passing of the Married Women's Property Acts) own the persons
or property of other human beings, commercial companies do have owners.
Their shareholders have an economic interest in their commercial success.
Although the shareholders do not own their company's assets, a wrong to the
company (if uncompensated) may cause them economic loss. But in general the
shareholders will have no direct right of action in respect of such loss (see
Prudential Assurance Co Ltd v Newman Industries Ltd (No 2) [1982] 1 All ER 354 at 367,
[1982] Ch 204 at 223). This point was not mentioned in argument, being neither
controversial nor directly relevant; but I think it worth mentioning both in order
to identify and distinguish another corporate 'double recovery' problem which
does not arise here, and because it leads on to the topic of intra-group
indebtedness, which is directly relevant in this case.

The third point is that where there is a group of companies and they are all
solvent, a claim by one group company against another, even though sound in
law, is likely to have only marginal economic effects (it may have some, for
instance in connection with taxation). But as soon as both companies go into
insolvent liquidation, any claim between them assumes much greater importance
(unless by an extraordinary coincidence both have identical creditors with
identical claims, which is certainly not the case here). That is, I think, the point

a that Lord Wilberforce must have had in mind when he said in *Ford & Carter Ltd v Midland Bank Ltd* (1979) 129 NLJ 543 at 544:

'When creditors become involved, as they do in the present case, the separate legal existence of the constituent companies of the group has to be respected.'

b This important effect of group insolvency needs to be underlined because it has sometimes been suggested (e g in *Barclays Bank Ltd v TOSG Trust Fund Ltd* [1984] 1 All ER 628 at 637–637, [1984] AC 626 at 636–637 per Oliver LJ) that it is useful to test a disputed case of double proof by reference to the situation as it would be if all parties were solvent. In circumstances of all-round group insolvency that may not be a wholly reliable test. It is not now open to PPI's administrators to pay off

c the bondholders in full and, by doing so, to discharge its obligation to PPIF (and, simultaneously, PPIF's obligation to the bondholders).

Issue 1(a): was PPIF an agent or nominee?

In *Salomon v Salomon & Co* the House of Lords roundly rejected the conclusion

d of the lower courts that Salomon & Co was a 'mere nominee or agent' of Mr Aron Salomon, or his 'alias', or that his fellow shareholders were 'dummies' (see [1897] AC 22 at 35, 42, 43, [1895–9] All ER Rep 33 at 39, 43). There are of course many cases in which it has been held, on the facts, that a company has acted as an agent or nominee, either for its principal shareholder or for some other party, and several of them were cited to me (e g *Canada Rice Mills Ltd v R* [1939] 3 All ER 991

e and *Firestone Tyre and Rubber Co Ltd v Lewellin (Inspector of Taxes)* [1957] 1 All ER 561, [1957] 1 WLR 464). But neither agency nor nomineeship—nor, still less, sham or something akin to sham—is to be inferred simply because a subsidiary company has a small paid-up capital and has a board of directors all or most of whom are also directors or senior executives of its holding company.

f Mr Kosmin does not, as I understand his submissions, contend that the arrangements between PPI, PPIF and the lead mangers were a sham (I will return below to 'cipher' and 'facade'). He does contend that a variety of factors lead to an inference of agency or nomineeship. The most important of these factors (which are all set out in the detailed skeleton argument prepared by Mr Kosmin and Mr Chivers) are the following: (i) PPIF was incorporated solely for the

g purpose of the bond issues; (ii) it had no separate, independent management; (iii) it had a very small paid-up capital; (iv) it did not pay the costs of the transactions and could not have done so; (v) it had no normal bank account and no separate financial records (in practice PPI saw to everything and acted as PPIF's banker and bookkeeper); (vi) the terms of the on-loan were not independently negotiated, did

h not serve any commercial purpose and in any case were never finally agreed, nor was the ¼% turn paid otherwise than as a paper transaction; and (vii) no lender could or would have relied on PPIF's covenant, as opposed to PPI's (which could substitute itself as principal debtor if it got the approval of the principal paying agents).

j In short, Mr Kosmin submits that PPIF had only a nominal role in the arrangements, and that as a matter of substance PPI should be recognised as having borrowed direct from the original bondholders, so depriving the on-loan of any legal significance (or indeed existence). To come to that conclusion I would have to find that that was the effect, not merely of what was informally arranged in the boardroom at 42 Berkeley Square, but also of the formal legal documents which were entered into on the occasion of each bond issue. On the second SwF issue (which is typical since it was the first issue of non-convertible bonds) the formal documents consisted of (i) a public bond issue agreement between PFIF, *a* PPI and Warburg SA as lead managers on behalf of a consortium including 26 other banks (the agreement annexed the form of the bearer bonds and the terms of their issue); (ii) a guarantee agreement between PPI, Warburg SA and the consortium; and (iii) a 42-page prospectus. All these documents made clear that the bond issue was to be made by PPIF and that PPIF's obligations were to be guaranteed by PPI subject to the provision for substitution which I have already *b* mentioned. The documentation on the later loans was essentially similar, subject to small variations (already mentioned) on the DM issue.

In the face of these documents I find it impossible to conclude that the factors that Mr Kosmin relies on establish a relationship of agency or nomineeship. Mr Moss referred me to some passages from the speeches in *McEntire v Crossley Bros Ltd* [1895] AC 457, [1895–9] All ER Rep 829 quoted by Dillon LJ in *Welsh* *c* *Development Agency v Export Finance Co Ltd* [1992] BCLC 148 at 160–161. Lord Herschell LC said:

'... there is no such thing, as seems to have been argued here, as looking at the substance, apart from looking at the language which the parties have used. It is only by a study of the whole of the language that the substance can *d* be ascertained.' (See [1895] AC 457 at 463, [1895–9] All ER Rep 829 at 831.)

Similarly Lord Watson said:

'The substance of the agreement must ultimately be found in the language of the contract itself. The duty of the court is to examine every part of the *e* agreement, every stipulation which it contains, and to consider their mutual bearing upon each other; but it is entirely beyond the function of a court to discard the plain meaning of any term in the agreement unless there can be found within its four corners other language and other stipulations which necessarily deprive such term of its primary significance.' (See [1895] AC 457 *f* at 467, [1895–9] All ER Rep 829 at 834.)

(It is interesting to note that less than three weeks after judgment was given in *McEntire v Crossley Bros*, Lord Herschell LC said almost exactly the same thing in another well-known case, *Helby v Matthews* [1895] AC 471 at 475, [1895–9] All ER Rep 821 at 823; and it was his observations in the latter case that were cited to and *g* discussed by the House of Lords in the leading tax case on the substance of a transaction, *IRC v Duke of Westminster* [1936] AC 1 at 20, [1935] All ER Rep 259 at 268. The on-loan in this case might be thought to have at least a passing resemblance to the on-transfer that was considered by the House of Lords in another leading tax case, *Furniss (Inspector of Taxes) v Dawson* [1984] 1 All ER 530, *h* [1984] AC 474. But neither counsel suggested that I could get any guidance from that specialised and difficult area of authority, and probably they were right not to do so.)

Some of the factors on which Mr Kosmin relies do tend to show that the Polly Peck personnel who were concerned with the matter at 42 Berkeley Square were (to say the least) less than meticulous in their administrative procedures. I make *j* no specific finding about that. But even blatant and reprehensible 'cutting of corners' (if it occurred) could not, it seems to me, retroactively alter the character of the transactions embodied in the formal documents by which the bond issues were effected. The factors which Mr Kosmin relies on cannot and do not in my judgment establish PPIF's role as that of agency or nomineeship, and so they do not eliminate the on-loan as a significant part of the composite transaction.

Issue 1(b): sham, pretence, cipher, facade

a

My conclusion that there was no conventional relationship of agency or nomineeship is not conclusive of the case, because Mr Kosmin had further submissions. On what I have called his point (1)(b) and his point (2) I was referred to quite a lot of authority touching on what is sometimes called lifting (or piercing) the corporate veil. That is a vivid but imprecise metaphor which has

b possible application in several different contexts, some far removed from this case. The most relevant, it seems to me, is where corporate personality is (in the words of Lord Keith in *Woolfson v Strathclyde Regional Council* 1978 SLT 159 at 161) used as 'a mere facade concealing the true facts'.

Sham, pretence, cipher and facade are all (as was said by Dixon J in the passage already quoted) 'bad names' implying a value judgment of disapprobation.

c 'Sham' was at least half way to becoming a term of art (requiring an intention common to all parties) but has now, it seems, been supplanted (at least in the context of licence or tenancy) by 'pretence' (see *Aslan v Murphy (Nos 1 and 2)*, *Duke v Wynne* [1989] 3 All ER 130 at 133, [1990] 1 WLR 766 at 770 and *AG Securities v Vaughan, Antoniades v Villiers* [1988] 3 All ER 1058 at 1067–1069, [1990] 1 AC 417 at

d 462–465). Mr Kosmin did not rely on sham or pretence. He did submit (orally) that PPIF was a 'cipher' and (in his skeleton argument) that it was a 'facade'. I think that his use of 'cipher' was to add colour and force to his submission on agency or nomineeship (which I have already considered). 'Facade' (or 'cloak' or 'mask') is perhaps most aptly used where one person (individual or corporate) uses a company either in an unconscionable attempt to evade existing obligations

e (*Gilford Motor Co Ltd v Horne* [1933] Ch 935, [1933] All ER Rep 109 and *Jones v Lipman* [1962] 1 All ER 442, [1962] 1 WLR 832) or to practise some other deception (a sort of unilateral sham, since the corporate facade has no independent mind). In *Adams v Cape Industries plc* [1991] 1 All ER 929, [1990] Ch 433 the establishment and interposition of the Liechtenstein corporation referred to as AMC was a

f facade in this sense, and 'no more than a corporate name', though the new Illinois corporation, CPC, was not. But the notion that regular sales of large volumes of South African asbestos to an United States purchaser were being effected through a lawyer's office in Vaduz is to my mind of a quite different order of artificiality from the function of PPIF as a single-purpose financial vehicle (I am not overlooking the two other isolated transactions entered into by PPIF; but they add

g little to its independent reality). In my judgment PPIF was more than a mere facade.

Issue (2): single economic unit

h It is on this part of the case that I have found Mr Kosmin's submissions most persuasive, though I am not ultimately persuaded by them. The arguments for considering a closely-integrated group of companies as a single economic unit were fully considered (principally in the context of corporate presence as founding jurisdiction) in *Adams v Cape Industries plc* [1991] 1 All ER 929 at 965, [1990] Ch 433 at 476–477, both by Scott J and, with a full citation of authority, in the judgment

j of the Court of Appeal (see [1991] 1 All ER 929 at 1016–1020, [1990] Ch 433 at 532–537). Both passages merit careful study. The Court of Appeal concluded that—

'save in cases which turn on the wording of particular statutes or contracts, the court is not free to disregard the principle of *Salomon v Salomon & Co Ltd* [1897] AC 22, [1895–9] All ER Rep 33 merely because it considers that justice so requires.' (See [1991] 1 All ER 929 at 1019, [1990] Ch 433 at 536.)

Mr Kosmin seeks to add to these exceptions (turning on particular statutes or contracts) a further exception where a rule of law founded in public policy (the rule against double proof) would be frustrated by ignoring the economic reality of the single group. In that submission Mr Kosmin can and does call in aid the words of Oliver LJ in *Barclays Bank Ltd v TOSG Trust Fund Ltd* [1984] 1 All ER 628 at 636–637, [1984] AC 626 at 636 that the test is 'a much broader one which transcends a close jurisprudential analysis of the persons by and to whom the duties are owed'.

Nevertheless I am not persuaded by the argument. I can accept that as a matter of economic reality the bondholders (whose presumed intentions may be material) must have intended to rely on the credit-rating and covenant of PPI, whether as guarantor or (after substitution) as principal obligor. It is doubtful whether even the most far-sighted of them can have calculated that in the event of a crash, PPIF might have fewer unsecured creditors than PPI, and a claim against PPI under an on-loan. It was perfectly possible, consistently with each prospectus, that the proceeds of some or all of the bond issues would be loaned on, not to PPI, but to other group subsidiaries. It is also possible, though less likely, to imagine a situation in which PPIF lent on to another subsidiary, with PPI guaranteeing that borrowing also, and the second subsidiary then lending on to PPI. Each of those sequences of events would be likely to produce a different result in the event of a crash of the whole group, whether or not the rule against double proof has any application. The possibility of there being subsidiaries which were not wholly-owned subsidiaries adds to the range of imaginable variations.

Were I to accede to Mr Kosmin's submission it would create a new exception unrecognised by the Court of Appeal in *Adams v Cape Industries plc* and that is not open to me. Moreover I think that Mr Kosmin is in one sense assuming what he seeks to prove, since the unjust or inequitable result which he asserts does not occur unless the group is recognised as being in substance a single economic entity, whose constituent members' internal rights and obligations are to be disregarded. But the authorities to which I have already referred show that substance means legal substance, not economic substance (if different), and that (as Lord Wilberforce said in *Ford & Carter Ltd v Midland Bank Ltd*) the separate legal existence of group companies is particularly important when creditors become involved. Injustice may be in the eye of the beholder, but I do not perceive any obvious injustice—certainly not such as the court can remedy—in the unpredictable consequences that may follow from the unforeseen insolvency of a large international group of companies such as the Polly Peck group.

Conclusion

For these reason I will answer the question posed in para (1) of the preliminary issue in terms of sub-para (i)—that is, that both claims should be admitted in full as scheme liabilities.

As I understand it para (2) then also falls to be answered in terms of sub-para (i)—that is that a dividend should be paid on both claims. But I do not recall any submissions specifically directed to para (2), and if there is some subtlety that I have missed, counsel will no doubt explain it to me.

Order accordingly.

Carolyn Toulmin   Barrister.

a   # Miller and another v Stapleton and another

QUEEN'S BENCH DIVISION

CARNWATH J

b   20, 21 DECEMBER 1995, 25 JANUARY 1996

Pension – Pension scheme – Maladministration of pension scheme – Jurisdiction of Pensions Ombudsman – Trustees offering pension or transfer value guaranteed for three months – Beneficiary applying for transfer value to be paid to new scheme within guarantee period – Transfer value reduced – Effect of guarantee – Whether application
c   *for transfer value valid – Whether Pensions Ombudsman having jurisdiction to award compensation for distress and inconvenience – Pension Schemes Act 1993, ss 95, 151.*

On the termination of S's employment he acquired a right under the relevant pensions legislation (now s 94[a] of the Pension Schemes Act 1993) to a cash
d   equivalent of any benefits which had accrued to him under the group pension scheme of which he was a member. That right could only be exercised by an application in writing to the trustees of the scheme requiring them to use the cash equivalent in whichever of the ways, specified in s 95[b] of the 1993 Act, was chosen by the applicant; under s 95(2) S was entitled to acquire transfer credits allowed
e   under the rules of another pension scheme, provided that the trustees of that scheme were 'able and willing' to accept payment. The scheme administrator later wrote to S requesting him to indicate, pending a final assessment of the scheme assets available to secure benefits, whether he would prefer a paid-up pension of £3,126, or a transfer value of £16,387 which was expressed to be guaranteed for three months, after which it would be recalculated to reflect the
f   true value of S's benefits at the date of transfer. Two months later S wrote to the scheme administrator advising that he had decided to join a new pension plan to be set up by the new owners of his former employer and would be transferring his benefits over to it in due course. The trustees subsequently advised S that, for transfer purposes, the value of his benefits had been revised down to £11,496, but that, taking account of actuarial advice, a restricted transfer value of £9,197 would
g   be offered. The Pensions Ombudsman upheld S's subsequent complaint against the trustees on the basis that S had, by his letter, exercised his right to transfer under s 95(1) of the 1993 Act by a valid application in writing within the three-month period guaranteed to him, and that the trustees' failure (a) to comply thereafter with the requirements of the Act and (b) to pay the original
h   transfer value amounted to maladministration. The trustees were directed under s 151[c] of the Act to make good the original transfer value with interest and to pay £750 to S to compensate him for the injustice suffered as a result of the trustees' maladministration. The trustees appealed.

j   **Held** – (1) Although there was no specific provision for guarantees in the 1993 Act, the practice of giving guarantees for transfer values was well established; and when a transfer value was stated as being 'guaranteed', the use of that word was

---

a   Section 94, so far as material, is set out at p 456 *g*, post
b   Section 95, so far as material, is set out at p 456 *j* to p 457 *a*, post
c   Section 151, so far as material, is set out at p 458 *j*, post

inconsistent with anything other than a binding commitment during the period
for which it was given (seep 458 *b*, p 459 *d e* and p 466 *d*, post).

(2) A valid application to transfer value to another pension scheme under
s 95(2) of the 1993 Act could not be made until the trustees of the new pension
scheme were ready to accept the transfer. On the facts, S's letter was not a valid
application, because the new scheme did not come into existence until just before
the end of the guarantee period, and there was no evidence that it was 'willing
and able' to accept transfers before that date. The ombudsman was accordingly
wrong to hold that S had made a valid application under s 95 and the appeal
would therefore be allowed (see p 460 *b c h j* and p 466 *d*, post).

Per curiam. The ombudsman has no power under s 151 of the 1993 Act to
direct compensation for distress and inconvenience for maladministration in the
ordinary sense, such as rudeness, incompetence, insensitive handling of complaints etc, since the language of s 151, under which trustees could be directed to
'take, or refrain from taking ... steps', naturally implied some pre-existing
obligation or right of a specific nature which the ombudsman was empowered to
enforce; it is also reasonable to expect that any power to make an award for
distress or inconvenience would have been created by express words (see p 465 *d*
to *j* and p 466 *c d*, post).

Notes

For occupational pension schemes generally, see 33 *Halsbury's Laws* (4th edn)
para 973.

Cases referred to in judgment

Hamar v Pensions Ombudsman (18 October 1995, unreported), QBD.
Hawksley v May [1955] 3 All ER 353, [1956] 1 QB 304, [1955] 3 WLR 569.
Hayes v James & Charles Dodd (a firm) [1990] 2 All ER 815, CA.
R v Investors Compensation Scheme Ltd, ex p Bowden [1995] 1 All ER 214, [1995] QB
    107, [1994] 3 WLR 1045, CA; *rvsd* [1995] 3 All ER 605, [1996] 1 AC 261, [1995]
    3 WLR 289, HL.
R v Comr for Local Administration, ex p Eastleigh BC [1988] 3 All ER 151, [1988] QB
    855, [1988] 3 WLR 113, CA.
Stannard v Fisons Pension Trust Ltd [1992] IRLR 27, CA.
Watts v Morrow [1991] 4 All ER 937, [1991] 1 WLR 1421, CA.

Appeal

The trustees of the Rockwood Holdings plc Group Pension Scheme (Thomas
Forrest, Roger George Miller and KC Independent Trustees Ltd) appealed, by
way of a notice of motion, from the decision of the second respondent, the
Pensions Ombudsman, on 7 February 1995, whereby he upheld a complaint by
the first respondent, John Thomas Stapleton, against the trustees alleging
maladministration of the pension scheme. Thomas Forrest was discharged as
trustee before the hearing of the appeal. The facts are set out in the judgment.

Josephine Hayes (instructed by *Hammond Suddards*) for the trustees.
Christopher Nugee (instructed by *Paisner & Co*) for the respondents.

Cur adv vult

a   25 January 1996. The following judgment was delivered.

CARNWATH J. This is an appeal from a determination of the Pensions
Ombudsman dated 7 February 1995 on a complaint by John Stapleton. The
appeal raises important points of law relating on the one hand to the application
of the provisions of the Pension Schemes Act 1993 dealing with transfer values in
b   cases where a fund is in deficit; and on the other hand to the functions of the
Pensions Ombudsman.

Facts

   Mr Stapleton was an employee of a company called Bond's Delivery Service
Ltd (the old employer). That company was a subsidiary of Rockwood Holdings
c   plc, which operated a group pension scheme, the Rockwood Holdings plc Group
Pension Scheme (the Rockwood scheme). In July 1990 receivers were appointed
over the companies in the Rockwood group, and the old employer was sold to
Bondelivery Ltd. Bondelivery Ltd was a subsidiary of Inter Forward Ltd. At this
time Mr Stapleton's employment with the old employer was terminated.
d   The Rockwood scheme is a trust set up by trust deed and has about 940
beneficiaries at present. The relevant deed is dated 8 June 1990. For present
purposes I am concerned only with the provisions relating to termination of the
scheme. By cl 27.1 the employer's liability to pay contributions to the scheme
stops if, inter alia, 'the principal company informs the Trustees in writing that
contributions by the employer shall stop'. By cl 33 (the definition clause) the
e   'termination date' is defined as the date the employer's liability to contribute
ends. Termination beneficiaries are defined as persons who on the termination
date are employed by the employer or who, when they were last employees,
were employed by an employer. Clause 30 deals with 'deficit or surplus on
termination'. Rule 30.1 provides that if the main fund share in relation to an
f   employer less administrative costs cannot secure the benefits in the categories
listed as (1) to (5) in respect of the termination beneficiaries, the available assets
are to secure benefits in the order in which they appear in the five categories.
Where benefits in one of the categories can only be partly secured, the trustees
shall reduce the benefits in that category as they think fit. The five categories are
then set out being: (1) pensioners and their dependants; (2) persons other than
g   pensioners who have reached normal retirement date and their dependants; (3)
guaranteed minimum pensions; (4) graduated scheme pensions; and (5) members
who have not reached normal retirement date.
   Notice under cl 27 was given terminating the payments by the employer as
from 10 August 1990, which accordingly became the 'termination date'.
h   Although not so described in the deed, it is common ground that this date
represents the commencement of the process of 'winding up' of the scheme,
where that term is relevant (e g in s 94(1)(a)).
   Mr Stapleton's employment had ended on 3 August 1990 but he remained a
member of the scheme, and a 'termination beneficiary', because his last
j   employment had been with the company. He had not reached his normal
retirement date, which would be 9 January 2009, and therefore he came within
the lowest priority category (apart from his guaranteed rights). Clause 31 of the
deed provides for the various possible methods for securing benefits. The 'main
fund share' is defined broadly as being that part of the fund, other than assets
deriving from voluntary contributions, which is attributable to the termination
beneficiaries concerned (cl 33).

The person principally concerned with the administration of the scheme on behalf of the trustees was a Mr Chris Delacombe. There was a meeting to discuss the future of the scheme on 13 November 1990. It was anticipated that the winding-up procedure would take at least two years, and that until all the benefits had been calculated it would not be possible to establish whether or not the scheme had any surplus. The last actuarial valuation of the scheme had been carried out in April 1989, but this had been concerned with a global picture of all the pension schemes in the Rockwood group. At that time the scheme was considered to be 101% funded. It was anticipated that a new valuation would be carried out as at 6 April 1991 and that by Easter 1991 Mr Delacombe would have the information necessary to calculate benefits. At that time Inter Forward did not have a group pension scheme but one was to be set up.

The next important step was a letter dated 9 April 1991 from Mr Delacombe to Mr Stapleton, enclosing a quotation of options. Since this letter forms the foundation of the ombudsman's finding of maladministration, it is necessary to set it out in some detail. It stated:

'For your information the Trustees are in the process of winding-up the Rockwood Holdings PLC Group Pension Scheme and this includes realising assets and identifying all liabilities of The Scheme. The Trustees also have the discretionary power to use any surplus assets of The Scheme to provide additional benefits to members and, of course, should The Scheme prove to be in deficit, then the reverse situation would apply.'

It was said that the process of winding up would take some time and that recipients should consult their own financial advisers. The letter referred to an enclosed 'statement', and said:

'Your action in returning the duplicate second page of your personal statement is simply an indication of your preferred option and can subsequently be varied by you until you confirm that a final decision has been reached. Once the Trustees, together with their advisors, are satisfied with the likely ultimate funding level of The Scheme, the members will be advised of any variation in options available to them. The Trustees have been informed that the Scheme's assets must be realised in a controlled manner. Therefore if a substantial number of members request an immediate transfer the Trustees reserve the formal right to suspend the payment of transfer values if investment conditions make it necessary to do so.'

The enclosure was headed: 'QUOTATION OF OPTIONS ON LEAVING SERVICE'. It gave details of Mr Stapleton's date of birth and employment, and continued:

'2. Options Available (A) A paid-up pension of 3,126·59 payable from NRD. (B) A transfer value of £16,387·31, of which £5,442·45 represents the value of the Guaranteed Minimum Pension (GMP)—see note 7 overleaf.'

Note 7 explained that the guaranteed minimum pension is the pension that the trustees are required to provide by law in replacement of the earnings related element of the state pension. I need only refer to the notes dealing with option (B). As to this, paras 4 and 6 are relevant; they state:

a
'4. If you elect Option (B): The transfer value can be transferred: (B1) To a new employer's scheme, if suitable or ... (B2) To an individual policy with an insurance company or a personal pension plan ...
6. The transfer value quoted in this statement is guaranteed for 3 months. After 3 months it will be recalculated to reflect the true value of your benefits at the date of transfer.'

b
On 2 May 1991 Mr Stapleton returned a copy of the form, having ticked option B2. He appears to have made inquiries of the Wesleyan Assurance Society and the Guardian Royal Exchange, both of which companies submitted applications to the trustees on his behalf. However, on 15 May 1991 he received from the old employer a letter inviting him to join the new Inter Forward pension plan, which
c it was said would be open from 1 July 1991; membership would be backdated to July 1990 for former members of the Rockwood pension scheme. On 20 May 1991 Mr Stapleton wrote to Mr Delacombe saying that he had received details of the Inter Forward scheme and was still making up his mind what to do. On 23 May 1991 Mr Delacombe replied indicating that the trustees were currently—

d
'overwhelmed with transfer applications which are taking three to four months to process. There is therefore plenty of time before your file comes to the top of the "queue" for you to make up your mind about the Inter Forward Scheme which is being set up.'

On 14 June Mr Stapleton wrote again saying that he had decided to join the Inter
e Forward scheme and would be transferring his benefits over to it when it is possible to do so.
There matters rested for the time being as far as Mr Stapleton was concerned. The Inter Forward group pension plan was established by interim trust deed on 27 June 1991 but no immediate steps seem to have been taken to enable transfers
f into the new scheme to take place. (The Inter Forward trustees' letter to the ombudsman dated 14 June 1994 makes clear that there was no possibility of transfers taking place before 11 July 1991, which was the end of the three-month guarantee referred to in the April letter.) On 20 November 1991, in response to a telephone call from Mrs Stapleton, Mr Delacombe wrote to the Stapletons indicating that he would be writing in December with an updated valuation of
g the benefits within the scheme. He advised them that if they wished to proceed with the transfer to the Inter Forward scheme they should apply formally through the Inter Forward scheme trustees.
On 30 December 1991 the trustees of the scheme wrote to Mr Stapleton referring to the completion of the actuary's valuation of the scheme as at 6 April
h 1991, the purpose of the letter being to advise them of the benefits following the actuarial valuation. The actuary had advised that the amount of transfer values offered should be restricted at the present time, for two reasons: first, because a substantial proportion of the assets were invested in property and it was not possible to predict when they would be sold, and secondly because it would be necessary at the final stage to purchase annuity policies for those members who
j retained their benefits in the scheme, and the cost of purchasing them would be dependent on interest rates at the time.
Under the heading 'Benefits', the letter stated that, although great care had been taken in establishing the basis of the benefits set out—

'the amount of benefit that can ultimately be provided is dependent on the assets available and the annuity rates prevailing at the final date of wind-up, and therefore it is not possible to guarantee the precise amount of your benefit. Nevertheless the Trustees feel confident that the basis set out in the letter is the final basis on which all benefits will be calculated.'

It indicated that, according to the April 1991 valuation, the assets of the scheme were sufficient to meet all future instalments of pensions currently in payment, and to provide revised benefits as detailed below for members who had not yet reached normal retirement age. For transfer purposes the value of these benefits was stated to be £11,496·41, but taking the actuary's advice into account the trustees were prepared to offer a restricted transfer value of £9,197·13 (80%). The letter continued:

'Should you proceed with a transfer at this stage the Trustees will reconsider your case again before RHGPS is finally wound-up, and, if adequate further funds are available, they will top up your transfer value with a further payment.'

Following this letter there was some discussion on Mr Stapleton's behalf of the reasons for the reduced value. In a letter from the trust's solicitors, Messrs Allen & Overy, dated 11 March 1992 (referring to the position of another beneficiary, Mr Scadden) it was explained that the original figures were based on the 1989 valuation which assumed that various other pension schemes of Rockwood subsidiaries would be amalgamated; that amalgamation had not taken place. The new figures were derived from the revaluation in April 1991, based on the assets actually available to the scheme.

The mechanics of transferring values to the Inter Forward scheme were not completed until the end of 1992. On 4 November 1992 Mr Delacombe sent to the Inter Forward representatives a form for signature to allow the transfer to proceed. The full cash equivalent of the benefits was stated to be as in the December letter, and the same restricted value was offered. Mr Stapleton signed the form on 15 December 1992.

In the meantime on 11 November 1992 he had written to the ombudsman asking him to investigate the circumstances leading to the delay in transfer, and the substantial reduction in the amount. He was uncertain whether the responsibility lay with the Rockwood trustees or the Inter Forward trustees. The ombudsman accepted the complaint and in due course treated it as a complaint to be dealt with jointly against Rockwood and Inter Forward. Representations were submitted and exchanged, and the ombudsman's provisional determination was issued on 17 January 1995. Following comments from the Rockwood trustees, the ombudsman issued his final determination on 7 February 1995.

I should set out his conclusions in full:

'11. I uphold the complaint against the Trustees but not against the New Company. The Complainant acquired a right to a cash equivalent (the term used for a transfer value under the Act) under what has since been consolidated into Part IV, Chapter IV, Section 94 of the Act. In his letter of 14 June 1991, he specified that he wished the transfer value to be paid to the Plan and thus exercised this right by application in writing within Section 95(1) of the Act, and he did so within the three months guarantee period indicated to him. It is not correct to argue, as the Trustees did, that an application had to be made by the trustees of the Plan since this is not required by the Act. The Trustees' failure to comply with the requirements of the Act clearly amounted to maladministration.

a   12. If my conclusion that the Complainant's letter of 14 June 1991 was a valid and effective application were found to be strictly incorrect, nevertheless the Trustees must still be held guilty of maladministration in failing to pay the original transfer value, having led the Complainant to believe, quite reasonably, that he had done all that was necessary to secure payment of the amount that they originally quoted. In concluding that the Complainant's belief was reasonable I take into account the fact that the Trustees volunteered payment of a transfer value, and that the Complainant made his position clear to them in his letter. His actions were entirely consistent with the Trustees' letter of 9 April 1991 ... in which he was asked to complete his preferred option on the basis that he was not committed to it, and told that he could vary it at any stage until he confirmed that a final decision had been reached. This is exactly what he did.

c   13. Further, the Trustees ought to have adhered to the figure quoted in the attachment to the letter of 9 April 1991. I do not accept that the words "After three months it will be recalculated ..." could reasonably have been understood as meaning that the transfer value actually had to be paid within three months for the guarantee to apply. The Complainant believed that in confirming his intention within the three months guarantee period he had fixed the figure at the quoted level, and in my view his belief was entirely justified. The Trustees' assertion that the guarantee only applied if the transfer value was paid in the three month period is entirely incompatible with the Administrator's statement that there was a "queue" of three to four months ... This being so, the guarantee, on the Trustees' reading of it, would have been worthless, and I do not accept that this can be taken as intended.

    14. In its letter to the Complainant of 30 December 1991, the Independent Trustee said that the transfer value would need to be restricted due to difficulties in selling property assets. Sections 97 and 99 of Part IV, Chapter IV of the Act do not allow for the payment of interim cash equivalents. The Pension Schemes Office of the Inland Revenue does not approve the payment of restricted transfer values but states, in its Notes on approval (IR12) in Section 10.21 "a transfer payment should represent the whole of a member's benefits under the transferring scheme". The Trustees could have applied to the Occupational Pensions Board for an extension of time limits for payment of cash equivalents (and later did so) but such extension relates to the whole cash equivalent, and does not permit the action taken by the Trustees. Quite simply, only the full cash equivalent should have been paid.

    15. For the reasons given above, I uphold the complaint against the Trustees. I do not uphold the complaint against the New Company since it was not required to initiate any action in relation to the transfer. In so far as any delay by the New Company in providing membership data could amount to maladministration, it plainly did not occasion injustice: at the time the transfer request was made, the Trustees had calculated the Complainant's benefits and were therefore in a position to act on his request.'

He accordingly directed the trustees in effect to make good the original transfer value of £16,387·31, increased by interest between 14 June 1991 and the date of payment, giving credit for the amounts already paid. He concluded:

'The complainant has suffered injustice beyond pecuniary loss involving
distress and inconvenience as a result of the Trustees' maladministration. a
The Trustees are to pay £750 to the complainant to compensate him fully for
the injustice.'

Finally, I should refer to an affidavit from Mr Earnshaw on behalf of the
trustees of the Rockwood scheme. He explains that under the valuation carried
out as at 6 April 1991 the estimated deficit was £2,625,300. A further valuation b
was carried out as at 6 April 1994 which indicated a deficit of £5,423,200. He
produces a copy of the April 1994 valuation. This also indicates that in December
1992 the Occupational Pensions Board agreed to a suspension of transfer values
following annual reviews. According to Mr Earnshaw, this extension currently
runs until 31 January 1996.   c

Issues
The questions for my consideration can be grouped under the following
headings: (1) the effect in law of the 'guarantee' contained in the letter of 9 April
1991; (2) the relationship of such a guarantee and the priority rules in the trust
deed; and (3) the award of damages for maladministration.   d

Statute
The relevant statutory law was consolidated (as from 7 February 1994) in the
Pension Schemes Act 1993. The appeal from the ombudsman arises under s 151
of that Act. Although the facts which I have set out arose against the background e
of the earlier legislation, it is not suggested that there is any material difference
between those provisions and those of the 1993 Act, and it is convenient to refer
to the latter, which follow a more orderly sequence.

I am concerned principally with the provisions of the Act dealing respectively
with transfer values (Pt IV, Ch IV), the relationship between those requirements
and scheme rules (Pt VIII), and the office and functions of the Pensions f
Ombudsman (Pt X).

The relevant provisions on transfer values begin at s 94, by which, subject to
the following provisions of the chapter—

> 'a member of an occupational pension scheme acquires a right, when his
> pensionable service terminates, to the cash equivalent at the relevant date of g
> any benefits which have accrued to or in respect of him under the applicable
> rules ...'

The 'relevant date' is defined as the date of the 'relevant application' (or, if later,
the termination of his employment). The 'relevant application' means an h
application made by the member under s 95. By that section, a person who
acquires a right to a cash equivalent—

> 'may only take it by making an application in writing to the trustees or
> managers of the scheme requiring them to use the cash equivalent to which
> he has acquired a right in whichever of the ways specified in subsection (2) j
> or, as the case may be, subsection (3) he chooses ...'

For present purposes I need only refer to sub-s (2)(a) under which one of the
specified 'ways' is:

> '... for acquiring transfer credits allowed under the rules of another
> occupational pension scheme—(i) the trustees or managers of which are able

a   and willing to accept payment in respect of the member's accrued rights, and
    (ii) which satisfies prescribed requirements ...'

    Section 97 provides for the calculation of cash equivalents, which are to be
    'calculated and verified in the [manner] prescribed [by regulations]'. The
    regulations may, inter alia, provide 'that in prescribed circumstances a cash
    equivalent shall be increased or reduced'. The circumstances which may be so
b   prescribed include 'the state of the funding of the scheme' (s 97(3)(c)).

    By s 99, where a member has exercised his option under s 95 and the trustees
    have done what is needed to carry out what the member requires, the trustees
    are discharged from any obligation to provide benefits to which the cash
    equivalent related (there are some exceptions which are not relevant here).
c   Section 99(2) provides that the trustees must do what is needed to carry out what
    the member requires within 12 months of the date on which they receive the
    application. By sub-s (4), however, the Occupational Pensions Board may in
    specified circumstances grant an extension of the period within which the
    trustees are obliged to carry out these steps. One of the circumstances is where
d   'the scheme is being wound up or is about to be wound up' (s 99(4)(a)(i)).
    Another is where—

        'the member has not taken all such steps as the trustees or managers can
        reasonably expect him to take in order to satisfy them of any matter which
        falls to be established before they can properly carry out what he requires ...'
e   (See s 99(4)(a)(iv).)

    The regulations in force at the relevant time were the Occupational Pension
    Schemes (Transfer Values) Regulations 1985, SI 1985/1931. Regulation 3 dealt
    with the manner of calculation and verification of cash equivalents. The methods
    and assumptions must be certified by an actuary to be consistent with the
f   requirements of the Social Security Pensions Act 1975 and with the document
    'Retirement Benefit Schemes—Transfer Values (GN11)' published by the
    Institute of Actuaries. Regulation 4 provides for increases and reductions of cash
    equivalents. Where from the latest actuarial statement or from an actuary's
    certificate it appears that—

g   'the scheme does not have sufficient assets to meet its liability in respect of
        the whole or any specified part of the accrued rights to benefit of members,
        the cash equivalent, or, as the case may be, the part of that cash equivalent
        which corresponds with that specified part of those accrued rights, may be
        reduced by the percentage by which the scheme is so shown to be deficient.'

h   By reg 4(4), if the trustees of the scheme fail without reasonable excuse to do
    what is needed in response to an application within six months of the relevant
    date, the member's cash equivalent is increased by an amount reflecting interest.
    I have been referred to the document GN11, mentioned in the regulations.
    Paragraph 4.1 explains that if, in the actuary's opinion, the scheme's assets would
j   be insufficient to cover liabilities and if the immediate payment of a transfer value
    would further reduce the security for the benefits of other members, the actuary
    should advise the trustees as to any reduced transfer value which would be
    appropriate having regard to reg 4(3); he may also advise that member's interest
    might be better served by deferring the taking of the transfer until a later date.
    I should note also para 7.2, which says:

'The actuary should note that the legislation requires that the cash
equivalent is to be calculated as at the date it is validly requested by the
member. Where there is a practice of guaranteeing a quotation for a period
of time, and the financial conditions have changed since the quotation was
prepared resulting in a change in the basis of the calculation of the cash
equivalent, a revised figure will need to be calculated as at the date of request
if this produces a higher cash equivalent figure.'

This confirms that, although there is no specific provision for 'guarantees' in the
legislation, the practice of giving guarantees was well established. More recently,
the Pensions Act 1995 has, by amendment of the 1993 Act, imposed upon trustees
a specific duty, on the application of a member, to provide a written statement of
the amount of the cash equivalent at a 'guarantee date'; and has conferred upon
the member who makes a relevant application within three months of the
guarantee date a right to a payment of the guaranteed cash equivalent. This
provides some confirmation of the practical utility of such guarantees. It does not
assist in determining whether, prior to the 1995 Act, there was power to give such
guarantees, and, if so, their effect.

Returning to the 1993 Act, s 129 (in Pt VIII) is headed 'Overriding requirements'. This provides, inter alia, that Ch IV of Pt IV is to be regarded generally
as overriding any provision of a scheme to the extent of any conflict. There are
certain exceptions, referred to as 'protected provisions', one of which is: 'any
provision of a scheme to the extent that it deals with priorities on a winding up'
(s 129(3)(b)). (The predecessor of this provision was para 18(2) of Sch 1A to the
1975 Act: 'This Part of this Schedule does not override any provision of a scheme
to the extent that it deals with priorities on a winding-up.')

Part X deals with the Pensions Ombudsman. The office with that name is
established by s 145 'For the purpose of conducting investigations in accordance
with this Part ...' His functions are described by s 146 as follows:

'(1) The Pensions Ombudsman may investigate and determine any
complaint made to him in writing by or on behalf of an authorised
complainant who alleges that he has sustained injustice in consequence of
maladministration in connection with any act or omission of the trustees or
managers of an occupational pension scheme or personal pension scheme.
(2) The Pensions Ombudsman may also investigate and determine any
dispute of fact or law which arises in relation to such a scheme between—(a)
the trustees or managers of the scheme, and (b) an authorised complainant,
and which is referred to him in writing by or on behalf of the authorised
complainant ...'

The subsequent provisions set out the procedure to be adopted on such an
investigation. Section 151 deals with determinations of the Pensions Ombudsman. He is required to send a written statement of his determination to the
parties and any such statement 'shall contain the reasons for his determination'.
By s 151(2):

'Where the Pensions Ombudsman makes a determination under this Part
... he may direct the trustees or managers of the scheme concerned to take,
or refrain from taking, such steps as he may specify in the statement referred
to in subsection (1) or otherwise in writing.'

a His determination is final and binding, subject to the appeal on a point of law to the High Court. A determination or direction of the ombudsman is enforceable in a county court 'as if it were a judgment or order of that court' (s 151(5)(a)).

Effect of 'guarantee'

b The ombudsman held that Mr Stapleton was entitled to the amount specified in the letter of 9 April 1991 because he exercised his right by application under s 95(1) within the three-month guarantee period indicated to him. Alternatively, he held that the trustees were guilty of maladministration in failing to pay the original value, having led him to believe that he had done all that was necessary to secure payment. The trustees challenge this reasoning on two main grounds. c First, as a matter of construction of the letter of 9 April and its enclosure, they contend that the guarantee was to be read as operating only if the sum in question is paid within the three-month period. Secondly, they contend that the ombudsman was wrong to hold that the letter of 14 June 1991 was a valid and effective application, having regard to the requirements contained in the 1993 Act.

d On the first point, I am inclined to agree with the ombudsman. Certainly, the letter of 9 April, taken with the enclosure, does not give a very clear picture of what is intended. However, para 6 of the enclosure specifically states that the transfer value quoted in the statement is being 'guaranteed' for three months. This word, to my mind, is inconsistent with anything other than a binding e commitment during that period. Although the letter indicates that in certain circumstances the benefits may be adversely affected if the scheme should prove to be in deficit, it does not state that this is intended to detract from the 'guarantee' contained in the enclosure.

The more difficult point is to determine what has to happen within the three months if the guarantee is to take effect. Within the statutory scheme, the natural f expectation is that the sum is being guaranteed provided the statutory application is made within the three-month period—that is 'the relevant date' as defined. It is true that para 6 indicates that the recalculation, following the guarantee period, is to reflect the value 'at the date of transfer'. This might suggest that it is the transfer date rather than the application date which is the trigger. However, this g seems inconsistent with s 94, which requires the calculation to be made as at the 'relevant date' (unless there is a general power to override that pursuant to s 129). Further, if the guarantee was dependent upon the transfer being effected within three months, the matter would have been entirely out of the control of the applicant, and dependent on the time scale within which the trustees were able to process the application. In practice, as the ombudsman points out, the three h to four month queue which they were operating would make it worthless.

The second submission of the trustees has more substance, although it does not seem to have been pursued in detail in argument to the ombudsman. It is given weight by the judgment of Collins J in *Hamar v Pensions Ombudsman* (18 October 1995, unreported). As has been seen, a valid application under s 95 must j be in writing and must indicate one of the statutory ways in which the right to a cash equivalent may be taken. The 'way' which is relevant here is under s 95(2)(a), which refers to transfer credits allowed under the rules of another occupational pension scheme '(i) the trustees or managers of which are able and willing to accept payment in respect of the member's accrued rights, and (ii) which satisfies prescribed requirements'. As Collins J said in *Hamar*'s case:

'It is perfectly clear from s 95(1) and (2)(a) that the option could only be
exercised if there is an existing other occupational pension scheme to which   *a*
the money can be transferred and which must be a scheme which itself
satisfies prescribed requirements ... and is one in respect of which the
trustees or managers are willing and able to accept payment.'

If that is right, Mr Stapleton's letter of 14 June 1991 was not a valid application,   *b*
because the Inter Forward scheme was not in existence at that time. The
ombudsman was wrong to say that, at the time of the transfer request, 'the
trustees were in a position to act on his request'. Although the scheme came into
existence on 1 July, just before the end of the guarantee period, there is no
evidence that it was 'willing and able' to accept transfers before that date.
Therefore, even if the trustees had spelled out the position in detail for Mr   *c*
Stapleton on the receipt of his letter, he would not have been able to improve his
position within the three-month period by making a valid application.

Mr Nugee, on behalf of the ombudsman, sought to persuade me that Collins J
had overstated the requirement for a valid application. This was in spite of the
fact that the reasoning in *Hamar's* case was largely a reflection of Mr Nugee's own   *d*
submissions on behalf of the successful appellant in that case. He submitted that
it was unnecessary, as a matter of construction, that the new scheme should
satisfy sub-s (2)(a) at the time of the application; it was sufficient if it did so within
the 12 months allowed for the trustees to comply with the requirements.

I am unable to accept that contention. I agree with Collins J that the statutory
language is clear. Furthermore, the time limits allowed for the trustees' action   *e*
under the 1993 Act—that is both the six-month period before interest begins to
be payable and the 12-month period ultimately allowed—are designed to run
from a date at which they are in a position to comply with the application. Mr
Nugee accepted that, on his argument, even if the requirements of sub-s (2)(a)
were only fulfilled on the last day of the 12-month period, the application would   *f*
still have to be treated as valid. His answer to that was that the trustees could seek
an extension of time under s 99(4). However, the circumstances would not, as I
see it, fall within any of the paragraphs of that subsection. In particular,
s 99(4)(a)(iv), to which Mr Nugee referred, only applies where the member has
not taken all such steps as can reasonably be expected of him. In the
circumstances postulated by Mr Nugee the member would have done everything   *g*
within his power, and the only problem would be the fact that the scheme in
question had not been established by those responsible for it.

It follows that, on this short point, I must allow the appeal. The ombudsman
was in my view wrong to hold that Mr Stapleton, by his letter of 14 June 1991,
made a valid application under s 95(1). Furthermore, his alternative basis,   *h*
namely that the trustees had led the complainant to believe that he had done all
that was necessary to secure payment, presupposes that it was possible for him to
take advantage of the guarantee within the context of the Inter Forward scheme.
On the view I have taken, however, it was not possible to make a valid
application until the scheme was ready to accept transfer. Thus, even if one   *j*
accepts the finding of maladministration in relation to the advice given (to which
I will come), it did not cause the loss identified by the ombudsman.

Relationship of guarantee with the priority rules in the trust deed

The above conclusion makes it unnecessary to reach a final decision on the
submissions made to me as to the overriding effect of the priority rules in the

a   trustee. Miss Hayes, for the trustees, submitted that it would be inconsistent with s 129 of the 1993 Act (or its predecessor) to give effect to a guarantee such as this, if the effect is to give Mr Stapleton a greater share of the assets of the scheme than he would be entitled to under the priority rules in the trust deed. This appeared to raise the question whether the trustees had power to give a binding guarantee at all; or, in any event, whether such a guarantee once given could be effective in *b*   circumstances where the scheme was shown by later valuations to be in deficit, or in more serious deficit than had at first appeared.

Mr Nugee submitted that s 129 has to be read in the context of the rest of the 1993 Act. Section 97 contains specific provision for the cash equivalent to be reduced having regard to the state of funding of the scheme, and this is reflected in the regulations to which I have referred. As he says, it is quite clear (for *c*   example from s 99(4)(a)), that the transfer provisions are intended to operate while a scheme is being wound up, although the right is lost once the winding up is completed (s 98(6)). Thus, he says, the mechanism is provided within the Act for both the funding of the scheme, and the priorities which arise in the event of a deficit, to be taken into account in calculating the cash equivalent which is to be *d*   offered. Alternatively, the trustees can seek an extension of time from the Occupational Pensions Board. It would frustrate the scheme of the Act if that cash equivalent, once fixed under s 97, were liable to a possible reduction. There is nothing in the Act or the regulations which contemplates such a reduction, or provides a machinery for it to be carried out. Further, he says, the trustees must, by implication, have power to guarantee the cash equivalent for a sufficient *e*   period to enable the beneficiary to arrive at an informed decision under s 95.

While I see force in Mr Nugee's submissions, I do not find the answer clear cut and I prefer not to express a concluded view. Apart from the 1993 Act, the trustees have a duty to the general body of beneficiaries to make payments out of the scheme on the basis of up-to-date valuations (see e g *Stannard v Fisons Pension* *f*   *Trust Ltd* [1992] IRLR 27). This is particularly important in a winding up when there is a risk of deficit and where there is a need to maintain a fair balance between the beneficiaries, having regard to the priority rules in the trust deed. Section 129 makes that duty overriding, notwithstanding the specific powers in the 1993 Act and the regulations. Therefore it is not easy to see how the mere fact that a cash equivalent has been fixed under the Act (even if some adjustment *g*   has been made under reg 4(3)) can give that beneficiary a higher priority if in the event, when payment comes to be made, the figure proves more than is justified by the funding of the scheme and the priority rules.

Damages for maladministration

h   Miss Hayes, on behalf of the trustees, challenged the award of compensation for distress and inconvenience on the basis, first, that there was no power for the ombudsman to make such an award, and, secondly, that the facts as found by him could not reasonably justify the award he made. Although I have already found that the basis of the ombudsman's decision cannot be supported in law, I have *j*   been asked to deal with this issue and I have heard argument upon it. There is some controversy as to the power of the ombudsman to award such damages, and the present ombudsman (Professor Farrand) is anxious to have an authoritative ruling on the point. Unlike his predecessor, he takes the view that he has such power, and I have been shown an article by him in which he discusses the arguments, 'Pensions Ombudsman v Courts—a curious case' (1995) 63 Pension Lawyer 1. He notes that the government has recently rejected the recommendation of the Pension Law Review Committee under the chairmanship of Professor Roy Goode QC (*Pension Law Reform* (Cm 2342) (1993)) that there *a* should be a power to direct compensation payment for 'distress, delay and inconvenience caused, as well as actual financial loss' (see vol I, para 152, pp 39, 439). The reason given for rejection was:

> 'The Pensions Ombudsman can already order restitution for financial loss. As the powers which allow the courts to award compensation for distress are *b* very limited, and apply to circumstances which would not arise in connection with the administration of pension schemes, it is not considered appropriate to allow the Ombudsman to order the payment of compensation. It will, however, remain open for the Ombudsman to encourage schemes to consider making such payments.' (See government White *c* Paper: *Security, Equality, Choice—The Future for Pensions* (Cm 2594), vol II, 1994.)

Professor Farrand criticises this reasoning, and draws attention to the specific provisions in the Courts and Legal Services Act 1990 (s 23(2)(d)) for the award of compensation for distress caused by handling of complaints by professional *d* bodies in that context.

It is desirable first to say something about the term 'maladministration'. The Pensions Ombudsman is unusual in that he has power both to investigate complaints of maladministration and to decide points of fact or law which arise in relation to a pension scheme. The latter function is similar to that of a court, and it is not surprising therefore that his decisions are enforceable in the same *e* way as court judgments. Investigation of maladministration, on the other hand, is not the normal function of a court. Maladministration as such does not give rise to a cause of action in law. In this respect, he is acting in a manner similar to that of so-called 'ombudsmen' under other statutes, for example the Parliamentary Commissioner for Administration or the Local Commissioners for *f* Administration. There is no statutory definition of 'maladministration', either under this or under other, similar Acts. The Parliamentary Commissioner has been guided by what is known as the 'Crossman Catalogue'. When the Parliamentary Commissioner Bill was being taken through Parliament, Mr Crossman, as Leader of the House of Commons, gave examples of maladministration (see 734 HC Official Report (5th series) col 51). He referred to *g* bias, neglect, inattention, delay, incompetence, ineptitude, perversity, turpitude, arbitrariness, and so on. More recently, the Parliamentary Commissioner has suggested other examples, such as rudeness, refusing to answer reasonable questions, knowingly giving advice which is misleading or inadequate, faulty procedures, and so on. The courts have not attempted a definition. In *R v Comr* *h* *for Local Administration, ex p Eastleigh BC* [1988] 3 All ER 151 at 155, [1988] QB 855 at 863 Lord Donaldson MR said:

> '... administration and maladministration, in the context of the work of a local authority, is concerned with the *manner* in which decisions by the authority are reached and the *manner* in which they are or are not *j* implemented ... Administration and maladministration have nothing to do with the nature, quality or reasonableness of the decision itself.' (Lord Donaldson MR's emphasis.)

Although these may provide some parallel for 'maladministration' in the context of the 1993 Act, there are material differences of subject matter. In a particular, it must be borne in mind that the Parliamentary Commissioner and the Local Commissioner are dealing with authorities operating in the public sphere. The Pensions Ombudsman, unusually, is investigating the performance of those involved in schemes established under private law. The framework within which the trustees are acting is essentially one of contract or trust law, although the statute imposes certain requirements and provides certain

b additional rights and obligations. In particular, the courts have taken a restrictive view of the trustees' legal duty to advise beneficiaries of their rights under such schemes. I have in that context been referred to another part of Collins J's judgment in *Hamar*'s case, where he deals with the duty of the trustees in relation to the giving of advice. He referred to the judgment of Havers J in *Hawksley v May* [1955] 3 All ER 353, [1956] 1 QB 304, where it was held that in general a trustee

c has no duty to give a beneficiary legal advice. Collins J continued:

> 'What is suggested here is that there was a duty on the trustees not only to inform of rights, but also to inform as to how those rights could be properly exercised or, more importantly perhaps, that those rights were not being properly exercised. It seems to me that that is to extend, beyond anything
> d that has hitherto been suggested, the supposed duties of trustees. It is certainly the case that there is an obligation to give information to a beneficiary of the existence of the trust and, by showing him documents, to give information. What is, in my judgment, not supported by the authorities is a duty to go further and to give explanations. No doubt the trustees
> e frequently will, but they do not have to ... It is a statutory right that is here under consideration. It is a right in respect of which the beneficiary who wishes to effect the transfer may seek advice. It is up to him to follow the correct statutory procedure ...'

In the present case, the ombudsman has identified the 'maladministration' in
f question as either 'the trustees' failure to comply with requirements of the Act', or their failure 'to pay the original transfer value having led the complainant to believe quite reasonably that he had done all that was necessary to secure payment for the amount that they originally quoted'. In the last paragraph of his decision he holds that the complainant 'has suffered injustice beyond pecuniary loss involving distress and inconvenience as a result of the trustees' mal-
g administration'. For that injustice he awards compensation of £750.

These conclusions are open to the criticism that they fail to distinguish clearly between the two separate functions under s 146. If the ombudsman were correct on his first ground, that would be a finding of fact and law which would entitle the complainant to the same relief as if that finding had been made by a court. It
h does not seem correct to characterise that as a finding of 'maladministration'. If the trustees, acting on proper advice, believed their view of the law to be correct, they were entitled to assert that position before the ombudsman. That is a normal and proper part of good administration. It might be otherwise if they had adopted a perverse stance, or failed to take appropriate legal advice. But there is
j no suggestion of that here.

The second ground of the ombudsman's decision comes closer to what might normally be regarded as 'maladministration', since it is addressed to the way in which the trustees responded to the complainant's letter of 14 June, against the background of the advice given in their letter of 9 April. However, again it seems to me to be open to the criticism that it fails to distinguish between the bona fide giving of advice which is reasonably believed to be correct in law, but ultimately turns out not to be; and the giving of advice which is knowingly misleading, or otherwise tainted by incompetence. The former would not normally, in my view, amount to maladministration.

This is not to say that the trustees' conduct of the matter in this case is above criticism. I have already referred to the somewhat confusing impression given by the 9 April letter and its enclosure. Even if pension trustees are under no legal duty to give advice to beneficiaries, it is generally good practice for them to do so; and, when they do, it should be as clear and accurate as possible. Furthermore, they could be open to criticism if they purported to offer 'guaranteed' cash equivalents before an up-to-date valuation had been completed. Depending on the facts, such criticisms might justify a finding of maladministration. But that is not the basis of the ombudsman's decision in this case.

Mr Nugee attempted to uphold the finding of maladministration by reference to the whole course of dealing between the complainant and the trustees, as evidenced by the correspondence. However, that approach is not supported by the decision itself. The ombudsman was required to state his reasons for his finding of maladministration. Apart from the two matters to which I have referred, both of which concern the treatment of the letter of 14 June, he has not criticised the way the matter was dealt with by the trustees, either then or subsequently.

Miss Hayes, for the trustees, attacks the award of compensation principally on the ground that there is no power to compensate for distress and inconvenience. She refers to the general principle of law that damages are not recoverable for distress and inconvenience: (i) for breach of contract, unless the object of the contract was to provide peace of mind or freedom from distress, or (ii) for negligence, unless the result of reasonably foreseeable physical consequences of the breach. She also refers me to *Hayes v James & Charles Dodd (a firm)* [1990] 2 All ER 815 at 823, where Staughton LJ said:

'Damages awarded for negligence or want of skill, whether against professional men or anyone else, must provide fair compensation, but no more than that. And I would not view with enthusiasm the prospect that every shipowner in the Commercial Court, having successfully claimed for unpaid freight or demurrage, would be able to add a claim for mental distress suffered while he was waiting for his money.'

He added (at 824) that classes of cases where damages for mental distress are recoverable in contract—

'should not, in my judgment, include any case where the object of the contract was not comfort or pleasure, or the relief [of] discomfort, but simply carrying on a commercial activity with a view to profit.'

To the same effect is the decision of the Court of Appeal, *Watts v Morrow* [1991] 4 All ER 937, [1991] 1 WLR 1421, where the authorities were fully considered. In the light of that decision, in *R v Investors Compensation Scheme Ltd, ex p Bowden* [1995] 1 All ER 214, [1995] QB 107 it was conceded that, under the rules applying to the board, it had correctly refused compensation for distress, anxiety and inconvenience. Although the matter was kept open in the Court of Appeal, it was not pursued before the House of Lords ([1995] 3 All ER 605, [1996] 1 AC 261).

There appear to me to be three separate points: first, whether there is power at all under the 1993 Act to award compensation for the consequences of maladministration; secondly, if so, whether such compensation extends to mere a distress and inconvenience, as opposed to 'actual financial loss'; thirdly, whether it extends to what might be called 'litigation distress'. As to the first, the Goode Committee, and the government in their response, seem to have assumed that there was power to direct 'restitution' for actual financial loss. I have heard no argument in that respect and I express no view.

b Only the third point appears to arise directly in this case. The distress and inconvenience for which the ombudsman awarded £750 appears to be nothing more than the natural result of the disagreement between the trustees and Mr Stapleton as to the effect of the so-called 'guarantee'. If that had been dealt with by a court, and if Mr Stapleton's position had been upheld, he would not have been awarded anything for the inconvenience and anxiety inevitably involved in
c litigation. The courts have taken the view that that is not an appropriate head of compensation, even where a cause of action is established. There is no reason why a complainant should be in a better position because the dispute happens to be litigated before the ombudsman rather than before a court. Thus, even assuming the ombudsman has power to award compensation for distress and inconvenience, it would not, in my view, justify the award made by him in this
d case.

The more difficult question is whether the ombudsman has power to direct compensation for distress and inconvenience caused by maladministration in its ordinary sense, for example rudeness, incompetence, insensitive handling of complaints and so on. The fact that damages for such action would not be
e available in a court of law is not a sufficient answer. By conferring a power to investigate maladministration, Parliament has implicitly accepted the need to provide a remedy in matters which might not give rise to an action at law. It is the well-established practice of the Parliamentary Commissioner and the Local Commissioner to make recommendations for the award of compensation for
f maladministration in that sense. Although those recommendations are not binding, they are generally accepted by those concerned as an appropriate way of remedying maladministration where it has been found. Parliament would have been aware of that practice when enacting the 1993 Act or its predecessor. Mr Nugee relies on the widely expressed power of the ombudsman to 'direct the trustees or managers ... to take ... such steps as he may specify'. It is clear that
g such 'steps' may take the form of the payment of money, for example where it is held that the trustees have failed to make some payment which they were in law obliged to make. Thus, it is argued, the words are wide enough to cover a payment of monetary compensation for distress. Furthermore, if mal-administration cannot be reflected in a monetary award, it is hard to see what
h other remedy is available. The function of investigating maladministration would be rendered nugatory unless it was intended to result in an effective remedy where maladministration is found.

I am reluctant to express a final view on this difficult point, given that it does not in the event arise on the facts. However, I am inclined to agree with the
j previous ombudsman's view. The trustees may be directed to 'take, or refrain from taking ... steps'. The language, to my mind, naturally implies some pre-existing obligation or right of a specific nature—whether positive or negative—which the ombudsman is empowered to enforce. Given that, in the law generally, the award of damages for distress or inconvenience is the exception rather than the rule, I would have expected a power to make such an award to have been created by express words.

Furthermore, it is important to bear in mind who is going to bear the cost of any compensation that is awarded. The trustees are operating the pension scheme on behalf of all the beneficiaries. They are protected from liability for their actions, except in the case of personal dishonesty (trust deed cl 24) and they are entitled normally to recover the expenses of operating the scheme from the funds within the scheme itself (see cll 15 to 17). As the trustees explained in their comments on the ombudsman's provisional decision (letter of 6 February 1995), they had been advised that the award of damages would rank with the payment of expenses under the fund as a priority liability, and that any additional payment to compensate Mr Stapleton could only be at the expense of other beneficiaries. In effect, the ombudsman is robbing Peter to pay Paul.

There can of course be no concern if the ombudsman limits himself to awards reflecting the legal entitlement of the parties. Each beneficiary is entitled, as against the other beneficiaries, to the due and prompt performance of legal obligations inherent in the deed. However, it is a different thing to impose upon the general body of beneficiaries an obligation to compensate their fellows for distress or inconvenience caused by the actions of the trustees. In the context of what is essentially a private law scheme, I doubt that the words of this statute are sufficiently specific to have that effect.

Conclusion

For the above reasons, I allow the appeal.

Order accordingly.

Dilys Tausz   Barrister.

a   # Westminster City Council v Haywood and another

QUEEN'S BENCH DIVISION

b   ROBERT WALKER J

30, 31 JANUARY, 1, 2, 22 FEBRUARY 1996

Pension – Pension scheme – Maladministration of pension scheme – Complaint to Pensions Ombudsman – Jurisdiction of Pensions Ombudsman – Local authority operating severance and compensation scheme in addition to statutory pension scheme
c   *– Local authority reducing monthly payments to pensioner under own scheme after receiving legal advice as to legality of payments – Pensioner alleging misinformation as to pension entitlement – Pensions Ombudsman finding maladministration and directing local authority to reinstate payments and pay compensation for distress and inconvenience – Whether ombudsman having jurisdiction to entertain complaint –*
d   *Limit to ombudsman's payment order.*

In November 1991 H, who was employed by a local authority, elected to take voluntary redundancy effective from his fiftieth birthday in April 1992, whereupon he would qualify for payments under his employer's severance and compensation scheme in addition to a pension payment from funds subject to the
e   pension regulations. Before H left his employment, the local authority, which was aware of doubts about its severance and compensation scheme, reassured him that his entitlement was not under threat. Thereafter, H took redundancy and received an immediate lump sum and pension under the pension regulations, a statutory redundancy payment and compensation (comprising a lump sum and an annuity) under the local authority's scheme. However, in February 1993 the
f   local authority, acting on legal advice obtained following the outcome of litigation on the lawfulness of severance payments, informed H that his monthly compensation payment would be reduced by £158. H complained to the Pensions Ombudsman pursuant to the provisions of the Pension Schemes Act 1993. The ombudsman found that the local authority was guilty of
g   maladministration on the grounds that it had failed to warn H about doubts which it ought to have had as to the validity of its severance and compensation scheme and had therefore given him misleading or at least incomplete advice. He directed the local authority to reinstate H's monthly payments to their former level and to pay him £1,000 compensation for distress and inconvenience. On
h   appeal, the local authority challenged the jurisdiction of the ombudsman to entertain H's complaint and contended, principally, (i) that he had erred in law in directing the local authority to resume payments to H which it could not lawfully make and (ii) that he had no power to award compensation for distress and inconvenience.

j   **Held** – The appeal would be allowed in part for the following reasons—
(1) Construing the Pensions Ombudsman's jurisdiction as broadly as possible, it was clear he had correctly classified H's approach as a complaint of maladministration which he had jurisdiction to investigate under s 146(1)[a] of the

---

a   Section 146(1), so far as material, is set out at p 475 *e*, post

1993 Act, even though the payments that had been reduced were payments out of the general rate fund, not payments out of funds subject to the pension regulations (see p 477 *b* to *d j* to p 478 *e g*, post). *a*

(2) Compensation for negligent misrepresentation amounting to mal-administration should put a plaintiff in the same position as if his informant had provided correct information; it should not put him where he would have been, had the incorrect information been correct.   On the facts, the Pensions *b* Ombudsman was entitled to conclude that there had been maladministration on the part of the local authority; but there was no pecuniary loss established as injustice sustained by H in consequence of that maladministration.   In the absence of such loss, there was no lawful basis on which the ombudsman could direct the local authority to pay H a pension larger than that to which he (or any other pensioner in his position) was lawfully entitled.   That part of the *c* ombudsman's decision directing reinstatement of the monthly payments to H to their former level would accordingly be set aside (see p 482 *j* and p 483 *b d* to *f*, post).

(3) The steps which the Pensions Ombudsman could direct under s 151(2)[b] of the 1993 Act included the payment of reasonable compensation for distress and *d* inconvenience, notwithstanding the fact that the power to make such awards had not been expressly created by Parliament.   Indeed, if monetary compensation could not be awarded for non-monetary injustice, many complainants might be left without an effective remedy and the statutory function of the ombudsman would be frustrated.   The award of £1,000 made to H in the instant case, although high, was not so excessive as to be wrong in law (see p 484 *j* to p 485 *b f* to *h* and *e* p 486 *a c*, post); dictum of Carnwath J in *Miller v Stapleton* [1996] 2 All ER 449 at 465 considered.

Per curiam. Taking and acting on a wrong view of the law may be maladministration if the decision-maker knows or ought to know that the state of the law is uncertain and that those who may be adversely affected by the *f* uncertainty need to be warned about it; it is wrong however to assume that any mistake made by a local authority employer as to the scope of its statutory powers is necessarily maladministration (see p 482 *c f*, post).

Notes

For occupational pension schemes generally, see 33 *Halsbury's Laws* (4th edn) *g* para 973.

Cases referred to in judgment

Allsop v North Tyneside Metropolitan BC (1991) 90 LGR 462, DC; *affd* [1992] ICR 639, CA.   *h*
Associated Provincial Picture Houses Ltd v Wednesbury Corp [1947] 2 All ER 680, [1948] 1 KB 223, CA.
Banque Bruxelles Lambert SA v Eagle Star Insurance Co Ltd [1995] 2 All ER 769, [1995] QB 375, [1995] 2 WLR 607, CA.
Crédit Suisse v Allerdale BC [1995] 1 Lloyd's Rep 315.
Dundee General Hospitals Board of Management v Walker [1952] 1 All ER 896, HL.   *j*
Hazell v Hammersmith and Fulham London BC [1991] 1 All ER 545, [1992] 2 AC 1, [1991] 2 WLR 372, HL.
Holsworthy UDC v Holsworthy RDC [1907] 2 Ch 62.

b   Section 151(2), so far as material, is set out at p 475 *g*, post

a *Mangin v IRC* [1971] 1 All ER 179, [1971] AC 739, [1971] 2 WLR 39, PC.
  Miller v Stapleton [1996] 2 All ER 449.
  Norwich Provident Insurance Society, Re, Bath's Case (1878) 8 Ch D 334, CA.
  Pepper (Inspector of Taxes) v Hart [1993] 1 All ER 42, [1993] AC 593, [1992] 3 WLR
    1032, HL.
  R v Comr for Local Administration, ex p Eastleigh BC [1988] 3 All ER 151, [1988] QB
b   855, [1988] 3 WLR 113, CA.
  R v Insurance Ombudsman, ex p Aegon Life Assurance Ltd [1995] LRLR 101, DC.
  R v Investors Compensation Scheme Ltd, ex p Bowden [1995] 1 All ER 214, [1995] QB
    107, [1994] 3 WLR 1045, CA; *rvsd* [1995] 3 All ER 605, [1996] 1 AC 261, [1995]
    3 WLR 289, HL.
  R v Local Comr for Administration for the North and East Area of England, ex p Bradford
c   *Metropolitan City Council* [1979] 2 All ER 881, [1979] QB 287, [1979] 2 WLR 1,
    CA.
  Rhyl UDC v Rhyl Amusements Ltd [1959] 1 All ER 257, [1959] 1 WLR 465.
  Roome v Edwards (Inspector of Taxes) [1981] 1 All ER 736, [1982] AC 279, [1981] 2
    WLR 268, HL.
d *Rowling v Takaro Properties Ltd* [1988] 1 All ER 163, [1988] AC 473, [1988] 2 WLR
    418, PC.
  Securities and Investments Board v Pantell SA (No 2) [1993] 1 All ER 134, [1993] Ch
    256, [1992] 3 WLR 896, CA.

Cases also cited or referred to in skeleton arguments

e *Australian Consolidated Press Ltd v Australian Newsprint Mills Holdings Ltd* (1960) 105
    CLR 473, Aust HC.
  British Basic Slag Ltd's Agreements, Re [1963] 2 All ER 807, [1963] 1 WLR 727, CA.
  Howell v Falmouth Boat Construction Ltd [1951] 2 All ER 278, [1951] AC 837, HL.
  Manning v Eastern Counties Rly Co (1843) 12 M & W 237, 152 ER 1185.
f *Morgan Grenfell & Co Ltd v Sutton London BC* (1995) 93 LGR 554.
  R v Dairy Produce Quota Tribunal for England and Wales, ex p Lifely [1988] 2 EGLR 1.
  Steed's Will Trusts, Re [1960] 1 All ER 487, [1960] Ch 407, CA.
  Westdeutsche Landesbank Girozentrale v Islington London BC, Kleinwort Benson Ltd v
    Sandwell BC [1994] 4 All ER 890, [1994] 1 WLR 938, QBD and CA.
  XCO Pty Ltd v Comr of Taxation of the Commonwealth of Australia (1971) 124 CLR
g   343, Aust HC.

Appeal

h By notice dated 16 January 1996 (as amended) Westminster City Council (Westminster) appealed from the decision of the second respondent, the Pensions Ombudsman, made on 25 July 1995, whereby he directed Westminster (i) to reinstate the level of their monthly gross payments of pension to the first respondent, Jeffrey James Haywood, to what it would have been, had it not been reduced in February 1993, (ii) to pay back such reductions with interest, and (iii) to pay him £1,000 compensation for distress and inconvenience. The facts are set out in the judgment.

j

Elizabeth Slade QC and Charles Bear (instructed by Colin Wilson) for Westminster.
Andrew Arden QC and Andrew Dymond (instructed by Paisner & Co) for the Pensions Ombudsman.
Mr Haywood did not appear.

Cur adv vult

22 February 1996. The following judgment was delivered.

ROBERT WALKER J.

THE PARTIES TO THE APPEAL

This is an appeal by Westminster City Council (Westminster) from a determination made and directions given on 25 July 1995 by the Pensions Ombudsman. The first respondent to the appeal is Mr Jeffrey Haywood, the 'authorised complainant' who brought the matter before the Pensions Ombudsman. Mr Haywood has taken no part in the appeal, although he has been present in court throughout the hearing. The second respondent is the Pensions Ombudsman himself, who has resisted the appeal. I do not criticise him for doing so. The appeal raises important and difficult questions as to the nature of the Pensions Ombudsman's jurisdiction and powers, on which it was most desirable for me to hear argument from both sides.

THE PRIMARY FACTS

The factual situation out of which Mr Haywood's complaint arose is described in the second part of the Pensions Ombudsman's written determination (the decision). Since the appeal is on points of law only the following outline of the primary facts is taken from that part of the decision, supplemented by some further undisputed background material as to local authorities' pension, severance and compensation arrangements.

At the end of 1991 Mr Haywood worked as a senior structural engineer in Westminster's surveyors department. He was then 49 years of age and a member of the Local Government Superannuation Scheme regulated by the Superannuation Act 1972 and (as they then were) the Local Government Superannuation Regulations 1986, SI 1986/24 (the pension regulations).

At the end of 1991 Westminster was seeking quite a large number of voluntary redundancies and Mr Haywood was among those considering that course. Mr Haywood's fiftieth birthday was not far off—12 April 1992—and on 20 November 1991 he wrote to the personnel development manager mentioning this and asking: 'Would it therefore be possible for me to be employed until I am 50 to qualify for early retirement and associated benefits?' This was arranged and Mr Haywood left Westminster's service on 12 April 1992, his fiftieth birthday.

The age of 50 was important because it was the earliest age at which a local government employee could in any circumstances begin to receive an immediate retirement pension (and a lump sum in lieu of a part of the pension) under the pension regulations. An employee who left service before 50 had to wait until the age of 60 before being entitled to receive either a pension or a lump sum under the pension regulations.

The age of 50 was also of some significance in connection with payments to which employees made redundant by Westminster might become entitled otherwise than under the pension regulations, and in addition to their ordinary statutory redundancy payments. As a matter of terminology Westminster (in the relevant policy document) referred to 'severance' payments on redundancy before the age of 50 and 'compensation' payments on redundancy at or after 50. More importantly, severance payments were simply lump sums, whereas compensation payments comprised both lump sums and additional periodical payments. All severance and compensation payments came from the general rate fund, not from separate funds which are subject to the pension regulations (and are held on statutory trusts). But periodical payments of compensation to a   those made redundant after 50 were in practice paid together with their pensions, and both payments were (as from age 55) enhanced by index linking under the Pensions (Increase) Act 1971 as amended. So to the non-expert observer they closely resembled pensions.

As the decision records, the choice quoted to Mr Haywood was between: (i) on redundancy under 50—(a) a deferred pension of £6,890 pa and lump sum of
b   £20,690 under the pension regulations; (b) statutory redundancy of £11,200; and (c) a severance lump sum of £21,000; and (ii) on redundancy at 50—(a) an immediate pension of £7,376 pa and lump sum of £22,129 under the pension regulations; (b) statutory redundancy of £11,544; and (c) a compensation lump sum of £8,509 and a compensation annuity of £3,950 pa.

These figures are not completely comparable because the first quotation ((i)
c   above) was prepared in November 1991 and Mr Haywood later had a salary increase of about £17 per month, but the effect of that is negligible. In his decision the Pensions Ombudsman aggregated the lump sums and periodical payments at (ii) above. He added: 'No reference was made to any judicial proceedings or to the possibility that the quotations might be affected by lack of authority.'

d   This leads on to the issues of ultra vires which (together with issues of jurisdiction) lie at the heart of this appeal. It is not only in connection with interest rate swaps that problems have arisen in relation to local authorities' statutory powers (and, in particular, the scope of the powers conferred by s 111 of the Local Government Act 1972 to do whatever is incidental to the discharge of their functions). A similar question arose in relation to the 'enhanced
e   voluntary severance scheme' established by the North Tyneside Metropolitan Borough Council, and this was referred to the court by the auditor. The case came before the Divisional Court on 16 October 1991 (see *Allsop v North Tyneside Metropolitan BC* (1991) 90 LGR 462). On a preliminary issue, the court held that the local authority had no power under ss 111 or 112 of the Local Government
f   Act 1972 to make payments in excess of those permitted by s 81 of the Employment Protection (Consolidation) Act 1978 or by the regulations specifically relating to redundancy and premature retirement. There was then an appeal to the Court of Appeal, which was dismissed on 3 March 1992 (see [1992] ICR 639).

g   In para 4 of his decision the Pensions Ombudsman at least inclines to the view—there is an issue as to whether it is a finding of fact—that Mr Haywood received reassuring advice (from Westminster's superannuation section) to the effect that the litigation posed no threat 'to the lump sum and pensions of those people taking premature retirement due to redundancy'.

h   Following the decision of the Court of Appeal in *Allsop*'s case Westminster's director of personnel issued a special bulletin dated 11 March 1992. The bulletin began as follows (part of this being quoted in para 6 of the Pensions Ombudsman's decision):

j   'Following the *Allsop v North Tyneside* case about the lawfulness of severance payments I wrote to staff last October to say that under special powers available to London Boroughs [Westminster's] scheme was to continue. Although the North Tyneside case has no direct bearing on [Westminster] the Audit Commission have now issued guidelines about the way in which London councils can lawfully make severance payments, and we have had to modify our arrangements to comply. The major changes are as follows: we *cannot* operate a fixed scheme, so we have had to withdraw the scheme from the Personnel Handbook. We *can* use the scheme but purely as a guide and must consider each case on its merits ... We *cannot* make severance payments as well as statutory redundancy payments to staff who have no rights to ill health benefits under the Local Government Superannuation Scheme or who have less than one year's service.' (Westminster's emphasis.)

The special powers referred to are conferred by s 31 of the London County Council (General Powers) Act 1921, as applied to Westminster by the Greater London Council (General Powers) Act 1968. The limit set by s 31(1) of the 1921 Act by reference to ill-health benefit explains the reference in the bulletin to ill-health benefits under the Local Government Superannuation Scheme. As I have said, Mr Haywood retired on his fiftieth birthday, 12 April 1992. At the end of January 1993 he became aware from television news that his pension (in common with those of up to 600 others) might be reduced. He then received a letter (dated 8 February 1993) from Westminster's finance department notifying him that 'your gross pension will be reduced by approximately £158 per month'. This reduction came exclusively out of Mr Haywood's monthly compensation payment (initially £329·16) from the general rate fund, and not out of the monthly pension payment (£614·71) from funds subject to the pension regulations. The letter dated 8 February referred to *Allsop's* case and said: 'Whilst the circumstances of that case were different from those of this Council, it brought into focus the whole question of severance payments and how they are calculated.' It also referred to advice to Westminster from two leading counsel. The Pensions Ombudsman has criticised the summary of their advice as neither accurate nor complete. I have heard no argument either against or in support of that criticism.

Mr Haywood then made his complaint to the Pensions Ombudsman by a letter dated 1 March 1993. After some preliminary inquiries there was a delay while the Pensions Ombudsman awaited the final drafting and coming into force of the Local Government (Compensation for Redundancy) Regulations 1994, SI 1994/3025. The delay was necessary because the 1994 regulations (which came into force on 24 December 1994) might have removed, retrospectively, at least the main financial burden of Mr Haywood's complaint. But they merely alleviated it and on 19 December 1994 the Pensions Ombudsman informed Mr Haywood that he was accepting his complaint for investigation. On 5 January 1995 the Pensions Ombudsman sent to Westminster a summary, prepared within his office, of Mr Haywood's complaint.

The relevant part of the 1994 regulations is Pt IV, which applies to local government employees who (apart from other requirements) were made redundant between 1 April 1980 and 1 October 1992. By reg 14 a local authority was given a temporary power to pay lump sum compensation up to a maximum calculated by a formula. The maximum was the amount by which 127% (approximately) of annual remuneration exceeded statutory redundancy actually paid. Westminster decided to pay the maximum to all its ex-employees who came within Pt IV of the 1994 regulations, and Mr Haywood received about £19,770, less income tax at 40%.

For reasons that I shall have to come back to, the Pensions Ombudsman has directed Westminster to reinstate Mr Haywood's monthly payment to its former level, and to pay to him, with interest, the reductions made since February 1993, but that Westminster can set off against its payments the lump sum compensation paid to him under the 1994 regulations. The Pensions

a   Ombudsman has also directed a payment by Westminster to Mr Haywood of
    £1,000—

> 'as compensation for the distress and inconvenience constituting injustice
> beyond pecuniary loss which he has suffered in consequence of
> [Westminster's] maladministration.'

b
ISSUES ON THE APPEAL

Although Miss Slade QC and Mr Bear (for Westminster) put forward no fewer
than nine grounds of appeal in the amended notice of appeal and in their skeleton
argument, there are four main issues of law to which most of the argument has
been addressed. These are as follows.

c   (1) The first jurisdiction issue is whether the Pensions Ombudsman had
jurisdiction to entertain the complaint since the only payments to Mr Haywood
that were reduced (and the subject matter of the only possible misrepresentations
to Mr Haywood) were payments of compensation out of the general rate fund,
not payments out of funds subject to the pension regulations.

d   (2) The second jurisdiction issue is whether the Pensions Ombudsman was
prevented from hearing the complaint by para 3(b) of the Personal and
Occupational Pension Schemes (Pensions Ombudsman) Regulations 1991, SI
1991/588.

(3) If jurisdiction is established, the main issue of law—though it ramifies in
various directions—is whether the Pensions Ombudsman was right to direct
e   Westminster to resume payment to Mr Haywood (as compensation for injustice
in consequence of maladministration) of periodical payments which (on
unchallenged advice to Westminster from two leading counsel) it could not
lawfully pay as compensation for loss of his employment.

(4) A distinct but subsidiary issue of law is whether the Pensions Ombudsman
f   has power to direct a person against whom he has upheld a complaint to pay a
sum as compensation for distress and inconvenience, apart from any demonstrable financial loss.

THE PENSIONS OMBUDSMAN

I will in due course deal with these four issues in turn. But since the jurisdiction
g   and powers of the Pensions Ombudsman are entirely the recent creation of
statute, and since the relevant statutory provisions are not entirely easy to follow
(either in isolation or when compared with other legislation in more or less
similar fields), I think it may be worth starting with a rather general look at the
legislative history and purpose of ombudsmen.

h   The first in the field was of course the Parliamentary Commissioner for
Administration himself, established by the Parliamentary Commissioner Act
1967 at a time when judicial review was a good deal less developed than it is now.
His investigations are limited to action in the exercise of administrative functions
by central government and a variety of statutory bodies, subject to important
j   exceptions, one exception being the existence of a right of appeal, reference or
review. The investigation is into a complaint of 'injustice in consequence of
maladministration'. That is a common factor in all the statutory public sector
jurisdictions and it also applies to the Pensions Ombudsman, though he has a
second string to his bow. There is no appeal from the Parliamentary
Commissioner, though he is subject to judicial review. Nor is there any
machinery for the enforcement of his decisions, which are embodied in reports

to Parliament. The reporting procedure itself is assumed to be an adequate   *a*
means of remedying maladministration.

In the period of nearly 30 years since the 1967 Act many other ombudsmen of
different sorts have appeared. They can be loosely classified under four heads.

(1) There are statutory officials concerned solely with administration or
services in the public sector: the health service commissioners (established by the
National Health Service (Scotland) Act 1972 and the National Health Service   *b*
Reorganisation Act 1973); the local commissioners for administration (estab-
lished by the Local Government Act 1974 and the Local Government (Scotland)
Act 1975); and in Northern Ireland, the Northern Ireland Parliamentary
Commissioner for Administration and the Northern Ireland Commissioner for
Complaints (established by Acts passed in 1969 by the Northern Ireland   *c*
Parliament).

Except in Northern Ireland, the pattern of these ombudsmen's jurisdictions
and powers has followed that of the Parliamentary Commissioner: other legal
remedies have (in general) to be exhausted, there is no right of appeal, and no
machinery for direct enforcement of decisions. The failure by some local
authorities to act on the reports of local commissioners caused concern during   *d*
the 1980s and changes were made by the Local Government and Housing Act
1989; but adverse publicity still remains the final sanction. By an earlier
amendment made in 1978 to s 31 of the Local Government Act 1974, where a
local authority decides that a payment should be made to a person who has
suffered injustice in consequence of maladministration, it has power to incur that
expenditure. That statutory power is of some interest on the ultra vires issue.   *e*

(2) There are statutory officials concerned with administration or services
which, though of public concern, lie wholly or mainly within the private sector:
the Legal Services Ombudsman and the Conveyancing Ombudsman (established
by the Courts and Legal Services Act 1990) and the Pensions Ombudsman
(established by the Social Security Act 1990). The Legal Services Ombudsman   *f*
has the limited function of investigating allegations about the way in which
complaints to lawyers' professional bodies are dealt with: his function is to report
and the ultimate sanction is adverse publicity. However, his recommendations
may include a payment for loss, inconvenience, distress or costs (see the Courts
and Legal Services Act 1990, s 23(2)(d) and (e)).

The Conveyancing Ombudsman has a jurisdiction determined by the   *g*
Conveyancing Ombudsman Scheme. That scheme confers on him power to
require a conveyancing practitioner to pay compensation for loss suffered by, or
inconvenience or distress caused to, any person by any matter under
investigation, though the practitioner complained of may if he chooses decline to
pay and expect adverse publicity instead (see the Courts and Legal Services Act   *h*
1990, Sch 7). There is an appeal by way of case stated to the High Court on a
question of law. I will come back to the Pensions Ombudsman.

(3) Some statutes (dealing with matters in the private sector, but of public
concern) require the establishment of a scheme for dealing with complaints, but
do not create any public office for the person who is to adjudicate on them. An   *j*
example is the provisions of Pt IX of and Schs 12 and 13 to the Building Societies
Act 1986. Permitted matters of complaint are to be prescribed and are not in
terms grounded in maladministration, though that is the general flavour. Under
Sch 12, para 5(1)(a) a scheme must empower the adjudicator to order a building
society to pay to a complainant a sum by way of compensation for loss, expense
or inconvenience. Under s 84(3), (4) and (5) an adjudication is final (except so far

a as a society may be authorised to choose adverse publicity rather than pay compensation) subject to an appeal by way of case stated to the High Court on a question of law.

(4) Finally, there are wholly non-statutory ombudsmen established and paid for by participants in particular industries—such as banking and insurance. Even if recognised by regulatory agencies they have powers derived from contract, not *b* statute, and (unlike, it seems, all the statutory ombudsmen referred to above) they are not susceptible to judicial review (see *R v Insurance Ombudsman, ex p Aegon Life Assurance Ltd* [1995] LRLR 101).

I have thought it worthwhile to make a quick survey of the whole field of ombudsmen because it seems unlikely that Parliament, in enacting s 12 of and Sch 3 to the Social Security Act 1990 (and so creating the office of Pensions *c* Ombudsman), did not have well in mind the general scheme, and to some extent the language, of the provisions creating earlier ombudsmen or comparable adjudicators.

The Social Security Act 1990 inserted a new Pt IVA into the Social Security Pensions Act 1975, and those provisions are now re-enacted as Pt X of the Pension *d* Schemes Act 1993. The most important general features of the Pensions Ombudsman's jurisdiction and powers (which in some respects mirror, but in other respects are in contrast to, those of other statutory ombudsmen) seem to me to be the following (references being to the 1993 Act).

(a) *Scope of jurisdiction*   The Pensions Ombudsman may not only 'investigate and determine any complaint' alleging 'injustice in consequence of mal-*e* administration' (s 146(1)); he may also investigate and determine any dispute of fact or law (s 146(2)). In each case there must be an authorised complainant and the complaint or dispute must fall within the specified field.

(b) *Exhaustion of legal remedies*   There is no such requirement, and existing legal proceedings may be stayed (s 148; cf s 146(6)(a)).

f   (c) *Right of appeal*   There is an appeal (not by way of case stated) on a question of law only; in addition the Pensions Ombudsman may refer any question of law direct to the High Court (s 151(4); s 150(7)).

(d) *Powers on making determination*   The Pensions Ombudsman may on making a determination 'direct the trustees or managers of the scheme concerned to take, or refrain from taking, such steps as he may specify' (s 151(2)). *g* This is at first blush wide language apt to include ordering the payment of money (see *Securities and Investments Board v Pantell SA (No 2)* [1993] 1 All ER 134 at 138, 148–149, [1993] Ch 256 at 271, 284). It is to be noted that by the effect of s 146(4)(a) and reg 2 of the 1991 regulations the Pensions Ombudsman's jurisdiction and powers now extend to employers (in relation to an occupational *h* pension scheme) as they do to trustees and managers.

(e) *Procedure and direct enforcement*   The Pensions Ombudsman has the powers of the county court as regards oral and documentary evidence (s 150) and any determination or direction of his is enforceable as if it were a judgment or order of the county court (s 151(5)).

j   It is, I think, easy to see the general legislative purpose behind these wide provisions, including the Pensions Ombudsman's unusual powers (not shared by other ombudsmen) to decide questions of law and to give directions that are enforceable. A very important part of the legislative purpose was to provide a quick, inexpensive and informal means of settling complaints and disputes about occupational pensions, especially where an individual or a small group of individuals (whether employees or pensioners) find themselves in conflict with

trustees who have large resources and may sometimes (rightly or wrongly) be
thought to be more attentive to the views of the employer than to those of the
employees or pensioners. The provisions relating to disputes on questions of
law, to references of questions of law to the High Court, and to appeals on
questions of law, can be seen as a recognition that however desirable quick,
inexpensive and informal procedures are, complaints and disputes about pension
rights do often raise difficult questions of law as well as questions of fact. The
relevant provisions of primary and subordinate legislation are often lengthy and
obscure, and the same is unfortunately true of many pension schemes' trust
deeds and rules. Countless ill-drafted amending deeds, hurriedly executed in the
late 1970s in an attempt to comply with the complexities of the Social Security
Pensions Act 1975, or in the 1980s in the heat of take-over battles, are out there
somewhere like rusty unexploded land mines. The Pensions Ombudsman's task
in delivering rapid, unlegalistic justice, without cutting too many legal corners, is
a dauntingly difficult one.

As I have said, I think the *general* legislative purpose behind Pt X of the 1993 Act
is reasonably clear. But the statutory provisions raise many difficult questions,
some of which I have to decide. These include the question whether the Pensions
Ombudsman can do whatever he thinks fair (I will not speak of his dispensing
'palm tree justice') regardless of the principles which would guide the court if the
matter had come straight to court. In particular, how does the concept of
maladministration by trustees fit in with the traditional view of their duties, and
their proper performance of them, being determined by the law of fiduciary
obligations? Can the 'steps' open to the Pensions Ombudsman include a
direction to trustees to pay to a complainant benefits greater than those to which
he is entitled under the scheme, because the trustees have made a mistake in
informing him of his entitlement to benefits? Can they include a direction to pay
compensation for distress and inconvenience? I shall have to come back to these
points in the course of considering the four main issues on the appeal.

THE FIRST JURISDICTION ISSUE

To be within the Pensions Ombudsman's jurisdiction a complaint or dispute
must relate to an occupational pension scheme or to some act or omission of the
trustees or managers (or, under reg 2 of the 1991 regulations, the employer) in
their capacity as such. The words 'in connection with' in s 146(1) of the 1993 Act
link the alleged maladministration with some act or omission of the trustees or
managers (or employers) as such. They do not in my judgment loosen the
requirement for the act or omission to be that of the trustees or managers (or
employer) as such.

The expression 'occupational pension scheme' is defined in s 1 of the 1993 Act
as—

'any scheme or arrangement which is comprised in one or more
instruments or agreements and which has, or is capable of having, effect in
relation to one or more descriptions or categories of employments so as to
provide benefits, in the form of pensions or otherwise, payable on
termination of service, or on death or retirement, to or in respect of earners
with qualifying service in an employment of any such description or
category ...'

'Scheme' and 'arrangement' are abstract nouns with a wide and elastic scope. (I
have been shown a number of citations, which I need not list, to that effect.) A

a scheme or arrangement is in this context a legal concept abstracted from one or more written instruments, ranging in formality from Acts of Parliament through statutory instruments, trust deeds and scheduled rules and contracts of employment to circulars or other notices to employees. (If it were relevant to this case I do not think I would accept Miss Slade's submission that an occupational pension scheme could never be found in a simple contract of employment,
b though such a scheme plainly could not secure official approval for contracting-out or tax purposes.)

Miss Slade submits that the scheme of which Mr Haywood was a member was to be found in the Superannuation Act 1972 and the pension regulations, and that Westminster's severance and compensation scheme should be regarded as a separate scheme. She places particular importance on the fact (which is not
c disputed) that payments under the severance and compensation scheme (whether consisting of lump sums or periodical payments) came from Westminster's general rate fund and not from its pension funds, which are held on statutory trusts.

This is a powerful submission but I am not convinced that it must be decisive.
d The question must, I think, be taken in the round. There is at least a distant analogy in the law applicable to family trusts, as to whether a particular state of affairs should be regarded as a single settlement or (whether serially or simultaneously) more than one settlement. In *Roome v Edwards (Inspector of Taxes)* [1981] 1 All ER 736 at 739, [1982] AC 279 at 292–293 Lord Wilberforce said: 'There are a number of obvious indicia which may help to show whether a
e settlement, or a settlement separate from another settlement, exists.' Lord Wilberforce then gave examples of such indicia, but continued:

'There are so many possible combinations of fact that, even where these indicia or some of them are present, the answer may be doubtful, and may depend upon an appreciation of them as a whole. Since "settlement" and
f "trusts" are legal terms, which are also used by business men or laymen in a business or practical sense, I think that the question whether a particular set of facts amounts to a settlement should be approached by asking what a person, with knowledge of the legal context of the word under established doctrine and applying this knowledge in a practical and commonsense
g manner to the facts under examination, would conclude.'

So I think I must try to look at all the relevant facts in a practical manner. The source from which benefits are paid is important but may not be decisive. A scheme which provides for additional voluntary contributions does not thereby automatically have to be regarded as two schemes. It is possible to imagine a
h pension scheme trust deed under which an employer undertakes to make supplementary payments direct to pensioners in certain circumstances. Such a provision might run into difficulties with the Inland Revenue, but practical considerations of that sort must be disregarded in a general inquiry as to the meaning of the definition.

j There are to my mind a number of indications that Westminster's severance and compensation scheme, even though funded in a different way, could and should be regarded as part of the same scheme as the pension scheme (in the stricter sense). The definition in s 1 of the 1993 Act recognises that a scheme may be comprised in more than one instrument. It also contemplates that a scheme will or may provide 'benefits, in the form of pensions or otherwise, payable on termination of service, or on death or retirement'. This treatment of benefits payable on 'termination of service' as potentially different from those payable on 'retirement' suggests that payments of compensation for loss of office are seen as properly within the scope of an occupational pension scheme. The same thought seems to be the explanation of the otherwise puzzling reg 7(2), inserted by amendment in 1993, of the Transfer of Undertakings (Protection of Employment) Regulations 1981, SI 1981/1794.

The statutory authorities for payment of pensions (strictly so called) and for payment of compensation for loss of office were different: s 7 of the Superannuation Act 1972 and the pension regulations on the one hand; s 31 of the 1921 Act (as applied to Westminster, but unfortunately not fully understood or observed by Westminster) on the other hand. But there is no reason to suppose that more than a handful of Westminster's employees or pensioners would have known or cared about this difference (until it came to make a practical difference in a reduction of their monthly receipts). Moreover, s 24 of the Superannuation Act 1972 does enable payments of compensation for loss of office to be authorised by statutory instrument. Section 31 of the 1921 Act could therefore be seen as a local variant of something also found in s 24 of the 1972 Act. It was under s 24 that the 1994 regulations were made and Mr Haywood received a payment as already mentioned.

What to my mind tips a nicely poised balance is that Westminster itself seems, in communicating with its employees and pensioners, to have drawn little or no distinction between the two types of payment. Without (at this stage) going into the disputed finding about 'reassuring advice', I note that pension payments and periodical compensation payments were paid together, being distinguished only by a code number on the payslip; both qualified for index-linking (see s 8 of the Pensions (Increase) Act 1971); and Westminster's letter of 8 February 1993 (intended to break to Mr Haywood the news that he had already heard on television) referred, more than once, to a reduction in his pension.

In the circumstances it is hardly surprising that Mr Haywood made his complaint to the Pensions Ombudsman. The local commissioner for administration would not in any case have had jurisdiction over a local authority's personnel matters. Jurisdiction cannot be conferred by estoppel any more than by consent, but I think that I should construe the Pensions Ombudsman's jurisdiction as broadly as I can, consistently with principle; and I am narrowly persuaded that Westminster fails on the first jurisdiction issue.

THE SECOND JURISDICTION ISSUE

The effect of reg 3(b) of the 1991 regulations (read in conjunction with the definitions of 'complaint' and 'dispute' in reg 1(1)) is that the Pensions Ombudsman has jurisdiction to investigate a complaint (under s 146(1) of the 1993 Act) in relation to a public service pension scheme, but not a dispute (under s 146(2)) in relation to a public service pension scheme.

'Public service pension scheme' is defined in s 1 of the 1993 Act. I think it clear beyond argument that Westminster's pension scheme is within that definition, even on the footing (as I have held) that it includes the severance and compensation arrangements. Mr Arden QC (who appeared with Mr Dymond for the Pensions Ombudsman) argued that the written guidelines about those arrangements prepared by Westminster were 'particulars' not 'set out in, or in a legislative instrument made under, an enactment, Royal warrant or charter'; but guidelines with no mandatory effect cannot be regarded as essential particulars of a scheme.

a   That leaves the more difficult question of the relationship between a complaint of maladministration under s 146(1) and a dispute under s 146(2). There is a considerable degree of overlap between the two subsections. Most complaints of maladministration will involve disputed questions of fact and law (including, it may be, the proper ambit, in a pensions context, of 'maladministration'). That is reflected in the terms of s 150(7) of the 1993 Act.

b   In view of the overlap between the two subsections it is quite surprising to find such a sharp distinction made between them for the purpose of the jurisdiction over public service pension schemes (it has been pointed out to me that a similar though converse distinction is drawn in Sch 1 to the Tribunals and Inquiries Act 1992 in relation to the jurisdiction of the Council on Tribunals: it is to review the work of the Pensions Ombudsman in respect of his function under s 146(2) only).

c   In practice, it is probably only a small minority of individuals who, in approaching the Pensions Ombudsman, specify whether their approach is with a complaint under s 146(1) or a dispute under s 146(2). But in practice the Pensions Ombudsman probably has little difficulty in classifying most approaches as falling naturally under one head or the other; and it seems likely that what he classifies

d   as complaints under s 146(1) easily outnumber what he classifies as disputes under s 146(2). An obvious example of a simple dispute would be where trustees, without adopting or acting on any final view on an issue of fact or law, suggested to a member that it should be referred to the Pensions Ombudsman for decision, and the member agreed to make the reference (as he must under s 146(2)). That dispute might however have turned into a complaint, so as to fall under s 146(1),

e   if the trustees had themselves taken a final view and acted on it in a way which was said to make the complainant sustain injustice in consequence of maladministration.

       Mr Haywood did not actually refer to maladministration in his first letter (dated 1 March 1993) to the Pensions Ombudsman, but he did in his second letter

f   (dated 27 April 1993). In any case, I think the whole tenor of his approach was a complaint of maladministration, and that the Pensions Ombudsman was obviously right to classify it in that way in his letter of 19 December 1994 agreeing to accept the complaint for investigation.

       The only way of making sense of reg 3(b) of the 1991 regulations is, it seems to me, by recognising that this sort of classification has to be made, in practice by the

g   Pensions Ombudsman himself, and that most approaches will be properly classified as complaints even though they raise issues of fact or law. Otherwise the Pensions Ombudsman's jurisdiction over public service pension schemes would be so attenuated as to be derisory (limited, perhaps, to complaints about indisputable rudeness or delay in correspondence).

h   For these reasons Westminster fails on the second jurisdiction issue.

MALADMINISTRATION BY TRUSTEES

       Until the coming into force of the relevant provisions of the Social Security Act 1990 the obligations of pension scheme trustees were founded in the law of trusts

j   (statutory trusts in the case of Westminster and other local authorities holding funds subject to the pension regulations). The general obligation of trustees to comply with the terms of their trust instrument is affected, in the case of private sector pension scheme trustees, by various statutory provisions peculiar to pension schemes, such as Pt IV of the 1993 Act (protection for early leavers). But the effect of those provisions is in general to add to, or modify, the terms that the trustees must comply with rather than imposing new statutory duties on the trustees themselves. That will, however, change with the full coming into force of the Pensions Act 1995. Some of the provisions of Pt IV of the 1993 Act were considered by Carnwath J in *Miller v Stapleton* [1996] 2 All ER 449. That was an appeal from the Pensions Ombudsman (in which, as in this case, he was the only active respondent) and I shall have to come back to it.

Now pension scheme trustees must be regarded as also under a statutory duty not to cause injustice by maladministration. That by itself is not a very startling proposition. Causing injustice by maladministration is plainly a bad thing to do, and any right-minded body of trustees (like Calvin Coolidge's preacher on the subject of sin) must be against it. Although this is the first time that Parliament has in terms imported the concept of maladministration into an area which extends to the private sector, the notion that it is 'concerned with the *manner* in which decisions by the authority are reached and the *manner* in which they are or are not implemented', can quite readily be applied to the duties of trustees of pension schemes whether in the private or (as with Westminster) in the public sector (see *R v Comr for Local Administration, ex p Eastleigh BC* [1988] 3 All ER 151 at 155, [1988] QB 855 at 863; Lord Donaldson MR's emphasis). The decisions which pension scheme trustees have to take and implement (on such matters as application of actuarial surplus, quantum of transfer payments, early retirement for ill-health and so on) have at least as much in common with decisions of official administrators as they have with decisions of trustees of family settlements. Lord Reid's observations about trustees' decision-making in *Dundee General Hospitals Board of Management v Walker* [1952] 1 All ER 896 at 905 are not very far from Lord Greene MR's observations about administrative decision-making in *Associated Provincial Picture Houses Ltd v Wednesbury Corp* [1947] 2 All ER 680 at 682–683, [1948] 1 KB 223 at 229.

What is perhaps more surprising is that, on the first occasion when Parliament has given an ombudsman jurisdiction over private sector activities and has made his determinations and directions enforceable like orders of the county court, it has given so little guidance to the Pensions Ombudsman as to the range and scale of remedies available to him. The provision of means of direct enforcement recognises that in the private sector adverse publicity may on its own be an inadequate sanction (as arguably it has been, on occasions, with local authorities). The steps that the Pensions Ombudsman may direct are not limited to exhortation or censure.

Nevertheless, the Pensions Ombudsman must (except so far as Parliament has clearly given him wider powers) act in accordance with established legal principle. The concept of 'injustice' has been left undefined in the 1993 Act, as in other statutes establishing ombudsmen, no doubt in order not to restrict its scope unduly. But any remedy for injustice must be appropriate and proportional, and not such as to risk creating some new injustice. Even if Parliament has created a new statutory tort of maladministration (which is the view expressed by the present Pensions Ombudsman in a lecture which attracted wide attention last year) it must be borne in mind that remedies for tort have traditionally been concerned either with restraint or with monetary compensation, and exemplary damages are very rare.

I should perhaps add that it was not suggested that on these points I could get any assistance from Hansard under the principle in *Pepper (Inspector of Taxes) v Hart* [1993] 1 All ER 42, [1993] AC 593.

The ultra vires doctrine

a   In her submissions on behalf of Westminster Miss Slade rightly emphasised that local authorities are (apart from a point on royal charters that need not divert me) creatures of statute. They can lawfully do nothing except what has been authorised, expressly or impliedly, by Parliament. Local authorities' powers to make severance or compensation payments on termination of their officers' or
b   workers' employment were reviewed by the Court of Appeal in *Allsop v North Tyneside Metropolitan BC* [1992] ICR 639 as already mentioned. It was after that decision, and after taking legal advice on its significance, that Westminster decided that it must reduce its payments to Mr Haywood and others in the same position. It has not been suggested that Westminster was wrongly advised, or had any alternative to limiting severance and compensation payments to what
c   was authorised by the 1921 Act (or, retrospectively, by the 1994 regulations made under the Superannuation Act 1972).

   Mr Arden did however argue that Westminster, having (as Mr Arden said) misled Mr Haywood about his pension entitlement, must have had power to right the wrong done to him by agreeing, by way of compromise, to pay
d   compensation. In response to this, Miss Slade referred me to what Lord Templeman said in *Hazell v Hammersmith and Fulham London BC* [1991] 1 All ER 545 at 562, [1992] 2 AC 1 at 38. After setting out what Jessel MR said in *Re Norwich Provident Insurance Society, Bath's Case* (1878) 8 Ch D 334 at 340, Lord Templeman went on:

e   'In my opinion it would be a startling proposition that an individual or a corporation may always avoid having resort to litigation by agreeing, by way of compromise, to carry out an unlawful act. The position was made abundantly clear by Warrington J in *Holsworthy UDC v Holsworthy RDC* [1907] 2 Ch 62. He decided that a compromise agreement entered into bona fide by
f   two councils was not rendered invalid by the fact that one of the claims included in the compromise subsequently proved to be unfounded in law. Warrington J said (at 73): "... a compromise, if entered into bona fide, and *if it does not involve the doing of an act by one of the parties which is itself ultra vires*, may be made by and may be binding on a corporation just as on any individual ..." (I have emphasised the important words.)'

g   So here Westminster could not lawfully have agreed, by way of compromise, to pay to Mr Haywood sums which are not authorised by statute, and which are unrelated to compensation for financial loss which might have been awarded as damages by the court. Nor could a similar result be reached by estoppel (see *Rhyl UDC v Rhyl Amusements Ltd* [1959] 1 All ER 257 at 265–266, [1959] 1 WLR 465 at
h   474–475 and *Crédit Suisse v Allerdale BC* [1995] 1 Lloyd's Rep 315 at 356, 367).

The Pensions Ombudsman's decision

   After the second part of the decision setting out the primary facts the Pensions Ombudsman begins the third part (headed 'Conclusions') as follows (para 11):
j
       'An employer entering into an agreement with an employee which is necessarily ultra vires and void as a contract would undoubtedly be guilty of maladministration.'

   I cannot agree. I consider that the Pensions Ombudsman has here made an error of law. It is not necessarily maladministration for a decision-maker to take a

wrong view of the law; as the Privy Council said in *Rowling v Takaro Properties Ltd*
[1988] 1 All ER 163 at 173, [1988] AC 473 at 502—

> 'As is well known, anybody, even a judge, can be capable of misconstruing
> a statute; and such misconstruction, when it occurs, can be severely criticised
> without attracting the epithet "negligent."'

Indeed, in *R v Local Comr for Administration for the North and East Area of England,
ex p Bradford Metropolitan City Council* [1979] 2 All ER 881 at 902, [1979] QB 287 at
317, Eveleigh LJ said that a faulty decision may amount to maladministration, but
that there cannot be a conclusion adverse to the decision-maker based on the
finding of a faulty or wrong decision 'unless the decision was linked to some other
act of maladministration'.

Taking and acting on a wrong view of the law may be maladministration if the
decision-maker knows, or ought to know, that the state of the law is uncertain
and that those who may be adversely affected by the uncertainty need to be
warned about it. That seems to be the point that the Pensions Ombudsman is
making in the rest of para 11 of the decision. But then para 12 begins with the
words, 'However, that is not exactly this case ...' In the course of the hearing of
the appeal various submissions were made about these rather delphic words. I
must say that I do not find it easy to follow the reasoning of the decision at this
point, and Mr Arden accepts that the reference to Westminster 'completely
removing any compensatory element' from the payments to Mr Haywood must
be mistaken.

I do not think that minute analysis of paras 11 and 12 of the decision is helpful
since, as Lord Donaldson MR said in *Ex p Eastleigh BC* [1988] 3 All ER 151 at 157,
[1988] QB 855 at 866, an ombudsman's report is not a statute or a judgment and
ought not to be examined as if it were. I am however driven to the conclusion
that the decision is wrong in law in assuming that any mistake made by a local
authority employer as to the scope of its statutory powers is necessarily
maladministration.

I am also driven to the conclusion that the Pensions Ombudsman has erred in
failing to identify the injustice which he considered Mr Haywood to have suffered
in consequence of maladministration on the part of Westminster; and that this
failure led him to direct Westminster to take steps which could not possibly be
justified as appropriate or proportionate compensation for any injustice suffered.
Reading paras 3 to 7 (inclusive) and 11 of the decision as a whole I think that they
do contain findings that Westminster failed to warn Mr Haywood about doubts
which it should have had (as to the validity of the severance and compensation
scheme which it was then operating) and so gave him misleading or at least
incomplete advice; and that these findings lead to the conclusion that this
amounted to maladministration on the part of Westminster. I do not think it can
be said that these findings and conclusion were perverse or unsupported by any
evidence.

But there is in my judgment a gap in the reasoning of the decision between the
conclusion of maladministration and the compensation directed. Compensation
for negligent misrepresentation (to which the Pensions Ombudsman equated the
maladministration) should put the plaintiff in the same position as if the
informant had performed his duty and provided correct information, not put him
in the position in which he would have been if the incorrect information had been
correct. That basic principle is illustrated in the numerous recent cases on

a negligent property valuations and explains the distinction between 'no-transaction' and 'successful-transaction' situations drawn in those cases (see *Banque Bruxelles Lambert SA v Eagle Star Insurance Co Ltd* [1995] 2 All ER 769 at 840, [1995] QB 375 at 404).

In this case there is no suggestion in the facts found by the Pensions Ombudsman that Mr Haywood suffered any quantifiable pecuniary loss as a result of being misinformed by Westminster. He might, for instance, have
b chosen for his retirement home rented accommodation which he could not afford on his reduced pension, so that he had the expense of moving. There is no suggestion that Mr Haywood (despite the so-called voluntary redundancy scheme) could have kept his job until normal retirement. There is some suggestion in the decision (para 4 of which quotes and presumably accepts Mr
c Haywood's statement that he was 'persuaded that taking premature retirement was the best and safest course of action') that Mr Haywood would have done better in financial terms to have left Westminster's employment just before his fiftieth birthday. But Miss Slade demonstrated convincingly that the financial consequences of Mr Haywood's leaving employment before his fiftieth birthday
d would have been worse.

So on the facts found by the Pensions Ombudsman there was, it seems to me, no pecuniary loss established as injustice sustained by Mr Haywood in consequence of maladministration. In the absence of such loss being established I cannot accept that the remedying of injustice can require, or even be consistent with, the payment to a local authority pensioner of a pension larger than that to
e which he (or any other pensioner in his position) is lawfully entitled, simply because of an error (however culpable) on the part of the local authority. The Pensions Ombudsman has directed such payments either on the strength of a contract or estoppel between Westminster and Mr Haywood, or as compensation for misrepresentation. But for the reasons already stated, neither
f contract, nor estoppel, nor compromise can be a lawful foundation for unlawful payments; nor can the analogy with negligent misrepresentation justify compensation where monetary loss is not established.

COMPENSATION FOR DISTRESS OR INCONVENIENCE

I now come to the last of the four main issues on the appeal; and I do so having
g already come to the conclusion that unless Westminster can be directed to pay compensation to Mr Haywood for the distress and inconvenience which he may have suffered, his successful complaint is going to bring him nothing except the meagre satisfaction of knowing that Westminster has suffered something of a reprimand (and might, I suppose, have been directed to send him a written
h apology). Sometimes an apology is all that a complainant wants, but it is clear that in this case Mr Haywood has been looking for more than that.

This point was considered and tentatively answered by Carnwath J in *Miller v Stapleton* [1996] 2 All ER 449 though he did not have to decide the point, as the appeal succeeded on other grounds. Carnwath J said ([1996] 2 All ER 449 at 465):

j   'The more difficult question is whether the ombudsman has power to direct compensation for distress and inconvenience caused by mal-administration in its ordinary sense, for example rudeness, incompetence, insensitive handling of complaints and so on. The fact that damages for such action would not be available in a court of law is not a sufficient answer. By conferring a power to investigate maladministration, Parliament has implicitly accepted the need to provide a remedy in matters which might not give rise to an action at law.   It is the well-established practice of the Parliamentary Commissioner and the Local Commissioner to make recommendations for the award of compensation for maladministration in that sense.   Although those recommendations are not binding, they are generally accepted by those concerned as an appropriate way of remedying maladministration where it has been found.   Parliament would have been aware of that practice when enacting the 1993 Act or its predecessor. [Counsel for the pensioner] relies on the widely expressed power of the ombudsman to "direct the trustees or managers ... to take ... such steps as he may specify".   It is clear that such "steps" may take the form of the payment of money, for example where it is held that the trustees have failed to make some payment which they were in law obliged to make.   Thus, it is argued, the words are wide enough to cover a payment of monetary compensation for distress.   Furthermore, if maladministration cannot be reflected in a monetary award, it is hard to see what other remedy is available.   The function of investigating maladministration would be rendered nugatory unless it was intended to result in an effective remedy where maladministration is found.   I am reluctant to express a final view on this difficult point, given that it does not in the event arise on the facts. However, I am inclined to agree with the previous ombudsman's view.   The trustees may be directed to "take, or refrain from taking ... steps".   The language, to my mind, naturally implies some pre-existing obligation or right of a specific nature—whether positive or negative—which the ombudsman is empowered to enforce.   Given that, in the law generally, the award of damages for distress or inconvenience is the exception rather than the rule, I would have expected a power to make such an award to have been created by express words.'

It is not clear from the judgment whether Carnwath J was referred to statutory provisions (such as those of s 23 of and Sch 7 to the Courts and Legal Services Act 1990 and Sch 12 to the Building Societies Act 1986) which expressly authorise compensation for distress or inconvenience; or to s 66(4) of the Sex Discrimination Act 1975 (damages for unlawful discrimination may include compensation for injury to feelings)—a provision which is, paradoxically, expressed to be for the avoidance of doubt.

Earlier in his judgment Carnwath J ([1996] 2 All ER 449 at 464) had referred to the decision of the Court of Appeal in *R v Investors Compensation Scheme Ltd, ex p Bowden* [1995] 1 All ER 214, [1995] QB 107.   That decision was not cited to me, probably because it turned on the construction of the detailed definitions in the Financial Services (Compensation of Investors) Rules 1990, the context of which was compensation for financial loss.   I do not think it gives me any guidance as to the construction of the 1993 Act.

So Carnwath J noted the practice of other ombudsmen in making unenforceable recommendations, which Parliament would have been aware of.   He also noted that if monetary compensation cannot be awarded for non-monetary injustice such as distress and inconvenience, many complainants might be left without an effective remedy and the Pensions Ombudsman's function would be frustrated.

Those are to my mind formidable arguments.   Against them must be set the linguistic argument (why did not Parliament say it expressly?) and a practical a argument which Carnwath J then went on to consider (whose pocket is the compensation going to come out of?).

The linguistic argument carries some weight, but I do not think it can be decisive. Styles of drafting change over the years, even in statutory drafting. As Lord Wilberforce said (in a dissenting opinion but a comparable context) in *Mangin v IRC* [1971] 1 All ER 179 at 189, [1971] AC 739 at 755, 'an anonymous

b draftsman's hypothetical belief as to tautology can hardly make a canon of construction'.

The practical argument as to who ultimately bears the cost of the compensation may seem to carry less weight in the case of a large local authority like Westminster, but it calls for consideration as bearing on Parliament's likely intention in the generality of cases. *Miller v Stapleton* [1996] 2 All ER 449 was

c concerned with a pension scheme where a share of the fund had to be (in effect) wound up: there were to be no more employer's contributions, and the share of the fund was insufficient to meet all the claims of the pensioners and members. Had compensation been payable, it would (as the Pensions Ombudsman and Carnwath J both accepted) have come out of the inadequate share of the pension

d fund and not out of the individual trustees' own pockets. In those circumstances Carnwath J's reference to 'robbing Peter to pay Paul' was apposite (see [1996] 2 All ER 449 at 466). Rudyard Kipling wrote of 'robbing selected Peter to pay for collective Paul'. This would be the other way round: robbing collective (and uncomplaining) Peter to pay off selected (and complaining) Paul. With a solvent private sector scheme and a solvent employer, on the other hand, the burden of

e any compensation directed by the Pensions Ombudsman would be likely to fall ultimately on the employer, who would usually have covenanted to pay the balance of the overall cost of the scheme. That may do rough justice in most cases.

In deciding what level of compensation to direct the Pensions Ombudsman

f will undoubtedly be anxious not to remedy one injustice by creating another, and the ultimate burden of any compensation directed must therefore be a relevant consideration for him in considering the facts revealed by any particular investigation. But in the end I am not persuaded that either the linguistic argument or this practical argument is strong enough to overcome my strong inclination to construe what the 1993 Act says about the Pensions Ombudsman's

g powers in such a way as to effectuate, rather than frustrate, what I take to be the legislative purpose. I am naturally diffident about taking a view contrary to even the tentative view of Carnwath J, whose experience of Crown Office work is much greater than mine, but I have to come to the conclusion that the steps which the Pensions Ombudsman may direct under s 151(2) of the 1993 Act

h include the payment of reasonable compensation for distress and inconvenience.

Miss Slade's final argument was that the amount directed by the Pensions Ombudsman as compensation under this head (£1,000) was so high as to be perverse, unreasonable and wrong in law. I am inclined to think that the award was on the high side. I think it important that the Pensions Ombudsman should

j have in mind that responsible trustees and employers may feel (after a successful complaint against them) that they should consider doing the same (if they lawfully can, as to which I express no view) for any other pensioners or employees who are in similar circumstances, but have not complained to the Pensions Ombudsman. It would be unfortunate if an investigation by the Pensions Ombudsman produced much worse consequences for responsible and conscientious trustees and employers than for those who are less responsible and conscientious. Nevertheless, I am not persuaded that to pay £1,000 (roughly a month's national average earnings) to an ex-employee with 24 years' service who is found to have sustained injustice, is so excessive as to be wrong in law.

CONCLUSIONS

My conclusions are therefore as follows. (1) Westminster fails on the first jurisdiction issue (meaning of 'occupational pension scheme'). (2) Westminster fails on the second jurisdiction issue (limited jurisdiction over public service pension schemes). (3) Westminster's appeal succeeds on the main substantive issue, and I will set aside the part of the decision (embodied in para 14) directing the reduced monthly payments to Mr Haywood to be restored to their former level. (4) Westminster's appeal fails as to the part of the decision (embodied in para 15) directing a payment to Mr Haywood of £1,000 in respect of distress and inconvenience.

Appeal allowed in part.

K Mydeen Esq   Barrister.

a # Glengate-KG Properties Ltd v Norwich Union Fire Insurance Society Ltd and others

COURT OF APPEAL, CIVIL DIVISION

b NEILL, AULD LJJ AND SIR IAIN GLIDEWELL

30, 31 OCTOBER, 1 NOVEMBER, 21 DECEMBER 1995

Insurance – All risks insurance – Consequential loss policy – Construction – Policy covering loss of anticipated rent arising from damage to property used by insured property
c *developers for purposes of business – Policy containing material damage proviso requiring insurance of insured's interest in the property – Fire destroying site office and architects' drawings – Resulting delay in completion of project and loss of rental income – Whether loss arising from damage to property used by insured for purposes of its business – Whether insured having an insurable interest in drawings – Whether proviso operating to exclude indemnity.*
d

In March 1985 the plaintiff property developer took out a consequential loss policy with the defendant insurer for the purposes of a redevelopment project. Under the policy the insurer agreed to indemnify the insured for loss of anticipated rent if 'any building or other property or any part thereof used by the
e Insured at the premises ... for the purpose of the Business' suffered damage other than by excluded cause. The insurance effected by the policy was subject to a material damage proviso, which stipulated that, at the time of any damage, 'there shall be in force ... insurance covering the interest of the Insured in the property at the Premises against such Damage'. In September 1995 a fire on the site destroyed the temporary office in which the architects for the development had
f been working and a large number of documents, including the architects' work-in-progress drawings, which were not insured. As a result, the architects had to reconstruct many drawings and the development was delayed by 22 weeks, causing the plaintiff to suffer a substantial loss of rental income. The plaintiff's subsequent claim under the policy was declined by the insurer.
g Thereafter, the plaintiff commenced proceedings against the insurer and the firm of brokers which had placed the insurance. The judge held, in favour of the plaintiff, that (i) the architects' drawings constituted property used by the plaintiff at the premises for the purposes of its business within the meaning of the policy, and (ii) while the drawings had not been insured, the plaintiff had no insurable interest in them under the material damage proviso. The defendants
h appealed and the plaintiff cross-appealed.

Held – The appeal and cross-appeal would be dismissed for the following reasons—

(1) In the case of an insured property development company which carried
j out its business mainly by the employment of independent contractors who designed and constructed the buildings, the words 'property used by the insured at the premises' in a consequential loss policy could not properly be restricted to property owned by the developer or physically in its possession. Accordingly, the architects' drawings, which formed an integral part of the development, constituted property used by the plaintiff at the premises for the purposes of its

business within the meaning of the policy (see p 495 *d* to *g*, p 500 *j* to p 501 *a* and
p 503 *b*, post).

(2) (Sir Iain Glidewell dissenting) On its true construction, the phrase 'the
interest of the insured in the property' in a material damage proviso did not cover
an insurable interest which was not a personal property interest of the insured.
In the context of insurance, the word 'interest' could mean any insurable interest
in a broad sense, such as a contractual right in respect of insured goods which
would be affected if the goods were lost or damaged, or an insurable interest of
a more limited kind; it depended on the particular context. In the circumstances,
the reference to 'interest' in the proviso was a reference to an interest in the
narrower sense, and the plaintiff had no such interest in the architects' drawings,
even though it might have a licence to use the designs and might one day have
acquired the property in the drawings. At the time of the fire, the drawings were
clearly the property of the architects and it was their responsibility to replace
them if destroyed. The plaintiff was therefore under no obligation to insure the
drawings itself. The judge was accordingly correct in finding that the material
damage proviso did not operate to exclude indemnity (see p 497 *g*, p 498 *b* to *d*,
p 499 *b* to *d* and p 500 *j* to p 501 *a*, post); *Petrofina (UK) Ltd v Magnaload Ltd* [1983]
3 All ER 35 applied.

Notes
For consequential loss insurance generally, see 25 *Halsbury's Laws* (4th edn
reissue) para 785.

Cases referred to in judgments
Anderson v Morice (1876) 1 App Cas 713, HL; *affg* (1875) LR 10 CP 609, Ex Ch.
Beacon Carpets Ltd v Kirby [1984] 2 All ER 726, [1985] QB 755, [1984] 3 WLR 489,
  CA.
Constitution Insurance Co of Canada v Kosmopoulos (1987) 34 DLR (4th) 208, Can
  SC.
Goulstone v Royal Insurance Co (1858) 1 F & F 276, 175 ER 725.
Lucena v Craufurd (1806) 2 Bos & PNR 269, 127 ER 630, HL.
Macaura v Northern Assurance Co Ltd [1925] AC 619, [1925] All ER Rep 51, HL.
Mumford Hotels Ltd v Wheler [1963] 3 All ER 250, [1964] Ch 117, [1963] 3 WLR 735.
National Oilwell (UK) Ltd v Davy Offshore Ltd [1993] 2 Lloyd's Rep 582.
Petrofina (UK) Ltd v Magnaload Ltd [1983] 3 All ER 35, [1984] QB 127, [1983] 3 WLR
  805.
Rowlands (Mark) Ltd v Berni Inns Ltd [1985] 3 All ER 473, [1986] QB 211, [1985] 3
  WLR 964, CA.
Stone Vickers Ltd v Appledore Ferguson Shipbuilders Ltd [1991] 2 Lloyd's Rep 288; *rvsd*
  [1992] 2 Lloyd's Rep 578, CA.
Sharp v Sphere Drake Insurance plc, The Moonacre [1992] 2 Lloyd's Rep 501.
Waters v Monarch Fire and Life Assurance Co (1856) 5 E & B 870, [1843–60] All ER
  Rep 654, 119 ER 705.

Cases also cited or referred to in skeleton arguments
Anderson v Commercial Union Assurance Co (1885) 55 LJ QB 146, CA.
Blair v Alan S Tomkins and Frank Osborne (t/a Osborne & Tomkins (a firm)) [1971] 1
  All ER 468, [1971] 2 QB 78, CA.
Gibbon v Pease [1905] 1 KB 810, [1904–7] All ER Rep 454, CA.

a   *King (decd), Re, Robinson v Gray* [1963] 1 All ER 781, [1963] Ch 459, CA.
    Lek v Mathews (1927) 29 Ll L Rep 141, HL.
    Lonsdale & Thompson Ltd v Black Arrow Group plc [1993] 3 All ER 648, [1993] Ch 361.
    McLean Enterprises Ltd v Ecclesiastical Insurance Office plc [1986] 2 Lloyd's Rep 416.
    Margaronis Navigation Agency Ltd v Henry W Peabody & Co of London Ltd [1964] 3
b   All ER 333, [1965] 2 QB 430, CA.
    Pleasurama Ltd v Sun Alliance and London Insurance Ltd [1979] 1 Lloyd's Rep 389.
    Quicke's Trusts, Re, Poltimore v Quicke [1908] 1 Ch 887.
    Reynolds v Phoenix Assurance Co Ltd [1978] 2 Lloyd's Rep 440.
    Simpson v Scottish Union Insurance Co (1863) 1 H & M 618, 71 ER 270.

c
Appeal and cross-appeal

By notices dated 12 August and 28 September 1994 respectively the first defendant, Norwich Union Fire Insurance Society Ltd (Norwich Union), and the third defendant, Lowndes Lambert UK Ltd (Lowndes), appealed from the order of Phillips J ([1995] 1 Lloyd's Rep 278) made on 7 July 1994 and revised on 2
d   February 1995, whereby he determined in favour of the plaintiff, Glengate-KG Properties Ltd (Glengate), several questions of construction of a consequential loss policy No 85A35008 entered into between the parties in 1985, the effect of which was that Glengate was entitled to recover for consequential loss suffered as a result of a fire under the policy. By notice dated 6 October 1994 Glengate
e   cross-appealed, seeking affirmation of the decision of Phillips J on additional grounds. The second defendant, Scottish Union and National Insurance Co, was dismissed from the action before the hearing of the appeal. The facts are set out in the judgment of Neill LJ.

Roger Ter Haar QC and *James Holdsworth* (instructed by *Greenwoods*) for Norwich
f   Union.
Jeremy Cooke QC and *Dominic Kendrick* (instructed by *Cameron Markby Hewitt*) for Lowndes.
Charles Falconer QC and *Andrew Moran* (instructed by *Berwin Leighton*) for Glengate.

g
Cur adv vult

21 December 1995. The following judgments were delivered.

NEILL LJ.
h   *Introduction*
    This appeal raises questions as to the proper construction of three clauses in a consequential loss policy effected by Glengate-KG Properties Ltd (Glengate) with Norwich Union Fire Insurance Society Ltd (Norwich Union). At least one of the questions is of some general importance.
j   Glengate is the plaintiff in the action. Norwich Union is the first defendant. The second defendant (another insurance company) has been dismissed from the action. Lowndes Lambert UK Ltd (Lowndes), the third defendant, was the broker who placed the insurance.
    The appeal comes before the court in somewhat unusual circumstances. As Phillips J ([1995] 1 Lloyd's Rep 278) explained in his judgment dated 7 July 1994,

when the action was set down for trial it was intended that there would be a single trial of all issues relating to liability. By the time that the trial date was reached, however, it had become apparent that the time allocated for the trial would not be adequate. It was therefore agreed that the judge should use the time available to resolve issues of construction that arose on the pleadings. In the end the judge resolved additional issues which had not been pleaded.

The trial of the issues took place in February 1994. At the hearing the only oral evidence called was that of an expert witness called by Glengate and an expert witness called by Lowndes. These witnesses gave evidence as to market practice. The only other evidence was that contained in the bundles of documents.

At the conclusion of the hearing the judge prepared a draft judgment. In the course of his preparation of his judgment, the judge 'was attracted by an approach to one of the issues of construction which had not been advanced in argument'. The judge therefore invited further argument on the draft judgment which he had prepared. The final judgment was handed down in July 1994. By the order dated 7 July 1994 it was ordered that the draft judgment should be handed down, that Glengate's action against Norwich Union on quantum should be transferred to the Official Referee, and that leave should be granted to Lowndes to reamend their defence.

The matter came back before Phillips J again on 2 February 1995. By the judgment dated 2 February 1995 it was recorded that the parties had agreed that the previous order dated 7 July 1994 should be revised to the extent set out in the judgment. The judgment then contained declarations and orders on the eight issues of construction identified in the judgment. The judgment further recorded the basis upon which the issues of construction had been determined. It was stated that the issues of construction had been 'addressed on the premise and assumption that the facts derived from the documents before the court were correct, with (a) the plaintiffs being at liberty to adduce evidence to establish those facts at a further hearing, (b) the defendants being at liberty to challenge them, and (c) the later tribunal not being bound by the summary contained in the judgment herein'.

For the purposes of this judgment it is not necessary to refer further to the eight issues identified in the order dated 2 February 1995. Only three issues were argued in this court and it is important to emphasise that they were argued on assumed facts. Before turning to consider the three issues therefore I should first refer to the relevant documents and set out the assumed facts.

The insurance policies

In or about March 1985 Glengate purchased the former Bourne & Hollingsworth department store building in Oxford Street, London with a view to redeveloping it into a complex of offices and retail outlets to be known as The Plaza. For the purpose of the redevelopment, Glengate took out two policies of insurance with Norwich Union. These two policies took effect on 4 September 1985. The first policy was a material damage policy (No 85A35007). The second policy was a consequential loss policy (No 85A35008). It would have been possible for Glengate to have obtained the same cover under a single policy because the two policies were in the same form and were both entitled 'All Risks Insurance Policy' and were described as covering both material damage and/or consequential loss. In both policies section 1 related to material damage and section 2 related to consequential loss.

a In the present case we are concerned with the consequential loss policy, but nevertheless I must make some reference to the material damage policy and the provisions relating to section 1 cover.

By section 1 of the material damage policy Norwich Union agreed, subject to the terms, additions and exclusions specified, that if during the currency of the policy—

b
'any of the property insured described in the Schedule hereto be accidentally lost, destroyed or damaged (accidental loss, destruction or damage being hereinafter termed Damage) other than by an excluded cause, [it would] pay to the Insured the value of the property at the time of the Damage or, at its option, reinstate or replace such property or any part
c thereof, in accordance with the provisions contained in Section 1 of the specification forming part of the Schedule ...'

The material damage policy, however, contained a number of exclusion clauses. In particular exclusion 9 excluded—

d 'Damage to (a) goods held in trust or on commission, documents, manuscripts, business books, computer systems records, patterns, models, moulds, plans, designs, explosives, unless specifically mentioned as insured by this Section ... (d) property or structures in course of construction or erection and materials or supplies in connection with all such property in course of construction or erection ...'
e
In the specification to the policy, the property insured was defined. 'Item No. 1' was defined as the existing building as at the commencement of the refurbishment. 'Item No. 2' was defined as 'Extensions, additions and alterations for which the Insured are responsible to the above existing building but not such
f existing building itself'.

Attached to the policy were some typed memoranda. Memorandum 2 provided:

'The insurance by Item No 2 of this policy extends to include so far as the same are not otherwise insured temporary erections, plant, equipment,
g tools and materials (including printed books, unused stationery, plans and designs and other contents of temporary offices) the property of the Insured or for which he is (they are) responsible at the site of the aforesaid building(s) and used in connection therewith. The liability of the Company under this Memorandum and the policy in respect of any item shall in no case exceed
h the sum insured by such item.'

I can turn next to the consequential loss policy.

By the consequential loss policy Norwich Union agreed, subject to the terms conditions and exclusions specified, that if during the currency of the policy—

j 'any building or other property or any part thereof used by the Insured at the premises described in the Schedule hereto for the purpose of the Business suffers Damage other than by an excluded cause, [it would] pay to the Insured the amount of loss resulting from interruption of or interference with the Business carried on by the Insured at the Premises in consequence of the Damage (such loss being hereinafter termed Consequential Loss) in accordance with the provisions contained in Section 2 of the specification forming part of the Schedule ...'

In the appendix to the policy, the item insured was defined as being the anticipated rent which was stated to be £10,950,000. The maximum indemnity period was stated to be 36 months. It will be convenient to return later to set out the average clause relating to the loss of anticipated rent.

The insurance effected by the consequential loss policy was, however, subject to two provisos. Proviso (2) was in these terms:

'In respect of the insurance under Section 2, at the time of the happening of the Damage there shall be in force, under Section 1 or otherwise, an insurance covering the interest of the Insured in the property at the Premises against such Damage and that (i) payment shall have been made or liability admitted therefor, or (ii) payments would have been made or liability would have been admitted therefor but for the operation of a proviso in such insurance excluding liability for losses below a specified amount.'

I come next to the events which gave rise to the present proceedings.

The assumed facts

The purchase of the Bourne & Hollingsworth store by Glengate received some publicity. As a result, the architects who had been responsible for the original building and for a number of subsequent additions wrote to Glengate to say that apart from their own drawings they had retained all the original structural drawings dating from 1921. Discussions then followed, and in May 1985 Glengate bought the portfolio of record drawings for £15,000. The purchase of the record drawings was a substantial benefit to Glengate because it enabled the development to proceed without much of the preliminary survey work which would otherwise have been necessary.

Archer Boxer Partners were appointed the architects for the development.

Glengate wished the development to proceed with as little delay as possible. It was therefore agreed that a temporary office should be established on the first floor of the redevelopment which could be used by the architects as well as by the other professional advisers who were involved. It was thought that if the architects and the other professional teams worked together in one office co-operation between the various disciplines would be facilitated and the copying of documents could be greatly reduced. On 4 June 1985 the architects wrote to Glengate to inform them that they would be moving into the 'team base' in time for work to commence on Monday, 10 June 1985. The writer added: 'As we shall be taking all record drawings with us, we shall, as agreed, retain a print copy of each at our Hatfield office.'

During the next three months the architects and others carried out a great deal of design work in the office which formed the team base. In the course of this work a large number of drawings and other documents were created. On Saturday evening, 7 September 1985, however, a serious fire broke out at the Bourne & Hollingsworth site. The vast majority of the drawings in the architects' office at the team base were destroyed in the fire, as was much of the temporary office itself. The destroyed drawings were of two classes: (a) the record drawings, and (b) the drawings prepared by the architects during the previous few months (the architects' drawings). Copies of the record drawings had been retained at Hatfield. Save, however, for some copies of drawings which a had already been sent to Glengate, the architects' drawings and any copies which had been made of them for use at the team base were destroyed in the fire.

The destruction of the architects' drawings led to inevitable delay. Glengate assert that the redevelopment was set back by 22 weeks and that most of this delay was caused by the need to redraw the architects' drawings. As a result of the delay in the completion of the redevelopment there was a very substantial
b loss of rental income.

Following the fire it came to light that, though the architects had insured their drawing boards and other equipment, the work in progress had not been insured. It seems that this was due to an oversight by the broker instructed by the architects. Glengate then made a claim against Norwich Union under the consequential loss policy. The claim was disputed and Glengate brought
c proceedings. In these proceedings, which were commenced by a writ issued from the Admiralty and Commercial Registry of the High Court on 20 March 1991, Glengate also claimed damages against Lowndes for failing to effect the necessary insurances.

d *The hearing before the judge*

In the course of his judgment handed down on 7 July 1994, Phillips J considered four main issues: (a) whether the drawings were 'property used by the insured at the premises for the purpose of the business'; (b) whether there was any insurance in force covering the drawings; (c) the construction of proviso (2) in the consequential loss policy; and (d) the construction of the average
e clause.

On the first issue the judge recorded that it was not until the first day of the trial that Norwich Union made it plain that they denied that the architects' drawings constituted property 'used by the insured at the premises for the purpose of the business' within the meaning of the consequential loss policy.
f The point had not been pleaded nor was it suggested in the skeleton argument lodged on behalf of Norwich Union. In these circumstances the judge agreed to deal with the issue but dealt with it on assumed facts and on the basis that the facts set out in the documents were correct.

The judge decided this issue in favour of Glengate. He said ([1995] 1 Lloyd's Rep 278 at 283):
g

'Those contractors were using the design centre for the purpose of the business just as they were using the drawings in the design centre. In my judgment the property being used by the independent contractors at the premises for the purpose of the development constituted, on a true
h construction of the policy, "property being used by the Insured for the purposes of the business" whether owned by the plaintiffs or not. Insofar as the professional consultants were referring to the drawings in order to perform their contractual duties in relation to the development, the drawings fell within the scope of the business interruption cover.'

j On the second issue the judge held that there was no insurance in force covering the drawings at the time of the fire. It is to be noted that the fire occurred during the initial period of cover between 4 September 1985 and 12 August 1986.

In their respondent's notice Lowndes seek to contend that there was no evidence that the architects had not taken out material damage insurance on

their drawings. We declined, however, to consider this issue. The final order
dated 2 February 1995 made it clear that questions of fact could be the subject of
further evidence to be considered at a subsequent hearing. As I have already
stated, the judge's decision was based on assumed facts. Accordingly, I do not
propose to say any more about this issue.

The third issue before the judge was the construction of what he described in
his judgment as the 'material damage proviso'. I can summarise his conclusions
as follows.

(a) *The record drawings* Glengate had a proprietary interest in these drawings
which they could have insured. In the context of the sum insured under the
material damage policy (£25,000,000), the value of the record drawings (about
£15,000) was without significance. The judge said (at 287):

'I have no doubt that the "de minimis" principle applies so as to prevent
the first defendants from successfully contending that the absence of
insurance against material damage to the record drawings invalidated the
business interruption cover.'

(b) *The architects' drawings* The judge concluded that none of the matters
relied upon by Norwich Union or Lowndes gave Glengate an interest in the
architects' drawings which they were required to insure under the material
damage proviso. He pointed out that the drawings were owned by the architects
and remained in their possession. They formed part of the architects' work in
progress which would normally have been insured by the architects. He
concluded (at 287):

'They did not form part of the property on the insured premises in which
the plaintiffs had a personal interest and in respect of which the proviso
required that there should be in existence material damage cover.'

The fourth issue related to the construction of the average clause. It will be
convenient if I consider the judge's decision on this issue at the end of this
judgment when I have set out the material parts of the policy.

I turn therefore to the first of the issues which were argued on the appeal.

Were the architects' drawings 'property used by the insured'?

It is clear that the consequential loss provisions in the policy only came into
effect if damage was suffered by 'property or any part thereof used by the Insured
at the premises ... for the purpose of the Business'. It was argued on behalf of
Norwich Union that the architects' drawings, save for a comparatively small
number, did not fall into this category.

Some months after the fire, the architects wrote to Glengate on 12 November
1986 to explain what had happened to the drawings. They wrote:

'At the time of the fire, some 1–100 scale scheme and general arrangement
drawings had been issued, and therefore retrievable, and subsequently
retraceable. All other drawings being worked up, together with survey
sketches, notes, schedules, etc were irretrievably lost, which effectively
meant that we had to start from scratch.'

Norwich Union accepted that copies of the drawings which had been issued to
Glengate were capable of being used by Glengate for the purpose of their
business. But the great majority of the destroyed drawings did not fall into this

a   category. Some of the unissued drawings were still in an unfinished state and some of the sketches might never have been used in the development at any stage. Indeed Glengate might have disapproved of some sketched designs.

Many of the unissued drawings and sketches were being used by the architects alone. Some were also being used by other independent contractors, such as the engineers. The property in the unissued drawings was vested in the architects. *b*   In addition, as was made clear by cl 3.15 of the Royal Institute of British Architects (RIBA) Conditions of Engagements, the architects had reserved the copyright in the drawings and designs, though they granted a licence to Glengate to reproduce the designs after completion of work stage D of the contract between the architects and Glengate.

c   Counsel for Norwich Union drew attention to memorandum 2 of the material damage policy, which I have already set out. In this memorandum reference was made to 'the property of the Insured or for which he is ... responsible at the site'. He submitted that the architects' work in progress was not the property of Glengate, nor was the company responsible for it. At the stage when the drawings were still 'work in progress', the purpose for which they were being *d*   used was to enable the architects to carry out their contractual responsibilities.

In my judgment, however, it is important to remember, as counsel for Glengate pointed out, that Glengate is a property development company. It therefore carries out its business mainly by the employment of independent contractors who design and construct the buildings. It follows that in the context the words *e*   'property used by the insured at the premises' cannot properly be restricted to property owned by the developer or physically in the possession of the developer. The temporary office was constructed on the site so that all the professional consultants could work together to prepare their individual parts of the development. The drawings and sketches formed an integral part of that development. But Glengate were the developers.

f   In my opinion, any other construction would lead to absurd results. It would be necessary to consider each individual drawing to see whether it had been issued and whether any member of Glengate's own staff had made use of it at the premises. I am satisfied that the judge's approach was correct. In my judgment, the architects' drawings which were destroyed in the fire constituted property *g*   used by Glengate at the premises for the purpose of the business within the meaning of the consequential loss policy.

I turn therefore to the issues which relate to proviso (2), which the judge called the material damage proviso.

h   *The material damage proviso*

It will be convenient to repeat the material words of the proviso:

> 'In respect of the insurance under Section 2, at the time of the happening of the Damage there shall be in force, under Section 1 or otherwise, an insurance covering the interest of the Insured in the property at the Premises *j*   against such Damage ...'

Two issues arise relating to this proviso: (a) the effect of the fact that the record drawings were not insured by Glengate; (b) whether Glengate had an 'interest' in the architects' drawings within the meaning of the proviso.

I propose to deal with these issues in turn.

It will be remembered that on the first of these issues the judge held that the
de minimis principle applied so as to prevent Norwich Union from successfully
contending that the absence of insurance against material damage to the record
drawings invalidated the business interruption cover. He drew attention to the
fact that the sum insured under the material damage policy was £25,000,000,
whereas the value of the record drawings was, in his words, 'without
significance'. The record drawings had cost Glengate £15,000, but they had been
copied and the information was preserved at Hatfield.

It was argued on behalf of Norwich Union that the judge was in error in
applying the de minimis principle. It was said that the question was not whether
the original cost of buying the drawings was de minimis but whether the cost of
replacing them was de minimis. To replace the record drawings would have
required a fresh survey of the building and then further drawing. It was not to
the point that there was a spare set of drawings in the architects' offices at
Hatfield. Moreover, it was a condition of the policy that there should be in
existence an insurance covering the interest of the insured in any property at the
premises. Norwich Union were entitled to rely on the warranty that all the
conditions on the policy would be observed.

I consider that in the circumstances of the present case the judge was entitled
to apply the de minimis principle. But I would prefer to decide this issue on the
alternative argument advanced on behalf of Glengate to the effect that on its true
construction the proviso was concerned with the 'property' which caused the
consequential loss. Following the fire, 285 drawings had to be redrawn. These
were, however, the architects' drawings. They did not include the record
drawings. There was no material delay which flowed from the destruction of the
originals of the record drawings.

If Glengate had made a claim based on the destruction of the originals of the
record drawings, the proviso would have barred that claim. But the relevant
damage was that suffered by the architects' drawings.

I come therefore to the most difficult problem in this case.

The question for decision can be stated very shortly. Did Glengate have 'an
interest' in the architects' drawings within the meaning of the proviso? The
judge held that they did not. He said ([1995] 1 Lloyd's Rep 278 at 287):

> 'The drawings fell within the ambit of responsibility of the architects, not
> of the plaintiffs. They did not form part of the property on the insured
> premises in which the plaintiffs had a personal interest and in respect of
> which the proviso required that there should be in existence material
> damage cover.'

It was argued in support of the appeal that in the context the word 'interest' in
the proviso meant an insurable interest and that Glengate clearly had an
insurable interest in the architects' drawings. The argument was developed on
the following lines.

(1) The word 'interest' occurred in an insurance policy and accordingly the
natural meaning of 'interest' was 'insurable interest'.

(2) The classic definition of 'insurable interest' was that given by Lawrence J
in *Lucena v Craufurd* (1806) 2 Bos & PNR 269 at 302, 127 ER 630 at 643, where he
said:

> 'A man is interested in a thing to whom advantage may arise or prejudice
> happen from the circumstances which may attend it ... And whom it

a   importeth, that its condition as to safety or other quality should continue ...
To be interested in the preservation of a thing, is to be so circumstanced
with respect to it as to have benefit from its existence, prejudice from its
destruction.'

b   This definition was cited with approval by Kerr LJ in *Mark Rowlands Ltd v Berni Inns Ltd* [1985] 3 All ER 473 at 481, [1986] QB 211 at 228.

(3) In addition, Glengate had a right 'derivable out of' a contract relating to
the architects' drawings. We were referred to a passage in the speech of Lord
Eldon in *Lucena v Craufurd* 2 Bos & PNR 269 at 321, 127 ER 630 at 650, which is
cited in *McGillivray and Parkington on Insurance Law* (8th edn, 1988) para 116.
Glengate had an implied licence to use the designs represented by the drawings
c   and the property in the drawings (though not the copyright) would have passed
to Glengate after the completion of the project.

(4) By cl 4.37 of the RIBA Standard Terms of Appointment, which formed
part of the contract between Glengate and the architects, the risk of damage to
the drawings fell upon Glengate. So far as relevant, cl 4.37 provided:

d   'Where the architect is involved in extra work and expense for reasons
beyond the architect's control and for which the architect would not
otherwise be remunerated additional fees are due. Any of the following is
likely to involve the architect in extra work and expense ... (d) Any other
cause beyond the architect's control.'

e   It followed that the cost of redrawing the plans and other documents
destroyed in the fire fell on Glengate.

(5) The position of Glengate was similar to that of a tenant with only a limited
interest in a building. In such a case the financial value of the tenant's property
interest in the building may be quite small but he has an interest in having the full
f   reinstatement of the premises.

(6) In any event, Norwich Union were entitled to have an assurance that any
property, damage to which might have an impact on the risk covered by the
consequential loss policy, was properly insured.

These are formidable arguments, but I have come to the conclusion that the
g   judge was right.

It is well established that a landlord can insure premises to cover not only his
own interest but the interests of his tenants. A tenant can therefore insist on the
reinstatement of the insured property (see *Mumford Hotels Ltd v Wheler* [1963] 3
All ER 250, [1964] Ch 117). In the same way a bailee can insure goods in his
h   possession for their full value, holding the proceeds of the insurance in trust for
the owner of the goods. And there are other cases where the person who has
effected the insurance and recovers more than the value of his own interest will
be obliged to hold the balance in trust for the other interests represented.

In *Petrofina (UK) Ltd v Magnaload Ltd* [1983] 3 All ER 35, [1984] QB 127 Lloyd J
j   considered the question of insurance in the context of a building or engineering
contract where numerous different sub-contractors might be engaged. He said
([1983] 3 All ER 35 at 42, [1984] QB 127 at 136):

'I would hold that a head contractor ought to be able to insure the entire
contract works in his own name and the name of all his sub-contractors, just
like a bailee or mortgagee, and that a sub-contractor ought to be able to

recover the whole of the loss insured, holding the excess over his own
interest in trust for the others.'   *a*

In the course of the hearing we were referred to a number of cases which
demonstrated that a person may have an 'insurable interest' in property even
though he is not the owner. Persons having such an insurable interest include
not only those persons to whom I have already referred but also persons having
a contractual licence to use property, and pledgees.   *b*

But these cases and others clearly show that the word 'interest' in the context
of insurance can have more than one meaning. It can mean *any* 'insurable
interest' in the wide sense explained by Lawrence J in *Lucena v Craufurd* in the
passage I have cited. But it can also mean an insurable interest of a more limited
kind. It depends on the context. In this case the judge came to the conclusion   *c*
that as the architects' drawings were not property in which Glengate had a
personal interest, the proviso did not apply.

I can refer again to *Petrofina*. In that case Lloyd J, when referring to 'the excess
over his own interest', was referring to 'interest' in the more limited sense.

The point is well illustrated in the landlord and tenant cases. For example, in   *d*
Beacon Carpets Ltd v Kirby [1984] 2 All ER 726, [1985] QB 755 warehouse premises
were insured in the names of the landlords and the tenants. Both had an
insurable interest in the premises. The premises were destroyed by fire. It was
decided that the property would not be rebuilt and a question arose as to the
rights to the insurance moneys. Browne-Wilkinson LJ said ([1984] 2 All ER 726 at
732, [1985] QB 755 at 765):   *e*

'I have come to the conclusion that the moneys belonged to the landlords
and the tenants in shares proportionate to their respective interests in the
property insured.'

It is also useful to consider the cases relating to the sale of goods. In *Anderson*   *f*
v Morice (1876) 1 App Cas 713 a cargo of rice which a merchant had contracted to
buy was lost when the vessel in which the cargo was being carried sank near
Rangoon. At the time of the loss neither the risk nor the property had passed to
the buyer and he had neither paid the price nor taken possession of it. It was held
by the Court of Exchequer Chamber ((1875) LR 10 CP 609) that the buyer had no   *g*
insurable interest in the rice when the loss occurred and this decision was
affirmed because on the further appeal to the House of Lords the Lords were
equally divided. The buyer had only a contingent interest in the rice. But I think
Mr Colman QC was correct when, in his valuable judgment in *Sharp v Sphere
Drake Insurance plc, The Moonacre* [1992] 2 Lloyd's Rep 501 at 511–512, he said that
Anderson v Morice fell into that category of cases in which the assured's relation to   *h*
the goods is not such as to confer on him a sufficient certainty of benefit from
their preservation or to impose upon him any certain exposure to the risk of
liability in respect of their loss.

But the position will be different if at the time of the loss the insured already
has rights in respect of the insured goods which may be affected if the goods are   *j*
lost or damaged. In the event of such loss or damage he may lose the profits from
a forward sale for which a contract has already been made. He can insure against
that loss of profits if he has rights in existence at the time of the loss of the goods,
and it can be said that he has an insurable interest in the goods in the wider sense
explained by Lawrence J in *Lucena v Craufurd*. But in my view the right to insure

a against the loss of profits does not mean that the buyer has an 'interest in the property' in the sense contemplated by the material damage proviso.

I return to the proviso in this case.

I have come to the clear conclusion that in the context the reference to 'interest' in the proviso was a reference to an interest in the narrower sense. Glengate had no such interest in the architects' drawings, even though they
b might have a licence to use the designs and might one day have acquired the property in the drawings. At the time of the fire the drawings were the property of the architects and in my judgment it was the architects' responsibility to replace them if destroyed.

The reference in the proviso to 'Section 1 or otherwise' is clearly a reference to a material damage policy. Furthermore, I find some assistance in memo-
c randum 2 in the material loss policy effected by Glengate which extended the insurance to include 'the property of the Insured or for which he is (they are) responsible at the site'. The architects were responsible for their drawings and for their other work in progress.

I have therefore reached the same conclusion as the judge that the word
d 'interest' in the proviso was used in a limited sense and that Glengate were under no obligation to insure the architects' drawings themselves.

I turn therefore to the last issue.

The average clause

e The sum insured under the consequential loss policy was £10,950,000. In the appendix to section 2 the indemnity period was defined as follows:

> 'The period commencing with the date upon which but for the Damage the premises would have been available for occupation by tenants and ending not later than 36 months thereafter during which the results of the
f business shall be affected in consequence of the Damage.'

Glengate contended that the indemnity period would have commenced on 15 June 1987. Rental would then have become payable at a total rate, assuming that the premises were fully occupied by tenants, of £6,866,283 per annum.

The appendix to section 2, however, contained the following proviso:

g
> '... if the sum insured ... be less than the annual Rent which it is estimated would have been earned during the twelve months following the damage had the damage not occurred (or a proportionately increased multiple thereof where the maximum indemnity period exceeds twelve months) the
h amount payable shall be proportionately reduced.'

'Annual rent' was defined elsewhere in the appendix as 'The Rent which would be payable to the Insured had the premises been fully tenanted for a period of twelve months'.

It is clear that this proviso was inserted in order to protect Norwich Union
j against under-insurance. Before the judge, Glengate argued that Norwich Union could obtain no protection from this proviso because no annual rent would have been earned during the twelve months following the damage. The judge rejected this argument on the basis that it ignored the fact that the annual rent was a notional rent to be calculated on the basis that the premises were fully tenanted. The judge continued ([1995] 1 Lloyd's Rep 278 at 288):

'Plainly the proviso would have been much easier to operate if the *a* estimated rent had fallen to be calculated on the basis of the estimated rent for the first 12 months of the indemnity period. It does not follow, however, that it is impossible to operate the proviso in accordance with its terms. What must be done, in my judgment, is to estimate the annual rent that would have been earned if the premises had been fully tenanted the day after the fire. This necessarily involves assuming that the development was *b* completed on that day. I have no doubt that the exercise can be done with the aid of the appropriate indices on the basis of the rentals that were subsequently agreed. Having regard to the market movements, I apprehend that the annual rent calculated on this basis will be somewhat lower than the figure agreed for tenancies that began nearly two years later. The annual rent thus calculated must be multiplied by three and, if this exceeds the sum *c* insured, the plaintiffs' recovery must be proportionately reduced.'

The judge's construction of this average clause is challenged by both Glengate and Lowndes.

It was argued in support of the cross-appeal that the averaging provision was *d* only to apply if the sum insured was 'less than the annual rent which it is estimated would have been earned during the twelve months following the damage, had the damage not occurred'. The period to be covered by the estimate was the period of twelve months after the date of the fire, that is, the twelve months beginning on 8 September 1985. During that period the premises *e* would have been incomplete and there would have been no rent. There was no reason, it was argued, to make an estimate of the rent that might have been earned had the building been completed and had the premises been fully let. Moreover, if the proviso was ambiguous it should be construed contra proferentes. The wording was that of Norwich Union. Alternatively, if an assumption had to be made because of the definition of 'annual rent' the rent *f* should be calculated on the basis that though the premises were fully tenanted they were incomplete.

The proviso is not happily worded and I have had to consider whether it is a case of sufficient ambiguity to require the application of the contra proferentes rule. It seems to me, however, that one must construe the proviso in the context of *g* the policy as a whole. Glengate were developers and the policy was designed to protect them during the development. The indemnity period was three years. The cover was against the loss of anticipated rent, and the appendix included the following definition of 'estimated rent': 'The rent which might reasonably be expected to have been earned during the Indemnity Period had the Damage not *h* occurred.'

As I stated earlier, the proviso was inserted to guard against under-insurance. Against the background of a development of this nature, it is not surprising that the calculation envisaged by the proviso was based on a hypothesis. The hypothesis was introduced by the definition of 'annual rent' and by the use of the *j* words 'annual rent' in the proviso.

As the judge said, this construction necessarily involves assuming that the development was completed on the day after the fire. In my judgment, however, this assumption has to be made if proper effect is to be given to the proviso.

In these circumstances I would dismiss both the appeal and the cross-appeal.

a **AULD LJ.** I have read the judgments of Neill LJ and Sir Iain Glidewell in draft. I agree with Neill LJ that the appeal and the cross-appeal should be dismissed for the reasons he has given. I add a few words on the issue whether Glengate had at the time of the fire an insurable interest in the architects' drawings within the meaning of the material damage proviso in the consequential loss policy.

b Phillips J ([1995] 1 Lloyd's Rep 278 at 286) construed the word 'interest' in the proviso as referring to 'the insured's own interest in the property ... rather than any wider insurable interest he may have'. With respect, I do not consider that it is necessary to draw such a distinction when determining the applicability of the proviso. Although the term 'insurable interest' may have a constancy of meaning in the broad sense stated by Lawrence J in *Lucena v Craufurd* (1806) 2 Bos & PNR 269 at 302, 127 ER 630 at 643, the nature of the insurable interest in each case must depend on the type of cover in issue.

c

In the case of insurance against cost of repair or reinstatement of damaged property, the insured's relationship to the property, to qualify as an insurable interest, must normally be of a proprietary or contractual nature. *Mark Rowlands Ltd v Berni Inns Ltd* [1985] 3 All ER 473, [1986] QB 211 is an example of both a
d proprietary and contractual relationship, and Kerr LJ's reliance on the broad proposition of Lawrence J in *Lucena v Craufurd* was unnecessary on the facts of the case. Bailees are a long-established and special example of a possessory insurable interest (see *Waters v Monarch Fire and Life Assurance Co* (1856) 5 E & B 870, [1843–60] All ER Rep 654). But not every contractual interest in property creates an insurable interest in it for the purpose of material damage cover. The
e authorities do not suggest that contractual licensees have such an interest for that purpose as a general rule. However, a contractual licensee, or even one at will, may have it if he is in joint occupation of property with the licensor (see *Goulstone v Royal Insurance Co* (1858) 1 F & F 276, 175 ER 725). Different considerations apply to cover for consequential loss such as interruption of business.

f

I say that insurable interest for material damage cover must 'normally' be proprietary or contractual because the courts have acknowledged the presence of an insurable interest in other circumstances. See, for example, *Petrofina (UK) Ltd v Magnaload Ltd* [1983] 3 All ER 35 at 42, [1984] QB 127 at 136, in which Lloyd J expressed the view that a sub-contractor had an insurable interest in the main
g contract works analogous to that of a bailee in goods bailed to him. Colman J followed that reasoning in two cases in which he held that a supplier of property involved in a common project with the person to whom the property has been supplied may have an insurable interest in the property. The first was *Stone Vickers Ltd v Appledore Ferguson Shipbuilders Ltd* [1991] 2 Lloyd's Rep 288 at 301,
h in which (sitting then as Mr Anthony Colman QC, a deputy judge of the High Court) he stated that a risk of being 'materially adversely affected by loss of or damage to' the contract works 'by reason of the incidence of any of the perils insured against' was capable of amounting to 'a sufficient [insurable] interest in the whole contract works' (reversed on another point [1992] 2 Lloyd's Rep 578). The second was *National Oilwell (UK) Ltd v Davy Offshore Ltd* [1993] 2 Lloyd's Rep
j 582 at 611, in which he held that an insurable interest could be found in 'the assured's proximate physical relationship to the property in question'. In both cases he could, as his own treatment in each makes plain, have justified his conclusion on the narrower basis that the insurable interest derived from the supplier's potential entitlement and/or liability under the contract with the person supplied. See also *Sharp v Sphere Drake Insurance plc, The Moonacre* [1992]

2 Lloyd's Rep 501 at 512, where Colman J held that two powers of attorney granted by a company to its effective owner to enjoy the use of the company's boat exclusively for his own purposes was 'a valuable benefit' constituting an insurable interest in the boat (compare *Macaura v Northern Assurance Co Ltd* [1925] AC 619, [1925] All ER Rep 51).

Such extensions of the normal rule may make commercial sense, but they should, in my view, be closely defined, at least where material damage cover is concerned. I incline to the view urged by Mr Falconer QC, for Glengate, in his submissions on Phillips J's comment that to give a broad meaning to the proviso would 'produce a result that was unreasonable, if not unworkable'. Mr Falconer submitted that it would be unreasonable because it would impose on a person insured under a consequential loss policy the burden of insuring against material damage to other persons' property; it would be unworkable because of the inevitable uncertainty of what and whose property he should so insure to secure his consequential loss cover. I believe that the trend of jurisprudence in the United States and Canada may be against that line of reasoning (see e g *Constitution Insurance Co of Canada v Kosmopoulos* (1987) 34 DLR (4th) 208, a decision of the Supreme Court of Canada, noted in [1987] JBL 309.) Nevertheless, Mr Falconer's reservations about enlarging the notion of insurable interest in relation to material damage cover make good sense to me, and they appear to reflect the present state of English law.

But where the insurance cover in issue is against some loss consequential on damage to property, there is no reason why there should be so close a legal relationship between the insured and the property damaged. The insurable interest is in the event insured against rather than in the property the damage to which causes that event. See *MacGillivray and Parkington on Insurance Law* (8th edn, 1988) p 54, para 129 and *Anderson v Morice* (1875) LR 10 CP 609 at 722, 723 per Lord Chelmsford.

Here, the insurable interest in question under the proviso was that in respect of damage to property under the material damage policy, that is 'the property of the insured or for which ... they are responsible', not that in respect of loss of rent resulting from such damage under the consequential loss policy. That is why the proviso requires that 'there shall be in force, under Section 1 or otherwise, an insurance covering the interest of the Insured in the property ... against such Damage'. In my view, the proviso only required Glengate to insure against material damage to its own property or that in respect of which the cost of repair or replacement would fall on it. I do not consider that Glengate's possible licence to use the design represented by the drawings or its expectation of ownership of the drawings on completion of the project or its contingent liability under cl 4.37 of the RIBA Conditions of Appointment to pay the architects for the work of preparing replacement drawings gave it a sufficient proprietary or contractual interest in the drawings themselves to make them an insurable interest under the material damage policy. I adopt Phillips J's reasoning in this respect.

SIR IAIN GLIDEWELL. I have read the judgment of Neill LJ in draft. I gratefully adopt his summary of the facts agreed or assumed on which Phillips J ([1995] 1 Lloyd's Rep 278) reached his decision.

The issues which arise on this appeal related to the proper interpretation and application of clauses in the consequential loss policy. They have been usefully summarised by Neill LJ.

Issue 1

a   The consequential loss policy provided that the insurers would pay to Glengate the amount of loss resulting from the interruption of their business carried on at the premises if—'any building or other property ... used by the Insured at the premises ... for the purpose of the Business suffers Damage ...' The first issue is whether the architects' drawings were 'property ... used by the Insured at the b   premises ... for the purpose of the Business' within the meaning of this clause. I agree with Phillips J and Neill LJ that, on the assumed facts, the architects' drawings did come within this description.

Issues 2 and 3

    These arise out of the proviso to the policy. This required that, if the c   consequential loss insurance was to be enforced—

> 'at the time of the happening of the Damage there shall be in force ... an insurance covering the interest of the Insured in the property at the Premises against such Damage ...'

d   On the second issue, Phillips J found, on the assumed facts, that there was no such insurance in force at the relevant time. Again I agree.

    Issue 3 I need to consider in more detail later. Before doing so I can say shortly that issue 4 concerns the construction of the average clause in the policy. I agree with the construction placed on this clause by Phillips J for the reasons he gave in his judgment.

e   I would phrase issue 3 as follows: 'Did Glengate have an interest in the drawings within the proper meaning of the exclusion clause?' When considering this issue, the different types of drawings must be considered separately.

The record drawings

f   Glengate owned these drawings and therefore clearly had an interest in them. Nevertheless Phillips J held in relation to these drawings that the proviso did not apply because their value, in relation to the whole value of the contract, was so small that the lack of material damage insurance of these drawings could be disregarded. I disagree that this would be a valid reason for not applying the proviso.

g   However, I do agree with Neill LJ that the proviso applied only to those parts of the property, the destruction of which caused the consequential loss. No loss resulted from the destruction of the record drawings, and there was therefore no claim in respect of such loss. The fact that the record drawings were uninsured did not therefore bring the proviso into force so as to bar a claim for h   consequential loss resulting from the architects' drawings. In relation to these drawings, I therefore arrive at the same conclusion as Phillips J although by a different route.

Architects' drawings

j   I turn to consider whether, as found by Phillips J on issue 2, the fact that there was no material damage insurance in force covering these drawings brought the proviso into force so as to bar a claim for consequential loss arising from the destruction of these drawings. This is the remaining question on which this appeal turns.

    In deciding this issue, Phillips J said ([1995] 1 Lloyd's Rep 278 at 287):

'The drawings fell within the ambit of responsibility of the architects, not
of the plaintiffs. They did not form part of the property on the insured   *a*
premises in which the plaintiffs had a personal interest and in respect of
which the proviso required that there should be in existence material
damage cover. For these reasons I hold that the material damage proviso
was satisfied and the plaintiffs are entitled to recover under the
consequential loss policy ...'   *b*

In his judgment, Neill LJ has described an interest of this kind as a 'personal
property interest'. In relation to these drawings, such an interest would be that
of an owner or bailee of the drawings. On the assumed facts it is clear that
Glengate had no such interest.

It is, however, a fundamental principle of insurance law that a person who has   *c*
no personal property interest may nevertheless have an insurable interest in
property. Indeed, he must have such an interest to be entitled to insure the
property.

In *Mark Rowlands Ltd v Berni Inns Ltd* [1985] 3 All ER 473, [1986] QB 211 this
court specifically adopted and approved the classic definition of an insurable
interest given by Lawrence J in *Lucena v Craufurd* (1806) 2 Bos & PNR 269 at 302,   *d*
127 ER 630 at 643:

'A man is interested in a thing to whom advantage may arise or prejudice
happen from the circumstances which may attend it ... And to whom it
importeth, that its condition as to safety or other quality should continue ...
To be interested in the preservation of a thing, is to be so circumstanced   *e*
with respect to it as to have benefit from its existence, prejudice from its
destruction.'

Clearly an insurable interest so defined will include, but is wider than, a
personal property interest.

The issue for our decision can therefore be expressed as whether 'the interest   *f*
of the Insured in the property' within the proviso includes an insurable interest
which is not a personal property interest. In respectful disagreement with Neill
LJ, I see no reason why it should not. In my judgment, the phrase 'the interest
of the Insured in the property' in its context in a policy of insurance covers
whatever interest the insured has, including an insurable interest which is not a   *g*
personal property interest.

I do not find that the authorities cited to us on this issue lead to a contrary
conclusion, or indeed are of much assistance. In *Petrofina (UK) Ltd v Magnaload
Ltd* [1983] 3 All ER 35, [1984] QB 127 the sub-contractors had no property interest
in the works in progress but they had an insurable interest in the continued   *h*
existence of those works. It was to that latter interest that Lloyd J in his judgment
must have been referring. In *Beacon Carpets Ltd v Kirby* [1984] 2 All ER 726, [1985]
QB 755 both the landlord and the tenant had property interests in the building
which was destroyed by fire. This court decided that, when the building was not
reconstructed, the insurance moneys should be divided between the parties in
shares proportionate to the values of their respective property interest. No   *j*
question arose in that case relating to any wider insurable interest.

On the facts of the present case, Glengate clearly had an interest in the
continued existence of the architects' drawings. In my judgment they therefore
had an insurable interest in those drawings. I see no unfairness or illogicality
resulting from my conclusion. Since Glengate had an insurable interest, they

a could themselves have insured the architects' drawings under the material damage policy. Alternatively (and more probably) they could have required the architects themselves to take out such insurance, which would have satisfied the proviso. In the absence of any such insurance, however, it is my judgment that the proviso applied and was not satisfied.

For these reasons, I would allow the appeal.

b

Appeal and cross-appeal dismissed. Leave to appeal to House of Lords refused.

1 April 1996. The Appeal Committee of the House of Lords (Lord Goff of Chieveley, Lord Mustill and Lord Nicholls of Birkenhead) refused leave to appeal.

Paul Magrath Esq   Barrister.

Ismail and another v Richards Butler (a firm)   *a*

QUEEN'S BENCH DIVISION

MOORE-BICK J

5, 6, 7, 16 FEBRUARY 1996

b

Solicitor – Lien – Retaining lien – Jurisdiction of court to grant relief in equity against exercise of solicitor's lien – Whether jurisdiction superseded by rules of court – RSC Ord 29, r 6.

Solicitor – Lien – Retaining lien – Solicitor discharging himself in course of action – *c* *Non-payment of costs – Solicitor instructed in respect of several matters some of which had previously been concluded – Solicitor having concurrent lien over live and dead cases – Whether client having general right to order that solicitor hand over papers to new solicitor against undertaking to preserve lien without providing further security – Whether exceptional circumstances existing justifying conditions as to provision of security in return for papers being handed over.*   *d*

The plaintiffs, well-known importers of Egyptian potatoes, had for many years engaged the defendant firm to act as their London solicitors in disputes and litigation with shippers, shipowners, hauliers and others involved in the carriage and handling of the potatoes. In 1995 the partner in charge of the plaintiffs' work *e* wrote to them proposing certain hourly charges and billing on a quarterly basis or when substantial disbursements were incurred. The plaintiffs' principal considered the charges to be unjustified and excessive and replied that the plaintiffs refused to pay them. He claimed further that, in 1992, it had been agreed with the former senior partner (now retired) that the defendants' charges would not exceed £175 per hour. The defendants denied knowledge of any such *f* agreement and demanded payment of outstanding bills in default of which they would cease working on all the plaintiffs' cases. The plaintiffs then instructed other solicitors, who offered to pay some £175,000 to the defendants on account of outstanding bills, subject to taxation of such bills, and the immediate release of all papers relating to the plaintiffs' cases. The defendants refused that offer and insisted on payment of their bills in full before releasing any papers. When the *g* plaintiff's new solicitors offered their personal undertaking to hold any papers released to the order of the defendants, thereby preserving their lien, the defendants replied demanding payment of £250,000 immediately and a bank guarantee for £200,000 and subsequently issued a writ against the plaintiffs seeking to recover the outstanding fees, interest and costs. The plaintiffs, who *h* required the papers urgently for the imminent trial of three claims for damage to cargo and also for taxation in another case, issued a summons for immediate delivery up of all papers in their cases. The master ordered delivery up on condition that the plaintiffs pay £150,000 to the defendants within four days and a further £310,000 into court. The plaintiffs appealed, contending that where a *j* solicitor terminated his retainer, as the defendants had, the court should require the solicitor to deliver the papers to another firm instructed by the client against an undertaking by that firm to redeliver them at the conclusion of the case, thereby preserving the first solicitor's lien, and that there was nothing exceptional about the present case to warrant the imposition of terms on a client seeking the release of his papers. The defendants contended, inter alia, (i) that the matter was

a governed exclusively by RSC Ord 29, r 6[a], under which a court might order
payment into court in full in a claim for the recovery of specific property over
which a lien was asserted, and therefore the court could only order the
defendants to deliver up the papers which they held against the payment into
court of the full amount of the claim, and (ii) that they were entitled from their
retainers in completed matters to exercise a general lien over all papers which
b they currently held, regardless of who terminated the retainer.

Held – (1) It had long been recognised that, subject to any agreement to the
contrary, a solicitor was entitled to exercise a general lien in respect of his costs
on any property belonging to his client which properly came into his possession
c in his capacity as a solicitor. The basic rule was that a solicitor had the general
right to embarrass his client by withholding papers in order to force him to pay
what was due and the court would not compel him to produce them at the
instance of his client. However, a solicitor who had discharged himself was not
allowed so to exert his lien as to interfere with the course of justice, and the
established jurisdiction of the court to grant relief in equity against the exercise of
d a solicitor's lien had not been removed by the introduction of what was now RSC
Ord 29, r 6 (see p 514 e to h, p 516 g and p 519 j to p 520 a d, post); *Gamlen Chemical
Co (UK) Ltd v Rochem Ltd* [1980] 1 All ER 1049 applied.

(2) Where a solicitor terminated his retainer, the fact that he was entitled to a
e lien over papers in closed cases in respect of unpaid costs, thereby giving him a
concurrent lien over the papers in live cases, did not affect the client's general
entitlement to an order that papers required for the conduct of pending litigation
be delivered to the client's new solicitors against an undertaking to restore them
at the end of the litigation, without being required to provide any further security
in respect of outstanding costs, since it was the solicitor's action in discharging the
f live retainer and ceasing to act which caused the lien to have practical effect and
gave rise to the hardship and injustice which the court sought to mitigate.
However, in exceptional cases the court could attach conditions to such an order
to meet the overall justice of the case (see p 521 b to f and p 523 d e, post).

(3) The refusal by a solicitor to continue to act unless he was put in funds was
g generally treated by the court as the effective discharge of his retainer. Since the
defendants had effectively brought their retainers to an end by requiring payment
of their outstanding costs as a condition of continuing to act, the plaintiffs were
entitled to an order that papers required for the conduct of pending litigation be
delivered to their new solicitors. However, having regard to all the circum-
h stances, including the nature of the case, the stage which the litigation had
reached, the conduct of the parties, the fact that the value of the defendants' lien
was likely to be very considerably diminished if the papers required for the
pending litigation were handed over, and the interests of justice, the plaintiffs
would not to be ordered to make any immediate payment to the defendants, but
j would be required to provide security in the sum of £450,000 for the defendants'
claim by way of payment into court, bank guarantee or other acceptable means
(see p 522 h j, p 523 b to d, p 524 a to e and p 525 b to e h to p 526 a, post); *Robins v
Goldingham* (1872) LR 13 Eq 440 and *Gamlen Chemical Co (UK) Ltd v Rochem Ltd*
[1980] 1 All ER 1049 followed; *A v B* [1984] 1 All ER 265 distinguished.

---

a   Rule 6, so far as material, is set out at p 518 b c, post

Notes

For a solicitor's retaining lien on documents, see 44(1) *Halsbury's Laws* (4th edn   *a* reissue) paras 245–253, and for cases on the subject, see 44 *Digest* (Reissue) 341– 357, 3728–3899.

Cases referred to in judgment

A v B [1984] 1 All ER 265.   *b*
Colegrave v Manley (1823) Turn & R 400, 37 ER 1155, LC.
Faithfull, Re, Re London Brighton and South Coast Rly Co (1868) LR 6 Eq 325.
Galland, Re (1885) 31 Ch D 296, Ch D and CA.
Gamlen Chemical Co (UK) Ltd v Rochem Ltd [1980] 1 All ER 1049, [1980] 1 WLR 614, CA.
Gebruder Naf v Ploton (1890) 25 QBD 13, CA.   *c*
Heslop v Metcalfe (1837) 3 My & Cr 183, 40 ER 894, LC.
Hughes v Hughes [1958] 3 All ER 179, [1958] P 224, [1958] 3 WLR 500, CA.
Robins v Goldingham (1872) LR 13 Eq 440.
Segbedzi v Glah (1989) 139 NLJ 1303, CA.

                                                    d
Case also cited or referred to in skeleton arguments

Lord v Wormleighton (1822) Jac 580, 37 ER 969, LC.

Interlocutory appeal

The plaintiffs, Dr Fawzi Ahmed Abou Ismail and Aratra Potato Co Ltd, appealed from the order of Master Pollard dated 9 January 1996, pursuant to a summons *e* issued by the plaintiffs on 28 December 1995 in proceedings in which they claimed delivery up of all papers belonging to them in the possession of the defendants, Richards Butler (a firm of solicitors), the delivery of final bills of costs and an order for taxation of those bills, whereby he ordered that upon payment by the plaintiffs within four days of the sum of £150,000 to the defendants, and a further sum of £310,000 into court, the defendants should deliver to the plaintiffs' *f* solicitors all papers in their possession belonging to the plaintiffs. The appeal was heard in chambers but judgment was given by Moore-Bick J in open court. The facts are set out in the judgment.

Robert Deacon (instructed by *Mishcon de Reya*) for the plaintiffs.   *g*
Graham Charkham (instructed by *Richards Butler*) for the defendants.

                                                Cur adv vult

16 February 1996. The following judgment was delivered.

                                                  h
MOORE-BICK J. This matter comes before the court by way of an appeal by the plaintiffs from an order of Master Pollard made on 9 January 1996 whereby he ordered that upon payment by the plaintiffs within four days of the sum of £150,000 to the defendants and a further sum of £310,000 into court the defendants should deliver to the plaintiffs' solicitors all papers belonging to the *j* plaintiffs relating to six matters mentioned in the order. He also directed that the order should be stayed until agreement that there should be no appeal or until further order of the court. That order was made on a summons issued by the plaintiffs in proceedings begun by originating summons in which they claim delivery up of all papers belonging to them in the possession of the defendants, the delivery of final bills of costs and an order for taxation of those bills under the

a Solicitors Act 1974. Having regard to the nature of the issues raised on this appeal, all of which were fully argued, I considered that it would be appropriate for judgment to be delivered in open court and the parties have agreed to that being done.

The plaintiffs, Dr Ismail and Aratra Potato Co Ltd, are well-known importers into the United Kingdom of new potatoes from Egypt. In the course of that

b business they have from time to time inevitably become involved in disputes with shippers, shipowners, hauliers and others involved in the carriage and handling of the potatoes. Many of these disputes have led to litigation. For many years the plaintiffs instructed Messrs Richards Butler to act on their behalf in connection with these disputes. (For convenience I shall refer throughout to Dr Ismail and Aratra Potato Co Ltd together as 'the plaintiffs', without prejudice to

c the dispute which I understand exists between Dr Ismail and Richards Butler concerning his personal position.) The relationship between them appears to have originated in contacts between Dr Ismail and Mr Elmslie, who was then a partner in Richards Butler; certainly Dr Ismail appears to have had particular confidence in Mr Elmslie, which was no doubt fostered by his handling of the

d plaintiffs' affairs over many years. Apart from a brief interlude between 1988 and 1992 Mr Elmslie and Richards Butler continued to act for the plaintiffs until the autumn of 1995, when their relationship came to an end in circumstances which I shall have to deal with in more detail in a moment. First, however, it is necessary to say something more about the arrangements that were made between them in 1992 when the plaintiffs decided to return to instructing

e Richards Butler as their London solicitors.

The plaintiffs resumed their relationship with Richards Butler in about February 1992. By then Mr Elmslie had become senior partner. At that stage, the plaintiffs say, it was agreed that the previous billing arrangement would apply, namely that Mr Elmslie would charge a maximum of £175 per hour for work

f which he carried out and that Richards Butler would bill the plaintiffs only when cases were concluded by judgment or settlement. That arrangement does not appear to have been reduced to writing, but it is common ground that it was superseded shortly thereafter and nothing turns on it as far as this application is concerned. Mr Elmslie retired as senior partner of Richards Butler in April 1992, but before he did so he suggested that he should continue to handle the plaintiffs'

g work, but at a much reduced hourly rate payable on a monthly basis. According to Dr Ismail there was a meeting on 5 June 1992 between himself, Mr Elmslie, Mr Bush (then a partner in Richards Butler) and Mr Cock (an assistant solicitor), at which it was agreed that Richards Butler would continue to act for the plaintiffs after Mr Elmslie's retirement but on the basis that most of the work would be

h done by Mr Elmslie, with Mr Bush and Mr Cock undertaking a supporting and administrative role. He says that it was agreed on that occasion that Mr Bush would charge a maximum of £175 per hour, Mr Cock a maximum of £90 per hour and Mr Elmslie £40 per hour. Dr Ismail also says that it was agreed that in addition to billing the plaintiffs at the end of each case Richards Butler would

j render interim bills annually at the end of August or beginning of September. That some terms were agreed at about that time between Dr Ismail, Mr Elmslie and Mr Bush is not in dispute, but Richards Butler do not accept that the terms were as Dr Ismail says. In particular, they deny that there was any agreement as to the rates which would be charged in respect of work carried out by Mr Bush and Mr Cock. Again, it appears that that agreement was never reduced to writing.

Some time later (the precise date does not matter) Mr Bush gave notice to
retire from Richards Butler and did so with effect from 30 April 1994. Mr Cock *a*
left Richards Butler at about the same time. In February 1994, therefore, another
of Richards Butler's partners, Mr Francies, was introduced to Dr Ismail with a
view to taking over responsibility for the plaintiffs' affairs. That led in due course
to a further agreement being made at some time in April 1994 between Dr Ismail,
Mr Elmslie and Mr Francies, now acting on behalf of Richards Butler, which set *b*
out the basic terms on which the plaintiffs' work would be handled. This time
the agreement was reduced to writing. It provided as follows:

'Dr. Ismail wishes Richards Butler to be his (and his company's) solicitors
acting on the specific instructions of Mr. K.G. Elmslie. Richards Butler will
conduct routine correspondence and instruct counsel and experts as *c*
necessary, but with regard to court applications and correspondence of
significance will act as requested by Mr. Elmslie. Mr. Elmslie will, when
available, do the detailed work, save where a vessel is to be arrested. In the
event of Mr. Elmslie not being available for any reason, Dr. Ismail will
instruct Mr. Francies or Mr. Rudkin of Richards Butler and they will continue
to act on Dr. Ismail's instructions until Mr. Elmslie again becomes available. *d*
Richards Butler will invoice Dr. Ismail in respect of active cases annually on
31st August each year, save that they will invoice him when a case is closed
and in respect of disbursements when incurred.'

It can be seen that the agreement contained no reference to the charging rates of
either Mr Elmslie or Richards Butler themselves. *e*
By the middle of 1994 Mr Francies had already started to become concerned at
the way in which these arrangements were working in practice and as a result Mr
Elmslie's position was changed to one of consultant for Dr Ismail. Thereafter
Richards Butler acted on his instructions or those of Dr Ismail and according to
Mr Francies the arrangement seemed to work satisfactorily. *f*
On 31 July 1995 Mr Francies wrote to Dr Ismail with some general comments
on the approach to handling disputes. In the course of that letter he made some
suggestions as to ways in which funds spent on litigation could be used more
efficiently in future, and in that context he referred to the rates charged ordinarily
by Richards Butler for their work. He mentioned specifically the hourly rates at
which his time and that of his assistants was charged. He also made the point that *g*
an effective solicitor whose charging rate is higher may be more cost effective
than a solicitor whose hourly charging rate is lower but who spends more time
on the work. Finally in that letter he raised the matter of billing procedure and
suggested that the time had come to introduce interim billing on a monthly or
three-monthly basis. It may be relevant to note in view of what subsequently *h*
occurred that when he responded to that letter on 2 August Dr Ismail did not take
issue with the charging rates mentioned by Mr Francies.
There followed a meeting between Dr Ismail and Mr Francies towards the end
of October 1995 in which the matter of billing and (I infer) charging rates was
discussed. On 26 October Mr Francies wrote to Dr Ismail summarising the terms *j*
on which, as he understood it, Richards Butler would act for the plaintiffs in the
future. There was to be billing quarterly, or when a case was closed, or when any
substantial disbursements were incurred. In the same letter Mr Francies harked
back to his letter of 31 July and proposed certain hourly charging rates for himself
and his assistant. This time there was a strong reaction from Dr Ismail. In a letter
dated 15 November he replied to Richards Butler saying that he refused to pay

a charges at the level suggested, which he considered to be out of all proportion. In that letter he stated for the first time that he had agreed originally with Mr Elmslie, and subsequently with Mr Bush, that Richards Butler's charges would not exceed £175 per hour. Accordingly, he asked Mr Francies to re-examine all the bills submitted recently and to adjust them to ensure that they reflected that maximum hourly charge. This letter contained a thinly-veiled threat that if b Richards Butler did not comply with his demands he would withdraw the plaintiffs' account from them.

On 17 November Mr Francies replied in a letter which included the following passages:

c '... I think this is the first time you have told me you had an understanding with Ken Elmslie and Philip Bush that we would only charge you £175 per hour. Presumably this means only for my time and you make no mention of any junior solicitors. I am not aware of any such agreement and this was not a point you raised in August 1994 when we rendered you the bills for that year ... I am not sure how I should interpret your reply, and of course I d would like to continue doing your work. But we cannot do it at rates which are less than our competitors, less than we would obtain from a taxing master and which would drive us into bankruptcy. You owe us a very substantial amount of money which includes fees we are liable to pay to counsel. It is not possible for us to continue working for you in these circumstances. Unless we receive payment of these accounts forthwith, we e will have to cease working on all your cases. As regards "SATAMARU", "YOUSEF" and "DIAMOND REEFER", I am not prepared to incur any further liability towards counsel for their fees and I will not ask them to attend the proposed meeting at your offices on 27th November. Nor can I contemplate sending them a brief for the hearing in January. If necessary, I must ask you to nominate other solicitors to take over the handling of these cases and let f me know who they are so that I can transfer the papers to them. This is a drastic step to take and I am fully resolved to do it if I have to. However, I know you are a fair man and I appeal to your sense of honour and justice. I am ready and willing to come to your offices and sort out all these problems, and you know I will be back in the office next Thursday. Please let me find g some good news on my return.'

On 22 November Dr Ismail responded as follows:

'Thank you for your letter of 17th November. It is clear to me from your letter that the differences between us are such that it would not be fair to h either of us to continue with the existing arrangements. I have therefore decided to instruct other solicitors to take over the handling of all my cases with immediate effect, and Holmes Hardingham have agreed to accept instructions. Duncan Rudkin will be contacting you to arrange for collection of my papers from your office. Although we are now to go our separate j ways, I believe that in all fairness I am entitled to expect that the transfer can be arranged quickly and efficiently, so that the preparation of my cases will not suffer. This can be achieved if all concerned act fairly and with good will.'

There followed a further letter from Mr Francies sent by fax on 23 November in which he said:

'I attach a list of our outstanding bills. They are all long overdue, and we
have received nothing towards settlement of any of them. This has two
consequences: 1. Unless we receive payment of all of them within 7 days,
we shall have to consider commencement of court proceedings. 2. If
payment is not made, we shall have to come off the court record in the
following cases: [he then lists six pending matters]. 3. In any event I cannot
agree to instruct counsel or brief them on any hearings, or incur liability for
any other disbursements until full payment is made of all the outstanding
costs. If Holmes Hardingham serve notice of change of solicitor in all cases
where we are on the record, this may avoid any application by us to get off
the record. If they fail to take this course of action, I shall have to proceed as
indicated. You would then be unrepresented so that judgment in default
could be entered against you with costs. It is only "PACIFIC QUEEN" and
"OCEAN ICE" in which proceedings have not been commenced, but a time bar
is approaching. The Club, in both cases, have asked us not to issue a writ,
but these cases will need attention one way or the other in the near future.
Therefore I would appreciate your specific instructions on each case ...
While our bills remain unpaid, Fawzi, you have to believe me when I say my
partners insist that I take the action threatened above. However, your name
is well known to almost every partner here, you have been a good client for
a long time, and you are regarded with respect and affection. We do not
wish to sever the relationship ... we really cannot continue acting for you in
the present circumstances, and I am hoping, daily, that you will resolve it
favourably for us.'

On 24 November Messrs Holmes Hardingham, who had been instructed by
the plaintiffs, offered on their behalf to pay Richards Butler the sum of
£175,151·51 on account of the outstanding bills on certain conditions which
included the taxation of the outstanding bills and, more importantly, the
immediate release of all the plaintiffs' papers which Richards Butler were then
holding. That proposal was not acceptable to Richards Butler, however, who
insisted on payment of their bills in full before releasing any papers. Holmes
Hardingham wrote again on 27 November stating that in the plaintiffs' view the
hourly rates being charged by Richards Butler were unreasonably high and also
that they had charged for an unreasonably high number of hours, and on the
same day they offered their personal undertaking to hold any papers released to
them to the order of Richards Butler, thereby preserving their lien. That was
unacceptable to Richards Butler, however, who wanted to receive payment
rather than mere security in the form of a lien which might be worth very little
at the conclusion of the cases. On 8 December 1995 Richards Butler issued a writ
against the plaintiffs seeking to recover the outstanding fees, interest and costs.

Meanwhile it had become apparent to all concerned that Mr Rudkin of Holmes
Hardingham (who had previously been an assistant of Mr Francies at Richards
Butler) was a potential witness in relation to the dispute between the plaintiffs
and Richards Butler and that there were therefore difficulties in the way of
Holmes Hardingham's continuing to act for the plaintiffs. Accordingly, early in
December the plaintiffs instructed their present solicitors, Messrs Mishcon de
Reya. By letter dated 12 December Mishcon de Reya also offered a personal
undertaking to hold the papers to the order of Richards Butler, but that remained
unacceptable to Richards Butler for the same reasons as before. Their minimum
demand was for a payment of £250,000 immediately, together with a bank

a guarantee in the sum of £200,000. In their letter of 12 December Mishcon de
Reya also described briefly the complaints they understood the plaintiffs to be
making, namely that Richards Butler's costs were unjustified or excessive and
that work had been done without the plaintiffs' authority or in the alternative
negligently. In a later letter to Richards Butler they said:

b '... after a full hearing of our clients' defences and counterclaims and an
assessment of damages it is entirely possible that your firm will end up
indebted to our clients.'

By this time pressure on the plaintiffs was mounting. The trial in the actions
concerning the vessels 'Yousef', 'Satamaru' and 'Diamond Reefer' in which the
plaintiffs were making claims for alleged damage to cargo was fixed to begin on
c 16 January 1996. Moreover, some of the papers being held by Richards Butler
were required for the purpose of a taxation of costs in another matter and the
plaintiffs had been ordered to produce them by 29 December. Further
negotiations between the parties proved fruitless and so, on 20 December 1995,
the plaintiffs issued the originating summons seeking an order that Richards
d Butler deliver up all the plaintiffs' papers in their possession, that final bills of costs
be delivered and that those bills be taxed. On 28 December the plaintiffs issued a
summons in those proceedings seeking an order for the immediate delivery up of
the papers on such terms as the court might think just, and it was on the hearing
of that summons that Master Pollard made the order against which this appeal is
brought.
e The documents currently held by Richards Butler fall into two categories:
those relating to litigation which has been completed, and those relating to
litigation which is still pending, or, in some cases, is yet to be commenced. The
three actions concerning the 'Yousef', 'Satamaru' and 'Diamond Reefer' were
still technically pending when the appeal came on for hearing, though agreement
f on terms had been reached in principle.
Mr Deacon, who appeared for the plaintiffs, submitted that the principles
which govern the court's approach to the exercise of a solicitor's lien when he
himself has terminated the retainer (as he submits Richards Butler did in this case)
have been well established for many years. They can be conveniently found in
g the decisions in *Heslop v Metcalfe* (1837) 3 My & Cr 183, 40 ER 894, *Robins v
Goldingham* (1872) LR 13 Eq 440 and *Gamlen Chemical Co (UK) Ltd v Rochem Ltd*
[1980] 1 All ER 1049, [1980] 1 WLR 614. In his submission these authorities
establish that in such a case the court will require the solicitor to deliver the
papers to another firm instructed by the client against an undertaking by that firm
to redeliver them at the conclusion of the case, thereby preserving the first
h solicitor's lien. The court, he submitted, imposes a restriction on the solicitor's
exercise of his lien in that way to avoid the injustice which the client would
otherwise suffer if he were prevented from pursuing the litigation. Although he
accepted that in exceptional cases the court can and will impose terms upon the
client seeking the release of his papers, he submitted that there was nothing
j exceptional about the present case. Accordingly, he submitted on the basis of
these authorities that the master was wrong to require the plaintiffs to pay a
substantial sum of money to Richards Butler and an additional sum into court in
order to obtain the release of the documents. He submitted that Richards Butler
should be ordered to deliver up the documents unconditionally, or at worst
against the payment of a sum of money into court by the plaintiffs to stand as
security for their claim.

The submissions made by Mr Charkham on behalf of the defendants can be summarised under four heads. First, he submitted that an application of the kind now being made by the plaintiffs falls within the scope of, and is governed exclusively by, the provisions of RSC Ord 29, r 6 and that therefore the court can only order Richards Butler to deliver up the papers which they hold against the payment into court of the full amount of their claim. Secondly, he submitted that in any event Richards Butler were separately retained by the plaintiffs in relation to each of the several different matters in question, some of which had long since been completed (although fees and disbursements remained outstanding) by the time the relationship between them and the plaintiffs broke down. Each of those retainers, he submitted, gave rise to a general lien which could not later become qualified merely as the result of Richards Butler's subsequently terminating other retainers in relation to uncompleted matters. Therefore, he argued, Richards Butler are entitled to exercise a lien derived from their retainers in those completed matters over all papers which they currently hold, regardless of whether they or the plaintiffs terminated the relationship. Thirdly, he submitted that it was the plaintiffs rather than Richards Butler who terminated the relationship, and so in accordance with established principles the court should not interfere with the exercise of their lien. Finally, even if he is wrong about all that, he submitted that considerations of justice do not require that in this case Richards Butler should be required to deliver up the papers which they hold unconditionally, or indeed at all.

It is convenient to begin by examining the law in relation to the exercise of the solicitor's lien as it has developed through the decided cases. This has been influenced by that fact that solicitors are officers of the court and therefore subject to its supervisory jurisdiction in a way not shared by others who may come before it. It has long been recognised that, subject to any agreement to the contrary, a solicitor is entitled to exercise a general lien in respect of his costs on any property belonging to his client which properly comes into his possession in his capacity as a solicitor (see 44(1) *Halsbury's Laws* (4th edn reissue) para 244, *Cordery on Solicitors*, para L [933] and *Snell's Equity* (29th edn, 1990) Pt IV, ch 10, pp 457ff, which contains a useful summary of the nature of liens at law and in equity generally, and of the position in relation to solicitors in particular). The solicitor's possessory lien may be exercised over any property of the kind just mentioned, whether or not it came into his possession in connection with the matter in respect of which the costs were incurred. The basic rule is that a solicitor has the general right to embarrass his client by withholding papers in order to force him to pay what is due and the court will not compel him to produce them at the instance of his client (see *Re Faithfull, Re London Brighton and South Coast Rly Co* (1868) LR 6 Eq 325 and *Hughes v Hughes* [1958] 3 All ER 179, [1958] P 224). This much was common ground in the present case.

Although the existence of such a lien has long been regarded as generally in the interest of litigants themselves, it was quickly realised that the unfettered right to exercise a lien on papers relating to current litigation could cause hardship and injustice. In *Heslop v Metcalfe* (1837) 3 My & Cr 183, 40 ER 894 the plaintiff had employed a solicitor, Blunt, to conduct an action on his behalf. About 16 months after proceedings had been commenced Blunt had run out of funds, so he applied to the plaintiff for a payment to cover his outstanding costs and costs to be incurred in future. When no payment was forthcoming he said that he would not proceed any further with the action unless his request for payment was complied with within a certain time. The plaintiff thereupon instructed another solicitor, a Green, to act on his behalf, but Blunt refused to part with the papers until his costs were paid. He did, however, offer to make them available to Green for the purposes of the litigation. The plaintiff made an application to the court for an order that the papers be delivered to Green against his undertaking to return them to Blunt after the case had been heard. Lord Cottenham LC giving judgment considered a number of earlier authorities decided by Lord Eldon LC

b in which the court had declined to allow a solicitor who had discharged himself from the retainer to insist on his lien if to do so would prevent the client from proceeding with his action. He quotes Lord Eldon LC in *Colegrave v Manley* (1823) 1 Turn & R 400, 37 ER 1155 as follows:

c 'His Lordship says "... Now, where the solicitor discharges himself, the rule is quite different from what it is where the solicitor is discharged by the client;" and afterwards he adds, "so far as the use of papers is concerned, the suitor, when his solicitor discharges himself, must have his business conducted with as much ease and celerity, and as little expense, as if the connection of solicitor and client had not been dissolved."' (See 3 My & Cr

d 183 at 187, 40 ER 894 at 896.)

These considerations were considered sufficient to justify as a general rule making an order requiring the solicitor to deliver the papers to the new solicitor to enable the client to continue the proceedings.

Referring to that principle, Lord Cottenham LC said (3 My & Cr 183 at 188, 40

e ER 894 at 896):

'Undoubtedly, that doctrine may expose a solicitor to very great inconvenience and hardship, if, after embarking in a cause, he finds that he cannot get the necessary funds wherewith to carry it on. But, on the other hand, extreme hardship might arise to the client, if—to take the case which

f is not uncommon in the smaller practice in the country—a solicitor, who finds a poor man having a good claim, and having but a small sum of money at his command, may go on until that fund is exhausted, and then, refusing to proceed further, may hang up the cause by withholding the papers in his hands. That would be a great grievance and means of oppression to a poor

g client, who, with the clearest right in the world, might still be without the means of employing another solicitor. The rule of the Court must be adapted to every case that may occur, and be calculated to protect suitors against such conduct.'

h Lord Cottenham LC, having concluded that Blunt had in fact terminated the retainer, said (3 My & Cr 183 at 190, 40 ER 896 at 897):

'I think the principle should be, that the solicitor claiming the lien should have every security not inconsistent with the progress of the cause. But it is clear that there will neither be, to use the expression of Lord Eldon, the same

j ease and celerity, nor as little expense, in the conduct of it, if the new solicitor is merely to have access to the papers, as where they are placed in his hands, upon his undertaking to restore them after the immediate purposes of the production have been served.'

Robins v Goldingham (1872) LR 13 Eq 440 was another case in which a solicitor declined to continue with an action unless put in funds by the client to enable him to pay counsel's fees. Malins V-C, giving judgment on the client's application for delivery up of his papers, stated the rule in this way (at 442):

> 'Now it is well settled that where a solicitor is discharged by the client he has a lien for his costs upon the papers in his hands, and can retain them until he is satisfied; but it is different where the discharge is by the solicitor ... it is clear that a solicitor is not entitled to stop litigation, because he cannot obtain funds to enable him to carry it on. There is no injustice in this view, because when the papers are in the hands of the new solicitor, Mr. *Suckling* [the original solicitor] will retain any lien to which he is entitled.'

He then applied the rule laid down in *Colegrave v Manley* and *Heslop v Metcalfe* and ordered delivery of the papers to the new solicitor against his undertaking to return them at the end of the proceedings.

This approach has been considered in a number of more recent cases, most notably *Gamlen Chemical Co (UK) Ltd v Rochem Ltd* [1980] 1 All ER 1049, [1980] 1 WLR 614 and *A v B* [1984] 1 All ER 265. In the *Gamlen Chemical Co* case the Court of Appeal considered the line of authority which includes *Heslop v Metcalfe* and *Robins v Goldingham* as well as a number of the other authorities. Goff LJ cited the following passage from the judgment of Oliver J at first instance, who had based himself on *Robins v Goldingham*:

> 'The principles, I think, are fairly clear; that is to say, that if a client discharges a solicitor the solicitor's lien endures and the court has no right (or no title) to call for the documents to be handed over. But, if the solicitor has discharged himself in the course of an action, then the order which is sought on this motion seems to follow as a course ...' (See [1980] 1 All ER 1049 at 1054, [1980] 1 WLR 614 at 620.)

Goff LJ clearly had some initial misgivings about the approach to be found in the nineteenth century cases, but he regarded *Heslop v Metcalfe* as a decision of the utmost significance because the court had clearly adverted to the effect an order to deliver up the documents would have on the solicitor's lien. He was satisfied, therefore, that it would not be right to overrule *Robins v Goldingham* and he cast no doubt on Oliver J's formulation of the principles to be derived from it. It should be noted, however, that Goff LJ regarded the overriding principle to be that a solicitor who has discharged himself is not allowed so to exert his lien as to interfere with the course of justice (see [1980] 1 All ER 1049 at 1057–1058, [1980] 1 WLR 614 at 623).

Templeman LJ agreed with Goff LJ. He put the matter in this way ([1980] 1 All ER 1049 at 1058, [1980] 1 WLR 614 at 624):

> 'If before the action is ended, the client determines the retainer, the solicitor may, subject to certain exceptions not here material, exercise a possessory lien over the client's papers until payment of the solicitor's costs and disbursements ... The solicitor himself may determine his retainer during an action, for reasonable cause, such as the failure of the client to keep the solicitor in funds to meet his costs and disbursements; but in that case the solicitor's possessory lien ... is subject to the practice of the court which, in order to save the client's litigation from catastrophe, orders the solicitor to hand over the client's papers to the client's new solicitors, provided the new solicitors undertake to preserve the original solicitor's lien and to return the

a   papers to the original solicitors, for what they are worth, after the end of the litigation.'

Then, having said that there are convincing reasons why that practice should still be followed, he said ([1980] 1 All ER 1049 at 1058–1059, [1980] 1 WLR 614 at 624–625):

b   'Where the solicitor has himself discharged his retainer, the court then will normally make a mandatory order obliging the original solicitor to hand over the client's papers to the new solicitor against an undertaking by the new solicitor to preserve the lien of the original solicitor. I wish to guard myself against possible exceptions to this general rule. The court in fact is
c   asked to make a mandatory order obliging the original solicitors to hand over the client's papers to the new solicitors. An automatic order is inconsistent with the inherent, albeit judicial, discretion of the court to grant or withhold a remedy which is equitable in character. It may be, therefore, that in exceptional cases the court might impose terms where justice so required. For example, if the papers are valueless after the litigation is ended
d   and if the client accepts that he is indebted to the original solicitor for an agreed sum and has no counterclaim, or accepts that the solicitor has admittedly paid out reasonable and proper disbursements, which must be repaid, the court might make an order which would only compel the original solicitor to hand over the papers to the new solicitor, on the usual terms
e   preserving the lien but providing that in the first place the client pays to the original solicitor a sum, fixed by the court, representing the whole or part of the moneys admittedly due from the client to the original solicitor. Much would depend on the nature of the case, the stage which the litigation had reached, the conduct of the solicitor and the client respectively, and the balance of hardship which might result from the order the court is asked to
f   make.'

A v B [1984] 1 All ER 265 provides a modern example of exceptional circumstances leading to a departure from the usual practice. In that case the original solicitors had discharged themselves for good cause, the client having failed to pay their costs. By the time the matter came before the court on the
g   client's application for an order that the solicitors should deliver up the papers, the solicitors had already obtained a default judgment for their costs which remained unsatisfied. Leggatt J held that the overriding principle is that the court should make such order as is most conducive to the interests of justice and that in order to do so it is necessary to weigh up two matters: (a) that a litigant should
h   not be deprived of material relevant to the conduct of his case and so driven from the judgment seat, if that would be the result of permitting the lien to be sustained, and (b) that litigation should be conducted with due regard to the interests of the court's own officers, who should not be left without payment for what is justly due to them. In that case Leggatt J considered that there was a clear
j   analogy between the case where the client admits a sum or sums to be due to his solicitor and the case where there is a default judgment in respect of outstanding costs. It was also a case where the conduct of the client compared very unfavourably with that of the solicitors who, he found, had acted impeccably. In the event the lien was allowed to stand and the client's application was dismissed.

With these authorities in mind I turn to consider the arguments of the parties in the present case. It is convenient to begin with Mr Charkham's submission

that the matter is now governed exclusively by Ord 29, r 6. This is the current
successor of the rule which first saw the light of day as Ord L, r 8 in the Rules of *a*
the Supreme Court 1883, which came into effect on 1 January 1884. The material
parts of Ord 29, r 6 (which for present purposes does not differ in substance from
the original Ord L, r 8) provide:

> 'Where the plaintiff ... claims the recovery of specific property ... and the *b*
> party from whom recovery is sought does not dispute the title of the party
> making the claim but claims to be entitled to retain the property by virtue of
> a lien ... the Court ... may order that the party seeking to recover the
> property be at liberty to pay into Court ... the amount of money in respect
> of which the security is claimed and such further sum (if any) for interest and
> costs as the Court may direct and that, upon such payment being made, the *c*
> property claimed be given up to the party claiming it.'

In *Gebruder Naf v Ploton* (1890) 25 QBD 13 the plaintiff sought to obtain delivery
of goods held by the defendant who was asserting the right to exercise a lien over
them. The goods were worth about £656; the defendant was claiming £942. The
question arose whether the court had jurisdiction to order that the goods be *d*
delivered against payment into court of any sum greater than the value of the
goods themselves, or indeed any sum less than the full amount being claimed by
the defendant. The Court of Appeal held that the terms of the rule were clear:
fraud apart, it required that the whole sum claimed by the defendant should be
paid into court as a condition of ordering delivery of the goods. The same
construction of the present Ord 29, r 6 was adopted, albeit with obvious *e*
reluctance, by the Court of Appeal in *Segbedzi v Glah* (1989) 139 NLJ 1303. The
plaintiffs were the administrators of the estate of one Kpomasi Segbedzi whose
assets included property in this country. The defendant was a barrister and
solicitor of the Supreme Court of Ghana and a practising member of the English
Bar. Dr Glah had accepted instructions to act for the administrators in *f*
connection with the realisation of the deceased's assets in this country, for which
he had paid himself substantial sums of money on account of fees and expenses
and in respect of which he claimed that further substantial sums remained owing
to him. Dr Glah claimed to exercise a lien over various documents belonging to
the estate which he refused to deliver except against payment of the sums he
claimed were due to him. The administrators therefore applied to the court for *g*
an order under Ord 29, r 6 and in due course an order was made for the
immediate delivery of the documents without any corresponding order for a
payment into court of the sums claimed by Dr Glah. In the Court of Appeal
Bingham LJ (with whom Parker LJ agreed) clearly had doubts about Dr Glah's
right to be paid the sums he claimed and considered that it was 'in the highest *h*
degree uncertain' that he was entitled to assert a lien of any kind. However, he
held, following *Gebruder Naf v Ploton*, that under Ord 29, r 6 the court was
precluded from inquiring into the merits of the alleged right to exercise a lien or
from ordering delivery of the documents to the administrators against a suitable
undertaking from them in relation to proceeds of the property. Since there was *j*
no suggestion of any fraud on Dr Glah's part the only order that could properly
be made was for delivery of the documents against payment into court of the full
amount of his claim.

Basing himself on these authorities Mr Charkham submitted that since the
present application fell squarely within Ord 29, r 6 the court could not order
delivery of the documents held by Richards Butler, regardless of whether they or

a the plaintiffs terminated the retainers, except against payment into court of the full amount of their claim and such sum as might be appropriate in respect of interest and costs. He submitted that the cases concerning solicitors' liens, in particular *Gamlen Chemical Co (UK) Ltd v Rochem Ltd*, were decided per incuriam, in that no consideration was given to the impact of Ord 29, r 6, which has statutory force. Although he accepted that in the ordinary way I would none the

b less be bound to follow that decision, he submitted that it is inconsistent with the decision in *Segbedzi v Glah* (which is also binding on me) and that I therefore have to choose between these conflicting decisions of the Court of Appeal. That being so, he naturally submitted that I should follow *Segbedzi v Glah*.

It was not disputed that if the application does fall to be dealt with under Ord 29, r 6, and on no other basis, the court in this case has no power to order delivery

c of the documents otherwise than against payment into court of the full amount of Richards Butler's claim. Mr Deacon submitted, however, that the application does not fall to be dealt with exclusively under Ord 29, r 6 because the plaintiffs are entitled to invoke an equitable jurisdiction which had developed before the rules were formulated and which the introduction of the original Ord L, r 8 and

d the current Ord 29, r 6 did nothing to diminish. In support of that proposition he drew my attention to a number of cases decided since the introduction of Ord L, r 8 in 1884, in none of which does it appear to have occurred to anyone that the previous practice had been swept away. He also drew my attention to s 50 of the Solicitors Act 1974 which deals with the court's jurisdiction over solicitors generally and to s 68(1) which deals specifically with the court's power to order a

e solicitor to deliver a bill of costs and to deliver up documents.

The practice of the court in cases where the solicitor discharges himself, as described in *Heslop v Metcalfe* (1837) 3 My & Cr 183, 40 ER 894 and established through subsequent cases, involves the granting of a remedy that is equitable in character. That was expressly recognised by Templeman LJ in *Gamlen Chemical*

f *Co (UK) Ltd v Rochem Ltd* [1980] 1 All ER 1049 at 1058, [1980] 1 WLR 614 at 624. The jurisdiction to grant relief of that kind appears to have been limited to solicitors' liens, perhaps because of the fact they are officers of the court and therefore directly amenable to its control, but probably because the hardship which the rule seeks to alleviate is one which, in the past at any rate, has been peculiar to the exercise of a solicitor's lien. This equitable jurisdiction has been

g regularly exercised over the past 150 years since *Heslop v Metcalfe* and the principles upon which the court exercises it have been developed over the course of time to meet new situations. Despite their diligence in this case, counsel were unable to shed any additional light on the purpose behind the introduction of Ord L, r 8, but in my view it was clearly intended, then as now, to give the court

h power to provide interim relief by ordering the release of property held under an assertion of lien against the provision of alternative security. As such it provided a form of remedy available in all cases where a right to exercise a possessory lien was asserted. That it might be invoked in the case of a solicitor's lien seems to me uncontroversial since it is only in the relatively narrow class of cases to which

j I have drawn attention that it was clearly established that the court could intervene under its equitable jurisdiction (see *Re Galland* (1885) 31 Ch D 296 where the scope of the court's inherent jurisdiction to make an order of the kind permitted by the new Ord L, r 8 was in dispute).

I am unable to accept that the introduction of Ord L, r 8, presumably to alleviate difficulties caused by the exercise of possessory liens in general, was intended to, or did, sweep away the established jurisdiction of the court to grant

relief in equity against the exercise of a solicitor's lien. I can see nothing in the
language of the rule itself to suggest that it was meant to subsume that a
jurisdiction and it would be surprising if that had been the intention. I say that,
first, because it would have removed from the court a valuable discretion, as is
apparent from *Segbedzi v Glah*, and secondly, because it would have rendered the
client whose solicitor had discharged himself significantly worse off than under
the existing law, in that in every case it would be necessary for him to pay into b
court the full amount of his former solicitor's claim in order to recover his papers.
I do not think that the decision in *Segbedzi v Glah* assists Mr Charkham's
argument. The application in that case appears to have been made under Ord 29,
r 6 and it does not appear that the line of authority dealing with solicitors' liens
was drawn to the court's attention. That is not surprising, if only because Dr
Glah was not an English solicitor and therefore fell outside the established scope c
of the equitable jurisdiction. I should also say that I find it difficult to accept that
all those who have been involved in the many cases which have come before the
court since 1884 have failed to realise that the jurisdiction which they were
purporting to exercise had ceased to exist by virtue of what is now Ord 29, r 6.
For the reasons I have given I am satisfied that it had not and that *Gamlen Chemical* d
Co (UK) Ltd v Rochem Ltd was not therefore decided per incuriam.

Mr Charkham's second line of argument was based on the fact that Richards
Butler had been retained by the plaintiffs in a number of matters in addition to
those to which the papers covered by their application related. Exhibited to Mr
Miller's affidavit is a schedule of the matters in respect of which Richards Butler
are seeking payment. Twelve separate cases are included and it is common e
ground that each of these matters gave rise to a separate retainer. The plaintiffs
admit that four of these have been finally concluded and that agreement appears
to have been all but reached in relation to three more. Mr Charkham pointed out
that in all the cases to which I have referred the court was concerned with a
solicitor who had been retained to conduct a single piece of litigation which was f
still pending, whose lien therefore arose only from that retainer, and who was
seeking to recover the costs incurred in relation to that litigation. To that extent,
therefore, the present case raises questions which did not arise for consideration
in any of the previous cases.

Mr Charkham's submission was to this effect. In the case of each retainer
which expired naturally (so-called 'dead' cases) the plaintiffs obtained a general g
lien for their costs which entitled them to retain any of the plaintiffs' papers still
in their possession, including, of course, papers relating to other matters in which
litigation was currently pending ('live' cases). Since those retainers had expired
naturally, it follows that they had not been discharged by Richards Butler.
Accordingly, one of the essential grounds of the court's jurisdiction to restrict the h
exercise of the liens arising under those retainers was missing, nor could those
liens be affected by the discharge of any other retainers, whether that was
brought about by the plaintiffs or by Richards Butler themselves. Therefore,
even if Richards Butler were responsible for the discharge of their retainers in the
live cases so as to bring the liens under those retainers within the rule laid down j
in *Heslop v Metcalfe*, they could none the less retain the papers through the
exercise of their liens arising under the dead cases.

In order to decide whether this argument is correct it is necessary to return to
the principles underlying the equitable jurisdiction relating to solicitors' liens. Mr
Charkham is right in saying that the cases show that the court has not in the past
been willing to interfere with the exercise of the lien, even where the papers

a concerned are required for pending litigation, in cases where the client has discharged the solicitor (see *Hughes v Hughes* [1958] 3 All ER 179 at 180, [1958] P 224 at 227 per Hodson LJ and *Gamlen Chemical Co (UK) Ltd v Rochem Ltd* [1980] 1 All ER 1049 at 1054–1055, 1058, [1980] 1 WLR 614 at 620, 624 per Goff and Templeman LJJ). However, the problem has always been seen as essentially a practical one of doing justice as between solicitor and client, and when the court b did interfere it did so because it considered it necessary in order to protect the client from the hardship and injustice which would otherwise result from the solicitor's action in terminating his retainer. In my judgment, where the solicitor terminates his retainer in relation to a live case the essential nature of the problem is not altered by the fact that he has previously been instructed on a matter which has by then become dead and thereby has a concurrent lien over the papers in the c case which is still live. It is still the solicitor's action in discharging the retainer and ceasing to act which causes the lien to have a practical effect and give rise to the hardship and injustice which the court seeks to mitigate. That being so, for the court to restrict the exercise of the lien which arises under an earlier retainer in the same manner as the lien arising under the current retainer is consistent d with the principle underlying the exercise of the equitable jurisdiction established in the decided cases. There is, therefore, in my view jurisdiction in such cases to make an order of the kind made in *Gamlen Chemical Co (UK) Ltd v Rochem Ltd* and the earlier cases, and the court should normally do so unless exceptional circumstances indicate otherwise. The lien in respect of outstanding costs in the dead matter would, of course, be equally protected by the redelivery of the e papers at the conclusion of the live action, and if for some reason there were a peculiar value to retaining possession of any of the papers in the live matter in relation to obtaining payment of outstanding costs in the dead matter, that is no doubt something which the court could take into account in the exercise of its discretion. For these reasons I do not consider that the mere fact that Richards f Butler were entitled to exercise a lien under their retainers in a number of dead matters prevents the court from making an order of the kind sought.

In these circumstances it becomes necessary to decide whether in the present case it was the plaintiffs or Richards Butler who terminated the retainers. In fact, of course, the plaintiffs and Richards Butler were drawing apart because the plaintiffs were unwilling to pay costs at the rates which Richards Butler sought to g charge, both for work already carried out and for work to be done in the future, and Richards Butler were unwilling to continue acting as the plaintiffs' solicitors if their costs were not paid. No doubt each case has to be decided on its own facts, but the plaintiffs submit that the decided cases give some indication of the way in which the court will approach the question. In *Heslop v Metcalfe* (1837) 3 My & Cr h 183, 40 ER 894 the solicitor told his client that he would not continue to act unless he received payment (which had been requested some months earlier) the next day. The client thereupon instructed another solicitor to take over the case. The court considered that the solicitor's action amounted to discharging himself. In *Robins v Goldingham* (1872) LR 13 Eq 440 the facts were similar. The solicitor j asked his client for funds to pay counsel's fees which the client declined to provide. Eventually the solicitor wrote a letter pointing out that it was unreasonable of the client to expect him to fund counsel's fees and continued 'I really must decline to increase my liabilities on your account unless some satisfactory arrangements be made as to costs' (see LR 13 Eq 440 at 441). The client thereupon appointed a new solicitor. It was argued that the solicitor had not discharged himself in that he was quite willing to go on if provided with

funds, but the court held otherwise, even though it did not consider that any
blame was to be attached to the solicitor. In *Gamlen Chemical Co (UK) Ltd v Rochem
Ltd* the situation was a little more complicated. In February 1979 the solicitor had
told the client—

"'unless my firm's bill is paid in the very near future, then we shall have no
alternative but to apply to the Court to be removed from the record ... I must ask
you to accept this letter as formal notice ... that if the balance of my firm's costs
and disbursements ... is not paid to us by Friday the 2nd March 1979, we will issue
a Summons ...'" (See [1980] 1 All ER 1049 at 1053, [1980] 1 WLR 614 at 618.)

However, they did not carry out that threat, the client took no steps to instruct
other solicitors and the original solicitors continued to act for the time being. On
25 June, however, their patience ran out. They wrote to the client saying that
they had no alternative but to apply to have themselves removed from the record
and could no longer act unless their position as regards costs was satisfactorily
secured. The same day they issued a summons. On 3 July they wrote to the client
enclosing a copy of the summons and reiterating that they could not continue to
act unless their position as regards costs was secured; but that if their costs were
paid before the hearing of the summons, they would be happy to continue to act.
Oliver J at first instance considered the case to be indistinguishable from *Robins v
Goldingham* and held that by issuing the summons and by indicating in their letter
of 3 July that they were not prepared to go on unless some arrangement was
made as to their costs the solicitors had discharged themselves.

Mr Deacon for the plaintiffs submitted that the present case was really on all
fours with *Gamlen Chemical Co (UK) Ltd v Rochem Ltd.* Although Richards Butler
were willing to continue to act for the plaintiffs, they made it clear in their letter
of 17 November that they would only do so if their costs were paid, and virtually
invited the plaintiffs to instruct other solicitors if they were not willing to do that,
an invitation which Dr Ismail on behalf of the plaintiffs accepted in his letter of 22
November. It was Richards Butler who thereby brought the retainers to an end,
he submitted, and their willingness to continue if their costs were paid does not
detract from that position. Mr Charkham, on the other hand, submitted that it
was the plaintiffs who terminated the retainers, not Richards Butler. Drawing a
parallel between Richards Butler's letter of 17 November and the solicitors' letter
of 23 February in *Gamlen Chemical Co (UK) Ltd v Rochem Ltd*, he submitted that it
was nothing more than an early warning. Richards Butler made it clear that they
did wish to continue to act for the plaintiffs and hoped to find a satisfactory
solution through discussions. It was clear from Dr Ismail's letter of 22 November
that it was he, not Richards Butler, who terminated the retainer.

It is interesting to see that an argument very similar to that of Mr Charkham
was advanced in *Gamlen Chemical Co (UK) Ltd v Rochem Ltd* but failed to impress
the court. The fact is that the authorities to which I have referred do not support
the conclusion that the client is considered to have discharged his solicitors
simply because he takes them at their word and instructs new solicitors rather
than accede to what may be quite justified requests for payment. Rather, the
court has generally treated the refusal by the solicitor to continue to act unless he
is put in funds as the effective discharge of his retainer (see [1980] 1 All ER 1049
at 1055, [1980] 1 WLR 614 at 621 per Goff LJ).

In the present case, if one reads Mr Francies' letter of 17 November 1995 as a
whole it makes Richards Butler's position quite clear: although they would like
to have continued to act for the plaintiffs, they were not willing to take any

a   further steps in any of the current matters unless and until their costs were paid or some satisfactory arrangement was made. As far as the cases involving the 'Satamaru', 'Yousef' and 'Diamond Reefer' were concerned, Mr Francies spelled the alternative out to the plaintiffs in quite unequivocal terms: they would have to instruct new solicitors. Dr Ismail's letter of 22 November shows that he took Mr Francies at his word. Mr Charkham submitted that the correspondence as a

b   whole does not support the view that Richards Butler unilaterally terminated the relationship on 17 November and I can see the force in that, but none the less when one looks at the matter objectively it seems clear to me that it was Richards Butler who, no doubt quite reasonably, brought matters to a head and who, by requiring payment of their outstanding costs as a condition of continuing to act, effectively brought their retainers to an end. Although the present case differs in

c   some respects on the facts, it is in my view indistinguishable in substance from *Robins v Goldingham* and *Gamlen Chemical Co (UK) Ltd v Rochem Ltd*. Once the plaintiffs accepted that position, as they did by the letter of 22 November and by instructing new solicitors straight away, the retainers were discharged and it is clear that despite further correspondence and negotiations they were never

d   renewed.

In these circumstances the plaintiffs would in the ordinary way be entitled as of course to an order that papers required for the conduct of pending litigation be delivered to their new solicitors against an undertaking, which those solicitors are willing to give, to restore them at the end of the litigation and without being required to provide any further security in respect of the outstanding costs.

e   However, it was recognised in *Gamlen Chemical Co (UK) Ltd v Rochem Ltd* that the court can, and in exceptional cases will, attach conditions to such an order to meet the overall justice of the case. Is this, then, an exceptional case, and if so, what conditions should the court impose?

Mr Charkham submitted that this is, as the master held, an exceptional case

f   and that the circumstances are such as to justify the order which he made, including the payment of £150,000 to Richards Butler. He based that submission partly on the general nature of the relationship between these parties and partly on the particular way in which the plaintiffs have behaved in relation to the bills submitted to them. As to the former, he submitted with some justification that this case is a far cry from the type of case considered by the court in *Heslop v*

g   *Metcalfe*, involving, as it does, experienced and sophisticated litigants who have enjoyed a good relationship for many years with a large and very reputable firm of solicitors. At any given time Richards Butler were acting for the plaintiffs in several matters which had progressed to different stages. Litigation of the kind in which the plaintiffs became involved was inevitably expensive and it would be

h   impracticable in this kind of relationship for solicitors to require clients to fund each case separately in advance. The relationship has to operate on the basis of mutual trust. There is no evidence that the plaintiffs cannot pay or provide adequate security for the outstanding costs, and in such cases the court ought to impose terms to ensure justice between the parties rather than allow its officers

j   to be exploited. As to the conduct of the plaintiffs in the present case, he pointed out that although bills rendered by Richards Butler in 1994 had been calculated on the same basis, the plaintiffs had not made any complaint about charging rates until after the 1995 bills were rendered. Moreover, complaints about the quality of the service provided by Richards Butler had been raised for the first time in December 1995 after the writ had been issued, and then only in the most general of terms. The plaintiffs had at one stage offered to pay a substantial sum (though still considerably less than the full amount outstanding) to settle the matter, so it could hardly be said that they were unable to raise the funds.

Mr Deacon submitted that there are no exceptional reasons in the present case for departing from the usual practice. He relied in particular on the judgment of Templeman LJ in *Gamlen Chemical Co (UK) Ltd v Rochem Ltd* where it is made clear that the fact that the solicitors may have had reasonable grounds for discharging themselves does not of itself provide sufficient reason for departing from the usual practice even under modern conditions. In the light of the Court of Appeal's reaffirmation in that case of the approach adopted in *Heslop v Metcalfe,* I do not think that the general considerations urged on me by Mr Charkham would themselves be sufficient to justify my departing from the normal practice in this case. I do, however, think that there is some force in Mr Charkham's other points. The reality of this case is that the value of the lien to Richards Butler is likely to be very considerably diminished if the papers currently required for the various pieces of live litigation are handed over now. Although I cannot form any conclusion at this stage about the merits of the plaintiffs' complaints, I think I am entitled to take into account the time and manner in which they have been raised and, at least as regards complaints about the quality of Richards Butler's work, the fact that only a few days earlier the plaintiffs were actively discussing with Richards Butler the terms upon which they might resume their relationship. In all the circumstances I can understand why the master felt it appropriate to make the order he did, though for reasons which I shall come to in a moment I think he went further than was justified in this case.

In *Gamlen Chemical Co (UK) Ltd v Rochem Ltd* Templeman LJ adverted to the possibility of requiring the client to pay sums admitted to be due in respect of costs, and in *A v B* [1984] 1 All ER 265 Leggatt J did impose a term of that kind. That was a strong case because, as the judge found, although the solicitors had discharged themselves (again because the client would not pay their costs), they had behaved impeccably and, moreover, by the time the application came before the court they had already obtained a default judgment against the client for the costs in question. The present case is rather different, but it is clear from the judgment of Templeman LJ that in exercising its discretion the court is entitled to take into account all the circumstances of the case, including the nature of the case, the stage which the litigation has reached, the conduct of the solicitor and client respectively, and the balance of hardship.

I can deal briefly with one point made in argument on behalf of the plaintiffs, namely that some of the bills which they have refused to pay were rendered around the middle of August 1995 rather than at the end of the month, contrary to the terms of Richards Butler's retainer, and that the costs to which they related were therefore not due at all at that time. There is little merit in that argument since it is admitted that the bills were due to be rendered at the end of August in any event, and having seen the explanation given in Mr Francies' affidavit I am satisfied that they were delivered early with the plaintiffs' approval. In fact, almost half the outstanding costs were incurred in relation to matters which are now dead and a further quarter in relation to the three actions in which agreement has all but been reached. As I have said, the plaintiffs do not appear to have made any complaint in the past about Richards Butler's charges or the quality of their work. However, the fact remains that the plaintiffs do not admit that any sum is due to Richards Butler when these matters have been taken into account, and on the material before me I cannot decide whether at the end of the day Richards Butler will be held entitled to recover the full amount of their claim, a or indeed any particular amount. I understand that they have issued a summons seeking summary judgment or an interim payment, so that is a question which will have to be considered in those proceedings. That distinguishes the present case from *A v B* [1984] 1 All ER 265 and from the type of case contemplated by Templeman LJ, and I do not think that it would be right under these circumstances to order the plaintiffs make any payment to Richards Butler at this stage.

b However, when I consider the other aspects of this case I do think that some departure from the normal practice is called for in the interests of justice. I can see no basis for criticising Richards Butler's conduct in this matter, and such indications as there are suggest that in some respects the plaintiffs' attitude may owe more to negotiating tactics than to a real sense of grievance. I accept that the plaintiffs require the immediate delivery of the papers in the three matters

c mentioned in their summons which remain fully live, but if Richards Butler are required to hand over the papers on the usual terms their lien is likely to prove of little value when the papers are returned to them. It has not been suggested, on the other hand, that the plaintiffs are likely to suffer any real hardship if they are required to provide security of another kind other than the general effect on their

d cash flow of having to fund a payment into court. That is a difficulty which can probably be largely overcome by providing security in some other recognised form. Taking all these matters into account I am satisfied that the interests of justice in this case require that the plaintiffs provide some security for Richards Butler's claim.

Before deciding in what form and in what amount it would be appropriate to

e require security, there is one other matter to be considered. Among the documents held by Richards Butler are a number of P & I Club letters of undertaking and bank guarantees which provide for payment to Richards Butler as the plaintiffs' solicitors of sums which may be adjudged or agreed to be due to them. It was common ground that Richards Butler would have an equitable lien in

f respect of their costs on the fruits of litigation obtained by their efforts and that the letters of undertaking therefore indirectly provide them with a measure of security for their outstanding costs. Mr Deacon was inclined to accept, correctly in my view, that these documents were not required for the conduct of pending litigation and could properly be excluded from the order he is seeking. In my judgment it is appropriate that they should be excluded from the order and in the

g ordinary way the value of such security is something which can be taken into account in deciding what additional security the plaintiffs should be required to provide. The difficulty I am faced with in this case, however, is that there is no material before me which would enable me to form any reliable view of the likely value of that security.

h If the plaintiffs are to be required to provide security for Richards Butler's claim as the price of obtaining delivery of their papers, as I think they should, I can see no satisfactory basis for fixing the amount of that security at anything short of the full amount of the claim. The total amount claimed by Richards Butler in their writ issued on 8 December is £439,254·50, to which I think it appropriate to add

j a small allowance for further interest and costs. In the light of all these matters I consider that the appropriate order in this case is that upon provision by the plaintiffs of security in the sum of £450,000 for the defendants' claim for outstanding costs the defendants do deliver to the plaintiffs' solicitors the documents referred to in the notice of appeal, except for the letters of undertaking issued in the cases of the 'Satamaru', 'Yousef', 'Diamond Reefer', 'Oceanic Ice' and 'Pacific Queen'. The security can be provided by way of payment into court, bank guarantee, or any other means which the parties may agree or which, in the absence of agreement, the court considers acceptable. I will hear counsel on this before finally settling the terms of the order.

Finally, before leaving this matter I should like to express my gratitude to both counsel for the admirable quality of their arguments and the assistance which they have given me.

Order accordingly.

K Mydeen Esq   Barrister.

a
Wraith v Sheffield Forgemasters Ltd

QUEEN'S BENCH DIVISION
POTTER J SITTING WITH MASTER WRIGHT AND MR P SYCAMORE AS ASSESSORS
15 DECEMBER 1995, 31 JANUARY 1996

b

Costs – Taxation – Solicitor – Contentious business – Level of fees allowable – Whether reasonable for plaintiff to instruct London solicitors in case proceeding in Sheffield – Whether costs recoverable at London or Sheffield rates – RSC Ord 62, r 12(1).

c The plaintiff was injured in an industrial accident in Sheffield in the course of his employment by the defendant and issued a claim for compensation with the assistance of his trade union, which recommended and instructed on his behalf their London solicitors. The case was commenced in London, but at an early stage was transferred to Sheffield by consent. Judgment was given for the plaintiff with costs and his solicitors thereafter produced a bill for taxation *d* claiming, in respect of profit costs, the total sum of £53,526. Their charging rates were stated to be in accordance with the 'broad average cost' of litigation in the Holborn and Westminster area and were allowed by the deputy district judge who conducted the taxation. The defendant lodged an objection, contending that, since the case had proceeded in the Sheffield District Registry and was heard *e* at Sheffield, the bill of costs should be taxed on the hypothesis that a Sheffield solicitor had acted. The deputy district judge refused to interfere with the amounts allowed on the taxation on the ground that the bill did not include any increased costs occasioned by the location of the solicitors and that their rate was appropriate to the work carried out. The defendant thereafter applied for a review of the taxation, contending principally that in view of the discrepancy *f* between the broad costs of litigation in London and in Sheffield, the London solicitors' costs were not 'costs reasonably incurred' within the meaning of RSC Ord 62, r 12(1)ᵃ, or if such costs were reasonably incurred from the point of view of the plaintiff, then none the less the 'reasonable amount' to be allowed in respect of them should be no more than an amount assessed in accordance with the Sheffield rates.

g

Held – When assessing costs under RSC Ord 62, r 12(1) a taxing master should consider, first, whether the costs claimed were reasonably incurred by the plaintiff for his own purposes in the litigation and, second, what costs it was reasonable for the paying party to be required to meet. While on the first *h* question it was in principle open to the paying party to object that the costs claimed were not reasonably incurred, the taxing master, in deciding whether such an objection was sustainable in practice, should focus primarily on the reasonable interests of the plaintiff and assess whether, having regard to the extent and importance of the litigation to a reasonably minded plaintiff, a *j* reasonable choice had been made. If he was satisfied that it had, the second question then imported consideration of the appropriate rate or fee for a solicitor or counsel of the status and type retained. On the facts, it was reasonable for the plaintiff to have consulted with and placed his case in the hands of his trade union

---

a   Rule 12(1), so far as material, provides: 'On a taxation of costs on the standard basis there shall be allowed a reasonable amount in respect of all costs reasonably incurred ...'

and, through them, to have instructed the London solicitors they recommended; and since the solicitors' costs were in accordance with the broad average costs of solicitors in their area, it was not therefore appropriate to impose a lower rate of charge than that approved by the deputy district judge. The application would accordingly be dismissed (see p 534 *d* to p 535 *a e* to *j*, post).

KPMG Peat Marwick McLintock v HLT Group Ltd [1995] 2 All ER 180 considered.

Notes

For taxation and assessment of costs generally, see 37 *Halsbury's Laws* (4th edn) paras 726–732, 744–753, and for cases on the subject, see 37(3) *Digest* (Reissue) 286–296, 301–327, 4623–4680, 4724–4927.

Cases referred to in judgment

Ajanaku, Re (28 October 1991) referred to in Butterworths Costs Service N 399.
KPMG Peat Marwick McLintock v HLT Group Ltd [1995] 2 All ER 180.
R v Dudley Magistrates' Court, ex p Power City Stores Ltd (1990) 154 JP 654, DC.
R v Goodwin (January 1984) referred to in Taxing Compendium S7.
R v Wilkinson [1980] 1 All ER 597, [1980] 1 WLR 396.
Smith v Butler (1875) LR 19 Eq 473, [1874–80] All ER Rep 425.

Summons for review of taxation

By summons dated 15 December 1994 the defendants, Sheffield Forgemasters Ltd, applied under RSC Ord 62, r 35(1) for a review of the taxation of Deputy District Judge Thompson made on 17 November 1994, whereby he disallowed an objection by the defendants to his taxation on 19 August 1994 of the costs claimed by the London solicitors to the plaintiff, Trevor Wraith, in respect of a personal injury action brought by him against the defendants in the Queen's Bench Division of the High Court at Sheffield. The summons was heard and judgment was given in chambers. The case is reported by permission of Potter J. The facts are set out in the judgment.

Jeremy Morgan (instructed by *Nelson & Co*, Leeds) for the defendant.
Paul Kilcoyne (instructed by *Russell Jones & Walker*) for the plaintiff.

Cur adv vult

31 January 1996. The following judgment was delivered.

POTTER J. This is the hearing of a summons under RSC Ord 62, r 35 to review the allowance on taxation by Deputy District Judge Thompson of the hourly rates of charge claimed by the plaintiff's solicitors. The question is whether the plaintiff, who instructed London solicitors to conduct a case which proceeded in the Sheffield District Registry and was heard at Sheffield, should be allowed to recover costs at London or Sheffield rates. At trial, the plaintiff obtained judgment by consent for £271,500 plus costs on the standard basis in respect of his personal injuries claim. On the third day of the hearing, agreement was reached to settle the plaintiff's case in the sum of £350,000, the judgment sum being the balance of that settlement figure after taking into account an earlier interim payment. The judgment and order for costs are dated 19 May 1993.

The case concerned an industrial accident in 1985 when the plaintiff, in the course of his employment by the defendants, slipped and fell from the walkway of an overhead crane to the shop floor below. It was not an unduly complicated a claim but there were a large number of witnesses and some complications in relation to quantum, the plaintiff being confined to a wheelchair and having suffered some brain damage and psychological disturbance. At the interlocutory stage there had been an application for specific discovery and for an interim payment. Leading and junior counsel appeared at the trial.

b The plaintiff was a member of a trade union into whose hands he placed his claim for compensation. The union advised him in relation to the proceedings and supported his case, recommending and instructing on his behalf their London solicitors who specialised in personal injury claims and who usually handled their cases, Messrs Russell Jones & Walker. The case was commenced in London, but early in its interlocutory history it was transferred to Sheffield by consent.

c The solicitors produced their bill for taxation, claiming in respect of profit costs the total sum of £53,526. Their charging rate, as stated in the bill, was £75 per hour in respect of costs prior to 1 April 1991 and £90 per hour in respect of costs incurred thereafter, on the basis that the action justified a partner having its conduct throughout. The rates were stated to be in accordance with the 'broad average cost' of litigation in the Holborn and Westminster area as set out in a d Central London Law Society survey for that area.

The deputy district judge allowed the hourly rates contended for, although he disallowed various items and amounts under heads which are irrelevant on this review.

e On 8 September 1994 the defendants lodged an objection in these terms:

'The Plaintiff's address on the writ is in Sheffield. He or his Trades Union on his behalf has instructed London solicitors. The distant solicitor rule applies and the bill of costs should be taxed on the hypothesis that a Sheffield solicitor has acted. The accident occurred in 1985 when hourly charging f rates allowed in Sheffield were £32 per hour and trial took place in 1993 for which date Senior Solicitors are being allowed upon taxation the sum of £65 per hour. Upon that basis and dealing with the matter by averaging the expense rates over the period of time in question the costs in Part 1 of the Bill should be allowed at £40 per hour and in Part 2 at £60 per hour.'

g On 30 September 1994 the plaintiff replied to the objection.

On 17 November 1994 the deputy district judge gave written reasons pursuant to Ord 62, r 34(4). He reviewed authorities to which he had been referred by the defendants which were not directly in point, relating as they did to the question h of whether or not a paying party should be obliged to pay costs directly increased by reason of the solicitor's distance from the party instructing him, or the witnesses concerned, or the court of trial (eg travelling time and expense), as opposed to whether the paying party was obliged to pay costs in respect of work properly and reasonable carried out by the successful party's solicitor in the area in which his office was located. In that respect the deputy district judge said (and j it has not been challenged before me):

'9. Having considered the bill of costs in full at the original taxation I was satisfied that the bill did not include any increased costs occasioned by any extra work or expense directly caused by the fact that the Plaintiff's Solicitors were in London ...'

After reference to *Re Ajanaku* (28 October 1991), referred to in Butterworths Costs Service N 399, to which I shall refer further below, the deputy district judge went on to state:

> '… there was no issue on the taxation or the review concerning the hourly charging rates for London solicitors or Sheffield solicitors for the period involved. The issue was whether the plaintiff's solicitors, who are in London and who did their work in London, should be allowed an hourly charging rate as though they were in Sheffield and did their work in Sheffield. I disagree with the defendants' objection No 1. The London hourly charging rate allowed by me on the taxation is appropriate to apply to the work carried out by the plaintiff's solicitors. 14. I did not at the taxation nor do I now consider it to have been unreasonable for the plaintiff to consult the solicitors he did. Such consultation may very well have led to an increase in the "solicitor and own client" costs owing to the distance between the two. I am however satisfied that those costs have not been claimed by the plaintiff against the defendants in this taxation. 15. For the reasons given above I am not prepared to interfere with amounts allowed by me on the taxation on 19 August 1994.'

The submission of Mr Morgan for the defendants on this application can be shortly stated. It is as follows. (1) Sheffield was the natural forum for the case. The parties resided there, as did all or almost all of the witnesses. It was also the locus of the accident. (2) There are a substantial number of solicitors in Sheffield or Leeds (which is reasonably nearby) who regularly and competently handle work of this kind. (3) There were no special features of the case which meant that it could be handled more advantageously in London or by London solicitors, nor any requiring or specially indicating trial in the Royal Courts of Justice. (4) There was no evidence before the deputy district judge that London solicitors in general, or the plaintiff's solicitors in particular, handled such cases any more expertly than those in Sheffield or Leeds. (5) The position has now been reached where there is such a large discrepancy between the broad costs of litigation in London and in Sheffield that, whatever the position between a party and his own solicitor, it is not reasonable to expect the opposite paying party on a standard basis taxation to pay for a London solicitor at London rates in respect of litigation in Sheffield which could equally well be conducted by a Sheffield solicitor.

Mr Morgan submitted that, in a case of this kind, when assessing 'a reasonable amount in respect of all costs reasonably incurred' (Ord 62, r 12(1)), it is open to the taxing officer either to take the view that the amount of the discrepancy yielded by application of the rival rates is such that the London solicitor's costs are not 'costs reasonably incurred' by the plaintiff, or (if such costs were reasonably incurred from the point of view of the plaintiff) then none the less the 'reasonable amount' to be allowed in respect of them should be no more than an amount assessed in accordance with the Sheffield rates.

It was conceded by Mr Morgan for the defendants that, if this application is decided in his favour, it will break new ground and have considerable repercussions. It will break new ground because taxing masters and district judges have hitherto generally proceeded on the basis that, in carrying out their task in determining 'the broad average direct cost of work done … in the relevant area at the relevant time' (*R v Wilkinson* [1980] 1 All ER 597 at 604, [1980] 1 WLR 396 at 404), the 'relevant area' is the area in which the work was done (*Re Ajanaku* (28 October 1991), referred to in Butterworths Costs Service N 399). Those a principles have recently been recited and applied in *KPMG Peat Marwick McLintock v HLT Group Ltd* [1995] 2 All ER 180. It will have widespread repercussions because there are a number of insurers and trades unions who are accustomed to instruct particular firms of London solicitors for litigation conducted outside London as well as in the Royal Courts of Justice on the basis that experience and efficiency, as well as economy and ease of administration, are thereby achieved b in their litigation 'across the board', albeit individual cases might be adequately conducted by local firms.

It is Mr Morgan's submission that none of the hitherto decided cases, when closely examined, preclude the submissions which he makes in this case. The judgment in *Re Ajanaku* was either very brief or is very sparsely reported. However, it relates to a case in the Family Division of the High Court which was c originally a Manchester case, in which it was appropriate that Manchester solicitors were instructed, but which had been transferred at some stage to London where it was heard. The district judge carrying out the taxation had applied rates applicable in the London area. It was held on review that the Manchester rate was the appropriate rate to apply. However, the case did not d turn upon the general question of whether or not it was reasonable to instruct solicitors in an area substantially more expensive than the 'natural locus' for the litigation.

In the *KPMG* case, while it was held that the solicitors' costs on taxation should be taxed by reference to the broad average direct costs in the area for such a firm, and the fact that the party could have obtained the same services at a much lower e price elsewhere was irrelevant, the decision was premised on a finding that it was reasonable for the plaintiffs to have instructed the City of London solicitors who were retained rather than solicitors located nearby in the City of Westminster and Holborn, where the broad average direct hourly costs of litigation in the area were substantially less. In giving judgment Auld J said ([1995] 2 All ER 180 at 185– f 186):

> 'The plaintiffs contend first that Master Ellis ... was clearly reluctant to allow rates applicable to the area in which the work was done, the City of London, because he considered that it was unreasonable to allow such rates. Whilst he did not expressly say so, his reasoning necessarily required him to g conclude that it was unreasonable of the plaintiffs to instruct City solicitors of the calibre of Travers Smith Braithwaite in the matter. The plaintiffs maintain that, as a leading firm of City accountants facing allegations of professional negligence, they were entitled to instruct City solicitors of such calibre to act for them in that litigation. The defendant maintains that the h expertise of City solicitors was not required for this case, and that the mere fact that the plaintiffs and their solicitors were located in the City does not mean that it should have to pay higher rates than it would have to pay for solicitors instructed outside the City. In my view, Master Ellis was wrong to regard as unreasonable "the broad average direct costs" of City of London j solicitors for such a case. His approach was contrary to authority and was, in any event, inappropriate to the circumstances of this case, in particular the standing and location of the plaintiffs meeting allegations of professional negligence in a case with commercial undertones. If, as I find, it was reasonable for the plaintiffs to have instructed Travers Smith Braithwaite in the litigation, then the firm's costs on taxation should be taxed by reference to the broad average direct costs for such a firm in the area. The fact that the

plaintiffs could have obtained the same services at a much lower price than
that average elsewhere is irrelevant (cf *R v Dudley Magistrates' Court, ex p
Power City Stores Ltd* (1990) 154 JP 654 on the question of the reasonableness
of instructing leading counsel).'

Mr Morgan submitted that it was plain that the remark of Auld J that the
availability of the same services at a lower price elsewhere was irrelevant, was
premised on the assumption of a need for the plaintiff to prove that it was
reasonable to have instructed the particular firm in the first place and, in relation
to that question, did not exclude as an element in the reasonableness of the
plaintiff's decision its likely impact on the defendant as the paying party in the
event that the plaintiff was successful in the litigation.

Mr Morgan also relied upon the authoritative booklet published by the Lord
Chancellor's Department in 1984 and written by former Chief Taxing Master
Matthews, *Notes for Guidance on the Taxation of Civil Costs*. Under the heading
'distant solicitors', paras 66 and 67 of that booklet state as follows:

> '66. Two separate problems arise; first where a solicitor is instructed who
> practises at a distance from the locus and the client or secondly where the
> solicitor practises at a distance from counsel's chambers or the court. The
> first problem arises most often where a plaintiff is represented by a trade
> union solicitor or a defendant is represented by an insurance solicitor and
> unless there are exceptional and compelling reasons to the contrary the costs
> should be taxed on the hypothesis that a local solicitor had acted and any
> increased costs (e.g. the time and expense in travelling to interview the client
> or witnesses or view the locus) should be reduced or disallowed. 67. The
> second problem usually arises in cases where a "distant" solicitor is
> nominated to act for the client under a civil aid certificate or where a case is
> transferred to London or another District Registry or to a distant town for
> trial. Here consideration should be given to the employment of a solicitor
> agent in order to avoid the extra cost and expenses which would be involved
> if the principal travelled to undertake the work himself.'

Mr Morgan argued that the logic which applies to disallowance of costs directly
increased by reason of the distance of a solicitor from the client, witnesses or
locus should be extended to increased costs incurred by reason of the fact that the
particular locus of the solicitor instructed is one which generates higher rates for
the broad costs of litigation. In this connection he also referred to *R v Goodwin*
(January 1984) referred to in Taxing Compendium S7 (regs 5 and 6: travelling and
waiting and instruction of a distant solicitor), in which a taxing master held under
the Legal Aid in Criminal and Care Proceedings (Costs) Regulations 1968, SI
1968/1231 (now the Legal Aid in Criminal and Care Proceedings (Costs)
(Amendment) Regulations 1990, SI 1990/488) that the amounts allowed on
taxation for travelling and waiting time to a solicitor whose practice was based
about 100 miles from his legally aided client's home and the local court where the
case was heard, were properly to be assessed on the basis of what should
reasonably have been allowed to a local solicitor.

Mr Morgan emphasised that, for purposes of taxation, there is a well-
recognised distinction between the costs which it is reasonable for a plaintiff to
incur for his own purposes in the litigation and the costs which it is reasonable for
the paying party to be required to meet. This is the essential difference between
the standard and indemnity basis of taxation and between costs inter partes and

a   solicitor and own client costs (see Ord 62, rr 12(1), (2) and 15). He submitted that a similar type of distinction is recognised and preserved in Ord 62, r 12(1) by use of the phrase 'a reasonable amount in respect of all costs reasonably incurred'.

While the reasoning in the authorities to date, including the *KPMG* case, does not appear specifically to have analysed Ord 62, r 12(1) in the terms of such a distinction, it does seem to me that the way in which the sub-paragraph is phrased
b   invites a twofold approach on those lines. It would certainly reflect the approach stated to be required by Woolf LJ in *R v Dudley Magistrates' Court, ex p Power City Stores Ltd* (1990) 154 JP 654 (referred to by Auld J in *KPMG*) when dealing with the provisions of s 16(6) of the Prosecution of Offences Act 1985 and regulations relating thereto in respect of orders for costs out of central funds made by magistrates' courts when dismissing cases dealt with summarily. The case
c   concerned the expenses incurred by a defendant in retaining leading counsel in a case in which the clerk to the magistrates, in assessing the amount to be paid under their order, disallowed the claim for leading counsel's fees on the grounds that the case could more than adequately have been dealt with by senior solicitor or junior counsel.

d   Section 16(6) provided:

> '... for the payment out of central funds ... of such amount as the court considers reasonably sufficient to compensate him for any expenses properly incurred by him in the proceedings.'

In considering that question, Woolf LJ said of the taxing officer's task (at 657–
e   658):

> '... he has to ask himself, first of all, whether the expenses are ones which are properly incurred by the defendant. Looking at the situation in this case the cost of instructing leading counsel, in my view, could not be described as other than expenses properly incurred, subject to the amount of those costs
f   being reasonable. Having regard to the nature of the case, which I have already described, it is quite impossible for it to be said that the defendants were acting improperly in instructing leading counsel. Having come to the conclusion that the expenses are properly incurred the court's next task is to consider the amount which is reasonably sufficient to compensate the
g   defendants for those costs. That is a question of quantum.'

Woolf LJ went on to consider reg 7 of the Costs in Criminal Cases (General) Regulations 1986, SI 1986/1335, which applied to the determination of the costs payable. Regulation 7(1) required to be allowed—

h   'such costs in respect of—(a) such work as appears to have been actually and reasonably done ... as it considers reasonably sufficient to compensate the applicant for any expenses properly incurred by him in the proceedings.'

Regulation 7(3) provided:

j   'When determining costs for the purpose of this regulation, there shall be allowed a reasonable amount in respect of all costs reasonably incurred and any doubt which the appropriate authority may have as to whether the costs were reasonably incurred or were reasonable in amount shall be resolved against the applicant.'

It will be noted that the wording of reg 7(3) is effectively in identical terms to that of Ord 62, r 12(1) so far as the costs to be allowed are concerned.

In this context Woolf LJ observed that, in relation to the retention of leading *a* counsel, the taxing officer had asked himself the wrong question:

> 'What he was asking himself was this: could a junior counsel or a senior solicitor reasonably have conducted the case on behalf of the applicants? ... Mr. Inman submits that ... the applicants acted reasonably in employing leading counsel, which is an entirely different question ... If it was *b* reasonable for him to employ leading counsel, then in the language of s.16 the expenses were properly incurred. It seems to me the criticism which is made by Mr. Inman ... is justified. If the justices' clerk had asked himself the right question he would undoubtedly have come to a different conclusion from that which he did.' (See 154 JP 654 at 659–660.)

In directing the justices' clerk to reconsider the matter on the basis that it was *c* reasonable to engage leading counsel, Woolf LJ made clear that the separate question of quantum, namely the consideration of what fees were properly recoverable in respect of the instruction of leading counsel, was a matter for separate assessment by the taxing officer.

In my view, the cases, and in particular the decision in the *KPMG* case, *d* recognise that in relation to the first question, Were the costs reasonably incurred?, it is in principle open to the paying party, on a taxation of costs on the standard basis, to contend that the successful party's costs have not been 'reasonably incurred' to the extent that they have been augmented by employment of a solicitor who, by reason of his calibre, normal area of practice, status or location, amounts to an unsuitable or 'luxury' choice, made on grounds *e* other than grounds which would be taken into account by an ordinary reasonable litigant concerned to obtain skilful, competent and efficient representation in the type of litigation concerned (cf the remarks of Malins V-C in *Smith v Butler* (1875) 19 LR Eq 473 at 475, [1874–80] All ER Rep 425 at 426, since when the test of 'necessity' has been replaced by that of 'reasonableness'). *f*

However, in deciding whether such an objection is sustainable in practice, the focus is primarily upon the reasonable interests of the plaintiff in the litigation, so that, in relation to broad categories of costs, such as those generated by the decision of a plaintiff to employ a particular status or type of solicitor or counsel, or one located in a particular area, one looks to see whether, having regard to the extent and importance of the litigation to a reasonably minded plaintiff, a *g* reasonable choice or decision has been made. If satisfied that the choice or decision was reasonable, it is the second question, What is a reasonable amount to be allowed?, which imports consideration of the appropriate rate or fee for a solicitor or counsel of the status and type retained. If not satisfied that the choice or decision was reasonable, then the question of 'reasonable amount' will fall to *h* be assessed on the notional basis of the costs reasonably to be allowed in respect of a solicitor or counsel of the status or type which should have been retained.

In either case, solicitors' hourly rates will be assessed, not on the basis of the solicitor's actual charging rates, but (in a case where the decision to retain was reasonable) on the basis of the broad costs of litigation in the area of the solicitor *j* retained or (in a case where the choice made was not reasonable) of the type or class of solicitor who ought to have been retained.

Applying that process of reasoning on this review, I consider (as the deputy district judge considered) that it was reasonable for the plaintiff (or his trade union on his behalf) to instruct their London solicitors in this case. From the personal point of view of the plaintiff, it was entirely reasonable to consult and a place his case in the hands of his trade union and, through them, to instruct whatever solicitor they recommended. From the point of view of the trade union acting on the plaintiff's behalf, it was reasonable for them to instruct the solicitors who regularly and usually handled their substantial personal injury work and in whom they had confidence borne of a long-standing relationship.

b This was an important case from the plaintiff's point of view (even if not unduly complicated). Viewed on its own, despite the location of the defendants, it justified the initial view that a hearing in London was appropriate and it is noteworthy that, prior to the agreement to transfer it to Sheffield, which was made on the plaintiff's solicitors' initiative, no objection or contrary suggestion (let alone any application to transfer) had been made by the defendants.

c Whilst no doubt there were firms of solicitors in Sheffield or Leeds well qualified to do the work, it has not been argued that (for any reason other than the effect of London charging rates upon the defendants if they lost the case) there was any requirement of reasonableness resting upon the plaintiff to appoint a local solicitor. Nor does any such requirement seem to me to arise simply on the basis that Sheffield was some kind of 'forum conveniens' for the hearing. In this country, distances are not great and communication is easy; the solicitors were prepared to travel and the plaintiff (or his trade union) to meet any increase in costs such as travelling time and expense on a solicitor and own client basis.

d I now turn to consider whether, despite my decision that it was reasonable to instruct London solicitors, and despite the (unchallenged) view of the deputy district judge that the hours allowed on taxation were reasonably incurred and the rates of charge reasonable for London work, the proper course, taking into account the interests of the paying party, is to impose a lower (Sheffield) rate of charge.

e Looked at in the light of the *KPMG* case, it seems plain that course is not appropriate. In that case it was stated that, where it is reasonable for the plaintiff to have instructed the solicitors concerned in the litigation, the firm's costs on taxation should be taxed by reference to broad average direct costs for such a firm in that area (see [1995] 2 All ER 180 at 186). Such a ruling does not only rest on the authority of *Re Ajanaku* but also in common sense, since the reasonable costs of a solicitor engaged in litigation depend to a large extent on local conditions in terms of the levels of rent, rates, staff salaries etc obtaining within the area.

g Furthermore, while the 'reasonable costs' allowable in respect of any individual category or item in a particular bill are conventional rather than actual, they are at least based upon the principle of an inter partes indemnity for costs properly and reasonably incurred by the solicitor in question, the underlying principle being that the successful party is entitled to be compensated for his reasonable

h costs by the paying party. In that respect, as further stated in the *KPMG* case, once it has been determined that the plaintiff acted reasonably in retaining the solicitor he did, the fact that the plaintiff could have obtained elsewhere the same services at a lower price than the average direct costs for a firm in the area of the solicitor retained is to be disregarded.

j That is enough to dispose of this review in favour of the plaintiff.

I would only add this. The main thrust of the defendants' application was essentially that the discrepancy between London and provincial rates of charge is now so great that, in any case where the 'natural forum' is a provincial court centre and the successful party has retained a London solicitor for a case which has no features which make it peculiarly appropriate for trial in London, and which is a case which could be conducted equally competently by a provincial solicitor, the successful party's costs should be taxed on the basis of charging rates local to the natural forum.

On the present state of the law such a broad proposition is unacceptable because (a) it fails to take account of the various other considerations which may reasonably guide a party in the selection of a London solicitor in the first place, and (b) it would, if applied, lead to wholesale inroads into the principle that a party is entitled to recover his solicitor's costs based on the broad average cost of litigation in the area in which the solicitor practises and in which his services are largely performed.

If, in future, the discrepancy between charging rates continues to widen, then it may become appropriate for taxing officers to attach more emphasis to that consideration when assessing the reasonableness of the winning party's choice of solicitor. It may even be that at some future time requirements of policy will dictate judicial or statutory intervention so as to modify the principle that a solicitor retained on grounds judged to be objectively reasonable in the interests of the winning party should nonetheless have his charging rates assessed on a basis which involves departure from the underlying concept of compensation in respect of costs reasonably incurred by the plaintiff.

However, so far as this review is concerned, I have no material before me of the kind which would be necessary or sufficient even to contemplate such an exercise; nor, in the light of the previous decisions to which I have referred, do I think it would be proper for me to do so. I do not know how far the discrepancy between London and Sheffield rates spoken to in this case is typical of other court centres; I do not even know on what material those Sheffield rates which throw up such discrepancy were agreed. Unless or until an exercise is conducted which demonstrates on a reliable basis the size and nature of the problem across the spread of provincial centres in relation to which any change of approach would fall to be applied, a submission advanced on the broad ground set out above does not seem to me to merit application as a general principle of taxation.

The defendants' application is refused.

Application dismissed.

K Mydeen Esq   Barrister.

a
Re Campbell (a bankrupt)

CHANCERY DIVISION

KNOX J

b   19, 20 OCTOBER 1995

Bankruptcy – Property available for distribution – Bankrupt receiving award from Criminal Injuries Compensation Board – Application for award made before bankruptcy order – Action by trustee in bankruptcy claiming award – Whether award part of bankrupt's estate at time of bankruptcy order – Whether award representing a
c *future or contingent interest in 'property' – Insolvency Act 1986, ss 283, 436.*

The respondent suffered serious injuries as a result of a criminal assault and was awarded £200,000 in compensation by the Criminal Injuries Compensation Board. Prior to the award, the respondent had been adjudicated bankrupt, with
d the result that, on receiving the sum of £182,150 (a deduction having been made in respect of an interim payment), her solicitors informed the Official Receiver of receipt of the award. The trustee in bankruptcy thereafter obtained an order of examination under the Insolvency Act 1986. Following the examination, the court ordered that the respondent should pay over the sum of £182,150 with interest to the trustee, on the ground that the award fell within the definition of
e 'property' in s 436[a] of the 1986 Act and therefore, under s 283[b], formed part of the bankrupt's estate at the time of the bankruptcy order. The respondent applied to rescind the order, contending that an award made to an applicant who became bankrupt after applying for compensation, but prior to its award, could not form part of the bankrupt's estate at the time of the bankruptcy order. The order was
f rescinded and the trustee appealed, contending that at the time of the bankruptcy order there was, vested in the bankrupt, either a future or contingent interest in 'property' within the meaning of the 1986 Act.

Held – On its true construction, the word 'property' when used in the definition of property in the 1986 Act was not intended to describe anything other than an
g existing item; it could not refer to something which did not exist at the time of the bankruptcy order but might possibly come into existence on the occurrence of some uncertain event in the future. That situation was distinct from one involving a future or contingent interest arising out of or incidental to property because there was no underlying existing property which (or the proceeds of sale
h of which) was susceptible to the existence of a proprietary interest, even a future one. Given that, at the date of the bankruptcy order, the respondent had only a prospect of receiving an award by the Criminal Injuries Compensation Board, to describe such a prospect as an interest in property would be to enlarge the concept of property contained in the Act beyond that which was intended. It
j followed that that prospect was not, at the date of the bankruptcy order, part of the respondent's property in such a way as to vest in the trustee in bankruptcy when she became bankrupt. The appeal would accordingly be dismissed (see p 539 *f*, p 540 *e* to *j* and p 543 *j* to p 544 *c*, post).

---

a   Section 436, so far as material, is set out at p 540 *b*, post
b   Section 283, so far as material, is set out at p 539 *j*, post

Notes

For meaning of 'bankrupt's estate', see 3(2) *Halsbury's Laws* (4th edn reissue) para 204, and for vesting of property in trustee, see ibid para 380.

For the Insolvency Act 1986, ss 283, 436, see 4 *Halsbury's Statutes* (4th edn) (1987 reissue) 925, 1051.

Cases referred to in judgment

Beckham v Drake (1849) 2 HL Cas 579, 9 ER 1213.
Brunsden v Humphrey (1884) 14 QBD 141, [1881–5] All ER Rep 357, CA.
Heath v Tang, Stevens v Peacock [1993] 4 All ER 694, [1993] 1 WLR 1421, CA.
Howard v Crowther (1841) 8 M & W 601, 151 ER 1179.
Wilson v United Counties Bank Ltd [1920] AC 102, [1918–19] All ER Rep 1035, HL.

Cases also cited or referred to in skeleton arguments

Isaacs v Robertson [1984] 3 All ER 140, [1985] AC 97, PC.
Metroinvest Anstalt v Commercial Union Assurance Co plc [1985] 2 All ER 318, [1985] 1 WLR 513, CA.

Appeal

The trustee in bankruptcy, Henry Robert Guest, appealed from the order of Deputy District Judge Glover dated 12 July 1995, whereby he, inter alia, set aside the order of District Judge Jackson made on 16 January 1995 that the bankrupt, Mrs Jane Elizabeth Campbell, pay the sum of £182,150, received by her from the Criminal Injuries Compensation Board, together with interest to the trustee in bankruptcy. The facts are set out in the judgment.

Ian McCulloch (instructed by *John Healey & Co*, Brighton) for the trustee in bankruptcy.
Marcia Shekerdemian (instructed by *Smart & Spicer*, Eastbourne) for Mrs Campbell.

KNOX J. This is an appeal from a decision of Deputy District Judge Glover on 12 July 1995. By that order he ordered that an order made on 16 January 1995 should be rescinded. Going back in time that order was made by District Judge Jackson. It recited that it was made on the application of Mr Guest, who is the trustee in bankruptcy of Mrs Jane Elizabeth Campbell, who is the bankrupt in this matter. There was a recital that Mrs Campbell had in her examination taken that day admitted that she had received a sum of £182,150 and the district judge ordered that she, Mrs Campbell, should pay that sum with interest to the trustee. A similar order, although not in the same figure, was made in respect of Mr Campbell, Mrs Campbell's husband, on the basis of an admission that he had made in the course of the same examination. Those examinations were conducted, as I say, on 16 January 1995, there having been an originating application for an examination under s 366 of the Insolvency Act 1986 on 25 October 1994 which produced an order for that examination which was in fact made on 22 November 1994.

The point that arises is brought about by a singularly sad story of the events that had occurred. Mrs Campbell suffered very serious injuries as a result of a criminal assault some considerable time ago, long before the bankruptcy. She made an application to the Criminal Injuries Compensation Board for an award to be made to her. That was equally a very long time before she was made a bankrupt. The indications are that the attack on her was in 1984 and her application to the board was in 1985—the precise dates do not matter.

On 11 December 1990 a bankruptcy order was made in respect of Mrs Campbell and that is the relevant bankruptcy order. Subsequent to that, and indeed not very far off two years subsequent to it, an award was made in her favour on that application that had been made by her a number of years, of the

b order of seven years, previously, whereby she actually received over £182,000. She was awarded £200,000 and the deduction was in respect of an interim payment which had been made in the meanwhile. The solicitors acting for her actually received the sum in question, £182,150, in mid-September 1992 and it is common ground between the parties that they wrote to the Official Receiver telling him of that receipt.

c The question which has been argued before me so far is one of two questions that arose when the order that is under appeal was made in July 1995. The first question was not the one that I am presently concerned with and that was concerning the validity of the examination process that I have mentioned and whether it was right or wrong for it to be held as it was in public. The second

d question, which is what I am presently concerned with, was equally fundamental to the trustee's case, namely whether the entitlement of Mrs Campbell to the award that ultimately was made in her favour in September 1992 was or represented something which vested in the trustee in bankruptcy when she was made bankrupt.

e Of course at that date it was only a prospect of receiving an award from the board and it is again common ground between the parties that, unlike the situation that obtains when a person has a right to sue for trespass for personal injuries, as no doubt Mrs Campbell had as against the criminal in question, when it is a Criminal Injuries Compensation Board award that is in issue there is no right either to sue for the award or when the award is made to recover the award.

f The latter does not really signify. What matters is that there is no right in a citizen who suffers injuries as a result of a criminal assault to enforce any form of award from the board.

The prospect of getting such an award has variously been described in argument as a hope and a spes, which is the Latin word for the same thing, but it

g is not, and this is again common ground, a thing in action or, to speak law French for a second, a chose in action.

The law in the 1986 Act on what vests and what does not vest in a bankrupt's trustee on the making of a bankruptcy order is to be found in a combination of sections in that Act. One starts conveniently at s 306(1), which states:

h   'The bankrupt's estate shall vest in the trustee immediately on his appointment taking effect or, in the case of the official receiver, on his becoming trustee.'

One then needs to find out what a bankrupt's estate is and that is defined in

j s 283(1) of the 1986 Act, which reads:

      'Subject as follows, a bankrupt's estate for the purposes of any of this Group of Parts comprises—(a) all property belonging to or vested in the bankrupt at the commencement of the bankruptcy, and (b) any property which by virtue of any of the following provisions of this Part is comprised in that estate or is treated as falling within the preceding paragraph.'

Subsection (2) makes various qualifications and exceptions to that vesting for
such matters as tools of the trade and clothing, bedding and furniture etc. The *a*
term 'property' is also the subject of a specific statutory definition, in s 436 of the
1986 Act, where one finds (it is somewhat circular in part):

> '... "property" includes money, goods, things in action, land and every
> description of property wherever situated and also obligations and every
> description of interest, whether present or future or vested or contingent, *b*
> arising out of, or incidental to, property ...'

It is the use of that final word 'property' that makes me describe the definition, if
that is what it really is, as somewhat circular, because it will be recalled that what
is actually being defined is just that word 'property'.

The submission that was made by Mr McCulloch for Mr Guest, the trustee *c*
who is the appellant, is that although the prospect of recovering under an award
by the board is not a thing in action, it was or represented something which did
come within the definition of property and the way he put that claim, as I
understood it, was to say that there was an interest vested in Mrs Campbell which
was either future or contingent and arose out of or was incidental to property. *d*
The property which he identified as being the relevant asset was the money that
was prospectively going to be paid if and when an award was made.

Treating the matter purely as a matter of construction, I am quite unable to
accept that the word 'property' when it is used in the definition of property is
intended to describe anything other than an existing item. In other words, I do *e*
not accept that it is susceptible of referring to something which has no present
existence but may possibly come into existence on some uncertain event in the
future. There seems to me to be a very clear distinction between two situations.
The first is when there is a contingent interest in property, for example, the right
to receive £50,000 under a legacy contingently on attaining the age of 'x' years
when one is 'x' minus 'y' years old. That is an interest which is contingent and *f*
future but, if there is a trust fund—which I assume in my example there is—there
is existing property in respect of which there is a contingent interest. That seems
to me to be quite different from the second situation, the possibility of achieving
an interest in something which presently does not exist but may exist in the
future.

Examples might perhaps be the owner of a lottery ticket in relation to the prize *g*
that may, perhaps, at the end of the following week arise in his or her possession.
Similarly, the person who has filled in a coupon on the football pools might
perhaps become entitled to property should that coupon have been successfully
filled. In neither case there can it be described as a future or contingent interest
arising out of or incidental to property because there is no underlying existing *h*
property which, or the proceeds of sale of which, are susceptible to the existence
of a proprietary interest, even a future one. It seems to me that the trustee's
argument purely as a matter of construction of the 1986 Act and the definition or
enlargement of the concept of property which is contained in it cannot succeed.

I was, however, referred to authority—not on the basis that there was any *j*
authority on the present particular problem whether the prospect of an award
from the board is something which vests in a trustee in bankruptcy when the
award is made after the bankruptcy order, because there is, I am told, no such
authority. There is a good deal of authority which is to the effect that although
the definition of property which I have read and do not repeat includes things in
action, it does not include every thing in action.

a Certain things in action are, nevertheless, excluded. That is a very old and well-established doctrine. The oldest authority to which I was referred is one taken from 1841, when the matter came before the Exchequer of Pleas in a case called *Howard v Crowther* 8 M & W 601, 151 ER 1179. The action there was an action by the plaintiff for damages for the seduction of his sister which was, in accordance with the practice in those days, supported by an averment that she

b was his servant and that in consequence of her pregnancy he had lost and been deprived of her services.

The defence was that the plaintiff became bankrupt before the commencement of the action and the issue that came before the court on a demurrer was whether or not that right of action vested in the assignee—as it was in those days—in bankruptcy, rather than the modern equivalent of a trustee in

c bankruptcy. The court upheld the claim that the demurrer failed because it took the view that it is not every right of action that passes to an assignee in bankruptcy but only those which are concerned with rights of action for injury to property.

Lord Abinger CB said (8 M & W 601 at 604, 151 ER 1179 at 1180):

d 'Nothing is more clear than that a right of action for an injury to the property of the bankrupt will pass to his assignees; but it is otherwise as to an injury to his personal comfort. Assignees of a bankrupt are not to make a profit of a man's wounded feelings; causes of action, therefore, which are, as in this case, purely personal, do not pass to the assignees, but the right to sue remains with the bankrupt.'

e The other three members of the court agreed with that view. That of course was an action for damages for loss of services.

Another authority to which I was taken was *Wilson v United Counties Bank Ltd* [1920] AC 102, [1918–19] All ER Rep 1035. That was a case where there were two claims made by a certain Major Wilson against the respondents, the United

f Counties Bank Ltd. One was that he had suffered damage and loss to his credit and reputation and the other was that he had suffered loss to his estate by the negligent failure of the bank to look after his business while he was away on military service, presumably in the 1914–18 war.

The House of Lords upheld the argument that the claim to damages for the

g injury to his credit and reputation had not passed to the trustee in bankruptcy, because he had become bankrupt in the meanwhile at the time when he had not yet recovered damages for the injuries that had been suffered by him. It is in relation to the claim with regard to the injury caused to his credit and reputation that the speeches in the House of Lords were referred to before me. The issues, such as they were, with regard to the other matter were not relevant to anything

h I have to decide because it was not suggested that that loss to his estate did not in fact pass to the trustee in bankruptcy.

Their Lordships all referred, either expressly or by adopting each other's judgments, to earlier authority and I can conveniently take a passage that Mr McCulloch particularly relied upon in the speech of Lord Atkinson, where he

j quoted what had been said by Erle J in the earlier decision of *Beckham v Drake* (1849) 2 HL Cas 579 at 604, 9 ER 1213 at 1222. Lord Atkinson states:

'In *Beckham v. Drake* Erle J. said: "The right of action does not pass where the damages are to be estimated by immediate reference to pain felt by the bankrupt in respect to his body, *mind, or character*, and without immediate reference to his rights of property. Thus it has been laid down that the assignees cannot sue for breach of promise of marriage, for criminal conversation, seduction, *defamation, battery, injury to the person by negligence,* as by not carrying safely, not curing, not saving from imprisonment by process of law." Maule J. said (2 HL Cas 579 at 621, 9 ER 1213 at 1228): "There is no doubt that the right to bring an action for an injury to the person, *character,* or feelings of a bankrupt, does not pass to the assignees, and that the right to bring an action for the payment of money agreed to be paid to a bankrupt does pass. And it appears to me that the present action is in effect an action on a contract to pay money."' (See [1920] AC 102 at 130, [1918–19] All ER Rep 1035 at 1039; Lord Atkinson's emphasis.)

The speech of Lord Atkinson also refers to *Brunsden v Humphrey* (1884) 14 QBD 141, [1881–5] All ER Rep 357, where it was held by a majority of the Court of Appeal that an action could be brought not only in the county court, as at first it was for damage to the property of the plaintiff (his cab) which had been caused by the negligent driving of the defendant's servant, but that having succeeded in that action it was open to the plaintiff to bring a second action claiming damages for personal injury in respect of the same incident. The basis upon which it was held that those two actions could both be maintained in succession was that they constituted infringements of distinct and different rights creating distinct and different causes of action and that consequently the successful prosecution of the first suit raised no bar to the institution of the second one.

That decision was applied by analogy to the case before Lord Atkinson when he said that he thought that by parity of reasoning it would seem to follow that the negligence of the defendant, that is to say the bank, gave rise to two distinct causes of action: one consisting of injury to the bankrupt's estate, the other personal and consisting of injury to his character, credit and repute. On that basis the House of Lords were unanimous in deciding that the right to the £7,500 remained in the bankrupt, Major Wilson.

In my judgment, before there can be an effective severance on those lines, it has to be possible to come to the conclusion that there has been an infringement of distinct and different rights creating different and distinct causes of action. The only severance which has been suggested as being conceivably possible in this case is the subdivision of the £200,000 because it does appear that the award made it clear that it was divided as to £30,000 in respect of physical injuries, as to £55,000 in respect of past loss of earnings, and as to £115,000 in respect of future loss of earnings. There can, I think, be no doubt but that the cause of action and the right that was infringed, assuming there was one, was a single right and a single cause of action. There is no separate right to past earnings and a separate right to future earnings and a separate right not to be physically injured. The right of the citizen is not to be criminally assaulted.

A criminal assault may, of course, lead to a variety of unfortunate consequences, some physical and some economic. They all fall under the same cause of action and they all, as I see it, constitute infringements of a particular right, the right not to be assaulted by third parties.

Accordingly, I do not myself see any basis upon which it can validly be suggested that there could properly be an apportionment of the £200,000. This, however, is not, I think, the main point that was relied upon by Mr McCulloch in the old authorities and new ones to which he referred me because he made it clear in referring to the latest and last of the authorities what it was that he was mainly asserting. That latest authority was *Heath v Tang, Stevens v Peacock* [1993] *a* 4 All ER 694, [1993] 1 WLR 1421, where the issue was whether a bankrupt could appeal against the judgment for a liquidated sum on which the bankruptcy petition which had caused him to be adjudicated bankrupt had been founded. In each case the Court of Appeal in a judgment delivered by Hoffmann LJ held that there was no such right vested in the bankrupt because it was a right that had vested in his trustee.

b Hoffmann LJ referred to earlier authority in the following terms. He stated ([1993] 4 All ER 694 at 697, [1993] 1 WLR 1421 at 1423):

> 'The property which vests in the trustee includes "things in action": see s 436 of the 1986 Act. Despite the breadth of this definition, there are certain causes of action personal to the bankrupt which do not vest in his trustee. *c* These include cases in which—"the damages are to be estimated by immediate reference to pain felt by the bankrupt in respect of his body, mind, or character, and without immediate reference to his rights of property." (See *Beckham v Drake* (1849) 2 HL Cas 579 at 604, 9 ER 1213 at 1222 per Erle J. See also *Wilson v United Counties Bank Ltd* [1920] AC 102, [1918–19] All ER *d* Rep 1035.) [Hoffmann LJ was referring to the passage in *Beckham v Drake* which I have already quoted.] Actions for defamation and assault are obvious examples. The bankruptcy does not affect his ability to litigate such claims. But all other causes of action which were vested in the bankrupt at the commencement of the bankruptcy, whether for liquidated sums or unliquidated damages, vest in his trustee.'

e

Mr McCulloch pointed to the expression 'without immediate reference to his rights of property' in passing but he referred much more often and more forcefully to the expression 'damages ... to be estimated by immediate reference to pain'. He sought to draw a distinction between that which is immediately *f* referable to pain, under which heading I think he would put the £30,000 paid in respect of physical injuries to Mrs Campbell, and what he described as consequential damages, which covered both past and future loss of earnings in the much larger sum, of course, of £170,000.

The emphasis upon 'immediate reference to pain' leaves out of account the latter half of the sentence which is 'and without immediate reference to his rights *g* of property'. Both have to be satisfied. If there is something which is immediately referable to pain but nevertheless refers to rights of property—it may perhaps be difficult to contemplate but it must be theoretically possible—it would vest, as I understand it, in the trustee in bankruptcy. The real touchstone is whether the asset is properly to be described as part of the bankrupt's estate. *h* That has to be resolved in the light of the definition of his or her property.

These authorities that I was referred to seem to me to be concerned with the limitation that the courts over the years have read into things in action which vest in a trustee. I am not concerned with these because everyone is agreed that a Criminal Injuries Compensation Board award is not a thing in action, nor is the *j* right to receive it or the hope of receiving it a thing in action. Strictly speaking, therefore, all this is by the way.

The requirement of immediate reference to pain is in my judgment not something that should be looked at as though it was part of an Act of Parliament and stood by itself because that seems to me to leave out of account what was in fact included by not only Hoffmann LJ but also Erle J, the requirement that there should be a reference to rights of property, and for the reasons that I gave earlier

and do not repeat I am not satisfied that a future item of property which may or
may not come into existence is properly to be described as 'property'.

Accordingly, I have come to the conclusion that the hope that Mrs Campbell
had of being awarded an award, which in fact fructified two years later, was not
at the date when she became bankrupt part of her property in such a way as to
vest in the trustee in bankruptcy when she became bankrupt. On that basis it
seems to me that the decision of the district judge from which this appeal is
brought was, on the ground with which I have dealt, unimpeachable. That
makes it unnecessary, I think, as I understand it—although I will hear counsel on
this subject—for me to express views about the procedural point and the fact that
the examination that occurred was in public and not in private and I prefer, in
those circumstances, to say nothing about it.

Appeal dismissed.

Celia Fox   Barrister.

a Citi-March Ltd and another v Neptune Orient Lines Ltd and others

QUEEN'S BENCH DIVISION

b COLMAN J

8 DECEMBER 1995, 29 JANUARY 1996

Practice – Service out of the jurisdiction – Bill of lading containing exclusive foreign jurisdiction clause – Time limit for bringing action in foreign court expiring – Service of English proceedings out of jurisdiction in breach of jurisdiction clause – Whether service of English proceedings to be set aside – Whether strong cause shown as to why English jurisdiction should be maintained – Reasonableness of plaintiffs' conduct in ignoring time bar in contractual forum – RSC Ord 11, r 4(2).

d The first defendant, a company incorporated and carrying on business in Singapore, issued bills of lading for consignments of clothing which were to be shipped to London for delivery to the plaintiffs. The bills of lading contained exclusive jurisdiction clauses, which provided that all disputes should be determined by the courts of Singapore. When the containers were opened, following delivery in London, a total of 800 cartons of clothing were discovered to be missing. Thereafter the plaintiffs initiated proceedings in the United *e* Kingdom against the first defendant and three other companies (which had stored the containers in their respective premises prior to delivery to the plaintiffs) in respect of the missing consignments. They also obtained leave under RSC Ord 11, r 4(2) to serve proceedings out of the jurisdiction on the first defendant, which could be served only in Singapore. At no time did the plaintiffs issue a protective *f* writ in Singapore, with the result that once the 12-month limitation period applicable under the Hague Rules had expired, the first defendant would have a complete defence to any action commenced in that jurisdiction. The first defendant applied to set aside service of the English proceedings outside the jurisdiction. The issue arose whether, as a matter of discretion, the plaintiffs should be permitted to invoke the jurisdiction of the English courts, *g* notwithstanding the fact that they had contracted by way of an exclusive foreign jurisdiction clause to refer all disputes to the courts of a foreign jurisdiction where the claim had become contractually time-barred.

Held – (1) In a case involving an exclusive foreign jurisdiction clause, the court *h* would judge the reasonableness of the plaintiff's conduct in ignoring the time bar in the contractual forum by reference to the principle that a stay would be granted or service of the writ set aside unless strong cause in favour of English jurisdiction was demonstrated, and not merely by reference to the forum non conveniens test that the English courts were clearly the appropriate forum. *j* Where, but for the time bar, there was strong cause for English jurisdiction, a stay would not be ordered or service set aside even if the plaintiff had consciously decided not to preserve time in the contractual forum, for in so conducting himself he could not be said to have acted unreasonably. However, where no such cause could be shown, the plaintiff might be able to rely on the prejudice to him by reason of a time bar in the contractual forum if he could show that he had not acted unreasonably in failing to take steps to prevent the claim in the foreign

jurisdiction from becoming time-barred; and whether the omission was a
unreasonable would depend on all the circumstances of the case (see p 551 j and
p 552 f to j, post); *Aratra Potato Co Ltd v Egyptian Navigation Co, The El Amria* [1981]
2 Lloyd's Rep 119, *Spiliada Maritime Corp v Cansulex Ltd, The Spiliada* [1986] 3 All
ER 843 and *The Pioneer Container, KH Enterprise (cargo owners) v Pioneer Container
(owners)* [1994] 2 All ER 250 considered.

(2) Leaving aside the time bar defence, if the plaintiffs were obliged to pursue b
their claim in Singapore, it was probable that separate proceedings would be
pursued in London. If the proceedings were to be so split, there would be a clear
risk of inconsistent decisions on the facts; the plaintiffs would also lose the benefit
of a composite trial and would be precluded from having the benefit (given the
subject matter of the dispute) of getting the evidence of all four defendants before
the same court. Strong cause had therefore been shown in favour of English c
jurisdiction and, in the circumstances, the plaintiffs' decision not to incur further
costs by protecting their position in Singapore was not unreasonable. It followed
that the time bar had not been allowed to develop unreasonably and that the
relevant factors were overwhelmingly in favour of the maintenance of English
jurisdiction. The application to set aside service of the writ would accordingly be d
dismissed (see p 553 d to j, p 554 g and p 555 b to j, post).

Notes
For service out of the jurisdiction, see 8(1) *Halsbury's Laws* (4th edn reissue) paras
650–651, 671, and for cases on the subject, see 37(2) *Digest* (Reissue) 279–318,
1801–1993. e

Cases referred to in judgment
Aratra Potato Co Ltd v Egyptian Navigation Co, The El Amria [1981] 2 Lloyd's Rep
    119, CA; *affg* [1980] 1 Lloyd's Rep 390.
Blue Wave, The [1982] 1 Lloyd's Rep 151. f
Eleftheria, The [1969] 2 All ER 641, [1970] P 94, [1969] 2 WLR 1073.
Eschersheim, The [1976] 1 All ER 920, [1976] 1 WLR 430, HL.
Halifax Overseas Freighters Ltd v Rasno Export, The Pine Hill [1958] 2 Lloyd's Rep
    146.
Pioneer Container, The, KH Enterprise (cargo owners) v Pioneer Container (owners)
    [1994] 2 All ER 250, [1994] 2 AC 324, [1994] 3 WLR 1, PC. g
Spiliada Maritime Corp v Cansulex Ltd, The Spiliada [1986] 3 All ER 843, [1987] AC
    460, [1986] 3 WLR 972, HL.
Taunton-Collins v Cromie [1964] 2 All ER 332, [1964] 1 WLR 633, CA.

Cases also cited or referred to in skeleton arguments h
Ali (Abdullah) Almunajem Sons Co v Recourse Shipping Co Ltd, The Reefer Creole [1994]
    1 Lloyd's Rep 584.
Adolf Warski, The [1976] 2 Lloyd's Rep 241, CA; *affg* [1976] 1 Lloyd's Rep 107.
Caribbean Gold Ltd v Alga Shipping Co Ltd, The Nova Scotia [1993] 1 Lloyd's Rep 154.
Dong Wha Enterprise Co Ltd v Crownson Shipping Ltd [1995] 1 Lloyd's Rep 113. j
Payabi v Armstel Shipping Corp, The Jay Bola [1992] 3 All ER 329.

Application
The first defendants, Neptune Orient Lines Ltd, a company incorporated and
carrying on business in Singapore, applied under RSC Ord 12, r 8(4) to set aside
the decision of Rix J on 14 September 1994 giving the plaintiffs, Citi-March Ltd

a and Hamlet International plc, leave under Ord 11, r 4(2) to serve proceedings out of the jurisdiction on the first defendants in Singapore in breach of an exclusive foreign jurisdiction clause. The second, third and fourth defendants, Russell Davies Container Transport Ltd, Hays Storage Services Ltd and Hays Distribution Services Ltd, took no part in the proceedings. The application was heard in chambers but judgment was given in open court. The facts are set out
b in the judgment.

Nigel Jacobs (instructed by *Clyde & Co*) for the plaintiffs.
James Turner (instructed by *Bentleys Stokes & Lowless*) for the defendants.

Cur adv vult

c
29 January 1996. The following judgment was delivered.

COLMAN J. This is an application on behalf of the first defendants under RSC Ord 12, r 8(4) to set aside an order of Rix J dated 14 September 1994. He gave leave to issue a concurrent writ in the Commercial Court and to serve it on the
d first defendants in Singapore where they are incorporated and carry on business. I am giving judgment in open court at the request of both parties in view of the importance of the point in issue in relation to the application of the discretion under Ord 11, r 4(2) to permit service overseas of proceedings brought in the English courts in breach of an exclusive foreign jurisdiction clause.
e   The first defendants were the carriers on board the Humber Bridge of consignments of clothing from Hong Kong to London under eleven bills of lading issued on 16 June 1993. The containers were discharged from the vessel at Felixstowe in July 1993.
    The containers were then collected by the second defendants and taken first to their own premises at West Thurrock, Essex, then to the third and fourth
f defendants' bonded warehouse at Dagenham, Essex, for a customs inspection, then carried back to the second defendants' premises and then carried on to the second plaintiffs' agents' premises in London. When the containers were opened, following delivery in London, a total of 800 cartons of clothing were missing from all three containers. The loss was discovered on 26–28 July 1993. A writ was issued against all four defendants on 6 April 1994. The second, third and
g fourth defendants could all be served in this country, but the first defendants could be served only in Singapore. Hence the order by Rix J.
    The claim against the first defendants as carriers who issued the bills of lading was subject to Singapore law and Singapore exclusive jurisdiction clauses:

h   '29 *LAW AND JURISDICTION*
    (a) *Governing Law*
    Insofar as anything has not been dealt with by the terms and conditions of this Bill of Lading, Singapore law shall apply. Singapore law shall in any event apply in interpreting the terms and conditions hereof.
    (b) *Jurisdiction*
j   All disputes relating to this Bill of Lading shall be determined by the Courts of Singapore to the exclusion of the jurisdiction of the Courts of any other country PROVIDED ALWAYS that the Carrier may in its absolute discretion invoke or voluntarily submit to the jurisdiction of the Courts of any other country which, but for the terms of this Bill of Lading, could properly assume jurisdiction to hear and determine such disputes.'

That claim against the first defendants was also subject to the Hague Rules 12-month limitation period, which expired on about 26–28 July 1994. At no time did the plaintiffs issue a protective writ in Singapore. It follows that if service is set aside on the grounds of a Singapore jurisdiction clause, the defendants will have a complete defence to any action now commenced in Singapore.

Accordingly, this application raises an important point on the way in which the court should exercise its discretion to set aside service outside the jurisdiction when the claim has become contractually time-barred in the contractual forum. In particular, what is the correct discretionary approach to the three fundamental considerations: (i) the existence of an exclusive jurisdiction clause in respect of the courts of a foreign jurisdiction; (ii) the general principles of forum non conveniens; and (iii) there being an accrued contractual time bar defence in the contractual forum?

The authorities in which the courts have considered the relationship between these fundamental considerations have been concerned with applications to stay English proceedings, to restrain foreign proceedings or to set aside service outside the jurisdiction of the English courts. It is, in my judgment, apparent from the speech of Lord Goff of Chieveley in *Spiliada Maritime Corp v Cansulex Ltd, The Spiliada* [1986] 3 All ER 843 at 860–861, [1987] AC 460 at 483–484 and from the judgment of the Privy Council in *The Pioneer Container, KH Enterprise (cargo owners) v Pioneer Container (owners)* [1994] 2 All ER 250 at 268–269, [1994] 2 AC 324 at 348–349 that the considerations material to the exercise of the court's discretion whether to stay an action properly commenced in England by reason of an exclusive foreign jurisdiction clause do not differ in substance from the considerations material to the exercise of the court's discretion upon an application to set aside service under Ord 11 by reason of such a clause. It would indeed be surprising if substantially different considerations applied depending upon the procedural framework of the applications. In both cases the essential issue is whether as a matter of discretion the plaintiff should be permitted to invoke the jurisdiction of the English courts notwithstanding his having contracted to refer all disputes to a foreign court.

It is therefore appropriate in considering what is material to the exercise of the court's discretion on an application such as this to have regard to the same matters which have been regarded by the courts as material to applications to stay English proceedings.

The starting point must therefore be the decision of the Court of Appeal in *Aratra Potato Co Ltd v Egyptian Navigation Co, The El Amria* [1981] 2 Lloyd's Rep 119 and in particular the judgment of Brandon LJ, who, in reiterating the principles which he had set out in his judgment in *The Eleftheria* [1969] 2 All ER 641, [1970] P 94, stated:

'(1) Where plaintiffs sue in England in breach of an agreement to refer disputes to a foreign Court, and the defendants apply for a stay, the English Court, assuming the claim to be otherwise within its jurisdiction, is not bound to grant a stay but has a discretion whether to do so or not. (2) The discretion should be exercised by granting a stay unless strong cause for not doing so is shown. (3) The burden of proving such strong cause is on the plaintiffs. (4) In exercising its discretion the Court should take into account all the circumstances of the particular case. (5) In particular, but without prejudice to (4), the following matters, where they arise, may properly be regarded: (a) In what country the evidence on the issues of fact is situated, a or more readily available, and the effect of that on the relative convenience and expense of trial as between the English and foreign Courts. (b) Whether the law of the foreign Court applies and, if so, whether it differs from English law in any material respects. (c) With what country either party is connected, and how closely. (d) Whether the defendants genuinely desire trial in the foreign country, or are only seeking procedural advantages.

b (e) Whether the plaintiffs would be prejudiced by having to sue in the foreign Court because they would: (i) be deprived of security for their claim; (ii) be unable to enforce any judgment obtained; (iii) be faced with a time-bar not applicable in England; or (iv) for political, racial, religious or other reasons be unlikely to get a fair trial.' (See [1981] 2 Lloyd's Rep 119 at 123–124.)

c
The substance of the approach to discretion thus identified is therefore that where the plaintiffs have failed to comply with a foreign jurisdiction clause they can avoid a stay only if they show *strong cause* for keeping the proceedings in the English courts, having regard to all the circumstances of the case, including the d para (5) considerations. The concept that the plaintiff should be required to show 'strong cause' involves, as expressed earlier by Brandon LJ on the same page of his judgment in *The El Amria*, that the inclusion of an exclusive foreign jurisdiction clause gives rise to a 'strong prima facie case for a stay', which reflects what he said in *The Eleftheria* [1969] 2 All ER 641 at 648, [1970] P 94 at 103:

e   'I think that it is essential that the court should give full weight to the prima facie desirability of holding the plaintiffs to their agreement. In this connection, I think that the court must be careful not just to pay lip service to the principle involved, and then fail to give effect to it because of a mere balance of convenience.'

f   Amongst the specific relevant considerations identified by Brandon LJ is whether the plaintiffs could be prejudiced were a stay to be granted because they could be met by a time bar in the contractual forum. Unlike all the other specific considerations, this one is not concerned with any of the intrinsic characteristics of the dispute or of the means of trying it, such as the whereabouts of the evidence, the applicable law, the connection of the parties to the dispute with the g contractual forum or with this country or the procedure for security, trial or enforcement of judgment of the foreign court. The feature of the time bar consideration which differentiates it from all the others is that its existence arises from the omission of the plaintiff to take the steps necessary to preserve time in the courts of the contractual jurisdiction. Therefore, when having failed to take h such steps, he invites the English court to refuse a stay on the grounds that he would be prejudiced by the claim then being time-barred in the contractual forum, what he is really doing is praying in aid of the jurisdiction of an uncontractual forum his own failure to pursue his claim in the contractual forum in sufficient time. In essence, his prejudice is self-induced.

j   Why, in such a case, should the plaintiff ever be entitled to rely on his own self-induced prejudice? To this the answer is that the jurisdiction, in origin equitable, to stay English proceedings is exercised by reference to discretionary principles; similarly the jurisdiction to set aside service outside the jurisdiction. Amongst those principles is included the concept that in international commercial litigation, where in the interests of all the parties and the ends of justice between the parties it is substantially more appropriate that the issues between the parties should be determined in the English courts than in the contractual forum, a stay will not be ordered merely to protect the defendants' right to the contractual forum. Accordingly, if a plaintiff utilises the English courts and, in so doing, ignores the contractual forum and permits the claim to become time-barred there, it is open to the English court, when asked to stay the proceedings, to look at the plaintiffs' conduct in permitting the time bar to arise in order to ascertain whether such conduct was justifiable. In that context his conduct cannot be justifiable merely by reference to the jurisdiction clause in his contract, but it may be justifiable by reference to the place where in the interests of all the parties and of justice it is then appropriate that the issues should be tried. In other words, if, notwithstanding the foreign jurisdiction clause, there are factors such as the features of the dispute or of the means of trying it or of enforcing security or a judgment which, in the interests of justice and all the parties, provide strong cause for treating the English courts as the appropriate forum, the plaintiff's omission to protect time in the contractual forum will not condemn him to a stay of the English action. In such a case his self-induced prejudice or, putting it obversely, the defendants' accrued defence, is merely a consequence of the plaintiff's having given effect by his own conduct to the principles which underlie the exercise by the court of its own discretion. For the court to take into account against a plaintiff a time bar arising in such circumstances would involve an inconsistency of approach which cannot be justified in principle.

Where, however, factors other than the time bar in the contractual forum cannot be shown to provide strong cause for trial in the English courts, but indicate either that there is equal convenience in the English courts and in the contractual forum or that the latter is the appropriate forum, the plaintiff will be in greater difficulty in seeking to rely on the prejudice to him of the time bar which he has permitted to arise. In the former case, it may be appropriate to give weight in the plaintiffs' favour to the fact that the action has become time-barred in the contractual forum, provided that the plaintiff can show that he did not act unreasonably in omitting to issue protective proceedings in that forum. He has, after all, brought his claim within the applicable time limit in an available jurisdiction, albeit inconsistently with his contract, and the interests of justice and of all parties may well require that in such a case he should not be wholly deprived of the right to claim if his conduct in failing to preserve time has not been unreasonable. This was the approach adopted by Sheen J in *The Blue Wave* [1982] 1 Lloyd's Rep 151 at 156 in which, having decided that there was little to choose in terms of convenience between England and Greece, the contractual forum, he laid emphasis in refusing a stay on the fact that—

'the plaintiffs were not guilty of conduct deliberately designed to allow the time limit in Greece to expire so that they could pray in aid the time bar as a reason for contending that proceedings instituted in this country should not be stayed.'

In *The Spiliada* [1986] 3 All ER 843 at 860, [1987] AC 460 at 483–484 Lord Goff of Chieveley discusses how the principle of forum non conveniens should be applied—

'in a case in which the plaintiff has started proceedings in England where his claim was not time-barred, but there was some other jurisdiction which, *a* in the opinion of the court, is clearly more appropriate for the trial of the action, but ... where his claim is now time-barred.'

He said:

b 'Now, to take some extreme examples, suppose that the plaintiff allowed the limitation period to elapse in the appropriate jurisdiction, and came here simply because he wanted to take advantage of a more generous time-bar applicable in this country; or suppose that it was obvious that the plaintiff should have commenced proceedings in the appropriate jurisdiction, and yet he did not trouble to issue a protective writ there; in cases such as these, I

c cannot see that the court should hesitate to stay the proceedings in this country, even though the effect would be that the plaintiff's claim would inevitably be defeated by a plea of the time-bar in the appropriate jurisdiction. Indeed, a strong theoretical argument can be advanced for the proposition that, if there is another clearly more appropriate forum for the trial of the action, a stay should generally be granted even though the

d plaintiff's action would be time-barred there. But, in my opinion, this is a case where practical justice should be done. And practical justice demands that, if the court considers that the plaintiff acted reasonably in commencing proceedings in this country, and that, although it appears that (putting on one side the time-bar point) the appropriate forum for the trial of the action is elsewhere than England, the plaintiff did not act unreasonably in failing to

e commence proceedings (for example by issuing a protective writ) in that jurisdiction within the limitation period applicable there, it would not, I think, be just to deprive the plaintiff of the benefit of having started proceedings within the limitation period applicable in this country. This approach is consistent with that of Sheen J in *The Blue Wave* [1982] 1 Lloyd's

f Rep 151. It is not to be forgotten that, by making its jurisdiction available to the plaintiff, even the discretionary jurisdiction under RSC Ord 11, the courts of this country have provided the plaintiff with an opportunity to start proceedings here; accordingly, if justice demands, the court should not deprive the plaintiff of the benefit of having complied with the time-bar in this country. Furthermore, as the applicable principles become more clearly

g established and better known, it will, I suspect, become increasingly difficult for plaintiffs to prove lack of negligence in this respect. The fact that the court has been asked to exercise its discretion under RSC Ord 11, rather than that the plaintiff has served proceedings on the defendant in this country as of right, is, I consider, only relevant to consideration of the plaintiff's

h conduct in failing to save the time-bar in the other relevant alternative jurisdiction.'

It will be observed that by his reference to *The Blue Wave* Lord Goff does not distinguish between the approach to be adopted in foreign jurisdiction clause

j cases and forum non conveniens cases. However, it must, in my view, be correct, in principle, that in a foreign jurisdiction clause case the court should judge the reasonableness of the plaintiffs' conduct in ignoring the time bar in the contractual forum by reference to the principle that a stay will be granted or service of the writ will be set aside unless strong cause in favour of English jurisdiction is demonstrated and not merely by reference to the forum non conveniens test that the English courts are clearly the appropriate forum.

The Pioneer Container [1994] 2 All ER 250, [1994] 2 AC 324 was a case where the
judge had held that, apart from the time bar, Taiwan, the contractual forum, was
the appropriate forum, being the place from which shipment was effected and
where the loss of the cargo occurred. He held that the plaintiffs had none the less
acted reasonably in starting proceedings in Hong Kong by arresting a sister ship
there and allowing time to expire in Taiwan, because in Taiwan they would have
had to put up security for costs at a certain percentage of their claim and counter
security for the full amount of the claim if a vessel were arrested. The Hong Kong
Court of Appeal, with which the Judicial Committee of the Privy Council agreed,
reversed the judge's decision, holding that in deliberately ignoring the time bar in
the contractual forum the plaintiffs had acted unreasonably. Godfrey J said
([1994] 2 All ER 250 at 268, [1994] 2 AC 324 at 348–349):

> "'If you find yourself bound to litigate in a forum which is more expensive
> than the one you would prefer, deliberately to choose the latter rather than
> the former seems to me (although the judge thought otherwise) to be forum
> shopping in one of its purest and most undesirable forms. And if in
> pursuance of your deliberate decision to litigate here instead, you let time
> run out in the jurisdiction in which you are bound to litigate, without taking
> the trouble (because of the expense) even to issue a protective writ there,
> you are not, as I think, acting reasonably at all; you are gambling on the
> chance of a stay being refused here and you cannot complain if you then lose
> that gamble. That may seem to you at the time a justifiable commercial risk
> to take. But that, in the context of the litigation, does not make your decision
> a reasonable one.'"

The approach in these cases is, in my judgment, consistent with the view that
in an exclusive jurisdiction clause case, where a plaintiff has failed to issue
protective proceedings in the contractual forum, a stay will not be ordered or
service set aside unless strong cause is shown why English jurisdiction should be
maintained. In a case where, but for the time bar, there is strong cause for English
jurisdiction, a stay will not be ordered or service set aside in spite of the plaintiffs'
having consciously decided not to preserve time in the contractual forum, for in
so conducting himself he cannot be said to have acted unreasonably and it is in
the circumstances inappropriate that he should be shut out from pursuing his
claim by reason of the foreign jurisdiction clause. In a case where, however, but
for the time bar, strong cause in favour of English jurisdiction cannot be shown,
a plaintiff may be able to rely on the prejudice to him by reason of a time bar in
the contractual forum if he can show that he did not act unreasonably in failing
to issue protective proceedings in order to prevent time running against him.
Whether his omission is unreasonable will depend on all the circumstances of the
case, including his awareness of the potential time bar, the explanation for his
omission to preserve time and the extent to which the contractual forum is also,
time bar apart, the appropriate forum for the adjudication of the dispute in
question. At the end of the day the court must consider whether in the interests
of justice it is more appropriate to permit a plaintiff to proceed in England,
although he has omitted to preserve time in the contractual forum, and although
England is not clearly the more appropriate forum than to deprive him of all
opportunity of pursuing his claim in any forum.

I now turn to the facts in this case.

a The first defendants are the only party incorporated or carrying on business in Singapore. The first plaintiffs—the shippers—are incorporated in Hong Kong. The other parties are all incorporated in England and carry on business here.

The essential issue is whether the goods were lost in breach of the duty, contractual or otherwise, of any, and if so, which of the four defendants. That will involve investigation of the number of cartons shipped in Hong Kong and of b the care of the containers and their contents during the period when they were in the possession of each of the defendants. Thus, the evidence as to the quantity delivered into the first defendants' custody will have to come from Hong Kong and the evidence as to what happened subsequent to arrival at Felixstowe will be in England. There is no evidence to suggest that the law of Singapore, by which the bill of lading contract was governed, differs in any material respect from c English law with regard to the application of the Hague Rules, art III, r 6 time bar. Accordingly, the first defendants would certainly have a good defence to any proceedings now commenced in Singapore. If the other defendants were entitled to rely on the Hague Rules by reason of the terms of the bill of lading and of their relationship to the first defendants, they too would have a good defence. It is not d suggested that there is any material difference between English and Singapore substantive law or procedure.

Leaving aside the time bar defence, if the plaintiffs were obliged to pursue their claims in Singapore, the English witnesses would be unlikely to attend voluntarily and could not be compelled to attend the trial and to give evidence and even if they were called by the plaintiffs, they could not be cross-examined e unless they could be treated as hostile. Furthermore, the preponderance of the oral evidence is likely to come from English witnesses and to be based on discovery of documents in England and a trial in Singapore would therefore involve more movement of witnesses and documents and therefore probably greater administrative costs than a trial in London.

f There is, however, one matter which is, in my judgment, highly relevant to the exercise of discretion on this application and that is the fact that if, as may well be the case, the second, third and fourth defendants cannot be compelled to participate in an action against all the defendants in Singapore, there will arise a highly unsatisfactory procedural situation in which the action against the first defendants must be pursued in Singapore, whereas the English action against the g second, third and fourth defendants must be continued here, for there is no reason to believe that those defendants will be persuaded to submit voluntarily to Singapore jurisdiction. In that event, the plaintiffs would be left in the position where they could not advance their alternative claims against the four defendants all in the same forum. Not only would this be inconvenient; but it would be h potentially unjust, for it would preclude the plaintiffs from having the benefit of getting the evidence of all four defendants before the same court. Where, as here, the underlying issue is which, if any, of the several defendants was responsible for the loss and the evidence as to how the goods were cared for is exclusively in the possession of the defendants, a plaintiff who is precluded from joining all the j defendants in the same proceedings is placed in what is potentially an extremely detrimental position, for he may be prevented from deploying the strength of the evidence of one or more of the defendants to make good his claim against another defendant.

In addition, there is the risk, if actions in respect of the same loss must be brought in different jurisdictions, that there will be inconsistent decisions on the facts. Great weight was put on this feature by the Court of Appeal in *The El Amria*

[1981] 2 Lloyd's Rep 119. In that case the plaintiff cargo interests had proceeded *a*
in rem against the shipowners, claiming damages for breach of duty and/or
contract whereby the cargo of potatoes had become damaged. However,
following the issue of the shipowners' notice of motion to stay on the grounds of
the jurisdiction clause in the bills of lading which referred all disputes to the
courts of the carrier's principal place of business (Egypt), the plaintiffs issued a
writ against the Mersey Docks and Harbour Co claiming damages against them *b*
on the basis of the failure by their stevedores to discharge the cargo with
reasonable despatch. This was apparently in consequence of the shipowners
having attributed the cargo damage to slow discharge by the stevedores. With
reference to this second action Brandon LJ observed (at 128):

> 'This circumstance was, as I said earlier, one of the subsidiary reasons *c*
> relied on by the learned Judge for dismissing the defendants' application for
> a stay. With regard to it he said at ([1980] 1 Lloyd's Rep 390 at 392):
> "Furthermore in view of the allegations made by the defendants that the
> deterioration of the cargo took place as a result of unreasonably slow
> discharge of the cargo, the plaintiffs have issued a writ against the Mersey
> Docks and Harbour Company. Obviously, it will be a matter of great *d*
> convenience if that action can be tried at the same time as this action." I
> agree entirely with the learned Judge's view on that matter, but would go
> rather further than he did in the passage from his judgment quoted above.
> By that I mean that I do not regard it merely as convenient that the two
> actions, in which many of the same issues fall to be determined, should be *e*
> tried together; rather that I regard it as a potential disaster from a legal point
> of view if they were not, because of the risk inherent in separate trials, one
> in Egypt and the other in England, that the same issues might be determined
> differently in the two countries. See as to this *Halifax Overseas Freighters Ltd.
> v. Rasno Export; Technoprominport; and Polskie Linie Oceaniczne P.P.W. (The
> Pine Hill)* ([1958] 2 Lloyd's Rep 146) and *Taunton-Collins v. Cromie & Others* *f*
> ([1964] 2 All ER 332, [1964] 1 WLR 633).'

In concluding that a stay was correctly refused by the judge, Brandon LJ
expressed the view that the existence of the second action against the Mersey
Docks and Harbour Co was one of two 'dominant' considerations which led to
that conclusion (see [1981] 2 Lloyd's Rep 119 at 128–129). *g*

In the present case it is also appropriate that considerable weight should be
given to the risk of inconsistent decisions if proceedings were to be split between
Singapore and London. I would also attach equal weight to the injustice of
requiring a plaintiff in a case on facts such as these to sue in separate jurisdictions
different defendants in respect of the same loss thereby causing him to lose the *h*
benefit of a composite trial. In that connection I would add that the practice
which has developed in relation to the exercise of the court's discretion in the
analogous case of applications to stay under s 4(1) of the Arbitration Act 1950 is
that if an action has been properly commenced against more than one defendant
in respect of the same loss, a stay will not generally be granted upon the *j*
application of one defendant in reliance on his arbitration clause: see *The
Eschersheim* [1976] 1 All ER 920, [1976] 1 WLR 430.

Mr James Turner, on behalf of the first defendants, has argued that there is
indeed no risk of inconsistent decisions because, if his application succeeds and
service is set aside, the plaintiffs will in reality never commence proceedings
against the first defendants in Singapore for such proceedings would be futile by

a reason of the time bar defence. The only proceedings would therefore be against the other three defendants in the present action. He submits that, accordingly, no weight should be given to the risk of separate trials producing inconsistent decisions. If service of the writ were allowed to stand, not only would the first defendants be deprived of the enforcement of the exclusive jurisdiction clause but they would be deprived of the benefit of their accrued time bar defence.

b   Consideration of those factors (other than the time bar defence) material to the question whether England, as distinct from the contractual forum, is the place where in the interests of justice and of all the parties the disputes ought to be tried lead, in my judgment, to the view that strong cause is shown for a trial in England. The existence of the time bar defence arises because those advising the plaintiffs had reached that conclusion. In his affidavit Mr Salisbury of the c plaintiffs' solicitors has deposed as follows:

'The decision was taken to proceed in England alone because all the connecting factors pointed to England as the proper and more convenient forum. The cargo was discharged and delivered in England. The claim was to be pursued against three other English Defendants. Multiplicity of d proceedings was considered to be inherently undesirable.'

That was, in my judgment, an entirely reasonable view to take at the time when action would have been necessary if time was to be preserved in Singapore. The factors in favour of English jurisdiction were strong enough to justify the belief that service outside the jurisdiction could be justified and held on an Ord e 12, r 8 application. In the circumstances it cannot be maintained that the omission to incur further costs in order to preserve time in Singapore was unreasonable. Consequently, the first defendants cannot rely on the fact that proceedings in Singapore have subsequently become time-barred in order to cut away from the relevant considerations the risk of inconsistent decisions if a stay f is granted or to justify setting aside service on the grounds that they would otherwise lose the benefit of an accrued defence. This is because there was indeed a risk of inconsistent decisions at the time when the plaintiffs took the decision which gave rise to the time bar. At the end of the day that time bar has developed because and only because the plaintiffs by their own conduct gave effect to the very principles which the English courts apply in deciding how the g discretion as to their jurisdiction should be exercised. If in the circumstances existing prior to the effluxion of time in the contractual forum strong cause can be shown in favour of maintaining the proceedings in England, a plaintiff is entitled to take the view that it is unnecessary for him to take steps to preserve time in the contractual forum. Where, however, his ability to show strong cause h is in doubt, he omits to preserve time at his peril, as *The Pioneer Container* demonstrates.

For these reasons I conclude that the first defendants' application to set aside service of the writ fails. The relevant factors are overwhelmingly in favour of the maintenance of English jurisdiction.

j *Application dismissed.*

K Mydeen Esq   Barrister.

Count Tolstoy-Miloslavsky v Lord Aldington   *a*

COURT OF APPEAL, CIVIL DIVISION
ROSE, ROCH AND WARD LJJ
11, 12, 13 DECEMBER 1995

b

Solicitor – Payment of costs by solicitor personally – Costs incurred unreasonably or improperly – Jurisdiction to order solicitor to pay wasted costs – Solicitors ordered to pay personally opponent's costs – Whether solicitors' conduct unreasonable – Whether wasted costs order appropriate – Supreme Court Act 1981, s 51(1)(3)(6)(7).

The plaintiff's solicitors, acting without fee, issued a writ against the defendant, *c* seeking to set aside an award of libel damages which he had obtained against the plaintiff on the ground of fraud. The writ was not preceded by any letter before action; nor was legal aid for the plaintiff (who appeared to be impecunious) applied for. The statement of claim was served, apparently settled by and bearing the signatures of leading and junior counsel, who also provided their services to *d* the plaintiff free of charge. The defendant's subsequent application to strike out the statement of claim as an abuse of process was successful, the judge having determined that there was no reasonable possibility that the new evidence might be relevant to the fraud allegation. The defendant thereafter applied for an order that the plaintiff's solicitors pay his costs, on the grounds (i) that the costs which he had incurred were 'wasted costs' within the meaning of s 51(6) and (7)[a] of the *e* Supreme Court Act 1981 which the solicitors should be ordered to bear due to their 'improper' and 'unreasonable' conduct in bringing the fresh proceedings, and (ii) that by agreeing to act without fee the solicitors had put themselves in the position of 'third party funders' of the litigation and should therefore be ordered to pay his costs pursuant to the general discretion conferred by s 51(1) and (3) of *f* the Act. The judge rejected the first ground but accepted the second, and ordered the solicitors to pay 60% of the defendant's costs. The solicitors appealed. The defendant sought to affirm the judge's order on the additional ground that he should have made a wasted costs order.

Held – (1) The court had no jurisdiction under s 51(1) and (3) of the 1981 Act to *g* make an order for costs against legal representatives when acting as legal representatives. There were only three categories of conduct which could give rise to an order for costs against a solicitor: (i) if it was within the wasted costs jurisdiction of s 51(6) and (7); (ii) if it was otherwise a breach of duty to the court such as could found an order (e g if he acted, even unwittingly, without authority *h* or in breach of an undertaking); and (iii) if he acted outside the role of solicitor (e g in a private capacity or as a third party funder for someone else). The judge had accordingly erred in founding jurisdiction on, and ordering costs pursuant to, s 51(1) and (3) of the 1981 Act (see p 563 *h* to p 565 *h* and p 570 *b* to *d f* to *j*, post); *Aiden Shipping Co Ltd v Interbulk Ltd, The Vimeira* [1986] 2 All ER 409 distinguished. *j*

(2) The jurisdiction to make a wasted costs order under s 51(6) and (7) of the 1981 Act had to be exercised with care and the question whether a solicitor had properly discharged his duty to the court to conduct litigation with due propriety depended on the circumstances of the particular case. Acting without fee and

---

a   Section 51, so far as material, is set out at p 561 *h* to p 562 *a*, post

a doing so in a hopeless case or even in a case struck out for abuse of process was not conduct which itself would justify the making of a wasted costs order. In the instant case, the solicitors' conduct in instituting the proceedings could properly be characterised as unreasonable and clearly constituted the unjustifiable conduct of litigation against which the wasted costs regime was aimed. Moreover, counsel's role in signing the pleading did not exonerate the solicitors from their

b obligation to exercise their own judgment to consider whether the plaintiff's claim could properly be pursued. The order for costs made against the solicitors was therefore correct and the appeal would be dismissed accordingly (see p 563 g, p 565 h, p 566 h to p 567 g, p 568 a b, p 569 f to p 570 a e, p 571 f to j and p 572 c, post); Ridehalgh v Horsefield [1994] 3 All ER 848 applied.

c **Notes**

For the jurisdiction of the court to order costs against a legal representative personally, see 37 Halsbury's Laws (4th edn) para 719 and 44 ibid paras 259–262, and for cases on the subject, see 44 Digest (Reissue) 421–422, 4587–4600.

For the Supreme Court Act 1981, s 51, see 11 Halsbury's Statutes (4th edn) (1991

d reissue) 1217.

Cases referred to in judgments

Aiden Shipping Co Ltd v Interbulk Ltd, The Vimeira [1986] 2 All ER 409, [1986] AC 965, [1986] 2 WLR 1051, HL.

Bishopsgate Investment Management Ltd (in prov liq) v Maxwell [1992] 2 All ER 856,
e [1993] Ch 1, [1992] 2 WLR 991, CA.

Clyne v New South Wales Bar Association (1960) 104 CLR 186, Aust HC.

Davy-Chiesman v Davy-Chiesman [1984] 1 All ER 321, [1984] Fam 48, [1984] 2 WLR 291, CA.

Fisher, Re [1894] 1 Ch 450, CA.

f Fozal v Gofur (1993) Times, 9 July, [1993] CA Transcript 680.

Gupta v Comer [1991] 1 All ER 289, [1991] 1 QB 629, [1991] 2 WLR 494, CA.

Locke v Camberwell Health Authority [1991] 2 Med LR 249.

McFarlane v E E Caledonia Ltd (No 2) [1995] 1 WLR 366, [1995] 1 Lloyd's Rep 535.

Mills' Estate, Re, ex p Works and Public Buildings Comrs (1886) 34 Ch D 24.

Myers v Elman [1939] 4 All ER 484, [1940] AC 282, HL; rvsg sub nom Myers v
g Rothfield [1938] 3 All ER 498, [1939] 1 KB 109, CA.

Orchard v South Eastern Electricity Board [1987] 1 All ER 95, [1987] QB 565, [1987] 2 WLR 102, CA.

Ridehalgh v Horsefield [1994] 3 All ER 848, [1994] Ch 205, [1994] 3 WLR 462, CA.

Steele Ford & Newton (a firm) v CPS [1993] 2 All ER 769, [1994] 1 AC 22, [1993] 2
h WLR 934, HL.

Symphony Group plc v Hodgson [1993] 4 All ER 143, [1994] QB 179, [1993] 3 WLR 830, CA.

Udall v Capri Lighting Ltd [1987] 3 All ER 262, [1988] QB 907, [1993] 3 WLR 830, CA.

j Wild v Simpson [1919] 2 KB 544, [1918–19] All ER Rep 682, CA.

Cases also cited or referred to in skeleton arguments

Al-Kandari v J R Brown & Co (a firm) [1988] 1 All ER 833, [1988] QB 665, CA.

Aratra Potato Co Ltd v Taylor Joynson Garrett (a firm) [1995] 4 All ER 695.

Ashmore v British Coal Corp [1990] 2 All ER 981, [1990] 2 QB 338, CA.

Bourne v Colodense Ltd [1985] ICR 291, CA.

Bradlaugh v Newdegate (1883) 11 QBD 1.

Business Computers International Ltd v Registrar of Companies [1987] 3 All ER 465, [1988] Ch 229.

Fox (John) (a firm) v Bannister King & Rigbeys (a firm) [1987] 1 All ER 737, [1988] QB 925, CA.

Giles v Thompson [1993] 3 All ER 321, [1994] 1 AC 142, CA and HL.

Harris v Brisco (1886) 17 QBD 504, [1886–90] All ER Rep 564, CA.

Hayward v Giffard (1838) 4 M & W 194, 150 ER 1399.

Hunter v Chief Constable of West Midlands [1981] 3 All ER 727, [1982] AC 529, HL.

Jennings v Johnson (1873) LR 8 CP 425.

Jones, Re (1870) LR 6 Ch App 497, LC.

Kelly v London Transport Executive [1982] 2 All ER 842, [1982] 1 WLR 1055, CA.

Ladd v London Road Car Co (1900) 110 LT Jo 80.

Land and Property Trust Co plc, Re [1991] 3 All ER 409, [1991] 1 WLR 601, CA.

Mainwaring v Goldtech [1991] CA Transcript 0048.

Orchard v South Eastern Electricity Board [1987] 1 All ER 95, [1987] QB 565, CA.

Orme v Associated Newspapers [1980] CA Transcript 809.

R v Bow Street Metropolitan Stipendiary Magistrate, ex p Mirror Group Newspapers Ltd, R v Bow Street Metropolitan Stipendiary Magistrate, ex p British Broadcasting Corp [1992] 2 All ER 638, [1992] 1 WLR 412, DC.

R v Horsham DC, ex p Wenman [1994] 4 All ER 681, [1995] 1 WLR 680.

Rich v Cook (1900) 110 LT Jo 94, CA.

Rondel v Worsley [1967] 3 All ER 993, [1969] 1 AC 191, HL.

Rooks Rider (a firm) v Steel [1993] 4 All ER 716, [1994] 1 WLR 818.

Shah v Karanjia [1993] 4 All ER 792.

Sievwright v Ward [1935] NZLR 43, NZ SC.

Singh v Observer Ltd [1989] 2 All ER 751; rvsd [1989] 3 All ER 777, CA.

Taylor v Pace Developments Ltd [1991] BCC 406, CA.

Tharros Shipping Co Ltd v Bias Shipping Ltd (No 3) [1995] 1 Lloyd's Rep 541.

Thistleton v Hendricks (1992) 32 Con LR 123.

Ward v Procter (1891) 7 TLR 244, DC.

Wiggins v Lavy (1928) 44 TLR 721.

Appeal

Messrs Schilling & Lom appealed with leave from the order of Collins J made on 16 December 1994, whereby he ordered, on the application of the defendant, Lord Aldington, that the solicitors should personally pay 60% of Lord Aldington's costs incurred in connection with libel proceedings brought against him by their client, Count Nikolai Tolstoy-Miloslavsky, pursuant to s 51(1) and (3) of the Supreme Court Act 1981. By a respondent's notice, Lord Aldington sought to affirm Collins J's order on the ground that he should have made a wasted costs order against the solicitors under s 51(6) and (7) of the 1981 Act. The Registrar of Civil Appeals ordered pursuant to RSC Ord 59, r 8 that the notice of appeal and respondent's notice be served on the Bar Council and the Law Society to enable them to appear at the hearing of the appeal and to make submissions. Count Tolstoy took no part in the appeal. The facts are set out in the judgment of Rose LJ.

Guy Mansfield QC and Adrienne Page (instructed by Barlow Lyde & Gilbert) for the solicitors.

Charles Gray QC (instructed by Allen & Overy) for Lord Aldington.

a *Duncan Matheson QC* and *Gregory Chambers* (instructed by *Diane Burleigh* and *Janice Bye*) for the Law Society and the Bar Council.

ROSE LJ. This is an appeal by leave of the judge, Collins J, by solicitors for the plaintiff against that part of his order made on 16 December 1994 whereby he ordered under s 51(1) and (3) of the Supreme Court Act 1981 that the solicitors
b should personally pay 60% of the defendant's costs in connection with the proceedings. By a respondent's notice the defendant contends that the order should be affirmed on the additional ground that the judge should have made a wasted costs order under s 51(6) and (7) of the Act.

Because issues of general concern to the Bar and the Law Society were raised
c by the appeal the Registrar of Civil Appeals ordered, pursuant to RSC Ord 59, r 8, that the notice of appeal and the respondent's notice should be served on the Bar Council and the Law Society to enable them to appear at the hearing of the appeal and to make submissions. That they have done.

The background to the present litigation was an action for libel brought by the
d present defendant, Lord Aldington, initially against a man called Watts, the present plaintiff, Count Tolstoy, being joined as co-defendant at his own request. The libel was, in essence, that Lord Aldington was a major war criminal who had arranged every detail of the massacre of 70,000 men, women and children. If untrue this was obviously a very grave libel. The defence was justification, particularised over 80 pages of pleadings. The main issues in the pleadings all
e related to events before 22 May 1945. The trial lasted two months. On 30 November 1990 the jury found for Lord Aldington. He was awarded £1·5m damages and costs. His reputation was vindicated. But in financial terms it was a pyrrhic victory. Watts has paid £10,000 and Count Tolstoy not a penny. Count Tolstoy sought to appeal but was unable to provide security for costs as required
f by an order of the Court of Appeal in July 1990. That court was highly critical of the merits of the appeal and questioned the value of 'new' evidence he wished to rely on in the form of two letters written by Lord Aldington which supposedly threw light on the date of his departure from Austria. On 3 August 1990 the appeal was dismissed because no security was provided. With the appellant solicitors acting for, and apparently paid by, him, Count Tolstoy instituted other
g proceedings, which failed at first instance before Morritt J. He failed on appeal to the Court of Appeal, where the solicitors were not acting for him. He claimed that an agreement by Lord Aldington to release Watts, on payment of the sum of £10,000, from claims resulting from the libel proceedings applied to him also.

The writ in the present proceedings was issued on 21 February 1994. Count
h Tolstoy sought an order that the judgment of 30 November 1990 be set aside on the grounds of fraud. That cause of action, which had vested in his trustee in bankruptcy, was assigned to Count Tolstoy for £10 and notice of that assignment was given by the appellant solicitors to Lord Aldington in December 1993. The writ was issued by the appellant solicitors, who had acted for Count Tolstoy since
j about April 1991. The writ was not preceded by any letter before action. Legal aid was not applied for or, apparently, even contemplated prior to proceedings. On 14 March the statement of claim was served, apparently settled by and bearing the signatures of leading and junior counsel, the leader having represented Count Tolstoy in the original defamation proceedings. Both counsel and the appellant solicitors provided their services to Count Tolstoy free of charge.

On 29 March 1994 Lord Aldington applied for an order that the statement of
claim be struck out and the action dismissed on the ground that it was frivolous,
vexatious and otherwise an abuse of the process of the court. In October 1994 the
matter came before Mr Andrew Collins QC sitting as a deputy judge of the High
Court. Neither of the counsel who had signed the statement of claim appeared
for Count Tolstoy; he was represented by another leading counsel. It was
conceded on behalf of Count Tolstoy that the fraud allegation was arguable if and
only if he could establish his case in relation to a phantom log and certain
observations by Brigadier Tryon-Wilson, which were said to demonstrate
perjury on the part of Lord Aldington as to the date in May 1945 when he had left
Austria. He had testified in the libel proceedings that he left by air on the morning
of 22 May and this account was corroborated by the evidence of Brigadier
Tryon-Wilson and to a very limited extent by a journal of Brigadier de
Fonblanque. The phantom log appeared to show that Lord Aldington had left on
23 May. It had been common ground at the trial that he could not have left on
that day because the airfield was closed. The phantom log had been in the
possession of Count Tolstoy since December 1990 and had been available in the
Public Records Office at the date of the libel trial. The observations by Brigadier
Tryon-Wilson were contained in an interview with Dr Smith of the Imperial War
Museum in 1990 which Count Tolstoy contended showed that Lord Aldington
had attended a corp commanders' conference in Austria on the morning of 22
May; plainly they did not show this. Although a good deal of time had been
devoted in the libel proceedings to the date of Lord Aldington's departure from
Austria it was not one of the 23 key issues identified by Count Tolstoy's counsel
in his closing speech to the jury in those proceedings.

On 14 October 1994 Mr Collins QC, in a reserved judgment, held that Count
Tolstoy was unable to establish 'even a reasonable possibility that the new
evidence ... may show that Lord Aldington committed perjury'. The date of
departure was not a key issue, the log was not decisive and it was not established
that the log could not have been discovered by reasonable diligence. He
concluded that the claim was utterly hopeless and ordered that it be struck out as
an abuse of process. Lord Aldington then indicated that he was considering an
application for an order that Count Tolstoy's legal representatives should pay the
costs of the proceedings. The deputy judge adjourned further questions as to
costs and gave directions.

On 21 October 1994, by written notice, Lord Aldington applied for an order
that the appellant solicitors should pay his costs. The grounds of the application
were (a) that, by acting without fee, the solicitors had maintained the action and
thus exposed themselves to an order for costs and (b) the action had no realistic
prospect of success and, in those circumstances, the solicitors should be liable for
costs.

The application was heard by Collins J (as he had then become) on 30
November 1994. The main thrust of the oral argument differed from that set out
in the written notice. In summary, it was based on two main grounds: (a) that
the costs incurred by the defendant were 'wasted costs' as defined by s 51(6) and
(7) of the 1981 Act, as amended by the Courts and Legal Services Act 1990, and
the solicitors should be ordered to bear them, their conduct having been
'improper' and 'unreasonable'; and (b) by agreeing to act without fee the
solicitors put themselves in the position of 'third party funders' of the litigation
and should therefore be ordered to pay the defendant's costs pursuant to the
general discretion conferred by s 51(1) and (3) of the Act, as explained in *Aiden*

a *Shipping Co Ltd v Interbulk Ltd, The Vimeira* [1986] 2 All ER 409, [1986] AC 965. In a reserved judgment on 16 December Collins J rejected the first ground but accepted the second and ordered the solicitors to pay 60% of Lord Aldington's costs.

The judge first considered the wasted costs jurisdiction and, in particular, the judgment of this court delivered by Sir Thomas Bingham MR in *Ridehalgh v*
b *Horsefield* [1994] 3 All ER 848, [1994] Ch 205 and he also referred to the judgment of Balcombe LJ in *Symphony Group plc v Hodgson* [1993] 4 All ER 143, [1994] QB 179. He rejected an argument that when, in *Ridehalgh v Horsefield* [1994] 3 All ER 848 at 863, [1994] Ch 205 at 234, Sir Thomas Bingham MR referred to 'abuse of process', he was giving that term a different meaning from that which it ordinarily bears in RSC Ord 18, r 19. He held that there had been a serious error
c of judgment by the solicitors. Nevertheless, in all the circumstances, he concluded that, although it was a borderline case, it would not be right to make a wasted costs order.

As to the alternative ground, he dismissed the argument that s 51(6) and (7) now defines the circumstances in which costs orders can be made against
d solicitors and, having discussed the concepts of maintenance and funding, he concluded that, in general, it is no longer necessary to have regard to maintenance in view of the decision in *Aiden Shipping*. In the light of that authority he said it had become clear that—

> *e* 'the court has jurisdiction to order a third party to pay costs under the wide provisions of s 51(1) and (3) of the 1981 Act. It is a jurisdiction which will, except where the funding arises in what might be called a business context (e g by insurers or trade unions), be very sparingly exercised.'

After referring to other authorities he concluded that there was no reason in principle why 'solicitors who choose to fund a client's litigation by acting for no
f fee should not be treated as third party funders and so be liable to pay the other side's costs'. Finally, he reached the conclusion that, in the wholly exceptional circumstances, an order should be made against the solicitors and he took the broad view that the amount they should be ordered to pay was 60%.

From that order the solicitors appeal. An application for leave to appeal the
g judgment of 14 October 1994 striking out the plaintiff's claim stands adjourned. It is common ground that the present appeal should be considered on the basis that the judgment of 14 October was correct.

Section 51 of the 1981 Act, as amended by the 1990 Act, is, in material parts, in these terms:

h '(1) Subject to the provisions of this or any other enactment and to rules of court, the costs of and incidental to all proceedings in—(a) the civil division of the Court of Appeal; (b) the High Court; and (c) any county court, shall be in the discretion of the court …

(3) The court shall have full power to determine by whom and to what
j extent the costs are to be paid …

(6) In any proceedings mentioned in subsection (1), the court may disallow, or (as the case may be) order the legal or other representative concerned to meet, the whole of any wasted costs or such part of them as may be determined in accordance with rules of court.

(7) In subsection (6), "wasted costs" means any costs incurred by a party—(a) as a result of any improper, unreasonable or negligent act or omission on

the part of any legal or other representative or any employee of such a
representative; or (b) which, in the light of any such act or omission *a*
occurring after they were incurred, the court considers it is unreasonable to
expect that party to pay.'

For the solicitors, Mr Mansfield QC submits that the judge had no jurisdiction
to make an order under s 51(1) and (3). The court can only make costs orders *b*
against solicitors either under the wasted costs provisions of sub-ss (6) and (7) or
under its inherent jurisdiction in relation to breaches of duty to the court. Before
and since the Judicature Acts the court's inherent jurisdiction over solicitors as
officers of the court has depended not on blameworthiness in the ordinary sense,
but on breach of duty to the court, e g in acting without authority or in breach of
an undertaking (see *Ridehalgh v Horsefield* [1994] 3 All ER 848 at 856–857, [1994] *c*
Ch 205 at 227); it is this which distinguished the position of solicitors from that of
other non-parties prior to *Aiden Shipping*. Section 5 of the Supreme Court of
Judicature Act 1890 (see *Re Mills' Estate, ex p Works and Public Buildings Comrs*
(1886) 34 Ch D 24 and *Re Fisher* [1894] 1 Ch 450) and its subsequent manifestations
did not, and s 51(3) does not, apply to solicitors; hence when, in *Myers v Elman* *d*
[1939] 4 All ER 484, [1940] AC 282, the House of Lords considered the courts'
jurisdiction to order solicitors to pay costs, s 50 of the Supreme Court of
Judicature (Consolidation) Act 1925 (the successor to s 5 of the 1890 Act) was not
referred to. When the forerunner of the present wasted costs regime was
introduced by RSC Ord 62, r 8(1) in 1960 it was unrelated to the jurisdiction under
s 50 of the 1925 Act. *Aiden Shipping* was not concerned with solicitors. The *e*
concurrent enactment of the conditional fee provisions of s 58 of the 1990 Act and
s 51(6) and (7) is inconsistent with any intention on the part of Parliament to
widen the liability of solicitors to costs orders save under the wasted costs regime.
The judge was wrong to found jurisdiction under s 51(1) and (3) on an analogy
with acting without authority, particularly as he found no breach of any duty to *f*
the courts. He was also wrong to hold that a solicitor acting without fee was to
be equated to a third party funder, and that acting without fee in a case both
without merit and constituting abuse of process gave rise to impropriety. The
credibility of Lord Aldington was crucial to his success in the libel proceedings
and the appearance of the phantom log lent documentary challenge to his
accuracy in saying that he had left Austria on 22 May. As to causation, the judge *g*
was not justified in finding that the defendant would have acted for himself if the
plaintiff had acted in person. The judge was right not to make a wasted costs
order because the solicitors' conduct was not 'plainly unjustifiable': see *Ridehalgh
v Horsefield* [1994] 3 All ER 848 at 866, [1994] Ch 205 at 237. This court should be
very slow to interfere with his findings when refusing such an order. *h*

For the Law Society and the Bar Council, Mr Matheson QC confines his
submissions to the general principles, without taking up any position on the facts
or merits of this particular case. He submits that, apart from the inherent
jurisdiction over solicitors as officers of the court, the whole jurisdiction to award
costs against legal representatives is contained in s 51(6) and (7). Alternatively, *j*
even if *Aiden Shipping* confers a jurisdiction in relation to solicitors, a decision that
a wasted costs order is not called for should normally be conclusive against resort
to s 51(1) and (3). Legal representatives who provide their services free should
not be equated with third party funders. The instant decision has serious
implications for pro bono work and conditional fee agreements. He makes
similar submissions to Mr Mansfield on the history of s 51(1) and (3). Resort to

a sub-ss (1) and (3) undermines *Ridehalgh v Horsefield*. If these subsections confer a jurisdiction in relation to solicitors, neither Balcombe LJ in *Symphony Group v Hodgson* [1993] 4 All ER 143 at 150–152, [1994] QB 179 at 190–192, nor Lord Bridge (who had presided in *Aiden Shipping*) in *Steele Ford & Newton (a firm) v CPS* [1993] 2 All ER 769 at 772, [1994] 1 AC 22 at 30–31, would have expressed themselves as they did. Alternatively, in the light of those observations, even if there is such a
b jurisdiction, it would be wrong to exercise it against a legal representative against whom a wasted costs order could not be made. Further, legal representatives who act without fee do not put themselves into the position of third party funders. The long and honourable tradition of lawyers providing their services without charge is of particular importance at a time of increasing debate about access to justice and would be undermined if a legal representative acting without
c charge thereby exposed himself to the risk of an adverse order for costs. Conditional fee agreements having been approved by Parliament as being in the public interest, it would be curious if a legal representative who acted without fee were in a potentially worse position then one acting for a contingent fee.

For the defendant Mr Gray QC submits that four particular matters support an
d order for costs, whether under s 51(3) or (6): the case was hopeless; it was an abuse of process from its inception, as the judge found; the solicitors knew of Count Tolstoy's impecuniosity, bankruptcy and inability to pay costs if he lost; and yet they funded the litigation by making their services available free. The failure to consider applying for legal aid, the absence of a letter before action and the harassing of Lord Aldington by hopeless proceedings all point to unreason-
e ableness on the solicitors' part. The principles underlying pro bono work are unaffected by the exceptional circumstances of the present case. In the light of *Aiden Shipping*, s 51(3) is wide enough to confer jurisdiction in relation to solicitors. These solicitors funded a hopeless case which was an abuse of process and a breach of their duty to the court. Cases in relation to maintenance support
f this: see *McFarlane v E E Caledonia Ltd (No 2)* [1995] 1 WLR 366, [1995] 1 Lloyd's Rep 535 and *Bishopsgate Investment Management Ltd (in prov liq) v Maxwell* [1992] 2 All ER 856, [1993] Ch 1. Alternatively, the solicitors behaved improperly and unreasonably and a wasted costs order should have been made against them. The judge's conclusions in relation to causation and discretion are unassailable.

g In my judgment, Collins J reached the right conclusion, but did so by the wrong route.

Section 51(1) and (3) of the 1981 Act does not confer jurisdiction to make an order for costs against legal representatives when acting as legal representatives. I say this for six reasons.

h First, the provisions of these subsections have appeared in virtually identical form since the enactment of s 5 of the 1890 Act. It is clear from *Re Mills' Estate* that s 5 did not confer a new jurisdiction but regulated the way in which, on transfer of various jurisdictions to the High Court, costs were there to be dealt with: see (1886) 34 Ch D 24 at 33, 36, 37 and 41 per Cotton, Bowen and Fry LJJ
j respectively. Prior to the Supreme Court of Judicature Acts 1873 and 1875 the court had jurisdiction over solicitors as officers of the court based on their duty to the court and this duty continues: see eg in *Myers v Elman* [1939] 4 All ER 484 at 508–509, 510, [1940] AC 282 at 319, 321 per Lord Wright and *Udall v Capri Lighting Ltd* [1987] 3 All ER 262 at 268–269, [1988] QB 907 at 916–918 per Balcombe LJ. But s 5 was not needed to confer any jurisdiction in relation to solicitors acting in breach of duty to the court.

The amendment to s 51(1) brought about by the 1990 Act extended the court's century-old discretionary powers in relation to costs in proceedings in the county court as well as in the Civil Division of the Court of Appeal and the High Court. The new provisions as to wasted costs orders against legal representatives, by way of sub-ss (6) and (7), were introduced by s 4(1) at the same time. It is to my mind inconceivable that Parliament, which is presumed to know the law, would have thought it necessary to introduce such a regime in relation to legal representatives if the courts' powers, under sub-ss (1) and (3), were already sufficiently wide to enable it to make orders against solicitors. The conclusion is reinforced by the fact that *Aiden Shipping* was decided by the House of Lords four years before the 1990 Act, so Parliament presumably did not regard that decision as applying to legal representatives; had it done so sub-ss (6) and (7) would have been otiose.

Secondly, there is no authority, so far as I am aware, prior to 1990, wherein it was accepted by the court, that s 51(1) and (3), or their statutory precursors, conferred jurisdiction in relation to legal representatives. There are observations in *Gupta v Comer* [1991] 1 All ER 289 at 293, 294, [1991] 1 QB 629 at 635–636, 637 per Lord Donaldson MR and Balcombe LJ which might lend support to a contrary view, but they were obiter; the history of the legislation does not appear to have been considered in that case as it has in this; the 1990 Act has since come into force correcting the anomaly referred to; and Lord Bridge's speech in *Steele Ford & Newton (a firm) v CPS* casts light on *Aiden Shipping* which was not available at the time of *Gupta v Comer*. The maintenance cases relied on by Mr Gray do not relate to solicitors, who, as Atkin LJ pointed out in *Wild v Simpson* [1919] 2 KB 544 at 562, [1918–19] All ER Rep 682 at 691, obviously intermeddle with litigation and may lawfully do so provided they have no direct interest in receiving part of the proceeds of the litigation. In *Clyne v New South Wales Bar Association* (1960) 104 CLR 186 at 203 the High Court of Australia, presided over by Dixon CJ, put the matter in this way:

> '... it is obvious that, in relation to maintenance, special considerations must apply to a solicitor, since it is, in a sense, the business of a solicitor to maintain litigation for his clients. It would appear indeed to be impossible for a solicitor to be held, in relation to legal proceedings conducted for a client, to be guilty of maintenance except perhaps in two cases, one of which might amount to champerty. For a solicitor could hardly be held guilty of a crime in respect of conduct which is recognized by the law as perfectly proper professional conduct. And it seems to be established that a solicitor may with perfect propriety act for a client who has no means, and expend his own money in payment of counsel's fees and other outgoings, although he has no prospect of being paid either fees or outgoings except by virtue of a judgment or order against the other party to the proceedings. This, however, is subject to two conditions. One is that he has considered the case and believes that his client has a reasonable cause of action or defence as the case may be. And the other is that he must not in any case bargain with his client for an interest in the subject-matter of litigation, or (what is in substance the same thing) for remuneration proportionate to the amount which may be recovered by his client in a proceeding ...'

That passage now, of course, has to be read in this country subject to the contingent fee provisions of the 1990 Act.

a Thirdly, there is clear authority, binding on this court, that s 4 of the 1990 Act was not retrospective (*Fozal v Gofur* (1993) Times, 9 July and *Ridehalgh v Horsefield* [1994] 3 All ER 848 at 877, [1994] Ch 205 at 250) and there was previously no jurisdiction to make orders against barristers: see *Davy-Chiesman v Davy-Chiesman* [1984] 1 All ER 321 at 328, [1984] Fam 48 at 58 and *Orchard v South Eastern Electricity Board* [1987] 1 All ER 95 at 99, 106, [1987] QB 565 at 571–581 per
b Donaldson MR and Dillon LJ. There was no suggestion in *Orchard's* case that *Aiden Shipping* had changed the position in relation to solicitors.

Fourthly, ss 111 and 112 of the 1990 Act amend, respectively, the Prosecution of Offences Act 1985 and the Magistrates' Courts Act 1980 so as to introduce a wasted costs regime like s 51(6) and (7) into criminal proceedings and civil proceedings in magistrates' courts. This indicates that Parliament intended the
c same test of liability by legal representatives to costs orders to be applied in all courts and is inconsistent with the notion that such liability already existed by virtue of s 51(1) and (3).

Fifthly, although *Aiden Shipping* was referred to in argument in *Ridehalgh v Horsefield* [1994] Ch 205 at 214, the Court of Appeal in that case proceeded on the
d basis that s 51(6) and (7) contained the only statutory provisions applicable to costs orders against legal representatives. It is to be noted that in *Steele Ford & Newton (a firm) v CPS* [1993] 2 All ER 769 at 772, [1994] 1 AC 22 at 31 Lord Bridge of Harwich, with whose speech all other members of the House agreed, firmly rejected the suggestion that *Aiden Shipping* established an unlimited jurisdiction to order any person to pay costs. Furthermore, Balcombe LJ's analysis of *Aiden*
e *Shipping* and his principles for guidance in *Symphony Group plc v Hodgson* [1993] 4 All ER 143 at 150–154, [1994] QB 179 at 190–194 do not suggest that *Aiden Shipping* has any application to legal representatives.

Sixthly, as was analysed in *Ridehalgh v Horsefield* [1994] 3 All ER 848 at 856–860, [1994] Ch 205 at 226–231, the origins of s 51(6) and (7) lay in the provisions of
f what, by 1986, became RSC Ord 62, r 11, which reflected the court's inherent jurisdiction in relation to solicitors. It was not suggested that s 51(1) and (3) reflects such inherent jurisdiction.

In my judgment Mr Mansfield is correct in his submission that there are only three categories of conduct which can give rise to an order for costs against a solicitor (i) if it is within the wasted costs jurisdiction of s 51(6) and (7); (ii) if it is
g otherwise a breach of duty to the court such as, even before the Judicature Acts, could found an order (e g if he acts, even unwittingly, without authority or in breach of an undertaking); (iii) if he acts outside the role of solicitor (e g in a private capacity or as a true third party funder for someone else).

There is in my judgment no jurisdiction to make an order for costs against a
h solicitor solely on the ground that he acted without fee. It is in the public interest and it has always been recognised that it is proper for counsel and solicitors to act without fee. The access to justice which this can provide, for example in cases outside the scope of legal aid, confers a benefit on the public. Section 58 of the 1990 Act, which legitimises conditional fees, inferentially demonstrates
j Parliament's recognition of this principle. For it would be very curious if a legal representative on a contingent fee and, therefore, with a financial interest in the outcome of litigation, could resist an order for costs against himself but one acting for no fee could not. Whether a solicitor is acting for remuneration or not does not alter the existence or nature of his duty to his client and the court, or affect the absence of any duty to protect the opposing party in the litigation from exposure to the expense of a hopeless claim. In neither case does he have to

'impose a pre-trial screen through which litigants must pass': see *Orchard v South Eastern Electricity Board* [1987] 1 All ER 95 at 100–101, [1987] QB 565 at 572–574 per Donaldson MR.

If I am wrong about this and s 51(1) and (3) confers jurisdiction in relation to legal representatives, it is not a jurisdiction which has been, nor in my judgment in the light of the wasted costs code now provided by the 1990 Act should it now be, exercised in relation to legal representatives. *Ridehalgh v Horsefield* comprehensively deals with the way in which the courts should approach applications for costs against legal representatives, save where a solicitor acts in either of the ways identified in (ii) or (iii) above.

I turn to the defendant's respondent's notice and the question as to whether a wasted costs order should have been made under sub-ss (6) and (7) of s 51.

Three questions arise. First, was the judge correct to conclude that the solicitors' conduct, although on the borderline, was 'not improper' or 'unreasonable'? Secondly, if not, did their conduct cause costs to be incurred by the defendant? Thirdly, should an order have been made in the exercise of discretion?

It is the answer to the first question which is crucial.

The solicitors rely on the affidavit of Mr Thomson, who swears that they decided to act because they considered Count Tolstoy 'had a cause of action ... which he wished to pursue for bona fide reasons'. They would not have acted if they had not taken the view it was proper to represent the plaintiff. They also took the view that it was 'proper' to place the plea of fraud on the record. In the absence of waiver of privilege they can 'say no more'. They accept that they have a duty to the court to conduct litigation with due propriety.

The proper discharge of that duty must, as it seems to me, depend on the circumstances of the particular case. The background to the present litigation was unusual in a number of respects. The plaintiff was not initially sued in the libel proceedings; he was joined as co-defendant at his own request. The trial took two months, so the costs, like the damages awarded by the jury, were enormous. Count Tolstoy had not and still has not the means or, apparently, the intention to satisfy either. I set out at the beginning of this judgment the course of subsequent events. The appellant solicitors knew of all these matters. They chose to act for the plaintiff without fee. More than four years after the trial, without a letter before action and without applying for, or apparently considering applying for, legal aid they issued proceedings on the plaintiff's behalf. The action was a collateral attack on the decision of a court of competent jurisdiction which, it is conceded, was prima facie an abuse. There was no, or so little, evidence of fraud and perjury that the proceedings were struck out as 'utterly hopeless' and an abuse of process under RSC Ord 18, r 19. The pleading was signed by counsel, 'surprisingly' as the judge found. I am astonished, though it is right that I should emphasise that no submissions on behalf of the counsel in question have been made in the course of these proceedings. Counsel's role, however, did not exonerate the solicitors from their obligation to exercise their own independent judgment to consider whether the claim could properly be pursued; they were not entitled to follow counsel blindly: see *Davy-Chiesman v Davy-Chiesman* and *Locke v Camberwell Health Authority* [1991] 2 Med LR 249 at 254. They had to apply their 'own expert professional mind to the substance of the advice received': see *Ridehalgh v Horsefield* [1994] 3 All ER 848 at 858, [1994] Ch 205 at 228.

a   In my judgment these facts show a lack of due propriety in the conduct of the litigation and an abuse of process of the court in the wider sense in which that phrase was used in *Ridehalgh v Horsefield* [1994] 3 All ER 848 at 863, [1994] Ch 205 at 234. (I comment, in passing, that the judge was wrong to conclude that the court was there using that phrase in the same sense as in RSC Ord 18, r 19; the examples given show that the court was using the phrase in a wider sense.) I

b   emphasise that acting without fee, and doing so in a hopeless case, or even in a case struck out for abuse of process under RSC Ord 18, r 19, is not conduct which itself would justify the making of a wasted costs order. But when all the other circumstances which I have identified are added, the appellant solicitors' conduct in the present case is, in my judgment, properly to be characterised as 'unreasonable' in the way in which that word is defined in *Ridehalgh v Horsefield*

c   [1994] 3 All ER 848 at 861, [1994] Ch 205 at 232. In particular: (i) this was the second if not the third occasion on which Count Tolstoy had sought by litigation to defeat Lord Aldington in relation to the same matters and it was to this extent at least potentially vexatious: indeed, as Mr Makie's affidavit shows, Lord Aldington has been harassed by the litigation; (ii) Count Tolstoy was not merely

d   impecunious but he had not satisfied, and had taken steps to avoid satisfying, the existing judgment against him and was only able to proceed because he had bought the cause of action from his trustee in bankruptcy; (iii) the Court of Appeal had already been highly critical of other 'new' evidence relating to the date of leaving Austria; (iv) the proceedings were prima facie an abuse because they were a collateral attack on the judgment of a court of competent

e   jurisdiction; (v) the allegation of perjury and fraud was made on a manifestly insubstantial basis: even if the phantom log was capable of calling Lord Aldington's accuracy into question it did not begin to demonstrate perjury in relation to events 45 years earlier.

f   Bearing in mind that the jurisdiction to make a wasted costs order must be exercised with care and only in a clear case, these features, in my judgment, gave rise to 'the unjustifiable conduct of litigation' against which the wasted costs regime is aimed: see *Ridehalgh v Horsefield* [1994] 3 All ER 848 at 860, [1994] Ch 205 at 231. In my judgment, no solicitor in the position of the appellants, taking these factors into account, could, notwithstanding that counsel had put their

g   names to the statement of claim, reasonably have instituted these proceedings.

Collins J concluded that the solicitors' conduct was surprising, an error of judgment and possibly due to their inability to take an objective view. He concluded, however, clearly having in mind the judgment in *Ridehalgh v Horsefield* [1994] 3 All ER 848 at 866, [1994] Ch 205 at 237, that they should be

h   given the benefit of the doubt, apparently because Count Tolstoy's refusal to waive privilege had made it difficult for them to defend themselves and they had taken the view that it was proper to represent him; in consequence the judge was not satisfied that there was no reasonable explanation. In this respect, it seems to me, he fell into error in applying the principles of *Ridehalgh v Horsefield* to the

j   facts. He had to decide the case on the evidence before him. Having regard to the circumstances of this case he made undue allowance for the possibility of an exculpatory account if privilege had been waived. If, in the absence of further explanation, the circumstances clearly pointed, as in my view they did, to unreasonableness, such a conclusion could not be avoided by the solicitors asserting that they were acting properly. It is for the court, not the solicitors themselves, to judge this.

On the evidence before the court the institution of these proceedings in the *a* circumstances earlier identified was conduct which did not permit a reasonable explanation and the judge should so have found.

As to causation and, so far as it arises, discretion, the judge's conclusions on these matters in relation to the order he made under s 51(1) and (3) are in my view unassailable and apply mutatis mutandis in relation to an order under sub-ss (6) and (7). *b*

Although, as I have sought to explain, I differ from the reasoning of the judge, the order which he made was, in my view, correct. I would dismiss this appeal.

ROCH LJ. This was an exceptional action to bring. The first feature which made it exceptional was the fact that Count Tolstoy had already had his day in court. *c* Indeed, it could be said that he had had several days in court before the commencement of these proceedings. The second feature is that he had not originally been a party to the first action by Lord Aldington for libel; he had become a party because he had applied to be joined. The third unusual feature was that although Count Tolstoy had lost the initial libel action, he had not paid a penny of the damages or the costs awarded against him. On the contrary, he *d* had had himself made bankrupt. The fourth unusual feature was that before these proceedings got under way the Court of Appeal, on 18 July 1990, had expressed a view that Count Tolstoy had no reasonable chance of making good his grounds of appeal against the jury's verdict in the defamation action or any of them. There was no merit in them. One of those grounds was that there was *e* fresh evidence, albeit not the alleged fresh evidence relied on in these proceedings. The observation of the members of the Court of Appeal on that occasion anticipated the conclusions reached by the deputy High Court judge in the application of Lord Aldington to strike out the action which forms the basis of these proceedings.

The fifth unusual circumstance was that the original defendant in the libel *f* proceedings had given undertakings to Lord Aldington and had reached a compromise with him. Count Tolstoy had not. Count Tolstoy had, however, relied on that arrangement in an attempt to obtain a release from the orders for damages and costs made against him in the libel action. That attempt was pursued to the Court of Appeal and was unsuccessful both at first instance and on *g* appeal.

The sixth unusual feature was that in order to be in a position to commence this action Count Tolstoy had to take an assignment of the cause of action from his trustee in bankruptcy. The cause of action was assigned to Count Tolstoy by his trustee in bankruptcy for the princely sum of £10. Then there were the *h* unusual features that the action was commenced without a letter before action and without an application for legal aid being made. The absence of a legal aid application was curious because those acting for Count Tolstoy knew that he was unable to pay any costs if this action was lost either to those acting for him or to Lord Aldington. The safeguards for a proposed defendant afforded by the Legal *j* Aid Scheme were not brought into play.

The eighth feature was that in this action a further serious allegation was being made against Lord Aldington, namely that he was a fraud and a perjurer and he had used such means to obtain the jury's verdict in the first action.

Finally, these proceedings were a collateral attack on the jury's verdict in the libel action, following an unsuccessful attempt to appeal that verdict.

a   In those circumstances, which, as Mr Gray QC points out, are unlikely to be present together in other cases, there was a duty on those acting for Count Tolstoy to investigate with the greatest care his motives and the strength of the material on which these fresh and serious allegations against Lord Aldington were to be made. Failure to do that, in my judgment, would amount to improper or unreasonable behaviour by those legal representatives of a kind to found a b wasted costs order under s 51(6) of the Supreme Court Act 1981 and s 4 of the Courts and Legal Services Act 1990.

The deputy High Court judge, on Lord Aldington's application to strike out this action as an abuse of process, found that the action was hopeless and struck it out as an abuse of process; the abuse of process being created by the hopelessness of the case. Following a careful examination of the new material, c the deputy judge expressed his conclusion on the phantom log entry in these terms:

'In my judgment the phantom log entry does not begin to raise even a possibility of persuading any court that Lord Aldington committed perjury.'

d   On the other piece of evidence, namely Brigadier Tryon-Wilson's answers in interview, the judge said:

'It seems to me that in the light of that material it is quite impossible for Count Tolstoy to place any reliance on the Tryon-Wilson interview as an indication, let alone possible proof of perjury.'

e

The deputy judge further found that the phantom log had been available at the trial of the libel action and therefore would not have passed the test for the admissibility of new evidence.

This court, in my opinion, must proceed, as should Collins J have proceeded, f on the basis that all the evidence and material on which this action was based was deployed before him to resist Lord Aldington's application to strike out the action as an abuse of process. The fact that counsel signed the statement of claim and gave advice cannot raise a presumption that there may have been more evidence or material which for some reason was not placed before the deputy judge in October 1994.

g   Considering the evidence and material that was placed before the deputy judge on that occasion, in my judgment it must have been glaringly obvious to any competent legal representative that there was no basis for this second action and that the second action had no prospect of success; that to commence these proceedings would be a clear case of an unjustifiable conduct of litigation. This h claim, to use the words of Collins J, who, as Mr Mansfield QC has submitted and I accept, had an unrivalled detailed knowledge of these proceedings, was 'wholly without merit and amounted to an abuse of process'. The knowledge of Count Tolstoy's legal representatives must have been equivalent to that of the judge and their appreciation of the action should have been the same as his. They should j not have lent themselves to these proceedings in the particular circumstances of this case which I have listed. During his judgment Collins J said:

'I am convinced that there was a serious error of judgment. It may be that the advisers have lived with the case and more particularly with Count Tolstoy's enthusiasm for his point of view for so long that they were unable to take an objective view.'

It seems to me that those are inescapable conclusions on the facts of this case
and that those conclusions should have led the judge to making a wasted costs
order against Count Tolstoy's legal representatives. I agree with Rose LJ that the
judge made undue allowance for the possibility of an exculpatory account
emerging if privilege had been waived.

On the question whether a costs order could be made against the solicitors
under s 51(1) and (3) of the Act, in my judgment, on the facts in this case, such an
order could not be made. A person who is not a party to proceedings can be
ordered to pay costs in those proceedings if he has made himself a quasi-party, for
example, by being a party to separate proceedings which have been heard
together with the proceedings in which the costs order is sought, or by funding
the proceedings or by initiating them for some purpose of his own and it is
reasonable and just to make the order. The legal representative who acts as a
legal representative does not make himself a quasi-party and no jurisdiction to
make an order for costs against him under s 51(1) and (3) arises. However, a legal
representative who goes beyond conducting proceedings as a legal representative
and behaves as a quasi-party will not be immune from a costs order under s 51(1)
and (3) merely because he is a barrister or a solicitor.

In this case, in my judgment, neither solicitor nor counsel acted in a way which
made them liable to the jurisdiction of this court under s 51(1) and (3) to make a
costs order against a person who is not a party to the proceedings. Acting pro
bono is not, of itself, sufficient to make a legal representative a quasi-party. More
is required.

On the issue of causation I, like Rose LJ, consider the judge's findings to be
unassailable.

I would dismiss this appeal.

WARD LJ. As I see it, the legislative purpose of s 51(6) and (7) of the Supreme
Court Act 1981, as amended, was to provide the framework which would enable
the court to order all litigators to bear some or all of the costs of an action in the
same manner as solicitors alone had borne them when their work fell short of the
standard of competence which the court expected of them within their province
as officers of the court to further the ends of justice. These provisions, and the
rules made thereunder, now contain a code which governs all awards of costs
against solicitors and other legal representatives when acting as such. It may be,
though it is not necessary to express more than a tentative view about it, that
even if a solicitor is in breach of an undertaking or begins proceedings without
authority, then, if an order for costs is to be imposed upon him, his liability should
be judged under s 51(6) and (7) and the inherent jurisdiction of the court may
then be limited to such other control or discipline over solicitors as may be
necessary to ensure their due compliance with their duties as officers of the court.

For the six reasons given by Rose LJ, with which I entirely agree, s 51(1) and (3)
has no application to solicitors acting as such. Their liability for costs, when
acting as solicitors, should be judged by the same criteria when their fees are paid
as when they act pro bono.

Lord Aldington's claim for wasted costs against Count Tolstoy's solicitors is
brought under those limbs of s 51(7) which relate to costs resulting from the
improper and/or unreasonable conduct of the solicitors. But one should not lose
sight of the observations of this court in *Ridehalgh v Horsefield* [1994] 3 All ER 848
at 862, [1994] Ch 205 at 233:

a   'Conduct which is unreasonable may also be improper, and conduct which is negligent will very frequently be (if it is not by definition) unreasonable. We do not think any sharp differentiation between these expressions is useful or necessary or intended.'

Whilst, therefore, focusing on what seems to me to be the material allegation here, namely the unreasonableness of the solicitors' conduct, I judge it necessary

b   to view that conduct in the round against the background of all the circumstances, including, of course, the whole history of this sorry case which is, as Rose and Roch LJJ have pointed out, a wholly exceptional one.

With that broad approach I ask myself whether this litigation was unreasonably initiated and prosecuted in a manner which was vexatious and

c   designed to harass Lord Aldington, and whether the solicitors lent assistance to proceedings which in the broad sense and not in the narrow meaning of RSC Ord 18, r 19 went so far beyond the court's expectation of reasonable conduct as to constitute an abuse of process. I must make due allowances for the difficulties confronting the solicitors who cannot explain their conduct by revealing

d   privileged information and I must give them the benefit of all doubts. But I must not suspend my judgment absolutely. I must still inquire whether there is a reasonable explanation for their conduct, judging what is reasonable by reference to what the reasonably well informed, competent member of the profession would have done had he been placed in the circumstances of these particular solicitors. The reasonable explanations advanced here are: (1) that the solicitors

e   relied on fully instructed and very experienced, respected leading counsel who put his name to a statement of claim seeking to set aside a jury's findings by alleging that Lord Aldington was guilty of perjury and fraud, counsel having extensive knowledge of the background of the case; (2) that they satisfied themselves that the 'plea of fraud' to be advanced gave rise to 'a reasonable cause of action' which was properly arguable; and (3) that they satisfied themselves that

f   Count Tolstoy 'wished to pursue the claim for bona fide reasons'.

As to the first, this does not absolve the solicitors exercising their independent judgment nor allow them to close their eyes to the blindingly obvious. Their eyes ought to have been opened by the judgment of the Court of Appeal when they were put fully on their guard and were made alive to the difficulties in

g   reopening this case, whatever the fresh evidence might be.

As to the second, I recognise that the critical judgment to be made is that of the lawyer's assessment, which is made before the proceedings commence and is then kept under regular review, of the strength of the arguments, as much of law as of fact, that were to be deployed before the deputy judge, with due allowances

h   being made, in accordance with the guidance expressed in *Ridehalgh v Horsefield*, for running the hopeless case.

As to the third, I accept the genuineness of the solicitors' belief in their client's bona fides, but the reasonable justification for their belief is a matter which the court must itself assess.

j   In the light of that approach I have come to the firm conclusion that their conduct was unreasonable, for the reasons already given by Rose and Roch LJJ and especially, in my judgment, because:

(1) Making all due allowances for ineffable forensic optimism, any reasonable solicitor, assessing the prospects of success of this action, would have realised, as the deputy judge in fact found, that the evidence demonstrated 'the flimsiness of Count Tolstoy's case', that 'the phantom log entry does not begin to raise the

possibility of persuading any court that Lord Aldington committed perjury', and
that 'it is quite impossible for Count Tolstoy to place any reliance on the
Tryon-Wilson interview as an indication, let alone possible proof of perjury'. As
hopeless cases go, this really was plumbing the depths. Even so, that by itself may
not have been enough. But I am further satisfied that:

(2) Against the background of the previous history, and the known
impecuniosity of Count Tolstoy, this new round of litigation was clearly
vexatious. It heaped fraud and perjury upon the vicious calumny of the allegation
of being a war criminal.

(3) The action was instituted to harass Lord Aldington. No reasonable
solicitor could conclude otherwise than that this writ was issued to feed Count
Tolstoy's obsession with his perception of justice.

I am satisfied that this litigation was so unreasonably conducted, at consequent
cost to Lord Aldington, as to be an abuse of the procedure and that the solicitors
allowed themselves to be dragged outside that broad province where their
actions could reasonably be said to further the ends of justice.

Accordingly, I too would dismiss this appeal.

Appeal dismissed. Leave to appeal to the House of Lords refused.

*1 May 1996. The Appeal Committee of the House of Lords (Lord Jauncey of Tullichettle,
Lord Steyn and Lord Hoffmann) refused leave to appeal.*

Paul Magrath Esq   Barrister.

a   # Thomas Witter Ltd v TBP Industries Ltd

CHANCERY DIVISION

JACOB J

3–6, 9–13, 16, 19, 20, 23, 24 MAY, 13–16 JUNE, 8, 15 JULY 1994

b

Misrepresentation – Fraudulent misrepresentation – Sale of company – Misrepresentation inducing contract – No dishonesty in making misrepresentation – Whether damages can be claimed for fraudulent misrepresentation if no dishonesty in making misrepresentation.

c   *Misrepresentation – Negligent misrepresentation – Sale of company – Misrepresentation inducing contract – Damages – Award of damages where plaintiff entitled to rescind contract by reason of innocent misrepresentation inducing contract – Whether damages can be awarded if rescission no longer a viable remedy – Misrepresentation Act 1967, s 2(1)(2).*

d   The defendants, a large conglomerate, acquired a business which included the plaintiff company, a carpet manufacturing business, and after absorbing those parts of the business it wished to retain it decided to sell the carpet business. In August 1989 P, the owner of a company which also manufactured carpets, expressed interest in purchasing the carpet business. In preliminary negotiations between the parties, the defendants provided P with audited and management

e   accounts for 1988 and stated that estimated profits for 1989 would be £750,000 to £760,000. They also provided P with a sight of the October 1989 management accounts and indicated that they were prepared on the same basis as the audited accounts but included a special one-off expense of £120,000 because of problems with carpets supplied to one customer. On 24 November P made a preliminary

f   offer of £4m to purchase the plaintiff company and agreed to an 'earn-out' element payable to the defendants on the 1990 profits in excess of £650,000. The defendants indicated that such an offer would be acceptable to them. At a further meeting on 29 December to consider a draft contract the defendants produced a disclosure letter in which it was revealed, for the first time, that there had been a

g   change of accounting policy from 1 January 1989 whereby expenditure on producing pattern books (which lasted for 24 months) was spread over 24 months instead of being immediately written off when the expenditure was incurred. The disclosure letter also referred to the special one-off expense of £120,000 included in the October management accounts. Later the same day, the parties signed a contract for the sale and purchase of the plaintiff company. The contract

h   included a clause (cl 17.2) which stated that the contract set forth the entire agreement between the parties and, in particular, that the purchaser acknowledged that it had not been induced to enter into the agreement by any representation or warranty, and a contractual limitation clause (cl 12.3(a)) which stated that the defendants would not be liable for a breach of the agreement or a

j   claim in respect of a warranty unless written notice was given by 1 January 1992. The contract also stated in cl 5.2 that the 1989 accounts were to be prepared on the same basis as for 1988. On 22 May 1990 solicitors for the plaintiff company, by then owned by P, wrote to the defendants giving notice of a claim for misrepresentation in respect of the one-off expense of £120,000 included in the October management accounts. That claim was rejected by the defendants, and in June 1990 the plaintiff company issued a writ claiming, inter alia, rescission of

the contract on the ground of misrepresentation or alternatively damages
pursuant to s 2(2)^a of the Misrepresentation Act 1967 or for breach of the
agreement. The plaintiff alleged, inter alia, that P had made his offer of £4m on
the basis of the October management accounts, that the defendants had
misrepresented those accounts by (i) stating that they included the special one-off
expense of £120,000 (from which it was to be implied that the underlying or
maintainable profits would be higher) when the actual amount of that expense
was no more than £50,000, and (ii) by not disclosing that they included deferred
pattern book expenditure, which had the effect of decreasing the profit figure on
which P had made his offer. The plaintiff further alleged that those misrepresentations were fraudulent or negligent and that P had relied on them in
making his offer to buy the business.

Held – (1) Damages could not be claimed in deceit on the basis of recklessness
alone since the essence of deceit was dishonesty. Accordingly, in order to
establish fraudulent misrepresentation by the defendant it had to be shown that
his recklessness in making a false representation was such as to amount to a
disregard of the truth to the extent that he should be regarded as fraudulent. On
the facts, the defendants had been negligent in not disclosing to P that the
October management accounts contained deferred pattern book expenditure and
in stating that those accounts contained a one-off expense of £120,000 when they
had obtained only a rough, instead of a detailed, estimate of that expense, but
they had not been dishonest as regards those discrepancies in the accounts (see
p 587 f to j and p 588 e, post); dictum of Lord Herschell in *Derry v Peek* [1886–90]
All ER Rep 1 at 22–23 applied.

(2) Rescission was not a practical remedy in the circumstances, since it was not
available where it was not possible to restore the parties to their position before
the contract, and although P had kept the plaintiff company separate from his
other businesses there had been significant changes to the business since the
purchase and third parties would be affected if the business was handed back to
the defendants (see p 588 f to j, post).

(3) The power to award damages under s 2(2) of the 1967 Act where the
plaintiff was entitled to rescind a contract by reason of an innocent misrepresentation which induced him to enter into the contract did not depend on the right to
rescind still being extant but on the plaintiff having had such a right in the past.
Accordingly, the fact that rescission was no longer a viable remedy was not a bar
to the award of damages under s 2(2). Moreover, damages were available under
s 2(2) even when damages could not be awarded under s 2(1) because the
defendant misrepresentor was able rely on the 'innocence' defence in s 2(1), ie
that he believed on reasonable grounds that the facts represented were true.
However, damages awarded under s 2(2) were discretionary and, having regard
to the fact that the court had to take into account the nature of the
misrepresentation, the loss occasioned by it if the contract was upheld, and the
loss which rescission would cause to the misrepresentor, any damages awarded
under s 2(2) were likely to be lower than under s 2(1). On the facts, the
defendants were guilty of negligent misrepresentation in stating that pattern
book expenditure was written off as it was incurred when in fact it was deferred
and in overstating the one-off expense caused by faulty carpets supplied to one
customer by £70,000; and in the circumstances in which the misrepresentations

---

a   Section 2 is set out at p 589 *e* to *j*, post

a were made the defendants were not entitled to rely on the 'innocence' defence in s 2(1). Furthermore, P had relied on those misrepresentations in determining the amount of his offer for the defendants' carpet business (see p 590 *j*, p 591 *b* to *e g* to p 592 *d*, p 593 *c* to *h* and p 594 *f* to p 595 *d*, post).

(4) A contractual term purporting to confine the parties' agreement to the terms of the contract had to make it manifestly clear that the purchaser had agreed only to have a remedy for breach of warranty and that the vendor's liability for damaging untrue statements was excluded before it was effective in excluding liability for pre-contractual misrepresentations. Furthermore, under s 1[b] of the 1967 Act, an exclusion clause which intended to exclude liability for misrepresentation was ineffective if the misrepresentation had become a warranty of the agreement. Accordingly, cl 17.2 of the contract did not have the purported effect of excluding liability or remedies for misrepresentation, but even if it had done so it would have been ineffective under s 3[c] as being neither fair nor reasonable because it purported to exclude all forms of misrepresentation, including fraudulent misrepresentation. Likewise, the contractual limitation clause, cl 12.3(a), did not have the effect of excluding liability for misrepresentations which induced P to enter into the contract, since it only applied to breaches of the agreement or claims in respect of warranties in the contract. On the facts, the plaintiff had given sufficient notice of the prospective claim in respect of the one-off expense of £120,000 included in the October management accounts in their solicitors' letter of 22 May 1990, but in any event the statements about the one-off expense amounted to a misrepresentation inducing the contract and therefore no notice of that claim was required under cl 12.3(a) (see p 595 *j* to p 596 *d*, p 597 *b* to *j*, p 598 *c* to *e*, p 599 *e* to *g* and p 601 *e* to *h*, post).

(5) The plaintiff was entitled to damages for breach of contract or misrepresentation in respect of the deferred pattern book expenditure and the overstatement of the one-off expense. In the circumstances, the measure of damages for breach of contract or misrepresentation was the same. The plaintiff was also entitled to damages for breach of cl 5.2 of the contract, because, if the 1989 accounts had been drawn up on the same basis as the 1988 accounts, the pattern book expenditure would have been written off as it occurred, as had happened in previous years, which would have resulted in the net assets being less by £251,316, being the amount deferred to 1990. It followed that the plaintiff was entitled to damages of £251,316 for breach of cl 5.2 and £775,000 for misrepresentation (see p 601 *h j*, p 602 *h* to p 603 *b*, p 607 *c* to *j* and p 608 *b c*, post).

Notes

For damages for misrepresentation, see 31 *Halsbury's Laws* (4th edn) paras 1099–1103, 1107–1113.

For the Misrepresentation Act 1967, ss 1, 2, 3, see 29 *Halsbury's Statutes* (4th edn) (1995 reissue) 978, 979, 980.

Cases referred to in judgment

A / S Rendal v Arcos Ltd [1937] 3 All ER 577, (1937) 58 Ll L Rep 287, HL.
Alman v Associated Newspapers Ltd (20 June 1980, unreported), Ch D.
Atlantic Lines and Navigation Co Inc v Hallam Ltd, The Lucy [1983] 1 Lloyd's Rep 188.

b   Section 1 is set out at p 597 *c*, post
c   Section 3 is set out at p 597 *h j*, post

Babanaft International Co SA v Avant Petroleum Inc, The Oltenia [1982] 3 All ER 244, [1982] 1 WLR 871, CA; *affg* [1982] 1 Lloyd's Rep 448.

Bisset v Wilkinson [1927] AC 177, [1926] All ER Rep 343, PC.

Brownlie v Campbell (1880) 5 App Cas 925, HL.

Cremdean Properties Ltd v Nash (1977) 244 EG 547, CA.

Derry v Peek (1889) 14 App Cas 337, [1886–90] All ER Rep 1, HL.

Esso Petroleum Co Ltd v Mardon [1976] 2 All ER 5, [1976] QB 801, [1976] 2 WLR 583, CA.

Hedley Byrne & Co Ltd v Heller & Partners Ltd [1963] 2 All ER 575, [1964] AC 465, [1963] 3 WLR 101, HL.

Metalimex Foreign Trade Corp v Eugenie Maritime Co Ltd [1962] 1 Lloyd's Rep 378.

Pepper (Inspector of Taxes) v Hart [1993] 1 All ER 42, [1993] AC 593, [1992] 3 WLR 1032, HL.

Riverlate Properties Ltd v Paul [1974] 2 All ER 656, [1975] Ch 133, [1974] 3 WLR 564, CA.

Tradax Export SA v Italcarbo Societa di Navigazione SpA, The Sandalion [1983] 1 Lloyd's Rep 514.

Action and counterclaim

By writ dated 5 June 1990 the plaintiff, Thomas Witter Ltd, claimed against the defendants, TBP Industries Ltd, inter alia, rescission of an agreement made between the defendants and Nathu Puri on 29 December 1989 for the sale and purchase of the plaintiff's business of manufacturing and marketing floor coverings, alternatively damages pursuant to s 2(2) of the Misrepresentation Act 1967 or for misrepresentation inducing Mr Puri to enter into the agreement, alternatively damages for fraudulent or negligent misrepresentation, or alternatively damages for breach of the agreement. The defendants counterclaimed for payment of £157,000 due under the contract and unpaid. The facts are set out in the judgment.

Martin Mann QC and *Richard Perkoff* (instructed by *D J Freeman*) for the plaintiff.
Roger Kaye QC and *David Foxton* (instructed by *Masons*) for the defendants.

Cur adv vult

15 July 1994. The following judgment was delivered.

JACOB J. This is an action and counterclaim about the purchase of a carpet business called Thomas Witter Ltd. In substance the seller was Tarmac plc (Tarmac), the buyer Melton Medes Ltd. However, in the contract, concluded on 29 December 1989, Tarmac was not the actual vendor and Melton Medes was not the purchaser. How this came about emerges from the history of the negotiations.

A. INTRODUCTION

In about 1980 Tarmac acquired Thomas Witter Ltd, then a conglomerate. Parts of its business (e g in bitumen) were of interest to Tarmac. Those parts were duly absorbed within other parts of Tarmac, leaving only a carpet business. Tarmac's legal and business structures were different. At the time of the sale to Melton Medes the legal structure was thus: the assets of the business were formally owned by TBP Industries Ltd (TBPI), the actual defendants. The business was run by Thomas Witter Ltd as agent for TBPI. Both these companies *a* were subsidiaries of Tarmac Industrial Products Ltd (TIPL), itself a subsidiary of Tarmac. The business structure was different. TBPI formed part of the Insulation and Building Chemicals Group (IBC) of Tarmac Industrial Products Division, which formally took the form of another subsidiary, TIPL.

b For the purposes of this case the details of the set-up within Tarmac are not important. The seller of the business was Tarmac (the witnesses generally so described it). Those concerned within Tarmac for the Thomas Witter business were an accountant, Andrew Lloyd, and Peter Simpson, a chemist turned manager. Mr Simpson was managing director of IBC, he was also chairman of the board of Thomas Witter. Both he and Mr Lloyd were concerned with many other businesses of Tarmac. Also within Tarmac and concerned with advising it in relation to acquisitions and disposals was another accountant, Mr Clough.

c For accounting purposes Thomas Witter Ltd was treated as a branch of TBPI. The accounts were prepared as that of a single business with its own assets. At Thomas Witter there was a managing director, Mr Francis. Formally reporting to Mr Lloyd was a Mr Hogarth, who, though not formally qualified, held the job of chief accountant. Reporting to Mr Hogarth was a Mr Ainscow. All of these, *d* save for Mr Francis, were called as witnesses by the plaintiff. Some time after the acquisition, Mr Francis left Thomas Witter, I was told on bad terms. He was unwilling to give evidence for the plaintiff, which (not surprisingly) did not subpoena him. Mr Francis at some point supplied some information to the defendants, so the plaintiff suggested I should draw some adverse inference against the defendants because they did not call him. I decline to do so. It is *e* possible he might have been able to cast some light about what Mr Simpson or Mr Francis knew at various times, but I am not convinced of this. I regard Mr Francis's absence as neutral.

f The upshot is that the Tarmac negotiating team were Messrs Simpson, Lloyd and Clough, who obtained their information about Thomas Witter from Messrs Francis, Hogarth, and Ainscow.

g Melton Medes is a private company owned by Mr Nathu Puri. After a period of study as an engineer and working with an engineering company (and a gap of some years which was not gone into) he founded Melton Medes. This was in 1983. This company, together with another holding company of his, has been the vehicle for a very successful series of business acquisitions, principally if not wholly, in the field of manufacture. By the date of acquisition of the Witter business Mr Puri was a successful and experienced acquirer of businesses. He had dealt with many vendors, both large and small. Mr Puri's companies now employ about 5,000 people around the world, mostly in the UK. A wide range of *h* products are made by the various companies.

j One subsidiary of Melton Medes was Georgian Goodacre, who made good and top quality woven carpet. Thomas Witter made carpet for the bottom end of the market. Despite a suggestion to the contrary, I accept Mr Puri's evidence that his purchase of Witter was not influenced by a desire to obtain some beneficial synergy by ownership of a company whose carpets were complementary in quality to Georgian Goodacre. Witters was purchased for what it was, a business on its own account, with its own manufacturing facilities, customers, employees and so on.

The key witnesses from Melton Medes were Mr Puri, who was concerned with all the negotiations, and Mr Cooke, an accountant employed by Melton Medes. He, however, only came in at the later stages. Also called was an engineer, Mr

Newton, who inspected the Witter factory. He advised Mr Puri that the
machinery was outdated and dilapidated, 'rubbish' is the word Mr Puri used.   *a*

Mr Puri first came to hear that Witter was for sale when a middleman
contacted him in August 1989. Mr Puri had several years earlier briefly
considered an acquisition of Witter but rejected the idea then on the grounds of
its then poor performance. The middleman suggested that things had improved
and supplied Mr Puri with a performance summary for the years 1985–88. This   *b*
indicated growing profits and cash generation. It indicated a low asset base and
a capacity to generate a substantial return on capital—53% was the figure given.
The document claimed that the 'improvement in performance in 1988 has
continued into 1989'. It had been sent by Mr Lloyd to the middleman (originally
for some other potential buyer). I have no doubt it was intended to present a rosy
view of Witter as a business, even though, of course, a buyer would want much   *c*
more information.

Mr Puri asked for and, under cover of a letter from Mr Simpson of 25
September, was given more information. This included the audited accounts for
1988 and management accounts to July 1989. There was an indication that the
latter were reliable, in that the letter said: 'There is no difference between the   *d*
audited accounts and Period 12 Management accounts to December 1988.'

Moreover, in my judgment that passage clearly indicated that the audited
accounts and management accounts were prepared on essentially the same basis.

There is a bit of dispute as to whether at that time Mr Puri received a further
performance summary and a monthly statistics summary. He says he did,   *e*
whereas Mr Simpson says not—the documents were supplied later. I cannot
think why the documents would have been held back if they existed at the time,
but whether or not they were supplied then or later does not matter.

On the basis of what he received Mr Puri decided to proceed further. The July
management accounts indicated profits to date of £322,000 and cash of £317,000.   *f*
There was a short pause whilst Mr Puri was busy with other things but in early
November he contacted Mr Simpson to set up a meeting. He requested further
financial information and also planned a view of the factory. Messrs Puri and
Simpson met at Melton Medes' offices on 8 November. Mr Simpson supplied Mr
Puri with the September management account balance sheet and profit
statement. Operating profits were stated to be £443,000 and cash £695,000. So   *g*
the picture continued to appear rosy.

I will defer until later the disputes as to what was said or represented at the
meeting of 8 November in relation to the key topics of 'pattern book expenditure'
and the 'Allied problem' for these subjects are said to form misrepresentations
inducing the contract. Things were said about these at later points before the   *h*
contract was finally made and it is better to deal with them as a whole. It is of
course the state of mind of the parties about those subjects at that time of contract
which matter so far as misrepresentation is concerned.

It is common ground, however, that Mr Simpson gave Mr Puri a figure of his
estimate of profits expected in 1989, namely £750,000 to £760,000. Mr Puri says   *j*
he doubted this figure and in any event did not have enough information to make
an offer at that point. What is clear is that Mr Simpson's estimate was predicated
on the basis that the same principles of accountancy would be used for 1989 as
had been used in 1988. I also think it was clear from the outset that since Mr Puri
was buying a business and not merely assets, he would be concerned throughout
the negotiations with the underlying profitability of the business. That always

a remained the position even though, as will be seen, ultimately the contract took the form of an assets plus goodwill purchase.

Following the meeting on 8 November there were some telephone conversations between Messrs Puri and Simpson. There was something of a dispute as to what was said on the telephone, and as to what Mr Puri wrote down at the time. To my mind little of this matters in view of what happened later. But *b* I must note that Mr Puri expected substantial cash in the business (£800,000–£900,000) which was consistent with the management accounts he had seen.

The parties agreed to meet again, this time at the Thomas Witter premises. The meeting was on 24 November. This was the occasion when Mr Newton (of Melton Medes) inspected the machinery and told Mr Puri (in private) that the *c* machinery as such, was poor. Attending the meeting at various points in time were Mr Francis, Mr Simpson, Mr Hogarth and Mr Lloyd. Mr Hogarth only came into the meeting for a short while and played no part in the negotiations. Mr Lloyd arrived late in the day.

There are disputes as to what was said at the meeting, particularly about pattern book expenditure and the Allied problem. It is not in dispute that Mr Puri *d* was allowed to see the key pages of the October management accounts, namely the profit statement and balance sheet and was given copies of these. Nor is it disputed that Mr Simpson gave a profit estimate for year end of £750,000 whereas Mr Lloyd said £650,000. As I have said, it was manifest to all concerned that Mr Puri was concerned with the underlying profitability of Witter. He was told *e* about a special expense of £120,000 (the 'Allied problem'—see below) and took that into account in making his offer. There was some haggling, the upshot of which was that Mr Puri made an offer of £4m. There is an immaterial dispute as to whether that was to be all on completion or was to be £3·5m on completion and £500,000 with the profit-related consideration. Mr Puri's account would be consistent with an offer with an inbuilt negotiation ploy—namely the giving up *f* of the delayed payment of £500,000. A witness who could have assisted on when he instructed Mr Lloyd to insist upon the full £4m on completion, Mr Myatt (Messrs Lloyd and Simpson's senior at Tarmac), was not called. Mr Puri says that Mr Lloyd telephoned him with an indication that Mr Myatt would accept the offer provided all the money was paid at once. It is suggested that this never *g* happened on a Sunday, as Mr Puri thought was the case (but was not '101% sure'). He may have been wrong about the day, but I rather think there was a telephone conversation about that time to the effect contended by Mr Puri. It does not really matter, for the offer soon became the full £4m on completion. In addition there was to be an 'earn-out' on the 1990 results. This was agreed on 24 November. The 'earn out' would be to a maximum of £750,000 profits. The *h* earn-out ultimately took the form of cl 6.3 of the contract, namely:

'The Profit Related Consideration shall be the amount equal to £2.50 for every £1 of Net Profits in excess of £650,000 subject to a maximum payment of £750,000.'

j

The significance of the earn-out provision for present purposes is that it shows the sort of profit being considered in November for the year end. £650,000 is the bottom end, but if profits were higher Tarmac would get more—by £2·50 for every £1 extra profit. I have no doubt that so far as Mr Puri was concerned that order of profit (taken with the special 'Allied' one-off cost—see later) amounted to what he saw as the maintainable profit of the business.

On 24 November the parties envisaged that the transaction would take the   *a*
form of a 'hive-down', i e that Tarmac would put all the assets of the business into
one company and Melton Medes would buy the shares in that.

Solicitors were instructed on both sides. They fairly soon concluded that a
'hive-down' was not appropriate for tax reasons. Instead, the machinery of
purchase was to be as follows. Melton Medes were to use a subsidiary company
for the acquisition. That company would acquire the assets and goodwill and   *b*
everything concerning Witter from Tarmac companies. Then the acquiring
company would change its name to Thomas Witter. That was the structure of
the contract of 29 December 1989. The vendor was TBPI, selling as beneficial
owner of the assets and goodwill and agreeing to procure that these would be
vested in the purchaser (some assets were owned legally, if not beneficially, by
other Tarmac companies, particularly Thomas Witter & Sons Ltd). The   *c*
purchaser was a Melton Medes owned company then called Maxi-Reverse Ltd.
Melton Medes was guarantor. Maxi-Reverse in due course changed its name and
is now the plaintiff. The defendants are the formal sellers under the contract,
TBPI.

I must return to developments leading to the contract. On 5 December Mr   *d*
Puri sent Mr Simpson a fax of draft heads of agreement. It is to be noted that he
specifically repeated that Mr Simpson had estimated profits to the year end to be
about £750,000. This again shows to my mind both that Mr Puri was buying on
the basis of anticipated underlying profits and that Tarmac knew this. Moreover
the fax referred to the October management accounts.

Mr Simpson replied by letter of 7 December. In relation to the October   *e*
accounts he said:

> 'You refer in your letter to the October 1989 management accounts. These
> show pre-interest profits of £980,000 for the first 10 months and Capital
> Employed of £2,387,000, but you will appreciate that the Balance Sheet does   *f*
> not purport to represent the likely year-end position.'

There was no qualification of the profit figure for the first ten months, which,
as I have said, showed an operating profit of £499,000 (the remainder of the
£980,000 was shown as profit on an asset sale). Nor was there any qualification
of the budget figure shown in the accounts.   *g*

There is a dispute about the extent to which Mr Puri asked for and was refused
'due diligence', i e inspection of the accounts of Thomas Witter by accountants.
In substance he says he did and this was refused. The defendants say it was not
refused as such, but there was concern about disclosure of confidential
information to a potential competitor should the deal not go ahead. To some   *h*
extent I think the defendants fobbed Mr Puri off. For instance Mr Lloyd wrote an
internal note of 20 December 1989, which said:

> '[Melton Medes] want to look at the audit files tomorrow, 21st December
> 1989. Following discussion with D. Watson I have resisted, pending
> settlement of all outstanding matters.'   *j*

Mr Lloyd said due diligence would have been granted to independent
accountants—but he does not say he offered this. In the end there was no due
diligence. To my mind that should have made it all the more apparent to Tarmac
that Melton Medes were relying upon the financial information being given to
them as substantially accurate.

a   On 14 December there was a further meeting. It was between Mr Puri (in the morning), Mr Cooke (who took over for Mr Puri), for Melton Medes, and Messrs Simpson, Clough and Lloyd for Tarmac. It became apparent that corporation tax had to be considered. If Thomas Witter had already been one company when Mr Puri made his offer of £4m based on the October accounts, then he would have bought the company with that liability. So he readily agreed that Melton Medes

b   would have to accept that liability. There was a short dispute over what period. Mr Puri said his offer was based on the October position and he would pay a further sum for the tax due on the profits up to then. This was agreed to amount to a sum of £157,000. In due course this entered the contract as cl 6.1: 'The Purchaser shall transfer into the Vendor's Bank Account the sum of £157,000 on 1st October 1990' (1 October was when the tax would be due from the vendor).

c   I think discussion is important in relation to the pattern book expenditure question for reasons I will explain later. (Actually the ultimate consideration was £4m less £157,000 tax, but there was a corresponding reduction in the net assets to be transferred.)

   It was at that meeting that the non-hive down route was settled, or nearly so.

d   It became necessary therefore to value the assets for the purpose of an asset sale. This exercise was not carried out by the use of any valuation expert. The estimates of value were made more sketchily than that. The estimates did not really have great significance in the context of the whole agreement where Melton Medes were paying £4m plus the earn-out. I do not think it necessary to go further into the detail here.

e

   Negotiations continued on the telephone and by fax until the final meetings on 28 and 29 December 1989. The parties' solicitors were present. Mr Puri was present for the afternoon of the 29th whilst Mr Cooke was there all the time. Messrs Clough and Simpson were present for Tarmac. The contract took shape through a number of drafts. Comparatively late in the day (on the morning of the

f   29th) a disclosure letter was produced by Tarmac. It contained the following passages:

> '2. This is the Disclosure Letter referred to in the Agreement. This letter makes disclosures limiting the scope of the warranties and representations
>
> g   referred to in the Agreement and Schedules 6 and 7 thereof (herein called "the Warranties") ...
>
> *The 1988 Accounts*   The 1988 Accounts in the Agreed Form are Disclosed Document 20. The Management Accounts in the Agreed Form are Disclosed Document 11 [these were the October management accounts].
>
> h   The accounting policies for stock, work in progress and depreciation are referred to in Disclosed Document 30 ...
>
> (Change of policy on pattern books) see Rider X ...'

   Rider X, which was handwritten, stated:

j

> 'A change in the accounting policy relating to pattern books (samples) was proposed and adopted in November 1989 and implemented with effect from 1st January 1989. The change allows for the costs associated with the production and distribution of pattern books to be spread evenly over 24 months in line with the expected normal life of a carpet range.'

Conduct of business

During the period September/October 1989 a routine quality inspection by Allied Carpets highlighted a number of carpets of unacceptable quality. Witter staff examined the claim and put in place the necessary work to overcome the problems observed, with special attention to the secondary backing process. This necessitated changes in working practices and an increase in the number of people handling the carpet at this stage. Over the next two months every carpet supplied to Allied Carpets was inspected by the customer but after the remedial steps were put in hand the inspection criterion was reduced to its pre-September level and orders have been placed for the winter sale period for current and new ranges. The charge to September and October profit and loss was some £120,000. The capital expenditure planned to improve the backing line is intended further to improve the ability to produce acceptable carpet. No further complaint has been received.

The significance of these disclosures is discussed below. However, I must deal with Mr Puri's reaction to the disclosure about pattern book expenditure, Rider X. He says when he saw this:

'I thought it was another one of their bloody tricks. I am sorry, my Lord, for my language, but that is what I was thinking, that they were trying to create some assets which would reduce the transfer of assets at the year end and, secondly, that it is going to hurt me next year to create a consideration where none would exist. I have done a calculation. I do have one copy and I can show how they were trying to cheat at the last minute.'

Mr Puri did not say he showed his reaction angrily at the time. Nor was he asked whether he had. The other witnesses who had been at the meeting were asked whether he showed angry reaction and all said he did not. That, to my mind, means nothing. Mr Puri, whilst clearly capable of showing anger, is a skilled enough negotiator not to show his reaction if he does not want it seen. Besides he immediately set about dealing with the problem by devising a clause to deal with pattern book expenditure. This became cl 6.4 of the agreement, which I consider further below.

It is common ground that nothing was said about the October management accounts. To my mind, anyone seeing the rider would expect those accounts to have been done on the basis of an immediate write-off of pattern book expenditure.

Finally, therefore, I come to the agreement itself. Apart from provisions I have already quoted, or provisions with which I deal separately below, the material provisions are as follows:

'1. *Interpretation*

1.1. In this Agreement and the Schedules hereto unless the context otherwise requires the following expressions have the following meanings: "*Accounts*" means the audited balance sheet and profit and loss account relating to the Business as at the Accounts Date; "*Accounts Date*" means 31st December 1989; "*the 1990 Account*" means the profit and loss account of the Purchaser in respect of the calendar year 1990 as determined in accordance with Clauses 6.4 to 6.7 inclusive … "*Disclosure Letter*" means the letter of even date from the Vendor to the Purchaser in the Agreed Form … "*Net Assets*" means the total amount shown in a certificate to be given by the Vendors Auditors (and which shall be derived from the Accounts) as comprising the a total written down value for accounting purposes as at 31st December 1989 of all the assets less the liabilities of the Business but excluding fixed assets and goodwill. For this purpose *"fixed assets"* shall mean the Property, the fixtures and fittings and the equipment shown in the Plant Register together with any other equipment of like nature used in the Business; *"Net Profits"* means the net profits for the calendar year 1990 as determined pursuant to

b Clause 6 ... *"Profit Related Consideration"* means the sum determined in accordance with Clause 6.3 ... *"SSAP's"* means Statements of Standard Accounting Practice ...

2. *Sale of the Business and Assets*

   2.1. The Vendor as beneficial owner shall on Completion sell, transfer or assign (and procure to be sold, transferred and assigned) free from all liens,

c charges and encumbrances and the Purchaser shall purchase on the terms and conditions herein contained [here were specified all the assets and goodwill etc of the Thomas Witter business].

3. *Consideration*

   3.1. The aggregate consideration payable for all the Assets shall be

d £4,000,000 plus the Profit Related Consideration plus the assumption by the Purchaser of the Liabilities plus any amount which may become payable pursuant to Clause 5.5 which shall be apportioned as follows [details were set out].

4. *Completion*

   4.1. Providing approval of the Major Projects Committee of Tarmac Plc

e referred to in Clause 19 has been given Completion shall take place within 7 days of the date of this Agreement ... (b) the Purchaser shall pay to the Vendor by telegraphic transfer the sum of £3,843,000.

5. *The accounts*

   5.1. The Vendor shall procure that the Accounts shall be produced and

f audited by 2nd February 1990.

   5.2. The Accounts shall be prepared by the Vendor's Auditors using the principles, standards and assumptions employed in the preparation of, and on the same bases as the accounts for the Vendor were prepared in respect of the year ending 31st December 1988 in respect of that part of its business

g which comprised the Business which principles etc. were (save as disclosed in the Disclosure letter) in accordance with SSAP's and generally accepted accounting practice.

   5.3. The Vendor shall be responsible for the costs of auditing the Accounts and for giving a certificate in relation to the Net Assets (*"the Certificate of Net*

h *Assets"*) and no provision in respect of such costs shall be included therein ...

   5.5. If the total of the Net Assets exceeds £1,887,000 the Purchaser shall pay to the Vendor an amount equal to the excess within 10 working days of receipt of the Certificate of the Net Assets and such additional amount shall form an additional part of the Consideration payable under item (d) of

j Clause 3.1.

   5.6. If the total of the Net Assets referred to in Clause 5.5 shall be less than £1,887,000, the Vendor shall repay to the Purchaser an amount equal to the amount by which the Net Assets are less than £1,887,000 together with interest on such amount at the rate of 1% above base lending rate of Lloyds Bank Plc from Completion until payment and such amount shall be paid to the Purchaser by the Vendor within 10 working days of receipt of the

Certificate of Net Assets and shall reduce the consideration payable under item (d) of Clause 3.1.

[Clauses 5.5 and 5.6 were collectively called the 'pound for pound adjustment clause']

6. *Post-Completion Payments*

6.1. The Purchaser shall transfer into the Vendor's Bank Account the sum of £157,000 on 1st October 1990.

6.2. Subject to Clauses 6.7. and 6.8., the Purchaser shall not later than the Last Payment Day transfer into the Vendor's Bank Account the Profit Related Consideration.

6.3. The Profit Related Consideration shall be the amount equal to £2.50 for every £1 of Net Profits in excess of £650,000 subject to a maximum payment of £750,000.

6.4. Subject to Clauses 6.5. and 6.9., a draft profit and loss account estimating the net profits of the Business for the Calendar Year 1990 will be prepared and audited by the Purchaser's Auditors (the *"Draft Account"*) in accordance with the principles, standard and assumptions employed in the preparation of, and on the same bases as the Accounts save that the base values for calculating depreciation on the fixed assets sold as part of this Agreement shall be those which would have applied at 31st December 1989 had the Business continued to be carried on by the Vendor in 1990, and so that the basis of comparison of the Business in the Accounts and in the Draft Account shall be the same. The cost of making up pattern books (samples) has been written off in the year it was incurred. However if such cost in the year to December 1990 is higher than such cost was in 1989 then 50% of the amount of the increase in such cost shall be discounted for the purpose of preparation of the Draft Account e g if such cost in 1990 was £60,000 more than in 1989 then £30,000 of the total cost will be discounted ...

12. *Warranties and Representations*

12.1. Subject to Clause 12.2 the Vendor hereby warrants and represents to the Purchaser in respect of the Business and Assets that each of the statements in Schedule 6 (*"the Warranties"*) is true at the date hereof.

12.2. The Warranties shall be qualified by reference to the disclosures contained in the Disclosure Letter and not otherwise.

12.3. [This is considered separately below] ...

14. *Interest*

If any sum due to or from the Vendor or to the Purchaser pursuant to the provisions of this Agreement shall not be paid in full within thirty days of written demand therefor, then such sum or the amount thereof remaining unpaid shall bear interest (which shall accrue from day to day after as well as before any judgment for the same) at the rate per annum equal to the base or prime lending rate (or equivalent published rate) of Lloyds Bank PLC plus two per cent from the day following such demand to and including the day of actual payment of such sums (or the next business day if such day of actual payment is not a business day), compounded quarterly on the usual quarter days, and the amount of all such interest accrued shall be paid to or by the Vendor by or to the Purchaser as the case may be from time to time on written demand therefor ...

17.2. [This is considered separately below] ...

SCHEDULE 6 (referred to in Clause 12)

Warranties and Representations ...

The 1988 Accounts

4.1 The accounts for the Business for the year ending 31 December 1988 (*"the 1988 Accounts"*) which have been produced to the Purchaser and are in the Agreed Form: (a) comply (insofar as it is practical for branch accounts) with the requirements of the Companies Act 1985, all current SSAP's and generally accepted accounting practice; (b) have been prepared on the basis set out in the notes to the 1988 Accounts and have been prepared on the same basis as the corresponding accounts for the preceding 2 financial years; (c) show a true and fair view of the state of affairs of the Vendor in relation to the Business as at 31 December 1988 and of the results of the Business for the accounting period ending on 31 December 1988 and at that date were not (save as shown therein) affected by any extraordinary or exceptional items ...

The Management Accounts

4.4 The Management Accounts for the period ending 29 October 1989 (*"the Management Accounts"*) which have been produced to the Purchaser and are in the Agreed Form: (a) were carefully prepared in accordance with good accounting practice, and were based upon the balance sheet in the 1988 Accounts; (b) were prepared on the basis set out in the notes to the 1988 Accounts [those notes say nothing about pattern book expenditure]; (c) give a reasonable view of the state of affairs of the Vendor in relation to the Business as at 29 October 1989 and of the results of the Business for the accounting period up to that date and at that date were not (save as shown therein) affected by any extraordinary or exceptional items ...

6.5 The stock take carried out in November 1989 did not reveal any material difference from the book values for stock shown in the Management Accounts after allowing for stock movements in November 1989.

Records

7.1 The accounting and other books and records of the Vendor in connection with the Business (including the Records and in particular the Plant Register) have been written up and maintained in accordance with generally accepted commercial principles and standards ...

Conduct of Business since Accounts Date

8. Since the 31st December 1988 (but disregarding the sale hereby agreed) ... (c) there has been no materially adverse change in the financial or trading position of the Business and the Business has been carried on in the ordinary course and in the same manner (including nature and scale) as immediately before the 31st December 1988 ...

Disclosure Letter

11.1 All statements of fact made in the Disclosure Letter (but not including the Disclosed Documents as defined therein) are true and accurate in all material respects and are not misleading in any material respect (including by reason of any omissions therefrom) ...'

B. THE MATTERS IN DISPUTE

There are a host of matters in dispute. The plaintiff produced a document which doubtless was intended to be a helpful summary but I have to say I found it very difficult to follow. More helpful were Mr Kaye QC's written submissions. I will set forth the points I believe to be in dispute in the order in which I propose to deal with them.

Misrepresentation

(a) Introduction to fraudulent misrepresentation; (b) the legal test for fraudulent misrepresentation; (c) findings of fact in relation to fraudulent misrepresentation; (d) rescission; (e) innocent and negligent misrepresentation: the Misrepresentation Act 1967, s 2; (f) findings in relation to non-fraudulent misrepresentation; (g) misrepresentations of fact or opinion? (h) reliance; (i) estoppel/acquiescence/settlement; (j) the effect of the 'whole agreement' clause, cl 17.2; (k) s 3 of the 1967 Act and the Unfair Contract Terms Act 1977; (l) overall effect of misrepresentation.

Contract

(a) Clause 12.3: the contract limitation period; (b) the contract counterclaim for £157,000; (c) cl 5.2: the claim and counterclaim; (d) the interest under cl 5.2 claim; (e) breach of warranty: general; (f) breach of warranty: the October management accounts; (g) warranty 8(c): material adverse change; (h) warranty 11.1: the disclosure letter; (i) how much cash would be included in assets purchased?

C. MISREPRESENTATION

(a) *Introduction to fraudulent misrepresentation ·*

There is no dispute that if Tarmac were guilty of fraudulently making representations of fact which induced the plaintiff to enter the contract, then the plaintiff is entitled to damages and (subject to the court's discretion) to rescission of the contract.

Now it is not suggested that any of the Tarmac team told Messrs Puri or Cooke a deliberate lie. The case advanced was one of recklessness. In relation to pattern book expenditure the recklessness is said to arise in two ways: (i) by supplying the management accounts with undisclosed deferrals, the recklessness consisting of not knowing about those deferrals; and (ii) by Mr Simpson giving (in conjunction with the documents supplied) first a profit estimate on one basis (ie no deferrals) and then later estimates on a different basis (ie with deferrals) without telling Mr Puri of the changed basis.

The alleged recklessness in relation to the Allied problem is simpler. It is simply that Mr Simpson failed to check or cause to be checked the figure of £120,000 cost of the 'one-off' problem. It is said that this was obviously so important that it was utterly reckless for Mr Simpson first to supply the figure on the basis of a casual inquiry of Mr Hogarth only, or, having supplied the figure on that basis, not to have caused a proper check to be made.

These points are also of relevance to the claim in negligent misrepresentation for, the argument runs, even if not amounting to fraud, the self-same points do amount to negligence. I shall return to them under that head.

(b) *The legal test for fraudulent misrepresentation*

First then deceit. Mr Mann QC relied upon part of the classic speech of Lord Herschell in *Derry v Peek* (1889) 14 App Cas 337 at 375–376, [1886–90] All ER Rep 1 at 22–23:

'The ground upon which an alleged belief was founded is a most important test of its reality. I can conceive many cases where the fact that an alleged belief was destitute of all reasonable foundation would suffice of itself to convince the Court that it was not really entertained, and that the *a* representation was a fraudulent one. So, too ... if I thought that a person making a false statement had shut his eyes to the facts, or purposely abstained from inquiring into them, I should hold that honest belief was absent, and that he was just as fraudulent as if he had knowingly stated that which was false.'

b He further submitted that where a person has made a representation of fact and, before the contract is concluded, comes to learn of its falseness, that person comes under a duty to correct the representation and, if he fails to do so, then is taken to be fraudulent. Mr Mann relied upon the speech of Lord Blackburn in *Brownlie v Campbell* (1880) 5 App Cas 925 at 950:

c 'I quite agree in this, that whenever a man in order to induce a contract says that which is in his knowledge untrue with the intention to mislead the other side, and induce them to enter into the contract, that is downright fraud; in plain English, and Scotch also, it is a downright lie told to induce the other party to act upon it, and it should of course be treated as such. I further agree in this: that when a statement or representation has been made in the *d* *bonâ fide* belief that it is true, and the party who has made it afterwards comes to find out that it is untrue, and discovers what he should have said, he can no longer honestly keep up that silence on the subject after that has come to his knowledge, thereby allowing the other party to go on, and still more, inducing him to go on, upon a statement which was honestly made at the time when it was made, but which he has not now retracted when he has *e* become aware that it can be no longer honestly persevered in. That would be fraud too, I should say, as at present advised.'

This argument related to the changed basis of profit forecast point. It was argued that Mr Simpson, having given to Mr Puri profit forecasts on one basis of *f* pattern book expenditure, knew his later forecast was on a different basis and should be taken as fraudulent for not disclosing that fact.

In my judgment Mr Mann's argument is wrong in law. He takes the reference to 'recklessness' out of context—divorcing it from the heart of the tort of deceit, namely dishonesty. One only has to read earlier in the speech of Lord Herschell to see that this is so:

g '... there has always been present, and regarded as an essential element, that the deception was wilful either because the untrue statement was known to be untrue, or because belief in it was asserted without such belief existing ... I cannot assent to the doctrine that a false statement made *h* through carelessness, and which ought to have been known to be untrue, of itself renders the person who makes it liable to an action for deceit.' (See (1889) 14 App Cas 337 at 369, 373, [1886–90] All ER Rep 1 at 19, 21.)

(c) *Findings of fact in relation to fraudulent misrepresentation*
j So what I have to decide is whether Mr Simpson or Mr Lloyd deliberately set out to mislead Mr Puri, not by a deliberate untruth (for that is not alleged) but by its equivalent, such recklessness as to amount to a disregard for the truth. I have no difficulty in acquitting these witnesses of any such intent. I must explain why.

So far as pattern book expenditure deferrals in the October management accounts are concerned, I accept Mr Simpson's evidence that he did not know of these right up until the time of the contract. Nor did Mr Lloyd. By the time of

the contract both thought that until November pattern book expenditure was
written off as it was incurred. No one had ever suggested that the management
accounts sometimes had ad hoc deferrals for 'smoothing' purposes.

In relation to the Allied problem the facts are broadly these. Mr Simpson told
Mr Puri of the existence of the problem on 8 November and that it had been
cured. So much is not in dispute. The purpose of telling Mr Puri was manifest—
that he was to regard the problem as a one-off (so that underlying or maintainable
profits would be higher). There is a dispute as to whether Mr Simpson gave Mr
Puri a figure on that date. Mr Puri says he did—£130,000. Mr Simpson says he
did not, that he did not know the figure. I marginally prefer Mr Puri's evidence,
for I cannot see how a sensible discussion about the matter could have proceeded
without a figure being mentioned. It may well be that Mr Simpson gave only a
very qualified estimate then. The point does not matter, because it is clear that
by the time of the contract the representation had been defined as set out in the
disclosure letter, namely £120,000 charged to the September and October
accounts.

What does matter is whether Mr Simpson was so reckless in the estimate that
he should be regarded as fraudulent. He says he was given the figure of £120,000
by Mr Hogarth as a 'fag packet' calculation at a Witter board meeting on 21
November. Mr Hogarth has no recollection whatever of the cost of the Allied
problem being discussed. There appears never to have been a detailed estimate
of the figure being worked out. Now I accept Mr Simpson's evidence that he got
a rough estimate from Mr Hogarth. It was obviously important. So I think he
was negligent not to get a proper estimate, or to tell Mr Puri that he had not got
a proper estimate. But it was not dishonest of him to give that rough estimate to
Mr Puri. He believed it, but knowing there was no proper check, his belief was
not reasonable.

(d) *Rescission*

Mr Mann tied his claim to rescission to the claim in fraud. I never was quite
sure why, since rescission is available also for innocent misrepresentation. Even
if I had found fraud, however, I would not have granted rescission. This remedy
is not available where it is not possible to restore the parties to their position
before the contract. Although Melton Medes kept the Witter business separate,
it is unrealistic to regard it as the same as the business conveyed. There have been
numerous changes to staff and personnel (including the departure of Mr Francis
who had exceptional sales skills). Those personnel who have stayed have been in
different pension schemes, there are mortgagees of the business and so on. Time
has moved on and third parties would, I think, be affected.

Mr Mann's actual submission was that it was not shown that third parties
would be affected. So he was suggesting that the onus was on the defendants to
avoid rescission by showing innocent third parties would be affected. I cannot
think that is right. The Thomas Witter business has been in the hands of Melton
Medes for four years. It is they who would know who or what might be affected
by a transfer back to Tarmac.

(e) *Innocent and negligent misrepresentation: s 2 of the 1967 Act*

The law concerning a non-fraudulent misrepresentation which induces a party
to enter into a contract is that embodied under the common law (including
equity) as modified by the 1967 Act as amended by 1977 Act. Before the 1967 Act
the remedy where a non-fraudulent misrepresentation of fact had been made and

a relied upon lay in equity. Equity could not provide damages: it provided rescission where this was possible. It was not in some cases for certain; in others there was doubt as to the law. It remains the law that a misrepresentation as to law, opinion, or a mere puff will not give rise to a remedy. The misrepresentation must be one of fact, not a mere unfulfilled promise. Nor is there a remedy unless the representee relies upon the representation. By 1967 there may also have been
b a remedy in negligence, where the misrepresentation of fact was negligently made and there was some kind of special relationship between the parties. *Hedley Byrne & Co Ltd v Heller & Partners Ltd* [1963] 2 All ER 575, [1964] AC 465 had recently been decided. Liability for negligent misrepresentation had become part of the law but its scope was not fully resolved.

c The 1967 Act essentially widened the remedies available. By s 1 it was made clear that the remedies are available even if the misrepresentation has become a term of the contract (a point doubtful before) or if the contract has been performed. By s 2 a remedy in damages was created, both for negligent and non-negligent misrepresentation. As a result it now seldom matters whether a misrepresentation is made fraudulently or not: the 1967 Act confers substantial
d remedies in respect of non-fraudulent misrepresentation. The principal difference may now lie in relation to clauses attempting to exclude liability for misrepresentation—a matter I consider below.

I turn to the provisions concerned. Section 2 provides:

e '(1) Where a person has entered a contract after a misrepresentation has been made to him by another party thereto and as a result thereof he has suffered loss, then, if the person making the misrepresentation would be liable to damages in respect thereof had the misrepresentation been made fraudulently, that person shall be so liable notwithstanding that the misrepresentation was not made fraudulently, unless he proves that he had
f reasonable ground to believe and did believe up to the time the contract was made that the facts represented were true.

(2) Where a person has entered into a contract after a misrepresentation has been made to him otherwise than fraudulently, and he would be entitled, by reason of the misrepresentation, to rescind the contract, then, if it is claimed, in any proceedings arising out of the contract, that the contract
g ought to be or has been rescinded the court or arbitrator may declare the contract subsisting and award damages in lieu of rescission, if of opinion that it would be equitable to do so, having regard to the nature of the misrepresentation and the loss that would be caused by it if the contract were upheld, as well as to the loss that rescission would cause to the other party.

h (3) Damages may be awarded against a person under subsection (2) of this section whether or not he is liable to damages under subsection (1) thereof, but where he is so liable any award under the said subsection (2) shall be taken into account in assessing his liability under the said subsection (1).'

j Both ss 2(1) and 2(2) provide for damages for misrepresentation. Section 2(1) provides a defence for the misrepresentor—a defence which I shall for brevity call 'innocence' but which involves proof of belief and reasonable grounds for belief that the representation was true. Thus, it is sometimes said that s 2(1) relates to 'negligent' misrepresentation in the sense that it has the 'innocence' defence. Section 2(2) provides no such defence. However, damages are only available 'in lieu of rescission'.

The defendants here argued that they had a defence of innocence both in relation to pattern book expenditure and in relation to the Allied problem, and so escaped s 2(1). I reject that on the facts (see below). But even if the 'innocence defence' applies, then s 2(2) comes into play. Mr Kaye argued that it could not do so because rescission is no longer available. He argued that the discretion under s 2(2) to award damages crucially depends upon the rescission remedy remaining extant at the time the court comes to consider the question. Whether that argument is right has been a moot point since the Act was passed. The leading article of the time, Atiyah and Treitel 'Misrepresentation Act 1967' [1967] MLR 369, noticed the point at once. I found the argument unattractive: rescission might or might not be available at the time of trial depending on a host of factors which have nothing to do with behaviour of either party. I was not surprised to find that the authors of *Chitty on Contracts* (27th edn, 1994) para 6–058, p 372 found the suggested construction 'strange' even though Mustill J had apparently accepted it obiter in *Atlantic Lines and Navigation Co Inc v Hallam Ltd, The Lucy* [1983] 1 Lloyd's Rep 188 and one of the plaintiffs conceded it in *Alman v Associated Newspapers Ltd* (20 June 1980, unreported).

The argument assumes that the Act is referring to the remedy of 'rescission', though this is not clear. If it were only the remedy referred to then it is difficult to understand the reference to 'has been rescinded' in the section. It seemed to me that the reference might well be to a claim by the representee that he was entitled to rescission, in which case it would be enough for the court to find that the agreement was 'rescissionable' at least by the date when the representee first claimed rescission or at any time. There was enough ambiguity here to look to see what was said in Parliament at the time of the passing of the Act, pursuant to the limited new-found freedom given by *Pepper (Inspector of Taxes) v Hart* [1993] 1 All ER 42, [1993] AC 593. Mr Foxton found what the Solicitor General of the time said in the House of Commons. Even though it was against his and Mr Kaye's case, in the usual fine tradition of the Bar, he drew it to my attention. The Solicitor General said (741 HC Official Report (5th series) cols 1388–1389, 20 February 1967):

> '... the hon. Gentleman put to me the case of the sale of a house. He asked me to suppose that there had been the sale of a house, some defect was discovered afterwards, it might be that a third party had come into the matter, and it might be entirely unjust or inequitable to insist on rescission in such a case. I suggest that in such a case, as the Lord Chancellor said, the conveyance is unlikely to be rescinded because of the impossibility of restitution. My answer is that a case of that sort would be covered by Clause 2(2) which says [here the material words of the present section were read]. That is the option which is given to the court, and in the sort of case which has been put to me ... it would follow that the court or arbitrator would almost certainly award damages in lieu of rescission. Therefore that matter is really fully covered.'

So the Solicitor General told the House of Commons that it was his view that damages could be awarded under s 2(2) when there was an impossibility of restitution. Accordingly, I hold that the power to award damages under s 2(2) does not depend upon an extant right to rescission—it only depends upon a right having existed in the past. Whether it depends upon such a right existing at any time, or depends upon such a right subsisting at the time when the representee first claims rescission, I do not have to decide. It was here first claimed by letter

of 25 April 1990 which is only some four months from the contract date. In
a principle, however, I would have thought that it is enough that at any time a right
to rescind subsisted. It is damages in lieu of that right (even if barred by later
events or lapse of time) which can be awarded.

Given that construction of s 2(2), it may be asked: what is the difference
between s 2(2) and s 2(1)? In particular, since s 2(1) has a defence of 'innocence'
b is that in practical terms useless because damages can be had under s 2(2)? There
is, of course, overlap between the two subsections on any construction, and s 2(3)
explicitly recognises this. But if my construction covered all the cases covered by
s 2(1) then the latter would be pointless and my construction would probably be
wrong. However, I do not think there is complete overlap. First, under s 2(1)
damages can be awarded in addition to rescission. So if there is 'innocence' the
c representor cannot have both remedies and never could, whatever the date of the
decision. Secondly, the question of an award of damages under s 2(2) is
discretionary and the court must take into account the matters referred to in the
concluding words of the subsection. Thirdly, the measure of damages under the
two subsections may be different—s 2(3) certainly contemplates that this may be
d so and moreover contemplates that s 2(1) damages may be more than s 2(2)
damages and not the other way round. It is fair to say, as *Chitty* para 6–059, p 373
observes, that 'the Act gives little clue as to how damages are to be assessed under
this subsection if they are not to be assessed in the same way as under subsection
(1)'. However both *Chitty* and Treitel *Law of Contract* (8th edn, 1991) p 326 (see
also Atiyah and Treitel [1967] MLR 369 at 376) suggest that damages under s 2(2)
e may be limited to the loss in value of what is bought under the contract whereas
s 2(1) damages may also include consequential loss.

I reach my conclusions under s 2(2) without misgivings: as between the person
making the innocent misrepresentation and his misrepresentee, the 'merits'
favour the latter. The constant and justified academic criticism of the Act
f indicates a subject well worth the attention of the Law Commission.
Fortunately, so far as I am concerned, in the circumstances of this case there can
be no difference between the two subsections, for no consequential loss is
claimed.

g ### (f) *Findings in relation to non-fraudulent misrepresentation*

The misrepresentations are said to be: (i) that the basis of all profit forecasts and
budget estimates given to Mr Puri orally and in writing are the same, namely that
pattern book expenditure was written off as incurred; (ii) that there were no
deferrals in the October management accounts; (iii) that the Allied problem cost
£120,000 charged to the September/October accounts and was non-recurring,
h and (iv) that when the business was transferred, a substantial amount of cash
would be included because the October management accounts showed a large
sum.

I can deal briefly with the last point. It amounts really to an allegation of a
promise and no more. Moreover Mr Puri was warned that the year-end position
j as regards the balance sheet might well be different. This misrepresentation
claim fails.

As to the others, however, I think all of these were made out. Item (i) (basis of
all profit forecasts and budget estimates) was disputed. My reasons for my finding
appear below. As to (ii), it is conceded that there were ad hoc deferrals of
£120,000 pattern book expenditure in the October management accounts and
that Mr Puri was never told of this. As to (iii), it is conceded that the figure of

£120,000 cost of the Allied problem was not justified. The plaintiff's expert accountant, Mr Barford, puts the figure at £29,000; the defendants' expert accountant, Mr Hughes, puts it at £49,000 or about £80,000 if the cumulative cost for the year is what matters. I have no doubt that the representation as ultimately made (both in the 24 November meeting and the disclosure letter) related to September/October and conveyed, and was intended to convey, that profits otherwise would be higher by £120,000 on a continuing basis. Whether the figure is £49,000 or £29,000 is difficult to decide, depending as it does on a complicated assessment of how much of the carpet supplied to and returned by Allied was in fact of good quality and was thus resold at full price, how much was sold cheaply and how much sold as scrap. I was tempted to split the difference, but on reflection I must remember that the onus lies on the plaintiff, so I shall take the higher figure of costs. To round figures, the cost of the Allied problem was overstated by £70,000.

Moreover, I hold that these misrepresentations were negligently made or continued down to the date of the contract. By 'negligent' I mean that the defendants have failed to satisfy me of the proviso to s 2(1). I turn to consider this further.

So far as failure by either of Messrs Lloyd or Simpson to tell Mr Puri that their 24 November profit estimates took into account deferrals, it is accepted that they did not do so expressly. What they both say is that Mr Puri was told of a Witter board policy decision made three days earlier on 21 November. The board minutes read:

> 'Pattern Books M J Hogarth proposed a new accounting policy to be effective retrospectively regarding the treatment of pattern book expenditure. Due to our strategic plan to increase sales revenue through wholesale distribution outlets the volume of pattern books produced, particularly during the latter part of the year, has been very significant. It would be unrealistic to absorb the total cost of these books in the current year and it is proposed to spread this cost over the considered life span of carpet ranges. The accounting policy will therefore state: "The cost of pattern books is spread over two years in order to reflect the future increase which is generated by the books. The unamortised amount is carried forward as deferred expenditure."'

The proposal was agreed and accepted by the meeting.

According to Messrs Lloyd and Simpson, they got a rough estimate of the pattern book expenditure—£300,000. On the basis that half would be deferred but that the figure was higher than usual, this augmented profits by £150,000. On the other hand, there was the Allied cost. One roughly cancelled the other out and so the profit estimate given before remained about the same. It is not suggested that Mr Puri was told any of this at any time. It is, however, said by both Mr Lloyd and Mr Simpson, that Mr Simpson told Mr Puri of the change of pattern book expenditure policy on 24 November. He agrees something was said. He says he was told only that the company was considering a change in the manner in which the expenditure was written off, and remarked that was how it was done in his carpet company, Georgian Goodacre. He understood the position to be that the policy would be changed if he did not buy the company. I accept Mr Puri's evidence of his understanding at that meeting. I think Mr Simpson intended to convey more, but I think he failed to do so. Mr Lloyd already knew of the policy change and so an incomplete explanation might well a have seemed complete to him. Since Mr Simpson was giving a profit estimate on a different basis from the basis which had been given previously he could easily have made this explicit. That was never done. Mr Simpson thinks Mr Puri, as a businessman, could have worked this out for himself. Mr Lloyd says he was surprised that Mr Puri did not ask about the amount of such expenditure. I am sure he would have done if the true effect of what was intended had been spelled

b out properly. It all depends on how well the information was conveyed. It would have been so simple, for instance, when he examined and later took away the management accounts for October, to warn him that they were on a different basis.

Now it might not have mattered if what Mr Simpson had said had been ambiguous at the time, provided he had not already made an earlier

c representation on a different basis. But given that (coupled with supply of the October accounts), it became essential to make sure there was no misunderstanding. Mr Simpson knew that as a result of the policy change as he understood it was going to be implemented the basis of his original representation of profits estimate was no longer true. Unless that representation was clearly withdrawn it would continue in effect. And Mr Simpson could not, in relation to that

d representation, satisfy the innocence defence of s 2(1).

Next there is Mr Simpson's letter of 7 December, which qualified the balance sheet in the manner I have indicated above. There was a golden opportunity, not taken, to say that it was Mr Simpson's view that the new policy affected the basis of the profit figure given.

e Moreover, there is the meeting of 14 December to be considered. In particular there was the discussion about tax. Mr Simpson took part in estimating the tax on the 10-month figures to October. Yet on the new basis those figures would be different. He had ample opportunity to warn Mr Puri that reliance on the October figures as such was no longer appropriate—to withdraw explicitly the

f earlier representation.

Further, there was the insistence by Melton Medes, in the absence of due diligence, that the October accounts be warranted. This again ought to have alerted those at Tarmac to Melton Medes's reliance on that document.

Finally there is Mr Puri's reaction at the final meeting. If he had known all

g along of the pattern book deferral policy change then he would hardly have reacted as he says he did. Moreover, he would not have needed, on the spot, to start drafting a clause to deal with those deferrals. He would surely have told his solicitors earlier about them and arranged for appropriate draft clauses to deal with them—he may even have pulled out of the whole negotiation.

h I would add this as a general comment: both parties' expert accountants agreed that if one were to change the policy, one should not only do this for 1989 but also go back a year and do it for 1988—so as to include for 1989 that which would have been deferred from 1988. Plainly no one at Tarmac ever considered this: they had not thought through what the change of policy really involved. This to my mind

j indicates a level of muddle, which is consistent with the effect of the policy not being properly set out for Mr Puri to consider.

Another example of sloppiness concerns the ad hoc deferrals which were in the October accounts. I accept Mr Simpson's evidence that he did not know of these until well after the contract. But he should have done, after all he was the chairman of the 'company'. Shortly before he first met Mr Puri he received from Mr Hogarth the September 1989 financial report. This included under the head

'profit' (a head which one really might expect the chairman to read) the
following:

> 'Total expenses after provision for Management Charges, overhead
> movement and write back of MD's discretion were favourable by £4,000,
> although this does not reflect the full charge of significant sampling costs
> which will be recovered over the final quarter of the year.'

That, as plain as can be, says pattern book expenditure has been deferred. I
accept Mr Simpson's evidence that he did not in fact read it. But as chairman of
Witter and the person negotiating with, and supplying information to, the buyer,
he ought to have done. I think the truth is that Mr Simpson just had too many
responsibilities within Tarmac at the time.

Whether Mr Simpson told Mr Puri on 8 November that there were no
deferrals is in dispute. In the end this does not matter for, by the time of the
contract, it was the clear implication of Rider X that there were no deferrals
before November. Likewise I think that was the representation earlier. (I reject
the submission that one might have considered the possibility of ad hoc deferrals
all being sorted out by the year end. This would have occurred to no one, and it
was not suggested it should have done.) Mr Puri says that on 8 November he
raised the question of pattern books. He would have been aware of the
importance of these as a significant cost of a carpet business from his other carpet
business (where the policy was a two-year write-off). Mr Puri says that since he
saw no express reference to these books in the accounts he inferred that they
were treated as stocks, as they were treated in his carpet company. Mr Puri says
he raised the question in relation to the stocks of Witter which he thought were
low. Mr Puri says Mr Simpson said that at Witter the business wrote off the cost
as it was incurred and so the stocks did not include pattern books. Mr Simpson
denies that pattern book expenditure was discussed on 8 November. He says he
did not even know the policy about these until the board meeting of 21
November. Although ultimately it may not matter (and I certainly do not think
Mr Simpson was deliberately giving erroneous evidence) I prefer Mr Puri's
evidence on this point. Pattern book expenditure is an obvious factor potentially
affecting profits. Mr Puri's account of how it came to be raised is convincing. I
do not think, however, that it formed a major point of discussion at the time and
I rather think Mr Simpson may have given no more than a hazy answer.
Moreover, at the meeting of 24 November, whether one accepts the Puri or
Simpson/Lloyd version of what was said, the clear implication is that pattern
book expenditure up to that point had been written off as incurred.

As to negligence in relation to the cost of the Allied problem, I have already
given my reasons for holding that the misrepresentation was negligently made or
at least negligently continued down to the time of the contract.

(g) Misrepresentations of fact or opinion?

I should say that I consider the representations as to profit forecasts to involve
more than representations of opinion. It is clear that a representation of fact may
be inherent in a statement of opinion: *Bisset v Wilkinson* [1927] AC 177 at 182,
[1926] All ER Rep 343 at 346 per Lord Merrivale. Here there was an implicit
representation of fact in the estimates: namely that the basis of the forecast being
given was the same basis as for earlier forecasts given orally and was the same
basis as in the budget forecasts contained in the documents supplied. The
October management accounts showed a profit to date of £499,000 (as against a

a   budget of £550,000). Mr Simpson knew Mr Puri saw these figures. For a later forecast to assume deferrals (which would bump up profits) without making sure that Mr Puri realised what was being done was to mislead him as to fact.

The representation that there were no deferrals in the October management accounts was clearly a representation of fact. So also with the Allied cost—the nature of the representation is clearly one of fact as set out in the disclosure letter.

b   Thus I conclude that although Mr Puri made his own profit estimate, he was doing so on the basis of facts which he thought were true when they were not.

(h) *Reliance*

It was suggested there was no reliance on these misrepresentations. The suggestion was that by insisting upon warranties as to the October accounts and
c   other appropriate warranties, Melton Medes were indicating that they were not relying upon the representations as such. This is but an echo of the pre-1967 doubts as to whether there was a remedy for a pre-contractual misrepresentation which had become a contractual term. I have no doubt that Melton Medes relied upon the misrepresentations. The fact that they were warranted too makes no
d   difference, indeed insistence upon warranties shows reliance.

(i) *Estoppel / acquiescence / settlement*

This was but faintly urged. It was suggested that as a result of some discussions in about April 1990 Mr Puri had agreed not to pursue the claim. These discussions did not lead to any positive agreement and the defence fails.
e

(j) *The effect of the 'whole agreement' clause, cl 17.2*

Clause 17.2 of the contract provides:

f   'This Agreement sets forth the entire agreement and understanding between the parties or any of them in connection with the Business and the sale and purchase described herein. In particular, but without prejudice to the generality of the foregoing, the Purchaser acknowledges that it has not been induced to enter into this Agreement by any representation or warranty other than the statements contained or referred to in Schedule 6.'

g   The defendants say this prevents any liability for misrepresentation. A similar clause was relied upon in *Alman v Associated Newspapers Ltd* (20 June 1980, unreported). In that case the clause provided simply that the written contract constitutes 'the entire agreement and understanding between the parties'. Browne-Wilkinson J held the clause was ineffective to exclude liability for misrepresentation. It did not refer to pre-contract representations. He suggested,
h   obiter, that a clause acknowledging that the parties had not relied on any representations in entering the contract would do. That suggestion is apparently the basis of the second sentence of the present clause.

The first thing to do is to construe the clause. As in the *Alman* case, in my judgment the first sentence does not operate to exclude remedies for
j   pre-contractual misrepresentations. It simply does not say it does. If it said, for instance, 'The vendor agrees that he will have no remedy in respect of any untrue statement made to him upon which he relied in entering this contract and that his only remedies can be for breach of contract' the clause would probably have done the job. Then, if he is sold a pup, he will have no remedy unless it is a contractually warranted pup (I here gratefully adapt the language of Shaw LJ in *Esso Petroleum Co Ltd v Mardon* [1976] 2 All ER 5 at 26, [1976] QB 801 at 832).

Unless it is manifestly made clear that a purchaser has agreed only to have a remedy for breach of warranty I am not disposed to think that a contractual term said to have this effect by a roundabout route does indeed do so. In other words, if a clause is to have the effect of excluding or reducing remedies for damaging untrue statements then the party seeking that protection cannot be mealy-mouthed in his clause. He must bring it home that he is limiting his liability for falsehoods he may have told.

I am reinforced in my view by the second sentence. This by clear implication suggests positively that the purchaser was induced to enter into the contract by any representation contained in or referred to in schedule 6. Now schedule 6 contains a cl 11.1, which reads:

> 'All statements of fact made in the Disclosure Letter (but not including the Disclosed Documents as defined therein) are true and accurate in all material respects and are not misleading in any material respect (including by reason of any omissions therefrom).'

So any representation of fact in that letter is referred to in schedule 6, and, if untrue, can found a misrepresentation.

I should add that I was much pressed by the practice of solicitors in relation to this type of clause. I was referred to a number of textbooks on company acquisition where learned authors comment on clauses intended to exclude liability for misrepresentation and what the authors perceive as their general desirability. Thus Knight *The Acquisition of Private Companies* (6th edn, 1992) p 123 says:

> 'It is suggested that in a normal company acquisition, the inclusion in the contract of an acknowledgment by the purchaser that he has not entered into the contract on the basis of any representation other than those contained in the contract should be effective. If a representation has been made by the vendor, and the purchaser is relying upon it, then he has this opportunity to include it as an express warranty in the contract. If he does not do so, then in subsequent proceedings it will be difficult to show, having regard to the acknowledgment, that the contract was entered into in reliance upon the representation. It can be said that a provision of this nature is not subject at all to the Misrepresentation Act 1967, s 3, and that it is not the case that liability is excluded or restricted by the contractual provision, but that no liability arises because of the state of affairs of which the acknowledgment is a record. It is unlikely, however, that this argument will find sympathy with the court. In *Cremdean Properties v Nash* (1977) 244 EG 547 at 551, Bridge LJ indicated that, in his view, exclusion clauses which purported to deny the very existence of a representation did not avoid the effect of s 3. Nevertheless, in a commercial transaction such as an acquisition, when the parties on each side are businessmen who take advice, it is difficult to see why the provision should not be regarded by the court as fair and reasonable in a normal case.'

Wine and Beswick *Buying and Selling Private Companies and Businesses* (4th edn, 1992) p 85 say:

> 'Where, however, the agreement provides that the purchaser is relying on no representations other than those incorporated as warranties, it is thought

a that a vendor's liability in tort for misrepresentation will be excluded and the purchaser's remedy will be a contractual one.'

Both *Practical Commercial Precedents* and the *Encyclopaedia of Forms and Precedents* contain standard form clauses of the type wherein the purchaser acknowledges that it has not been induced to enter the agreement by any representation or warranty other than warranties set out in the agreement.

b To my mind, if those clauses are intended to exclude liability for misrepresentation if that misrepresentation has become a warranty of the agreement, they are ineffective. Section 1 of the Misrepresentation Act 1967 specifically deals with this. It reads:

c 'Where a person has entered into a contract after a misrepresentation has been made to him, and—(a) the misrepresentation has become a term of the contract; or (b) the contract has been performed; or both, then, if otherwise he would be entitled to rescind the contract without alleging fraud, he shall be so entitled, subject to the provisions of this Act, notwithstanding the matters mentioned in paragraphs (a) and (b) of this section.'

d The authors do not mention this provision in their discussion of this type of clause. I think that where a man has been sold a pup, even if it is a warranted pup, there is nothing, unless the contract expressly says so, from the man also treating it as a misrepresented pup, if that was indeed the case. What he relied upon is a question of fact.

e Of academic importance here would be a misrepresentation of fact not contained or referred to in schedule 6. Would the second sentence preclude the purchaser from saying he had relied upon this? I rather doubt it. Again, the point of exclusion of liability is not made explicit. It is perfectly possible to read the clause as doing no more than attempting to set out such representations as the purchaser thinks he was relying on at the time. He may have difficulty later in

f proof of any further representation, but if he can prove one, then his acknowledgement that there was no other may amount to no more than an acknowledgement of what he thought was the position at the time.

(k) *Section 3 of the 1967 Act and the 1977 Act*

g Even if I were wrong on the meaning of cl 17.2 and it does have the purported effect of excluding liability or remedies for misrepresentation, it bumps into s 3 of the 1967 Act, as substituted by s 8 of the 1977 Act. This provides:

'If a contract contains a term which would exclude or restrict—(a) any liability to which a party to a contract may be subject by reason of any

h misrepresentation made by him before the contract was made; or (b) any remedy available to another party to the contract by reason of such a misrepresentation, that term shall be of no effect except in so far as it satisfies the requirement of reasonableness as stated in section 11(1) of the Unfair Contract Terms Act 1977; and it is for those claiming that the term satisfies

j that requirement to show that it does.'

Section 11(1) of the 1977 Act defines the requirement of reasonableness as follows:

'In relation to a contract term, the requirement of reasonableness for the purposes of ... section 3 of the Misrepresentation Act 1967 ... is that the term shall have been a fair and reasonable one to be included having regard to the circumstances which were, or ought reasonably to have been, known to or in the contemplation of the parties when the contract was made.' *a*

This makes it plain that the test is retrospective—was the term reasonable at the time? Mr Kaye urged that a clause excluding liability for misrepresentation was in widespread use and was therefore to be considered reasonable. He relied upon the views of the authors I have mentioned and evidence from the defendants' solicitor to establish that such clauses were indeed in common use. I *b* note that Browne-Wilkinson J in *Alman's* case found as a fact that skilful and reputable solicitors commonly include clauses of the type he was considering in share purchase agreements and I make the same finding in relation to cl 17.2 here.

But I have to say that even if cl 17.2 had exclusionary effect it would to my mind be neither fair nor reasonable. The problem is its scope. The 1967 Act calls *c* for consideration of the *term* as such. And it refers to 'any liability' and 'any misrepresentation'. It does not call for consideration of the term so far as it applies to the misrepresentation in question or the kind of misrepresentation in question. The term is not severable: it is either reasonable as a whole or not. So one must consider its every potential effect. The clause does not distinguish between fraudulent, negligent, or innocent misrepresentation. If it excludes *d* liability for one kind of misrepresentation it does so for all. I cannot think it reasonable to exclude liability for fraudulent misrepresentation—indeed Mr Kaye accepted it would not work in the case of fraud. It may well be, with a different clause, reasonable to exclude liability for innocent misrepresentation or even negligent misrepresentation. But since the width of this clause is too great I *e* would have held it failed the requirement of reasonableness and so was of no effect.

A possible route around this latter objection would be to construe the clause so that it did not apply to a fraudulent misrepresentation. This approach is artificial. It is unnecessary now that the 1977 Act exists to destroy unreasonable exclusion clauses. The construction involves creating an implied exception in the *f* case of fraud. What about an implied exclusion of negligence? Or gross negligence? It is not for the law to fudge a way for an exclusion clause to be valid. If a party wants to exclude liability for certain sorts of misrepresentations, it must spell those sorts out clearly.

g

(1) *Overall effect of misrepresentation*

In the result I conclude as follows. The October management accounts gave a figure of profit for the year to date of £499,000. It contained undisclosed deferrals of pattern book expenditure of £120,000. There was a misrepresentation in respect of the true cost of Allied, represented to be a one-off, now solved, *h* problem. It was said to be £120,000 when in fact it was about £50,000, an overstatement of £70,000.

D. CONTRACT

(a) *Clause 12.3(a): contractual limitation period*

Clause 12.3(a) of the contract provides: *j*

'Notwithstanding anything in this Agreement to the contrary the Vendor shall not be liable (by way of damages or otherwise) in respect of a breach of this Agreement or claim by the Purchaser in respect of a Warranty unless the Vendor shall have been given written notice by the Purchaser of such breach or claim on or prior to 1st January 1992. Such notice shall be in writing and a shall contain the Purchaser's then best estimate of the amount claimed and the basis on which such estimate is made. Any liability in respect of a breach or claim of which notice is given as aforesaid shall cease unless proceedings in respect of such breach or claim are issued and served within 6 months of the date of the written notice (unless liability has been agreed in the interim).'

b This is a contractual limitation clause. The first thing to note is that it only applies in respect of 'a breach of this Agreement or claim ... in respect of a Warranty'. In my judgment, as indeed was conceded by Mr Kaye, the clause can have no effect upon any misrepresentation which induced the contract. The claim in misrepresentation is not touched by this clause. Secondly, there was no
c attack on the clause pursuant to the provisions of the 1977 Act. I was a little surprised by this because I would have thought that to the extent to which the clause prevents a claim based on what in the law of limitation is called 'concealed fraud' it might be unreasonable.

The defendants say, so far as the claim is founded in breach of contract, that a number of the aspects of the claim are barred by cl 12.3(a). The most significant
d of these is the claim in relation to the Allied problem. Matters of much less significance are also said to be barred, for instance, the treatment of the proceeds of sale of Dacca Street (see later) and some other minor matters.

Now it is common ground that the clause should be construed strictly in the sense that liability is only excluded if the language says so clearly. On that basis
e Mr Mann first argued that all that was necessary to comply with the clause is that there should be a general written notice of 'any breach or claim' before 1 January 1992. He likened the degree of notice required to that called for in a writ. In relation to Allied, he said, the fact that any notice which mentioned an Allied problem would be sufficient. I do not agree with Mr Mann's submission. I believe the purpose of the clause is not merely to warn the vendor that there is a
f claim being made but that the Vendor must be given at least some basis to support the claim. This follows from the requirement that the purchaser must provide his best estimate and the basis on which such estimate is made. It is not good enough to say, for example that 'I have a claim in respect of the warranty that the cost of the Allied problem was £120,000. I estimate the amount to be £x
g without giving any basis whatever for the claim'.

Alternatively, Mr Mann submits that sufficient notice of the Allied problem was in fact given. He relies upon the letter of 22 May 1990 wherein the plaintiff's solicitors said:

h 'The true profits of the business to October 1989 were further misrepresented in the October Management Accounts, in so far as they failed to reflect considerable charges which had arisen as a consequence of carpet, supplied to Allied Maples Limited by your clients, being rejected on quality grounds and credit notes issued.

j At meetings between Mr. Puri and Mr. Simpson on 8th and 26th November 1989, Mr. Simpson represented that these charges were reflected in the October Management Accounts and even after completion, Mr. Simpson continued to maintain this was the case. For example, in his letter to Mr. Puri of 27th March 1990, he stated "as we discussed within the 1989 accounts, there are substantial non-recurring charges which we had accepted in September and October to put to rights our service with a major retail customer".

Notwithstanding these representations however, our clients recently discovered that credit notes, amounting to some £40,000, were not reflected in the October accounts, but were only issued in November and December 1989.'

a

Mr Kaye says that notice was not good enough. Although it complains about the Allied Maples problem it provides detail which ultimately was not relied upon at all. The original detail is contained in the third paragraph I have just quoted. The complaint is now quite different says Mr Kaye, namely that the true cost of the Allied problem was nowhere near £120,000 as represented both before the contract and in the disclosure letter.

b

Now the purpose of cl 12.3(a) is to give notice to the vendor of a claim so that he can assess its validity at an early stage. Mr Kaye relied upon *Babanaft International Co SA v Avant Petroleum Inc, The Oltenia* [1982] 3 All ER 244, [1982] 1 WLR 871. In that case there was a similar, but tighter, clause. Liability was discharged 'unless a claim has been presented ... in writing with all available supporting documents, within 90 (ninety) days from completion of discharge of the cargo'. The Court of Appeal unanimously approved the judgment of Bingham J ([1982] 1 Lloyd's Rep 448) to the effect that the requirement for 'all supporting documents' meant what it said. The plaintiff in that case had not supplied such documents so the claim was barred. Bingham J said (at 453):

c

d

'The commercial intention underlying this clause seems to me plainly to have been to ensure that claims were made by the owners within a short period of final discharge so that the claims could be investigated and if possible resolved while the facts were still fresh (cf. *Metalimex Foreign Trade Corporation v. Eugenie Maritime Co. Ltd.* ([1962] 1 Lloyd's Rep 378 at 386 per McNair J)). This object could only be achieved if the charterers were put in possession of the factual material which they required in order to satisfy themselves whether the claims were well-founded or not. I cannot regard the expression "all available supporting documents" as in any way ambiguous ... The interpretation of any clause must of course be governed very largely by the language of the clause itself, but I find some support for my approach to this clause in the House of Lords decision in *A/S Rendal v. Arcos Ltd.* ([1937] 3 All ER 577, 58 Ll L Rep 287). The clause in question, (24) in that case, was less rigorous than cl. M.2, in that it provided for notice of a claim to be given within 12 months, with no requirement that supporting documents be submitted. The question was considered whether there had been compliance with the clause if notice had been given of a claim for delay and consequential expenses caused by lack of ice-breaker assistance but not of damage caused by ice to the ship itself. Lord Wright said ([1937] 3 All ER 577 at 580, 58 Ll L Rep 287 at 292): "It is convenient first to state how I construe Clause 24. That clause requires 'notice of claim'. That in my opinion does not merely mean a precisely formulated claim with full details, but it must be such a notice as will enable the party to whom it is given to take steps to meet the claim by preparing and obtaining appropriate evidence for that purpose. Thus, in the present case there was a claim for damages for breach of the ice clause, with particulars so far as damages were claimed in respect of delay and consequent expenses. The further claim for damage to the ship herself was a claim in respect of the same cause of action, that is, breach of the ice clause, but it involved different issues of fact, estimates of damage, ship surveys, repair accounts and so forth. I think, therefore, that

e

f

g

h

j

a   Clause 24 requires a separate notice in respect of such a claim, if the purpose of Clause 24 is to be fulfilled."'

Similarly in *Tradax Export SA v Italcarbo Societa di Navigazione SpA, The Sandalion* [1983] 1 Lloyd's Rep 514 at 517 Lloyd J said of a similar clause:

b   'The clause requires the claim to be made in writing within 12 months, and continues—"... where provision is not complied with the claim shall be deemed to be waived and absolutely barred." It seems to me clear, both on the language of the clause, and also by reason of the commercial purpose which it was intended to serve, that the claim must be identified in terms precise enough to enable the other party to know what claim it is he has to meet.'

c

Mr Mann accepted that the claim as originally formulated, based upon in effect an overstatement of £40,000, has been considerably modified. But, he said, the notice given required, or at least gave, the purchaser the opportunity of d investigating the claim as then formulated. That would necessarily involve going into the Allied problem, and examining all the accounts in relation to it. From this the true position would emerge just as it in fact did when Mr Barford of Touche Ross set about examining the claim as originally formulated. So sufficient notice of the claim had been given. With some hesitation I think this is right. The point is that the vendor under the notice given in the letter would have e to examine the Allied problem and the claim as then formulated to see if it was right. He would clearly have an opportunity of doing that. Necessarily he would, assuming he investigated the matter properly, come up with the true facts because he would investigate credit notes from Allied and what happened in fact. I regard the Allied claim, as now formulated, as an amendment of the claim as f originally formulated, albeit a very substantial one. I therefore think that sufficient notice was given under cl 12.3(a).

As regards the minor matters such as Dacca Street, the position is different. Mr Mann overstretched his argument for these. In effect, he said, whilst investig-ating the accounts generally these matters would also be turned up. That to my mind does not mean that the claim was made at all in respect of those matters, g and whilst the vendor may have found these, he may not have done because he would not have been looking for them. They are barred by cl 12.3(a).

It is not disputed that so far as the pattern book expenditure side of the case is concerned, that sufficient notice was given and so cl 12.3(a) has no application to that.

h
In any event, by virtue of my holding that the Allied problem can be the subject of a claim in misrepresentation my decision in relation to cl 12.3(a) is essentially academic. I say this because as far as I can discern there is no difference in the quantum of damage whether the matter should be regarded as one of breach of contract or as damages for misrepresentation in the circumstances of this case. j This is a matter to which I shall return under the heading of damages.

(b) *The contract counterclaim for £157,000*

There is an amount of £157,000 which the plaintiff did not pay and which was due under the contract. It is agreed that this can be set off against any damages payable to the plaintiff.

(c) *Clause 5.2: the claim and counterclaim*

I begin with the dispute under cl 5.2. Although I have quoted it above it is convenient to requote it here:

> 'The Accounts shall be prepared by the Vendor's Auditors using the principles, standards and assumptions employed in the preparation of, and on the same bases as the accounts for the Vendor were prepared in respect of the year ending 31st December 1988 in respect of that part of its business which comprised the Business which principles etc. were (save as disclosed in the Disclosure Letter) in accordance with SSAP's and generally accepted accounting practice.'

The defendants suggest it should be construed so as to have the effect that the 1989 accounts were to be drawn up taking into account the Rider X of the disclosure letter, namely by writing off pattern book expenditure over two years. Moreover, they say this should be done as accountants would do it properly (even though neither party contemplated this), namely by redoing the 1988 accounts to find out how much pattern book expenditure was deferred from that year. This would mean that they had overpaid by nearly £200,000 under the adjustment clause, cl 5.6.

I reject this construction. The qualification in parenthesis relates to the principles in accordance with SSAPs (ie Statements of Standard Accounting Practice) and generally accepted accounting practice used for the 1988 accountants. In effect the defendants want to move the qualification so as to be a qualification of the principles etc to be used for the 1989 accounts. It just is not such a qualification as matters stand.

So, say the defendants alternatively, the clause should be rectified. But the evidence does not remotely suggest that there was a common mistake in writing down that which had in fact been agreed between the parties, the normal basis for a rectification claim. Alternatively, it is suggested that there is a unilateral mistake by TBP (thinking they were to prepare the 1989 accounts on the new policy), that the plaintiff knew this and is guilty of 'sharp practice' in taking advantage of the mistake. Reliance is placed on the principles in *Riverlate Properties Ltd v Paul* [1974] 2 All ER 656 at 661, [1975] Ch 133 at 140 in relation to the unilateral mistake claim. I reject it. Far from establishing that Mr Puri thought the 1989 accounts were to be drawn up for the purposes of the agreement with pattern book expenditure deferrals for 1989, the evidence establishes precisely the opposite, both at the time of the contract and, by way of corroboration, shortly thereafter when he indicated they should be drawn up without deferrals.

So the counterclaim under cl 5 fails. That leaves the plaintiff's claim under this clause to be considered. The plaintiff says it overpaid by £251,316. It says that the 1989 accounts should have been drawn by writing pattern book expenditure off as it incurred, as had happened in previous years. This would have resulted in the net assets being less by the amount claimed, which is the amount deferred to 1990.

So how should the 1989 accounts have been drawn up—with pattern book expenditure deferred or not? Clause 5.2 says on the same basis as 1988. But Rider X speaks of the adoption in November of a different policy for 1989 having been adopted. That to my mind records what was done, it does not override cl 5.2, which provides a complete code for drawing up the accounts. The factual matrix supports this construction. Clause 5.2 existed in draft before the disclosure letter

a
was supplied. No one said to Mr Puri at the time that the last-minute Rider X would have the significant effect contended for by the defendants. He made special provision at the time in relation to pattern book expenditure in relation to the earn-out (see cl 6.4). Then was the time for the defendants to seek provision in relation to cl 5.2. If they had, then probably the whole true position in relation to pattern book expenditure would have come out.

b   So the claim relating to the construction of cl 5.2 succeeds.

(d) *Interest under the cl 5.2 claim*

That does not end the dispute in relation to over- or underpayment. The plaintiff says that cl 5.6 governs the rate of interest up until the due date of payment under the clause (ie 1% above Lloyds Bank base rate, simple interest).
c   Thereafter the rate of interest is governed by cl 14 which provides for 2% above that rate, compound. The defendants say cl 5.6 provides its own complete code for interest due on payments under it—the special derogating from the general.

I think the plaintiff is clearly right about this. Clause 5.6 sets the rate of interest until a sum is due. Clause 14 governs the position when money due is not paid
d   timeously.

(e) *Breach of warranty—general*

A variety of these is pleaded. In most important respects they overlap with the claim in misrepresentation. By cl 12.1 the vendors warranted that the statements in schedule 6 were true. There was a qualification in relation to the disclosure
e   letter, but not otherwise (cl 12.2). So attention is focused on the schedule 6 statements of fact.

(f) *Breach of warranty—the October management accounts*

I have already set forth cl 4.4 of schedule 6, which relates to the October
f   management accounts. I turn to consider the alleged breaches of warranty in respect of that paragraph.

Warranty 4.4(a): good accounting practice

There was failure to comply with good accounting practice in respect of pattern book expenditure. Good accounting practice requires consistency of
g   treatment. There was an argument that 'good accounting practice' is not the same as 'generally accepted accounting practice'. That may be so, but it does not mean that inconsistency can be 'good practice' of any kind. Ad hoc deferral of items, whilst perfectly rational when used for the purposes of management by those who know of the deferrals, is not good accountancy practice. I wish to
h   make it plain here that I in no way criticise Mr Hogarth who was responsible for the deferrals. He knew what he was doing and was never told that his internal accounts were going to be represented and warranted as complying with good accountancy practice in general.

There was a further breach of this warranty in relation to some minor items
j   (depreciation and the redundancy of a Mr Atherton). But I have held that these items are barred by cl 12.3. In any event they are comparatively trivial.

There was also an alleged breach in that a large cheque from Allied Maples was included whereas it may in fact have been received very early in the following month. The evidence is that a large cheque was received every month and Mr Hogarth included it in the management accounts every month, even if it arrived slightly late. Otherwise some months might have two cheques whilst others

none. I cannot consider the inclusion of this cheque as a failure to exercise good
accountancy practice. The policy was consistently applied.

Warranty 4.4(b): on the basis of the notes to the 1988 accounts

As already noted, the notes to the 1988 accounts say nothing about pattern
book expenditure. So the ad hoc deferrals are not inconsistent with the notes.
Things would be different if the clause had simply said on the basis of the 1988
accounts.

Warranty 4.4(c): reasonable view; no extraordinary or exceptional items

It is worth repeating this warranty in respect of the management accounts,
namely that they—

'give a reasonable view of the state of affairs of the Vendor in relation to
the Business as at 29 October 1989 and of the results of the Business for the
accounting period up to that date and at that date were not (save as shown
therein) affected by any extraordinary or exceptional items.'

There was considerable dispute between the experts here. It was pointed out
that 'reasonable view' is not the same as 'true and fair view' (cf warranty 4.1(c)
and the use of the phrase in statute—see the Companies Act 1985, ss 226, 227).
So, it was argued, a 'reasonable view' represents something less than 'true and
fair'. The latter provide for a margin of error of 5% so more would do here, say
10%. There was a less than 10% error in the balance sheet which the defendants
equate to the 'state of affairs' but more than that in relation to the 'results' which
the defendants equate to profits.

I think there was a breach of this warranty. The 'results' given did not provide
a reasonable view of the profits. I do not see how it can sensibly be argued
otherwise. It was suggested that because cl 12.2 expressly qualifies the warranties
in schedule 6 by anything in the disclosure letter, the October management
accounts were qualified by Rider X. This makes no sense to me. The October
accounts were done before the adoption of the changed policy. No one would
have thought that the October accounts should in some way include deferrals of
pattern book expenditure, ad hoc or otherwise.

As to the balance sheet, I think there was a failure to give a reasonable view in
that there was included (probably in stock) a substantial item (pattern book
expenditure) with no realisable value. It is not just a question of percentages as
the defendants suggest.

I do not regard the inclusion of the Allied Maples monthly cheque as a failure
to provide a reasonable view of either the state of affairs or of the profitability. As
I have said the inclusion of this monthly item was consistently applied.

There is one other possible breach of this warranty. It is not pleaded as such,
the point arising more by way of reply to a point taken by way of defence. I do
not think this matters because the defendants had fair notice of the point in Mr
Barford's first report. The point is this: the defendants say that the pattern book
expenditure for 1989 was unusually high on a one-off basis. This is because the
company was attacking the wholesale market and more books were needed for
the initial attack than would be wanted in later years. Particular reliance was
placed on the re-examination of Mr Ainscow to establish this. To this the plaintiff
ripostes firstly that the pattern book expenditure was not in fact unusually high if
one bears in mind sales also (see below). Alternatively, they say that if the

a   expenditure was unusually high it was an 'exceptional item' and there was a breach of this warranty. I think both ripostes are right.

(g) *Warranty 8(c): no material adverse change*
     Warranty 8(c) provides:

b   '... there has been no materially adverse change [since 1988] in the financial or trading position of the Business and the Business has been carried on in the ordinary course and in the same manner (including nature and scale) as immediately before the 31st December 1988.'

     There was a dispute as to the meaning of this warranty. Did 'financial or trading position' mean merely the balance sheet or did it include current
c   profitability? I have little doubt it included the latter—everything that a purchaser would want to know about the business, especially current profitability and performance against budget. 'Material' must be viewed through the eyes of the purchaser: what is 'material' to him is what matters.

     On that basis there was indeed a material change. The business was not
d   making as much profit as in 1988 by a substantial amount. The defendants say this is not good enough because what has to be affected is the long-term likely profitability—the maintainable profits. They say what happened to pattern book expenditure in 1989 was special—arising from the attempt to target wholesalers. The result was a one-off increase in pattern book expenditure for that year. Hence, they say, no affect on maintainable profits. I do not find so. Pattern book
e   expenditure is related to sales. Mr Barford shows that in relation to sales, pattern book expenditure was not particularly unusual for 1989. Expenditure went up, so did sales. There was some argument that the sales which matter are the sales for the next year, but to my mind this was entering too much into the field of speculation.

f   Accordingly I hold that there was a breach of warranty 8(c).

(h) *Warranty 11.1: the disclosure letter*
     So far as the Allied problem is concerned I have already held that the disclosure letter was misleading: suggesting a one-off cured cost of £120,00 for September/
g   October whereas the true cost was at best £50,000. So there was a breach of warranty too.

(i) *How much cash would be included in the assets purchased?*
     Mr Puri plainly expected cash. He said so and the October management accounts indicated that cash was there at the time. He calculated that although
h   the price he offered was £4m he would immediately get about £700,000 back in cash. But I can find no express warranty that there would be cash in the business—and I have already excluded liability for misrepresentation as to a cash promise. It should also be remembered that there is the adjustment provision, cl 5. This has the effect that, if cash has gone, it must be replaced by other assets,
j   or, if not, will be compensated by the adjustment. Further, I have to say that I cannot really find any pleading about this cash point, a pleading which faces the defendants squarely with it.

     That is not to say that cash does not matter. It plainly does when one considers the actual effective price paid for the business, or the effective price Mr Puri thought he was paying for the business. But that goes to damages to which I must now turn.

E. DAMAGES

I have already dealt with the contractual claim under cl 5. I must now deal a with the damages claim otherwise. There is little dispute as to the applicable legal principles, either for misrepresentation or breach of contract. In principle there is a difference between the two. Damages for misrepresentation cover all damage which foreseeably flows from the misrepresentation, including consequential loss. Possibly, so far as the claim is made under s 2(1) of the 1967 b Act, even unforeseeable damage flowing from the misrepresentation may be covered, as would probably be the case if the misrepresentation were fraudulent. Damages for breach of contract seek to put the injured party in the position he would have been if there had been no breach. Here that would mean damages to put the plaintiff in the same position as if the warranties broken had been true.

In relation to misrepresentation there are, in this case, no consequential losses c claimed. Given that rescission is not available, the aim must therefore be to put the plaintiff in the same position financially as he would have been if the contract had not been made. Suppose the plaintiff owns the business (actual value '£X' at time of acquisition). Suppose he paid '£Y'. Then the damages are £(Y–X). In relation to contract the algebra works out this way: price paid £Y for a business d on assumption that warranties are true; actual value of business, the warranties being untrue, £X°. So damages are £(Y–X°). There is in this case a minor difference between X and X° in that the latter cannot include the small items excluded from consideration by cl 12.3. For practical purposes there is no difference between the two formulae here. (I should say that the plaintiff seemed to think there was a difference in date to be taken into account. I did not e understand the point and in any event the difference was trifling.)

Before I go further in assessing damages I must make some general observations. One cannot be terribly precise about the numbers (as the accountants sometimes seem to suggest). As soon as one starts making assumptions, or figures are not precisely measurable, error, or rather f impossibility of precision, comes in. There is a danger whenever numbers are given to many apparently significant figures of assuming that those numbers are accurate—a spurious impression of exactness is given. It would often be more helpful if numbers in calculations—especially damages calculations—were given to the nearest figure the accountant considered significant—together with his estimate of the accuracy of the figure and why. '± X%' is used both by engineers g and scientists to indicate margins of accuracy. Accountants could usefully do the same. Here I have some intricate calculations by both sides which give figures which are apparently precise to a far greater degree than can conceivably be justified. Dr Johnson may have said 'round numbers are always false' but then he was not familiar with the ways of the modern accountant. Lord Rutherford used h to tell students that the value of π is 3. He knew more about numbers than Dr Johnson.

So the above bits of algebra are all very well in theory, but they involve considerable dispute as to the values of X and Y. One only has to dip into the voluminous expert reports to see that fundamental to these are a series of j assumptions one way or another. For instance in calculating the value of the company, one can estimate its true maintainable profitability and apply a multiplier. This exercise itself involves marked room for error and dispute— what is 'true profitability', what is the appropriate multiplier? I have to say that the expert evidence on both sides to a large extent involved matters of conjecture and surmise.

a　I was conscious of the considerable difficulties here. So I wondered whether there was a different route and asked Mr Barford, the plaintiff's expert, about it. Suppose a man pays £A for a business represented to have a profit stream of £P. In fact the profit stream is £Q. Then Mr Barford accepted that the 'damage' could be said, to a first order, to be £[A–(A x Q/P)]. As he pointed out this could only be a first order approximation, upwardly biased somewhat depending on the

b　disparity between P and Q and the actual net assets of the company. For instance if the profits were actually zero, the damage would be the entire price paid, even if the company owned substantial assets, which is a nonsense. Despite this, however, I remained attracted by the simplicity of the formula as a first order approximation at least as a guide to the uppermost figure for damages.

　This requires determination of A, P and Q. I begin with a very rough approach.

c　Crudely one may say here the price, £A, was £4m. £P is more difficult. The represented profits for ten months was £499,000 (£500,000). So for the year (assuming straight line continuation of profits) the figure is £600,000. One adds the £120,000 Allied problem to end up with a 'represented' profit (ie a profit one might reasonably assume on the basis of the factual representations) of £720,000.

d　The actual, maintainable profit, £Q, is, on the same crude approach £600,000 – £120,000 (deferrals) + £50,000 (actual cost of Allied), namely £530,000. So the crude sum gives a figure of £1·05m. By way of rough comparison, if one takes the profit figure actually assumed by Mr Puri, namely £650,000 for the year, to which is added £120,000 (Allied), the figure comes to £1·25m.

　Mr Kaye attacked the figures for A and Q. First Q, the actual maintainable

e　profit. He said that because pattern book expenditure was exceptionally high for 1989, even though it was deferred, the 'excess' should be regarded as a 'one-off' not affecting maintainable profits. I have already considered this and reject it. Mr Kaye also said I should take a 'weighted average' for the profits. His expert, Mr Hughes, thought this more appropriate because a single year was an unsafe

f　guide. Mr Barford thought the most recent figures were the best thing to take precisely because they were the most recent. I prefer the latter approach in this case where the profits had been consistently on the rise and were represented as such from the outset.

　Then Mr Kaye attacked £A, the price paid. I think he was on better ground here. Mr Puri was only expecting to pay net about £3·3m ± £0·1m. £3·3m is the

g　effective price according to Mr Hughes, £3·6m according to Mr Barford. I prefer Mr Hughes' evidence on this, for Mr Barford's figure depends upon assumptions about average bank credits and the taking into account of a holding back of cheques which gets taken up in the price adjustment clause. From Mr Hughes' figure one must also deduct what I have held to be a necessary repayment under

h　the adjustment clause, £0·25m. The effective price is, I hold, £3·05m. The formula then gives a result of £0·805m. This seems to me to be of the right order. I will take a figure of £0·775m to allow for the fact that the formula is biased upwardly. I do not believe greater accuracy of estimation is possible.

　Now the expert accountants did not use this formula. They tried to find the

j　actual market value of the company. This involved not only estimating its future profitability but also other estimates, such as the multiplier. The complicated calculation of the plaintiff is to be found as particulars under para 45 of the statement of claim. Figures of £1·8 and £1·5m are claimed depending on the multiplier. As to contractual damages, the particulars give figures of £1·5 and £1·35m. In relation to both contractual and non-contractual claims there are assumptions and inclusions of minor items which I have ruled out as

inadmissible. I do not propose to delve into this further—it only leads to assessing
whether one expert's valuation technique is better than another's in a situation
where there was, so far as the evidence goes, no open market. I do not regard this
as any safer than the first approximation method I have referred to, which Mr
Barford accepted as such and which, with suitable caveats, Mr Kaye in argument
also accepted as a permissible method of assessment.

CONCLUSION

1. The plaintiff is entitled to judgment: (a) in the sum claimed in under cl 5.6,
namely £251,316 plus interest at the cl 5.6 rate until payment was due, thereafter
at the cl 14 rate; (b) in the sum of £775,000 by way of damages for misrepresentation, alternatively for breach of contract, plus interest as agreed by the parties.

2. The defendants are entitled to set off in the sum of £157,000, plus interest as
agreed by the parties.

Order accordingly.

Celia Fox   Barrister.

a Dhak v Insurance Co of North America (UK) Ltd

COURT OF APPEAL, CIVIL DIVISION

NEILL, ALDOUS LJJ AND SIR JOHN BALCOMBE

15, 16 JANUARY, 6 FEBRUARY 1996

b

Insurance – Accident insurance – Perils insured against – Accidental injury resulting in death – Causation – Whether asphyxia caused by inhalation of vomit following deliberate excessive drinking amounting to bodily injury – Whether resulting death caused by accidental means.

c The plaintiff's wife, a nurse, suffered severe back pain while lifting a heavy patient. The pain persisted despite treatment and thereafter she started to drink heavily to relieve the pain. About six months after her accident she died in her sleep after consuming a considerable quantity of alcohol, probably more than the equivalent of a bottle of gin, over a relatively short period. The plaintiff, who was sleeping d in another room, was not aware of how much his wife had drunk. An inquest recorded a verdict of death by misadventure and the cause of death was stated as acute alcoholism and misadventure. The plaintiff's wife was insured under a personal accident policy which provided for payment of £50,000 in respect of, inter alia, 'bodily injury resulting in death ... caused directly or indirectly by the accident'. 'Bodily injury' was defined in the policy as 'Bodily injury caused by e accidental means'. The plaintiff, as his wife's executor, made a claim under the policy but it was rejected by the insurers. The plaintiff then brought proceedings against the defendant insurers to recover the amount under the policy. The judge found that the cause of death was asphyxia resulting from the inhalation of vomit and dismissed the claim on the grounds that asphyxia in those circumstances did f not amount to bodily injury. The plaintiff appealed to the Court of Appeal, contending that his wife had sustained a bodily injury and that she had done so as the result of an accident since no distinction was to be drawn between an accidental result and accidental means, but even if such a distinction were drawn, the proximate, or effective or dominant, cause of death was the inhalation of vomit, not the deliberate ingestion of alcohol.

g

Held – (1) In order to make a successful claim under the policy the plaintiff had to establish (i) that his wife sustained a bodily injury, (ii) that her bodily injury resulted in death, and (iii) that the bodily injury was caused by accidental means. Bodily injury was not restricted to injury to the exterior of the body and could h include the introduction of some foreign matter into the body or into a particular part of the body which caused harmful physiological changes in the structure of the body. Accordingly, asphyxia resulting from the inhalation of vomit was just as much a bodily injury as asphyxia caused by a blockage of the windpipe by foreign matter such as a peanut. The plaintiff's wife had accordingly sustained a bodily injury which had resulted in death (see p 614 h, p 616 h to p 617 b and p 622 j, j post); *Life and Casualty Insurance Co of Tennessee v Brown* (1957) 95 Ga App 354, *Johnson v Mutual of Omaha Insurance Co* (1982) 139 DLR (3d) 358 and dictum of Brennan J in *Australian Casualty Co Ltd v Federico* (1986) 160 CLR 513 at 535 considered.

(2) The terms of the policy, by referring to bodily injury 'caused by accidental means', required the court to concentrate on the cause of the injury and to inquire whether the injury was caused by accidental means. An injury was caused by an

accident if it was the natural result of a fortuitous and unexpected cause or the *a* fortuitous or unexpected result of a natural cause, but not if it was the natural result of a natural cause or if it was the natural and direct consequence of a deliberate act done or a calculated risk taken by the assured. Where an insured embarked deliberately on a course of conduct which led to some bodily injury, the questions which the court had to consider were (i) whether the insured intended to inflict some bodily injury to himself, (ii) whether the insured took a calculated *b* risk that if he continued with that course of conduct he might sustain some bodily injury, (iii) whether some bodily injury was the natural and direct consequence of the course of conduct, and (iv) whether some fortuitous cause intervened. On the facts, the plaintiff's wife, as a nurse with many years of experience, must have been well aware of the consequences and dangers of drinking alcohol to excess and was to be regarded as having foreseen what might happen in the event of her *c* drinking to excess and to have taken a calculated risk of sustaining some bodily injury. In those circumstances her injury and death were not the result of some fortuitous cause and were not 'caused by accidental means' within the terms of the policy. The appeal would therefore be dismissed (see p 619 *j* to p 620 *j*, p 621 *f* and p 622 *c* to *j*, post). *d*

Notes

For accident insurance, see 25 *Halsbury's Laws* (4th edn reissue) paras 567–588, and for cases on the subject, see 29(2) *Digest* (2nd reissue) 237–251, 4638–4722.

Cases referred to in judgments

Australian Casualty Co Ltd v Federico (1986) 160 CLR 513, Aust HC. *e*
Beller (Marcel) Ltd v Hayden [1978] 3 All ER 111, [1978] QB 694, [1978] 2 WLR 845.
Candler v London and Lancashire Guarantee and Accident Co of Canada [1963] 2 OR 547, Ont HC.
Clidero v Scottish Accident Insurance Co Ltd (1892) 19 R 355, Ct of Sess.
De Souza v Home and Overseas Insurance Co Ltd [1995] LRLR 453, CA. *f*
Fenton v J Thorley & Co Ltd [1903] AC 443, HL.
Gray v Barr (Prudential Assurance Co Ltd, third party) [1971] 2 All ER 949, [1971] 2 QB 554, [1971] 2 WLR 1334, CA.
Hamlyn v Crown Accidental Insurance Co Ltd [1893] 1 QB 750, CA.
Johnson v Mutual of Omaha Insurance Co (1982) 139 DLR (3d) 358, Ont HC; *affd* (1984) 8 DLR (4th) 640, Ont CA. *g*
Koch v Empire Life Insurance Co (1981) 124 DLR (3d) 161, Alta QB.
Landress v Phoenix Mutual Life Insurance Co (1934) 291 US 491, US SC.
Life and Casualty Insurance Co of Tennessee v Brown (1957) 95 Ga App 354, Ga Ct of Apps; *rvsd* (1957) 213 Ga 390, Ga SC.
Long v Colonial Mutual Life Assurance Society Ltd [1931] NZLR 528 NZ SC; *rvsd* *h* [1931] NZLR 536, NZ CA.
National and General Insurance Co Ltd v Chick [1984] 2 NSWLR 86, NSW CA.
Scarr and General Accident Assurance Corp, Re [1905] 1 KB 387, [1904–7] All ER Rep 566.
Tracy-Gould v Maritime Life Assurance Co (1992) 89 DLR (4th) 726, NS SC; *affd* (1992) *j* 98 DLR (4th) 741, NS CA.
Trew v Railway Passengers Assurance Co (1861) 6 H & N 839, 158 ER 346, Ex Ch.
United London and Scottish Insurance Co, Re, Brown's Claim [1915] 2 Ch 167, CA.
Winspear v Accident Insurance Co Ltd (1880) 6 QBD 42, CA.

Cases also cited or referred to in skeleton arguments

Aguilar v London Life Insurance Co (1990) 70 DLR (4th) 510, Man CA.

a   *Barrett v Ministry of Defence* [1995] 3 All ER 87, [1995] 1 WLR 1217, CA.
    CNA Assurance Co v MacIsaac (1979) 102 DLR (3d) 160, NS SC.
    Columbia Cellulose Co Ltd v Continental Casualty Co (1963) 40 DLR (2d) 297, BC CA;
        affd (1963) 42 DLR (2d) 401n Can SC.
    DPP v Majewski [1976] 2 All ER 142, [1977] AC 443, HL; *affg* [1975] 3 All ER 296,
        [1977] AC 443, CA.
b   *Gay v Pacific Mutual Life Insurance Co* (1956) 237 F 2d 448, US Ct of Apps (5th Cir).
    Glenlight Shipping Ltd v Excess Insurance Co Ltd 1983 SLT 241.
    Harmon v Travellers Insurance Co (1937) 2 DLR 175, Alta SC.
    Jason v Batten (1930) Ltd, Jason v British Traders' Insurance Co Ltd [1969] 1 Lloyd's Rep
        281, CA.
    Jones v Allstate Insurance Co of Canada (1980) 40 NSR (2d) 469, NS SC.
c   *Jones v Prudential Insurance Co of America* [1972] OR 101, Grey Cty Ct (Ont).
    Leontowicz v Seaboard Life Insurance Co (1984) 16 DLR (4th) 95, Alta CA.
    Milashenko v Co-op Fire and Casualty Co (1968) 1 DLR (3d) 89, Sask CA; *rvsd* (1970)
        11 DLR (3d) 128, Can SC.
    Mutual Omaha Insurance Co v Stats (1978) 87 DLR (3d) 169, Can SC.
d   *Powley v Equitable Life Assurance Society of the US* (1939) 257 App Div 324 NY SC; *affd*
        (1940) 284 NY 664, NY Ct of Apps.
    Sloboda v Continental Casualty Co [1938] 3 DLR 166, Alta SC.
    Smith v British Pacific Life Insurance Co (1965) 51 DLR (2d) 1, Can SC.
    Tamelin v Pioneer Life Assurance Co (1990) 39 CCLI 306, BC SC.
e   *Voison v Royal Insurance Co of Canada* (1988) 66 OR (2d) 45, Ont CA.
    Wyman v Dominion of Canada Gen Ins Co [1936] 2 DLR 268, Ont SC.

Appeal

By notice dated 24 March 1994 the plaintiff, Kashmir Singh Dhak, appealed as administrator of the will of his wife, Inderjit Kaur Dhak (deceased), from the order
f   of Judge Malcolm Lee QC sitting as a judge of the High Court in the Queen's Bench Division at Birmingham on 28 February 1994, whereby he ordered that Mr Dhak's claim for recovery under a personal accident policy held by the deceased with the defendant, the Insurance Co of North America (UK) Ltd, should be dismissed and judgment entered for the defendant. The facts are set out in the judgment of Neill LJ.

g
Michael Spencer QC and Richard Hone (instructed by Graham Pearce & Co, Solihull)
    for the plaintiff.
Crawford Lindsay QC and David Pittaway (instructed by Barlow Lyde & Gilbert) for
    the defendant.

h   *Cur adv vult*

6 February 1996. The following judgments were delivered.

NEILL LJ. This is a tragic case. Indeed, no one could read the papers without feeling the greatest sympathy for Mr Kashmir Dhak, who lost his wife in such
j   distressing circumstances. At the same time, however, one has to recognise that the case raises important questions of law in the field of personal accident insurance.

Mrs Inderjit Dhak was aged 43 at the time of her death on 28 October 1986. She was a ward sister at the General Hospital in Birmingham, and had had many years of experience as a hospital nurse. In May and June 1986 Mrs Dhak suffered severe back pain which had been brought on as a result of lifting a heavy patient. She had a short period of treatment as an in-patient in a hospital in Solihull but then went

back to work. However, she continued to suffer significant pain. She began to
drink alcohol in the hope of relieving the pain, though there was no evidence that
she ever drank on a day when she had to go to work. Mr Dhak told the trial judge
that before his wife sustained the injury to her back she had only drunk socially.
After about June 1986, however, he said that there were occasions when she drank
to excess and he noticed that her speech would be slightly slurred.

About the beginning of October 1986 Mr and Mrs Dhak went on holiday for
two weeks. During the holiday Mrs Dhak only drank with meals and certainly not
to excess. On return from the holiday Mrs Dhak went back to work, but after a
few days she contracted a heavy cold or 'flu and had to remain at home. She was
off work from Sunday, 19 October and was due to go back to work on the evening
of Tuesday, 28 October 1986.

In the latter part of October Mr Dhak was working in London. It was necessary
for him to get up very early in the morning to catch a train at about 6 am and he
did not return until about 7 pm. In the evidence contained in his witness
statement Mr Dhak gave this account of what he observed during the week ended
25 October:

> 'I suspect that in the week she was off work, she was drinking during the
> day-time. I was at work, but noticed when I returned home most days, that
> she had been drinking. When I came home on each of those days, we ate a
> meal together, talked and went to bed between 10.30 and 11 pm.'

Mr Dhak then dealt with the events of Monday, 27 October and Tuesday, 28
October:

> 'On Monday 27 October, I went to work as usual, returning home about
> 7 pm. My wife had been drinking during that day. I could tell that she had
> had a few. Her speech was quite slurred. Probably as bad as any time I had
> heard her. She was still well under control however, and was not falling
> about. We ate a meal about 8 pm. She ate normally and seemed perfectly
> normal, apart from obviously having had some alcohol. She did not seem
> depressed and she was very much looking forward to returning to work the
> next day. We went to bed that evening between 10.30 and 11 pm. My wife
> suggested that I sleep in another bedroom so that she would not disturb me
> if she were tossing and turning. I do not believe that she had any more to
> drink that evening, nor after I had gone to bed. I am a very light sleeper and
> I am sure I would have heard if she had got up and was moving around. I
> woke up at my usual time the following morning, about 4.30 am. I had a
> shower and before I was due to go out I went in to see if she would like a cup
> of tea or coffee. Sometimes she did in the morning. I could not wake her and
> immediately became concerned. I called for an ambulance and for the doctor
> but it was too late. The doctor certified her dead at our home.'

A post mortem was carried out and an inquest was held. At the inquest evidence
was given by a pathologist to the effect that the blood/alcohol concentration in
Mrs Dhak's body showed a very high level. The verdict of the inquest as recorded
on 19 December 1987 was death by misadventure. On the death certificate dated
22 December 1986 the cause of death was shown as: '1. Acute alcoholism
2. Misadventure.'

I come now to the present proceedings. At the time of her death Mrs Dhak had
a personal accident policy which had been effected on her behalf as part of block
insurance arrangements made by the Royal College of Nursing with the Insurance

a Co of North America (UK) Ltd. The insurance policy specified the events for which benefits under it were payable as follows:

'Bodily injury resulting in Death or Injury within 12 months of the accident occurring during the Period of Insurance and caused directly or indirectly by the accident.'

b The benefit table specified that the sum payable on death was £50,000.

The policy contained a definition of the term 'Bodily Injury'. The definition was in these terms: 'Bodily Injury caused by accidental means, which shall include Disappearance and Exposure.' The policy also included an exclusion clause. The only potentially relevant exclusion was in these terms: 'This policy does not cover Bodily Injury caused by or resulting from ... suicide, any intentional self inflicted

c injury or sickness ...' The commencement date of the insurance was 30 June 1986.

In due course Mr Dhak obtained letters of administration of his late wife's estate and made a claim under the insurance policy. Liability, however, was repudiated. On 25 October 1990 the writ in these proceedings was issued.

On 18 December 1990 the defence was served. Though the pleading is not

d altogether clear it seems that it raised four issues. (1) The mechanism of death. It was said that the cause of death was the toxic effect of the deliberate ingestion of a very large quantity of alcohol. (2) Whether the deceased had suffered any bodily injury? This was denied. (3) Whether, if any bodily injury had been caused, this had been caused by accidental means? This too was denied. (4) Whether the insurers were entitled to rely on the exclusion clause on the basis

e that, if the bodily injury resulted from the deliberate ingestion by the deceased of a very large quantity of alcohol, it was caused by suicide and/or an intentional self-inflicted injury and/or sickness?

I can dispose of the fourth issue at once. It is clear that no reliance was placed on the exclusion clause before the judge, though he made a reference to it. In this

f court counsel for the insurers expressly disclaimed any reliance on the exclusion clause. He said, quite rightly as it seems to me, that the words 'intentional self-inflicted injury' related to circumstances where there was an actual intention to inflict injury.

The action was heard at Birmingham on 31 January and 1 February 1994 by Judge Malcolm Lee QC sitting as the designated mercantile judge. He gave

g judgment on 28 February 1994.

The judge heard evidence from Mr Dhak and from three distinguished pathologists, Dr Henry Thompson, Dr Roger Protheroe (who had carried out the original post-mortem examination) and Professor Usher.

Before turning to the issues which were debated in this court it will be

h convenient to set out the judge's findings of fact including his finding on the issue as to the mechanism of death. It is important to remember, however, when considering some of the evidence given in this case, that a substantial part of the expert evidence was directed to the question whether Mrs Dhak died as a result of the toxic effects of the alcohol or as a result of asphyxiation due to the inhalation

j of vomit.

The judge made the following findings:

'(1) At the time of her death the deceased had consumed a great quantity of alcohol. The precise amount of alcohol in her bloodstream cannot be measured with accuracy because the sample of blood was taken from the heart and that in the light of what is now known within pathology, might have been contaminated by leakage of the contents of the stomach.

(2) However, the deceased had at least 350 mg of alcohol per cent in her blood and probably a higher figure than that. I find that she had drunk so much alcohol that she had entered two danger zones. First, that she might inhale her vomit, and, secondly, that her brain might cease to function. Although Professor Usher had not himself encountered such a case, a well recognised and respected modern work on pathology "Forensic Pathology", published in 1991 by Professor Knight, spoke of death from such a mechanism as being possible with a reading of more than 350 mg per cent. (3) It is impossible to say precisely when the deceased died, between retiring to bed at 11 pm and being found at 4.30 am ... (4) I find that she must have consumed a considerable quantity of alcohol that night before she died and after the husband's return. She must have done so secretly, that is without the husband's knowledge, both before she went to bed and after she went to bed, and she must have been a great deal more drunk than she appeared to be at the time she went to bed, or must have consumed a considerable quantity of alcohol after that time. Light sleeper though the husband may have been, if asleep he might not have heard the deceased get up. There was no evidence before me as to what drink there had been in the house or where it was kept or what receptacles which had contained drink or might have contained drink were found and where. (5) She must have drunk at least the contents of a bottle of gin over a relatively short period and, as an intelligent woman and nursing sister when sober and in the early stages of intoxication, must have appreciated that such drinking presented a real danger to the drinker, in that vital bodily functions might be impaired or interrupted. (6) As to the precise mechanism of death I find that for the reasons advanced by Dr Thompson the immediate cause of death was the inhalation of vomit. In my judgment, Dr Thompson and Dr Protheroe are likely to be right about that and Professor Usher made a significant concession about the views he had originally held once he knew that the sample of blood came from the heart ... The death of the deceased in the instant case was closely and intimately related to the consumption of alcohol. There was a continuum leading from the ingestion of alcohol to an advanced stage of intoxication, to the dangerous relaxation of the body's reflexes, to inhalation of the contents of the stomach, to asphyxia and death.'

I come then to the issues which were argued in this court.

In order to bring the claim within the terms of the insurance policy it was necessary for Mr Dhak to establish: (1) that Mrs Dhak sustained a bodily injury; (2) that this bodily injury resulted in death; and (3) that this bodily injury was caused by accidental means.

It will be remembered that one of the important issues at the trial was whether Mrs Dhak died from the toxic effects of the ingestion of alcohol or whether she died through asphyxiation. It may be that it was for this reason that the question whether the inhalation of foreign matter which leads to asphyxiation does or does not involve some bodily injury was not fully explored when the three pathologists gave their evidence. Accordingly, in considering the questions whether Mrs Dhak suffered a bodily injury and whether that injury resulted in death, one must bear this point in mind.

In his report on the autopsy dated 6 November 1986 Dr Protheroe included the following finding under the heading 'Histological examination': 'Lungs show chronic passive venous congestion and pulmonary oedema.'

a   Sections of the lung were preserved for examination and in November 1992 Dr Protheroe and Dr Thompson reviewed these sections. They then found that there were some intra-alveolar asphyxial haemorrhages which Dr Protheroe had not previously commented on. These haemorrhages were later described in the course of the evidence as petechial haemorrhages.

b   Dr Thompson gave evidence about the condition of the lungs. He referred to Dr Protheroe's report of November 1986 and no doubt also took account of the review in November 1992. He said:

> '... in the lungs there is evidence of intense congestion of the blood vessels and also small intra-alveolar haemorrhages in the lungs which are consistent with asphyxia.'

c   He was then asked about these haemorrhages and replied:

> 'The term "alveoli" represents the respiratory [sic], a breathing compart-ment of the lungs, and large numbers of alveoli, tiny little sacs, microscopic sacs, and these sacs are lined by capillaries which, in the state of asphyxia and *d*   congestion, can rupture, leading to intra-alveolar haemorrhages.'

He said that both he and Dr Protheroe had examined the sections and agreed as to what could be observed.

In the course of his judgment the judge referred to the submissions on the question of bodily injury. He said:

e
> 'Mr Hone (on behalf of the husband) submitted to me that no clear external sign of injury is necessary for an injury to amount to bodily injury, and some internal injury would be enough. He gave as examples of such internal injuries, cardiac arrest, asphyxia, petechial haemorrhages the result of asphyxia, oedema, and, generally, the toxic effects of the ingestion of alcohol. *f*   Eventually he submitted that death itself and the bodily changes which necessarily occur at and following death amount to bodily injury.'

The judge then referred to some of the authorities which had been drawn to his attention and stated his conclusion:

g
> 'I conclude that the phrase "bodily injury resulting in death" should be given meaning as an ordinary phrase in the English language used in the context of this policy of insurance. It is not to be equated, in meaning, with death itself; otherwise the words "bodily injury resulting in" would be otiose. Nor are bodily changes consequent upon death or symptomatic of death or of a mechanism by which death has occurred sufficient to come within the *h*   meaning of the phrase. There must be resulting in death something which amounts to bodily injury. Here death came about as the result of the effect on the body and the reflex actions of the body of the ingestion over a period of time of an excessive amount of alcohol, and the immediate mechanism of death was asphyxia caused by regurgitation of the contents of the stomach of *j*   the deceased into her lungs. I do not find on those facts that there was here any bodily injury resulting in death, and the claim of the husband must fail by reason of that finding.'

Counsel for the insurers supported the judge's finding. In his helpful submissions he drew attention to the fact that in many of the authorities the court seemed to have assumed that some bodily injury had been caused, and the argument had been directed to whether the injury had been caused by accidental means. There had been no detailed analysis of what 'bodily injury' meant in the context of an accident policy.

Among the cases to which we were referred on the question of bodily injury were *Trew v Railway Passengers Assurance Co* (1861) 6 H & N 839, 158 ER 346, *Clidero v Scottish Accident Insurance Co Ltd* (1892) 19 R 355, *Hamlyn v Crown Accidental Insurance Co Ltd* [1893] 1 QB 750, *Re Scarr and General Accident Assurance Corp* [1905] 1 KB 387, [1904–7] All ER Rep 566 and *Re United London and Scottish Insurance Co, Brown's Claim* [1915] 2 Ch 167. In *Scarr's* case and *Clidero's* case the cause of death was heart failure brought on by some extra exertion. The basis of those decisions was that the 'injury' was not caused by accidental means.

The decision in *Trew's* case, however, is of more assistance. In that case the deceased went bathing in the sea. He disappeared. Some weeks later a body was found in the water and it was assumed that it was the body of the deceased. It was argued on behalf of the insurers that in order to recover under an accident policy it had to be proved that death had been caused by some outward and visible means capable of satisfactory proof. This argument was rejected by the Exchequer Chamber. Cockburn CJ said ((1861) 6 H & N 839 at 845, 158 ER 346 at 348–349):

> 'If [the jury] found that he died in the water, they might reasonably presume that he died from drowning. It is true, that death occurs in the water in some instances from natural causes, as apoplexy or cramp in the heart— but such cases are rare and bear a small proportion to the number of deaths which take place from the action of the water. We think it ought to be submitted to the jury to say whether the deceased died from the action of the water or natural causes. If they are of opinion that he died from the action of the water causing asphyxia, that is a death from external violence within the meaning of this policy,—whether he swam to a distance and had not strength enough to regain the shore, or on going into the water got out of his depth.'

The case was sent for a new trial.

It was argued on behalf of the insurers in the present case that asphyxia alone does not constitute bodily injury. Furthermore, the congestion of the lungs and the oedema were consequent upon asphyxia. Counsel added that he wished to reserve the question whether death by drowning involved any bodily injury resulting in death. He referred us to the evidence of the pathologists at the trial and submitted that all that had been established was that the signs found after death were features symptomatic of asphyxia.

I would reject these arguments. I am quite satisfied that Mrs Dhak's death resulted from bodily injury within the meaning of this policy. I can state my reasons quite shortly. (1) Counsel for the insurers was prepared to admit that in certain circumstances the swallowing of a peanut causing asphyxiation and death might involve bodily injury. But in such an event the mechanism of death would be similar to that in the present case. The blockage of the windpipe would lead to apnoea and after a short time to congestion of the lungs. This would be followed or accompanied by petechial haemorrhages and the absence of oxygen would then cause damage to the brain by anoxaemia. (2) Bodily injury will often involve some external trauma. But, in the absence of express words, I see no reason why bodily injury should be restricted to some injury to the exterior of the body. The introduction of some foreign matter into the body or into a particular part of the body which causes harmful physiological changes in the structure of the body can in my view amount to a bodily injury. I am unable to distinguish this case from the case referred to in argument of a peanut becoming lodged in the a trachea or windpipe, or the case considered by Judge Townsend in *Life and Casualty Insurance Co of Tennessee v Brown* (1957) 95 Ga App 354 (which was cited in *Koch v Empire Life Insurance Co* (1981) 124 DLR (3d) 161) where the insured, while being administered ether, vomited and the food particles in his stomach lodged in his windpipe causing anoxaemia of the brain resulting in his death. In *Brown*'s case the judge held, as I think rightly, that the patient was injured by the b lodging of food particles in his windpipe. (3) I find support for this view in the judgment of Brennan J in the High Court of Australia in *Australian Casualty Co Ltd v Federico* (1986) 160 CLR 513 at 535:

c 'The policy definition of "injury" is satisfied by a proximate cause of bodily injury which is both accidental and internal. Provided "injury" is understood as covering a pathological condition caused by any accidental force or event, the cover which the policy provides is probably the cover which an uninstructed purchaser of the sickness and accident policy would have expected to obtain ...'

(4) This conclusion is also consistent with the decision of Labrosse J in *Johnson v* d *Mutual of Omaha Insurance Co* (1982) 139 DLR (3d) 358, one of the comparatively few cases where the words 'bodily injury' have been considered quite separately from the cause of the bodily injury. In that case a sum was payable under an accident insurance policy on the death of the insured from accidental bodily injuries. The insured, a physician, died from suffocation caused by the voluntary inhalation of an anaesthetic. The judge considered first the argument that the e asphyxiation did not amount to 'bodily injuries' within the meaning of the policy. He said (at 364):

'Very little authority can be found as to the meaning of "bodily injuries". Most of the case-law appears to treat the phrase "accidental bodily injuries" as a unit and focuses on the question of accident, implicitly assuming or f accepting bodily injuries.'

The judge then referred to some dictionary definitions of 'bodily' and 'injury', and to two previous Canadian cases, in one of which it had been held that asphyxia could constitute an injury within the meaning of the policy. The judge concluded (at 365):

g 'In my view, the asphyxiation fatally injured the body of the deceased and his death was not caused by natural causes, illness or disease. I therefore conclude that death resulted from bodily injuries. The real issue is whether or not they were accidental.'

h I turn therefore to the most difficult issue in this case.

It will be remembered that 'bodily injury' was defined in the policy as 'bodily injury caused by accidental means'. It was argued on behalf of Mr Dhak that Mrs Dhak's death was plainly an accident. We were referred to the definition of 'accident' given by Lord Macnaghten in *Fenton v J Thorley & Co Ltd* [1903] AC 443 j at 448: 'an unlooked-for mishap or an untoward event which is not expected or designed.'

Counsel developed his argument on the following lines.

(1) The question to be answered in this case was: did Mrs Dhak die as a result of an accident? English law did not distinguish between an accidental result and accidental means.

(2) It was true that in some other jurisdictions the law did draw a distinction between an accidental result and accidental means, but this distinction was not

part of the law of England. The passages in the judgment of Mustill LJ in *De Souza v Home and Overseas Insurance Co Ltd* [1995] LRLR 453, relied upon by the insurers, were obiter dicta and were not necessary for the decision in that case.

(3) The proposition contended for was supported by the decision of the Court of Appeal in *Hamlyn v Crown Accidental Insurance Co* [1893] 1 QB 750. In that case the policy effected by the plaintiff was to secure compensation in case he sustained 'any bodily injury caused by violent, accidental, external, and visible means'. The plaintiff, who was a tradesman, was standing by the counter in his shop when a customer came in with a child. The child dropped a marble which rolled away on the sloping floor. The plaintiff stooped to pick it up and in doing so wrenched his knee. He was disabled for some time. Counsel drew attention to a passage in the judgment of Lord Esher MR where, in referring to the movement of the plaintiff to pick up the marble, he said (at 753):

'He seems to have done this awkwardly; at all events, in doing it he wrenched his knee, and that did the mischief, and that wrench was the cause of the injury. That that was accidental I cannot doubt.'

In addition counsel drew attention to a sentence in the judgment of Lopes LJ where he said (at 754): 'The cause of the injury was accidental in the sense that the injury was a casualty and unforeseen and unexpected.' In this passage, it was said, Lopes LJ was plainly drawing no distinction between an accidental result and an accidental cause.

In this context we were also referred to a note in 25 *Halsbury's Laws* (4th edn reissue) para 576:

'If the phrase "accidental means" is used in the policy, it seems that it is synonymous with, or at any rate adds nothing to, the phrase "by accident": see *Hamlyn v Crown Accidental Insurance Co* ...'

(4) In his powerful dissenting judgment in *Landress v Phoenix Mutual Life Insurance* (1934) 291 US 491 Justice Cardozo deplored the attempted distinction between accidental results and accidental means. In an apparent reference to Milton's *Paradise Lost* he said (at 498–500, para 3): 'The attempted distinction between accidental results and accidental means will plunge this branch of the law into a Serbonian Bog.' A little later he added: 'When a man has died in such a way that his death is spoken of as an accident, he has died because of an accident, and hence by accidental means.'

(5) Alternatively, if English law does draw a distinction between accidental results and accidental means, it is then necessary to look at the 'proximate cause', that is, the effective or dominant cause of the injury. Counsel accepted that 'proximate cause' did not mean the cause which was the nearest in time to the relevant occurrence, but that which was the effective or dominant cause (see *Gray v Barr (Prudential Assurance Co Ltd, third party)* [1971] 2 All ER 949 at 955, [1971] 2 QB 554 at 567). In the present case, it was submitted, the proximate cause was the inhalation of the vomit. The ingestion of alcohol was merely part of the background.

(6) The examples given by Gibbs CJ in the *Federico* case were instructive. He said (160 CLR 513 at 521):

'The words "caused by an accident" naturally refer to the proximate or direct cause of the injury, and not to a cause of the cause, or to the mere occasion of the injury. Thus ... if a man while walking stumbles and sprains his ankle, the injury is caused by an accident—the stumbling—and not by the a   deliberate act of walking. Or a person goes swimming, becomes exhausted and drowns—surely the death is caused by an accident.'

The decision of the Court of Appeal in *Winspear v Accident Insurance Co Ltd* (1880) 6 QBD 42 was also of assistance. In that case the deceased was an epileptic. The policy against accidental injury contained a proviso that the insurance should not extend to any injury caused by or arising from natural disease or weakness or

b   exhaustion consequent upon disease. While crossing a stream near Birmingham the deceased was seized by an epileptic fit and fell down in the stream and was drowned. Lord Coleridge CJ, in a judgment with which the other members of the court agreed, said (at 45): 'The death was not caused by any natural disease or weakness or exhaustion consequent upon disease, but by the accident of

c   drowning.'

(7) It was accepted that 'accidental means' did not extend to the case where the proximate cause was the deliberate taking of an appreciated risk. An example of a case involving a calculated risk was provided by the decision of Grant J in *Candler v London and Lancashire Guarantee and Accident Co* (1963) 40 DLR (2d) 408. In that case the insured, to show his nerve to a friend, went out to the patio of his

d   13th-floor hotel suite and sat on the coping round the patio with his feet drawn up. While trying to balance himself he slipped and fell to his death. The deceased had been drinking. The judge described the deceased's conduct as foolhardy and attended with the most obvious danger (see 40 DLR (2d) 408 at 423).

In the present case, however, Mrs Dhak did not take a calculated risk. The

e   judge was wrong to conclude that Mrs Dhak must have appreciated that her drinking presented a real danger. There was no evidence to this effect. In any event it was to be remembered that the drinking was to relieve pain and that, whatever the position may have been in the early stages, Mrs Dhak's judgment would have been seriously affected at the crucial time when her intoxication became dangerous.

f   (8) The judge was wrong to rely on the principle that 'a man is taken to intend the natural consequences of his acts'. As Judge Edgar Fay QC recognised in *Marcel Beller Ltd v Hayden* [1978] 3 All ER 111 at 119, [1978] QB 694 at 704–705 the law did not require the application of an objective test of risk-running. Furthermore, this view of the law was supported by a passage in the judgment of Samuels JA in

g   *National and General Insurance Co v Chick* [1984] 2 NSWLR 86 at 103:

'I do not perceive the relevance of invoking the somewhat dubious principle that a man must be taken to intend the ordinary consequence of his acts.'

h   These arguments were put forward most clearly and cogently. I have also taken account of the fact that, on Mr Dhak's uncontradicted evidence, Mrs Dhak was looking forward to her return to work. In ordinary language it could well be said that Mrs Dhak's death was indeed a tragic accident.

I have come to the conclusion, however, that it has not been established that the bodily injury to Mrs Dhak was 'caused by accidental means' within the

j   meaning of the policy. In reaching this conclusion I have been persuaded that the words 'caused by accidental means' are a clear indication that it is the cause of the injury to which the court must direct its attention.

I can turn at once to the judgment of Mustill LJ in *De Souza* [1995] LRLR 453 at 458–459. Mustill LJ adopted as representing his own opinion the summary of the law set out in Welford *The Law Relating to Accident Insurance* (1923) pp 295–296, 299:

'The word "accident" involves the idea of something fortuitous and
unexpected, as opposed to something proceeding from natural causes; and
injury caused by accident is to be regarded as the antithesis to bodily infirmity
by disease in the ordinary course of events. An injury is caused by accident in
the following cases, namely: (1) Where the injury is the natural result of a
fortuitous and unexpected cause, as, for instance, where the assured is run
over by a train, or thrown from his horse whilst hunting, or injured by a fall,
whether through slipping on a step or otherwise; or where the assured drinks
poison by mistake, or is suffocated by the smoke of a house on fire or by an
escape of gas, or is drowned whilst bathing. In this case the element of
accident manifests itself in the cause of the injury. (2) Where the injury is the
fortuitous or unexpected result of a natural cause, as, for instance, where a
person lifts a heavy burden in the ordinary course of business and injures his
spine, or stoops down to pick up a marble and breaks a ligament in his knee,
or scratches his leg with his nail whilst putting on a stocking, or ruptures
himself whilst playing golf. In this case the element of accident manifests
itself, not in the cause, but in its result. On the other hand, an injury is not
caused by accident when it is the natural result of a natural cause as, for
instance, where a person is exposed in the ordinary course of his business to
the heat of a tropical sun and in consequence suffers from sunstroke, or
where a person with a weak heart injures it by running to catch a train, or by
some other intentional act involving violent physical exertion. In this case
the element of accident is broadly speaking absent, since the cause is one
which comes into operation in the ordinary course of events, and is
calculated, within the ordinary experience of mankind, to produce the result
which it has in fact produced. In considering whether an injury is caused by
accident, it is necessary to take into consideration the circumstances in which
the injury is received.'

Mustill LJ then referred to the examples given by *Welford* and a little later
continued with the quotation:

'The same principles apply where the injury is the result, not of natural
causes, but of the intervention of human agency. Two cases have to be
distinguished, namely: (1) Where the injury is caused by the act of a third
person ... (2) Where the injury is caused by the act of the assured himself. An
injury may be caused by accident within the meaning of the policy, although
it is caused by the act of the assured. The following cases must be
distinguished, namely ... (ii) An injury which is the natural and direct
consequence of an act deliberately done by the assured is not caused by
accident. A man must be taken to intend the ordinary consequences of his
acts, and the fact that he did not foresee the particular consequence or expect
the particular injury does not make the injury accidental if, in the
circumstances, it was the natural and direct consequence of what he did,
without the intervention of any fortuitous cause. Thus, where physical
exertion, deliberately intended, such as, for instance, running to catch a train,
throws a strain upon his heart at a time when it is in a weak and unhealthy
condition, in consequence of which the assured dies, his death is not to be
regarded as accidental merely because the assured did not know of his
condition and therefore did not foresee the effect, provided that it was the
natural and direct consequence of a strain being put upon a heart in that
condition.'

a   It is to be noted that these passages were repeated by Mr Welford in the second edition of his book published in 1932 (see pp 268–269, 272–273).

I am unable to accept the submission that Mustill LJ's summary of the law was obiter. The judgment, with which the other members of the Court of Appeal agreed, was given in the context of a claim by the wife of the insured who had been on holiday in Torremolinos where he sustained heat stroke by reason of
b   excessive exposure to the sun and subsequently died. Mustill LJ's examination of the principles to be applied and of the relevant authorities was directed to dealing with the question whether the insured had sustained 'accidental bodily injury' within the meaning of his insurance policy. Mustill LJ said ([1995] LRLR 453 at 463):

c   'Did Mr. De Souza suffer an "injury"? I cannot see that he did. To my mind he unfortunately became ill and died. Where was the element of "accident" in his illness? The plaintiff has never identified what the accident was, or when it happened. So far as we know there was normal sun, normal heat, and normal exposure to them, which for some reason sadly led to Mr. De Souza's death.'
d

    In the course of the argument we were referred to a number of cases on 'accidental' injuries decided not only in this country but also in Australia, Canada, the United States and New Zealand. Some of the decisions are impossible to reconcile.

e   In a number of the Canadian decisions the distinction between accidental means and accidental results has been rejected. The conflicting authorities were considered by Nunn J in his judgment in *Tracy-Gould v Maritime Life Assurance Co* (1992) 89 DLR (4th) 726. Nunn J concluded that the distinction between 'accidental bodily injury' and 'bodily injury caused by an accident' was not a real distinction (89 DLR (4th) 726 at 732).

f   In my judgment, however, whatever the position may be in some other jurisdictions, the terms of this policy require a court in this country to concentrate on the cause of the injury and to inquire whether the injury was caused by accidental means. Furthermore, this approach is consistent with a number of the Commonwealth cases to which we were referred, including the decision of the
g   Court of Appeal in New Zealand in *Long v Colonial Mutual Life Assurance* [1931] NZLR 536 at 538.

    It will be remembered that it was argued on behalf of Mr Dhak that the decision of the Court of Appeal in *Hamlyn v Crown Accidental Insurance Co Ltd* [1893] 1 QB 750 supported the proposition that English law drew no distinction between an accidental result and an accidental cause. I have come to the conclusion,
h   however, that the judgments of Lord Esher MR and A L Smith LJ do not support this argument. The policy under consideration included the words 'any bodily injury caused by violent, accidental, external, and visible means'. Lord Esher MR referred to 'the cause of the injury' and then considered 'was the cause of the injury something violent?' (see [1893] 1 QB 750 at 753). Later he added 'because
j   the cause of the injury was not internal it must have been "external"'. It is clear that he was concentrating on the word 'cause'. The judgment of A L Smith LJ is even more explicit. He said (at 755):

         'By what means was the plaintiff injured and his knee put out? There cannot be a question that the means were violent. They were also accidental, for getting into the particular position in which the injury could happen was not done on purpose. Then, were they external? I think the word must be understood as meaning the opposite of internal. The means by which the injury was caused were the stooping on the part of the plaintiff and his grabbing at the marble to pick it up ...'

I would therefore reject Mr Spencer's first argument.

I turn to his argument on proximate cause. It was common ground between counsel that a proximate cause meant the effective or dominant cause. The point at issue was the application of the law to the facts. The submission on behalf of Mr Dhak was that the excessive intake of alcohol was a part of the background, but not the effective cause of the injury.

In my judgment, however, the correct approach to the question of cause in this case is to adopt the analysis approved by Mustill LJ in *De Souza*. In addition one should consider whether the insured took a calculated risk. I would put the matter as follows.

Where an insured embarks deliberately on a course of conduct which leads to some bodily injury one has to consider the following questions. (a) Did the insured intend to inflict some bodily injury to himself? (b) Did the insured take a calculated risk that if he continued with that course of conduct he might sustain some bodily injury? (c) Was some bodily injury the natural and direct consequence of the course of conduct? (d) Did some fortuitous cause intervene?

In this case there is no suggestion whatever that Mrs Dhak intended any bodily injury to herself. One has therefore to examine the other three questions. At the same time one must take account of all the circumstances including the state of knowledge or presumed state of knowledge of the insured. In considering what could be foreseen one must apply the standard of foresight of the reasonable person with the attributes of the insured.

It was strongly argued on behalf of Mr Dhak that the inhalation of vomit was unforeseen and unforeseeable. I have considered this argument with the greatest of care but I have come to the conclusion that the judge was justified in finding that Mrs Dhak must have been well aware of the consequences and dangers of drinking alcohol to excess and that she must be taken to have foreseen what might happen in the event of someone drinking to excess. She was a ward sister with many years of experience as a nurse. The judge found as a fact that Mrs Dhak must have drunk at least the contents of a bottle of gin over a relatively short period. I am satisfied that there must have been a point at which she would have realised that any further drinking would be dangerous and that vital bodily functions might be impaired or interrupted.

As I said at the outset of this judgment one feels the greatest sympathy for Mr Dhak at his tragic loss. I feel quite unable to say, however, that Mrs Dhak's injury and death were the result of some fortuitous cause. It was the direct consequence of her drinking to excess. Indeed, I feel bound to say that for someone with her knowledge and experience she must be regarded as having taken a calculated risk of sustaining some bodily injury.

For these reasons I would dismiss this appeal.

ALDOUS LJ. I agree.

SIR JOHN BALCOMBE. I also agree.

Appeal dismissed. Leave to appeal refused.

Paul Magrath Esq   Barrister.

a # Ernst & Young (a firm) v Butte Mining plc

CHANCERY DIVISION

ROBERT WALKER J

23, 26 FEBRUARY, 6 MARCH 1996

b *Practice – Discontinuance of action – Discontinuance by plaintiff – Plaintiff obtaining judgment in default – Defendant applying to set aside – Affidavit in support exhibiting defence and counterclaim – Parties agreeing consent order setting aside default judgment with unconditional liberty to serve defence and counterclaim – Plaintiff's solicitors obtaining carriage of consent order – Plaintiff discontinuing action*
c *immediately – Whether defendant's counterclaim surviving discontinuance – Whether consent order excluding plaintiff's right to discontinue – Whether service of notice of discontinuance an abuse of process – RSC Ord 15, r 2(3).*

In 1992 the plaintiff firm commenced proceedings against the defendant company claiming some £315,000 in unpaid professional fees for its work as auditor and
d reporting accountant for the defendant's flotation on the stock exchange. In March 1995 the plaintiff entered judgment in the fees action in default of a defence. In support of its subsequent application to set aside the judgment, the defendant filed an affidavit exhibiting a draft defence and counterclaim for £1·9m, alleging breach of duty (including conspiracy) in connection with its earlier acquisition of another company. A further affidavit was later filed which exhibited a fuller defence and
e counterclaim for damages of around £100m. The parties' solicitors later conducted without prejudice discussions with a view to setting aside the default judgment on terms, during which reference was made to directions in the fees action. Neither solicitor referred expressly to the possibility of discontinuance. On 31 January 1996 the court sealed a consent order setting aside the default judgment and providing
f that the defendant 'be at liberty unconditionally' to serve its defence and counterclaim on the plaintiff. The plaintiff's solicitors, who had obtained carriage of the order, received it soon after midday on 1 February and at 1.20 pm they faxed a notice of discontinuance to the defendant's solicitors, followed at 1.50 pm by a copy of the perfected order. At 2.20 pm they served both the order and the notice of discontinuance on the defendant's solicitors. At 3.45 pm the defendant's solicitors
g served the defence and counterclaim, in the same form as that exhibited to the affidavit, on the plaintiff's solicitors. The defendant applied to set aside service of the notice of discontinuance as an abuse of the process of the court.

Held – (1) The general rule that a counterclaim could be set up only when a
h pleading in the form of a counterclaim, or some equivalent document, was served, could be widened to include cases where a defendant had formally placed before the court evidence of sufficient weight, backed by sufficient undertakings, to persuade the court to grant relief appropriate on the basis that the defendant was making (and would in the near future formally complete the making of) a counterclaim. On that test, the defendant had not made a counterclaim, either by the swearing of the
j affidavit with its exhibited draft or by that affidavit and exhibit in combination with the consent order, which would survive the plaintiff's notice of discontinuance under RSC Ord 15, r 2(3)[a] (see p 633 *d* to *j* and p 640 *f*, post); *Impex Transport Aktieselskabet v A G Thames Holdings Ltd* [1982] 1 All ER 897 and *Fakih Bros v A P Moller (Copenhagen) Ltd* [1994] 1 Lloyd's Rep 103 considered.

---

a   Rule 2, so far as material, is set out at p 628 *j*, post

(2) When litigants agreed through their legal representatives to a consent order of an interlocutory nature, there was seldom (at least in routine cases) an enforceable contract apart from their bare consent to or concurrence in the terms of the order. In the instant case, the consent order was not a routine matter; however, on the balance of probability, it was not clear that the solicitors had intended to conclude any larger agreement than that embodied in the agreed consent order. Construed naturally, without reference to the solicitors' actual intention, the consent order did not, either expressly or by necessary implication, exclude the plaintiff's ordinary right to serve a notice of discontinuance (see p 636 *d* to *f*, p 637 *b c* and p 640 *g*, post).

(3) Even in the most hostile litigation solicitors had to be scrupulously fair and not take unfair advantage of obvious mistakes, particularly where the solicitor in question had been a major contributing cause of the mistake. In the circumstances, the fact that the defendant's solicitor had readily agreed to the plaintiff's solicitors having carriage of the consent order was the clearest indication that she had come to believe that the plaintiff was not going to discontinue the action in the near future, and the misleading conduct of the plaintiff's solicitor during the discussions was the major cause of that mistaken belief. It followed that service of the plaintiff's notice of discontinuance was an abuse of process and would be set aside unconditionally (see p 639 *e f j* and p 640 *g h*, post).

Notes

For counterclaim against the plaintiff, see 37 *Halsbury's Laws* (4th edn) para 248.

For discontinuance and withdrawal, see ibid paras 280–284, and for cases on the subject, see 37(2) *Digest* 419–422, 2565–2583.

Cases referred to in judgment

Artoc Bank and Trust Ltd v Prudential Assurance Co plc [1984] 3 All ER 538, [1984] 1 WLR 1181.

Bildt v Foy (1892) 9 TLR 34, DC; *affd* (1892) 9 TLR 83, CA.

Castanho v Brown & Root (UK) Ltd [1981] 1 All ER 143, [1981] AC 557, [1980] 3 WLR 991, HL; *affg* [1980] 3 All ER 72, [1980] 1 WLR 833, CA.

CSI International Co Ltd v Archway Personnel (Middle East) Ltd [1980] 3 All ER 215, [1980] 1 WLR 1069, CA.

Derby & Co Ltd v Weldon (No 8) [1990] 3 All ER 762, [1991] 1 WLR 73, Ch D and CA.

Fakih Bros v A P Moller (Copenhagen) Ltd [1994] 1 Lloyd's Rep 103.

Fox v Star Newspaper Co Ltd [1900] AC 19, HL; *affg* [1898] 1 QB 636, CA.

General Accident Fire and Life Assurance Corp Ltd v IRC [1963] 1 All ER 618, [1963] 1 WLR 421.

General Railway Syndicate, Re, Whiteley's Case [1900] 1 Ch 365, CA.

Gniezno, The, Owners of the Motor Vessel Popi v Owners of the Steamship or Vessel Gniezno [1967] 2 All ER 738, [1968] P 418, [1967] 3 WLR 705.

Impex Transport Aktieselskabet v A G Thames Holdings Ltd (t/a John Gibb & Sons) [1982] 1 All ER 897, [1981] 1 WLR 1547.

Prenn v Simmonds [1971] 3 All ER 237, [1971] 1 WLR 1381, HL.

Salybia, The [1910] P 25.

Saxicava, The [1924] P 131, CA.

Siebe Gorman & Co Ltd v Pneupac Ltd [1982] 1 All ER 377, [1982] 1 WLR 185, CA.

Cases also cited or referred to in skeleton arguments

Commission for the New Towns v Cooper (GB) Ltd [1995] 2 All ER 929, [1995] Ch 259, CA.

Goldsmith v Sperrings Ltd [1977] 2 All ER 566, [1977] 1 WLR 478, CA.

a   *Stirling v Maitland* (1864) 5 B & S 840, [1861–73] All ER Rep 358, 122 ER 1043.
Trentham (G Percy) Ltd v Archital Luxfer Ltd [1993] 1 Lloyd's Rep 25, CA.

Motion

By notice of motion issued on 6 February 1996 the defendant, Butte Mining plc (Butte), applied for an order that service of a notice of discontinuance given on 1 February 1996 by the plaintiff, Ernst & Young, a firm of chartered accountants, of its *b*   action against the defendant for unpaid professional fees, be set aside as an abuse of the process of the court. The facts are set out in the judgment.

Alan Boyle QC and *Douglas Close* (instructed by *Frere Cholmeley Bischoff*) for Butte.
Jonathan Hirst QC and *Neil Calver* (instructed by *Barlow Lyde & Gilbert*) for Ernst &
     Young.
c
                                                                    Cur adv vult

6 March 1996. The following judgment was delivered.

ROBERT WALKER J. I have before me a notice of motion issued on 6 February 1996 on behalf of Butte Mining plc, the defendant in the proceedings. The most *d*   substantial and controversial relief sought by the notice of motion is the setting aside of a notice of discontinuance given on 1 February 1996 on behalf of the plaintiff, Ernst & Young, the well-known accountants.

The claim to set aside the notice of discontinuance raises some technical questions about the making of counterclaims. It also raises some non-technical questions about what is acceptable or unacceptable in solicitors' conduct of hostile *e*   litigation. For that reason I did, exceptionally on an interlocutory application, allow cross-examination of two of the deponents on their affidavits. But I must first explain the way in which these questions have arisen.

THE BACKGROUND

f   Four sets of proceedings—three in this country and one in the United States—come into the story. They are, in chronological order of commencement, as follows.

(1) An action (the Montana action) was commenced on 20 May 1992 by Butte and three co-plaintiffs in a United States federal court, that is the United States District Court for the district of Montana, against over 70 defendants, including *g*   Ernst & Young and Simon Engineering plc.

(2) This present action (the fees action) was commenced by Ernst & Young against Butte (they being the only parties) on 26 May 1992.

(3) On 14 February 1995 (shortly after the Montana action had failed at first instance for want of subject matter jurisdiction) Ernst & Young commenced an *h*   action (the anti-suit action) in the Commercial Court in England to restrain Butte from pursuing an appeal in the Montana action. Simon had a few days before begun a similar anti-suit action.

(4) On 21 July 1995 Butte commenced an action (the Gramcol action) in the Chancery Division in England claiming damages against Ernst & Young as accountants and auditors of Butte in connection with its acquisition of a company *j*   called Gramcol Zircon Ltd.

Of this litigation only the anti-suit action has been finally disposed of, although for practical purposes the Montana action is at an end so far as Ernst & Young and Simon are concerned. The course taken by the anti-suit action (and Simon's similar action) was that Rix J granted Ernst & Young an interlocutory injunction (restraining Butte from appealing in the Montana action) on 27 February 1995. Butte did not agree to treat this as the trial of the action and the action was heard at

the end of July 1995 by Miss Barbara Dohmann QC, sitting as a deputy judge of the
High Court. She granted a final injunction on 3 October 1995. An appeal to the *a*
Court of Appeal from her order was abandoned only a week before the hearing of
this motion, and that has for practical purposes permanently halted any appeal to
the United States Court of Appeals in the Montana action so far as Ernst & Young
and Simon are concerned.

The judgments of Rix J and Miss Dohmann QC are reported ([1996] 1 Lloyd's Rep *b*
104 and 91 respectively) and reference can be made to those reports for a detailed
account of this complicated litigation. What follows is a very brief summary.

The Montana action arose out of events of 1987 and 1988 when Arthur Young
(a firm of accountants who became part of Ernst & Young) were Butte's auditors
and acted as reporting accountants for Butte's flotation. Butte was incorporated on
12 August 1987 and floated on the London Stock Exchange on 1 October 1987. *c*
There was then a further issue of shares made by Butte for the acquisition (on 26
April 1988) of another English company, North Butte Investments Ltd.

The Montana action was therefore an action by an English company (its
co-plaintiffs were mere shells) against English accountants over work done mostly
in England in connection with an English flotation. The grounds on which Butte *d*
nevertheless sought to establish Montana as the forum, and its reasons for doing so,
appear from Miss Dohmann QC's judgment (Mr Lloyd-Jacob has been the chairman
of Butte since May 1991, and is the driving force behind the Montana action; the
Robertson companies produced reports for the listing particulars and were later
acquired by Simon):

    'After Mr. Lloyd-Jacob had come on to the scene Butte began to prepare for *e*
litigation in the United States on the basis, inter alia, that Robertson companies
had been promoters of Butte and shareholders in land owning companies in
Montana which were sold to Butte at great, allegedly secret, profit.   In
February, 1992 contingency fee terms were agreed with U.S. attorneys.   On
Apr. 29, 1992 Butte's board approved Mr. Lloyd-Jacob's and another director's *f*
right to receive a percentage of the net proceeds of the United States litigation.
On May 20, 1992 Butte filed a complaint in the United States District Court for
the district of Montana against some 77 defendants, of whom 27 are residents
of, or companies incorporated in, England and Wales. The defendants of real
or the greatest substance are Simon and Ernst & Young. Federal causes of
action are required to launch a claim in a Federal Court. Butte accordingly *g*
relied on alleged securities fraud contrary to United States Securities Exchange
Act, 1934 and claimed treble damages under the Racketeering Influenced and
Corrupt Organisations Act ("RICO"). The alleged causes of action not based
on a United States statute include fraud, breach of contract, negligence, breach
of duty, negligent misrepresentation, constructive trust and secret profits.' (See *h*
[1996] 1 Lloyd's Rep 91 at 93.)

It was in these circumstances that Butte decided, as their leading counsel is recorded
as having told Miss Dohmann QC, to 'live or die' by its decision to sue in Montana
(see [1996] 1 Lloyd's Rep 91 at 100).

I need not go further into the issues in the Montana action except to say that the *j*
claims against Ernst & Young included claims which plainly could not be pleaded
against that firm in this country, and the damages claimed (in reliance on the
Racketeering Influenced and Corrupt Organisations Act) were enormous: of the
order, it is suggested, of US $2b. In comparison to that claim the sums involved in
the other claims, although substantial by any normal standards, are relatively
modest: about £315,000 (plus interest) in the fees action; about £5·5m in the

a Gramcol action, and a figure of the order of perhaps £100m for the claims in the defunct Montana action, which (shorn of triple damages and other excesses) Butte now seeks to bring by way of counterclaim in the fees action. These are only rough figures, but they give an idea of the scale of the various claims and cross-claims. This is needed in order to understand the tactical planning and manoeuvring on which both sides have been engaged during the past few months.

b THE FEES ACTION

I must now return, in a little more detail, to the history of the fees action. Ernst & Young claimed a liquidated sum of about £315,000 for professional fees (in respect of a period spanning 1990 and 1991, that is, later than the events raised in the Montana action) and also an account. Soon after the fees action had been started

c (and before Butte had put in a defence) Ernst & Young was enjoined by the United States federal court in Montana from taking any further steps in the fees action, and the injunction was upheld by the United States Court of Appeals. This standstill continued until 31 January 1995, when Chief Judge Hatfield dismissed the whole of the Montana action, with immediate effect, for lack of subject matter jurisdiction. Ernst & Young served notice of intention to proceed on 3 February 1995, and on 7

d March 1995 entered judgment in default of defence on the strength of its liquidated claim (the claim for an account being abandoned). On the same day Butte issued a summons for a stay of execution. It will be in mind that this was shortly after Rix J had granted an interlocutory injunction, but with Butte intending to go to trial, in the anti-suit action.

e Butte's application to set aside the default judgment was supported by two short affidavits sworn by Mr Steven Loble, the solicitor then acting for Butte. He deposed that the omission to serve a defence in the fees action had been inadvertent. On 7 April 1995 Mr Lloyd-Jacob swore an affidavit exhibiting a draft defence and counterclaim which Butte wished to put in in the fees action. These alleged breaches of duty, including conspiracy, on the part of Ernst & Young in connection

f with the acquisition of Gramcol (which took place in the second half of 1989). The draft counterclaim claimed 'at least £1·9m'. The draft counterclaim made no reference to the issues in the Montana action (which arose, it will be in mind, from events of 1987 and 1988). Mr Loble's affidavits had made no reference to any allegation of a conspiracy.

g Mr Michael Lynch-Bell (a partner in Ernst & Young) swore an affidavit in opposition in 28 April 1995 in which he said, of the allegation of conspiracy:

> 'The reason why it was never mentioned until the draft Defence was exhibited to Mr Lloyd-Jacob's affidavit is that the claim is wholly spurious and belatedly raised in a transparently dishonest attempt to have a simple judgment
h of long-outstanding fee notes for work done by a reputable firm of accountants and auditors set aside.'

This is one of many possible illustrations of the fact that (as Mr Jonathan Hirst QC for Ernst & Young put it, and as Mr Alan Boyle QC for Butte does not dispute) this litigation has been conducted with the utmost vigour, and with no quarter asked for

j or given on either side.

The application to set aside the default judgment had been fixed for 2 May 1995. It was, however, adjourned generally, and soon afterwards Butte instructed their present solicitors, Messrs Frere Cholmeley Bischoff (FCB).

On 24 July 1995 (just before the trial of the anti-suit action before Miss Dohmann QC) Mr Lloyd-Jacob made a second long affidavit which referred to the commencement of the Gramcol action as a separate action ('in order to insure that

no limitation periods passed'). It set out at length the defence which Butte wished
to rely on in the fees action. It did not refer to any possible counterclaim in the fees *a*
action (Butte's complaints about the Gramcol episode, shorn of allegations of
conspiracy, being now raised in the Gramcol action).

The hearing of the summons to set aside the default judgment was further
adjourned, by consent. It was relisted for 30 January 1996, that is a few weeks before
the date for the hearing of Butte's appeal in the anti-suit action. Then on 21 *b*
December 1995 Mr Lloyd-Jacob swore a third and even longer affidavit, setting out
the nature of its claims against Ernst & Young which had formed part of its claims
in the Montana action, and exhibiting a draft defence and counterclaim which was
said to have superseded the draft exhibited to Mr Lloyd-Jacob's first affidavit. The
matters raised in the draft counterclaim had not previously been raised in any
English proceedings, and the damages claimed were (as I have already mentioned) *c*
of the order of perhaps £100m. There was also an affidavit sworn on 21 December
1995 by Mr Frederick Jackson, a partner in Price Waterhouse, deposing to his belief
in the substance of the proposed counterclaim. Mr Lloyd-Jacob's third affidavit was
not filed (the same may be true of other affidavits which I have mentioned, but Mr
Lloyd-Jacob's third affidavit is the crucial affidavit for present purposes). *d*

That is how matters stood at the beginning of 1996, and the events which are
directly material to this motion took place within the space of ten days at the end of
January and the beginning of February 1996. In bare summary, there were without
prejudice discussions between the parties' solicitors which led to a consent order
being obtained, without a hearing, setting aside the judgment in default. Ernst &
Young's solicitors, Messrs Barlow Lyde & Gilbert (BLG) had the carriage of this *e*
order. The perfected order (the consent order) bore the date 25 January 1996, but it
was not sealed by the court until 31 January 1996. The sealed order was obtained by
BLG soon after midday on 1 February. At 1.20 pm on that day BLG faxed a notice
of discontinuance to FCB. At 1.50 pm BLG faxed a copy of the perfected order to
FCB. At 2.20 pm BLG served or re-served on FCB the order and the notice of *f*
discontinuance. At 3.45 pm FCB served the defence and counterclaim on BLG. (I
have omitted 'purportedly'(s) but as may be imagined such expressions recur in the
skeleton arguments and submissions.) The counterclaim was (apart from some
trivial corrections) in the same form as that exhibited to Mr Lloyd-Jacob's third
affidavit.

g
DISCONTINUANCE

Discontinuance is the process by which a plaintiff (or plaintiff by counterclaim)
may put an end to the whole of his claim in the proceedings in question. It has
featured in the Rules of the Supreme Court for well over a century, having
superseded older procedures such as non-suit or voluntary dismissal of a bill in *h*
chancery (see *Fox v Star Newspaper Co Ltd* [1900] AC 19; *affg* [1898] 1 QB 636).

Discontinuance of an action is now provided for by RSC Ord 21, rr 2 to 5. Notice
of discontinuance can in general be given without leave at any time not later than
14 days after service of the defence. Otherwise the leave of the court is required and
may be given 'on such terms as to costs, the bringing of a subsequent action or
otherwise as it thinks just.' *j*

RSC Ord 15, r 2 permits a defendant to counterclaim against the plaintiff. Order
15, r 2(3) provides:

'A counterclaim may be proceeded with notwithstanding that judgment is
given for the plaintiff in the action or that the action is stayed, discontinued or
dismissed.'

a   A plaintiff's apparently unfettered right to discontinue before or within 14 days after defence is, however, subject to the overriding rule that discontinuance will not be permitted if it is an abuse of process. That was established by the House of Lords in *Castanho v Brown & Root (UK) Ltd* [1981] 1 All ER 143, [1981] AC 557. Although the House of Lords affirmed the decision of the Court of Appeal ([1980] 3 All ER 72, [1980] 1 WLR 833), they preferred the first instance judgment of Parker J and the

b   dissenting judgment of Lord Denning MR on this issue. Lord Scarman referred to the view of Shaw LJ ([1980] 3 All ER 72 at 88, [1980] 1 WLR 833 at 864) that it was 'an inversion of logic to speak of an act which purports to terminate a process as being an abuse of that process' and continued:

c   'I am not sensitive to the logical difficulty. Even if it be illogical (and I do not think it is) to treat the termination of legal process as an act which can be an abuse of that process, principle requires that the illogicality be overridden, if justice requires. The court has inherent power to prevent a party from obtaining by the use of its process a collateral advantage which it would be unjust for him to retain; and termination of process can, like any other step in

d   the process, be so used. I agree, therefore, with Parker J and Lord Denning MR that service of a notice of discontinuance without leave, though it complies with the rules, can be an abuse of the process of the court.' (See [1981] 1 All ER 143 at 148, [1981] AC 557 at 571.)

THE LIMITATION ASPECT

e   Often it is a matter of relative indifference to a defendant in civil proceedings who has a cross-claim against the plaintiff whether to make his claim by way of counterclaim or by way of a new action. Sometimes the choice will depend on whether the subject matter of the cross-claim is the same as, or closely linked to, the subject matter of the plaintiff's claim. But in two situations it may be of practical

f   importance. One is where the defendant might have difficulty in getting leave to serve out. The other (which is of the highest practical importance in this case) is where the cross-claim, if brought by way of a new action, would be statute-barred, but if brought by way of a counterclaim, would get the advantage of s 35 of the Limitation Act 1980, and so escape being statute-barred. The potential advantages of s 35 are particularly striking in this case, as the fees action was begun in 1992 and

g   then went into a state of suspended animation (with neither defence nor counterclaim) for the best part of three years.

Since the damages claimed in the draft counterclaim exhibited to Mr Lloyd-Jacob's third affidavit were hundreds of times larger than the sum awarded by the default judgment (even allowing for interest on that sum), it is understandable that

h   Ernst & Young and their advisers might have come to the conclusion that they would willingly relinquish the default judgment and put an end to the fees action by discontinuance, if they could do so without letting in the counterclaim. Conversely, Butte and its advisers might have come to the conclusion that Ernst & Young should (if possible) be stopped from discontinuing the fees action unless and until Butte's counterclaim had been made. Once made it would survive discontinuance under

j   Ord 15, r 2(3).

Both parties did indeed have these thoughts. It is quite clear, from the affidavit evidence and the oral evidence that I have heard on this motion, that the two litigation partners concerned (Miss Caroline Bassett at FCB and Miss Clare Canning at BLG) were both well aware, as one would expect, of the implications of the position. So long as the default judgment remained and had not been set aside, there was (from Butte's point of view) no action in which to counterclaim and (from Ernst

& Young's point of view) no action which needed to be, or could be, discontinued. As I have said, Miss Bassett and Miss Canning were both well aware of the implications; but neither was sure that the other was equally aware of them. That (and not much more than that) is the matrix of fact against which the exchanges and events leading up to the consent order have to be assessed. They are an unusually vivid illustration of the general point made by Lord Wilberforce in *Prenn v Simmonds* [1971] 3 All ER 237 at 241, [1971] 1 WLR 1381 at 1385:

> 'The words used may, and often do, represent a formula which means different things to each side, yet may be accepted because that is the only way to get "agreement" and in the hope that disputes will not arise. The only course then can be to try to ascertain the "natural" meaning.'

THE ISSUES

There are essentially three issues that have been argued before me. In the order addressed by Mr Hirst (which is, I think, the most logical order) they are as follows.

(1) Had Butte, at the time of service of the notice of discontinuance, already made a counterclaim so as to be able to take advantage of Ord 15, r 2(3)? If so, the other issues do not arise.

(2) Did the parties, through their solicitors, make an agreement that Ernst & Young would not serve notice of discontinuance until Butte had had seven days to put in a defence and counterclaim? If so, it is accepted on behalf of Ernst & Young that it would be an abuse of process to breach such an agreement.

(3) Even in the absence of such an agreement, did Miss Canning mislead Miss Bassett in such a way as to amount to an abuse of process? If so, how should the court exercise its discretion in relation to the notice of discontinuance?

I will take these three issues in turn.

The first issue: had Butte made a counterclaim?

There is a good deal of authority on this point and I was taken quite fully thorough the authorities: *Bildt v Foy* (1892) 9 TLR 34; affd (1829) 9 TLR 83; *Re General Railway Syndicate, Whiteley's Case* [1900] 1 Ch 365; *The Salybia* [1910] P 25; *The Saxicava* [1924] P 131; *The Gniezno, Owners of the Motor Vessel Popi v Owners of the Steamship or Vessel Gniezno* [1967] 2 All ER 738, [1968] P 418; *Impex Transport Aktieselskabet v A G Thames Holdings Ltd (t/a John Gibb & Sons)* [1982] 1 All ER 897, [1981] 1 WLR 1547; *Artoc Bank and Trust Ltd v Prudential Assurance Co plc* [1984] 3 All ER 538, [1984] 1 WLR 1181; and *Fakih Bros v A P Moller (Copenhagen) Ltd* [1994] 1 Lloyd's Rep 103.

Of these cases, five (*Bildt v Foy, The Salybia, The Saxicava, The Gniezno* and *Fakih Bros v Moller*) were actually concerned with the interrelation of discontinuance and counterclaiming in an action commenced by writ (in *The Gniezno* the plaintiffs wished to discontinue—see [1967] 2 All ER 738 at 742, [1968] P 418 at 421). The other cases were concerned with related or analogous points, such as (in *Impex Transport*) when an action by way of counterclaim was commenced for the purposes of art 32 of the Convention on the Contract for the International Carriage of Goods by Road (set out in the schedule to the Carriage of Goods by Road Act 1965). Moreover, only the two most recent of the five cases most in point were concerned with the Rules of the Supreme Court in their modern form. I think (with all respect to what Brandon J said in *The Gniezno* [1967] 2 All ER 738 at 749, [1968] P 418 at 433) that the alterations in the language of the rules were intended to make some significant change, at least by removing the ambiguity in the expression 'set up' to which Bankes LJ drew attention in *The Saxicava* [1924] P 131 at 135.

The Salybia and *The Saxicava* undoubtedly establish that the mere announcement
or assertion of a counterclaim, in correspondence between solicitors, is not enough
to enable the claim to survive discontinuance by the plaintiff. Nor, as Brandon J
decided in *The Gniezno* [1967] 2 All ER 738 at 756, [1968] P 418 at 443), is the filing of
notice of counterclaim in an Admiralty action in rem in which the writ has not yet
been served. These cases illustrate that 'a counterclaim can only be born of a living
action' (see *The Salybia* [1910] P 25 at 171 per Bigham P), and that when there is a
living action a counterclaim can come into existence only with some degree of
formality. The difficulty is discerning what degree of formality is required. The
formulation by Bankes LJ in *The Saxicava* [1924] P 131 at 135 that—

'Order XXI., r. 16 [the predecessor of Ord 15, r 2(3)], in speaking of "setting
up", must refer to a setting up in a pleading, or, at any rate, in some proceeding
which is recognized or directed by the rules, and which becomes part of the
record, or something which is filed in the Court',

raises as many questions as it answers. It is to be contrasted with the stricter view of
Robert Goff J in *Impex Transport* [1982] 1 All ER 897 at 905, [1981] 1 WLR 1547 at
1556:

'It follows, in my judgment, that, on the balance of authority under the old
rules, a counterclaim could be "set up" for the purposes of Ord 21, r 16, when
a pleading in the form of a counterclaim was served, or when some equivalent
document which was ordered to take the place of a pleading was served. If that
is right, I can see no reason to apply any different construction to the present
Ord 15, r 2(3).'

The only modern case which seems to recognise a counterclaim as having come
into existence (so as to survive the plaintiff's discontinuance) otherwise than by
actual service of the counterclaim as a pleading is *Fakih Bros v A P Moller (Copenhagen)
Ltd* [1994] 1 Lloyd's Rep 103. That case concerned a dispute on a shipping contract
providing for the English court to have exclusive jurisdiction. The plaintiffs issued
a writ on 30 January 1992 and served it on 19 March. On 31 March the defendants
acknowledged service. On the same day the plaintiffs (in breach of a club guarantee
furnished to them) arrested one of the defendants' vessels and (in breach of the
jurisdiction clause) commenced proceedings in Freetown, Sierra Leone. On 1 April
Waller J granted the defendants Mareva relief in respect of a proposed counterclaim
and ordered the plaintiffs to discontinue the foreign action. The plaintiffs did not do
so. On 3 April the plaintiffs served notice of discontinuance, and on 6 April the
defendants applied to set it aside.

Hobhouse J held that the notice of discontinuance, given at a time when the
plaintiffs were in contempt of court, was an abuse of process. He noted (at 109) five
points on *Castanho v Brown & Root* (which I shall have to come back to). He then
went on to consider shortly, as an alternative ground of decision, the question when
the counterclaim could be said to have been made. After referring to several of the
authorities mentioned, and also to the decision of the Court of Appeal in *CSI
International Co Ltd v Archway Personnel (Middle East) Ltd* [1980] 3 All ER 215, [1980] 1
WLR 1069, Hobhouse J said (at 110):

'Here, it would not have been proper to grant a *Mareva* injunction at all to the
defendants except on the basis that a counterclaim was being made in the
action. Waller J could have required the service of a counterclaim forthwith;
instead he took an undertaking that the points of defence and counter-claim
would be served within seven days. It may well be that where such an order is

made by the Court this creates a third exception to the requirement that a
pleading must actually be served before it can be said that a counterclaim has
been made in the action. Where a *Mareva* is granted to a plaintiff on an
undertaking to issue and serve a writ, there is inevitably an interval of time
before the writ is actually issued, maybe as long as over a bank holiday
weekend. In the present case, the order of Mr. Justice Waller followed a similar
logic and also provides an analogy with the O. 14 cases where the Court may
give directions which vary the effect of O. 15, r. 2(1).'

Hobhouse J's reference to a third exception is little puzzling, since the judgment
does not identify the first two exceptions. It was suggested to me that they are to be
found in Brandon J's judgment in *The Gniezno* [1967] 2 All ER 738 at 756, [1968] P 418
at 442, where he said:

'I have already indicated that there may be exceptional cases where a
counterclaim is raised at a stage in an action earlier than the stage of service of
a defence and counterclaim. One such case is in proceedings under R.S.C., Ord.
14, and another such case seems to me to be where the defendant in an
Admiralty action seeks to obtain security for an intended counterclaim by the
arrest of the plaintiff's ship or by the obtaining of bail in order to avoid such
arrest.'

This does seem the most likely identification of the first two exceptions, but
Hobhouse J had been referred to *Impex Transport* and must have seen the passage in
which Robert Goff J criticised (to my mind compellingly) what Brandon J had said
about affidavits put in under Ord 14 (see [1982] 1 All ER 897 at 905, [1981] 1 WLR
1547 at 1555–1556, ending with the conclusion which I have already set out). So the
three exceptions must, in my view, be revised to some extent and stated as (i) cases
where an affidavit or other document is ordered (whether under Ord 14 or
otherwise) to stand as a counterclaim; (ii) cases under the special Admiralty security
procedure; and (iii) cases where Mareva relief is granted in anticipation of, and on an
undertaking to serve, a counterclaim. That is what occurred in *Fakih Bros v A P
Moller (Copenhagen) Ltd* [1994] 1 Lloyd's Rep 103 (see the undertakings set out at 106);
and in such a case the nature and strength of the proposed counterclaim is sure to
be scrutinised quite closely by the court which grants the Mareva relief.

I must here note Mr Hirst's submission that what Hobhouse J said on this point
was not part of his decision. I think that Mr Hirst is probably right about this. An
alternative ground of decision, even if shortly expressed, can be part of the ratio of a
case; but Hobhouse J would not, I think, have said 'it may well be' had he intended
to express a final view. But even a tentative view of Hobhouse J calls for respectful
attention.

As I have already indicated, there is a considerable difference of view between
Brandon J in *The Gniezno* and Robert Goff J in *Impex Transport*, especially as regards
the significance of the three rather difficult cases of *Bildt v Foy*, *Whiteley's Case* and
The Saxicava. In relation to *Bildt v Foy* and *Whiteley's Case*, I respectfully prefer the
views of Robert Goff J; in particular I think it reasonably clear that in *Whiteley's Case*
Lindley MR ([1900] 1 Ch 365 at 369, in the context of an action against a shareholder
for a call on his shares) thought that the shareholder had *not* made a counterclaim,
but had done 'all that could be reasonably expected to assert in a legal proceeding
his right to repudiate' his shares.

As to *The Saxicava*, I think that the point is reached (perhaps quite quickly) at
which it becomes idle to speculate on exactly what Bankes LJ meant in his
judgment, or whether Sergeant LJ was correct in supposing ([1924] P 131 at 139) that

a   Bankes LJ agreed with him (as Mr Hirst points out, Sergeant LJ was in a better position to judge that on 13 February 1924 than anyone is today). Nevertheless, my own tentative view is that Bankes LJ was (at 135) making the obviously valid point that 'set up' in the old Ord 14, r 4 plainly included setting up by affidavit and had a different meaning from 'sets up' in the old Ord 21, r 16 (where it pointed to the use of a pleading or—to beg the question—something like a pleading). Thus far, I think,

b   Bankes LJ and Sergeant LJ probably were in agreement. Bankes LJ (in an extempore judgment after the respondents had not been called on) then went on (at 136) to consider the authorities which had been cited and referred to *Bildt v Foy* as a case (not under Ord 14) where it was sufficient for the defendant to secure the exercise of the court's discretion if he made an affidavit asserting a counterclaim. The reference to discretion is, I think, important; it fits in with the appellant's counsel's argument in

c   *The Saxicava* [1924] P 131 at 133, that *Bildt v Foy* was disposed of on equitable grounds. The next sentence, in which Bankes LJ says that the Divisional Court and the Court of Appeal took the same view on the 'setting up' point, seems unsustainable on the basis of the only known report.

   The conclusion that I draw from these rather difficult authorities is that although
d   the informal or semi-formal assertion of a counterclaim may in particular circumstances form a ground for the exercise of discretion (a point which may be of significance in connection with abuse of process) it does not amount to the making of a counterclaim. The balance of authority supports the narrower conclusion drawn by Robert Goff J in *Impex Transport* (and it follows, I think, that Robert Goff J did not accidentally make an omission as suggested by Falconer J in *Artoc Bank and*
e   *Trust Ltd v Prudential Assurance Co plc* [1984] 3 All ER 538 at 545, [1984] 1 WLR 1184 at 1190). But this narrower view should, I consider, be widened a little so as to let in cases in which a defendant has formally placed before the court evidence of sufficient weight, backed by sufficient undertakings, to persuade the court to grant relief appropriate only on the footing that the defendant is making (and will in the
f   near future formally complete the making of) a counterclaim. That would let in the Mareva relief in support of an intended counterclaim granted in *Fakih Bros v Moller* and may also let in comparable procedures peculiar to Admiralty law (on which I heard no submissions). It opens the door a little wider, but not much wider.

   On that test, which I take to be the correct test, Butte did not make a counterclaim, either by the swearing of Mr Lloyd-Jacob's third affidavit with its exhibited
g   draft, or by that affidavit and exhibit in combination with the consent order. The affidavit had not been filed at the time when the consent order was made. Even if it had been, there is no reason to suppose that it could have been read, still less carefully considered, by Master Winegarten (whose name appears on the consent order). The terms of the consent order were no doubt checked in Chancery
h   Chambers to see that they met formal requirements (as appears from small textual changes from the draft order signed by BLG and FLB; one of these changes distorted the agreed time for service of the defence and counterclaim and it is agreed that this should be corrected under the slip rule). The consent order itself is of course on the court file. But the process by which the consent order came into being, and the
j   extent of any judicial recognition (through the consent order) of the existence of a serious counterclaim, was quite different from what happened when Mareva relief was granted in *Fakih Bros v Moller*. I cannot therefore accept Mr Boyle's submission on the first issue.

The second issue: was there an agreement that Ernst & Young would not discontinue?

   Mr Boyle submits on this point that BLG (in the person of Miss Canning, on behalf of Ernst & Young) agreed with FCB (in the person of Miss Bassett, on behalf

of Butte) that Ernst & Young would not serve a notice of discontinuance before the
expiry of the time limit for service of Butte's defence and counterclaim. Mr Boyle's *a*
primary submission is that this agreement was an oral agreement reached in the
course of a telephone conversation on 25 January 1996 and including (but not
limited to) the terms of the consent order as eventually perfected; his fall-back
position is that such an agreement is to be found in the terms of the consent order
itself, construed in the light of relevant surrounding circumstances. As to the right *b*
approach to construing a consent order, Mr Hirst submits, and Mr Boyle does not
dispute, that surrounding circumstances are admissible to the same extent as with
other contracts, but that evidence of subjective intention is inadmissible (see *General
Accident Fire and Life Assurance Corp Ltd v IRC* [1963] 1 All ER 618 at 627, [1963] 1 WLR
421 at 430–431).

I must therefore now look rather more closely at the events leading up to the *c*
making of the consent order as they appear from the affidavits and exhibits and from
the oral evidence. These events are material to the issue of abuse of process also,
and to avoid repetition I will cover some events which are not admissible in relation
to the issue of what was agreed, but are material to the abuse of process issue.

The first telephone conversation between Miss Bassett and Miss Canning took *d*
place on 23 January 1996, one week before the date finally fixed for the much-
adjourned summons to set aside the default judgment. The appeal to the Court of
Appeal (from the judgment of Miss Dohmann QC) had not yet been abandoned.
Miss Bassett made the call (to inquire about further evidence) but Miss Canning
asked to have a 'without prejudice' conversation, to which Miss Bassett agreed.
Miss Canning said that her clients were minded to agree to the default judgment *e*
being set aside on terms, including payment of their costs. Miss Bassett asked
whether Miss Canning had an estimate of the costs; Miss Canning said that she did
not, but would try to get one. Miss Canning said that the matter was urgent because
she was being pressed on brief fees for the hearing in the following week.

There is no real dispute about this first conversation except for some difference *f*
about how far terms (other than costs) were discussed; but some reference was
made to directions in the fees action, as appears from both solicitors' manuscript
attendance notes. Miss Bassett and Miss Canning agree that nothing was said
expressly about discontinuance. On the Butte side, the background to Miss
Canning's approach (which is admissible and relevant only on the abuse of process
issue) was that strategy and tactics had been considered at a consultation with *g*
leading counsel on 15 January 1996. At this consultation it was decided that Ernst &
Young would if possible discontinue the fees action in order to get rid of the huge
counterclaim asserted in Mr Lloyd-Jacob's third affidavit, a claim which appeared to
be statute-barred unless it could be asserted as a counterclaim in the fees action.

From the consultation there emerged what Miss Canning called Plan A and Plan *h*
B (I do not know whether these terms were used in the consultation). Plan A was
to get agreement to set aside the default judgment and then to discontinue. It was
part of Plan A for BLG to obtain carriage of the consent order. Plan B was a more
vague fall-back plan to be resorted to if Miss Canning was asked for an undertaking
not to discontinue, or had to meet inquiries about discontinuance: it amounted to
going back to the drawing-board and, probably, fighting the summons to set aside *j*
the default judgment.

Miss Bassett for her part deposes (and this too is relevant, if at all, to abuse of
process rather than to the issue of agreement) that, because she was well aware of
the implications of discontinuance, she thought that if Butte were to agree to set
aside the judgment it must be on terms that it would have the right to defend and
counterclaim. But it seems clear (from what followed) that Miss Bassett thought

a that this could be achieved without her coming out plainly with the words—'no discontinuance'—which were on her mind.

On Mr Boyle's application, and without real opposition from Mr Hirst, I made an order for cross-examination of Miss Bassett and Miss Canning on their affidavits, while indicating that the scope and duration of the oral evidence should be restricted (in the event both witnesses were cross-examined and re-examined in just under

b two hours). These two witnesses were both giving evidence about events of barely a month ago, which is a refreshing change from most witness actions. It is nevertheless almost impossible to remember or reconstruct correctly the exact words and nuances of any but the simplest and shortest conversation.

It is no criticism of Miss Bassett to say that her evidence illustrated this. In her first affidavit she said (of the second telephone conversation) that she 'stressed that Butte

c must be allowed to defend and counterclaim'. In her oral evidence she used the expressions 'entitled', 'able' and 'will be allowed'. I think that Miss Bassett was doing her best to assist the court, but in giving her evidence she was obviously (and understandably) upset about the whole episode. She must have rerun it in her mind many times in the last month. I have difficulty in accepting her answer to a question

d which was repeatedly put to her, in varying terms, by Mr Hirst: why she did not ask for an undertaking about non-discontinuance to be included in the consent order, or at least to be recorded in correspondence? To this repeated question Miss Bassett replied, in much the same terms, that it was not necessary; that if the agreement had extended only to setting aside the default order and dealing with costs, it would have been necessary; but that as the agreed directions provided for defence and

e counterclaim and other pleadings, there was an on-going action and she had no need to raise the question of discontinuance expressly. I cannot accept this as a complete answer. I find that Miss Bassett must have made a deliberate decision not to mention discontinuance, in case she put in Miss Canning's mind a thought which was not already there (if the agreed terms were so unequivocal, and if the thought of discontinuance was already in Miss Canning's mind, there was nothing to be lost

f by spelling it out).

Miss Canning, by contrast, appeared untroubled by the whole episode. She was candid about Plan A and Plan B, but denied that she had in any way misled Miss Bassett. So far as the primary facts are concerned (as opposed to the view which the court should take of them) I have little difficulty in accepting her evidence.

g I must return to the facts and the important telephone conversation which took place on 25 January 1996. Miss Bassett made the call. The exhibits include her contemporaneous manuscript note and a typed attendance note which Miss Bassett actually dictated on 2 February; and Miss Canning's contemporaneous manuscript note and a typed attendance note prepared within a day or two.

h It is common ground that the conversation took between five and ten minutes and that much of it was taken up with Miss Bassett reading out a draft consent order which she had prepared. The first three paragraphs of the draft were as follows:

'1. The default judgment dated 7 March 1995 be set aside.

2. The defendant do have unconditional leave to defend and counterclaim.

j 3. The defendant do serve a defence and counterclaim within 7 days of the date of this order.'

These paragraphs were followed by further directions as to pleadings and costs, with liberty to apply.

Miss Bassett's evidence was that after reading the draft she returned to para 2 and reiterated or emphasised it (I have already referred to some of her evidence on this point). Miss Canning had no recollection one way or the other as to whether Miss

Bassett returned to the point, but she firmly denied that Miss Bassett said that she
wanted to be sure that Butte could defend and counterclaim. None of the *a*
attendance notes cast any clear light on this except that Miss Bassett's manuscript
note says 'Agree to c/c'; this appears in the typed note as 'Confirmed agreement to
counterclaim and defence'.

In the course of the conversation there was also discussion of costs, the Gramcol
action, and the preparation of the consent order. Miss Canning had still not got an *b*
estimate of costs, but that does not seem to have been an obstacle. The solicitors
discussed the possibility of consolidating the fees action and the Gramcol action, but
Miss Canning did not indicate any definite agreement to that course. She did
indicate her agreement to the directions to be given in the Gramcol action mirroring
those embodied in the draft consent order. Miss Canning proposed that her
assistant Miss Jenny Brown should prepare the draft order (on which she was, Miss *c*
Canning said, already engaged) and that BLG should have carriage of the order.
Miss Bassett said that she agreed to this (although the summons to set aside was
Butte's application) because she no longer saw discontinuance as a threat.

When litigants agree (through their solicitors or counsel) to a consent order of an
interlocutory nature there is seldom (at least in routine cases) any enforceable *d*
contract apart from their bare consent to or concurrence in the terms of the order,
with all the possibilities of the order being varied, or affected by other interlocutory
steps, inherent in a non-peremptory order (see *Siebe Gorman & Co Ltd v Pneupac Ltd*
[1982] 1 All ER 377, [1982] 1 WLR 185). In this case the consent order was not a
routine matter. Nevertheless, I am not satisfied, on the balance of probability, that
the solicitors intended to conclude any larger agreement than that embodied in the *e*
draft consent order which was signed on behalf of both firms and submitted to
Chancery Chambers for perfection. The solicitors did also reach a measure of
accord about the course of the Gramcol action, but I doubt whether that amounted
to an enforceable agreement. If it did, it is not relevant to this issue.

So it comes down to construing the consent order itself in the light of admissible *f*
surrounding circumstances. Those surrounding circumstances include the importance to the parties (because of the limitation aspect) of whether or not Ernst &
Young would be able to discontinue before Butte counterclaimed. But the more
important that question is recognised as being, the more puzzling it is (to an
observer who knows the general background, but does not know about Miss
Canning's Plan A or Miss Bassett's tacit assumptions) that the consent order does *g*
not address the matter expressly. Instead it reproduces in these terms the first three
paragraphs of Miss Bassett's original draft (which had been compressed into two by
Miss Brown):

'IT IS BY CONSENT ORDERED *h*
(1) that the default judgment dated 7 March 1995 be set aside
(2) that the defendant be at liberty unconditionally on or before [a date which
is to be corrected under the slip rule] to serve on the plaintiff its defence and
counterclaim',

followed by the agreed directions as to further pleadings and costs. *j*

In this form of order the single word 'unconditionally' is the only hint that this is
anything other than a normal order setting aside a default judgment. Such an order
would not normally carry any implication of the plaintiff's right of discontinuance
being excluded or restricted. Nor is the word 'unconditionally' particularly
surprising, since under Ord 13, r 9 the court may set aside a judgment on such terms
as it thinks just (for instance, the court may impose the condition of a payment-in).

But the word 'unconditionally', if inserted for that reason, would naturally be found in para 1 rather than para 2.

a

It seems to me that this was a situation in which (in the words of Lord Wilberforce in *Prenn v Simmonds* [1971] 3 All ER 237 at 241, [1971] 1 WLR 1381 at 1385 to which I have already referred) 'unconditionally' was a formula which meant different things to each side. To Miss Bassett it was all-important; to Miss Canning

b it was unimportant. In such a situation the only course, as Lord Wilberforce says, is to try to ascertain the natural meaning. Construed naturally, without reference to the solicitors' actual intention, the consent order does not in my judgment, either expressly or by necessary implication, exclude Ernst & Young's ordinary right to serve a notice of discontinuance. I should add that I was referred to a number of well-known authorities on the implication of contractual terms. The principles

c which they state are not in dispute, but I do not think they assist me in the interpretation of the consent order.

The third issue: abuse of process

It is therefore necessary to consider the third issue, abuse of process. The proposition that a notice of discontinuance may be an abuse of process was novel in

d *Castanho v Brown & Root (UK) Ltd* [1981] 1 All ER 143, [1981] AC 557 as appears from the difference of judicial opinion and the paucity of authority cited (on that point) in different courts. Moreover, apart from *Fakih Bros v Moller* [1994] 1 Lloyd's Rep 103 there seems to have been little authority since. In *Fakih Bros v Moller* (at 109) the third of Hobhouse J's five points was that, in considering whether or not the service

e of the notice was an abuse of process, it is necessary to have regard to the overall position of the parties, and what the plaintiff is trying to achieve by discontinuance. Looking at the overall position cannot in my view exclude looking at any allegation that one side has misled the other and has thereby put itself in a position to serve a notice of discontinuance which it might not otherwise have been able to serve.

f   Mr Boyle did not shrink from submitting, in unequivocal terms, that BLG deliberately (and at several stages) misled FCB as to Ernst & Young's intentions. The deception which Mr Boyle asserts was practised (if it was practised by anyone) by Miss Canning; and Miss Canning herself did not in her oral evidence seek to disclaim responsibility, though she did refer to the plan (which I take to mean Plan A, or if it failed, Plan B) being discussed at the consultation on 15 January. In the

g course of his submissions Mr Hirst candidly said that if the plan was improper, he apologised because he had advised on it. I have no idea how far the detail of the plan was discussed in consultation, and in any case I am not prepared to say that the plan, as a plan, was improper.   But it was to my mind imprudent because of the predictable difficulty, which in the event occurred, of carrying out Plan A without

h prevarication, and in particular of deciding when proper professional conduct required Plan A to be aborted, whatever its attractions in the client's interests.

The first matter that calls for consideration is the telephone conversation on 23 January. Miss Canning readily agreed in her oral evidence that she did not mention Ernst & Young's intention to discontinue, because she did not want to alert Miss Bassett to the idea. That by itself is plainly unexceptionable; Miss Bassett did just the

j same. But Miss Canning agreed that the discussion of directions would give the impression that the action was to continue.   The transcript of cross-examination provided to me by Mr Boyle (from which Mr Hirst did not dissent, and which largely coincides with my note) records these exchanges:

'Q. At [Miss Canning's manuscript note of the 23 January call] there is a reference to a timetable for directions and the conduct of the action. You must

have known it would have created the impression for Miss Bassett that you
would continue with the action? *A.* I suppose it would.

    Q. Miss Bassett was misled? *A.* In so far as she would not realise that we
were planning to discontinue.

    Q. You were prepared to mislead her? *A.* I did not look at it like that. I did
not know we were going to discontinue until the final decision. We might have
changed our minds if we were not able to pursue Plan A.

    Q. You would only have changed your mind if you could not achieve Plan
A? *A.* Yes.'

So Miss Canning went some way to accepting that the discussion of directions on 23
January gave Miss Bassett a misleading impression.

    There was further discussion of directions, both for the fees action and for the
Gramcol action, during the second telephone conversation on 25 January. This was
the subject of cross-examination.

    '*Q.* You agreed in your first conversation that reference would be made to
directions for further conduct so you expected Miss Bassett would telephone
you to discuss terms of an agreement? *A.* The debate on terms was only
whether Butte would pay costs.

    Q. Not terms? *A.* I did not look upon future directions as "terms".
Obviously we were going to agree directions. I was aware of my intention to
stop the action in its tracks as soon as the order was made.

    Q. You were prepared in the conversation on 25 January to agree further
conduct of the action although you knew your client would stop the action the
moment the order was made? *A.* Yes.

    Q. You knew the discussion would mislead Miss Bassett? *A.* No, because the
important thing was not to confirm we were not going to discontinue.

    Q. What would be the point of discussing directions if they were not going
to be carried out? *A.* One would normally agree directions.

    Q. The real reason was you wanted Miss Bassett to believe that your clients
would continue with the action? *A.* I did not care what she believed as long as
I gave no confirmation that we were not going to discontinue.'

    In relation to the Gramcol action Miss Canning was referred to her typed
attendance note of this conversation which recorded her as commenting 'that she
could see no obvious difficulty with it—and would consider it as a possibility'. She
was asked whether this was a fair statement:

    '*A.* I cannot remember saying it but I take my attendance note as accurate.
It was dictated after the conversation for my assistants.

    Q. So a discussion about consolidation would not be misleading but agreeing
to it would be? *A.* Yes I treated it the same way as directions.

    Q. If you had agreed it would have been misleading? *A.* Yes because it
would imply an intention to continue and one can only consolidate a live
action.

    Q. Exactly. *A.* We were solicitors talking in hypotheticals about the concept
of consolidation.

    Q. You draw a distinction between agreement and discussion? *A.* Yes.

    Q. Should solicitors be able to trust what other solicitors say? *A.* It depends
on the circumstances, the conversation they are having.'

a A third matter which calls for special mention is Miss Canning's success in seeing that BLG obtained the carriage of the consent order. This was an important part of Plan A, as Miss Canning acknowledged:

'*Q*. You wanted to have carriage of it? *A*. Yes, because then we would know when it was sealed.

b *Q*. Did you have that in mind during your conversation on 25 January? *A*. It was my preference.

Q. You expressed that preference to Miss Bassett in your second conversation? *A*. Yes, it was not debated, she just agreed.

Q. Having regard to your strategy, Plan A, you realised that it was crucial that she agreed? *A*. It helped.

c *Q*. It was crucial? *A*. It was what I wanted. I had not thought of what would happen if there was not agreement.

Q. You wanted the discontinuance before they got their counterclaim in? *A*. Yes, I intended to serve the notice of discontinuance and the order at the same time.'

d

The practice as to which solicitor has carriage of an order is a procedural nicety on which I was not referred to any authority (it is touched on, but not fully explained, in the Chancery Division practice directions in *The Supreme Court Practice 1995* vol 2, para 810(d)). But Mr Hirst did not dispute Mr Boyle's submission that in *e* having carriage of an order a solicitor would be acting as an officer of the court, and should not use that responsibility in order to secure some partisan advantage. But that is, as I must conclude, what Miss Canning tried to achieve in this case. The fact that Miss Bassett readily agreed to Miss Canning having carriage of the consent order is to my mind the clearest indication that she had come to believe that Ernst & Young were not going to discontinue in the near future. I must also regretfully *f* conclude that misleading conduct on the part of Miss Canning was the major cause of Miss Bassett's mistaken belief. It is to Miss Canning's credit that she was so candid on these matters in her oral evidence.

In deciding whether the service of the notice of discontinuance in these circumstances amounted to an abuse of process, and if so what should be done *g* about it, I have well in mind Mr Hirst's submission (put colloquially, but then developed) that Ernst & Young did not owe Butte any favours. I have well in mind that Butte's initiation and conduct of the Montana action has been characterised by Rix J and Miss Dohmann QC as oppressive, and that that is why Ernst & Young were successful in the anti-suit action. But it is a commonplace that two wrongs do not *h* make a right.

Heavy, hostile commercial litigation is a serious business. It is not a form of indoor sport and litigation solicitors do not owe each other duties to be friendly (so far as that goes beyond politeness) or to be chivalrous or sportsmanlike (so far as that goes beyond being fair). Nevertheless, even in the most hostile litigation (indeed, especially in the most hostile litigation) solicitors must be scrupulously fair and not *j* take unfair advantage of obvious mistakes: see the decision of the Court of Appeal in *Derby & Co Ltd v Weldon (No 8)* [1990] 3 All ER 762, [1991] 1 WLR 73 (this was not cited by counsel but the general principle is, I think, uncontroversial). The duty not to take unfair advantage of an obvious mistake is intensified if the solicitor in question has been a major contributing cause of the mistake.

For these reasons I conclude that the service of the notice of discontinuance was, in all the circumstances, an abuse of process.

THE RELIEF TO BE GRANTED

Although there has been an abuse of process, I still have a discretion whether to *a* set aside the notice of discontinuance entirely, or to leave it to stand, conditionally or unconditionally. The test adopted in *Castanho v Brown & Root* was to consider what the court's attitude would have been if leave to discontinue had required the court's leave (this is Hobhouse J's fifth point in *Fakih Bros v Moller* [1994] 1 Lloyd's Rep 103 at 109).

I find it difficult to adopt that test here, because if I ask myself what ought properly *b* to have happened, the answer seems to be that Plan A (if ever entertained at all) should have been aborted once Miss Bassett started talking to Miss Canning about directions and possible consolidation; and that the likely outcome would have been no consent order, but instead a contested hearing of the summons to set aside. At such a contested hearing the issue of the proposed counterclaim, and possible *c* discontinuance, could hardly have remained unacknowledged any longer. I have considered whether I ought to decide, notionally, how a contested hearing of the summons would have gone, and to exercise my discretion whether or not to set aside the notice of discontinuance accordingly. Another possibility would be to set aside the notice, but only on terms that the consent order was also set aside.

I have, however, come to the conclusion that where there has been an abuse of *d* process, I ought not to try either to restore the status quo as it was at the beginning of the year, or to rewrite history on a hypothetical basis by taking a view of the outcome of a contested hearing which never happened. In my judgment the right course is simply to set aside the notice of discontinuance as being, in all the circumstances, an abuse of process. *e*

The effect will be to leave the consent order in place and the defence and counterclaim as properly served on 1 February 1995. I will consider extending the time limits in the consent order. I should also record that I have heard no developed argument and I express no view on some other objections to the counterclaim (which Mr Hirst merely outlined). *f*

SUMMARY

In brief, therefore, my conclusions are as follows.

(1) Butte did not, before or on the making of the consent order, have a subsisting counterclaim within Ord 15, r 2(3).

(2) The parties did not agree through their solicitors, or by the consent order, that Butte would not serve notice of discontinuance before the expiry of the time for *g* defence and counterclaim.

(3) Nevertheless, the service of the notice was an abuse of process and must be set aside.

(4) Butte's defence and counterclaim stands, subject to possible attack on other grounds. *h*

Order accordingly.

Celia Fox   Barrister.

a
R v Parole Board, ex parte Watson

COURT OF APPEAL, CIVIL DIVISION
SIR THOMAS BINGHAM MR, ROSE AND ROCH LJJ
19, 20 FEBRUARY, 4 MARCH 1996

b
Prison – Release on licence – Refusal to release on licence – Review by Parole Board –
Prisoner serving discretionary life sentence released on licence – Secretary of State
revoking licence and recalling prisoner – Parole Board giving extra-statutory
confirmation of recall prior to formal review – Statutory review by Parole Board – Board
refusing to order re-release of prisoner – Whether board's earlier confirmation resulting
c *in procedural irregularity or bias – Whether board applying correct test on review –*
Criminal Justice Act 1991, ss 34(4), 39(2)(4).

W was released from prison on licence after serving 18 years of a discretionary life
sentence in respect of convictions for sexual offences against young boys.
d Following reports from his probation officers and a consultant psychiatrist
indicating concern that W was associating with youths under the age of consent,
it emerged that he had been cohabiting with a 17-year-old boy. In March 1994 the
Secretary of State for the Home Department revoked W's licence under s 39(2)[a]
of the Criminal Justice Act 1991 and his recall to prison was considered and
subsequently confirmed by the Parole Board in a letter dated 30 March 1994. In
e July 1994 the board held a full review of W's case under s 39(4) of the Act, at
which W was represented by counsel and substantial documentary material was
placed before it. The board however declined to direct W's release on licence,
not being satisfied, as required by s 34(4)[b] of the Act, that W's confinement was
no longer necessary for the protection of the public. W's application for judicial
f review of the board's decision was dismissed and he appealed to the Court of
Appeal. The issues arose: (i) whether the extra-statutory confirmation of W's
recall by the board on 30 March 1994 pre-empted or unfairly influenced the
board's formal review under s 39(4) or created a likelihood of bias; and (ii)
whether the public safety test in s 34(4) to be applied by the board when
considering the initial release of a discretionary life sentence prisoner also applied
g to a review under s 39(4).

Held – (1) The extra-statutory practice whereby by the board confirmed a
decision by the Secretary of State to recall to prison a discretionary life prisoner
who had been released on licence did not compromise the independence and
h objectivity of the board in the exercise of its powers of review under s 39(4) of the
1991 Act. It followed that there had been no procedural irregularity or danger of
bias in the board's review of W's case, particularly in view of the fact that it had
considered fuller material than that available in March (see p 649 *d* to *g*, p 651 *g h*
and p 652 *d* to *f h*, post.)

j   (2) The public safety test which s 34(4) of the 1991 Act required the board to
apply when considering the initial release of a discretionary life sentence prisoner
was equally applicable where the board reviewed, under s 39(4), the case of such
a prisoner who had been released on licence but later recalled on revocation of
that licence. In exercising its practical judgment, the board was bound to

---

a   Section 39, so far as material, is set out at p 647 *g* to *j*, post
b   Section 34, so far as material, is set out at p 647 *b* to *e*, post

approach its task under the two sections in the same way, balancing the hardship
and injustice of continuing to imprison a man who was unlikely to cause serious
injury to the public against the need to protect the public against a man who was
not unlikely to cause such injury. The board had therefore applied the right test
on the review of W's case. Further, there was material before the board on which
it could found a reasonable apprehension of serious injury to the public if W were
released on licence at that time. The appeal would accordingly be dismissed (see
p 650 g to j, p 651 c d j to p 652 a d and p 653 d to g, post).

Notes

For parole of prisoners serving life sentences, see 37 *Halsbury's Laws* (4th edn)
paras 1187–1192, and for a case on the subject, see 37(3) *Digest* (Reissue) 406, *5341*.

Cases referred to in judgments

Associated Provincial Picture Houses Ltd v Wednesbury Corp [1947] 2 All ER 680,
    [1948] 1 KB 223, CA.
R v Gough [1993] 2 All ER 724, [1993] AC 646, [1993] 2 WLR 883, HL.
R v Parole Board, ex p Lodomez (1994) 26 BMLR 162, DC.

Cases also cited or referred to in skeleton arguments

Hannam v Bradford City Council [1970] 2 All ER 690, [1970] 1 WLR 937, CA.
McInnes v Onslow Fane [1978] 3 All ER 211, [1978] 1 WLR 1520.
R v Barnsley Metropolitan BC, ex p Hook [1976] 3 All ER 452, [1976] 1 WLR 1052, CA.
R v Oxford Regional Mental Health Review Tribunal, ex p Mackman (1986) Times, 2
    June.
R v Parole Board, ex p Bradley [1990] 3 All ER 828, [1991] 1 WLR 134, DC.
R v Secretary of State for the Home Dept, ex p Benson (1988) Independent, 16
    November, DC.
R v Secretary of State for the Home Dept, ex p Evans (2 November 1994, unreported),
    DC.
R v Secretary of State for the Home Dept, ex p Singh (No 1) (1993) Times, 27 April, DC.
Singh v UK (11 October 1994, unreported), E Com HR.
Thynne v UK (1990) 13 EHRR 666, ECt HR.

Appeal

By notice dated 14 November 1995 David Adam Watson, a discretionary life
sentence prisoner, appealed with leave from the order of Popplewell J on 16
October 1995 dismissing his application for judicial review of the decision of the
Parole Board dated 25 July 1994, taken on the review of his case under s 39(4) of
the Criminal Justice Act 1991, not to direct his immediate re-release on licence
following his recall to prison by the Secretary of State for the Home Department
under s 39(2) of the 1991 Act on 26 March 1994. The facts are set out in the
judgment of Sir Thomas Bingham MR.

Edward Fitzgerald QC (instructed by *B M Birnberg & Co*) for Mr Watson.
Steven Kovats (instructed by the *Treasury Solicitor*) for the Parole Board.

Cur adv vult

4 March 1996. The following judgments were delivered.

SIR THOMAS BINGHAM MR. Mr Watson received a discretionary sentence of
life imprisonment. After serving a long term in prison he was released on licence.
After just over a year at liberty his licence was revoked and he was recalled to
prison. The Parole Board informally confirmed this recall. Having later

a considered his case in detail the Parole Board decided not to direct his release and he remains in prison. He obtained leave to challenge the lawfulness of this decision by the Parole Board. His challenge was rejected by Popplewell J. Mr Watson renews his challenge in this court.

I

b Mr Watson is now aged 53. In April 1975 he was convicted on four counts of buggery and five of indecent assault and was sentenced to life imprisonment on each of the counts of buggery and to seven years concurrently on each of the counts of indecent assault. The offences were committed against schoolboys and were accompanied by beatings and other sadistic acts. At the time of these convictions Mr Watson had previous convictions of indecent assault on boys c aged nine and thirteen and buggery of a boy aged nine.

On 29 January 1993 the Home Secretary directed Mr Watson's release on licence and he was released on 1 February 1993. He had been in prison (including a period on remand) for over 18 years. His licence contained terms which required him to place himself under the supervision of a probation officer and to report in accordance with that officer's instructions. In August 1993 he was d advised by his solicitor that there was no reason why two young men named James Wilson and Stephen Goodall should not stay with him as his guests. His probation officers, however, were concerned at his association with these young men, one of whom was 18 and the other (Goodall) 17. They were also concerned at reports of contacts between Mr Watson and a 14-year-old boy who had e absconded from a children's home. The probation officers had elicited information from Mr Watson about his contacts with this boy, and had also warned him of the inappropriateness of his seeking to establish a parental or supervisory relationship with these young men. Reports were written on 10 and 13 December 1993 recording these concerns. It was decided to seek a report from Dr Mendelson, a consultant forensic psychiatrist.

f Dr Mendelson reported in writing on 16 February 1994. In the course of his report, he said :

'I am particularly concerned by his refusal to associate with a more age-appropriate group of homosexuals. Instead, he still indulges his interest in young men and is eagerly looking forward to the proposed age reduction g of consenting homosexuals. However, he still denies having any sexual fantasies or urges towards young boys. He claims that he is mixing with the youths, as you no doubt heard from his Probation Officer, only to fulfil his needs to care for others. Yet he admits that he finds these dependent relationships somewhat rewarding. They are of course partly reminiscent h of his original behaviour surrounding the index offences.'

Dr Mendelson referred to a meeting at which he and the probation officer had impressed their concerns on Mr Watson and he expressed a hope (described as 'slim') that this might have some influence on him. Dr Mendelson continued:

j 'I cannot say that David Watson is in imminent danger of reoffending. However, I regret that he is failing to make the progress that either his Probation Officer or I would wish. Moreover, by maintaining his association with youths, he is inevitably going to come into contact with boys and situations of temptation. In his seemingly arrogant way, he will not consider that this is a risk, nor that he need not even take it. I fear that unless he can change his attitude it is likely that he will fall into further trouble. He is of course extremely vulnerable to allegations and I doubt whether the

youngsters he chooses to mix with will be that long in discovering the
potential to blackmail him. However, he remains confident this will not be
the case, despite discussing our frank concerns with him.'

Dr Mendelson believed that Mr Watson had the potential to develop adequately
and minimise the risk of re-offending and did not consider that there were
grounds for his recall to prison at that time.

At the instigation of the probation officers, Mr Watson's case was referred to
the Parole Board, who recommended the addition of a further condition to his
licence. The Secretary of State on 17 March 1994 accordingly directed that a
condition be added that Mr Watson should not entertain at his residence male
persons under the age of consent nor engage in any activity involving such
persons without the permission of his probation officer. A letter was written to
Mr Watson warning him about his future conduct and informing him of this new
condition. The letter was handed to Mr Watson on 23 March 1994 and he signed
a written copy of the condition. It appears that on being notified of this condition
Mr Watson told Goodall to leave his bedsitter, in which Goodall had for some
time been living, but Mr Watson did not tell the probation officer that Goodall
had been doing so.

On the same day, 23 March 1994, Goodall went to Mr Watson's probation
officer and made a report. The effect of the report (later recorded in a written
statement) was that Mr Watson had asked Goodall to get hold of a gun and had
suggested that the two of them should take Wilson to the New Forest, beat him
up and kill him. The probation officers were concerned to learn not only the
details of this proposed plan, but also that Goodall had been living at Mr Watson's
address without the knowledge or permission of the probation officer. It was
agreed that the Home Office should be informed and that Mr Watson's recall
should be recommended. This recommendation was accepted. On 26 March
1994 Mr Watson's licence was revoked by the Secretary of State for the Home
Department and he was recalled to prison.

Reasons for his recall were given to Mr Watson in prison in these terms:

'The Secretary of State revoked your life licence on 26 March 1994, under
section 39(2) of the Criminal Justice Act 1991. This action was taken after
evidence was received indicating that you had allegedly suggested that a
firearm be obtained on your behalf. It was also alleged at a later date, that
you spoke of a plan to attack, and possibly kill a young man. These recent
developments have followed earlier events and concerns expressed by the
Probation Service and Dr Mendelson, which resulted in the conditions of
your licence being varied. In addition you have concealed from your
supervising officer the fact that you had been co-habiting with a 17 year old
boy since January 1994. Having regard to all the circumstances, in particular
the offences for which you were sentenced to life imprisonment, the
Secretary of State considered that your presence in the community no longer
constituted an acceptable risk to the safety of others. For that reason, he
decided to immediately revoke your life licence and recall you to prison.'

On 30 March 1994 the Parole Board considered and confirmed Mr Watson's
recall. Its reasons were:

'1. The pattern of your conduct since release on licence belies the
assurances that you gave to the Board and falsifies the belief then held that
you could be released without risk to the public. 2. This conduct has already
led to changes in the conditions of your licence and [you] have received one

a warning letter on 23 March 1994. 3. Finally your offering accommodation to a boy of seventeen and hiding this fact from your Probation Officer makes recall inevitable.'

Arrangements were put in train for a formal review of Mr Watson's recall by the Parole Board. For this review, a considerable body of documentary material was placed before the board, including copies of reports by probation officers, the

b statement by Goodall, the letter of Dr Mendelson, the board's recommendation of 30 March 1994, statements by a governor and chaplain at Winchester Prison, written representations by and on behalf of Mr Watson, a letter from his solicitors and testimonials to his character. The review took place on 22 July 1994 when Mr Watson was represented by counsel. On 25 July 1994 the Parole Board wrote

c to Mr Watson giving its reasons for not recommending his release. This letter is of importance and its terms should be quoted in full:

'Discretionary Lifer Panel—22 July 1994
1. On 26 March 1994 the Secretary of State revoked your life licence and recalled you to prison. This decision was confirmed by the Parole Board on

d 30 March 1994. Pursuant to Section 39(4) of the Criminal Justice Act 1991, a panel of the Parole Board convened on 22 July 1994 to consider your representations against recall. The Act requires the Board to direct your release only if it is satisfied that it is no longer necessary for the protection of the public that you be confined. The panel were not so satisfied and have therefore rejected your representations.   2. The panel carefully

e considered:—(a) your history of offending, in particular your convictions for sexual offences against boys, some of them involving acts of violence; (b) your history whilst in hospital and in prison; (c) the reports and statements in the dossier, excluding the statement of Stephen Goodall which was disregarded by the panel following submissions by your Counsel; (d) your

f representations and other statements submitted by you; (e) the evidence of Ms Robinson, your Probation Officer; and (f) your evidence and the evidence of Mr Edwards, your legal representative, and the full submissions of your Counsel. 3. In rejecting your representations against your recall, the panel were wholly convinced, on the totality of the evidence that they heard, that you continue to present a very real risk to the public and that there is a

g substantial risk that if you were released you would again commit serious sexual offences against males under the age of consent. 4. The panel accepted and took into account the fact that you have not committed any criminal offence since your release on licence and that there was no condition in your life licence that you should not associate with male persons

h under the age of consent. Nonetheless, on the evidence, the panel was satisfied that by reason of your association with young men aged 17, with criminal convictions, drug addiction and no settled way of life, you exposed them and young members of the public and yourself to a substantial potential risk. They accepted the contention that you created an undesirable

j dependency of those youths on you. They took the view that the risk of these associations leading to serious sexual offending was very high. You were not honest and open with your supervising officer. You concealed the extent of your associations from her and then did not heed her advice and warnings that you must associate with more appropriate persons. You accommodated a young person, aged 17, in your room for a period of some months without disclosing this to your supervising officer or seeking her advice. 5. In coming to their conclusion, the panel took into account all the evidence that they heard, but particularly:—(a) your own evidence. You told the panel that the young people with whom you were associating with were, during the association, committing criminal offences to feed their drug and alcohol addiction. The panel had no doubt that you had no insight into or understanding of the risks you were running or the reasons why these associations were inappropriate; (b) the evidence of Mrs Robinson, whose evidence they accepted. She told the panel that she did advise you on a number of occasions that you should associate with more age appropriate persons and that you should not associate with criminally orientated youths, but that you ignored this advice and the warnings given to you by her. She said that she had told you that you must have an open and honest relationship with her but that you had concealed from her the extent of your associations and the fact that Stephen Goodall was living in your room with you; (c) the reports of Dr Mendelson. In his report of 16 February 1994, Dr Mendelson said that he was particularly concerned with your refusal to associate with more age appropriate homosexuals. You were eagerly looking forward to the proposed reduction in the age of consent for homosexuals. You were failing to make the progress that the Doctor and the Probation Officer would wish. It is right that Dr Mendelson said "I cannot say that David Watson is in imminent danger of reoffending" but he went on to say that by maintaining your association with youths you are inevitably going to come into contact with boys and situations of temptation. Dr Mendelson said that you would not consider that there was a risk and that until you can change your attitude it is likely that you will fall into further trouble. The panel agreed with this view and detected no change of substance in your views. Until there is evidence of change you will continue to be a risk; (d) the statement of Mr Hearn, the Governor V, that you make no secret of your association with young males and that this makes you a risk; and (e) the statement of the Chaplain that it is your stubbornness to do things your way which gives greatest cause for concern. 5. The panel considered that it is essential that you should receive further assessment and treatment to lead to an understanding and insight into your potential for reoffending, with a view to your eventual release. They recommended to the Secretary of State that on completion of any assessment and treatment that is considered necessary your case should again be reviewed to see whether it is appropriate to transfer you to open conditions. 6. The decision of the panel not to direct your release is binding upon the Secretary of State. However it is a matter for him to decide whether to accept the recommendations that you undertake further assessment and treatment and that your case be referred back to the Board for a further review upon completion of such treatment.'

II

Section 32(2) of the Criminal Justice Act 1991 provides:

'It shall be the duty of the Board to advise the Secretary of State with respect to any matter referred to it by him which is connected with the early release or recall of prisoners.'

The board is required by s 32(3) to make recommendations on consideration of documents given to it by the Secretary of State and any other oral or written information obtained by it, and it may interview the person to whom the case relates. Section 32(6) requires the Secretary of State, in giving directions to the board, to have regard in particular to the need to protect the public from serious harm from offenders and the desirability of preventing the commission by them of further offences and of securing their rehabilitation. Section 34 of the 1991 Act, so far as material, reads:

'(1) A life prisoner is a discretionary life prisoner for the purposes of this Part if—(a) his sentence was imposed for a violent or sexual offence the sentence for which is not fixed by law; and (b) the court by which he was sentenced for that offence ordered that this section should apply to him as soon as he had served a part of his sentence specified in the order.

(2) A part of a sentence so specified shall be such part as the court considers appropriate taking into account—(a) the seriousness of the offence, or the combination of the offence and other offences associated with it; and …

(3) As soon as, in the case of a discretionary life prisoner—(a) he has served the part of his sentence specified in the order ('the relevant part'); and (b) the Board has directed his release under this section, it shall be the duty of the Secretary of State to release him on licence.

(4) The Board shall not give a direction under subsection (3) above with respect to a discretionary life prisoner unless—(a) the Secretary of State has referred the prisoner's case to the Board; and (b) the Board is satisfied that it is no longer necessary for the protection of the public that the prisoner should be confined.

(5) A discretionary life prisoner may require the Secretary of State to refer his case to the Board at any time—(a) after he has served the relevant part of his sentence …'

Section 37(3) of the 1991 Act provides that where a life prisoner is released on licence, his licence shall, unless previously revoked under s 39(1) or (2), remain in force until his death.

Section 39 of the 1991 Act is one of a series of three sections headed 'Misbehaviour after release'. So far as material, it provides:

'(1) If recommended to do so by the Board in the case of a long-term or life prisoner who has been released on licence under this Part, the Secretary of State may revoke his licence and recall him to prison.

(2) The Secretary of State may revoke the licence of any such person and recall him to prison without a recommendation by the Board, where it appears to him that it is expedient in the public interest to recall that person before such a recommendation is practicable.

(3) A person recalled to prison under subsection (1) or (2) above—(a) may make representations in writing with respect to his recall; and (b) on his return to prison, shall be informed of the reasons for his recall and of his right to make representations.

(4) The Secretary of State shall refer to the Board—(a) the case of a person recalled under subsection (1) above who makes representations under subsection (3) above; and (b) the case of a person recalled under subsection (2) above.

(5) Where on a reference under subsection (4) above the Board—(a) directs in the case of a discretionary life prisoner … his immediate release on licence under this section, the Secretary of State shall give effect to the direction …'

The scheme of these provisions is clear. Once a discretionary life sentence
prisoner has served the penal or tariff term of his sentence he may require the   *a*
Secretary of State to refer his case to the board and the Secretary of State must do
so. If the board is satisfied that it is no longer necessary for the protection of the
public that the prisoner should be confined, it will direct his release and the
Secretary of State must then release him on licence.

The recall to prison of a discretionary life sentence prisoner released on licence   *b*
may be effected in one or other of two ways. If recall is recommended by the
board, the Secretary of State may revoke the prisoner's licence and recall him. If
a prisoner so recalled makes representations in writing with respect to his recall,
the Secretary of State must refer the case to the board. Alternatively, the
Secretary of State may revoke the prisoner's licence and recall him without a
recommendation by the board if it is expedient in the public interest to do so and   *c*
it is impracticable to obtain a recommendation. This procedure is plainly
appropriate only in cases where there is thought to be urgent need to protect the
public. Where it is adopted, the case must be referred to the board whether
representations are made or not. If (whichever recall procedure is adopted and
whether a case is referred under s 39(4)(a) or (b)) the board directs the immediate   *d*
release on licence of the discretionary life sentence prisoner, the Secretary of State
must give effect to that direction.

In Mr Watson's case the emergency procedure under s 39(2) was followed. His
case had to be referred to the board, but in any event he made written
representations.

Since Mr Watson was recalled under s 39(2), there was no statutory obligation   *e*
on the Secretary of State to consult the board at that stage or at any time before
the reference under s 39(4). But the evidence is that in practice he does so, after
recall of the prisoner under s 39(2), and if the board considers the recall to have
been unreasonable the Secretary of State will consider releasing the prisoner.
This extra-statutory procedure is recognised in the Parole Board Rules 1992.   *f*
These prescribe the information and reports which the Secretary of State must
serve on the board and the prisoner on a reference under s 39(4) and there is
included:

'The details of any memorandum which the Board considered prior to
making its recommendation for recall under section 39(1) of the Act or   *g*
confirming the Secretary of State's decision to recall under section 39(2) of
the Act, including the reasons why the Secretary of State considered it
expedient in the public interest to recall that person before it was practicable
to obtain a recommendation from the Board.' (See schedule 2A, para 9.)

h

III
Mr Watson's first challenge was to the lawfulness of this extra-statutory
confirmation of his recall by the Parole Board on 30 March 1994. Mr Fitzgerald
QC on his behalf submitted that this procedure compromised the Parole Board's
standing as a review body independent of the executive by involving it in the
process of recall; denied Mr Watson any right at that stage to a fair hearing or an   *j*
opportunity to make representations; pre-empted or unfairly influenced the
review of the Parole Board under s 39(4); and gave rise to a real danger of bias
within the test laid down in *R v Gough* [1993] 2 All ER 724, [1993] AC 646.

Mr Kovats for the board pointed out that since, in the absence of an
emergency, the Act provided for the board to recommend recall under s 39(1)
and later review the case under s 39(4) there could under the Act (the European

a   Convention for the Protection of Human Rights and Fundamental Freedoms (Rome, 4 November 1950; TS (1953); Cmd 8969) apart) be no objection to the less formal involvement of the board in confirming recall rather than recommending it. But his main answer rested on the substantial merits of the procedure involved. This extra-statutory consultation of the board at the time of recall, pending review under s 39(4), could only work to the advantage of the prisoner,

b   by giving him a chance of accelerated release; it could not work to his disadvantage. The board was not (in contrast to its role under s 39(1)) involved in making a decision to recall, but was merely acting as an extra-statutory watchdog. There was no call for the prisoner to be heard at that stage, since a full hearing, at which the prisoner would enjoy full rights to be heard, would inevitably follow when a prisoner had been recalled under s 39(2). The board's

c   informal confirmation could not in practice pre-empt or unfairly influence the s 39(4) review, since the members conducting that review would always be different from those giving the earlier confirmation; and they would appreciate that the confirmation had been provisional and tentative, given on a partial hearing of only one side of the case, without the benefit of the full materials and

d   representations available at the later review. There was no real danger of bias, since those conducting the later review would inevitably form their own judgment on all the materials presented to them.

   I do not regard the confirmation procedure adopted here as objectionable. To condemn it could only work to the disadvantage of discretionary life prisoners recalled under s 39(2). It would not make sense to impose the requirements of a

e   full hearing on a step which is clearly intended to be tentative and provisional. I would regard the procedure as objectionable if there were any reason to suppose that those conducting the later review would feel that they could not direct release on licence without appearing to disagree with, or implicitly criticise, those who had earlier confirmed the recall. In my view there is no such reason. No one

f   who reaches a decision on full argument and evidence following a hearing between the parties accuses of error or impliedly criticises the maker of a preliminary decision taken on hearing one party alone. The standing of those conducting the review under s 39(4), under judicial chairmanship, is sufficient guarantee of complete independence and objectivity. The earlier confirmation will be seen as part of the history, but in itself of no weight at all. There is in my

g   opinion no danger of bias whatever.

IV

   The board's letter of 25 July 1994, quoted above, makes clear in its first paragraph the test which the board applied in considering Mr Watson's release under s 39(4):

h

> 'The Act requires the Board to direct your release only if it is satisfied that it is no longer necessary for the protection of the public that you be confined.'

j   This is the test which s 34(4)(b) requires the board to apply when considering the initial release of a discretionary life sentence prisoner. Is the same test applicable on a review under s 39(4)?

   Mr Fitzgerald strongly argued that it is not. At the stage of considering initial release, he pointed out, a discretionary life prisoner was serving a sentence imposed by a judge who must (to justify passing the sentence) have concluded that the prisoner was likely to be a danger to the public for the foreseeable future. That judgment would stand unless and until displaced. It would be displaced

only when the board concluded under s 34(4)(b) that it was no longer necessary
for the protection of the public that the prisoner should be confined. But once
that conclusion had been reached and the prisoner had been released on licence,
he was substantially (if not technically) at liberty. There was no longer a
presumption in favour of continued imprisonment (see *R v Parole Board, ex p
Lodomez* (1994) 26 BMLR 162). Ground had now to be shown for depriving the
former prisoner of the freedom he had been held entitled to enjoy. Accordingly,
the board should confine itself to determining the validity of the reasons for recall
given by the Home Secretary. Alternatively, the board should apply a different
test: whether it was positively satisfied that recall was necessary to prevent the
commission of (in Mr Watson's case) further serious sexual assaults of the kind
that had led to the original sentence.

These submissions are not unattractive, and they have the practical justification that if a prisoner has been released because the board was satisfied under
s 34(4)(b), and nothing has changed, it would be absurd and oppressive if,
following recall and review under s 39(4), the board were not to direct immediate
release. There must in practice be some relevant new material to justify the
board's reconsideration of the substance of the case. I do not, however, conclude
that either of Mr Fitzgerald's arguments is sound.

It would, in my view, be subversive of the review regime established by the Act
if the board confined itself to reviewing the validity of the Secretary of State for
the Home Department's reasons for recall. It is the judgment of the board as an
independent quasi-judicial review body, not the judgment of the Secretary of
State as an arm of the executive, which matters. He is a party to the review, and
of course his evidence and submissions must be received and weighed. But the
board must make its own mind up, and give its own reasons. It would seriously
undermine the integrity of the system if the board were to defer to the Secretary
of State's view unless it were shown to be wrong. It is itself the primary
decision-maker.

I find Mr Fitzgerald's alternative argument more persuasive, but I reject it for
these reasons.

(1) Even when released on licence, a discretionary life sentence prisoner
remains subject to that sentence, passed because of the likelihood of danger to the
public.

(2) By the time the Parole Board conducts its review under s 39(4) the prisoner
is back in prison, continuing to serve his sentence.

(3) Section 39(4) prescribes no statutory test which the board is to apply. But
the board's function under s 39(5) is almost exactly the same as that under s 34(3),
namely to direct (or not) the prisoner's release. In the absence of express
statutory provision, it is to be assumed that the same test is applicable.

(4) In exercising its practical judgment the board is bound to approach its task
under the two sections in the same way, balancing the hardship and injustice of
continuing to imprison a man who is unlikely to cause serious injury to the public
against the need to protect the public against a man who is not unlikely to cause
such injury. In other than a clear case this is bound to be a difficult and very
anxious judgment. But in the final balance the board is bound to give
preponderant weight to the need to protect innocent members of the public
against any significant risk of serious injury. This is the test which s 34(4)(b)
prescribes, and I think it is equally appropriate under s 39(4).

Had the board adopted a test more favourable to Mr Watson, it appears from
the letter that it would none the less have held that test to be met on the facts
here. But, in my view, the board applied the right test.

V

a   Thirdly, Mr Fitzgerald challenged the merits of the board's decision. He pointed out, correctly, that Mr Watson had committed no criminal offence and broken no condition of his licence. His association with youths of 17 and 18 (it was said) showed no propensity to commit offences against the much younger boys who had been the victims of his original offences. He had done nothing *b*   whatsoever to encourage the 14-year-old absconder. No reliance could be placed on the suspicion of intended violence which had prompted Mr Watson's emergency recall.

These are fair points. But they were matters for the board. It is not for the court to second-guess the judgment of a specialist tribunal. It is evident from the board's letter that the board reviewed the case fully, paying regard to the *c*   evidence it heard and the submissions it received. Even disregarding, as the board did, the allegation of intended violence, there was material before it (much of it rehearsed in the letter) which could found a reasonable apprehension of serious injury to members of the public if Mr Watson were released on licence at that time.

d   I would dismiss the appeal. In my judgment the judge reached the right answer for the right reasons.

ROSE LJ. I gratefully adopt the recital of the facts, issues and submissions in the judgment of Sir Thomas Bingham MR.

As to alleged procedural irregularity and bias, it is to be noted that the Home *e*   Secretary's consultation of the Parole Board on 30 March 1994 was a step which was potentially in the applicant's interest. It afforded to that independent body an immediate opportunity, which the Home Secretary was not obliged to give at that stage, to advise as to the propriety of his decision to revoke the applicant's licence. The advice then given by the board without, at that urgent stage, having *f*   heard representations from the applicant, was that recall was appropriate. The board's reasons for that view were made known to the applicant, as is apparent from the terms of his letter of 20 May, well before the hearing on 22 July. There is no allegation or evidence to suggest that the discretionary lifer panel on 22 July was actually biased. I am unable to accept that 'there was a real danger of bias' (*R v Gough* [1993] 2 All ER 724 at 737–738, [1993] AC 646 at 670 per Lord Goff of *g*   Chieveley). Those who then sat were not the same members of the board who had considered the matter on 30 March. They were experienced professionals chaired by a judge. The material which they considered was much fuller, and included, for example, reports from the governor and chaplain which had not been available in March. The hearing was inter partes. The applicant made *h*   representations through counsel. In my judgment, it is impossible in these circumstances to contend that there was any unfairness in the July panel knowing of the March decision or the reasons for it.

As to the test applied, I see no warrant for the suggestion that a different test should be applied by the board when reviewing a decision to recall a discretionary *j*   lifer under s 39(4)(b) from that applicable when determining whether to direct initial release under s 34(3) and (4). In both cases the prisoner is in custody by virtue of a life sentence imposed by the trial judge and the question is whether, having served the tariff part of his sentence, he should continue to be confined. In both cases the need to protect the public is paramount. The only test specified in the Act is in s 34(4)(b) namely 'that it is no longer necessary for the protection of the public that the prisoner should be confined'. That test is as apt for cases of re-release as for cases of initial release. There is nothing in the English authorities or in the decisions of the European Court of Human Rights to suggest that different tests are appropriate. Accordingly, the judge was right to reject the contention that a different test should be applied in re-release cases.

As to the merits of the decision, there was in my judgment abundant evidence to justify the panel's conclusion that in 1994 the applicant continued 'to present a very real risk to the public' and that his association with youths with criminal connections, drug addiction and no settled way of life, created an undesirable dependency of those youths on him so that 'the risk of those associations leading to serious sexual offending was very high'. An association with such people was established by the applicant's own evidence; it was persisted in, despite advice and warnings from the probation officer, from whom the applicant sought to conceal it; it involved the applicant locking a 17-year-old in his premises and visits from others under 16, in the context of the applicant looking forward to a reduction in the age of consent; it displayed a lack of insight on the part of the applicant into the risks he was running and a stubborn refusal to change; and it led Dr Mendelson, who could not say there was an imminent risk of re-offending, to conclude that, until the applicant changed his attitude, it was likely he would fall into further trouble.

Accordingly, and for the other reasons given by Sir Thomas Bingham MR, I agree that this appeal should be dismissed.

ROCH LJ. I agree.

The reference by the Secretary of State of his decision to recall the appellant to prison to the Parole Board and the discharge by the board of their duty under s 32(2) of the Criminal Justice Act 1991 to advise the Secretary of State does not, in my judgment, render the board partisan or mean that the board ceases thereafter in the appellant's case to be an independent body which can exercise a judicial function independent of the executive. Mr Fitzgerald did not go so far as that in argument, because the remedy he was seeking was the quashing of the decision of 25 July 1994 and a reference of the appellant's case to a different discretionary lifer panel who would not be informed of the board's confirmation on 30 March 1994 of the Secretary of State's decision to recall the appellant to prison or for their reasons for that confirmation. Mr Fitzgerald did not submit that the board had become incapable of dealing judicially with the appellant's representations against his recall. It is also to be observed that no suggestion was made that the confirmation of the Secretary of State's revocation of the appellant's licence was unreasonable on the material available to the board or that the reasons the board gave could be criticised.

Did the fact that the discretionary lifer panel knew of the board's decision of 30 March and the reasons for that decision create a real danger of bias in the panel, although its members were different from those who had acted on 30 March? Again, in my judgment, the answer is, No it did not. The proof is there in the panel's decision letter. The panel clearly listened to the submissions of the appellant's counsel and of the appellant and accepted some of them. The panel excluded the statement of Stephen Goodall, for example. It was not suggested either to this court or to Popplewell J that the panel had behaved in a biased manner.

Section 39(4)(b) of the 1991 Act placed a duty on the Secretary of State to refer to the board the case of the appellant, he having been recalled to prison by the Secretary of State under s 39(2). Section 39(5) obliges the Secretary of State to give effect to the board's direction that a recalled discretionary life prisoner be released immediately on licence. Section 39 does not expressly confer on the *a* board authority to direct the immediate release on licence of a discretionary life prisoner. That authority derives from s 32 and s 34(3). It is of considerable importance, in my opinion, that s 32(6) enables the Secretary of State to give the board directions as to the matters to be taken into account by the board in discharging its functions under Pt II of the Act (Early Release of Prisoners). Parliament requires the Secretary of State if he chooses to give such directions, to

b have particular regard to—

> '(a) the need to protect the public from serious harm from offenders; and (b) the desirability of preventing the commission by them of further offences and of securing their rehabilitation.'

Section 34(4) provides:

c
> 'The Board shall not give a direction under subsection (3) above with respect to a discretionary life prisoner unless ... (b) The Board is satisfied that it is no longer necessary for the protection of the public that the prisoner should be confined.'

d That provision is not repeated in s 39, in my judgment, because there was no need that it should be repeated. The power of the board to direct the release of a discretionary life prisoner is a single statutory power which can be exercised at any time after the expiration of the specified part of the sentence, whether the Secretary of State is referring the life prisoner's case to the board under s 34(4) or under s 39(4). The test that the board has to apply in both situations is the same:

e that the board has to be satisfied that further confinement of the prisoner is no longer necessary for the protection of the public. That this is the test in all cases is consistent with the intention of Parliament as manifested in the language of s 32(6). The test is justified if the protection of innocent people is to be placed above the personal liberty of one who has been guilty of grave offending and who

f may still represent a danger to others. In my opinion, it is incontrovertible that Parliament in the 1991 Act has manifested an intention to put the protection of the public as the overriding consideration. It follows that, in my judgment, the board directed itself correctly as to the test it had to apply.

On Mr Fitzgerald's third submission, that the board's conclusion was *Wednesbury* unreasonable (see *Associated Provincial Picture Houses Ltd v Wednesbury*

g *Corp* [1947] 2 All ER 680, [1948] 1 KB 223), I agree with the judgments of Sir Thomas Bingham MR and Rose LJ on that issue, and would simply refer to para (2) of the grounds of the appellant's notice of appeal, which reads:

> 'It is submitted that, if the correct test were applied, there was insufficient evidence of renewed dangerousness to justify recall ...'

h
That sentence implies: first, that there was evidence, albeit it is said that the evidence was insufficient, and secondly, that if the test applied by the board was the correct test, then the evidence of renewed dangerousness was sufficient.

j *Appeal dismissed. Leave to appeal to the House of Lords refused.*

L I Zysman Esq   Barrister.

Sheppard & Cooper Ltd v TSB Bank plc and others

CHANCERY DIVISION

BLACKBURNE J

25, 26 MARCH, 3 APRIL 1996

Company – Debenture – Demand made under debenture – Money payable on demand – Creditor demanding payment at meeting with directors of debtor company – Director stating that company unable to meet demand – Creditor appointing administrative receivers not more than 60 minutes after making demand – Whether creditor allowing sufficient time to pass between making of demand and appointment of receivers.

In January 1990 the plaintiff company executed a debenture in favour of a bank whereby it granted a fixed and floating charge over its assets and undertaking to secure its indebtedness to that bank. By cl 1 the plaintiff covenanted to pay or discharge its indebtedness on demand; cl 8A further provided that the bank might appoint administrative receivers of the charged assets at any time after all or any of the indebtedness became immediately payable. The bank was later acquired by the first defendant, along with its assets rights and liabilities, including the rights and obligations under the debenture and the debts secured by it. By early 1996 the plaintiff was substantially in debt to the defendant. In the course of a meeting between the parties on 7 February, at about 9.15 am or 9.30 am, the defendant's representatives handed to the plaintiff's directors a written demand requiring repayment of the plaintiff's indebtedness to the bank, which was stated to be £618,083·58. One of the plaintiff's directors thereupon stated that the plaintiff was not in a position to meet the demand and that the best that he could hope to achieve would be to pay half the excess on the overdraft over the next seven days. The meeting ended at or shortly after 10 am. At 10.15 am the same day the bank appointed the second and third defendants as administrative receivers of the plaintiff's assets and undertaking. The question arose whether the defendant had allowed sufficient time to pass between making its demand of the plaintiff and its purported appointment of the administrative receivers not more than 60 minutes later.

Held – Where money was payable on demand and the debtor failed to make payment, he would not be in default until he had had a reasonable opportunity of implementing whatever reasonable mechanics of payment he might need to employ to discharge the debt. The requirement that sufficient time be permitted to elapse to enable the debtor to make the necessary arrangements for payment assumed that that was the period needed if the debtor had the funds available. If, however, the debtor had made it clear to the creditor that the required funds were not available, that admission established the necessary default and there was thus no need for the creditor to allow any time to elapse before treating the debtor as in default. It followed that the time allowed between the effective making of the demand on the plaintiff by the first defendant and the purported appointment of the administrative receivers of the plaintiff pursuant to the demand was sufficient (see p 657 *f g*, p 658 *a*, p 660 *a b*, p 661 *c* and p 663 *d*, post).

Massey v Sladen (1868) LR 4 Exch 13, *Cripps (Pharmaceuticals) Ltd v Wickenden, R A Cripps & Sons Ltd v Wickenden* [1973] 2 All ER 606 and *Bank of Baroda v Panessar* [1986] 3 All ER 751 considered.

Notes

a For appointment of receiver by debenture holder, see 7(2) *Halsbury's Laws* (4th edn reissue) para 1157.

Cases referred to in judgment

Bank of Baroda v Panessar [1986] 3 All ER 751, [1987] Ch 335, [1987] 2 WLR 208.

b *Brighty v Norton* (1862) 3 B & S 305, 122 ER 116.

Cripps (Pharmaceuticals) Ltd v Wickenden, R A Cripps & Sons Ltd v Wickenden [1973] 2 All ER 606, [1973] 1 WLR 944.

Hawtin & Partners Ltd v Pugh (25 June 1975, unreported), Ch D.

Massey v Sladen (1868) LR 4 Exch 13.

Moore v Shelley (1883) 8 App Cas 285, PC.

c *Toms v Wilson* (1863) 4 B & S 442, 122 ER 524.

Cases also cited or referred to in skeleton arguments

Civil Service Co-operative Society Ltd v McGrigor's Trustee [1923] 2 Ch 347, [1923] All ER Rep 595.

d *Horsey Estate Ltd v Steiger* [1899] 2 QB 79, [1895–9] All ER Rep 515, CA.

Motion

By notice of motion dated 6 March 1996 the plaintiff, Sheppard & Cooper Ltd, applied under RSC Ord 14A for determination of the question whether the first defendant, TSB Bank plc, had allowed sufficient time to pass between making its
e demand of the plaintiff on 7 February 1996 pursuant to the terms of a debenture dated 8 January 1990 and its purported appointment of the second and third defendants, Iain John Allan and Richard Anthony Oirschot, as administrative receivers of the plaintiff not more than 60 minutes later. The fourth defendant, the Registrar of Companies, took no part in the proceedings. The facts are set out
f in the judgment.

Gabriel Moss QC and *Geoffrey Zelin* (instructed by *Withers*) for the plaintiff.
Philip Heslop QC and *Orlando Fraser* (instructed by *Hammond Suddards*) for the defendants.

g
Cur adv vult

3 April 1996. The following judgment was delivered.

BLACKBURNE J. On 8 January 1990 the plaintiff, Sheppard & Cooper Ltd,
h which trades in ancient and antique glass, executed a debenture in favour of Hill Samuel Bank Ltd, whereby it granted a fixed and floating charge over its assets and undertaking to secure its indebtedness to that bank. By cl 1 the plaintiff covenanted to pay or discharge its indebtedness on demand. By cl 8A it was provided that, at any time after all or any of the indebtedness should have become
j immediately payable, Hill Samuel might appoint administrative receivers of the charged assets.

Hill Samuel has since been acquired by the first defendant, TSB Bank plc (the bank), to which, by Act of Parliament, its assets rights and liabilities have been transferred. Those assets rights and liabilities include the rights and obligations under the debenture of 8 January 1990 and, in particular, the debts secured by it.

By early 1996 substantial indebtedness had built up on the plaintiff's account with the bank. On 7 February a meeting took place at the bank's Lower Thames

Street premises attended by representatives of the bank and by Mr Christopher
Sheppard and Mr Christopher Cooper on behalf of the plaintiff. Mr Sheppard and a
Mr Cooper are directors of the plaintiff and their respective families own the
whole of the plaintiff's issued share capital.

During the course of the meeting, a written demand was handed by one of the
bank's two representatives at the meeting to Mr Sheppard and Mr Cooper
demanding repayment of the plaintiff's indebtedness to the bank. The amount b
of the indebtedness was stated, as at close of business the previous day, to be
£618,083·58. There is a difference of recollection as to when the demand was
handed over. The bank says it was 9.15 am. The plaintiff says it was around 9.30
am. The difference between the two is not material. The undisputed evidence
is that Mr Sheppard stated to the bank's two representatives that the plaintiff was
not in a position to meet the demand and that the best that he could hope to c
achieve would be half the excess on the overdraft over the next seven days from
sales made in New York. The meeting ended at or shortly after 10 am. At 10.15
am the same day the bank appointed the second and third defendants, licensed
insolvency practitioners and partners in the firm of Smith & Williamson, to be
administrative receivers of the plaintiff's assets and undertaking. Following that d
appointment the second and third defendants took possession of the plaintiff's
premises.

The plaintiff took the view that the period of time between demand and the
appointment of the second and third defendants as administrative receivers was
insufficient with the result that the appointment was invalid. It also took the view
that the appointment was in breach of the terms of a letter of appointment dated e
1 February 1993, addressed to the plaintiff by Smith & Williamson on the
occasion of Smith & Williamson's appointment to undertake an investigation
into the plaintiff's affairs. It was a term of that appointment that Smith &
Williamson would not undertake any responsibility for the management of the
plaintiff's affairs either then or in the future. f

Accordingly, six days later, on 13 February, the plaintiff applied ex parte to
Harman J and obtained an injunction restraining the second and third defendants
until after 16 February from acting as administrative receivers of the plaintiff. On
the inter partes hearing on 16 February Harman J refused to continue the
injunction. He took the view that the period of time between demand and
appointment was not insufficient and that, on the balance of convenience, it g
would not be right to restrain the second and third defendants from acting upon
their appointment notwithstanding the terms of the letter of 1 February 1993. By
now the writ in the action had been issued. In it the plaintiff claims a declaration
that the appointment of the second and third defendants as administrative
receivers was invalid, an order that they resign as such receivers, an inquiry as to h
damages and other relief.

On 26 February the plaintiff successfully appealed Harman J's decision.
Subject to various cross-undertakings by the plaintiff and Mr Sheppard and Mr
Cooper, including cross-undertakings as to damages, the second and third
defendants undertook to resign as administrative receivers on or before 4 pm on j
29 February and an injunction was granted, in the meantime, restraining them
from acting upon their appointment. The basis of the Court of Appeal's decision
was that Smith & Williamson, including the second and third defendants as
partners of that firm, were disabled by contract from accepting appointment as
administrative receivers of the plaintiff and there was no reason why that
agreement should not be enforced. The court declined, however, to express any

a view on whether, additionally, the appointment was invalid as having been made before sufficient time had elapsed following demand. It refused to do so, taking the view that the point at issue was complex and that, in the circumstances, it was unnecessary to decide the point having regard to its decision on the issue of the contractual disability.

On 27 February the bank served a fresh demand on the plaintiff. Two days

b later, on 29 February at 1.40 pm the second and third defendants resigned as administrative receivers and 20 minutes later two partners of Messrs Levy Gee were appointed as administrative receivers of the plaintiff's assets, effectively in their place. The validity of the replacement appointment is challenged on the ground that the fresh demand of 27 February and the replacement appointment were made before the second and third defendants had restored the plaintiff to

c possession of its assets.

On the basis that the validity of the administrative receivership turns on whether the bank had allowed sufficient time to pass between making its demand of the plaintiff on 7 February and its purported appointment of the second and third defendants as administrative receivers not more than 60 minutes later,

d application under RSC Ord 14A was made to, and an order granted by, Rattee J on 11 March for that question to be determined. It is that question which is now before me. The relevant facts, as I have related them, are not in dispute. The question is one of law.

The case raises once again the question how much time must pass following demand by a creditor, where money is payable on demand, before the debtor,

e who fails to make payment, can be said to be in default.

In *Bank of Baroda v Panessar* [1986] 3 All ER 751 at 759–760, [1987] Ch 335 at 348 Walton J, repeating a test which he had formulated in his earlier decision in *Hawtin & Partners Ltd v Pugh* (25 June 1975, unreported), stated as follows:

f '"Money payable 'on demand' is repayable immediately on demand being made ... Nevertheless, it is physically impossible in most cases for a person to keep the money required to discharge the debt about his person. He may in a simple case keep it in a box under his bed; it may be at the bank or with a bailee. The debtor is therefore not in default in making the payment demanded unless and until he has had a reasonable opportunity of implementing whatever reasonable mechanics of payment he may need to

g employ to discharge the debt. Of course, this is limited to the time necessary for the mechanics of payment. It does not extend to any time to raise the money if it is not there to be paid."'

Walton J was also following the approach of Goff J in *Cripps (Pharmaceuticals) Ltd*

h *v Wickenden, R A Cripps & Sons Ltd v Wickenden* [1973] 2 All ER 606, [1973] 1 WLR 944, who, in turn, had applied a line of authority, also referred to by Walton J, beginning with a dictum of Blackburn J in *Brighty v Norton* (1862) 3 B & S 305 at 312, 122 ER 116 at 118 and followed by a passage from the judgment of Lord Cockburn CJ in *Toms v Wilson* (1863) 4 B & S 442 at 453, 122 ER 524 at 529 which

j had been adopted and applied by Sir Barnes Peacock in the Privy Council in *Moore v Shelley* (1883) 8 App Cas 285 at 293.

In stating the so-called mechanics of payment test to be the appropriate test, Walton J was concerned to reject what he described as a slightly different approach adopted in certain Commonwealth jurisdictions where the amount of time to be allowed for a debtor to comply with the demand had been stated to be 'a reasonable time', meaning a reasonable time in all the circumstances. Walton

J criticised that test as wholly imprecise and undesirable in a commercial context which is where the question usually arises.

It is not in dispute that the mechanics of payment test is the correct test. What is in dispute is its application in the circumstances of the present case.

For the plaintiff Mr Moss submitted that the mechanics of payment test involves both the making of a demand and the elapse of a period of time. He described those twin requirements as a condition precedent to the bank's right to treat the plaintiff's failure to make payment as a default entitling it to appoint administrative receivers. In the instant case, he said, the effective period of time was no more than 15 minutes calculated from the time when the meeting between the two directors and the bank's representatives ended, which was at or shortly after 10 am, to the time of the purported appointment of the second and third defendants as administrative receivers at 10.15 am. The period of 30 to 45 minutes between the time when the demand was delivered (at either 9.15 am or 9.30 am) and the end of the meeting was to be disregarded, he said, because, until the two directors were able to get away from the meeting and set in train the mechanics of paying the bank's demand, it could not realistically be said that the period within which to implement the mechanics of payment had begun. He submitted that no case has ever held that *no* time need elapse. In the instant case, he said, there is no meaningful difference between the 15 or so minutes effectively allowed to elapse and no time at all. Without stating what minimum period would have been appropriate in the instant case he submitted that 15 minutes was altogether insufficient. He pointed out that in *Panessar's* case [1986] 3 All ER 751, [1987] Ch 335, which involved demands on two companies, the shortest period accepted by Walton J was 45 minutes, and that in the *Cripps* case [1973] 2 All ER 606, [1973] 1 WLR 944 it was approximately 60 minutes.

He submitted that the whole point of Walton J's mechanics of payment test is the application of objective criteria and that it is not dependent upon what he described as the subjective vagaries of a 'reasonable time in all the circumstances' approach. Moreover, he said, it proceeds on the footing that the necessary moneys are available with which to effect payment, whether or not in fact they are. For these reasons, he submitted, the relevant time cannot be made to depend upon the subjective knowledge of the true position which the creditor may possess, whether that knowledge is to be derived, as here, from an admission by the plaintiff of an inability to pay, or from other circumstances. The admission, although not disputed, could not amount to a waiver of the condition precedent, as he described it, and, anyway, he said, the defendants have not sought to say that it did. Short of waiver or an invitation by the plaintiff to appoint a receiver, there is no principled basis, he submitted, for the court to disregard the need for the condition precedent to be fulfilled before the creditor can be permitted in law to act on the default.

He went on to submit that there are good reasons why the admission of an inability to pay should be disregarded in the application of the mechanics of payment test. For example, debtors might be discouraged from being honest with their creditors, pretending to be able to pay when they could not (so as not to forfeit the time otherwise available to them), and disputes might arise as to just what the debtor had admitted and whether, even if the admission was clear, it was one that the directors had authority to make or was one which should have been made. If it were open to a creditor, knowing that the debtor could not make payment, to make a demand followed immediately by the appointment of a receiver, the prospect might arise of what Mr Moss luridly described as a new *a* type of 'dawn raid'—of debtors being roused from their beds at dead of night to be faced with demands that could not be met, followed immediately by appointments of receivers, or of out-of-hours demands made of companies at their registered offices followed by appointments of receivers who would immediately take possession, with directors turning up to work later that morning only to find the company's premises already occupied by the receivers.

b Such a prospect would, he said, be appalling and uncivilised and one that the court should not contemplate. On the other hand, he said, there are good practical reasons why, whether or not he has the necessary moneys, the debtor should have the benefit of the period of time following demand allowed by the mechanics of payment test. Such reasons include the opportunity to consider his position, take advice and establish the authority of the person, if not the creditor *c* himself, who makes the demand.

Alternatively, Mr Moss submitted, the matter may be viewed simply as one of construction in that the expression 'on demand' as used in the debenture means that the plaintiff is to be provided with a sufficient time, following demand, to effect the mechanics of payment. The length of the time must be judged from *d* the point of view of the parties at the time the contract was made—ie when the debenture was given—and not at the time of demand or subsequently. The contract assumes, he submitted, that the moneys would be there to effect the necessary payment following demand, not that they would not, and the only question, therefore, is what the time is that is needed to effect such payment. On that basis neither the creditor's knowledge of absence of funds nor any statement *e* to him of the absence of any funds can alter the nature of the condition precedent.

In my view, the question how much time must elapse after demand before a debtor can be said to be in default is essentially a practical one. As Goff J observed in the *Cripps* case [1973] 2 All ER 606 at 616, [1973] 1 WLR 944 at 955:

f '... the cases show that [where money is payable on demand] all the creditor has to do is to give the debtor time to get it from some convenient place, not to negotiate a deal which he hopes will produce the money.'

What that time is must, in my view, depend on the circumstances of the case. If the sum demanded is of an amount which the debtor, if he has it, will be likely to have in a bank account—which will be the position in 99 cases out of 100—the *g* time permitted must be reasonable in all the circumstances to enable the debtor to contact his bank and make the necessary arrangements for the sum in question to be transferred from his bank to the creditor. If the demand is made out of banking hours, the period of time is likely to be longer—involving waiting until banks reopen—than if the demand is made during banking hours. In so stating I *h* do not consider that I am abandoning the mechanics of payment test in favour of some wider and less precise approach. In his unreported decision in *Hawtin,* referred to in *Panessar*'s case, Walton J himself said that the debtor is not in default in making payment 'unless and until he has had a reasonable opportunity of implementing whatever reasonable mechanics of payment he may need to *j* employ to discharge the debt'. This, I venture to suggest, is no more than the application of practical common sense. Nothing is gained by investing the proposition with the status of a condition precedent to the existence of an actionable default and, as Mr Heslop QC pointed out, the matter has never been analysed in the authorities on that basis.

Where I part company from Mr Moss is in the suggestion that, short of waiver or an invitation by the debtor to the creditor to treat his failure to pay following demand as a default on his part (by, for example, inviting the creditor to appoint a receiver), the court must in all circumstances allow a minimum period to elapse before the debtor's default can be established. The requirement that sufficient time be permitted to elapse to enable the debtor to effect the mechanics of payment assumes that that is the period needed if the debtor has the necessary moneys available. If, however, he has made it clear to the creditor that the necessary moneys are not available, then, provided a proper demand has been made, I cannot see that the creditor need allow any time to elapse before being at liberty to treat the debtor as in default.

The authorities, the few that there are, are entirely consistent with this view.

In *Massey v Sladen* (1868) LR 4 Exch 13 the plaintiff executed in favour of the defendants a bill of sale of certain machinery at his mill premises to secure his indebtedness. The bill was redeemable if he should pay the sums due 'instantly on demand, and without any delay on any pretence whatsoever'. The bill provided that the demand might be made personally on the plaintiff—

> 'or by giving or leaving verbal or written notice to or for him at his present or last known place of business ... or at the residence or last known residence of him, so nevertheless that a demand be in fact made.' (See LR 4 Exch 13 at 14.)

The bill also provided that on default the defendants might enter and seize and sell the property thereby assigned but that, until default, the plaintiff should remain in possession of it. The defendants' solicitor made demand of the plaintiff's son at the plaintiff's premises at a time when the plaintiff himself was absent. The son stated that the demand could not be met whereupon the solicitor took immediate possession. Later that same day the defendants made demand of the plaintiff personally. It was held that the defendants were not entitled to enter and seize the plaintiff's goods when they did. In the view of three of the four members of the court (Kelly CB, Channell and Pigott BB), as the plaintiff was absent when the demand was made it was necessary, before seizure could lawfully be effected, that notice should be given or left to or for the debtor in such a manner that it might fairly be supposed that it would reach him. As this had not happened by the time seizure was effected, the seizure was unlawful. In the view of the fourth member of the court (Cleasby B), the demand was defective through failing to state the amount claimed (a ground which would probably not be good in law today). It was clear, therefore, that, in the view of all four members of the court, as no proper demand had been made of the plaintiff before seizure had been effected, the seizure was invalid.

In the course of his judgment Kelly CB said (LR 4 Exch 13 at 17):

> '... if a personal demand could not be made by reason of the plaintiff's absence from his place of business, then that notice should be left or given in such a way that, if reasonable diligence were used, it might without substantial delay come to his knowledge. It is true that the deed provides that instantly on the demand being made the plaintiff must pay. But this must refer to a personal demand to be made in case he is found upon the premises, and cannot apply to the alternative demand to be made in his absence; and for this reason, if he is on the premises he must make some answer to the demand, either offering to pay at once, or, if he were unable to do so, admitting his inability; in which latter case the defendants would have been entitled to seize at once.'

a In the view of Kelly CB, therefore, the defendants could lawfully have seized the plaintiff's property without waiting if, having made demand of him personally, the plaintiff had admitted his inability to pay.

In the course of his judgment, Channell B said (at 18–19):

b 'It may be, that if a personal service had been made on the plaintiff, the defendants might have seized immediately afterwards, making the seizure in effect concurrent with the default. But it is unnecessary to decide this, for there was here clearly no personal service before the seizure.'

It would therefore seem that he too envisaged seizure following immediately upon demand without the necessity for allowing any time to pass to enable the debtor to effect the mechanics of payment. Neither of the other two members of c the court expressed any separate view on the point. In my view, *Massey v Sladen* supports the proposition that, where demand is made and the debtor admits that he cannot pay, the creditor need not wait before acting. The necessary default is established by the admission of the inability to pay.

The *Cripps* case involved the validity of the appointment by a bank of a receiver d of two companies, a parent and its subsidiary, pursuant to debentures under which money was repayable on demand. One of the issues in the case was whether the bank had allowed sufficient time between demand and appointment. The evidence established that the demands had been made at or shortly before 11 am and that the appointments had been made at or shortly after midday. Having held (in the passage which I have cited (see [1973] 2 All ER 606 e at 616, [1973] 1 WLR 944 at 955)) that all that a creditor has to do is to give the debtor time to get the money from some convenient place, not to negotiate a deal which he hopes will produce the money, Goff J went on to consider whether, on the facts, the bank had allowed the two companies sufficient time. He said ([1973] 2 All ER 606 at 617):

f 'It is abundantly plain that Cripps [ie the two companies] had not got the money and had no convenient place to which they could go to get it. Two passages in the evidence will suffice here. First, Mr Stapleton [the chairman of the parent company] in chief said: "At one time Mr Stokoe [the bank's district manager] asked if there was any more money likely to be coming g from me or anyone else. He asked, 'from me'. Can't really say if he said, 'or others'. There were others who helped put up the earlier money. I replied as far as I was concerned I was not prepared to do anything. I did not say I thought someone else would. In fairness I could not have led him to think any likelihood of money coming from anywhere else." Secondly, Mr Yarnell h [a director of both companies] in cross-examination was asked this question: "Apart from a sale to someone who might put in money, what other sources of further capital were available?" and he answered: "No immediate sources." In my judgment, therefore, the plaintiffs cannot object on the ground that they were not given time to find the money or that the interval of time between 11 am, or shortly before, when the demands were made and j midday, or later, when the receiver was appointed was too short.'

The reference to the evidence of Mr Stapleton is to what he said at a meeting which took place when the demands were delivered to Mr Stapleton.

In other words, given the admission by Mr Stapleton that the companies did not have the money, the judge considered the period of one hour or so which elapsed between demand and appointment was not too short.

Another issue in the case was whether Mr Stapleton had authority to accept the
demand on behalf of the subsidiary company (he being a director of the parent   *a*
company but not of the subsidiary). After holding that Mr Stapleton had
authority to act for the subsidiary, Goff J went on to find that the demand had in
fact been delivered to the subsidiary at around midday which was at or around
the very time that the appointment had been made. Having held, if necessary by
reliance upon a legal presumption as to the order in which events occurred, that   *b*
the letter of demand reached the subsidiary just before the appointment, Goff J
reached the following conclusion ([1973] 2 All ER 606 at 618, [1973] 1 WLR 944
at 956):

> 'On this basis the interval between demand and appointment is still shorter
> but not, I think, unreasonable having regard to the passages in the evidence   *c*
> to which I have drawn attention.'

That is a reference to the passages which I have earlier quoted.

It is clear, therefore, that, as Mr Heslop submitted, Goff J was prepared to
accept that, given the admission to the bank by the chairman of the parent
company that the companies could not pay, the interval of time between demand   *d*
and appointment, on this basis no more than minutes, was sufficient.

Mr Moss sought to suggest that, in that passage, Goff J was employing a
different approach to the one that he had earlier adopted. I do not agree. He was
merely saying that, if the company admits that it cannot pay, it cannot object that
the bank, having made demand, fails to give it any further time. That, as Mr
Heslop pointed out, is this case.   *e*

In *Panessar*'s case [1986] 3 All ER 751, [1987] Ch 335, as I have mentioned, the
period between demand and appointment of a receiver was, on one view at least,
no more than 45 minutes. That was a period not significantly shorter than the
time it took for the demand to be delivered by the bank's messenger to the offices
of the company in question. Even then, the demand was left in a sealed envelope   *f*
on the counter on the ground floor of the company's premises. In the case of the
other company the period between demand and appointment was 75 minutes.
The sum claimed does not appear from the judgment but it would seem from the
amount claimed against the defendants in the action, guarantors of the
company's indebtedness, namely just over £830,000, that the amount must have
been extremely substantial. There was no suggestion in the evidence that the   *g*
companies were able to pay the amounts claimed. Walton J took the view that
'the time allowed by the bank to the companies was, in both cases, amply
sufficient' (see [1986] 3 All ER 751 at 760, [1987] Ch 335 at 348). That suggests that
he would have regarded a lesser period as sufficient. In his judgment, after having
referred to the passage from his earlier decision in the *Hawtin* case, Walton J said   *h*
([1986] 3 All ER 751 at 760, [1987] Ch 335 at 348):

> 'In practice, in 99 cases out of 100, all this is completely academic, because
> the debtor has not got the money available anyway and the demand is only
> a step towards some other end, e g bringing an action, appointing a receiver
> in the case of a company, and so forth. In this case the debtor cannot possibly   *j*
> claim any additional time as, there being no payment that he can make, there
> can be no pretence that he requires any additional time to implement the
> mechanics of payment.'

There was much debate before me as to what precisely Walton J meant in that
passage. Even taking the passage at its most favourable from the plaintiff's point

a of view, namely that in appropriate circumstances a debtor might seek to obtain time additional to what would otherwise ordinarily be sufficient in order to effect the mechanics of payment, I cannot see that where, so far from asking for additional time, the debtor indicates to the creditor that he cannot pay (with the result that no time is needed because no payment can be effected), this is something which the court must nevertheless wholly disregard.

b   In his judgment in the present case, when the motion for interlocutory relief was before him on 16 February, Harman J said:

'As it seems to me ... if the debtor admits that the debtor cannot pay, it is clearly unnecessary for the creditor to allow time for the mechanics of payment which he knows cannot have any point. The law does nothing in
c   vain and it will be pointless to require time to be allowed for an act that cannot happen.'

In my judgment, in so stating, Harman J was entirely correct.

I propose therefore to answer the question raised by para 2 of the notice of motion by declaring that, in the events that have happened as set out in the
d statement of claim, the time allowed between the effective making of the demand on the plaintiff by the first defendant on 7 February 1996 and purported appointment of the second and third defendants as administrative receivers of the plaintiff pursuant to that demand was sufficient.

Order accordingly.

Celia Fox   Barrister.

Re Schuppan (a bankrupt)

a

CHANCERY DIVISION

ROBERT WALKER J

8, 15 MARCH 1996

b

Solicitor – Duty – Conflict of interest – Acting for both parties in transaction – Bankruptcy – Trustee in bankruptcy appointing petitioning creditor's solicitors to advise on administration of bankrupt's estate – Outstanding matters in relation to earlier proceedings involving bankrupt and petitioning creditor and its solicitors – Whether retention of petitioning creditor's solicitors by trustee creating conflict of **c** *interest – Whether outstanding matters giving rise to conflict of interest.*

The petitioning creditor obtained judgment against the debtor in a contested action in which the debtor was found guilty of fraud and dishonesty. The debtor was later adjudicated bankrupt following his failure to satisfy the judgment. *d* Certain matters in connection with the main action remained outstanding, including an application for a wasted costs order, an inquiry as to damages in associated proceedings in the Isle of Man and an action for slander brought by the debtor against the petitioning creditor's solicitors. Nevertheless, the district judge authorised the trustee in bankruptcy to retain the petitioning creditor's solicitors to advise and assist him in the administration of the debtor's estate, *e* subject to an exception requiring another firm to be retained in relation to the unfinished business. The debtor objected to the trustee in bankruptcy being advised by the petitioning creditor's solicitors on the grounds that a conflict of interest existed and applied to set aside the district judge's authorisation. The application was dismissed and the debtor appealed.

f

Held – (1) It was not unreasonable for the trustee in bankruptcy to retain the petitioning creditor's solicitors, particularly where the anticipated difficulties related to the identification, tracing and recovery of assets for the bankrupt's estate; in that situation, the retainer of solicitors who were already aware of those difficulties could be advantageous to all the creditors, not just the petitioning *g* creditor. If the petitioning creditor was the largest creditor and no difficulties were expected in quantifying the provable debts, the risk of a conflict of interest would appear to be only a distant possibility. If, however, a conflict of interest was identified, but there was no real risk of confidential information miscarrying or being misused, or any identified risk could be averted by a division of *h* responsibility, a balancing exercise might be appropriate to determine whether the conflict was something which the court might cour.tenance (see p 668 *g* to *j* and p 669 *f* to *j*, post); *Re Maxwell Communication Corp plc* [1992] BCLC 465 applied.

(2) Although the risk of a conflict of interest was fairly remote, the retainer of a separate firm of solicitors to deal with the Manx inquiry and the wasted costs *j* application, which involved the trustee in bankruptcy on one side and the solicitors on the other, was a sensible course which averted any risk of a conflict of interest. As regards the slander action, any improper advantage arising from the solicitors' access to the debtor's papers could be appropriately resolved by an undertaking from the solicitors not to use in that action any documents which they saw in their capacity as solicitors to the trustee without leave. It followed

a that the district judge had not erred in the exercise of his discretion. The appeal would accordingly be dismissed (see p 668 *j* to p 669 *fj* to p 670 *aj* to p 671 *b*, post).

Notes

For a solicitor acting for opposing interests, see 44(1) *Halsbury's Laws* (4th edn reissue) para 150, and for cases on the subject, see 44 *Digest* (Reissue) 126–129,
b *1227–1261.*

Cases referred to in judgment

Crest Homes plc v Marks [1987] 2 All ER 1074, [1987] AC 829, [1987] 3 WLR 293, HL.
English and American Insurance Co Ltd v Herbert Smith [1988] FSR 232.
c *Gilmartin (a bankrupt), Re, ex p the bankrupt v International Agency and Supply Ltd* [1989] 2 All ER 835, [1989] 1 WLR 513.
Goddard v Nationwide Building Society [1986] 3 All ER 264, [1987] QB 670, [1986] 3 WLR 734, CA.
Heath v Tang [1993] 1 WLR 1421, CA.
d *Maxwell Communication Corp plc, Re* [1992] BCLC 465.
Polly Peck International plc (No 1), Re [1991] BCC 503.
Rakusen v Ellis Munday & Clarke [1912] 1 Ch 831, [1911–13] All ER Rep 813, CA.
Solicitors, Re a firm of [1992] 1 All ER 353, [1992] QB 959, [1992] 2 WLR 809, CA.
Solicitors, Re a firm of [1995] 3 All ER 482.
Supasave Retail Ltd v Coward Chance (a firm), David Lee & Co (Lincoln) Ltd v Coward
e *Chance (a firm)* [1991] 1 All ER 668, [1991] Ch 259, [1990] 3 WLR 1278.

Case also cited or referred to in skeleton arguments

Packaging Direct, Re [1994] BCC 213.

f **Appeal**

Vernon John Schuppan appealed from the order of District Judge Jolly made on 22 February 1996 in the Slough County Court in Bankruptcy, dismissing his application to set aside the order of District Judge Burgess made on 16 February 1996 in the same court whereby he authorised the trustee in bankruptcy of Mr Schuppan, Mark Pearce Riley, to retain the same firm of solicitors who were
g acting for the petitioning creditor to advise him in administration of Mr Schuppan's estate. The facts are set out in the judgment.

David Wolfson (instructed by *Stockler Charity*) for Mr Schuppan.
Robin Knowles (instructed by *Travers Smith Braithwaite*) for the trustee in
h bankruptcy.

Cur adv vult

15 March 1996. The following judgment was delivered.

j **ROBERT WALKER J.** This is an appeal from an order of District Judge Jolly made on 22 February 1996 in the Slough County Court in Bankruptcy. By that order District Judge Jolly dismissed an application to set aside an order of District Judge Burgess made on 16 February 1996 in the same court. District Judge Burgess's order had authorised Mr Mark Riley, as trustee in bankruptcy of Mr Vernon Schuppan, to continue to retain a well-known firm of London solicitors as solicitors to advise and assist him in the administration of Mr Schuppan's estate. This order was subject to an exception which I shall come back to. The appeal is a true appeal (see *Re Gilmartin (a bankrupt), ex p the bankrupt v International Agency and Supply Ltd* [1989] 2 All ER 835, [1989] 1 WLR 513). *a*

The background to this matter is an exceptionally hard-fought Queen's Bench Division action which, after much interlocutory skirmishing, was tried last autumn by Buckley J. A Japanese corporation, Art Corp, was the plaintiff, and Mr Schuppan and Race Corp Ltd, a British Virgin Islands company controlled by or *b* for the benefit of Mr Schuppan, were the defendants. Before the trial, Art had on 24 November 1993 obtained summary judgment against Mr Schuppan in a sum denominated in yen, the sterling equivalent of which, with accrued interest, is now in excess of £2·5m. Execution was stayed on this judgment pending trial of a counterclaim by Mr Schuppan. The trial before Buckley J occupied some seven weeks. On 18 December 1995 Buckley J dismissed Mr Schuppan's counterclaim. *c* He found Mr Schuppan guilty of fraud and dishonesty. He also gave judgment against Race. After giving judgment Buckley J granted worldwide Mareva relief against both defendants. Mr Schuppan has failed to satisfy the judgment and he has been made bankrupt on the petition of Art. The solicitors acted for Art throughout the Queen's Bench Division action. *d*

It is now known that there is to be no appeal against the decision of Buckley J. There are, however, three items of unfinished business connected with the action, and these are the main basis of the strong objections which Mr Schuppan raises, on this appeal, to the solicitors acting for Mr Riley, the trustee in bankruptcy. Mr Riley, however, has a strong preference, subject to the court's *e* approval, for retaining the solicitors to act for him. He says in a report to the court:

> '[Art] appears to be the largest unsecured creditor of the estate. It has a substantial interest in the successful administration of the estate. It is inevitable that [Art] will be called upon to provide substantial funding for *f* that administration. [The solicitors] have, by reason of their having acted for [Art] in its litigation against the Bankrupt, substantial familiarity with the affairs of the Bankrupt. I have ascertained that the litigation involved over 50 interlocutory applications and a seven week trial. The judgment at trial (of Buckley J.) makes clear that the trial addressed questions concerning the assets of the bankrupt. The judgment contains a finding of fraud against the *g* Bankrupt and reference to [his] having taken steps to put his assets beyond the reach of his creditors. I am accordingly very concerned to undertake the most detailed and rigorous investigation in order to identify and recover assets for the benefit of the insolvent estate. This is an urgent priority. The introduction of a new firm of solicitors to assist in this task would involve *h* substantial cost as that firm familiarises itself with the material available. [Art] is (as am I) reluctant to see that cost incurred. I am also concerned to have the close familiarity of [the solicitors] with the affairs of the Bankrupt available to me at first hand in the circumstances of this particular case.'

Mr Riley then refers to correspondence in which Mr Schuppan's objections, and *j* the solicitors' answer to them, are set out.

The three items of unfinished business are: an application for a wasted costs order, an inquiry as to damages under an undertaking given in associated proceedings in the Isle of Man, and a pending action for slander brought by Mr Schuppan against the solicitors and an individual (then an employed solicitor but *a* now a partner) in the solicitors. All three items reflect the hostility with which the Queen's Bench Division action was fought.

The application for a wasted costs order arises out of an early stage of the action at which an order granting Mareva relief against the defendants was discharged by Sir Peter Pain (sitting as a judge of the High Court) on grounds including material non-disclosure. Art was ordered to pay the costs on an *b* indemnity basis but (although Art's capacity to pay the costs is not in doubt) Mr Schuppan decided to seek wasted costs orders against the solicitors and against leading counsel then acting for Art. The order of Sir Peter Pain was made on 14 December 1993 and the summons for a wasted costs order was issued on 10 January 1994, so that it cannot be said to have been issued with Mr Schuppan's imminent bankruptcy in mind. It was adjourned to be heard after the conclusion *c* of the action. I should add that at the time of Sir Peter Pain's order Mr Schuppan was (surprisingly, as he was a successful racing driver) legally aided. There was an inconclusive discussion before me as to whether (because of set-off rules) the trustee does or does not have a financial interest in obtaining an order against the solicitors and against leading counsel. For the purposes of this appeal I shall *d* assume that he may have such an interest.

At an early stage in the main action Art also obtained Mareva relief under an order made on 12 November 1993 in the High Court of the Isle of Man. This contained an undertaking in damages. The injunction was discharged by consent on 15 December 1993. On 7 July 1995 the High Court of the Isle of Man ordered that the undertaking should be enforced, and the inquiry as to damages is fixed to *e* be heard in the Isle of Man on 4 April 1996. Buckley J has already decided that no damages are payable under the comparable undertaking in the English action, but Mr Schuppan does not accept that the same outcome will necessarily follow in the Isle of Man.

The slander action is connected with the main action in that it concerns what *f* the individual solicitor is alleged to have said about Mr Schuppan's honesty in telephone calls, made on two separate occasions, to a Slough bank manager and a Nottingham solicitor. The proceedings were commenced on 21 December 1993. Pleadings have been exchanged and the proceedings were on 29 June 1994 stayed until the conclusion of the main action. Mr Schuppan's cause of action in slander, if he has one, has not vested in his trustee in bankruptcy (see *Heath v Tang* *g* [1993] 1 WLR 1421 at 1423). So there is the possibility of Mr Schuppan proceeding, perhaps as a litigant in person, with his slander action. Any decision about proceeding with, abandoning or compromising the wasted costs application and the Isle of Man inquiry, on the other hand, would plainly be for the trustee in bankruptcy (Race is not concerned in either of these matters).

h Mr David Wolfson (for Mr Schuppan) relies on these three particular matters as creating a conflict of interest. That conflict was, he says, recognised in the order of District Judge Burgess, which made an exception for 'those matters concerning the liability of the estate to [Art] and the liability of [Art] to the estate where [another well-known firm of London solicitors—"the other firm"] shall *j* continue to be retained'. Mr Wolfson argues that this conflict of interest, once recognised, should have been treated as determinative, and that District Judge Jolly erred in law in treating it, not as determinative, but as calling for a balancing exercise. Alternatively, he argues that the district judge exercised his discretion unreasonably. Mr Wolfson made clear that he was not making any attack on the solicitors' integrity or suggesting that they would be guilty of any deliberate impropriety.

Mr Robin Knowles (for the trustee in bankruptcy) meets Mr Wolfson's submissions by arguing that they do not sufficiently analyse the nature and implications of conflict of interest in this situation: properly analysed, he says, the situation gives rise to no conflict of interest which is not adequately catered for either by the retainer of the other firm under the existing order, or by the other firm acting (as I am told they will) in connection with the wasted costs application if it proceeds, or by an undertaking which the solicitors are willing to give in connection with the slander action.

I have also heard short but useful submissions from Mr Pugh, the Official Receiver with responsibility for this bankruptcy. He told me that it is his own practice, over many years of experience, not to retain the solicitors acting for the petitioning creditor, even when the petitioning creditor presses for this. This practice was, Mr Pugh said, founded in his perception of the importance of the Official Receiver being demonstrably impartial in his treatment of debtors and creditors. He acknowledged that this was not an official practice in the sense of being prescribed for Official Receivers generally, and that it is a more stringent practice than what is required by the official guidance to insolvency practitioners (see the 'Guidance Notes on Professional Conduct and Ethics for Persons Authorised by the Secretary of State to Act as Insolvency Practitioners'; these notes refer to what is proper for the insolvency practitioner himself, not for his advisers, but they provide guidance by analogy).

The matter does indeed call for analysis. It seems to me that there are, on analysis, three different issues which are (in descending order of generality).

(1) Is it generally acceptable (and fair as between the petitioning creditor and other unsecured creditors) for the trustee in bankruptcy to retain the petitioning creditor's solicitors to act for him?

(2) If so, is it made unacceptable in this case because of the trustee in bankruptcy's possible claims against Art (the Isle of Man inquiry as to damages) and against the solicitors personally (the wasted costs application)?

(3) Is the slander action by Mr Schuppan against the solicitors personally a further or final reason for depriving the trustee in bankruptcy of the solicitors of his choice?

On the first and most general point Mr Pugh's practice is, as I have said, to regard the retainer of the petitioning creditor's solicitors as unacceptable in every case. However, that seems to me to be a counsel of perfection which need not necessarily be followed by all insolvency practitioners in all circumstances. In a case where the real difficulties that are foreseen are in connection with the identification, tracing and recovery of assets for the bankrupt's estate, the retainer of solicitors who already have a good grasp of these difficulties can be of great advantage to all the creditors, not just the petitioning creditor. Mr Riley deposes that that would be the case here. If in such a case the petitioning creditor is very much the largest creditor, and no difficulties are expected in quantifying the provable debts of either the petitioning creditor or the other creditors, the risk of a conflict of interest would appear to be, in the words of Hoffmann J in *Re Maxwell Communication Corp plc* [1992] BCLC 465 at 468, 'a mere distant possibility'.

In this case the petitioning creditor, Art, is the largest creditor. There is no evidence that it is very much the largest creditor, but the size of its claim (both the judgment and the dismissal of Mr Schuppan's counterclaim no longer being open to appeal) suggests that that is likely. There is no evidence of any particular difficulty being expected in quantifying the provable debts of other creditors. Apart from the Isle of Man inquiry and the wasted costs application, therefore, *a* the risk of conflict of interest does seem to be fairly remote. Mr Riley's report to the court contains nothing to indicate that he, as an experienced insolvency practitioner, takes a different view.

Next I must consider the two particular matters that do involve the trustee in bankruptcy on one side and the solicitors (as agents, in the Manx inquiry, or as principals, in the wasted costs application) on the other side. I must assume that *b* the trustee in bankruptcy cannot and will not simply drop these matters, but will need to take legal advice about them. That legal advice plainly cannot be given by the solicitors. It will be given by the other firm. That is provided for by the order of District Judge Burgess in relation to the Manx inquiry (which is one of the 'matters concerning the liability of [Art] to the estate') and it is accepted in an open letter (written by the solicitors on 16 February 1996) in relation to the *c* wasted costs application.

Mr Wolfson made the general point that the retainer of two different firms (or even three, if a comparable arrangement in relation to Race has to be used in practice) is undesirable and likely to lead to unnecessary expense, duplication of work, and confusion. He mentioned some instances of confusion which have *d* already occurred. These do not seem to have been very serious. I can readily accept that the retainer of more than one firm is in general undesirable, for the reasons which Mr Wolfson has mentioned, and that it is an expedient to be adopted only in exceptional circumstances. But *Re Maxwell Communication Corp plc* [1992] BCLC 465 at 469 and also *Re Polly Peck International plc (No 1)* [1991] BCC 503 show that in exceptional circumstances a division of responsibility may be the *e* best solution.

The Manx inquiry and the wasted costs application are both self-contained matters of limited scope, and they are both likely to be disposed of in weeks rather than months. The bankruptcy as a whole, on the other hand, is likely to be protracted and difficult, for reasons already mentioned. The retainer of more *f* than one firm of solicitors is in the circumstances a sensible course.

I should at this point return to Mr Wolfson's general point, that conflict of interest is something which the court will not countenance, and that if conflict of interest is identified it must be treated as determinative, rather than being the starting point for a balancing exercise. This is an attractive general proposition, *g* but I cannot accept it without a good deal of qualification. As Mr Knowles said, it is not the law that a solicitor or a firm of solicitors can never act for and against a client, even in the same matter. The law and practice in England is less inflexible than in (for instance) the United States (see *Re a firm of solicitors* [1995] 3 All ER 482 at 488–489, where Lightman J said 'The basis of the court's intervention is not a possible perception of impropriety: it is the protection of *h* confidential information', followed by citations from *Rakusen v Ellis Munday & Clarke* [1912] 1 Ch 831 at 845, [1911–13] All ER Rep 813 at 820, *Supasave Retail Ltd v Coward Chance (a firm)*, *David Lee & Co (Lincoln) Ltd v Coward Chance (a firm)*, [1991] 1 All ER 668 at 674, [1991] Ch 259 at 268 and *Re a firm of solicitors* [1992] 1 All ER 353 at 365–366, [1992] QB 959 at 974). Where there is a real risk of *j* confidential information miscarrying or being misused, the court will treat that as paramount and will not embark on a balancing exercise. That appears, for instance, from *Supasave Retail Ltd v Coward Chance (a firm)*, *David Lee & Co (Lincoln) Ltd v Coward Chance (a firm)* [1991] 1 All ER 668, [1991] Ch 259, a decision of Browne-Wilkinson V-C. But if there is no real risk, or if any identified risk can be averted by a division of responsibility, then a balancing exercise may be appropriate. The retainer of the other firm to advise Mr Riley on the Manx

inquiry and the wasted costs application does in my judgment avert any risk, *a*
since it is not suggested that the solicitors (as the past and current solicitors acting
for Art) have any information that is confidential to the trustee in bankruptcy.
The suggestion that Mr Riley might be embarrassed in deciding (on the advice of
the other firm) what to do about the wasted costs application, because of the
cordial relationship which he has or hopes to have with the solicitors, seems to
me to underrate both the objectivity of the advice which the other firm can be *b*
expected to give, and the robustness of Mr Riley's own professional judgment.

So I come to the last and most particular matter, the slander action by Mr
Schuppan against one of the partners in the solicitors, and the solicitors
themselves. The effect of the bankruptcy on the pending action for slander is to
sever the bare cause of action (if it exists) from the rest of Mr Schuppan's assets,
including his business papers. If the action proceeds that may throw up some odd *c*
questions of practice, for instance in connection with discovery. But for present
purposes I am concerned only with whether the solicitors' access to Mr
Schuppan's papers, as and when they come into the trustee's hands, would give
them an improper advantage in the defence of the slander action and, if so, how
the court should prevent that.   *d*

There is some affinity here to the familiar problem of the implied undertaking
given on obtaining discovery, and the principles on which the court may release
or modify an undertaking (see *Crest Homes plc v Marks* [1987] 2 All ER 1074, [1987]
AC 829). Indeed, it seems likely that the majority of any documents which the
solicitors might wish to use in the defence of the slander action— if the pleadings
are amended to plead justification—should already have come to the notice of *e*
the solicitors in the course of discovery in the main Queen's Bench Division
action, so as to be covered already by the implied undertaking.

Mr Knowles drew my attention to a passage near the end of Lightman J's
judgment in *Re a firm of solicitors* [1995] 3 All ER 482 at 492:

> 'Where there has been the previous relationship of solicitors and client and *f*
> the solicitor at the date of his proposed new retainer possesses relevant
> confidential information, in the ordinary course the court will in my view
> grant an injunction restraining the solicitor acting ... But in the case where
> without any such previous relationship a party's solicitor illegitimately
> becomes possessed of confidential information of the other party to the suit *g*
> or dispute, in the ordinary course the court will merely grant an injunction
> restraining the solicitor making use of that information; it will not prohibit
> his continuing to act (see *English and American Insurance Co Ltd v Herbert Smith*
> [1988] FSR 232 and *Goddard v Nationwide Building Society* [1986] 3 All ER 264,
> [1987] QB 670).'   *h*

That distinction in practice is in my judgment appropriate here (except that the
mention of information being illegitimately obtained tends, in this context, to
blur the issue; it would be information obtained legitimately but for a restricted
purpose, as with documents properly disclosed on discovery). I understand that
the solicitors are willing to undertake not without leave to use in the slander *j*
action any documents which they see in their capacity as solicitors to the trustee
in bankruptcy (this undertaking being given in addition to the subsisting implied
undertaking on obtaining discovery in the main action) and that is in my
judgment the appropriate way to resolve this problem.

There is a detailed note (approved by the district judge) of the judgment of
District Judge Jolly. The submissions made to him seem to have followed much

a the same lines as before me (though without citation of authority). The district judge does seem to have viewed the matter as a balancing exercise but I am not satisfied that he erred in law in the exercise of his discretion. If (contrary to my view of the note of his judgment) he did exercise his discretion on a wrong principle, so that I have to exercise my own discretion, I would exercise it in the same way. It is implicit in this that I do not accept Mr Wolfson's alternative

b submission that the exercise of discretion was wholly unreasonable.

If Mr Knowles (as the solicitors' counsel for this purpose) can confirm the undertaking in relation to the slander action I will dismiss the appeal, and so the order of District Judge Burgess will not be set aside. I doubt whether there is any need to modify it so as to make reference to the wasted costs application, but I will hear any submissions that counsel wish to make about the precise form of

c order that is appropriate.

Appeal dismissed.

Celia Fox   Barrister.

Foster and others v Spencer   *a*

CHANCERY DIVISION

JUDGE PAUL BAKER QC SITTING AS A JUDGE OF THE HIGH COURT

1, 2, 25 MAY 1995
                                                                          b

Trust and trustee – Remuneration of trustee – Order of court – Circumstances in which court will exercise jurisdiction to award remuneration – Trustees making unremitting efforts over 20-year period to sell trust land – Whether trustees entitled to expenses with interest thereon – Whether trustees entitled to remuneration for past and future services.   *c*

In 1969 the three plaintiffs became trustees of land used as a cricket club and held on the trusts declared by an indenture made in 1921. The club's membership was by that time declining and it had insufficient income to maintain the grounds, which fell into decay. The trustees therefore decided, with the unanimous support of the contributors, to sell the grounds for development and look for *d* another site. There were a number of obstacles in doing so: the land was zoned as open space; it was not clear from the documents whether the trustees had power to sell; and later there were difficulties in evicting squatters and securing the land against further invasions. The trustees made vigorous efforts over the years to resolve those matters and to secure the sale of the land, the main burden *e* falling on F, a chartered surveyor whose expertise was particularly valuable in marketing the site, and on S, who had useful business experience as a building contractor and was the only trustee to live near the site. At the end of 1992 the land was sold to a developer for over £900,000. The trustees subsequently brought proceedings against a representative beneficiary, seeking an order authorising them to be paid out of the trust funds (i) the sum of £40,396 each in *f* respect of out-of-pocket expenses incurred by them together with interest pursuant to s 35A[a] of the Supreme Court Act 1981, or under the court's general equitable jurisdiction; (ii) remuneration for F and S at an hourly rate for their services in bringing about the sale of the land; and (iii) remuneration for all three trustees for the tasks which they had yet to perform in determining the beneficial *g* ownership of the funds.

Held – (1) The right of trustees to be reimbursed their expenses out of the trust estate was well established and had been given statutory form by s 30(2)[b] of the Trustee Act 1925. However, there was no entitlement to claim interest thereon *h* under s 35A of the 1981 Act, since the proceedings were not proceedings for the recovery of a debt or damages, the trustees having come to court simply to gain approval of the exercise of their right of retainer so as to forestall any future allegations of breach of trust. Further, it was contrary to established practice to allow interest on ordinary costs and expenses that had accrued in a piecemeal fashion. It followed that the court would authorise payment of the trustees' *j* out-of-pocket expenses but no interest thereon (see p 677 *e*, and p 678 *b* to *d f* to *j*, post).

---

a   Section 35A, so far as material, is set out at p 678 *c*, post
b   Section 30(2) provides: 'A trustee may reimburse himself or pay or discharge out of the trust premises all expenses incurred in or about the execution of the trusts or powers.'

(2) Although a trustee was not entitled to any allowance for his time and
a trouble except as authorised by the trust instrument, the court had power under
its inherent jurisdiction to allow a trustee to retain remuneration for his services
according to its assessment of what was reasonable in the circumstances. The
right of the trustee to remuneration for past services did not depend on the
circumstance that, at the time he sought it, his services were further required so
b that he was in a position to demand remuneration for the past as a condition of
continuing in office; indeed, in cases where there were no funds out of which to
pay remuneration at the time of the trustees' appointment and a true
appreciation of the extent of the task was not possible, a prospective application
would be impracticable, if not impossible. In the circumstances, the services
rendered by the trustees had been wholly outside their contemplation when
c appointed and had made great demands on the expertise of F and S in particular.
An hourly rate for their services was not appropriate, but a suitable remuneration
for F would be a 5% commission on the net proceeds of the sale of the land (ie
£45,560), and for S, an annual fee of £5,000 for his ten years of activity before the
sale (see p 678 *j* to p 679 *a*, p 681 *b* to *e* and p 682 *a* to *d*, post); *Re Duke of Norfolk's*
d *Settlement Trusts* [1981] 3 All ER 220 applied.

(3) The task remaining to the trustees was quite different from those leading
to the disposal of the ground; it consisted in resolving the question of the
beneficial ownership of the land, which did not call for any special expertise on
their part. The continued service of the trustees was not therefore necessary for
the good administration of the trust and their application for future remuneration
e would be refused accordingly (see p 682 *e* to *h*, post).

Notes

For remuneration of trustees, see 48 *Halsbury's Laws* (4th edn reissue) paras 811–
815, and for cases on the subject, see 48 *Digest* (Reissue) 345–353, *3105–3197.*
f   For the Trustee Act 1925, s 30, see 48 *Halsbury's Statutes* (4th edn) (1995 reissue)
287.

For the Supreme Court Act 1981, s 35A, see 11 *Halsbury's Statutes* (4th edn)
(1991 reissue) 998.

Cases referred to in judgment
g *Beulah Park Estate, Re, Sargood's Claim* (1872) LR 15 Eq 43.
Finch v Pescott (1874) LR 17 Eq 554.
Gordon v Trail (1820) 8 Price 416, 146 ER 1248.
Norfolk's (Duke of) Settlement Trusts, Re [1981] 3 All ER 220, [1982] Ch 61, [1981] 3
WLR 455, CA; *rvsg in part* [1978] 3 All ER 907, [1979] Ch 37, [1978] 3 WLR 655.
h *Salmen, Re, Salmen v Bernstein* (1912) 107 LT 108, Ch D and CA.

Cases also cited or referred to in skeleton arguments
Boardman v Phipps [1966] 3 All ER 721, [1967] 2 AC 46, HL.
Buckton, Re, Buckton v Buckton [1907] 2 Ch 406.
j *Clarkson v Robinson* [1900] 2 Ch 722.
Forster v Ridley (1864) 4 De G J & Sm 452, 46 ER 993.
Grimthorpe's (Baron) Will Trusts, Re [1958] 1 All ER 765, [1958] Ch 615.
Hallows v Lloyd (1888) 39 Ch D 686.
Harris v Sleep [1897] 2 Ch 80, Ch D and CA.
Macadam, Re, Dallow v Codd [1945] 2 All ER 664, [1946] Ch 73.
McDonald v Horn [1995] 1 All ER 961, CA.

Malcolm v O'Callaghan (1837) 3 My & Cr 52, 40 ER 844.
Marshall v Holloway (1820) 2 Swan 432, [1814–23] All ER Rep 395, 36 ER 681, LC.   a
Wells (decd), Re, Wells v Wells [1962] 2 All ER 826, [1962] 1 WLR 874, CA.
Worthington (decd), Re, ex p Leighton v Macleod [1954] 1 All ER 677, [1954] 1 WLR
    526.

Summons   b
The plaintiffs, Anthony Burrington Foster, David George Bone and Gordon
William Joseph Sealy, who were the trustees of Elmers End Cricket Club, applied
for remuneration for their services, both past and future, and for expenses (with
interest) incurred in carrying out the trusts of an indenture under which a
five-acre field at Elmers End, near Beckenham, Kent was purchased. The
defendant was Claude William Spencer, a representative beneficiary. The facts   c
are set out in the judgment.

Alexandra Mason (instructed by *Cowles & Co*) for the trustees.
William Henderson (instructed by *Cowles & Co*) for the beneficiaries.

Cur adv vult   d

25 May 1995. The following judgment was delivered.

JUDGE PAUL BAKER QC. This is an application by the plaintiff trustees for the
payment of remuneration for their services, both past and future, in carrying out   e
the trusts of an indenture of 16 March 1921. They also apply for the court's
approval to the expenses which they claim to have expended in carrying out
those duties.
    The trustees' duties related to the Elmers End Cricket Club. The club had its
own ground, a field of some five acres near Beckenham in Kent. In addition to
the pitch, there were some tennis courts and a pavilion with a bar. The ground   f
had been acquired by purchase in 1921. The price of £700 was defrayed out of a
sum of £742 raised by subscription from the then members of the club and
well-wishers. The minimum subscription was £5, but some subscribed more.
The land was conveyed on 6 January 1921 to five of the subscribers as joint
tenants in fee simple. Those five, describing themselves as trustees, then entered   g
into the indenture already mentioned declaring the trusts on which the land was
to be held. It has been subsequently modified. As the original subscribers
resigned from the club or died they or their personal representatives were paid
out by new members.
    In their younger days, the plaintiffs were playing members of the club. As time   h
passed they became increasingly involved in its management. In 1969 they were
persuaded to become trustees of the club along with a continuing trustee who has
since died. Unfortunately, as they soon discovered, if they did not know it
already, all was not well with the club. Membership, and consequently income,
was declining. There was no capital reserve. The third plaintiff, Mr Sealy, puts it
thus in para 7 of his affidavit: j

    'At the time of our acceptance of office it was becoming impossible,
    through lack of funds, to keep up the Cricket table on the Field, the tennis
    courts which had been sited on another part of the Field had become
    overgrown and the pavilion itself was taking on the appearance of a
    ramshackle shed. For some time football was played on the Field, but this

a   eventually ceased and the only activity which remained centred round the bar in the old pavilion which acquired a bad reputation.'

The trustees fairly soon came to the conclusion that the best chance of reviving interest in the club and obtaining some funds was to attempt to sell the ground for development and look for another site. That proposal was put to a meeting
b   of the contributors on 7 April 1972, who gave it their unanimous support. There were, however, formidable obstacles, some recognised at the time, others emerging later. At the time it was realised that the field was subject to planning blight in that there was a proposal to route a new road through the land. That was later abandoned, but the land remained zoned as open space. That would have to be altered if a reasonable price was to be obtained from a developer.
c   Then it was not clear from the documents whether the trustees had power to sell, and who all the beneficiaries were. Later there was much trouble in evicting squatters and securing the land against further invasions.

The trustees tackled these problems vigorously and unremittingly for the next 20 years until at the end of 1992 they managed to achieve a sale to a developer,
d   Crest Homes (Southern) Ltd, for over £900,000.

At this point I will describe the trustees individually. As already mentioned, as young men they played for the club, having been brought up in the area. Mr Sealy still lives nearby. At the critical period he was the managing director of a company of building contractors. As the trustee nearest to the site and with that background he was in the best position to monitor what was going on there. The
e   first plaintiff, Mr Foster, is a chartered surveyor. He works as a freelance consultant. His home is in the area, but during most of the critical period he was supervising a substantial development in Malaysia, though making frequent visits to this country. His expertise has been particularly valuable in marketing the site. The second plaintiff, Mr Bone, lives in Colchester in Essex, but spends much of
f   his time in Brussels. He is a businessman, a director of a company engaged in film and television commercial advertising. All three submitted affidavits upon which they were cross-examined by Mr Henderson, counsel for the defendant, Mr Spencer, a representative beneficiary. I was impressed by them all and have no hesitation in accepting their evidence.

I now pass to the main events which followed the meeting of 1972. Within a
g   year of that meeting, the trustees had found a developer who was prepared to pay £25,000 as a non-returnable deposit for an option to run for five years. During that time the developer, assisted as necessary by the trustees, attempted to get an acceptable planning permission. Despite going to appeal, the attempt failed, and the deposit was forfeit to the trustees. This episode provided much-needed funds
h   but it exposed the uncertainties both of obtaining an acceptable planning permission and the ability of the trustees to make title on a sale. In the meantime on the ground sporting activities came virtually to an end, and the pavilion degenerated into an undesirable drinking den. Other unauthorised and undesirable activities such as car breaking and squatting began. All this resulted
j   in complaints from the residents of adjoining properties and notices from the local authority. The trustees were advised to apply to the court for assistance on clarifying their title and regaining possession of the land.

In 1982 proceedings were commenced in the Chancery Division of the High Court which came on before Harman J in 1988. I note that the judge opens his judgment by saying that the originating summons had been amended three times and raised 'extremely difficult issues concerning the title to and beneficial

ownership of some five acres of land at Elmers End', not all of which he was able
to resolve at that stage. According to his judgment, he did not lay any blame on   *a*
the trustees for delay in bringing the matter on; nor do I. In fact, by this time, as
Mr Foster says in para 10 of his first affidavit, the trustees were having to fund 'out
of their own pockets all the other costs of meetings, travel, legal consultations,
telephone, fax, postage, stationary [sic] and negotiations with consultants,
professional advisors and developers'.   *b*

Harman J held positively that the land was vested in the trustees as trustees for
sale and that they were entitled to sell and convey it for the best price reasonably
obtainable in the open market. He made an order for possession in their favour.
Negatively, he held that the land was not held on charitable trusts—a matter
strongly canvassed before him—and that various clauses in the indenture of 16
March 1921 were void. He left unanswered questions directed to determining   *c*
the beneficial ownership on the assumption that the trusts were not charitable,
adjourning the originating summons to allow further evidence to be adduced.
Accordingly, the trustees still have a lot to do in getting this matter resolved.

The order for possession was executed, but in the following year, 1989, the
field was invaded by some 60 or 70 gypsies with numerous lorries and caravans. *d*
In para 10 of his affidavit, Mr Sealy says of this episode:

'This occasioned much local hostility and my co-Plaintiffs and myself had
serious difficulties in having them evicted. My co-Plaintiffs and myself and
our solicitors had much trouble dealing with the protests of the residents of
the houses surrounding the field. The local press devoted several leading   *e*
articles and news columns reporting that [sic] the nuisance caused by this
unlawful occupation of the field. There was implied criticism of us as owners
of the land and my co-Plaintiffs and I were called upon to take action to evict
the squatters and to develop the ground. We ultimately obtained an order
for possession against them on the 31st. July 1989. We were then faced with   *f*
the worry of securing the field by strong fencing and erecting a barrier to
ensure that they did not return.'

This was an exceptionally difficult time for Mr Sealy. Hence his fellow trustees
were particularly concerned to give him support. Mr Bone said in the course of
his cross-examination: *g*

'Mr Sealy lived closest to the ground. He bore the brunt of direct contact
with everybody. He felt under personal threat. I attended the eviction to
support him. He felt at risk and required some back up. He organised the
securing of the field. Matters were very fraught and he was trying to run his   *h*
own business.'

With the title clarified, the trustees were free to renew their efforts to sell the
land. All were involved, but the main burden fell on Mr Foster who had the
necessary expertise. They approached a large number of companies possibly
interested in developing the land. Serious negotiations ensued with nine of them. *j*
Eventually Crest Homes took an option and proceeded to tackle the obtaining of
a suitable planning permission. In this they were successful and the land was sold
to them as I have already stated. Though I have said that in this phase Mr Foster
had the main burden, the contribution of Mr Sealy should not be overlooked. He
told me, and I accept: 'My knowledge of land transactions and local contacts did
go some way to persuade the local authority to change its mind over zoning.'

a   Also Mr Sealy's business experience as a building contractor was of considerable assistance in connection with the tender documents.

As a result of their efforts, the trustees are now in possession of a substantial sum of cash. As at 5 April 1993, after deduction of all payments to third parties, and a sum of nearly £70,000 on account of the trustees' own expenses, the balance was a little over £750,000. Interest is accruing on it, but there will have to be met
b   capital gains tax estimated at around £200,000, and the costs of these proceedings together with those of the further proceedings to resolve the beneficial interest.

At the outset of this judgment I referred briefly to the applications which the trustees are making for payment and reimbursement from the funds which have now become available. I must now return to them. They fall under two main heads, remuneration and expenses, to which, of course, different principles apply.
c   I propose to start with the claim relating to expenses. The order sought is as follows:

> 'An Order authorising the Plaintiffs as the present trustees of the said Indenture to be paid and retain out of funds subject to the said Indenture the sum of £40,396 each in respect of out of pocket expenses incurred by them
d   and each of them between 7th May 1969 and 5th April 1993, alternatively such sums as the Court shall think proper together with interest on such sums at such rate and for such periods as the Court shall think fit.'

The right of trustees to be reimbursed their expenses out of the trust estate has long been established and is now statutory: the Trustee Act 1925, s 30(2). Owing
e   to the long period which has elapsed without funds being available to meet the expenses as they occurred, the trustees have not retained receipts or vouchers to substantiate a good part of it. Furthermore, the trustees have incurred travelling expenses in meeting together and going to see professional advisers and attending court which are now very difficult to quantify. This especially applies to Mr Bone
f   and Mr Foster who have had to come from afar. In these circumstances they have instructed accountants to prepare an estimate of their expenses. Mr Bone has been mostly responsible for collecting the available data and information for feeding to the accountants. The total of the estimated costs is £121,188. This contains some heavy items such as six trips from Malaysia at business class rates for Mr Foster and secretarial services for Mr Sealy of over £17,000 which at first
g   sight seem surprising. They were rightly the subject of cross-examination by Mr Henderson as were a number of other items. I have, however, come to the conclusion that the items criticised in this way were justified.

While he was in Malaysia, Mr Foster made many trips to this country. For most of them he came either on leave or on other business. On many of them he
h   was able to attend meetings of the trustees and deal with trust affairs generally. On a few occasions he had to make a special trip. These occurred during the six-year period, 1987 to 1992, which included the hearing before Harman J and culminated in the sale. They averaged about one a year. He normally travelled in the business class, and I do not see why he should not use that class if he had
j   to come home in connection with the affairs of the trust. I do not forget that he incurred this expenditure when there was no guarantee that he would recover it.

There is no doubt that Mr Sealy, and to a less extent the others, were involved in very heavy secretarial work. I have seen the voluminous files. It was reasonable that Mr Sealy should get paid assistance to cope with it.

Reading the accountants' report and hearing the evidence, especially from Mr Bone, I am satisfied that they have set about preparing the assessment on a

conservative basis and in a responsible and careful way. Hence I do not see much a
point in going through the estimate in detail, much less ordering an inquiry. The
consequence is that I shall authorise the retainer or a further sum of £51,720
which, together with the sum of £69,468 already retained and paid on account,
makes up the sum of £121,188 in the assessment. I do not apportion the sum
equally or in any other way between the plaintiffs as the originating summons
suggests. That is a matter for them to agree between themselves. b

The plaintiffs claim interest on the amount of the out-of-pocket expenses.
Their counsel primarily relies on s 35A of the Supreme Court Act 1981.
Subsection (1) provides:

'Subject to rules of court, in proceedings (whenever instituted) before the
High Court for the recovery of a debt or damages there may be included in c
any sum for which judgment is given simple interest ...'

I am unable to accept that submission. These proceedings are not proceedings
for the recovery of a debt or damages. No party can be ordered to pay them. The
trustees are entitled to the expenses out of the trust estate, and only out of the
trust estate. They come to court simply to gain approval of their exercise of their d
right of retainer so as to forestall any future allegations of breach of trust.

Alternatively, Miss Mason submits that the court has power to award interest
under its general equitable jurisdiction in taking accounts. The difficulty facing
her here is the old decision of *Gordon v Trail* (1820) 8 Price 416, 146 ER 1248. An
executor applied for interest on the costs of an action brought by him on behalf e
of the estate, and of actions defended by him, which he had paid out of his own
pocket at a time when he had no money of the estate in his hands. Richards CB,
refusing the application, said (8 Price 416, 146 ER 1248): '... notwithstanding the
frequent hardships of such a case, it was contrary to the established course of
practice to allow interest on costs, under such circumstances.'

An exception to this rule is where an executor or trustee pays off an f
interest-bearing debt of the estate: see *Re Beulah Park Estate, Sargood's Claim* (1872)
LR 15 Eq 43 and *Finch v Pescott* (1874) LR 17 Eq 554. The judgments are extremely
brief. The exception has been rationalised on the ground that the trustee stands
in the shoes of the creditor by way of subrogation (see Underhill's *Law of Trusts
and Trustees* (14th edn, 1987) p 706 and Seton's *Forms of Decrees, Judgments and
Orders in Equity* (7th edn, 1912) p 1334). Yet in both cases interest was allowed at g
a higher rate than the rate payable under the original debt. An alternative
rationalisation would regard the advance as a lien on the trust fund which carried
interest as any other equitable charge or mortgage. However that may be, I
would not extend the exception to the case of ordinary costs and expenses which
accrue in a piecemeal fashion. I regard the decision in *Gordon v Trail* as based on h
convenience, to avoid having interest accrue as each item of expenditure is
incurred. Where, as in this case, the costs have mounted up over a considerable
period, some hardship or injustice may occur, as Richards CB particularly noted.
I thus conclude that I have no jurisdiction to award interest in the circumstances
of this case. j

I now come to the application for remuneration. This falls into two parts.
First, an application by Mr Sealy and Mr Foster for their services in bringing about
the successful sale. Secondly, an application by all three for remuneration for the
tasks which they have yet to perform.

It is trite law that a trustee is entitled to no allowance for his time and trouble
unless it is authorised by the trust instrument. However, the court has power

a under its inherent jurisdiction to allow a trustee to retain remuneration. It also has statutory powers in relation to particular types of trustees. For example, under s 42 of the 1925 Act, the court has power on appointing a corporation as trustee to authorise 'the corporation to charge such remuneration for its services as trustee as the court may think fit'.

The claim here is made under the inherent jurisdiction. The leading case is
b now *Re Duke of Norfolk's Settlement Trusts* [1981] 3 All ER 220, [1982] Ch 61, decided at first instance by Walton J and by the Court of Appeal. In view of the arguments addressed to me, I should look at the judgments in both courts.

The trustees of this settlement were an individual and a trust corporation. There was a normal professional charging clause which did not apply to the individual trustee. The corporate trustee was entitled to remuneration in
c accordance with its usual scale fees as they stood at the date of the settlement. The estate contained land which became subject to a scheme of substantial redevelopment. That involved the trustees in work entirely outside anything which could reasonably have been foreseen when they took office. They applied for remuneration for past and future services including an increase, in the case of
d the corporation, in the scale of charges from that specified in the settlement to the then current scale. Walton J summarised the principles as follows ([1978] 3 All ER 907 at 924–925, [1979] Ch 37 at 58):

'(i) The jurisdiction is a wholly exceptional one, to be exercised sparingly. (ii) Subject to (iii) below, the only ground on which the court has ever acted,
e so far as the reported cases go, has been the necessity for obtaining the services either of some particular individual trustee, whose services were of special value to the trust, or of obtaining the services of some particular kind of trustee, such as, for example, a trust corporation. (iii) It was indicated by Eve J in *Re Salmen* (1912) 107 LT 108, and the Court of Appeal approved the
f reasoning in his judgment, that remuneration might be awarded if the circumstances of the case were such as to raise an implied promise to pay it on behalf of the beneficiaries ... (iv) There has never been a case in which the court has ever altered the general level of remuneration fixed by the trust instrument, once the trust has been unconditionally accepted ... (v) The court has always shown marked reluctance to award any remuneration
g unless the application has been made very promptly on assumption of office or where there has been a radical change in the circumstances.'

Applying these principles, Walton J held that the trustees were entitled to a proper allowance, on the basis of an implied promise, in respect of their services in connection with the redevelopment scheme. That decision was not appealed.
h He held, however, that the court had no jurisdiction to alter the general level of the corporation's fees specified in the trust instrument. That decision was appealed.

The leading judgment in the Court of Appeal was delivered by Fox LJ; Brightman and Cumming-Bruce LJJ, the other members of the court, expressly
j agreed with it. In the opinion of Fox LJ, Walton J 'took too narrow a view of the inherent jurisdiction' (see [1981] 3 All ER 220 at 228, [1982] Ch 61 at 75). He dissented from the view that the trustees' right to remuneration had a contractual basis, saying ([1981] 3 All ER 220 at 228–229, [1982] Ch 61 at 76–77):

'The position, it seems to me, is this. Trust property is held by the trustees on the trusts and subject to the powers conferred by the trust instrument and

by law. One of those powers is the power to the trustee to charge
remuneration. That gives the trustee certain rights which equity will enforce
in administering the trust. How far those rights can properly be regarded as
beneficial interests I will consider later. But it seems to me to be quite unreal
to regard them as contractual. So far as they derive from any order of the
court they simply arise from the court's jurisdiction and so far as they derive
from the trust instrument itself they derive from the settlor's power to direct
how the property should be dealt with.'

Other points on which they differed from Walton J were the effect of express
provision for remuneration in the trust instrument and the timing of the
application for remuneration. Fox LJ said ([1981] 3 All ER 220 at 230, [1982] Ch
61 at 78–79):

'As to principle, it seems to me that, if the court has jurisdiction, as it has,
on the appointment of a trustee to authorise remuneration though no such
power exists in the trust instrument, there is no logical reason why the court
should not have power to increase the remuneration given by the
instrument. In many cases the latter may involve a smaller interference with
the provisions of the trust instrument than the former. Further, the law has
not stopped short at authorising remuneration to a trustee only if he seeks
the authority at the time when he accepts the trusts.'

On the true foundation of the jurisdiction Fox LJ had this to say ([1981] 3 All
ER 220 at 230–231, [1982] Ch 61 at 79):

'I appreciate that the ambit of the court's inherent jurisdiction in any
sphere may, for historical reasons, be irrational and that logical extensions
are not necessarily permissible. But I think that it is the basis of the
jurisdiction that one has to consider. The basis, in my view, in relation to a
trustee's remuneration is the good administration of trusts ... I conclude
that the court has an inherent jurisdiction to authorise the payment of
remuneration of trustees and that that jurisdiction extends to increasing the
remuneration authorised by the trust instrument. In exercising that
jurisdiction the court has to balance two influences which are to some extent
in conflict. The first is that the office of trustee is, as such, gratuitous; the
court will accordingly be careful to protect the interests of the beneficiaries
against claims by the trustees. The second is that it is of great importance to
the beneficiaries that the trust should be well administered. If therefore the
court concludes, having regard to the nature of the trust, to the experience
and skill of a particular trustee and to the amounts which he seeks to charge
when compared with what other trustees might require to be paid for their
services and to all the other circumstances of the case, that it would be in the
interests of the beneficiaries to increase the remuneration, then the court
may properly do so.'

Mr Henderson for the beneficiaries submitted that the trustees here were not
entitled to remuneration either for the past or for the future. He drew from the
judgment of Fox LJ the proposition that before one could award remuneration
one had to find that the interests of the beneficiaries required the services of
particular trustees who would not act unless remunerated. The alternative basis
of an implied contract relied on by Walton J had been expressly disapproved of
by the Court of Appeal. In the present case, he said, the trustees had completed

a the task for which their skill and time were required. For the remaining tasks there is no need to obtain the services of any particular trustee. Hence they are not entitled to be paid remuneration for their past services as the only basis on which it could be justified has been disapproved.

I regard this as too narrow a reading of the decision of the Court of Appeal. It fails to take account of the passages of the judgment of Fox LJ where he expressly indorses earlier cases allowing remuneration for past services (see [1981] 3 All ER
b 220 at 230, [1982] Ch 61 at 78–79). Where, as in this case, there were no funds out of which to pay remuneration at the time of their appointment, nor was a true appreciation of the extent of the task possible, a prospective application would be impracticable, if not impossible. The refusal of remuneration on the grounds suggested by Mr Henderson would result in the beneficiaries being unjustly
c enriched at the expense of the trustees. The right of the trustee to remuneration for past services cannot depend upon the circumstance that at the time he seeks it, his services are further required so that he is in a position to demand remuneration for the past as a condition of continuing in office.

The services rendered by the trustees were wholly outside their contemplation
d when appointed. They were appointed as trustees of a cricket club which had its own ground. They found themselves obliged by unforeseen circumstances to dispose of the ground. This proved far more difficult than would normally be expected and made great demands on the expertise of Mr Sealy and of Mr Foster, and on the time of all of them. I have no doubt that if they had realised what they were in for, they would have declined to act unless remunerated in some way.
e The authorities provide little or no guidance on the issue of quantum. As might be expected, it is left to the discretion of the court. The size of the trust fund is one obvious factor. The cost of engaging outside professional help, the amount of time spent are all relevant. In the end, however, the judge must try to assess what is reasonable in all the circumstances. Mr Sealy had little idea of what
f he thought he should have and left it entirely to the court to say what is reasonable. Mr Foster, on the other hand, prepared an assessment for himself and Mr Sealy which he introduces in para 19 of his first affidavit. After producing it he continues:

g 'It must be admitted that the total appears very substantial. However, having regard to the considerable amount of time expended by us and the professional expertise which Mr Sealy and myself have used for the good of the club as referred to in the preceding paragraphs of this affidavit we ask this Honourable Court to grant us each a reasonable sum as remuneration for the work which we have done over and above what a trustee of a sports club
h would normally be expected to do.'

The assessment is presented as for professional services rendered by Mr Foster as a chartered surveyor, and by Mr Sealy as the managing director of a construction company. In it Mr Foster estimates the time each has spent on such activities and applies an hourly rate based on the charges which Mr Sealy's company would
j have charged over the period for professional services. This leads to a total assessment for the two of them of £252,600, that is about a half of the available funds without allowing for interest.

I do not accept that approach in the circumstances of this case. Yet I am anxious, as are the parties, that I should not adjourn the case for further evidence, or order an inquiry in chambers, thereby adding to the costs. I consider that I have sufficient material to determine this issue.

I take the case of Mr Foster first. His input, albeit over a long period, was *a* necessarily sporadic and principally confined to the planning problems and the negotiations for sale. The proper way to remunerate him, as I see it, is by a commission on the purchase price achieved which I would fix at 5%, about double the normal rate of commission an estate agent earns, to recognise the great effort in securing a suitable planning permission before the property could be marketed. The net proceeds amounted to £911,188 so 5% would be £45,560, *b* rounded up to the nearest pound.

Mr Sealy's position is different. He alone was on the spot throughout. His contribution through his construction company was important, but not the whole story. He had to deal with the squatters, with the neighbours, with the local authority, with the police, with the press. In his affidavit he eschewed any intention to seek compensation in respect of work already carried out but later *c* changed his mind. The period of his most intense activity was the ten-year period before the sale at the end of 1992. The appropriate form of remuneration in his case is an annual fee which I would set at £5,000, giving £50,000 for the whole period.

On these amounts, under the court's equitable jurisdiction, I would award *d* interest at 8% pa from 15 December 1992, being the date when the funds became available.

Finally I come to the application for future remuneration, which is sought on behalf of all three trustees. The suggestion here is that I should make an order in the form of the normal wide professional charging clause.

I am unable to do that. The present position is that owing to the efforts of the *e* trustees, the trust assets are now in the form of cash and deposits. The tasks remaining are quite different from those leading to the disposal of the ground. They consist of restoring the originating summons to determine the beneficial interests. I do not see that that calls for any special expertise on the part of the trustees. They have said that they are not willing to continue if not allowed to *f* charge. It was submitted in reply that the experience of the trustees is very important and difficult to replace with anybody who would not charge. I am not persuaded of this. It may be that the knowledge of the trustees is important for the purpose of placing evidence before the court in determining the beneficial interest, but the duties of the trustees at this stage would not appear to be onerous. The burden will fall on solicitors who will be paid. There may be other *g* beneficiaries who could be persuaded to take over if the plaintiffs insist on resigning. I do not say that if the burden proves too onerous than at present seems likely, a further application would be excluded. But as things stand, I cannot say that the continued services of these trustees is necessary for the good administration of the trusts, whether these take the form of a distribution among *h* the contributors or the refounding of the cricket club elsewhere.

Order accordingly.

Celia Fox   Barrister.

a # Long v Tower Hamlets London Borough Council

CHANCERY DIVISION

b JAMES MUNBY QC SITTING AS A DEPUTY JUDGE OF THE HIGH COURT

20, 21 FEBRUARY, 20 MARCH 1996

Limitation of action – Land – Adverse possession – Period of adverse possession – Landlord confirming grant of quarterly tenancy by letter – Tenant in possession for many years without paying rent – Tenant claiming beneficial entitlement to premises –
c *Whether letter a 'lease in writing' – Whether letter sufficient to create leasehold estate in land – Limitation Act 1980, Sch 1, para 5(1).*

Landlord and tenant – Lease – Statutory requirements – Parol lease – Lease taking effect in possession for a term not exceeding three years – Whether letter confirming tenancy
d *to commence three weeks later operating as a lease 'taking effect in possession' – Law of Property Act 1925, s 54(2).*

On 4 September 1975 the agents acting for one of the local authority's predecessors in title wrote to L confirming that they were prepared to grant L a quarterly tenancy of shop premises. The relevant terms were that the rent was
e £55 a quarter and that the tenancy would commence on 29 September 1975. On 8 September 1975 L indorsed a copy of the letter (the tenancy document) to the effect that he agreed to abide by the terms and conditions of the tenancy and returned it to the landlord. L took possession of the premises three weeks later and in 1977 ceased to pay rent. He remained in possession, notwithstanding a
f notice to quit served by the local authority, and in 1995 commenced proceedings against the local authority, seeking a declaration that he was beneficially entitled to the premises and rectification of the proprietorship register on the basis that he had obtained title by adverse possession. The deputy master subsequently granted the local authority's application to strike out L's claim. On appeal, L contended that since he had paid no rent since 1977 the landlord's right of action
g to recover the premises was treated as having accrued at the latest by 1 January 1978 (in accordance with para 5[a] of Sch 1 to the Limitation Act 1980) and was therefore statute-barred by virtue of the 12-year limitation period prescribed by s 15(1)[b] of the 1980 Act. The local authority, however, contended that the tenancy document was a 'lease in writing' within para 5 of Sch 1 to the 1980 Act so that
h the limitation period began to run, not when L stopped paying rent, but on 25 March 1984, when his tenancy was brought to an end by the expiry of the notice to quit.

Held – (1) A written document was not a 'lease in writing' for the purposes of
j para 5(1) of Sch 1 to the 1980 Act if the writing, whatever its terms and however comprehensively it set out the terms of the lease, merely evidenced the existence of a lease; the document had to be dispositive in that it created at law, of and by itself, a leasehold estate in land. Since the tenancy document was not executed as

---

a   Paragraph 5, so far as material, is set out at p 686 *j* to p 687 *a*, post
b   Section 15(1) is set out at p 686 *h*, post

a deed, it could take effect as a lease creating a legal estate in land only if it operated in accordance with s 54ᶜ of the Law of Property Act 1925 as a 'lease taking effect in possession for a term not exceeding three years' (see p 692 e to h, p 693 b to d g h and p 694 c, post); Doe d Landsell v Gower (1851) 17 QB 589 and Moses v Lovegrove [1952] 1 All ER 1279 applied.

(2) A lease of less than three years which conferred no immediate right to possession was not a lease 'taking effect in possession' and was excluded from the ambit of s 54(2) of the 1925 Act; it was therefore void for the purpose of conveying and creating a legal estate unless made by deed. It followed that the tenancy document, which did not confer on L an immediate right to take possession, was a reversionary lease not made by deed and was incapable of taking effect as a parol lease under s 54(2) and had not therefore created a legal estate in land. Since the tenancy document was not a 'lease in writing', and in the absence of any other arguable grounds on which L's claim could be struck out, L was entitled to have his claim determined at trial. The appeal would accordingly be allowed (see p 694 d to p 695 a, p 701 b to d, p 702 g and p 704 f g, post).

Notes

For limitation of actions and tenancies from year to year or without written lease, see 28 Halsbury's Laws (4th edn) paras 752–753, and for cases on the subject, see 32(2) Digest (2nd reissue) 325–326, 2413–2422.

For requisites for demise by lease for three years or less, see 27(1) Halsbury's Laws (4th edn reissue) para 78, and for cases on the subject, see 31(1) Digest (2nd reissue) 223–224, 1822–1831.

For the Law of Property Act 1925, s 54, see 37 Halsbury's Statutes (4th edn) 155.

For the Limitation Act 1980, s 15, Sch 1, para 5, see 24 Halsbury's Statutes (4th edn) (1989 reissue) 664, 697.

Cases referred to in judgment

Bolton (Lord) v Tomlin (1836) 5 Ad & El 856, 111 ER 1391.
Buckinghamshire CC v Moran [1989] 2 All ER 225, [1990] Ch 623, [1989] 3 WLR 152, CA.
Doe d Landsell v Gower (1851) 17 QB 589, 117 ER 1406.
Edge v Strafford (1831) 1 Cr & J 391, 148 ER 1474.
Foster v Reeves [1892] 2 QB 255, CA.
Hand v Hall (1877) 2 Ex D 355, CA.
Inman v Stamp (1815) 1 Stark 12, 171 ER 386, NP; subsequent proceedings (1815) 2 Selwyn NP 759.
Kingsmill v Millard (1855) 11 Exch 313, 156 ER 849.
Kushner v Law Society [1952] 1 All ER 404, [1952] 1 KB 264, DC.
Martin v Smith (1874) LR 9 Exch 50.
Moses v Lovegrove [1952] 1 All ER 1279, [1952] 2 QB 533, CA.
Parker v Briggs (1893) 37 SJ 452, CA.
Parker v Taswell (1858) 2 De G & J 559, 44 ER 1106, LC.
Rawlins v Turner (1699) 1 Ld Raym 736, 91 ER 1392, NP.
Rollason v Leon (1861) 7 H & N 73, 158 ER 398, Ex Ch.
Ryley v Hicks (1725) 1 Stra 651, Bull NP 177, 93 ER 760.
Smirk v Lyndale Developments Ltd [1975] 1 All ER 690, [1975] Ch 317, [1975] 2 WLR 495, CA; rvsg in part [1974] 2 All ER 8, [1975] Ch 317, [1974] 3 WLR 91.

---

c   Section 54 is set out at p 691 e f, post

a
Tress v Savage (1854) 4 E & B 36, 119 ER 15.
Walsh v Lonsdale (1882) 21 Ch D 9, CA.
Wright v Macadam [1949] 2 All ER 565, [1949] 2 KB 744, CA.

Appeal

b
The plaintiff, Ronald James Long, appealed from the decision of Deputy Master Wall made on 26 September 1995, whereby, on a summons issued by the defendant, Tower Hamlets London Borough Council (LBTH), on 21 March 1995, he struck out Mr Long's originating summons issued on 13 January 1995 seeking a declaration that he was beneficially entitled to premises at 21 Turners Road, Tower Hamlets, London E3 by adverse possession, and rectification of the proprietorship register of title No 255264. The facts are set out in the judgment.

c

Philip Walter (instructed by *Wallace Bogan & Co*) for Mr Long.
Sara Hargreaves (instructed by *Russell Power*) for LBTH.

Cur adv vult

d
20 March 1996. The following judgment was delivered.

JAMES MUNBY QC. This case raises the question what is meant by the words 'tenancy from year to year or other period, without a lease in writing' in para 5(1) of Sch 1 to the Limitation Act 1980. It also, at least on one view of the matter,
e
raises the question what is meant by the words 'creation by parol of leases taking effect in possession for a term not exceeding three years' in s 54(2) of the Law of Property Act 1925—a question which, in turn, involves consideration of the law relating to reversionary leases. Both questions are of some interest and importance.

f
The matter comes before me on an appeal by the plaintiff, Ronald James Long, from an order made by Deputy Master Wall on 26 September 1995. The master had before him an application by the defendant, Tower Hamlets London Borough Council (LBTH), by summons dated 21 March 1995, to strike out the originating summons which the plaintiff had issued on 13 January 1995. The master struck out the originating summons on the ground that Mr Long's claim
g
was doomed to fail.

THE FACTS
The facts which are relevant to the main question that I have to decide lie within a very narrow compass. The dispute relates to the ground floor shop and a maisonette on the upper floors at 21 Turners Road, Tower Hamlets, London
h
E3. The premises are part of the property registered at HM Land Registry under title number 255264. On 4 September 1975 agents acting for the then owner of the premises, Mr Jacobs, wrote a letter to Mr Long in the following terms:

'Dear Sir,

j
21 Turners Road E3, Ground Floor. We confirm on behalf of our client, Mr H Jacobs, that we are prepared to grant you a quarterly tenancy of the above upon the following terms: (1) the rent to be £55 per quarter, payable on the usual quarter days in advance, exclusive of general and water rates payable in respect of this part of the property; (2) the premises are to be held by R J Long, Esq, trading as Long Bros, Upholstery, in connection with his business as an upholsterer; (3) the tenant is not to sublet the whole or any

part of the premises; (4) the tenant is to maintain the interior and shop front *a* in good decorative repair and condition; (5) the tenant is to give four weeks notice in writing before vacating the premises; (6) the tenancy is to commence on Monday, 29 September 1975 on a quarterly basis.
Yours faithfully …'

On 8 September 1975 Mr Long made the following indorsement on a copy of *b* the letter: 'I, Ronald James Long, agree to abide by the terms and conditions of the tenancy set out herein. (Signed) R J Long. Date 8 September 1975.' The copy letter indorsed by Mr Long (the tenancy document) was returned to the landlord. It was retained by the landlord and his successors in title, being eventually produced from its files by LBTH after the present litigation had been commenced. *c*

On or about 29 September 1975 Mr Long took possession of the shop. On 24 September 1976 Mr Jacobs' successor in title completed the sale of the freehold of the premises to the Greater London Council (the GLC). On 13 October 1976 the GLC was registered as proprietor of the premises. In or about September 1983 the GLC gave Mr Long notice to quit the shop. The notice expired on 25 March 1984. On 25 August 1988 the freehold of the premises was transferred under *d* statutory powers to LBTH as the successor authority to the GLC. LBTH has since been registered as proprietor of the premises.

THE ISSUES
It is common ground that Mr Long has paid no rent for the shop for many *e* years. According to Mr Long he stopped paying rent in 1977. LBTH accepts that rent has been neither demanded nor paid since March 1984. When precisely rent was last paid is a matter which can only be resolved at trial. Mr Long claims to have taken possession of the maisonette in 1977 at a time when, he says, it was unoccupied. LBTH, on the other hand, has produced documents which prima facie establish that the maisonette was lawfully occupied by Mr Taylor as tenant *f* of the GLC until 20 February 1978, when he was rehoused by the GLC elsewhere. Precisely when and to what extent Mr Long ever made use of the maisonette is in dispute between the parties, as is the extent to which he has, in recent years, been in occupation of the shop. These also, however, are matters which can only be resolved at trial. *g*

At trial the case will turn on the application to the facts, whatever they may be found to be, of s 15(1) and (6) of and paras 5 and 8 of Sch 1 to the Limitation Act 1980. Section 15(1) and (6) is in the following terms:

'(1) No action shall be brought by any person to recover any land after the expiration of twelve years from the date on which the right of action accrued *h* to him or, if it first accrued to some person through whom he claims, to that person.

(6) Part I of Schedule 1 to this Act contains provisions for determining the date of accrual of rights of action to recover land in the cases there mentioned.' *j*

Paragraph 5 of Sch 1 provides as follows:

'(1) Subject to sub-paragraph (2) below, a tenancy from year to year or other period, without a lease in writing, shall for the purposes of this Act be treated as being determined at the expiration of the first year or other period; and accordingly the right of action of the person entitled to the land subject

a
to the tenancy shall be treated as having accrued at the date on which in accordance with this sub-paragraph the tenancy is determined.
(2) Where any rent has subsequently been received in respect of the tenancy, the right of action shall be treated as having accrued on the date of the last receipt of rent.'

b
Paragraph 8(1) of Sch 1 provides:

'No right of action to recover land shall be treated as accruing unless the land is in the possession of some person in whose favour the period of limitation can run (referred to below in this paragraph as "adverse possession"); and where under the preceding provisions of this Schedule any
c
such right of action is treated as accruing on a certain date and no person is in adverse possession on that date, the right of action shall not be treated as accruing unless and until adverse possession is taken of the land.'

Mr Long's case is simple. He says that he is and has been ever since 1977 continuously in possession of the whole of the premises (that is, of both the shop
d
and the maisonette); that he has paid no rent since 1977 for any part of the premises and has, ever since then, been in adverse possession of the premises within the meaning of para 8(1); that in accordance with para 5(2) the GLC's right of action to recover the premises is to be treated as having accrued at the latest by 1 January 1978; and that, in consequence, any claim by LBTH to recover the premises became statute-barred, in accordance with s 15(1), at the latest by 1
e
January 1990, some five years before the present proceedings were commenced. On this footing Mr Long seeks: (i) a declaration that he is entitled beneficially to the premises; and (ii) rectification of the proprietorship register of title number 255264 to remove the premises from that title and to open a new title for the premises under which he is the registered proprietor.

f
LBTH denies that Mr Long can prove either the factual possession or the animus possidendi which are necessary to found adverse possession (see *Buckinghamshire CC v Moran* [1989] 2 All ER 225, [1990] Ch 623). Moreover, LBTH says that Mr Long last paid rent in March 1984, less than 12 years before the proceedings were commenced on 13 January 1995. Accordingly, says LBTH, its claim to recover the premises is not yet statute-barred.
g
As I have already said, the factual disputes between the parties can only be resolved at trial. On what basis, therefore, does LBTH seek to strike out Mr Long's claim? Three arguments are put forward by Miss Sara Hargreaves, counsel on behalf of LBTH. Each, in substance, proceeds on the footing that, whatever may be the eventual resolution of the factual disputes to which I have
h
referred, there are other grounds on which LBTH can establish that time cannot on any view have begun to run in Mr Long's favour until 1984 at the earliest.

Before considering Miss Hargreaves' arguments there is one preliminary matter which I must address. It will be appreciated that the tenancy document related only to the shop. There is no suggestion that Mr Long was ever granted
j
a tenancy of the maisonette or that he has ever paid any additional rent for the maisonette. On what basis, then, does Miss Hargreaves seek to resist Mr Long's claim in so far as it relates to the maisonette? She relies upon the principle that if a tenant occupies land belonging to the landlord but not included in the demise, that land is presumed to be an addition to the land demised to the tenant, so that it becomes subject to the terms of the tenancy and must therefore be given up to the landlord when the tenancy ends (see *Smirk v Lyndale Developments Ltd* [1975]

1 All ER 690, [1975] Ch 317; *rvsg in part* [1974] 2 All ER 8, [1975] Ch 317). Mr Philip *a*
Walter, counsel on behalf of Mr Long, seeks to confine the principle, which
otherwise he accepts, in two ways: first, he says it is limited to cases where the
encroachment is on land which is waste; secondly, he says that it is limited to
cases where the tenant is estopped by words or conduct from denying that the
additional land is within the demise. Neither condition, he says, is satisfied in the
present case.   *b*
    I cannot accept either of Mr Walter's submissions.   In *Smirk v Lyndale*
Developments Ltd [1974] 2 All ER 8 at 12, 13, 16, 20, [1975] Ch 317 at 323, 324, 329,
332 Pennycuick V-C considered all the relevant authorities, which, as he said, had
got into something of a tangle, and concluded that the law had been correctly
stated by Alderson and Parke BB in *Kingsmill v Millard* (1855) 11 Exch 313, 156 ER
849. His decision on the point was not challenged on appeal and was accepted as *c*
correct by the Court of Appeal (see [1975] 1 All ER 690 at 693, 695, 696, [1975] Ch
317 at 337, 340, 341). The law as laid down in those two cases I take to be clear
and binding on me. They show that the principle applies whether or not the land
encroached upon is waste. They show, moreover, that the principle is based on
a presumption, albeit a rebuttable presumption, which, although it may be *d*
considered to operate in a manner akin to an estoppel, is not dependent upon
proof, as Mr Walter I think would have it, of any active representation to the
landlord by the tenant. On the contrary, the presumption is treated as applying
unless the tenant, during the term, communicates with the landlord in such a way
as to show that he is asserting his own title as against the landlord or, as
Alderson B put it, that he is setting the landlord at defiance. There is nothing in *e*
the evidence before me in the present case which even begins to suggest that Mr
Long, in his dealings with the GLC and LBTH, ever sought to distinguish
between the shop and the maisonette or ever sought to assert that, whilst he
occupied the shop as tenant, his occupation of the maisonette was in some
different character. Accordingly, in my judgment, Miss Hargreaves is entitled to *f*
say that, on the evidence as it stands, the presumption is wholly unrebutted and
that the principle as laid down in *Smirk v Lyndale Developments Ltd* applies. It
follows that, for present purposes, no distinction is to be drawn between Mr
Long's claim as it relates to the shop and his claim as it relates to the maisonette.
    I turn therefore to consider the three issues identified by Miss Hargreaves as
justifying the striking out of Mr Long's claim.   *g*

ISSUE 1—'LEASE IN WRITING'
    In the first place, and this is her principal argument, Miss Hargreaves submits
that the tenancy document is a 'lease in writing' within the meaning of para 5(1)
of Sch 1 to the 1980 Act; that time accordingly did not begin to run in favour of *h*
Mr Long when he stopped paying rent (whenever that was) but only when his
tenancy was brought to an end by notice to quit; and that the only relevant notice
to quit was that which expired on 25 March 1984, less than 12 years before the
commencement of the present proceedings.
    Mr Walter denies that the tenancy document is, or as a matter of law is capable *j*
of being, a 'lease in writing' within the meaning of para 5(1). Put shortly, his *J*
argument can be summarised as follows.
    (1) A document cannot be a 'lease in writing' within the meaning of para 5(1)
unless it is dispositive, that is, as Mr Walter put it in argument, the document
must be one which at law creates, of and by itself, a leasehold estate in land.
    (2) As the tenancy document was not executed as a deed, it could take effect
as a lease only if it fell within the exception in s 54(2) of the Law of Property Act

a   1925, that is if it '[took] effect in possession' for a term not exceeding three years. It did not, says Mr Walter, because it took effect, if at all, as a reversionary lease.

At first blush, the use in para 5(1) of the words 'tenancy from year to year or other period, without a lease in writing' is rather puzzling to anyone familiar with the scheme of the 1925 Act and its distinction between those leases which are required by s 52 to be made by deed and those leases which s 54(2) permits to be

b   created by parol, in other words without the need even for writing. The provisions of the 1925 Act itself are also, at first, rather puzzling. Notwithstanding the reference in s 52(2)(d) to 'leases or tenancies ... not required by law to be made in writing', the Act does not itself, so far as I am aware, require any class of lease to be made in writing, though certain leases made under the Settled Land Act 1925 which would otherwise be required by s 42(1)(i) of that Act

c   to be made by deed are permitted by s 42(5)(ii) to be made by writing under hand.

(1) The historical background

The explanation for these seeming oddities is historical. As Mr Walter pointed out, para 5 of Sch 1 to the 1980 Act reproduces provisions first enacted as s 8 of

d   the Real Property Limitation Act 1833 and later re-enacted as s 9(2) of the Limitation Act 1939. Section 8 of the 1833 Act provided as follows:

> 'And be it further enacted, That when any Person shall be in Possession or in Receipt of the Profits of any Land, or in Receipt of any Rent, as Tenant from Year to Year or other Period, without any Lease in Writing, the Right
>
> *e*   of the Person entitled subject thereto, or of the Person through whom he claims, to make an Entry or Distress or to bring an Action to recover such Land or Rent shall be deemed to have first accrued at the Determination of the first of such Years or other Periods, or at the last Time when any Rent payable in respect of such Tenancy shall have been received (which shall last
>
> *f*   happen).'

As Mr Walter also pointed out, the context in which the 1833 Act was enacted was that of the Statute of Frauds 1677. However, in order to understand the exceedingly interesting and instructive arguments that have been so skilfully deployed by Mr Walter and Miss Hargreaves it is necessary to go even further

g   back than that and to consider, albeit briefly, the relevant principles of the common law.

At common law a lease could be granted in any way, even orally (see Megarry and Wade *The Law of Real Property* (5th edn, 1984) p 636). Moreover, there was at common law no restraint upon the grant of a reversionary lease, that is, a lease to take effect *in* reversion on some future day, however distant, and conferring no

h   right to take possession in the meantime. Such a lease (to be contrasted with a concurrent lease, that is, a lease *of* the reversion (see *Megarry and Wade* pp 664–665)) gave the lessee an immediate vested legal *interest* in the land, that interest being known as an interesse termini, though until the date when the lease was due to take effect this interest was vested in interest and not in possession. On

j   the other hand, the lessee under a reversionary lease acquired no *estate* in the land until he had actually entered, that is, taken possession in accordance with the lease; until then all he had was an interesse termini (see *Megarry and Wade* pp 231, 637, 647–648).

In 1677 the Statute of Frauds was enacted 'For Prevention of many fraudulent Practices, which are commonly endeavoured to be upheld by Perjury and Subornation of Perjury'. Section 1 of the Statute of Frauds provided:

'... all Leases, Estates ... or Terms of Years ... made or created by Livery *a* and Seisin only, or by Parol, and not put in Writing, and signed by the Parties so making or creating the same, or their Agents thereunto lawfully authorised by Writing, shall have the Force and Effect of Leases or Estates at Will only, and shall not either in Law or Equity be deemed or taken to have any other or greater Force or Effect; any Consideration for making any such Parol Leases or Estates, or any former Law or Usage, to the contrary *b* notwithstanding.'

Section 2 of the Statute of Frauds excepted from the operation of s 1:

'... all Leases not exceeding the Term of Three Years from the making thereof, whereupon the Rent reserved to the Landlord, during such Term, shall amount unto Two third Parts at the least of the full improved Value of *c* the Thing demised.'

Section 4 of the Statute of Frauds provided, so far as is material:

'... no Action shall be brought ... to charge any Person ... upon any Contract or Sale of Lands ... or any Interest in or concerning them ... unless *d* the Agreement upon which such Action shall be brought, or some *Memorandum* or Note thereof, shall be in Writing, and signed by the Party to be charged therewith, or some other Person thereunto by him lawfully authorized.'

Accordingly, when the 1833 Act was enacted the distinction was not, as it now *e* is, between those leases required to be made by deed and those which may be created by parol, but rather between those leases required by s 1 of the Statute of Frauds to be 'put in Writing' and those which, by virtue of s 2 of the Statute of Frauds, could still be created at common law by parol.

The modern requirement of a deed was first imposed by s 4 of the Transfer of *f* Property Act 1844, which provided:

'That no Lease in Writing of any ... Land ... shall be valid as a Lease ... unless the same shall be made by Deed; but any Agreement in Writing to let ... any such Land shall be valid and take effect as an Agreement to execute a Lease ... and the Person who shall be in the Possession of the Land in *g* pursuance of any Agreement to let may, from Payment of Rent or other Circumstances, be construed to be a Tenant from Year to Year.'

The drafting of s 4 of the 1844 Act was soon perceived to have been defective (see *Tress v Savage* (1854) 4 E & B 36 at 43, 119 ER 15 at 17 per Coleridge J). Section 4 was therefore repealed by s 1 of the Real Property Act 1845. Section 3 of the latter *h* Act provided: 'That ... a Lease, required by Law to be in Writing ... shall ... be void at Law, unless made by Deed ...' Sections 1, 2 and 4 of the Statute of Frauds remained in force.

Thus, from 1845, the combined effect of the Statute of Frauds and the 1845 Act was that those leases which, prior to the 1844 Act, had been required by s 1 of the *j* Statute of Frauds to be in writing were now required by s 3 of the 1845 Act to be made by deed; but that those leases which had been excepted by s 2 of the Statute of Frauds from the operation of s 1 of the Statute of Frauds remained excepted from the operation of s 3 of the 1845 Act.

Although the effect of s 3 of the 1845 Act was to make a written lease which did not fall within s 2 of the Statute of Frauds 'void', that did not deprive the written document of all legal effect. At *law*, as soon as the tenant took possession, and *a* rent was paid and accepted, a yearly or other periodic tenancy arose. That periodic tenancy was a legal estate which was treated as being held on such of the terms set out in the written document as were applicable to and not inconsistent with a periodic tenancy (see *Tress v Savage* and *Martin v Smith* (1874) LR 9 Exch 50). In *equity*, the imperfect lease was treated as a contract to grant a lease and, moreover, provided there was valuable consideration and a sufficient act of part

b performance, a contract of which specific performance would, in principle, be granted under the rule in *Parker v Taswell* (1858) 2 De G & J 559, 44 ER 1106 and *Walsh v Lonsdale* (1882) 21 Ch D 9.

Sections 1 and 2 of the Statute of Frauds and s 3 of the 1845 Act were replaced by ss 52 and 54 of the 1925 Act. Section 4 of the Statute of Frauds, so far as is material, was replaced by s 40 of the 1925 Act, itself since repealed by s 2(8) of the

c Law of Property (Miscellaneous Provisions) Act 1989. Section 52 of the 1925 Act, replacing s 3 of the 1845 Act, provides so far as is material, as follows:

'(1) All conveyances of land or of any interest therein are void for the purpose of conveying or creating a legal estate unless made by deed.

(2) This section does not apply to ... (d) leases or tenancies or other
d assurances not required by law to be made in writing ...'

'Conveyance' is defined by s 205(1)(ii) of the 1925 Act as including a lease. Section 54 of the 1925 Act, replacing ss 1 and 2 of the Statute of Frauds, is in the following terms:

e '(1) All interests in land created by parol and not put in writing and signed by the persons so creating the same, or by their agents thereunto lawfully authorised in writing, have, notwithstanding any consideration having been given for the same, the force and effect of interests at will only.

(2) Nothing in the foregoing provisions of this Part of this Act shall affect the creation by parol of leases taking effect in possession for a term not
f exceeding three years (whether or not the lessee is given power to extend the term) at the best rent which can be reasonably obtained without taking a fine.'

The words 'taking effect in possession' are not defined as such, though 'term of years absolute' is defined by s 205(1)(xxvii) of the 1925 Act in such a way as to
g distinguish a 'term of years taking effect in possession' from a 'term of years taking effect in reversion': '"Term of years absolute" means a term of years (taking effect either in possession or in reversion whether or not at a rent) ...' 'Possession' is defined by s 205(1)(xix) of the 1925 Act as including receipt of rents or profits or the right to receive the same.

h It will be observed that ss 52 and 54 of the 1925 Act follow very closely, and in large part perpetuate the language of, their statutory precursors. As is pointed out in *Megarry and Wade* p 637:

'The provisions of the two previous Acts were repeated by the Law of Property Act 1925 but with certain alterations. No attempt has been made
j to state the combined effect of the earlier Acts: section 54 follows the Statute of Frauds 1677 and section 52 follows the Real Property Act 1845 so that their differing provisions still stand side by side. This is presumably because they had become so familiar that it was thought best to preserve them.'

Thus, ss 52(2)(d) and 54(1) preserve fossilised references to leases in writing which, though they may reflect the formal requirements imposed in 1677 by the Statute of Frauds (and still representing the law when the 1833 Act was enacted),

had been overtaken by the formal requirement of a deed imposed by the 1844   *a*
Act.

However, as is also pointed out in *Megarry and Wade* p 637, and as appears from
a comparison of s 54(2) of the 1925 Act with s 2 of the Statute of Frauds, s 54(2)
did make two changes. The first, on which nothing turns for present purposes,
was to substitute for the reference in the Statute of Frauds to a rent not less than
two-thirds of the full improved value, reference to the best rent reasonably   *b*
obtainable without taking a fine. The second, which is crucial to Mr Walter's
argument, was to substitute for the reference in the Statute of Frauds to a lease
not exceeding three years 'from the making thereof' in s 54(2), to a lease 'taking
effect in possession' for a term not exceeding three years.

The 1925 Act made two other changes to the law which are material for
present purposes: first, ss 149(1) and (2) abolished the doctrine of interesse   *c*
termini and the rule that a lessee took no estate until he had actually entered;
secondly, s 149(3) limits to 21 years the time that may elapse before the term
under a reversionary lease begins; a reversionary lease postponed for more than
21 years is void. The effect of s 149, therefore, is to give the lessee under a
reversionary lease, so long as it is not postponed for more than 21 years, an   *d*
immediate estate, rather than a mere interest, in the land—though until the date
when the lease is due to take effect that estate will be vested in interest only and
not in possession.

(2) Paragraph 5(1): 'Lease in writing'

Before the master, Mr Walter argued that, notwithstanding the use of the   *e*
words 'lease in writing', the exception under para 5(1) of Sch 1 to the 1980 Act
applies only if the lease has been made by deed. That submission, which in my
judgment is clearly wrong, was not pursued before me. Mr Walter and Miss
Hargreaves were at one in agreeing that the word 'writing' in para 5(1) has the
meaning given to it by s 5 of and Sch 1 to the Interpretation Act 1978:   *f*

'"Writing" includes typing, printing, lithography, photography and other
modes of representing or reproducing words in a visible form, and
expressions referring to writing are construed accordingly.'

I agree. A written document does not have to be a deed in order to be a 'writing'
for the purposes of para 5(1), though on the other hand, a document which is a   *g*
deed will also be a 'writing' for the purposes of para 5(1).

As I have said, Mr Walter's argument is that a document is not a 'lease in
writing' unless it is dispositive, that is a document which at law creates, of and by
itself, a leasehold estate in land. A document which is merely an agreement for a
lease, or merely evidential of the terms of a lease is not, he submits, a 'lease in   *h*
writing'. Miss Hargreaves' submission is that this is much too subtle and
technical an approach. She contends for a simple and practical approach,
suggesting that the reason why para 5(1) distinguishes between those leases
which are, and those leases which are not, 'in writing' is evidential. She asserts, I
have no doubt correctly, that Mr Long acquired, at the latest when he took   *j*
possession and started paying rent on or about 29 September 1975, a periodic
tenancy at law and that that tenancy is to be treated at law as having been held
on the terms of the tenancy document. She says, again no doubt correctly, that
equity would in principle treat the tenancy document as a specifically enforceable
agreement for a lease, so that Mr Long had what is often called an equitable lease.
Thus far, I did not understand Mr Walter to challenge Miss Hargreaves' analysis
of the effect of the tenancy document in the events which had happened. So, says

a   Miss Hargreaves, there plainly was a lease, all the terms of the lease are to be found set out in a written document, and there is, therefore, a 'lease in writing'. It is, says Miss Hargreaves, as simple and straightforward as that. No, says Mr Walter, Miss Hargreaves' argument does not go far enough. She has to show that the tenancy agreement itself was dispositive and created a legal estate in land. An equitable lease is not, he says, a lease and does not of itself create an estate in land.

b   In my judgment, Mr Walter's submission on this point is correct.

In the light of the historical background, and bearing in mind the familiar distinction, drawn for example in ss 9 and 7 of the Statute of Frauds (now s 53(1)(c) and 53(1)(b) of the 1925 Act), between those transactions required to be 'in' writing, that is where the writing required by the statute is dispositive, and those requiring only to be 'manifested and proved by some writing', that is where

c   the writing required by the statute need be no more than evidential, one's initial impression is that the 'writing' referred to in para 5(1) of Sch 1 to the 1980 Act must be dispositive and not merely evidential. Paragraph 5(1), after all, refers to a 'lease *in* writing'. Indeed, as a matter of simple English language, that is what one would expect the words to mean.

d   But the matter does not rest there, because I have been referred to two authorities which, in my judgment, indicate that this is indeed the correct meaning of the words. In *Doe d Landsell v Gower* (1851) 17 QB 589, 117 ER 1406 the question was whether an entry in a vestry book, signed by the tenant and by one, but not by all, of the parish officers, was a 'lease in writing' within the meaning of s 8 of the 1833 Act. It was held by the Court of Queen's Bench

e   (Patteson, Coleridge and Wightman JJ) that it was not, because only one of the parish officers had signed the vestry book and he had not professed to sign on behalf of all. The facts of the case were very far removed indeed from the facts of the present case, but the reasons given by the judges for arriving at their decision are apposite. They are all to the same effect. Patteson J made it clear

f   that, in his opinion, what s 8 required was an 'actual lease', that is '... not ... a document, generally, but ... a lease ... something which is to pass an interest'. Coleridge J said that what s 8 required was 'a lease in writing: that is, not merely an instrument which would be evidence of the conditions of holding, but one passing an interest'. Wightman J said that s 8 'requires an instrument in writing that may operate as a lease'. (See 17 QB 589 at 598, 599, 600, 117 ER 1406 at 1410,

g   1411.)

In my judgment this is clear authority for the proposition that there was no 'lease in writing' for the purposes of s 8 of the 1833 Act, and thus there is no 'lease in writing' for the purposes of para 5(1) of Sch 1 to the 1980 Act, if the 'writing' is merely evidential. If there is to be a 'lease in writing' the writing must itself at law

h   'pass an interest' (to use the words of Patteson and Coleridge JJ) and 'operate as a lease' (to use Wightman J's words).

Moses v Lovegrove [1952] 1 All ER 1279, [1952] 2 QB 533, the only other authority on the point to which I was referred, is to the like effect. One of the questions in that case was whether a rent book was a 'lease in writing' within the meaning of

j   s 9(2) of the Limitation Act 1939. The Court of Appeal held that it was not. Evershed MR said ([1952] 2 QB 533 at 536, cf [1952] 1 All ER 1279 at 1280):

'The alleged lease in writing consisted of the rent book, which was put in evidence. The judge rejected the view that the rent book was such a lease in writing within the meaning of the Act, and I think he was entirely right in that conclusion. The rent book is, I think, what it purports to be, and what it is called, a rent book, that is, a book containing acknowledgments for

payment of weekly sums of rent, and containing also, in pursuance of the
terms of the legislation, a reference to the conditions on which the tenant
was holding his tenancy. I think that on the face of it, it was not intended to
be, and is not a contract for granting a tenancy, still less a lease creating an
estate. It is, I think, at most what it was intended to be, and what it is on the
face of it called, a book evidencing the terms on which the tenant held.'

Romer LJ ([1952] 1 All ER 1279 at 1285, [1952] 2 QB 533 at 543) said that he
entirely agreed with Evershed MR.

These authorities make it clear, in my judgment, that a written document,
whatever its terms, however clearly referable to the existence of a lease, and
however comprehensive it may be in setting out the terms of the lease, is not a
'lease in writing' for the purposes of para 5(1) of Sch 1 to the 1980 Act unless at
law the document itself operates to 'pass an interest' (the words used by Patteson
and Coleridge JJ), itself 'operates as a lease' (the words used by Wightman J) or
itself 'creates an estate' (the words used by Evershed MR).

(3) Section 54(2): 'taking effect in possession'

That being so, the next question which arises is whether the tenancy document
operated to create a leasehold estate. It plainly did not take effect as a deed. The
question therefore is whether or not it operated in accordance with s 54(2) of the
1925 Act as a 'lease taking effect in possession for a term not exceeding three
years'.

Mr Walter accepts that, notwithstanding the reference in s 54(2) to the creation
of leases 'by parol', a lease which otherwise satisfies the requirements of s 54(2)
can be created either by parol or in writing. This is plainly correct: see e g *Wright
v Macadam* [1949] 2 All ER 565 at 568, [1949] 2 KB 744 at 747 per Jenkins LJ; and
Kushner v Law Society [1952] 1 All ER 404 at 407, [1952] 1 KB 264 at 272 per Lord
Goddard CJ. Mr Walter concedes that the tenancy document, properly
construed, purported to take effect as a tenancy and not as a mere agreement to
grant a tenancy: see *Rollason v Leon* (1861) 7 H & N 73, 158 ER 398 and *Hand v Hall*
(1877) 2 Ex D 355. He also accepts that the tenancy document, since it stipulated
for a quarterly tenancy, was for a 'term not exceeding three years' as that phrase
is used in s 54(2).

However, submits Mr Walter, the tenancy did not 'tak[e] effect in possession'
and the tenancy document was therefore not, as required by s 54(2), a 'lease taking
effect in possession'. Although the tenancy document was executed on 8
September 1975, the tenancy was not to commence immediately but rather on a
future date, 29 September 1975, and Mr Long had no right to take possession until
the latter date. Therefore, says Mr Walter, it took effect, if at all, as a reversionary
lease. Whatever may have been the position at common law or prior to 1925, he
says, the inclusion in s 54(2) of the words 'taking effect in possession' has the effect
of excluding altogether from the ambit of s 54(2) reversionary leases conferring no
immediate right to take possession. Thus, he submits, a reversionary lease can
only take effect if made by deed. If that is right then it follows, says Mr Walter,
that a reversionary lease cannot be a 'lease in writing' for the purposes of para 5(1)
of Sch 1 to the 1980 Act unless it is made by deed. Mr Walter submits that the only
tenancy which ever came into existence in the present case was not one created by
the tenancy document. It arose, he says, by operation of law as a result of Mr Long
taking possession on or about 29 September 1975 and paying rent. The tenancy
document, says Mr Walter, is not a lease. It is no more than a document whose
terms, so far as they are consistent with a periodic tenancy, will be treated as the

a   terms on which Mr Long held the periodic tenancy which arose by operation of law on or about 29 September 1975.

Miss Hargreaves, on the other hand, disputes that reversionary leases were excluded from the exception in s 2 of the Statute of Frauds or that they are excluded from the ambit of s 54(2). She accepts that the three-year period, referred to both in s 2 of the Statute of Frauds and in s 54(2), provides what she

b   calls the basic measure of computation, and that the computation of the three-year period is from the date of the parol grant. But that, according to Miss Hargreaves, is the only limit imposed by s 54(2). The fundamental principle, common both to s 2 of the Statute of Frauds and to s 54(2), she says, is this: the term, whether it is to commence immediately or at some date in the future, must take effect in possession within three years from the date of the parol grant and

c   must not extend beyond three years from the date of the parol grant. So long as it satisfies this condition it matters not, she submits, whether the term takes effect in possession at the date of the parol grant. It is implicit in this argument that the words 'taking effect in possession' in s 54(2) are descriptive only of the quality of the lease at the date when the term commences and not of the quality of the lease

d   at the date of the parol grant. She suggests that the restrictions on the grant of reversionary leases are to be found in s 149 of the 1925 Act, and not in s 54(2).

(a) The Statute of Frauds

Before turning to consider the question as it arises in relation to s 54(2), I must first examine certain older authorities on s 2 of the Statute of Frauds. The first

e   case is *Rawlins v Turner* (1699) 1 Ld Raym 736, 91 ER 1392. The report is very short:

> 'No lease by parol is good which imports to convey an interest for more than three years from the time of the making. It was ruled by *Holt* chief justice at *Lent* assizes at *Kingston* 1699, that such lease for three years of land,
>
f   > as will be good without deed within the [Statute of Frauds] *s*. 2, must be for three years, to be computed from the time of the agreement; and not for three years to be computed from any day after.'

The second case is *Ryley v Hicks* (1725) 1 Stra 651, 93 ER 760. Again the report is very short:

g
> '*In* Middlesex, coram Raymond, *Chief Justice*. Leases by parol for less than three years from the making, to commence at a future day, are not within Statute of Frauds. The plaintiff declares, that 24 *February* 1723, she demised to the defendant a chamber, a cellar, and half a shop, *habendum* from *Lady-day* then next for a quarter of a year, and so from quarter to quarter, so long as

h   > both parties shall please, at 5l. *per*. quarter. It was objected by *Whitaker*, that this being to commence at a future day, was but a lease at will since the Statute of Frauds. The Chief Justice at first thought it a good objection, but upon farther consideration he was of opinion, that the exception was not confined to leases that were to commence from the time of making, but was

j   > general as to all leases that were not to hold for above three years from the making. So the plaintiff had a verdict.'

The case is also reported in Buller's Nisi Prius p 177:

> 'A lease by parol for a year and an half, to commence after the expiration of a lease which wants a year of expiring, is a good lease within the statute of frauds, for it does not exceed three years from the making.'

It will be seen that the two reports differ in their summary of the relevant facts. As observed in Selwyn *An Abridgment of the Law of Nisi Prius* (13th edn, 1869) vol 2, p 759, the report in Strange is 'probably from a different note'. But the statement of principle is the same in both reports.

Ryley v Hicks was criticised by Dampier J in *Inman v Stamp* (1815) 1 Stark 12, 171 ER 386, reported on this point only in *Selwyn* (p 759):

'In *Inman v Stamp* ... Dampier J said the practice had been with the foregoing case of *Ryley v Hicks*, although he rather inclined to think that the 2nd section of the [Statute of Frauds], taken with section 4 [of the Statute of Frauds], was confined to leases executed by possession, on which two-thirds of the improved rent was reserved.'

In *Edge v Strafford* (1831) 1 Cr & J 391, 148 ER 1474 it was argued that *Ryley v Hicks* had in effect been overruled by *Inman v Stamp*. The argument was rejected by Bayley B, giving the judgment of the Court of Exchequer, who appears to have treated *Ryley v Hicks* as good authority for the proposition that 'a lease, though it were to commence *in futuro*, would be within the exception in the statute of frauds, if it did not exceed three years from the making' (see 1 Cr & J 391 at 396, 148 ER 1474 at 1476–1477.) A similar argument in *Lord Bolton v Tomlin* (1836) 5 Ad & El 856, 111 ER 1391 fared little better, though the court in that case managed to avoid deciding, or even expressing any opinion on, the point.

In *Hand v Hall* (1877) 2 Ex D 355 an agreement was made on 26 January 1876 for a tenancy until midsummer 12 months from 14 February 1876. It was held by the Court of Appeal, reversing the Exchequer Division, that the agreement operated as a devise within the exception in s 2 of the Statute of Frauds. As was pointed out in Foa *The Relationship of Landlord and Tenant* (6th edn, 1924) p 11, the decision of the Court of Appeal is consistent only with the view that *Ryley v Hicks* was correctly decided, although that case seems not to have been referred to and the contrary appears not to have been argued.

The next case to which I was referred is *Foster v Reeves* [1892] 2 QB 255. In that case an agreement was made on 12 May 1890 for a tenancy for three years to commence on 24 June 1890 and thereafter from year to year until determined. The landlord sued to recover rent after the tenant had given up possession. It seems to have been common ground that there was no lease at law, and the argument in the Court of Appeal was as to the power of the county court, under the legislation then in force, to grant specific performance of the agreement under the rule in *Walsh v Lonsdale*. Each of the judges, however, referred, albeit briefly, to the position at law. Lord Esher MR said (at 257):

'When the agreement is looked at, it is found that it assumes to create a tenancy for three years, to begin at a subsequent date. Such a tenancy can at common law only be created by deed ... If, therefore, we look to the common law alone, this claim cannot be supported.'

Fry LJ said (at 258–259):

'[The debt] was a sum which could be recovered in equity, provided the agreement under which it was claimed was one that would be enforced by a court of equity. Independently of this, there was no right to sue for it.'

Lopes LJ said (at 259):

'By the joint operation of the Statute of Frauds and [the Real Property Act 1845], a lease for more than three years must be by deed. Here the a   agreement purports to create a term of more than three years, and it is clear that rent could not, at common law, have been recovered under that agreement.'

At first, Mr Walter was minded to argue that Lord Esher MR's observations (though not, he accepted, those of Lopes LJ) were authority for the proposition that a tenancy to begin at a subsequent date could at law only be created by deed.
b   On reflection, and having considered *Ryley v Hicks*, Mr Walter accepted that this was not what Lord Esher MR had meant. In my judgment Mr Walter was entirely correct to make that concession. When Lord Esher MR said that 'Such a tenancy can at common law only be created by deed', the tenancy he was referring to was, as the immediately preceding words make clear, 'a tenancy *for*
c   *three years*, to begin at a subsequent date' (my emphasis). Read thus, Lord Esher MR was making the same point as Lopes LJ, and indeed the very same point that had been made by Lord Holt CJ as long ago as 1699: a tenancy for three years to commence at a future date was not within s 2 of the Statute of Frauds, and thus at law could only be made in writing from 1677 or, from 1844, by deed. This was not because the tenancy was to commence at a future date, for *Ryley v Hicks*
d   shows that, even after the enactment of the Statute of Frauds, there was nothing objectionable in that. It was because the tenancy was to last for a period expiring more than three years from the date of the agreement, and it had been established by *Rawlins v Turner* (1699) 1 Ld Raym 736, 91 ER 1392 that such a lease fell outside the exception in s 2. There is, in my judgment, nothing in *Foster v Reeves* to
e   suggest that the Court of Appeal was seeking to overturn established authority, although in that case, as previously in *Hand v Hall*, *Ryley v Hicks* seems not to have been referred to. *Foster v Reeves* is, therefore, in my judgment, no authority for the proposition that, after the enactment of the 1845 Act, a lease for less than three years to commence at a future date could at law only be created by deed.

Be that as it may, the matter appears to have been resolved the following year
f   in *Parker v Briggs* (1893) 37 SJ 452, a decision of the Court of Appeal reported only, and there rather inadequately, in the Solicitors Journal:

'... the appellants contend[ed] ... that a parol lease to commence at a future date was in point of law and in fact an agreement for a lease, and as such must be in writing under section 4 of the Statute of Frauds, even though the lease agreed to be granted were for a less period than three years (*Edge* v. *Strafford*)
g   ((1831) 1 Cr & J 391, 148 ER 1474) ... The court, however, decided against the appellants ... two of the learned judges holding that it was possible to create a parol lease to commence in the future (*Ryley* v. *Hicks*) ...'

h   Accordingly, Mr Walter was, in my judgment, correct not to press the argument that, after the enactment of the 1845 Act, a lease to commence at a future date could at law only be created by deed, even if it would otherwise fall within the exception in s 2 of the Statute of Frauds. The contrary is, in my judgment, clear from the authorities to which I have referred. That *Ryley v Hicks* remained good law until the coming into force of the 1925 Act appears, moreover, to have been
j   the general view of the commentators: see 18 *Halsbury's Laws* (1st edn) para 830, Foa *The Relationship of Landlord and Tenant* p 11 and Redman *The Law of Landlord and Tenant* (8th edn, 1924) pp 121, 439–440).

It follows, in my judgment, that prior to the coming into force of the 1925 Act Mr Walter's argument would have failed. So far as concerns the effect of the exception in s 2 of the Statute of Frauds, Miss Hargreaves correctly relies upon *Rawlins v Turner* and *Ryley v Hicks* to make good her submissions. Unless,

therefore, the effect of s 54(2) of the 1925 Act was, as Mr Walter asserts, to change *a*
the law as previously laid down in *Ryley v Hicks*, the tenancy document will, as it
seems to me, constitute a 'lease in writing' for the purposes of para 5(1) of Sch 1
to the 1980 Act.

Before turning to consider the meaning of s 54(2) there is another aspect of the
Statute of Frauds on which Mr Walter placed some reliance and to which I must
briefly advert. Cases such as *Inman v Stamp, Edge v Strafford* and *Lord Bolton v* *b*
Tomlin show that if there was an oral letting in futuro for less than three years
from the date of the agreement, there was no remedy in contract, though an
action could be brought on the lease once possession had been taken, so that
what had previously been a mere interesse termini had become an estate in the
land. The reason for the divergent treatment was, as Mr Walter points out, that
such an oral transaction was caught, qua contract, by s 4 of the Statute of Frauds *c*
but, falling as it did within the exception in s 2, was not caught, qua lease, by s 1
of the Statute of Frauds. As Mr Walter observes, the law as formulated in
particular in *Edge v Strafford* was unsatisfactory in treating very differently the
enforceability of the same transaction qua contract and qua demise. Given that
the exception in s 2 of the Statute of Frauds extended to oral demises, it could be *d*
a fine point whether a particular oral transaction was a mere agreement, and thus
wholly unenforceable by virtue of s 4, or a demise, and thus effective qua lease
under the exception in s 2.

(b) Section 54(2)

As I have already mentioned, the words 'taking effect in possession' which *e*
appear in s 54(2) of the 1925 Act were not to be found in s 2 of the Statute of
Frauds. There appears to be no judicial authority as to the effect (if any) of this
change—certainly I was referred to none. The question is canvassed by some of
the commentators, though unhappily for Mr Long and LBTH, who as a result
have been driven to litigate the matter, the commentators do not speak with one *f*
voice.

Foa *General Law of Landlord and Tenant* (7th edn, 1947) p 10 puts the point very
clearly:

'A parol lease might be made under the exception in the Statute of Frauds
... to take effect in futuro, provided that it came to an end within three years *g*
from the making thereof (*Ryley v Hicks* (1725) 1 Stra 651, 93 ER 760). The
present statute seems to except only those taking effect immediately in
possession.'

The same view is expressed in *Megarry and Wade* p 637, where it is said: 'A lease *h*
taking effect in possession is to be contrasted with one taking effect in reversion,
e.g. a lease granted today to *take effect in 19 days' time'. Emmet on Title* (19th edn,
1986) vol 2, para 26.006 expresses the same view as *Megarry and Wade* in very
similar language. Hill and Redman's *Law of Landlord and Tenant* (18th edn, 1988)
vol 1, pp A 264–265, paras A[631]–[639], is to the same effect, drawing a
distinction between: *j*

'(a) reversionary leases, that is leases to take effect in reversion at the time
of the grant, possession being postponed to a future date (which are outside
the s 54(2) exception); and (b) leases which take effect in possession at once
but where the term is calculated from a future date (which are within the
exception).'

a These plainly support Mr Walter's argument. Miss Hargreaves referred me to the contrary view expressed in 27(1) *Halsbury's Laws* (4th edn reissue) para 78, where it says of s 54(2):

b 'The three years are computed from the day of the making of the lease; and, if the term does not commence at once, it must expire, or be capable of expiring, within three years from that day (*Rawlins v Turner* (1699) 1 Ld Raym 736, 91 ER 1392; *Foster v Reeves* [1892] 2 QB 255, CA per Lord Esher MR). The exception to the requirement of a deed is not confined to leases commencing at the time they are made (*Ryley v Hicks* (1725) 1 Stra 651, 93 ER 760).'

c One's confidence in that view might be somewhat greater were it not for the fact that the passage has remained unchanged since before 1925 (cf 18 *Halsbury's Laws* (1st edn, 1911) para 830). Miss Hargreaves also referred me to Woodfall's *Law of Landlord and Tenant* (1994) vol 1, p 5/2, para 5.003, where *Ryley v Hicks* is still referred to as good authority, albeit not for the point at present in issue. Again, the passage in question has remained virtually unchanged since before 1925 (cf *Woodfall's Law of Landlord and Tenant* (21st edn, 1924) p 158). Moreover, *d* elsewhere in the current edition the view appears to be expressed that a lease takes effect in possession for the purposes of s 54(2) only if it is to commence immediately and not at a future date (see *Woodfall*, vol 1, p 6/8, para 6.019).

The preponderance of the commentaries therefore supports Mr Walter. That fact, though suggestive, can hardly be decisive. There are, however, in my judgment three reasons why Mr Walter's argument is indeed correct.

e In the first place, the words 'in possession', when used as part of the phrase 'taking effect in possession for a term not exceeding three years', in my judgment have their normal legal meaning. They connote an estate or interest in the land which is vested 'in possession' rather than merely vested 'in interest'. This reading is powerfully reinforced by the distinction drawn in s 205(1)(xxvii) of the *f* 1925 Act between a 'term of years taking effect in possession' and a 'term of years taking effect in reversion'. The words 'taking effect in possession' in s 54(2) are, in my judgment, used in the same sense in which those words are used in s 205(1)(xxvii) and thus, and this is the critical point, in distinction to the words 'taking effect in reversion'. This, as it seems to me, demonstrates that, as Mr Walter submits, reversionary leases were not intended to come within the ambit *g* of s 54(2). Putting the same point rather differently, the words 'taking effect in possession' are used in s 54(2) in such a way as to achieve the same result as that contended for by Dampier J in *Inman v Stamp* when he sought to argue that the exception in s 2 of the Statute of Frauds applied only to leases 'executed by possession' (see *Selwyn* p 759).

h Secondly, it is very difficult, if Miss Hargreaves' argument is correct, to see what was the purpose of including the words 'in possession' in s 54(2) at all. It is implicit in her argument that the words 'taking effect in possession' in s 54(2) are descriptive of the quality of the lease at the date when the term commences and not of the quality of the lease at the date of the parol grant. Given the definition of 'possession' in s 205(1)(xix) of the 1925 Act, however, it would seem that any *j* lease, even a concurrent lease, must necessarily take effect 'in possession' at the date when the term commences. So, if Miss Hargreaves is correct, the words 'in possession' add nothing to what would otherwise be the effect of s 54(2).

The third reason is, in my judgment, decisive. It will be remembered that those leases which fell within the exception in s 2 of the Statute of Frauds were defined, so far as is material for present purposes, as being 'Leases not exceeding the Term of three Years from the making thereof.' In contrast, those leases which fall within the exception in s 54(2) are defined, so far as is material for present purposes, as being 'leases taking effect in possession for a term not exceeding three years.'

It will be seen that the three-year period referred to in s 2 of the Statute of Frauds is *not* the same as the three-year period referred to in s 54(2). Under the Statute of Frauds the three-year period was the period 'from the making' of the lease, in other words the period of three years from the date of the parol grant. Thus, whether or not the language of s 2 implicitly required the term of the lease to commence on 'the making thereof' (the point on which Dampier J in *Inman v Stamp* thought that *Ryley v Hicks* had been wrongly decided), the words 'not exceeding the Term of Three Years from the making thereof' plainly meant that, as held by Holt CJ in *Rawlins v Turner*, no lease by parol could be good which imported to convey an interest for more than three years from the time of the making. Under s 54(2), on the other hand, the three-year period is the period of the term comprised in the lease. Moreover, there has been omitted from s 54(2) any express reference to the date of 'the making' of the lease. Thus, if Miss Hargreaves' argument is correct, there is no limit expressed in s 54(2) to the period which may elapse before the lease 'tak[es] effect in possession', the only requirement being that the lease, when eventually it does 'tak[e] effect in possession', must be 'for a term not exceeding three years'. On this footing the only limit to the period which might elapse before the term 'tak[es] effect in possession' would be the period of 21 years specified in s 149(3) of the 1925 Act. Miss Hargreaves, of course, recoils from going this far. Her argument acknowledges that the term, whether it is to commence immediately or at some date in the future, must not extend beyond three years from the date of the parol grant. However, it is impossible to find that limitation in the language of s 54(2) unless it is to be found, as I think it is to be found, in the crucial words 'taking effect in possession', those words then being understood, as they have to be understood, in the sense which I have already indicated. Indeed, Miss Hargreaves comes very close to recognising how far the logic of her argument drives her when she suggests that the restrictions on the grant of reversionary leases are to be found in s 149 of the 1925 Act, and not in s 54(2). But this, in my judgment, is quite impossible. There is simply no basis for suggesting that what Parliament envisaged when it repealed s 2 of the Statute of Frauds and enacted s 54(2) was the grant of parol leases which might not come into effect for 21 years and might not come to an end for 24 years. It makes sense to suggest, as is implicit in Mr Walter's argument, that Parliament intended to clarify the law and, by adopting Dampier J's approach, to abolish the gloss to *Rawlins v Turner* represented by the somewhat controversial decision in *Ryley v Hicks*. It is a very different thing indeed to suggest that Parliament intended to sweep away the basic principle articulated in *Rawlins v Turner* and to widen so drastically the class of leases excepted from the operation of what are now ss 52(1) and 54(1) of the 1925 Act.

One final comment on the matter is perhaps appropriate. As Mr Walter points out, the effect of construing s 54(2) in the way for which he contends is to put an end to the distinction, based on ss 2 and 4 of the Statute of Frauds and illustrated by cases such as *Edge v Strafford*, of an oral letting in futuro being enforceable qua lease but not qua contract. If his construction of s 54(2) is correct, the effect of the 1925 Act was to make equally unenforceable both an oral executory agreement to grant a lease (s 40) and an oral attempt to grant a lease taking effect in possession in the future (s 54(2)), and, accordingly, to put an end to the need to distinguish between those oral transactions for a future tenancy which, as a matter of construction, took effect as mere agreements, and were thus

a unenforceable by virtue of s 4 of the Statute of Frauds, and those oral transactions which, as a matter of construction, took effect as leases, and thus fell within the exception in s 2 of the Statute of Frauds. It is tempting to think that this was, indeed, Parliament's intention when it replaced s 2 of the Statute of Frauds with s 54(2) of the 1925 Act, but the temptation, which rests on mere speculation, must in my judgment be resisted. Be that as it may, it is of some comfort to note that,
b accepting Mr Walter's submission, as I do, this is indeed the effect of the legislation.

Accordingly, Mr Walter is correct, in my judgment, when he submits that reversionary leases conferring no immediate right to take possession are altogether excluded from the ambit of s 54(2) of the 1925 Act and that such reversionary leases can take effect only if made by deed. It follows that the
c tenancy document (which it is common ground was a reversionary lease not made by deed and not conferring on Mr Long an immediate right to take possession) was incapable of taking effect as a parol lease under s 54(2). Thus, as Mr Walter submits, the tenancy which undoubtedly came into existence was not one created by the tenancy document but rather one which arose by operation of
d law. From this it follows, in my judgment, that the tenancy document is not a 'lease in writing' within the meaning of para 5(1) of Sch 1 to the 1980 Act. Accordingly, and as a matter of law, Miss Hargreaves fails in her first argument for striking out Mr Long's claim.

ISSUE 2—THE LANDLORD AND TENANT ACT 1954
e Miss Hargreaves' second argument is based on the provisions of the Landlord and Tenant Act 1954. She submits that Mr Long's tenancy was a tenancy to which Pt II of the 1954 Act applied. Section 24(1) of that Act provides that: 'A tenancy to which this Part of this Act applies shall not come to an end unless terminated in accordance with the provisions of this Part of this Act;' an event
f which, she says, did not occur in the present case until the notice to quit given to Mr Long in or about September 1983 expired on 25 March 1984. She points out that s 24(2) of the 1954 Act does not include the operation of the 1980 Act amongst the list of matters which, notwithstanding s 24(1), are expressed not to prevent a tenancy to which the Act applies coming to an end. In short, she submits, the effect of the clear and mandatory language of s 24(1) is to make it
g impossible for the tenant under a tenancy to which Pt II of the 1954 Act applies to be in adverse possession within the meaning of para 8(1) of Sch 1 to the 1980 Act until such time as the tenancy has been terminated in accordance with the provisions of Pt II of the Act. The argument is entirely novel: neither Miss Hargreaves nor Mr Walter was able to point me to any authority in which the
h point has been canvassed let alone decided.

A similar argument in the context of the Rent Acts was rejected in *Moses v Lovegrove*. I have to confess that my initial reaction to Miss Hargreaves' argument reflected that of Evershed MR, when he said ([1952] 2 QB 533 at 537, cf [1952] 1 All ER 1279 at 1280–1281):

j 'Such a view, if well founded, is, I think, somewhat startling, for it would necessarily follow therefrom that in a case of premises controlled or covered by the Rent Restriction legislation, unless the statutory period under the Limitation Act, 1939, had expired before they came under the control, no Limitation Act could ever run in favour of the tenant, or could ever run at all, so long as the Rent Restriction legislation remains on the statute book. There is a further reason for thinking such a conclusion surprising, and it was a reason noticed by my brother Romer during the argument: the Rent *a* Restriction legislation is intended to protect tenants. If [counsel] is right, it would, in this instance, have the peculiar and oblique effect of preserving to the landlord a right in respect of this property, which she would indubitably, on the argument, otherwise have lost.'

Miss Hargreaves points out, however, that there is a fundamental difference *b* between the operation of the Rent Acts and the operation of Pt II of the 1954 Act. Whereas the Rent Acts do not prevent the termination of the tenancy by a common law notice to quit, and thus confer on the protected tenant no more than what has been described as a 'personal status or statutory right of irremovability', Pt II of the 1954 Act continues the common law tenancy, albeit with a statutory variation as to the mode of determination. What Miss *c* Hargreaves says as to the distinction between the two statutory schemes of protection is, of course, entirely correct. For my part, however, I doubt that the distinction which Miss Hargreaves draws really bears upon the reasoning which underlay the decision of the Court of Appeal in *Moses v Lovegrove* or that it is sufficient, for the purposes of the proper application of the 1980 Act, to justify *d* distinguishing the two types of case in the way she suggests.

Be that as it may (and I wish to emphasise that I am expressing no final view on Miss Hargreaves' submissions), there is, in my judgment, a fundamental flaw in her argument which makes it impossible for her to succeed at this stage in the litigation. This is that her argument assumes that Mr Long's tenancy was a tenancy to which Pt II of the 1954 Act applied at the material times. However, *e* Pt II of the Act applies only to tenancies where the property comprised in the tenancy is or includes premises occupied by the tenant for the purposes of a business carried on by him or for those and other purposes (see s 23(1)). Given the factual disputes between the parties to which I have already referred, and the general paucity of the evidence at present before the court, it would not, in my judgment, be appropriate to assume for the purposes of this striking out *f* application, as on Miss Hargreaves' case I have to, that Mr Long was at the material times occupying the whole or some part of the premises for the purposes of a business being carried on by him.

Accordingly I reject Miss Hargreaves' second argument for striking out Mr Long's claim.   *g*

ISSUE 3—ACKNOWLEDGMENT

Miss Hargreaves' final argument is that Mr Long acknowledged the GLC's title to the premises in 1984, that is less than 12 years before the present proceedings were commenced. In this connection she relies upon ss 29 to 31 of the 1980 Act. *h* She accepts that the acknowledgment must be in writing. She puts her case in two ways.

First, she relies upon a letter dated 12 January 1984 written to the GLC by Messrs Jones Son & Day, a firm of estate agents and valuers who Mr Walter accepts were acting as Mr Long's agents. The letter was in the following terms: *j*

'Long Brothers, Clemence Street Site, 11/19 & 21 Turners Road. We refer to your letter of 14 September with enclosure. Since it would appear our clients are entitled to compensation for disturbance we shall be obliged if [an] appropriate claim form [could] be forwarded. As our clients would prefer alternative accommodation they ask if your Council have any lock-up type store in the area to let of 500/600 square feet.'

a   Neither the letter of 14 September 1983 nor its enclosure was in evidence before me. Both seem to have been lost. Deputy Master Wall thought that the reference to compensation might have been to statutory compensation following the service of a compulsory purchase order. Miss Hargreaves was able to demonstrate to my satisfaction that this cannot have been the case, and Mr Walter does not seek to argue the contrary. Miss Hargreaves and Mr Walter are

b   at one in accepting that the enclosure to the missing letter of 14 September 1983 was in all probability a notice to quit served in accordance with Pt II of the 1954 Act, and in accepting that the reference to compensation in the letter of 12 January 1984 was in all probability a reference to compensation payable under that Act. Mr Walter, however, draws attention to the fact that, whilst the letter of 12 January 1984 referred to two other properties in addition to the premises,

c   namely numbers 11 and 19 Turners Road, it referred to the letter of 14 September 1983 as having apparently contained only a single enclosure. Therefore, he says, it is not shown with that degree of probability necessary to justify the striking out of Mr Long's claim, either that the letter of 14 September 1983 contained a notice to quit the premises, as opposed to a notice to quit one or other or both of the other properties, or that the letter of 12 January 1984 was written with reference

d   to the premises.

Furthermore, says Mr Walter, the letter of 12 January 1984 did not constitute an acknowledgment of the GLC's title to anything because it was not making any definite assertion. The critical words 'it would appear' are, he says, suggestive of no more than an inference derived from a document just received rather than an

e   assertion or admission of fact. The letter of 12 January 1984 merely assumes for the sake of argument that something said in the missing letter of 14 September 1983 may be correct, but without acknowledging that it necessarily is. It amounts, he says, to nothing more than a comment to the effect that 'on the basis of what you say in your letter, and assuming for the sake of argument that it is

f   correct, it would appear ...' The request for a claim form cannot, he says, be read as an admission of anything. He points out that it is difficult to construe the letter of 12 January 1984 without knowing what had been said in the letter of 14 September 1983 and without knowing the precise form of its enclosure. He relies upon the subjunctive use of the word 'would' which, he says, is not consistent with an unequivocal acknowledgment.

g   I can see the force of Mr Walter's arguments. The point, in a sense, is a short one, but at the end of the day, and not having seen either the letter of 14 September 1983 or its enclosure, I am not prepared to hold that the letter of 12 January 1984 constituted an acknowledgment by Mr Long of the GLC's title to the premises.

h   In the alternative, Miss Hargreaves relies upon the following letter written to the GLC by Mr Long on 1 March 1984:

'As explained to your dept on many many times we are exempt from water rates, we have no toilets, no running water at all. One of your men came round and had a look at the premises later part of last year to see for himself

j   what I said was correct.'

Miss Hargreaves says, on the evidence I have seen no doubt correctly, that the GLC's practice was to collect water rates on behalf of Thames Water only in respect of *tenanted* properties. Therefore, she says, the very fact that in 1984 the GLC was, as the evidence shows, trying to collect water rates from Mr Long indicates that he must still have been paying rent to the GLC for the shop. That may or may not be so, but as I have already said the date when Mr Long last paid

rent is a matter which can only be resolved at trial. More to the point, however,   *a*
Miss Hargreaves submits that there would have been no purpose in Mr Long
approaching the GLC with the complaint about the water supply set out in his
letter of 1 March 1984 unless he had thought that the GLC was responsible for the
water supply by reason of his tenancy. Therefore, she says, the letter of 1 March
1984 constitutes an acknowledgment by Mr Long of the GLC's title to the
premises.   *b*

Mr Walter says that the letter of 1 March 1984 cannot possibly be construed as
an acknowledgment of the GLC's title as freeholder. The only admission, he
says, is that the GLC was demanding payment of the water rate. I agree. It is, in
my judgment, nothing to the point that the GLC's practice was to collect water
rates only from tenanted properties and that the GLC may therefore have
thought that Mr Long was its tenant. There is nothing in the evidence I have seen   *c*
to show that Mr Long either knew of the GLC's practice or had any reason to
believe that the reason why the GLC was demanding payment of the water rates
was because it was treating him as its tenant. There is, in my judgment, no
warrant for Miss Hargreaves' assertion that Mr Long must have thought that the
GLC was responsible for the water supply *by reason of his tenancy*. Absent   *d*
knowledge of the GLC's practice, there is any number of reasons why someone
in Mr Long's position may have thought that the GLC, a local authority
exercising many public functions, was responsible for collecting water rates.
Acknowledgment by Mr Long that the GLC had some form of responsibility for
the water supply to the premises cannot of itself and without more ado, in my
judgment, constitute an acknowledgment by him of the GLC's title to the land.   *e*
Someone like Mr Long is as likely to have thought that the GLC was exercising
its functions as local authority as to have thought that its involvement was as
owner of the land.

CONCLUSION

Accordingly, in my judgment, Miss Hargreaves has failed to make out any of   *f*
the grounds she relies upon to justify striking out Mr Long's claim. It may be that,
at trial, she will succeed in making good one or other of the matters on which I
have held there to be triable issues. But she has failed to show, as she must if it is
to be struck out at this stage, that Mr Long's claim is doomed to fail. Mr Long is
entitled to go to trial to have his claim determined.   *g*

It follows, in my judgment, that Mr Long's appeal must be allowed. I shall
therefore set aside the order made by Deputy Master Wall on 26 September 1995
and dismiss the summons issued by LBTH on 21 March 1995.

Appeal allowed.   *h*

Celia Fox   Barrister.

a R v Central Criminal Court, ex parte Guney

HOUSE OF LORDS

LORD GOFF OF CHIEVELEY, LORD JAUNCEY OF TULLICHETTLE, LORD SLYNN OF HADLEY, LORD STEYN, LORD HOFFMANN

b 14 DECEMBER 1995, 9 MAY 1996

Criminal law – Bail – Recognisance – Forfeiture – Effect of defendant's arraignment – Arraignment taking place at preparatory hearing – Defendant pleading not guilty to indictment at arraignment – Agreement between counsel that defendant not required to surrender to custody of court for arraignment – Defendant subsequently fleeing jurisdiction – Whether surety's liability continuing after defendant arraigned – Whether surety discharged on indictment.

In January 1991 the respondent stood surety in the sum of £1m for a defendant charged with offences of fraud and false accounting. On 22 June 1992 at the preparatory hearing in the Crown Court the defendant was arraigned and pleaded not guilty to the indictment. On that occasion the prosecution and defence privately agreed that it would not be necessary for the defendant to surrender to the custody of the court. In May 1993 the defendant fled the country and in July 1993 the respondent was ordered to forfeit the sum of £650,000 within six months with two years' imprisonment in default of payment. The respondent applied for judicial review of the forfeiture order, contending, inter alia, that it had been made without jurisdiction since his obligations under the recognisance had come to an end on 22 June when the defendant had been arraigned and had surrendered to the custody of the court for that purpose. The court dismissed the application on the ground, inter alia, that there was nothing in the process of arraignment which in law required, or in fact amounted to, a surrender to the custody of the court. The Court of Appeal allowed the respondent's appeal and the Serious Fraud Office appealed to the House of Lords.

Held – When a defendant who had not previously surrendered to custody was arraigned he thereby surrendered to the custody of the court and from that moment the defendant's further detention lay solely within the discretion and power of the judge. There was no justification for applying a different rule to cases governed by the Criminal Justice Act 1987; neither could a judge deprive an arraignment of its legal effect, nor could an agreement between the parties divest it of its effect on bail. On the facts, the defendant was validly arraigned. It followed that he had thereby surrendered to custody and that the respondent simultaneously ceased to be bound by his recognisance. The appeal would accordingly be dismissed (see p 706 *f g*, p 709 *d* to *g* and p 710 *b* to *f*, post).

Decision of the Court of Appeal [1995] 2 All ER 577 affirmed.

j Notes

For remand on bail in criminal proceedings, see 29 *Halsbury's Laws* (4th edn) para 349.

For meaning of arraignment, see 11(2) *Halsbury's Laws* (4th edn reissue) para 961.

For the Criminal Justice Act 1987, see 12 *Halsbury's Statutes* (4th edn) (1994 reissue) 1100.

Case referred to in opinions   *a*
DPP v Richards [1988] 3 All ER 406, [1988] QB 701, [1988] 3 WLR 153, DC.

Appeal
The Serious Fraud Office (the SFO), as an interested party and an effective
respondent to the application for judicial review by Ramadan Hussein Guney,
appealed with leave from the decision of the Court of Appeal (Peter Gibson LJ   *b*
and Sir Michael Mann; Sir Thomas Bingham MR dissenting) ([1995] 2 All ER 577,
[1995] 1 WLR 576) delivered on 1 February 1995 reversing the decision of the
Queen's Bench Divisional Court (Ralph Gibson LJ and Smith J) ([1994] 2 All ER
423, [1994] 1 WLR 438) on 26 January 1994 dismissing Mr Guney's application for
judicial review of the decision of Tucker J made on 30 July 1993 requiring Mr   *c*
Guney, as a surety for the bail of Mr Asil Nadir, a defendant who had fled the
jurisdiction, to forfeit £650,000 of his recognisance in the sum of £1m within six
months or in default be committed to prison for two years. The facts are set out
in the opinion of Lord Steyn.

Robert Owen QC, David Calvert-Smith and *Simon Browne-Wilkinson* (instructed by   *d*
    the *Serious Fraud Office*) for the SFO.
Edmund Lawson QC and *Russell Houston* (instructed by *Kaim Todner*) for Mr Guney.

Their Lordships took time for consideration.
                                                       e

9 May 1996. The following opinions were delivered.

LORD GOFF OF CHIEVELEY. My Lords, I have had the advantage of reading
in draft the speech prepared by my noble and learned friend Lord Steyn. For the
reasons he gives I too would dismiss this appeal.   *f*

LORD JAUNCEY OF TULLICHETTLE. My Lords, I have had the advantage
of reading in draft the speech of my noble and learned friend Lord Steyn. For the
reasons he gives I too would dismiss this appeal.

LORD SLYNN OF HADLEY. For the reasons given in the speech prepared by   *g*
my noble and learned friend Lord Steyn, I too would dismiss this appeal.

LORD STEYN. My Lords, on this appeal the general question of law arises
whether a defendant on bail, who is under a duty to surrender to the custody of
the court but neglects to do so before arraignment, does so by operation of law   *h*
upon his formal arraignment.

MR NADIR AND MR GUNEY

    On 16 December 1990 Mr Asil Nadir was charged with a number of offences of
theft and false accounting. On 17 December 1990 the Bow Street Magistrates'   *j*
Court remanded Mr Nadir on bail. The conditions of his bail included provisions
that Mr Nadir had to deposit £2m; that he had to provide five sureties in the sum
of £1·5m; and that he had to live and sleep at a London address. Mr Nadir was
admitted to bail. The grant of bail was continuous so long as the proceedings
remained in the magistrates court, and extended until Mr Nadir first surrendered
to the custody of the Crown Court.

a   On 28 January 1991 Mr Ramadan Guney signed a form of recognisance for sureties in criminal cases. It bore the heading of the Bow Street Magistrates' Court. It described Mr Nadir as the accused, and Mr Guney as the surety. The form read as follows:

b   'I acknowledge my obligation to pay the court the sum specified opposite my signature if the accused fails to surrender to the custody of the above-named court [Bow Street Magistrates' Court] on 23 April 1991 at 2 pm; and custody at every time and place to which during the course of the proceedings the hearing may from time to time be adjourned as may be notified to the accused by the appropriate officer of that court.'

c   Mr Guney signed the form opposite the figure of £1m. By his recognisance Mr Guney undertook the obligation to ensure that Mr Nadir surrendered to the custody of the court when required to do so. If Mr Nadir did so, Mr Guney ceased to be bound by his recognisance.

      On 25 October 1991, after Mr Nadir had been charged with further offences, Bow Street Magistrates' Court wrote to Mr Guney to inquire as to his willingness
d   to continue to act as surety. On 1 November 1991 Mr Guney confirmed his willingness to continue as surety.

      In February 1992 the prosecution decided to use the special procedures introduced by the Criminal Justice Act 1987 for the management of serious fraud cases. On 7 February 1992 the charges against Mr Nadir were transferred to the Central Criminal Court. Under the 1987 Act there was no need for committal
e   proceedings. The proceedings against Mr Nadir were assigned to Tucker J. On 28 February 1992, and at the Central Criminal Court, Tucker J held a preliminary hearing. Mr Nadir and his advisers were present. The judge fixed 22 June 1992 as the date of the first 'preparatory hearing' under the provisions of s 7 of the 1987 Act. It was common ground on the appeal to your Lordships' House that Mr
f   Nadir was required to surrender to the custody of the court on 22 June 1992.

      On 22 June 1992 the preparatory hearing was held at Chichester Rents. That building has no cells. It also has no custody area set aside for persons surrendering to bail to report to an official or a particular office. The courtroom has no dock. Mr Nadir, accompanied by his advisers, was present throughout the preparatory hearing. After some preliminary exchanges the judge said that the
g   preparatory hearing would start. He asked Mr Nadir to stand up. The arraignment commenced. The counts in the indictment were then put to Mr Nadir. He pleaded not guilty to them. At no stage during the preparatory hearing was any reference made to Mr Nadir's bail. The fact that Mr Guney was not present to agree to any extension of his recognisance caused counsel for the
h   prosecution and counsel for Mr Nadir to agree that it was not necessary for Mr Nadir to surrender to the custody of the court on that occasion. Both counsel bona fide believed that their agreement effectively kept Mr Guney's recognisance in force. Tucker J was not informed of this arrangement.

      Subsequent events do not affect the outcome of the appeal and can be
j   summarised briefly. Further preparatory hearings were held on 7 September and 14 to 17 December 1992. On the latter occasion Mr Nadir sought, and was refused, a variation of his bail conditions in order to enable him to visit Northern Cyprus. At the end of April 1993 Mr Guney took steps to withdraw his recognisance, but he abandoned his application before it was considered by the court. On 4 May 1993 Mr Nadir fled the country. He went to Northern Cyprus. He has been a fugitive from justice ever since.

a

Mr Guney was called upon to show cause why he should not forfeit £1m. Tucker J ruled that in view of the agreement between counsel that Mr Nadir should not surrender to his bail on 22 June he must be regarded as not having surrendered to bail on that occasion. Tucker J also added, for what it was worth, that he never regarded Mr Nadir as having surrendered to his custody. The judge ordered that Mr Guney should forfeit £650,000 and that in default of payment within six months Mr Guney should serve two years' imprisonment. Mr Guney applied for judicial review. The principal issue was whether by virtue of his arraignment Mr Nadir had surrendered to custody. Giving the judgment of the Queen's Bench Divisional Court Ralph Gibson LJ ruled that it was possible in law for an arraignment to take place without surrender of the defendant to the custody of the court, and he ruled that that is what happened in this case (see [1994] 2 All ER 423 at 432, [1994] 1 WLR 438 at 447–448). The application for judicial review was dismissed.

b

c

Mr Guney appealed. In the Court of Appeal ([1995] 2 All ER 577, [1995] 1 WLR 576) there was a difference of opinion between the members of the court on the central question. In agreement with the Divisional Court, Sir Thomas Bingham MR held that there is nothing in the process of arraignment which in law requires, or in fact amounts to, a surrender to the custody of the court (see [1995] 2 All ER 577 at 584, [1995] 1 WLR 576 at 584). The majority thought differently. Peter Gibson LJ concluded ([1995] 2 All ER 577 at 590, [1995] 1 WLR 576 at 590):

d

'In my judgment a surrender to the custody of the court occurs when a defendant on bail and under a duty so to surrender is required to attend the court and responds by attending the court and overtly subjecting himself to the directions of the court. This he does at the latest when he is arraigned at the commencement of the trial, but he may do so earlier ...'

e

Sir Michael Mann agreed with Peter Gibson LJ, and said ([1995] 2 All ER 577 at 588, [1995] 1 WLR 576 at 588): 'Arraignment provides a clearly identifiable moment of surrender (which may, however, in some cases occur earlier).'

f

Before I turn directly to the issues arising on this appeal, it is necessary briefly to explain the statutory framework. In granting bail and taking Mr Guney's recognisance the magistrates' court was validly exercising powers conferred by s 3 of the Bail Act 1946 and s 128 of the Magistrates' Courts Act 1980. Section 3 of the 1976 Act provides that a person granted bail in criminal proceedings shall be under a duty to surrender to custody, and that the duty is enforceable in accordance with s 6 of the Act. Section 2(2) provides that 'surrender to custody' means, in relation to a person released on bail, 'surrendering himself into the custody of the court ... at the time and place for the time being appointed for him to do so'. The critical hearing in the present case was a preparatory hearing under s 7(1) of the 1987 Act, that being a hearing for the judge to give directions to facilitate the effective and expeditious conduct of the trial. Section 8(1) provides that the trial shall begin with the preparatory hearing and s 8(2) provides that arraignment shall accordingly take place at the start of the preparatory hearing.

g

h

j

While Mr Robert Owen, who appeared for the Serious Fraud Office, advanced the appeal on a narrow basis, it is right that their Lordships should also address directly the reasoning of Tucker J, the Divisional Court and Sir Thomas Bingham MR. It will be convenient to discuss the issues in the following order: (1) whether a there is a rule that a defendant in criminal proceedings, who is on bail and does not otherwise surrender to bail, does so by operation of law upon his formal arraignment; (2) if so, whether a different rule obtains under the 1987 Act; (3) whether any applicable rule can be varied or relaxed by order of the judge or agreement between the parties or counsel; (4) the correct disposal of the appeal.

b (1) *The effect of arraignment upon bail*

The duty of a defendant who has been granted bail by the magistrates' court is to surrender to the custody of the court at the required time and place. Depending on arrangements at various trial centres, a person desiring to surrender to bail may be required to report to a particular office or a particular official (see *DPP v Richards* [1988] 3 All ER 406 at 412, [1988] QB 701 at 711).

c Through the years the arrangements have been simplified. Nowadays a defendant is usually simply required to go to a particular courtroom where he may surrender to a dock officer, if there is one, or to a court official, such as the usher. It also has to be borne in mind that in a small but significant number of cases a defendant will be required to surrender to custody in a courtroom not

d equipped for the hearing of criminal cases, ie without cells or a dock.

The present appeal raises the question of what happens when the defendant, although present in court, is not officially asked to surrender but is formally arraigned. Does he remain on bail after arraignment until the judge orders otherwise? If the answer is in the affirmative, and there is an adjournment, short or long, the defendant is presumably free to leave unless the judge directs

e otherwise. That in my judgment is a position which is calculated to create uncertainty, confusion and practical difficulties. There will always be cases where the system for surrender before arraignment breaks down. The situation demands a clear-cut rule. It is imperative that there should be an objectively ascertainable formal act which causes a defendant's bail to lapse at the beginning

f of a trial. In my judgment that formal act can only be the arraignment of a defendant. The arraignment of a defendant involves: (1) calling the defendant to the bar by name; (2) reading the indictment to him; and (3) asking whether he is guilty or not (see Archbold *Criminal Pleading, Evidence and Practice* (1995 edn) vol 1, p 1/465, para 4–84). When a defendant who has not previously surrendered to custody is so arraigned he thereby surrenders to the custody of the court. From

g that moment the defendant's further detention lies solely within the discretion and power of the judge. Unless the judge grants bail the defendant will remain in custody pending and during his trial. This is a readily comprehensible system which causes no problems for the administration of justice.

h (2) *Does a different rule obtain under the 1987 Act?*

Given that s 8 of the 1987 Act expressly provides that a trial shall begin with a preparatory hearing, and that arraignment shall take place at the start of the preparatory hearing, there is no justification for applying a different rule to cases governed by the Act. There is nothing in the provisions of the Act, or in its

j purposes, which in any way alters the legal effect on bail of an arraignment. The reason for the general rule applies equally to cases governed by the Act.

(3) *Varying or relaxing the rule*

Mr Calvert-Smith, who appeared with Mr Owen QC on behalf of the Serious Fraud Office, informed their Lordships that there have been cases where trial judges have ruled that, notwithstanding an arraignment, a defendant will be deemed not to have surrendered. Mr Calvert-Smith is Senior Treasury Counsel *a* at the Central Criminal Court. I readily accept his assurance that such cases have occurred. In the present case the judge was unaware of the agreement between counsel. But Mr Owen argued that the general rule, which before your Lordships' House he did not challenge, may validly be displaced by an appropriate ruling of the judge and, therefore, by analogy pursuant to the agreement of the parties. I reject these submissions. Given that arraignment *b* operates in law as a surrender to custody, the judge may not in law abdicate his responsibility in respect of the custody of the defendant. He cannot deprive an arraignment of its legal effect. A fortiori the agreement of the parties cannot divest an arraignment of its effect on bail. Whatever may mistakenly have been thought and done in rare cases in the past, the rule is that where a defendant has not previously surrendered to custody his arraignment amounts in all cases as a *c* matter of law to a surrender by the defendant to the custody of the court.

(4) *The disposal of the appeal*

It is plain that the judge and counsel thought that Mr Nadir had not surrendered to custody. Their mistaken belief is devoid of legal consequences. *d* But at one stage Mr Owen appeared to argue that it is a distinguishing feature of this case that Mr Nadir was not arraigned in a dock. That cannot be right. The application of the rule cannot depend on the vagaries of the physical arrangements in various courtrooms. It is sufficient that Mr Nadir was validly arraigned. It follows that Mr Nadir surrendered to custody, and that Mr Guney simultaneously ceased to be bound by his recognisance. *e*

CONCLUSION

I would dismiss the appeal.

LORD HOFFMANN. My Lords, I have had the advantage of reading in draft the speech of my noble and learned friend Lord Steyn. For the reasons he gives I too *f* would dismiss this appeal.

Appeal dismissed.

Celia Fox   Barrister.

a # R v Chief Constable of the Devon and Cornwall Constabulary, ex parte Hay

R v Chief Constable of the Devon and Cornwall Constabulary, ex parte Police Complaints Authority

b

QUEEN'S BENCH DIVISION (CROWN OFFICE LIST)

SEDLEY J

c 8, 13, 21 NOVEMBER 1995

Police – Discipline – Disciplinary proceedings – Judicial review of decision in disciplinary proceedings – Two officers charged with disciplinary offences – Chief constable permitting retirement of one officer prior to hearing – Charges against officer
d *withdrawn – Charges against second officer dismissed as an abuse of process – Whether officer facing disciplinary process able to avoid adjudication by retiring – Whether decision to dismiss proceedings against second officer justified.*

In October 1993 a man was shot dead in an operation mounted by police officers under the command of A and M. The Police Complaints Authority later
e recommended that disciplinary proceedings be commenced against A and M, but charges were not preferred against them until January 1995. The applicant, the dead man's brother, was informed and requested permission to attend the disciplinary hearing. That request was refused on the ground that neither the applicant nor his family had made a formal complaint against the police officers
f concerned. In April 1995, some five weeks before the scheduled hearing, the chief constable accepted the advice of police doctors that there was a likelihood that M's appearance before the disciplinary hearing would hasten his complete mental breakdown and permitted M, who had been on sick leave since the shooting, to retire due to ill-health. The disciplinary charges against M were therefore withdrawn. The chief constable subsequently amended the charges against A,
g following an unsuccessful attempt to persuade the authority to permit a complete withdrawal of the charges in view of the absence of M's crucial evidence. At the disciplinary hearing on 30 May 1995 the presiding chief constable granted A's application to dismiss the proceedings as an abuse of process, on the grounds that the late notice of the amended charges combined with the delay in the
h disciplinary hearing had prejudiced his defence. The applicant and the authority applied separately for judicial review of the decision to dismiss the charges against A; the applicant also sought review of two other matters, including the chief constable's decision to withdraw the disciplinary proceedings against M on his resignation from the force.

j
Held – (1) A chief officer of police had power either to require or to refuse to require the retirement of an officer who was threatened with or faced disciplinary proceedings. In order to exercise that power lawfully, the chief officer had to consider not only the evidence tendered to him in support of retirement, but also the fact that he was not obliged to accede to it if there was good reason for refusal, and had to go on to consider whether the interest of the police service and the

public in seeing any disciplinary proceedings against the officer to their end   *a*
outweighed, for the time being, the case for his retirement. Although, on the
evidence, that process had not been properly undertaken, the court in its
discretion would not now make an order which would undo the effects of
retirement (see p 724 *j* to p 725 *c* and p 726 *d* to *g*, post).

(2) The chief constable had erred in law and taken extraneous matters into
account in deciding to dismiss the disciplinary proceedings as an abuse of process.   *b*
There had been no serious or culpable delay, nor was there any evidence that A
had suffered any identifiable prejudice by reason of any delay or the late
amendment of the charges. The applicants were entitled to an order of certiorari
to quash the decision and an order of mandamus directing the chief constable to
hear and determine the disciplinary charge against A on its substantive merits (see
p 731 *b* to *h* and p 732 *d e*, post); *A-G's Reference (No 1 of 1990)* [1992] 3 All ER 169   *c*
followed.

Per curiam. The charging and judicial functions of a chief constable need to be
kept separate not only from one another, but from the overall administrative
function of the chief constable as the head of his force (see p 732 *f* and p 733 *a*,
post).   *d*

Notes

For complaints against the police, the conduct of disciplinary hearings, and for
judicial review of police disciplinary proceedings, see 36 *Halsbury's Laws* (4th edn)
paras 275–283, 289, and for cases on the subject, see 37(1) *Digest* (Reissue) 331–
333, 2129–2136.   *e*

Cases referred to in judgment

A-G of Hong Kong v Cheung Wai-bun [1993] 2 All ER 510, [1994] 1 AC 1, [1993] 3
    WLR 242, PC.
A-G's Reference (No 1 of 1990) [1992] 3 All ER 169, [1992] QB 630, [1992] 3 WLR 9,   *f*
    CA.
Irani v Southampton and South West Hampshire Health Authority [1985] ICR 590.
Miles v Wakefield Metropolitan DC [1987] 1 All ER 1089, [1987] AC 539, [1987] 2
    WLR 795, HL.
R v Bow Street Stipendiary Magistrate, ex p Cherry (1990) 91 Cr App R 283, DC.
R v Chief Constable of Northumbria Police, ex p Charlton (1994) Times, 6 May.   *g*
R v Chief Constable of Thames Valley Police, ex p Police Complaints Authority (13 October
    1995, unreported), QBD.
R v Chief Constable of the Merseyside Police, ex p Merrill [1989] 1 WLR 1077, CA.
R v Lord Chancellor's Dept, ex p Nangle [1992] 1 All ER 897, [1991] ICR 743, DC.

    h

Cases also cited or referred to in skeleton arguments

Hughes v Southwark London Borough [1988] IRLR 55.
Multi Guarantee Co Ltd v Cavalier Insurance Co Ltd (1986) Times, 24 June.
Powell v Brent London BC [1988] ICR 176, CA.
Wadcock v Brent London Borough [1990] IRLR 223.   *j*

Applications for judicial review

R v Chief Constable of the Devon and Cornwall Constabulary, ex p Hay
The applicant, Robert Howard Soltau Hay, applied with leave of the judge for
judicial review of (i) the decision of Mr Walter Girven, the Chief Constable of
Wiltshire acting as agent for the Chief Constable of the Devon and Cornwall

a Constabulary, made on 31 May 1995 whereby he dismissed disciplinary charges which had been brought against Chief Insp Alan Paul McArthur of the Devon and Cornwall Constabulary as an abuse of process, and (ii) the decisions of the Chief Constable of Devon and Cornwall made in April 1995 whereby he (a) refused to record the applicant's written complaint dated 19 April 1995 as a formal complaint against the police force and (b) withdrew disciplinary charges against
b Supt Roger Mechan following his retirement from the force due to ill-health. The relief sought was orders of certiorari to quash the above decisions. The facts are set out in the judgment.

R v Chief Constable of the Devon and Cornwall Constabulary,
ex p Police Complaints Authority

c The Police Complaints Authority applied with leave of the judge for judicial review of the decision of Mr Walter Girven, the Chief Constable of Wiltshire acting as agent for the Chief Constable of the Devon and Cornwall Constabulary, made on 31 May 1995 whereby he dismissed disciplinary charges which had been brought against Chief Insp Alan Paul McArthur of the Devon and Cornwall
d Constabulary as an abuse of process. The relief sought was an order of certiorari to quash that decision. The facts are set out in the judgment.

Philip Sapsford QC and *Philip Engelman* (instructed by *Bevan Ashford*, Bristol) for Mr Hay.

e *James Turner* (instructed by the *Treasury Solicitor*) for the Police Complaints Authority.

Anthony Donne QC and *Sue Campbell* (instructed by *Jim Rea*, Exeter) for the chief constable.

Martin Picton (instructed by *Russell Jones & Walker*, Bristol) for Chief Insp McArthur.
f
Cur adv vult

21 November 1995. The following judgment was delivered.

g **SEDLEY J.** On 13 October 1993 at Crabadon Manor near Diptford, in Devon, Ian Fitzgerald Hay was shot dead, in what can be shortly described as siege conditions, by officers of the Devon and Cornwall Constabulary under the immediate command of Chief Insp Alan Paul McArthur and the overall command of Supt Roger Mechan. On the same day the chief constable referred the incident to the Police Complaints Authority (the authority). Pursuant to its
h statutory functions the authority appointed an investigating officer, Mr Hugo Pike, Assistant Chief Constable of Avon and Somerset. His remit was: 'To investigate the incidents culminating in the death of Ian Fitzgerald Hay and all attendant circumstances.' Five days after the incident the coroner opened his inquest. Some four weeks after this, on 15 November 1993, Chief Insp McArthur
j was served with a notice under reg 7 of the Police (Discipline) Regulations 1985, SI 1985/518, alleging that as a tactical firearms adviser he had failed to ensure that adequate planning was carried out prior to the deployment of authorised firearms officers involved in the incident.

    At the beginning of February 1994 Mr Pike submitted a report recommending that there should be no criminal proceedings against any officer. Some seven weeks later, on 25 March 1994, he submitted a full report recommending, among

other things, that there should be disciplinary proceedings against both Chief Insp   *a*
McArthur and Supt Mechan for neglect of duty. The latter had been on sick leave
ever since the incident. The Chief Constable of Devon and Cornwall, acting
through his assistant chief constable, Mr Keith Portlock, told the authority in June
1994 that, pending and subject to the decision of the Director of Public
Prosecutions as to whether any criminal proceedings should be brought, the chief
constable's view was that disciplinary proceedings ought to be brought against   *b*
Supt Mechan but not against Chief Insp McArthur. The authority did not agree
in relation to the latter, and negotiations followed, resulting at the end of October
1994 in the deferral of a final decision on disciplinary proceedings until the inquest
was concluded.

The inquest occupied four days, from 9 to 12 December 1994. For the first
time much material evidence became public. The jury returned a verdict of   *c*
lawful killing. Some further discussion with the authority followed, but on 28
December the chief constable, again speaking through Mr Portlock, expressed
the view that no disciplinary proceedings or other adverse measures were called
for in relation to Chief Insp McArthur:

> 'Given the failures of Superintendent MECHAN in this operation it is difficult   *d*
> to criticise Chief Inspector McARTHUR. This point becomes even more
> poignant when it is unlikely, in my view, that Superintendent MECHAN will
> return from sick leave and face discipline for his neglect.'

A week later the investigating officer, Mr Pike, reaffirmed his recommendation   *e*
to the contrary. The following day, 4 January 1995, the authority wrote to Mr
Portlock reiterating Mr Pike's criticisms of Chief Insp McArthur and now
invoking its powers under s 93(1) of the Police and Criminal Evidence Act 1984
(PACE) to recommend that a charge of neglect of duty be preferred against him.
The letter identified four main areas of concern: a want of initial planning and
intelligence, a failure to acquire the information necessary for containment, an   *f*
unauthorised change of role during the operation, and a failure to consult the
deceased man's mother before deploying his team. These allegations, which the
letter spelt out in rather more detail, but which were fully particularised in Mr
Pike's report, were formulated by Mr Portlock as an allegation that Chief Insp
McArthur had—   *g*

> 'failed to plan properly the armed containment of Crabadon Manor and in
> particular:—(a) Failed to take into account the local geography of the area (b)
> Failed to consider the available knowledge in respect of Mr FITZGERALD-HAY
> with respect to its relevance to an armed containment. (c) Failed to liaise
> properly with Silver Command.'   *h*

This disciplinary charge was contained in a letter to the authority dated 26
January 1995 and, it is to be inferred, was conveyed then or not long afterwards
to Chief Insp McArthur. It was followed a few days later by a further letter to the
authority setting out the charge of neglect of duty which it was proposed to lay
against Supt Mechan.   *j*

Meanwhile the authority had been keeping the deceased man's brother, Mr
Robert Hay, and his mother informed. On 1 February, writing on behalf of both
of them, Mr Hay asked the authority—

> 'if the family could be represented at the hearing. Inevitably questions and
> answers will emerge which may not have been apparent at the Inquest and I

a
feel that this will go some way to assist my family to come to terms with the loss of Ian ... Although we are grateful for your offer to come and discuss procedural aspects of the disciplinary proceedings with us, I really feel that a family presence at the disciplinary proceedings, even in an observer role, will be the better course to follow.'

b
For the authority, Mr Peter Moorhouse, the deputy chairman (discipline), pointed out that because neither Mr Hay nor his mother had lodged a formal complaint they had no right to attend, but assured them that the authority would make 'strong representations' in favour of permission to attend. This was done by a letter of 6 February, from which it also appears that no appointment of an officer to hear the charge on behalf of the chief constable had yet been made, but
c
that it was hoped that Mr Walter Girven, the Chief Constable of Wiltshire, would hear the charge 'on a date yet to be agreed'. Mr Portlock (in a letter of considerable length, possibly rehearsing extensive and not entirely relevant legal advice which he had received) refused. The letter, which is dated 7 March 1995, says:

d
'We must bear in mind that we are talking about an incident which occurred in October, 1993 and with the inquest only having been completed in December, 1994. The dates I currently have from the Chief Constable of Wiltshire take me into June, 1995.'

e
In addition to reasons of law, to which I will come, the letter gives reasons why it is thought inappropriate that the family should be able to observe the disciplinary process. In spite of further correspondence this position was maintained, with the result that on 19 April 1995 Mr Hay wrote to the authority:

f
'I was disturbed to learn that there is an objection to the presence of myself or my family at the forthcoming disciplinary hearing; I understand that this is because the family have not made an official complaint. Accordingly, in order to comply with the regulations, you may treat this letter as a complaint; I rely upon the evidence given at the recent Inquest into the death of my late brother which overwhelmingly confirms the lack of police management of the operation leading ultimately to his death.'

g
Mr Portlock replied directly to Mr Hay. He quoted ss 85(1) and 84(6) of PACE, to which I shall come, and continued:

h
'I have to decide on behalf of the Chief Constable whether or not to record your complaint as a formal complaint against police. Given that the events referred to occurred on 13 October 1993 and that all the circumstances were exhaustively investigated by the Avon and Somerset Police, under supervision of the Police Complaints Authority, and examined minutely at the inquest it is apparent that your complaint has been made after your meeting with the Police Complaints Authority merely to circumvent the provision of Section 22 of the Police and Criminal Evidence Act of 1984
j
which precludes your attendance at the Police Discipline hearings being conducted against Superintendent R. MECHAN and Chief Inspector A. McARTHUR. Further, it is clear that your complaint relates wholly to matters which are now the subject of disciplinary proceedings and therefore the provisions of Section 85[1] of the Act do not apply. I have also taken account of the [effect] this late recording of a complaint could have on the pending discipline proceedings, due to commence on 30 May, in which those

representing the accused officers could seek to show that the introduction of this element at such a late stage is an abuse of process which could invalidate or at least undermine those proceedings. Throughout this matter I believe you have had the benefit of legal advice and therefore, no doubt, you have been aware of the complaints procedure. Therefore, given the circumstances of a most thorough investigation conducted by the Avon and Somerset Police, the opportunity you have had to make such a complaint against police had you wished to do so and the circumstances under which you now make such a complaint, I am led inevitably to the conclusion that this is an abuse of the Police Complaints system and it is not therefore my intention to record this matter formally as a complaint against police under Part IX of the Police and Criminal Evidence Act 1984.'

The reference to s 22 of PACE is conceded to be an error for reg 22 of the 1985 regulations.

At this stage further correspondence from Mr Portlock shows that consideration was being given to the feasibility of conducting a disciplinary hearing against Supt Mechan even if he were to retire on medical grounds before it took place. The evidence now makes clear that it was on 24 April 1995 that the decision was taken to allow Supt Mechan to retire. Dr John Whitehead, the force medical officer for Devon and Cornwall, deposes that on consideration of reports from two other doctors together with his own examination on 21 March 1995, he concluded and advised that Supt Mechan was permanently unfit to serve or to prepare for a hearing, and that although he was physically fit to appear before such a hearing, there was a likelihood that it would hasten a complete mental breakdown. The chief constable, Mr John Evans, deposes—and Dr Whitehead confirms—that it was on 24 April that the former accepted the latter's advice. On 27 April 1995 the chief constable gave Supt Mechan notice that he was to retire on 7 June with an ill-health pension.

Because of his diary commitments Mr Girven was unable to fix the disciplinary hearing against Chief Insp McArthur until 30 May 1995. At the end of March, however, the legal adviser to the Devon and Cornwall Constabulary, Mr James Rea, sent to the investigating officer's force a copy of the disciplinary charges against both officers, asking for any comments. On 10 April Mr Pike wrote to Mr Portlock pointing out that the second and third heads of particulars in the charge did not reflect any criticisms which he had made of Chief Insp McArthur in his report, and that in his view there was no evidence to support them. As to the first of the particulars, he was critical of its obscurity, concluding:

'... does (a) include Mr McArthur's failure to manage the containment placed upon Crabadon Manor? It was the issues in this paragraph that formed the basis of my recommendation in respect of Mr McArthur.'

The charges were not promptly amended. Instead, a fortnight later, Mr Portlock wrote to the authority pointing out that the basis of the draft charge was the authority's own letter, and continuing:

'In my view the contents of ACC [Pike's] letter fatally undermines the charge against Chief Inspector McARTHUR and morally at least calls into question the viability of seeking to institute disciplinary proceedings at all. I would go even further and suggest that in the circumstances ACC [Pike] is clearly indicating that the entire evidence will not lead to a disciplinary *a* finding against Chief Inspector McARTHUR, even given the breadth of the allegations as charged.'

He went on to argue the case for aborting the disciplinary proceedings against Chief Insp McArthur. In response to a prompt reply from the authority saying that its remit was at an end unless there was a formal request for withdrawal of charges, Mr Portlock on 9 May made such a formal request. His letter said 'we *b* always held the gravest reservations with respect to any charge in this matter', and went on to argue that Supt Mechan's absence through ill-health was going to deprive the inquiry against Chief Insp McArthur of an essential witness. He added:

c   'I have also to indicate that the lawyer presenting the case feels totally compromised by both the failure of Superintendent MECHAN to attend the hearing and the observations of Assistant Chief Constable [Pike]. He has indicated that the ethics of a lawyer are that they should not attempt to obtain a conviction by any means at their command; they should be fair and impartial. Given the comments made now in the case by Avon and Somerset *d* it is clear that the only way the charges could be proved would be by the art of advocacy rather than by the substance of the evidence.'

The authority, having consulted Mr Pike, refused to agree to the withdrawal of charges and suggested instead that the 'mismatch' might be cured by amendment. In prompt response, on 17 May, Mr Portlock confirmed that it was *e* proposed to prefer an amended charge against Chief Insp McArthur. The offence alleged was still neglect of duty, but the particulars more closely matched the key criticisms in Mr Pike's report. It is to be inferred that Chief Insp McArthur and those representing him were given notice of the proposed amendment at the same time.

f   Mr Girven sat on 30 May 1995 to conduct the disciplinary inquiry. Mr Rea appeared as 'prosecutor' on behalf of the chief constable and Chief Insp McArthur was represented by Supt Walker, who on 24 March had written to require the attendance at the hearing of 18 named persons, none of whom was Supt Mechan. Supt Walker advanced as a preliminary point the submission that the proceedings were an abuse of process. Mr Girven, having heard argument, reserved his *g* decision overnight and the following morning accepted the submission and—giving reasons to which I will come in due course—dismissed the case on the ground of abuse of process. The chief constable thereupon issued a press release expressing disappointment that 'the issues have not been fully aired', but in the next sentence describing the disciplinary proceeding as 'unnecessary and wholly *h* inappropriate given the lack of evidence to support the charge'.

The applications for judicial review

Unknown to each other, the authority and Robert Hay issued applications for leave to apply for judicial review within two days of one another, Mr Hay on 8 *j* August 1995 and the authority on 10 August. Both seek to challenge the legality and propriety of Mr Girven's decision to dismiss the proceedings as an abuse of process (the third decision). Additionally, Mr Hay challenges Mr Portlock's refusal to record his complaint (the first decision) and the chief constable's decision to withdraw the disciplinary proceedings against Supt Mechan upon his resignation from the force (the second decision). Before me, the chief constable and Chief Insp McArthur have been separately represented as respondents.

On 20 October 1995 both applications for leave came on before Popplewell J, *a* who adjourned them with a direction that notice be given to Mr Girven and to both accused officers. In the event neither Mr Girven nor Supt Mechan has appeared or been separately represented before me, but the chief constable has spoken in fact as well as in law for Mr Girven. Popplewell J also directed that the adjourned hearing for leave should be followed immediately by the full inter partes hearing if leave were granted, and he expedited the hearings. *b*

It was appreciated belatedly before Popplewell J that the affidavit of Mr Moorhouse for the authority had exhibited to it a document, Mr Pike's report, which belonged to a class covered by public interest immunity. Accordingly, leave was given for the exhibit to be withdrawn, and when the case came on before me an application was made for leave to adduce the report on the ground that the interests of justice in the present proceedings were such as to override the *c* immunity which the document would ordinarily attract in the public interest. Because the report was clearly material to much of the correspondence with which I am concerned, and because it was referred to at the hearing before Mr Girven, I ruled—effectively with the assent of all parties—that the document might be referred to in evidence, together with the transcripts of the proceedings *d* before Mr Girven if (which I doubt) public interest immunity otherwise attaches to them.

For the chief constable the point is taken that Mr Hay's application in respect of the second decision (which was made on 24 April) puts Mr Hay some two weeks out of time in relation to that decision. He further submits (and the submission is adopted on behalf of Chief Insp McArthur) that none of the *e* applications has been made promptly as required by RSC Ord 53, r 4. I will return to these points as well as to Mr Hay's locus when I have considered the substantive issues.

The law *f*

Part IX of PACE makes comprehensive provision for the statutory system governing police complaints and discipline. Section 88 makes it possible for the authority to become involved without the making of any formal complaint by a member of the public if, as happened here, the chief constable considers that there may have been a criminal offence or an offence against discipline which by reason of its gravity or of exceptional circumstances ought to be referred to the *g* authority. It is a precondition of any such referral, however, that the matter 'is not the subject of a complaint'. The initiation of complaints is provided for by s 84(6), which provides:

'If any conduct to which a complaint wholly or partly relates is or has been *h* the subject of criminal or disciplinary proceedings, none of the provisions of this Part of this Act which relate to the recording and investigation of complaints have effect in relation to the complaint in so far as it relates to that conduct.'

There then follows (in ss 85 to 87) provision for the processing of complaints, *j* beginning with s 85(1):

'If a chief officer determines that he is the appropriate authority in relation to an officer about whose conduct a complaint has been made and who is not a senior officer [viz an assistant or deputy chief constable], he shall record it.'

a Subsection (3) requires the chief officer to appoint an investigating officer—in this case Assistant Chief Constable Pike of the Avon and Somerset force—and s 90 makes detailed provision for the action to be taken by the chief constable on receipt of the report, including the sending of a memorandum to the authority setting out his proposed action, if any, in response to the report. The memorandum in the present case rejected the bringing of any disciplinary
b proceedings against Chief Insp McArthur, but recommended bringing them against Supt Mechan.

Section 93 equips the authority with powers, of central relevance to these proceedings, enabling it to intervene at this point:

c '(1) Where a memorandum under section 90 above states that a chief officer of police has not preferred disciplinary charges or does not propose to do so, the Authority may recommend him to prefer such disciplinary charges as they may specify.

(2) Subject to subsection (6) below, a chief officer may not withdraw charges which he has preferred in accordance with a recommendation under
d subsection (1) above.

(3) If after the Authority have made a recommendation under this section and consulted the chief officer he is still unwilling to prefer such charges as the Authority consider appropriate, they may direct him to prefer such charges as they may specify ...

e (6) The Authority may give a chief officer leave ... (b) not to proceed with charges with which ... subsection (2) ... above would otherwise oblige him to proceed ...'

In the present case, as has been seen, the charge against Chief Insp McArthur was preferred pursuant to a recommendation under s 93(1).
f Section 94 gives the authority power, among other things, to direct in exceptional cases that the disciplinary hearing be conducted by a tribunal chaired by the relevant chief officer of police (who may act by a proxy, as was done here) together with two members of the authority itself.

Procedure is provided for by the 1985 regulations. Regulation 9, in the light of
g the statutory provisions which I have cited, permits the withdrawal of a charge by the chief officer of police, but not without the authority's leave in a s 93 case such as that against Chief Insp McArthur. In the present case the authority refused leave to withdraw.

Regulation 10(1)(b) entitles the accused officer to a copy of the report on which the charge is based, or as much of it as relates to him. I am told that Chief Insp
h McArthur's representative received Mr Pike's report, or as much of it as was material to him, some two weeks before the hearing, but at the hearing waived any point on time in relation to it.

Regulation 18 provides:

j '*Procedure at hearing* (1) The accused shall be ordered to attend at the hearing of the case.

(2) The hearing shall be in private: Provided that it shall be within the discretion of the officer conducting the hearing to allow any member of the Authority, any solicitor or any such member or members of a police force as he considers desirable to attend the whole or such part of the hearing as he

may think fit, subject to the accused or his representative not objecting to the attendance of the person or persons in question.'

Regulation 18(10) requires a verbatim transcript to be taken.

Regulation 21 provides for the conduct of a hearing in the absence of the accused. Regulation 22 then provides:

> 'Attendance of complainant at hearing (1) This Regulation shall apply in relation to [the] hearing of a charge against a member of a police force where the charge is in respect of a complaints matter.
>
> (2) Notwithstanding anything in Regulation 18(2) but subject to paragraph (4), the officer conducting the hearing shall allow the complainant to attend the hearing while witnesses are being examined, or cross-examined, on facts alleged in the charge …'

There follow provisions qualifying the complainant's right to attend in the interests of an orderly hearing. A 'complaints matter', which is referred to in reg 22(1), is defined by reg 4 as meaning the matter or matters dealt with in a report of an investigation sent to the authority under s 90(9) of PACE, which relates to investigations conducted in response to complaints but not supervised by the authority.

Certain other provisions need to be noticed because they bear on the argument in reply on behalf of Mr Hay. For purposes which do not at present matter, the 'police force concerned' is specified in the 1985 regulations and is defined in reg 4 as: 'in relation to a person who may have committed, or has been accused of, an offence, the police force of which he is a member …' The regulations throughout speak of an officer who is a 'member' of a police force. Regulation 24 provides for a range of punishments, including dismissal from the force, requirement to resign, reduction in rank and reduction in pay. Regulation 27(1) provides that pending disciplinary proceedings 'the chief officer concerned may suspend that member [of a police force] from membership of the force and from his office as constable'.

The first decision

It is accepted by Mr Donne QC for the chief constable that the intended reference by Mr Portlock in his response to Mr Hay to reg 22 was no more apt than the actual reference to s 22 of PACE. Regulation 22, far from being something which Mr Hay wanted to circumvent, was a provision of which he wanted to take advantage. It was reg 18, as Mr Donne accepts, that Mr Portlock ought to have referred to, for it is this which provides that a disciplinary hearing shall be in private (subject to the consensual admission of certain outsiders, not including complainants).

For Mr Hay, Mr Sapsford QC argues that to use the right which reg 22 affords a complainant to attend a hearing as a reason for rejecting the complaint, is deliberately to frustrate the very purpose for which the Home Secretary has made the regulation. Moreover, to the extent that the refusal is also founded on the fact that the authority and the coroner had both conducted exhaustive inquiries, Mr Sapsford submits that this cannot militate against the validity of the complaint; indeed, it was only what emerged at the inquest that enabled Mr Hay to know that he had legitimate grounds of complaint at all. In so far as the response founds upon the pendency of disciplinary proceedings, Mr Sapsford points out that by the date of the letter (10 May 1995) the chief constable had *a* already decided not to pursue disciplinary proceedings against Supt Mechan and Mr Portlock was actively canvassing the withdrawal of proceedings against Chief Insp McArthur.

While Mr Sapsford accepts that the lateness of the complaint, to which the letter also refers, is capable of having a bearing on its acceptance, the bulk of the grounds given for rejection are in his contention entirely inadmissible. When one

b reads the correspondence passing between Mr Hay, the authority and Mr Portlock, he submits, one sees that the complaint was an entirely reasonable step taken in the face of a refusal by the chief constable, without even making reference to the officer who was to conduct the hearing or to the accused who had the power to object, to allow Mr Hay to attend.

c Mr Donne begins by meeting Mr Sapsford on this ground. He submits that there is a discretion in a chief officer of police, notwithstanding the peremptory wording of s 85(1), to decline to record a complaint if he reasonably believes it to be an abuse of the system. While, for reasons to which I will come, I do not have to decide what is the threshold of refusal to record a complaint, I have no hesitation in rejecting the argument that the statute confers any discretion

d properly so called upon the chief officer who receives the complaint. That there may be complaints which are plainly mala fide or unhinged I do not doubt, nor that this court would refuse mandamus—whether for reasons of law or discretion—in the event of a refusal to record such a complaint. But Mr Hay's letter of complaint could on no conceivable view fall into this category. Although

e laconic, it was specific in its reference to 'the lack of police management of the operation' and in its citation of the evidence given at the inquest in support of the allegation. Nor was there anything devious about it: Mr Hay was perfectly open about his reason for making the complaint. I need not therefore deal with Mr Donne's arguments in defence of Mr Portlock's view that the complaint was an abuse of the statutory process, except to say that in my view the concept has no

f place in the functions allocated to a chief officer of police on receipt of a complaint. If it did, then I would accept Mr Sapsford's argument that the exercise, whether of discretion or of judgment, was vitiated by the irrationality of using the right of attendance given to a complainant by reg 22 as a reason for refusing to record the complaint.

g Mr Donne's other two arguments, however, are more formidable. The first of them is that while a complaint, in order to come within s 85(1), can naturally include more than one officer, it must still relate to identifiable officers, and if it fails to do so it falls outside the statutory provision. The phrase 'lack of police management', he contends, is quite unspecific in this regard. If, however, it is taken to mean Chief Insp McArthur and Supt Mechan—whose disciplinary

h hearings it was, after all, Mr Hay's wish to attend as a complainant—then s 84(6) disapplies the whole procedure for recording and investigating complaints in so far as the complaint relates to conduct which 'is or has been the subject of ... disciplinary proceedings'. At the date when the complaint was made the conduct of both officers was the subject of disciplinary proceedings; and by the time Mr

j Portlock replied, Supt Mechan's conduct no longer was, but had been the subject of disciplinary proceedings.

Replying in Mr Sapsford's absence, Mr Engelman sought to extricate himself from this Morton's fork by submitting that 'has been the subject of ... disciplinary proceedings' means that disciplinary proceedings have been brought to a proper conclusion and have not merely aborted. As a complainant, he submits, Mr Hay

is entitled to step into the shoes of the authority, since nothing in the language of *a*
s 88, couched as it is in the present tense ('is not the subject of a complaint'), shuts
out a chief constable's reference if a complaint has already been made, but not
vice versa.

In my judgment, the statutory scheme is unequivocal. The combined effect of
ss 88 and 84(6) is that if a complaint is made first, there is no room for the chief
constable to refer the matter to the authority himself unless the complaint is *b*
withdrawn—at which point the matter 'is not [although previously it was] the
subject of a complaint' and so falls, provided the other tests are met, within s 88.
If, however, the chief constable has in the absence of a complaint made a s 88
referral which has resulted in disciplinary proceedings, then s 84(6) comes into
operation not only for as long as the disciplinary proceedings are pending, but in
perpetuity, for the bar operates where the material conduct 'is or has been the *c*
subject of ... disciplinary proceedings'. This does not mean that a complaint
ceases to be a complaint—simply that the duty under s 85(1) to record it and
thereafter to act on it ceases to exist. The reason for the use of the past tense as
well as the present in s 84(6), in contrast to s 88, is that while a complainant can
voluntarily withdraw proceedings at any time even where the chief constable *d*
thinks a referral should be proceeded with, a chief constable is under a series of
explicit and implicit obligations to see a disciplinary process to its end unless a
factor recognised by law supervenes—a proposition which has a bearing on other
aspects of this case.

If, in answer to Mr Hay's letter of complaint, Mr Portlock had confined *e*
himself, as he should have done, to pointing out that s 84(6) prevented him from
recording the complaint in so far as it related to the conduct of the two officers,
which was by then the subject of the very disciplinary proceedings which Mr Hay
perfectly reasonably wanted to observe, it would have been unanswerable. In so
far as the complaint might have referred to other officers, the terms of Mr Hay's
short letter made it clear that he was not interested in these but in the two officers *f*
charged, so that Mr Portlock had no need to concern himself further with the
possible breadth of the complaint. Instead, as I have recounted, a letter was sent
which, having correctly referred to s 84(6), proceeded irrelevantly to treat the
power to record the complaint as discretionary and sought to impugn Mr Hay's
motives (which were perfectly reasonable and honourable ones, and which he
had not sought to conceal) and to characterise his complaint as an abuse of the *g*
system.

While, therefore, it is unsurprising that Mr Hay wished to contest the decision,
the fact is that the recording of his complaint was precluded by law. The contrary
seems to me, with respect to the arguments advanced, to be unarguable. It is
therefore unnecessary to consider Mr Donne's further submissions that the *h*
application in relation to the first decision was not made promptly and that in any
event no relief could properly be granted at this time of day. In relation to the
first decision I would decline to grant Mr Hay leave to move.

The second decision   *j*
This issue, by contrast, is in my judgment arguable. Although its formulation
has metamorphosed in the course of argument, this is no criticism of counsel but
only a reflection of the difficulty which the issue presents. It involves, in strictly
legal terms, the question whether officers who are threatened with or facing
disciplinary process can avoid adjudication by retiring. This differs from the

a wider public debate, with which the court is not concerned, as to whether they ought to be able to do so.

In the present case, it will be recalled, the view was taken and acted on by the chief constable that he was obliged on medical advice to permit Supt Mechan to retire and that upon his retirement any disciplinary process pending against him would cease. It is contended upon Mr Hay's behalf that either retirement has no *b* such legal effect or, if it does, it is unlawful to permit an officer to retire until the disciplinary proceedings have been completed. As subsidiary arguments in reply, Mr Engelman sought to argue that the chief constable's purpose in accepting the resignation was the unlawful purpose of enabling Supt Mechan to avoid the disciplinary process against him and, beyond this, of improving the case for the withdrawal of proceedings against Chief Insp McArthur. The first of these *c* allegations, which is set out in the originating application, simply does not square with the consistent evidence that the chief constable had considered throughout that Supt Mechan ought to be called to account in disciplinary proceedings. The second, which was unpleaded, is an allegation of considerable gravity which cannot properly be introduced by way of reply, and which I therefore discount in *d* relation to this part of the case.

The argument of principle for the applicant is that there are, on authority, elements of the employment relationship which can and do survive the termination of the contract. The obligation of confidentiality is a recognised example, but authority shows that disciplinary provisions can also survive, at least where they may operate for the protection of the employee (see *Irani v* *e* *Southampton and South West Hampshire Health Authority* [1985] ICR 590).

Before I return to this interesting argument, which Mr Engelman developed in reply, I turn to Mr Donne's response, which is short and sharp. Supt Mechan, he submits, was charged on the recommendation of the authority pursuant to s 93(1) of PACE, so that the chief constable had no power of withdrawal under *f* reg 9 and was bound by s 93(2) not to withdraw the charge without the leave of the authority, which was not sought. He therefore submits that the single question is whether on Supt Mechan's retirement the disciplinary charge against him lapsed by operation of law, and that the answer is that it did. Mr Engelman, replying, agrees that this is the first question but if it is answered against him he *g* submits, as I have indicated, that the corollary is that the chief constable may not accept an officer's retirement if it is going to have this effect.

Although he has pursued the argument in reply with great skill, much of Mr Engelman's reasoning is question-begging. He points, for example, to the use throughout the regulations of the word 'member' to describe the relationship of *h* an officer to his force; but this does not tell one what is to happen when membership ceases. He is not helped, in my view, by the definition in reg 4 of 'police force concerned' (a phrase which recurs at various points in the regulations) as meaning the police force of which the officer 'is a member'; nor by the provision of reg 18(1) that the accused officer 'shall be ordered to attend at the hearing of the case', which is difficult to apply to an officer no longer subject *j* to police discipline; nor by reg 24, which includes among the available punishments dismissal from the force, enforced resignation, reduction in rank and reduction in pay. But in the ordinary way delegated legislation is not an aid to statutory construction. As to the statutes themselves, Mr Engelman points out with some force that there is nothing in either the Police Act 1964 or in PACE, Pt IX which even begins to suggest that Parliament supposed that resignation was or should be an escape from disciplinary process. But the nub of his argument is *a* that there is in the statutory scheme (see s 33(2) of the 1964 Act) an explicit distinction between membership of a police force and the office of constable. There is no doubt that the statute, and the discipline regulations correspondingly, use the two phrases in juxtaposition, strongly suggesting that unless the text is to be taken as tautologous these are two different things. If so, the argument goes, then while the office of constable is on first constitutional principles a status *b* under the Crown carrying only such incidents as the common law or statute may invest it with, membership of a police force is, precisely, an employment relationship. The novelty of this proposition does not detract from its cogency, for when one looks at s 146(2) and (3) of the Employment Protection (Consolidation) Act 1978, Parliament has gone to the trouble of excluding police officers from the employment rights which, it is to be inferred, Parliament *c* considered that the legislation would otherwise accord them. Against this, as I pointed out in argument, there is s 48 of the Police Act 1964 which is predicated on the opposite assumption, namely that a police officer has no employer, making it necessary for his chief officer to be deemed to be his employer for the purpose of creating vicarious liability for his torts. *d*

If it rested there, the inquirer might be baffled. But while statute can modify the common law it cannot, by revealing Parliament's or the draftsman's view of the common law, determine what the common law is. For reasons of principle, therefore, and not merely of bafflement, one has to return from the statutory provision to the relationship itself. Although, as I accept, it contains many of the incidents of ordinary contractual employment, and although the superimposition *e* on such incidents of a variety of statutory elements in no way negatives the contractual nature of the relationship, there is no apparent answer to the question posed by Mr Donne: who then is the officer's employer? Neither the chief officer nor the Police Authority can realistically be taken to fulfil this role. While the balance of modern authority now favours the proposition that the employment *f* of the bulk of Crown servants is contractual (see *R v Lord Chancellor's Dept, ex p Nangle* [1992] 1 All ER 897, [1991] ICR 743) and while it has been held that the tenure of an office does not exclude the incidents of an employment relationship (see *Miles v Wakefield Metropolitan DC* [1987] 1 All ER 1089, [1987] AC 539), it is a further step to deduce from the tenure of office under the Crown an employment relationship with the Crown. *g*

Even if, however, an employment relationship were held to exist for serving police officers, it is a further and equally difficult step to contend that its disciplinary incidents survive not for the benefit of the officer but to his potential detriment, enabling him to be disciplined—with potentially adverse effects on his pension—after retirement. *h*

Although I am conscious that it has not been possible fully to explore this difficult question within the four corners of the present proceedings, my present view is that a police officer is not, in addition to being the holder of the office of constable, a party to a contract of employment by virtue of his service.

This being so, has a chief officer of police any power to refuse to require the *j* resignation of an officer? The answer is plainly, Yes—for example in a case where an officer seeks without any or adequate supporting evidence to retire on medical grounds. But this is not the present case: here the evidence is that the chief constable had before him the unanimous views of three doctors to the effect that Supt Mechan was mentally ill, had indeed been mentally ill at the time of the a incident, and could suffer a breakdown if compelled to face disciplinary process. This without doubt was capable of furnishing grounds upon which the chief constable might call upon the officer to retire. In such circumstances this court has held that the chief constable has a choice: he may decide not to require the officer to resign by reason of unfitness, in which case the officer's service continues and the disciplinary process with it, or he may require the officer to

b resign by reason of his unfitness, in which case he cannot postpone the effective date of retirement pending completion of the disciplinary process (see *R v Chief Constable of Northumbria Police, ex p Charlton* (1994) Times, 6 May). It follows that in order to take a lawful decision which does not leave relevant matters out of account, a chief officer of police who is invited to require the retirement of one of his officers must consider not only the evidence tendered to him in support of

c retirement, but also the fact that he is not obliged to accede to it if there is a good reason for refusal, and must go on to consider, for example, whether the interest of the police service and the public in seeing any disciplinary proceedings against the officer to their end outweighs for the time being the case for his retirement.

In the present case the chief constable, Mr John Evans, describes in his affidavit

d the decisive point of time:

'On 24 April 1995 I became aware that the medical view was that Superintendent MECHAN was not fit enough to withstand the rigours of disciplinary proceedings and was certainly not fit enough to prepare his defence. After very careful consideration and being fully aware of the

e implications of my decision I decided that I had no alternative but to recommend that Superintendent MECHAN be discharged as medically unfit and without recourse to disciplinary proceedings which in the circumstances undoubtedly would have been oppressive ... it was clear from the reports I received that Superintendent MECHAN would be most unlikely to be fit in the

f future to return to duty or face disciplinary proceedings and I felt that I had no alternative in these circumstances but to proceed as recommended by the Force Medical Officer ...'

This evidence is not easy to interpret. The first passage might be taken as

g meaning that the wider interests of the force and public were properly taken into account; but the second passage suggests that they were not. One does not like to decide questions like this on onus, but the fact is that the only person who can describe his process of reasoning is the chief constable himself, and I do not consider that he has satisfactorily done so. The evidence points on balance to his having concluded that in spite of the fact that the disciplinary proceedings would

h abort, he had no option in the face of the medical evidence presented to him but to require Supt Mechan to retire.

In the light of the foregoing I turn to the question of Mr Hay's locus. Does he have, as Mr Donne contends he has not, a 'sufficient interest' within Ord 53, r 3(7) in the matter to which the present application relates? Mr Donne submits that

j these are domestic proceedings between a chief constable and one of his officers in which the applicant has no more interest than any other member of the public. I disagree. Not only does Mr Hay have a personal concern as a close relative of the man whose death prompted the disciplinary process; the operation of s 84(6), which shuts out the recording of his complaint by reason of the bringing of disciplinary proceedings, gives him a very immediate interest as a potential complainant whose entitlement under Pt IX of PACE has been supplanted for good, not merely for their duration, by the bringing of disciplinary proceedings. *a*

Next Mr Donne takes a point on time. The decision to require Supt Mechan's retirement was taken at the latest on 27 April 1995, putting the date of the application for judicial review some two weeks out of time. Mr Sapsford, while accepting that it was in April that grounds for the application first arose (see Ord 53, r 4(2)), submits that it is only from 13 May, when the family learned of it, that *b* time should be treated as running. In that event, Mr Donne contends, the application was still not made promptly as required by r 4(1). It is true that thereafter Mr Hay's solicitor does not appear to have instructed counsel until late in July. Nevertheless, because there was by then the major issue, which has also brought the authority to this court, of Mr Girven's dismissal of the proceedings *c* against Chief Insp McArthur, I think it is right not to hold against Mr Hay the want of swifter action in relation to the second decision. There is, in my view, good reason for extending by some two weeks the period within which his application under this head is to be made, and this I do.

This brings me to Mr Donne's final ground of resistance—that it would be a wrong exercise of the court's discretion to grant any relief which might have the *d* effect of nullifying Supt Mechan's retirement. From 8 June he has ceased to be a serving officer, and it was known by the date when Mr Girven sat to hear the case against Chief Insp McArthur that Supt Mechan was unfit and had been required to retire. I accept this submission. For better or for worse the only information which this court has about Supt Mechan is that to compel him to face a *e* disciplinary process would precipitate a breakdown in his mental health. To wind the film back to April or May in order to put him back in service would involve payment of his salary for the whole intervening period and onward to such time as he finally left the service. I do not think that this is something which the court can properly undertake. I bear in mind, too, that even after a full appraisal of the competing personal and public interests affecting the question of *f* retirement it would be open to the chief constable to come to the same decision as he has already reached. While I do not suggest for a moment that it is a foregone conclusion that he would do so, the possibility and legitimacy of his doing so is a further reason for not granting either the order of certiorari which is sought or any other formal relief. *g*

The third decision

For the authority, Mr Turner, whose submissions Mr Sapsford adopts, contends that Mr Girven, exercising the adjudicative function in the name of the Chief Constable of Devon and Cornwall, erred in law in dismissing in limine the *h* charge of neglect of duty laid against Chief Insp McArthur.

It is common ground that, although there is no express provision in either the statute or the regulations for the dismissal of a disciplinary charge on the ground of abuse of process, it is a necessary incident of the disciplinary jurisdiction that in a proper case the tribunal not only can but must dismiss in limine a proceeding *j* which it is inherently unfair to the accused to continue with. This power, as Owen J has held in *R v Chief Constable of Thames Valley Police, ex p Police Complaints Authority* (13 October 1995, unreported), is a residual power furnished by the common law, with the result that it is to be exercised in accordance with principles laid down from time to time by the courts of common law. These a include a classic passage of Lord Donaldson MR in *R v Chief Constable of the Merseyside Police, ex p Merrill* [1989] 1 WLR 1077 at 1085:

'The Chief Constable had no need to concern himself with "abuse of process." As a judicial tribunal, he had a discretionary power to dismiss the charge without hearing the full evidence if he was satisfied that, whatever the evidence might reveal, it would be unfair to proceed further. b "Unfairness" in this context is a general concept which comprehends prejudice to the accused, but can also extend to a significant departure from the intended and prescribed framework of disciplinary proceedings or a combination of both.'

c As Lord Donaldson MR mentions, and as the Privy Council has more recently spelt out in *A-G of Hong Kong v Cheung Wai-bun* [1993] 2 All ER 510 at 515, [1994] 1 AC 1 at 7, the power is one which is to be exercised before the evidence is heard. It is Mr Turner's submission that Mr Girven erred fundamentally, first in allowing the defence to travel a considerable distance into the substantive merits of the disciplinary case, and secondly—and no doubt because neither advocate brought d the correct authority to his attention—in failing to apply the principles of law which by 1995 had been clearly established by the Court of Appeal in *A-G's Reference (No 1 of 1990)* [1992] 3 All ER 169, [1992] QB 630.

As to the first limb of the argument, I have before me the full transcript of the proceedings in relation to the preliminary point of abuse of process. The e amended charge was put, without objection, to Chief Insp McArthur, but at the request of Mr Rea, the prosecuting solicitor, no plea was entered, and at the invitation of Mr Rea, supported by Supt Walker for Chief Insp McArthur, the investigating officer, Assistant Chief Constable Pike, was called and extensively questioned. Supt Walker had first unsuccessfully submitted (a) that the first and second particulars of the amended charge were bad for duplicity, and (b) that the f charge as a whole fell outside the ambit of the reg 7 notice which had specified only: 'Failing to ensure that adequate planning was carried out prior to the deployment of authorised firearms officers at Crabadon Manor.' Mr Walker now moved to a substantial submission on the law of abuse of process. Citing authorities up to about 1990—a period in which a sudden mushrooming of applications to stay a criminal process for abuse had led to sometimes discrepant g decisions—he developed his argument, praying in aid the fact that he had only 11 days' notice of the amended charge but had waived his right to 21 days' notice, and contending that Chief Insp McArthur's situation was for this and other reasons severely prejudiced.

At page 16 of the transcript Assistant Chief Constable Pike is called. Five pages h later he embarks, at Supt Walker's invitation, upon the verbatim reading of the greater part of his report, running to 60 pages of transcript. This is followed by questioning by Supt Walker, which begins:

'Can we just start off by, could I ask you if there is any suggestion j anywhere in your report that the alleged failings of Mr McArthur had any effect on the final tragic outcome of this incident?'

For the next 28 pages of transcript, without any objection from Mr Rea, Supt Walker cross-examines Mr Pike about the substantive issues raised by his report and the disciplinary charge—to which, be it remembered, Chief Insp McArthur had not yet pleaded.

Mr Rea is then recorded as saying:

'First of all can I indicate that I do not take issue with Superintendent Walker's interpretation of the case and in fact I would have to quote from *R v Chief Constable of the Merseyside Police, ex p Merrill* ([1989] 1 WLR 1077) where [Lord Donaldson MR] indicated that the public interest in complaints against the police officers being fully investigated and adjudicated is undoubted but it must be speedily. I also have to concede the case [of] *R v Bow Street Stipendiary Magistrate, ex p Cherry* ((1990) 91 Cr App R 283) where in the [Divisional] court it was indicated [that] there is ample precedent for the proposition that delay which gives rise to prejudice and unfairness may by itself amount to an abuse of process and that there has to be a demonstration that they caused genuine prejudice and unfairness, and I concede that any delay here might have to justify that, and I have to prove beyond reasonable doubt that no prejudice has occurred to the chief inspector before I can be allowed to continue. In total, I understand, sir, that I have 17 months to justify from the date of the incident, 13 October 1993, to today's date.'

With help like this from his opponent, it is unsurprising that Chief Supt Walker succeeded without having to say another word. When it came to Supt Mechan, Mr Rea said:

'Naturally it would be possible for me to concede certain omissions with respect to Superintendent Mechan in terms of his responsibility, sir, and this could diminish any potential prejudice you may feel, but his omission is serious at this stage.'

Mr Girven reserved his decision to the following day. When he gave it, he spelt out his reasons for it, and I will set them out in full:

'This is the resumed hearing of a discipline matter at the Devon and Cornwall Police Headquarters, there is before the disciplinary tribunal a charge of "Neglect of Duty" against Alan Paul McArthur—Chief Inspector in the Devon and Cornwall Constabulary and I am Walter Girven—Chief Constable of Wiltshire dealing with the matter on behalf of the Chief Constable. Those present are those who are here at the commencement of the hearing yesterday together with Mr May, a member of the Police Authority who is appearing as an independent representative. Yesterday Superintendent Walker made several submissions to me regarding the charge which was then placed against Chief Inspector McArthur; argument was put by both Superintendent Walker and Mr Rea with evidence provided on the background and investigation procedures by Mr Pyke who is the Assistant Chief Constable of the Avon and Somerset Constabulary who led the Investigation. I shall briefly indicate my response to those issues raised by Superintendent Walker. First, initially, he submitted that the first two specified items in the charge marked little (i) and (ii) were prejudicial, I did not agree that a failure to ensure the implementation of a call-out of staff was prejudicial, and so rejected that recommendation. Mr Walker then submitted that the actions alleged in the current charge set out at items little (i), (ii) and (iv), did not fall within the ambit of the allegation alleged in the reg 7 Notice on Chief Inspector McArthur's form served on him on 11 November 1993. I found that the reg 7 Notice alleging failure to ensure a adequate planning prior to deployment of firearms officers at Crabadon Manor did encompass the four listed matters set out in the charge. The final submission by Superintendent Walker was that the slow progress and proceedings adopted and leading to the charge against Chief Inspector McArthur were an abuse of process which prejudiced his ability to prepare his defence. Superintendent Walker argued cogently quoting authorities

b that the decision sought was within my discretion to make that unreasonable delay had occurred, that the accused officer had not contributed to that delay, that on the balance of probabilities at least he will be prejudiced. In particular the prejudice would arise due to the lengthy period which had passed to the stress caused to the accused by that period of time and also by the adverse publicity which has accompanied that time. Particularly the late

c notification of detail of changes, sorry, charges on the absence of a Superintendent Mechan who was deemed an essential witness by the accused. Mr Pyke the ACC's testimony outlined the procedures followed and the decisions made. Mr Rea provided a very full and useful exposition of the salient dates relative to the proceedings, he explained the time

d sequences and delays, conceding the prosecution needs to justify were they considered unreasonable and this he sought to do. I'm conscious that the investigation into a death at police hands required a thorough and detailed inquiry, the criminal inquiry was completed within three months with a report to the Director of Prosecutions submitted on 24 January 1994 and the investigation procedurally with a report to the Police Complaints Authority

e on 25 March 1994. The Director of Public Prosecution's decision to take no action on 13 June 1994 was not in my view an unreasonable delay. It is unfortunate therefore that there was then a delay to the end of 1994 and following the Coroner's inquest before the Police Complaints Authority indicated action against Chief Inspector McArthur. No further inquiries had been pursued during this period, nor was any fresh evidence gained,

f similarly the change of charge details only days before this hearing could not be attributed to any fault of the accused officer, I consider the delay from at least June 1994 to be unreasonable and accordingly prejudicial. The recent non-availability of Superintendent Mechan is critical in allegations of neglect in the provision of support to the sole commander which post he held. I am

g conscious that the nature of the alleged failings, if they were admitted, were deemed to merit no more than an admonishment. In the circumstances it is difficult to perceive that the seriousness justified the delays which occurred. I find that there has been a delay and that the delay has prejudiced the defence's position to put forward a case. Under the circumstances the charge

h will be dismissed.'

In these proceedings Mr Girven has sworn an affidavit which not only repeats these reasons but gives a number of further reasons for his conclusion. It is sufficient to say that, while admissible, its reasoning is manifestly ex post facto and Mr Donne has wisely not founded upon it.

j It is Mr Turner's submission that if, instead of a list of authorities beginning with Magna Carta and ending in 1991, Mr Girven had put before him the law which by then was summarised in *Archbold's Pleading, Evidence and Practice in Criminal Cases* (45th edn, 1995) para 4-44a together with the decisive authority, *A-G's Reference (No 1 of 1990)* [1992] 3 All ER 169, [1992] QB 630, he would not have been sidetracked into an extensive consideration of the substantive defence case and would have been unable to conclude that there was any such unfairness as rendered the proceedings an abuse of process.

In *A-G's Reference (No 1 of 1990)* a Court of Appeal presided over by Lord Lane CJ gave a definitive decision, which is sufficiently summarised for present purposes in the headnote ([1992] QB 630 at 631):

'... (1) a stay for delay or any other reason was to be imposed only in exceptional circumstances; that, even where delay could be said to be unjustifiable, the imposition of a permanent stay was to be the exception rather than the rule; and that even more rarely could a stay properly be imposed in the absence of fault on the part of the complainant or the prosecution, and never where the delay was due merely to the complexity of the case or contributed to by the defendant's actions ... (2) That no stay was to be imposed unless the defendant established on the balance of probabilities that, owing to the delay, he would suffer serious prejudice to the extent that no fair trial could be held, in [other words] that the continuation of the prosecution amounted to a misuse of the process of the court ...'

This unitary set of principles, it is submitted, leaves no room for a preliminary appraisal of the strength or weakness of the case against the accused. What it does require is not only a consideration of the reasons for any delay in addition to its length, but also a careful appraisal of any prejudice which the accused can establish. None of these elements, Mr Turner submits, was satisfied in the present case.

Mr Picton for Chief Insp McArthur, adopting for the most part Mr Donne's submissions, concedes that the anticipated strength or weakness of the case for the prosecution is irrelevant to whether it is fair to proceed, but describes it as 'irresistible in reality', so that Mr Girven should not be criticised for considering it. Mr Donne accepts that the cross-examination of Mr Pike went well beyond any question of delay. But he submits that both prosecution and defence legitimately considered that Mr Girven required a detailed knowledge of the case in order to decide the two preliminary questions (duplicity and the ambit of the reg 7 notice) and the major question of unfairness. If there was delay, he submits that the weakness of the case can be added to it in order to demonstrate the unfairness of proceeding. He points to Lord Donaldson MR's phrase 'without hearing the *full* evidence' (my emphasis), submitting that the hearing of some evidence is therefore permissible on an application to stay for abuse. The late amendment of the charge and the late service of two witness statements in support of it were also, Mr Donne submits, legitimate elements for Mr Girven to consider, and so was the absence through sickness of Supt Mechan.

As to the latter both Mr Donne and Mr Picton have argued energetically that Supt Mechan was a crucial witness in the proceedings against Chief Insp McArthur and that his unavailability through sickness—albeit that this ran from the very day of the incident—made it impossible for Chief Insp McArthur to get a fair hearing.

As to why Mr Girven was not shown the Court of Appeal decision in *A-G's Reference (No 1 of 1990)*, Mr Donne, having taken instructions at my invitation from Mr Rea, told me that there was liaison between Mr Rea and Supt Walker. Of the list of authorities put before Mr Girven and used as the basis of both sides' submissions, he said:

a   'They felt these were the authorities which would assist him to reach the right conclusion. Neither of them seems to have felt that *Attorney-General's Reference (No 1 of 1990)* ([1992] 3 All ER 169, [1992] QB 630) was an appropriate one to be included in the list.'

I reject the respondents' submissions in their entirety. In my judgment:

b   (1) The substantive merits of the case against Chief Insp McArthur were irrelevant to the submission that to proceed would be an abuse of process, with the result that Mr Girven was induced to err in law in taking them into account.

(2) By reason of the citation of incomplete and largely out of date authority and the omission to cite the single authority which would have given him the guidance he needed, Mr Girven was led to approach the entire question of abuse
c   of process upon a legally faulty basis.

(3) The submission by Supt Walker and the concession by Mr Rea that Supt Mechan would, but for his unavailability, have been an essential witness was unreal. Although both Mr Picton and Mr Donne have tried valiantly to justify the contention, there is no way in which it could have been sensibly proposed that, but for his illness, Supt Mechan would have been a key witness either for or
d   against Chief Insp McArthur. McArthur's defence was, in effect, that the failure of command was Mechan's and not his. Mechan was not a potential witness for the prosecution, both because Assistant Chief Constable Pike's criticisms of McArthur depended not at all upon what Mechan had to say, and because to have called Mechan as a prosecution witness (as a serving officer he would have been
e   compellable) would have been to invite him to condemn himself out of his own mouth. To have called him as a witness for the defence would, barring an unpredictable bout of self-criticism, have been of no help at all to McArthur's case. The submission, apart from being founded on the hypothesis that Mechan was well, when everybody knew that he was said to be seriously and indefinitely ill, was a factitious argument with which Mr Rea ought to have had no truck.

f   (4) There was no serious or culpable delay; all the time which had passed could be well accounted for, and much of the time which had elapsed since the completion of the inquest in December 1994 had resulted from the state of Mr Girven's diary.

(5) Not only was the burden of showing prejudice—contrary to Mr Rea's
g   concession—upon the accused officer; there was much assertion but no evidence that he had suffered any identifiable prejudice by reason of the delay, or of the late amendment of the charge and late service of some further evidence in support of it. As Mr Girven had held, the amended charge lay within the four corners of the reg 7 notice which had been served on Chief Insp McArthur shortly after the
h   incident itself. I am told also that the defence asked for and were given the relevant parts of the Pike report some 14 days before the hearing.

Consequently, I hold that in reaching the decision to dismiss as an abuse of process the proceedings against Chief Insp McArthur, Mr Girven was misdirected in law and took extraneous matters into account.

Before I turn to the question of relief, I must mention Mr Donne's submission
j   that in relation to this decision, as in relation to the second, Mr Hay has no sufficient interest to mount a challenge. His grounds for making the submission are the same as in relation to the second decision, and my grounds for rejecting it are also the same.

Mr Donne also contends that neither application was promptly made. The decision was given on 31 May, but the applications were not made until 8 and 10

August respectively. While I do not lose sight of the requirement of RSC Ord 53
r 4 for promptness, irrespective of the formal time limit, the practice of this court
is to work on the basis of the three-month limit and to scale it down wherever the
features of the particular case make that limit unfair to the respondent or to third
parties. Mr Donne submits that this is such a case, given the magnitude of the
consequences for Chief Insp McArthur. While I do not underestimate how
serious it is for an officer to find himself once again facing a charge which he
thought had been disposed of, I am quite satisfied that the balance of interests,
including the public interest in the issue, is not such that the present applications
should be dismissed for lack of promptness.

Consequently I grant leave to the authority and to Mr Hay (who already has
leave in relation to the second decision). With the consent of all parties I abridge
entirely the time limited for service of evidence, dispense with further service and
treat the argument for and against leave in both cases as the argument upon the
substantive matters on which I have granted leave.

In my judgment both applicants are entitled to the principal relief which they
seek, namely an order of certiorari to bring up and quash the decision of Mr
Walter Girven given on 31 May 1995 to dismiss the disciplinary charge against
Chief Insp McArthur. On the view which I take of the law and the facts, the only
decision open to Mr Girven was that there was no unfairness in proceeding with
the charge, and I propose accordingly, if asked, to make an order of mandamus
directed to the Chief Constable of Devon and Cornwall to hear and determine on
its substantive merits the disciplinary charge laid against Chief Insp McArthur.

Postscript

This case has highlighted the relevance of the remark of Owen J in *R v Chief
Constable of Thames Valley Police, ex p Police Complaints Authority* (13 October 1995,
unreported) about 'the necessity for separation of the charging and judicial
functions' to which, incidentally, the Home Office's own guidance notes draw
attention. It is a necessity which is not only reflected, as in the present case, in the
appointment of an outside chief constable to adjudicate in the name of the chief
officer of the Devon and Cornwall force, but which needs also to be reflected in
a clear separation of the prosecutorial function from the overall administration of
the force. A chief constable has duties, whether legal or moral, of loyalty to his
officers, which in turn call for him to support them except where he is satisfied
that their conduct merits censure. In the chief constable's view, as repeatedly
expressed by Mr Portlock to the authority, Chief Insp McArthur was an officer
deserving of support and not of censure. It is a misfortune that his legitimate
stance as the chief officer of the force in support of Chief Insp McArthur was
allowed, as in my view it clearly was, to invade the prosecutorial function which
the chief constable had a separate responsibility to fulfil in response to the
statutory intervention of the authority. The unhappy result can be seen in Mr
Rea's approach to the presentation of the case against Chief Insp McArthur. I do
not dissent from Mr Rea's advice, as recorded by Mr Portlock, that it is a
prosecutor's duty to be scrupulously fair and balanced; but the manner in which
the record shows him to have conducted the disciplinary proceedings carried Mr
Rea far beyond the call of this duty, leading him to take bad points against himself
and in effect wrongly to concede the case on abuse of process. In doing so he may
well have reflected the official view within the force of Chief Insp McArthur's role
in the incident, but through him the chief constable was failing to carry out his

a separate statutory obligation to prosecute the disciplinary charge which he had brought on the express recommendation of the authority. To expand Owen J's formulation, if I may, the charging and judicial functions need to be kept separate not only from one another, but from the administrative function of the chief constable as the head of his force. The endeavour of Mr Portlock to be allowed to withdraw the charge against Chief Insp McArthur appears, when leave was

b refused, to have coloured the conduct of the disciplinary proceedings, as it should not have done.

Order accordingly.

Dilys Tausz   Barrister.

Biggs v Somerset County Council

COURT OF APPEAL, CIVIL DIVISION

NEILL, AULD LJJ AND SIR IAIN GLIDEWELL

6, 7 NOVEMBER 1995, 26 JANUARY 1996

Employment – Discrimination against a woman – Unfair dismissal and redundancy payments – Part-time worker – Time limit for making claim – Claim made by part-time employee 18 years after dismissal – Applicant only aware of right to make claim after House of Lords ruling in other proceedings that statutory provisions relating to redundancy and unfair dismissal for part-time workers contrary to Community law – Whether applicant's claim time-barred – Whether industrial tribunal bound by Community law to disallow statutory time limits – Whether applicant having directly enforceable right under Community law to present claim – EC Treaty, art 119 – Employment Protection (Consolidation) Act 1978, s 67(2).

In 1976 the appellant was dismissed from her job as a part-time science teacher at a school under the control of the defendant council. At the time the existing statutory provisions provided that an employee employed under a contract of employment for less than 21 hours a week had no right to make a claim to an industrial tribunal for unfair dismissal. The appellant had been employed to work only 14 hours a week. In 1994 the House of Lords ruled that the provisions of the Employment Protection (Consolidation) Act 1978 (replacing the earlier provisions) disqualifying employees who worked for fewer than 16 hours per week from claiming redundancy pay and compensation for unfair dismissal were respectively contrary to art 119[a] of the EC Treaty and Council Directive (EEC) 75/117 (the equal pay directive) and to Council Directive (EEC) 76/207 (the equal treatment directive). Two months after the House of Lords decision the appellant lodged a claim with an industrial tribunal for unfair dismissal. The chairman of the tribunal held that the tribunal had no jurisdiction to hear the claim because it had not been made within three months of the termination of the employment as prescribed by s 67(2)[b] of the 1978 Act. The appellant's appeal to the Employment Appeal Tribunal was dismissed. The appellant appealed to the Court of Appeal, contending (i) that on the state of the law as it was perceived to be prior to the House of Lords decision it was not reasonably practicable for her to have presented her claim within three months following her dismissal in 1976, (ii) that the industrial tribunal was bound by Community law to disallow the time limits imposed by s 67(2) because they made it impossible to enforce a Community right, and (iii) that the appellant was entitled to rely on her directly enforceable rights under art 119 of the EC Treaty (to which the time limits in s 67(2) did not apply).

Held – The appeal would be dismissed for the following reasons—

(1) An industrial tribunal had no jurisdiction to consider an unfair dismissal claim lodged by a part-time worker outside the prescribed time limit after the House of Lords ruling in 1994 that the restrictions on part-time workers making such claims were contrary to art 119 of the EC Treaty and the equal pay and equal

---

a   Article 119, is set out at p 745 *a b*, post

b   Section 67(2), so far as material, is set out at p 738 *c*, post

a treatment directives. The provision in s 67(2) of the 1978 Act for extending the time limit within which to submit a claim for unfair dismissal or redundancy, if it had not been 'reasonably practicable' to present the claim within three months of dismissal, was directed to difficulties or a temporary impediment or hindrance, such as illness, faced by an individual claimant. The appellant's mistake as to what her rights were was a mistake of law, not fact, and it would be contrary to

b the principle of legal certainty to allow past transactions to be reopened and limitation periods circumvented because the existing law at the relevant time had not yet been explained or had not been fully understood. It was therefore 'reasonably practicable' for the appellant to have made her claim within the time prescribed (see p 742 *f j* to p 743 *e* and p 746 *e f*, post); *Equal Opportunities Commission v Secretary of State for Employment* [1994] 1 All ER 910 considered.

c (2) The time limit imposed by s 67(2) of the 1978 Act did not itself offend Community law and was compatible with the principle of legal certainty. The appellant's failure to make a claim within the time limit was not the result of applying the time limit, but of her ignorance of her right in 1976 to present a claim by invoking Community law and s 2^c of the European Communities Act 1972 so

d as to ensure that the restriction on claims by part-time workers was disapplied (see p 744 *f* to *h* and p 746 *e f*, post).

(3) Although art 119 of the EC Treaty prohibited sex discrimination and therefore, assuming that compensation for unfair dismissal was 'pay' for the purposes of art 119, a person of either sex had a right under art 119 not to be unfairly dismissed by reason of unfair discrimination, art 119 itself did not provide

e any direct remedy for breach of that right. The only remedy was the statutory right to make a claim to an industrial tribunal for unfair dismissal and that remedy was only available subject to the time limit laid down in s 67(2) of the 1978 Act (see p 745 *c* to *e* and p 746 *b* to p 747 *c*, post).

f **Notes**

For time limits in proceedings before industrial tribunals, see 16 *Halsbury's Laws* (4th edn reissue) paras 356, 505, and for cases on the subject, see 20 *Digest* (Reissue) 414–419, 3393–3410.

For the principle of equal pay for equal work in Community law, see 52 g *Halsbury's Laws* (4th edn) paras 21.11–21.13.

For the European Communities Act 1972, s 2, see 17 *Halsbury's Statutes* (4th edn) (1993 reissue) 37.

For the Employment Protection (Consolidation) Act 1978, s 67, see 16 *Halsbury's Statutes* (4th edn) (1990 reissue) 293.

h

Cases referred to in judgments

Amministrazione delle Finanze dello Stato v SpA San Giorgio Case 199/82 [1983] ECR 3595.

Brasserie du Pêcheur SA v Germany, R v Secretary of State for Transport, ex p Factortame j *Ltd* Joined cases C-46/93 and C-48/93 [1996] All ER (EC) 301, ECJ.

Defrenne v Sabena Case 43/75 [1981] 1 All ER 122, [1976] ECR 455, ECJ.

Emmott v Minister for Social Welfare Case C-208/90 [1991] ECR I-4269.

---

c   Section 2, so far as material, provides: 'All such rights, powers, liabilities, obligations and restrictions from time to time created or arising by or under the Treaties ... are without further enactment to be given legal effect ...'

Equal Opportunities Commission v Secretary of State for Employment [1994] 1 All ER   *a*
910, [1995] 1 AC 1, [1994] 2 WLR 409, HL.
Francovich v Italy Joined cases C-6/90 and C-9/90 [1991] ECR I-5357.
Johnson v Chief Adjudication Officer (No 2) Case C-410/92 [1995] All ER (EC) 258,
[1994] ECR I-5483, ECJ.
Palmer v Southend-on-Sea BC [1984] 1 All ER 945, [1984] 1 WLR 1129, CA.
Rewe-Zentralfinanz eG v Landwirtschaftskammer für das Saarland Case 33/76 [1976]   *b*
ECR 1989.
Singh v Post Office [1973] ICR 437, NIRC.

Cases also cited or referred to in skeleton arguments
Arbeiterwohlfahrt der Stadt Berlin v Bötel eV Case C-360/90 [1992] ECR I-3589.
Barber v Guardian Royal Exchange Assurance Group Case C-262/88 [1990] 2 All ER   *c*
660, [1991] 1 QB 344, [1990] ECR I-1889, ECJ.
Bilka-Kaufhaus GmbH v Weber von Hartz Case C-170/84 [1986] ECR 1607.
EC Commission v France Case 169/87 [1988] ECR 4093.
EC Commission v Germany Case 29/84 [1985] ECR 1661.
Factortame Ltd v Secretary of State for Transport (No 2) Case C-213/89 [1991] 1 All ER   *d*
70, [1991] 1 AC 603, [1990] 3 WLR 818, [1990] ECR I-2433, ECJ and HL.
Macarthys Ltd v Smith [1981] 1 All ER 111, [1981] QB 180, [1980] ECR 1275 ECJ and
CA.
Marshall v Southampton and South West Hampshire Area Health Authority (No 2) Case
C-271/91 [1993] 4 All ER 586, [1994] QB 126, [1993] ECR I-4367, ECJ; *ruling*   *e*
applied [1994] 1 All ER 736, [1994] AC 530, HL.
Mediguard Services Ltd v Thame [1994] ICR 751, EAT.
R v Secretary of State for Employment, ex p Seymour-Smith [1996] All ER (EC) 1, CA.
Rankin v British Coal Corp [1995] ICR 774, EAT.
Secretary of State for Scotland v Wright [1991] IRLR 187, EAT.
Steenhorst-Neerings v Bestuur van de Bedrijfsvereniging voor Detailhandel, Ambachten   *f*
en Huisvrouwen Case C-338/91 [1993] ECR I-5475.
Vroege v NCIV Instituut voor Volkshuisvesting BV Case C-57/93 [1995] All ER (EC)
193, [1994] ECR I-4541, ECJ.

Appeal   *g*
By notice dated 17 July 1995 Mrs Mary Biggs appealed with leave from the order
of the Employment Appeal Tribunal ([1995] ICR 811) on 6 July 1995 dismissing
her appeal from the decision of the chairman of the industrial tribunal sitting at
Exeter dated 22 September 1994 that Mrs Biggs' complaint that she had been
unfairly dismissed from her part-time employment in August 1976 by her   *h*
employers, Somerset County Council, was barred by the time limit in s 67(2) of
the Employment Protection (Consolidation) Act 1978, notwithstanding that her
complaint (although made almost 18 years after she was dismissed) was made
within three months of a decision of the House of Lords declaring that qualifying
thresholds for claims by part-time workers were incompatible with Community   *j*
law. The facts are set out in the judgment of Neill LJ.

James Goudie QC (instructed by *Bindman & Partners*) for Mrs Biggs.
David Pannick QC and *Paul Golding* (instructed by *Andrew North*, Taunton) for the
council.

Cur adv vult

a   26 January 1996. The following judgments were delivered.

NEILL LJ. On 3 March 1994 the House of Lords made two declarations which were of great significance in the field of employment law. The declarations, which were made in judicial review proceedings instituted in June 1990 by the Equal Opportunities Commission, were in the following terms (see *Equal*
b   *Opportunities Commission v Secretary of State for Employment* [1994] 1 All ER 910 at 923–924, [1995] 1 AC 1 at 31–32 (the *EOC* case)):

'(1) That the provisions of the Employment Protection (Consolidation) Act 1978 whereby employees who work for fewer than 16 hours per week are subject to different conditions in respect to qualification for redundancy
c   pay from those which apply to employees who work for 16 hours per week or more are incompatible with art 119 of the EEC Treaty and Council Directive (EEC) 75/117 of 10 February 1975 (the equal pay directive). (2) That the provisions of the Employment Protection (Consolidation) Act 1978 whereby employees who work for fewer than 16 hours per week are subject to different conditions in respect of the right to compensation for
d   unfair dismissal from those which apply to employees who work for 16 hours per week or more are incompatible with the Council Directive (EEC) 76/207 of 9 February 1976 (the equal treatment directive).'

In the present proceedings it is necessary to consider the impact of the *EOC* case and of the relevant EU legislation on Mrs Biggs' claim for a finding that she
e   was unfairly dismissed by the Somerset County Council.

Mrs Biggs commenced employment with the council as a part-time science teacher at Whitstone School, Shepton Mallet, in April 1975. She was dismissed on 31 August 1976. At the time of her dismissal the right not to be unfairly dismissed was contained in para 4 of Sch 1 to the Trade Union and Labour
f   Relations Act 1974. By para 9(1)(f) of Sch 1, however, it was provided that para 4 did not apply to any employment 'under a contract which normally involves employment for less than twenty-one hours weekly'. Mrs Biggs was employed to work for only 14 hours per week. The provisions in the 1974 Act were later replaced by comparable provisions in subsequent legislation. The relevant provisions at the time of the *EOC* case were contained in Sch 13 to the
g   Employment Protection (Consolidation) Act 1978.

Before turning to consider Mrs Biggs' claim in more detail it is necessary to note: (a) that Council Directive (EEC) 76/207 (the equal treatment directive) did not come into force until 9 August 1978, that is after the date of Mrs Biggs' dismissal. It seems clear that she cannot rely on this directive; (b) that in the *EOC*
h   case the House of Lords did not reach a final conclusion as to whether or not compensation for unfair dismissal was 'pay' within the meaning of art 119 of the EC Treaty and of Council Directive (EEC) 75/117 (the equal pay directive) (see [1994] 1 All ER 910 at 923, [1995] 1 AC 1 at 31 per Lord Keith); (c) but that in the present case it is accepted, at any rate for the purpose of this appeal, that
j   compensation for unfair dismissal is 'pay' within the meaning of art 119; (d) that in the *EOC* case the House of Lords did not decide (and was not asked to decide) what effect, if any, its decision had on time limits for the bringing of claims by part-time workers either for a redundancy payment or for unfair dismissal.

The House of Lords announced its decision in the *EOC* case on 3 March 1994. On 1 June 1994 Mrs Biggs' application for compensation for unfair dismissal was received at the Central Office of Industrial Tribunals. In her application form it was stated that the time limits for the presentation of claims contained in s 67(2) *a* of the 1978 Act had no application to her claim and that accordingly the industrial tribunal had jurisdiction to hear it under s 67(1).

On 9 September 1994 the chairman of the industrial tribunal sitting at Exeter held a preliminary hearing to decide whether the tribunal had jurisdiction to hear her claim. In his reserved decision, which was sent to the parties on 22 September 1994, the chairman referred to the statutory time limit within which a claim is to *b* be presented. He noted that the limit of three months specified in s 67(2) of the 1978 Act was the same as that contained in Sch 1 to the 1974 Act. Section 67(2) is in these terms:

'... an industrial tribunal shall not consider a complaint under this section unless it is presented to the tribunal before the end of the period of three *c* months beginning with the effective date of termination or within such further period as the tribunal considers reasonable in a case where it is satisfied that it was not reasonably practicable for the complaint to be presented before the end of the period of three months.'

The chairman found that the claim had not been presented within three *d* months of the effective date of termination of her employment and that it had not been reasonably practicable for Mrs Biggs to present her claim within that time. He said that she had been prevented from doing so by Sch 13 to the 1978 Act and its predecessor in the 1974 Act—that is the provisions which excluded part-time employees from bringing claims for compensation for unfair dismissal. He then turned to consider whether any further period for the presentation of the claim *e* was reasonable. In the course of his decision he expressed this general opinion:

'It seems to me that it is impossible to suppose that it is now just to permit a claim for unfair dismissal to be presented 18 years after the events took place. Memories will have faded, probably completely. Those responsible for the employment may have retired or died, or changed posts. Records *f* may have been destroyed. Businesses may have changed ownership— possibly more than once. The very identity of the applicant may be unknown to the respondent.'

He concluded that he did not think that any further period was reasonable. *g*

In addition the chairman, in his careful decision, dealt with a number of other arguments which had been addressed to him, but in the end decided that Mrs Biggs' claim was barred by the time limit in s 67(2) and he dismissed her application.

Mrs Biggs then appealed to the Employment Appeal Tribunal. The appeal was heard on 23 February 1995. Meanwhile on 6 February 1995 the Employment *h* Protection (Part-time Employees) Regulations 1995, SI 1995/31, came into force. These regulations removed the provisions of the 1978 Act and the Trade Union and Labour Relations (Consolidation) Act 1992 which excluded part-time employees from rights under those Acts. The regulations thus ensured compliance with art 119 and with the equal pay directive and the equal treatment *j* directive. The regulations were made under s 2(2) of the European Communities Act 1972.

The judgment of the Employment Appeal Tribunal ([1995] ICR 811) was delivered on 6 July 1995.

The appeal to the Appeal Tribunal was on two main grounds. First, that the chairman erred in law in applying UK domestic law time limits to a claim under a art 119 of the EC Treaty. Second, if domestic law time limits did apply, it was perverse of the chairman and therefore an error of law to refuse to extend the time limit so as to enable the applicant to bring her claim for unfair dismissal.

In the course of the judgment of the Employment Appeal Tribunal, Mummery J underlined the importance of the EOC case and the impact that it might have on a wide variety of claims. Among the examples he gave were: (a) cases by
b claimants like Mrs Biggs who had not brought any earlier proceedings because their normal weekly hours of work were below the statutory minimum for claims for unfair dismissal; (b) cases which had been brought by part-time workers but which had failed because of the statutory threshold. In such cases questions might arise as to whether leave to appeal could be granted out of time and whether the principle of res judicata might bar any fresh claim; and (c) cases
c where claimants might wish to bring proceedings for damages for failure to implement fully into the domestic law of the United Kingdom the provisions of the equal treatment directive. The judgment was therefore wide-ranging in its consideration of the relevant principles of Community law and we are grateful to Mummery J for the light which his judgment has cast on this difficult subject.

d For the purposes of this judgment, however, I think it is sufficient to state the main conclusions which were reached by the Employment Appeal Tribunal. I can do this by referring to passages in the judgment, where Mummery J said ([1995] ICR 811 at 826–828):

e '(1) The applicant's claim against the council, as her former employer, is a private law claim for compensation for unfair dismissal ...

(2) Prima facie, a claim for unfair dismissal is brought under United Kingdom domestic law. There is no Community right not to be unfairly dismissed ... The [domestic] legislation lays down the conditions, including time limits for the making of claims, relevant to the enforcement of the right.

f (3) The domestic legislation also designates the courts to which the complaints of unfair dismissal may be presented, i.e., an industrial tribunal under section 67(1) of the Act of 1978, and places limits on the jurisdiction of that tribunal. The industrial tribunal has no general (or inherent) jurisdiction, separate and apart from that conferred by domestic statutes ... It has no jurisdiction to entertain claims for unfair dismissal presented
g outside the time limit of three months, unless that period is extended in appropriate cases to such period as the tribunal considers reasonable. Thus, if the claim is not made under the Act of 1978 and is not made within the time limit in that Act, as extended, it cannot be decided by the industrial tribunal.

(4) An industrial tribunal may, within the scope of its statutory
h jurisdiction, administer, apply and enforce not only United Kingdom domestic law but also Community law ... Thus, in the exercise of its statutory jurisdiction, the industrial tribunal is bound to apply and enforce relevant Community law, and disapply an offending provision of United Kingdom domestic legislation to the extent that it is incompatible with
j Community law, in order to give effect to its obligation to safeguard enforceable Community rights.

(5) In 1976 the industrial tribunal had a jurisdiction, at the suit of those with directly effective rights, to disapply the qualifying threshold conditions for weekly hours in the Act of 1978 and previous legislation incompatible with Community law ... The industrial tribunal has jurisdiction to disapply other provisions in United Kingdom domestic law, such as those relating to

procedure, compensation, time limits and so on if they offend against, and *a* are incompatible with, Community law.

(6) Prima facie, the time limits contained in United Kingdom domestic law apply to unfair dismissal claims, even where those claims invoke directly enforceable Community rights such as those conferred by article 119. In accordance with general principles of Community law, Community rights enforced in the national courts are subject to the procedural conditions and *b* time limits laid down by national rules.

(7) The time limits contained in the employment legislation, such as the Act of 1978, are not incompatible with Community law. The industrial tribunal chairman was right not to disapply them. There are no relevant time limits in domestic law or Community law expressly stated to apply to *c* article 119. That does *not* mean that there are *no* time limits. In accordance with the principles of Community law, the time limits are those applicable to "similar actions of a domestic nature."... The domestic law time limits apply, unless it can be shown that they are less favourable than those relating to similar actions of a domestic nature or are such as to make it impossible in practice to exercise the rights under article 119. That has not been shown in *d* this case. The time limits are of general application. They do not discriminate between claims for unfair dismissal under the domestic law and claims which invoke Community law. It was not in practice impossible to invoke the rights under article 119. It was possible by virtue of the decision in *Defrenne v. Sabena* (Case 43/75) ([1981] 1 All ER 122, [1976] ECR 455) ... for *e* the applicant to present her complaint of unfair dismissal to the industrial tribunal within three months of her being dismissed and to argue then that the qualifying conditions in United Kingdom domestic law at that time were ineffective barriers to her claim by reason of their incompatibility with article 119. It was recognised in the E.O.C. case ([1994] 1 All ER 910, [1995] 1 AC 1) that the claim in that case made by the individual, Mrs. Day, would fall *f* within the jurisdiction of the industrial tribunal which would have power to disapply the qualifying conditions which offended against article 119 so that effect could have been given to her claim. The applicant relies on the declaration in the E.O.C. case as having retrospective effect, enabling her to complain of a dismissal before 3 March 1994. It is implicit in that *g* retrospectivity that she could have brought her case when she was dismissed or within three months. She did not.' (Mummery J's emphasis.)

Mrs Biggs' appeal was therefore dismissed. It is clear that the Employment Appeal Tribunal considered that it had been reasonably practicable for Mrs Biggs to have presented her complaint within three months of her dismissal in 1976. *h*

THE CASE FOR MRS BIGGS ON HER APPEAL

The argument for Mrs Biggs was advanced under three headings. (a) That it was not reasonably practicable for her to have presented her claim within three months following her dismissal in 1976. She presented her claim within a *j* reasonable period thereafter. (b) Alternatively, that the industrial tribunal was bound by principles of Community law to disapply the time limits imposed by s 67(2) of the 1978 Act. (c) Alternatively, that Mrs Biggs can rely on her rights (which are directly enforceable rights) under art 119, to which s 67 has no application.

It will be convenient to deal with these arguments in turn.

a   *Whether it was reasonably practicable to present a claim in 1976*
      Mr Goudie QC developed his argument on behalf of Mrs Biggs as follows.
      (1) In 1976 any claim for a finding of unfair dismissal was doomed to failure
      because the right not to be unfairly dismissed did not apply to any employment
      under a contract which normally involved employment for less than 21 hours
      weekly (see para 9(1)(f) of Sch 1 to the Trade Union and Labour Relations Act
b   1974).
      (2) In 1976 Mrs Biggs could not reasonably have been expected to be aware of
      the existence of her directly effective rights under art 119 or of her right to assert
      that para 9(1)(f) should be disapplied.
      (3) The fact that Mrs Biggs would have been unaware of her rights was
      because the United Kingdom was in breach of its obligations under art 5 of the
c   EEC Treaty in failing to ensure that the provisions of national legislation were
      efficient to make individuals fully aware of their rights.
      We were referred to art 5, which is in these terms:

d   'Member States shall take all appropriate measures, whether general or
      particular, to ensure fulfilment of the obligations arising out of this Treaty or
      resulting from action taken by the institutions of the Community. They shall
      facilitate the achievement of the Community's tasks. They shall abstain
      from any measure which could jeopardize the attainment of the objectives
      of this Treaty.'

e   I see the force of this argument. Moreover in 1976 the impact and importance
      of s 2 of the European Communities Act 1972 was not widely known. Nor was
      the decision in *Defrenne v Sabena* Case 43/75 [1981] 1 All ER 122, [1976] ECR 455
      fully understood or taken into account even by the legal profession.
      It is also necessary to consider the way in which the words 'reasonably
      practicable' in s 67(2) have been construed in other cases. In *Palmer v*
f   *Southend-on-Sea BC* [1984] 1 All ER 945, [1984] 1 WLR 1129 the Court of Appeal,
      in a judgment delivered by May LJ, considered a number of the earlier cases in
      which the meaning of the words had been examined. The court summarised the
      matter as follows:

g   'In the end, most of the decided cases have been decisions on their own
      particular facts and must be regarded as such. However we think that one
      can say that to construe the words "reasonably practicable" as the equivalent
      of "reasonable" is to take a view too favourable to the employee. On the
      other hand "reasonably practicable" means more than merely what is
      reasonably capable physically of being done, different, for instance, from its
h   construction in the context of the legislation relating to factories ... In the
      context in which the words are used in the 1978 consolidation Act, however,
      ineptly as we think, they mean something between these two. Perhaps to
      read the word "practicable" as the equivalent of "feasible" as Brightman J did
      in [*Singh v Post Office* [1973] ICR 437] and to ask colloquially and
j   untrammelled by too much legal logic, "Was it reasonably feasible to present
      the complaint to the industrial tribunal within the relevant three months?" is
      the best approach to the correct application of the relevant subsection.
      What, however, is abundantly clear on all the authorities is that the answer
      to the relevant question is pre-eminently an issue of fact for the industrial
      tribunal and that it is seldom that an appeal from its decision will lie.
      Dependent on the circumstances of the particular case, an industrial tribunal

may wish to consider the manner in which and reason for which the employee was dismissed, including the extent to which, if at all, the employer's conciliatory appeals machinery has been used. It will no doubt investigate what was the substantial cause of the employee's failure to comply with the statutory time limit; whether he had been physically prevented from complying with the limitation period, for instance by illness or a postal strike, or something similar. It may be relevant for the industrial tribunal to investigate whether at the time when he was dismissed, and if not then when thereafter, he knew that he had the right to complain that he had been unfairly dismissed; in some cases the tribunal may have to consider whether there has been any misrepresentation about any relevant matter by the employer to the employee. It will frequently be necessary for it to know whether the employee was being advised at any material time and, if so, by whom; of the extent of the advisers' knowledge of the facts of the employee's case; and of the nature of any advice which they may have given to him. In any event it will probably be relevant in most cases for the industrial tribunal to ask itself whether there has been any substantial fault on the part of the employee or his adviser which has led to the failure to comply with the statutory time limit. Any list of possible relevant considerations, however, cannot be exhaustive and, as we have stressed, at the end of the day the matter is one of fact for the industrial tribunal taking all the circumstances of the given case into account.' (See [1984] 1 All ER 945 at 955, [1984] 1 WLR 1129 at 1141–1142.)

Moreover, it is right to take account of the fact that in the cases decided before and since *Palmer's* case the words 'reasonably practicable' have been construed quite liberally.

In the end, however, I have been driven to the conclusion that, if the words 'reasonably practicable' are properly construed in their context, Mummery J was correct in concluding that it was reasonably practicable for Mrs Biggs to have made her claim within the time prescribed. Her mistake as to what her rights were was, as has now been made clear, a mistake of law. It was not a mistake of fact.

The decision in the *EOC* case [1994] 1 All ER 910, [1995] 1 AC 1 was declaratory of what the law has always been ever since the primacy of Community law was established by s 2 of the 1972 Act. Indeed, as Mummery J pointed out, Mrs Biggs relies on the retrospective effect of the *EOC* case. Accordingly, since 1 January 1973, and certainly since the decision of the Court of Justice in *Defrenne v Sabena*, there was no legal impediment preventing someone who claimed that he had been unfairly dismissed from presenting a claim and arguing that the restriction on claims by part-time workers was indirectly discriminatory.

It seems to me that in the context of s 67 the words 'reasonably practicable' are directed to difficulties faced by an individual claimant. Illness provides an obvious example. In the case of illness the claimant may well be able successfully to assert that it was not 'reasonably practicable' to present a claim within three months. But the words 'reasonably practicable', when read in conjunction with a 'reasonable' period thereafter, point to some temporary impediment or hindrance. It is to be noted that in the *EOC* case Lord Keith expressed the view that Mrs Day, who was an individual party to the proceedings, could bring her private law claim for a redundancy payment before an industrial tribunal and argue there that the restrictions imposed on part-time workers were not

a objectively justified and should be disapplied (see [1994] 1 All ER 910 at 917–918,
   [1995] 1 AC 1 at 25). Mrs Biggs could have taken a similar course in 1976.
      I have found this to be an anxious point because Mrs Biggs' employment came
   to an end in 1976. At that time it had been the generally accepted doctrine for
   centuries that courts and tribunals were required to apply the law as passed by
   Parliament. The fact that after 1 January 1973 Acts of Parliament and other UK
b legislation might have to yield to provisions determined by a different and
   superior system of law was, I suspect, fully appreciated only by a comparatively
   small number of people. But in my view it would be contrary to the principle of
   legal certainty to allow past transactions to be reopened and limitation periods to
   be circumvented because *the existing law* at the relevant time had not yet been
   explained or had not been fully understood.
c   If this analysis is correct, it follows that the fact that it was not until 3 March
   1994 that the House of Lords declared that the threshold provisions in the 1978
   Act were indirectly discriminatory, unless objectively justified, cannot be taken
   into account as a ground for arguing that it was not 'reasonably practicable'
   before that date to present a claim within the time limit.
d   If, however, this analysis is not correct, I would respectfully agree with the
   chairman of the industrial tribunal that the claim by Mrs Biggs was not presented
   within a reasonable period after the expiry of the time limit. In deciding what is
   a reasonable further period for the purpose of para 21(4) of Sch 1 to the 1974 Act
   and s 67(2) of the 1978 Act, the tribunal has to take all the circumstances into
   account in order to achieve a fair balance. At this stage the tribunal is not
e concerned only with the difficulties faced by the claimant. An extended further
   period may be unreasonable if the employer were to face difficulties of substance
   in answering the claim.
      I would therefore reject Mr Goudie's first argument.

f *Whether the industrial tribunal should have disapplied the time limits*
      It was argued in the alternative on behalf of Mrs Biggs that whatever the
   position might be according to the UK legislation if considered in isolation,
   domestic tribunals and courts had to disapply time limits if the application of the
   limits made it impossible in practice to enforce a Community right. In this
g context we were referred to a number of cases decided by the Court of Justice.
      In *Rewe-Zentralfinanz eG v Landwirtschaftskammer für das Saarland* Case 33/76
   [1976] ECR 1989 the Court of Justice was concerned with customs duties. The
   first question for consideration was whether a member state, which had, in
   breach of Community law, exacted from a trader a charge having an effect
   equivalent to a customs duty, might rely on a limitation period prescribed by its
h own national law. In dealing with this question the court said ([1976] ECR 1989
   at 1997–1998 (para 5)):

      '... in the absence of Community rules on this subject, it is for the domestic
      legal system of each Member State to designate courts having jurisdiction
j   and to determine the procedural conditions governing actions at law
      intended to ensure the protection of the rights which citizens have from the
      direct effect of Community law, it being understood that such conditions
      cannot be less favourable than those relating to similar actions of a domestic
      nature ... The position would be different only if the conditions and
      time-limits made it impossible in practice to exercise the rights which the
      national courts are obliged to protect ... The laying down of such time-limits

with regard to actions of a fiscal nature is an application of the fundamental   a
principle of legal certainty protecting both the tax-payer and the
administration concerned.'

A similar principle limiting the right of national courts to restrict the recovery
of charges levied contrary to Community law was considered in *Amministrazione
delle Finanze dello Stato v SpA San Giorgio* Case 199/82 [1983] ECR 3595. In that
case the member state had made the repayment of charges conditional upon   b
proof that those charges had not been passed on to other persons. The Court of
Justice held that Community law did not prevent a national legal system from
disallowing the repayment of charges where to do so would entail unjust
enrichment of the recipients, but added that the conditions as to recovery—

'may not be less favourable than those relating to similar claims regarding   c
national charges and they may not be so framed as to render virtually
impossible the exercise of rights conferred by Community law.' (See [1983]
ECR 3595 at 3612 (para 12).)

Statements to the same effect can be found in other cases including *Johnson v*   d
Chief Adjudication Officer (No 2) Case C-410/92 [1995] All ER (EC) 258 at 276,
[1994] ECR I-5483 at 5509 (para 21) and *Francovich v Italy* Joined cases C-6/90 and
C-9/90 [1991] ECR I-5357 at 5416 (para 43), where it was said that the conditions
for reparation of loss and damage laid down by the national law 'must not be so
framed as to make it virtually impossible or excessively difficult to obtain
reparation'.   e

It was therefore argued on behalf of Mrs Biggs that the statutory time limit
should be disapplied because its application would run counter to the principle
that it must not be impossible or extremely difficult to present a claim.

In my judgment, however, this argument too must be rejected. Section 2 of
the 1972 Act recognises the primacy of Community law. Accordingly, as I have   f
already stated, persons in the position of Mrs Biggs were able to present a claim
by invoking Community law and s 2 of the 1972 Act so as to ensure that the
restriction on claims by part-time workers was disapplied. Furthermore, the time
limit itself does not offend Community law and indeed is compatible with the
principle of legal certainty.

I appreciate the hardship which may be caused to individual claimants, but I   g
can see no satisfactory basis for disapplying a time limit to enable a claim to be
advanced which as a matter of law was capable of being enforced at the moment
of dismissal. I am not persuaded that one can relax a time limit to assist a claimant
who was ignorant of the law, when the same time limit would have to be
enforced against a claimant in a similar situation who was fully aware of his or her   h
legal rights including the right to rely on the principle in *Defrenne v Sabena* Case
43/75 [1981] 1 All ER 122, [1976] ECR 455.

Whether Mrs Biggs can rely on her rights under art 119

In the further alternative it was argued that Mrs Biggs could rely on her directly   .
enforceable rights under art 119. Neither s 67(2) of the 1978 Act (nor its   j
predecessor) has any application to directly enforceable Community rights. In
addition it was argued that in any event no time limits could be relied upon until
UK legislation had been brought into line with Community law. This was not
done until the 1995 regulations came into force on 6 February 1995.

Article 119 is in these terms:

a 'Each Member State shall during the first stage ensure and subsequently maintain the application of the principle that men and women should receive equal pay for equal work.

For the purposes of this Article, "pay" means the ordinary basic or minimum wage or salary and any other consideration, whether in cash or in kind, which the worker receives, directly or indirectly, in respect of his
b employment from his employer.

Equal pay without discrimination based on sex means: (a) that pay for the same work at piece rates shall be calculated on the basis of the same unit of measurement; (b) that pay for work at time rates shall be the same for the same job.'

c   As I have already noted, it is accepted for the purpose of the present proceedings that compensation for unfair dismissal constitutes 'pay' within the meaning of art 119. But it does not seem to me that art 119 assists Mrs Biggs in the present case. It is true, on the concession which has been made, that art 119 prohibits sex discrimination in relation to compensation for unfair dismissal. The
d article, however, does not confer a right to compensation for unfair dismissal where there is no sex discrimination. The difficulty in Mrs Biggs' path is the procedural rule of limitation which governs the bringing of a claim, but this rule by itself does not involve any element of sex discrimination.

In 1976 Mrs Biggs could have relied on art 119 to circumvent the rule as to the disqualification of part-time workers. But art 119 does not provide a separate
e claim for compensation for unfair dismissal. Moreover, even if such a separate basis of claim existed, it would not fall within the jurisdiction of an industrial tribunal.

I turn therefore to the argument based on *Emmott v Minister for Social Welfare* Case C-208/90 [1991] ECR I-4269. In that case Mrs Emmott brought proceedings
f against the Minister for Social Welfare in Ireland claiming that the relevant domestic legislation had not correctly transposed the principle of equal treatment of men and women in matters of social security contained in Directive 79/7 on the progressive implementation of the principle of equal treatment for men and women in matters of social security. The question which was referred to the Court of Justice was whether the member state could rely on a time limit laid
g down in national law to preclude Mrs Emmott from initiating proceedings. In an important decision the court held:

'... until such time as a directive has been properly transposed, a defaulting Member State may not rely on an individual's delay in initiating proceedings against it in order to protect rights conferred upon him by the provisions of
h the directive and that a period laid down by national law within which proceedings must be initiated cannot begin to run before that time.' (See [1991] ECR I-4269 at 4299 (para 23).)

In reliance on *Emmott's* case it was argued on behalf of Mrs Biggs that the
j council could not rely on any time limit until UK law had been brought into conformity with Community law.

It is necessary to consider this argument first in relation to art 119. It is clear from the decision of the Court of Justice in *Francovich v Italy* Joined cases C-6/90 and C-9/90 [1991] ECR I-5357 that even where a directive is capable of having direct effect, an individual cannot rely on its terms while the directive is unimplemented. Until implemented it has no force of law in the relevant

jurisdiction, though the fact that it has not been implemented may give rights to   *a*
compensation. The nature of these rights are at present under consideration by
the Court of Justice in *R v Secretary of State for Transport, ex p Factortame Ltd*; it is to
be noted that the Advocate General delivered his opinion in this case on 28
November 1995.[d] But a provision in the Treaty itself which has direct effect
stands on a different basis. Thus, the validity of art 119 in UK law does not depend
on any implementation by the UK Parliament; it is part of UK law. It follows   *b*
therefore in my view that the principle set out in *Emmott's* case has no application
to a claim involving art 119. Indeed it is to be noted that in the judgment in
Emmott's case [1991] ECR I-4269 at 4298 (para 17) attention was drawn to the
'particular nature of directives'.

     I turn next to the equal pay directive (Directive 75/117). Can it be argued that
a separate claim may be made under the equal pay directive which is not subject   *c*
to any time limit until UK law has been brought into conformity with
Community law? I am satisfied that such an argument must be rejected. The
principle that men and women should receive equal pay was set out in art 119 of
the Treaty. The equal pay directive was adopted in order to implement the
principle in art 119. In these circumstances it does not seem to me that the equal   *d*
pay directive conferred any new or separate right. It follows that in the
circumstances of this case I can see no room for the application of the *Emmott*
principle to the equal pay directive.

CONCLUSION
     For these reasons I consider that the Employment Appeal Tribunal reached the   *e*
correct decision. I would dismiss the appeal.

AULD LJ. I agree.

SIR IAIN GLIDEWELL. I agree that this appeal should be dismissed for the   *f*
reasons set out in the judgment of Neill LJ, which I have read in draft. I wish,
however, to add a short observation on the third issue, namely whether Mrs
Biggs is entitled to rely on a directly enforceable right given her by art 119 of the
EC Treaty, to which the time limits contained in s 67(2) of the Employment
Protection (Consolidation) Act 1978 have no application.   *g*
     Article 119 is transposed into English law by s 2(1) of the European
Communities Act 1972. The effect of the decision of the House of Lords in *Equal
Opportunities Commission v Secretary of State for Employment* [1994] 1 All ER 910,
[1995] 1 AC 1 (the *EOC* case) is that, by virtue of art 119, any person of either sex
has a right not to be discriminated against unfairly in relation to a claim for
redundancy pay. On the assumption accepted for the purposes of this appeal but   *h*
not as yet decided, that compensation for unfair dismissal is 'pay' within the
meaning of art 119, a person of either sex also has a right not to be unfairly
dismissed by reason of unfair discrimination.
     What art 119 does not do is to provide any remedy for breach of this right. The
remedy is provided by national law in this country by the 1978 Act, which   *j*
provides the procedure for a claim for unfair dismissal (see *Rewe-Zentralfinanz eG
v Landwirtschaftskammer für das Saarland* Case 33/76 [1976] ECR 1989 and the *EOC*

---

d   The Court of Justice has since given its decision in *Factortame* (see *Brasserie du Pêcheur SA v Germany,
R v Secretary of State for Transport, ex p Factortame Ltd* Joined cases C-46/93 and C-48/93 [1996] All ER
(EC) 301).

a case [1994] 1 All ER 910 at 917–918, [1995] 1 AC at 25 per Lord Keith of Kinkel in relation to the claim of Mrs Day). Such a claim, however, is subject to the time limits in s 67(2) of the 1978 Act.

In my judgment, therefore, whether the correct analysis of the application of art 119 to the facts of the present case is that it disapplies the restrictive provisions contained in para 9 of Sch 1 to the Trade Union and Labour Relations Act 1974,

b or that the article grants a right which is directly enforceable, the effect is the same. On either analysis, the remedy is the statutory right to make a claim for unfair dismissal, now contained in the 1978 Act. For the reasons explained by Neill LJ, that remedy is and was available to Mrs Biggs only subject to the time limits in s 67(2).

c *Appeal dismissed. Leave to appeal to the House of Lords refused.*

Paul Magrath Esq   Barrister.

Barber v Staffordshire County Council

COURT OF APPEAL, CIVIL DIVISION

NEILL, AULD LJJ AND SIR IAIN GLIDEWELL

6, 7 NOVEMBER 1995, 26 JANUARY 1996

Estoppel – Issue estoppel – Dismissal of application – Applicant withdrawing application – Whether applicant estopped from raising same issue in second action – Whether applicant estopped from raising new issue which could have been raised in original application.

Industrial tribunal – Procedure – Decision – Res judicata – Tribunal decision dismissing application without hearing evidence or argument – Whether principles of issue and cause of action estoppel applicable.

In 1992 B was dismissed from her employment as a part-time teacher at two of the local authority's schools. She lodged a claim with the industrial tribunal seeking a redundancy payment, but did not seek compensation for unfair dismissal. In order to satisfy the relevant statutory conditions relating to the minimum hours of work per week required to support a claim, B aggregated her hours of work from the separate contracts of employment. However, before the hearing B was advised that she was not entitled to aggregate the hours under separate concurrent contracts with the same employer. B therefore elected to withdraw her claim and at the hearing in May 1993 the industrial tribunal dismissed the proceedings without hearing any evidence or argument. In May 1994, following a House of Lords decision that the relevant statutory provisions were incompatible with provisions of Community law relating to part-time workers, B presented a further application, seeking a redundancy payment and also compensation for unfair dismissal. The tribunal held that the principle of res judicata did not prevent B from proceeding with her claim. The Employment Appeal Tribunal allowed the local authority's subsequent appeal, holding that the principles of cause of action and issue estoppel applied to an application which had been withdrawn and that B was precluded from pursuing her claim for unfair dismissal by the doctrine of res judicata in the wider sense, namely that it would be an abuse of the process of the court to raise in subsequent proceedings matters which could and should have been litigated in earlier proceedings. B appealed.

Held – The appeal would be dismissed for the following reasons—

(1) The principles of cause of action or issue estoppel applied to an industrial tribunal application which had been formally dismissed following its withdrawal by the applicant, and the fact that the tribunal had heard no evidence or argument on the issues of fact and law did not prevent such a decision operating by way of res judicata. It followed that the order of May 1993 was a judicial decision made by the industrial tribunal in the exercise of its statutory powers and not a mere administrative act, and in the absence of any exceptional circumstances B was thereby prevented from bringing a further claim for a redundancy payment (see p 756 *a* to *c* and p 757 *h*, post); *SCF Finance Co Ltd v Masri (No 3) (Masri, garnishee)* [1987] 1 All ER 194 and *Arnold v National Westminster Bank plc* [1991] 3 All ER 41 applied.

a   (2) It was possible in special circumstances to allow a claim to be put forward which was not the subject of res judicata in the strict sense but which could have been brought forward in some earlier proceedings, where it would in effect be an abuse of process if permission were refused. However, relaxation of the rule did not assist B, since the qualifying conditions for her claim for a redundancy payment were the same as those for a claim for compensation for unfair
b   dismissal, so that it was not the statutory provisions which had prevented the addition of the second claim (see p 757 *c* to *h*, post); *Arnold v National Westminster Bank plc* [1991] 3 All ER 41 considered.

Notes

For the doctrine of res judicata and issue estoppel, see 16 *Halsbury's Laws* (4th edn
c   reissue) paras 953, 974–982, and for cases on the subject, see 21(2) *Digest* (2nd reissue) 12–14, 70–81, 95, 45–54, 406–445, 536–537.

Cases referred to in judgments

Arnold v National Westminster Bank plc [1991] 3 All ER 41, [1991] 2 AC 93, [1991] 2
d   WLR 1177, HL.
Biggs v Somerset CC [1995] ICR 811, EAT; *affd* [1996] 2 All ER 734, CA.
Blaik v Post Office [1994] IRLR 280, EAT.
Brasserie du Pêcheur SA v Germany, R v Secretary of State for Transport, ex p Factortame Ltd Joined cases C-46/93 and C-48/93 [1996] All ER (EC) 301, ECJ.
Emmott v Minister for Social Welfare Case C-208/90 [1991] ECR I-4269.
e   *Equal Opportunities Commission v Secretary of State for Employment* [1994] 1 All ER 910, [1995] 1 AC 1, [1994] 2 WLR 176, HL.
Francovich v Italy Joined Cases C-6/90 and C-9/90 [1991] ECR I-5357.
Henderson v Henderson (1843) 3 Hare 100, [1843–60] All ER Rep 378, 67 ER 313, V-C.
f   *Hines v Birkbeck College (No 2)* [1991] 4 All ER 450, [1992] Ch 33, [1991] 3 WLR 557, CA.
Khan v Goleccha International Ltd [1980] 2 All ER 259, [1980] 1 WLR 1482, CA.
SCF Finance Co Ltd v Masri (No 3) (Masri, garnishee) [1987] 1 All ER 194, [1987] QB 1028, [1987] 2 WLR 81, CA.
g   *Surrey CC v Lewis* [1987] 3 All ER 641, [1988] AC 323, [1987] 3 WLR 927, HL.
Talbot v Berkshire CC [1993] 4 All ER 9, [1994] QB 290, [1993] 3 WLR 708, CA.
Thoday v Thoday [1964] 1 All ER 341, [1964] P 181, [1964] 2 WLR 371, CA.

Cases also cited or referred to in skeleton arguments

h   *Brisbane City Council v A-G for Queensland* [1978] 3 All ER 30, [1979] AC 411, PC.
Carl-Zeiss-Stiftung v Rayner and Keeler Ltd (No 2) [1966] 2 All ER 536, [1967] AC 853, HL.
Coates v C J Crispin Ltd [1973] ICR 413, NIRC.
EC Commission v France Case 169/87 [1988] ECR 4093.
j   *EC Commission v Germany* Case 29/84 [1985] ECR 1661.
Factortame Ltd v Secretary of State for Transport (No 2) Case C-213/89 [1991] 1 All ER 70, [1991] 1 AC 603, [1990] ECR I-2433, ECJ and HL.
Hoystead v Taxation Comr [1926] AC 155, [1925] All ER Rep 56, PC.
Land v Land [1949] 2 All ER 218, [1949] P 405, DC.
Macarthys Ltd v Smith Case 129/79 [1981] 1 All ER 111, [1981] QB 180, [1980] ECR 1275, ECJ and CA.

Marshall v Southampton and South West Hampshire Area Health Authority (No 2) Case
  C-271/91 [1993] 4 All ER 586, [1994] QB 126, [1993] ECR I-4367, ECJ; *ruling*   *a*
  applied [1994] 1 All ER 736, [1994] AC 530, HL.
Munir v Jang Publications Ltd [1989] ICR 1, CA.
Setiya v East Yorkshire Health Authority [1995] ICR 799, EAT.
South American and Mexican Co Ltd, Re, ex p Bank of England [1895] 1 Ch 37, [1891–4]
  All ER Rep 680, CA.   *b*
Thomas v University of Bradford [1986] 1 All ER 217, [1986] Ch 381, CA; *rvsd* [1987]
  1 All ER 834, [1987] AC 795, HL.
Times Newspapers Ltd v Fitt [1981] ICR 637, EAT.
Yat Tung Investment Co Ltd v Dao Heng Bank Ltd [1975] AC 581, [1975] 2 WLR 690,
  PC.   *c*

Appeal
By notice dated 2 November 1995 Mary Andra Roberta Barber appealed with
leave from the decision of the Employment Appeal Tribunal (Mummery J, Mr J
A Scouller and Mr A C Blyghton) on 30 October 1995 whereby it allowed an   *d*
appeal by the respondent, Staffordshire County Council (Mrs Barber's former
employer), from the decision of an industrial tribunal held at Birmingham dated
10 November 1994 that Mrs Barber was entitled to proceed with a claim seeking
redundancy payments and compensation for unfair dismissal before the tribunal
under provisions of Community law and that her claim was not subject to res
judicata. The facts are set out in the judgment of Neill LJ.   *e*

James Goudie QC (instructed by *Bindman & Partners*) for Mrs Barber.
T Brendan Hegarty QC and *Joanne Connolly* (instructed by *David Wright*) for the
  council.

Cur adv vult   *f*

26 January 1996. The following judgments were delivered.

NEILL LJ. On 3 March 1994 the House of Lords, in a decision of great
significance in the field of employment law, made declarations that certain   *g*
provisions of the Employment Protection (Consolidation) Act 1978 relating to
part-time employees were incompatible with art 119 of the EC Treaty, Council
Directive EEC 75/117 (the equal pay directive) and Council Directive EEC 76/
207 (the equal treatment directive). The declarations were made in judicial
review proceedings instituted in June 1990 by the Equal Opportunities   *h*
Commission (see *Equal Opportunities Commission v Secretary of State for Employment*
[1994] 1 All ER 910, [1995] 1 AC 1 (the EOC case)).
     On 3 May 1994 Mrs Barber instituted the present proceedings against
Staffordshire County Council seeking redundancy payments and awards of
compensation for unfair dismissal. The claims were based on the termination of   *j*
three contracts of part-time employment whereby Mrs Barber was formerly
employed by the council as a teacher. The three contracts of employment related
to her employment at (a) Manifold Primary School from 1 September 1984 to 31
August 1992; (b) St Leonard's Primary School, Ipstones, from 1 September 1989
to 31 August 1992; and (c) St Bartholomew's Primary School, Longnor, from
1 September 1986 to 31 August 1993. This appeal is concerned only with the

termination of Mrs Barber's employment at Manifold Primary School and at St
a Leonard's Primary School.

At the time of her dismissal from Manifold Primary School Mrs Barber was
required to work there for three hours a week. At St Leonard's Primary School
she was required to work for about three and a half hours a week. Following her
dismissal from these two schools on 31 August 1992 Mrs Barber sought legal
b advice from her union. She was advised that her hours of work could be
aggregated and that in this aggregation account could also be taken of the fact
that at St Bartholomew's Primary School she was required to work for about
seven hours a week. Accordingly, on 2 November 1992 Mrs Barber presented an
originating application to the industrial tribunal. Her complaint was that she had
been dismissed from her posts in the two schools by reason of redundancy. She
c had sought, but had not received, a redundancy payment. No claim was made
by Mrs Barber for compensation for unfair dismissal.

The claim for a redundancy payment was listed for hearing on 5 May 1993. On
4 May 1993, however, the representative acting for Mrs Barber became aware of
the decision of the House of Lords in *Surrey CC v Lewis* [1987] 3 All ER 641, [1988]
d AC 323, where it was held that it was impermissible to aggregate the hours
worked per week under separate concurrent contracts with the same employer.
There then followed some discussion between Mrs Barber and the council, and
as a result Mrs Barber stated that she would withdraw her claim. On the same
day a letter was sent on behalf of the council to the regional office of the industrial
e tribunal in Birmingham stating:

'... [Mrs Barber's representative] has indicated his intention to withdraw
the application due to be heard tomorrow, 5 May ... and in turn I have
indicated I would have no application to make on behalf of Staffordshire
County Council. Therefore, on the understanding that in these
f circumstances the application will now be dismissed I do not propose to
attend tomorrow's hearing.'

Accordingly, at the hearing on 5 May 1993 Mrs Barber's application was
withdrawn, and in accordance with r 12(2)(c) of Sch 1 to the Industrial Tribunals
g (Rules of Procedure) Regulations 1985, SI 1985/16, the tribunal dismissed the
proceedings. The reason why Mrs Barber withdrew her claim was because
without aggregation she could not satisfy the statutory conditions relating to the
minimum hours of work per week required to support a claim.

The hearing on 5 May 1993 was before a chairman and two lay members. No
h evidence was heard. It is clear, however, that the tribunal reached a decision and
that the decision was signed by the chairman in accordance with the industrial
tribunal rules. The decision was entered in the register and copies were sent to
the parties on 18 May 1993. The decision as recorded was in these terms: 'The
unanimous decision of the Tribunal is that this application is dismissed on
j withdrawal by the applicant.'

As I have already mentioned, following the decision in the *EOC* case, on 3 May
1994 Mrs Barber presented a further application. On 22 June 1994 the council
submitted a notice of appearance resisting the claim and stating that Mrs Barber
was fairly dismissed on the ground of redundancy. In addition the council raised
a plea of res judicata which was framed in these terms:

'(2) The application relates to the same termination of employment as was dealt with in application 61096/92, an application that was dismissed on *a* withdrawal by the applicant.'

It is to be noted that Mrs Barber did not make any application to the industrial tribunal to exercise its powers to review the decision of 5 May 1993 'in the interests of justice'.

Mrs Barber's application came before the chairman of the industrial tribunal *b* sitting alone on an interlocutory hearing held on 24 August 1994.

On 10 November 1994 copies of the chairman's decision were sent to the parties. By his decision the chairman concluded that no part of the proceedings was subject to res judicata and that no question of cause of action or issue estoppel arose. He held therefore that Mrs Barber was entitled to proceed with a *c* claim under art 119 of the EC Treaty, the equal pay directive and the equal treatment directive. In his extended reasons, to which one must pay tribute for their clarity and for their careful identification of the issues, the chairman set out the grounds on which he had reached his decision. In para 11 of the reasons the chairman referred to a passage in the opinion of Lord Keith of Kinkel in the *EOC* case [1994] 1 All ER 910 at 917–918, [1995] 1 AC 1 at 25, where he said, in relation *d* to the claim by Mrs Day, who had been joined in the proceedings:

'If the discriminatory measures in the 1978 Act are not objectively justified, Mrs Day has a good claim for redundancy pay against her employers, the Hertfordshire Area Health Authority, under art 119, which by virtue of s 2(1) *e* of the 1972 Act prevails over the discriminatory provisions of the 1978 Act. She would also have a good claim under the equal pay directive and the equal treatment directive, which are directly applicable against her employers as being an emanation of the state ...'

The chairman concluded that Mrs Barber did not have and never had had a claim *f* directly under the provisions of the 1978 Act for unfair dismissal or for a redundancy payment.

Having referred to the decision in *Blaik v Post Office* [1994] IRLR 280, the chairman continued in para 14 of his reasons:

'The relevance of *Blaik v Post Office* ([1994] IRLR 280) is in relation to the *g* possibility of pursuing proceedings under European legislation where UK domestic law does not provide a sufficient remedy. That is Mrs Barber's situation. She cannot pursue a claim under the UK domestic law that she is entitled to a redundancy payment or to compensation for unfair dismissal. That is precisely the type of claim which in my view, can proceed in separate *h* and distinct litigation under European law.'

The council then appealed to the Employment Appeal Tribunal, which allowed the appeal.

The decision of the Employment Appeal Tribunal   *j*
The arguments before the Employment Appeal Tribunal followed a different course from that followed before the chairman of the industrial tribunal. Thus it was accepted on behalf of Mrs Barber that in the light of the decision in *Biggs v Somerset CC* [1995] ICR 811 it was not possible to argue, at any rate below the Court of Appeal, that the claims for unfair dismissal and redundancy could be brought as causes of action under art 119 and the two directives. In his judgment

a Mummery J identified the two questions which had been addressed by the parties as follows:

> '(1) Whether the principles of cause of action estoppel and issue estoppel are applicable to a case where an application has been withdrawn and dismissed without any argument or reasoned decision on the merits of the
b case; and (2) if those principles are applicable, whether, on the particular facts of this case, Mrs Barber can rely on an exception which would otherwise preclude her from continuing with her second application.'

The Employment Appeal Tribunal came to the conclusion that the principles of cause of action estoppel and issue estoppel did apply to an application which had
c been withdrawn. Mummery J drew attention to the wording of r 12(2)(c) of Sch 1 to the 1985 regulations, which were in these terms:

> 'A tribunal may, if it thinks fit … (c) if the applicant shall at any time give notice of the withdrawal of his originating application, dismiss the proceedings …'

d
He pointed out that the rule conferred a discretion on the tribunal whether or not to dismiss the proceedings. Accordingly, it was not a mere administrative act.

Mummery J also referred to the decisions of the Court of Appeal in *SCF Finance Co Ltd v Masri (No 3) (Masri, garnishee)* [1987] 1 All ER 194, [1987] QB 1028 and *Khan v Goleccha International Ltd* [1980] 2 All ER 259, [1980] 1 WLR 1482.
e On the second question the Employment Appeal Tribunal concluded that there were no exceptional circumstances which entitled Mrs Barber to continue with her application. Mummery J referred to *Henderson v Henderson* (1843) 3 Hare 100, [1843–60] All ER Rep 378 and to other more recent cases where the question of special circumstances has been examined. He said that Mrs Barber was
f precluded from pursuing her claim for unfair dismissal on the doctrine of res judicata in the wider sense, namely that it would be an abuse of the process of the court to raise in subsequent proceedings matters which could and should have been litigated in earlier proceedings. He continued:

> 'There is no good reason why she could not have included in her claim
g presented in November 1992 a complaint of unfair dismissal, as well as a claim for redundancy. The same requirements for continuity of employment and qualifying hours had to be satisfied.'

The appeal
h It will be convenient to deal first with the argument that Mrs Barber can bring her claims in the industrial tribunal under art 119 and under the directives.

Article 119 of the Treaty is in these terms:

> 'Each Member State shall during the first stage ensure and subsequently
j maintain the application of the principle that men and women should receive equal pay for equal work. For the purposes of this Article, "pay" means the ordinary basic or minimum wage or salary and any other consideration, whether in cash or in kind, which the worker receives, directly or indirectly, in respect of his employment from his employer. Equal pay without discrimination based on sex means: (a) that pay for the same work at piece rates shall be calculated on the basis of the same unit of

measurement; (b) that pay for work at time rates shall be the same for the   *a*
same job.'

It was established in the *EOC* case that a redundancy payment is 'pay' for the
purpose of art 119, and I shall assume that compensation for unfair dismissal also
is to be regarded as 'pay'.

As I pointed out, however, in my judgment in *Biggs v Somerset CC* [1996] 2 All   *b*
ER 734 at 745, art 119 does not confer any right to a redundancy payment or any
right to compensation for unfair dismissal. Its provisions are directed to ensuring
that men and women should receive equal pay for equal work. In my view,
therefore, it follows that Mrs Barber cannot rely on a cause of action created by
art 119. I believe the true position to be as was explained by Mummery J in his
valuable judgment in *Biggs v Somerset CC* [1995] ICR 811 at 830, where he   *c*
summarised the position as follows:

'(a) The industrial tribunal has no inherent jurisdiction. Its statutory
jurisdiction is confined to complaints that may be made to it under specific
statutes, such as the Employment Protection (Consolidation) Act 1978, the
Sex Discrimination Act 1975, the Race Relations Act 1976, the Equal Pay Act   *d*
1970 and any other relevant statute. We are not able to identify the legal
source of any jurisdiction in the tribunal to hear and determine disputes
about Community law generally. (b) In the exercise of its jurisdiction the
tribunal may apply Community law. The application of Community law
may have the effect of displacing provisions in domestic law statutes which   *e*
preclude a remedy claimed by the applicant. In the present case the remedy
claimed by the applicant is unfair dismissal. That is a right conferred on an
employee by the Act of 1978 and earlier legislation. If a particular applicant
finds that the Act contains a barrier which prevents the claim from
succeeding but that barrier is incompatible with Community law, it is
displaced in consequence of superior and directly effective Community   *f*
rights. (c) In applying Community law the tribunal is not assuming or
exercising jurisdiction in relation to a "free-standing" Community right
separate from rights under domestic law. In our view, some confusion is
inherent in or caused by the mesmeric metaphor, "free-standing".
"Free-standing" means not supported by a structural framework, not   *g*
attached or connected to another structure. This is not a correct description
of the claim asserted by the applicant. She is not complaining of an
infringement of a "free-standing" right in the sense of an independent right
of action created by Community law, unsupported by any legal framework
or not attached or connected to any other legal structure. Her claim is within   *h*
the structural framework of the employment protection legislation, subject
to the disapplication of the threshold qualifying provisions in accordance
with the *EOC* case ([1994] 1 All ER 910, [1995] 1 AC 1) ...' (Mummery J's
emphasis.)

Article 119 can be relied upon by an applicant to disapply barriers to a claim   *j*
which are incompatible with Community law. The statutory conditions which
have to be satisfied before compensation can be obtained can therefore be
disapplied if they are discriminatory and contrary to Community law. Moreover,
it was held in *Emmott v Minister for Social Welfare* Case C-208/90 [1991] ECR I-4269
that a member state cannot rely on the limitation period for the bringing of a
claim to protect rights conferred on the claimant by the provisions of a directive

a until such time as the directive has been properly transposed into domestic law. But, as I understand the matter, the impact of Community law on claims brought before industrial tribunals is that Community law can be used to remove or circumvent barriers against or restrictions on a claim, but that it does not create rights of action which have an existence apart from domestic law. We are not of course concerned in this case with a claim for compensation such as that which *b* was considered by the Court of Justice of the European Communities in *Francovich v Italy* Joined Cases C-6/90 and C-9/90 [1991] ECR I-5357. The nature and extent of such a claim has recently been examined by the Court of Justice in the last stage of the *Factortame* litigation (see *Brasserie du Pêcheur SA v Germany, R v Secretary of State for Transport, ex p Factortame Ltd* Joined cases C-46/93 and C-48/93 [1996] All ER (EC) 301). But, unless Parliament otherwise decided, such a *c* claim would not come within the jurisdiction of an industrial tribunal.

I turn therefore to the question of estoppel.

The argument on behalf of Mrs Barber was developed on the following lines.

(1) Mrs Barber's claim for redundancy payment was not barred by any principle of res judicata or by any cause of action or issue estoppel. The order of *d* the industrial tribunal dated 5 May 1993 was a purely administrative act. The tribunal, though in theory exercising a judicial discretion, was bound to dismiss Mrs Barber's claim on withdrawal because she could not satisfy the qualifying conditions set out in the 1978 Act. The tribunal heard no evidence and made no adjudication on either an issue of law or fact. The case was similar to a case of discontinuance or alternatively to a case where an action may be dismissed on the *e* sole ground that a particular court has no jurisdiction. We were referred to the decision of the Court of Appeal in *Hines v Birkbeck College (No 2)* [1991] 4 All ER 450, [1992] Ch 33.

(2) Mrs Barber's claim for compensation for unfair dismissal was not barred by the principle of res judicata or cause of action or issue estoppel because: (a) the *f* claim for unfair dismissal was not a claim which she should, with due diligence, have advanced in the earlier proceedings; and (b) the provisions contained in the 1978 Act and the subsequent decision in the *EOC* case constituted special circumstances which prevented the application of the estoppel doctrine.

(3) In any event, Mrs Barber's claims under Community law were not barred by any principle of res judicata or estoppel because such principles did not apply *g* to Community claims.

I can deal at once with the third argument. I have already considered whether Mrs Barber has any separate causes of action under Community law and have decided that she has not. In these circumstances, as it seems to me, the third argument is bound to fail.

h I turn therefore to the claim for a redundancy payment.

A cause of action estoppel was defined by Diplock LJ in *Thoday v Thoday* [1964] 1 All ER 341 at 352, [1964] P 181 at 197 as follows:

> '[A cause of action estoppel] is that which prevents a party to an action from asserting or denying, as against the other party, the existence of a *j* particular cause of action, the non-existence or existence of which has been determined by a court of competent jurisdiction in previous litigation between the same parties. If the cause of action was determined to exist, i.e., judgment was given on it, it is said to be merged in the judgment ... If it was determined not to exist, the unsuccessful plaintiff can no longer assert that it does; he is estopped per rem judicatam.'

The argument for Mrs Barber was that on 5 May 1993 the industrial tribunal made no relevant determination; it simply dismissed her claim by means of an administrative action or, at any rate, without any consideration of its merits.

In my judgment, however, Mummery J was correct when he said that there was nothing in the principles of cause of action or issue estoppel which stipulated that they could only apply in cases where a tribunal has given a reasoned decision on the issues of fact and law in the previous litigation. Section 140 of the 1978 Act contains provisions which render void any agreement to preclude a person from bringing proceedings before an industrial tribunal. A tribunal has therefore to be satisfied that a withdrawal is properly made.

I am satisfied that the order which was made by the industrial tribunal on 5 May 1993 was a judicial decision made by the industrial tribunal in the exercise of its powers under the 1978 Act and the 1985 regulations. It was not a mere administrative act.

It is true that no evidence was heard by the tribunal but that fact does not prevent the decision operating by way of res judicata. In *SCF Finance Co Ltd v Masri* [1987] 1 All ER 194, [1987] QB 1028 the Court of Appeal considered the earlier decision in *Khan v Goleccha International Ltd* [1980] 2 All ER 259, [1980] 1 WLR 1482, where it had been held that an express admission and a subsequent order by consent could give rise to an issue estoppel. The court continued:

'The decision in *Khan's* case makes it clear that an order dismissing proceedings is capable of giving rise to issue estoppel even though the court making such order has not heard argument or evidence directed to the merits ... If a party puts forward a positive case, as the basis of asking the court to make the order which that party seeks, and then at trial declines to proceed and accepts that the claim must be dismissed, then that party must, in our view, save in exceptional circumstances, lose the right to raise again that case against the other party to those proceedings.' (See [1987] 1 All ER 194 at 208, [1987] QB 1028 at 1047.)

Before leaving this part of the case I should deal with the subsidiary argument advanced on behalf of Mrs Barber to the effect that there were exceptional circumstances which prevented the application of the ordinary rules of res judicata and cause of action estoppel. It seems to me, however, that this argument is bound to fail. It is sufficient to refer to a passage in the opinion of Lord Keith in *Arnold v National Westminster Bank plc* [1991] 3 All ER 41 at 46, [1991] 2 AC 93 at 104:

'Cause of action estoppel arises where the cause of action in the latter proceedings is identical to that in the earlier proceedings, the latter having been between the same parties or their privies and having involved the same subject matter. In such a case the bar is absolute in relation to all points decided unless fraud or collusion is alleged, such as to justify setting aside the earlier judgment. The discovery of new factual matter which could not have been found out by reasonable diligence for use in the earlier proceedings does not, according to the law of England, permit the latter to be reopened.'

I come finally to Mrs Barber's claim for compensation for unfair dismissal. I have found this part of the case the most difficult.

The council relied on the classic statement of principle set out by Wigram V-C in *Henderson v Henderson* (1843) 3 Hare 100 at 114–115, [1843–60] All ER Rep 378 at 381–382:

'... I believe I state the rule of the Court correctly, when I say, that where a given matter becomes the subject of litigation in, and of adjudication by, a court of competent jurisdiction, the Court requires the parties to that litigation to bring forward their whole case, and will not (except under special circumstances) permit the same parties to open the same subject of litigation in respect of matter which might have been brought forward as part of the subject in contest, but which was not brought forward, only because they have, from negligence, inadvertence, or even accident, omitted part of their case. The plea of res judicata applies, except in special cases, not only to points upon which the Court was actually required by the parties to form an opinion and pronounce a judgment, but to every point which properly belonged to the subject of litigation, and which the parties, exercising reasonable diligence, might have brought forward at the time.'

This statement of principle has been applied in a number of more recent cases. As Stuart-Smith LJ explained in *Talbot v Berkshire CC* [1993] 4 All ER 9 at 13, [1994] QB 290 at 294, the rule as stated in *Henderson's* case is in two parts:

'The first relates to those points which were actually decided by the court; this is res judicata in the strict sense. Secondly, those which might have been brought forward at the time, but were not. The second is not a true case of res judicata but rather is founded upon the principle of public policy in preventing multiplicity of actions, it being in the public interest that there should be an end to litigation ...'

In *Arnold's* case the House of Lords considered what 'special circumstances' would allow the reopening of an issue which had already been decided inter partes. It was held that the doctrine of issue estoppel was not inflexible and a disputed issue can be reopened where it would in effect be an abuse of process if permission were refused.

It seems to me to follow from *Arnold's* case that it would be possible in special circumstances to allow a claim to be put forward which was not the subject of res judicata in the strict sense but which could have been brought forward in some earlier proceedings. I have come the conclusion, however, that this possible relaxation of the rule does not assist Mrs Barber in the present case. The qualifying conditions for her claim for a redundancy payment were the same as those for a claim for compensation for unfair dismissal. It was not the provisions of the 1978 Act which prevented the *addition* of the second claim.

In these circumstances I have been driven to the conclusion that Mrs Barber's appeal must be dismissed.

AULD LJ. I agree.

SIR IAIN GLIDEWELL. I also agree.

Appeal dismissed. Leave to appeal to the House of Lords refused.

Paul Magrath Esq   Barrister.

Mulcahy v Ministry of Defence   *a*

COURT OF APPEAL, CIVIL DIVISION
NEILL, McCOWAN LJJ AND SIR IAIN GLIDEWELL
30, 31 JANUARY, 21 FEBRUARY 1996

b

Negligence – Duty to take care – Serviceman – Soldier engaging enemy in battle conditions – Soldier sustaining personal injury – Injury caused by negligence of fellow soldier – Whether soldier owing duty of care to fellow servicemen when engaging enemy during hostilities.

The plaintiff was a soldier serving with a British Army artillery unit during the   *c*
Gulf War. While his unit was deployed in Saudi Arabia firing a howitzer into Iraq he was ordered by the gun commander to fetch some water from in front of the gun carriage. While he was in front of the gun the gun commander negligently caused the gun to fire. The discharge knocked the plaintiff off his feet and adversely affected his hearing. He brought an action against the Ministry of   *d*
Defence as his employer for damages for personal injury, alleging res ipsa loquitur and that the department was vicariously liable for the gun commander's negligence or alternatively that, by causing or permitting the gun to be fired while the plaintiff was not standing in the safety position required by gun drill, the department was in breach of its duty to adopt and maintain a safe system of work. The department applied to strike out the claim on the ground that it disclosed no   *e*
cause of action, but the county court judge dismissed the application. The department appealed to the Court of Appeal.

Held – A serviceman owed no duty of care to his fellow servicemen in battle conditions, since as a matter of common sense and policy it would not be fair, just   *f*
and reasonable to impose on a soldier a duty of care in his conduct towards a fellow soldier when engaging the enemy during hostilities, even if proximity and foreseeability of damage were proved. Since the plaintiff had been in a war zone, taking part in warlike operations by being a member of a gun crew which was engaged in firing shells on enemy targets when he was injured, neither the gun commander nor the department as the plaintiff's employer owed him a duty of   *g*
care. The appeal would therefore be allowed and the claim struck out (see p 770 *j* to p 771 *b d* to p 772 *c j* to p 773 *a c*, post).

Shaw Savill and Albion Co Ltd v Commonwealth (1940) 66 CLR 344, dictum of Lord Reid and of Lord Pearce in *Burmah Oil Co (Burma Trading) Ltd v Lord Advocate* [1964] 2 All ER 348 at 360, 394, dictum of Gibbs CJ in *Groves v Commonwealth of*   *h*
Australia (1982) 150 CLR 113 at 195 and *Hughes v National Union of Mineworkers* [1991] 4 All ER 278 considered.

Notes

For res ipsa loquitur, see 34 *Halsbury's Laws* (4th edn) paras 57–61, and for cases   .
on the subject, see 36(1) *Digest* (2nd reissue) 359–367, 2852–2894.   *j*

Cases referred to in judgments

Burmah Oil Co (Burmah Trading) Ltd v Lord Advocate [1964] 2 All ER 348, [1965] AC
  75, [1964] 2 WLR 1231, HL.
Canterbury (Lord) v R (1843) 12 LJ Ch 281.
Dyson v A-G [1911] 1 KB 410, CA.

a *Groves v Commonwealth of Australia* (1982) 150 CLR 113, Aust HC.
Hedley Byrne & Co Ltd v Heller & Partners Ltd [1963] 2 All ER 575, [1964] AC 465, [1963] 3 WLR 101, HL.
Hill v Chief Constable of West Yorkshire [1988] 2 All ER 238, [1989] AC 53, [1988] 2 WLR 1049, HL.
Home Office v Dorset Yacht Co Ltd [1970] 2 All ER 294, [1970] AC 1004, [1970] 2 WLR 1140, HL.

b *Hughes v National Union of Mineworkers* [1991] 4 All ER 278.
Hydra, The [1918] P 78.
Knightley v Johns [1982] 1 All ER 851, [1982] 1 WLR 349, CA.
Lonrho plc v Fayed [1991] 3 All ER 303, [1992] 1 AC 448, [1991] 3 WLR 188, HL.
Marais v General Officer Commanding the Lines of Communication, ex p Marais [1902]

c AC 109, PC.
Marc Rich & Co AG v Bishop Rock Marine Co Ltd, The Nicholas H [1995] 3 All ER 307, [1996] 1 AC 211, [1995] 3 WLR 227, HL.
Shaw Savill and Albion Co Ltd v The Commonwealth (1940) 66 CLR 344, Aust HC.
Thomas v R (1874) LR 10 QB 31.

d *Weaver v Ward* (1616) Hob 134, 80 ER 284.
X and ors (minors) v Bedfordshire CC, M (a minor) v Newham London BC, E (a minor) v Dorset CC [1995] 3 All ER 353, [1995] 2 AC 633, [1995] 3 WLR 152, HL; *rvsg in part* [1994] 4 All ER 640, [1995] 2 AC 633, [1994] 3 WLR 853, CA.

Cases also cited or referred to in skeleton arguments.

e *Ancell v McDermott* [1993] 4 All ER 355, CA.
Anns v Merton London Borough [1977] 2 All ER 492, [1978] AC 728, HL.
Caparo Industries plc v Dickman [1990] 1 All ER 568, [1990] AC 605, HL.
Elguzouli-Daf v Comr of Police of the Metropolis [1995] 1 All ER 833, [1995] QB 335, CA.

f *Evans v London Hospital Medical College (University of London)* [1981] 1 All ER 715, [1981] 1 WLR 184.
Fraser v Balfour (1918) 34 TLR 502, HL.
Murphy v Brentwood DC [1990] 2 All ER 908, [1991] AC 398, HL.
Rowling v Takaro Properties Ltd [1988] 1 All ER 163, [1988] AC 473, PC.
Saif Ali v Sydney Mitchell & Co [1978] 3 All ER 1033, [1980] AC 198, HL.

g *Spring v Guardian Assurance plc* [1994] 3 All ER 129, [1995] 2 AC 296, HL.
Tilling v Whiteman [1979] 1 All ER 737, [1980] AC 1, HL.
Yuen Kun-Yeu v A-G of Hong Kong [1987] 2 All ER 705, [1988] AC 175, PC.

Appeal

h By notice dated 30 November 1994 the defendants, the Ministry of Defence, appealed with leave of Rose LJ dated 21 November 1994 from the decision of Judge Walker sitting in the Dewsbury County Court on 22 September 1994, refusing their application to strike out the claim of the plaintiff, Richard Mulcahy, for damages for negligence, as disclosing no reasonable cause of action. The facts

j are set out in the judgment of Neill LJ.

Philip Havers QC and *Ian Burnett* (instructed by the *Treasury Solicitor*) for the defendants.
Simon Hawkesworth QC and *David Gripton* (instructed by *Wilkinson Woodward & Ludlam*, Halifax) for the plaintiff.

Cur adv vult

21 February 1996. The following judgments were delivered.   *a*

NEILL LJ.

Introduction

This is an appeal by the defendants, the Ministry of Defence, from the order dated 22 September 1994 of Judge Walker sitting in the Dewsbury County Court refusing the defendants' application to strike out the plaintiff's claim. The *b* application was made on the basis that the plaintiff's claim as formulated disclosed no cause of action. Leave to appeal to this court was given by Rose LJ on 21 November 1994.

In view of the nature of the application it is necessary to refer to the plaintiff's pleaded case, because for the purpose of an application to strike out, the facts *c* alleged by the plaintiff are assumed to be true. I should therefore start by referring to parts of the amended particulars of claim, which were further amended by leave of the Court of Appeal during the course of the hearing. The rereamended particulars of claim are in these terms:

'1. At all material times the plaintiff (Richard Mulcahy) was a serving *d* soldier in the employ of the defendant, being a member of 32 Heavy Artillery Regiment, 74 Battalion. 2. In or about February/March 1991 during the course of his employment with the defendant, the plaintiff was part of a team manning an M110 8 inch howitzer gun and his particular job was to swab out the breech of the gun after each firing and, for that purpose, he was provided with a bucket and a mop. 3. One Sergeant Warren was in charge of the *e* team and was the only person in the team allowed to fire the gun. 4. (a) At the time of the matters hereinafter complained of the gun was deployed at a location in Saudi Arabia and was firing into Iraq. (b) The plaintiff does not know the date on which he was injured but recalls that, on that day, his unit was visited by Kate Adie and a B.B.C. television crew. (c) No return fire *f* from any quarter had been experienced in the days leading up to the day of the plaintiff's injury, none was experienced on that day or on any of the days thereafter. 5. (a) At a time when the gun was ready for firing, the gun commander—the said Sergeant Warren—ordered the plaintiff to fetch a jerrican of water for the mop bucket which required him to go from the position where he stood when the gun was about to be fired to the front of *g* the gun carriage where the jerricans were stored. (b) The plaintiff was to the front of the gun when the gun commander negligently caused the gun to fire and the discharge knocked the plaintiff off his feet whereafter he was temporarily unable to focus properly, was disorientated and his hearing was adversely affected. (c) The plaintiff says res ipsa loquiter. (d) Further, or in *h* the alternative, by causing or permitting the gun to be fired while the plaintiff was not standing in the safety position required by gun drill the defendants were in breach of their duty to adopt and maintain a safe system of work ...'

Before turning to the judge's judgment and to the questions of law which were argued before us it is first necessary to deal with two preliminary matters. This *j* is an application to strike out pursuant to CCR Ord 13, r 5(1)(a). The principles on which an order can be made are the same as in the High Court. It is therefore important to remember that the summary procedure for striking out pleadings is only to be used in plain and obvious cases. One must also take account of the fact that in *Dyson v A-G* [1911] 1 KB 410 at 414 Cozens-Hardy MR, in a passage approved by Lord Bridge of Harwich in *Lonrho plc v Fayed* [1991] 3 All ER 303 at a 313, [1992] 1 AC 448 at 469, said that the procedure 'ought not to be applied to an action involving serious investigation of ancient law and questions of general importance'. At the same time it is necessary to have regard to some recent statements as to the correct approach. In *E (a minor) v Dorset CC* [1994] 4 All ER 640 at 649, [1995] 2 AC 633 at 693–694 Sir Thomas Bingham MR said:

b 'I share the unease many judges have expressed at deciding questions of legal principle without knowing the full facts. But applications of this kind are fought on a ground of a plaintiff's choosing, since he may generally be assumed to plead his best case, and there should be no risk of injustice to plaintiffs if orders to strike out are indeed made only in plain and obvious cases. This must mean that where the legal viability of a cause of action is

c unclear (perhaps because the law is in a state of transition), or in any way sensitive to the facts, an order to strike out should not be made. But if, after argument, the court can be properly persuaded that no matter what (within the reasonable bounds of the pleading) the actual facts the claim is bound to fail for want of a cause of action, I can see no reason why the parties should be required to prolong the proceedings before that decision is reached.'

d When the *Dorset* case reached the House of Lords, together with other cases (reported compendiously as *X and ors (minors) v Bedfordshire CC, M (a minor) v Newham London BC, E (a minor) v Dorset CC* [1995] 3 All ER 353, [1995] 2 AC 633), Lord Browne-Wilkinson expressed his approval of this approach. He said ([1995] 3 All ER 353 at 373, [1995] 2 AC 633 at 740–741):

e 'Actions can only be struck out under RSC Ord 18, r 19 where it is clear and obvious that in law the claim cannot succeed. Where the law is not settled but is in a state of development (as in the present cases) it is normally inappropriate to decide novel questions on hypothetical facts. But I agree with Sir Thomas Bingham MR ... that there is nothing inappropriate in

f deciding on these applications whether the statutes in question confer private law rights of action for damages: the answer to that question depends upon the construction of the statutes alone. Much more difficult is the question whether it is appropriate to decide the question whether there is a common law duty of care in these cases. There may be cases ... where it is

g evident that, whatever the facts, no common law duty of care can exist. But in other cases the relevant facts are not known at this stage ... I again agree with Sir Thomas Bingham MR that if, on the facts alleged in the statement of claim, it is not possible to give a certain answer whether in law the claim is maintainable, then it is not appropriate to strike out the claim at a

h preliminary stage but the matter must go to trial when the relevant facts will be discovered.'

It follows therefore that before a court can consider whether a claim should be struck out on the ground that it discloses no cause of action the court must first be satisfied that all the relevant facts are before it. Furthermore, save perhaps in

j an exceptional case, the court should give the plaintiff an opportunity to amend his claim to include any other appropriate cause of action. In addition, the court will want to consider whether the parties have had a proper opportunity to put before the court any arguments or authorities on which they may wish to rely. Where, however, the court is satisfied that additional facts will not change the framework of the claim and that the opposing arguments have been fully deployed the court should not shrink from deciding whether the application to

strike out is well-founded in law. At the same time the court must take account
of Lord Browne-Wilkinson's admonition that it is normally inappropriate to
decide novel questions on hypothetical facts. But the novelty of the question of
law is not an absolute barrier. It is to be remembered that the resolution of a
question of law at an early stage in proceedings may result in a very substantial
saving of costs.

I turn therefore to the second preliminary matter. It was argued on behalf of
the plaintiff that an application to strike out was in any event inappropriate
because further facts needed to be elucidated. It was said that the exact
circumstances in which the gun was being fired should be investigated. Indeed at
one stage in the course of the argument it was suggested that the firing of the gun
might have been part of a training exercise. It is therefore necessary to look at the
pleaded facts and at any explanations which were given to the judge.

It is common ground that the plaintiff's battalion formed part of the allied
forces in what is known as the Gulf War. The plaintiff formed part of a gun crew
at a location in Saudi Arabia. At the moment when he sustained his injury and
for some days before the gun was firing live rounds into Iraq. Furthermore it was
accepted by counsel for the plaintiff before the judge that the Gulf War involved
warlike operations.

The judge accepted the argument that further facts had to be established. He
said:

> '... it has to be established on the basis of [the facts pleaded in paras 4(a) and
> 4(c) of the particulars of claim] whether the degree of involvement in warlike
> activities was such as to allow the Crown to argue that it was in fact a heat of
> battle situation. The Crown says: "Well, this is precisely the situation where
> there should be no investigation because it is contrary, in a sense, to public
> policy to be investigating the circumstances on the field of battle." But that
> begs the question. The question is—was it the field of battle? The plaintiff
> will seek to argue that it was not the field of battle, although it was firing at
> the enemy. There are obviously degrees of involvement in warlike activities,
> some of which have been canvassed by me to counsel on a hypothetical
> basis. What is the situation of somebody involved in firing a guided missile
> a hundred miles? What is the situation in somebody arming a bomber? All
> that has to be determined and ... I am not going to confuse the issue by
> having this strike out taken on appeal returned here for a finding of the facts.'

It is right to say that counsel for the plaintiff did not persist in his suggestion
that the gun might have been fired as part of a training exercise. But he said that
this case was plainly distinguishable from a case of hand-to-hand combat. He also
said that the precise circumstances in which Sgt Warren had given the order to
fire the gun should be determined by the calling of evidence.

I have come to the conclusion that the facts are sufficiently clear to enable one
to decide whether or not on those facts Sgt Warren owed a duty of care to the
plaintiff or whether the defendants were in breach of their duty to adopt and
maintain a safe system of work.

I do not consider that it is necessary to examine whether a duty would be owed
when someone was involved in firing a guided missile over a distance of a
hundred miles or when someone was arming a bomber. These were two
situations mentioned by the judge in the course of his judgment. Nor do I
consider it to be necessary to reach a conclusion as to what, if any, duty would be
owed by a driver of a vehicle bringing ammunition to the front line from a rear

a echelon. The plain facts of this case were that the plaintiff was in a war zone taking part in warlike operations and he was a member of a gun crew which was engaged in firing shells on enemy targets. It is on that substratum of fact that I approach this application to strike out.

The liability of the Crown in tort
b

It is to be remembered that the primary claim by the plaintiff against the defendants is on the basis that the defendants are liable vicariously for the negligence of Sgt Warren. Nevertheless, it is necessary to consider the law relating to the liability of the Crown in tort because the relevant legislation and the decided cases may throw light on the questions raised in this appeal and
c because the plaintiff's alternative claim is a direct claim against the defendants.

Until 1947 actions against the Crown were inhibited by two principles of ancient though doubtful origin. The first was that the King could not be impleaded in his own courts. The effect of the application of this principle was that until the nineteenth century proceedings against the Crown, so far as they
d were available at all, had to be brought by various complicated procedures including a petition of right. These procedures were simplified by the Petitions of Right Act 1860, and it was held in *Thomas v R* (1874) LR 10 QB 31 that proceedings by way of petition of right were available to recover unliquidated damages against the Crown for breach of contract. But proceedings for damages
e for tort were inhibited or rather prevented by the application of the second ancient principle, the principle that the King could do no wrong. It may be that at one time the maxim 'the King can do no wrong' meant that the King was not privileged to commit illegal acts, but it came to be understood to be a rule barring actions in tort against the Crown. Thus in *Lord Canterbury v R* (1843) 12 LJ Ch 281 an ex-Speaker failed in his claim for compensation from the Crown for damage
f done to his furniture in the fire which destroyed the Houses of Parliament in 1834 caused, it was alleged, by the negligence of certain Crown servants.

The consequences of the immunity of the Crown against proceedings in tort were mitigated by the practice whereby, for example, if a claim were brought for damages for negligent driving against a Crown servant acting in the course of his
g employment, the Crown, in what were considered to be appropriate cases, would pay the damages on an ex gratia basis. But the system attracted widespread criticism and both Lord Haldane and Lord Birkenhead made proposals for reform. Furthermore, in Australia and New Zealand the matter was largely rectified by statute by the beginning of this century.
h
The pre-1947 law, however, throws little light on the rights of servicemen rather than civilians to make claims. It seems probable that, irrespective of the rule as to Crown immunity, if one serviceman had made a claim for damages for personal injuries against another serviceman the Crown could have resisted liability under the doctrine of common employment. The researches of counsel
j brought to our attention the decision in *Weaver v Ward* (1616) Hob 134, 80 ER 284 where it was held on demurrer that an action of trespass would lie if in the course of military exercises a soldier were injured by another unless the latter could prove that the injury had been 'utterly without his fault'. But it is clear that the military exercise was being undertaken in peace time conditions.

I must turn therefore to the Crown Proceedings Act 1947.

The 1947 Act
The immunity of the Crown against proceedings in tort was fundamentally changed by s 2 of the 1947 Act. Section 2, so far as is material, is in these terms:

'(1) Subject to the provisions of this Act, the Crown shall be subject to all those liabilities in tort to which, if it were a private person of full age and capacity, it would be subject:—(a) in respect of torts committed by its servants or agents; (b) in respect of any breach of those duties which a person owes to his servants or agents at common law by reason of being their employer ... Provided that no proceedings shall lie against the Crown by virtue of paragraph (a) of this subsection in respect of any act or omission of a servant or agent of the Crown unless the act or omission would apart from the provisions of this Act have given rise to a cause of action in tort against that servant or agent or his estate.'

The 1947 Act, however, contained special provisions relating to the armed forces. These provisions were set out in s 10, which so far as is material was in these terms:

'(1) Nothing done or omitted to be done by a member of the armed forces of the Crown while on duty as such shall subject either him or the Crown to liability in tort for causing the death of another person, or for causing personal injury to another person, in so far as the death or personal injury is due to anything suffered by that other person while he is a member of the armed forces of the Crown if—(a) at the time when that thing is suffered by that other person, he is either on duty as a member of the armed forces of the Crown or is, though not on duty as such, on any land, premises, ship, aircraft or vehicle for the time being used for the purposes of the armed forces of the Crown; and (b) [the Secretary of State] certifies that his suffering that thing has been or will be treated as attributable to service for the purposes of entitlement to an award under the Royal Warrant, Order in Council or Order of His Majesty relating to the disablement or death of members of the force of which he is a member: Provided that this subsection shall not exempt a member of the said forces from liability in tort in any case in which the court is satisfied that the act or omission was not connected with the execution of his duties as a member of those forces ...
(3) ... a Secretary of State, if satisfied that it is the fact:—(a) that a person was or was not on any particular occasion on duty as a member of the armed forces of the Crown; or (b) that at any particular time any land, premises, ship, aircraft, vehicle, equipment or supplies was or was not, or were or were not, used for the purposes of the said forces; may issue a certificate certifying that to be the fact; and any such certificate shall, for the purposes of this section, be conclusive as to the fact which it certifies.'

It will be seen that the effect of s 10 of the 1947 Act was to prevent proceedings being brought in respect of the death of, or personal injury to, a member of the armed forces caused by the negligence of another member of the armed forces provided that the Secretary of State issued a certificate that the death or injury was attributable to service for the purposes of entitlement to a war pension.

The Crown Proceedings (Armed Forces) Act 1987
Few cases involving the operation of s 10 of the 1947 Act came before the courts. As time passed, however, there was growing dissatisfaction that s 10

a acted as a bar to claims in tort even in peacetime conditions. A wide disparity was perceived between the level of pensions awarded and the sums that would have been obtained had an action for damages been available. A further cause for concern was the restricted rights of dependent parents to make a claim for a war pension.

b In 1987 the Crown Proceedings (Armed Forces) Act 1987 was passed to remove the blanket protection of s 10 of the 1947 Act. Section 1 of the 1987 Act was in these terms:

'Subject to section 2 below, section 10 of the Crown Proceedings Act 1947 (exclusions from liability in tort in cases involving the armed forces) shall cease to have effect except in relation to anything suffered by a person in
c consequence of an act or omission committed before the date on which this Act is passed.'

Provision was made, however, for the revival of s 10 in certain circumstances. Thus, s 2 of the 1987 Act provided:

d '(1) Subject to the following provisions of this section, the Secretary of State may, at any time after the coming into force of section 1 above, by order—(a) revive the effect of section 10 of the Crown Proceedings Act 1947 either for all purposes or for such purposes as may be described in the order; or (b) where that section has effect for the time being in pursuance of an order made by virtue of paragraph (a) above, provide for that section to cease
e to have effect either for all of the purposes for which it so has effect or for such of them as may be so described.

(2) The Secretary of State shall not make an order reviving the effect of the said section 10 for any purposes unless it appears to him necessary or expedient to do so—(a) by reason of any imminent national danger or of any great emergency that has arisen; or (b) for the purposes of any warlike
f operations in any part of the world outside the United Kingdom or of any other operations which are or are to be carried out in connection with the warlike activity of any persons in any such part of the world.

(3) Subject to subsection (4) below, an order under this section describing purposes for which the effect of the said section 10 is to be revived, or for
g which that section is to cease to have effect, may describe those purposes by reference to any matter whatever and may make different provision for different cases, circumstances or persons.

(4) Nothing in any order under this section shall revive the effect of the said section 10, or provide for that section to cease to have effect, in relation
h to anything suffered by a person in consequence of an act or omission committed before the date on which the order comes into force.

(5) The power to make an order under this section shall be exercisable by statutory instrument subject to annulment in pursuance of a resolution of either House of Parliament.'

j It will be seen that under s 2(2)(b) the Secretary of State is empowered to make an order reviving the effect of s 10 of the 1947 Act for 'the purposes of any warlike operations in any part of the world outside the United Kingdom'. It will also be seen that under s 2(3) an order reviving s 10 can be restricted to any particular circumstances or persons which the Secretary of State considers appropriate. Accordingly, it seems plain that the Secretary of State *could* have made an order reviving s 10 for the purposes of the Gulf War and have restricted the operation

of s 10 to certain specified areas in the Middle East or to certain specified *a*
activities. But no order was made under s 2 of the 1987 Act.

The appeal

It was accepted on behalf of the defendants that there was no direct English
authority to support the proposition that no duty of care in tort is owed by one
soldier to another when engaging the enemy in battle conditions. Reliance was *b*
placed, however, on: (a) the decisions of the High Court of Australia in *Shaw
Savill and Albion Co Ltd v The Commonwealth* (1940) 66 CLR 344 and *Groves v
Commonwealth of Australia* (1982) 150 CLR 113; (b) dicta in *Burmah Oil Co (Burmah
Trading) Ltd v Lord Advocate* [1964] 2 All ER 348, [1965] AC 75; and (c) cases
involving injuries to police officers while engaged on operational duty. These *c*
cases included *Hughes v National Union of Mineworkers* [1991] 4 All ER 278.

I should refer first to the *Shaw Savill* case. In that case the plaintiff company
sued the Commonwealth of Australia for damages in consequence of a collision
which occurred between HMAS Adelaide and a motor vessel owned by the
plaintiff. In the defence the Commonwealth pleaded that at the time of the
collision and at all material times there existed a state of war in which the *d*
Commonwealth of Australia was engaged. Paragraph 23 of the defence was in
these terms:

> 'The plaintiff's supposed cause of action consisted solely in acts, matters
> and things done or occurring in the course of active naval operations against
> the King's enemies by the armed forces of the Commonwealth.' (See (1940) *e*
> 66 CLR 344 at 348)

The Commonwealth sought to set the service of the writ aside or, in the
alternative, an order that the action should be stayed. The High Court refused to
dismiss or stay the action and held that the question whether at the time of the
collision the warship was engaged in active operations against the enemy was an *f*
issue which the court could decide for itself. In the course of the judgments,
however, consideration was given to whether a duty of care was owed if the
warship had been engaged on active operations. Dixon J said (at 361–362):

> 'Outside a theatre of war, a want of care for the safety of merchant ships *g*
> exposes a naval officer navigating a King's ship to the same civil liability as if
> he were in the merchant service. But, although for acts or omissions
> amounting to civil wrongs an officer of the Crown can derive no protection
> from the fact that he was acting in the King's service or even under express
> command, it is recognised that, where what is alleged against him is failure
> to fulfil an obligation of care, the character in which he acted, together, no *h*
> doubt, with the nature of the duties he was in the course of performing, may
> determine the extent of the duty of care ... It could hardly be maintained
> that during an actual engagement with the enemy or a pursuit of any of his
> ships the navigating officer of a King's ship of war was under a common law
> duty of care to avoid harm to such non-combatant ships as might appear in *j*
> the theatre of operations. It cannot be enough to say that the conflict or
> pursuit is a circumstance affecting the reasonableness of the officer's conduct
> as a discharge of the duty of care, though the duty itself persists. To adopt
> such a view would mean that whether the combat be by sea, land or air our
> men go into action accompanied by the law of civil negligence, warning
> them to be mindful of the person and property of civilians. It would mean

a that the courts could be called upon to say whether the soldier on the field of battle or the sailor fighting on his ship might reasonably have been more careful to avoid causing civil loss or damage. No one can imagine a court undertaking the trial of such an issue, either during or after a war. To concede that any civil liability can rest upon a member of the armed forces for supposedly negligent acts or omissions in the course of an actual
b engagement with the enemy is opposed alike to reason and to policy. But the principle cannot be limited to the presence of the enemy or to occasions when contact with the enemy has been established. Warfare perhaps never did admit of such a distinction, but now it would be quite absurd. The development of the speed of ships and the range of guns were enough to show it to be an impracticable refinement, but it has been put out of question
c by the bomber, the submarine and the floating mine. The principle must extend to all active operations against the enemy. It must cover attack and resistance, advance and retreat, pursuit and avoidance, reconnaissance and engagement. But a real distinction does exist between actual operations against the enemy and other activities of the combatant services in time of
d war. For instance, a warship proceeding to her anchorage or manoeuvring among other ships in a harbour, or acting as a patrol or even as a convoy must be navigated with due regard to the safety of other shipping and no reason is apparent for treating her officers as under no civil duty of care, remembering always that the standard of care is that which is reasonable in the circumstances. Thus the commander of His Majesty's torpedo-boat
e destroyer *Hydra* was held liable for a collision of his ship with a merchant ship in the English Channel on the night of 11 February 1917, because he failed to perceive that the other ship, which showed him a light, was approaching on a crossing course ... obviously the *Hydra* was on active service and war conditions obtained (*H.M.S. Hydra* ([1918] P 78)). It may not be easy under
f conditions of modern warfare to say in a given case upon which side of the line it falls. But, when, in an action of negligence against the Crown or a member of the armed forces of the Crown, it is made to appear to the court that the matters complained of formed part of, or an incident in, active naval or military operations against the enemy, then in my opinion the action must fail on the ground that, while in the course of actually operating against the
g enemy, the forces of the Crown are under no duty of care to avoid causing loss or damage to private individuals.'

Rich ACJ and McTiernan J agreed with the judgment of Dixon J. Starke and Williams JJ concurred in the result. Starke J said (at 355–356):

h

'... there is no doubt that the executive government and its officers must conduct operations of war, whether naval, military, or in the air, without the control or interference of the courts of law. Acts done in the course of such operations are not justiciable and the courts of law cannot take cognizance
j of them. In my judgment, the case of *Ex parte D. F. Marais* ([1902] AC 109) so decided.'

Williams J reached a similar conclusion. He too referred to *Marais v General Officer Commanding the Lines of Communication, ex p Marais* [1902] AC 109 and said that if it were proved that actual hostilities were in progress at the time 'the alleged cause of action would not be justiciable' (see (1940) 66 CLR 344 at 366).

It is apparent from the later decision of the High Court of Australia in *Groves'* *a* case, that when the claim by Shaw Savill came to trial the action succeeded on the ground that the captain of the *Adelaide* had steered a wrong course (see (1982) 150 CLR 113 at 123). Presumably the trial judge found that at the material time the warship was not engaged in actual operations against the enemy. But Gibbs CJ (at 117) affirmed as correct what had been said by Dixon J in the *Shaw Savill* case. Gibbs CJ added: *b*

> 'To hold that there is no evil liability for injury caused by the negligence of persons in the course of an actual engagement with the enemy seems to me to accord with common sense and sound policy.'

The plaintiff in *Groves'* case was an airman in the RAAF who was injured when *c* leaving a stationary aircraft being used to transport civilians in a time of peace. The accident occurred when a folding ladder collapsed beneath him as a result of the absence of locking pins. The High Court held that as the case arose out of routine duties in time of peace the plaintiff was entitled to the same protection of the common law as would protect other members of the community, and that *d* the Commonwealth were vicariously liable for the negligence of other members of the crew. In a joint judgment of four members of the court led by Stephen J references were made to the *Shaw Savill* decision. As I read the judgment, however, the support given to *Shaw Savill* was less emphatic than in the judgment of Gibbs CJ. It was said (150 CLR 113 at 134):   *e*

> 'Nor do we have occasion to consider the position of servicemen engaged in combatant activities in time of war or in training for such activities. It would not be wise, in the abstract, to attempt to mark out whatever line may be thought to exist between one act of military duty and another. Public policy may require that, at some point in the continuum from civilian-like duties performed by servicemen in peacetime to active service in wartime, *f* what would otherwise involve actionable negligence should not give rise to a cause of action. If so, the definition of liability would seem to be pre-eminently a case for legislation, preceded by evaluation and report by law reform agencies.'

On the other hand, in other passages in the judgment and in the judgment of *g* Murphy J there seems to have been a recognition of the fact that warlike activities fell into a special category (see 150 CLR 113 at 125, 136). Looking at the case as a whole I do not consider that it throws any doubt on the proposition affirmed in the *Shaw Savill* case that no duty exists where a serviceman is engaged in actual *h* operations against the enemy.

   Counsel for the defendants also referred us to the decision in *Burmah Oil Co (Burmah Trading) Ltd v Lord Advocate* [1964] 2 All ER 348, [1965] AC 75. In that case installations belonging to the appellant companies near Rangoon had been destroyed by the army in order to prevent them falling into the hands of the enemy. It was held that as the demolitions had taken place otherwise than in the *j* course of actual military operations compensation was payable. The speech of Lord Reid contains an interesting account of the general rule that where property was taken or destroyed in the exercise of the Royal prerogative compensation was payable. But Lord Reid recognised the exception of what had been called 'battle damage'. He said ([1964] 2 All ER 348 at 360, [1965] AC 75 at 110):

a
'Such damage must include both accidental and deliberate damage done in the course of fighting operations. It cannot matter whether the damage was unintentional or done by our artillery or aircraft to dislodge the enemy or by the enemy to dislodge our troops; and the same must apply to destruction of a building or a bridge before the enemy actually capture it. Moreover, it would be absurd if the right to compensation for such a building or bridge

b
depended on how near the enemy were when it was destroyed.'

In the House of Lords the decision of the First Division of the Court of Session was reversed by a majority on the basis that the destruction of the installations was not so intimately tied up with the actual fighting as to be regarded as battle damage. It seems quite plain, however, that Lord Reid would have upheld the

c
decision if he had reached the same conclusion as the Court of Session on the facts.

Lord Pearce adopted a similar approach to that of Lord Reid. He said ([1964] 2 All ER 348 at 394, [1965] AC 75 at 162):

d
'In respect of a house that has the misfortune to be in the centre of a battle field and is inevitably demolished by the Crown's artillery, it is clear, on the principles which have been almost unanimously set out, that the subject can have no claim. In respect of a house that is demolished by the Crown with wise forethought, long before any battle, to provide a fort or a clear field of fire in case of threatened invasion I think it is equally clear that the subject

e
should obtain compensation. Cases which lie close to that line, wherever it be drawn, must depend on fact and degree ... I would define the line as excluding damage done in the battle or for the necessities of the battle. If an evacuating army destroys as it goes, I would exclude from compensation any damage which it does for the purposes of its survival, for example, ammunition which will be turned against it by the enemy, or petrol which

f
will be used by the enemy to pursue it, or food which will sustain the enemy during their attacks on it.'

It is to be noted that Lord Upjohn too recognised the distinction between the taking of property to prevent it being of use to the enemy and the destruction of property caused by artillery in, for example, retaking a town from the enemy (see

g
[1964] 2 All ER 348 at 399, [1965] AC 75 at 169). The House accepted that the relevant law was the law of Burma but the case was decided on the basis that the law of Burma in 1941 had to be assumed to be the same as the law of England.

It was therefore submitted in this court that the decision in the *Burmah Oil* case, though it was concerned with compensation for loss of property, was some

h
support for the proposition that a claim could not be based on damage sustained in the course of military operations against the enemy.

The third strand of authority relied upon by the defendants related to actions against the police. In particular, our attention was directed to the decision of May J in *Hughes v National Union of Mineworkers* [1991] 4 All ER 278. In that case the

j
plaintiff, who was a police officer, was injured during disturbances at a colliery in North Yorkshire in 1984. The plaintiff brought an action against the union and also against the Chief Constable of the North Yorkshire Police. He alleged that there had been a failure to provide him with adequate protection, that there had been inadequate co-ordination of the police forces available and that he had been exposed to the risk of injury. On the application by the chief constable to strike the action out the judge referred to a number of cases involving the police

including *Hill v Chief Constable of West Yorkshire* [1988] 2 All ER 238, [1989] AC 53. Having considered these authorities, the judge expressed his conclusion:

> '... in my judgment, as a matter of public policy, if senior police officers charged with the task of deploying what may or may not be an adequate force of officers to control serious public disorder are to be potentially liable to individual officers under their command if those individuals are injured by attacks from rioters, that would be significantly detrimental to the control of public order. It will no doubt often happen that in such circumstances critical decisions have to be made with little or no time for considered thought and where many individual officers may be in some danger of physical injury of one kind or another. It is not, I consider, in the public interest that those decisions should generally be the potential target of a negligence claim if rioters do injure an individual officer, since the fear of such a claim would be likely to affect the decisions to the prejudice of the very task which the decisions are intended to advance.' (See [1991] 4 All ER 278 at 288.)

It was said that *Hughes'* case was another illustration of the rule that in what may be called 'battle conditions' those who take part in an attempt to control events should not be made liable for damages in civil proceedings.

It was argued on behalf of the plaintiff on the other hand that until the facts had been fully investigated it was not possible to say whether 'battle conditions' existed at the relevant time. One of the matters which would have to be investigated was whether, in allowing the plaintiff to go forward, Sgt Warren had been in breach of some recognised rule or standing instruction. Thus, as was demonstrated by the decision of the Court of Appeal in *Knightley v Johns* [1982] 1 All ER 851, [1982] 1 WLR 349, a police officer might be held liable in negligence to one of his subordinates if, even in an emergency, he acted in breach of an explicit standing order.

It was further submitted on behalf of the plaintiff that some passages in the judgments in the *Shaw Savill* case 66 CLR 344 went too far. Attention was drawn to the criticisms of the decision by Professor Hogg in *Liability of the Crown* (1971) p 95. The right approach, it was suggested, was to allow the claim to proceed and then to have an investigation at the trial into the particular circumstances surrounding the firing of the gun to see whether there had been any breach of a duty of care. The exigencies of battle might well provide an excuse for what in other circumstances would constitute a breach of duty.

Furthermore, it was submitted, it would be wrong to invoke public policy to provide the defendants with a defence. Parliament had empowered the Secretary of State to reintroduce the immunity conferred by s 10 of the 1947 Act to cover hostilities in a particular war zone. No action had been taken under s 2 of the 1987 Act and the common law had no part to play.

Conclusions

In my judgment the circumstances in which the plaintiff was injured clearly constituted 'battle conditions' in the sense contemplated by Lord Reid, Lord Pearce and Lord Upjohn in the *Burmah Oil* case [1964] 2 All ER 348, [1965] AC 75. Furthermore, I consider that an English court should approach this claim in the same way as the High Court of Australia in the *Shaw Savill* case. I do not accept Professor Hogg's criticisms of that decision. Moreover, I would observe that in *Liability of the Crown* (2nd edn, 1989) p 137, Professor Hogg acknowledged that his a   earlier criticism did not 'seem to have won any converts'. As I said earlier, I do not find it necessary to explore the territorial limits of this immunity. It is sufficient to say that in my view it covers the present situation where, in the course of hostilities against an enemy, a howitzer of the plaintiff's battalion was engaging the enemy and the plaintiff was a member of the gun team.

b   In addition it may be helpful if I state what my conclusions would be even in the absence of the Australian decisions and the *Burmah Oil* case. It is true that the Secretary of State, by conferring his powers under s 2 of the 1987 Act could have reintroduced the immunity conferred by s 10 of the 1947 Act. But in the absence of this statutory protection one still has to consider the position at common law. It is therefore necessary to consider whether at the relevant time Sgt Warren owed a duty of care to the plaintiff at common law.

c   In *Marc Rich & Co AG v Bishop Rock Marine Co Ltd, The Nicholas H* [1995] 3 All ER 307 at 326, [1996] 1 AC 211 at 235 Lord Steyn drew attention to the fact that since the decision in *Home Office v Dorset Yacht Co Ltd* [1970] 2 All ER 294, [1970] AC 1004 it has been settled law that the elements of foreseeability and proximity as well as considerations of fairness, justice and reasonableness are relevant to all d   cases of alleged negligence whatever the nature of the harm sustained by the plaintiff.

In the present case it is accepted on behalf of the defendants that two of these components of a duty of care, proximity and foreseeability of damage, are present. The issue to be determined is whether it is fair, just and reasonable that a duty of care should be imposed on one soldier in his conduct towards another e   when engaging the enemy during hostilities. In the light of the recent amendment to the plaintiff's pleading the same question has to be asked in relation to the alleged duty to maintain a safe system of work.

It is plain from the decision of the House of Lords in the *Marc Rich* case that in order to decide whether it is fair, just and reasonable to impose a duty of care one f   must consider all the circumstances including the position and role of the alleged tortfeasor and any relevant policy considerations. In this context one should bear in mind the dictum of Lord Pearce in *Hedley Byrne & Co Ltd v Heller & Partners Ltd* [1963] 2 All ER 575 at 615, [1964] AC 465 at 536:

g   'How wide the sphere of the duty of care in negligence is to be laid depends ultimately upon the courts' assessment of the demands of society for protection from the carelessness of others.'

This dictum was cited by Lord Diplock in the *Dorset Yacht* case [1970] 2 All ER 294 at 324, [1970] AC 1004 at 1058. In the absence of legislative guidance the question of policy has to be resolved by the courts.

h   I am satisfied that in a hypothetical case a court would require proof that the injury was sustained in battle conditions. But here, as it seems to me, the plaintiff's pleaded case makes the position clear. The question then becomes: 'Is a duty of care to be imposed in such conditions so as to make one serviceman liable for his negligent act towards another?' In my opinion, despite the careful j   arguments addressed to us on behalf of the plaintiff, there is no basis for extending the scope of the duty of care so far. I would echo the words of Gibbs CJ in *Groves'* case (1982) 150 CLR 113 at 117:

'To hold that there is no civil liability for injury caused by the negligence of persons in the course of an actual engagement with the enemy seems to me to accord with common sense and sound policy.'

I reach the same conclusion on the plaintiff's alternative claim. In my opinion   *a*
there was no duty on the defendants in these battle conditions to maintain a safe
system of work.

I would therefore allow the appeal and make an order to strike out the
statement of claim and to dismiss the action.

McCOWAN LJ. I entirely agree with the judgment of Neill LJ and have nothing   *b*
to add.

SIR IAIN GLIDEWELL. I have had the advantage of reading the judgment of
Neill LJ in draft. For the reasons he gives, I agree that this appeal should be
allowed, the statement of claim struck out and the plaintiff's action dismissed.   *c*
As, however, we are differing from the decision of Judge Walker. I think it right
to express my own views shortly.

Mr Havers QC, for the defendants, defined the issue before the court in these
words: 'Does one soldier owe to another a duty of care when engaging the enemy
in the course of hostilities?' I agree that, on the pleadings and in the argument   *d*
before the judge, this is a correct formulation of the issue.

It may seem surprising that this question has not previously been decided by a
court in this country, but the reason is not far to seek. An action in negligence by
one member of the armed forces of the Crown against another would have been
barred by the doctrine of common employment until that doctrine was abolished
by the Law Reform (Personal Injuries) Act 1948. When that happened, the   *e*
Crown Proceedings Act 1947 was already in force. Neill LJ has set out in his
judgment the terms of s 10 of that Act. The terms of that section clearly required
the question posed by Mr Havers to be answered No. Thus it was not until s 10
of the 1947 Act was itself suspended by s 1 of the Crown Proceedings (Armed
Forces) Act 1987 that the answer to the question depended, for the first time, on   *f*
the general common law principles of the law of negligence.

Mr Havers accepts that, if the plaintiff proves the facts alleged in his statement
of claim (as, for the purposes of this appeal, we must assume he can do) the first
two criteria for establishing that Sgt Warren owed the plaintiff a duty of care,
namely proximity between the parties and foreseeability of damages, are
satisfied. Thus, such a duty of care would be owed unless considerations of public   *g*
policy require that, in the course of hostilities, it should not.

Like Neill LJ, it is in my judgment clear that public policy does require that,
when two or more members of the armed forces of the Crown are engaged in the
course of hostilities, one is under no duty of care in tort to another. Indeed, it
could be highly detrimental to the conduct of military operations if each soldier   *h*
had to be conscious that, even in the heart of battle, he owed such a duty to his
comrade. My reasons are thus in essence those expressed by Dixon J in the
passage from his judgment in *Shaw Savill and Albion Co Ltd v The Commonwealth*
(1940) 66 CLR 344, which Neill LJ has quoted. If during the course of hostilities
no duty of care is owed by a member of the armed forces to civilians or their   *j*
property, it must be even more apparent that no such duty is owed to another
member of the armed forces. This conclusion is wholly consistent with, and
supported by, the decision of the House of Lords in *Burmah Oil Co (Burmah
Trading) Ltd v Lord Advocate* {1964] 2 All ER 348, [1965] AC 75 and depends upon
similar reasoning to that adopted by May J in relation to police officers in *Hughes
v National Union of Mineworkers* [1991] 4 All ER 278. In my judgment, therefore,

a at common law, one soldier does not owe to another a duty of care when engaging the enemy in the course of hostilities.

Mr Hawkesworth QC, for the plaintiff, sought to amend his pleading to allege that the defendants were not merely vicariously liable for any breach of duty (if duty there was) by Sgt Warren, but also directly liable for failure to maintain a safe system of work. I agree with Neill LJ however that such an amendment

b makes no difference. The reasons which result in the first question being answered 'No' result in the same answer to the second issue. Having reached this decision as a matter of principle, I agree with Neill LJ that the plaintiff's claim is pleaded with sufficient clarity to make it clear that no further process of fact finding could result in success in his action.

For these reasons, which do no more than underline the detailed reasoning of

c Neill LJ, I agree that this appeal should be allowed and the plaintiff's claim be struck out.

Appeal allowed. Leave to appeal to the House of Lords refused.

Paul Magrath Esq   Barrister.

Possfund Custodian Trustee Ltd and another v Diamond and others (McGrigor Donald (a firm), third party)

Parr and others v Diamond and others (McGrigor Donald (a firm), third party)

CHANCERY DIVISION

LIGHTMAN J

20–22, 25, 26 MARCH, 2 APRIL 1996

Negligence – Information or advice – Knowledge third party might rely on information – Company – Prospectus for initial allotment of shares and after-market purchase on unlisted securities market – Prospectus allegedly misrepresenting company's financial position – Plaintiffs making after-market share purchases in reliance on prospectus – Plaintiffs suffering loss – Whether persons issuing prospectus owing duty of care to purchasers of after-market shares.

On 19 April 1992 the defendant company, D plc, issued a prospectus in connection with the flotation of its shares on the unlisted securities market. The prospectus specifically stated that, as part of the same exercise as allotment, the facility would be available for shares to be dealt with subsequently on the unlisted securities market. The majority of the plaintiffs were subscribers at the time of the placing of the shares; the others made subsequent purchases of shares in the unlisted securities market during the period 2 May to 11 July 1989 (the after-market purchases). D plc subsequently went into receivership and in 1992 two of the plaintiffs commenced proceedings against D plc, the company's directors at the time of the placing of shares, and its financial advisors and auditors, claiming, inter alia, damages for deceit and negligence in relation to material misrepresentations contained in the prospectus as to D plc's financial position which they had relied on and in consequence of which they had suffered financial loss. In 1995 a second action was commenced against the defendants by a number of other plaintiffs. The two actions were consolidated and thereafter three of the defendants applied under RSC Ord 18, r 19 to strike out the plaintiffs' claims in respect of the after-market purchases as disclosing no cause of action, on the basis that the common law duty of care in respect of the issue of a company's prospectus was limited to the initial subscription and did not extend to subsequent purchasers of the company's shares in the unlisted market.

Held – It was arguable that persons responsible for the issue of a company's share prospectus owed a duty of care to, and could be liable in damages at the instance of, subsequent purchasers of that company's shares on the unlisted securities market, provided that the purchaser could establish that he had reasonably relied on representations made in the prospectus and reasonably believed that the representor intended him to act on them, and that there existed a sufficient direct connection between the purchaser and the representor to render the imposition of such a duty fair, just and reasonable. If the plaintiffs in the instant case could establish that, at the date of preparation and circulation of the original share

a prospectus, the defendants intended to inform and encourage after-market purchasers, in addition to those investors who relied on the prospectus in making a decision whether to accept the allotment offer thereby made, it was at least arguable that the defendants had assumed and owed a duty of care to those investors who relied on the contents of the prospectus in making after-market purchases. The plaintiffs' claim therefore merited full consideration at trial. The
b applications would accordingly be dismissed (see p 786 g, p 787 a b e f and p 798 a b e to p 789 d, post).

Peek v Gurney [1861–73] All ER Rep 116 and Al-Nakib Investments (Jersey) Ltd v Longcroft [1990] 3 All ER 321 considered.

Notes

c For negligence in relation to statements, see 34 Halsbury's Laws (4th edn) para 53.

Cases referred to in judgment

Al-Nakib Investments (Jersey) Ltd v Longcroft [1990] 3 All ER 321, [1990] 1 WLR 1390.
Andrews v Mockford [1896] 1 QB 372, CA.
d Caparo Industries plc v Dickman [1990] 1 All ER 568, [1990] 2 AC 605, [1990] 2 WLR 358, HL.
Chanel Ltd v F W Woolworth & Co Ltd [1981] 1 All ER 745, [1981] 1 WLR 485, CA.
Derry v Peek (1889) 14 App Cas 337, [1886–90] All ER Rep 1, HL.
Dombey & Son v Playfair Bros [1897] 1 QB 368, CA.
Galoo Ltd (in liq) v Bright Grahame Murray (a firm) [1995] 1 All ER 16, [1994] 1 WLR
e 1360, CA.
Hedley Byrne & Co Ltd v Heller & Partners Ltd [1963] 2 All ER 575, [1964] AC 465, [1963] 3 WLR 101, HL.
Henderson v Merrett Syndicates Ltd [1994] 3 All ER 506, [1995] 2 AC 145, [1994] 3 WLR 761, HL.
f House of Spring Gardens Ltd v Waite [1990] 2 All ER 990, [1991] 1 QB 241, [1990] 3 WLR 347, CA.
Morgan Crucible Co plc v Hill Samuel Bank Ltd [1991] 1 All ER 148, [1991] Ch 295, [1991] 2 WLR 655, CA.
Peek v Gurney (1873) LR 6 HL 377, [1861–73] All ER Rep 116.
Scott v Dixon (1859) 29 LJ Ex 62n.
g Williams & Humbert Ltd v W & H Trade Marks (Jersey) Ltd [1986] 1 All ER 129, [1986] AC 368, [1986] 2 WLR 24, HL.

Summonses

By summonses issued on 6 December 1995, 13 December 1995 and 4 March 1996
h respectively the ninth, tenth and seventh defendants, Allied Provincial Corporate Services Ltd (APCS), Arthur Andersen & Co (a firm) (AA) and George Brian Phillips, applied under RSC Ord 18, r 19 to strike out the claims in two consolidated actions brought by the plaintiffs, Possfund Custodian Trustee Ltd, Britel Fund Trustees Ltd (CH 1992 P 4177) and Irene Maud Parr (CH 1995 P 1919)
j and 75 other subscribers and/or purchasers of shares in the eighth defendant company, Diamond Group Holdings plc, on the unlisted securities market, as disclosing no cause of action in respect of after-market purchases of shares allegedly made in reliance on the company's share prospectus. The remaining defendants, Victor Derek Diamond, Clive Brown Miller, Ian King, Michael John Vernon Housley, James Kenneth Downes and Robert Barr Marshall, and the third party, McGrigor Donald (a firm), took no part in the proceedings. The

summonses were heard in chambers, but judgment was given by Lightman J in   a
open court. The facts are set out in the judgment.

Charles Falconer QC and *Martin Moore* (instructed by *Maxwell Batley*) for the
plaintiffs.
Robin Potts QC and *Philip Gillyon* (instructed by *Richards Butler*) for APCS.
Mark Barnes QC and *Rhodri Davies* (instructed by *Herbert Smith*) for AA.   b
Andrew Thornton (instructed by *Simmons & Simmons*) for Mr Phillips.

Cur adv vult

2 April 1996. The following judgment was delivered.

c

LIGHTMAN J.

I. INTRODUCTION

A. *Nature of claims in actions*

The applications before me raise the novel and important question of law   d
whether it is arguable today that those responsible for the issue of a company's
prospectus owe a duty of care to subsequent purchasers of that company's shares
on the market.
    These two actions commenced in 1992 and 1995 by different plaintiffs against
the same defendants arise (i) out of a placing of shares in the eighth defendant,   e
Diamond Group Holdings plc (Diamond), on the unlisted securities market (the
USM) in April 1989 (the placing) in respect of which the majority of the plaintiffs
were subscribers and (ii) out of subsequent purchases by certain of the plaintiffs
of Diamond's shares (the after-market purchases) on the USM.   5,177,726
ordinary 5p shares in Diamond were placed at 85p per share. The shares placed
amounted to 27·51% of the issued share capital of Diamond, as enlarged by the   f
issue.
    Diamond's main business was the provision and arranging of mechanical
breakdown insurance for the purchase of new and used cars. On 19 April 1989
Diamond issued a prospectus in connection with the flotation of its shares on the
USM. The plaintiffs contend that (1) when subscribing for and purchasing shares   g
in Diamond (shares which in truth were valueless), they relied on (as they were
intended to) the prospectus; (2) the prospectus materially misrepresented
Diamond's financial position (in the main because it very substantially
understated its liabilities by failing to disclose adequately, or at all, Diamond's
liability to pay substantial extra premiums to the syndicates at Lloyds); and (3) the
first to seventh defendants (the directors at the time of the placing), the eighth   h
defendant, Diamond, the ninth defendant, Allied Provincial Corporate Services
Ltd (APCS) (the financial advisers for the placing), and the tenth defendant,
Arthur Andersen & Co (a firm) (AA) (Diamond's auditors and the reporting
accountants for the placing), in respect both of the placing and after-market
purchases owed them duties of care which they broke and thereby caused the   j
plaintiffs' loss. In both actions the plaintiffs claim: (1) against all the defendants in
respect of the shares subscribed in the placing, statutory compensation under s 67
of the Companies Act 1985; (2) in respect of the shares subscribed in the placing
and the after-market purchases, common law damages for: (a) deceit against the
first four defendants and Diamond; (b) negligence against the first to ninth
defendants in causing or procuring the publication of the prospectus; and (c)

a negligence against AA in respect of their financial report which they consented to being included in the prospectus.

The plaintiffs define the term 'after market' to mean the period after the placing during which the most recent published financial information relating to Diamond was contained in the prospectus and, as so defined, the after market in relation to Diamond extended over the period from 2 May to 11 July 1989.

b Diamond is in receivership. Judgment in default of defence has been entered against the second defendant, Mr Miller, who lives in Florida. Third party proceedings have been commenced against Messrs McGrigor Donald, a firm of solicitors, who were the solicitors to the placing.

c **B. History of proceedings**

In the 1992 action (begun on 1 May 1992) the plaintiffs, Possfund Custodian Trustee Ltd (Possfund) and Britel Fund Trustees Ltd (Britel), allege that they subscribed for 250,000 shares in the placing at a total cost of £213,112 and that thereafter they purchased a further 670,000 shares by 16 purchases in the market at a total cost of £618,752. In 1993 AA applied by summons to strike out the
d paragraphs in the statement of claim containing the allegations against them of a breach of a common law duty of care in respect of the placing and the after-market purchases, on the ground that the statement of claim disclosed no reasonable cause of action. Argument was however confined to the issue whether the claim in respect of after-market purchases was maintainable. The hearing before Harman J took place on 16 November 1993. At the preliminary
e stage, after a hearing lasting about half a day, Harman J dismissed the application with costs. In his judgment he expressed 'grave doubts about the soundness of the claims advanced' but stated that he could not 'be satisfied upon this particular application by one of these ten defendants that substantial savings will be caused' by striking out the paragraphs in question. The critical factor was that the same
f allegations were made against APCS as against AA and APCS (plainly with full knowledge of AA's application) decided not to join in the application, and, since APCS had not joined in the application, whatever its outcome, the same areas of fact and law would still have to be investigated at the trial. He rejected an application by AA after judgment for an opportunity to join APCS and in effect have another chance: AA had already had its bite of the cherry and it was too late.
g The 1995 action was commenced on 31 March 1995 (effectively on the last day before expiration of the statute of limitation). Originally there were 94 plaintiffs, but there are now (following various amendments) 75 plaintiffs or joint plaintiffs, including three nominee companies (the 12th, 49th and 94th plaintiffs). In brief: (1) the total claim in the 1995 action is for about £935,000, of which about
h £270,000 relates to after-market purchases: (2) nine plaintiffs, and eleven beneficiaries of nominee plaintiffs, are solely concerned with after-market purchases.

Service of proceedings was delayed until July 1995. By letter dated 24 August 1995, the defendants requested particulars, in particular as to which of the
j plaintiffs made claims in respect of the placing and which in respect of after-market purchases, and intimated that an application would be made to strike out all after-market claims. These particulars were given on 14 November 1995. APCS issued a summons seeking an order under RSC Ord 18, r 19 striking out the claims in the two actions in respect of after-market purchases as disclosing no cause of action (ie bound in law to fail) on 6 December 1995. AA followed suit on 13 December 1995, and the seventh defendant, Mr Phillips (formerly a

non-executive director of Diamond), evidently a late convert to this course of
action, did likewise on 4 March 1996. At the hearing before me his counsel
sensibly only made a fleeting appearance to adopt in advance the arguments of
counsel for AA and APCS.

For completeness I should add that by order dated 29 August 1995, the two
actions were consolidated. The pleadings in the two actions remain separate, but
(save to the extent I indicate later) the two statements of claim are practically
identical.

II. THE APPLICATIONS TO STRIKE OUT: THE PRELIMINARY STAGE

A. *The principles*

The House of Lords in *Williams & Humbert Ltd v W & H Trade Marks (Jersey)
Ltd* [1986] 1 All ER 129, [1986] AC 368 held that there should be two stages on an
application to strike out involving (as does the present application) a prolonged
and serious argument. There is the preliminary stage, when the court has to
decide whether to allow the application to proceed. If the court decides to allow
the application to proceed, there is then the substantive stage when the court
hears the application on its merits. The preliminary stage operates as a filter
designed to ensure that the court's time and the parties' costs are not wasted on
inappropriate or oppressive (often lengthy and expensive) applications.

The relevant principles were stated by Lord Templeman ([1986] 1 All ER 129
at 139, [1986] AC 368 at 435–436):

'My Lords, if an application to strike out involves a prolonged and serious
argument the judge should, as a general rule, decline to proceed with the
argument unless he not only harbours doubts about the soundness of the
pleading but, in addition, is satisfied that striking out will obviate the
necessity for a trial or will substantially reduce the burden of preparing for
trial or the burden of the trial itself.'

Lord Mackay then stated ([1986] 1 All ER 129 at 143, [1986] AC 368 at 441):

'If on an application to strike out it appears that a prolonged and serious
argument will be necessary there must, at the least, be a serious risk that the
court time, effort and expense devoted to it will be lost since the pleading in
question may not be struck out and the whole matter will require to be
considered anew at the trial. This consideration, as well as the context in
which Ord 18, r 19 occurs and the authorities on it, justifies a general rule
that the judge should decline to proceed with the argument unless he not
only considers it likely that he may reach the conclusion that the pleading
should be struck out, but also is satisfied that striking out will obviate the
necessity for a trial or will so substantially cut down or simplify the trial as to
make the risk of proceeding with the hearing sufficiently worth while.'

B. *Application of the principles*

Mr Falconer QC for the plaintiffs submitted that at the preliminary stage the
defendants' summonses should be dismissed and accordingly should not proceed
to the substantive stage. After full argument I rejected this submission, but
indicated that I would give my reasons in this judgment, which I now do. Mr
Falconer relied on four grounds, and I shall deal with each in turn.

a

(1) Abuse of process

Mr Falconer contended that to bring a second application to strike out on the same grounds as the earlier application dismissed by Harman J was an abuse of process. In the special circumstances of this case I disagree.

Whilst the doctrine of res judicata may at least ordinarily be inapplicable in respect of an earlier interlocutory decision (see *Dombey & Son v Playfair Bros* [1897]

b 1 QB 368), in *Chanel Ltd v F W Woolworth & Co Ltd* [1981] 1 All ER 745 at 751, [1981] 1 WLR 485 at 492–493 Buckley LJ stated:

> 'Even in interlocutory matters a party cannot fight over again a battle which has already been fought unless there has been some significant change of circumstances, or the party has become aware of facts which he could not
> *c*   reasonably have known, or found out, in time for the first encounter.'

This principle applies where in the previous battle the substantive issue between the parties has been decided, and not where on account of some remediable procedural error or omission the substantive issue has had to be left undecided (as in *Dombey v Playfair*). The substantive issue was decided by

d Harman J: he decided it on the merits as fought by AA: the absence of APCS was not a technicality, but a matter of substance critically affecting the balancing exercise the judge was required to make. This is reflected in the judge's refusal after judgment to allow a further hearing after efforts had been made to secure the consent of APCS to their joinder in the application. The principle stated by Buckley LJ accordingly precluded a fresh application by AA unless one of the

e stated conditions could be satisfied.

Where one defendant has made an application, e g to strike out, and another defendant, to whom a like application on the same ground is available, deliberately refrains from joining in the application, and the application is refused, then ordinarily that other defendant will be subject to a similar bar

f (consider *House of Spring Gardens Ltd v Waite* [1990] 2 All ER 990, [1991] 1 QB 241). APCS, as Mr Potts QC put it, (and no doubt Mr Phillips) made the tactical decision not to join in the application by AA. APCS and Mr Phillips can be in no better position in this regard than AA. This principle therefore, as it seems to me precluded a second application to strike out the 1992 action by AA, APCS or Mr Phillips unless one of the stated preconditions for a fresh application could be

g satisfied.

After anxious consideration I have however reached the conclusion that the commencement of the 1995 action and its consolidation with the 1992 action constitute a sufficient change of circumstances. The mere fact that a fresh action is brought by a new plaintiff maintaining the same claim is not necessarily

h sufficient to release a defendant from such a constraint in a previous action. Indeed the circumstances may justify the extension of the constraint to the new action and prevent a striking out claim in both actions. It is likely that justice and convenience will require that the question of law be decided in both actions at the same time and accordingly that there be a joint hearing or no hearing. The

j decision in each case must be reached on consideration of the facts of that case and with regard to the considerations of justice and convenience. Justice to AA, APCS and Mr Phillips does require that they be entitled to proceed with the application in the 1995 action because of the substantial value of the claim made and number of the plaintiffs making the claim, each of which claim will require (or at least may require) detailed investigation at trial unless the application succeeds. There would be a substantial objection to the judge deciding the

question of law on a striking out application in the 1995 action without at the   *a*
same time allowing it to be decided at the same time in the 1992 action.

Some reinforcement of this conclusion (if needed) may be found in the fact that
Harman J saw much in the merits of the application before him, and only
dismissed it with some obvious regret because of the non-joinder of APCS, an
obstacle not present on the current joint applications by AA and APCS (together
with Mr Phillips) in both actions.   I am not persuaded that there is any   *b*
counter-veiling disadvantage to the plaintiffs, save that an adverse decision on the
application to strike out is likely to prejudice their negotiating position in any
settlement discussions. As regards this factor, I see every reason and advantage
in negotiations taking place (if this is possible) on a realistic (and indeed correct)
basis as to the prospects of a plaintiff's claims.   *c*

(2) Soundness of statements of claim
   Mr Falconer submitted that the court should not harbour any doubts as to the
soundness of the statements of claim on the ground that they are plainly sound.
Mr Potts (for APCS) and Mr Barnes QC (for AA) submitted that the court should
not harbour any doubts, for they are plainly unsound. At this stage (since I shall   *d*
go into this matter in detail later) I shall only say that for the purposes of applying
the principles in the *Williams* case I was in serious doubt as to the soundness of
the pleadings as they then stood.

(3) Saving of costs or simplification of trial   *e*
   The observations of Lord Templeman and Lord Mackay in *Williams* were
made in the context where there were only two parties to the proceedings, and
they did not need to consider whether it was sufficient to justify proceeding to the
substantive stage that an application (if successful) would achieve a substantial
saving in the costs of one of numerous defendants, or simplify and reduce the
burdens of the trial for that defendant, even if it did not have any substantial effect   *f*
on the trial as a whole. Harman J does appear to have taken the view that it was
insufficient: the application before him would plainly have achieved savings and
reduced the burdens for AA, but since the overall costs and burdens of the trial
would not be substantially reduced, he dismissed the application. I understand
however that the contrary was not argued. In my view, the court can and should
consider the effect of applications (if successful) both on the trial as a whole and   *g*
on the particular defendant making the application, and if the beneficial impact
on the particular defendant is substantial, then that defendant can satisfy this
requirement and the court should not refuse to proceed to the substantive stage
because of the limited effect of the order (if made) on the trial as a whole.

   On the facts of this case, I am amply satisfied that the application (if successful)   *h*
will effect substantial savings and reduce the burdens of the trial for each of
APCS, AA and Mr Phillips.   In respect of the after-market purchases, these
defendants will be saved the need: (1) to examine the relevant plaintiffs'
documents revealed on discovery; (2) to test or investigate their evidence as to
reliance; or (3) to adduce or test expert evidence as to the value of the shares at   *j*
the dates of the various after-market purchases. The application, if successful,
will open the way to negotiations for settlement better informed as to the
plaintiffs' prospects at trial as against them (and the other defendants) if (as is at
least possible) the parties want to settle. If necessary I would also have decided
that the applications (if successful) would achieve substantial savings in respect of
the trial as a whole.

a (4) Importance of questions of law

There is no doubt that the court will consider how far it is appropriate on an application under Ord 18, r 19 to decide an important issue of law which requires detailed and considered examination appropriate to a trial or a trial of a preliminary issue of law.

b In this case, the question whether persons in the position of the defendants can be under a duty to after-market purchasers is by common consent important, and involves careful consideration of the authorities. But, as will appear later, on the pleadings as they stood when I had to decide whether to proceed to the substantive stage, the issue whether the plaintiffs' claim disclosed a cause of action did not appear particularly difficult, or inappropriate to be dealt with, at this interlocutory stage. This factor in the circumstances did not appear an *c* objection of any real weight to proceeding to the substantive stage.

III. THE APPLICATIONS TO STRIKE OUT: THE SUBSTANTIVE STAGE

It is common ground for the purposes of these applications that the plaintiffs' pleadings disclose a cause of action in respect of the placing. The issue is whether *d* such a cause of action is disclosed in respect of the after-market purchases.

I propose to approach this question in three stages. First, I shall consider in outline the common law and statutory schemes providing protection to investors in respect of prospectuses. Second, I shall examine the pleadings. Third, I shall look in more detail at the authorities so far as they provide guidance on the scope of the common law duty of care owed to investors and in particular whether it is *e* arguable that the tort of negligence provides the protection pleaded by the plaintiffs.

(A) *The common law and statutory scheme*

In the nineteenth century when the issue of prospectuses first became a *f* common feature of commercial life, the common law allowed a claim in damages to the investor who incurred a loss after investing in reliance on the contents of a false or misleading prospectus (in the absence of a breach of a fiduciary or contractual duty owed to the investor) only if he could establish the tort of deceit (see *Derry v Peek* (1889) 14 App Cas 337, [1886–90] All ER Rep 1). The prospectus was an invitation issued to the public to subscribe for shares, and not to purchase *g* shares in the market, and without more the prospectus could only found liability if relied on for the purpose for which it was issued, namely making the decision whether to subscribe, and not if relied on for the purpose of deciding whether or not to make purchases in the market (see *Peek v Gurney* (1873) LR 6 HL 377, [1861–73] All ER Rep 116). The principle was graphically expressed in the expression *h* that the representations contained within the prospectus were exhausted upon the allotment being completed.

The legislature evidently considered that the common law provided inadequate protection to placees, and the Directors Liability Act 1890 provided that: (1) directors, promoters and persons authorising the issue of a prospectus *j* should be liable to pay compensation to all persons who should subscribe for shares on the faith of a prospectus for the loss or damage they sustained by reason of any untrue statement in the prospectus; and (2) they should have a statutory defence (in respect of which the onus should be upon them) that they had reasonable grounds to believe and did believe that the statement was true or the fair representation of the views of an expert. No statutory protection was afforded to after-market purchasers.

The provisions of the 1890 Act were brought into the mainstream of *a*
companies legislation in 1908 in the form of s 84 of the Companies (Consolidation) Act 1908 and re-enacted by s 37 of the Companies Act 1929, in each case
without any material change.

The Companies Act 1948 supplemented the previous statutory provisions in
three relevant respects. First, it provided that it should be unlawful to make an
invitation to the public to subscribe for shares without issuing a prospectus *b*
containing certain specified information. Secondly, it added experts who
consented to the use of their reports in the prospectus to the class of those liable
to persons subscribing on the faith of a prospectus, and such experts were
likewise afforded a statutory defence if they could prove the existence of
reasonable grounds for believing their statements to be true. Thirdly, s 45(1)
introduced the provision (now in s 58 of the Companies Act 1985) whereby the *c*
protection previously afforded to subscribers was extended to cover the loophole
that might otherwise exist where shares were first allotted to an issuing house for
sale to the public. This was done by deeming the offer for sale to the public to be
an offer for subscription and the purchasers to be subscribers.

In 1963 the House of Lords in *Hedley Byrne & Co Ltd v Heller & Partners Ltd* *d*
[1963] 2 All ER 575, [1964] AC 465 established that at common law a cause of
action exists enabling the recovery of damages in respect of a negligent
misrepresentation occasioning damage and loss where the necessary proximity
exists between the representor and representee. It is clearly established (and
indeed common ground on these applications) that in a case such as the present, *e*
where the defendants have put a document into more or less general circulation
and there is no special relationship alleged between the plaintiffs and the
defendants, foreseeability by the defendants that the plaintiffs would rely on the
prospectus for the purpose of deciding whether to make after-market purchases
is not sufficient to impose upon the defendants a duty of care to the plaintiffs in
respect of such purchases (see *Caparo Industries plc v Dickman* [1990] 1 All ER 568, *f*
[1990] 2 AC 605). The imposition of a duty of care in such a situation requires a
closer relationship between representor and representee, and its imposition must
be fair, just and reasonable. I shall come back to consider whether in this context
the existence of an intention on the part of the defendants that investors should
rely on the prospectus for this purpose is sufficient to establish the necessary *g*
proximity, for that is the crux of the present applications.

The Companies Act 1985 (in force at the time of the prospectus) in ss 56 to 71
re-enacted the provisions of the 1948 Act (for present purposes) without any
material change. Section 67 contains the provisions for payment of compensation to placees.

Following Professor Gower's review, there was enacted the Financial Services *h*
Act 1986. This Act drew a sharp distinction between listing particulars (which
effectively replace prospectuses) in respect of shares to be admitted to the official
list of The Stock Exchange (listed securities) and prospectuses in respect of
unlisted securities, which include shares to be listed on the USM. Part IV of the
Act related to listed and Pt V to unlisted. Part IV was brought into force, but Pt *j*
V never was. In the case of listed securities, the Act and the listing rules (which
the Act required to be complied with) required listing particulars to be constantly
updated in respect of any information affecting, inter alia, the value of the listed
securities. Section 150 gave a remedy against the 'persons responsible' for listing
particulars—

a   'to any person who has acquired any of the securities in question [ie the listed securities] and suffered loss in respect of them as a result of any untrue or misleading statement in [the listing particulars] or the omission from them of any matter required to be included ...'

In short, protection was afforded to all purchasers of listed securities (whether placees or after-market purchasers) relying on the continuing and updated
b   representations in the listing particulars and the updates.

In the case of unlisted securities, there is no equivalent statutory provision for updating the prospectus, but the USM does in fact require an undertaking to like effect from a company admitted to the USM. Section 166 provides that persons responsible for a prospectus—

c   'shall be liable to pay compensation to any person who has acquired the securities to which the prospectus relates and suffered loss in respect of them as a result of any untrue or misleading statement in the prospectus ...'

For the purpose of determining the ambit of the duty of care under the tort of negligence, I have been invited to consider whether s 166 (albeit not brought into
d   force, but later repealed and re-enacted in 1995) gave a statutory cause of action to after-market purchasers. All I shall say is that as present advised, I do not think that it does. The reference to the 'person who has acquired the securities to which the prospectus relates', as it seems to me, naturally refers to the placee in respect of the shares originally allotted to him.

e   To complete the legislative history, the Public Offers of Securities Regulations 1995, SI 1995/1537, made pursuant to Council Directive (EEC) 89/298 (in force on 19 June 1995) on co-ordinating the requirements for the drawing-up, scrutiny and distribution of the prospectus to be published when transferable securities are to be offered to the public, laid down a detailed regime in respect of public offers of securities. Any public offer must be accompanied by a prospectus to be
f   made available to the public during the period of the offer, a supplementary prospectus must be published in the event of any significant change or matter arising during the period of the offer, and a remedy in respect of misleading statements in prospectuses for unlisted securities is provided 'to any person who has acquired the securities to which the prospectus relates'. This provision for
g   compensation is to like effect to that contained in s 166 and is, I think, likewise limited in operation and scope.

(B) *Pleadings*

Since these applications turn on the sufficiency of the pleadings, I think it right
h   to set out the relevant passages in the pleadings in the two actions.

(1) The 1992 action

(a) The statement of claim in 1992 action (so far as material) reads as follows:

'PART IV: THE PURPOSE OF THE PROSPECTUS

j   5.1 The purpose and object of the Prospectus was to provide information on the Company and its subsidiaries to prospective placees and provide encouragement to prospective placees to invest in the shares of the Company by participating in the Placing. Prospective placees were persons to whom the Prospectus was sent (whether directly or as a result of an inquiry made by the recipient however prompted). The Plaintiffs were prospective placees.

5.2 Further and in the alternative, the purpose and object of the Prospectus was to provide the financial background to the Company and its subsidiaries on the strength of which or in the context of which a market in the shares of the Company was established and maintained, and, in particular, to induce or encourage the persons mentioned in para 5.3 below to purchase shares on the Aftermarket, so as to ensure or attempt to ensure a satisfactory market in the shares after the commencement of dealings at least until further or other financial information was provided to the public by or on behalf of the Company.

5.3 In any event, and for the aforesaid purposes or either of them, the persons to whom such information was to be given and who were intended to consider and act upon the statements made in the Prospectus were prospective placees (as defined in para 5.1 above) who either: 5.3.2 would purchase further shares in the Aftermarket notwithstanding that they obtained their desired number of shares in the Placing, or 5.3.3 would obtain in the Placing less than the number of shares desired and would purchase further shares in the Aftermarket, or 5.3.4 would not seek to participate in the Placing but would purchase further shares in the Aftermarket.'

The plaintiffs then go on to set out the facts and matters relied on in support of the allegations contained in paras 5.1 and 5.2. It is sufficient to say that the substance of these particulars amounted to the following: (1) the advantages of permission being granted to deal with the shares in the USM for placees in respect of the marketability of their shares and for Diamond in respect of access to the equity capital markets; and (2) the references in the prospectus to: (a) the future prospects of Diamond and certain imminent acquisitions; (b) the agreement by the directors (other than Mr Phillips), in order to maintain an orderly market in the shares in Diamond, to restrict for a period the sales of their own holdings and not to compete with Diamond.

None of the particulars provided any support for the allegation of purpose and intent pleaded in paras 5.2 and 5.3. The particulars merely reflect inducements to prospective investors to take up the invitation proffered with the prospectus and communicate the information required to be provided to such investors to enable an informed decision to be made whether to do so.

(b) Further and better particulars in the 1992 action were served at the request of the ninth and tenth defendants. These took the matter no further.

(c) Voluntary further and better particulars were served supplementing the particulars already given to the tenth defendant. These contained only one relevant and potentially supportive particular under para 5.2. It reads as follows:

'7(a)(ii) The fact that the purpose set out in Paragraph 5.2 of the Amended Statement of Claim is acknowledged by those experienced as advisors in relation to the flotation of companies as one of the purposes of a Prospectus issued in connection with a placing, the other purpose being as set out in Paragraph 5.1 of the Amended Statement of Claim.'

I should add that the defendants have long made discovery in the 1992 action and accordingly there is no scope for that frequently met excuse for serving inadequate particulars that full particulars cannot be served until after discovery.

a (2) The 1995 action

The statement of claim in the 1995 action contains provisions identical to paras 5.1 and 5.2 in the 1992 action, but para 5.3 is in different terms. It reads as follows:

> *b* '5.3 In any event, the persons to whom such information was given and who were intended to consider and act upon the statements made in the Prospectus were all or any of the following: (i) members of the public (including the Group B Plaintiffs); (ii) members of the public who were employees of the Company or its subsidiaries (including Group B Plaintiffs); (iii) connected brokers (including those of the Group A Plaintiffs); (iv) stockbrokers and other financial institutions and intermediaries (including *c* those of the Group A Plaintiffs) who would purchase shares.'

The plaintiffs then proceed to set out identical particulars to those to be found in the 1992 statement of claim, but do not incorporate para 7(a)(ii) of the voluntary particulars.

d (3) Sufficiency of pleadings

Leaving aside the voluntary particulars, the particulars relied on (as I have said) were quite inadequate to establish any properly arguable or pleadable purpose of the prospectus or intention upon the part of the defendants to induce after-market purchases. The one paragraph in the voluntary particulars alone went any way in this direction, but (1) the voluntary particulars were relied on *e* only in the claim against AA in the 1992 action and were not relied on against the other defendants in the 1992 action or in the 1995 action at all; and (2) para 7(a)(ii) appeared objectionable as close to unintelligible and totally uncommunicative. Unfortunately no request for particulars was ever made in respect of these particulars. Perhaps AA had abandoned hope of any sensible clarification.

f When it became apparent from the plaintiffs' submissions that para 7(a)(ii) and the (as yet unrevealed) expert evidence in support intended to be adduced at the trial, constituted essentially the whole thrust of their case on the applications before me, of my own motion I directed the plaintiffs to provide full further and better particulars of para 7(a)(ii), and in the exceptional circumstances of this case (in order to show the substance and bona fides of this contention as to which the *g* earlier pleadings left me in some real doubt), I also ordered the plaintiffs to file an affidavit from their expert substantiating their case on this score. Mr Falconer objected to the order for service of the affidavit: such an order (he said) was quite novel on such an application—it was a procedural innovation. But everything is new once. In future, the same order may be made again if the exceptional *h* circumstances justify it. Such order will then not be novel, but it will be none the better or worse for that. Not only do I possess jurisdiction to make such an order, but I ought to exercise such jurisdiction when, as in this case, justice and convenience so require.

Mr Falconer after an adjournment provided both the particulars and the *j* affidavit. Put very shortly, his case thus revealed is that, whatever the situation at the time of the decision in *Peek v Gurney* (1873) LR 6 HL 377, [1861–73] All ER Rep 116, by 1989 company and commercial practice in respect of prospectuses and market conditions and perceptions had changed and with them the purpose of a prospectus: the established purpose of a prospectus and its contents were no longer confined to inducing investors to become placees, but extended to inducing the public to make after-market purchases. A significant factor in this

context was the requirement of The Stock Exchange for the entire prospectus to   *a*
be printed on Extel cards for Extel Statistical Services Ltd for the purposes of that
company making them available to all subscribers and investors who want to
look at them. Read in this light and against this background, the intention of the
defendants reasonably to be inferred and as reasonably understood by the
plaintiffs was to induce the plaintiffs, as well as to accept shares on the allotment,
to make after-market purchases. The affidavit in support is from Mr John   *b*
Herring, a director of Kleinwort Benson Securities Ltd. His affidavit verifies the
particulars and is to the effect that in the market today a prospectus is perceived
as intended to be acted upon for the purposes of after-market purchases and that
indeed is the intention of those who prepare and are responsible for them.

Mr Barnes for AA accepted that the particulars did now furnish a sufficiently
pleaded case that the purpose of the prospectus and the intention of the   *c*
defendants was to induce such purchases. Mr Gillyon for APCS objected to the
pleadings as still insufficiently particularising the facts relied on in support of the
contention. I think that the pleading is sufficient.

The plaintiffs case, as Mr Falconer made clear and as is now apparent from the
pleadings, is one applicable to any ordinary prospectus today and turns   *d*
exclusively on expert evidence as to the perception in current practice of the
purpose of a prospectus. The defendants know sufficiently the case they have to
meet from the particulars, supplemented by the affidavit of Mr Herring.

(C) *Intent and proximity*   *e*
The issue before me is accordingly whether it is arguable that persons
responsible for a prospectus owe a duty of care to (and may be liable in damages
at the instance of) an after-market purchaser if it is established that such
purchaser was intended to rely on the prospectus for this purpose, and in
particular whether the necessary proximity exists in such a situation between
those responsible for the prospectus and the purchaser.   *f*

(1) Intention
For the purpose of the torts of deceit and negligent misrepresentation, it is
necessary to establish a material misrepresentation intended to influence, and
which did in fact influence the mind of the representee and on which the   *g*
representee reasonably relied.

There has been much argument before me whether the required intention of
the representor should be objectively ascertained, as the intention reasonably to
be inferred from his words or action (or inaction), or whether the subjective
intention of the representor to induce is sufficient. The authorities and textbooks
do not provide any clear guidance. For example, in 31 *Halsbury's Laws* (4th edn)   *h*
para 1042 it is stated that the intention may be actual or presumptive. Whilst in
Clerk and Lindsell on Torts (17th edn, 1995) para 7.65 it is categorically stated: 'The
defendant's intention must be assessed objectively.' A footnote makes reference
to a dictum of Lord Goff in *Henderson Syndicates Ltd v Merrett* [1994] 3 All ER 506
at 521, [1995] 2 AC 145 at 181 to the effect that in determining whether a party   *j*
has 'assumed responsibility' an objective test of intention must be applied.

Whether or not theoretically a subjective intention is sufficient, for all practical
purposes, as it seems to me, the intention must in all cases be objectively
established. Such intent is objectively established if the representor expressly
communicates intent to the representee. On the other hand, where it is not
expressly communicated, the representee must establish that he reasonably relied

a on the representation and that he reasonably believed that the representor intended him to act upon it. Accordingly, if the subjective intention of the representor is not expressly communicated to him, the existence of a subjective intention alone is insufficient to found an action unless the existence of such an intention on the part of the representor was reasonably to be inferred by the representee: ie the objective test must be satisfied. If in all cases the objective test b must be satisfied, the subjective (uncommunicated) intention of the representor adds nothing as a matter of law. As a matter of fact, if established it may perhaps assist in establishing what reasonable inference should be drawn from his conduct; and of course it is relevant if the actual state of mind of the representor is in issue (eg a fraudulent intent).

c (2) Proximity

The law has drawn a distinction between representations made to specific persons for specific purposes and representations to the public (or sections of the public eg investors). In the case of the former, in general it is sufficient to establish a duty on the part of the representor that he should reasonably have d foreseen that the persons concerned would rely on his representation for the purposes in question. But in the latter, generally it is necessary to establish a proximity between the representor and representee beyond the mere foreseeability of reliance by the representee to render it fair, just and reasonable that such a duty be imposed in respect of the representation. As it seems to me, it is at least well arguable that the necessary proximity in such a case is established e if the reliance by the members of public for the purpose in question is intended by the representor. Intention, if not sufficient to establish the necessary proximity, is at the least a very important factor (see *Morgan Crucible Co plc v Hill Samuel Bank Ltd* [1991] 1 All ER 148 at 160, [1991] Ch 295 at 320 per Slade LJ). The requirements for imposition of a duty of care of fairness, justice and f reasonableness are to a large degree directed to protecting against potential far reaching foreseen, but unintended, consequences: where the consequences are intended, rarely can the representor on these grounds object to his being held responsible for the deliberate consequences of his words. Some support for this view may be found in passages in the judgments of the Court of Appeal in *Morgan Crucible v Hill Samuel* and *Galoo Ltd (in liq) v Bright Grahame Murray (a firm)* [1995] g 1 All ER 16 at 37–38, [1994] 1 WLR 1360 at 1382–1383.

(3) Negligence and prospectus

In *Peek v Gurney* the House of Lords held that (at common law) the object of a prospectus was to provide the necessary information to enable an investor to h make an informed decision whether to accept the offer thereby made to take up shares on the proposed allotment, but not a decision whether to make after-market purchases. The later legislation (including the 1948 and 1965 Act which required and regulated the contents of prospectuses) had the same objective. The 1986 Act recognises a wider object in the case of listing particulars j in respect of listed securities: the object includes properly informing after-market purchasers and creates a corresponding duty of care. Parliament refrained from so widening the object of a prospectus in unlisted securities. The question before me is whether it is properly arguable that the common law can in changed market conditions recognise a duty of care in case of prospectuses for unlisted securities which is substantially equivalent to the duty of care statutorily created in respect of listed securities, but statutorily withheld from unlisted.

The starting point in determining the ambit of the duty of care in respect of a *a* prospectus is the statutory purpose of the prospectus. In the same way the starting point in determining the ambit of the duty of auditors in respect of their audit and audit report is the limited statutory purpose of that statutory requirement, namely to enable shareholders to exercise their class rights in general meeting in an informed manner (see *Caparo v Dickman* [1990] 1 All ER 568 at 582–583, [1990] 1 AC 605 at 629–630). But that is only the beginning: it is not *b* necessarily also the end. It does not necessarily preclude a super-added purpose if a super-added purpose can positively be shown to exist. The burden of establishing such a super-added purpose may be heavy or indeed overwhelming, but whether the burden can or cannot be discharged is a matter for the trial.

The plaintiffs say the prospectus must be examined in the light of changed *c* market practice and philosophy current at its date of preparation and circulation. The plaintiffs claim that there has developed and been generally recognised an additional purpose, an additional perceived intention on the part of the issuer and other parties to a prospectus, namely to inform and encourage after-market purchasers, and that this is the basis for the pleaded purpose attributed by the plaintiffs to the prospectus. If this is established, then it does seem to me to be at *d* least arguable that a duty of care is assumed and owed to those investors who (as intended) rely on the contents of the prospectus in making such purchases. No doubt the court should think carefully before recognising a duty in case of unlisted securities which has been withheld by the legislature. Though the plaintiffs may find some support in the recurring provision in the legislation that it should not affect any liability which a party may incur apart from the legislation *e* (see e g s 160 of the 1986 Act), I do not think that it provides the complete answer. What is significant is that the courts have since 1873 (before any legislation) recognised a duty of care in case of prospectuses when there is a sufficient direct connection between those responsible for the prospectuses and the party acting in reliance (see *Peek v Gurney*), and the plaintiffs' claim may be recognised as *f* merely an application of this established principle in a new fact situation. It is highly questionable whether (as contended for by the defendants) recognition of such a duty involves recognition of a novel category of negligence or a massive extension of a duty of care.

I can find nothing in the authorities or textbooks which precludes the finding *g* of such a duty and at least some potential support in them.

(a) As regards the authorities, in the decisions limiting the duty of care to placees, the only pleaded allegation of the purpose of the issue of the prospectus was the inducement to take up the allotted shares (see e g *Peek v Gurney* (1873) LR 6 HL 377 at 395–396, [1861–73] All ER Rep 116 at 124–125 and *Al-Nakib Investments (Jersey) Ltd v Longcroft* [1990] 3 All ER 321, [1990] 1 WLR 1390). In *Peek* *h* *v Gurney* itself, support may be found in the speech of Lord Chelmsford for the proposition that the necessary direct connection between issuers and after-market purchasers may be found where the intention is established that after-market purchasers rely on the prospectus (see (1873) LR 6 HL 377 at 398–400, [1861–73] All ER Rep 116 at 125–127). Support for the proposition is also *j* found in the speech of Lord Cairns (see LR 6 HL 377 at 412–413, [1861–73] All ER Rep 116 at 134). How the intention is manifested, whether by sale of the prospectus to prospective after-market purchasers (as in *Scott v Dixon* (1859) 29 LJ Ex 62n), or by other means (as in *Andrews v Mockford* [1896] 1 QB 372), surely cannot be crucial. Both these last two cases cited are cases of fraudulent misrepresentation, but it is not self-evident to me that, if the issuers of a *a* prospectus intend investors to rely on it, the issue of proximity should depend on whether the representation was fraudulent or negligent. In case of fraudulent representations, the authorities cited above do support the proposition that intended reliance is sufficient (see also *Clerk and Lindsell* para 14.02).

(b) In *Gower on Company Law* (5th edn, 1992) p 498 the view is expressed that, once prospectuses specifically stated that one of their purposes was to lead to an *b* admission to listing on The Exchange, the decision limiting the scope of the duty of care adopted in *Peek v Gurney* seems outmoded and the decision in *Al-Nakib* should be reviewed by a higher court. This passage in this authoritative work supports the view that the plaintiffs' claim as to the purpose of the prospectus and the duty of care owed today in respect of the prospectus—a prospectus which specifically states that, as part of the same exercise as allotment, the facility will *c* be available for shares in Diamond to be dealt with on the USM—sufficiently merits full consideration at trial.

IV. CONCLUSION

I accordingly refuse the defendants the relief which they seek. I cannot however part with this case without expressing my deep indebtedness to all *d* counsel involved, who have saved me from worse errors than may be apparent in this judgment.

Order accordingly.

Celia Fox   Barrister.

Bate v Chief Adjudication Officer and another   *a*

HOUSE OF LORDS

LORD GOFF OF CHIEVELEY, LORD JAUNCEY OF TULLICHETTLE, LORD BROWNE-
WILKINSON, LORD SLYNN AND LORD HOFFMANN

11, 12 MARCH, 16 MAY 1996   *b*

*Social security – Income support – Disability premium – Entitlement to severe disability
premium – Claimant being denied premium on basis of residence with parents in their
house – Subsequent decision granting premium to other claimants in same
circumstances – Claimant seeking review – Effect of subsequent decision on earlier*   *c*
*decision – Whether earlier decision reviewable as erroneous in law – Whether claimant
'residing with' parents – Whether claimant in 'joint occupation' with parents – Social
Security Act 1975, s 104(1A)(7)(8) – Income Support (General) Regulations 1987, reg 3,
Sch 2, para 13(2)(a)(ii).*

B, who was severely disabled and lived with her parents in a house owned by   *d*
them, received income support under the Social Security Act 1986 with effect
from 11 April 1988 when it became payable, but was excluded from entitlement
to a severe disability premium. In 1990, following a social security
commissioner's decision that two other claimants in a similar position were
entitled to the premium, B sought a review of the decision in her case pursuant   *e*
to s 104(1A)ᵃ of the Social Security Act 1975 on the basis that it was erroneous in
law. Her application was dismissed, but on appeal a social security tribunal
reviewed the initial decision and awarded her the premium. In 1993 the
commissioner allowed an appeal by the adjudication officer and held that B was
not entitled to the premium. The Court of Appeal allowed B's appeal, and first
considered the effect of s 104(7) and (8) of the Act on B's right to a review. Those   *f*
subsections required 'any question arising on the review' of a decision, which, in
consequence of a subsequent determination by a commissioner or court, would
otherwise fall to be revised on a review under s 104(1A), to be determined as if
the decision subject to the determination had not been found to be erroneous in
point of law. The court held that it had jurisdiction under s 104(1A) to decide that   *g*
the original decision of the adjudication officer on B's claim to a severe disability
premium was wrong in law, since s 104(7) and (8) had no application to the
decision of an appellate court or the commissioner on the issues of law arising out
of B's review; in its view, s 104(7) only applied to a 'question arising on a review'
and not an appeal from a refusal to entertain a review, and s 104(8) did not confer   *h*
the status of law on the erroneous decision, it merely required the commissioner
to assume that the adjudication officer's decision had been correctly determined
in law. Secondly, the court held that B was entitled to a severe disability premium
because her parents were not 'persons who jointly occupy' her dwelling within
the meaning of reg 3(2)ᵇ of the Income Support (General) Regulations 1987 and
were not 'persons who normally reside with a claimant' for the purposes of the   *j*
reg 3(1) definition, with the result that B satisfied the criterion in para 13(2)(a)(ii)ᶜ
of Sch 2 to the 1987 regulations that she had no 'non-dependents' aged 18 or over

_____

a   Section 104, so far as material, is set out at p 793 *j* to p 794 *c*, post
b   Regulation 3, so far as material, is set out at p 797 *j* to p 798 *b*, post
c   Paragraph 13, so far as material, is set out at p 797 *f* to *h*, post

a residing with her. The Chief Adjudication Officer and the Secretary of State for Social Services appealed to the House of Lords.

Held – The appeal would be allowed for the following reasons—

(1) On a true construction of s 104(7) and (8) of the 1975 Act, the decision to refuse a claimant an income support severe disability premium had to be treated
b as correct at all stages of the claim process, notwithstanding that a social security commissioner had subsequently decided that two other claimants in a similar position were entitled to the premium. B was not therefore entitled to seek a review of the earlier decision not to award her a severe disability premium (see p 792 *b c*, p 795 *f g*, p 796 *g j* to p 797 *b d* and p 800 *j*, post).

c (2) There was no indication in reg 3(1) of the 1987 regulations that 'resides with' was to be given any meaning other than its ordinary meaning; it meant no more than that the claimant for a severe disability premium and the other person lived in the same residence or dwelling. The phrase 'resides with a claimant' therefore included the situation where the household in a broad sense was that of the claimant, and the situation where the household was that of the other person;
d who had the ownership or tenancy was irrelevant. It followed that B could not be treated as a severely disabled person entitled to the premium under para 13(2)(a)(ii) of Sch 2 to the 1987 regulations by virtue of having no non-dependants residing with her unless her parents were persons who 'jointly [occupied] the claimant's dwelling' for the purposes of reg 3(2) (see p 792 *b c*, p 798 *j* to p 799 *d* and p 800 *j*, post).
e (3) The term 'jointly occupies' in reg 3(2) was a technical expression connoting a legal relationship and did not involve merely factual co-residence, and in the absence of such a legal relationship between B and her parents, B did not qualify for a severe disability premium as at 11 April 1988 (see p 792 *b c* and p 799 *j* to p 800 *c j*, post); dictum of Hoffmann LJ in *Fulwood v Chesterfield BC* (1993)
f 92 LGR 160 at 164 applied.

Notes

For income support, see 33 *Halsbury's Laws* (4th edn) para 856A.

As from 1 July 1992, s 104(7) and (8) of the Social Security Act 1975 was
g replaced by ss 25(2) and 69(1) and (2) of the Social Security Administration Act 1992. For ss 25 and 69 of the 1992 Act, see 40 *Halsbury's Laws* (4th edn) 824, 867.

Cases referred to in opinions

Chief Adjudication Officer v Foster [1993] 1 All ER 705, [1993] AC 754, HL.
h *Fulwood v Chesterfield BC* (1993) 92 LGR 160, CA.

Appeal

The Chief Adjudication Officer and the Secretary of State for Social Services appealed from the decision of the Court of Appeal (Glidewell, Mann and Millett
j LJJ) ([1994] 23 BMLR 155) on 30 November 1994 allowing an appeal by Miss Ann Marie Bate, appearing by her next friend Mavis Bate, from a decision of the social security commissioner on 13 January 1993, whereby he allowed an adjudication officer's appeal from the decision of a social security appeal tribunal on 20 November 1990 which had reviewed his decision and awarded Miss Bate an income support severe disability premium as from 9 October 1989. The facts are set out in the opinion of Lord Slynn of Hadley.

Stephen Richards and *Richard McManus* (instructed by *P K J Thompson*) for the Chief   a
Adjudication Officer and the Secretary of State.
David Pannick QC and *Bethan Harris* (instructed by *David Thomas*) for Miss Bate.

Their Lordships took time for consideration.

16 May 1996. The following opinions were delivered.   b

LORD GOFF OF CHIEVELEY. My Lords, I have had the advantage of reading
in draft the speech of my noble and learned friend Lord Slynn of Hadley and for
the reasons he gives I too would allow the appeal.
     c
LORD JAUNCEY OF TULLICHETTLE. My Lords, I have had the advantage
of reading in draft the speech of my noble and learned friend Lord Slynn of
Hadley and for the reasons he gives I too would allow the appeal.

LORD BROWNE-WILKINSON. My Lords, I have had the advantage of
reading in draft the speech of my noble and learned friend Lord Slynn of Hadley   d
and for the reasons he gives I too would allow the appeal.

LORD SLYNN OF HADLEY. My Lords, this case concerns the entitlement of
Miss Bate, the respondent to this appeal, to an allowance as a severely disabled
person which it is common ground that she is.   e
     The appeal raises two distinct issues, one as to the interpretation of s 104 of the
Social Security Act 1975 as amended in 1983, 1986 and 1990 (now ss 25(2) and
69(1) and (2) of the Social Security Administration Act 1992); the other as to the
meaning of reg 3 of the Income Support (General) Regulations 1987, SI 1987/
1967, which were made pursuant to the Social Security Act 1986.
     As a somewhat discouraging introduction to the case, it is to be recalled that   f
Glidewell LJ in the Court of Appeal said ((1994) 23 BMLR 155 at 158):

> 'Even for this legislation, they [sub-ss (7) and (8) of s 104 of the 1975 Act, as
> amended] are particularly obscure in their meaning. It is no wonder in my
> view that an experienced [social security] appeal tribunal has formed a
> different view of the proper meaning of these provisions from that formed   g
> by the [social security] commissioner. I comment, not merely in relation to
> these provisions, but to the regulations which we have to consider in relation
> to the second issue, that it is deplorable that legislation which affects some of
> the most disadvantaged people in society should be couched in language
> which is so difficult for even a lawyer trained and practising in this field to   h
> understand.'

Whether in the event your Lordships agree wholly with that view it is underlined
in the Court of Appeal by the fact that Millett LJ (with whom, in the result,
Glidewell and Mann LJJ agreed) found that the construction of the statute
adopted by the commissioner 'is not only unwarranted by the wording of   j
[sub-s (8)], but is unacceptable in its effect and capricious in its application' (see 23
BMLR 155 at 167).
     The 1986 Act provided for the payment of 'income support' in place of
'supplementary benefit' and s 22(3) (now s 135(5) of the Social Security
Contributions and Benefits Act 1992) provided:

a 'In relation to income support, housing benefit and any community charge benefit, the applicable amount for a severely disabled person shall include an amount in respect of his being a severely disabled person.'

The 'applicable amount' for the purpose of calculating the benefit was to be prescribed by regulations. Income support and the severe disability premium (the premium) became payable with effect from 11 April 1988. Miss Bate received income support from that date but initially was not paid the premium which she had claimed.

b

According to the agreed statement of facts 'At all material times she lived with her parents in a house owned by them [ie the parents]'. Following a commissioner's decision on 17 May 1990 that two other claimants in a similar position to Miss Bate (Miss Trotman and Miss Crompton, who also lived with

c their parents without being joint owners of the property with their parents) were entitled to the allowance, Miss Bate applied for a review of the award of income support without the premium. The adjudication officer decided that the earlier decision should not be reviewed; a social security tribunal on 20 November 1990 reviewed the initial decision and awarded the premium from 9 October 1989; on

d 13 January 1993 the commissioner allowed the adjudication officer's appeal against the decision of the tribunal and held that Miss Bate was not entitled to the premium. The Court of Appeal allowed Miss Bate's appeal.

Whether there was and is jurisdiction to review the initial decision to award Miss Bate income support without the premium in the light of the decision in

e Trotman/Crompton is the first issue in this appeal and depends on the correct interpretation of s 104 of the 1975 Act as amended in particular by para 7(1) of Sch 6 to the Social Security Act 1990. By s 104(1) of the 1975 Act:

'Any decision under this Act of an adjudication officer, a social security appeal tribunal or a commissioner may be reviewed at any time by an adjudication officer, or, on a reference by an adjudication officer, by a social

f security appeal tribunal ...'

Such a review may take place where the decision was given in ignorance of, or was based on a mistake as to, some material fact, or where there has been a relevant change of circumstances; by sub-s (1A) (as added by s 25(1) of and Sch 8,

g Pt II, para 3 to the Health and Social Services and Social Security Adjudication Act 1983 and amended by s 52(1) of and Sch 5, Pt I, para 10(b) to the 1986 Act)—

'Any decision of an adjudication officer may be reviewed, upon the ground that it was erroneous in point of law, by an adjudication officer or, on a reference from an adjudication officer, by a social security appeal tribunal.'

h

Subsection (1) is not relied on here but it is said that on the basis of the decision in Trotman/Crompton the adjudication officer's initial decision in 1988 in Miss Bate's case was erroneous in law. Accordingly, if sub-s (1A) had stood alone, Miss Bate was entitled to have that initial decision in her case reviewed.

Subsections 104(7) and (8) as introduced by the 1990 Act (s 21(1) and Sch 6,

j para 7(1)), however, provided:

'(7) Subsection (8) below applies in any case where—(a) on the determination, whenever made, of a Commissioner or the court (the "relevant determination"), a decision made by an adjudicating authority is or was found to have been erroneous in point of law; and (b) in consequence of that determination, any other decision—(i) which was made before the date of that determination; and (ii) which is referable to a claim made or treated as made by any person for any benefit, falls (or would, apart from subsection (8) below, fall) to be revised on a review carried out under subsection (1A) above after the coming into force of this subsection.

(8) Where this subsection applies, any question arising on the review referred to in subsection (7)(b) above, or on any subsequent review of a decision which is referable to the same claim, as to any person's entitlement to, or right to payment of, any benefit—(a) in respect of any period before the date of the relevant determination; or (b) in the case of widow's payment, in respect of a death occurring before that date, shall be determined as if the decision referred to in subsection (7)(a) above had been found by the Commissioner or court in question not to have been erroneous in point of law.'

By sub-s (10) 'adjudicating authority' and 'the court' have the same meaning as in s 165D of the 1975 Act (added by s 21(1) of and Sch 6, para 7(2)). Subsection (4) of the latter section provides that 'adjudicating authority' means '(a) an adjudication officer, the Attendance Allowance Board, a social security appeal tribunal and a medical appeal tribunal.' 'The court' means, so far as England and Wales are concerned, the High Court, the Court of Appeal, the House of Lords or the Court of Justice of the European Community.

The social security commissioner appointed pursuant to s 97 of the 1975 Act is not in either category, though an appeal to him is provided by s 101 of the 1975 Act.

Miss Bate accepts that, where a decision is taken by a commissioner or by a court that the decision of the adjudicating authority is wrong in law, the assumption is to be made in other cases (contrary to the fact) that the adjudicating authority's decision was correct in law. It follows that, so far as the first two levels in the hierarchy are concerned, decisions cannot be reopened because of a subsequent decision that they were wrong, because by statute they are to be taken as being right. It is said, however, that this does not affect the power of the commissioner or of a court to set aside earlier decisions when they have been shown to be wrong. Such a result is said to flow from the language of the section and from the fact that the appellate bodies, the commissioner and the courts, are not part of the review process; it is also said to be inherent in the power of the higher court to make sure that the law is observed. If there is ambiguity in the language it is said that s 104(7) and (8) should be given the narrowest construction so as to ensure that claimants can have the social security benefit to which they are on a proper construction of the legislation entitled. Alternatively, it is said by Miss Bate that the use of the words 'found to have been erroneous in point of law' make it clear that the provisions of s 104(7) and (8) are only to apply where a commissioner or a court has reversed a previous decision which was binding on the adjudicating authority. Until such a decision was taken the adjudicating authority could not have known that its decision was erroneous in point of law or dealt with such an error since he was bound by higher authority. It is only when the adjudicating authority has followed previous wrong but binding decisions that public funds should be protected from claims being reopened. Here, *Trotman/Crompton* did not overrule any previously binding authority so that s 104(7) and (8) do not apply.

The Court of Appeal accepted that s 104(7) and (8) had no application to the decision of the court or the commissioner on the issues of law arising out of the

a
review sought by Miss Bate. The principal judgment on this part of the case was given by Millett LJ, the other members of the court expressing agreement. It was held that s 104(7) only applies to a 'question arising on the review.' That is limited to review by the adjudicating officer and the social security appeal tribunal in Miss Bate's case. The commissioner and the court are not conducting a review—in the case like the present they are dealing with matters 'on an appeal from a refusal to entertain a review.' Moreover, the Court of Appeal held that the effect of the statutory assumption was no more than that the decisions of the adjudication officers in the earlier cases were to be treated as having been correctly determined in law and not that, by statute, the adjudicators' decisions were correct in law so that they would be binding on other commissioners and the court. Millett LJ said:

'In my judgment the effect of sub-s (8) is that the adjudication officer in the present case was bound by the decision which he was required to assume the commissioner had made in the earlier cases to reject the claimant's application for a review; but that even if the subsection was directed to him the commissioner was not bound to do so. Moreover, there is nothing in the subsection to preclude this court from reaching its own conclusion on the meaning of para 3(2)(c) of the Regulations, whatever the commissioner in the earlier cases may have or must be assumed to have decided; or from deciding that, even if the tribunals below were bound to reject the claimant's application for a review, their decisions were wrong in law ... On this construction, the subsection can be given a limited and rational application. It requires an application for review under s 104(1A) to begin, in effect, at an appellate level for which leave is required, thus preventing frivolous or repeated applications.'

As I see it, s 104(7) applies where: (1) in case B, the commissioner or the court determines that an adjudicating authority has made a decision in that case which was erroneous in law; (2) in case A, decided earlier than case B, a decision has been based on the same error of law so that, but for sub-s (8), the earlier decision would fall to be revised on a review for error of law under s 104(1A).

The effect of sub-s (8) is that if a question arises on the review of case A as to a person's entitlement to benefit, the determination of the commissioner or the court is taken as being that the decision was not erroneous in point of law in respect of any period before the date of the determination.

The result is that the claimant in case A cannot take advantage of the determination in case B retrospectively.

These provisions introduced a substantial change in the law. Prior to that time there had been a limit on the period in respect of which claimants could claim if they succeeded on a review of a previous decision. Thus by the Supplementary Benefits (General) Regulations 1977, SI 1977/1141, a commissioner was given by reg 9 power to review a determination made by a commissioner or by an appeal tribunal on the right to or the amount of pension or allowance in respect of any period on the grounds stated. Where the review arose from a mistake as to a material fact or a relevant change of circumstances of which a claimant was aware but of which he had failed to notify the secretary of state then—

'if that review would result in an increase in the amount of pension or allowance payable, that increase should not be payable from a date earlier

than 52 weeks before the week in which the claimant first furnished that *a*
information'. (See reg 9(2).)

By reg 9(5):

'Any determination made by the [Supplementary Benefits] Commission
on a matter specified in the preceding paragraphs of this regulation may be
reviewed by them if they are satisfied that it was based on a mistake as to the *b*
law but any such review shall not be made in respect of a period of more than
52 weeks before the date on which a claimant requested or the date on which
the Commission made the review, whichever is the earlier.'

Regulation 69(1) of the Social Security (Adjudication) Regulations 1986, SI
1986/2218, provided: *c*

'... a determination on a claim or question relating to income support shall
not be revised on review under section 104 of the 1975 Act so as to make
income support payable or to increase the amount of income support
payable in respect of—(a) any period which falls more than 12 months before
the date on which the review was requested or, where no request is made, *d*
the date of the review ...'

The provisions allowing for decisions to be reopened on review (which go
back in one form or another to the Supplementary Benefit (General) Regulations
1966, SI 1966/1065) are in a sense a concession since, contrary to the practice in
the courts, they allow cases closed by, for example, the decision of an adjudica- *e*
tion officer, to be reopened before an adjudication officer or, on a reference by
him, by a social security appeal tribunal. It is, therefore, perhaps not surprising
that some limit was introduced in the regulations to the retrospective effect of
subsequent decisions on the law.

Subsections (7) and (8) of s 104 are on any view more radical, however *f*
tortuous the method adopted to make the change. The question, however, is
whether Parliament intended to limit the effect of the subsequent determination
to decisions on review, on the ground of error of law, by the adjudication officer
and the social security appeal tribunal or whether this provision was intended to
apply across the board.

For my part, I am not persuaded by the argument that 'review' is different from *g*
'appeal,' the former being carried out by the adjudication officer and the tribunal,
the latter by the commissioner and the court. It seems to me that the various
stages of reconsideration at each level, including the court, are part of one
process—to see whether in the adjudication officer's decision there was an error
of law. The process is still one of review whether the body further up in the *h*
hierarchy accepts or rejects the application for a review. The reference in
sub-s (8) to 'any subsequent review of a decision which is referable to the same
claim' is wide enough to include decisions by a higher jurisdiction and is not
limited to a second bite at the cherry on different grounds before the same
jurisdiction. *j*

I do not accept that the object of the legislation was simply to allow review to
begin at the appellate level, for which leave was required, and thereby to prevent
frivolous or repeated applications, as the Court of Appeal thought. On the face
of it this amendment was intended to exclude claims based on a change in the law
following a subsequent decision by the statutory authorities or by the courts.
Nor do I think that it is right to say, if a commissioner decides that there has been

a an error of law in the case before him, that its effect on the earlier case is simply that there has been a deemed decision that the adjudication officer was right in law which can be appealed to a court. The intention, in my view, was that that deemed decision in the earlier case is to be treated as correct at all stages of the process and that claims for benefit arising prior to the subsequent determination should be excluded. If that means adopting in case A a fiction that the decision in case B was to the opposite effect, then that on the wording of the statute must be

b accepted. I am satisfied that this was what was intended; if such a result is 'unacceptable in its effect' it is for Parliament to change it.

I accept the submission of Mr Richards that there is no warrant for limiting the effect of the subsection to cases where a previous decision binding on the adjudication officer has been reversed. Mr Pannick QC's argument based on the

c word 'found' I would reject, forcefully and skilfully though he argued it. 'Found' is used in the general sense of declared and I decline to draw a legalistic distinction between 'found' for facts and 'held' for law in this particular subsection.

I do not see that this is any way interfering with the proper functioning of the judicial hierarchy, nor as preventing the proper interpretation of the law. The

d decision in case A above was wrong; for the future the law as declared in case B must apply; entitlement to benefit in respect of the past, however, has been excluded by Parliament.

Accordingly on this point I consider that the commissioner was right and that the Court of Appeal were in error. I am not persuaded by Mr Pannick that this result is incompatible with Community law.

e Two other issues have been raised as to Miss Bate's entitlement to the allowance under the regulations. By para 13(2) of Sch 2 to the 1987 regulations a person is to be treated as being a severely disabled person if and only if—

f '(a) in the case of a single claimant ... (i) he is in receipt of attendance allowance, and (ii) subject to sub-paragraph (3), he has no non-dependants aged 18 or over residing with him, and (iii) no-one is in receipt of an invalid care allowance under section 37 of the Social Security Act [1975] in respect of caring for him ...

(3) For the purposes of sub-paragraph (2)(a)(ii) ... no account shall be

g taken of—(a) a person receiving attendance allowance; or (b) a person to whom regulation (3) (non-dependants) applies; or (c) subject to sub-paragraph (4) a person who joins the claimant's household for the first time in order to care for the claimant or his partner and immediately before so joining the claimant or his partner was treated as a severely disabled person.

h (4) Sub-paragraph (3)(c) shall apply only for the first 12 weeks following the date on which the person to whom that provision applies first joins the claimant's household.'

A challenge to the vires of para 13(2)(a)(ii) and (iii) was rejected by your

j Lordships' House in *Chief Adjudication Officer v Foster* [1993] 1 All ER 705, [1993] AC 754.

'Non-dependant' is defined in reg 3 of the 1987 regulations as follows:

'(1) In these Regulations, 'non-dependant' means any person, except someone to whom paragraph (2) applies, who normally resides with a claimant.

(2) This paragraph applies to ... (c) a person who jointly occupies the *a*
claimant's dwelling ...
(4) For the purposes of this regulation a person resides with another only
if they share any accommodation except a bathroom, a lavatory or a
communal area.
(5) In this regulation 'communal area' means any area (other than rooms)
of common access (including halls and passage ways) ...'   *b*

The effect of this is that a claimant cannot be treated as a severely disabled
person if someone other than one of the persons specified in reg 3(2) is 'residing
with him', since for the purposes of reg 13(2)(a)(ii) that person is a
non-dependant, the assumption apparently being that such a person is likely to
assist the claimant to cope with his severe disability so that the premium to *c*
provide assistance is not required. But a person is not to be treated as a
non-dependant if he 'jointly occupies the claimant's dwelling.'
     The Court of Appeal in the present case followed an earlier decision of that
court in *Fulwood v Chesterfield BC* (1993) 92 LGR 160. There it was held that in
reg 3(2)(d) of the Housing Benefit (General) Regulations 1987, SI 1987/1971, the *d*
words 'a person who jointly occupies the claimant's dwelling' connoted a legal
relationship between joint occupiers who occupied premises by virtue of the
same legal right. Accordingly the court concluded that on the facts of the present
case Miss Bate's parents were not persons who jointly occupied her dwelling for
the purposes of the Income Support (General) Regulations 1987. They were,
therefore, not excluded from the definition of 'non-dependants' by virtue of *e*
reg 3(2)(c). The Court of Appeal, however, concluded, on a point apparently
raised for the first time by the court, that the ordinary meaning of 'resides with a
claimant' (reg 3(1)) connoted someone who resided with a householder and was
not apt to cover the situation of a householder having someone else to live in his
house. Millett LJ said (23 BMLR 155 at 169):   *f*

     'In the case of severe disability premium likewise one begins with the
     claimant and asks whether he has anyone residing with him, ie sharing his
     accommodation with his consent. If so, he will normally be deprived of
     severe disability premium because if he has allowed someone to reside with
     him it is reasonable to expect him to have made arrangements for that *g*
     person to help look after him in return for accommodation. The exceptions
     are all cases where that expectation would not be justified.'

They did not reside with her because 'both as a matter of ordinary language and
in the context of the 1987 regulations, a householder does not reside with the
persons with whom he shares his accommodation; they reside with him.' *h*
Accordingly the Court of Appeal held that Miss Bate had no non-dependants
residing with her and she was entitled to the premium.
     The scheme of the legislation as I see it is that if a claimant has to make
arrangements to enable him to deal with his disability (not just to be housed) then
the premium is payable, but that if someone is living with him and able to look *j*
after him (or who may be assumed to be likely to look after him) then the
premium is not payable.
     I do not see any indication in the regulation that 'resides with' is to be given
any meaning other than its ordinary meaning. It seems to me to mean no more
than that the claimant and the other person live in the same residence or
dwelling. There is no need to read into the phrase 'resides with a claimant' the

a qualification that the household has to be that of the claimant or that the dwelling must be one in which the claimant has the legal interest and that the other person is there in a subordinate position (it is not his household) or without any legal interest before that person can reside with the claimant. Glidewell J suggested that for a husband and wife the normal phrase would be that they 'live together'; that is no doubt right but the act of living together means that he lives (or resides) b with her and she lives (resides) with him.

The phrase 'resides with a claimant' thus includes the situation where the household in a broad sense is that of the claimant (as contemplated in para 13(3)(c) and (4) of Sch 2 to the 1987 regulations) and also where it is that of the other person. Who has the ownership or the tenancy, for the purpose of deciding whether a person resides with a claimant, is irrelevant. Regulation 3(4) c gives some indication of the nature of 'residing with'; it imposes the qualification that a person resides with another only if they share 'any' accommodation except, for example, a bathroom. It does not limit it to the situation where the other person shares 'the claimant's' sitting-room.

Accordingly Miss Bate cannot show that she has no non-dependants residing d with her unless her parents are persons who 'jointly occup[y] the claimant's dwelling.'

In the Trotman/Crompton case, the commissioner, Mr R A Sanders, ruled that 'jointly occupies' did not have a technical meaning. On the basis that there was nothing in the severe disability premium to suggest 'that a claimant ought to get the premium if she and her mother jointly own the property but not if they e jointly occupy their home as owner and licensee,' he concluded that 'the provision applies if in fact the persons in question who normally reside together jointly occupy the premises in the sense of equality of access and use as distinct from a situation where restrictions are imposed in relation to those matters.'

His view was rejected by the Court of Appeal in Fulwood v Chesterfield BC (1993) f 92 LGR 160 at 164, where Hoffmann LJ, with whom other members of the court agreed, said that 'jointly occupied' did not have any 'ordinary and generally understood meaning' but was 'a technical expression, which connotes a legal relationship, either between two or more people and a third party, or between two or more people and an item of property.'

That case concerned the Housing Benefit (General) Regulations 1987 and it is g clear that different considerations may apply, since the purpose of housing benefit is to assist people who cannot afford to house themselves and who need help related to their income, whereas severe disability premium is to help with the extra cost likely to be incurred by reason of the disability.

Mr Pannick submits that the Court of Appeal were wrong to follow Fulwood in h the present case and 'that a person "jointly occupies" a dwelling with another if they live there together on terms of equal sharing, whether or not their joint occupation has specific legal characteristics.' Whilst accepting that Fulwood was correct in relation to housing benefit, he contends:

j 'In the context of severe disability premium, however, it is impossible to understand why there should be a link between the legal status of the co-resident and the entitlement of the severely disabled person to extra money for living expenses.'

Though, like Glidewell LJ, I have sympathy with the submission, it is not one which I can accept. It does not follow, I accept, that a phrase used in the Housing Benefit Regulations necessarily has the same meaning as in regulations dealing with severe disability premium. But it is not possible to ignore that these *a* regulations were made at the same time pursuant to the same statute. What is perhaps more important is that in reg 3 a distinction is drawn between 'resides with' and 'jointly occupies the claimant's dwelling' which does not apply in the Housing Benefit Regulations. I do not think it is possible to construe 'jointly occupies' as meaning merely 'resides in' or the same words would have been used. They were not used because the result would not have made sense since a *b* person would have been a non-dependant for the purposes of reg 3(1) but for exactly the same reason and solely on the same basis would have been exempted by reg 3(2). Nor is it possible to accept that there is a distinction solely in that 'jointly occupies' is intended to cover residence where there is equal access or use. If that had been intended it would have been expressed in relation to residence; again it was not done because the result would have been bizarre—if *c* a person having precisely equal access was not a non-dependant whereas someone who had less or more than equal access was a non-dependant. I conclude therefore, as Hoffmann LJ said in *Fulwood*, that 'jointly occupies' involves a legal relationship; it does not involve merely factual co-residence.

With effect from 2 December 1994 by virtue of the Income-related Benefits *d* Schemes (Miscellaneous Amendments) (No 6) Regulations 1994, SI 1994/3061, following the Court of Appeal's judgment in the present case on 30 November 1994, reg 3(1) of the 1987 regulations was amended (by reg 2(1) and (2)) by adding after the words 'who normally resides with the claimant' the words 'or with whom a claimant normally resides' and para 13(2)(a)(ii) of Sch 2 to the 1987 regulations was consequentially amended (by reg 2(1) and (3)) by substituting for *e* 'residing with him' the words 'normally residing with him or with whom he is normally residing.' The present question was thus answered for the future but in my opinion the provision always had that meaning.

With effect from 9 October 1989 reg 3(2)(c) of the 1987 regulations was amended (by reg 3 of the Income Support (General) Amendment No 3 *f* Regulations 1989, SI 1989/1678) by adding after the words 'person who jointly occupies the claimant's dwelling' the words:

'and either is a co-owner of that dwelling with the claimant or his partner (whether or not there are other co-owners) or is liable with the claimant or his partner to make payments in respect of his occupation of the dwelling.' *g*

So once again from that date the requirement of a legal relationship between the claimant and the other person is specified.

Miss Bate's case has however to be determined as of 11 April 1988; and your Lordships have been told that a significant number of cases will turn on the interpretation of the legislation regardless of these amendments. *h*

In my opinion the appeal should be allowed but on the terms agreed that the appellants will pay Miss Bate's costs of this appeal and not seek to disturb the order for costs in the Court of Appeal.

LORD HOFFMANN. My Lords, I have had the advantage of reading in draft the *j* speech of my noble and learned friend Lord Slynn of Hadley and for the reasons he gives I too would allow the appeal.

Appeal allowed.

Celia Fox   Barrister.

a Bristol and West Building Society v May May & Merrimans (a firm) and others

CHANCERY DIVISION AT BRISTOL

b CHADWICK J

23–27, 30, 31 OCTOBER, 1, 2 NOVEMBER 1995, 16 APRIL 1996

Solicitor – Duty – Breach of trust – Mortgage transaction – Solicitor acting for both borrower and society – Advance paid to solicitor to enable completion of purchase of property – Solicitor's obligation to disclose facts not relevant to title – Solicitor's *c* *obligation as a fiduciary – Payment away in breach of instructions – Misrepresentation in breach of fiduciary duty – Evidence required on application for summary judgment – Whether necessary to establish that if lender had known of undisclosed fact advance could not have been made.*

d The plaintiff building society brought actions against the defendants, a number of firms of solicitors; the actions arose out of loans made by the society for the purchase of domestic property in which the defendants had acted for the society in taking security over the property. The loans were made between 1988 and 1991, at a time when loans equivalent to 90% and more of the purchase price of the property were not unusual. A number of the society's borrowers defaulted *e* on their repayment obligations and the society realised its security by possession and sale of the mortgaged property. In many cases the proceeds of realisation were insufficient to cover the borrower's indebtedness. There was little hope of recovering the shortfall from the borrowers and the society sought to make recovery from the defendants. In each case, the defendants were retained upon *f* terms contained in standard form documentation. The solicitor's letter contained an offer by the society to retain the solicitors as its solicitors for the purpose of the mortgage transaction described in the offer of advance. Paragraph 2 of the solicitor's instructions required that any matters which might prejudice the society's security or which were at variance with the offer of advance should be notified to the society in writing immediately they became known. The report *g* on title and request for advance cheque included a warranty that the details of the transaction in respect of which the solicitor sought authority to proceed accorded exactly with the particulars in the offer of advance. There were two features common to all the actions. First, the society instructed the borrower's solicitor to act in relation to the taking of its security; and in accepting those instructions *h* the solicitor became solicitor to the parties on each side of the lending transaction. Secondly, the society made no direct payment to the borrower, but paid the amount of the advance to the solicitor for the purpose of enabling the purchase of the property to be completed. On completion the funds were paid over by the solicitor in exchange for a transfer executed by the vendor and a *j* mortgage executed by the borrowers. The issues arose: (i) how far the defendants were obliged to disclose to the society facts which, if they had not also been acting for the borrower, they would have been unlikely to know; (ii) whether the solicitor committed a breach of trust if he paid over funds received from the society on completion in circumstances where the completion had taken place following a failure by the solicitor to disclose to the society some fact which, on a proper understanding of his obligations, he ought to have disclosed;

and (iii) whether it was necessary for the society to establish not only that there had been a failure to disclose some fact which the solicitor ought to have disclosed before completion, but also that, if that fact had been disclosed, the society would not have authorised the advance, or alternatively would have withdrawn its offer of advance.

Held – (1) Information obtained in the course of investigating title or in the course of preparing for completion which was not confidential and which a reasonably competent solicitor would realise might be of significance to his client, as lender, ought to be disclosed to him (see p 814 *h*, post).

(2) In cases where a solicitor received funds from a building society following a request based upon a warranty or representation which he knew, or must be taken to have known, to be misleading in some material respect, equity would give a remedy based upon breach of fiduciary duty in respect of any loss which the society suffered as a result of its payment in reliance upon that request. Where necessary, the remedy would take the form of the imposition of a constructive trust on those funds to enforce the solicitor's obligation to return them to the society forthwith, which overrode any express or implied trust which might otherwise have arisen out of any instructions given by the client when the money was paid to the solicitor. Cases where the solicitor knew nothing, prior to the receipt of the advance cheque, which ought to have led him to qualify the report which he signed were governed by rules applicable under s 32 of the Solicitors Act 1974 prescribing the obligations of a solicitor in relation to clients' money and did not require the imposition of a constructive trust by way of equitable remedy (see p 818 *d* to *f h*, post); *Target Holdings Ltd v Redferns (a firm)* [1995] 3 All ER 785 considered.

(3) For the purpose of an application for summary judgment, where the breach of trust lay in paying over the mortgage funds at a time when the solicitor knew of a matter which ought to be reported prior to completion, ie in paying over the funds on completion without authority and in breach of the solicitor's instructions, it had to be established that the society would not have authorised the solicitor to proceed if it had known the facts (see p 823 *e f* and p 825 *d*, post).

(4) Accordingly, in those cases, the society was entitled to succeed on the issue of liability, since the payment on completion had been made in breach of its instructions. However, the society also had to prove that it would not have proceeded with the transaction if the matter in question had been reported to it. In the cases before the court, it was not appropriate to determine that issue on summary judgment, and the defendants would be granted unconditional leave to defend on the issue of causation (see p 834 *e f j* to p 835 *b d* to *g*, post).

(5) The principle that a fiduciary who had failed to disclose material facts could not rely on the defence that disclosure would not have altered the decision to proceed with the transaction applied to those cases where the solicitor had received the advance cheque in response to a request made on the basis of a warranty or representation which he knew, or must be taken to have known, was misleading. In such cases, the question what would the society have done if it had been told the true facts was not relevant (see p 826 *h* and p 827 *e f*, post); *Brickenden v London Loan and Savings Co* [1934] 3 DLR 465 applied.

(6) Accordingly, where the defendant solicitors had received the mortgage funds from the society in response to a request based on a misleading warranty or representation, it was unnecessary to try the question whether the society would have made the advance if it had been told the true facts. That question was

a irrelevant and, accordingly, the society was entitled to judgment (see p 834 *e j* and p 835 *d* to *g*, post).

(7) In those cases where the alleged breach of duty consisted of a failure to make inquiries or to report facts to the society, but it was not clear that the defendants ought to have realised that they should have made those inquiries or reported those facts, the defendants would be granted unconditional leave to

b defend, since there was some issue in dispute which ought to be tried in relation to liability (see p 834 *e f* and p 835 *b* to *g*, post).

Notes

For the extent of liability for breach of trust, see 48 *Halsbury's Laws* (4th edn reissue) paras 960–961, and for cases on the subject, see 48 *Digest* (Reissue) 657–

c 661, 6044–6072.

For the Solicitors Act 1974, s 32, see 41 *Halsbury's Statutes* (4th edn) (1995 reissue) 55.

Cases referred to in judgment

d *Alliance and Leicester Building Society v Edgestop Ltd* (18 January 1991, unreported), Ch D.

A-G for Hong Kong v Reid [1994] 1 All ER 1, [1994] 1 AC 324, [1993] 3 WLR 1143, PC.

Barclays Bank Ltd v Quistclose Investments Ltd [1968] 3 All ER 651, [1970] AC 567, [1968] 3 WLR 1097, HL.

e *Bartlett v Barclays Bank Trust Co Ltd (No 2)* [1980] 2 All ER 92, [1980] Ch 515, [1980] 2 WLR 430.

Bishopsgate Investment Management Ltd (in liq) v Maxwell (No 2) [1994] 1 All ER 261, CA; *affg* [1993] BCLC 814.

Brickenden v London Loan and Savings Co [1934] 3 DLR 465, PC.

f *Bristol and West Building Society v Evans Bullock & Co (a firm)* (6 October 1995, unreported), Judge Jack QC.

Bristol and West Building Society v Kramer & Co (a firm) (1995) Times, 6 February.

Bristol and West Building Society v Mothew (27 July 1995, unreported), Ch D.

Bristol and West Building Society v Read & Rogers (7 September 1995, unreported), Judge Weeks QC.

g *Bristol and West Building Society v Singh & Ruparell (a firm)* (6 October 1995, unreported), Judge Jack QC.

Caffrey v Darby (1801) 6 Ves 488, [1775–1802] All ER Rep 507, 31 ER 1159.

Chesterfield (Earl of) v Janssen (1750) 2 Ves Sen 125, 28 ER 82.

Clough v Bond (1838) 3 My & Cr 490, 40 ER 1016, LC.

h *Colchester Estates (Cardiff) v Carlton Industries plc* [1984] 2 All ER 601, [1986] Ch 80, [1984] 3 WLR 693.

Commonwealth Bank of Australia v Smith (1991) 102 ALR 453, Aust Fed Ct.

Dawson (decd), Re, Union Fidelity Trustee Co Ltd v Perpetual Trustee Co Ltd [1966] 2 NSWR 211, NSW SC.

j *Derry v Peek* (1889) 14 App Cas 337, [1886–90] All ER Rep 1, HL.

Hospital Products Ltd v United States Surgical Corp (1984) 156 CLR 41, Aust HC.

Kelly v Cooper [1993] AC 205, [1992] 3 WLR 936, PC.

Miller's Deed Trusts, Re (1978) 75 LS Gaz 454.

Moody v Cox [1917] 2 Ch 71, [1916–17] All ER Rep 548, CA.

Mortgage Express Ltd v Bowerman & Partners [1996] 2 All ER 836, CA.

Nestle v National Westminster Bank plc [1994] 1 All ER 118, [1993] 1 WLR 1260, CA.

Nocton v Lord Ashburton [1914] AC 932, [1914–15] All ER Rep 45, HL.   *a*
Target Holdings Ltd v Redferns (a firm) [1995] 3 All ER 785, [1995] 3 WLR 352, HL;
     rvsg [1994] 2 All ER 337, [1994] 1 WLR 1089, CA.
Tennant (Lady Anne) v Associated Newspapers Group Ltd [1979] FSR 298.

Summonses and appeals
The plaintiff, Bristol and West Building Society, brought separate proceedings *b*
against the defendants, May May & Merrimans (a firm), and 12 other defendants
(being either firms of solicitors or individual solicitors) who had acted for the
society in connection with a number of loans made between 1988 and 1991 for
the purchase of property, seeking to recover the shortfall between the proceeds
of sale of the repossessed properties and the borrowers' indebtedness in respect
of capital and interest. The actions in which the present summonses and appeals *c*
arose had common elements and were commenced in Bristol. The facts are set
out in the judgment.

Michael Burton QC, Paul Lowenstein, Timothy Higginson, William Bojczuk and
     Christopher Semken (instructed by *Osborne Clarke*, Bristol, *Eversheds* and *Veale* *d*
     Wasborough, Bristol) for the society.
Nicholas Davidson QC, Patrick Lawrence and *Elizabeth Weaver* (instructed by *Pinsent
     Curtis*) for the defendant solicitors.

Cur adv vult

e

16 April 1996. The following judgment was delivered.

CHADWICK J. These actions arise out of loans made for the purchase of
domestic property by the plaintiff, Bristol and West Building Society. The
defendants are solicitors who acted for the society in taking security over that *f*
property.
     The loans were made during the years 1988 to 1991. Those years included (or,
in part, followed) a period during which the market price of domestic property
had been rising steeply. There was a belief, widely held amongst house
purchasers and some others, that prices could only continue to rise. There was a
desire to take advantage of that trend; alternatively, a fear that failure to do so *g*
would make it difficult, if not impossible, to enter the housing market in the
future. The market was extremely active. The society was an active—the
defendants would say aggressive—lender in that market. Loans equivalent to
90% and more of the price at which the property was to be purchased by the
borrower were not unusual.   *h*
     A number of the society's borrowers defaulted on their repayment obligations.
The society realised its security by possession and sale of the mortgaged property.
Default, and the subsequent realisation of security, are familiar incidents of
mortgage lending. On a rising market a lender could expect to recover in full out
of the proceeds of realisation. But, by the end of 1991, the market for domestic
property had begun to collapse. House prices fell. In many cases the proceeds of *j*
realisation were insufficient to cover the borrower's indebtedness in respect of
capital and interest. The society was left with a shortfall. There was little hope
of recovering the shortfall from the borrower under his covenants for payment.
     In those circumstances the society has sought to identify some other source or
sources from which to make recovery. One potential source of recovery is

a   solicitors the who acted for the society in connection with the loan transactions. The actions with which I am concerned in this judgment represent only a small proportion of those commenced by the society against solicitors in the Bristol District Registry of the Chancery Division of the High Court.

In some of these actions the matter has come before me by way of appeal from a decision of a district judge on an application under RSC Ord 14. In the other

b   actions it is the Ord 14 application itself which is before me de novo. I directed that these matters (and other matters not the subject of this judgment) be heard together. That appeared to me appropriate and desirable for a number of reasons. First, although each case does, of course, turn on its own facts, there are issues which recur in most of these actions. In particular, there is the common element that the defendants were retained upon terms contained in standard

c   form documentation. Secondly, the number of actions commenced by the society is such that, unless both the society and solicitor defendants have some reasonably comprehensive guidance as to the way in which the court is likely to approach applications for summary judgment, there is a real danger that the district judges in this district registry will be overwhelmed by such applications.

d   Thirdly, there are existing decisions on appeals from the district judges which are perceived to be inconsistent. That perception makes the task of the district judges unreasonably burdensome; and encourages appeals from their decisions in cases of this nature however they decide. It is essential that any perceived inconsistency is resolved. Fourthly, there is a common plaintiff, the society, in all these actions; and there is, in substance, a common defendant. Although the

e   defendants sued are individual firms of solicitors, the Solicitors' Indemnity Fund stands behind those individual firms. In substance, the dispute in these actions is between the society and the fund.

The direction that these matters be heard together led to a high degree of co-operation between the different firms of solicitors and counsel already instructed by the society, and between the solicitors and counsel already instructed on

f   behalf of the defendants. Each side has found it possible to direct its arguments on the main issues of principle through one leading counsel. Junior counsel have addressed me on the particular facts in those cases for which each had had specific responsibility. I pay tribute to the way in which solicitors and counsel on both sides have co-operated in preparing and arguing these matters before me. That

g   co-operation must, undoubtedly, have led to a considerable overall saving in costs.

It is, I suspect, a feature common to most building society lending—and it is certainly a feature common to the matters before me—that the building society instructs the borrower's solicitor to act in relation to the taking of its security.

h   Typically, the borrower will have instructed a solicitor to act for him at or about the time when, as purchaser, he agrees terms with his vendor. The borrower gives the name of that solicitor to the building society at the time when he applies for an advance. If the application is approved, the building society sends a copy of its offer of advance to the solicitor, together with its own instructions inviting the solicitor to act on its behalf. In accepting those instructions the solicitor

j   becomes solicitor to the parties on each side of the lending transaction. This may have advantages of convenience and economy; but the solicitor's dual role can lead to difficulties. In accepting instructions to act for the society, the solicitor assumes an obligation to disclose to the society facts which, as solicitor to the borrower, he might not have disclosed; and which, if the society and the borrower were separately advised, the society's solicitor would have been

unlikely to discover. A solicitor who accepts instructions to act for both lender a
and borrower needs a clear understanding as to the obligations which he assumes
in relation to each of his clients. A question in dispute in a number of the matters
now before me is how far the defendants were obliged to disclose to the society
facts which, if they had not also been acting for the borrower, they would have
been unlikely to know.

A second feature common to the matters before me is that the society made no b
direct payment to the borrower. The society paid the amount of the advance to
the defendant solicitor for the purpose of enabling the purchase of the property
to be completed. On completion the moneys were paid over by the defendant
(usually, but not invariably, to the vendor's solicitor) in exchange for a transfer
executed by the vendor and a mortgage executed by the borrower. It has been
accepted in argument before me that moneys received by the defendant solicitor c
from the society for the purpose of enabling a mortgage loan to be completed
were, on receipt, held by the solicitor upon trust for the society. This would
normally be reflected by the credit of those moneys in the solicitors' own
accounts to a client account in the name of the society; and by the payment of
those moneys into the solicitors' client account at their bankers. A question in d
dispute in the matters before me is whether the solicitor commits a breach of
trust in all cases—and, if not, then in which cases—if he pays over those moneys
on completion in circumstances in which the completion has taken place
following a failure by the solicitor to disclose to the society some fact which, on
a proper understanding of his obligations, he ought to have disclosed.

The third main issue is whether it is necessary for the society to establish in e
every case—and, if not, then in which cases—not only that there has been a
failure to disclose some fact which the solicitor ought to have disclosed before
completion, but also that, if that fact had been disclosed, the society would not
have authorised the advance; alternatively, would have withdrawn its offer of
advance. In other words, must the society establish that, if the lender had known f
of that fact, the advance would not have been made. If so, then what evidence
does the society need to adduce on an application for summary judgment? Is it
safe for the court to act on the uncontradicted (but untested) assertion in an
affidavit that—to use counsel's description of the evidence adduced in these
cases—the society 'would not have touched this transaction with a bargepole'?

The necessary starting point from which to examine these issues is, of course, g
the society's own documentation. It is on the basis of the documents sent to him
by the society that the solicitor accepts instructions to act as its solicitor in the
proposed mortgage transaction.

THE SOCIETY'S STANDARD DOCUMENTATION   h
A short description of the usual procedure will be sufficient to introduce the
standard documents. The prospective borrower, having agreed the purchase
with the vendor on a 'subject to contract' basis, made an application to the society
for a mortgage advance. The application named the solicitor who was to act for
the applicant in the purchase. It also stated the purchase price. If the society was j
willing to offer an advance, after making such inquiries as to the value of the
property and the status of the borrower as it thought necessary, it sent to the
applicant a formal offer of advance. At the same time the society sent to the
applicant's solicitor a standard letter (the solicitor's letter) together with (i) a copy
of the offer of advance and (ii) a document described as 'solicitor's instructions'.
Uncompleted copies of the mortgage deed/standard security and the report on
title were also sent with the solicitor's letter.

a   The standard solicitor's letter was in these terms:

'Please investigate the title and prepare the Mortgage Deed/Standard Security in accordance with the terms of the enclosed offer of advance and Solicitors Instructions. The society should be advised immediately of any discrepancy or variation in the details of the transaction. Notification of material changes must not be left until Report on Title stage as completion
b   may well be delayed. The Report on Title should be received by the society's Head Office/Scottish Regional Office at least three working days before the cheque is required. If a Valuer's final inspection is necessary before completion, an additional four working days must be allowed. The Solicitor is responsible for ensuring that the policy or policies as set out in the offer of
c   advance are in full force at the date of completion, even if the society is arranging the policy.'

The offer of advance contained (on p 1) particulars of (i) the applicant, with his address, (ii) the solicitor, described in the copy sent to the solicitor as the 'society's solicitor', (iii) the property to be charged, with a description of the nature and
d   tenure of the property as well as the address, (iv) the purchase price, (v) if leasehold, the unexpired term of the lease, (vi) the total advance, (vii) the repayment term, (viii) the interest rate, (ix) the monthly contractual payment and (x) the actual amount to be paid each month by the borrower (which, in the case of an endowment mortgage, would be less than the contractual payment). Also shown on p 1 of the offer of advance was an amount—described as 'the amount
e   ... payable by the borrower to the society's Solicitor at the time of completion of the advance'—which was to be deducted by the society from the advance cheque. That amount might include, typically, a single premium in respect of any mortgage indemnity guarantee which the society proposed to take from a third party and the first periodic premium in respect of buildings and contents
f   insurance in respect of the property to be charged.

In cases where the society proposed to take a mortgage indemnity guarantee from a third party the offer of advance also contained, on p 1, a notice, said to be given under s 28 of the Building Societies Act 1962, in these terms:

'Whereas the Bristol and West Building Society is prepared to consider
g   making an advance to you of [say, £X] to assist you in defraying the purchase price of the above property. And whereas the society proposes to take the said property as security for the advance Notice is hereby given that: (1) the maximum amount which the society would consider proper to advance upon the security of the property if no other security were taken by the
h   society is [say, £Y] (2) the amount by which the advance exceeds the said maximum amount is £[X-Y] (3) the society proposes to take security for the advance from a third party, particulars of which are: A guarantee given by [naming the third party].'

The reverse side of p 1 of the offer of advance contained printed special
j   conditions. These were incorporated, as required, by a provision on the third page (numbered p 2). It appears from the documents which I have seen that it was the society's usual practice to incorporate special conditions 1 and 2 in the offer of advance. Those special conditions were incorporated in each of the cases which are before me. Special condition 1 was in these terms, so far as material:

'1.(a) All information on the application form being correct, acceptance of the terms and conditions set out in the society's form of mortgage and the title of the proposed security being acceptable to the society's solicitors. If *a* the offer of advance is not accepted within 21 days of the date hereof or the mortgage is not completed within three months from such date or any question arises or any event happens which in the view of the society renders it undesirable for an advance to be made the society reserves the right to withdraw the offer ... (c) The Applicant providing from his own resources (without further borrowing) the whole of the balance of purchase money *b* except with the prior consent of the society ... (e) The valuation report has been prepared by the society, as required by section 13 of the Building Societies Act 1986, to enable it to assess the adequacy of the property as security for the proposed advance ...'

Page 2 of the offer of advance contained provision for the incorporation of *c* further conditions ('supplementary conditions') specific to the proposed transaction and not included in the printed special conditions. At the foot of p 2 in the copy sent to the solicitor there was a notice in the following terms:

'SOLICITORS INSTRUCTIONS   This sheet forms part of the offer of advance. Please advise the society immediately of any discrepancy or variation in the *d* above details or those shown on the offer of advance. Notification of material changes must not be left until Report on Title stage as completion may well be delayed.'

The solicitor's instructions were set out on two sides of a further sheet of paper. The instructions commenced with a notice in these terms: 'IMPORTANT: *e* The society's offer of advance forms an integral part of these instructions.'

Paragraph 2 of the solicitor's instructions was in these terms (so far as material):

'2 MATTERS WHICH MUST BE REPORTED TO THE SOCIETY   Any matters which might prejudice the society's security or which are at variance with *f* the offer of advance should be notified to the society in writing immediately they become known. Completion should not be arranged until the society has indicated its willingness to proceed.'

Paragraph 10 (renumbered as para 11 in later versions of the instructions) explained the procedure for obtaining the advance cheque: *g*

'10 REPORTING ON TITLE AND REQUESTING THE ADVANCE CHEQUE   The Report on Title should be received by the society at least three clear working days before the cheque is required. If a Valuer's inspection is necessary before completion an additional four working days must be allowed. The society will draw a crossed cheque in favour of the firm of Solicitors. Any *h* amount shown on the copy offer of advance as payable to the society on completion will be deducted from the Advance cheque. If completion has not taken place within seven days of the date of issue, the Advance moneys should be returned to the society. Interest is charged from the date of the cheque. A new cheque will be issued on notice of intention to complete *j* being received by the society.'

A document described as 'report on title and request for advance cheque' was sent to the solicitor, as an uncompleted printed form, at the same time as the other documents which I have described. The form contained space for the insertion of the name of the borrower, the address of the property, particulars of certain provisions in any lease under which the property was held, the date of *a* completion and the date (being a date not more than seven days before the date of completion) upon which the society's cheque was to be posted. The form then continued in these terms:

> 'I/We hereby confirm that the details of the transaction accord exactly with the particulars in the offer of advance and the requirements of the Solicitors Instructions (If not, please give full details). I/We have investigated the title of this property and report that I/We consider the title to be good and marketable and that it may be safely accepted by the society.'

b

On completing the report and request the solicitor signed the form immediately under the text which I have just set out.

If the report and request were completed to the satisfaction of the society, the *c* society sent to the solicitor its cheque for the advance on or about the date requested. The cheque was accompanied by two further documents. These were headed 'release of advance cheque' and 'notification of completion of advance'. The two documents, which were prepared by the society, contained identical particulars of deductions and retentions so as to reconcile the amount of *d* the agreed advance to the amount of the society's cheque. The first did no more than notify the solicitor that the cheque (in the amount computed as shown) was enclosed. The second was for the solicitor to return (having inserted the completion date) immediately after completion of the mortgage.

THE SOLICITOR'S CONTRACT OF RETAINER

e The primary duties of the solicitor to the society, as his client, must be found in the contract between them. The correct analysis, as it seems to me, is that the solicitor's letter contains an offer by the society to retain the solicitor as its solicitor for the purpose of the mortgage transaction described in the offer of advance. The scope of the work which the solicitor is to be retained to do is *f* defined by the solicitor's letter. It is 'to investigate the title and prepare the Mortgage Deed', and (where relevant) '[to ensure] that the policy or policies as set out in the offer of advance are in full force at the date of completion'. Prima facie, the purpose of the solicitor's instructions is to define what the solicitor is required to do in the course of investigating title and preparing the mortgage deed. The retainer is to investigate title and prepare the mortgage deed 'in *g* accordance with ... the Solicitors Instructions'.

The society's offer to retain the solicitor, contained in the solicitor's letter, is one which, again prima facie, can be accepted by conduct. It is unnecessary, in the circumstances with which I am concerned, to decide whether acceptance is effective as soon as the solicitor begins to investigate title. It is sufficient to *h* recognise that the offer is accepted, at the latest, when the solicitor returns the report on title and request for advance cheque. At that stage, if not before, there is a contract between the society and the solicitor. Further, in signing and returning the report on title, the solicitor warrants or represents that his principal obligation under the contract has been performed—'I/We have investigated the title of this property and report that I/We consider the title to be good and *j* marketable and that it may be safely accepted by the society'.

It is, I think, beyond argument that a solicitor who had not investigated title at all or who had not investigated the particular matters which the solicitor's instructions require to be investigated—see, in particular, para 4 (searches), para 5 (vacant possession and rights of persons in occupation) and para 7 (leasehold securities)—would be in breach of his contract with the society if he were to sign and return the report on title without qualification. Alternatively, by returning the report on title without qualification, he would be in breach of warranty or guilty of misrepresentation. So, also, the solicitor would be in breach of his contract with the society if he had failed to exercise the required degree of care and skill in carrying out his investigation. Further, the solicitor would be in breach of contract, in breach of warranty or guilty of misrepresentation, if he were to sign and return the report on title without qualification in circumstances where, having made a full investigation of the title, he did not consider the title to be good and marketable. Yet further, he would be in breach of contract if, having made a full investigation of the title, he were to sign and return the report on title without qualification in circumstances in which a reasonable conveyancing solicitor, exercising the required degree of care and skill, could not have reached the conclusion that the title was good and marketable on the material   available.

The breaches of contract to which I have just referred may be described as breaches of the obligation to investigate and report on title. There are examples, in the cases before me, of conduct by defendant solicitors which fall within this description. But, in most of the cases before me, the conduct of which the society complains cannot be regarded as a breach of the obligation to investigate and report on title in the sense to which I have referred. Rather, it is said the defendant solicitor knew of some fact—not relevant to title—which would or might have influenced a lender in its decision to lend and which the solicitor did not disclose to the society.

THE SOLICITOR'S OBLIGATION TO DISCLOSE FACTS NOT RELEVANT TO TITLE

The society relies upon the warranty or representation contained in the first of the two paragraphs which appear immediately above the solicitor's signature on the report and request: 'I/We hereby confirm that the details of the transaction accord exactly with the particulars in the offer of advance and the requirements of the Solicitors Instructions ...'

It is, I think, relevant to keep in mind that, whatever may have been the obligations assumed by the solicitor at the time when he began an investigation of title following receipt of the solicitor's letter, the return of the completed report and request marks a progression in the relationship between the solicitor and the society. By returning the report and request the solicitor (a) confirms that he has fulfilled one of his contractual obligations—to investigate and report on title—and (b) invites the society to authorise him to proceed to completion of the mortgage transaction by putting him in funds for that purpose. The request for authority to proceed to completion is founded not only upon the report on title but also upon the warranty or representation that the transaction which is to be completed does accord exactly with the particulars in the offer of advance and the requirements of the solicitor's instructions.

The 'particulars in the offer of advance' include, inter alia, particulars of the property to be charged—including, if leasehold, particulars of the unexpired term of the lease—and a statement of the purchase price. It is, I think, beyond argument that a solicitor who knew that the property which was to be the subject of the mortgage deed which he was to prepare for the purpose of completion was not exactly as described in the offer of advance could not, properly, sign and return the report and request without qualification. So, also, if the solicitor knew that the true purchase price payable by the purchaser/borrower to the vendor was not the purchase price stated in the offer of advance. Further, as it seems to me, a solicitor who signs and returns the report and request without qualification is, at the least, warranting to the society that he has taken some steps to satisfy

a

himself that the mortgage transaction in respect of which he is seeking authority to proceed to completion does accord exactly with the transaction which was the subject of the society's offer of advance; and that he knows of no reason why he cannot give the confirmation in the absolute and unqualified terms in which it appears in the report and request to which he has put his signature.

The solicitor's confirmation as to the details of the mortgage transaction in respect of which he is seeking authority to proceed is not limited to confirmation that those details accord exactly with 'the particulars in the offer of advance'. It includes confirmation that those details accord exactly with 'the requirements of the solicitors instructions'. The solicitor's instructions include, at para 2, a requirement that the solicitor report to the society immediately they become known 'Any matters which might prejudice the society's security or which are at variance with the offer of advance'. The offer of advance itself includes, at special condition 1(c), the requirement that the borrower should provide 'from his own resources (without further borrowing) the whole of the balance of purchase money except with the prior consent of the society'.

Again, it appears to me beyond argument that a solicitor who knew that the borrower was intending to fund the balance of the purchase money from further borrowing—for example, by borrowing upon the security of a second mortgage on the property to be purchased—or that the balance of the purchase money was to be left outstanding by way of loan from the vendor could not, properly, sign and return the report and request without qualification. Again, as it seems to me, a solicitor who signs and returns the report and request without qualification is, at the least, warranting to the society that he knows of no reason why he cannot give a confirmation in absolute terms to the effect that the mortgage transaction in respect of which he is seeking authority to proceed will be completed in accordance with the terms in special condition 1(c) of the offer of advance.

The society is not content to rely only upon the words 'Any matters ... which are at variance with the offer of advance' in para 2 of the solicitor's instructions. It seeks to rely also upon the words 'Any matters which might prejudice the society's security'. This raises the question whether, in that context, the phrase 'the society's security' means (as the defendants contend) no more than the security by way of mortgage over the property described in the offer of advance or has some wider meaning. The society contends that the phrase is capable of extending the solicitor's reporting obligation (a) to matters which might throw doubt on the valuation of the property upon which the society relied in deciding whether and in what amount to offer an advance, and (b) to matters which might affect the borrower's credit.

If the matter turned only on the construction of the relevant words in para 2 of the solicitor's instructions, I would not find it easy to hold that the reporting obligation does extend to matters which might throw doubt on the valuation of the property or affect the borrower's credit. First, the words are 'matters which might prejudice the society's security' not 'matters which might affect the value of the society's security'. Secondly, the relevant words must be construed in the context of the solicitor's instructions as a whole, and with due regard to the terms of the solicitor's letter and the offer of advance. The solicitor's letter requests the solicitor to investigate title and prepare the mortgage deed. Prima facie, the solicitor's instructions are ancillary to that request. The offer of advance contains nothing which would inform the solicitor either (a) what valuation advice the society had received in respect of the property to be mortgaged or (b) what criteria the society had taken into account in assessing the creditworthiness of the borrower. In so far as the offer of advance refers to 'the security' it is clear that

the reference is to the property to be mortgaged or to the third party guarantee—
see, in particular, special conditions 1(a) and 1(e) and the notice under s 28 of the *a*
Building Societies Act 1962. Other references to 'the security' in the solicitor's
instructions are references to the property to be mortgaged—see, in para 2 itself,
'persons ... in occupation of the mortgage security'. If I were to treat the
reporting obligation as turning only on the narrow question of construction,
without regard to the general law, I would be likely to reach the conclusion that *b*
the words 'matters which might prejudice the society's security' were not apt to
extend the reporting obligation beyond matters affecting title.

The society contends that this approach would be too narrow. I was referred
to the recent decision of the Court of Appeal in *Mortgage Express Ltd v Bowerman
& Partners* [1996] 2 All ER 836. I take the following summary of facts from the
judgment of Sir Thomas Bingham MR (at 840): *c*

'At the time of both exchange and completion Mr Gilroy [a partner in the
defendant firm of solicitors] was acting for both Mortgage Express and Mr
Hadi [the borrower]. He knew that Mr Hadi was buying for £220,000 a flat
valued at £199,000 on the security of which Mortgage Express was lending *d*
£180,000. He knew that Mr Hadi was buying from Mr Arrach, who was at
the same time buying the flat for £150,000. He knew that the vendor to Mr
Arrach had bought the flat on 2 November 1990 [ie some five weeks before
exchange of contracts between Mr Arrach and Mr Hadi] at a price which he
did not know but which that vendor's solicitor was reluctant to disclose and
which (according to his oral evidence) he thought it "obviously quite likely" *e*
was less than the figure of £150,000 which Mr Arrach was paying. He knew
that at this time the housing market in London was not rising and if anything
was falling.'

In those circumstances the plaintiff, Mortgage Express Ltd, contended that the *f*
defendant solicitors, through Mr Gilroy, had acted in breach of their duty to it in
failing to draw attention to the simultaneous purchase by Mr Arrach and the price
at which he was buying. It was argued for the defendant solicitors that their duty
was to do what was necessary to report to Mortgage Express on title, no more
and no less. The Court of Appeal rejected that contention. Sir Thomas Bingham
MR explained the principle (at 842): *g*

'A client cannot expect a solicitor to undertake work he has not asked him
to do, and will not wish to pay him for such work. But if in the course of
doing the work he is instructed to do the solicitor comes into possession of
information which is not confidential and which is clearly of potential *h*
significance to the client, I think that the client would reasonably expect the
solicitor to pass it on and feel understandably aggrieved if he did not. I would
accordingly reject the submission originally made on behalf of the solicitors
as to the narrow ambit of the duty, as the judge did, and accept, as I
understand her to have done, the submission of Mortgage Express. This was *j*
that if, in the course of investigating title, a solicitor discovers facts which a
reasonably competent solicitor would realise might have a material bearing
on the valuation of the lender's security or some other ingredient of the
lending decision, then it is his duty to point this out.'

Millett LJ posed the question for the court in these terms (at 845):

a
'… whether a solicitor of ordinary competence would have regarded the information in question as information which might cause the plaintiffs to doubt the correctness of the valuation which they had obtained.'

There were two features present in the facts before the Court of Appeal in *Mortgage Express Ltd v Bowerman & Partners* which are not reflected in the facts of any of the cases which I have to consider. First, the 'standing instructions to solicitors', which were sent by Mortgage Express to Mr Gilroy with the initial letter of instructions, contained the express provision that: 'These instructions are not intended to be exhaustive and do not in any way limit the normal duties of a solicitor when acting for a mortgagee.'

b

Secondly, there was enclosed with the initial letter of instructions, a 'valuation report' which disclosed the valuation (£199,000) upon which the lender was relying. Sir Thomas Bingham MR described that document as 'central to this appeal'.

c

I do not think that, in the cases before me, the defendant solicitors can take comfort from the absence of an express provision in the solicitor's instructions disclaiming any intention to limit the normal duties of a solicitor when acting for a mortgagee. It is obvious that the solicitor's instructions are not intended to contain an exhaustive statement of all that the solicitor is to do in the course of investigating title. For example, para 4 refers to 'the usual searches'; para 5 refers to the need to make 'such enquiries as are reasonable and appropriate'; para 7 puts on the solicitor the burden of identifying 'unsatisfactory or unduly onerous provisions in [a] lease'. The solicitor is to exercise his skill and judgment in carrying out the normal duties of a solicitor when instructed to investigate title. The Court of Appeal has held that those duties include a duty to inform the lender of facts discovered in the course of investigating title which a reasonably competent solicitor would realise might have an effect on the valuation of the security upon which the lender has relied when deciding to offer the advance. It would be perverse to construe the solicitor's instructions so as to exclude a duty to which a solicitor instructed to investigate title is subject under the general law. The society's concern as to matters affecting valuation is apparent from para 7(1)(c) of the instructions:

d

e

f

g
'… any escalation clause [in a lease] which could result in a substantial increase in the ground rent, or which is considered unduly onerous, should be referred to the Advances Manager immediately as it could adversely affect valuation.'

The absence of any valuation report from the documents supplied by the society to the solicitor is, however, a relevant factor. In considering whether some fact which has come to his knowledge in the course of investigating title—for example, the price payable by the intermediate vendor who is selling on to the society's borrower by way of sub-sale—would or ought to have caused the solicitor to doubt the valuation (alternatively, would or ought to have caused him to realise that the lender might question the valuation) it cannot be without relevance that the solicitor does not know what valuation advice the society has received in respect of the property. But the relevance, as it seems to me, is that in particular cases it may be more difficult to say that the solicitor ought to have realised that knowledge of the particular fact might have caused the lender to question the valuation. In the context of an application for summary judgment under Ord 14 it must, I think, be necessary for the society to show that the fact which the solicitor knew but did not disclose—for example, the price payable by

h

j

the vendor—was so obviously inconsistent with the amount of the advance that   a
any competent solicitor would realise that the lender must be acting upon a
valuation which would be called into question once that fact was known.

The decision in *Mortgage Express Ltd v Bowerman & Partners* was as to the duty
to disclose known facts which the reasonably competent solicitor would realise
might cause the lender to question the valuation upon which he was relying. But,
in the course of reaching that decision, Sir Thomas Bingham MR ([1996] 2 All ER   b
836 at 842) referred to the guidance on mortgage fraud given in Annex 24L of the
1990 *Guide to the Professional Conduct of Solicitors*:

> 'Solicitors must not withhold information relevant to a transaction from
> any client and for a lender this includes not only straightforward price
> reductions but may also include other allowances (e g for repairs, payment of   c
> costs, the inclusion of chattels in the price and incentives of the kind offered
> by builders such as free holidays and part-subsidisation of mortgage
> payments) which amount to a price reduction and which would affect the
> lender's decision to make an advance. Solicitors should not attempt to
> arbitrate on whether the price change is material but should notify the
> lender. It is recommended that solicitors advise their clients as soon as   d
> practicable that it would be regarded as fraud to misrepresent the purchase
> price and that a solicitor is under a duty to inform the lender of the price
> being paid for a property.'

Sir Thomas Bingham MR described guidance in those terms as a distillation, or
codification, of existing good practice. He approved it as sound practice. It is, I   e
think, a foundation of his observation, in the passage which I have already cited,
that—

> 'if in the course of doing the work he is instructed to do the solicitor comes
> into possession of information which is not confidential and which is clearly
> of potential significance to the client, I think that the client would reasonably   f
> expect the solicitor to pass it on and feel understandably aggrieved if he did
> not.' (See [1996] 2 All ER 836 at 842.)

In the cases which are before me the warranty, in the report and request, that
the details of the transaction in respect of which the solicitor seeks authority to
proceed accord exactly with the particulars in the offer of advance, and the   g
express obligation, in para 2 of the solicitor's instructions, to report any matter
which is at variance with the offer of advance are likely to be sufficient to catch
anything which amounts to a price reduction in the wide sense described in the
guidance note to which I have referred. But it is, I think, not irrelevant that those
provisions reflect, and perhaps extend, what would be the position under the   h
general law. Information obtained in the course of investigating title or in the
course of preparing for completion which is not confidential and which a
reasonably competent solicitor would realise might be of significance to his
client, as lender, ought to be disclosed to him.

In many cases the existence of facts (if any) which, upon a proper understanding of his duty to disclose, ought to be reported to the lender, will have   j
become known to the solicitor before he signed and returned the report and
request. But there are examples, in the cases which are before me, where the
relevant fact did not become known to the solicitor until after he had received the
advance cheque, that is to say, until a time shortly before completion. In those
cases the society cannot rely directly on the warranty or representation in the
report and request; but it can rely on the instruction, in para 2 of the solicitor's

a instructions, that 'Matters which might prejudice the society's security or which are at variance with the offer of advance must be notified to the society immediately they become known', and that, once such a matter has become known, 'Completion should not be arranged until the society has indicated a willingness to proceed'. A solicitor who learns of a matter which ought to be notified to the society, will be in breach of that instruction—and so in breach of

b his contract of retainer—if he proceeds to complete without having first obtained further authority from the society.

THE SOLICITOR'S OBLIGATIONS AS A FIDUCIARY

Contractual and fiduciary relationships may co-exist between the same parties (see *Barclays Bank Ltd v Quistclose Investments Ltd* [1968] 3 All ER 651 at 656, [1970]

c AC 567 at 581–582). The principle governing the interrelation of contractual and fiduciary relationships was explained by Mason J in *Hospital Products Ltd v United States Surgical Corp* (1984) 156 CLR 41 at 97, an appeal in the High Court of Australia, in a passage cited by Lord Browne-Wilkinson in *Kelly v Cooper* [1993] AC 205 at 215, [1992] 3 WLR 936 at 942:

d 'That contractual and fiduciary relationships may co-exist between the same parties has never been doubted. Indeed, the existence of a basic contractual relationship has in many situations provided a foundation for the erection of a fiduciary relationship. In these situations it is the contractual foundation which is all important because it is the contract that regulates the

e basic rights and liabilities of the parties. The fiduciary relationship, if it is to exist at all, must accommodate itself to the terms of the contract so that it is consistent with, and conforms to, them. The fiduciary relationship cannot be superimposed upon the contract in such a way as to alter the operation which the contract was intended to have according to its true construction.'

f It is not open to doubt that a solicitor stands in a fiduciary relationship to his client (see *Nocton v Lord Ashburton* [1914] AC 932 at 952, [1914–15] All ER Rep 45 at 52 per Viscount Haldane LC). The scope of the fiduciary duty owed by a solicitor to a lender for whom he acts must be defined by the terms of the retainer; but that duty cannot be cut down (in the absence of an express term in that retainer) by the fact that the solicitor, to the knowledge of the lender, acts

g also for the borrower. A solicitor who acts for two parties in the same transaction is not released from his obligations to the one by the fact that, in performing those obligations, he may be in breach of his obligations to the other. The solicitor who puts himself in the position in which he cannot advance the interests of one client without failing in his duty to another has only himself to blame (see *Moody v Cox*

h [1917] 2 Ch 71 at 81, [1916–17] All ER Rep 548 at 551 per Lord Cozens-Hardy MR).

The nature of fiduciary obligations was explained in the judgment of the Full Court in *Commonwealth Bank of Australia v Smith* (1991) 102 ALR 453 at 477, an appeal in the Federal Court of Australia:

j 'Not only must the fiduciary avoid, without informed consent, placing himself in a position of conflict between duty and personal interest, but he must eschew conflicting engagements. The reason is that, by reason of the multiple engagements, the fiduciary may be unable to discharge adequately the one without conflicting with his obligation in the other ... In such a case, it is not to the point that the fiduciary himself may not stand to profit from the transaction he brings about between the parties. The prohibition is not against the making of a profit (though many cases of breach of fiduciary duty involve the wrongful acquisition of a profit, rather than the infliction of a loss) but of the avoidance of conflict of duties … Nor, of course, is it to the point that the appellants did not act with fraudulent intent: *Nocton v Lord Ashburton* ([1914] AC 932 at 957, [1914–15] All ER Rep 45 at 54).'

Where a solicitor has received moneys from one client for the benefit or advantage of himself or another client on the basis of a warranty or representation which he knows, or ought to know, is misleading, equity will require him to restore those moneys forthwith. It is not necessary to establish that the misleading representation was made fraudulently, in the sense required to found an action for deceit at common law. The principle was explained by Viscount Haldane LC in *Nocton v Lord Ashburton* [1914] AC 932 at 951–952, [1914–15] All ER Rep 45 at 51–52:

'My Lords, it is known that in cases of actual fraud the Courts of Chancery and of Common Law exercised a concurrent jurisdiction from the earliest times. For some of these cases the greater freedom which, in early days, the Court of Chancery exercised in admitting the testimony of parties to the proceedings made it a more suitable tribunal. Moreover, its remedies were more elastic. Operating in personam as a Court of conscience it could order the defendant, not, indeed, in those days, to pay damages as such, but to make restitution, or to compensate the plaintiff by putting him in as good a position pecuniarily as that in which he was before the injury. But in addition to this concurrent jurisdiction, the Court of Chancery exercised an exclusive jurisdiction in cases in which, although classified in that Court as cases of fraud, yet did not necessarily import the element of dolus malus. The Court took upon itself to prevent a man from acting against the dictates of conscience as defined by the Court, and to grant injunctions in anticipation of injury, as well as relief where injury had been done. Common instances of this exclusive jurisdiction are cases arising out of breach of duty by persons standing in a fiduciary relation, such as the solicitor to the client, illustrated by Lord Hardwicke's judgment in *Chesterfield* v. *Janssen* ((1750) 2 Ves Sen 125, 28 ER 82). I can hardly imagine that those who took part in the decision of *Derry* v. *Peek* ((1889) 14 App Cas 337, [1886–90] All ER Rep 1) imagined that they could be supposed to have cast doubt on the principle of any cases arising under the exclusive jurisdiction of the Court of Chancery …'

Viscount Haldane LC went on to examine the circumstances in which the Court of Chancery would exercise what he had described as its exclusive jurisdiction. He said ([1914] AC 932 at 955–957, [1914–15] All ER Rep 45 at 53–54):

'… fraud as the term was employed by the Court of Chancery … applied to breach of special duty by a person who erred, not necessarily morally but at all events intellectually, from ignorance of a special duty of which the Courts would not allow him to say that he was ignorant. Such a special duty may arise from the circumstances and relations of the parties. These may give rise to an implied contract at law or to a fiduciary obligation in equity … My Lords, the solicitor contracts with his client to be skilful and careful. For failure to perform his obligation he may be made liable at law in contract or even in tort, for negligence in breach of a duty imposed on him … There was a time when in cases of liability for breach of a legal duty of this kind the Court of Chancery appears to have exercised a concurrent jurisdiction …

a But later on, after the action of assumpsit had become fully developed, I think it probable that a demurrer for want of equity would always have lain to a bill which did no more than seek to enforce a claim for damages for negligence against a solicitor ... This, however, does not end the matter. When, as in the case before us, a solicitor has had financial transactions with his client, and has handled his money to the extent of using it to pay off a

b mortgage made to himself, or of getting the client to release from his mortgage a property over which the solicitor by such release has obtained further security for a mortgage of his own, a Court of Equity has always assumed jurisdiction to scrutinize his action. It did not matter that the client would have had a remedy in damages for breach of contract. Courts of Equity had jurisdiction to direct accounts to be taken, and in proper cases to

c order the solicitor to replace property improperly acquired from the client, or to make compensation if he had lost it by acting in breach of a duty which arose out of his confidential relationship to the man who had trusted him ...'

Lord Atkinson and Lord Shaw of Dunfermline expressly agreed with the judgment of Viscount Haldane LC. Lord Dunedin also agreed, in these words

d ([1914] AC 932 at 964–965, [1914–15] All ER Rep 45 at 58):

'If, then, we turn to the solicitor's position we may look at it in two aspects, which is not to look at two different things, but to look at the same thing from two different points of view. He has contracted to be diligent; he is

e negligent. Law will give a remedy. It may well be that if a bill had been filed with a bald statement to the effect above, there might have been a demurrer for want of equity. He has not contracted that all representations made by him, if not negligently made, shall be true; and consequently, fraud apart, he cannot, on the law of *Derry v. Peek*, be made answerable at law for his representation. But from the other point of view he may have put himself in

f a fiduciary position, and that fiduciary position imposes on him the duty of making a full and not a misleading disclosure of facts known to him when advising his client. He fails to do so. Equity will give a remedy to the client. This it does quite apart from the doctrine of *Derry v. Peek*, for in that case there was no fiduciary relationship, and the action had to be based on the representation alone.'

g

It may well be that, in the circumstances which I have to consider, the solicitor could, now, be made liable at law in tort as well as in contract for representations made negligently in the report and request; but that change in the law since *Nocton v Lord Ashburton* does not affect the equitable remedy based on breach of

h fiduciary duty which the House of Lords affirmed in that case.

It is clear, from the judgment of Viscount Haldane LC, that not every allegation of misrepresentation against a solicitor will attract the jurisdiction of a Court of Equity. What is required is some circumstance which enables the court to intervene 'to prevent a man from acting against the dictates of conscience as defined by the Court' (see [1914] AC 932 at 952, [1914–15] All ER Rep 45 at 52).

j The circumstances in *Nocton v Lord Ashburton* included the fact that the solicitor himself had an interest in the transaction which was to be effected in reliance on his advice. But there can be no doubt that the requirement of unconscionable conduct is present where a solicitor who is acting for both borrower and lender misrepresents to the lender some fact which he knows, or must be taken to know, will or may affect the lender's decision to proceed with the loan. In those circumstances the solicitor is abusing his fiduciary relationship with one client, the lender, to obtain an advantage for his other client, the borrower. It is as much *a* 'against the dictates of conscience' for a solicitor knowingly to prefer the interests of one client over those of another client as it is for him to prefer his own interests over those of his client. This was the foundation of the decision in *Commonwealth Bank of Australia v Smith* (1991) 102 ALR 453 at 477 as appears from the passages to which I have already referred.

In circumstances in which a Court of Equity does intervene on the basis of a *b* breach of fiduciary duty, it may do so by imposing a constructive trust on the property which has been acquired as a result of that breach of duty. In the recent decision of the Privy Council in *A-G for Hong Kong v Reid* [1994] 1 All ER 1 at 4–5, [1994] 1 AC 324 at 331, Lord Templeman explained the position in these words:

> 'As soon as the [property] was received it should have been paid or *c* transferred instanter to the person who suffered from the breach of duty. Equity considers as done that which ought to have been done. As soon as the [property] was received, whether in cash or in kind, the false fiduciary held the [property] on a constructive trust for the person injured.'

For the reasons which I have set out I am satisfied that in those cases where *d* moneys have been received by the solicitor from the society following a request based upon a warranty or representation which he knew, or must be taken to have known, to be misleading in some material respect, equity will give a remedy in respect of any loss which the society may suffer as a result of its payment in reliance upon that request. That will be a remedy based upon breach of fiduciary duty and may, where necessary, take the form of the imposition of a constructive *e* trust on those moneys to enforce the solicitor's obligation to return them to the society forthwith. The constructive trust imposed by equity to enforce the obligation to make immediate restitution overrides any express or implied trust which might otherwise arise out of any instructions given by the client when the money is paid to the solicitor. No reliance can be placed on authority purportedly *f* conferred by those instructions, because they are vitiated by the breach of duty by which they were obtained. In particular, the solicitor has no authority, under the constructive trust, to apply the moneys in payment to, or to the order of, the borrower against the security of a mortgage over the property to be purchased. In the absence of some fresh instructions, given by the society after full disclosure of the matters in respect of which it has been misled, the only course properly *g* open to the solicitor is to repay the moneys to the society with interest.

BREACH OF TRUST

Cases where the solicitor knew nothing, prior to the receipt of the advance cheque, which ought to have led him to qualify the report which he has signed *h* are in a different category. In those cases there is nothing in the circumstances in which the moneys are received to require the imposition of a constructive trust by way of equitable remedy. Those cases are governed by rules applicable under s 32 of the Solicitors Act 1974, which prescribe the obligations of a solicitor in relation to clients' money. At the relevant time the applicable rules were the Solicitors' Accounts Rules 1986 and, subsequently, the Solicitors' Account Rules *j* 1991. Clients' money must be paid by the solicitor into a client account. Money may be withdrawn from a client account only for the purposes now prescribed by r 7 of the 1991 rules. These include (i) money properly required for a payment to or on behalf of the client; (ii) money properly required in full or partial reimbursement of money expended by the solicitor on behalf of the client, and (iii) money drawn on the client's authority. The solicitor's obligation (if any) to a   pay interest to a client in respect of money held in a client account is, itself, prescribed by the Solicitors' Account Rules (see s 33 of the 1974 Act). In *Target Holdings Ltd v Redferns (a firm)* [1995] 3 All ER 785 at 795, [1995] 3 WLR 352 at 362 Lord Browne-Wilkinson made it clear that he accepted that moneys held by solicitors on client account are trust moneys. Absent any express trust imposed by the client at the time that the moneys are paid to the solicitor, it

b   seems to me that the trust which attaches to clients' moneys (in cases within this second category) is an implied trust imposed in order to give effect to the Accounts Rules made under s 32 of the 1974 Act. The solicitor's obligations under that trust are the obligations imposed by the rules. It follows that a payment made out of clients' moneys to or to the order of a third party which is not authorised by, or 'properly required' on behalf of, the client is a payment

c   made in breach of trust.

I have already pointed out, in an earlier section of this judgment, that para 2 of the solicitor's instructions required that any matters which might prejudice the society's security or which were at variance with the offer of advance should be notified to the society in writing immediately they became known. The

d   paragraph continues: 'Completion should not be arranged until the society has indicated its willingness to proceed'. It is made clear by that instruction that the solicitor does not have authority to proceed to complete the mortgage—and, in particular, does not have authority to pay the whole or any part of the proceeds of the advance cheque received from the society to or to the order of the borrower—until any matter which ought to be reported to the society has been

e   reported and the society has indicated its willingness to proceed. A payment made to the vendor's solicitor at a time when the solicitor knows of a matter which ought to be reported to the society will, prima facie, be a payment made in breach of trust. It will be no answer to the allegation of breach of trust that the payment was made in order that the borrower could complete and execute the

f   mortgage upon the security of which the society intended to lend. The society has limited the solicitor's authority to proceed to completion in order to reserve to itself the opportunity to consider whether it wishes to proceed with a transaction which, ex hypothesi, differs from that contemplated at the time when it sent its advance cheque in response to the report and request.

g   THE 'TARGET' LITIGATION

The judgments in the Court of Appeal ([1994] 2 All ER 337, [1994] 1 WLR 1089) in *Target Holdings* were delivered on 8 November 1993. The decision of the House of Lords ([1995] 3 All ER 785, [1995] 3 WLR 352), reversing the Court of Appeal, was given on 20 July 1995. The actions with which I am concerned were

h   commenced during the period between those two dates.

The facts of the *Target* case are set out in the dissenting judgment of Ralph Gibson LJ ([1994] 2 All ER 337 at 339–343, [1994] 1 WLR 1089 at 1092–1096). It is unnecessary to rehearse them fully in this judgment. It is sufficient to note the following features of that case.

j   (1) There was no formal report on title. The solicitor defendants, Messrs Redferns, accepted instructions to act in the transaction on behalf of Target, as lender, on 23 June 1989 by letters which did not disclose that, as they knew, the purchaser (Crowngate) had agreed (subject to contract) to purchase two properties from the vendor (Mirage) at a price (£775,000) which was very substantially less than the sum of the valuations (£2m) which had been sent to Target. The claim in respect of that non-disclosure was put only in negligence, not as a breach of fiduciary duty. The judge, Warner J ([1994] 2 All ER 337 at 343–

344, [1994] 1 WLR 1089 at 1095–1097), gave unconditional leave to appeal in *a* relation to that claim in negligence and his decision on that point was not appealed.

(2) The amount of the advance (£1,525,000) was transferred by Target to Redferns on 28 June 1989. There were no express instructions as to the circumstances in which those moneys were to be released. It was accepted in the Court of Appeal that the effect was that Redferns held those moneys upon a bare *b* trust for Target, subject only to Redferns having implied authority to transmit the moneys to Crowngate or at Crowngate's direction, but then only upon receipt of executed transfers and mortgages to complete the security which Target intended to take ([1994] 2 All ER 337 at 342, 348, [1994] 1 WLR 1089 at 1095, 1101). In the House of Lords it was held that the trust was a bare trust, arising 'as but one incident of a wider commercial transaction involving agency'. Lord *c* Browne-Wilkinson explained the position in these terms ([1995] 3 All ER 785 at 795, [1995] 3 WLR 352 at 362):

'The depositing of money with the solicitor is but one aspect of the arrangements between the parties, such arrangements being for the most *d* part contractual. Thus, the circumstances under which the solicitor can part with money from client account are regulated by the instructions given by the client: they are not part of the trusts on which the property is held.'

Neither the Court of Appeal nor the House of Lords was invited to deal with the matter on the basis that, by reason of the non-disclosure prior to 28 June 1989, *e* Redferns held the moneys upon a constructive trust under which the only proper course open to them was to return those moneys immediately to Target. They could not be invited to deal with the matter on that basis because there was no appeal against the decision of Warner J that, on the material before him, Redferns were entitled to unconditional leave to defend on the question whether they had been under any duty to disclose what they knew about the circumstances in *f* which Crowngate appeared to paying £2m for properties which it had agreed to purchase for £775,000.

(3) Redferns transferred £1,250,000 out of the moneys in their hands to the intermediate purchaser (Panther) on 29 June 1989 without seeking or obtaining consent from Target; and without obtaining a transfer to Crowngate or a *g* mortgage from Crowngate. A further £240,000 was paid out to third parties on 3 July 1989. It was common ground that those payments were in breach of trust (see [1994] 2 All ER 337 at 342, 348, [1994] 1 WLR 1089 at 1095, 1101; [1995] 3 All ER 785 at 790, [1995] 3 WLR 352 at 356). The purpose of the transfer to Panther was, in part, to enable Panther to complete its purchase from Mirage on the *h* following day, 30 June 1989. Warner J made no finding whether, but for the transfer of Target's moneys to Panther, the purchase from Mirage would have taken place on 30 June 1989 or at all (see [1994] 2 All ER 337 at 343, 346, [1994] 1 WLR 1089 at 1095, 1098; [1995] 3 All ER 785 at 790, [1995] 3 WLR 352 at 357). If Panther could not have completed its purchase from Mirage without the Target moneys, then, as Lord Browne-Wilkinson pointed out the transaction would not *j* have gone through, Target would not have advanced any money at all and therefore Target would not have suffered any loss (see [1995] 3 All ER 785 at 790–791, [1995] 3 WLR 352 at 357–358, 366–367).

(4) The transfer by Panther to Crowngate and the mortgage by Crowngate in favour of Target were executed during July 1989. The security was perfected by registration on 26 November 1989.

a In summary, the position was described by Lord Browne-Wilkinson in these terms ([1995] 3 All ER 785 at 790, [1995] 3 WLR 352 at 356):

b 'In the course of acting as Target's solicitors Redferns had paid away the mortgage money in their client account to a stranger who had no contractual relationship with Crowngate and before completion of the purchase by Crowngate or the mortgages by Crowngate to Target. Such payments out of client account were otherwise than in accordance with Redferns' instructions from Target. It is common ground that the payments constituted a breach of trust by Redferns. On the other hand, Target had obtained exactly what it had originally intended to obtain, that is to say a loan to Crowngate secured by valid charges over the property.'

c The Court of Appeal (Ralph Gibson LJ dissenting) had held that Redferns came under an immediate duty to make restitution of the mortgage moneys when they paid those moneys away to Panther and others in breach of trust; that no inquiry as to causation was necessary because there was an immediate loss to Target when the moneys were paid away and the causal connection was obvious; and *d* that, accordingly, Target's loss was quantified in the amount of the moneys paid away, subject only to credit being given for the proceeds of realisation of the security.

The House of Lords reversed that decision. They accepted that a trustee who wrongly pays away trust money commits a breach of trust and comes under an immediate duty to remedy that breach; but the fact that there was an accrued *e* cause of action as soon as the breach was committed did not mean that the quantum of compensation payable had to be fixed as at the date when the breach occurred. As Lord Browne-Wilkinson put it ([1995] 3 All ER 785 at 796, 798, [1995] 3 WLR 352 at 363, 365):

f 'The quantum is fixed at the date of judgment, at which date, according to the circumstances then pertaining, the compensation is assessed at the figure then necessary to put the trust estate or the beneficiary back into the position it would have been in had there been no breach ... Equitable compensation for breach of trust is designed to achieve exactly what the word compensation suggests: to make good a loss in fact suffered by the *g* beneficiaries and which, using hindsight and common sense, can be seen to have been caused by the breach.'

On the facts which had to be assumed, namely that the property would have been transferred by Mirage to Panther even if the mortgage moneys had not been paid over by Redferns to Panther in breach of trust, the breach of trust had caused *h* no loss; because, (i) despite the breach of trust, Target obtained the security for its loan which it had intended to obtain, and (ii) Target would have made the loan and obtained the same security even if there had been no breach of trust.

It is, I think, implicit in the reasoning by which Lord Browne-Wilkinson (with whom each of the other members of the House of Lords agreed) reached the conclusion that Redferns' breach of trust had caused no loss, that he felt obliged *j* to assume, not only that the property would have been transferred by Mirage to Panther even if the mortgage moneys had not been paid over by Redferns to Panther in breach of trust, but also that Redferns would have committed no breach of trust, notwithstanding their knowledge of the circumstances, if they had completed the transaction regularly by paying over the mortgage moneys against receipt of an executed transfer to Crowngate and a mortgage from Crowngate. In other words, it would not have been a breach of trust to pay over the mortgage moneys on completion without having first made disclosure of the *a* facts which would or might have caused Target to doubt the valuations upon which it was relying and without having sought authority to proceed after disclosure of those facts. That was an assumption which had to be made in the light of the finding by Warner J, which had not been appealed, that there was a triable issue whether Redferns were under any duty to tell Target what they knew (see [1994] 2 All ER 337 at 343, [1994] 1 WLR 1089 at 1096). Further, Target *b* had given to Redferns no express instructions comparable to those in para 2 of the solicitor's instructions in the matters with which I am concerned. It is an assumption which, as it seems to me, is implicit in the reasoning because Lord Browne-Wilkinson could not have reached the conclusion that Target had suffered no loss by reason of the admitted breach of trust (that is to say, the payment of the mortgage moneys to Panther) unless he were prepared to assume *c* that the transaction could have been completed without any breach of trust. If it was inevitable that completion without prior disclosure would have involved a breach of trust, then it could not be right to make that assumption.

In the course of his judgment Lord Browne-Wilkinson restated the equitable rules of compensation for breach of trust in the following passage ([1995] 3 All ER *d* 785 at 793–794, [1995] 3 WLR 352 at 360):

'The equitable rules of compensation for breach of trust have been largely developed in relation to such traditional trusts, where the only way in which all the beneficiaries' rights can be protected is to restore to the trust fund what ought to be there. In such a case the basic rule is that a trustee in breach *e* of trust must restore or pay to the trust estate either the assets which have been lost to the estate by reason of the breach or compensation for such loss. Courts of Equity did not award damages but, acting in personam, ordered the defaulting trustee to restore the trust estate (see *Nocton v Lord Ashburton* [1914] AC 932 at 952, 958, [1914–15] All ER Rep 45 at 51, 55 per Viscount *f* Haldane LC). If specific restitution of the trust property is not possible, then the liability of the trustee is to pay sufficient compensation to the trust estate to put it back to what it would have been had the breach not been committed (see *Caffrey v Darby* (1801) 6 Ves 488, [1775–1802] All ER Rep 507 and *Clough v Bond* (1838) 3 My & Cr 490, 40 ER 1016). Even if the immediate cause of the loss is the dishonesty or failure of a third party, the trustee is liable to *g* make good that loss to the trust estate if, but for the breach, such loss would not have occurred (see Underhill and Hayton *Law of Trusts and Trustees* (14th edn, 1987) pp 734–736, *Re Dawson (decd), Union Fidelity Trustee Co Ltd v Perpetual Trustee Co Ltd* [1966] 2 NSWR 211 and *Bartlett v Barclays Bank Trust Co Ltd (No 2)* [1980] 2 All ER 92, [1980] Ch 515). Thus the common law rules *h* of remoteness of damage and causation do not apply. However, there does have to be some causal connection between the breach of trust and the loss to the trust estate for which compensation is recoverable, viz the fact that the loss would not have occurred but for the breach (see also *Re Miller's Deed Trusts* (1978) 75 LS Gaz 454 and *Nestle v National Westminster Bank plc* [1994] *j* 1 All ER 118, [1993] 1 WLR 1260).'

Lord Browne-Wilkinson went on to explain that, where the beneficiary was absolutely entitled to the trust fund, as against the trustee, the court would not, ordinarily, order reconstitution of the trust fund, but rather payment of compensation direct to the beneficiary. But the measure of compensation was the same; that is to say, the difference between what the beneficiary has in fact *a* received and the amount he would have received but for the breach of trust (see [1995] 3 All ER 785 at 794, [1995] 3 WLR 352 at 361).

CAUSATION: PAYMENT AWAY IN BREACH OF INSTRUCTIONS

The measurement of compensation by reference to what the beneficiary would have received but for the breach of trust requires, prima facie, an *b* examination of the question, necessarily hypothetical, what would have happened if the breach of trust had not been committed? In *Target* the relevant question was whether the moneys paid over by Redferns to Panther were essential to the carrying out of the transaction. If they were, then 'but for' Redferns' breach of trust in paying over those moneys the transaction would have failed before the time came for Target to make its advance and the advance *c* would not have been made. The House of Lords did not find it necessary to consider the possibility, obviously remote in that case, that, if the moneys were not available from another source to complete Panther's purchase from Mirage, they might have been paid by Redferns from the mortgage moneys with the consent of Target; that is to say, without any breach of trust. They did not need *d* to address, directly, the question what would have happened if Redferns had sought consent before making the payment to Panther.

The matters which I have to consider raise the question which it was unnecessary for the House of Lords to address directly. Where the breach of trust lies in paying over the mortgage moneys at a time when the solicitor knows of a matter which ought to be reported prior to completion—that is to say, in paying *e* over the mortgage moneys on completion without authority and in contravention of the solicitors instructions—an immediate and obvious answer to the question, 'What would have happened if the breach of trust had not been committed', is that the moneys would not have been paid over, the transaction would not have completed and the loan would not have been made. But it is *f* submitted on behalf of the defendants that that immediate and obvious answer is over-simplistic. What is required, in order to keep faith with the approach in *Target*, is an investigation into what would have happened if the solicitor had done all that he was required to do by the solicitors instructions; that is to say, if he had not only refused to complete but had taken the further step of making the disclosure and seeking authority. If, notwithstanding the matters disclosed, the *g* society would have decided to proceed with the loan, then (it is said) the breach of trust caused no loss.

I find that submission difficult to reconcile with the decision of the Court of Appeal in *Bishopsgate Investment Management Ltd (in liq) v Maxwell (No 2)* [1994] 1 All ER 261. The defendant, Mr Ian Maxwell, was held to be in breach of fiduciary *h* duty when, as a director of the plaintiff company, he executed stock transfer forms without the authority of a board resolution for the purpose of transferring, for nil consideration, to Robert Maxwell Group plc (a company which controlled his father's private interests) five parcels of publicly quoted shares. In a passage cited by Peter Gibson LJ in *Target* [1994] 2 All ER 337 at 353, [1994] 1 WLR 1089 *j* at 1106 Hoffmann LJ rejected the argument that it was not Mr Ian Maxwell's breach of duty which had caused the loss: 'It was the improper transfer which caused the loss and the necessary causal connection is therefore established' (see [1994] 1 All ER 261 at 266).

There is no suggestion in the judgments of the Court of Appeal in *Bishopsgate* that it was relevant to inquire what would have happened if Mr Ian Maxwell had refused, as he should have done, to sign the stock transfer forms. But that was, pre-eminently, a case in which the answer to such an inquiry might well have

been that the transfer would have been made anyway, following a board *a*
resolution procured for that purpose or on transfer forms signed by other
directors of the plaintiff company. At the least, the question what would have
happened if Mr Ian Maxwell had refused to sign, if relevant, was an issue to be
tried (see, in relation to similar issues in the same litigation, the comments in the
court below ([1993] BCLC 814) and the observations of the Court of Appeal
([1994] 1 All ER 261 at 264)). The conclusion must be that the Court of Appeal *b*
did not think it relevant to consider what would have happened if Mr Ian Maxwell
had refused to sign.

I can find nothing in the judgments of the House of Lords in *Target* which
suggests that *Bishopsgate* was wrongly decided. In commenting upon the decision
of the Court of Appeal in *Bishopsgate* Lord Browne-Wilkinson said:
c

'In that case, apart from one possibility, there was no doubt the shares were
irretrievably lost and that the value of the shares so lost was in excess of
£500,000. The only possibility of reducing that loss was that the plaintiff
might have a claim to recover the shares from the transferee on the grounds
that the transferee had notice of the impropriety ... The only way in which
the plaintiff company's loss could be less than the value of the shares wrongly *d*
transferred was if such hazardous litigation should be successfully pursued to
judgment ... The position is wholly different in the instant case where, on
the facts to be assumed, it is demonstrated that no loss has in fact been
incurred by reason of the breach of trust.' (See [1995] 3 All ER 785 at 798–
799, [1995] 3 WLR 352 at 365–366.)
e

There is nothing there which suggests that Lord Browne-Wilkinson thought
that the Court of Appeal ought to have considered what would have happened if
Mr Ian Maxwell had refused to sign the stock transfer forms.

The only support which I find in *Target* for the 'what if' approach advocated by
the defendants is in the passage in which Lord Browne-Wilkinson distinguished *f*
the decision of Hoffmann J in *Alliance and Leicester Building Society v Edgestop Ltd*
(18 January 1991, unreported). The relevant passage in the judgment of
Hoffmann J is set out in the judgment of Peter Gibson LJ ([1994] 2 All ER 337 at
351–352, [1994] 1 WLR 1089 at 1104). It is sufficient to cite the following:

'The society's instructions authorised the money to be advanced for the *g*
purpose of the purchases set out in the instructions and not for some
materially different transactions. It also required that the society should,
before completion, be notified of matters which ought reasonably to have
been brought to its attention. The solicitors knew or ought to have known
that the true nature of the transactions had been concealed from the society *h*
and I think that there can be no doubt that if the facts known to the solicitors
had been brought to the attention of the society before completion, it would
not have made any of the advances.'

Lord Browne-Wilkinson said ([1995] 3 All ER 785 at 798, [1995] 3 WLR 352 at
365):
j

'The plaintiff building society had paid moneys to solicitors in
circumstances similar to the present case and the solicitors had wrongly paid
them away in breach of their instructions. The building society obtained
orders for interim payment against the solicitors on the grounds that they
were liable for breach of trust. The case however is distinguishable because
of one crucial difference, viz the judge found that if the building society had

known the true facts it would not have made the advance, ie one of the facts
that has to be assumed to the contrary in the present case. In that case
therefore at the date of judgment a certain loss had been demonstrated in
that the breach of trust had caused the building society to enter into a
transaction in which they would not have participated had there been no
breach of trust.'

Lord Browne-Wilkinson could have chosen to distinguish the *Edgestop* case on
the ground that, as in *Bishopsgate*, the 'but for' test of causation was satisfied, in
that the connection between the payment and the loss was obvious. But he did
not take that course. There can be no doubt that he did regard it as relevant that,
in *Edgestop*, Hoffmann J had answered the question what would have happened
if the defendants had done what their instructions required; that is to say, had not
only refused to complete, but had brought the relevant facts to the attention of
the building society.

I cannot pretend that I find the apparent difference in the House of Lords'
treatment of the *Edgestop* and the *Bishopsgate* decisions easy to understand. Be
that as it may, for the purpose of an application for summary judgment, the
conclusion must be that the 'but for' test is not satisfied in a breach of instructions
case unless the answer to the question, 'what if', is that the society would not
have authorised the solicitors to proceed if it had known the facts.

CAUSATION: MISREPRESENTATION IN BREACH OF STATUTORY DUTY

Hitherto, I have been considering the position only in relation to cases in
which the breach of trust lies in paying over the mortgage moneys at a time when
the solicitor knows of a matter which ought to be reported prior to completion;
that is to say, in paying over moneys held upon an implied trust to give effect to
his instructions in circumstances which are a breach of those instructions. It is
necessary to consider how far the same principles apply where the remedy is
compensation for breach of fiduciary duty in respect of moneys paid away by a
solicitor who had received them from the society in response to a request based
upon a warranty or representation which he knew, or must be taken to have
known, was misleading.

There can be no doubt that the society must establish that it paid the moneys
to the solicitor in reliance on the warranty or representation. But that is likely to
be self-evident in a case in which the confirmation (which encapsulates the
warranty and representation) is contained in the standard document which the
society requires to be signed and returned by the solicitor before an advance
cheque will be released. The question is not whether the society must show that
it relied on the representation which was made, but whether it must go further
and establish that it would not have released the advance cheque if the true facts
had been disclosed by an appropriate qualification to the confirmation in the
report and request.

It would, as it seems to me, be a strange principle of equity which allowed a
solicitor who, in breach of the duty of good faith owed to his client, had given a
warranty which he knew to be false with the intention that the client should act
upon it, to say, in answer to a claim for compensation in respect of loss which had
resulted from the client relying on the warranty and acting as intended, that the
client must establish that he would not have so acted if he had been told the true
facts. After all, a common reason for giving a warranty which the warrantor
knows to be false is the fear that, without the false warranty, the lender will refuse
to proceed. If it were not for that fear the warrantor would have no reason to

withhold the truth. I am comforted, therefore, to find a decision of the Privy
Council, on appeal from the Supreme Court of Canada in *Brickenden v London*   *a*
Loan and Savings Co [1934] 3 DLR 465, which rejects any such principle.
The appeal in *Brickenden* arose out of a breach by the appellant of his duty as a
solicitor to the respondent loan company in connection with a mortgage advance
of $Can 13,500 made in November 1924 to other clients of his, Mr and Mrs Biggs.
It was not disclosed to the loan company, either in the application for the advance   *b*
or in the certificate of title prepared by the appellant, that part of the mortgage
moneys were to be used to discharge two existing loans, of $Can 2,000 and $Can
1,200, owed by Mr and Mrs Biggs to the appellant and secured on the property to
be mortgaged.
The judgment of the Privy Council was delivered by Lord Thankerton. He
held that the appellant's non disclosure of the two mortgages was a breach of his   *c*
duty as solicitor to the loan company. He went on to consider whether any
damage had been shown to result from that breach. He dismissed the argument
that disclosure would not have altered the loan company's decision to proceed
with the transaction in the following passage (at 469):

'When a party, holding a fiduciary relationship, commits a breach of his   *d*
duty by non-disclosure of material facts, which his constituent is entitled to
know in connection with the transaction, he cannot be heard to maintain
that disclosure would not have altered the decision to proceed with the
transaction, because the constituent's action would be solely determined by
some other factor, such as the valuation by another party of the property   *e*
proposed to be mortgaged. Once the Court has determined that the
non-disclosed facts were material, speculation as to what course the
constituent, on disclosure, would have taken is not relevant.'

That passage was cited and applied by the Federal Court of Australia in
Commonwealth Bank of Australia v Smith (1991) 102 ALR 453 at 479, to which I have   *f*
already referred in another context. It is material to note that the Full Court, in
that appeal, regarded the passage as an illustration of the principle, identified by
Street J in *Re Dawson (decd), Union Fidelity Trustee Co Ltd v Perpetual Trustee Co Ltd*
[1966] 2 NSWR 211 at 216 and recognised by Lord Browne-Wilkinson in *Target*
Holdings, that the obligation to make restitution which Courts of Equity imposed
on fiduciaries was of a more absolute nature than the common law obligation to   *g*
pay damages for tort or for breach of contract and that the equitable obligation
to make restitution was not necessarily limited by common law concepts of
foreseeability and remoteness (see 102 ALR 453 at 480).
In my view I should apply the principle identified by Lord Thankerton in
Brickenden—that, where a fiduciary has failed to disclose material facts, he cannot   *h*
be heard to say, in answer to a claim for equitable compensation, that disclosure
would not have altered the decision to proceed with the transaction—unless
satisfied that it is inconsistent with the decision of the House of Lords in *Target*.
Lord Browne-Wilkinson does not refer, in his judgment in *Target*, to *Brickenden*
or to the subsequent decision in the Federal Court of Australia. The *Brickenden*
principle was of no direct relevance to the question which the House of Lords had   *j*
to decide in *Target*; namely, whether in applying the 'but for' test of causation, for
the purpose of quantifying equitable compensation in respect of a payment made
in breach of trust it was relevant to look, with benefit of hindsight, at what would
have happened if there had been no breach of trust and so no payment. As I have
already indicated, the only support which I can find in his judgment for the
relevance of the question 'what if' in the context of failure to disclose material

a facts lies in his treatment of the decision in *Edgestop* (18 January 1991, unreported).

It is not open to me to speculate whether Lord Browne-Wilkinson had the *Brickenden* principle in mind when he distinguished *Edgestop* in the way that he did; nor to speculate whether, if his attention had been directed to the *Brickenden* principle, he would have distinguished *Edgestop* on the basis that that might be
b regarded as a case for the application of that principle. I cannot hold that a decision of the House of Lords on which the defendants rely was given per incuriam. I should not allow myself to wonder whether it might have been. I must accept that Lord Browne-Wilkinson's treatment of the *Edgestop* decision is inconsistent with the *Brickenden* principle having any application where the breach of trust lies in paying over money in breach of instructions. In such a case
c I must hold, for the reasons which I have already given, that the question what the society would have done if, in accordance with his instructions, a solicitor had asked for authority to proceed to completion, is a relevant question.

It does not follow that I must treat the *Brickenden* principle as overruled by *Target* in cases where the breach of fiduciary duty lies in the giving of a false
d warranty or representation for the purpose of obtaining the advance cheque. The decision in *Target* is not directed to that question. The House of Lords cannot be taken to have intended to overrule, as it were by a side wind, a decision of the Privy Council which had stood for sixty years, which had been applied recently by the Federal Court in Australia and to which its attention does not appear to have been drawn.

e I am satisfied that I should treat the *Brickenden* principle as applicable in those cases where the solicitor has received the advance cheque in response to a request made on the basis of a warranty or representation which he knew, or must be taken to have known, to be misleading in some material respect. In those cases the question what the society would have done if it had been told the true facts is
f not relevant.

EVIDENCE ON THE CAUSATION ISSUE

In those cases in which the question what the society would have done if it had been asked for authority to proceed to completion is a relevant question, the further question arises as to what evidence the society needs to adduce on that
g issue in order to satisfy the court on an application for summary judgment.

The society has taken the view that it is sufficient to rely upon an affidavit, usually from the branch manager or other officer who authorised the loan but, on occasion, by another deposing 'on information and belief', to the effect that if he or she had known of any one of a number of matters which, as alleged, ought
h to have been (but were not) reported, the loan would never have been authorised. Examples of the standard formula used in the affidavits are set out later in this judgment.

The defendants criticise this approach in a number of respects. First, they point out that the standard formula tends to lose credibility by repetition. It becomes
j apparent, after considering a number of these cases together, that the deponent has adopted a formula which has come off the word processor, rather than applying his mind to the facts of the individual case. Secondly, the standard formula tends to lose credibility through its all-embracing inclusiveness. When it is found that the deponent is prepared to depose that authority would not have been granted if any one of a number of non-disclosed matters had been reported, and that, amongst those matters there are some which appear to be of the utmost triviality, little confidence can be placed on the deponent's reliability. Thirdly,

the deponents have not supported their confident assertions as to the decisions
which they would have made some six or more years ago (in a market very
different to that prevailing when the affidavits were sworn) by reference to any
manual of standard procedures (such as a building society of this size might have
been expected to operate), so that there is no way of ascertaining how far any
particular decision was prescribed by internal rules or was a matter for the
discretion of the deponent. Fourthly, in so far as the decision was a matter for
discretion, there is no material against which the deponent's assertion as to the
way in which he or she would have exercised that discretion can be tested; in
particular there is no material which shows how discretion was exercised in
relation to comparable loan applications where similar matters were disclosed. In
short, the defendants contend that the question what would the society have
done if it had been asked for authority to proceed, cannot fairly be decided
without a trial; in preparation for which there would have to be very extensive
discovery.

I was, of course, pressed on behalf of the society with the well-known
observations of Megarry V-C in *Lady Anne Tennant v Associated Newspapers Group
Ltd* (1979) 5 FSR 298 at 303:

'A desire to investigate alleged obscurities and a hope that something will
turn up on the investigation cannot, separately or together, amount to
sufficient reason for refusing to enter judgment for the plaintiff. You do not
get leave to defend by putting forward a case that is all surmise and
Micawberism.'

I am quite satisfied that the defendants' desire to have a proper opportunity to
test the assertions made in affidavits sworn by deponents on behalf of the society
in the actions which are before me cannot be dismissed as Micawberism. One of
the advantages of hearing a number of applications together—with agreement
that the evidence in each may be read in every other—is that the court has a much
wider view of the picture than would be presented by the evidence in any
individual case. I have no doubt that, generally, it would be unsafe to act on the
basis of untested assertions in the society's affidavits that the society 'would not
have touched this transaction with a bargepole'. I think it may well turn out at a
trial that, in the relevant period (1988 to 1991), the society was a good deal less
fastidious in choosing its borrowers than it would now wish to recall.

Accordingly, where the question, 'what would the society have done if it had
been asked for authority to proceed to completion', is a relevant question, it is a
question which needs to be tried. If, as I suspect, that will necessitate very
extensive discovery—including discovery of comparable transactions authorised
(or not authorised) by the relevant loan officers and of much of the internal
procedures of the society—that will have to be faced; and, where appropriate,
managed by suitable directions made applicable to multi-party litigation.

THE OTHER BRISTOL AND WEST DECISIONS
I have mentioned, in the introduction to this judgment, existing decisions on
appeals from the district judges in this district registry which are perceived to be
inconsistent. It is, I think, necessary that I examine those decisions in an attempt
to resolve, so far as possible any perceived inconsistency. The relevant decisions,
which are unreported, are: (i) a decision of mine (delivered shortly after the
decision of the House of Lords in *Target*), *Mothew* (27 July 1995); (ii) a decision of
Judge Weeks QC, *Read & Rogers* (7 September 1995); and (iii) two decisions of

a Judge Jack QC, *Evans Bullock & Co (a firm)* (6 October 1995) and *Singh & Ruparell (a firm)* (6 October 1995).

In *Mothew,* the advance had been made by the Cheshunt Building Society, to the undertaking of which the Bristol and West Society had succeeded by a transfer of engagements effected under s 98 of the Building Societies Act 1986 with effect from 30 December 1991. The standing instructions to solicitors acting
b for the Cheshunt Society in mortgage transactions required the solicitor to report any proposal that the applicant might create a second mortgage in order to finance part of the purchase price. That requirement was no different in substance from the obligation, in the Bristol and West Society's own solicitors instructions, to report any matter which was at variance with the offer of advance. The defendant made a report on title to the society on 2 August 1988.
c In that report the defendant confirmed, in answer to a specific inquiry, that to the best of his knowledge and belief the balance of the purchase money was being provided by the applicants personally without resort to further borrowing. It was impossible to see how that answer could properly have been given by the defendant in the circumstances that he knew, at the time, that the balance of the
d purchase price was to be provided by a loan from Barclays Bank plc secured by a second mortgage on the property. Indeed, the defendant had, on 21 July 1988, given an undertaking to Barclays Bank to hold the title deeds to its order pending registration. The defendant offered no explanation as to the circumstances in which he had given the confirmation in the report on title. On 15 August 1988 the society sent to the solicitor an advance cheque in the sum of £59,000. I held:
e
'In those circumstances it seems to me beyond argument that the defendant solicitor received the cheque or cheques for £59,000 as a direct result of the misleading report which he had supplied to the society on 2 August 1988. The money was paid to the defendant by the society as a result of a misrepresentation made to the society by the defendant. The society
f was led to believe that there would be no further borrowing and no second charge; and so no contravention of general condition 16 in the offer of advance. That belief was induced by the misrepresentation in the report to which I have referred.'

g The effect, in my judgment, was that from the moment when each cheque for £59,000 was received by the defendant solicitor, he held it upon a constructive trust to return it forthwith to the society; unless authorised to retain, or dispose of, it after a full knowledge of the facts had been disclosed.

The decision of the district judge, from which the appeal was before me, had been given on 21 June 1995, shortly before the decision of the House of Lords in
h *Target.* She had, of course, applied the law as it was understood to be following the decision of the Court of Appeal in that case. It was submitted to me that, in the light of the decision of the House of Lords, it was necessary to be satisfied that the breach of trust had caused the damage of which the plaintiff complained. I held:

j
'Claims by building societies and other mortgage lenders against solicitors who act in contravention of the standing instructions upon which they are retained must turn on their own particular facts. The particular feature of this case—which, in my view, differentiates it both from *Target Holdings v Redferns* ([1995] 3 All ER 785, [1995] 3 WLR 352) and from *Bristol and West Building Society v Kramer* (Times, 6 February 1995)—is that the money required by the solicitor from the society was paid by the society as the direct

result of the defendant solicitor's misleading report of 2 August 1988. It was
that circumstance which gave rise to an immediate obligation to repay the *a*
money as soon as the defendant received it. The defendant had the money
from the moment of receipt upon a constructive trust to repay it forthwith
to the society; unless, of course, with full knowledge of the facts the society
authorised the defendant to do otherwise.   There were no other
circumstances in which payment to the vendor could have been an *b*
authorised application of the moneys in the defendant's hands. The society's
loss of the £59,000 was the direct result of the unauthorised payment to the
vendors of moneys which the defendant held upon trust to repay to the
society. I am satisfied, therefore, that there is nothing in the judgments in the
House of Lords in *Target Holdings v Redferns* which affords a defence to the
solicitor in the circumstances of this case.'   *c*

Later in that judgment, in answer to the defendant's contention that the plaintiff
could not establish, without a trial, that the society would not have made the
advance if it had known of the borrowing from Barclays Bank, I said:

'But that point affords no defence to the plaintiff's claim. It is nihil ad rem *d*
that if the true position had been disclosed to the society, the society might
or might not have issued an amended offer of advance. Liability to repay
arises in this case because the defendant solicitor received money from the
society as a result of his own misrepresentation. He cannot be heard to say
that he could retain that money against the society, or dispose of it to the *e*
vendors, because, in other circumstances, the society might have chosen to
make the advance notwithstanding the borrowing from Barclays.'

In *Read & Rogers* the advance was made by the society on the basis of its own
documentation. The offer of advance incorporated special condition 1(c). The
report on title was returned by the solicitor on 1 August 1988 and contained an *f*
unqualified confirmation that the transaction was in exact accord with the
particulars in the offer of advance. Completion was fixed for 30 August 1988. On
or about 22 August 1988 the solicitors learnt, for the first time, that the borrowers
might be intending to complete with the assistance of a top-up loan and
temporary bridging finance. The judge accepted that—
g

'by 25 August the solicitors had strong reason to believe that any previous
statement they had made to the effect that the borrowers were paying the
rest of the purchase price out of their own resources was no longer true, and
Ö there was a continuing duty on the solicitors to inform the building society
of the change in events as they saw it. It is common ground that they did not *h*
do so.'

The society sent its advance cheque to the solicitors on 25 August 1988.
The judge identified two issues to be tried. The first was whether the society
knew of the borrowers' intention to fund the balance of the purchase money by
further borrowing. On that issue alone the matter would have had to go to trial. *j*
The second issue was whether there was satisfactory evidence that the society
suffered a loss which it would not have suffered but for the solicitor's omission to
inform them, 'i.e. would the building society, even if it had been told that a top-up
loan or a bridging loan was to be obtained, have gone ahead with the advance?'
He was not satisfied with the evidence which had been adduced by the society on
that point.

a   There is nothing in the approach which I have set out above which I find inconsistent with my decision in *Mothew*. Judge Weeks QC was not dealing with a case in which it could be said that the solicitor had received the mortgage moneys from the society as a result of a warranty or representation which was known to be misleading at the time when it was given. He identified the distinction between his case and *Mothew* in the following passage: 'The

b   distinction is that the misrepresentation to the building society [in *Mothew*] was a positive one rather than an omission and was made before the cheque was received.'

On the basis of that distinction, the reasoning in *Mothew* had no application to the question which the judge had to decide. He could not have held, as I had done in *Mothew*, that liability to repay arose because the solicitor had received

c   money as a result of his own misrepresentation and could not be heard to say that he could dispose of that money to the vendors because, in other circumstances, the society might have chosen to make the advance notwithstanding the further borrowing. He was bound to regard the question, 'what if the society had been told', as a relevant question.

d   The judge did not regard the distinction as material. Accordingly, he went on to consider the reasoning in *Mothew* and expressed the view that there was great difficulty in reconciling that reasoning with the decision of the House of Lords in *Target*. He was spared the necessity of actually declining to follow *Mothew* by the concession, which he recorded in his judgment, that counsel for the defendant solicitor was not relying on *Mothew* as authority for the proposition that '*in the*

e   *present case*' the question of whether or not the building society would have made the advance if it had known the true facts was irrelevant. I think that concession was rightly made; on the factual basis on which the judge was proceeding— namely that there was no omission to inform the society of the true position prior to the receipt of the advance cheque—*Mothew* was not authority for the

f   proposition that the question 'what if' was irrelevant.

Evans Bullock & Co was also a case in which the advance was made by the society on the basis of its standard documentation. The facts were rather more complex than in the ordinary residential house mortgage. On 16 July 1990 James Williams had applied to the society for an advance of £232,000 to assist him in the purchase of Flat 6, Westside Court, Elgin Avenue, London W9. The purchase

g   price stated in the application was £290,000. On 24 August 1990 the society issued an offer of advance in the sum of £233,529—being the amount sought together with a mortgage indemnity guarantee (MIG) premium. It appears that an exactly parallel application was made by Peter Ferreday in relation to Flat 7, Westside Court, and a similar offer of advance issued in respect of that application.

h   On or about 5 February 1991 Mr Bullock, the partner in the defendant firm who were acting for the society and for the borrowers, received instructions that each flat was being sold by a common vendor, Jongems Ltd, at a price of £217,000. Flat 6 was to be sold by Jongems to Mr Ferreday and immediately sold on by Mr Ferreday to Mr Williams at a stated price of £290,000; and Flat 7 was to

j   be sold by Jongems to Mr Williams and immediately sold on by Mr Williams to Mr Ferreday at the same stated price, £290,000. On 13 February 1991 the society issued fresh offers of advance to Mr Williams (in respect of Flat 6) and to Mr Ferreday (in respect of Flat 7). The amended offers were in the same terms as those issued in August 1990. On 20 February 1991 Mr Bullock returned to the society reports on title in respect of each flat. Each report contained an unqualified confirmation that the details of the transaction were in exact accord with the particulars in the offer of advance and the requirements of the solicitor's

instructions. Mr Bullock did not inform the society of the reciprocal purchase
arrangements from Jongems which I have described above. The advance
cheques were sent by the society to the solicitors on 28 February 1991 and
completion of the purchases from Jongems, the reciprocal purchases between the
borrowers and the mortgages took place on that day. After payment to Jongems'
solicitors of £437,164 in respect of the two flats, there was a balance of some
£26,806 remaining out of the mortgage moneys; for which, after deducting their
own costs, the defendants accounted to Mr Williams.

Judge Jack QC held that the reciprocal sales between Mr Williams and Mr
Ferreday were sham transactions 'introduced by them for the purpose of
inducing the society to lend the amounts which it did, namely sums in excess of
the amounts actually required to purchase the properties'. He held, also, that the
defendant solicitors were in breach of their instructions in failing to inform the
society of the full facts. He rejected a submission that he could not be satisfied,
on the evidence, that the society would not have gone ahead even if it had been
told the full facts. He said:

'I am wholly satisfied that, if the society had known what was actually
going on, it would have withdrawn from the transactions. If the matter went
to trial and the relevant employees were cross-examined exhaustively, I can
see no other possible outcome.'

If I may say so, I think the contrary was unarguable. On that basis the judge
gave judgment for damages to be assessed on the claim for breach of contractual
duty; and ordered a substantial interim payment. He then went on to consider
the claim in breach of trust. After a detailed examination of Lord Browne-
Wilkinson's judgment in *Target* he reached the conclusion that—

'the defendants have an arguable defence to the claim in breach of trust
made on the ground of payment in breach of instructions, the ground of
arguable defence being that the payment was not in breach of an instruction
relating to payment.'

He then turned to consider my judgment in *Mothew*. He identified the
proposition for which that case was being advanced as authority in these terms:

'The submission of law has to be that, where money is paid by a principal
to his agent as part of a contractual arrangement with a third party and the
payment to him is induced by an innocent misrepresentation of fact by the
agent and so is made by mistake, the money is impressed with a constructive
trust in the hands of the agent requiring its immediate repayment to the
principal. It could be added to that the misrepresentation by the agent is
made in breach of his contractual duty to the principal.'

He took the view that that proposition was not so clearly established as the law
that he should give summary judgment on the basis that it was correct. Again, if
I may say so, given the width in which the proposition was apparently advanced,
I am not surprised that he took that view. *Mothew* could not be relied upon for
so wide a proposition. First, in *Mothew*, the 'agent' was a fiduciary who had put
himself in a position in which his duty to the lender was in conflict with the
interests of his other client, the borrower. Secondly, the misrepresentation could
not be described as innocent; the solicitor clearly had the knowledge which made
the representation false. It was unnecessary to establish an intention to deceive
in order to invoke the equitable remedy.

Finally, Judge Jack QC considered the argument that the breach of trust had
a not caused the loss claimed. Strictly, in the circumstances that he had found no
breach of trust established, that question did not arise. He dealt with it briefly:

'[Counsel] submitted that the principle set out by Lord Browne-Wilkinson
in *Target* ([1995] 3 All ER 785, [1995] 3 WLR 352) to the effect that a lender
could only recover his real loss was wide enough to cover a *Mothew* situation.
b Lord Browne-Wilkinson suggested that the principles of compensation for
breach of trust should not differ at least fundamentally from those applied at
common law (see [1995] 3 All ER 785 at 792, 794, [1995] 3 WLR 352 at 359,
361). It does seem to me that the principle that the loss would not have
occurred but for the breach must apply. If the lender would still have gone
c ahead if the correct position had been reported, in my view there is a serious
argument whether the lender can establish any loss.'

In *Singh & Ruparell* the borrower had applied to the society for an advance of
£270,000 against a stated purchase price of £330,000. The society issued an offer
of advance in the amount of £272,450, which included an MIG premium. The
d offer of advance included special condition 1(c). The defendant solicitors
completed and returned the report on title on 18 August 1989. The report
contained an unqualified confirmation in the usual terms. The solicitors did not
disclose that, as they knew, the vendor was prepared to accept only £265,000 on
completion; so that an amount in excess of £55,000 (after allowing for the deposit
of £9,750 said to have been paid direct to the vendor's solicitors) would be left
e outstanding on completion. The advance cheque was sent on 24 August 1989 and
completion took place on the same day.

Judge Jack QC held that the fact that a substantial sum was being left
outstanding on completion ought to have been reported to the society. He was
satisfied that, had that fact been reported, the society would not have proceeded
f with the transaction. He gave judgment for the society on its claim in contract,
with damages to be assessed. He gave leave to defend in relation to the claims
based on breach of trust, for the reasons which he had set out in his judgment,
given on the same day, in *Evans Bullock & Co.*

It is impossible to avoid the conclusion that both Judge Weeks and Judge Jack
have taken the view that they ought not to follow my decision in *Mothew*. In
g those circumstances it was submitted to me, very properly, that judicial comity
required that I should accept that *Mothew* was wrongly decided and, myself,
follow the decisions in *Read & Rogers* and in *Evans Bullock & Co.*

The principles which a judge of first instance should apply when faced with
two earlier inconsistent decisions of judges of co-ordinate jurisdiction are
h explained by Nourse J in *Colchester Estates (Cardiff) v Carlton Industries plc* [1984] 2
All ER 601 at 604–605, [1986] Ch 80 at 85. The general rule is that the later
decision is to be preferred, if it has been reached after a full consideration of the
earlier decision. But Nourse J recognised an exception to the general rule. He
said:

j   '... I would make an exception only in the case, which must be rare, where
the third judge is convinced that the second was wrong in not following the
first. An obvious example is where some binding or persuasive authority has
not been cited in either of the first two cases.'

I am satisfied that this is one of those rare cases in which I should depart from
the general rule. *Brickenden v London Loan and Savings Co* [1934] 3 DLR 465 is a
Privy Council decision of high persuasive authority which is directly on the point.

It was not cited in any of the earlier cases. Although I reflected the *Brickenden*   *a*
principle in my judgment in *Mothew*, I did not support that principle by reference
to the relevant authority; with the consequence that neither Judge Weeks nor
Judge Jack had the opportunity to consider that authority. Nor did I explain, in
Mothew, the principles, derived from *Nocton v Lord Ashburton* [1914] AC 932,
[1914–15] All ER Rep 45 and *Commonwealth Bank of Australia v Smith* (1991) 102
ALR 453, which, as it seems to me, lead to the conclusion that a party who pays   *b*
money to his solicitor in reliance on a representation known by the solicitor to be
false, has a remedy in respect of breach of fiduciary duty. These are matters
which, understandably, receive no analysis in the judgments which follow
Mothew. It has seemed to me right that I should examine the law at some length
in this judgment. Having done so, and having reached a firm conclusion upon it,
it would be would be wrong to refuse to give effect to that conclusion because   *c*
other judges have declined to follow an earlier ex tempore decision in which the
reasoning was not fully set out. If the question, 'what if', is irrelevant in what I
may, for convenience, call '*Mothew*' cases, then it is important that that be
recognised before a great deal of time and expense is expended in investigating
that question in each of what are likely to be many cases in which the society can   *d*
establish that it was misled by a misrepresentation, knowingly made by its
solicitor, in the report and request.

THE CURRENT APPLICATIONS
    The applications and appeals which are now before me fall into three main
groups: (i) those in which I am satisfied that the defendant received the mortgage   *e*
moneys from the society in response to a request based upon a warranty or
representation which the defendant knew, or must be taken to have known, to
be misleading; (ii) those in which I am satisfied that, in paying over the mortgage
moneys on completion, the defendant was in breach of the instructions contained
in the solicitor's letter but where there is an issue of causation to be tried; and (iii)   *f*
those in which the defendant's alleged breach of duty turns on some issue or
question in dispute which ought to be tried.

THE FIRST GROUP OF CASES
    In these cases I am satisfied that the society paid the advance cheque to the
defendant solicitors in response to a request based on a warranty or   *g*
representation which the defendant knew, or must be taken to have known, was
misleading. For the reasons which I have already set out, I am satisfied that it is
unnecessary to try the question whether the society would have made the
advance if it had been told the true facts in these cases because that question is
irrelevant. Accordingly, in these cases the society is entitled to judgment. The   *h*
cases are (i) *Bristol and West Building Society v May May & Merrimans (a firm)*; (ii)
Bristol and West Building Society v Spence and ors; (iii) *Bristol and West Building
Society v White*; (iv) *Bristol and West Building Society v Pillai Hassan & Corbin (a
firm)*; and (v) *Bristol and West Building Society v Sturgess and ors*. [His Lordship then
reviewed the facts in each case and gave his decision as indicated above and   *j*
continued:]

THE SECOND GROUP OF CASES
    These are cases in which I am satisfied that the society is entitled to succeed on
the issue of liability, in that the payment on completion was made in breach of its
instructions, but where the defendant should have unconditional leave to defend
in relation to the issue of causation. The cases in this group are (i) *Bristol and West*

a *Building Society v Bower Cotton & Bower (a firm)*; (ii) *Bristol and West Building Society v Leftley Blackwell (a firm)* (save as to £3,433 with interest, in respect of which the society is entitled to judgment); (iii) *Bristol and West Building Society v The Simkins Partnership (a firm)*; (iv) *Bristol and West Building Society v Dallas Brett (a firm)*; and (v) *Bristol and West Building Society v George H Coles (a firm)*. [His Lordship then reviewed the facts in each case and gave his decision as indicated above and
b continued:]

THE THIRD GROUP OF CASES
   The cases in which the defendant ought to have unconditional leave to defend on the ground that there is some issue or question in dispute which ought to be tried in relation to liability are these: (i) *Bristol and West Building Society v Alan
c Budds & Co (a firm)*; (ii) *Bristol and West Building Society v Fancy & Jackson (a firm)*; and (iii) *Bristol and West Building Society v Bhadresa*.

SUMMARY
   I dismiss the appeals in the following matters: (1) *Bristol and West Building Society v Spence and ors*, (2) *Bristol and West Building Society v White*; (3) *Bristol and
d West Building Society v Fancy & Jackson (a firm)*; and (4) *Bristol and West Building Society v Sturgess*.
   I allow the appeal in (5) *Bristol and West Building Society v Alan Budds & Co (a firm)*.
   I dismiss the summonses in the following matters: (6) *Bristol and West Building
e Society v Bower Cotton & Bower (a firm)*; (7) *Bristol and West Building Society v Leftley Blackwell & Co (a firm)* (save to the extent of £3,433 and interest, for which judgment may be entered; (8) *Bristol and West Building Society v The Simkins Partnership (a firm)*; (9) *Bristol and West Building Society v Dallas Brett (a firm)*; (10) *Bristol and West Building Society v George Coles (a firm)*; and (11) *Bristol and West Building Society v Bhadresa*.
f I refuse leave to defend and direct that judgment be entered, subject to computation, on the summonses in (12) *Bristol and West Building Society v May May & Merrimans (a firm)* and (13) *Bristol and West Building Society v Pillai Hassan & Corbin (a firm)*.
   I will hand down a separate judgment in those two of the other matters argued
g before me in which the lender was the Cheshunt Building Society; namely *Bristol and West Building Society v Berger Oliver & Co (a firm)* and *Bristol and West Building Society v Clive Travers & Co (a firm)*. I direct that all other matters argued before me be restored for further consideration.

Orders accordingly.

Celia Fox   Barrister.

Mortgage Express Ltd v Bowerman & Partners (a firm)

COURT OF APPEAL, CIVIL DIVISION

SIR THOMAS BINGHAM MR, MILLETT AND SCHIEMANN LJJ

10, 11 JULY 1995

Solicitor – Duty – Breach of duty – Solicitor acting for both purchaser and mortgagee in conveyancing transaction – Solicitor receiving information that vendor buying the property in simultaneous transaction – Vendor paying price much lower either than price being paid by purchaser or valuation of property – Solicitor communicating information to purchaser but not to mortgagee – Whether solicitor in breach of duty to mortgagee.

G, a partner in the defendant firm of solicitors, was instructed to act on behalf of the plaintiff mortgage lending company in respect of an application for a loan of £180,150 by H, who wished to purchase a property for £220,000. G was also instructed to act for H. Enclosed with the plaintiff's letter of instruction was a professional valuation, valuing the property at £199,000. G became aware that the vendor was himself purchasing the property for £150,000 and was selling on simultaneously to H. G drew to H's attention the discrepancies between the two purchase prices and the valuation figure. However, in his written report on title to the plaintiff, G did not mention the simultaneous sale of the property for £150,000. The plaintiff duly advanced the loan to H and the sales were completed. H defaulted on the loan after one payment and the property was repossessed and sold for £96,000. Thereafter, the plaintiff issued proceedings against the defendants, claiming damages for negligence on the basis that G had acted in breach of his duty in failing to draw to the plaintiff's attention the fact that there was a simultaneous sale of the property at a figure £50,000 below the valuation on which it was relying and £30,000 below its proposed advance. The judge found for the plaintiff on liability, but accepted the defendants' submissions as to the measure of damages. The plaintiff's appeal on damages was heard as one of a group of six similar cases, and the appeal was allowed. The defendants cross-appealed on the issue of liability.

Held – A solicitor who, in the course of investigating title, discovered facts which a reasonably competent solicitor would have realised might have a material bearing on the valuation of a lender's security, or some other ingredient of the lending decision, had a duty to point that out. There was, however, no general principle requiring a solicitor who acted for both purchaser and lender and who had given information to one party to pass that information on to the other; the question to whom he should pass the information depended on the relevant interests of each client. On the facts, it was clear that G would have failed in his duty to H if he had not disclosed to him the information that he was paying much more than the valuation and considerably more than the immediate vendor of the property. Moreover, as a question of fact and degree, it was impossible to escape the conclusion that, had he applied his mind to the facts, he would also have appreciated that that information might have caused the plaintiff to doubt the valuation of the property as security for its loan. G's failure to pass the a information to the plaintiff was therefore negligent, and his cross-appeal would, accordingly, be dismissed (see p 841 *g j* to p 842 *a e* to *g*, p 843 *e* to *j*, p 844 *a*, p 845 *g* and p 846 *b* to *d*, post).

Notes

For solicitor's obligations towards his client and liability for negligence, see 44(1)
b *Halsbury's Laws* (4th edn reissue) paras 152–155, and for cases on the subject, see 44 *Digest* (Reissue) 153–155, *1546–1570*.

Cases referred to in judgments

Anglia Hastings and Thanet Building Society v House & Son (Wetheralls, third party) (1981) 260 EG 1128.
c *Banque Bruxelles Lambert SA v Eagle Star Insurance Co Ltd* [1995] 2 All ER 769, [1995] QB 375, [1995] 2 WLR 607, CA.
Scholes v Brook (1891) 63 LT 837; *affd* (1891) 64 LT 674, CA.

Cross-appeal

d The defendant solicitors, Messrs Bowerman & Partners, cross-appealed from the decision of Arden J made on 11 May 1994 ([1994] 2 EGLR 156), whereby she determined, inter alia, the issue of liability in favour of the plaintiff mortgagee, Mortgage Express Ltd, in respect of an action for negligence brought against the solicitors, who had acted for both Mortgage Express and the borrower in a property purchase. Mortgage Express's appeal from Arden J's determination of
e the quantum of damages was allowed by the Court of Appeal (Sir Thomas Bingham MR, Rose and Morritt LJJ) ([1995] 2 All ER 769) on 20 February 1995, subject to the decision of the court on the solicitors' cross-appeal. The facts are set out in the judgment of Sir Thomas Bingham MR.

f *Christopher Gibson QC* and *Ben Patten* (instructed by *Pinsent Curtis*, Birmingham) for the solicitors.
Nicholas Patten QC and *Timothy Harry* (instructed by *Rosling King*) for Mortgage Express.

g **SIR THOMAS BINGHAM MR.** This is a cross-appeal by a firm of solicitors, Messrs Bowerman & Partners, against a finding of negligence made against one of their partners on 11 May 1994 by Arden J ([1994] 2 EGLR 156).
The partner involved is a Mr Gilroy, who was admitted in 1974 and practised in Cricklewood from 1976 to 1988. During that time he built up a local connection in that area. In 1988 Mr Gilroy became a partner in Bowerman &
h Partners. That firm had its office in Bicester, but a substantial proportion of Mr Gilroy's clients continued to be based in London and were referred to him through his old contacts. In this way he remained conversant with conditions in the London housing market. During 1990 a number of clients were referred to Mr Gilroy by Brondesbury Estates, a firm of estate agents and mortgage brokers.
j By a letter dated 21 November 1990, Mr Gilroy was instructed to act on behalf of Mortgage Express Ltd, a company specialising in lending on mortgage and the plaintiff in these proceedings. The letter related to an application for a loan by Mr A Hadi of 38 Queen's Court, Queensway, London W2. The leasehold flat which he wished to buy was 119 Queen's Court, Queensway, London W2. The purchase price was £220,000. The amount of the proposed loan was £180,150. The mortgage term and rate of interest were stated.

Enclosed with this letter of instruction was a copy of a letter from Mortgage
Express to Mr Hadi containing the offer of a loan. Mr Gilroy, and his firm's name
and address, appeared in this offer letter under the heading 'Solicitor'. It was plain
that Mr Hadi had nominated Mr Gilroy to Mortgage Express as the solicitor
whom he proposed to instruct. Also enclosed with the letter of instruction were
the special conditions of Mortgage Express, and its 'Standing Instructions to
Solicitors'. The first of the standing instructions provided:

> 'These instructions are not intended to be exhaustive and do not in any
> way limit the normal duties of a solicitor when acting for a mortgagee …'

The standing instructions made clear that Mortgage Express reserved the right to
withdraw its offer at any time before completion of the mortgage transaction.
    Also enclosed with the letter of instruction was a document central to this
appeal. It was headed 'Valuation report' and was a valuation of the flat which Mr
Hadi proposed to buy. The valuation was made by a valuer practising in Kilburn
Lane and valued the flat in its existing condition at £199,000. It was evident that
the loan of £180,150 which Mortgage Express had offered was based on this
valuation.
    Seeing the name and address of the purchaser, Mr Gilroy assumed that these
instructions resulted from an introduction by Brondesbury Estates, whom he
accordingly telephoned. He learned that the vendor of the flat was a Mr Arrach,
that his solicitor was Mr F G Litchfield and that the purchase price (as stated in his
instructions) was £220,000. It seems that Mr Gilroy then spoke to Mr Hadi and
agreed to act on his behalf.
    On 26 November 1990 Mr Gilroy received a fax from Mr Litchfield, which read
in material part:

> 'I have just been instructed by a Mr. Ahmed Arrach in relation to his
> proposed purchase of [119 Queen's Court] and its sub-sale to Mr. Ali Hadi for
> £220,000. I have been told that you are acting for Mr. Hadi and that he
> already has a Mortgage Offer. I phoned the Vendor's Solicitors, John Healy
> & Co, to ascertain the position and was advised that their Client had only
> recently purchased the property and they expect the Purchaser to register
> the Transfer to their Client …'

Mr Gilroy replied to Mr Litchfield by fax on the same day, confirming that he had
instructions from Mr Hadi and that he had a mortgage offer from Mortgage
Express.
    Also on 26 November, Mr Gilroy wrote to Mr Hadi (whom he had not up to
then met) as follows:

> 'Dear Mr. Hadi,
>   Re: 119 Queens Court
>   I am enclosing a copy of a fax from Mr Litchfield together with a copy of
> my reply. I will let you know as soon as I receive documentation. You will
> note that this is a sale on and accordingly it can be assumed that Mr Arrach
> is purchasing the property and is selling on to you immediately at a profit. I
> do not know the price that Mr Arrach is paying.'

The fax and reply referred to were those already quoted. But it seems that Mr
Gilroy then received a further message from Mr Litchfield, dated 26 November,

a enclosing a further letter from Messrs John Healy & Co, also of 26 November. In this letter John Healy & Co wrote to Mr Litchfield:

> 'We refer to our telephone conversation this morning and understand that you have been instructed by Mr. Ahmed Arrach who has agreed, subject to contract, to purchase the leasehold interest in [119 Queen's Court] from our Client at a price of £150,000. As you are aware, our Client has only recently
>
b > completed his purchase of the leasehold interest on 2nd November and the Transfer has yet to be stamped ...'

The letter went on to deal with the mechanics of the conveyancing, which was to be done very quickly. Receipt of a copy of this letter caused Mr Gilroy to add a postscript to his letter to Mr Hadi. This read:

c

> 'P.S. I enclose a copy of a fax from John Healy & Co dated 26th November. Please note the price being paid by Mr Arrach and the timetable required. I will be in touch as soon as I receive documents.'

In his written witness statement Mr Gilroy described his state of mind at this
d stage:

> '8. Whilst I considered that I should draw the fact of the sub-sale and the obvious discrepancy between the price being paid by Mr Arrach and the price being paid by Mr Hadi to his attention in case he was not aware of it, I did not regard this as particularly unusual or as a matter giving rise to any
e > cause for concern provided the purchasing client understood and accepted the situation. 9. In this case I was aware that Hadi was to pay £220,000 for the property when his immediate vendor Arrach was only paying £150,000. I was of course conscious that this was a large difference and recall that I discussed this with Mr Hadi and also pointed out to him the discrepancy between the valuation of £199,000 and the price he was paying. This caused
f > me the greatest concern since it appeared that Mr Hadi was paying too much. I was satisfied that he understood the position (his spoke perfect English). He said that he wanted a flat in that block and was prepared to pay the price and to accept that Arrach was making a substantial profit.'

g On the following day, 27 November, Mr Gilroy wrote to Mr Hadi giving details of what was required to carry out the purchase. He made no further reference to the price at which Mr Arrach had bought or to the sale to Mr Arrach or to the valuation of the flat. He also wrote to Mr Litchfield asking for a copy of the transfer to Mr Arrach. Mr Litchfield wrote back to him on 30 November, enclosing a copy of a letter of 28 November from John Healy & Co to Mr
h Litchfield. With this letter to Mr Litchfield John Healy & Co enclosed a copy of the transfer to their client, from whom Mr Arrach was buying the flat, but they wrote that 'until contracts have been exchanged our Client is unwilling to disclose the consideration'. From the transfer it was apparent that John Healy & Co's client was a Mr Rasool, who had bought the flat from a Mr Khedair.

j On 10 December 1990 contracts were exchanged for the sale by Mr Rasool to Mr Arrach at £150,000 and for the sale by Mr Arrach to Mr Hadi at £220,000.

Mr Gilroy made his written report on title to Mortgage Express on 11 December. The report was made on a form supplied by Mortgage Express and confirmed that the title was good and marketable and might safely be accepted as security. No mention was made of Mr Arrach's contemporaneous purchase at £150,000. Mortgage Express duly advanced £180,150 to Mr Gilroy on behalf of

Mr Hadi, and both sales were completed on 19 December. Mr Hadi provided, *a* apparently from his own resources, the difference between the mortgage advance and the purchase price.

At the time of both exchange and completion Mr Gilroy was acting for both Mortgage Express and Mr Hadi. He knew that Mr Hadi was buying for £220,000 a flat valued at £199,000 on the security of which Mortgage Express was lending £180,000. He knew that Mr Hadi was buying from Mr Arrach, who was at the *b* same time buying the flat for £150,000. He knew that the vendor to Mr Arrach had bought the flat on 2 November 1990 at a price which he did not know but which that vendor's solicitor was reluctant to disclose and which (according to his oral evidence) he thought it 'obviously quite likely' was less than the figure of £150,000 which Mr Arrach was paying. He knew that at this time the housing market in London was not rising and if anything was falling. *c*

Mr Hadi made only one interest payment to Mortgage Express, who repossessed the flat and sold it for £96,000, the best price then obtainable. On 15 April 1993 Mortgage Express issued proceedings claiming damages for negligence against Mr Gilroy's firm. Its central contention was that Mr Gilroy acted in breach of his duty to it in failing to draw attention to the simultaneous purchase *d* by Mr Arrach, and the price at which he was buying. The parties are agreed that the open market value of the flat at the time of this transaction was £120,000. The judge held (and her finding has not been challenged) that if Mortgage Express had been informed that Mr Arrach was simultaneously buying for £150,000 it would have arranged for a second valuation as a matter of urgency. The parties are agreed that if a second valuation had been performed the figure given would have *e* been sufficiently different from that on which Mortgage Express relied to have caused it to withdraw its offer of a loan to Mr Hadi. The learned judge found for Mortgage Express on liability but accepted the solicitors' submissions on the measure of damage. Mortgage Express appealed against that ruling and the solicitors cross-appealed on the issue of liability. *f*

The appeal of Mortgage Express was heard as one of a group of six cases raising the same or a similar issue on the measure of damages. In the result, the Court of Appeal allowed the appeal by Mortgage Express (see *Banque Bruxelles Lambert SA v Eagle Star Insurance Co Ltd* [1995] 2 All ER 769 esp at 862, [1995] QB 375 esp at 428). Thus, it is only now that the solicitors' cross-appeal on liability, although *g* logically prior to the appeal on damages, comes before us.

Before addressing the issues which fall for consideration in this appeal, it is helpful to clear out of the way matters which are not in issue.

1. No aspersion of any kind has been cast on Mr Gilroy's professional integrity. I must emphasise that this is not, and has never been presented as, the case of a solicitor shutting his eyes to nefarious practices of which he was or should have *h* been aware.

2. Mortgage Express has not advanced its case on the basis that Mr Hadi was engaged in any dishonest practice. It has not accused him of acting dishonestly, although it does not accept that he was necessarily acting honestly.

3. It is common ground that neither of Mr Gilroy's clients retained him to *j* advise on the commercial merits of the transaction. Thus, he was not asked to advise Mr Hadi on the wisdom or unwisdom of buying this flat at the proposed price, nor was he asked to advise Mortgage Express on the valuation of the security against which it was lending. Mr Gilroy was a solicitor not a valuer. He had no duty to second-guess the valuer. He knew, as any solicitor in his position would, that Mortgage Express would rely on the reliability of the valuation it had

a obtained, but he had no duty to investigate whether that valuation was reliable or not.

4. It was expressly accepted on behalf of Mr Gilroy in argument that the fact that he was acting for Mr Hadi did not reduce the duty he would have owed to Mortgage Express had he been acting for Mortgage Express alone. Mr Gilroy owed a full duty to Mortgage Express, as he did to Mr Hadi. What that duty
b required is the central issue in this cross-appeal. But we are not asked to, and do not, approach this case on the basis that Mr Gilroy's duty to Mortgage Express, whatever it may have been, was cut down as a result of his acting also for Mr Hadi.

5. The information which Mr Gilroy received concerning the sale to Mr
c Arrach at £150,000 and the sub-sale to Mr Hadi at £220,000 was information which Mr Gilroy received as solicitor to each of his respective clients. It was directly relevant to the conveyancing transaction he was carrying out for Mr Hadi since it went to show how and when Mr Arrach would acquire title to sell. For the same reason it was relevant to Mr Gilroy's instructions from Mortgage Express, who wanted to be sure that its borrower was obtaining a good and
d marketable title which might safely be accepted as security. The present case is not, therefore, one in which a solicitor acting for two parties receives information confidential to one of them. In such a case it may be necessary for the solicitor to obtain the consent of the client whose information it is to disclose it to the other and, if consent is refused, the solicitor may be obliged to cease to act for the other party or both parties. But that is not this case. It has not been suggested that Mr
e Gilroy would have been in breach of any duty to Mr Hadi if he had disclosed the information in question to Mortgage Express.

6. It was suggested in argument that Arden J had held that, as a matter of principle, any information which a solicitor in the position of Mr Gilroy, acting
f for both purchaser and lender, gives to one party he should give to the other. I do not, with respect, think that the learned judge laid down any such principle. Had she done so the principle would, in my view, have been manifestly wrong. Where a solicitor acting for purchaser and lender receives information common to both, the question whether he should pass it on to one client or the other or both or neither entirely depends on the relevant interest of each client which the
g solicitor is engaged to serve.

That leads on to the question which, in my view, lies at the heart of this cross-appeal. What duty did the solicitors, by Mr Gilroy, owe to Mortgage Express? Before the judge it was argued for the solicitors that the duty was to do what was necessary to report to Mortgage Express on title—no more and no less.
h There were problems about this contention. In the first place, it did not seem to accord with the standing instructions issued by Mortgage Express to solicitors acting for it. These referred to the 'normal duties of a solicitor when acting for a mortgagee' and did not suggest that the solicitor's duty began and ended with the report on title. Secondly, as Mr Gilroy's evidence made clear, this strict and
j rather legalistic approach did not accord with the realities of practice. Mr Gilroy acknowledged that matters might come to the notice of a solicitor in his position which he would be under a professional duty to report to the lender. For example, such a solicitor was not retained to second-guess the valuation on which the lender was relying, but if he received information of previous transactions so apparently inconsistent with that valuation as to give possible reasons for doubting its reliability, that might be something which he should report. Thus,

Mr Gilroy accepted that questions of fact and degree would affect the solicitor's *a* duty.

Thirdly, this strict approach does not, in my view, lie comfortably alongside the general guidance given to solicitors on professional conduct. In December 1990 guidance was given on mortgage fraud in Annex 24L of the *Guide to the Professional Conduct of Solicitors* in these terms:

> 'Solicitors must not withhold information relevant to a transaction from any client and for a lender this includes not only straightforward price reductions but may also include other allowances (e.g. for repairs, payment of costs, the inclusion of chattels in the price and incentives of the kind offered by builders such as free holidays and part-subsidisation or mortgage payments) which amount to a price reduction and which would affect the *c* lender's decision to make the advance.'

This guidance is not something which Mr Gilroy, in all probability, saw before completion of these transactions and he is not to be criticised for that. But guidance of this kind is not the product of parthenogenesis. It represents a *d* distillation, or codification, of existing good practice and it represents, as it seems to me, sound practical common sense. A client cannot expect a solicitor to undertake work he has not asked him to do, and will not wish to pay him for such work. But if in the course of doing the work he is instructed to do the solicitor comes into possession of information which is not confidential and which is clearly of potential significance to the client, I think that the client would *e* reasonably expect the solicitor to pass it on and feel understandably aggrieved if he did not.

I would accordingly reject the submission originally made on behalf of the solicitors as to the narrow ambit of the duty, as the judge did, and accept, as I understand her to have done, the submission of Mortgage Express. This was that *f* if, in the course of investigating title, a solicitor discovers facts which a reasonably competent solicitor would realise might have a material bearing on the valuation of the lender's security or some other ingredient of the lending decision, then it is his duty to point this out.

In reaching this decision I do not gain much help from previous authority. It *g* is, however, worthy of note that in *Scholes v Brook* (1891) 63 LT 837 a claim in negligence was made by a mortgagee against solicitors on the ground that they had failed to report to the mortgagee striking differences in the price paid for the property which had come to the solicitor's attention in the course of doing the legal work necessary to perfect the mortgage. The claim failed, but only on the basis that the solicitors had discharged their duty by reporting the discrepancies *h* to the valuers and, in effect, inviting them to reconsider their valuation. Romer J said (at 838):

> 'But it is said that they were guilty of default towards the plaintiff because, having ascertained the existence of some striking differences in the price paid *j* for the property, they ought to have called the attention of the plaintiff to it. In my judgment, knowing as they did that what the plaintiff relied upon was Brook and Dransfield's valuation, knowing that she would be guided by that in carrying out the transaction, they did what they ought to have done in calling Mr. Brook's attention to the discrepancies; and, when they had obtained from him a statement that, notwithstanding those discrepancies,

a   his valuation still stood unaffected, they discharged their duty, and were guilty of no negligence.'

One infers that the judge would have taken a different view had the solicitors done nothing.

b   In *Anglia Hastings and Thanet Building Society v House & Son (Wetheralls, third party)* (1981) 260 EG 1128 negligence was admitted by the defendant valuers and third party solicitors, and the issue was one of apportionment. The case is of interest only to the limited extent that the main complaint against the solicitors (who were ordered to bear the major share of the blame) was that they had failed to disclose to the plaintiff mortgagee facts of which they became aware in the course of performing their conveyancing duties.

c   What, then, did Mr Gilroy's duty as stated above require of him on the facts of this case? From the outset he knew that his client, Mr Hadi, was proposing to buy the flat at £20,000 over the professional valuation figure. That was possibly a little surprising in a flat or declining market, but perhaps not in itself remarkable. But he then learned that this was a sub-sale by a vendor who was simultaneously d buying the flat at £70,000 below what Mr Hadi was agreeing to pay and £50,000 below the valuation figure on which Mortgage Express was relying. Mr Gilroy thought it important to draw these facts to Mr Hadi's attention because, as he agreed in evidence, he was concerned that Mr Hadi might be paying too much for the flat. He was, after all, paying much more than the valuation and very considerably more than Mr Arrach.

e   It seems to me clear beyond argument that Mr Gilroy would have failed in his duty to Mr Hadi had he not alerted Mr Hadi to these new facts which had come to his attention, so that Mr Hadi could take such action, if any, as he wished.

It does not follow from that conclusion that it was necessarily Mr Gilroy's duty to pass the information to Mortgage Express. But I think any lender in Mortgage f Express's position would have been greatly concerned to learn of a simultaneous sale at a figure £50,000 below the valuation on which it was relying and £30,000 below its proposed advance. The transaction might, of course, be explained by special circumstances, but an obvious alternative explanation was that the flat had been significantly overvalued. A moment's reflection would, I think, have alerted Mr Gilroy to this second possibility and to the need to give Mortgage g Express the opportunity to review it. In fact, it is clear this second possibility did not occur to Mr Gilroy. He was aware that Mortgage Express had obtained its own valuation and regarded valuation as no concern of his. Up to a point he was right. But he rightly accepted a duty to report the facts to Mortgage Express if he had reason to doubt the valuation and, on the facts here, I find it impossible to h escape the conclusion that if he had applied his mind to these facts he would have appreciated that they might have caused Mortgage Express to doubt the valuation. The contemporary sale at a much lower value was itself evidence of value for Mortgage Express to assess. He should not be too harshly judged for this oversight in the course of a busy and, no doubt, pressured professional life, j but if his only client had been Mortgage Express and his only duty had been to them, I find it very hard to think he would not have recognised the need to alert it to these potentially significant facts.

In the course of his argument for the solicitors, Mr Christopher Gibson QC indicated that the judgment of Arden J had aroused widespread concern as to its implications for solicitors at large. Mr Patten QC for Mortgage Express suggested that the decision was one closely dependent on the facts of the case. I accept the

latter view. I do not think either the judge's decision or this judgment extends
the duties to which solicitors are subject. I would affirm the judge's decision and
dismiss the cross-appeal.

MILLETT LJ. Mr Gilroy, a conveyancing partner in the defendant firm of
solicitors, Messrs Bowerman & Partners, was instructed to act for Mr Ali Hadi in
connection with his purchase of a flat at 119 Queen's Court, Queensway, London
W2. Mr Hadi was buying the flat for £220,000 with the assistance of a mortgage
offer from the plaintiffs, Mortgage Express Ltd, of £180,150. The offer
represented approximately 90% of a professional valuation which the plaintiffs
had obtained and which valued the flat at £199,000.

As is common in such cases, Mr Gilroy was also instructed by the plaintiffs to
act for them in connection with the purchase and mortgage of the flat. The
plaintiffs forwarded to him copies of their mortgage offer to Mr Hadi (though not
of his mortgage application) and of the valuation.

Shortly after accepting his instructions to act, Mr Gilroy learned that the
registered proprietor was a Mr Khedair. He was not, however, the vendor from
whom Mr Hadi was buying the flat. Mr Hadi was buying from a Mr Arrach, who
had simultaneously agreed, subject to contract, to buy the flat for £150,000, not
from Mr Khedair himself but from someone (later identified as a Mr Rasool) who
had only recently completed his purchase from Mr Khedair and had not yet
registered his title, at a price which his solicitor was reluctant to disclose, but
which Mr Gilroy assumed was less than £150,000. Mr Gilroy informed Mr Hadi
that his vendor, Mr Arrach, had agreed, subject to contract, to buy the flat for
£150,000. He did not, however, pass this information on to the plaintiffs.

Contracts were exchanged for Mr Hadi's purchase on 10 December 1990. Mr
Gilroy gave a clear report on title to the plaintiffs on the same day. Following
receipt of the report on title the plaintiffs advanced £180,150 on 18 December
1990. Completion of the purchase and a legal charge in favour of the plaintiffs
followed on 19 December 1990.

Mr Hadi defaulted almost at once. Possession proceedings were commenced
and an order for possession was obtained in November 1991. In due course the
flat was sold. It realised only £96,000. In the present action the plaintiffs sue the
defendants for negligence and breach of duty as their solicitors in failing to inform
them of the fact that Mr Hadi's vendor was a person who agreed, subject to
contract, to buy the flat for only £150,000

At the trial it was common ground that in November 1990 the open market
value of the flat was only £120,000. The judge found that if Mr Gilroy had
informed the plaintiffs of the price which Mr Hadi's vendor was paying for the flat
they would have commissioned another valuation, that this would have
produced a figure not materially in excess of £120,000, and that the transaction
with Mr Hadi would not have proceeded. There is no appeal from those findings.
The judge also found that Mr Gilroy ought to have communicated the
information in question to the plaintiffs and that his failure to do so was negligent.
The defendants appeal that finding.

It is important at the outset to recognise that it would not have involved Mr
Gilroy in any breach of duty to his client, Mr Hadi, if he had communicated the
information in question to the plaintiffs. A solicitor who acts both for a purchaser
and a mortgage lender faces a potential conflict of duty. A solicitor who acts for
more than one party to a transaction owes a duty of confidentiality to each client,
but the existence of this duty does not affect his duty to act in the best interests of

the other client. All information supplied by a client to his solicitor is confidential
a and may be disclosed only with the consent, express or implied, of his client.
There is, therefore, an obvious potentiality for conflict between the solicitor's
duty of confidentiality to the buyer and his duty to act in the best interests of the
mortgage lender.

No such conflict, however, arose in the present case. It is the duty of a solicitor
b acting for a purchaser to investigate the vendor's title on his behalf and to deduce
it to the mortgagee's solicitor. He has the implied authority of his client to
communicate all documents of title to the mortgagee's solicitor. In the present
case, the information in question appeared on the face of the vendor's title, which
consisted of his agreement, subject to contract, to purchase the flat for £150,000.
Had the plaintiffs instructed other solicitors, Mr Gilroy would have had to
c provide them with a copy of that agreement. It would then have been for those
solicitors to consider whether they ought to inform their client of the price which
Mr Arrach was paying for the flat. In the present case Mr Gilroy was instructed
to act both for the buyer and the mortgagee and it was his duty to investigate the
vendor's title on behalf of each of his clients. He must, therefore, be taken to have
d been in possession of the documents of title, including Mr Arrach's purchase
agreement, not only as solicitor for Mr Hadi but also, with Mr Hadi's implied
authority, as solicitor for the plaintiffs. He then came under a duty to the
plaintiffs to consider whether he ought to disclose the information which that
documentation contained to them.

Mr Gilroy recognised as much. In cross-examination he said: 'If I had had any
e cause to doubt the valuation, that is something I should have passed on, but I did
not doubt the valuation.'

It might be thought from that answer that the question which the judge should
have asked herself was: 'Would a solicitor of ordinary competence have regarded
the information that Mr Arrach was paying only £150,000 for the flat as throwing
f doubt on the valuation of £199,000?' That, however, would not, in my opinion,
be an accurate formulation of the question. Mr Gilroy was not a valuer and it was
not his responsibility to doubt a professional valuation. The question which the
judge had to ask herself was whether a solicitor of ordinary competence would
have regarded the information in question as information which might cause the
plaintiffs to doubt the correctness of the valuation which they had obtained.
g The judge, in effect, answered this question in the affirmative. In my judgment, her conclusion is unassailable. Mr Hadi was paying £220,000, i e £20,000 or
10% more than the valuation. That was not something which should necessarily
arouse suspicion. But he was also paying £70,000 (or 50%) more than Mr Arrach
was paying, or than the price at which Mr Khedair and Mr Rasool were selling.
h At least two people (Mr Khedair and Mr Rasool) evidently thought that the flat
was not worth more than £150,000, that is to say, £50,000 less than the valuation
and £30,000 less than the mortgage advance.

The judge accepted Mr Gilroy's explanation that it never occurred to him to
doubt the valuation. I do not find it easy to follow Mr Gilroy's process of
j reasoning. He told the judge that he communicated the information in question
to Mr Hadi because he was concerned that Mr Hadi was paying too much for the
flat. But Mr Gilroy knew that Mr Hadi was aware of the valuation and that he
might be paying £20,000 too much for the flat. Mr Gilroy, then, must have been
concerned that Mr Hadi was not only consciously taking the risk of paying
£20,000 or 10% over the odds, but that he might unconsciously be taking the risk
of paying £70,000 or 50% over the odds. But that is only another way of saying

that Mr Gilroy realised that Mr Hadi might think that the information threw *a*
doubt on the correctness of the valuation.

Mr Gilroy did ask Mr Hadi about it, and told the judge that he was satisfied by
Mr Hadi's response. But Mr Hadi gave him no explanation why he was willing
to pay £220,000 for a flat which had been professionally valued at £199,000 and
which had twice recently changed hands at £150,000 or less, particularly when his
vendor had not even got a binding contract of purchase   *b*

Whether the information in question was of such a nature that it might have
caused the plaintiffs to doubt the correctness of the valuation depended upon the
size of the discrepancy between the price which Mr Arrach was paying for the flat
and the price at which he was selling it. It was, therefore, essentially a question
of fact and degree on which it is impossible to challenge the judge's finding.

In my judgment, her conclusion that a solicitor of ordinary competence would *c*
have passed the information to the lender and that Mr Gilroy's failure to do so
was negligent cannot be faulted. I would dismiss the cross-appeal.

SCHIEMANN LJ. For the reasons given by Sir Thomas Bingham MR and Millett
LJ, I agree that this cross-appeal should be dismissed.   *d*

Cross-appeal dismissed.

L I Zysman Esq   Barrister.

a

Desert Sun Loan Corp v Hill

COURT OF APPEAL, CIVIL DIVISION

STUART-SMITH, EVANS AND ROCH LJJ

b 25, 26 JANUARY, 15 FEBRUARY 1996

Conflict of laws – Foreign judgment – Enforcement – Action in England – Issue estoppel – Plaintiff obtaining judgment in foreign court – Defendant unsuccessfully challenging foreign court's jurisdiction – Plaintiff attempting to enforce judgment in England –
c *Whether decision of foreign court on procedural issue giving rise to issue estoppel – Whether defendant entitled to leave to defend.*

In 1990 the plaintiff bank issued proceedings in Arizona against a limited partnership for the amount due under a promissory note and against certain of the partners, including the defendant, as guarantors. By that time the defendant
d had sold his interest in the partnership and had left the United States; however, one of his former partners, G, authorised US attorneys to accept service of the proceedings on behalf of the defendant as well as the partnership and the other guarantors. The plaintiff obtained judgment in 1992 and the defendant (who was now resident in England) was held liable as guarantor for 19% of the partnership's
e liability. When he became aware of the judgment against him personally, the defendant instructed another US attorney to take steps to vacate the judgment on basis that he had not authorised G to instruct the US attorneys to accept service or to act on his behalf personally as guarantor and that the court therefore lacked personal jurisdiction over him. The motion was unsuccessful in the Arizona courts, where G gave evidence that the defendant had expressly authorised him
f to instruct US attorneys to accept service on his behalf. The defendant appealed to the Arizona Court of Appeals. Before the hearing, the plaintiff sought to enforce the judgment in England by way of summary judgment under RSC Ord 14. The deputy judge however gave the defendant unconditional leave to defend on the grounds that he had raised a triable issue in his defence and that it was at
g least arguable that the plaintiff could not rely on a plea of issue estoppel, ie that it could not assert that the question whether the defendant voluntarily submitted to the jurisdiction of the Arizona court by authorising the US attorneys to enter an appearance there was foreclosed by that court's own subsequent decision that such authority was given. The plaintiff appealed, and thereafter the Arizona Court of Appeals dismissed the defendant's appeal, holding that he had in fact
h submitted to the jurisdiction of the Arizona court by virtue of the fact that the attorney had entered an appearance on his behalf. On appeal, the plaintiff contended that the defendant was barred by the Arizona court's ruling from raising the same issue in the English proceedings.

j **Held** – (1) An issue estoppel could arise from an interlocutory judgment of a foreign court on a procedural, ie non-substantive, issue, thereby preventing a defendant from raising that issue in subsequent enforcement proceedings, where (i) there was express submission of the procedural or jurisdictional issue to the foreign court, (ii) the specific issue of fact had been raised before and decided by that court and (iii) caution was exercised in relation to practical considerations,

such as whether the issue was or should have been fully ventilated before the a
foreign court (see p 858 h j, p 862 h and p 863 d to f, post).

(2) In the circumstances, the judgment of the Arizona court did not give rise
to an issue estoppel: it was not sufficiently clear from that judgment that the
specific and narrower issue of fact which arose for decision in the enforcement
proceedings, namely whether or not the defendant had expressly authorised G to
instruct the US attorneys who were acting on behalf of the partnership to act in b
the proceedings on his behalf as a personal defendant, had been identified and
decided against the defendant in the foreign court. Moreover, the practical
considerations of particular relevance where an estoppel was said to arise out of
an interlocutory or procedural ruling could not be considered with the necessary
degree of certainty on an application for summary judgment. The appeal would
accordingly be dismissed and the defendant would be granted conditional leave c
to defend on payment of $US100,000 into court (see p 859 g to p 860 h, p 861 d e,
p 862 h j and p 864 b c, post).

Cases referred to in judgments

Adams v Cape Industries plc [1991] 1 All ER 929, [1990] 2 Ch 433, [1990] 2 WLR 657, d
CA.
Balkanbank v Taher [1995] 2 All ER 904, [1995] 1 WLR 1056, CA.
Black-Clawson International Ltd v Papierwerke Waldhof-Aschaffenburg AG [1975] 1 All
ER 810, [1975] AC 591, [1975] 2 WLR 513, HL.
Brinks Ltd v Abu-Saleh (No 1) [1995] 4 All ER 65, [1995] 1 WLR 1478.
Carl-Zeiss-Stiftung v Rayner & Keeler Ltd (No 2) [1966] 2 All ER 536, [1967] 1 AC 853, e
[1966] 3 WLR 125, HL.
Channel Tunnel Group Ltd v Balfour Beatty Construction Ltd [1993] 1 All ER 664,
[1993] AC 334, [1993] 2 WLR 262, HL.
Dept of Social Security v Butler [1995] 4 All ER 193, [1995] 1 WLR 1528, CA.
DSV Silo- und Verwastungsgesellschaft mbH v Sennar (owners), The Sennar [1985] 2 All f
ER 104, [1985] 1 WLR 490, HL.
Henderson v Henderson (1843) 3 Hare 100, [1843–60] All ER Rep 378, 67 ER 313,
V-C.
House of Spring Gardens Ltd v Waite [1990] 2 All ER 990, [1991] 1 QB 241, [1990] 3
WLR 347, CA.
Mercedes-Benz AG v Leiduck [1995] 3 All ER 929, [1996] 1 AC 284, [1995] 3 WLR g
718, PC.
Nouvion v Freeman (1889) 15 App Cas 1, HL.
Owens Bank Ltd v Bracco [1992] 2 All ER 193, [1992] 2 AC 443, [1992] 2 WLR 621,
HL; affg [1991] 4 All ER 833, [1992] 2 AC 443, [1992] 2 WLR 127, CA.
Owens Bank Ltd v Etoile Commerciale SA [1995] 1 WLR 44, PC. h
Talbot v Berkshire CC [1993] 4 All ER 9, [1994] QB 290, [1993] 3 WLR 708, CA.
Thoday v Thoday [1964] 1 All ER 341, [1964] P 181, [1964] 2 WLR 708, CA.
Williams & Glyn's Bank plc v Astro Dinamico Cia Naviera SA [1984] 1 All ER 760,
[1984] 1 WLR 438, HL.
Yorke (MV) Motors (a firm) v Edwards [1982] 1 All ER 1024, [1982] 1 WLR 444, HL. j

Appeal

By notice dated 3 May 1994, the plaintiffs, Desert Sun Loan Corp, appealed from
the decision of Mr Walter Aylen QC, sitting as a deputy judge of the High Court
in the Queen's Bench Division, made on 17 February 1994, whereby he granted

a the defendant, Daniel Hill, unconditional leave to defend the action brought by
the plaintiffs to enforce a judgment which they had obtained against the
defendant in the Arizona courts. The facts are set out in the judgment of
Evans LJ.

Charles Falconer QC (instructed by *Morgan Lewis & Bockius*) for the plaintiffs.
b *Christopher Semken* (instructed by *Rotheras*, Nottingham) for the defendant.

Cur adv vult

15 February 1996. The following judgments were delivered.

c **EVANS LJ.** The plaintiff bank obtained judgments in Arizona against a limited
partnership for the amount due under a promissory note and against certain of
the partners, including the present defendant, as guarantors. United States
attorneys acting for the partnership accepted service of the proceedings on behalf
of the defendant as well as the partnership and the other guarantors. The
defendant says that he did not authorise them to do this. He applied to the
d Arizona court to set aside the judgment, but his application failed. The plaintiffs'
claim in these proceedings is to enforce the judgment against the defendant, who
is now resident here. He denies that the attorneys were authorised to accept
service on his behalf. The plaintiffs say that the defendant is barred by the
Arizona court's ruling from raising the same issue here, and secondly, that he has
e no arguable defence in any event, so that they are entitled to summary judgment
under RSC Ord 14.

The deputy judge (as long ago as February 1994) gave unconditional leave to
defend, holding that it is at least arguable that the defendant is not estopped from
raising the issue in these proceedings. The plaintiffs now appeal.

Their plea of issue estoppel raises a question of some general interest and
f importance, and understandably it was presented as the first issue arising in the
appeal. Logically, however, the first question is whether the defendant does
show that he has an arguable defence. Only if he has, does it become necessary
to decide whether the rules regarding issue estoppel prevent him from raising the
defence in these proceedings.

g
The history

The judgment sued upon is that of the Superior Court for the State of Arizona
dated 2 January 1992. It records that 'this matter came on regularly for trial
before the court dated the 15th day of October 1991' and that the 'Defendants
h Lincoln Ranch Limited Partnership' and others including Vector Interests Ltd,
the general partner, and various guarantors, including the present defendant,
'were present through their representatives and through their attorneys', who
were two members of the firm of Messrs Gallagher & Kennedy. The first-named
guarantors were William J Graham and his wife, Kerry R Graham, who jointly
guaranteed 10% of the total amount. The formal judgment against the
j partnership was for $US1,324,675·78, described as the deficiency amount, plus
interest and costs but subject to a deduction of $310,655·02. Against the present
defendant, the judgment was for 19% of the resulting net total 'as his
proportionate share of the judgment amounts' and the sum claimed in these
proceedings is a total of $217,490·24 plus accrued interest, at rates up to 25% per
annum.

It is common ground that under English law the English court will only   *a*
enforce a judgment in personam given by a foreign court in a limited number of
cases, the third of which is 'if the judgment debtor, being a defendant in the
foreign court, submitted to the jurisdiction of the court by voluntarily appearing
in the proceedings': see *Dicey and Morris on the Conflict of Laws* (12th edn, 1993)
p 472. The defendant says that he did not voluntarily appear in the Arizona
proceedings.   *b*

It appears from evidence submitted to the Arizona court that the appearance
on behalf of the present defendant was made by William H Jury, of Gallagher &
Kennedy, who on 17 June 1991 deposed on oath as follows:

'1. That he is duly authorised to accept service of process on behalf of
defendants Lincoln Ranch Limited Partnership [and the other defendants   *c*
named in the proceedings, including the present defendant] in the above
captioned action. 2. That he hereby acknowledges receipt of a true and
correct copy of the complaint filed in the above-captioned action and does
hereby accept service of process on behalf of the defendants specified in
paragraph 1 hereof.'
    d

Mr Jury was authorised by Mr Graham to enter appearances for all the
defendants and to accept service of process on their behalf and it is not suggested
that Mr Jury exceeded this authority in any way. Mr Graham says that he was
expressly authorised by the defendant to instruct Mr Jury to do this in the course
of one or more transatlantic telephone conversations in mid-1991. This is   *e*
disputed by the defendant and it is here that the issue arises. The defendant
accepts, as I understand his evidence on affidavit, that he had a number of
telephone conversations with Mr Graham in 1990, when the Arizona proceedings
were first instituted, and in 1991, when the proceedings were served, and that the
proceedings were discussed between them, but he says that this was in his
capacity as a director of the corporation to which he had assigned his previous   *f*
interest as a limited partner, though not his liability as a part-guarantor. His
evidence is that he had no knowledge of any judgment against him, or that he was
being sued personally as guarantor, until he received a letter from the plaintiffs'
English solicitors claiming payment in June 1992, followed by service of the
present writ in July 1992.

The plaintiffs accept that it is necessary for them to establish, under English   *g*
law, that the defendant expressly authorised Mr Graham, and through him the
US attorney Mr Jury, to accept the service of proceedings on his behalf. He could
only do this if he knew that he was sued personally as a named defendant in the
US action. The plaintiffs say that this is established by Mr Graham's evidence and
by the defendant's admissions, but they do not rely upon any ostensible authority   *h*
which the defendant may have given to Mr Graham by reason of their former
partnership or in relation to partnership matters generally, including the
partnership's dealings with the plaintiffs which resulted in the proceedings in
which judgment was obtained. In this court it is a short issue of fact; did the
defendant expressly authorise Mr Graham to instruct US attorneys to accept   *j*
service on his behalf, as Mr Jury purported to do, on Mr Graham's instructions,
in June 1991?

Before referring to the accounts given by Mr Graham and the defendant,
respectively, it is necessary to say a little more about their relationship and the
background to their conversations. The defendant is Canadian and until about
1989, when he suffered severe injuries in a motor accident, he was resident or at

a least had a business base in Arizona. They and others formed the Lincoln Ranch Ltd Partnership to acquire and develop a piece of real estate and the plaintiffs made their advance to the partnership, secured by the promissory note, for this purpose. The promissory note is dated 7 December 1984 and the defendant's guarantee 13 December 1984. The partnership defaulted and then became liable for 'the deficiency amount', which was the sum due after giving credit for the value of the land. The general partner, Vector Interests Ltd, was personally liable *b* for the same amount but under the laws of Arizona the limited partners, including Mr and Mr Graham and the defendant, were not liable as such. They were liable, however, under their separate guarantees for the proportionate part of the liability of the partnership.

When he became aware of the judgment against him, the defendant instructed *c* another US attorney from Arizona, Lee Allen Johnson, who issued a motion to vacate judgment on his behalf. The grounds were that the court lacked personal jurisdiction over him. The application was supported by what was described as an affidavit by the defendant, but this was a document headed 'Declaration' which he signed under the following subscription: 'This Declaration made this 25 *d* day of June, 1993, at Berkshire, England, under penalty of perjury under the laws of the United Kingdom.' It may be inferred that this maladroit formula was not the work of an English lawyer. The document is not an affidavit under English law, and the Arizona court expressly rejected it as affidavit evidence which was required in support of the motion.

e The relevant parts of the declaration are these. The defendant, having referred to the letter he had received from the plaintiffs' London solicitors, said:

'3. Prior to receipt of this correspondence, I was unaware that judgment had been entered against me in this case. 4. ... From the judgment I learned that ... Gallagher & Kennedy had appeared in this action as my attorneys. 5. *f* I did not authorise such attorneys to make an appearance on my behalf, and at no time ... have I received any correspondence from any attorney or other employee of the law firm of Gallagher & Kennedy concerning this matter. 6. I had no prior indication that Gallagher & Kennedy was acting on my behalf, no one at that firm ever advised me of the status of the litigation, and the firm has never billed me for any services in connection with the case.'
g

This account of the defendant's knowledge of the proceedings was less than frank. He later accepts that he did know of proceedings against the partnership and that judgment had been given, his informant being Mr Graham. He maintains his denial, however, that he knew that judgment was entered 'against *h* me' or that the attorneys had purported to act in the proceedings on his behalf.

The plaintiffs responded by filing an affidavit from Mr Graham. This asserted that he had express authority from all of the limited partners, including the defendant, to act on their behalf in connection with the loan and the property; that there were extended negotiations with the plaintiffs following the *j* partnership's default, during which he kept the defendant and others appraised, although there were times following the defendant's motor accident when he was under medical care. When the plaintiffs brought their action, he informed the defendant of the action and entered into further negotiations through Mr Jury 'on behalf of the partnership and the general and limited partners', keeping the defendant informed as before. 'In particular, I had a regular series of telephone conversations with Mr Hill and he helped me make arrangements to pay his share

of our expert witness and attorney's fees by a separate entity to which he had   *a*
assigned his partnership interest (but not his guaranty obligation)'.

Mr Graham continues by saying that when the negotiations failed and the
plaintiffs proceeded with their action he instructed Mr Jury to accept service on
behalf of all the defendants, including Mr Hill. 'Mr Hill was given the option of
retaining his own counsel to represent his interests, or to retain Mr Jury and his
firm to represent the defendants on a group basis, and chose to retain Mr Jury.'   *b*
He says that throughout discovery and when judgment was entered he kept the
defendant informed during telephone conversations, and 'I continued to assess
and collect fees from the limited partners to cover litigation expenses, and had
regular conversations with Mr Hill on these topics'. He concluded: 'Mr Hill
specifically authorised me as an officer of the managing general partner to retain
Mr Jury to accept service and represent his interest in the action.'   *c*

There is no suggestion, however, that the defendant personally was billed for
or contributed towards any of the defence costs. Mr Graham's reference to
collecting fees from the limited partners means, presumably, the corporation to
which Mr Hill's interest was assigned. Mr Hill's evidence is that he had ceased
meanwhile to have any beneficial interest in the corporation, although he   *d*
remained a director of it.

The Superior Court of Arizona dismissed the defendant's motion on 17
September 1993. There followed an abortive application for review, which it
appears was misconceived, and then an appeal to the Arizona Court of Appeals.
Briefs were filed on behalf of both parties, and on 19 January 1995 the appeal was *e*
dismissed. The grounds will be summarised below.

The defendant swore an affidavit in reply to Mr Graham's in Arizona but this
was dated 30 September 1993 and was not before the Arizona court when the
motion was heard. He describes how he sold his limited partnership interest in
January 1987 to a corporation in which he had ceased to have any beneficial
interest by November 1988. Paragraph 9 of his affidavit reads as follows: *f*

'While Mr Graham may have had authority to act on behalf of the partners,
he had no authority to act on behalf of me personally because I was no longer
a partner. My discussions with Mr Graham from 1987 forward were only as
to the interest of the corporation. All discussions I had with Mr Graham,
related, I assumed, to the corporate limited partnership interest and my   *g*
position as director of that company. At no time did Mr Graham make
reference to a personal acceptance service for me as a guarantor. At all times,
as he says in his affidavit, he is only referring to his communication with
limited partners of which I was not one.'

                                                                                  h

This action

The plaintiffs rely solely upon the US judgment in their favour. They do not
assert any cause of action under the guarantee. They did not proffer evidence
that no payments have been made under the judgment principal debtors, but this
has been made clear by a further affidavit since the hearing of the appeal.   *j*

The defendant's first affidavit is dated 10 January 1994. He says that he gave
no express authority for anyone to accept service of the Arizona proceedings on
his behalf. After returning to England, following his motor accident in March
1988, he effectively ceased to have any connection with Lincoln Ranch. His
account of his telephone conversations with Mr Graham is in para 5:

a 'I had some contact with Mr Graham, who was also one of the Guarantors of Lincoln Ranch, but this was in connection with a whole range of business interests, not just Lincoln Ranch. I estimate that, from June 1991 I had in the region of 3 telephone conversations with Graham. Mr Graham did tell me about the litigation involving Lincoln Ranch, but my interest in this litigation was only to the extent that I had been a Limited Partner of Lincoln Ranch

b and the information imparted to me was only in that context, not regarding my position as Guarantor. I never told Mr. Graham that he had authority to nominate Lawyers to accept service. I was not aware that Graham had apparently informed American Lawyers that they could represent my personal interests. I was not told that any Judgment had been entered against me personally as a Guarantor.'

c
He exhibits an affidavit from Mr Johnson, which may have been put in evidence in support in his motion to vacate judgment in Arizona. This describes a conversation which Mr Johnson had with Mr Graham concerning the acceptance of service on the defendant's behalf. It reads in part as follows:

d '5. Mr Graham recounted that he was asked whether all of the partners to the litigation concurred in having the law firm of Gallagher & Kennedy represent their interests. He informed the attorneys at Gallagher & Kennedy that no one objected to joint representation by that firm. 6. To the best of Mr Graham's recollection, as he was able to recount it for me on July 12, 1993, this was the only discussion which related to execution of the

e acceptance of service. I specifically asked Mr Graham whether he had received permission from Daniel W. Hill to authorize an attorney to waive the requirements of service of process over Mr Hill and thereby submit Mr Hill to the jurisdiction of the Arizona Court. Mr Graham told me he had not received any such permission from Mr Hill.'

f
This affidavit has been verified by Mr Johnson for the purposes of these proceedings.

The plaintiffs' Ord 14 summons for summary judgment was heard by the deputy judge on 17 February 1994, before the hearing in the Court of Appeals. He held that the defendant was entitled to unconditional leave to defend, having

g raised a triable issue in his defence, and that it was at least arguable that the plaintiffs could not rely upon a plea of issue estoppel, ie that they could not assert that the question whether the defendant voluntarily submitted to the jurisdiction of the Arizona court by authorising the US attorneys to enter an appearance there was foreclosed by that court's own subsequent decision that such authority was

h given.

The plaintiffs now appeal, and Charles Falconer QC has submitted forcefully on their behalf (1) that issue estoppel does arise, (2) that no triable issue is raised in any event, and (3) that leave to defend, if granted, should be made conditional upon a payment into court of the whole of the sum which is now claimed.

j
Leave to defend

Logically, this question comes first and, as indicated above, in English law the issue raised is a straightforward question of fact; did the defendant expressly authorise Mr Graham to instruct the US attorney, Mr Jury, to accept service and enter an appearance on his behalf in the Arizona proceedings? The issue raised is a narrow one, because the defendant now accepts, although he did not volunteer

this initially to the Arizona court, that he did know of the existence of proceedings
against the partnership and that his interest in that action had caused Mr Graham a
to ask for his assent to Mr Jury being instructed to act on its behalf. But he says
that he was not told that he personally was a defendant, as guarantor, and that
because he had no contact at any stage with the attorneys he had no reason to
believe that his own personal interests, as distinct from his residual connection
with the partnership, were at risk in the litigation. He no longer had any b
beneficial interest in the partnership, or in the corporation to which his interest
was assigned, and there was no subsisting relationship which permitted Mr
Graham or the general manager to act on his behalf.

It is clear in my judgment that there is an area of dispute between Mr Graham
and the defendant, narrow though the issue may be. Mr Graham's evidence
throughout refers to the defendant as one of the limited partners and in one place, c
quoted above, he expressly distinguishes between the defendant's interests as
limited partner and as guarantor. Nowhere does he assert that he referred to the
distinction in his conversations with the defendant, and if it was not expressly
referred to then the defendant may not have realised that the proceedings were
also against the guarantors. This may give rise to a further question, which is d
whether he thought that he was named in the proceedings by reason of his
former status as a limited partner, in which case he might be said to have had
sufficient knowledge that he was a separate defendant. But he denies this and for
my part I would not hold that his evidence is incredible or that it should be
rejected at this interlocutory stage. Whether leave to defend should be
unconditional is a different matter to which I shall return below. e

Issue estoppel—English law

Issue estoppel has a long history, in England as well as other common law
countries (see Spencer Bower and Turner *The Doctrine of Res Judicata* (2nd edn,
1969) p 150), but it is usually thought only to have achieved authoritative f
recognition in English law by the House of Lords decision in *Carl-Zeiss-Stiftung v
Rayner & Keeler Ltd (No 2)* [1966] 2 All ER 536, [1967] 1 AC 853. It is an off-shoot
of what has been called 'cause-of-action estoppel' (see *Thoday v Thoday* [1964] 1
All ER 341 at 352, [1964] P 181 at 197 per Diplock LJ). In the international context,
the principle is based on recognition of the validity of a foreign judgment in
respect of the same claim or cause of action as between the same parties: see g
Owens Bank Ltd v Bracco [1992] 2 All ER 193 at 198, [1992] 2 AC 443 at 484 per Lord
Bridge.

The principle is that an issue of fact or law which necessarily was concluded in
favour of one party in the foreign proceedings cannot be reopened in further
proceedings between the same parties here. *Dicey and Morris* p 467 states as h
follows:

'For there to be such an issue estoppel, three requirements must be
satisfied: first, the judgment of the foreign court must be (a) of a court of
competent jurisdiction, (b) final and conclusive and (c) on the merits;
secondly, the parties to the English litigation must be the same parties (or j
their privies) as in the foreign litigation; and, thirdly, the issues raised must
be identical. A decision on the issue must have been necessary for the
decision of the foreign court and not merely collateral.'

The principle extends to issues which were not but which might have been
raised in the earlier proceedings. As *Spencer Bower and Turner* p 148 says, this

means that 'questions of considerable difficulty and nicety may arise'. But the rule is also restricted. One restriction is the requirement that the earlier (foreign) judgment which is relied upon in one party's favour must have been 'final' and 'on the merits'. Secondly, particularly in the case of issue estoppel, there are practical reasons why caution must be exercised before the rule is applied. This restriction was described by Lord Reid in *Carl-Zeiss* [1966] 2 All ER 536 at 555, [1967] 1 AC 853 at 918–919:

b

'I can see no reason in principle why we should deny the possibility of issue estoppel based on a foreign judgment, but there appear to me to be at least three reasons for being cautious in any particular case. In the first place, we are not familiar with modes of procedure in many foreign countries, and it c   may not be easy to be sure that a particular issue has been decided or that its decision was a basis of the foreign judgment and not merely collateral or obiter. Secondly, I have already alluded to the practical difficulties of a defendant in deciding whether even in this country he should incur the trouble and expense of deploying his full case in a trivial case: it might be d   most unjust to hold that a litigant here should be estopped from putting forward his case because it was impracticable for him to do so in an earlier case of a trivial character abroad with the result that the decision in that case went against him. These two reasons do not apply in the present case. The case for the Stiftung, or on this issue those who purported to represent it, was fought as tenaciously in West Germany as this case has been fought here, and e   it is not difficult to see what were the grounds on which the West German judgment was based. The third reason for caution, however, does raise a difficult problem with which I must now deal. It is clear that there can be no estoppel of this character unless the former judgment was a final judgment on the merits. But what does that mean in connexion with issue estopped? When we are dealing with cause of action estoppel it means that the merits f   of the cause of action must be finally disposed of so that the matter cannot be raised again in the foreign country. In this connexion the case of *Nouvion* v. *Freeman* ((1889) 15 App Cas 1) is important. There had been in Spain a final judgment in a summary form of procedure; but that was not necessarily the end of the matter because it was possible to reopen the whole question by g   commencing a different kind of action, so the summary judgment was not res judicata in Spain. I do not find it surprising that the House unanimously refused to give effect in England to that summary judgment.'

The natural meaning of 'final and on the merits' is that there has been a final, h as opposed to provisional, determination of the parties' substantive rights.

The present case raises what is, apparently, a novel question. Is there an issue estoppel when the decision of the foreign court was, using the words in their English meanings, interlocutory rather than final, and the rights in question were procedural, not substantive; in other words, when the decision was independent j of the 'merits' of the issues which were the subject matter of the foreign litigation?

In the absence of any reported authority, this has to be considered as a question of principle. A ruling in the plaintiffs' favour would be an extension of the existing law; but if the extension is shown to be justified in principle, and there are no countervailing factors, then there is no good reason why the ruling should not be made on the hearing of an Ord 14 summons.

The first point to make is that questions of procedure invariably are governed
by the lex fori, the law of the country in which the court is situated. So the foreign
court's decision will have resulted from applying the procedural laws of that
country, and it is difficult to conceive of circumstances where the English court
might be required to decide the same factual issues in accordance with the foreign
rather than English law. Apart from that possible exception, the decision of the
foreign court will be irrelevant to the (procedural) decision required of the
English court, and there will be no scope for the application of a rule equivalent
to 'cause of action' estoppel. However, this does not necessarily preclude the
application of issue estoppel, if the same factual issue arises here in a procedural
context as has been decided in a different context by a foreign court.

Secondly, it may be said as a general rule that interlocutory decisions of the
English courts are not binding on the court which decides the substantive issues
after trial. But this raises different questions, because issues decided at the
interlocutory stages are necessarily different from the substantive issues decided
at the trial, and even where some ruling is called for 'on the merits', for example
if the plaintiff seeks an interlocutory injunction, not only is the issue different but
the decision is provisional, not final.

Returning to the requirement that the foreign court's judgment must have
been 'final' and 'on the merits', the distinctions usually drawn by the English
court are between 'final and interlocutory ('interlocutory' in this context
including both definitive (eg leave to defend) and provisional (eg interlocutory
injunctions) rulings); between substantive and procedural; or between
substantive issues and, for example, a limitation defence (which was held not to
involve a decision 'on the merits' in *Black Clawson International Ltd v Papierwerke
Waldhof-Aschaffenburg AG* [1975] 1 All ER 810, [1975] AC 591). So it would seem
that the rule defined in terms of 'a final judgment on the merits' cannot apply
when there was no more than an interlocutory decision on a procedural and
non-substantive issue.

But there are strong contrary arguments. There is a difference between
submitting to the jurisdiction of a court or tribunal to decide the substantive
dispute, and on the other hand submitting only to its jurisdiction to decide
whether it has substantive jurisdiction or not: see *Williams & Glyn's Bank plc v
Astro Dinamico Cia Naviera SA* [1984] 1 All ER 760, [1984] 1 WLR 438. Here, the
defendant invoked the jurisdiction of the Arizona court to decide whether he was
subject to that court's jurisdiction in the proceedings in which the judgment was
given. If that question of jurisdiction involved the question of fact whether he
gave express authority to Mr Graham to instruct Mr Jury to act on his behalf, then
the defendant literally cannot deny that that issue was raised before and decided
against him by the Arizona courts.

Moreover, the fact that procedural or interlocutory issues do not involve
'causes of action' in the strict sense does not mean that their independent
existence cannot be recognised in appropriate circumstances. Their special
characteristics have been noticed recently in *Channel Tunnel Group Ltd v Balfour
Beatty Construction Ltd* [1993] 1 All ER 664 at 689, [1993] AC 334 at 365, where
Lord Mustill spoke of a 'free-standing item of ancillary relief', and in a different
procedural context in *Balkanbank v Taher* [1995] 2 All ER 904, [1995] 1 WLR 1067;
cf *Dept of Social Security v Butler* [1995] 4 All ER 193, [1995] 1 WLR 1528. The issues
are analysed in Lord Nicholls' (dissenting) opinion in *Mercedes-Benz AG v Leiduck*
[1995] 3 All ER 929, [1996] 1 AC 284 and it is noteworthy that the majority
opinion, delivered by Lord Mustill, did not differ from his analysis, finding it

a   unnecessary to decide the issue in that case. Lord Mustill also referred to the distinction between substantive and 'ancillary' and 'peripheral' proceedings and 'incidental' relief (see [1995] 3 All ER 929 at 936, 940–941, [1996] 1 AC 284 at 296–297, 302–303).

This echoes the distinction referred to by Lord Upjohn in *Carl-Zeiss* [1966] 2 All ER 536 at 574, [1967] 1 AC 853 at 948 between substantive and 'incidental'
b   proceedings.

There is also some support, though in my judgment very limited support, for the plaintiffs' submissions in *DSV Silo- und Verwastungsgesellschaft mbH v Sennar (owners), The Sennar* [1985] 2 All ER 104, [1985] 1 WLR 490. This is relied upon by Mr Falconer as a case where the House of Lords regarded themselves as bound by a decision of the Dutch court on a procedural issue where the court's
c   jurisdiction was involved. But essentially it was a decision as to the parties' substantive rights. The Dutch court held that the plaintiffs were bound by an express contractual provision to bring their claim before the courts of Sudan. In a blatant piece of 'forum shopping' the plaintiffs sought to bring their claim here (see [1985] 2 All ER 104 at 106, [1985] 1 WLR 490 at 493 per Lord Diplock). The
d   House of Lords held that the Dutch court's decision that the jurisdiction clause was binding gave rise to an issue estoppel; the plaintiffs could not raise the same issue here. Lord Diplock expressed the rule entirely in terms of 'cause of action' estoppel, which suggests that issue estoppel could not arise except in the context of a decision on substantive rights:

e   'To make available an issue estoppel to a defendant to an action brought against him in an English court on a cause of action to which the plaintiff alleges a particular set of facts give rise, the defendant must be able to show (1) that the same set of facts has previously been relied on as constituting a cause of action in proceedings brought by that plaintiff against that
f   defendant in a foreign court of competent jurisdiction and (2) that a final judgment has been given by that foreign court in those proceedings. It is often said that the final judgment of the foreign court must be "on the merits". The moral overtones which this expression tends to conjure up may make it misleading. What it means in the context of judgments delivered by courts of justice is that the court has held that it has jurisdiction
g   to adjudicate on an issue raised in the cause of action to which the particular set of facts give rise, and that its judgment on that cause of action is one that cannot be varied, reopened or set aside by the court that delivered it or any other court of co-ordinate jurisdiction although it may be subject to appeal to a court of higher jurisdiction.' (See [1985] 2 All ER 104 at 106, [1985] 1
h   WLR 490 at 493–494.)

Lord Brandon dealt specifically with this issue, referring to Mr Mance QC's submission that because the Dutch court's ruling was procedural no issue estoppel could arise. Lord Brandon did not say that the objection was wrong. Rather, he emphasised that the issue in question depended upon the parties'
j   substantive rights:

     'The argument in relation to the first contention was that the judgment of the Dutch Court of Appeal was procedural in nature, in that it consisted only of a decision that a Dutch court had no jurisdiction to entertain and adjudicate upon the appellants' claim, and did not pronounce in any way on the question whether the claim itself, or any substantive issue in it, if it were to be entertained and adjudicated on, would succeed or fall. In my opinion, this argument is based on a misconception with regard to the meaning of the expression "on the merits" as used in the context of the doctrine of issue estoppel. Looking at the matter negatively a decision on procedure alone is not a decision on the merits. Looking at the matter positively a decision on the merits is a decision which establishes certain facts proved or not in dispute, states what are the relevant principles of law applicable to such facts and expresses a conclusion with regard to the effect of applying those principles to the factual situation concerned. If the expression 'on the merits' is interpreted in this way, as I am clearly of opinion that it should be, there can be no doubt whatever that the decision of the Dutch Court of Appeal in the present case was a decision on the merits for the purposes of the application of the doctrine of issue estoppel. In my view, therefore, the argument for the appellants on this point is misconceived and should be rejected.' (See [1985] 2 All ER 104 at 110–111, [1985] 1 WLR 490 at 499.)

Whilst, therefore, Lord Brandon's formulation is wide enough to embrace a foreign court's decision on a purely procedural issue, I do not read his judgment as extending that far. If it did, it would go beyond Lord Diplock's definition, and the remaining three members of the House of Lords agreed with both speeches.

Similarly, Mr Falconer relies upon *House of Spring Gardens Ltd v Waite* [1990] 2 All ER 990, [1991] 1 QB 241, where the leading judgment in this court was given by Stuart-Smith LJ. There had been two earlier judgments of the Irish courts, the second being concerned with the specific issue whether the first judgment had been obtained by fraud. When the plaintiff brought proceedings to enforce the first judgment in England, the defendant sought to raise another of the recognised exceptions to the rule that the court will recognise and give effect to foreign judgments, namely where the foreign judgment was obtained by fraud. The existence of the exception was queried but was affirmed by the House of Lords for the purposes of that case in *Owens Bank Ltd v Bracco* [1992] 2 All ER 193, [1992] 2 AC 443, but so was this court's ruling in *House of Spring Gardens Ltd v Waite* that the Irish court's second judgment on the fraud issue should also be recognised. This too in my judgment was a substantive, not a procedural, issue and if so these judgments are not authority for the proposition that an issue estoppel arises in the case of rulings on non-substantive issues.

On balance, and regarding the question entirely as one of principle, I would be prepared to hold that an issue estoppel could arise from an interlocutory judgment of a foreign court on a procedural, ie non-substantive, issue, where the following conditions were fulfilled: (1) there was express submission of the procedural or jurisdictional issue to the foreign court; (2) the specific issue of fact was raised before and decided by the court; and (3) the need for 'caution' recognised by Lord Reid in *Carl-Zeiss* is carefully borne in mind. Practical considerations such as whether the issue was or should have been fully ventilated are likely to be especially relevant in relation to procedural, as distinct from substantive, issues and for this reason I would hesitate long before including issues which might have been, but were not in fact raised or decided by the foreign court (cf (2) above). Moreover, as Mr Semken submitted, there is some danger of injustice if an issue estoppel is based, not upon the foreign court's adjudication on a claim or cause of action which is sought to be raised for a second time here, but upon a specific issue which can only be identified within it *a* by a process of 'refining down' or, as he put it, of salami-slicing. As he might have said, Occam's razor can be taken too far.

Abuse of justice

b It may be, therefore, that in practice the scope for a plea of issue estoppel arising out of a procedural decision and in relation to non-substantive issues will be very small. At this stage a further consideration becomes relevant. It is well established that apart from issue estoppel the courts have power to prevent any abuse of justice which may be involved in an attempt to litigate matters for a second time. In *Owens Bank Ltd v Etoile Commerciale SA* [1995] 1 WLR 44 the Judicial Committee of the Privy Council found it unnecessary to decide whether the fraud exception to the recognition of foreign judgments permits the *c* defendant to raise an issue of fraud which has also been determined by the foreign court, because it held that the court has a general power of this kind. Lord Templeman said (at 51):

d 'No strict rule can be laid down; in every case the court must decide whether justice requires the further investigation of alleged fraud or requires that the plaintiff, having obtained a foreign judgement, shall no longer be frustrated in enforcing that judgment.'

This was also the second ground of decision in *House of Spring Gardens Ltd v Waite* [1990] 2 All ER 990 at 1000, [1991] 1 QB 241 at 254; see also *Brinks Ltd v Abu-Saleh (No 1)* [1995] 4 All ER 65, [1995] 1 WLR 1478.

e It appears therefore that reliance on the rules governing issue estoppel is unnecessary and superfluous where such an abuse of justice is established. Conversely, therefore, the cases where issue estoppel will become relevant are those where it cannot be said that there is an abuse of justice. Mr Semken in his thoughtful submission did not go so far as to suggest that, since issue estoppel is *f* said to depend upon fairness and justice, it is difficult to see why it should exist when no injustice exists in raising the issue for a second time. But in my judgment he is right in suggesting that this is or may be a potent factor in deciding whether or not the need for caution should prevail against allowing the plea of issue estoppel in a particular case.

g ### Issue estoppel—in this case

The relevant issue of fact which the defendant seeks to raise in these proceedings is whether or not he expressly authorised Mr Graham to instruct the US attorneys who were acting on behalf of the partnership to act in the proceedings on behalf of himself as a personal defendant.

h It is clear from the record of the US proceedings in which the defendant sought to have the judgment set aside that this was not the only issue raised. The plaintiffs relied, first, upon a rule of Arizona procedural law which, apparently, makes the formal entry of appearance by an attorney binding upon the party on whose behalf the attorney purported to act. The rule is said to derive from the *j* public status of the attorney, but it has no counterpart here. Mr Falconer accepts that a decision reached on this basis would not give rise to an issue estoppel, because a different issue was involved.

Secondly, the Arizona courts appear to have been influenced by the fact that the defendant's 'Declaration' filed by Mr Johnson on his behalf was not an affidavit as required by the rules, so that Mr Graham's affidavit evidence was formally unchallenged. But Mr Falconer points out that they went on to consider

the conflict of evidence, overlooking this technical objection, so that their *a*
decision was not based on that ground.

So the crucial part of their decision was where they considered the issue of
authority, which they defined in terms of Mr Jury's authority to act on behalf of
the defendant. The relevant part of the Court of Appeals judgment reads as
follows:

> 'In his affidavit, Graham, who managed all of the affairs of the partnership *b*
> dealing with the partnership property, stated that he had Hill's authority to
> hire attorneys to act on behalf of the limited partners who were also the
> guarantors in dealings with Desert Sun involving the defaulted loan.
> Graham retained the attorneys to represent the partnership and guarantors
> and the attorneys initially negotiated with Desert Sun in attempting to *c*
> modify or further extend the loan. Following the default, they continued to
> represent Hill and the other guarantors. Hill was notified of all negotiations
> and the litigation leading to the deficiency judgment. Hill paid his
> proportional share of the lawyer's fees. The attorneys Graham hired were
> authorized to accept service of process. Compliance with Ariz R Civ P 4(f),
> 16 ARS gave the court personal jurisdiction over Hill. Our de novo review *d*
> of Graham's affidavit leads us to the same conclusion the trial court reached.'

It seems from these passages that the Court of Appeals was prepared to consider
the question of authority in a wider context than is relevant for present purposes
under English law. In English terms, it may be that the defendant could be held *e*
to be barred by Mr Jury's entry of appearance on his behalf by virtue of the actual
authority which Mr Jury was given by the defendant to act generally on his behalf
in relation to partnership affairs, and specifically to negotiate a settlement of the
litigation, or by virtue of Mr Graham's apparent authority to instruct Mr Jury on
behalf of the defendant, derived from Mr Graham's status as the defendant's
partner or former partner or as his authorised agent to give instructions to *f*
negotiate with the plaintiffs.

The judge held that it was at least arguable by the defendant that the judgment
of the Arizona court did not give rise to an issue estoppel. Now that we have the
judgment of the Court of Appeals, with its authoritative statement of the grounds
of decision, I would hold that no issue estoppel does arise. It is not sufficiently *g*
clear, in my judgment, that the specific issue which arises for decision in these
proceedings was identified and decided against the defendant in the foreign court.
Moreover, to establish an issue estoppel it is necessary to take account of the
practical considerations referred to by Lord Reid in *Carl-Zeiss* and, I would
respectfully add, for the reasons which I have indicated above, these may be of
particular relevance when the estoppel is said to arise out of an interlocutory or *h*
a procedural ruling. This may well mean that in practice it will be a rare case
where the necessary degree of certainty arises on an application for summary
judgment.

Conditional leave *j*

The remaining question is whether the defendant should be given
unconditional leave to defend. This appears not to have been ventilated before
the judge, but before us Mr Falconer asserts that the suggested defence is
'shadowy' at best, and he relies upon what he says are inconsistencies in the
defendant's various accounts of his dealings and conversations with Mr Graham.
These include an apparent self-contradiction as to the date when the defendant

a   came to England from the United States after his motor accident and whether he returned to or even lived in Arizona before doing so.

If a condition requiring payment into court is justified, it remains necessary to consider whether the result would be to cause injustice in a case where the defendant could not afford to comply with it. The court's approach was described in *MV Yorke Motors (a firm) v Edwards* [1982] 1 All ER 1024, [1982] 1 WLR

b   444; cf *The Supreme Court Practice 1995* para 14/3–4/15. The defendant has submitted a further affidavit in which he says that he has no income and no assets. His living expenses at the house in which he lives with his wife at an address near Ascot, and the costs of sending his children to fee-paying schools are met, he says, by unspecified trusts in which he has no beneficial interest. On the other hand, he describes himself as a 'Business Consultant' without explaining whether or not

c   he is actively engaged as such, or how otherwise he occupies his time and he does not say whether or not he might be able to raise the sum claimed or any part of it from third party sources if required to do so.

It is particularly relevant in my judgment that the defence raised turns upon a narrow issue and that in relation to that issue the defendant initially was less than

d   frank, and perhaps even misleading in his first 'Declaration' to the Arizona court. He has failed in his objection before the Arizona courts. These factors, combined with the other matters raised by Mr Falconer, do make this, in my judgment, an appropriate case for a condition to be imposed, although not for payment into court of the whole of the sum claimed. I would give leave to defend conditional upon payment of $100,000 into court within 28 days or such other period as may

e   be determined after hearing further submissions from counsel.

I would dismiss the appeal against the grant of leave to defend but would make the leave conditional and to that extent would alter the judge's order accordingly.

ROCH LJ. The judgment that the appellants seek to enforce against Mr Hill was

f   obtained in the Superior Court for the State of Arizona on 2 January 1992. It was a judgment in personam. The basis on which the appellants seek to establish that they are entitled to enforce their judgment in this country is the common law.

Rule 36 in *Dicey and Morris on the Conflict of Laws* (12th edn, 1993) p 472 states:

g   'Subject to Rules 37 to 39, a court of a foreign country outside the United Kingdom has jurisdiction to give a judgment *in personam* capable of enforcement or recognition in the following cases ... If the judgment debtor, being a defendant in the foreign court, submitted to the jurisdiction of that court by voluntarily appearing in the proceedings.'

h   Where the defendant challenges the jurisdiction of the foreign court and appears before that court for that purpose, but for that purpose only, then s 33 of the Civil Jurisdiction and Judgments Act 1982 provides that he shall not be regarded as having submitted to the jurisdiction by reason only of the fact that he appeared in the foreign proceedings for that purpose. Thus the attempts by Mr Hill to have the judgment of 2 January 1992 set aside by the courts of Arizona on

j   the basis that the courts of Arizona did not have jurisdiction over him do not amount to a voluntary appearance conferring jurisdiction ex post facto on those courts.

Rule 42(1) of *Dicey and Morris* states (p 503):

'A foreign judgment is impeachable if the courts of the foreign country did not, in the circumstances of the case, have jurisdiction to give that judgment

in the view of English law in accordance with the principles set out in Rules *a*
36 to 40 inclusive.'

This rule repeats a principle stated by *Dicey and Morris* p 473 at the outset of
their exposition of r 36, namely:

'A fundamental requirement for the recognition or enforcement of a
foreign judgment in England at common law, is that the foreign court should *b*
have had jurisdiction according to the English rules of the conflict of laws.'

The second principle that *Dicey and Morris* p 474 derive from the Court of
Appeal decision in *Adams v Cape Industries plc* [1991] 1 All ER 929, [1990] Ch 433 is
that—   *c*

'in deciding whether the foreign court was one of competent jurisdiction,
the English court would apply, not the law of the foreign court, but English
rules of the conflict of laws.'

As I understand these principles, voluntary appearance in the foreign *d*
proceedings in a way accepted by English law as amounting to a voluntary
appearance has to be shown. To show that there was a voluntary appearance in
the proceedings in the eyes of the court of the foreign country whose judgment
the English court is being asked to enforce is not sufficient, unless it amounts to
a voluntary submission according to our rules.

Thus the failure to respond to a writ nailed to the door of the foreign *e*
courthouse cannot amount to a voluntary appearance even if the foreign court
were to decide that it was a voluntary appearance.

These principles may, in my view, exclude the application of issue estoppel in
this field based on the foreign court's decision that a defendant had voluntarily
submitted to its jurisdiction. The reason would be that it is always for the English *f*
court to inquire if there has been a voluntary appearance by the defendant before
the foreign court, as a result of his having acted in a way which would constitute
a voluntary appearance here.

The contrary conclusion would not necessarily result in any significant saving
of time, because it is always open to a defendant, where an issue estoppel is relied
upon by the plaintiff seeking to enforce a foreign judgment to establish that the *g*
defendant had appeared voluntarily before the foreign court, to contend that the
foreign court did not decide the precise issue which arises under English law.
However, it is not necessary to do more than express reservations about this
matter because in the present case I agree that it is not open to the appellants to
rely on the issue of estoppel for the reasons given by Evans LJ.   *h*

STUART-SMITH LJ. I agree that this appeal should be allowed in part to the
extent proposed in the judgment of Evans LJ, in that the defendant should only
have leave to defend on condition that $US100,000 is paid into court. I also agree,
for the reasons given by him, that the appeal should otherwise be dismissed. I *j*
only add a few observations of my own on issue estoppel, because this is the first
time that it has been sought to rely on a decision of a foreign court on a
procedural matter as giving rise to an issue estoppel.

The same principles of issue estoppel apply in the case of decisions of foreign
courts as they do to those of English courts, subject to the important qualification
enunciated most clearly by Lord Reid in *Carl-Zeiss-Stiftung v Rayner & Keeler Ltd*

a (*No 2*) [1966] 2 All ER 536, [1967] 1 AC 853, which has already been cited in the judgment of Evans LJ.

The rule is stated in *Dicey and Morris on the Conflict of Laws* (12th edn, 1993) vol 1, p 467 as follows:

b 'For there to be such an issue estoppel, three requirements must be satisfied: first, the judgment of the foreign court must be (a) of a court of competent jurisdiction, (b) final and conclusive and (c) on the merits; secondly, the parties to the English litigation must be the same parties (or their privies) as in the foreign litigation; and, thirdly, the issues raised must be identical. A decision on the issue must have been necessary for the decision of the foreign court and not merely collateral.'

c

Where these conditions are satisfied, a party in subsequent litigation in this country is precluded from asserting that an issue of fact or law is otherwise than was decided by the foreign court in the earlier proceedings.

There is no reason in principle why such an issue should not be decided in a *d* decision on a procedural matter as opposed to the final determination of the cause of action or proceedings. But the decision must be final and conclusive and not provisional or subject to revision. The expression 'interlocutory' is used in two distinct senses in English law, which can give rise to confusion unless the distinction is borne in mind. Some decisions or orders are interlocutory in the sense that they are made pending final determination of the case. The obvious *e* example of this is an interlocutory injunction pending trial. Such a decision cannot give rise to an issue estoppel because it is not final. The other use is to distinguish between those decisions where leave to appeal to the Court of Appeal is required and those where it is not. Some of the former decisions can determine finally the issue which is raised. I prefer therefore to use the expression *f* procedural in the sense that I have defined, rather than interlocutory.

In this case Mr Hill in seeking to challenge the jurisdiction of the Arizona court in his motion to set aside the judgment against him, and by appealing submitted the question of jurisdiction to be determined by the foreign court. It was a court of competent jurisdiction; its decision was final and conclusive and it was between the same parties. But the question for the Arizona court was: had Mr *g* Hill submitted to the jurisdiction of the Arizona court? Whereas the issue for the English court is narrower, namely whether the defendant expressly authorised Mr Graham to instruct Mr Jury to act on his behalf in the Arizona proceedings. If it was clear that the Arizona decision necessarily decided this issue as a question of fact against the defendant, then in my opinion there would be an issue estoppel *h* in this case. It is clear that the defendant did his best to challenge the jurisdiction in Arizona, which was the appropriate court in which to contest it. It is not a case, therefore, where a party in foreign proceedings decides either not to contest the question, or only do so half-heartedly because little is at stake. The defendant has rightly not sought to make any such case. Moreover, if the issue was decided by *j* the Arizona court, it is immaterial that Mr Hill did not adduce all the admissible evidence at his disposal, that the issue was determined without oral evidence or cross-examination, or that his attorney was at fault in the conduct of the case. This is well established: see *Henderson v Henderson* (1843) 3 Hare 100, [1843–60] All ER Rep 378 and *Talbot v Berkshire CC* [1993] 4 All ER 9, [1994] QB 290.

At one time it did appear to me that the factual issue whether the defendant did expressly authorise Mr Jury to act for him in the Arizona proceedings was

necessarily determined in the Arizona court. But Mr Semken has persuaded me, *a*
for the reasons given in the judgment of Evans LJ, that this is not clear.

The question of issue estoppel is very closely linked to abuse of process: see
House of Spring Gardens Ltd v Waite [1990] 2 All ER 990, [1991] 1 QB 241 and *Owens
Bank Ltd v Etoile Commerciale SA* [1995] 1 WLR 44. Mr Hill chose to contest the
issue of jurisdiction in the Arizona court. He could have waited till the plaintiffs
sought to sue on the judgment in this country and then contested the factual issue *b*
according to English law on the basis that he had given no express authority to
Mr Jury by way of Mr Graham. If, in the course of contesting the jurisdiction of
the foreign court in Arizona, that very question of express authority was clearly
decided, I think it would be an abuse of process to permit the defendant to litigate
it again here. But, as I have already indicated, I am left in doubt whether it was
so decided. *c*

Appeal dismissed.

Paul Magrath Esq   Barrister.

a # T v Secretary of State for the Home Department

HOUSE OF LORDS

LORD KEITH OF KINKEL, LORD BROWNE-WILKINSON, LORD MUSTILL, LORD SLYNN OF
HADLEY AND LORD LLOYD OF BERWICK

b 16, 20, 21 NOVEMBER 1995, 22 MAY 1996

*Immigration – Leave to enter – Refugee – Asylum – Applicant for asylum entering
country illegally on false documents – Applicant fearing threat to life or freedom in
home country – Applicant a member of illegal political organisation carrying out
terrorist activities in home country – Application for asylum refused on grounds of
applicant's involvement in 'serious non-political crimes' – Circumstances in which
crimes to be characterised as 'political' – Convention relating to the Status of Refugees
1951, art 1F.*

c

d T was an Algerian citizen who entered the United Kingdom as an illegal entrant
and later claimed political asylum. The Secretary of State refused his application.
T appealed to a special adjudicator on the ground that his removal would be
contrary to the United Kingdom's obligations under art 33(1)[a] of the Geneva
Convention relating to the Status of Refugees 1951 in view of the fact that his life
or freedom would be threatened on account of his political opinions if he were
e returned to Algeria. The special adjudicator accepted that T was a member of an
illegal political organisation (the FIS), which sought to secure power in Algeria by
any means including violence and that he had been involved in the planning of an
explosion at Algiers Airport (in which ten people had been killed) and a raid on a
military depot (in which one person had died). He accordingly dismissed the
appeal on the ground that T's involvement in those incidents brought him within
f the scope of art 1F[b] of the 1951 convention as a person with respect to whom
'there were serious reasons for considering' that he had committed a 'serious
non-political crime' before being admitted to the United Kingdom as a refugee
and was thereby not entitled to the protection of the convention. T's subsequent
appeal to the Immigration Appeal Tribunal was dismissed on the ground that the
terrorist offences could not be characterised as political crimes. T appealed
g further to the Court of Appeal, which held that it would be inappropriate to
characterise indiscriminate bombings which led to the deaths of innocent people
as political crimes and dismissed the appeal. T appealed to the House of Lords.

Held – The appeal would be dismissed for the following reasons—
h   (1) (Per Lord Keith, Lord Browne-Wilkinson and Lord Lloyd) A crime was a
political crime for the purposes of art 1F of the 1951 convention if it was
committed for a political purpose and there was a sufficiently close and direct link
between the crime and the alleged political purpose. In determining whether
such a link existed, the court would consider the means used to achieve the
j political end and, in particular, whether the crime was aimed at a military or
governmental target, or a civilian target, and in either event whether it was likely
to involve the indiscriminate killing or injuring of members of the public.
Although it was clear that the FIS was a political organisation and that T's motive

---

a   Article 33(1), so far as material, is set out at p 873 *f g*, post
b   Article 1F, so far as material, is set out at p 873 *e f*, post

in becoming involved in the airport bombing was to overthrow the government, the crime, as carried out, was almost bound to involve the indiscriminate killing of members of the public; the link between the crime and the political object which T was seeking to achieve was therefore too remote (see p 867 *f g* and p 899 *a* to *c d* to *j*, post).

(2) (Per Lord Mustill and Lord Slynn) Acts of violence which were likely to cause indiscriminate injury to innocent persons who had no connection with the government of the state did not constitute political crimes for the purposes of the 1951 convention and consequently the attacks on the airport and the barracks had been correctly characterised by the appeal tribunal as terrorist offences (see p885 *g* to p 886 *g* and p 888 *j* to p 889 *c*, post).

(3) It followed that the appeal tribunal and the Court of Appeal had been entitled to hold that there were serious reasons for considering that T had committed a serious non-political crime outside the United Kingdom and was therefore excluded from the protection of art 33(1) of the convention by virtue of art 1F(b) (see p 867 *f g*, p 886 *g*, p 889 *c* and p 899 *j* to p 900 *a*, post).

Decision of the Court of Appeal [1995] 2 All ER 1042 affirmed.

Notes

For control of immigration with respect to political asylum and refugees, see 4(2) *Halsbury's Laws* (4th edn reissue) para 82.

Cases referred to in opinions

Atta (Mahmoud Abed), Re (1989) 706 F Supp 1032, US Dist Ct, *affd* sub nom *Ahmed (Mahmoud Abed) v Wigen* (1990) 910 F 2d 1063, US Ct of Apps (2nd Cir).

Bugdaycay v Secretary of State for the Home Dept [1987] 1 All ER 940, [1987] AC 514, [1987] 1 WLR 155, HL.

Carron v McMahon, Carron v Governor of Portlaoise Prison [1990] IR 265, Ir SC.

Castioni, Re [1891] 1 QB 149, [1886–90] All ER Rep 640, DC.

Cheng (Tzu-Tsai) v Governor of Pentonville Prison [1973] 2 All ER 204, [1973] AC 931, [1973] 2 WLR 746, HL.

Doherty, Re (1984) 599 F Supp 270, US Dist Ct; *affd* sub nom *US v Doherty* [1986] F 2d 491, US Ct of Apps (2nd Cir).

Eain v Wilkes (1981) 641 F 2d 504, US Ct of Apps (7th Cir).

Ellis v O'Dea [1991] ILRM 346 Ir SC.

Folkerts v Public Prosecutor (1978) 74 ILR 498, Netherlands SC.

Gil and Minister of Employment and Immigration, Re (1994) 119 DLR (4th) 497, Can Fed CA.

Gross, Re, ex p Treasury Solicitor [1968] 3 All ER 804, sub nom *Re Extradition Act 1870, ex p Treasury Solicitor* [1969] 1 WLR 12.

Kolczynski, Re [1955] 1 All ER 31, sub nom *R v Governor of Brixton Prison, ex p Kolzynski* [1955] 1 QB 540, [1955] 2 WLR 116, DC.

McGlinchey v Wren [1982] IR 154, SC.

Mackin, Re (1981) 668 F 2d 122, US Ct of Apps (2nd Cir).

McMullen v Immigration and Naturalization Service (1981) 658 F 2d 1312, US Ct of Apps (9th Cir); *subsequent proceedings* (1986) 788 F 2d 591, US Ct of Apps (9th Cir).

Meunier, Re [1894] 2 QB 415, DC.

Ornelas v Ruiz (1896) 161 US 502, US SC.

Quinn v Robinson (1986) 783 F 2d 776, US Ct of Apps (9th Cir).

a *R v Governor of Pentonville Prison, ex p Budlong* [1980] 1 All ER 701, [1980] 1 WLR 1110, DC.

R v Governor of Winson Green Prison, Birmingham, ex p Littlejohn [1975] 3 All ER 208, [1975] 1 WLR 893, DC.

R v Secretary of State for the Home Dept, ex p Chahal [1995] 1 All ER 658, [1995] 1 WLR 526, CA.

b *Schtraks v Government of Israel* [1962] 3 All ER 529, [1964] AC 556, [1962] 3 WLR 1013, HL.

Wisconsin (State of) and Armstrong, Re (1973) 32 DLR (3d) 265, Can Fed CA.

Appeal

c T, an Algerian citizen who was an illegal entrant, appealed with leave from the decision of the Court of Appeal (Nourse, Glidewell and Simon Brown LJJ) ([1995] 2 All ER 1042, [1995] 1 WLR 545) delivered on 3 November 1994 dismissing T's appeal from the determination of the Immigration Appeal Tribunal made on 11 May 1994 dismissing his appeal from the determination of the special adjudicator promulgated on 29 March 1994, whereby the special adjudicator upheld the

d decision of the Secretary of State for the Home Department refusing his application for asylum. The facts are set out in the opinion of Lord Mustill.

Nicholas Blake QC and *Richard Scannell* (instructed by *Jane Coker & Partners*) for T. *David Pannick QC* and *Neil Garnham* (instructed by the *Treasury Solicitor*) for the

e Secretary of State.

Their Lordships took time for consideration.

22 May 1996. The following opinions were delivered.

f **LORD KEITH OF KINKEL.** My Lords, for the reasons given in the speech to be delivered by my noble and learned friend Lord Lloyd of Berwick, which I have read in draft and with which I agree, I would dismiss this appeal.

LORD BROWNE-WILKINSON. My Lords, for the reasons given by my noble

g and learned friend Lord Lloyd of Berwick I too would dismiss the appeal.

LORD MUSTILL. My Lords, during the nineteenth century those who used violence to challenge despotic regimes often occupied the high moral ground, and were welcomed in foreign countries as true patriots and democrats. Now, much has changed. The authors of violence are more ruthless, their methods

h more destructive and undiscriminating; their targets are no longer ministers and heads of state but the populace at large; and their aims and ideals are frequently no more congenial to the countries in which they take refuge than those of the regimes whom they seek to displace. The unsympathetic call them terrorists, and their presence is seen as both an affront and a danger. These fundamental

j changes in method and perception have not been matched by changes in the parallel, although not identical, laws of extradition and asylum. These laws were conceived at a time when political struggles could be painted in clear primary colours largely inappropriate today; and the so-called 'political exception' which forms part of these laws, and which is the subject of this appeal, was a product of Western European and North American liberal democratic ideals which no

longer give a full account of political struggles in the modern world. What I *a*
regard as the exceptional difficulty of this appeal is that the courts here, as in other
legal systems, must struggle to apply a concept which is out of date.

The appeal arises as follows. The appellant, identified throughout as T, is an
illegal immigrant, having entered the United Kingdom under a false name and
papers. He is a national of Algeria, and a member of a group named the Front
Islamique du Salut (the FIS) which, according to the account given in evidence on *b*
his behalf, was cheated of success in a democratic election and had recourse to
violent means aimed at displacing the ruling powers. Amongst the activities of
this group in which the appellant played a part was the detonation of a bomb at
an airport in Algeria. Ten people were killed, none of them having, so far as is
known, any connection with the opponents of the appellant's group, or with the
struggle in which the group was engaged. Unfortunately, the way in which this *c*
apparently random violence might have served the ends of the group was not
explored in these proceedings. We have little more than one or two statements
by the appellant in evidence that the objective of the bomb was to hit the national
economy, rather than to kill people. He also admitted to some degree of
involvement in an attack on an army barracks. *d*

These were the circumstances in which the appellant, having been arrested
and served by the Secretary of State with a notice that he would be returned to
Algiers, appealed to a special adjudicator, and thence to the Immigration Appeal
Tribunal and the Court of Appeal. He has failed at each stage, and now appeals
to your Lordships' House. *e*

I. PRELIMINARY

Four points of cardinal importance must at once be made. The first is that the
appeal is concerned with asylum, not with extradition. Algeria does not demand
the return of the appellant. There is no treaty of extradition which would permit
such a demand, and the United Kingdom would be in breach of no international *f*
obligation owed to Algeria if it allowed the appellant to remain within its
territories, or sent him somewhere else.

Secondly, and this is a most unusual feature, there is here no dispute, of the
kind which has become a common feature of the present flood of applications for
asylum, about the treatment which the asylum-seeker can expect if removed to *g*
another country. It is no longer questioned that if the appellant is returned to
Algeria his life or freedom would be threatened 'on account of his ... membership
of a particular social group or political opinion' (art 33(1) of the Convention
relating to the Status of Refugees (Geneva, 28 July 1951; TS 39 (1954); Cmd 9171).

Thirdly, although it is easy to assume that the appellant invokes a 'right of *h*
asylum', no such right exists. Neither under international nor English municipal
law does a fugitive have any direct right to insist on being received by a country
of refuge. Subject only to qualifications created by statute this country is entirely
free to decide, as a matter of executive discretion, what foreigners it allows to
remain within its boundaries. Under the law of asylum the United Kingdom can
choose to allow the appellant to reside here, rather than return him to Algeria to *j*
face the consequences of his admitted crimes. Conversely, it can expel him and
cause him to be transported to whatever country is willing to accept him. The
Secretary of State has made it plain that if the appellant can find a country other
than Algeria which will accept the appellant he will be sent there. No such
country has been suggested by the appellant. The Secretary of State does not

a wish to send the appellant back to Algeria, but as things now stand there is nowhere else for him to go.

Fourthly, although a refugee has no direct right to insist on asylum, there are certain statutory restrictions on the Secretary of State's freedom of choice as to the destination to which a person refused permission to remain may be sent, which may in practice achieve the same result. I will presently come to the *b* statutory provisions in detail. For the moment it is sufficient to say that the United Kingdom is under an international and municipal duty derived from art 33(1) of the 1951 convention not to return a fugitive to a place (like Algeria in the present instance) where he is liable to be persecuted. This duty (to which effect is given in English municipal law by r 334(ii) of the Statement of Changes in Immigration Rules (1980) (HC Paper (1994) No 395)), is subject to an exception, *c* whereby the protection against 'refoulement' (as it is called) is disapplied where the fugitive has, before coming to this country, committed a 'serious non-political crime', within the meaning of art 1F(b) of the 1951 convention. This expression is the source of the present appeal. That the bombing at the airport was a serious crime, and that the appellant took part in it, is beyond doubt. The question is *d* whether the crime was 'political' in character. If it was, the appellant must be given leave to remain. If not the Secretary of State may return him to Algeria, if all else fails.

II. THE APPELLANT'S CASE

On these simple facts the appellant founds a simple argument. If the elections *e* had been allowed to run their course, the incoming government would have been chosen by a contest between two or more parties or factions, plainly a political process. The undemocratic interference with this process left the appellant's associates with no choice but to adopt radically new methods to achieve the same political ends. True, these methods did not resemble those of *f* the Western democracies, but Algeria is not a democracy, and the Western model is not, and never has been, the only way of conducting politics. True also, that the methods were criminal, but an act may be none the less political for being criminal, as the expression 'non-political crime' itself recognises. And the degree of criminality is material only to the 'serious' element of the description 'serious non-political'. For the latter purpose it can logically make no difference how *g* many people suffered, or who they were. No doubt this bears on the acceptability of the fugitive's conduct to the ethical and social ideals of the receiving nation, but the test is not moral, and in any event is not to be judged by conditions and concepts remote from those of the place where the offence took place. Nor does it help to characterise the appellant as a terrorist, since, as is often *h* remarked, yesterday's terrorist is today's freedom fighter and perhaps tomorrow's head of state. In reality, so the argument concludes, the general character of the activities of the FIS was unchanged. It was as political after the abortive election as it had been before, and this character invests crimes committed under the aegis of the FIS with a character different from that which they would have had if committed, for example, in the course of criminal gang *j* warfare.

This is a powerful argument, the more so because it warns against the assumption that political action should be equated with the activities permitted to rival parties or groups seeking power under a parliamentary system of government such as exists in Europe and North America, and under other systems based on the same model. This being acknowledged, I believe that the appellant's argument goes too far, for it assumes that society, and the struggles *a* within it, have stood still for more than a century. Those who were intended to benefit from the political exception had taken up arms, having no other means, to relieve from oppression those who could not fend for themselves. The human rights of the individual who sought refuge in fear of persecution therefore coincided with those of the oppressed, and the evil of violence could be tolerated without threat to the world order in the greater interests of making the world a *b* better place. Whether this was sound thinking no longer matters, for the scene has changed. Those who use violence and fear to struggle against oppression may themselves be oppressors, causing as much suffering to the defenceless as those whom they seek to displace. When they flee to a foreign country the impulse to protect them from persecution remains, but it is muted. The community as a whole has a moral right to protection, which should not be *c* compromised by offering too ready a refuge to those who, having embroiled the population in violence, find themselves on the losing side. It must be acknowledged that although the words of the exception remain the same, the world has changed round it, and tests which may in the past have sufficed to settle the comparatively few cases where a criminal act required classification as *d* political or non-political are too inflexible, now that the motives and means of destructive violence have become so greatly enlarged.

For this reason, I would reject the simple logic of the appellant's primary argument, and also its exclusive reliance on the earlier authorities, to which I shall come in due course. To my mind, the whole trend of the more modern decisions *e* and writings is towards an acceptance that certain acts of violence, even if political in a narrow sense, are beyond the pale, and that they should not be condoned by offering sanctuary to those who commit them. Equally, the materials brought before the House concur in a very general ideal of where the boundary lies. The problem is to find a precise and intellectually sustainable test which will enable a line to be drawn in practice by those who are required to *f* make decisions, often under pressure of time with meagre factual materials. For this purpose I will examine the legislative background on the comparatively few authorities brought forward in argument, but must first set out the evidence and the proceedings leading to this appeal.

 g

III. PROCEEDINGS AND EVIDENCE

When the Secretary of State first came to consider the appellant's application for asylum, attention was concentrated on a number of issues no longer material, such as the questions whether the appellant had been in real peril before leaving Algeria; whether as he claimed he was concerned in the organisation of the FIS; *h* why he had not claimed asylum in Italy and France on leaving Algeria; why he had not claimed asylum immediately on arrival in England if he was a genuine asylum-seeker; whether he had been arrested in Algeria for a conspiracy to cause explosions; and whether he would be in danger if returned to Algeria. The scepticism of the Secretary of State on all these questions led him to decide that the appellant did not qualify for asylum, quite apart from whether he forfeited *j* any protection which he might otherwise have enjoyed because the attacks of which he had spoken were serious non-political crimes. Consequently this point was mentioned only in passing by the Immigration and Nationality Department of the Home Office in its letter dated 3 September 1993 giving the Secretary of State's reasons for refusing asylum.

a   It is not surprising therefore that the appellant had comparatively little to say about it in his grounds of appeal to the special adjudicator. According to this document, when the explosion took place the appellant had been present at the airport. He did not give any orders for the bombing to be carried out, but was simply the political organiser of the group. He was aware that the bombing was to take place, but was unaware of its exact details. The original plan had been for

b   the bomb to be placed outside and simply cause damage to the airport building, with the aim of causing economic damage to the government. But he became aware on the evening before that the group had been infiltrated by the government, with the result that the FIS would be classed as a terrorist organisation and exposed. It was too late for him to prevent the explosion from taking place.

c   As regards the attempt to get arms from the army barracks, the appellant planned the operation. One person was killed. Another was captured and gave the name of the appellant's cousin, who was arrested.

The appellant gave a further account in his oral evidence before the special adjudicator. The note of evidence is not verbatim, and may have suffered from difficulties of interpretation. At all events, it is very difficult to follow. The gist

d   seems to have been that although the appellant knew in advance that a bomb would be set off and that people would be injured he was not 'fully aware it was to be'. He was not involved in the planning of the explosion, and did not know where it was to be, except at the airport. By the time he reached the airport, where he was 'only passing by', the bomb had already been set off. The target for

e   the bomb was the economy of the state, since:

> 'After the anti constitutional dissolution of the FIS 80% of the population lost its voice. The council of FIS noticed the only way was to hit the State economy in a way to disturb it.'

f   The infiltration of the group by the security services caused the FIS to be regarded as a terrorist group.

The hearing before the special adjudicator concluded on 14 March 1993. His conclusions were as follows. He did not find the appellant to be a credible witness. Nevertheless, on balance of probabilities he accepted that the appellant was a member of the FIS. Also, on balance of probabilities, the appellant 'was

g   involved in the planning of the bombing at the airport and the raid to obtain arms.' If the account of the appellant was to be believed, he was aware of the planning of the bombing at the airport and he knew that the group had been infiltrated. If the special adjudicator accepted that account, the matter fell within art 1F of the 1951 convention. Similarly, the appellant had said in his grounds of

h   appeal that he was involved in the arms raid on the military establishment; one person was killed and another arrested. On this account the appellant again fell within art 1F. Accordingly, the appeal was dismissed.

The appellant appealed to the Immigration Appeal Tribunal. By this time the Secretary of State had accepted that apart from the exclusion in art 1F(b) the

j   appellant had a valid claim to asylum. Most of the issues of fact which had preoccupied the immigration officials, the special adjudicator and the appellant's advisers thereupon ceased to matter. The tribunal looked again at the facts which were now crucial, and made the following findings:

> 'We find as a fact, on the basis of that evidence that [T] was involved directly in the planning of an attack that led to the death of one person, and

he was involved in, and had prior knowledge of, a bomb attack in which ten a
people were killed. We do not accept [his counsel's] submission that his
degree of involvement was such that he was not personally and knowingly
involved. We conclude that [T], in common parlance was actively involved
in a terrorist organisation, one that was prepared to advance its aims by
random killings, and [T] was closely associated with one such incident.'

After a brief discussion of the relationship between terrorism and the 1951 b
convention the tribunal concluded that it would be against common sense and
right reason to characterise indiscriminate bombings which led to the deaths of
innocent people as political crimes so as to remove them from the exclusion
clause, and that it could not have been the intention of the 1951 convention to
accord protection to those who engaged in the 'terrorist activities' in which the c
appellant engaged. The appeal was therefore dismissed.

The appellant appealed to the Court of Appeal (Nourse, Glidewell and Simon
Brown LJJ) ([1995] 2 All ER 1042, [1995] 1 WLR 545). After anxious consideration
and not without some initial hesitation the court dismissed the appeal. The
thoughtful judgment, to which all members of the court contributed, examined
the authorities and in the light of them found the reasoning of the tribunal d
unsatisfactory because it proceeded simply on the basis that this was a case of
'terrorism' and as such must be outwith the political exception (a proposition
which the court did not accept), and gave no consideration to whether the
relevant offences were too remote from their alleged objective or otherwise
disproportionate to it. The court considered, however, that it was unnecessary e
to remit the matter to the tribunal, since the findings of fact were sufficient to lead
to a conclusion. This, the court expressed as follows:

'We too think it inappropriate "to characterise indiscriminate bombings
which lead to the deaths of innocent people as political crimes". Our reason
is not that all terrorist acts fall outside the protection of the convention. It is f
that it cannot properly be said that these particular offences qualify as
political. In our judgment the airport bombing in particular was an atrocious
act, grossly out of proportion to any genuine political objective. There was
simply no sufficiently close or direct causal link between it and T's alleged
political purpose. It offends common sense to suppose that the FIS's cause
of supplanting the government could be directly advanced by such an g
offence. Indeed, on the facts, T himself appears implicitly to recognise this
when he claims that the FIS group was infiltrated by the security services (ie
the government) and seeks to dissociate himself from the yet graver offence
which he acknowledges (indeed asserts) resulted from the infiltration—the
particular atrocity that led here to the deaths of ten innocent people. Despite h
therefore the deficient reasoning contained in the tribunal's own decision
and the real possibility that they asked themselves the wrong questions in
deciding whether the supposed offences were or were not political, we
accordingly dismiss this appeal.' (See [1995] 2 All ER 1042 at 1056, [1995] 1
WLR 545 at 559–560.) j

IV. NATIONAL AND INTERNATIONAL LEGISLATION
    That being the state of the dispute, I turn next to the international and national
legislation, which is relevant directly because it is the source of the problem, and
indirectly because it demonstrates to my mind a shift in the perceptions of the

a   international community about the degree of protection which should be given to refugees who have committed violent crimes to the harm of the public at large. It is convenient to arrange this material under the headings of asylum, extradition, the 'depoliticising' of offences and the prosecution in one country of crimes committed elsewhere.

b   *(1) Asylum*
    The legislation must be viewed against the background of a complete absence of any common law right, either national or international, for a refugee to insist on being admitted to a foreign country. For present purposes the starting point is the 1951 convention, which provides:

c   'Article 1 *Definition of the term "Refugee"*
        A. For the purposes of the present Convention, the term "refugee" shall apply to any person who: (1) Has been considered a refugee under the Arrangements of 12 May 1926 and 30 June 1928 or under the Conventions of 28 October 1933 and 10 February 1938, the Protocol of 14 September 1939 or the Constitution of the International Refugee Organization ... (2) ... owing
d   to well-founded fear of being persecuted for reasons of race, religion, nationality, membership of a particular social group or political opinion, is outside the country of his nationality and is unable or, owing to such fear, is unwilling to avail himself of the protection of that country ...
        F. The provisions of this Convention shall not apply to any person with
e   respect to whom there are serious reasons for considering that: (a) he has committed a crime against peace, a war crime, or a crime against humanity, as defined in the international instruments drawn up to make provision in respect of such crimes; (b) he has committed a serious non-political crime outside the country of refuge prior to his admission to that country as a refugee; (c) he has been guilty of acts contrary to the purposes and principles
f   of the United Nations ...
        Article 33 *Prohibition of expulsion or return ("refoulement")*
        1 No Contracting State shall expel or return ("*refouler*") a refugee in any manner whatsoever to the frontiers of territories where his life or freedom would be threatened on account of his race, religion, nationality,
g   membership of a particular social group or political opinion. 2 The benefit of the present provision may not, however, be claimed by a refugee whom there are reasonable grounds for regarding as a danger to the security of the country in which he is, or who, having been convicted by a final judgement of a particularly serious crime, constitutes a danger to the community of that country.'
h
    It is evident from the literature, which I need not cite, that the rather puzzling expression 'un crime de droit commun', often rendered as 'common crime', has nothing to do with the common law, but is equivalent to 'ordinary crime', or conduct recognised as criminal by the common consent of nations. Murder is a common crime; treason is not.
j   Turning to the United Kingdom legislation, effect is given to the 1951 convention by the Asylum and Immigration Appeals Act 1993, which provides, so far as material:

        '1. *Interpretation.*— In this Act—"the 1971 Act" means the Immigration Act 1971; "claim for asylum" means a claim made by a person ... that it would be contrary to the United Kingdom's obligations under the Convention for him to be removed from, or required to leave, the United Kingdom; and "the Convention" means the Convention relating to the Status of Refugees done at Geneva on 28th July 1951 and the Protocol to that Convention.

2 ... Nothing in the immigration rules (within the meaning of the 1971 Act) shall lay down any practice which would be contrary to the Convention ...

6 ... During the period beginning when a person makes a claim for asylum and ending when the Secretary of State gives him notice of the decision on the claim, he may not be removed from, or required to leave, the United Kingdom ...

8 ... (4) Where directions are given as mentioned in section 16(1)(a) or (b) of the 1971 Act for a person's removal from the United Kingdom, the person may apply to a special adjudicator against the directions on the ground that his removal in pursuance of the directions would be contrary to the United Kingdom's obligations under the Convention ...'

The 1993 Act operates by way of qualification to the Immigration Act 1971, paras 8 and 9 of Sch 2 to which provide:

'8.—(1) Where a person arriving in the United Kingdom is refused leave to enter, an immigration officer may ... (c) give [to the owners or agents of the ship or aircraft in which he arrives] directions requiring them to make arrangements for his removal from the United Kingdom in any ship or aircraft specified or indicated in the direction to a country or territory so specified, being either—(i) a country of which he is a national or citizen; or (ii) a country or territory in which he has obtained a passport or other document of identity; or (iii) a country or territory in which he embarked for the United Kingdom; or (iv) a country or territory to which there is reason to believe that he will be admitted ...

9. Where an illegal entrant is not given leave to enter or remain in the United Kingdom, an immigration officer may give any such directions in respect of him as in a case within paragraph 8 above are authorised by paragraph 8(1).'

Finally, practical effect is given to the 1951 convention by Pt I of the 1993 immigration rules, set out in the Statement of Changes in Immigration Rules, laid before Parliament on 23 May 1994 (HC Paper 1994 No 395). The relevant provisions are:

'328. All asylum applications will be determined by the Secretary of State in accordance with the United Kingdom's obligations under the United Nations Convention and Protocol relating to the Status of Refugees ...

329. Until an asylum application has been determined by the Secretary of State, no action will be taken to require the departure of the asylum applicant or his dependants from the United Kingdom ...

334. An asylum applicant will be granted asylum in the United Kingdom if the Secretary of State is satisfied that: (i) he is in the United Kingdom or has arrived at a port of entry in the United Kingdom; and (ii) he is a refugee, as defined by the Convention and Protocol; and (iii) refusing his application would result in his being required to go ... in breach of the Convention and Protocol, to a country in which his life or freedom would be threatened on

a   account of his race, religion, nationality, political opinion or membership of a particular social group.

335. If the Secretary of State decides to grant asylum to a person who has ... entered without leave, the Secretary of State will ... grant limited leave to remain ...

336. An application which does not meet the criteria set out in paragraph
b   334 will be refused.'

From what has already been said it will be plain that the appellant prima facie meets the criteria for non-refoulement to Algeria, and that in the absence of anywhere else to go he is entitled under r 334 to be given limited leave to enter the United Kingdom. But if his crime was not political he is not protected against
c   refoulement, his removal to Algeria would not be contrary to the United Kingdom's obligations under the convention, and he may be so removed under para 8(1)(a) of Sch 2 to the 1971 Act.

(2) *Extradition*

There is no need to prolong this opinion by setting out the history in detail, for
d   it is comprehensively described in the speech of Lord Simon of Glaisdale in *Tzu-Tsai Cheng v Governor of Pentonville Prison* [1973] 2 All ER 204, [1973] AC 931 (dissenting, but not on this aspect).

As I see it, the history discloses a series of oscillations. In earliest times one sovereign was most likely to ask that another should render up an offender when
e   the offence was directed at the sovereign and his apparatus of state; and the interests of comity made it most likely that a favourable response would be given when the offence was of that character. The changing face of political life in Europe, and later in the United States, brought about a reversal, so that whilst 'common crimes' now became the staple of formal extradition, there was a need for certain of such crimes to be exempt, when impressed with a political
f   character.

The result was a broad division, established by a series of bilateral treaties and a handful of decisions, into (a) 'common' crimes, (b) purely political crimes such as treason, and (c) 'relative' political crimes which are common crimes with a political overlay. This endured for a century with little strain. Conceptually, it
g   defied the commentators, but for so long as the only societies where in practice these questions were determined subscribed to the same broad principles of liberal democracy, there were few instances where the demand for extradition came close enough to the line to call for accurate judicial analysis.

In course of time this imprecision ceased to answer. A group of conflicting
h   impulses began to take effect. The first was the humanitarian impulse of hospitality to refugees, fuelled by the revealed horrors of totalitarian excess and by the acute political tensions of the post-war years. This impulse was repeatedly acknowledged by the United Nations in its early days, and was put into practice by the 1951 convention. The second impulse was to the contrary. Not all refugees were worthy of compassion and support. As art 1F of the convention
j   recognised, war criminals and offenders against the law of nations could properly be sent home to answer for their crimes, and there were others whose criminal habits made it unreasonable for them to be forced on to a host nation against its will. Such persons could not claim to be protected against refoulement, even where their lives or freedom were at risk. Significantly, they are referred to in the *Handbook on Procedures and Criteria for Determining Refugee Status under the 1951*

Convention and the Protocol relating to the Status of Refugees (1979) published by the
office of the UN High Commissioner for Refugees (hereafter 'the *UNHCR
Handbook*') as 'persons who are not considered to be deserving of international
protection' (2nd edn, 1988) para 140. Another, and rather different, impulse was
also opposed to the universal reception of refugees: namely the
acknowledgement that terror as a means of gaining what might be loosely
described as political ends posed a danger not only to individual states, but also to
the community of nations.

Thus, as long ago as 1937 the promoters of a League of Nations Convention
for the Prevention and Punishment of Terrorism made a concerted attempt to
reconcile the conflicting humanitarian impulses, calling on states to collaborate
in the punishment of what were called acts of terrorism. This convention was
unusual, and perhaps unique, in containing a useful definition. It was as follows:

> '"acts of terrorism" means criminal acts directed against a State and
> intended or calculated to create a state of terror in the minds of particular
> persons, or a group of persons or the general public.' (See art 1.2).

The 1937 convention never came into force, but in the post-war years advances
in technology and transportation have made the image of the lone assassin, with
pistol arm outstretched, hurling himself at the tyrant in defiance of an angry
crowd, seem out of date. The weapons have become more destructive, and less
discriminating; the targets, such as passenger aircraft, nuclear plants and off-shore
rigs, are more vulnerable; and the risks to the perpetrator are more easily evaded.
Furthermore, the simple world of the bad tyrants and the good patriots has
vanished. Those who struggle against odious regimes have now come to seem,
by their aims and methods, scarcely less odious than their oppressors. Yet it was
(and still is) hard to see why their crimes, however distasteful and heartless, are
any the less 'political' than those of the heroes of the Risorgimento. International
terrorism must be fought, but the vague outlines of the political exception are of
no help. Something more clear-cut is needed.

(3) *The depoliticising of crimes*

The first response to the problem was to define the boundaries of the political
exception by ignoring its intellectual basis and by listing those offences which,
without any regard to the factors which would otherwise be material, were not
for the purposes of extradition to be exempt. In the language of the text-writers,
these offences would be 'de-politicised'. A series of international conventions has
steadily enlarged this list, so that it embraces genocide, torture, the taking of
hostages, crimes against internationally protected persons and attacks on and acts
compromising the safety of aircraft, aerodromes, ships and marine installations;
and these specific instances have been the subject of legislation in the United
Kingdom which it is unnecessary to rehearse. Of particular importance,
however, is the European Convention on the Suppression of Terrorism
(Strasbourg, 27 January 1977; TS 93 (1978) Cmnd 7390), to which effect was given
in the United Kingdom by the Suppression of Terrorism Act 1978, now
re-enacted with enlargements by the Extradition Act 1989. The former Act not
only extended (as between the states party to the convention) the list of
extradition crimes, but also contained in Sch 1 a list (now carried into the 1989
Act) of offences which were not to count as political. These offences currently
include murder, manslaughter, offences against the person, and causing

a explosions likely to endanger life or property. Thus, if the appellant's activities had taken place within the territory of a European participating state (or in the United States, to which the convention and the statute have been extended), the anxious and difficult questions raised by this appeal would not have arisen.

(4) *Extra-territorial jurisdiction*

b Another weapon in the fight against terrorism has been the revival of the doctrine, propounded by Hugo Grotius (*De Jure Belli ac Pacis* lib 2, c 21, ss 3 and 4), 'aut dedere aut punire', that states are under an international obligation either to return criminals (or at least certain types of criminal) to the place where their crimes were committed, or to prosecute and if appropriate punish them locally. This idea was to a limited extent a feature of the 1937 League of Nations
c Convention (arts 9 and 10), and has now been given a more general effect by international and national legislation. Thus, by s 4(1) of the 1978 Act the United Kingdom has assumed extra-territorial jurisdiction over the long list of crimes contained in Sch 1: a list which, as already observed, is amply wide enough to cover the crimes of which the appellant is said to be guilty.

d The assumption of extra-territorial jurisdiction goes further. In relation to a much smaller group of activities, directed at particularly vulnerable targets, the United Kingdom has by statute assumed jurisdiction over criminal acts irrespective both of the offender's nationality and of the place where the acts are done. For present purposes the most conspicuous of these is the Aviation and Maritime Security Act 1990, s 1 of which makes it an offence triable in the United
e Kingdom—

> 'for any person by means of any device … to commit at an aerodrome serving international civil aviation any act of violence [defined in such a manner as to include murder, manslaughter, offences against the person and
f the use of explosive devices] which—(a) causes or is likely to cause death or serious personal injury and (b) endangers … the safe operation of the aerodrome or the safety of persons at the aerodrome.'

This appeal does not arise from a request for extradition by Algeria, and still less with any prosecution by the authorities under the 1990 Act; and it would be
g wrong to found any conclusion directly on a statute not examined in argument. Nevertheless the 1990 Act does serve to emphasise, in relation to activities resembling those of the appellant, the changed international perception of the relationship between sanctuary and acts of violence committed abroad.

V. THE AUTHORITIES

h (1) *Materials*

Although arising in the domestic context, this is essentially a case on public international law, a field in which the writings of scholars have always exerted great authority. Given both the intellectual difficulty of the present subject and the practical and moral problems which it presents, it was no surprise that a
j superficial survey after the close of the arguments disclosed an extensive literature, in which for more than 50 years writers have explored the political exceptions in depth, often with particular reference to issues arising on the present appeal. Some of this material was indeed brought forward, but the scale of citation was modest. Since it was neither practical to explore the writings in any depth, nor proper (in the context of an adversarial process) to rely upon

them, I have with regret left them out of account; with regret, because I believe
that they would have enabled a more systematic analysis than can be founded on *a*
the comparatively few, and by no means consistent, decisions of common law
courts relied upon before the House.

Nevertheless, that is how the matter stands, and to those decisions I now turn.
I include among them cases on extradition as well as asylum. There are
significant differences between the two doctrines; I have already mentioned one, *b*
and an account of several others may be found in the valuable judgment of
Hugesson J in *Re Gil and Minister of Employment and Immigration* (1994) 119 DLR
(4th) 497 in the Canadian Federal Court of Appeal. Nevertheless, the reference
to the 'serious non-political crime' in the 1951 convention must surely be an echo
of the political exception which had been a feature of extradition treaties for
nearly a century, and one may hope that decisions on the political exception *c*
would provide a comprehensive framework for the few and scattered decisions
on asylum.

(2) *Two categories of decision*

I have been unable to deduce from the cases and the literature any theory *d*
which accounts for all the decisions and dicta. It does, however, appear that the
authorities may be arranged in two groups. First, those which look to the
connection between the motive and political content of the crime and the
criminal act itself; and second those where attention is directed to the nature and
degree of the offence. These categories are not exclusive, and indeed one can see
both strands of reasoning in the passages quoted from the judgment of the Court *e*
of Appeal in the present case.

(3) *Context and motive*

This group includes all the English cases. It establishes one general
proposition, and a number of qualifications. The general proposition, which I *f*
believe is binding on this House as a matter of English law, is known in the
literature as the 'incidence' theory. The essence of this is that there must be a
political struggle either in existence or in contemplation between the
government and one or more opposing factions within the state where the
offence is committed, and that the commission of the offence is an incident of this *g*
struggle. Two cases in this House are in point. First, *Schtraks v Government of
Israel* [1962] 3 All ER 529 at 540, [1964] AC 556 at 591, in which Viscount Radcliffe
said:

> 'In my opinion the idea that lies behind the phrase "offence of a political
> character" is that the fugitive is at odds with the state that applies for his *h*
> extradition on some issue connected with the political control or
> government of the country.'

The second case, *Tzu-Tsai Cheng v Governor of Pentonville Prison* [1973] 2 All ER 204
at 209, [1973] AC 931 at 945, where Lord Diplock said— *j*

> 'even apart from authority, I would hold that prima facie an act committed
> in a foreign state was not "an *offence* of a political character" unless the only
> purpose sought to be achieved by the offender in committing it were to
> change the government of the state in which it was committed, or to induce
> it to change its policy, or to enable him to escape from the jurisdiction of a

a   government of whose political policies the offender disapproved but despaired of altering so long as he was there.' (Lord Diplock's emphasis.)

This principle underlies the major English decisions on extradition law. Thus, in *Re Meunier* [1894] 2 QB 415 an anarchist who had detonated a bomb in a café was refused the political exception because the essence of the anarchist philosophy is a denial of legitimacy to all forms of government and politics. An
b   anti-political gesture could not be political in nature. By contrast, in *Re Castioni* [1891] 1 QB 149, [1886–90] All ER Rep 640 extradition was refused where in the heat of an attack on an arsenal and the municipal palace of a Swiss canton by persons dissatisfied with the government the fugitive had shot and killed a member of the state council. It is notable that Hawkins J observed that things—

c   'may be done for the purpose of furthering and in furtherance of a political rising, even though it is an act which may be deplored and lamented, as even cruel and against all reason, by those who can calmly reflect upon it after the battle is over.' (See [1891] 1 QB 149 at 167, [1886–90] All ER Rep 640 at 649–650.)

d   In *Schtraks*, extradition was sought against the appellant by the State of Israel on charges of perjury and child-stealing. The evidence showed that the appellant had been concerned that his grandchild aged seven would not receive a religious education as an orthodox Jew if returned to his parents, and therefore refused to comply with an order for return made by the High Court of Israel. Although
e   there was a measure of difference between Lord Reid and Lord Radcliffe about the boundaries of the exception, all were agreed that this family quarrel was not within it, even though one political faction had taken up the appellant's cause.

The principle of incidence received emphatic indorsement in *Cheng*. The appellant was a member of a Formosan group opposed to the current regime in Taiwan. The son of the head of state visited the United States, and lodged in an
f   hotel, outside which there was a demonstration in which the appellant took part. In the course of the demonstration a pistol was discharged by another man who, together with the appellant, was indicted for attempted murder. The assailant pleaded guilty and the appellant was convicted. He absconded from bail whilst awaiting sentence, and was apprehended in this country. The United States
g   requested extradition, and the appellant raised the political exception. By a majority the House held that the exception did not apply. The principal ground was that a political offence must be an incident in a political struggle taking place in the country which requests the extradition: and the appellant had no aim to bring about any changes in the government of the United States. This reasoning
h   does not apply in an asylum case such as the present where there is no requesting state, and indeed the decision illustrates very well that the word 'political' does not have an identical meaning in the contexts of extradition and asylum. Nevertheless, the logic of the decision obviously demands that there cannot be a political crime in the absence of a struggle for power of which the crime is an element. To a similar effect is the decision of the Divisional Court in *R v Governor*
j   *of Pentonville Prison, ex p Budlong* [1980] 1 All ER 701, [1980] 1 WLR 1110, and the American cases cited in *McMullen v Immigration and Naturalization Service* (1986) 788 F 2d 591 at 595.

That the incidence test as applied in these authorities is not necessarily a complete account of the word 'political' is, however, shown by *Re Kolczynski* [1955] 1 All ER 31, [1955] 1 QB 540. Seven Polish seamen seized their vessel and

sought refuge in an English port. The Polish government requested extradition
for crimes of assault, malicious damage, and revolt on the high seas. The court
refused to grant extradition, notwithstanding that there was at the time no
political disturbance in Poland and that the seamen were not supporters of one
party at odds with another, Poland being a one-party state. The court was, I
believe, treating the situation as different from that which had prevailed when *Re
Castioni* was decided 60 years before (see [1955] 1 All ER 31 at 35, [1955] 1 QB 540
at 549 per Cassels J). In the words of Chapman J in *Re Gross, ex p Treasury Solicitor*
[1968] 3 All ER 804 at 809, [1969] 1 WLR 12 at 17—

> 'it may still be an offence of a political character if violent measures are
> taken to get away from a political ordering of society which is regarded as
> intolerable.'

With hindsight it may be thought that the decision could more convincingly have
been arrived at by holding that the offences for which extradition was claimed
were in reality 'pure' political offences, such as sedition, and that the totalitarian
regimes existing in Eastern Europe during the 1950s were not really different in
kind from those which had prompted the creation of the political exception.
However this may be, there is no suggestion in either *Schtraks* or *Cheng* that
Kolczynski was wrongly decided, and it must be taken to be the English law that
an offence may be political even where the possibility of struggle is excluded by
the presence of an overwhelmingly authoritative power, if the crime which they
commit is, in the words of Lord Goddard CJ, 'the only means open to them' (see
[1955] 1 All ER 31 at 36, [1955] 1 QB 540 at 541).

Thus far, the decided cases appear to lend support to an argument on the
following lines. There was at the material time a struggle for power in Algeria
which satisfied the requirements of *Schtraks* and *Cheng*. Unlike the crime in
Meunier the appellant's criminal act was part of this struggle. True, it involved
regrettable violence and loss of life, but this (as in *Castioni*) will often feature in a
fight against repression. The FIS would have adopted democratic means if the
ruling power had allowed it to do so, but (like the seamen in *Kolczynski*) had no
choice except to use the only available methods.

This is a powerful argument, but the cases show that it may be too simple. It
may be that another requirement—or perhaps two others, if they are not aspects
of the same concept—must be taken into account: namely that there must be a
causal link, and an absence of 'remoteness,' between the political situation of
which the refugee forms part and the crime which he has committed. This
conception draws its authority, if not its origin, from a passage in the speech of
Lord Diplock in *Cheng* [1973] 2 All ER 204 at 208–209, [1973] AC 931 at 944–945:

> 'My Lords, the noun that is qualified by the adjectival phrase "of a political
> character", is "offence". One must, therefore, consider what are the juristic
> elements in an offence, particularly one which is an extradition crime, to
> which the epithet "political" can apply. I would accept that it applies to the
> mental element: the state of mind of the accused when he did the act which
> constitutes the physical element in the offence with which he is charged. I
> would accept, too, that the relevant state of mind is not restricted to the
> intent necessary to constitute the offence with which he is charged; for, in
> the case of none of the extradition crimes, can this properly be described as
> being political. The relevant mental element must involve some less
> immediate object which the accused sought to achieve by doing the physical

a act. It is unnecessary for the purposes of the present appeal, and would, in my view, be unwise, to attempt to define how remote that object might be. If the accused had robbed a bank in order to obtain funds to support a political party, the object would, in my view, clearly be too remote to constitute a political offence. But if the accused had killed a dictator in the hope of changing the government of the country, his object would be

b sufficiently immediate to justify the epithet "political". For politics are about government. "Political" as descriptive of an object to be achieved must, in my view, be confined to the object of overthrowing or changing the government of a state or inducing it to change its policy or escaping from its territory the better so to do. No doubt any act done with any of these objects would be a "political act", whether or not it was done within the territory of

c the government against whom it was aimed. But the question is not simply whether it is political qua "act" but whether it is political qua "offence".'

This principle was applied in R v Governor of Winson Green Prison, Birmingham, ex p Littlejohn [1975] 3 All ER 208, [1975] 1 WLR 893; it is one of a battery of tests

d proposed in the UNHCR Handbook; and it has been adopted (at least as a theory) in North America. Yet I must own to serious problems. Historically, it seems unlikely that common law concepts such as remoteness, which even today are a well-recognised stumbling-block for lawyers from other traditions, should have been intended to play a part in the operation of an exception designed decades before these concepts began to be explored even in England. More importantly,

e the analysis seems to do no more than replace 'political' with another form of words. Leaving aside the trifling cases where the actor is moved only by malice, greed or a simple pathological desire to cause harm, how is the test of causation to be applied? Take the case of an insurgent group which attacks an army post, as part of a campaign to overthrow the government by force. This would plainly be a political offence, and on any ordinary understanding of causation it would be

f said that the desire to overthrow the government caused the attack to take place. Change the case now so that the soldiers, lacking the weapons needed for the attack, steal them from an arsenal. Would not this in ordinary language be described as a political offence, all of a piece with the subsequent attack, and would not the cause of the theft still be ascribed to the wish to bring down the

g government by force? If one changes the case once more, so that instead of stealing arms directly the insurgents steal from a bank the money with which to buy them, I can see that if the raiders intend to keep some of the proceeds for their own personal use it could well be held that the personal element of the crime is both non-political and serious enough to bring art 1F into play. But in the

h absence of such mixed motives I find it hard to see why the stealing of the money and its subsequent use to buy arms would not be a continuous causal chain of which all the links are political in nature; and if the logic is not clear I can foresee great difficulties in applying this criterion in practice. All the same, one must recognise that Schtraks and Littlejohn do recognise a test of causation; and the UNHCR Handbook, which, although without binding force in domestic or

j international law (see Bugdaycay v Secretary of State for the Home Dept [1987] 1 All ER 940, [1987] AC 514), is a useful recourse on doubtful questions, treats causation as one of the material factors (see the UNHCR Handbook para 152). To a similar effect are statements in McMullen v Immigration and Naturalization Service (1986) 788 F 2d 591 and Eain v Wilkes (1981) 641 F 2d 504. Reference may also be made to Re State of Wisconsin and Armstrong (1973) 32 DLR (3d) 265 at 286, where

Thurlow J assumed that the hypothetical bank robbery would not be a political a offence. All this being said however, the difficult decision on whether there is a sufficient discontinuity between the political aim and the crime to mean that the crime is to be treated as 'common' is not in my judgment made any easier by using the word 'causation' in a very special sense. I think it safer to rely on the words of the 1951 convention.

So also with 'remoteness.' I can see that even where the actor has no motive b other than to further his cause, the chain of events between the act and the achievement of the political goal may be so long that the two are disconnected. But to introduce into the international law of asylum and extradition a test derived from the specialist English law of damages seems to me to take the inquiry nowhere, except back to the central issue.

In short, to say that the political aim must cause the crime, or that the crime c must not be too remote from the aim, does no more than assert that the crime must be really political in nature to fall within the exception. This is the point which I understand Lord Diplock to have stressed. But to prescribe causation or remoteness as tests which must as a matter of law be applied, even though the political exception was conceived long before these notions became part even of d English law, only multiplies the problems. I prefer to do without them.

This negative opinion still leaves open the necessary connection between the subjective impulsion of the offender and the mental element of the offence. In recent years new criteria have been proposed. The first is one of 'proportionality'. Whilst there is substantial support for this test, on closer examination it is seen that the decisions and commentaries use the term in more e than one sense. The first, relied upon by the appellant, is that a crime cannot be political if the adverse consequences for the fugitive of using it as a basis for extradition or refoulement would be out of proportion to the gravity of the offence. I see no substance in this, and if *R v Secretary of State for the Home Dept, ex p Chahal* [1995] 1 All ER 658, [1995] 1 WLR 526 supports it, I must disagree. The f gravity of the offence is relevant to the question whether it is 'serious' for the purposes of art 1F(b). But the crime either is or is not political when committed, and its character cannot depend on the consequences which the offender may afterwards suffer if he is returned.

Another meaning of proportionality is more sound, but does not apply here. There are indications in the literature that the concept originally applied to what g are called 'délits complexes', where the same crime is impelled by more than one motive. So understood, the doctrine propounds only that the dominant motive determines the political character of the offence. This is rational, but of no help here, since it has not been suggested that the appellant had any motive for his acts other than to advance the cause of the FIS. At all events, the House has not had h the benefit of considering the relevant Swiss decisions and the matter cannot be pursued.

A different meaning of proportionality is also said to be relevant: namely that an offence will not qualify as political unless its nature and degree are in proportion to its political ends. This theory has academic support, is cited in the j UNHCR *Handbook* as one of the factors to be considered, and forms the centre-piece of the judgment given by the American Court of Appeals in *McMullen v Immigration and Naturalization Service* (1986) 788 F 2d 591 at 596–597:

'It appears to us that the [Board of Immigration Appeals'] interpretation of the statute is consistent with the [Geneva] Convention, and thus consistent

a   with congressional intent. A balancing approach including consideration of
the offense's "proportionality" to its objective and its degree of atrocity make
good sense ... Moreover, this approach better recognizes the type of crime
involved in this and most such cases. There is a distinction between "pure"
political crimes, such as sedition, treason, and espionage, and "relative"
political crimes, crimes that have both common law criminal aspects and
b   political aspects ... An approach that considers the proportionality and
atrocity of a particular course of conduct is better suited to the analysis of
"relative" political offenses under the Convention and Protocol.'

Notwithstanding its powerful support, I must own to real difficulty with this
doctrine. In the first place, I do not understand its logic. If the apparent
c   disproportion between ends and means is used simply as evidence that the
political motive has been fuelled by some other element, such as personal malice,
misanthropy, sadism, or mental unbalance, this is no more than a version of the
different proportionality doctrine to which I have already referred, which
requires a comparison between the political and non-political elements of the
motivation. Yet the proponents seem to advance a different theory, which
d   proceeds directly to an evaluation by the judge in the receiving country of
whether the fugitive has used more drastic methods than were necessary to
achieve his aim. I do not follow this. Provided that the extrinsic factors of malice,
etc, are absent, why should a crime which would have been political in nature be
turned into one which is not political, simply because the judge deems the
e   offender to have gone too far?

This leads to a second objection, that it will be hard for the judge of the
receiving state to decide whether the ends justified the means without applying
the notions of his own upbringing and environment in judging whether the
offender has overstepped the bounds of permissible political action. To my mind
this parochial approach is wrong in principle, and would yield absurd results. In
f   the Western democracies the use of assassination as a political instrument is
anathema; yet *Re Castioni* [1891] 1 QB 149, [1886-90] All ER Rep 640 shows that it
falls precisely within the political exception. In *Re Atta (Mahmoud Abed)* (1989) 706
F Supp 1032 at 1040 District Judge Korman stated:

> g   'Providing refuge for those who seek political change is one thing, making
> the United States a haven for those who engage in conduct that "violates our
> own notion of civilized strife" is quite another matter.'

It may be that this and similar pronouncements can be explained by the additional
requirement in the United States-Israel extradition treaty that the offence should
h   be '*regarded by the requested party*' as one of a political character (see 706 F Supp
1032 at 1038). If not, I must respectfully disagree.

Finally, I can envisage great difficulty in putting this theory into practice. To
strike a balance the official or adjudicator in the receiving state would have to
evaluate, amongst other facts: (i) the unacceptableness of the state of affairs
which the crime is designed to improve; (ii) the extent to which the crime would,
j   or at least might, bring about an improvement; (iii) the conformity or otherwise
of the crime with local conceptions of the way in which, if need be, political
change can be brought about; (iv) the practicability of achieving the same result
by other and less drastic means. Admittedly, there may be extreme cases where
the disproportion, or lack of it, is obvious; and others where the foreign state is
so close in geography and culture that the judge can make an assessment in the

light of his own general knowledge. But it is likely that in other instances an accurate appraisal would be possible, if possible at all, only to a specialist with years of experience. These decisions have to be made with speed, and in the light of the most fragmentary information. Algeria is far from being the most remote of the countries in respect of which questions of asylum may arise, and yet the special adjudicator and the Immigration Appeal Tribunal have had to make do with the evidence of the appellant's own account of the circumstances, events and motives; which the tribunal has found to be unreliable. A reasoned judgment on proportionality in such circumstances is surely out of the question.

Rejecting therefore the test of proportionality, I turn to another theme, which has appealed to judges in the United States and Canada, namely that those who have committed unpleasant crimes are unwelcome. This was put robustly in *Eain v Wilkes* (1981) 641 F 2d 504 at 520:

'We do not need [terrorists] in our society. We have enough of our own domestic criminal violence with which to contend without importing and harboring with open arms the worst that other countries have to export. We recognize the validity and usefulness of the political offense exception, but it should be applied with great care lest our country become a social jungle and an encouragement to terrorists everywhere.'

My Lords, many would agree with these responses, which may be relevant where the executive branch has an unfettered discretion on whether to allow an asylum-seeker to remain, but the present appeal is concerned with something altogether different: a decision on a mixed question of fact and law on whether the antecedent crime had a political character when and where committed. I am quite unable to see how the fact, if it is a fact, that the foreign crime shows the asylum seeker to be a wicked man of whom the country of refuge would be well rid can have any bearing on this question. Indeed the shape of the legislation shows that this is not so, for art 1F(b) of the 1951 convention assumes that a person who has committed a serious crime, which might make him just as unwelcome in the country of refuge, is immune from refoulement so long as his offence can be characterised as political.

Moreover, the argument overlooks art 33.2 of the 1951 convention, which it is timely to repeat:

'The benefit of the present provision may not, however, be claimed by a refugee whom there are reasonable grounds for regarding as a danger to the security of the country in which he is ...'

The state of refuge has sufficient means to protect itself against harbouring dangerous criminals without forcing on an offence, which either is or is not a political crime when and where committed, a different character according to the opinions of those in the receiving state about whether the refugee is an undesirable alien: opinions which may be shaped by considerations which have nothing to do with the political nature of the offence committed elsewhere.

Setting this argument aside, we arrive at what I believe to be the heart of the case. The Secretary of State contends, with much support from decided cases and texts, that the point at which criminal conduct which would otherwise be political loses this attribute is when it can be described as 'an atrocity' or 'terrorism'. The terminology is inexact. The words 'atrocity' and 'terrorism' reflect a similar impulse of revulsion from inhumanity, and there has for long *a* been a tendency to treat them as interchangeable. But they are not. The murders at Katyn Forest were atrocities by any standard, but they were not terrorism, for they were kept secret, and secret terrorism is a contradiction in terms. In the absence of any clear consensus in the texts and cases, and indeed any firm choice in the contentions of the Secretary of State, about which word more accurately describes the further exception impliedly superimposed on the political *b* exception, both must be examined.

I begin with 'atrocity'. This word reflects an impulse of revulsion which all must share from allowing the perpetrator of a repellent crime to insist on the hospitality and protection of any nation whose borders he can manage to penetrate. By way of illustration only (for they were not examined in argument) *c* one may instance *McGlinchey v Wren* [1982] IR 154 and *Carron v McMahon, Carron v Governor of Portlaoise Prison* [1990] IR 265. In the former, a group claiming affiliation to the self-styled Provisional Irish Republican Army fired Armalite weapons at a house from a moving car. Some occupants escaped death, but an old lady was, as the judgment put it, riddled with bullets. This crime, aptly described as revolting, was held to lie outside the political exception on the *d* ground that it was contrary to the basic requirements of political activity. In the later case, Finlay CJ described it as an illustration of the 'type of atrocity' which is outside any concept of a political offence. Whilst I respect this impulse, it is hard to accept as a reliable basis on which to apply the exception, for it posits that the community of nations has found it so clear that conduct which is political in the ordinary sense of the word may be deprived of that character by its atrocious *e* nature, that international legislation needs no express provision and no attempt to define what an atrocity entails. Can this really be so? When in the years since the 1939–45 war the international community had to grapple with war crimes, genocide and international terrorism it set out to do so explicitly by the exclusions contained in art 1F and in the conventions regarding depoliticisation *f* and extra-territorial jurisdiction to which I have referred. The respondents invite the House to accept that in addition there is a tacit qualification, the boundaries of which depend entirely on the personal reaction of the official or judge in the receiving state as to whether the act is 'atrocious' enough to merit special treatment. In a field which touches not only the life and liberty of the fugitive, *g* but also the social order of the two states and indirectly of the international community as a whole, one must surely look for a test more reliable than this.

I am, however, more persuaded by the idea of writing 'terrorism' into the modern concept of the political crime. To accept this requires, as must any model which involves departure from the concept of incidence, an important *h* step: the recognition that some characteristic of the crime can disconnect it from its political origins, using the word in its widest sense. Once this step is taken, as I believe it must be, I would prefer terrorism to atrocity as a test, because it concentrates on the method of the offence, rather than its physical manifestation. The terrorist does not strike at his opponents; those whom he kills are not the tyrants whom he opposes, but people to whom he is indifferent. They are the *j* raw materials of a strategy, not the objectives of it. The terrorist is not even concerned to inspire terror in the victims, for to him they are cyphers. They exist only as a means to inspire terror at large, to destroy opposition by moral enfeeblement, or to create a vacuum into which the like-minded can stride. It seems to me in a real sense that a political crime, the killing of A by B to achieve an end, involves a direct relationship between the ideas of the criminal and the victim, which is absent in the depersonalised and abstract violence which kills *a* twenty, or three, or none, it matters not how many or whom, so long as the broad effect is achieved. I find it hard to believe that the human rights of the fugitive could ever have been intended to outweigh this cold indifference to the human rights of the uninvolved.

There are two further reasons to think that this is the right answer. First, there is detectable in the international legislation and the debates surrounding it a *b* recognition that terrorism is an evil in its own right, distinct from endemic violence, and calling for special measures of containment. Secondly, the law of asylum fundamentally affects the lives of human beings, and yet must be applied at speed. Whether employed individually or as parts of a battery of tests, criteria such as remoteness, causation, atrociousness and proportionality seem too subjective to found the consistency of decision which must surely be essential in *c* a jurisdiction of this kind. By contrast, once it is made clear that terrorism is not simply a label for violent conduct of which the speaker deeply disapproves, the term is capable of definition and objective application. I quote again from the 1937 League of Nations Convention:

'"acts" of terrorism mean criminal acts directed against a State and *d* intended or calculated to create a state of terror in the minds of particular persons, or a group of persons or the general public.'

The convention never came into force, but the definition is serviceable, and I am content to adopt it.

e

VI. CONCLUSION

I return to the present appeal. A substantial point of difference between extradition and asylum is that where the former is in issue the political nature of the offence is an exception to a general duty to return the fugitive, whereas in relation to asylum there is a general duty *not* to perform a refoulement unless the *f* crime is non-political. This distinction may be of great practical importance where reliable information is at a discount. In the present instance, however, I am persuaded, whilst sharing the hesitations of the Court of Appeal, that the material does show the bombing at the airport to have been a terrorist offence, and that there were grounds on which the tribunal could properly find that the same conclusion applied to the attack on the barracks. Both offences therefore *g* are within the scope of art 1F, and the prohibition of refoulement does not apply.

Accordingly, although I would prefer the test applied by the tribunal to that laid down by the Court of Appeal, I arrive at the same conclusion and would dismiss the appeal.

h

LORD SLYNN OF HADLEY. My Lords, the Immigration Appeal Tribunal said in this case:

'We find as a fact, on the basis of that evidence that [T] was involved directly in the planning of an attack that led to the death of one person, and he was involved in, and had prior knowledge of, a bomb attack in which ten *j* people were killed. We do not accept [counsel's] submission that his degree of involvement was such that he was not personally and knowingly involved. We conclude that [T], in common parlance was actively involved in a terrorist organisation, one that was prepared to advance its aims by random killings and [T] was closely associated with one such incident.'

a   Nevertheless it is clear that the Front Islamique du Salut (the FIS) was a political organisation seeking to set up a fundamentalist Islamic regime in Algeria and that, since the second round of elections which was due to follow the first round (in which the FIS had gained a majority) was not held, the FIS was not able to pursue its aims through democratic election processes. T's activities were carried out against this background and in an effort to undermine the existing
b   government; there is no challenge to his claim that if he returns to Algeria he will be prosecuted.

Is he entitled to say that he is a refugee in the sense of one who—

'owing to well-founded fear of being persecuted for reasons of ...
membership of a particular social group or political opinion, is outside the
c   country of his nationality and is unable or, owing to such fear, is unwilling to avail himself of the protection of that country ...' (art 1 of the Convention relating to the Status of Refugees (Geneva 28 July 1951; TS 39 (1954) Cmd 9171),

d   or he is a person to whom the provisions of the 1951 convention do not apply since, pursuant to art 1F thereof—

'there are serious reasons for considering that ... (b) he has committed a serious non-political crime outside the country of refuge prior to his admission to that country as a refugee.'

e   These provisions of the 1951 convention are given effect to by para 334 of the Statement of Changes in Immigration Rules (HC Paper (1994) No 395) laid before Parliament on the 23 May 1994.

The meaning of 'serious non-political crime' has been considered in relation both to extradition and to asylum (different though they are) in many cases in the
f   courts of this country and in those of other countries, in particular of the United States and Canada. These cases have been analysed and considered in depth in the speeches of my noble and learned friends Lord Mustill and Lord Lloyd of Berwick, which I have had the advantage of reading. It is not necessary for me to repeat that analysis and it is sufficient to indicate the conclusions which I have
g   reached.

It is clear that the events of recent years having produced violent acts which in number, in extent and in character go far beyond the sort of cases which were considered in the nineteenth century when the concept of treating political acts, albeit criminal, differently from ordinary crimes was developed. It seems that in
h   consequence the international community has been striving to avoid giving the benefit of political asylum to those who can truly be categorised as terrorists. See, for example, the League of Nations Convention for the Prevention and Punishment of Terrorism, the European Convention on the Suppression of Terrorism (Strasbourg, 27 January 1977; TS 93 (1978) Cmnd 7390), given effect to in the United Kingdom by the Suppression of Terrorism Act 1978 and now by the
j   Extradition Act 1989. These provisions are also applicable to the United States. I say 'striving to', because no convention has yet been adopted which deals with this situation on a universal basis (or even in respect of states which are members of the United Nations), and a complete definition of 'terrorist act' which takes such acts outside the range of political crime may be very difficult to achieve and even more to obtain agreement to on the part of states.

In the course of argument a number of tests have been suggested to indicate *a*
whether a crime is or is not a political crime.

Decisions of this House in *Schtraks v Government of Israel* [1962] 3 All ER 529,
[1964] AC 556 and *Tzu-Tsai Cheng v Governor of Pentonville Prison* [1973] 2 All ER
204, [1973] AC 931 show that in order to be political an act must be an incident of
a dispute existing in a member state. As Viscount Radcliffe ([1962] 3 All ER 529
at 540, [1964] AC 556 at 591) said in the former case, the fugitive is 'at odds with *b*
the state that applies for his extradition on some issue connected with the political
control or government of the country'; in the latter, Lord Diplock ([1973] 2 All
ER 204 at 209, [1973] AC 931 at 945) says that the offence could not be political—

> 'unless the only purpose sought to be achieved by the offender in
> committing it were to change the government of the state in which it was *c*
> committed, or to induce it to change its policy, or to enable him to escape
> from the jurisdiction of a government of whose political policies the offender
> disapproved but despaired of altering so long as he was there.'

I am, for my part, not satisfied that in order to be a political offence the act has to
be directed against the government of the day; it is in a democratic society no less *d*
an attack on the state if the attacker seeks to destroy or to pressurise the
opposition party. In any event, on either of the ways of expressing the test which
I have quoted, the present appellant would seem to satisfy them.

I have doubts as to whether the test of remoteness which has been propounded
as a means of excluding some crimes from being 'political crimes' is satisfactory *e*
in itself. Whether there is a sufficiently direct link between the criminal act and
a political objective may pose an extremely difficult question to resolve and risks
fine lines being drawn. I am not, for example, at all certain that for a terrorist
group to rob a bank for the express and sole purpose of buying Semtex or guns to
achieve political ends, is clearly too remote or indirect to be regarded as a political
crime, as has been said in earlier cases. *f*

Nor do I find 'proportionality' in this context a suitable test. It may involve the
consideration of a situation which is wholly different from any experienced in this
country and imports inevitably a subjective element in the task of, and imposes a
difficult burden on, the official, tribunal or court considering the matter.

Paragraph 152 of the *Handbook on Procedures and Criteria for Determining Refugee* *g*
Status under the 1951 Convention relating to the Status of Refugees (1979) published by
the Office of the UN High Commissioner for Refugees, however, indicates that a
number of tests should be considered in each case—i e is the crime due to genuine
political motives, was there a close and direct cause or link between the crime and
its alleged political purpose, and do the political elements outweigh the common *h*
law character of the crime?

This is very much in accord with the judgment of the Court of Appeal in the
present case, and there may well be cases where it is possible to apply these tests
without difficulty. There are, however, likely to be other cases where the test
raises issues which it virtually impossible to decide and it must be remembered
that decisions as to asylum often have to be taken quickly. *j*

I do not wish to do anything to undermine the importance of genuine political
fugitives, even those who have committed serious crimes, from being granted
asylum here. I consider, however, that without resort to tests like remoteness
and proportionality 'serious non-political crime' as a matter of interpretation of
the convention and of the rules, includes acts of violence which are intended or

a   likely to create a state of terror in the minds of persons whether particular persons or the general public and which cause, or are likely to cause, injury to persons who have no connection with the government of the state. This is not intended to be a complete definition. There may be other acts which constitute terrorism which are far outside the concept of political crime, but in the present case the Immigration Appeal Tribunal was in my view entitled to conclude that—

b   'to characterise indiscriminate bombings which lead to the deaths of innocent people as political crimes so as to remove them from the exclusion clause [art 1F(b) of the convention] would be against commonsense and right reason. It cannot have been the intention of the Convention to accord protection to those who engage in such activities, and we would not so

c   conclude unless bound by high authority.'

Such bombing at the airport killing innocent citizens was 'totally beyond the pale' and outside the protection afforded by the 1951 convention. Although the attack on the barracks was more debatable, I conclude that the Immigration Appeal Tribunal was entitled to find that this was yet another 'random killing'.

d   I too would dismiss this appeal.

This does not mean that the appellant must be returned to Algeria; the Secretary of State has already made it plain that if he can find another state which will accept him he may go there. The Secretary of State was, however, entitled to say that he may not stay here.

e
LORD LLOYD OF BERWICK. My Lords, in this appeal your Lordships are concerned with the meaning of the words 'serious non-political crime' in art 1F(*b*) of the Convention relating to the Status of Refugees (Geneva, 28 July 1951; TS 39 (1954); Cmd 9171). Article 1 of the 1951 convention contains a definition of the term 'refugee.' Article 1F provides:

f   'The provisions of this Convention shall not apply to any person with respect to whom there are serious reasons for considering that: (a) he has committed a crime against peace, a war crime, or a crime against humanity ... (b) he has committed a serious non-political crime outside the country of refuge prior to his admission to that country as a refugee; (c) he has been

g   guilty of acts contrary to the purposes and principles of the United Nations.'

The facts are that T, an Algerian national, arrived in the United Kingdom on 14 March 1993, using a false French identity card. On 8 April he was arrested for theft. He was interviewed the following day by an immigration officer. In the

h   course of the interview he claimed asylum. Thereafter he was interviewed on four occasions between 21 April and 13 August. On 3 September the Secretary of State rejected his asylum claim, and on 17 September he gave directions for his removal to Algeria. On 23 September T appealed to a special adjudicator, as he was entitled to do, under s 8(4) of the Asylum and Immigration Appeals Act 1993. The special adjudicator, Mr John Fox, found on the balance of probabilities that

j   T was a member of the Front Islamique du Salut (the FIS), a revolutionary fundamentalist movement, and that he had been involved in the planning of two terrorist incidents.

The first incident was the planting of a bomb at Bône Airport, some 40 kilometres from Algiers, on 26 August 1992. Ten people were killed in the explosion. The second incident was an abortive attempt to steal arms from an

army barracks, in the course of which one person was killed. It is not clear
whether the casualty was a soldier, or a member of the FIS; probably the latter.
Mr Fox held in relation to both incidents that there were 'serious reasons for
considering' that Mr T had committed a serious non-political crime outside the
United Kingdom prior to his admission, so as to deprive him of the protection of
the convention.

T appealed to the Immigration Appeal Tribunal. At the hearing the Secretary
of State conceded that if the 1951 convention applied, then T had a valid claim for
asylum under r 334 of the Statement of Changes in Immigration Rules (HC Paper
(1994) No 395), on the ground that he had a well-founded fear of persecution if
he were to be returned to Algeria. The sole remaining issue for consideration was
whether the convention applied, or whether T was excluded by art 1F(b).

The Immigration Appeal Tribunal (Mr Maddison, Mr Froome and Mrs
Abrahams JP), found as a fact that T was directly involved in planning the attack
on the barracks, and that he was involved in and had prior knowledge of the
bomb attack at the airport. The tribunal did not accept a submission on his behalf
that his degree of involvement was such that he was not personally and
knowingly involved. The tribunal stated its conclusion as follows:

'We have to ask ourselves whether the terrorist activities in which we have
found as a fact he was involved were, in the terms of the Convention,
non-political crimes. There is a difficulty there because the only definition of
terrorism of which we are aware is that contained in the Prevention of
Terrorism (Temporary Provisions) Act 1989, in which it is defined as "the
use of violence for political ends" [s 20(1)]. That might at first sight suggest
that a terrorist crime was indeed a political crime. It seems to us however,
that to characterise indiscriminate bombings which lead to the deaths of
innocent people as political crimes so as to remove them from the exclusion
clause would be against commonsense and right reason. It cannot have been
the intention of the Convention to accord protection to those who engage in
such activities, and we would not so conclude unless bound by high
authority.'

From the decision of the Immigration Appeal Tribunal there is an appeal to the
Court of Appeal with leave, but only on a question of law. The question of law
is not very clearly identified. But the principal ground relied on, both on the
application for leave to appeal and in the notice of appeal itself, was that the
special adjudicator applied the wrong standard of proof. However, there was a
further ground of appeal. The Immigration Appeal Tribunal is said to have
concluded, wrongly, that because T was actively involved in a terrorist
organisation, and because the two incidents in which T was involved would
ordinarily be described as terrorist activities, it necessarily followed that the
crimes were non-political within the meaning of art 1F(b).

The Court of Appeal (Nourse, Glidewell and Simon Brown LJJ) ([1995] 2 All ER
1042, [1995] 1 WLR 545) dismissed the appeal in a judgment of the court
delivered by Glidewell LJ. While criticising the lack of satisfactory reasoning in
the decision of the Immigration Appeal Tribunal, the court, nevertheless,
reached the same conclusion. I quote from the judgment.

'We too think it inappropriate "to characterise indiscriminate bombings
which lead to the deaths of innocent people as political crimes". Our reason
is not that all terrorist acts fall outside the protection of the convention. It is

a that it cannot properly said that these particular offences qualify as political. In our judgment the airport bombing in particular was an atrocious act, grossly out of proportion to any genuine political objective. There was simply no sufficiently close or direct causal link between it and T's alleged political purpose. It offends common sense to suppose that the FIS's cause of supplanting the government could be directly advanced by such an offence. Indeed, on the facts, T himself appears implicitly to recognise this when he claims that the FIS group was infiltrated by the security services (ie the government) and seeks to dissociate himself from the yet graver offence which he acknowledges (indeed asserts) resulted from the infiltration—the particular atrocity that led here to the deaths of ten innocent people.' (See [1995] 2 All ER 1042 at 1056, [1995] 1 WLR 545 at 559–560.)

b

c I find myself in agreement with the reasoning of the Court of Appeal. There is no English authority on the meaning of 'non-political crime' in the 1951 convention. But it was common ground that the words must bear the same meaning as they do in extradition law. Indeed, it appears from the travaux préparatoires that the framers of the convention had extradition law in mind when drafting the convention, and intended to make use of the same concept, although the application of the concept would, of course, be for a different purpose.

d So far as English law is concerned the phrase 'offence ... of a political character' goes back to s 3(1) of the Extradition Act 1870, and is now to be found in s 6(1)(a) of the Extradition Act 1989. The most helpful English authorities are *Re Castioni* [1891] 1 QB 149, [1886–90] All ER Rep 640, *Re Meunier* [1894] 2 QB 415, *Schtraks v Government of Israel* [1962] 3 All ER 529, [1964] AC 556 per Lord Reid and Viscount Radcliffe and *Tzu-Tsai Cheng v Governor of Pentonville Prison* [1973] 2 All ER 204, [1973] AC 931 per Lord Diplock.

e

f *Re Meunier* is particularly helpful, since it was the first case in which the court had to consider whether a prisoner charged with indiscriminate violence aimed at members of the public could claim the protection of the political offence exception. It was held that he could not. The case is important since it concerned a type of terrorist offence which was still relatively uncommon in the nineteenth century, but has regrettably become more widespread in recent years. It has thus been much discussed in the numerous recent decisions in the United States and Canada.

g In a case concerning an international convention it is obviously desirable that decisions in different jurisdictions should, so far possible, be kept in line with each other. In the United States, recent cases include *Eain v Wilkes* (1981) 641 F 2d 504, *Quinn v Robinson* (1986) 783 F 2d 776, *McMullen v Immigration and Naturalization Service* (1986) 788 F 2d 591 and *Re Atta (Mahmoud Abed)* (1989) 706 F Supp 1032. In Canada the most recent decision is *Re Gil and Minister of Employment and Immigration* (1994) 119 DLR (4th) 497, a decision of the Federal Court of Appeal in Quebec. The Canadian case and *McMullen* (a decision of the United States Ninth Circuit Court of Appeals), are especially valuable since they are both refugee cases, and are therefore concerned with a similar background to the present case, and identical language.

h

j I return to the English cases. In *Re Meunier* [1894] 2 QB 415 the defendant was charged in France with causing two explosions. The first was at a café. Two members of the public were killed. The second was at a military barracks. The French authorities requested extradition. The defendant was committed by the

Bow Street magistrate with a view to his surrender under the Extradition Act 1870. He applied for a writ of habeas corpus. One of the grounds was that the crimes with which he was charged were offences of a political character within the meaning of s 3 of the 1870 Act. It was conceded that the explosion at the café could not be regarded as a political offence. But it was argued that the explosion at the barracks was on a different footing, since it was aimed at soldiers of the French government, and designed to destroy government property. The Divisional Court refused the application. The defendant was not seeking to impose his choice of government on the French. He was a member of the Anarchist movement, and therefore the enemy of all governments. Cave J said (at 419):

> 'Their efforts are directed primarily against the general body of citizens. They may, secondarily and incidentally, commit offences against some particular Government; but anarchist offences are mainly directed against private citizens.'

Although the offences in *Re Meunier* bear a strong resemblance to the offences in the present case, the difference is that T is not an anarchist. His case is that he was seeking to change the government of Algeria. To that extent his motive was clearly political. The question, as will be seen later, is whether this is enough to bring him within the political exception.

Schtraks v Government of Israel [1962] 3 All ER 529, [1964] AC 556 arose out of a dispute concerning the education of a seven-year-old boy in Israel. There were proceedings in the High Court of Israel brought by the boy's parents against his uncle, the appellant, and his grandparents, seeking an order for the boy's return. The uncle gave evidence in the proceedings. He was subsequently charged in Israel with offences of child-stealing and perjury. Meanwhile he had come to England. The Israeli government sought his extradition. One of the questions was whether the offences with which he was charged were political offences. There was evidence that in Israel the religious education of children is a political issue. The boy's future was the subject of questions and debates in the Knesset, where the uncle's actions received considerable political support. So the offences were committed in a political context. Nevertheless, it was held that the offences were not political offences. Lord Reid said ([1962] 3 All ER 529 at 536, [1964] AC 556 at 584):

> 'I am willing to assume that the accused did what he believed to be right, and that many people and even a whole political party agreed with him, but I cannot find any political character in the alleged offences. There is nothing to indicate that he acted as he did in order to force or even promote a change of government, or even a change of government policy, or to achieve a political objective of any kind. I do not say that every act done for such purposes would necessarily be of a political character, but without any such purpose it could only be in some exceptional case which I cannot foresee that the act could in my view be said to be of a political character.'

Viscount Radcliffe said ([1962] 3 All ER 529 at 540, [1964] AC 556 at 591):

> 'In my opinion the idea that lies behind the phrase "offence of a political character" is that the fugitive is at odds with the state that applies for his

a   extradition on some issue connected with the political control or government of the country.'

The essential idea, in Lord Radcliffe's view, was that of political opposition between the fugitive and the requesting state. That idea would be lost sight of—

b   'if one were to say that all offences were political offences, so long as they could be shown to have been committed for a political object or with a political motive or for the furtherance of some political cause or campaign. There may, for instance, be all sorts of contending political organisations or forces in a country, and members of them may commit all sorts of infractions of the criminal law in the belief that by so doing they will further their political ends: but if the central government stands apart and is concerned c   only to enforce the criminal law that has been violated by these contestants, I see no reason why fugitives should be protected by this country from its jurisdiction on the ground that they are political offenders.' (See [1962] 3 All ER 529 at 540, [1964] AC 556 at 591–592.)

d   On the facts, the case had become to some extent a political issue, as Lord Radcliffe accepted.   But the offences were not committed as part of a demonstration against government policy. They were more in the nature of incidents in a family quarrel.

In *Tzu-Tsai Cheng v Governor of Pentonville Prison* [1973] 2 All ER 204, [1973] AC 931 the appellant was a resident of the United States. He had been convicted of e   the attempted murder in the United States of the Vice-Premier of Formosa. The United States government sought his extradition from the United Kingdom. His case was that he was a member of an organisation known as the World United for Formosan Independence, and that his crime was therefore a political offence. The argument was rejected. Although the appellant was opposed to the regime in Formosa, he was not opposed to the government of the United States, where f   the offence was committed. To extend the concept of a political offence to crimes committed in a third country would, in the words of Lord Hodson be to 'create an impossible situation' (see [1973] 2 All ER 204 at 207, [1973] AC 931 at 943).

Lord Diplock, while accepting that the crime in question was a political *act*, held that it was not a political *offence*:

g   'I would not hold that an act constituted an *"offence of a political character"* in the ordinary meaning of that phrase appearing in a statute dealing with the trial and punishment of crimes committed in a foreign state if the only "political" purpose which the offender sought to achieve by it was not directed against the government or governmental policies of that state h   within whose territory the offence is committed and which is the only other party to the trial and punishment of the offence.' (See [1973] 2 All ER 204 at 209, [1973] AC 931 at 945; Lord Diplock's emphasis.)

The importance of the case for present purposes lies in Lord Diplock's discussion of the word 'political'. If the accused had killed a dictator in the hope of changing j   the government of the country, his object would be sufficiently immediate to justify the epithet 'political'.   For politics are about government.   But if the accused had robbed a bank in order to obtain funds to support a political party, the object would be too remote to constitute a political offence. In other words, a crime will only be regarded as a political offence if the relationship between the act and the effect on the government is sufficiently close.

This principle was applied in *R v Governor of Winson Green Prison, Birmingham,* *a*
ex p Littlejohn [1975] 3 All ER 208, [1975] 1 WLR 893. The government of the
Republic of Ireland sought the extradition of a member of the IRA on a charge of
armed robbery at a bank. There was an application for a writ of habeas corpus.
Lord Widgery CJ, giving judgment in the Divisional Court, held that despite the
applicant's connection with the IRA and despite the fact that the purpose of those
taking part in the robbery was to obtain money for the IRA and not for *b*
themselves, the crime was nevertheless a non-political offence.

I come now to some of the United States cases. The early decisions owed
much to the English decision in *Re Castioni* [1891] 1 QB 149, [1886–90] All ER Rep
640. An offence was treated as being of a political character if, but only if, it was
incidental to a political uprising. Applying this test, the US courts at first refused
extradition of members of the IRA accused of murdering British soldiers (see *c*
McMullen v Immigration and Naturalization Service (1981) 658 F 2d 1312 and *Re*
Mackin (1981) 668 F 2d 122. But by the beginning of the 1980s the traditional and
over-rigid approach of the US courts was beginning to break down. In *Eain v*
Wilkes (1981) 641 F 2d 504, a member of the Palestine Liberation Organisation
was accused of planting a bomb in a crowded market place in Israel, killing two *d*
boys and injuring many others. The State of Israel applied for extradition. The
accused relied on the political exception. The Seventh Circuit Court of Appeals
dismissed his appeal. The court was prepared to accept that there was a state of
conflict in Israel sufficient to lay the foundation for the political exception. But
the court went on to hold that the crime was not 'reasonably "incidental to"' the
state of conflict because of the indiscriminate nature of the attack (see 641 F 2d *e*
504 at 520). The court said (at 521):

'The exception does not make a random bombing intended to result in the
cold-blooded murder of civilians incidental to a purpose of toppling a
government, absent a direct link between the perpetrator, a political
organization's political goals, and the specific act. Rather, the indiscriminate *f*
bombing of a civilian populace is not recognized as a protected political act
even when the larger "political" objective of the person who sets off the
bomb may be to eliminate the civilian population of a country.'

The court then drew an important distinction between the political structure of *g*
a state, and its social fabric, quoting the English decision in *Re Meunier* [1894] 2 QB
415. The court commented (at 521–522):

'Anarchy presents the extreme situation of violent political activity
directed at civilians and serves to highlight the considerations appropriate for
this country's judiciary in construing the requirements of our extradition *h*
laws and treaties. But we emphasize that in this case, even assuming some
measure of PLO involvement, we are presented with a situation that solely
implicates anarchist-like activity, i.e., the destruction of a political system by
undermining the social foundation of the government. The record in this
case does not indicate that petitioner's alleged acts were anarchist-inspired. *j*
Yet the bombing, standing detached as it is from any substantial tie to
political activity (and even if tied, as petitioner insists, to certain aspects of the
PLO's strategy to achieve its goals), is so closely analogous to anarchist
doctrine considered in cases like *Re Meunier* ([1894] 2 QB 415) as to be almost
indistinguishable.'

a   Since the bombing was directed at the civilian population, 'without regard for political affiliation or governmental or military status of the victims', the accused was not entitled to the benefit of the political exception.

Eain v Wilkes was followed by the District Court of the Southern District of New York in Re Doherty (1984) 599 F Supp 270, which concerned an attack by a member of the Provisional IRA on a convoy of British soldiers in Northern

b   Ireland. The court rejected the United Kingdom's request for extradition. But it stated firmly that the political exception would not protect bombings in public places (see 599 F Supp 270 at 275).

The next important case was Quinn v Robinson (1986) 783 F 2d 776, a decision of the Ninth Circuit Court of Appeals. There is a very long and learned judgment of Judge Reinhardt, in which he traces the origin and development of the political

c   exception in the English, French, Swiss and US legal systems. The case arose out of the activities of the so-called 'Balcombe Street Four,' who were responsible for a series of terrorist incidents in 1974, directed at civilian targets in Great Britain, culminating in the shooting of PC Tibble in February 1975. Judge Reinhardt upheld the United Kingdom's request for extradition, but only on the narrow

d   ground that, although there was an uprising in Northern Ireland, the uprising did not extend to England, and so the terrorist incidents were not 'incidental' to any relevant uprising. This surprising conclusion was rejected by the other two members of the court. However, Judge Fletcher concurred in the result on other grounds. It is the other grounds which are relevant to the present purposes.

The thrust of Judge Reinhardt's judgment, with which Judge Fletcher agreed,

e   was to reverse the trend started by Eain v Wilkes. He did not accept that there was any distinction between military and civil targets. Nor did he attach any importance to the means used, whether discriminate or indiscriminate. He said (at 804–805, 810):

f   '... it is not our place to impose our notions of civilized strife on people who are seeking to overthrow the regimes in control of their countries in contexts and circumstances that we have not experienced, and which we can identify only with the greatest difficulty. It is the fact that the insurgents are seeking to change their governments that makes the political offense exception applicable, not their reasons for wishing to do so or the nature of

g   the acts by which they hope to accomplish that goal ... We believe the tactics that are used in such internal political struggles are simply irrelevant to the question whether the political offense exception is applicable ... It is for the revolutionaries, not the courts, to determine what tactics may help further their chances of bringing down or changing the government.'

h   Judge Fletcher said (at 819):

        'The new limitations imposed by the courts in Eain v. Wilkes ((1981) 641 F 2d 504) and in In Re Doherty ((1984) 599 F Supp 270) unnecessarily break from the traditional test by inquiring into [and] evaluating the legitimacy of given

j   political objectives and the conduct of internal political struggles.'

Not surprisingly, Mr Blake counsel for the appellant, set much store by Quinn v Robinson. But the minority judge, Judge Duniway, said that he could not concur in the 'lengthy opinion of Judge Reinhardt, or the very extensive dicta that it expounds'. He much preferred the rationale of Seventh Circuit Court of Appeals in Eain v Wilkes, where the court held that the political character of the offence

provision did not apply to 'the indiscriminate bombing' of a civilian populace. It *a*
is the minority view that has found favour in subsequent cases.

In *Re Atta (Mahmoud Abed)* (1989) 706 F Supp 1032 the US District Court for the
Eastern District of New York was concerned with an attack by three members of
the Abu Nidal Organisation on a bus in Israel. The driver was killed, and one of
the passengers en route for Tel Aviv was injured. One of the attackers escaped to
Venezuela, and thence to the United States. The government of Israel requested *b*
extradition. District Judge Korman certified accordingly. He summarised the
case law as sustaining the proposition that 'the United States does not regard the
indiscriminate use of violence against civilians as a political offense' (see 706 F
Supp 1032 at 1039). He dealt in short order with Judge Reinhardt's judgment in
Quinn v Robinson. He said (at 1040): *c*

'Setting aside the fact that the qualifications of the rule as set forth by Judge
Reinhardt cannot be reconciled with the sweeping rhetoric of his opinion, his
analysis is flawed for a number of reasons ... The decision to extradite
involves principally a decision regarding who may have refuge here.
Whether or not it is "our place to impose our notions of civilized strife on *d*
people who are seeking to overthrow the regimes in control of their
countries," it is plainly our place to decide who may obtain safe harbor in, or
passage through, the United States. Providing refuge for those who seek
political change is one thing, making the United States a haven for those who
engage in conduct that "violates our own notions of civilized strife" is quite
another matter.' *e*

When the case reached the Second Circuit Court of Appeals ((1990) 910 F 2d
1063) Judge Van Graafeiland agreed with District Judge Korman. He said (at
1066): *f*

'We agree that an attack on a commercial bus carrying civilian passengers
on a regular route is not a political offense. Political motivation does not
convert every crime into a political offense.'

All the US decisions so far considered have been extradition cases. I now come
to a refugee case. In *McMullen v Immigration and Naturalization Service* (1986) 788 *g*
F 2d 591 (a follow-up of the case referred to above) the Ninth Circuit Court of
Appeals were concerned with an application for deportation of a former member
of the Provisional IRA, who had committed numerous terrorist crimes between
1972 and 1974 in Northern Ireland and on the mainland. He relied on
s 243(h)(2)(C) of the Immigration and Nationalisation Act which corresponds *h*
exactly to art 1F(b) of the 1951 convention. In giving the leading judgment of the
court, Judge Wallace (at 595) quoted with approval the test stated in Goodwin-
Gill *The Refugee in International Law* (1983) pp 60–61:

'The nature and purpose of the offence require examination, including
whether it was committed out of genuine political motives or merely for *j*
personal reasons or gain, whether it was directed towards a modification of
the political organization or the very structure of the state, and whether
there is a close and direct causal link between the crime committed and its
alleged political purpose and object. The political element should in
principle outweigh the common law character of the offence, which may not

a
be the case if the acts committed are grossly disproportionate to the objective, or are of an atrocious or barbarous nature.'

The court held that there was a distinction between terrorist acts directed at military or official agencies of the state, and random acts of violence against ordinary citizens that are intended only '"to promote social chaos"' (*Eain v Wilkes* (1981) 641 F 2d 504 at 519), and citing *Re Meunier*. The court distinguished its own
b
previous decision in *Quinn v Robinson* 783 F 2d 776 on the unsatisfactory ground that the case was concerned with extradition (and as 'a distinction without a difference' (see 788 F 2d 591 at 598, 600 per Judge Goodwin)). There is then an extensive quotation from *Eain v Wilkes* 641 F 2d 504 at 520. The court concluded:

c
'the PIRA's random acts of violence against the ordinary citizens of Northern Ireland and elsewhere … are not sufficiently linked to their political objective and, by virtue of their primary targets, so barbarous, atrocious and disproportionate to their political objectives that they constitute "serious non-political crimes" …' (See 788 F 2d 591 at 598.)

d
There have, so far as I know, been no decisions of the Supreme Court of the United States since *Ornelas v Ruiz* (1896) 161 US 502. But the recent decisions of the Second, Seventh and Ninth Circuit Courts of Appeals to which I have referred are a sufficient indication that in US law any definition of 'serious non-political offence' would necessarily include the indiscriminate bombing of the civilian population. The contrary view stated by the divided court in *Quinn v Robinson*,
e
on which Mr Blake relied so strongly, can no longer be regarded as authoritative.

I come last, in this review of the authorities, to the Canadian case, *Re Gil and Minister of Employment and Immigration* (1994) 119 DLR (4th) 497 from which I have derived the greatest help. There is a full account of all the English and American authorities, to which I have myself referred. There is, in addition, a reference to *Folkerts v Public Prosecutor* (1978) 74 ILR 498 at 501, a decision of the
f
Supreme Court of the Netherlands, emphasising the objective nature of one aspect of the test:

g
'"In judging whether the political aspect of the offences concerned is of predominant importance, the court has at all times applied the following criterion: could the offenders reasonably have expected that the offences— separately or combined—would yield any result directly related to the ultimate political goal described above?"' (See 119 DLR (4th) 497 at 512).

There is also a useful reference to *Ellis v O'Dea* [1991] ILRM 346, in which the President of the High Court of Ireland echoed the prevailing American view as to
h
indiscriminate violence. All these cases, except *Quinn v Robinson*, point in the same direction. The facts of *Gil's* case were that the appellant, an Iranian citizen, came from a family which had supported the Shah. After the Ayatollah Khomeini came to power, he became a member of a group which planted bombs on the business premises of Khomeini's supporters in the bazaar, which resulted in the death of many innocent bystanders. Hugessen J rejected the appellant's
j
application for asylum. He said (119 DLR (4th) 497 at 515–516):

'There is, in my view, simply no objective rational connection between injuring the commercial interests of certain wealthy supporters of the regime and any realistic goal of forcing the regime itself to fall or to change its ways or its policies.'

At the end of his judgment, he drew a contrast between the plot against Hitler in *a*
1943 and the assassination of John F Kennedy. He then concluded (at 517–518):

'These considerations, however, do not come into play in the present case
for, although there is no doubt as to the extremely repressive nature of the
regime in Iran, the appellant's claim fails for other reasons: notably, the lack
of nexus between the crimes and any realistic political objective, and the fact
that the means employed are unacceptable as a form of political protest *b*
against any regime, no matter how repressive, totalitarian or dictatorial.'

The reasoning in *Gil's* case is in line with the recent authorities in the United
States. Your Lordships should, I think, hesitate long before rejecting this view of
the law.
   Another important source of law (though it does not have the force of law *c*
itself) is the UN *Handbook on Procedures and Criteria for Determining Refugee Status
under the 1951 Convention relating to the Status of Refugees* (1979) published by the
Office of the UN High Commissioner for Refugees.
   Paragraph 152 states:
                                                                              d
'In determining whether an offence is "non-political" or is, on the contrary,
a "political" crime, regard should be given in the first place to its nature and
purpose i.e. whether it has been committed out of genuine political motives
and not merely for personal reasons or gain. There should also be a close and
direct causal link between the crime committed and its alleged political
purpose and object. The political element of the offence should also *e*
outweigh its common-law character. This would not be the case if the acts
committed are grossly out of proportion to the alleged objective. The
political nature of the offence is also more difficult to accept if it involves acts
of an atrocious nature.'

   Finally, mention should be made of the European Convention on the *f*
Suppression of Terrorism (Strasbourg, 27 January 1977; TS 93 (1978) Cmnd 7390).
The convention is not, of course, directly relevant in the present case. But it
represents an attempt to limit by agreement among member states the
availability of the political exception in extradition cases. Under art 1, a number
of offences are not to be regarded as political offences, including any offence *g*
involving the use of a bomb. Under art 13.1, member states were entitled to
enter a reservation at the time of signing or depositing its instrument of
ratification; and a number of states, including France, did so. But such states
undertook to take into due consideration, when evaluating the character of an
offence, any particularly serious aspects of the offence, including:
                                                                              h
'(a) that it created a collective danger to the life, physical integrity or liberty
of persons; or (b) that it affected persons foreign to the motives behind it; or
(c) that cruel or vicious means have been used in the commission of the
offence.'

   Paragraph 21 of the Explanatory Report states: *j*

'The Convention applies only to particularly odious and serious acts often
affecting persons foreign to the motives behind them. The seriousness of
these acts and their consequences are such that their criminal element
outweighs their possible political aspects.'

a Taking these various sources of law into account one can arrive at the following definition. A crime is a political crime for the purposes of art 1F(b) of the 1951 convention if, and only if; (1) it is committed for a political purpose, that is to say, with the object of overthrowing or subverting or changing the government of a state or inducing it to change its policy; and (2) there is a sufficiently close and direct link between the crime and the alleged political

b purpose. In determining whether such a link exists, the court will bear in mind the means used to achieve the political end, and will have particular regard to whether the crime was aimed at a military or governmental target, on the one hand, or a civilian target on the other, and in either event whether it was likely to involve the indiscriminate killing or injuring of members of the public.

Although I have referred to the above statement as a definition, I bear in mind

c Lord Radcliffe's warning in *Schtraks v Government of Israel* [1962] 3 All ER 529, [1964] AC 556, that a question which was first posed judicially more than 100 years ago in *Re Castioni* [1891] 1 QB 149, [1886–90] All ER Rep 640 is unlikely now to receive a definitive answer. The most that can be attempted is a description of an idea. But to fall short of a description would, in Lord Radcliffe's words, be to

d abdicate a necessary responsibility, if the idea of a political crime is to continue to form part of the apparatus of judicial decision-making.

I now turn to apply the above 'definition' to the facts of the present case. As already briefly mentioned, the FIS is a political organisation which seeks to secure power in Algeria, in order to establish a fundamentalist Islamic regime in that country. In June 1991 the then government of Algeria declared a state of siege.

e Many people were detained, and some ill-treated. In September 1991 it was announced that elections would be held. In December 1991 the FIS secured a majority in the first round of the elections, and looked virtually certain to win the second and final round, and so form the next government. But the second round of elections never took place. A military clique was formed, and a new President

f appointed. This was followed by rioting and protests, in the course of which many members of the FIS were arrested. In March 1992 the FIS was declared an illegal organisation.

In the light of those facts it is clear that FIS is a political organisation which was thwarted in an attempt to become the government of Algeria by democratic means. T's motive in becoming involved in the bombing of the airport is not in

g doubt. He was attempting to overthrow the government by what he regarded as the only remaining available means. He therefore satisfies the first, or subjective, condition.

But does he satisfy the second, or objective, condition? On the findings of the Immigration Appeal Tribunal, T was an active member of a terrorist organisation

h which was prepared to advance its aims by random killing. He was closely associated with the attack on the airport. Although the airport itself could be regarded as a governmental target, the crime as carried out was almost bound to involve the killing of members of the public. The means used were indiscriminate, and therefore the link between the crime and the political object

j which T was seeking to achieve was too remote.

In the light of the above considerations, the Immigration Appeal Tribunal was entitled to hold that there were 'serious reasons for considering' that T had committed a serious non-political crime outside the United Kingdom. I can find no error of law in the conclusion at which they arrived, nor any error in the reasoning of the Court of Appeal, with which I agree.

It is unnecessary to consider whether the attack on the barracks was a serious *a*
non-political crime, and I say nothing on that issue.

I would dismiss the appeal.

Appeal dismissed.

Celia Fox   Barrister.

R v Secretary of State for the Home Department, ex parte Onibiyo

a

COURT OF APPEAL, CIVIL DIVISION

SIR THOMAS BINGHAM MR, ROCH AND SWINTON THOMAS LJJ

b

4, 5, 28 MARCH 1996

Immigration – Leave to enter – Refugee – Asylum – Fear of persecution held by overstayer – Home Department ordering overstayer's deportation – Overstayer applying for asylum on basis of father's political activities and claiming risk of
c *persecution – Home Secretary refusing application – Applicant giving notice of fresh application on basis of new material – Whether new material constituting a fresh 'claim for asylum' – Asylum and Immigration Appeals Act 1993, s 1.*

On 26 March 1995 the applicant, an overstayer from Nigeria, made a claim for asylum under s 1ᵃ of the Asylum and Immigration Appeals Act 1993 as a refugee
d within the 1951 Convention relating to the Status of Refugees. His claim for asylum, which was based on the political activities of his father and the situation in Nigeria, was refused and his subsequent appeal under s 8(3)(b)ᵇ of the 1993 Act was dismissed. Following his father's deportation to Nigeria, the applicant purported to make a fresh application for asylum on the basis of factors and circumstances that had not previously been considered, namely that he had a
e well-founded fear of persecution in Nigeria for reasons of membership of a particular social group and political opinion, being a supporter of the opposition movement there. In addition, the applicant submitted evidence that his father had disappeared since returning to Nigeria. The Secretary of State considered that the applicant's representations did not constitute a fresh claim for asylum
f and that his father's situation and the political climate in Nigeria remained the basis of his application. He accordingly treated the applicant's representations as relevant to the original claim, but declined to alter his decision refusing asylum and indicated that, since he had made no fresh decision, the applicant had no available avenue of appeal open to him. The applicant applied for judicial review of the Secretary of State's decisions, but the judge dismissed his application,
g holding that no more than one 'claim for asylum' within the meaning of s 1 of the 1993 Act could be made during a single uninterrupted stay in the United Kingdom. The applicant appealed.

Held – A person could during a single uninterrupted stay in the United Kingdom
h make more than one 'claim for asylum' for the purposes of s 1 of the 1993 Act. The test of what constituted a fresh 'claim for asylum' was whether, comparing the fresh claim with that earlier rejected, and excluding material on which the claimant could reasonably have been expected to rely in the earlier claim, the new claim was sufficiently different from the earlier claim to admit of a realistic
j prospect that a favourable view could be taken of the new claim, despite the unfavourable conclusion reached on the earlier claim. The question whether such a claim had been made was to be determined by the Secretary of State (in the first instance) and the immigration appellate authorities, whose

---

a   Section 1, so far as material, is set out at p 906 *h*, post
b   Section 8, so far as material, is set out at p 906 *j* to p 907 *d*, post

determinations were susceptible to challenge only on *Wednesbury* principles; the
court therefore had no power to review as an objective precedent fact the issue
whether a fresh 'claim for asylum' had been made or not. Since the applicant had
accepted before the judge that he could not impugn the Secretary of State's
decision as irrational, it followed that his appeal would be dismissed (see p 908 *j*,
p 909 *e* to *g*, p 910 *e*, p 911 *e f*, p 912 *d* to *j* and p 913 *j*, post).

> *Bugdaycay v Secretary of State for the Home Dept* [1987] 1 All ER 940 applied.
>
> *Khawaja v Secretary of State for the Home Dept* [1983] 1 All ER 765 considered.

Notes

For political asylum and refugees, see 4(2) *Halsbury's Laws* (4th edn reissue) para
82.

For asylum for refugees and stateless persons under the international
conventions, see 18 *Halsbury's Laws* (4th edn) paras 1717–1722.

For the Asylum and Immigration Appeals Act 1993, ss 1, 8, see 31 *Halsbury's
Statutes* (4th edn) (1994 reissue) 215, 224.

Cases referred to in judgments

Associated Provincial Picture Houses Ltd v Wednesbury Corp [1947] 2 All ER 680,
  [1948] 1 KB 223, CA.
Bugdaycay v Secretary of State for the Home Dept [1987] 1 All ER 940, [1987] AC 514,
  [1987] 2 WLR 606, HL.
Kalunga v Secretary of State for the Home Dept [1994] Imm AR 585, CA.
Khawaja v Secretary of State for the Home Dept [1983] 1 All ER 765, [1984] AC 74,
  [1983] 2 WLR 321, HL.
Ladd v Marshall [1954] 3 All ER 745, [1954] 1 WLR 1489, CA.
M v Secretary of State for the Home Dept [1996] 1 All ER 870, [1996] 1 WLR 507, CA.
R v Secretary of State for the Home Dept, ex p Kazmi [1995] Imm AR 73.
*Sandralingham v Secretary of State for the Home Dept, Rajandrakumar v Immigration
  Appeal Tribunal* [1996] Imm AR 97, CA.
Singh v Secretary of State for the Home Dept [1995] CA Transcript 1618; *affg* (18 July
  1995, unreported), QBD.

Cases also cited or referred to in skeleton arguments

Garlick v Oldham Metropolitan BC [1993] 2 All ER 65, [1993] AC 509, HL; *rvsg* sub
  nom *R v Tower Hamlets London BC, ex p Begum* [1993] 1 All ER 447, [1993] QB
  447, CA.
Khaboka v Secretary of State for the Home Dept [1993] Imm AR 484, CA.
R v Immigration Appeal Tribunal, ex p Enwia [1983] 2 All ER 1045, [1984] 1 WLR 117,
  CA.
R v Immigration Appeal Tribunal, ex p Secretary of State for the Home Dept [1990] 3 All
  ER 652, [1990] 1 WLR 1126, CA; *affg* [1990] Imm AR 166, DC.
R v Secretary of State for the Home Dept, ex p Fahmi [1994] Imm AR 447.
*R v Secretary of State for the Home Dept, ex p Sivakumaran (UN High Comr for Refugees
  intervening)* [1988] 1 All ER 193, [1988] AC 958, HL.
R v Secretary of State for the Home Dept, ex p Stefan [1995] Imm AR 410.
Secretary of State for the Home Dept v Savchenkov [1996] Imm AR 28, CA.
Tarling, Re [1979] 1 All ER 981, [1979] 1 WLR 1417, DC.

Appeal

By notice dated 20 February 1996 the applicant, Ademola Onibiyo, appealed with
leave from the decision of Latham J made on 19 January 1996 dismissing his

a application for judicial review of three decisions of the Secretary of State for the Home Department, whereby he (i) refused to issue a formal notice of refusal of asylum, (ii) refused to refer fresh material supplied by the applicant back to the immigration appellate authorities under s 21 of the Immigration Act 1971 and (iii) issued directions for the applicant's removal to Nigeria. The facts are set out in the judgment of Sir Thomas Bingham MR.

b
Nicholas Blake QC and *Duran Seddon* (instructed by *Fisher Meredith*) for the applicant.

Neil Garnham (instructed by the *Treasury Solicitor*) for the Secretary of State.

Cur adv vult
c

28 March 1996. The following judgments were delivered.

SIR THOMAS BINGHAM MR.   This appeal raises questions of general importance on the law and practice of asylum in the United Kingdom. If asylum
d has been claimed and refused, and the claimant has pursued his rights of appeal without success, may he make another claim for asylum, and if so in what circumstances and with what procedural consequences?

I

The applicant, Mr Ademola Onibiyo, is a Nigerian born on 7 December 1975
e and now aged 20.   On 29 August 1987 when he was aged 11 he arrived in the United Kingdom with his mother and two younger siblings, having flown from Nigeria via Frankfurt. His father had entered the United Kingdom in 1964 and had acquired settled status.   He had lost this status on returning to Nigeria between 1977 and 1983. But he had returned here in 1984 and had been granted
f leave to enter as a student for 12 months. Two of the applicant's older siblings had been born in this country and become United Kingdom citizens.

On his arrival in August 1987 the applicant was granted leave to enter as a visitor for six months until 29 February 1988.   That period was extended for a further six months until 29 August 1988. He applied out of time for leave to remain but leave was refused on 26 November 1991.
g
On 24 June 1993 the applicant was arrested as an overstayer and served with notice of intention to deport. He exercised his right of appeal, but at the hearing of the appeal it was conceded on his behalf that there was no ground for challenging the decision to deport. The appeal was accordingly dismissed, although the adjudicator recommended that the applicant be allowed to remain
h in the country until the end of that academic year. The applicant was, and has since (when at liberty) been, engaged in study at various colleges.

On 14 November 1994 an order was signed for the applicant to be deported and this order was served on him on 25 March 1995 when he was detained at Kennington Police Station.   Removal directions were given for 27 March 1995.
j On 26 March 1995 the applicant applied for asylum. In his then solicitors' letter of that date the application was put on the ground—

'that he is of the Tribe of Yoruba, the same as their leader, Mr Abiola. This particular tribe have been objects of hatred by the Abacha Government and are being persecuted intensely and he fears that his life will be in danger if he is returned to Nigeria.'

The applicant was interviewed: in answer to questions he referred, in general terms, to political activities of his father and made plain that his own claim for asylum was based on his father's political activities.

On 1 July 1995 the Secretary of State refused the applicant's claim for asylum. His reasons were set out in a long letter of that date. The Secretary of State did not find it credible that the applicant had a well-founded fear of returning to Nigeria because of his father's political activities and concluded that the claim for asylum had been concocted purely in an attempt to avoid removal from the United Kingdom. The applicant was served with a notice dated 11 July 1995 informing him that the Secretary of State had decided to treat his application as a request for the revocation of the deportation order previously made against him. He was told that the Secretary of State had refused his application for asylum and had accordingly refused to revoke the deportation order.

On 1 August 1995 the applicant exercised his right to appeal against this decision under s 8(3)(b) of the Asylum and Immigration Appeals Act 1993, to which reference is made below. He was released on bail. The applicant's appeal was heard on 18 September 1995, together with an appeal by his father (with his dependent wife and children), on whose behalf a claim for asylum had also been made. It was plain that the applicant could not succeed as a minor dependant of his father, since he was not under the age of 18. His claim for asylum therefore had to be judged on its own merits. It was conceded by counsel on his behalf that he could not establish a well-founded fear of persecution for a convention reason (see the Convention Relating to the Status of Refugees (Geneva, 28 July 1951; TS 39 (1954); Cmd 9171)). The special adjudicator observed:

'His application for asylum was made when it was quite clear from his interview that he could not hope to qualify for refugee status in his own right. It was quite rightly conceded straight away before me that he could not succeed. This, in my view, amounts in effect to an abuse of process and I conclude the application was only used as a means of delaying his departure and to seek a recommendation.'

The father's claim for asylum was also held to be entirely without merit and his appeal also was dismissed. The applicant was again detained. Both he and his father were refused leave to appeal to the Immigration Appeal Tribunal on 4 October 1995.

The applicant's father was returned to Lagos under escort on 26 October 1995. It is said that he was expected to make contact with his family and colleagues in this country on his return to Nigeria but has not done so. On the evidence before the court, nothing has been seen or heard of the father since his arrival at the airport in Lagos.

On 27 October 1995 the Secretary of State wrote to the applicant's solicitors informing them of his intention to deport the applicant. The solicitors made representations against this course, and by letter of 30 November 1995 gave notice of a fresh application for political asylum on behalf of the applicant. The grounds of this application were elaborated in a letter of 4 December 1995, in which it was stated that the application was a new one and based on factors and circumstances that had not previously been considered. The letter said that the applicant had a well-founded fear of being persecuted in Nigeria 'for reasons of membership of a particular social group and political opinion'. He was said to be a supporter of and associated with the opposition movement in Nigeria. Enclosed with the letter or sent at the same time were a statement of the applicant, a letter from the Nigerian Democratic Movement (UK), an extract a from a report of the Parliamentary Human Rights Group on the situation in Nigeria, an October 1995 report of the Refugee Council on the Home Office and Nigeria entitled 'Beyond Belief' (a critique of the Home Office's assessment of the human rights situation in Nigeria), and a report on Nigeria of a mission established pursuant to the Commonwealth Human Rights Initiative. Reference was made to recent events in Nigeria and in particular to the execution of Mr Ken b Saro-Wiwa and eight other Ogoni people.

By letters written on 5 and 6 December 1995 the applicant's solicitors urged the Home Office to defer the removal of the applicant, to give proper consideration to his claim for political asylum and to allow time for them to gather evidence. They asked that the request for political asylum should be read as including a request to revoke the deportation order in force against the applicant. The Home c Office replied in a letter of 6 December 1995. This letter acknowledged the applicant's solicitors' representations and enclosures, some of which the Home Office had already received and considered. The letter said:

d   'The Secretary of State has given careful consideration to the issues you have raised but is of the view that your representations of 4 December do not constitute a *fresh claim for asylum*. Although, it is now claimed that Mr Onibiyo is a supporter of and is associated with the opposition in Nigeria and that his political convictions would cause him difficulty it is still the situation of Mr Onibiyo's father and the political climate in Nigeria that remains the basis of his application. Accordingly your letter of 4 December 1995 has been e   treated as further information to Mr Onibiyo's original asylum claim.' (The Home Office's emphasis.)

The Home Office (it was said) had no evidence that the applicant's father was detained and no reason to believe that ordinary supporters of the pro-democracy movement or their relatives were likely to be subject to persecution. The f Secretary of State had carefully considered the applicant's request for revocation of the deportation order against him, but did not consider that there had been any material change in circumstances since the previous refusal decision sufficient to justify revocation and he was not prepared to delay further the deportation of the applicant. The applicant's solicitors took issue with this letter by a letter written g on the same date, 6 December 1995, and enclosed a notice of appeal to a special adjudicator under s 8(3)(b) of the 1993 Act. The Home Office maintained its position. In a letter of 7 December 1995 an official said:

h   'I am aware that you have treated my letter of 6 December as a refusal of asylum and have accordingly submitted notice of appeal to the Special Adjudicator. However, as explained in my letter of 6 December your representations of 4 December were not considered as a fresh asylum application but as further information to Mr Onibiyo's original asylum claim of 26 March 1995. Therefore, my letter of 6 December does not constitute a refusal of asylum but a consideration and dismissal of the further information j   you provided in your letter of 4 December. In the circumstances the Secretary of State has not made a fresh decision and your appeal of 6 December 1995 is invalid as there is no decision on which you have an avenue of appeal to the appellate authorities.'

The Home Office did, however, agree to a deferment of the applicant's removal. By letters written on 11 and 12 December the applicant's solicitors and the Home Office reiterated their respective positions.

On 13 December 1995 the applicant made an application for leave to move for
judicial review. The decisions which he sought to challenge were the refusal of
the Home Office on 12 December 1995 to issue a formal notice of refusal of
asylum, the decision of the Home Office of 12 December 1995 refusing to refer
the fresh material which the applicant had supplied back to the immigration
appellate authorities under s 21 of the Immigration Act 1971, and the directions
given for the removal of the applicant. Dyson J gave leave to move and the
application came before Latham J on 19 January 1996. He dismissed the
application and the applicant now appeals against that decision with the leave of
the judge.

II

The Geneva Convention, read with the 1967 Protocol (New York, 31 January
1967; TS 15 (1969); Cmnd 3906), provides in art 33(1):

'No Contracting State shall expel or return ("refouler") a refugee in any
manner whatsoever to the frontiers of territories where his life or freedom
would be threatened on account of his race, religion, nationality,
membership of a particular social group or political opinion.'

This is the overriding obligation to which states party to the convention commit
themselves. The risk to an individual if a state acts in breach of this obligation is
so obvious and so potentially serious that the courts have habitually treated
asylum cases as calling for particular care at all stages of the administrative and
appellate processes. By art 1A of the convention as amended by the protocol a
refugee is any person who—

'owing to well-founded fear of being persecuted for reasons of race,
religion, nationality, membership of a particular social group or political
opinion, is outside the country of his nationality and is unable or, owing to
such fear, is unwilling to avail himself of the protection of that country; or
who, not having a nationality and being outside the country of his former
habitual residence ... is unable or, owing to such fear, is unwilling to return
to it.'

The 1993 Act was passed to make provision for persons who claim asylum in
the United Kingdom. Section 1 of the Act defined a 'claim for asylum' as
meaning—

'a claim made by a person (whether before or after the coming into force
of this section) that it would be contrary to the United Kingdom's obligations
under the Convention for him to be removed from, or required to leave, the
United Kingdom ...'

Section 2 provides that nothing in the immigration rules shall lay down any
practice which would be contrary to the convention. Section 6 provides:

'During the period beginning when a person makes a claim for asylum and
ending when the Secretary of State gives him notice of the decision on the
claim, he may not be removed from, or required to leave, the United
Kingdom.'

Section 8, so far as material, reads:

'(1) A person who is refused leave to enter the United Kingdom under the
1971 Act may appeal against the refusal to a special adjudicator on the

a
ground that his removal in consequence of the refusal would be contrary to the United Kingdom's obligations under the Convention.

(2) A person who has limited leave under the 1971 Act to enter or remain in the United Kingdom may appeal to a special adjudicator against any variation of, or refusal to vary, the leave on the ground that it would be contrary to the United Kingdom's obligations under the Convention for him

b
to be required to leave the United Kingdom after the time limited by the leave.

(3) Where the Secretary of State—(a) has decided to make a deportation order against a person by virtue of section 3(5) of the 1971 Act, or (b) has refused to revoke a deportation order made against a person by virtue of section 3(5) or (6) of that Act, the person may appeal to a special adjudicator

c
against the decision or refusal on the ground that his removal in pursuance of the order would be contrary to the United Kingdom's obligations under the Convention; but a person may not bring an appeal under both paragraph (a) and paragraph (b) above.

(4) Where directions are given as mentioned in section 16(1)(a) or (b) of

d
the 1971 Act for a person's removal from the United Kingdom, the person may appeal to a special adjudicator against the directions on the ground that his removal in pursuance of the directions would be contrary to the United Kingdom's obligations under the Convention ...'

Schedule 2 to the Act contains supplementary provisions governing appeals

e
under s 8. Paragraph 2 of the schedule provides that a person may not bring an appeal on any of the grounds mentioned in s 8(1) to (4) of the Act unless, before the time of the refusal, variation, decision or directions (as the case might be) he had made a claim for asylum. Paragraph 3 provides that a special adjudicator hearing an appeal under s 8 of 1993 Act shall deal in the same proceedings with

f
appeals under the 1971 Act.

The Asylum Appeals (Procedure) Rules 1993, SI 1993/1661, were made a few days after the passing of the 1993 Act. These rules provide, in r 5(2)(b), for notice of appeal to be given in two days in a case where the Secretary of State certifies the claim to be without foundation. In such a case the special adjudicator is required by r 9(2) to determine the appeal not later than seven days after

g
receiving notice of the appeal, as compared with 42 days in other cases. By r 22(3) of these rules, r 35 of the Immigration Appeals (Procedure) Rules 1984, SI 1984/2041, applies to asylum appeals. Rule 35 of the 1984 rules reads:

'(1) Subject to the provisions of paragraph (2) below, where it appears to

h
an appellate authority that the issues raised on an appeal have been determined—(a) in the case of an appeal before an adjudicator, by the same or another adjudicator or by the Tribunal, or (b) in the case of an appeal before the Tribunal, by the Tribunal, under Part II of the Act in previous proceedings to which the appellant was a party, on the basis of facts which did not materially differ from those to which the appeal relates, the authority

j
may forthwith determine the appeal without a hearing.

(2) Before an appellate authority determines an appeal without a hearing in accordance with paragraph (1) above, the authority shall give the parties an opportunity of making representations to the effect that the appeal ought not be so determined.'

Rule 26 of the 1993 rules provides:

'In rule 35 of the 1984 Rules, the reference in paragraph (1) to "previous proceedings" shall be treated as including proceedings under the 1993 Act.' *a*

In the Statement of Changes in Immigration Rules (HC Paper (1994) No 395) (the 1994 rules) the Home Secretary laid down rules to govern the practice to be followed in the case of asylum applications. In r 327 an asylum applicant was defined as— *b*

'a person who claims that it would be contrary to the United Kingdom's obligations under the United Nations Convention and Protocol relating to the Status of Refugees for him to be removed from or required to leave the United Kingdom.'

Such cases were to be described in the rules as asylum applications. Rule 328 *c* provided:

'All asylum applications will be determined by the Secretary of State in accordance with the United Kingdom's obligations under the United Nations Convention and Protocol relating to the Status of Refugees. Every asylum application made by a person at a port or airport in the United Kingdom will *d* be referred by the Immigration Officer for determination by the Secretary of State in accordance with these Rules.'

Until an asylum application has been determined by the Secretary of State, no action will be taken to require the departure of the asylum applicant or his dependants from the United Kingdom (see r 329). Rule 346 provides: *e*

'When an asylum applicant has previously been refused asylum in the United Kingdom and can demonstrate no relevant and substantial change in his circumstances since that date, his application will be refused.'

Rule 347 reads: *f*

'When an asylum applicant has come to the United Kingdom from another country which is party to the United Nations Convention relating to the Status of Refugees or its Protocol and which has considered and rejected an application for asylum from him, his application for asylum in the United Kingdom may be refused without substantive consideration of his claim to *g* refugee status. He may be removed to that country, or another country meeting the criteria of paragraph 345, and invited to raise any new circumstances with the authorities of the country which originally considered his application.'

h

III

The first issue argued in this court was whether, as a matter of law, a person may during a single uninterrupted stay in the United Kingdom make more than one 'claim for asylum'. By 'claim for asylum' is meant a claim falling within the definition in s 1 of the 1993 Act. The applicant argued that after dismissal of a first claim, a fresh claim could in law be made. The Secretary of State took a different *j* view: he argued that once a person had made a 'claim for asylum', been refused by the Secretary of State and unsuccessfully exercised his rights of appeal under s 8 of the 1993 Act, that exhausted his legal rights. He could lay new material before the Secretary of State and the latter, if so advised, could in the exercise of his discretion refer such material to a special adjudicator or the tribunal under s 21 of the 1971 Act (applicable to asylum cases by virtue of para 4(2)(d) of Sch 2 to the *a* 1993 Act) for consideration by that person or body. But once there had been one claim for asylum and one appeal, there could be no further 'claim for asylum' unless the claimant had left the United Kingdom and returned before making the fresh application.

The judge accepted the Secretary of State's argument. After a careful review of the relevant provisions and authorities, and of the arguments addressed to him,
b he said:

> 'I have therefore come to the conclusion that the statutory scheme of the 1993 Act envisages a claim for asylum which becomes a historical fact entitling the asylum seeker to exercise a right of appeal under s 8 against any relevant administrative decision or action. Any further material submitted
> *c* or applications made by or on behalf of the asylum seeker are submitted or made in support of the original claim, whether they are made before or after the Secretary of State has made his decision on the claim or before or after any appeal under s 8. If the appeal is dismissed, then the material or applications will be considered by [the] Secretary of State in the exercise of the discretion which it is accepted that he has, to reconsider his decision, and
> *d* if he considers it appropriate, to refer any matter arising out of those materials or applications to an adjudicator under s 21 of the 1971 Act.'

I prefer the applicant's argument on this point. The obligation of the United Kingdom under the 1951 convention is not to return a refugee (as defined) to a country where his life or freedom would be threatened for any reason specified
e in the convention. That obligation remains binding until the moment of return. A refugee (as defined) has a right not to be returned to such a country, and a further right not to be returned pending a decision whether he is a refugee (as defined) or not. It would in my judgment undermine the beneficial object of the convention and the measures giving effect to it in this country if the making of an
f unsuccessful application for asylum were to be treated as modifying the obligation of the United Kingdom or depriving a person of the right to make a fresh 'claim for asylum'. It cannot, in my view, make any difference whether the person making the fresh 'claim for asylum' has left the country and returned or remained here throughout.

Any other construction would in my view be offensive to common sense.
g However rarely they may arise in practice, it is not hard to imagine cases in which an initial 'claim for asylum' might be made on insubstantial, or even bogus, grounds, and be rightly rejected, but in which circumstances would arise or come to light showing a clear and serious threat of a kind recognised by the 1951 convention to the life or freedom of the formerly unsuccessful applicant. A
h scheme of legal protection which could not accommodate that possibility would in my view be seriously defective.

Nothing in the convention or in the measures summarised in section II above in my view supports the Secretary of State's construction. By contrast, it appears to me that r 35 of the 1984 rules and r 26 of the 1993 rules give some support to
j the applicant. I do not accept, in the absence of any indication to that effect, that r 346 of the 1994 rules only applies where an applicant has left the United Kingdom and returned. Rule 347 of the 1994 rules plainly envisages that an applicant may raise new circumstances with the authorities of another country following an initial refusal by those authorities, although in this instance an intervening visit to the United Kingdom is postulated.

Neither side suggested that this question was concluded by authority, but in my view the applicant has much the best of such relevant references as there are in the cases. In *Kalunga v Secretary of State for the Home Dept* [1994] Imm AR 585 at 588, counsel for the Secretary of State accepted—

> 'that there can be, depending on the circumstances, second, or further successive, applications for asylum, and that fresh removal directions, or the refusal to revoke such directions subsequently to such further applications, would trigger a further right of appeal.'

Balcombe, Staughton and Rose LJJ were content to accept that view, although only in the course of refusing, on other grounds, a renewed application for leave to move for judicial review. In *R v Secretary of State for the Home Dept, ex p Kazmi* [1995] Imm AR 73 Dyson J based part of his judgment on the assumption, not (it would seem) challenged in argument, that there could in law be a fresh 'claim for asylum'. In *Singh v Secretary of State for the Home Dept* (18 July 1995, unreported); *affd* [1995] CA Transcript 1618 both Carnwath J and the Court of Appeal accepted the legal possibility of a fresh claim and considered whether on the facts there had been such. In *M v Secretary of State for the Home Dept* [1996] 1 All ER 870, [1996] 1 WLR 507 the court rejected the argument that a prior unsuccessful claim could deprive a person of his right to make a later fresh claim, although again the applicant failed on the facts.

I differ from the judge on this first issue.

IV

It is plain from s 8 of the 1993 Act that an appeal lies not against the refusal of asylum, but against a decision made or action taken or not taken pursuant to a refusal of asylum. If, contrary to the Secretary of State's central submission, there can in law be a fresh 'claim for asylum' following an earlier refusal or refusals, three main questions arise for consideration.

(1) What constitutes a fresh claim?

(2) How and by whom is it decided whether a claim is a fresh claim or not?

(3) What are the procedural consequences of a decision that a claim is or is not a fresh claim?

These questions must be considered in turn.

(1) *A fresh claim?*

It was accepted for the applicant that a fresh 'claim for asylum' could not be made by advancing an obviously untenable claim or by repeating, even with some elaboration or addition, a claim already made, or by relying on evidence available to the applicant but not advanced at the time of an earlier claim. There had, counsel acknowledged, to be a significant change from the claim as previously presented, such as might reasonably lead a special adjudicator to take a different view. If the fresh claim depended on new evidence, then it had to satisfy tests, analogous to *Ladd v Marshall* [1954] 3 All ER 745, [1954] 1 WLR 1489, of previous unavailability, significance and credibility.

Stuart-Smith LJ considered this matter in *Singh's* case, where he said (with the agreement of Rose LJ and Sir John Balcombe):

> 'In my opinion, in deciding whether or not a fresh claim to asylum is made, it is necessary to analyse what are the essential ingredients of a claim to asylum and see whether any of those ingredients have changed. A useful analogy is to consider a cause of action. In order to establish a cause of action a plaintiff must prove certain ingredients. How he proves them is a matter of evidence. If he changes the essential ingredients, he is asserting a different

a cause of action. What are the essential ingredients of a claim for asylum? First, that the applicant has a well-founded fear of persecution; secondly, that he has that fear in relation to the country from whence he came; thirdly, that the source of the persecution is the authorities of that state or, alternatively, some other group of local population where the actions of the group are knowingly tolerated by the authorities, or that the authorities refused or are b unable to offer effective protection (see the *Handbook on Procedures and Criteria for Determining Refugee Status* published by the United Nations High Comr for Refugees (1979) para 65); finally, that the persecution is by reason of the applicant's race, religion, nationality or membership of a particular social or political group. In my view, it is only if the applicant asserts that one or more of these essential ingredients is different from his earlier claim that c it can be said to be a fresh claim.'

I agree with this passage, and with the propositions (quoted above) accepted by counsel for the applicant. There is danger in any form of words, which can too easily be regarded as a binding formula. In *Singh's* case Carnwath J held that a change in the character of the application was required. I am content with that d statement, provided it is not taken to mean that there must necessarily be a change in the nature of the persecution said to be feared. The acid test must always be whether, comparing the new claim with that earlier rejected, and excluding material on which the claimant could reasonably have been expected to rely in the earlier claim, the new claim is sufficiently different from the earlier e claim to admit of a realistic prospect that a favourable view could be taken of the new claim despite the unfavourable conclusion reached on the earlier claim.

(2) *Who is to decide?*
It is plain from r 328 of the 1994 rules that all asylum applications will be determined by the Secretary of State in the first instance.
f

(3) *Procedural consequences*
If the Secretary of State decides on a fresh claim to grant asylum, and the claimant is accordingly granted limited leave to enter, no procedural difficulty is likely to arise.
g If the Secretary of State recognises a fresh claim as a 'claim for asylum', but nonetheless decides that asylum should not be granted, I see no reason why the same consequences should not follow as on refusal of an initial claim. The disappointed claimant can pursue his right of appeal under s 8.

The problematical situation is that in which, as here, the Secretary of State does h not recognise a claim as a fresh 'claim for asylum' and so declines to make any decision or to take or omit to take any action which would trigger a right of appeal under s 8. Neither party suggested that the asylum-seeker was without redress in this situation, and both accepted that redress could be obtained only by resort to the court. But there agreement ended. The applicant argued that whether or not a fresh 'claim for asylum' had been made was a matter of j precedent fact to be decided, in case of dispute, by the court. The Secretary of State argued that the question was one for him and his decision, while not immune from challenge, could be challenged only on grounds of irrationality. The cases already referred to contain tentative expressions of opinion both ways.

The judge did not rule on this question, and it is not clear to what extent it was argued before him. It was not raised in the notice of appeal, and not explored in the applicant's skeleton argument in this court. No authority was cited to us. For reasons given in section V below, I do not regard the answer to the question as determinative of this appeal. Since the issue is one of importance, and also in my opinion of considerable difficulty, I accordingly proffer a tentative answer only.

The role of the court in the immigration field varies, depending on the legislative and administrative context. Where an exercise of administrative power is dependent on the establishment of an objective precedent fact the court will, if called upon to do so in case of dispute, itself rule whether such fact is established to the requisite standard. Thus, for example, where power to detain and remove is dependent on a finding that the detainee is an illegal entrant, one who has entered clandestinely or by fraud and deceit, the court will itself rule whether the evidence is such as to justify that finding (see *Khawaja v Secretary of State for the Home Dept* [1983] 1 All ER 765, [1984] AC 74). By contrast, the decision whether an asylum-seeker is a refugee is a question to be determined by the Secretary of State and the immigration appellate authorities, whose determinations are susceptible to challenge only on *Wednesbury* principles (see *Bugdaycay v Secretary of State for the Home Dept* [1987] 1 All ER 940, [1987] AC 514). I am of opinion, although with some misgivings, that the judgment whether a fresh 'claim for asylum' has been made should be assimilated with the latter, and not the former, class of judgment. If the test propounded in (1) above is correct, the answer to the question whether or not a fresh 'claim for asylum' has been made, will depend not on the finding of any objective fact, nor even on a literal comparison of the earlier and the later claim, but on an exercise of judgment, and this is a field in which the initial judgments are very clearly entrusted to the Secretary of State. In giving effect, for example, to r 346 of the 1994 rules, it must be for the Secretary of State and not for the court to rule whether the applicant can demonstrate a relevant and substantial change in circumstances since his refusal of an earlier application. In a case such as the present, the judgment is not very different from that which the Secretary of State may make under s 21 of the 1971 Act.

I would accordingly incline to accept the Secretary of State's argument on this point, while observing that decisions reached by him are susceptible to challenge on any *Wednesbury* ground, of which irrationality is only one (see *Associated Provincial Picture Houses Ltd v Wednesbury Corp* [1947] 2 All ER 680, [1948] 1 KB 223).

V

The applicant accepted before the judge that he could not impugn the Secretary of State's decisions of 12 December 1995 as irrational, and no other ground of *Wednesbury* challenge was advanced save that considered in section VI below. If my answer to (3) in section IV above is correct, therefore, it must follow that (subject to section VI below) the applicant's appeal must fail.

If, contrary to my tentative view, the court has power to review as an objective precedent fact the issue whether a fresh 'claim for asylum' has been made or not, it is necessary for the court to apply the test propounded in (1) in section IV above to the facts of this case.

In contending that the basis of his November/December 1995 claim was sufficiently different from his March 1995 claim to be properly regarded as a fresh 'claim for asylum', the applicant relied on: evidence of his father's disappearance; additional evidence of civil rights abuses in Nigeria; new material supplied to the Home Office; newspaper publicity given to the cases of the applicant and his father; and a press statement issued by the Nigeria High Commission, critical of supporters of the Onibiyo family who had denigrated the Nigerian Government.

a The applicant is clearly right when he says that this is material which the special adjudicator had no opportunity to consider, the date of that hearing being the relevant date for present purposes (see *Sandralingham v Secretary of State for the Home Dept, Rajendrakumar v Immigration Appeal Tribunal* [1996] Imm AR 97).

There is, however, no evidence that the applicant's father has been detained, and the Nigeria High Commission has publicly asserted that he has not been *b* detained. More importantly, none of this material addresses the fundamental difficulty which has faced the applicant throughout, which is the extreme unlikelihood (in the absence of compelling evidence to the contrary) that there would be officially-inspired persecution of a young man who had not set foot in Nigeria since the age of 11 and who had not during his long stay in this country pursued any political activity of any kind. It was accepted for the applicant that *c* disappointed asylum-seekers were not as such a social group liable to per-secution. It was only if political opinions hostile to the Nigerian Government could be imputed to those seeking asylum that any persecution by the government could be apprehended. But the applicant's immigration history makes plain that he had been doing his utmost to remain in this country well *d* before any claim to asylum was made, and even then his claim was so threadbare as to be stigmatised as abusive. If the decision rested with this court I would hold, applying the test propounded above, that the applicant made no fresh 'claim for asylum' in November/December 1995.

VI

e On 9 December 1995 the applicant's mother was served with notice that she was to be removed to Nigeria on 14 December. She claimed asylum on 12 December 1995, relying on the disappearance of her husband, the applicant's father. No decision on her claim has yet been made, but if asylum is refused she will be entitled to appeal under the 1993 Act. The applicant submits that it is *f* irrational to proceed with his removal when the merits of his contentions will be investigated in his mother's case, with the risk of inconsistent decisions in the two cases. The Secretary of State answers that it is entirely rational for him to deal separately with independent claims made at different times by adult members of the same family, as and when such claims are made.

This issue must be approached on the assumption that the applicant applied for *g* asylum in March 1995, was refused and exhausted his right of appeal; that he has made no fresh 'claim for asylum' and has no further right of appeal; and that he is in law liable to be removed. Given the high threshold of irrationality, I cannot hold the Secretary of State to be irrational in declining to stay the removal of the applicant until the final outcome of his mother's claim is known.

h I would dismiss the applicant's appeal.

ROCH LJ. I agree.

SWINTON THOMAS LJ. I also agree.

j *Appeal dismissed. Leave to appeal to the House of Lords refused.*

L I Zysman Esq   Barrister.

Corbett v Newey and others   *a*

COURT OF APPEAL, CIVIL DIVISION

BUTLER-SLOSS, WAITE AND MORRITT LJJ

15, 16, 26 JANUARY 1996
                                                                 b

*Will – Construction – Intention of testator – Signed but undated will – Testatrix
intending that will should take effect on completion of inter vivos gifts – Whether
testatrix having necessary animus testandi to make valid will.*

Will – Condition – Conditional bequest – Evidence that will subject to condition and   *c*
that condition fulfilled – Testatrix intending that will only effective on completion of
*inter vivos gifts – Whether extrinsic evidence admissible to determine whether will
subject to condition and whether condition fulfilled.*

The testatrix owned two farms, one of which was let to a niece and the other to
a nephew. On 3 February 1989 the testatrix executed a valid will in which she   *d*
bequeathed the farms to the niece and nephew respectively and the residue of her
estate to the niece and nephew equally. The testatrix subsequently decided to
make inter vivos gifts of the farms to the niece and nephew and in July 1989,
aware of the effect that would have on her existing will, she instructed her
solicitor to change her will, omitting any reference to the two farms and   *e*
bequeathing her residuary estate to the niece's children.   The testatrix's
instructions made it clear that she intended that the inter vivos gifts and the new
will were interrelated transactions and that she did not intend to sign the new will
until the gifts were in place. There were delays in completing the conveyancing
of the gifts and in September the testatrix executed the new will but left it
undated, being under the impression that it was of no effect until dated. She   *f*
returned the signed and undated will to her solicitor with instructions that it was
to be dated when the gifts had been completed. The gifts were effected on 25
December and some days later the solicitor dated the new will 26 December.
After the testatrix died in February 1991, the nephew disputed the new will
claiming that it was not an effective will because it had not been signed by the   *g*
testatrix when she had the requisite animus testandi at the moment of signature.
The deputy judge dismissed the nephew's claim and held that the new will should
be admitted to probate, on the grounds that it was conditional on the inter vivos
gifts taking effect, that the testatrix had had the necessary animus to make a
conditional will and the condition had been fulfilled on completion of the gifts.   *h*
The nephew appealed.

Held – The appeal would be allowed for the following reasons—
    (1) The testatrix lacked the requisite animus testandi to execute an
unconditional will at the time she signed the new will, since the evidence clearly
showed that at the moment she signed the new will she did not intend to bring   *j*
into being a document which would operate with unconditional effect (see
p 920 *f g* and p 926 *c*, post).
    (2) In view of the requirement that every will had to be made with immediate
testamentary intent, a testator could not by words or conduct outside the terms
of the will impose upon his execution of the document a direction or condition

which would postpone or qualify its operation. It followed that, while it was
possible to have a will which was on its face conditional, a will which though
unconditional on its face purported, through a direction imposed externally by
the testator at the time of its execution, to be made conditional in its operation
was not a valid will. Accordingly, because the testatrix had executed the new will
with the intention that it should not be effective immediately but should be
effective only when the inter vivos gifts took effect, she did not have the
necessary animus testandi to make a will and the new will was therefore invalid
(see p 921 *a* to *g* and p 925 *h* to p 926 *c*, post); dictum of Mustill LJ in *Re Berger (decd)*
[1989] 1 All ER 591 at 599 applied.

(3) In any event, s 9[a] of the Wills Act 1837, which provided that a will had to
be in writing, signed by the testator and duly witnessed, made it impossible for
any condition to be introduced into a will which the testator had neither stated in
writing, nor signed, and therefore the conditional execution of a document
purporting to be a will (as opposed to the unconditional execution of a will which
in accordance with its terms was conditional in its operation) would be contrary
to the policy and requirements of the 1837 Act (see p 922 *j* to p 923 *a* and p 962 *c*,
post).

Per curiam. There is no requirement in law that a will should be dated and the
lack of a date or the inclusion of the wrong date cannot invalidate a will (see
p 920 *c*, p 923 *f* and p 926 *c*, post).

Decision of Eben Hamilton QC [1995] 1 All ER 570 reversed.

Notes

For necessity of testamentary intention, see 50 *Halsbury's Laws* (4th edn) para 250,
and for cases on the subject, see 50 *Digest* (1983 reissue) 94–97, 726–784.

For conditions attached to gifts in a will, see 50 *Halsbury's Laws* (4th edn) para
316, and for cases on the subject, see 50 *Digest* (1983 reissue) 21–22, 50–61.

For the Wills Act 1837, s 9, see 50 *Halsbury's Statutes* (4th edn) 154.

Cases referred to in judgments

Berger (decd), Re [1989] 1 All ER 591, [1990] Ch 118, [1989] 2 WLR 147, CA.
Ferguson-Davie v Ferguson-Davie (1890) 15 PD 109.
Govier (decd), Re [1950] P 237.
Horner, Re [1965] VR 177, Vict SC.
Hunt's Goods, Re (1875) LR 3 P & D 250.
*Le Cras v Perpetual Trustee Co Ltd, Far West Children's Health Scheme v Perpetual
Trustee Co Ltd* [1967] 3 All ER 915, sub nom *Re Resch's Will Trusts, Le Cras v
Perpetual Trustee Co Ltd, Far West Children's Health Scheme v Perpetual Trustee Co
Ltd* [1969] 1 AC 514, [1968] 3 WLR 1153, PC.
Lister v Smith (1863) 3 Sw & Tr 282, 164 ER 1282.
Meyer's Estate, Re [1908] P 353.
O'Leary v Douglass (1878) 3 LR IR 323, Ir CA.
Winn (decd)'s Goods, Re (1861) 2 Sw & Tr 147, 164 ER 949.

Cases also cited or referred to in skeleton arguments

Baxter's Goods, Re [1903] P 12.

---

a   Section 9, so far as material, provides: 'No will shall be valid unless—(a) it is in writing, and signed
    by the testator, or some other person in his presence and by his direction ...'

Cocke (decd), Re [1960] 2 All ER 289, [1960] 1 WLR 491.

Cowling (decd), Re, Jinkin v Cowling [1924] P 113, [1924] All ER Rep 469.

Finnemore (decd), Re [1992] 1 All ER 800, [1991] 1 WLR 793.

Gladstone v Tempest (1840) 2 Curt 650, 163 ER 538.

Greenough v Martin (1824) 2 Add 239, 162 ER 281.

Hugo's Goods, Re (1877) 2 PD 73.

King's Proctor v Daines (1830) 3 Hag Ecc 218, 162 ER 1136.

Lowthorpe-Lutwidge v Lowthorpe-Lutwidge [1935] P 151, [1935] All ER Rep 338.

Methuen v Methuen (1817) 2 Phillim 416, 161 ER 1186.

Meynell (decd), Re, Meynell v Meynell [1949] WN 273.

Milnes v Foden (1890) 15 PD 105.

Porter's Goods, Re (1869) LR 2 P & D 22.

Reffell v Reffell (1866) LR 1 P & D 139.

Slinn's Goods, Re (1890) 15 PD 156.

Smith's Goods, Re (1869) LR 1 P & D 717.

Spratt's Goods, Re [1897] P 28.

Stable (decd), Re, Dalrymple v Campbell [1919] P 7, [1918–19] All ER Rep 299.

Vines' Estate, Re, Vines v Vines [1910] P 147.

Webb (decd)'s Goods, Re (1864) 3 Sw & Tr 482, 164 ER 1362.

Appeal

By notice dated 20 June 1994, the plaintiff, William Harvey John Corbett, the joint residuary legatee under a will dated 3 February 1989 executed by his aunt, Nancie Armorel Tresawna (the testatrix), appealed from a decision of Mr Eben Hamilton QC ([1995] 1 All ER 570, [1994] Ch 388), sitting as a deputy judge of the High Court in the Chancery Division, made on 5 May 1994, whereby he upheld a will made in September 1989 by the testatrix. The defendants were: (1) John W Newey and (2) David P Bennett (the executors), (3) James and Jonathan Arthur, both minors appearing by their father, Nicholas Arthur, (4) Elsie Brew, (5) Molly Corbett, (6) Rosemary May Somerville and (7) Sarah Arthur, the testatrix's niece (and the mother of James and Jonathan), all of whom were beneficiaries under the September will. The facts are set out in the judgment of Waite LJ.

Quintin Iwi (instructed by *Sharpe Pritchard*, agents for *Nalder & Son*, Camborne) for William Corbett.

Francis Barlow (instructed by *Bevan Ashford*, Tiverton) for Mr Newey.

Patrick Powell (instructed by *Osborne Clark*, Bristol) for James, Jonathan and Sarah Arthur.

The second, fourth, fifth and sixth defendants did not appear.

Cur adv vult

26 January 1996. The following judgments were delivered.

WAITE LJ (giving the first judgment at the invitation of Butler-Sloss LJ). It is well established that a will may be executed with express conditional effect—that is to say with a condition stated on its face that the will is not to come into operation unless or until a particular contingency or condition has been satisfied. This appeal has involved consideration of a different question. Given the requirement that every will must be made with immediate testamentary intent ('animo testandi' in the traditional phrase), can a testator by words or conduct outside the a terms of the will impose upon his execution of the document some direction or condition which will postpone or qualify its operation?

The testatrix, Miss Nancie Tresawna, was aged 79 in the year 1989 and possessed assets consisting of her home, Myrtle Cottage, Grampound in Cornwall, two farms called Tolcarne Merrock Farm at St Mawgan (Tolcarne) and Lamellyn Farm at Probus (Lamellyn), a holding of land and property in the
b village of Probus, and a portfolio of quoted investments. The two farms were let to her nephew, William (Tolcarne) and her niece, Sarah (Lamellyn). William was unmarried and had no children. Sarah had two sons called James and Jonathan. On 3 February 1989 Miss Tresawna executed a will (the February will) under which Tolcarne and Lamellyn were bequeathed respectively to William and Sarah. Apart from small legacies, her remaining assets were devised and
c bequeathed to William and Sarah in equal shares.

During the course of that year she came to favour the idea, with assistance from her accountant, Mr Bennett, and surveyor, Mr Newey, of making an inter vivos gift to William and Sarah of the farms in their respective occupations. At
d the same time she decided to change her will, both to take into account the effect of those proposed gifts, and to change the destination of the residue—which, as she had by then decided, she wished to bequeath to her great-nephews, James and Jonathan (who were then, and still are, minors).

Her regular solicitor had recently ceased to practise, and in regard to these
e proposed arrangements she consulted a new firm of solicitors, Messrs Bond Pearce, where the proposed gifts of land were dealt with by Mr James and the proposed new will by Mr Nicholson. Miss Tresawna was an efficient and business-like person who, although lacking any legal or accountancy expertise, had a clear general grasp of the nature of the transactions she was proposing. She instructed Mr Nicholson that the new will should revoke the February will,
f should appoint Mr Newey and Mr Bennett to be her executors, should devise her land and property at Probus to Sarah and Myrtle Cottage to William, and should bequeath her residuary estate (subject to small legacies to others) to Jonathan and James. There would, of course, be no reference in the new will to Tolcarne and Lamellyn, because those farms would—so it was contemplated—have passed already to William and Sarah under the intended deeds of gift. Mr Nicholson
g obtained her approval of a draft will making those dispositions and prepared an engrossment for signature. This document (the September will) began with words in which a space was left for the date, reading thus: 'THIS WILL dated   1989 is made by me NANCIE ARMOREL TRESAWNA of Myrtle Cottage Old Hill Grampound ...' and after making the dispositions already mentioned,
h concluded with a common form clause for her signature in the presence of two witnesses.

The preparation of the deeds of gift for the farms proceeded more slowly than the drafting of the new will. The result was that by the time Mr Nicholson sent the engrossment of the September will to Miss Tresawna, on 8 September 1989,
j with instructions as to the formalities required for its due execution, the relevant deeds of gift were not yet ready to be executed. By 27 September 1989 it was becoming clear that the hoped-for arrangement, which had been to complete both the gifts and the will together at Michaelmas, would not be feasible. Miss Tresawna spoke by telephone that day to Mr Nicholson, who made two attendance notes. One related to the gifts and recorded that, because of difficulty

in tracing the necessary documents of title, the deeds could not be executed for some little time yet. The other concerned the will, and reads as follows:

> 'She has the Will and will take it to be signed shortly. However, she does not want to sign it until the Deeds of Gift are in place. She pointed out that if she signed the Will and dated it today and then died the property which she was giving would actually pass as residue. Agreed she was sensible on this point and she will not date the Will immediately as she does not wish it to take effect until the gifts are also complete.'

Within the next 48 hours Miss Tresawna made arrangements to execute the September will. It was duly signed and attested, but the space in the text for the date to be inserted was left blank. On 29 September she wrote to Mr Nicholson enclosing the executed engrossment of the September will bearing her signature and those of the attesting witnesses under cover of a letter, which, after referring to matters affecting the deeds of gift, concluded with this postscript: 'Can *you* date my will when Sarah and William have finally and legally accepted the gifts of the farm?' On 3 October Mr Nicholson replied, saying: 'As soon as the Deeds of Gift are completed I will complete your Will and confirm this to you by sending you a copy of course to keep at home.'

In due course, the deeds of gift of the two farms were drawn up and executed by Miss Tresawna. They were dated 25 December 1989. On 29 December 1989 Mr Nicholson wrote to her saying: 'As you know, I have been sitting on your Will, undated, but I have now dated it 26th December so that it is complete and I hold the original'. He referred to a request she had made in November to be supplied with a copy of the will, and inquired whether she wished to make any amendments to it. On 3 January 1990 Miss Tresawna replied:

> 'I note that you have now dated my Will. I cannot remember what alteration I had in mind in November. Anyway, I do not wish to make any amendments.'

Miss Tresawna died just over a year later on 6 February 1991 without having made any further testamentary or inter vivos dispositions. Her residuary estate comprised the assets remaining in her hands after the deeds of gift had been completed—that is to say her home and the properties in Probus, plus her portfolio of investments. If the September will was valid, Myrtle Cottage and the Probus properties would pass respectively to William and Sarah, and her investments and any other residue would pass to James and Jonathan. If it was invalid, all her assets would pass under the February will (which on that footing would constitute Miss Tresawna's unrevoked last will) to William and Sarah in equal shares.

William challenged the validity of the September will, and brought these proceedings for a declaration that it was invalid for want of any testamentary intent on the part of the testatrix at the moment of execution. The action was heard by Mr Eben Hamilton QC (sitting as a deputy judge of the High Court) on 16 and 17 March 1994. The representation of the parties was the same as it has been in this court. Mr Quintin Iwi appeared for William. Mr Barlow represented the executors of the September will with the support of Mr Powell, instructed on behalf of James and Jonathan, and also on behalf of their mother Sarah (who wishes to put their interests under the September will before her own as a residuary legatee under the February will).

a In his judgment given on 5 May 1994 ([1995] 1 All ER 570, [1994] Ch 388) the deputy judge ruled that the September will was valid and should be admitted to probate. He did so on the basis that although Miss Tresawna had no animus testandi to make an unconditional will, she did possess the necessary animus to make a conditional will. He held, further, that the September will (although unconditional on its face) falls to be treated as a conditional will giving effect to *b* that intention—and was to be admitted to probate as such—in the light of the evidence as to the circumstances of its execution, which is (he held) admissible not only to prove the animus of the testatrix but also to establish that the September will was a conditional will.

These holdings appear from the following two passages in his judgment. In one of them he was dealing with an argument by Mr Barlow that the September *c* will should, if necessary, be given unconditional effect. He said ([1995] 1 All ER 570 at 579, [1994] Ch 388 at 398):

> 'I should say that Mr Barlow submitted that it was not essential to his case to show that Miss Tresawna's will should be regarded as conditional. All he *d* had to do was to establish that the document in question was a will, and if evidence could not be introduced to show it was conditional it should take effect unconditionally. I do not accept this. Given the evidence before the court on the subject of Miss Tresawna's animus testandi to the clear effect the September will was executed with the intention that it should only become operative in the event of the gifts inter vivos being effected, it seems *e* to me that the September will can only take effect as a conditional will and that can only be an effective will if I am entitled to consider extrinsic evidence, and that evidence clearly establishes the condition and its fulfilment.'

f From there the judge went on to consider whether there was indeed evidence entitling him to treat the September will as operating in law (despite the absence of any condition upon its face) as a will taking effect conditionally upon completion of the deeds of gift. After referring to the textbooks and authorities he said:

> 'For my part, I fail to see the logic of the suggestion that the court is entitled *g* to consider extrinsic evidence to decide whether a document was executed animo testandi, but must stop short of considering whether the bequests made in the document were subject to a condition, albeit that such condition is not expressed in the document itself and whether such condition has been satisfied. In the present case it is quite clear that Miss Tresawna in executing *h* the September will intended that it should govern the distribution of her estate on her death, subject only to the completion of the inter vivos gifts to William and Sarah. I agree with Mr Barlow's submission that the imposition of such a condition is entirely consistent with Miss Tresawna having the requisite testamentary intention. In my judgment, the court is entitled to *j* consider extrinsic evidence and where the evidence is as clear as it is in the present case to hold that there is a valid conditional will and that the condition has been satisfied. I should add that I consider the dating of the will by Mr Nicholson to be irrelevant as, in my judgment, the September will was executed as a valid conditional will and would have been admitted to probate on proof of the condition having been fulfilled, even if it had not been dated by Mr Nicholson, albeit that Miss Tresawna may have misguidedly thought

it could only come into effect once dated.' (See [1995] 1 All ER 570 at 578, *a*
579–580, [1994] Ch 388 at 397, 398–399.)

The judge's conclusions can thus be summarised as follows.

(1) Miss Tresawna had no animus testandi to make an unconditional will.

(2) She did, however, have the animus to make a will conditional upon the
gifts inter vivos taking effect. *b*

(3) The evidence as to the circumstances in which she made the will is relevant
and admissible not only to ascertain her animus testandi at the moment of
execution, but also as justifying acceptance of the September will by a court of
probate as a will taking effect (notwithstanding the absence of any condition on
its face) subject to that condition.

Before coming to the arguments, I should state that it is common ground *c*
between all parties that there is no requirement in law that a will should be dated.
Lack of a date or the inclusion of the wrong date cannot invalidate a will. Mr
Nicholson gave evidence before the judge, but he is not a party to these
proceedings, and the judge rightly refrained from making any finding as to what
exactly was in his mind when he gave Miss Tresawna the advice he did regarding
the signing and dating of her will. This hearing has proceeded upon the agreed *d*
basis that Miss Tresawna mistakenly believed that the dating of her will was
essential to its operation, and that her instructions as to its subsequent dating by
her solicitor were given under that misapprehension. It is not the function of the
court in these proceedings to determine how far the misapprehension is one for
which Mr Nicholson or his firm must bear responsibility. It is enough, for present *e*
purposes, that the misapprehension existed.

Turning now to the submissions of the parties, Mr Iwi has no quarrel (so far as
it goes—though of course he says it does not go far enough) with the judge's first
conclusion. Mr Barlow has lodged a respondent's notice claiming that the judge
should in any event have treated the September will as a valid will taking
unconditional effect. He supported this by reliance on the presumption of due *f*
execution which applies to all wills appearing on their face to be validly signed
and attested. I would reject that submission. The evidence clearly shows that the
last thing Miss Tresawna intended at the moment of execution of the September
will was to bring into being a document which would operate with unconditional
effect. The judge was in my view right to hold that this testatrix had no animus *g*
to execute an unconditional will.

Mr Iwi does, however, challenge the second conclusion. He submits that the
evidence as to the circumstances in which Miss Tresawna came to execute the
September will admit of only one interpretation: she possessed at the moment of
execution no animus testandi—whether it be conditional or unconditional—at *h*
all. The only animus or intention she possessed at that moment was to put her
signature to a document which, while it remained undated, would have no effect
and would continue to have no effect unless or until her solicitor placed a date
upon it at some future date, depending upon an event which (however firm her
intention at the time regarding the deeds of gift) might never occur. Mr Barlow
argues that the judge was here making a finding of fact which is binding on this *j*
court. He was entitled to hold that, despite her misapprehension that a date on a
will is essential to its operation, Miss Tresawna had the necessary animus testandi
at the moment of execution to make at least a conditional will.

Although I have every sympathy with the judge in seeking to give effect to
intentions which Miss Tresawna had thought out carefully and clearly, and had

a made very plain to all concerned including her solicitor, I believe for my part that there is no escaping the correctness of Mr Iwi's submission, for the following reasons.

Animus testandi, or testamentary intent, means an intention to make 'a revocable ambulatory disposition of the maker's property which is to take effect on death' (see *Re Berger (decd)* [1989] 1 All ER 591 at 599, [1990] Ch 118 at 129 per
b Mustill LJ). A will, in other words, subjects the assets of the testator, from the moment of its execution, to a series of dispositions which, unless revoked, will operate at his death. It is true that those dispositions will remain inchoate until his death, but they operate immediately as ambulatory provisions varying in range or subject matter according as the assets in the ownership of the testator during his lifetime may change in nature value or extent. Since a will operates
c from the moment of execution, it necessarily follows that to possess the necessary animus testandi the testator must intend that this dispositive (though revocable and ambulatory) regime will be called into play immediately—and not postponed to, or made dependent upon, some future event or condition. That is why—surprising though the distinction may at first sight be to a layman—it is possible
d to have a will which is on its face conditional, and yet impossible to have a will which though unconditional on its face purports, through some direction imposed externally by the testator at the time of its execution, to be made conditional in its operation.

There was thus no possibility, in my judgment, on the evidence before the judge of attributing to Miss Tresawna, at the moment of execution of the
e September will, an intention that it should, from that moment, take dispositive effect. The most she could have intended, in view of the instructions given to her solicitor as to the future placing of a date on her will, was to bring into being a document which—depending on whether and when it was dated—would or might at some future date acquire a dispositive operation. The judge, though
f right to hold that she had no intention to execute an unconditional will, was wrong to hold that she had the alternative intention to execute (with the immediate effect that would have been essential to its validity) a will subject to the condition that he found. The only conclusion open to him on the evidence was that at the moment of execution Miss Tresawna (because of the misapprehension under which she was acting) lacked the animus to make any
g valid will—in the sense of a will intended to be immediately dispositive—at all.

That is sufficient to dispose of the appeal, but in view of the substantial argument directed to it, I should state my views also on the judge's third conclusion.

h Mr Iwi relied, as he did before the judge, upon the statement in *Mortimer on Probate, Law and Practice* (2nd edn, 1927) p 248 that a will may be expressed to take effect only in the event of some contingency or condition, but that 'it must plainly appear from the face of the will that the testator intended to limit its operation'. He submits that there is no support from authority for the statement in the successor work—Williams, Mortimer and Sunnucks *Executors, Administrators and*
j *Probate* (17th edn, 1993) p 124—that 'extrinsic evidence may be received to show that a will not expressed to be conditional was in fact so intended', and it has been common ground at this hearing that the authority cited in the text for that proposition (*Re Govier (decd)* [1950] P 237) does not support it. He relies further, sub silentio, upon the fact that in the long history of the probate jurisdiction in England and Wales, there is not a single reported instance of parole or other

extrinsic evidence being admitted to show that a will on its face unconditional   *a*
was in fact intended to be subject to a condition. He relies, finally, upon s 9 of the
Wills Act 1837 as making it impossible for any condition to be introduced into a
will which has not been incorporated into writing signed by the testator.

Mr Barlow acknowledges that there is no English authority in which the court
has held a will to be conditional in the light of external evidence as to the
testator's intention (as opposed to acting on indications gathered from the terms   *b*
of the will itself) but he submits that there is no logical justification for excluding
direct evidence to prove a condition as to operation, since such evidence forms
an essential part of the corpus of evidence going to animus testandi, which is
always admissible in probate proceedings. He relies on the Irish authority (not
cited to the judge) of *O'Leary v Douglass* (1878) 3 LR IR 323. In that case the   *c*
testator executed two testamentary papers, each duly attested, of different dates
but otherwise identical in their terms and each purporting to dispose of all his
property. The reason for it was that the first document had been brought into
being originally as a draft will only, but the testator became so ill that his solicitor
suggested that he should execute the draft as a will, notwithstanding that work
on the drawing up of the engrossment would still proceed. The testator followed   *d*
that suggestion. He executed the draft as a will, but then survived the immediate
crisis and executed the engrossment some seven weeks later. Following his death
it became necessary to determine which of the documents should be admitted to
probate. The court decided unanimously that probate should be granted of the
second document only. Ball C and Deasy LJ reached that conclusion on the   *e*
ground that the second document wholly superseded the first—an impression
primarily gained from the terms of the documents themselves, but confirmed by
the parole evidence of the testator's solicitor as to the circumstances of their
execution. Christian LJ preferred to base the conclusion on a different ground.
The parole evidence which had been properly admitted to determine whether or
not the first document had been executed with testamentary intent could also be   *f*
looked at, he said, to determine what exactly that intention had been. When so
examined, the parole evidence established that the first document had been
executed by the testator conditionally—ie subject to a condition that it should
come into operation only in the event (which did not happen) of the testator
dying without having executed the formal engrossment. Although that was a   *g*
view which he expressed with diffidence as a judge lacking familiarity with
probate law, it was one which he nevertheless held with sufficient confidence to
lead him to give it additional emphasis in a supplementary judgment which he
gave on the day after the original judgments had been delivered. It is a view
which provides, so Mr Barlow submits, a persuasive (though not of course a
binding) precedent for the decision of the judge in the present case to act upon   *h*
extrinsic evidence that the testatrix intended her will to be immediate in effect but
conditional upon the event (which did happen) of the deeds of gift of the farms
becoming duly executed.

On this issue, also, Mr Iwi's submission is in my judgment correct. Even if,   *j*
contrary to the view already expressed, the judge was right in his second
conclusion—that the testatrix had an immediate animus testandi to make a
conditional will—it was not an animus to which she ever succeeded in giving
effect, for the will she executed was unconditional. It would be against the
weight of authority and contrary to the express terms of the Wills Act 1837 to
allow extrinsic evidence as to her intentions to be used to write into her will, for

a probate purposes, a condition which she has neither stated in writing nor signed. In so far as the observations of Christian LJ in *O'Leary's* case tend to any contrary view, they should not be regarded as authoritative in this jurisdiction.

I repeat my regret that a lady of such evident clarity of mind and independence of judgment as Miss Tresawna should have been thwarted in her intention, clearly expressed in her lifetime, that her residuary estate should pass to James
b and Jonathan. The judge's desire to give effect to her wishes, if possible, is thoroughly understandable. But for the reasons already given, the evidence and the law are both too clear, in my judgment, to allow effect to be given to the September will on the basis that he adopted or at all. I would allow the appeal, discharge the order of the deputy judge, and direct that the February will be admitted to probate.

c Butler-Sloss LJ has already drawn attention to the court's concern as to the effect upon costs in this case of separate representation for parties arguing in the same interest. Counsel should be prepared to deal with the question whether any costs ordered to be paid out of the estate should provide for more than one set of costs as between the executors and the remaining defendants.

d
MORRITT LJ. The circumstances in which this appeal arises have been fully described by Waite LJ. I gratefully adopt his description. It is clear that when the testatrix signed what the judge called the September will she did not intend it to take effect as her will whenever she might die. If she had died the next day the gifts of the farms to the nephew and the niece respectively for which provision
e was made in cll 7 and 8 of the February will would not have been superseded by the gifts inter vivos for which she had given instructions but would be revoked by the September will.

The testatrix and her solicitor considered that her signature to the September will was ineffective, as the will itself was not dated. Both of them thought that it
f would become effective when the will was dated by the solicitor with the authority of the testatrix. In this they were both wrong, for it is common ground that the validity of a will does not depend on whether it is dated correctly or at all.

For the appellant it was submitted that the judge was wrong to conclude that the testatrix manifested the requisite animus testandi at the time she signed the September will. The appellant accepted that a will might be made conditionally
g or contingently if the condition or contingency was expressed in the will itself, but not otherwise.

For the respondents it was argued that as a will may be conditional or contingent the requisite animus testandi was only that the document should take effect as the will of the maker in the event of his death in circumstances in which
h the condition or contingency had been performed or otherwise satisfied. It was maintained that the law did not require that the condition or contingency should be expressed on the face of the will.

In my view the two points, animus testandi and whether the condition or contingency must be expressed in the will itself, are but two facets of the same
j problem. Each reflects on the other and both must be regarded in the light of the policy and requirements of the Wills Act 1837.

It is not disputed that under the 1837 Act, with the exception of privileged wills, a will must be in writing, signed by the testator and duly witnessed, as required by s 9. Further it may only be altered (s 21), or, subject to other statutory exceptions, revoked (s 20), by a subsequent will or codicil similarly executed.

Thus the plain and understandable emphasis is that the devolution of the estate a
of a testator should be written out for all to see in a document, which, so far as
possible, can be shown to be the product of the testator himself. The probate
procedure is designed to ensure that the document or documents which are
proved do record the intention of the testator. Accordingly, extrinsic evidence of
intention is freely admitted at that stage (cf *Le Cras v Perpetual Trustee Co Ltd, Far
West Children's Health Scheme v Perpetual Trustee Co Ltd* [1967] 3 All ER 915 at 925, b
[1969] 1 AC 514 at 547).

The authorities establish that if it is shown by extrinsic evidence that a
document which appears to be a will was not intended by the maker to operate
as such then it will not be admitted to probate. Thus, apparently regular wills
which were shams (*Lister v Smith* (1863) 3 Sw & Tr 282, 164 ER 1282 and
Ferguson-Davie v Ferguson-Davie (1890) 15 PD 109), or executed by the wrong c
person (*Re Hunt's Goods* (1875) LR 3 P & D 250 and *Re Meyer's Estate* [1908] P 353),
have been refused probate.

None of these cases deals with the situation in which the extrinsic evidence
shows that the testator intended the document to be his will not immediately but
at some future time as and when certain conditions or contingencies exist or have d
been satisfied. The nearest is *Re Horner* [1965] VR 177. In that case the testator
signed two wills without having then decided which of them was to govern the
devolution of his estate on his death. Later he decided and authorised the
destruction of that which had not been selected. Thus, before his death he had
decided that the surviving will was to constitute his will but he did not re-execute e
it. Hudson J decided that at the time of its execution there was no animus
testandi, for he did not then intend it to govern the devolution of his estate on his
death and nothing which occurred subsequently could remedy this deficiency.

The common feature of all these cases is that there was no intention at the time
the will was signed that it should operate immediately in the event of the death
of the maker. It seems to me that in principle the result should be the same when f
the intention was that the will should only take effect in the event of death and
the occurrence of one or more other conditions or contingencies.

It is necessary to consider the other aspect of the problem to which I have
referred before reaching any final conclusion. With two exceptions all the
authorities show that for a conditional will to be effective the condition must g
appear in the will itself. Thus, in *Mortimer on Probate* (2nd edn, 1927) p 248, the
last edition for which Dr Mortimer was responsible, he wrote:

'A will may be expressed so as to take effect only in the event of the
happening of some contingency or condition, and if such is the case, and the h
contingency does not happen or the condition fails, the will is not entitled to
probate. But in order that a will should be regarded as conditional or
contingent and probate refused on the ground that the contingency to which
the testator referred has not occurred, it must plainly appear from the terms
of the will that the testator intended to limit its operation, and that its
provisions were intended to take effect only in the event of the happening of j
the contingency and not otherwise ...'

The two indications to the contrary are the judgment of Christian LJ in *O'Leary
v Douglass* (1878) 3 LR IR 323 and a passage in Williams, Mortimer and Sunnucks
Executors, Administrators and Probate (17th edn, 1993) p 124.

a In *O'Leary v Douglass* there were two successive wills in identical terms. The
question was which one was effective, for the time at which the will was made
was relevant to the application of the Mortmain legislation. Ball C, Christian and
Deasy LJJ all concluded that it was a necessary implication from the terms of the
second will that it revoked the first. Christian LJ went further and concluded that
the first which was originally a draft and was executed lest the testator should not
b survive to execute the engrossed version was revoked by the execution of the
second, for that was the condition on which the first was originally executed. He
drew a parallel with the case in which the testator executes a will on the basis, not
expressed therein, that it is to be his will if he never returns to England but not
otherwise. He expressed the view that it would be valid if the testator died
abroad without having returned but not if he had returned to England and then
c died without having revoked it.

I do not think that the opinion of Christian LJ is in point on the facts of this case.
In this case the testatrix never intended that the September will should be
effective immediately but cease to be effective in the light of later events. By
contrast she did not intend it to be effective unless and until the gifts inter vivos
d had been perfected and the September will had been dated. But quite aside from
this distinction I do not think that the views of Christian LJ can be supported. It
is plain that he was in a minority and his opinion seems to me to be contrary to
the policy underlying the 1837 Act and the views in that respect of Cresswell J in
Re Winn (decd)'s Goods (1861) 2 Sw & Tr 147 at 149, 164 ER 949 at 950, where he
said:
e

'Again, can I, since the Wills Act, admit evidence of such declarations of the
deceased as are now before me? Would it not be making a will by word of
mouth.'

f In *Williams, Mortimer and Sunnucks* p 124, it is stated that 'extrinsic evidence
may be received to show that a will not expressed to be conditional was in fact so
intended'. The authority given in the footnote as authority for that proposition
is *Re Govier (decd)* [1950] P 237. But, as is common ground, that case is not
authority for the proposition stated in the text, as it concerned the admission of
extrinsic evidence to resolve an ambiguity appearing from the expression of the
g contingency in the will itself.

Accordingly, in my view there is no authority to support the view that a will
may be made conditional otherwise than in accordance with the conditions
expressed in it. The key to the understanding and resolution of the problem lies
in the distinction adverted to by Waite LJ in the course of argument between the
h conditional execution of a document described as a will and the unconditional
execution of a will which in accordance with its terms is conditional in its
operation. The former is not authorised by the 1837 Act. If it were to be
permitted then wills might be executed in escrow and the requirement that a will
be in writing substantially avoided by the conditions of the escrow. It was
j precisely this argument which the majority of the court rejected in *O'Leary v
Douglass*. In the latter case the will is executed unconditionally and will take
effect, so long as not revoked, in accordance with its terms including the
requirement that the condition expressed in it be performed or satisfied.

In my judgment both principle and authority require that a will be executed
with the intention or animus testandi that, subject only to the death of the maker,

the will should be of immediate effect at any time after its execution. Accordingly *a*
to be effective the condition must be expressed in the will.

Applying those principles to the facts of this case, it is in my judgment plain that
the testatrix did not have the requisite intention at the time she signed the
September will. She did not then intend that it should be effective immediately,
but only when her gifts inter vivos had been perfected and the appropriate date
inserted in the will. Nothing which occurred subsequently could give rise to a *b*
valid will for there was no further execution capable of complying with s 9 of the
1837 Act.

I agree with the judgment of Waite LJ and would allow this appeal.

BUTLER-SLOSS LJ. I agree with both judgments.

c

Appeal allowed.

Paul Magrath Esq   Barrister.

a

R v Christou

HOUSE OF LORDS

LORD GOFF OF CHIEVELEY, LORD GRIFFITHS, LORD BROWNE-WILKINSON, LORD TAYLOR
OF GOSFORTH AND LORD HOPE OF CRAIGHEAD

b   19 FEBRUARY, 9 MAY 1996

*Criminal law – Separate trials – Separate counts – Evidence – Admissibility on separate
counts – Sexual abuse of children – Severance of indictment – Whether counts should
be severed where evidence of one child complainant not so related to that of another
child complainant as to render it admissible on charges concerning other complainant
c   – Whether judge having discretion to order separate trials – Matters to be considered in
exercising discretion – Indictments Act 1915, s 5(3) – Indictment Rules 1971, r 9.*

The appellant was charged with sexual offences against his two young female
cousins and was indicted on various counts ranging from indecent assault to rape.
d   The counts concerning each complainant were tried together. The appellant was
found guilty and sentenced to three and a half years' imprisonment. He appealed
against his conviction on the grounds that the indictment should have been
severed and the counts in respect of each complainant tried separately. The
Court of Appeal dismissed the appeal but certified that the case raised a question
of general public importance, namely whether, having regard to s 5(3)[a] of the
e   Indictments Act 1915 and r 9[b] of the Indictment Rules 1971, the trial judge had a
discretion to order that all charges should be tried together where an accused was
charged with sexual offences against more than one person and the evidence of
one complainant was not so related to that of the other complainants as to render
it admissible on the charges concerning those other complainants. The appellant
f   appealed to the House of Lords, contending that although r 9 of the 1971 rules
provided for the joinder of charges in the same indictment if they were founded
on the same facts or formed part of a series of offences of the same or a similar
character, the court should always exercise the discretion which it had under
s 5(3) of the 1915 Act to order separate trials if the accused would be embarrassed
or prejudiced in his defence by the trial of more than one offence in the same
g   indictment in favour of severing counts relating to alleged sexual abuse of
children if the evidence of one child was not admissible to support the allegations
of another child.

Held – The question of severance of an indictment charging an accused with
h   sexual offences against more than one person where the evidence of one
complainant was not such as to be admissible on the charges concerning the
other complainants was a matter for the discretion of the trial judge. Where the
offences concerned sexual abuse of children, the judge was not obliged to exercise
that discretion in favour of severing the counts relating to different children, even
j   where the evidence of one child complainant was not so related to that of another
child complainant as to render it admissible on the charges concerning the other
complainant. In exercising his discretion the judge should seek to achieve a fair
resolution of the issues; and matters which the judge ought to take into account

---

a   Section 5(3) is set out at p 931 *b, post*
b   Rule 9 is set out at p 931 *a, post*

included, the extent to which the facts giving rise to the counts were discrete or
interrelated, the impact of ordering two or more trials on the defendant, his   *a*
family, the victims and their families and on press publicity, and importantly,
whether the judge's directions to the jury would suffice to secure a fair trial if the
counts were tried together. It followed that the trial judge had been entitled to
order that the counts against the appellant be tried together. The appeal would
therefore be dismissed (see p 929 *c f*, p 935 *d* to *f*, p 936 *e f* and p 937 *b* to *f*, post).   *b*

Dictum of Lord Lane CJ in *R v Cannan* (1990) 92 Cr App R 16 at 23 applied.

R v P [1991] 3 All ER 337 explained.

Notes

For separate trial of counts, see 11(2) *Halsbury's Laws* (4th edn reissue) para 933.   *c*

For corroboration, see 11(2) *Halsbury's Laws* (4th edn reissue) paras 1140–1145,
and for cases on the subject, see 15(2) *Digest* (2nd reissue) 106–107, *19059–19065*.

For admissibility of similar fact evidence, see 11(2) *Halsbury's Laws* (4th edn
reissue) paras 1091–1098, and for cases on the subject, see 15(1) *Digest* (2nd
reissue) 587–590, *17730–17751*.

For the Indictments Act 1915, s 5, see 12 *Halsbury's Statutes* (4th edn) (1994   *d*
reissue) 180.

For the Indictment Rules 1971, r 9, see 6 *Halsbury's Statutory Instruments* (1993
reissue) 20.

Cases referred to in opinions   *e*

Advocate, HM v Johnstone 1992 SLT 905, HC of Just.
Boardman v DPP [1974] 3 All ER 887, [1975] AC 421, [1974] 3 WLR 673, HL.
De Jesus v R (1986) 68 ALR 1, Aust HC.
Hoch v R (1988) 165 CLR 292, Aust HC.
Moorov v HM Advocate 1930 JC 68, HC of Just.   *f*
R v Blackstock (1979) 70 Cr App R 34, CA.
R v Brooks (1990) 92 Cr App R 36, CA.
R v Cannan (1990) 92 Cr App R 16, CA.
R v Dixon (1989) 92 Cr App R 43, CA.
R v Flack [1969] 2 All ER 784, [1969] 1 WLR 937, CA.   *g*
R v Grondkowski [1946] 1 All ER 559, [1946] KB 369, CCA.
R v P [1991] 3 All ER 337, [1991] 2 AC 447, [1991] 3 WLR 161, HL; *rvsg* (1990) 93
Cr App R 267, CA.
R v Sims [1946] 1 All ER 697, [1946] KB 531, CCA.
Sutton v R (1984) 152 CLR 528, Aust HC.   *h*

Appeal

George Christou appealed with leave of the Appeal Committee of the House of
Lords given on 13 July 1995 against the decision of the Court of Appeal, Criminal
Division (Farquharson LJ, Garland and Cazalet JJ) on 18 February 1994 dismissing   *j*
his appeal against his conviction in the Central Criminal Court before Judge
Steele and a jury on 12 August 1993 on charges of indecent assault on a female.
The Court of Appeal had certified pursuant to s 33(2) of the Criminal Appeal Act
1968 that a point of law of general public importance (set out at p 929, post) was
involved in the decision. The facts are set out in the opinion of Lord Taylor of
Gosforth.

a *Brian Higgs QC* and *Christopher Drew* (instructed by *Bernard Oberman & Co*) for the appellant.

Anthony Scrivener QC and *Jane Sullivan* (instructed by the *Crown Prosecution Service*) for the Crown.

b Their Lordships took time for consideration.

9 May 1996. The following opinions were delivered.

LORD GOFF OF CHIEVELEY. My Lords, I have had the advantage of reading in draft the speech of my noble and learned friend Lord Taylor of Gosforth. For *c* the reasons he gives I too would dismiss this appeal.

LORD GRIFFITHS. My Lords, I have had the advantage of reading the speech of my noble and learned friend Lord Taylor of Gosforth and agree that for the reasons he gives this appeal should be dismissed and the certified question answered in the affirmative.
d   I wish, however, to add a rider. Although the point was not argued, I am firmly of the opinion that the judge was wrong to rule that the evidence of the two complainants was not capable of corroborating one another. This was a case of a man successively sexually abusing his two young girl cousins whilst living as a member of their family in the same house. In such circumstances *R v P* [1991] 3 *e* All ER 337, [1991] 2 AC 447 is clear authority that should have led the judge to rule that the jury were entitled to regard the complainants' evidence as mutually corroborative. Had she done so the point argued in this appeal would, of course, never have arisen.

f **LORD BROWNE-WILKINSON.** My Lords, for the reasons given by my noble and learned friend Lord Taylor of Gosforth I agree that this appeal should be dismissed and the certified question answered in the affirmative.

LORD TAYLOR OF GOSFORTH. My Lords, this appeal arises from the conviction of the appellant on 12 August 1993 at the Central Criminal Court for *g* indecent assaults on his two young female cousins. The counts concerning each complainant were tried together. The appellant was sentenced to a total of three and a half years' imprisonment. The Court of Appeal, on 18 February 1994, dismissed the appellant's appeal which was based on the contention, inter alia, that the indictment should have been severed and the counts in respect of each *h* complainant tried separately. However, the Court of Appeal certified a point of general public importance in the following terms:

> 'Where an accused is charged with sexual offences against more than one person and the evidence of one complainant is not so related to that of the other complainants as to render it admissible on the charges concerning those other complainants, in accordance with the principle laid down in *R v* *j* *P* [1991] 3 All ER 337, [1991] 2 AC 447, has the trial judge a discretion to order that all charges should be tried together, having regard to the provisions of s 4 of the Indictments Act 1915 (as amended) and r 9 of the Indictment Rules [1971]?'

Your Lordships' House gave leave to appeal on 13 July 1995.

The facts
    The complainants were Chrisy, born in December 1964 and Maria, born in
October 1973. They are sisters and first cousins of the appellant. In 1972 the
appellant, aged 22, came from Cyprus to live as a lodger with his aunt and uncle,
the parents of the complainants. He became Maria's godfather and he lived with
the family until 1982 when he left to marry.
    The case for the Crown was that during the ten years he lodged in their home,
the appellant sexually abused both girls repeatedly, Chrisy from his arrival and
Maria from about 1978 when she was five. The girls made no complaint until
they went to the police in 1992. At the time of the trial Chrisy was 28, married
with three children. Maria was a 19-year-old student, unmarried but having a
sexual relationship with her boyfriend.
    Chrisy alleged the appellant had sexual intercourse with her on occasions
when she was about 8 years old (count 1, with its paired count of indecent assault,
count 2) and he kissed her breasts and private parts on one occasion when she was
9 or 10 (count 3). When she was about 10 or 11 and was reluctant to have sexual
intercourse she told the appellant he should not 'do anything to me at the front'.
In the result, the appellant committed what she alleged was buggery upon her
(count 4, with its paired count of indecent assault, count 5). Thereafter she
sought to avoid being alone with the appellant. Her final allegation was that the
appellant cornered her in the bathroom when she was about 15, pulled aside her
underclothes and raped her (count 6, with its paired count of indecent assault,
count 7).
    Maria said that the first incident with her was when the appellant caused her to
undress in a house to which the family had recently moved. Thereafter, she
alleged he had sexual intercourse with her (count 8, rape, with its paired count 9
of indecent assault) and buggered her (count 12, with its paired count of indecent
assault, count 13). These incidents occurred when she climbed into his bed. She
also alleged that on occasions when she returned from school the appellant had
intercourse with her on the sofa in the living room (count 10, rape, with its paired
count of indecent assault, count 11).
    At the close of the prosecution case, the trial judge upheld submissions of no
case to answer in respect of count 1 (rape) and count 6 (rape), in respect of Chrisy.
She also allowed submissions of no case in respect of Maria on count 14 (buggery)
and count 15 (indecent assault). The trial proceeded in respect of the remaining
11 counts.
    The appellant gave evidence. He was 42 years old, of previous good character
and he denied all the allegations of indecent conduct. Evidence was called on his
behalf. In the result, the jury convicted the appellant on five counts of indecent
assault, counts 3, 5 and 7 in respect of Chrisy and counts 11 and 13 in respect of
Maria. They acquitted the appellant of the other six counts. He was sentenced
to 18 months' imprisonment concurrently in respect of counts 3, 5 and 7 and two
years' imprisonment concurrently inter se, but consecutive to the 18 months in
respect of counts 11 and 13.
    It is convenient first to set out the effect of the statutory provisions and the
decision of your Lordships' House in *R v P* [1991] 3 All ER 337, [1991] 2 AC 447
which are mentioned in the certified question.

The statutory provisions
    Rule 9 of the Indictment Rules 1971, SI 1971/1253 (made under the
Indictments Act 1915), is in the following terms:

a
'Charges for any offences may be joined in the same indictment if those charges are founded on the same facts, or form or are a part of a series of offences of the same or a similar character.'

Section 5(3) of the 1915 Act provides:

b
'Where, before trial, or at any stage of a trial, the court is of opinion that a person accused may be prejudiced or embarrassed in his defence by reason of being charged with more than one offence in the same indictment, or that for any other reason it is desirable to direct that the person should be tried separately for any one or more offences charged in an indictment, the court may order a separate trial of any count or counts of such indictment.'

c
There was no dispute, nor could there be, that the counts in the present case relating to both alleged victims fell squarely within the scope of r 9. They were therefore properly joined in one indictment. Again, Mr Higgs QC accepted that s 5(3) of the 1915 Act gives the court a discretion as to whether or not counts on the same indictment should be separately tried. Prima facie, therefore, the
d
answer to the certified question as worded must quite simply be Yes. However, Mr Higgs sought to qualify and amplify the question. In cases of sexual abuse of children where the evidence of one child is not admissible in support of allegations by another child, he submits the judge's discretion should always be exercised in favour of severing the counts relating to those children. He seeks to rely principally on words used by Lord Mackay of Clashfern LC, in answering the
e
second of the two questions certified in R v P.

The decision in R v P
The defendant in that case was convicted on four counts of rape and four counts of incest in respect of each of his two daughters. Following the decision
f
of your Lordships' House in *Boardman v DPP* [1974] 3 All ER 887, [1975] AC 421 the test of whether the evidence of one complainant in such a case was admissible in support of the complaint of another had been whether there were striking similarities between the facts relating to each complaint. The central issue in *R v P* was whether such striking similarities were essential. The Court of Appeal ((1990) 93 Cr App R 267) had felt bound by authority to hold that they were and
g
accordingly they allowed the defendant's appeal. They certified two questions of general public importance as follows (at 271):

'(1) where a father or step-father is charged with sexually abusing a young daughter of the family, is evidence that he also similarly abused other young
h
children of the family admissible (assuming there to be no collusion) in support of such charge in the absence of any other "striking similarities"; and (2) where a defendant is charged with sexual offences against more than one child or young person, is it necessary, in the absence of "striking similarities" for the charges to be tried separately?'

j
Your Lordships' House unanimously reversed the decision of the Court of Appeal. Lord Mackay of Clashfern LC said ([1991] 3 All ER 337 at 346, [1991] 2 AC 447 at 460):

'As this matter has been left in *Boardman v DPP* ([1974] 3 All ER 887, [1975] AC 421) I am of opinion that it is not appropriate to single out "striking similarity" as an essential element in every case in allowing evidence of an offence against one victim to be heard in connection with an allegation against another.'

Lord Mackay LC said ([1991] 3 All ER 337 at 348, [1991] 2 AC 447 at 462):

'When a question of the kind raised in this case arises I consider that the judge must first decide whether there is material upon which the jury would be entitled to conclude that the evidence of one victim, about what occurred to that victim, is so related to the evidence given by another victim, about what happened to that other victim, that the evidence of the first victim provides strong enough support for the evidence of the second victim to make it just to admit it, notwithstanding the prejudicial effect of admitting the evidence. This relationship, from which support is derived, may take many forms and while these forms may include "striking similarity" in the manner in which the crime is committed, consisting of unusual characteristics in its execution the necessary relationship is by no means confined to such circumstances. Relationships in time and circumstances other than these may well be important relationships in this connection. Where the identity of the perpetrator is in issue, and evidence of this kind is important in that connection, obviously something in the nature of what has been called in the course of the argument a signature or other special feature will be necessary. To transpose this requirement to other situations where the question is whether a crime has been committed, rather than who did commit it, is to impose an unnecessary and improper restriction upon the application of the principle.'

Finally, in addressing the certified questions, Lord Mackay LC said ([1991] 3 All ER 337 at 348, [1991] 2 AC 447 at 462–463):

'I would answer the first question posed by the Court of Appeal by saying that the evidence referred to is admissible if the similarity is sufficiently strong, or there is other sufficient relationship between the events described in the evidence of the other young children of the family, and the abuse charged, that the evidence if accepted, would so strongly support the truth of that charge that it is fair to admit it, notwithstanding its prejudicial effect. It follows that the answer to the second question is No, *provided there is a relationship between the offences of the kind I have just described.*'

Mr Higgs relies on the last phrase in that passage, which I have emphasised. He contends its effect is to require counts concerning different complainants of sex abuse to be severed and separately tried unless, by the criteria laid down in R v P, the evidence of one complainant is admissible to support the complaint of another.

Before considering his submissions it is necessary to refer to earlier authorities so as to put Lord Mackay LC's words in context.

The earlier authorities

In R v Sims [1946] 1 All ER 697, [1946] KB 531 the defendant had been charged with homosexual offences committed on four separate occasions against four men who were unconnected. His appeal was rejected, the court ruling that the evidence of the victims was mutually supportive within the 'similar facts' principle. However, Lord Goddard CJ referred to s 5(3) of the 1915 Act and said ([1946] 1 All ER 697 at 699, [1946] KB 531 at 536):

a
'That section confers a discretion on the judge with which this court will not interfere unless it sees that justice has not been done: see *R. v. Grondkowski and Malinowski* ([1946] 1 All ER 559, [1946] KB 369) recently before this court. The appellant here says that justice has not been done because on a trial of the accused on the counts in respect of one man, evidence of offences in respect of the other men would not be admissible,

b
and that the accused was therefore improperly prejudiced by the joint trial. We agree with the contention to this extent, that if such evidence was not admissible, the accused would be prejudiced in his defence and it would be desirable to direct separate trials. We do not think that the mere fact that evidence is admissible on one count and inadmissible on another is by itself a ground for separate trials; because often the matter can be made clear in

c
the summing up without prejudice to the accused. In such a case as the present, however, it is asking too much to expect any jury when considering one charge, to disregard the evidence on the others, and if such evidence is inadmissible, the prejudice created by it would be improper and would be too great for any direction to overcome.'

d
Thus the court's approach was that the judge's exercise of his undoubted discretion would depend on the facts of the individual case and whether joint trial would create prejudice.

Mr Higgs relied upon a passage from the speech of Lord Cross of Chelsea in *Boardman*. The case concerned alleged offences of buggery of schoolboys by a

e
headmaster. Lord Cross said ([1974] 3 All ER 887 at 910–911, [1975] AC 421 at 459):

'When in a case of this sort the prosecution wishes to adduce "similar fact" evidence which the defence says is inadmissible, the question whether it is admissible ought, if possible, to be decided in the absence of the jury at the

f
outset of the trial and if it is decided that the evidence is inadmissible and the accused is being charged in the same indictment with offences against the other men the charges relating to the different persons ought to be tried separately. If they are tried together the judge will, of course, have to tell the jury that in considering whether the accused is guilty of the offence alleged against him by A, they must put out of mind the fact—which they know—

g
that B and C are making similar allegations against him. But, as the Court of Criminal Appeal said in *R v Sims* ([1946] 1 All ER 697, [1946] KB 531) it is asking too much of any jury to tell them to perform mental gymnastics of this sort. If the charges are tried together it is inevitable the jurors will be influenced, consciously or unconsciously, by the fact that the accused is

h
being charged not with a single offence against one person but with three separate offences against three persons.'

In *R v Blackstock* (1979) 70 Cr App R 34 the appellant was charged on four paired counts in respect of two robberies. It was conceded that the evidence on one

j
robbery was not admissible on the other. On appeal, the contention that the indictment should have been severed to allow separate trials in respect of each robbery was rejected. Roskill LJ said (at 38):

'We can see no reason at all, within the principles applicable to rule 9 of the Indictment Rules [1971] why these two robbery counts with the associated firearms counts should not have been joined and tried together. There was no injustice as a result, so long as the jury were told that the evidence on one pair of counts was not evidence on the other pair.'

In fact the jury acquitted the appellant on one pair of counts. It is right to note that the case did not involve sexual offences or children.

In *R v Brooks* (1990) 92 Cr App R 36 the appellant had been convicted of sexual offences against his three very young daughters. The judge had declined to sever the indictment and order separate trials. Mustill LJ having stated, contrary to the trial judge's directions, that the evidence of the daughters was not mutually corroborative or supportive, went on to say (at 42):

'So also it could not be right to try together in a case like this a series of offences in which the evidence on one series is not only inadmissible in relation to another, but casts a cloud of prejudice upon it.'

We were also referred to the Australian case of *De Jesus v R* (1986) 68 ALR 1 at 4, where Gibbs CJ quoted the judgment of Brennan J in *Sutton v R* (1984) 152 CLR 528 at 541–542 as follows:

'When two or more counts constituting a series of offences of a similar character are joined in the same information, a real risk of prejudice to an accused person may arise from the adverse effect which evidence of his implication in one of the offences charged in the indictment is likely to have upon the jury's mind in deciding whether he is guilty of another of those offences. Where that evidence is not admissible towards proof of his guilt of the other offence, some step must be taken to protect the accused person against the risk of impermissible prejudice. Sometimes a direction to the jury is sufficient to guard against such a risk; sometimes it is not. Where a direction to the jury is not sufficient to guard against such a risk, an application for separate trials should generally be granted.'

Although the members of the court in *De Jesus* did not agree in all respects, the views of the majority were encapsulated in the judgment of Brennan J (at 12):

'Suffice to say that when the admission of the evidence admissible on the charges joined in an indictment carries the risk of impermissible prejudice to the accused if the charges are tried together, separate trials should be ordered.'

That view was echoed in *Hoch v R* (1988) 165 CLR 292 at 298.

Clearly the authorities we have so far reviewed do not speak with one voice. However, the leading and most recent case on this topic, prior to *R v P*, was *R v Cannan* (1990) 92 Cr App R 16. There the appellant was charged with six offences against three women; rape and buggery on one, attempted kidnapping of another, abduction and murder of the third. The judge, whilst accepting that the three sets of offences were evidentially separate, declined to order severance. Lord Lane CJ, giving the judgment of the court, cited the passage quoted above from the speech of Lord Cross in *Boardman* and said (at 19): 'That of course is a dictum of great weight. But, as has been pointed out in subsequent cases, it is in fact an obiter dictum.'

Lord Lane CJ then reviewed a number of authorities including *R v Dixon* (1989) 92 Cr App R 43. That was a case involving sexual charges in which although the trial judge did not treat the evidence of the complainants as mutually supportive a under the 'similar facts' principle, he declined to sever the indictment. The Court of Appeal upheld his decision.

Lord Lane CJ referred finally to *R v Flack* [1969] 2 All ER 784, [1969] 1 WLR 937. There, the appellant was charged with sexual offences against his three sisters aged between 12 and 15. The trial judge took the view that all the counts could properly be tried together whether (as he initially thought) the evidence on each b was mutually supportive or (as he finally decided) the three sets of offences fell into water-tight compartments. Salmon LJ, giving the judgment of the court, said ([1969] 2 All ER 784 at 787–788, [1969] 1 WLR 937 at 943):

> 'This, no doubt, is a matter about which different judges might take different views. Certainly it would as a rule be better, in circumstances such c as these, that the counts should be tried separately. This court will not, however, interfere with the decision of the judge in such a matter unless satisfied there were no reasonable grounds upon which his decision could be supported, or that it may have caused a miscarriage of justice.'

After citing that passage, Lord Lane CJ went on ((1990) 92 Cr App R 16 at 23):

d
> 'It may well be that often the judge in sexual cases will order severance, as is clear from the various cases which we have already taken the liberty of citing ... But the fact remains that the Indictments Act 1915 gives the judge a discretion, and it is a well known fact, and a well known principle, as Salmon L.J. in his usual clear language sets out in the case of *Flack* ([1969] 2 e All ER 784, [1969] 1 WLR 937), that that is not a matter with which this court will interfere, unless it is shown that the judge has failed to exercise his discretion upon the usual and proper principles, namely, taking into account all things he should, and not taking into account anything which he should not.'

f Judgment in *R v Cannan* was given by Lord Lane CJ on 23 July 1990. Three days earlier, on 20 July, he had given the judgment of the Court of Appeal in *R v P* (1990) 93 Cr App R 267. It is clear from that judgment that the argument turned on whether the trial judge was right to find there were 'striking similarities' in the facts relating to each complainant and therefore the evidence of one was admissible to support the other. Whether, if the judge was wrong (as the court g held) the counts could nevertheless all be tried together was not argued (see 93 Cr App R 267 at 270). Lord Lane CJ said (at 271):

> 'It seems to us absurd that counsel and judge should be spending time searching through committal papers, which may in the upshot not represent h the evidence actually given, searching for "striking similarities" such as to justify allowing the jury to hear evidence of that which they would naturally and rightly consider themselves entitled to know, namely that the defendant is charged with abusing not merely one but two or more of his young daughters. We see force in the suggestion adumbrated in argument before j us that where the father has allegedly shown himself to be someone prepared to abuse sexually girls who are no more than children, in this case under the age of 13, girls who are moreover his own children, and to use his position of power over them in their own home to achieve those ends, this might provide a sufficient hallmark to render the evidence of one girl admissible in the case of the other where the danger of collusion can be discounted. In the current state of decided cases we are, we think, inhibited from so deciding.'

It was with those considerations in mind that the Court of Appeal certified the
two questions which were answered by your Lordships' House in *R v P* [1991] 3
All ER 337, [1991] 2 AC 447.

Scope of the decision in R v P

It is clear from the summary of counsel's submissions and from Lord
Mackay LC's speech that the case focused on the admissibility of one complainant's evidence to corroborate or support that of another complainant. More
specifically, it focused on whether or not 'striking similarities' were required to
render such evidence mutually supportive. The only mention, in counsel's
reported submissions, of separate trials where the evidence of one complainant is
not admissible on counts relating to another, is in a single sentence, tangential to
the main argument (see [1991] 2 AC 447 at 450–451). That was accompanied by
a reference to *R v Cannan*. But although *Cannan* was cited, and although it was
the most recent case on the topic, Lord Mackay LC made no mention of it in his
speech. If the words I have emphasised in his answer to the second certified
question were to have the meaning and significance Mr Higgs seeks to attach to
them, they would in effect have overruled the decision in *Cannan*. If that had
been intended, Lord Mackay LC would surely have said so in terms.

Conclusions

Since *R v Cannan* was not overruled and the point now at issue had not been
argued in *R v P* either in the Court of Appeal or in your Lordships' House, the
emphasised words must be regarded as obiter. In my judgment the proper
approach to the question of severance is that stated by Lord Lane CJ in his
judgment in *R v Cannan* (1990) 92 Cr App R 16 at 23, quoted above. My reasons
are as follows.

First, the statutory provisions undoubtedly give the trial judge a discretion. To
hold that he must decide the question of severance in a particular way would be
to fetter that statutory discretion.

Again, in what cases would the fetter apply? To all sexual offences? Or only,
as Mr Higgs argued, to sexual abuse of children? If so, children of what age?
Would such a fetter apply only where children were giving evidence or equally
(as here) where mature adults were giving evidence of abuse during their
childhood? No satisfactory answer of general application can be given to such
questions.

It is clear that no such fetter exists in the law of Scotland. Although
corroboration of a sexual complaint is required by Scottish law, counts may be
and are tried jointly even where the evidence on one is not corroborative of the
evidence on another (see eg *Moorov v HM Advocate* 1930 JC 68, cited approvingly
by Lord Mackay LC in *R v P* [1991] 3 All ER 337 at 347, [1991] 2 AC 447 at 461).

Looking specifically at sexual abuse of children, upon which Mr Higgs concentrated his argument, cases can vary greatly. A defendant may, for example, be
indicted for discrete incidents of sexual abuse of different children in different
places at different times, so that the allegations in respect of each count are in
'water-tight compartments'. By contrast, when, as here, the allegation is of a
continuous course of conduct within one household involving two or more
children over the same period and in similar circumstances, joint trial of all the
counts may well be appropriate. Indeed, in such cases the principles laid down in
R v P will often render the evidence of one child admissible to support the
evidence of the other.

a   The prosecution argued that was the case here. The trial judge did not accept that submission and directed the jury to consider the counts relating to the two complainants independently of each other. The Court of Appeal took the same view. We were not invited by the Crown on this appeal to depart from that view, as to do so would have rendered obiter our answer to the certified question.

b   Lord Lane CJ, in the quoted passage, refrained from specifying the factors a judge should consider when 'taking into account all things he should'. They will vary from case to case, but the essential criterion is the achievement of a fair resolution of the issues. That requires fairness to the accused but also to the prosecution and those involved in it. Some, but by no means an exhaustive list, of the factors which may need to be considered are: how discrete or interrelated are the facts giving rise to the counts; the impact of ordering two or more trials

c   on the defendant and his family, on the victims and their families and on press publicity; and importantly, whether directions the judge can give to the jury will suffice to secure a fair trial if the counts are tried together. In regard to that last factor, jury trials are conducted on the basis that the judge's directions of law are to be applied faithfully. Experience shows, as for example in *R v Blackstock* (1979)

d   70 Cr App R 34 and in the instant case, that juries, where counts are jointly tried, do follow the judge's directions and consider the counts separately.

Approaching the question of severance as indicated above, judges will often consider it right to order separate trials. But I reject the argument that either generally or in respect of any class of case, the judge must so order. Accordingly, I would answer the certified question, Yes, and dismiss this appeal.

e

LORD HOPE OF CRAIGHEAD. My Lords, I have had the advantage of reading in draft the speech of my noble and learned friend Lord Taylor of Gosforth. I also would answer the certified question in the affirmative and dismiss this appeal for the reasons which he has given.

f   I should like to add only a few words of my own with regard to the position in Scotland, to which Lord Taylor has made reference. Where an accused person comes before a criminal court in Scotland he frequently finds that he has more than one charge libelled against him. The question whether these charges should then be separated so that they may be tried separately is a matter for the trial judge to decide, in the exercise of a discretion under the common law. The test

g   to be applied is whether there is a material risk of real prejudice to the accused if all the charges were to proceed together under the same indictment. There is no fetter on the way in which that discretion is to be exercised. The principles to which Lord Lane CJ made reference in *R v Cannan* (1990) 92 Cr App R 16 at 23 apply. Where the trial judge fails to apply the proper test the matter will be open

h   for reconsideration by the Appeal Court, as in *HM Advocate v Johnstone* 1992 SLT 905. But the practice of trying all outstanding charges against the accused on a single indictment has been established for a long time. It is seen to be in the public interest as well as that of the accused, in order that justice may be done expeditiously.

j   It is inevitable, if a series of unconnected charges are allowed to go to trial at the same time, that evidence will be led in regard to one charge which is inadmissible in regard to another. A material risk of real prejudice to the accused is not thought, however, to arise merely because the charges relate to different kinds of crime committed at different times in different places and under different circumstances. Experience has shown that under proper directions juries are well able to consider each charge in an indictment separately. Their verdicts demonstrate time and time again that they have done so. In practice, motions for separation of charges are granted only in very clear cases, where fairness to the accused makes this necessary.

Cases of child sexual abuse, to a greater degree than is normal in cases of sexual misconduct, present difficulty for the prosecutor because of the rule which is still part of the criminal law of Scotland that the evidence of a single witness must be corroborated. Crimes of this kind are usually committed in private, so the complainer is frequently the only witness as to what was done and who was the perpetrator. The importance of *Moorov v HM Advocate* 1930 JC 68 in Scots law is that it enables the evidence of one complainer to be corroborated by the evidence of another complainer where the separate acts spoken to by each witness show such an underlying unity as to demonstrate that the accused was engaged on a course of criminal conduct which affected them both. Charges where mutual corroboration of this kind is in issue are invariably tried together on the same indictment, although it cannot be determined until the evidence has been heard at the trial whether the corroboration which is being looked for by the prosecutor is in fact available. The same is the case in regard to the admissibility of the evidence, which is determined on the same principle as that for corroboration, as Lord Mackay of Clashfern LC explained in *R v P* [1991] 3 All ER 337 at 347, [1991] 2 AC 447 at 461. Here again, experience has shown that juries follow the judge's directions and that they are well able to consider the charges separately.

My Lords, although the practice in the conduct of criminal trials in Scotland differs in some important respects from that in England and Wales, the essential underlying principle is the same, namely that of fairness. Experience in Scotland provides strong support for the view that the matter of severance may safely be left to the discretion of the trial judge, even where the evidence of one complainant is not so related to that of another complainant as to render it admissible on the charges concerning the other complainant.

Appeal dismissed.

Celia Fox   Barrister.

a
Turner v Plasplugs Ltd

COURT OF APPEAL, CIVIL DIVISION
SIR THOMAS BINGHAM MR, PETER GIBSON AND SCHIEMANN LJJ
17, 26 JANUARY 1996

b
Legal aid – Assisted person's liability to pay costs – Certificate limited to steps or procedures to be taken by legal advisers – Certificate limited to settling proceedings – Plaintiff issuing proceedings without obtaining extension of certificate – Proceedings later discontinued – Plaintiff's liability for costs for steps taken beyond scope of certificate – Legal Aid Act 1988, s 17.

c
In April 1993 the plaintiff consulted solicitors about commencing proceedings against the defendant for infringement of a patent of which he was the registered owner in the United Kingdom. On 10 June 1993 he was granted a legal aid certificate to take proceedings against the defendant for breach of patent rights.

d The certificate was expressed to be limited 'to obtaining further evidence and thereafter Counsel's Opinion as to merits and quantum, to include settling of proceedings ... if Counsel so advises'. Counsel instructed to advise on the merits advised that if the patent was valid the plaintiff had a good arguable case on infringement. Counsel was then instructed to settle a statement of claim and proceedings were issued at the end of November 1993. The defendant filed a

e defence challenging the validity of the patent and in the light of that defence the plaintiff's counsel felt unable to recommend any extension of the legal aid certificate. The plaintiff accordingly instructed his solicitors to discontinue the proceedings. They then applied to the court for his liability for costs to be limited under s 17ᵃ of the Legal Aid Act 1988, which provided that the liability of a legally

f aided party was not to exceed the amount which it was reasonable for him to pay. The plaintiff accepted that his legal aid certificate did not cover the issuing of proceedings, but contended that he was protected by s 17 from any order for payment of costs which the defendant sought to recover from him in respect of the costs of preparing and settling a defence to the proceedings, because until his legal aid certificate was discharged he continued to be a legally assisted person

g and therefore entitled to the protection of s 17. The county court judge held that s 17 did not apply, on the grounds that at the time the costs were incurred by the defendant the plaintiff's legal aid certificate was spent and he was no longer a legally assisted person. The judge accordingly awarded costs against the plaintiff, who appealed to the Court of Appeal.

h
Held – Where the steps for which a limited legal aid certificate had been granted had been accomplished, the certificate was spent without the need for a formal discharge of the certificate, and the assisted person could not be regarded as a 'legally assisted person' in respect of any procedural steps taken thereafter.

j Accordingly, a legally assisted party was not protected by s 17 of the 1988 Act from having a costs order made against him if he engaged in proceedings when his certificate was spent, in that the steps authorised by the certificate had already been completed. Since the plaintiff's certificate was spent by the time he issued the proceedings because it was limited to steps up to settling proceedings, he was not

---

a   Section 17, so far as material, is set out at p 942 *h*, post

entitled to the protection of s 17 against the costs awarded against him. The appeal
would therefore be dismissed (see p 943 *a* to *c*, p 945 *h j*, p 946 *b* and p 947 *a b*, post).
  Littaur v Steggles Palmer (a firm) [1986] 1 All ER 780 applied.
  Boorman v Godfrey [1981] 2 All ER 1012 distinguished.

Notes
For costs of legally assisted persons generally, see 27(2) *Halsbury's Laws* (4th edn
reissue) para 1985.
  For the Legal Aid Act 1988, s 17, see 24 *Halsbury's Statutes* (4th edn) (1989
reissue) 30.

Cases referred to in judgments
Boorman v Godfrey [1981] 2 All ER 1012, [1981] 1 WLR 1100, CA.
Dugon v Williamson [1963] 3 All ER 25, [1964] Ch 59, [1963] 3 WLR 477, CA.
Herbert (orse Bridgeman) v Herbert [1964] 1 All ER 915, [1964] 1 WLR 471.
King v T & W Farmiloe Ltd [1953] 1 All ER 614, [1953] 1 WLR 458.
Littaur v Steggles Palmer (a firm) [1986] 1 All ER 780, [1986] 1 WLR 287, CA.
Mills v Mills [1963] 2 All ER 237, [1963] P 329, [1963] 2 WLR 831, CA.

Appeal
By notice dated 13 December 1994 the plaintiff, Jeffrey Turner, appealed with
leave from the decision of Judge Ford in the Patents County Court on 5
September 1994 refusing his application for an order that his liability for costs, in
respect of an action for breach of patent rights against the defendant company,
Plasplugs Ltd, was limited as if s 17 of the Legal Aid Act 1988 applied. The facts
are set out in the judgment of Sir Thomas Bingham MR.

Gilead Cooper (instructed by *Mildred & Beaumont*) for the plaintiff.
Gregory Chambers (instructed by *Evershed Wells & Hind*, Nottingham) for the
  defendant.

Cur adv vult

26 January 1996. The following judgments were delivered.

SIR THOMAS BINGHAM MR. This appeal from a decision made in the Patents
County Court raises an issue of considerable practical importance on the legal
effect of a legal aid certificate granted to the plaintiff in these proceedings.
  Such an issue may arise in a number of different ways. The question may be
whether work which solicitors or counsel have done for a client is work for which
they are entitled to be paid by the Legal Aid Board. The answer will depend on
whether the work in question is work covered by the certificate granted to the
client. The question may also arise where a solicitor or counsel seeks to be paid
not by the board but by the client. That was the question in *Littaur v Steggles
Palmer (a firm)* [1986] 1 All ER 780, [1986] 1 WLR 287. What is now reg 64 of the
Civil Legal Aid (General) Regulations 1989, SI 1989/339, forbids solicitors and
counsel to receive payment from the client for work covered by a certificate. So
it may have to be decided whether the work for which payment is sought from
the client was work covered by the certificate.
  Sometimes the question arises when an opposing party in litigation seeks an
order for costs and the party against whom the order is sought seeks the
protection of what is now s 17 of the Legal Aid Act 1988. For example, a

a defendant or respondent may be granted legal aid to resist some claims made by a plaintiff or petitioner, but not others. That was the position in *Mills v Mills* [1963] 2 All ER 237, [1963] P 329 and *Herbert (orse Bridgeman) v Herbert* [1964] 1 All ER 915, [1964] 1 WLR 471. In those cases it had to be decided whether the claims or issues in relation to which the petitioner sought costs were claims or issues in relation to which the respondent was assisted by legal aid.

b A variant of this issue arises where a legal aid certificate is limited not by reference to particular claims or issues but by reference to specific procedural steps or stages. Limitations of this type fell for consideration in *Dugon v Williamson* [1963] 3 All ER 25, [1964] Ch 59 and *Boorman v Godfrey* [1981] 2 All ER 1012, [1981] 1 WLR 1100. In the first of those cases a respondent successful on appeal sought an order for costs against the unsuccessful appellant. In the second c of the cases a defendant successful on an interlocutory application sought an order for costs against the plaintiff. In each case the party against whom the order was sought claimed the protection of what is now s 17 of the 1988 Act. In each case it had to be decided whether the costs which the successful party was claiming were costs incurred at a time when, or in relation to a procedural stage d at which, the unsuccessful party was an assisted party.

The problem in this appeal is of the latter kind, as appears from a recital of the brief facts.

Mr Turner was the registered proprietor of a United Kingdom patent. In April 1993 he consulted solicitors about commencing proceedings against Plasplugs Ltd for infringement of his patent. The solicitors applied for legal aid on his e behalf. On 10 June 1993 he was granted a certificate 'To take proceedings against Plasplugs Ltd for breach of patent rights'. The certificate was subject to conditions and limitations which, so far as relevant, were:

f 'Limited to obtaining further evidence and thereafter Counsel's Opinion as to merits and quantum, to include settling of proceedings or a defence (and counterclaim) if Counsel so advises.'

Counsel was accordingly instructed to advise Mr Turner on the merits and generally. He was unable to advise whether Mr Turner's patent was valid, since he was not provided with details of any prior art, but he advised that, if the patent was valid, Mr Turner had a good arguable case on infringement. This advice was g given in writing on 12 October 1993. In view of counsel's positive advice he was instructed to settle a draft statement of claim to enable proceedings to be issued. He did so and sent a draft to Mr Turner's solicitors which reached them on 26 October 1993. Counsel's draft was then perfected and proceedings were issued at the end of November 1993.

h It is accepted on Mr Turner's behalf, obviously rightly, that the issue of proceedings was a step which was outside the scope of his legal aid certificate. The limitation imposed on this certificate was perhaps a little odd, since if favourable advice by counsel was to be treated as sufficient to warrant the settling of proceedings, one would have expected it to be sufficient warrant also for those j proceedings to be issued without further reference back to the legal aid committee for an extension of the certificate. The limitation was, however, expressed as quoted above, and there is no argument about its effect. Unfortunately, that effect was not noted by the assistant solicitor handling the case, and proceedings were thus issued without any further reference to the committee. Unfortunately, also, Mr Turner's solicitors failed to give notice to the defendant company of the issue of his legal aid certificate, as they were required

to do by reg 50 of the 1989 regulations. This did not deprive Mr Turner of any
protection to which he was or would have been entitled as an assisted person (see
King v T & W Farmiloe Ltd [1953] 1 All ER 614, [1953] 1 WLR 458). But it did mean
that the defendant company and its solicitors were unaware that any legal aid
certificate had been granted to Mr Turner, and of course deprived them of any
opportunity to point out that the certificate did not cover the issue of
proceedings.

The defendant company delivered a defence and counterclaim dated 4 March
1994. This defence denied infringement of Mr Turner's patent. Also, and more
importantly, it challenged the validity of that patent, placing reliance on prior art
not only in this country but also in Germany and the United States. Mr Turner's
counsel was invited to consider this defence, and in the light of it he felt unable to
recommend extension of the legal aid certificate. Mr Turner accordingly
instructed his solicitors to discontinue the proceedings, and they gave notice
under CCR Ord 18, asking that his liability for costs should be limited as if s 17 of
the 1988 Act applied. When the matter came before Judge Ford in the Patents
County Court it was argued that s 17 did apply. The issue the judge had to decide
was whether it did or not. He held that it did not. Distinguishing *Boorman v
Godfrey*, on which Mr Turner principally relied, the judge said:

'Once the steps authorised by a limited certificate have been taken, the
certificate is, if not extended (even retrospectively), spent. It would appear
to undermine the whole system of limiting certificates if the assisted person
could claim the same protection from liability for costs thereafter as if he had
obtained an extension. The possibilities of abuse of the system are even
greater if there is no sanction for failing to notify the Legal Aid Board, other
parties and the court of the position, preventing action being taken, if
necessary, to discharge the certificate.'

It is argued for Mr Turner on this appeal that the learned judge was wrong and
that Mr Turner was at all times, in the terminology of the 1988 Act, 'a legally
assisted person'. That expression is defined in s 2(11) of the 1988 Act to mean—

'any person who receives, under this Act, advice, assistance or
representation and, in relation to proceedings, any reference to an assisted
party or an unassisted party is to be construed accordingly.'

It is therefore argued that Mr Turner was entitled to the benefit of s 17(1), which
provides:

'The liability of a legally assisted party under an order for costs made
against him with respect to any proceedings shall not exceed the amount (if
any) which is a reasonable one for him to pay having regard to all the
circumstances, including the financial resources of all the parties and their
conduct in connection with the dispute.'

Mr Turner had been assessed as having a disposable income of nil and a
disposable capital of nil and had not been required to make any contribution
towards his legal aid expenditure. It has not been argued that any costs order
could or should have been made against him even if s 17 did apply in the
circumstances. So the question in this court, as before the judge, is whether s 17
did apply on the facts of this case. Does that section protect Mr Turner against
an order for payment of the costs which the defendant company seeks to recover

a against him, namely the costs of preparing and settling a defence to the proceedings issued by Mr Turner?

In the absence of authority, but having regard to the language of the 1988 Act and the 1989 regulations, I would for my part regard the answer to that question as clear. Mr Turner did not, as is accepted, have the benefit of a legal aid certificate to issue proceedings. That was, to express the same point in different

b words, something done without the benefit of legal aid. There is no suggestion that the defendant company incurred any significant costs before the issue of proceedings by Mr Turner. The defendant company incurred the relevant costs preparing and delivering a defence to proceedings which Mr Turner had no authority from the legal aid committee to issue. I cannot see how, in relation to those costs, Mr Turner is to be regarded as a legally assisted person. That is

c exactly what he was not. He had been such, for the accomplishment of three clearly defined procedural steps. Those steps had been accomplished. There was strictly no need to discharge the certificate. It was spent. Everything it authorised had been done.

It is argued for Mr Turner that *Dugon v Williamson* [1963] 3 All ER 25, [1964] Ch

d 59 and *Boorman v Godfrey* [1981] 2 All ER 1012, [1981] 1 WLR 1100 compel a different solution. They must therefore be examined.

In *Dugon* the sequence of events is important. A defendant to possession proceedings was unsuccessful before the trial judge. For that trial he had the benefit of legal aid. He gave notice of appeal himself without the benefit of legal

e aid. He set the appeal down for hearing. He was then granted a legal aid certificate which authorised him to continue his appeal, subject to limitations and conditions. These limited cover to obtaining a transcript of the judgment, preparing papers for counsel and obtaining counsel's opinion on the merits of the appeal and the prospects of success. The papers, including the transcript and counsel's opinion, were then to be returned to the area committee for the

f committee to consider whether the certificate should be amended or discharged. These conditions were complied with, and the papers were referred back to the committee. The committee declined to continue legal aid and discharged the certificate. The defendant therefore found himself without legal aid for his appeal. But having considered the matter, and obtained a deferment of the

g hearing, he decided to go on with the appeal on his own without the benefit of legal aid. He did so and his appeal failed. The successful respondent then asked for costs.

The defendant was plainly liable for the plaintiff's costs of the appeal before the legal aid certificate was granted for the appeal and after it was discharged. There

h was no argument about that. But what about the costs which the plaintiff had incurred in resisting the appeal during the period after the grant of the legal aid certificate and before its discharge? Unfortunately, because of the imminence of the hearing, the plaintiff incurred considerable costs during that period, when his solicitors prepared and delivered a brief to counsel, which amounted to the bulk

j of the costs.

The Court of Appeal held that the defendant was during that period an assisted person within the relevant provisions of the Act and the regulations. That decision was, as I respectfully think, plainly correct. The plaintiff incurred the costs in order to resist an appeal by a party who had legal aid to continue the appeal unless or until the certificate had been discharged or amended. The effect of the decision appears both clear and correct.

Boorman v Godfrey is more difficult. In November 1979 the plaintiff, Mr
Boorman, began county court proceedings to recover the balance of the price of
goods sold and delivered. He was not at that stage legally assisted. The
defendant, Mr Godfrey, counterclaimed for an injunction and also applied, in
circumstances which remain obscure, for a committal order. A hearing of the
defendant's application for an injunction and a committal order were both,
curiously, due to be heard on 1 July 1980. The defendant also applied for an order
for the delivery of further and better particulars of the particulars of claim. That
application was heard on 15 September 1980. It was successful. The plaintiff was
ordered to pay the defendant's costs of that application in any event.

Meanwhile the plaintiff had obtained the benefit of legal aid. On 30 June 1980
he was granted an emergency certificate to continue to take proceedings in the
county court in the plaint which was already proceeding. The emergency
certificate was subject to conditions and limitations, namely 'Limited to
representation on the Defendant's application for an Injunction and committal to
be heard on the 1st July 1980'. With effect from the issue of that certificate the
plaintiff was legally assisted. But it is as plain as it could be that he was legally
assisted for one proceeding only, namely the applications listed for 1 July 1980,
and that legal aid was limited to representation at that hearing.

That emergency certificate was superseded by an ordinary certificate issued on
22 July 1980, which must be read as having retrospective effect. Legal aid was
then granted to the plaintiff to enable him 'to continue to take proceedings in the
Lambeth County Court' in his existing plaint. Again, there were limitations and
conditions. These were:

> 'Limited to representation on the Defendant's application for an Injunction
> and committal to be heard on the 1st July 1980. Thereafter limited to
> preparation of papers for Counsel and obtaining Counsel's Opinion on
> evidence, merits and quantum after a conference at which the Assisted
> Person should attend. Papers and Counsel's Opinion to be referred to the
> Area Committee for decision whether Certificate be amended or
> discharged.' (See [1981] 2 All ER 1012 at 1014, [1981] 1 WLR 1100 at 1102.)

The first limitation or condition reproduced the terms of the emergency
certificate. It seems probable that that hearing had already taken place. The
second limitation or condition extended the scope of the emergency certificate to
cover: (1) preparation of papers for counsel; (2) the holding of a conference
attended by the assisted person; and (3) the giving of an opinion by counsel on
evidence, merits and quantum. When those three stages had been accomplished,
the papers and the written opinion of counsel were to be referred to the area
committee for a decision whether the certificate should be amended or
discharged.

That certificate, as already recorded, was issued on 22 July 1980. The
defendant's successful application for further and better particulars was made on
15 September 1980. The statement of the facts in the two reports of the case do
not record whether, by 15 September 1980, the three procedural stages specified
in the legal aid certificate had been accomplished or not. I infer that they had not.
I base that inference on the observation of Donaldson LJ ([1981] 2 All ER 1012 at
1017, [1981] 1 WLR 1100 at 1105):

> 'However little the assisted person's legal advisers may be authorised to
> do, until they have done it and the certificate has been discharged, the

a assisted person has the benefit of s 8(1)(e) of the [Legal Aid Act 1974] in relation to all costs incurred by the other party during that period.'

It is also worthy of note that the law reporter who composed the headnote of the All England report understood that the plaintiff had not obtained counsel's opinion, as authorised by the legal aid certificate, by 15 September (see [1981] 2 b All ER 1012 at 1013).

I should myself have been inclined to hold that the legal aid certificate granted to the plaintiff did not cover attendance on the application for particulars heard on 15 September 1980, since that was not one of the three procedural steps for which legal aid had been granted by the full certificate. That was certainly the view of the plaintiff's solicitors at the time, since they did not attend the hearing c on the ground that they had no legal aid cover to do so (see [1981] 2 All ER 1012 at 1015, [1981] 1 WLR 1100 at 1102). Donaldson LJ, however, held, with the agreement of Ackner LJ, that since the application for particulars was made during a period when the plaintiff was the beneficiary of a legal aid certificate which remained in force and had not been discharged, he was a legally assisted d person and so entitled to statutory protection in relation to the making of a costs order against him on that application. I have some reservations about the correctness of that decision, although I can understand the practical and administrative difficulties which might arise if, during the currency of a legal aid certificate, a party were covered by legal aid in relation to some procedural steps but not others. It seems to me somewhat anomalous if, on a particular e application, a party is protected against an award of costs to the other party because he is legally aided, but not entitled to representation because his legal aid certificate does not cover that application.

Even if one assumes, as one must, that the decision is correct, it is distinguishable. In that case the three procedural steps for which the certificate f provided had not, it seems, been accomplished. Here, on any showing, they had. If, therefore, *Boorman v Godfrey* is good authority for the proposition that a legal aid certificate protects the beneficiary against orders for costs during the currency of the certificate even though the certificate is limited to certain procedural steps and the costs in question were not incurred in relation to any of those steps, the case does not entitle Mr Turner to protection against costs in this case, unless the g case is also authority for the proposition that a legal aid certificate granted to cover certain procedural steps or stages protects the assisted party against an order for costs until the certificate is discharged. In my view that is not a sound proposition. *Littaur v Steggles Palmer (a firm)* [1986] 1 All ER 780, [1986] 1 WLR 287 shows that the legal aid certificate does not have to be discharged if it is spent. h In the present case, had counsel advised Mr Turner against proceeding and so declined to settle proceedings, it would in my view have been unnecessary to return to the legal aid committee to seek a discharge of the certificate. It had covered all that had been done and there was nothing more to do. It was now spent. The only purpose of returning to the committee would have been to j obtain an extension. This could have been done, and it is plain—in view of counsel's advice—that had application been duly made authority to issue proceedings would have been granted. But this was not done. So, from the time of issue onwards, Mr Turner held no relevant legal aid certificate. His solicitors were not, as they acknowledge, thereafter entitled to be paid by the board until a new certificate had been issued. And Mr Turner was not, as I think, entitled to the protection of s 17. It is quite true, as counsel for Mr Turner pointed out, that

in *Littaur* the description of the legal aid which was granted restricted the cover
to a specific application within the specified proceedings without any limitation
or condition, whereas here the grant was to take proceedings for breach of patent
rights and the restriction was by way of limitation or condition. But I do not see
why that distinction should be crucial. Much more significant, as it seems to me,
is the fact common to both cases, that everything which the current certificate
authorised to be done had been done.

In my view the judge came to the right conclusion. I would dismiss the appeal.

PETER GIBSON LJ. I agree with Sir Thomas Bingham MR.

SCHIEMANN LJ. I have found this case more difficult than Sir Thomas
Bingham MR and Peter Gibson LJ.

The question which arises is whether Mr Turner was 'an assisted party' at the
time when the defendant incurred costs, namely after proceedings were issued.
Section 17 of the Legal Aid Act 1988 refers both to a legally assisted 'party' and a
legally assisted 'person'. I can see no distinction between them or reason why the
draftsman should have employed two different terms. I proceed on the basis that
this difference does not matter for present purposes.

'Legally assisted person' is a term of art defined by s 2(11) as meaning—'any
person who receives, under this Act, advice assistance or representation'. I do not
find this definition helpful. It seems clear from the 1988 Act that a person can be
a legally assisted person at a time when, for good reason or bad, he is not actually
receiving anything. An example might be a situation where: (1) a certificate has
been issued and served on the other side who then proceed to incur costs; yet (2)
the assisted person's solicitors in fact do nothing.

I have found it difficult to define the precise point in time when, assuming that
the grant of legal aid is limited to advice, the certificate is spent. When the
solicitors receive the advice, assuming it to come from counsel? When they write
to the client enclosing it? What if the client wishes to discuss the advice with
solicitors? How long has the client got to consider whether to discuss the advice
with solicitors? Does the certificate cover the solicitors if they wish to ask counsel
to elaborate, qualify or explain the advice? How soon must the solicitors act
before the certificate is spent? These are points which can arise and may be
relevant to s 17 if the other side is meanwhile incurring costs.

Further, there are sections in the 1988 Act which appear to envisage that a
person can continue to be a legally assisted person notwithstanding that all has
been done which the certificate authorises. Thus ss 9(6) and 16(1) provide for
payment by 'a legally assisted person', at a time when all that has been authorised
by the certificate has been done. Clearly it was not desired that he should be in a
position to say 'I am no longer a "legally assisted person" and therefore I am not
one of the persons referred to in these subsections'.

But I am not persuaded that all of these problems—and similar problems
which can arise under the Civil Legal Aid (General) Regulations 1989, SI 1989/
339, made under the 1988 Act—would be avoided if we were to hold that a
person continued to be an assisted person until the certificate was formally
revoked or discharged.

Further, I can see no reason of policy why a party bringing proceedings
without the authorisation of the Legal Aid Board should receive the protection
which Parliament has sought by s 17 to give to those who do have that
authorisation. I appreciate that in the present case it seems highly probable that,

a had counsel's opinion been shown to the legal aid committee, they would have authorised proceedings, but I agree that this can make no difference to the problem we have to resolve.

Notwithstanding the potential problems which I have endeavoured to identify but which were not relied on by counsel in their submissions, given the decision in *Littaur v Steggles Palmer (a firm)* [1986] 1 All ER 780, [1986] 1 WLR 287, to which
b Sir Thomas Bingham MR has referred, I agree that this appeal ought to be dismissed.

Appeal dismissed. Leave to appeal to the House of Lords refused.

20 May 1996. The Appeal Committee of the House of Lords (Lord Keith of Kinkel, Lord
c *Mustill and Lord Nicholls of Birkenhead) refused leave to appeal.*

L I Zysman Esq   Barrister.

Doorbar v Alltime Securities Ltd   *a*

COURT OF APPEAL, CIVIL DIVISION
HIRST, PETER GIBSON LJJ AND FORBES J
2, 3, 30 NOVEMBER 1995

                                                                        b

Insolvency – Voluntary arrangement – Approval by creditors – Creditor having claims against debtor for past and future rent under lease – Chairman of creditor's meeting putting minimum estimated value on future rent without creditor's agreement – Whether creditor bound by arrangement in respect of future rent – Whether material irregularity at meeting – Whether unfair prejudice to creditor's interests – Insolvency Act 1986, s 262 – Insolvency Rules 1986, r 5.17.   *c*

The debtor submitted a proposal for a voluntary arrangement of his affairs, including his past and future liabilities to the creditor under a 20-year lease of business premises. At a creditors' meeting summoned to consider the arrangement, the chairman put an estimated minimum value of one year's rent on the   *d*
future liabilities under the lease, to enable the creditor to vote at the meeting in respect of its unascertained claim to future rent in accordance with r 5.17(3)[a] of the Insolvency Rules 1986. The creditor did not agree with the chairman's valuation and voted as creditor only in respect of its entitlement to the arrears of rent. Following the meeting's approval of the scheme, the creditor applied (i) for   *e*
a declaration that the scheme did not include the future rent and did not affect the debtor's future liabilities under the lease, and (ii) for revocation of the approval of the scheme under s 262(1)[b] of the Insolvency Act 1986, on the grounds that there was a material irregularity at the meeting and that the arrangement unfairly prejudiced its interests as a creditor. The creditor's applications were granted, but both decisions were reversed by the judge on the debtor's applications. The   *f*
creditor appealed.

Held – The appeals would be dismissed for the following reasons—
    (1) While a creditor could not vote in respect of an unliquidated or unascertained claim unless the chairman agreed to give it an estimated minimum value pursuant to r 5.17(3) of the 1986 rules, the chairman's agreement was not   *g*
expressed to be an agreement with the creditor or with anyone else, nor an agreement as to the value of the claim; it was sufficient if the chairman expressed his willingness to put, and did put, an estimated minimum value on the debt. It followed that, since the chairman had put an estimated value on the future liabilities, the creditor was bound by the arrangement in respect of all future rent   *h*
under the lease (see p 957 *b* to *e*, p 958 *c* and p 960 *c*, post); *Re Cranley Mansions Ltd* [1995] 1 BCLC 290 overruled.
    (2) There was no material irregularity in the chairman's estimate of the minimum value of future rent at less than the full number of years of the unexpired term of the lease. While the chairman should not have taken account   *j*
of any duty to mitigate, it was entirely realistic of him to have estimated what was likely to happen and to have made allowance for the possibility that the creditor would exercise its power of re-entry under the lease. Moreover, the creditor had

---

a   Rule 5, so far as material, is set out at p 950 *h* to p 951 *d*, post
b   Section 262, so far as material, is set out at p 951 *g*, post

not been unfairly prejudiced by the terms of the arrangement, because its right to require the surety to accept a lease (and thereby to recover all future rent) was a substitute for rather than a constituent part of the debtor's indebtedness, so that the creditor's interest was outside the ambit of s 262(1)(a) of the 1986 Act (see p 958 j to p 959 a j and p 960 b c, post).

Notes

For decisions of meetings, voting rights and majorities at creditors' meetings relating to individual voluntary arrangements, see 3(2) *Halsbury's Laws* (4th edn reissue) paras 93–99, and for cases on the subject, see 4(1) *Digest* (2nd reissue) 182–183, *1586–1607*.

For the Insolvency Act 1986, s 262, see 4 *Halsbury's Statutes* (4th edn) (1987 reissue) 905.

For the Insolvency Rules 1986, r 5.17, see 3 *Halsbury's Statutory Instruments* (1995 reissue) 380.

Cases referred to in judgments

Beverley Group plc v McClue [1995] 2 BCLC 407.
Bradley-Hole (a bankrupt), Re [1995] 4 All ER 865, [1995] 1 WLR 1097.
Cancol Ltd, Re [1996] 1 All ER 37.
Cranley Mansions Ltd, Re [1995] 1 BCLC 290, [1994] 1 WLR 1610.
Davis v Martin-Sklan [1995] 2 BCLC 483.
McKeen (a debtor), Re [1995] BCC 412.
Naeem (a bankrupt), Re (No 18 of 1988) [1990] 1 WLR 48.

Cases also cited or referred to in skeleton arguments

Company, Re a (No 00477 of 1986) [1986] BCLC 376.
Debtor, Re a (No 222 of 1990), ex p Bank of Ireland [1992] BCLC 137.
Debtor, Re a (No 259 of 1990) [1992] 1 All ER 641, [1992] 1 WLR 226.
Exchange Travel Agency Ltd v Triton Property Trust plc [1991] BCLC 396.
Olympia & York Canary Wharf Ltd, Re [1993] BCLC 453.
Weller (Sam) & Sons Ltd, Re [1990] Ch 682, [1989] 3 WLR 923.

Appeals

By notices dated 29 November 1994 and 21 August 1995 the debtor, Richard Leon Doorbar, appealed from the decisions of Knox J (i) on 3 November 1994 ([1995] 1 BCLC 316), setting aside the order of the District Judge Hollis dated 5 July 1994 whereby he declared that the debtor's proposal for a voluntary arrangement did not include future rent under a lease granted by the creditor, Alltime Securities Ltd, and (ii) on 16 June 1995 ([1995] 2 BCLC 513), setting aside the order of Deputy District Judge Gamba on 17 February 1995 whereby he revoked the approval of the voluntary scheme of arrangement. The facts are set out in the judgment of Peter Gibson LJ.

Amanda Tipples (instructed by *Tinklin Springall*, Beckenham) for the creditor.
Antony Zacaroli (instructed by *Charles Marlowe*, Brighton) for the debtor.

Cur adv vult

30 November 1995. The following judgments were delivered.   *a*

PETER GIBSON LJ (giving the first judgment at the invitation of Hirst LJ). Among the innovations introduced by the Insolvency Act 1986 were provisions in Pt VIII of the Act enabling an individual debtor to make a proposal to his creditors for a composition in satisfaction of his debts or a scheme of arrangement of his affairs (in either case called a voluntary arrangement), and for carrying that *b* voluntary arrangement into effect. There were corresponding provisions for corporate debtors in Pt I of the Act. These appeals raise questions as to the meaning of the statutory provisions and rules relating to individual voluntary arrangements and their effect in the particular circumstances of this case.

It is convenient to commence by summarising the statutory scheme for *c* individual voluntary arrangements. The debtor who intends to propose a voluntary arrangement is required to apply to the court for an interim order under s 253 of the 1986 Act. His proposal must provide for some person (the nominee) to act in relation to the voluntary arrangement as trustee or otherwise for the purpose of supervising its implementation. The matters to be dealt with in the proposal include his assets and their estimated values, any property, other *d* than the assets of the debtor himself, which is to be included in the voluntary arrangement, the nature and amount of his liabilities, the duration of the voluntary arrangement, and the functions which are to be undertaken by the supervisor of the voluntary arrangement (Insolvency Rules 1986, SI 1986/1925, r 5.3). Both the nominee and the supervisor have to be insolvency practitioners *e* (s 255(1)(d) and r 5.3(p)). If the court makes an interim order, no bankruptcy petition may be presented or proceeded with and no other proceedings and no execution or other legal process may be commenced or continued against the debtor without leave (s 252). The order ceases to have effect after 14 days and before it does the nominee must submit a report to the court, stating whether a creditors' meeting should be summoned to consider the debtor's proposal *f* (ss 255(6) and 256(1)). The debtor is required to submit to the nominee a statement of his affairs (s 256(2)). If the court is satisfied that there should be a creditors' meeting, the interim order is extended until the meeting (s 256(5)) and the nominee summons every creditor to the meeting (s 257). The creditors' meeting decides whether to approve the proposed voluntary arrangement and *g* may do so with modifications to which the debtor consents (s 258(1) and (2)). But the meeting shall not approve any proposal or modification which affects the right of a secured creditor to enforce his security, except with the creditor's concurrence (s 258(4)).

The nominee, if able to attend, is the chairman of the meeting (r 5.15(1)). *h* Voting rights are dealt with in r 5.17:

'(1) Subject as follows, every creditor who was given notice of the creditors' meeting is entitled to vote at the meeting or any adjournment of it.

(2) ... votes are calculated ... in Case 2 [relating to a case where the debtor *j* is other than an undischarged bankrupt] according to the amount of the debt as at the date of the meeting.

(3) A creditor shall not vote in respect of a debt for an unliquidated amount, or any debt whose value is not ascertained, except where the chairman agrees to put upon the debt an estimated minimum value for the purpose of entitlement to vote.

a
(4) The chairman has power to admit or reject a creditor's claim for the purpose of his entitlement to vote, and the power is exercisable with respect to the whole or any part of the claim.

(5) The chairman's decision on entitlement to vote is subject to appeal to the court by any creditor, or by the debtor.

b
(6) If the chairman is in doubt whether a claim should be admitted or rejected, he shall mark it as objected to and allow the creditor to vote, subject to his vote being subsequently declared invalid if the objection to the claim is sustained.

(7) If on an appeal the chairman's decision is reversed or varied, or a creditor's vote is declared invalid, the court may order another meeting to be summoned, or make such other order as it thinks just. The court's power to make an order under this paragraph is exercisable only if it considers that the matter is such as to give rise to unfair prejudice or a material irregularity.

c

(8) An application to the court by way of appeal under this Rule against the chairman's decision shall not be made after the end of the period of 28 days beginning with the day on which the chairman's report to the court is made under section 259.'

d

By r 5.18(1) for any resolution to pass approving any proposal or modification there must be a majority in excess of three-quarters in value of the creditors present in person or by proxy and voting on the resolution.

The effect of the approval is stated in s 260(2):

e

'The approved arrangement—(a) takes effect as if made by the debtor at the meeting, and (b) binds every person who in accordance with the rules had notice of, and was entitled to vote at, the meeting (whether or not he was present or represented at it) as if he were a party to the arrangement.'

f
Section 262(1) provides for challenges of the meeting's decision, allowing, amongst others, a person entitled to vote at the meeting to apply to the court on one or both of the following grounds:

'(a) that a voluntary arrangement approved by a creditors' meeting summoned under section 257 unfairly prejudices the interests of a creditor of the debtor; (b) that there has been some material irregularity at or in relation to such a meeting.'

g

The court, if satisfied on either of those grounds, may revoke or suspend any approval given by the meeting and may direct a further meeting to be summoned.

h
Where a voluntary arrangement takes effect, the supervisor performs the functions allotted to him by that arrangement. If the debtor or any creditor or other person is dissatisfied with any act, omission or decision of the supervisor, he may apply to the court under s 263(3).

j
By s 264(1)(c) the supervisor or any person (other than the debtor) who is for the time being bound by an approved voluntary arrangement may present a bankruptcy petition against the debtor, but a bankruptcy order will not be made on such petition unless the court is satisfied of a default by the debtor in connection with the voluntary arrangement (s 276(1)). In contrast, any creditor who is not bound by the approved arrangement may present a petition relying on his debt (s 264(1)(a)).

I turn to the facts. On 3 April 1981 the appellant, Alltime Securities Ltd, as the
landlord granted a lease of business premises, 343 Eden Park Avenue, Bromley,   *a*
to Menage Graphic Productions as the tenant for a term of 20 years at £7,500 per
annum subject to five-yearly rent reviews and an additional annual rent for
insurance. From 29 September 1990 the annual rent was increased to £13,830.
The tenant is in fact the respondent debtor, Mr Doorbar, by his trade name.
There was provision in cl 4 for re-entry by the landlord in usual form on the   *b*
failure to pay the rent thereby reserved for 21 days after becoming payable, or if
the tenant should become bankrupt or enter into any composition with his
creditors. Also named as parties to the lease were Mr Doorbar and his then wife,
who were called in the lease 'the Sureties'. By cl 5:

> 'If the Tenant shall go into liquidation and the liquidator shall disclaim this   *c*
> lease or if the Tenant shall be wound up or cease to exist (or if the Tenant for
> the time being shall be an individual and shall become bankrupt and the
> trustee in bankruptcy shall disclaim this Lease) and if the Landlord shall
> within three months after such disclaimer or other event putting an end to
> the effect of this Lease as aforesaid so far as concerns the Tenant by notice in
> writing require the Surety to accept a lease of the premises for a term   *d*
> commensurate with the residue which if there had been no disclaimer or if
> this Lease had continued to have had effect as aforesaid would have
> remained of the term hereby granted at the same rent and subject to the like
> covenants and conditions as are reserved by and contained in this Lease
> (with the exception of this clause) the said new lease and the rights and   *e*
> liabilities thereunder to take effect as from the date of the said disclaimer or
> of this Lease ceasing to have effect as aforesaid then and in such case the
> Surety shall pay the costs of and accept such new lease accordingly and will
> execute and deliver to the Landlord a counterpart thereof.'

Although that clause only refers to 'the Surety' in the singular, Mr Zacaroli for Mr   *f*
Doorbar does not dispute that if the conditions for the operation of cl 5 are
satisfied, Alltime may require Mrs Doorbar to take a lease for the remainder of
the term. It is to be noted that those conditions are more limited than the
conditions for forfeiture in cl 4, in particular in that they do not include the
condition, 'if the tenant should enter into any composition with his creditors'.
    Mr Doorbar fell into arrears with his rent and on 24 April 1993 Alltime served   *g*
a statutory demand on him, requiring payment of £7,434 arrears. Mr Doorbar did
not pay the sum demanded, but sought unsuccessfully to set aside the demand.
Alltime presented a bankruptcy petition based on that demand. The hearing was
fixed for 24 August 1993, but Mr Doorbar applied under s 253 for, and on 24
August 1993 obtained, an interim order on the basis of a proposal for a voluntary   *h*
arrangement. His statement of affairs, appended to his proposal, showed that his
only asset, a leasehold property, had a negative equity, while his liabilities were
some £35,000 (including a debt to Alltime of £7,434). That total proved to be a
gross underestimate. His proposal was based on monthly payments out of his
anticipated income. He proposed paying £250 per month for six months, £350   *j*
per month for the next six months and £500 per month for the remainder of the
term of the arrangement, which he proposed should last for four years. He
named Mr Kenneth Bradshaw as the nominee and Mr Michael Matthews as the
supervisor. The supervisor's functions were to include agreeing creditors' claims.
Dividends were to be paid to creditors where it was possible to pay at least 10p in
the pound on proved debts. Paragraph 12 stated: 'All future liabilities arising

a under the Guarantee on property owned by Alltime ... are to be included in the Arrangement'. It is common ground that the liability to Alltime of Mr Doorbar as tenant for future rent under the lease is covered by that paragraph.

A meeting of creditors was summoned by the nominee for 20 September 1993 but adjourned to 4 October 1993. Prior to the adjourned meeting Alltime had indicated to the nominee that it objected to the inclusion of para 12, but had not b put any value on its claim based on future rent under the lease. The nominee was chairman of the adjourned meeting.

At the meeting Alltime's managing director, Mr Springall, raised the question of the liability of Mr Doorbar for future rent. Mr Springall in his affidavit of 15 October said:

c   'whilst the Chairman permitted all future liabilities under the Lease to be included in the Voluntary Arrangement, he would not allow [Alltime], as Creditor, the value of this future liability for voting purposes.'

The nominee in his report to the court on the meeting said:

d   'Mr. Bradshaw was asked about Clause 12 of the Proposals, and it was confirmed that it was intended that any liabilities arising under the Lease of Premises should be included in the Arrangement. Mr. Springall suggested that the whole of the future Rent should therefore be included, but Mr. Bradshaw said that this could not be so because there had to be mitigation for the likelihood of the Property being re-let, and it was therefore not e   possible to quantify a Liquidated sum due. The only liquidated sum due at today's date was the figure claimed in Alltime Securities Ltd. Proof of Debt in the sum of £32,911·61. The most which would be accepted for future liability at this stage would be one year's future Rent.'

In his affidavit of 22 November 1993 the nominee amplified this:

f   'I invited the Applicant to submit a claim for the future rent liabilities in the sum of one year's rent. I would not accept a calculation of all the future rent because there was a duty to mitigate, but I would have been prepared to accept one year's future rent. The Applicant did not ask for such a sum to be included in the voting and as such its vote was in the sum of £32,911·61. g   Even if one year's rent (in the sum of £13,830·00) had been admitted for the purposes of voting, the proposal would still have been approved by the requisite majority.'

And a little later in that affidavit he said that he indicated to Mr Springall that he would allow Alltime to vote in relation to the future liabilities, restricted to the h future rent for the period of one year. But that was not acceptable to Mr Springall, who only voted for Alltime as creditor in respect of arrears of rent and interest thereon in the sum of £32,911·61.

Certain modifications of the proposed arrangement were approved, including the extension of the term of the arrangement to five years, and creditors with j debts of £226,898 approved the modified arrangement, only Alltime voting against; that is to say creditors with 87·34% of the total debts (on the footing that Alltime was a creditor in only the sum of £32,911·61) were in favour. The effect of the approved arrangement is that if it includes the future rent under the lease and Alltime is bound thereby, it cannot proceed with its bankruptcy petition to obtain a bankruptcy order against Mr Doorbar and so cannot invoke cl 5 of the lease to require Mrs Doorbar to take a lease for the remainder of the term.

On 18 October 1993 Alltime applied under s 262 of the 1986 Act in the *a* Eastbourne County Court, seeking by its amended summons three orders: (1) a declaration that the arrangement does not include future rent under the lease and does not affect Mr Doorbar's liability for the same; (2) the revocation of the approval given to the arrangement at the creditors' meeting on 4 October 1993, on the ground that the arrangement unfairly prejudiced the interests of Alltime as a creditor of Mr Doorbar; and (3) the revocation or suspension of that approval *b* on the ground that there was a material irregularity at the meeting.

On 5 July 1994 District Judge Hollis made the first order sought, saying that he could not see how a future debt, particularly where the amount was unliquidated, could be included in a voluntary arrangement unless there was agreement between the debtor and the creditor. He therefore did not deal with the second and third orders sought. Mr Doorbar appealed to the High Court. Knox J ([1995] *c* 1 BCLC 316) on 3 November 1994 allowed the appeal, holding that the voluntary arrangement did include the future rent under the lease and that Alltime was bound in respect of the same. He granted Alltime leave to appeal. Alltime then applied for the rest of its summons to be restored for hearing and on 17 February 1995 Deputy District Judge Gamba ordered that the approval to the arrangement *d* be revoked on the grounds stated in the second and third orders sought. He said that the inability to activate cl 5 of the lease constituted unfair prejudice to Alltime and that there was a material irregularity in that the chairman did not make a reasonable valuation of the future rent, but wrongly concerned himself with the duty to mitigate. Again that decision was the subject of an appeal by Mr Doorbar and this appeal too was allowed by Knox J ([1995] 2 BCLC 513) on 16 *e* June 1995. He held that the interests of Alltime were not prejudiced unfairly or at all. He further held that while there may have been an irregularity in that the chairman was wrong to rely, if he did, on a duty to mitigate, there was no material irregularity involved in the chairman's willingness to put upon Alltime's claim for future rent a minimum value of one year's rent. Again Knox J granted *f* leave to appeal.

Alltime now appeals to this court from both decisions of Knox J. It is not suggested by Miss Tipples, appearing for Alltime, that a future rent liability could not be included in a voluntary arrangement, nor that that liability does not fall within the words of r 5.17(3): 'a debt for an unliquidated amount, or any debt whose value is not ascertained.' She makes the following submissions on the *g* facts of this case. (1) Alltime was not bound by the arrangement in relation to the future rent liability because the chairman did not agree with Alltime to put upon that debt the estimated minimum value of one year's rent. (2) If it was bound, the court should revoke the approval given at the creditors' meeting of the voluntary arrangement on either or both of the following grounds: (a) the *h* chairman's valuation of the future rent liability was a material irregularity; (b) the arrangement unfairly prejudiced Alltime's interests.

I shall consider these submissions in turn.

(1) *Is Alltime bound by the arrangement?*   *j*

If Alltime was entitled to vote at the creditors' meeting in respect of the future rent liability owed to it, by virtue of s 260(2)(b) Alltime would be bound by the arrangement. The question whether Alltime was entitled to vote turns on the true construction of r 5.17(3) and in particular the word 'agrees'. Does it connote some element of bilateral concurrence between the chairman and the creditor, or an expression of willingness by the chairman?

The former was the conclusion of Ferris J in *Re Cranley Mansions Ltd* [1995] 1
a BCLC 290, [1994] 1 WLR 1610. That was a decision on a company voluntary
arrangement. As the corresponding rule (r 1.17(3)) of the 1986 rules uses the
same wording as r 5.17(3), it cannot be suggested that the two rules have different
meanings. In that case a leaseholder, Mrs Saigol, claimed damages against the
landlord company in respect of defects in works undertaken by the company to
b her property. A company voluntary arrangement was proposed. Mrs Saigol
lodged a claim in the sum of £900,000, but the chairman of the creditors' meeting
considered that the value of the debt was not ascertained and placed an estimated
minimum value of £1 on the debt for the purposes of entitlement to vote. If the
minimum value of her debt had been estimated at over £1,700 the proposal
would have been defeated. The proposal was approved by the creditors'
c meeting. Mrs Saigol sought an order revoking or suspending that approval. She
succeeded in her submission that there had been a material irregularity in the
conduct of the meeting in that the chairman had purported to admit her vote in
respect of £1, whereas r 1.17(3) was inapplicable, as no estimated minimum value
was agreed with her to be put on her debt.

d   Ferris J said ([1995] 1 BCLC 290 at 309–310, [1994] 1 WLR 1610 at 1628–1629):

'Both [counsel for the company] and [counsel for the chairman] pointed
out that unless the chairman is entitled to put a value upon the claim of a
creditor which is unliquidated or unascertained without regard to the wishes
of that creditor, the utility of the statutory provisions in respect of corporate
e   voluntary arrangements (and, indeed, individual voluntary arrangements
and other matters to be decided at meetings governed by rules as to voting
equivalent to r 1.17) would be greatly reduced. If a creditor is not entitled to
vote in respect of such a claim without a value being put upon the claim
under r 1.17(3) or its equivalent (which is a matter to be considered in a
f   moment) a disaffected creditor could stultify proposals for a voluntary
arrangement by the simple expedient of failing to concur in a value being put
on his claim. The arrangement might then be approved by the requisite
majorities of those entitled to vote on it, but it would not be binding on the
disaffected creditor. In most, if not all, cases there would be no point in
having an arrangement which is not binding upon all creditors. I see the
g   force of this submission, which causes me some anxiety because my decision
is likely to affect many other cases. Nevertheless I cannot escape the fact that
the relevant words of r 1.17(3) are "where the chairman agrees to put upon
the debt an estimated minimum value", not "where the chairman puts upon
the debt an estimated minimum value". Moreover I think it would be
h   perverse to say that the requirement imported by the word "agrees" can be
satisfied by an agreement between the chairman and someone other than the
creditor, such as the company, as was suggested in argument. In my
judgment "agrees" requires some element of bilateral concurrence between
the chairman and the creditor in question. If the creditor puts forward an
j   estimated minimum value without prejudice to a contention that his real
claim is much larger and if the chairman accepts this, the words of the rule
would, in my view, clearly be satisfied notwithstanding that there is nothing
in the nature of a contract between the chairman and the creditor. The same
would be the case if the chairman took the initiative in suggesting a value and
the creditor concurred in this suggestion for the purpose of r 1.17(3),
although not for the purpose of limiting the claim. The matter would be

more difficult if the chairman put forward a value for the purpose of r 1.17(3) and the creditor rejected this for all purposes but nevertheless insisted on voting. The outcome would, in my view, then depend upon an evaluation of precisely what was said and done.'

In the first of the decisions under appeal before us, Knox J took a different view of the meaning of r 5.17(3). He said:

'Mr Zacaroli invited me not to follow that decision and advanced a different argument from that which appears to have been advanced before Ferris J, namely that what the sub-rule requires is the chairman's agreement to put a minimum value and not an agreement upon or in relation to the minimum value. He submitted that an agreement by the chairman to put a value was satisfied on 4 October by Mr Bradshaw's expression of willingness to put a value of £13,830, one year's rent, upon the debt. The fact that that was not acceptable to Mr Springall does not detract from the effect of Mr Bradshaw's willingness to put a minimum value. In support of that construction Mr Zacaroli pointed out that the appeal machinery in r 5.17(5), which applies to sub-r (3) just as much as to sub-r (4), would be rendered effectively nugatory since it would only be if there was agreement that a minimum value could be placed upon the debt, and, if there was agreement, it is difficult to see how there could be an effective appeal. It is apparent that Ferris J himself was caused anxiety by what he took to be the inescapable requirement of bilateral concurrence between the creditor and the chairman, and I respectfully share that anxiety. I should, of course, normally follow what one of my brethren in this division has previously held but I am not bound to do so, and in the light of the argument addressed to me by Mr Zacaroli, which was not, so far as I could see, addressed to Ferris J, I have reached the conclusion that the only agreement that sub-r 5.17(3) requires is an expressed willingness by the chairman to put an estimated minimum value on the debt in question. If the sub-rule is thus interpreted it avoids the undesirable result that the relevant creditor can avoid the consequences of being in a minority of 25% or less and be bound by the 75% or more majority by the simple expedient of refusing to agree any minimum value for any purpose, and it gives the appeal procedure a proper field within which to operate.' (See [1995] 1 BCLC 316 at 331.)

Accordingly, he held that on the facts what the chairman did amounted to expressing a willingness to put a minimum value on Alltime's claim, and that therefore the exception in r 5.17(3) applied. In two subsequent cases, *Beverley Group plc v McClue* [1995] 2 BCLC 407 at 418 and *Re Cancol Ltd* [1996] 1 All ER 37, he adhered to his view of the word 'agrees' in the context of r 1.17(3).

Miss Tipples submitted that Ferris J's view was to be preferred to that of Knox J. She said that Knox J was construing the sub-rule as though it read 'except where the chairman puts upon the debt an estimated minimum value', and that gave no meaning to the word 'agrees'. She criticised Knox J's acceptance of the argument that the appeal machinery in r 5.17(5) would on her construction be rendered nugatory, pointing out that that machinery would still apply to r 5.17(3) on an appeal by a person other than the creditor in question, for example the debtor. In answer to the point that a creditor with an unliquidated claim could avoid being bound by not agreeing with the chairman, she submitted that it was in the commercial interest of the creditor to reach agreement in order to be bound by the arrangement and receive dividends thereunder. Although the creditor who is not bound by the arrangement might later make the debtor bankrupt, that in itself would not necessarily defeat the voluntary arrangement which would continue in operation, the assets subject to the arrangement being held by the supervisor on trust only for the creditors bound by the arrangement (see *Re McKeen (a debtor)* [1995] BCC 412 and *Re Bradley-Hole (a bankrupt)* [1995] 4 All ER 865, [1995] 1 WLR 1097).

I see the force of these submissions and of the considerations which led Ferris J to the construction which he put on the sub-rule, but I am not persuaded by them. The context of the crucial words in r 5.17(3) is that there is a general prohibition on voting by the creditor with an unliquidated or unascertained claim, to which prohibition there is an exception if the chairman agrees. That agreement, significantly, is not expressed to be with the creditor or anyone else. It is not an agreement on the value (that, in the voluntary arrangement, is for the supervisor who might arrive at a significantly higher value)–the chairman only agrees to put on the debt an estimated minimum value. That is an unlikely subject of a bilateral agreement and to my mind it suggests that it is left to the chairman alone to decide 'at the very least the claim is worth £X', rather than to arrive at an agreement with the creditor on that minimum value. Given that the chairman is not a lawyer but an insolvency practitioner at a meeting of creditors, it seems to me unlikely that the draftsman contemplated the necessity of agreement with the creditor on each debt of this character. It is sufficient if the chairman expresses his willingness to put, and puts, an estimated minimum value on the debt.

Knox J's interpretation seems to me to derive support from consideration of other parts of the legislation. For there to be a voluntary arrangement, there must be a composition in satisfaction of the debtor's debts or a scheme of arrangement of his affairs, and the intention must have been to bind all the creditors so far as possible even if creditors holding up to 25% in value of the debts do not agree. Of course the very wording of r 5.17(3) contemplates that the chairman may not agree to put an estimated minimum value on some unliquidated and unascertained claims, and so there may be some such creditors (as well as creditors inadvertently omitted) not bound by the arrangement; but it would in my opinion materially diminish the utility of voluntary arrangements if creditors with such claims were free not to be bound by the arrangement by simply choosing not to agree a minimum value which was not to their liking. A creditor not so bound is free to make the debtor bankrupt.

Mr Zacaroli, for the purposes of this appeal, did not challenge the correctness of the decisions in *Re McKeen* and *Re Bradley-Hole*, although both are first instance decisions. For completeness he drew to our attention the recent decision of Blackburne J in *Davis v Martin-Sklan* [1995] 2 BCLC 483, in which it was held that the making of a bankruptcy order on a petition presented by a petitioner within s 264(1)(c) automatically brought the arrangement to an end, and it may be that the decisions in *Re McKeen* and *Re Bradley-Hole* will on a future occasion need reconsideration. But I shall proceed like Mr Zacaroli did, on the footing that if a creditor not bound by the arrangement makes the debtor bankrupt, the arrangement will nevertheless not be terminated and the assets subject to the arrangement will remain subject to a trust from which the creditors not so bound are excluded. As Mr Zacaroli pointed out, it may be in such a creditor's commercial interest to petition for the debtor's bankruptcy, notwithstanding the existence of a voluntary arrangement, particularly in a case like the present where the only assets of the arrangement are to come from the debtor's future income. The trustee in bankruptcy can apply for an income payments order, claiming for the bankrupt's estate the bankrupt's surplus income (s 310). Such an order in a case like the present would imperil the arrangement, dependent as it is on the debtor's payments out of income to fund it. Any creditor not bound by the arrangement is therefore a threat to its efficacy.

Finally, r 5.17(5) seems to me to offer further support to Knox J's construction. It is plain that that sub-rule applies to r 5.17(3) and on its face, by allowing any creditor the right to appeal against the chairman's decision on entitlement, would give the creditor aggrieved by the chairman's decision on the estimated minimum value of his unliquidated claim the opportunity to appeal. On Miss Tipples' construction, that creditor could hardly appeal what he has agreed.

For these reasons, which are essentially those advanced by Mr Zacaroli in support of the first decision of Knox J, I would hold that Alltime was bound by the arrangement.

(2)(a) Was the chairman's valuation of the future liability a material irregularity?

Miss Tipples submitted that the whole of Mr Doorbar's future rent liability for the remaining seven years of the term of the lease should have been treated rateably for voting purposes. She said that instead, by being allowed to vote only in respect of one year's future rent, Alltime had been placed in the worst possible position: it had no voting power at the meeting and is now bound by the arrangement in respect of all the future rent liability. She complained that the chairman failed to make any real attempt to value Alltime's claim, that the chairman was wrong to make any allowance for what he may have considered to be the possibility of re-entry, and that he therefore failed to put an estimated minimum value on the claim. She points out that had Alltime been allowed to vote in respect of the whole of the future rent liability, the arrangement would not have been approved.

To take the last point first, any irregularity in the estimate of the minimum value would not be material unless that value was increased threefold. Only then would Alltime have had 25% or more of the voting power at the meeting. In considering this question it must be borne in mind that no attempt was made by Alltime to provide the chairman with any estimate or evidence of the then present value of its claim; it simply claimed the aggregate of the whole of the future rent. It is also not in dispute that the right of re-entry remained unaffected by the arrangement (s 258(4) and see *Re Naeem (a bankrupt) (No 18 of 1988)* [1990] 1 WLR 48). It was presently exercisable by Alltime at the time of the meeting by reason of the arrears of rent and would continue thereafter to be exercisable in relation both to the arrears and to the future rent reserved by the lease if it was not paid within 21 days of each payment being due. On the figures there was no possibility of such payments.

In those circumstances, while the chairman should not have taken account of any duty to mitigate, nor should he have considered, as he put in his report, 'the most which would be accepted for future liability', it was entirely realistic of him to put a minimum value on Alltime's claim by estimating what was likely to happen, and making allowance for the possibility that Alltime would exercise its power of re-entry. In my judgment Alltime's approach of treating the minimum value of the future rent liability as equal to the whole of that liability was wrong in principle. In agreement therefore with the judge, I do not see any material *a*   irregularity in the chairman's estimate of the minimum value which he put on Alltime's debt.

(2)(b) *Did the arrangement unfairly prejudice Alltime's interests?*

Miss Tipples submitted that the term 'interests' is one of wide import, by reference to the authorities on s 459 of the Companies Act 1985, where the
b   concept of unfair prejudice to a member's interests is found. However, it is common ground that the relevant interests in the context of s 262(1)(a) are the interests of the creditor as a creditor, and for my part I do not derive much assistance from consideration of the authorities on s 459 with its very different context. Miss Tipples said that Alltime's right arising under cl 5 of the lease was inextricably linked with its right to receive payment from Mr Doorbar of the
c   future rent liability and as such it was an interest of Alltime as creditor. Clause 5, she said, enabled Alltime, on Mr Doorbar's bankruptcy and the subsequent disclaimer by the trustee of the lease, to require the surety, Mrs Doorbar, to accept a lease and so Alltime had a legitimate expectation to recover from Mrs Doorbar all the future rent. She said that the unfairness in this case arises because
d   by reason of the voluntary arrangement Alltime is unable to proceed with its bankruptcy petition, and it is in a unique position in relation to all the other creditors because it had the means by cl 5 of suffering no loss in respect of its claim for future rent, and so, by being denied the ability to activate cl 5, it had been unfairly prejudiced by the terms of the arrangement.

e   I cannot do better on this point then refer to the analysis of the judge:

> 'The prejudice which is relied upon has the following features. First, it is a restriction of a right prospectively exercisable against a person other than the debtor. Second, it is the product of the statutory consequences of the approval of the voluntary arrangement, which includes the right to future rent, rather than the result of any particular term of the arrangement. Third,
> *f*   the right which is prejudicially affected is one which arises under the lease and therefore pre-exists the voluntary arrangement and has no connection with the voluntary arrangement save that its value increases if and to the extent that the debtor is insolvent. Fourth, the right which is prejudicially affected is not a right over the debtor's property but a contingent personal
> *g*   right against the third party, the debtor's ex-wife. Five, the right prejudicially affected is one to substitute in place of rights against the debtor corresponding rights against the debtor and another. It is therefore in practice a right to release the debtor and substitute another. The new covenant by the debtor ex hypothesi after his bankruptcy is practically worthless and would involve a merger of the debtor's existing covenant.
> *h*   Finally, there is no question of Alltime's rights of re-entry having been prejudiced by the voluntary arrangement.' (See [1995] 2 BCLC 513 at 522.)

The judge said that in the light of those characteristics and more especially of the fact that the right in question was one exercisable against a person other than the
j   debtor and arose on the determination through disclaimer by the trustee of the debtor's liability and was therefore a substitute for rather than a constituent part of the debtor's indebtedness, the interest of Alltime was outside the ambit of s 262(1)(a) of the 1986 Act and that therefore there was no prejudice of which it could complain. I agree with that analysis and that conclusion.

The judge also gave his answer to the question where the balance lies as between the prejudice to Alltime in having its right against the debtor's ex-wife restricted on the one hand, and the prejudice to the general body of creditors in being prevented from having the benefits of any voluntary arrangement which includes future payments of rent under the lease, on the other. He considered that the prejudice to Alltime would not in the circumstances be unfair, primarily because Alltime had its security against Mr Doorbar in the shape of the right of re-entry unaffected by the voluntary arrangement. That is a conclusion with which I would not think it right for this court to interfere, the judge having taken into account all the relevant circumstances.

For these reasons therefore, in my judgment, the judge came to unassailable conclusions in his second decision.

I would dismiss this appeal.

FORBES J. I agree.

HIRST LJ. I also agree.

Appeals dismissed.

Paul Magrath Esq   Barrister.

a # Westdeutsche Landesbank Girozentrale v Islington London Borough Council

HOUSE OF LORDS

LORD GOFF OF CHIEVELEY, LORD BROWNE-WILKINSON, LORD SLYNN OF HADLEY, LORD
b WOOLF AND LORD LLOYD OF BERWICK

10–13 JULY 1995, 22 MAY 1996

*Contract – Failure of consideration – Recovery of money paid – Lump sum payment
made by bank to local authority under interest rate swap agreement – Payments also
c made by local authority pursuant to agreement – Agreement being ultra vires the local
authority and void – Balance of lump sum recovered by bank – Whether local authority
liable to pay compound interest on balance from date sum paid – Whether local
authority holding funds on resulting trust – Whether bank entitled to simple interest
only.*

d
*Contract – Restitution – Interest rate swap agreement – Bank entering into interest rate
swap agreement with local authority – Agreement ultra vires the local authority –
Balance of lump sum recovered by bank – Whether compound interest recoverable from
date sum paid.*

e The plaintiff bank entered into a ten-year interest rate swap agreement with the
defendant local authority commencing on 18 June 1987. The interest payments,
which were payable half-yearly, were calculated on a notional principal sum of
£25m by reference to the difference between the fixed rate of interest (payable
by the bank) and the floating London Inter-Bank Offered Rate (payable by the
local authority). Additionally, the bank agreed to pay the local authority a lump
f sum of £2·5m on the commencement date as the first of the fixed rate payments.
By June 1989 the local authority had made four payments to the bank under the
swap agreement, totalling £1,354,474·07. However, on 1 November 1989 the
Divisional Court of the Queen's Bench Division held, in an unrelated case
subsequently upheld by the House of Lords in January 1991, that interest rate
g swap transactions were outside the powers of local authorities and void ab
initio. Thereafter the local authority made no further payments. The bank
subsequently brought an action against the local authority, claiming inter alia
repayment of £1,145,525·93, being the amount of the initial lump sum payment
of £2·5m less the payments made by the local authority, and interest as from 18
June 1987. The judge held that the bank was entitled to recover the principal
h sum plus compound interest from 1 April 1990. The Court of Appeal dismissed
the local authority's appeal and allowed the bank's cross-appeal from the judge's
decision that the interest should run from April 1990. The local authority
appealed to the House of Lords against the award of compound interest.

j **Held** – (1) In the absence of agreement or custom the court had no jurisdiction
to award compound interest either at law or under s 35A of the Supreme Court
Act 1981 and therefore, in a common law action for money had and received,
the bank was entitled to recover only simple interest under s 35A. Moreover,
in the absence of fraud, the courts of equity had never awarded compound
interest except against a trustee or other person owing fiduciary duties in cases

where the award was in lieu of an account of profits improperly made by the trustee. The local authority, as a recipient of money under a contract subsequently found to be void for mistake or as being ultra vires, did not hold the money under a resulting trust, and there was no other basis on which it could be regarded as owing fiduciary duties to the bank in relation to the upfront payment of £2·5m (see p 974 c to f, p 981 f, p 984 a c to e, p 985 e f, p 986 d to g, p 987 g to p 988 a, p 991 b c, p 992 b c, p 998 j to p 999 a, p 1002 h j and p 1018 j, post).

(2) (Lord Goff and Lord Woolf dissenting) A claim for money had and received under an ultra vires contract was a personal action based on the total failure of consideration; it was not based on an implied contract or on an equitable proprietary claim. Notwithstanding the strength of the bank's moral claim to receive full restitution, it would not be appropriate to develop the law and award compound interest on the ground that equity could act in aid of the common law; Parliament had twice considered what interest should be awarded on common law claims and had made it clear, both in s 3(1)ᵃ of the Law Reform (Miscellaneous Provisions) Act 1934 and its successor, s 35Aᵇ of the 1981 Act, that the award of compound interest was not authorised. It followed that the bank was entitled only to simple interest on the principal sum from the date of accrual of its cause of action (ie 18 June 1987) and not compound interest. The local authority's appeal would accordingly be allowed (see p 993 b, p 996 d to g, p 999 d to p 1000 d g, p 1001 b to d, p 1005 d, p 1018 h to p 1019 c and p 1022 b, post); President of India v La Pintada Cia Navegacion SA [1984] 2 All ER 773 applied; Chase Manhattan Bank NA v Israel-British Bank (London) Ltd [1979] 3 All ER 1025 considered; Sinclair v Brougham [1914] AC 398, [1914–15] All ER Rep 622 not followed.

Decision of the Court of Appeal [1994] 4 All ER 890 reversed.

Notes

For a local authority's power to incur expenditure, see 28 Halsbury's Laws (4th edn) paras 1245, 1247, and for cases on the subject, see 33 Digest (Reissue) 31–34, 96–104.

For the Law Reform (Miscellaneous Provisions) Act 1934, s 3, see 11 Halsbury's Statutes (4th edn) (1991 reissue) 789.

For the Supreme Court Act 1981, s 35A, see ibid 998.

Cases referred to in opinions

A-G v Alford (1855) 4 De GM & G 843, 43 ER 737, LC.
Afovos Shipping Co SA v Pagnan, The Afovos [1980] 2 Lloyd's Rep 469; rvsd [1982] 3 All ER 18, [1982] 1 WLR 848; affd [1983] 1 All ER 449, [1983] 1 WLR 195, HL.
Ames' Settlement, Re, Dinwiddy v Ames [1946] 1 All ER 689, [1946] Ch 217.
Armory v Delamirie (1722) 1 Stra 505, [1558–1774] All ER Rep 121, 93 ER 664.
Arnott v Redfern (1826) 3 Bing 353, 130 ER 549.
Atwool v Merryweather (1867) LR 5 Eq 464n.
Bankers Trust Co v Shapira [1980] 3 All ER 353, [1980] 1 WLR 1274, CA.
Barclays Bank Ltd v Quistclose Investments Ltd [1968] 3 All ER 651, [1970] AC 567, [1968] 3 WLR 1097, HL.

---

a   Section 3, so far as material, is set out at p 1013 b c, post
b   Section 35A, so far as material, is set out at p 1013 e, post

a *Barnes v Addy* (1874) LR 9 Ch App 244.
Birch v Blagrave (1755) Amb 264, 27 ER 176, LC.
BP Exploration Co (Libya) Ltd v Hunt (No 2) [1982] 1 All ER 925, [1979] 1 WLR 783;
    affd [1982] 1 All ER 925, [1981] 1 WLR 232, CA; *affd* [1982] 1 All ER 925, [1983]
    2 AC 352, [1982] 2 WLR 253, HL.
Burdick v Garrick (1870) LR 5 Ch App 233.
b *Chase Manhattan Bank NA v Israel-British Bank (London) Ltd* [1979] 3 All ER 1025,
    [1981] Ch 105, [1980] 2 WLR 202.
Childers v Childers (1857) 1 De G & J 482, 44 ER 810.
Comr of Stamp Duties v Livingston [1964] 3 All ER 692, [1965] AC 694, [1964] 3
    WLR 963, PC.
Cook (decd), Re, Beck v Grant [1948] 1 All ER 231, [1948] Ch 212.
c *De Havilland v Bowerbank* (1807) 1 Camp 50, 170 ER 872, NP.
Diplock's Estate, Re, Diplock v Wintle [1948] 2 All ER 318, [1948] Ch 465, CA; *affd*
    sub nom *Ministry of Health v Simpson* [1950] 2 All ER 1137, [1951] AC 251, HL.
Eddowes v Hopkins (1780) 1 Doug KB 376, 99 ER 242.
Fibrosa Spolka Akcyjna v Fairbairn Lawson Combe Barbour Ltd [1942] 2 All ER 122,
d   [1943] AC 32, HL.
Gittins v Steele (1818) 1 Swan 24, 199, 36 ER 283, 356, LC.
Goldcorp Exchange Ltd (in receivership), Re [1994] 2 All ER 806, [1995] 1 AC 74,
    [1994] 3 WLR 199, PC.
Hadley v Baxendale (1854) 9 Exch 341, [1843–60] All ER Rep 461, 156 ER 148.
Hallett's Estate, Re, Knatchbull v Hallett (1880) 13 Ch D 696, [1874–80] All ER Rep
e   793, CA.
Hazell v Hammersmith and Fulham London BC [1991] 1 All ER 545, [1992] 2 AC 1,
    [1991] 2 WLR 372, HL; *rvsg* [1990] 3 All ER 33, [1990] 2 QB 697, [1990] 2 WLR
    17, 1038, DC and CA.
Hungerfords v Walker (1988) 171 CLR 125, Aust HC.
f *Johnson v R* [1904] AC 817, PC.
Kleinwort Benson Ltd v South Tyneside Metropolitan BC [1994] 4 All ER 972.
Leslie (R) Ltd v Sheill [1914] 3 KB 607, [1914–15] All ER Rep 511, CA.
Lipkin Gorman (a firm) v Karpnale Ltd [1992] 4 All ER 512, [1991] 2 AC 548, [1991]
    3 WLR 10, HL.
London, Chatham and Dover Rly Co v South Eastern Rly Co [1893] AC 429, HL.
g *McCormick v Grogan* (1869) LR 4 HL 82.
Metall und Rohstoff AG v Donaldson Lufkin & Jenrette Inc [1989] 3 All ER 14, [1990]
    1 QB 391, [1989] 3 WLR 563, CA.
Montagu's Settlement Trusts, Re (1985) [1992] 4 All ER 308, [1987] Ch 264, [1987]
    2 WLR 1192.
h *Moses v Macferlan* (1760) 2 Burr 1005, [1558–1774] All ER Rep 581, 97 ER 676.
Muller, Re, Cassin v Mutual Cash Order Co Ltd [1953] NZLR 879, NZ SC.
Napier and Ettrick (Lord) v Hunter, Lord Napier and Ettrick v R F Kershaw Ltd [1993]
    1 All ER 385, [1993] AC 713, [1993] 2 WLR 42, HL.
National Bank of Greece SA v Pinios Shipping Co No 1, The Maira [1990] 1 All ER 78,
j   [1990] 1 AC 637, [1989] 3 WLR 1330, HL.
O'Sullivan v Management Agency and Music Ltd [1985] 3 All ER 351, [1985] QB 428,
    [1984] 3 WLR 448, CA.
Page v Newman (1829) 9 B & C 378, 109 ER 140.
Pavey & Matthews Pty Ltd v Paul (1987) 69 ALR 577, Aust HC.
President of India v La Pintada Cia Navegacion SA [1984] 2 All ER 773, [1985] AC
    104, [1984] 3 WLR 10, HL.

Scandinavian Trading Tanker Co AB v Flota Petrolera Ecuatoriana [1983] 2 All ER
763, [1983] 2 AC 694, [1983] 3 WLR 203, HL.   *a*
Sinclair v Brougham [1914] AC 398, [1914–15] All ER Rep 622, HL.
Stocks v Wilson [1913] 2 KB 235.
Vandervell v IRC [1967] 1 All ER 1, [1967] 2 AC 291, [1967] 2 WLR 87, HL.
Vandervell's Trusts, Re (No 2), White v Vandervell Trustees Ltd [1974] 3 All ER 205,
[1974] Ch 269, [1974] 3 WLR 256, CA.   *b*
Vinogradoff, Re, Allen v Jackson [1935] WN 68.
Wadsworth v Lydall [1981] 2 All ER 401, [1981] 1 WLR 598, CA.
Wallersteiner v Moir (No 2) [1975] 1 All ER 849, [1975] QB 373, [1975] 2 WLR 389,
CA.
West Sussex Constabulary's Widows, Children and Benevolent (1930) Fund Trusts, Re
[1970] 1 All ER 544, [1971] Ch 1, [1970] 2 WLR 848.   *c*
Woolwich Building Society v IRC (No 2) [1992] 3 All ER 737, [1993] AC 70, [1992] 3
WLR 366, HL.

Appeal
The defendant, Islington London Borough Council (the council), appealed with *d*
leave of the Appeal Committee of the House of Lords granted on 23 May 1994
from the decision of the Court of Appeal (Dillon, Leggatt and Kennedy LJJ)
([1994] 4 All ER 890, [1994] 1 WLR 938) made on 17 December 1993, whereby
inter alia it dismissed the council's appeal from the decision of Hobhouse J
([1994] 4 All ER 890) made on 12 February 1993 giving judgment for the *e*
plaintiff, Westdeutsche Landesbank Girozentrale (the bank), in the sum of
£1,145,525·93 with compound interest from 1 April 1990. The issue on appeal
was whether the court had jurisdiction to award compound interest. The facts
are set out in the opinion of Lord Browne-Wilkinson.

Trevor Philipson QC and *Brian Doctor* (instructed by *Nabarro Nathanson*) for the *f*
council.
Jonathan Sumption QC and *George Leggatt* (instructed by *Travers Smith
Braithwaite*) for the bank.

Their Lordships took time for consideration.   *g*

22 May 1996. The following opinions were delivered.

LORD GOFF OF CHIEVELEY. My Lords, this appeal is concerned with a
transaction known as an interest rate swap. Under such a transaction, one party *h*
(the fixed rate payer) agrees to pay the other over a certain period interest at a
fixed rate on a notional capital sum; and the other party (the floating rate payer)
agrees to pay to the former over the same period interest on the same notional
sum at a market rate determined in accordance with a certain formula. Interest
rate swaps can fulfil many purposes, ranging from pure speculation to more
useful purposes such as the hedging of liabilities. They are in law wagers, but *j*
they are not void as such because they are excluded from the regime of the
Gaming Acts by s 63 of the Financial Services Act 1986.
    One form of interest rate swap involves what is called an upfront payment,
ie a capital sum paid by one party to the other, which will be balanced by an
adjustment of the parties' respective liabilities. Thus, as in the present case, the

a fixed rate payer may make an upfront payment to the floating rate payer, and in consequence the rate of interest payable by the fixed rate payer is reduced to a rate lower than the rate which would otherwise have been payable by him. The practical effect is to achieve a form of borrowing by, in this example, the floating rate payer through the medium of the interest rate swap transaction. It appears that it was this feature which, in particular, attracted local authorities to enter *b* into transactions of this kind, since they enabled local authorities subject to rate-capping to obtain upfront payments uninhibited by the relevant statutory controls.

At all events, local authorities began to enter into transactions of this kind soon after they came into use in the early 1980s. At that time, there was thought *c* to be no risk involved in entering into such transactions with local authorities. Financially, they were regarded as secure; and it was assumed that such transactions were within their powers. However, as is well known, in *Hazell v Hammersmith and Fulham London BC* [1991] 1 All ER 545, [1992] 2 AC 1 your Lordships' House, restoring the decision of the Divisional Court ([1990] 3 All ER 33, [1990] 2 QB 697), held that such transactions were ultra vires the local *d* authorities who had entered into them. It is unnecessary for present purposes to examine the basis of that decision; though I wish to record that it caused grave concern among financial institutions, and especially foreign banks, which had entered into such transactions with local authorities in good faith, with no idea that a rule as technical as the ultra vires doctrine might undermine what *e* they saw as a perfectly legitimate commercial transaction. There then followed litigation in which banks and other financial institutions concerned sought to recover from the local authorities with which they had dealt the balance of the money paid by them, together with interest. Out of the many actions so commenced, two were selected as test cases. These were the present case, *Westdeutsche Landesbank Girozentrale v Islington London BC*, and *Kleinwort Benson* *f* *Ltd v Sandwell BC*. Both cases came on for hearing before Hobhouse J ([1994] 4 All ER 890). Your Lordships are concerned only with the former case. In a powerful judgment Hobhouse J held that the plaintiff (the bank) was entitled to recover from the defendant (the council) the net balance outstanding on the transaction between the parties, viz the difference between the upfront *g* payment of £2·5m paid by the bank to the council on 18 June 1987, and the total of four semi-annual interest payments totalling £1,354,474·07 paid by the council to the bank between December 1987 and June 1989, leaving a net balance of £1,145,525·93 which the judge ordered the council to pay to the bank. He held the money to be recoverable by the bank either as money had and received by the council to the use of the bank, or as money which in equity the *h* bank was entitled to trace into the hands of the council and have repaid out of the council's assets. He decided that the bank's right to restitution at common law arose from the fact that the payment made by the bank to the council was made under a purported contract which, unknown to both parties, was ultra vires the council and so void, no consideration having been given for the making of the payment. The decision by the judge, which was affirmed by the *j* Court of Appeal ([1994] 4 All ER 890, [1994] 1 WLR 938), raised important questions in the law of restitution, which are of great interest to lawyers specialising in this field. Yet it is an extraordinary feature of the present appeal to your Lordships' House that the judge's decision on the substantive right of recovery at common law does not fall for consideration by your Lordships'

House. The appeal of the council is confined to one point only—the question
of interest.   *a*

The judge ordered that the council should pay compound interest on the sum
awarded against them, calculated at six-monthly rests from 1 April 1990 to the
date of judgment. The Court of Appeal affirmed the judge's decision to award
compound interest but, allowing a cross-appeal by the bank, ordered that
interest should run from the date of receipt of the upfront payment. Both the   *b*
judge and the Court of Appeal held that they were entitled to invoke against the
council the equitable jurisdiction to award compound interest, on the basis that
the bank was entitled to succeed against the council in an equitable proprietary
claim. The foundation for the bank's equitable proprietary claim lay in the
decision of this House in *Sinclair v Brougham* [1914] AC 398, [1914–15] All ER
Rep 622. Since that decision has for long been controversial, the Appellate   *c*
Committee invited argument on the question whether the House should depart
from the decision despite the fact that it has stood for many years.

THE SHAPE OF THE CASE

Once the character of an interest swap transaction has been identified and
understood, and it is appreciated that, because the transaction was beyond the   *d*
powers of the council, it was void ab initio, the basic question is whether the law
can restore the parties to the position they were in before they entered into the
transaction. That is, of course, the function of the law of restitution. I feel
bound to say that, in the present case, there ought to be no difficulty about that
at all. This is because the case is concerned solely with money. All that has to   *e*
be done is to order that each party should pay back the money it has received—
or, more sensibly, to strike a balance, and order that the party who has received
most should repay the balance; and then to make an appropriate order for
interest in respect of that balance. It should be as simple as that. And yet we
find ourselves faced with a mass of difficult problems, and struggling to   *f*
reconcile a number of difficult cases.

I must confess that, like all the judges who have been involved in these cases,
I too have found myself struggling in this way. But in the end I have come to
realise the importance of keeping my eyes on the simple outline of the case
which I have just described; and I have discovered that, if one does that—if one
keeps one's eyes open above the thicket of case law in which we can so easily   *g*
become enclosed—the solution of the problem in the present case becomes
much more simple. In saying this, I do not wish in any way to criticise the
judges who have been grappling with the case at first instance and in the Court
of Appeal, within the confines of the doctrine of precedent by which they are
bound. On the contrary, they are entitled to our gratitude and respect. The   *h*
masterly judgment of Hobhouse J, in particular, has excited widespread
admiration. But it is the great advantage of a supreme court that, not only does
it have the great benefit of assistance from the judgments of the courts below,
but also it has a greater freedom to mould, and remould, the authorities to
ensure that practical justice is done within a framework of principle. The
present case provides an excellent example of a case in which this House should   *j*
take full advantage of that freedom.

THE THREE PROBLEMS

There are three reasons why the present case has become so complicated.
The first is that, in our law of restitution, there has developed an understanding

a that money can only be recovered on the ground of failure of consideration if that failure is total. The second is that because, in particular, of the well-known but controversial decision of this House in *Sinclair v Brougham*, it has come to be understood that a trust may be imposed in cases such as the present where the incapacity of one of the parties has the effect that the transaction is void. The third is that our law of interest has developed in a fragmentary and
b unsatisfactory manner, and in consequence insufficient attention has been given to the jurisdiction to award compound interest.

I propose at the outset to devote a little attention to each of these matters.

(1) *Total failure of consideration*

c There has long been a desire among restitution lawyers to escape from the unfortunate effects of the so-called rule that money is only recoverable at common law on the ground of failure of consideration where the failure is total, by reformulating the rule upon a more principled basis; and signs that this will in due course be done are appearing in judgments throughout the common law world, as appropriate cases arise for decision. It is fortunate, however, that in
d the present case, thanks (I have no doubt) to the admirable researches of counsel, a line of authority was discovered which had escaped the attention of the scholars who work in this field. This line of authority was concerned with contracts for annuities which were void if certain statutory formalities were not complied with. They were not therefore concerned with contracts void by
e reason of the incapacity of one of the parties. Even so, they were concerned with cases in which payments had been made, so to speak, both ways; and the courts had to decide whether they could, in such circumstances, do justice by restoring the parties to their previous positions. They did not hesitate to do so, by ascertaining the balance of the account between the parties, and ordering the repayment of the balance. Moreover, the form of action by which this was
f achieved was the old action for money had and received—what we nowadays call a personal claim in restitution at common law. With this precedent before him, Hobhouse J felt free to make a similar order in the present case; and in this he was self-evidently right.

The most serious problem which has remained in this connection is the
g theoretical question whether recovery can here be said to rest upon the ground of *failure* of consideration. Hobhouse J thought not. He considered that the true ground in these cases, where the contract is void, is to be found in the absence, rather than the failure, of consideration; and in this he was followed by the Court of Appeal. This had the effect that the courts below were not troubled by the question whether there had been a *total* failure of consideration.
h The approach so adopted may have found its origin in the idea, to be derived from a well-known passage in the speech of Viscount Simon LC in *Fibrosa Spolka Akcyjna v Fairbairn Lawson Combe Barbour Ltd* [1942] 2 All ER 122 at 129, [1943] AC 32 at 48, that a failure of consideration only occurs where there has been a failure of performance by the other party of his obligation under a contract
j which was initially binding. But the concept of failure of consideration need not be so narrowly confined. In particular, it appears from the annuity cases themselves that the courts regarded them as cases of failure of consideration; and concern has been expressed by a number of restitution lawyers that the approach of Hobhouse J is contrary to principle and could, if accepted, lead to undesirable consequences (see Professor Birks 'No Consideration: Restitution

after Void Contracts' (1993) 23 UWALR 195; W J Swadling in [1994] RLR 73; and Professor Burrows 'Swaps and the Friction between Common Law and Equity' [1995] RLR 15). However, since there is before your Lordships no appeal from the decision that the bank was entitled to recover the balance of the payments so made in a personal claim in restitution, the precise identification of the ground of recovery was not explored in argument before the Appellate Committee. It would therefore be inappropriate to express any concluded view upon it. Even so, I think it right to record that there appears to me to be considerable force in the criticisms which have been expressed; and I shall, when considering the issues on this appeal, bear in mind the possibility that it may be right to regard the ground of recovery as failure of consideration.

(2) *A proprietary claim in restitution*

I have already stated that restitution in these cases can be achieved by means of a personal claim in restitution. The question has however arisen whether the bank should also have the benefit of an equitable proprietary claim in the form of a resulting trust. The immediate reaction must be—why should it? Take the present case. The parties have entered into a commercial transaction. The transaction has, for technical reasons, been held to be void from the beginning. Each party is entitled to recover its money, with the result that the balance must be repaid. But why should the plaintiff bank be given the additional benefits which flow from a proprietary claim, for example the benefit of achieving priority in the event of the defendant's insolvency? After all, it has entered into a commercial transaction, and so taken the risk of the defendant's insolvency, just like the defendant's other creditors who have contracted with it, not to mention other creditors to whom the defendant may be liable to pay damages in tort.

I feel bound to say that I would not at first sight have thought that an equitable proprietary claim in the form of a trust should be made available to the bank in the present case, but for two things. The first is the decision of this House in *Sinclair v Brougham* [1914] AC 398, [1914–15] All ER Rep 622, which appears to provide authority that a resulting trust may indeed arise in a case such as the present. The second is that on the authorities there is an equitable jurisdiction to award the plaintiff compound interest in cases where the defendant is a trustee. It is the combination of those two factors which has provided the foundation for the principal arguments advanced on behalf of the bank in support of its submission that it was entitled to an award of compound interest. I shall have to consider the question of availability of an equitable proprietary claim, and the effect of *Sinclair v Brougham*, in some depth in a moment. But first I wish to say a few words on the subject of interest.

(3) *Interest*

One would expect to find, in any developed system of law, a comprehensive and reasonably simple set of principles by virtue of which the courts have power to award interest. Since there are circumstances in which the interest awarded should take the form of compound interest, those principles should specify the circumstances in which compound interest, as well as simple interest, may be awarded; and the power to award compound interest should be available both at law and in equity. Nowadays, especially since it has been established (see *National Bank of Greece SA v Pinios Shipping Co No 1, The Maira* [1990] 1 All ER 78, a [1990] 1 AC 637) that banks may, by the custom of bankers, charge compound interest upon advances made by them to their customers, one would expect to find that the principal cases in which compound interest may be awarded would be commercial cases.

Sadly, however, that is not the position in English law. Unfortunately, the power to award compound interest is not available at common law. The power

b is available in equity; but at present that power is, for historical reasons, exercised only in relation to certain specific classes of claim, in particular proceedings against trustees for an account. An important—I believe the most important—question in the present case is whether that jurisdiction should be developed to apply in a commercial context, as in the present case.

c EQUITABLE PROPRIETARY CLAIMS

I now turn to consider the question whether an equitable proprietary claim was available to the bank in the present case.

Ever since the law of restitution began, about the middle of this century, to be studied in depth, the role of equitable proprietary claims in the law of

d restitution has been found to be a matter of great difficulty. The legitimate ambition of restitution lawyers has been to establish a coherent law of restitution, founded upon the principle of unjust enrichment; and since certain equitable institutions, notably the constructive trust and the resulting trust, have been perceived to have the function of reversing unjust enrichment, they have sought to embrace those institutions within the law of restitution, if

e necessary moulding them to make them fit for that purpose. Equity lawyers, on the other hand, have displayed anxiety that in this process the equitable principles underlying these institutions may become illegitimately distorted; and though equity lawyers in this country are nowadays much more sympathetic than they have been in the past towards the need to develop a coherent law of restitution, and of identifying the proper role of the trust within

f that rubric of the law, they remain concerned that the trust concept should not be distorted, and also that the practical consequences of its imposition should be fully appreciated. There is therefore some tension between the aims and perceptions of these two groups of lawyers, which has manifested itself in relation to the matters under consideration in the present case.

g In the present case, however, it is not the function of your Lordships' House to rewrite the agenda for the law of restitution, nor even to identify the role of equitable proprietary claims in that part of the law. The judicial process is neither designed for, nor properly directed towards, such objectives. The function of your Lordships' House is simply to decide the questions at issue before

h it in the present case; and the particular question now under consideration is whether, where money has been paid by a party to a contract which is ultra vires the other party and so void ab initio, he has the benefit of an equitable proprietary claim in respect of the money so paid. Moreover, the manner in which this question has arisen before this House renders it by no means easy to address. First of all, the point was not debated in any depth in the courts below,

j because they understood that they were bound by *Sinclair v Brougham* to hold that such a claim was here available. But second, the point has arisen only indirectly in this case, since it is relevant only to the question whether the court here has power to make an award of compound interest. It is a truism that, in deciding a question of law in any particular case, the courts are much influenced by considerations of practical justice, and especially by the results which would flow from the recognition of a particular claim on the facts of the case before the court. Here, however, an award of compound interest provides no such guidance, because it is no more than a consequence which is said to flow, for no more than historical reasons, from the availability of an equitable proprietary claim. It therefore provides no guidance on the question whether such a claim should here be available.

In these circumstances I regard it as particularly desirable that your Lordships should, so far as possible, restrict the inquiry to the actual questions at issue in this appeal, and not be tempted into formulating general principles of a broader nature. If restitution lawyers are hoping to find in your Lordships' speeches broad statements of principle which may definitively establish the future shape of this part of the law, I fear that they may be disappointed. I also regard it as important that your Lordships should, in the traditional manner, pay particular regard to the practical consequences which may flow from the decision of the House.

With these observations by way of preamble, I turn to the question of the availability of an equitable proprietary claim in a case such as the present. The argument advanced on behalf of the bank was that the money paid by them under the void contract was received by the council subject to a resulting trust. This approach was consistent with that of Dillon LJ in the Court of Appeal (see [1994] 4 All ER 890 at 962, [1994] 1 WLR 938 at 947). It is also consistent with the approach of Viscount Haldane LC (with whom Lord Atkinson agreed) in *Sinclair v Brougham* [1914] AC 398 at 420–421, [1914–15] All ER Rep 622 at 632.

I have already expressed the opinion that, at first sight, it is surprising that an equitable proprietary claim should be available in a case such as the present. However, before I examine the question as a matter of principle, I propose first to consider whether *Sinclair v Brougham* supports the argument now advanced on behalf of the bank.

Sinclair v Brougham

The decision of this House in *Sinclair v Brougham* has loomed very large in both the judgments in the courts below and in the admirable arguments addressed to the Appellate Committee of this House. It has long been regarded as a controversial decision, and has been the subject of much consideration by scholars, especially those working in the field of restitution. I have however reached the conclusion that it is basically irrelevant to the decision of the present appeal.

It is first necessary to establish what the case was about. The Birkbeck Permanent Benefit Building Society decided to set up a banking business, known as the Birkbeck Bank. The banking business was however held to be ultra vires the objects of the building society; and there followed a spate of litigation concerned with solving the problems consequent upon that decision. *Sinclair v Brougham* was one of those cases.

The case has been analysed in lucid detail in the speech of my noble and learned friend Lord Browne-Wilkinson, which I have read (in draft) with great respect. In its bare outline, it was concerned with the distribution of the assets of the society, which was insolvent. There were four classes of claimants. First, there were two classes of shareholders—the A shareholders (entitled to repayment of their investment on maturity) and the B shareholders (whose shares were permanent). Next, there was a numerous class of people who had *a* deposited money at the bank under contracts which were ultra vires and so void. Finally, there were the ordinary trade creditors of the society. By agreement, the A shareholders and the trade creditors were paid off first, leaving only the claims of the depositors and the B shareholders. There were sufficient assets to pay off the A shareholders, but not the depositors and certainly not both. The question of how to reconcile their competing claims

b arose for consideration on a summons by the liquidator for directions.

The problem arose from the fact that the contracts under which the depositors deposited their money at the bank were ultra vires and so void. That prevented them from establishing a simple contractual right to be repaid, in which event they would have ranked with the ordinary trade creditors of the society in the liquidation. As it was, they claimed to be entitled to repayment

c in an action for money had and received—in the same way as the bank claimed repayment in the case now before your Lordships. But the House of Lords held that they were not entitled to claim on this ground. This was in substance because to allow such a claim would permit an indirect enforcement of the contract which the policy of the law had decreed should be void. In those days,

d of course, judges still spoke about the common law right to restitution in the language of implied contract, and so we find Lord Sumner saying in a much-quoted passage ([1914] AC 398 at 452, [1914–15] All ER Rep 622 at 648):

> 'To hold otherwise would be indirectly to sanction an ultra vires borrowing. All these causes of action are common species of the genus
e   assumpsit. All now rest, and long have rested, upon a notional or imputed promise to repay. The law cannot de jure impute promises to repay, whether for money had and received or otherwise, which, if made de facto, it would inexorably avoid.'

This conclusion however created a serious problem because, if the depositors
f had no claim, then, in the words of Lord Dunedin ([1914] AC 398 at 436, [1914–15] All ER Rep 622 at 640):

> 'The appalling result in this very case would be that the society's shareholders having got proceeds of the depositors' money in the form of investments, so that each individual depositor is utterly unable to trace his
g   money, are enriched to the extent of some 500 per cent.'

As a matter of practical justice, such a result was obviously unacceptable; and it was to achieve justice that the House had recourse to equity to provide the answer. It is, I think, apparent from the reasoning of the members of the
h Appellate Committee that they regarded themselves, not as laying down some broad general principle, but as solving a particular practical problem. In this connection it is, in my opinion, significant that there was a considerable variation in the way in which they approached the problem. Viscount Haldane LC, with whom Lord Atkinson agreed, did so on the basis that there arose in the circumstances 'a resulting trust, not of an active character' (see
j [1914] AC 398 at 421, [1914–15] All ER Rep 622 at 632). Lord Dunedin based his decision upon a broad equity of restitution, drawn from Roman and French law. He asked himself the question: 'Is English equity to retire defeated from the task which other systems of equity have conquered?'—a question which he answered in the negative (see [1914] AC 398 at 435, [1914–15] All ER Rep 622 at 639). Lord Parker of Waddington attempted to reconcile his decision with the

established principles of equity by holding that the depositors' money had been
received by the directors of the society as fiduciaries, with the effect that the
depositors could thereafter follow their money in equity into the assets of the
society (see [1914] AC 398 at 441–442, [1914–15] All ER Rep 622 at 643). Lord
Sumner considered that the case should be decided on equitable principles on
which there was no direct authority. He regarded the question as one of
administration, in which 'the most just distribution of the whole must be
directed, so only that no [recognised] rule of law or equity be disregarded' (see
[1914] AC 398 at 458, [1914–15] All ER Rep 622 at 651). Setting on one side the
opinion of Lord Parker, whose approach I find very difficult to reconcile with
the facts of the case, I do not discern in the speeches of the members of the
Appellate Committee any intention to impose a trust carrying with it the
personal duties of a trustee.

For present purposes, I approach this case in the following way. First, it is
clear that the problem which arose in *Sinclair v Brougham*, viz that a personal
remedy in restitution was excluded on grounds of public policy, does not arise
in the present case, which is not of course concerned with a borrowing contract.
Second, I regard the decision in *Sinclair v Brougham* as being a response to that
problem in the case of ultra vires borrowing contracts, and as not intended to
create a principle of general application. From this it follows, in my opinion,
that *Sinclair v Brougham* is not relevant to the decision in the present case. In
particular it cannot be relied upon as a precedent that a trust arises on the facts
of the present case, justifying on that basis an award of compound interest
against the council.

But I wish to add this. I do not in any event think that it would be right for
your Lordships' House to exercise its power under the *Practice Statement
(Judicial Precedent)* [1966] 3 All ER 77, [1966] 1 WLR 1234 to depart from *Sinclair
v Brougham*. I say this first because, in my opinion, any decision to do so would
not be material to the disposal of the present appeal, and would therefore be
obiter. But there is a second reason of substance why, in my opinion, that
course should not be taken. I recognise that nowadays cases of incapacity are
relatively rare, though the swaps litigation shows that they can still occur. Even
so, the question could still arise whether, in the case of a borrowing contract
rendered void because it was ultra vires the borrower, it would be contrary to
public policy to allow a personal claim in restitution. Such a question has arisen
in the past not only in relation to associations such as the Birkbeck Permanent
Benefit Building Society, but also in relation to infants' contracts. Moreover
there is a respectable body of opinion that, if such a case arose today, it should
still be held that public policy would preclude a personal claim in restitution,
though not of course by reference to an implied contract. That was the opinion
expressed by Leggatt LJ in the Court of Appeal (see [1994] 4 All ER 890 at 968,
[1994] 1 WLR 938 at 952) in the present case, as it had been by Hobhouse J; and
the same view has been expressed by Professor Birks (see Birks *An Introduction
to the Law of Restitution* (1985) p 374). I myself incline to the opinion that a
personal claim in restitution would not indirectly enforce the ultra vires
contract, for such an action would be unaffected by any of the contractual terms
governing the borrowing, and moreover would be subject (where appropriate)
to any available restitutionary defences. If my present opinion were to prove to
be correct then *Sinclair v Brougham* will fade into history. If not, then recourse
can at least be had to *Sinclair v Brougham* as authority for the proposition that,

a in such circumstances, the lender should not be without a remedy. Indeed, I cannot think that English law, or equity, is so impoverished as to be incapable of providing relief in such circumstances. Lord Wright, who wrote in strong terms indorsing the just result in *Sinclair v Brougham*, would turn in his grave at any such suggestion (see 'Sinclair v Brougham' [1938] CLJ 305). Of course, it may be necessary to reinterpret the decision in that case to provide a more

b satisfactory basis for it; indeed one possible suggestion has been proposed by Professor Birks in *Law of Restitution* p 396ff). But for the present the case should in my opinion stand, though confined in the manner I have indicated, as an assertion that those who are caught in the trap of advancing money under ultra vires borrowing contracts will not be denied appropriate relief.

c THE AVAILABILITY OF AN EQUITABLE PROPRIETARY CLAIM IN THE PRESENT CASE

Having put *Sinclair v Brougham* on one side as providing no authority that a resulting trust should be imposed in the facts of the present case, I turn to the question whether, as a matter of principle, such a trust should be imposed, the bank's submission being that such a trust arose at the time when the sum of £2·5m was received by the council from the bank.

d As my noble and learned friend Lord Browne-Wilkinson observes, it is plain that the present case falls within neither of the situations which are traditionally regarded as giving rise to a resulting trust, viz (1) voluntary payments by A to B, or for the purchase of property in the name of B or in his and A's joint names, where there is no presumption of advancement or evidence of intention to

e make an out-and-out gift; or (2) property transferred to B on an express trust which does not exhaust the whole beneficial interest. The question therefore arises whether resulting trusts should be extended beyond such cases to apply in the present case, which I shall treat as a case where money has been paid for a consideration which fails.

f In a most interesting and challenging paper, 'Restitution and Resulting Trusts' in *Equity and Contemporary Legal Developments, Papers Presented at the First International Conference on Equity* (ed Goldstein, 1992) p 335, Professor Birks has argued for a wider role for the resulting trust in the field of restitution, and specifically for its availability in cases of mistake and failure of consideration. His thesis is avowedly experimental, written to test the temperature of the

g water. I feel bound to respond that the temperature of the water must be regarded as decidedly cold (see e g Professor Burrows 'Swaps and the Friction between Common Law and Equity' [1995] RLR 15 and W J Swadling 'A new role for resulting trusts?' (1996) 16 LS 110).

In the first place, as Lord Browne-Wilkinson points out, to impose a resulting

h trust in such cases is inconsistent with the traditional principles of trust law. For on receipt of the money by the payee it is to be presumed that (as in the present case) the identity of the money is immediately lost by mixing with other assets of the payee, and at that time the payee has no knowledge of the facts giving rise to the failure of consideration. By the time that those facts come to light, and the conscience of the payee may thereby be affected, there will therefore be no

j identifiable fund to which a trust can attach. But there are other difficulties. First, there is no general rule that the property in money paid under a void contract does not pass to the payee; and it is difficult to escape the conclusion that, as a general rule, the beneficial interest to the money likewise passes to the payee. This must certainly be the case where the consideration for the payment fails after the payment is made, as in cases of frustration or breach of contract;

and there appears to be no good reason why the same should not apply in cases
where, as in the present case, the contract under which the payment is made is
void ab initio and the consideration for the payment therefore fails at the time
of payment. It is true that the doctrine of mistake might be invoked where the
mistake is fundamental in the orthodox sense of that word. But that is not the
position in the present case; moreover the mistake in the present case must be
classified as a mistake of law which, as at the law at present stands, creates its
own special problems. No doubt that much-criticised doctrine will fall to be
reconsidered when an appropriate case occurs; but I cannot think that the
present is such a case, since not only has the point not been argued but (as will
appear) it is my opinion that there is any event jurisdiction to award compound
interest in the present case. For all of these reasons I conclude, in agreement
with my noble and learned friend, that there is no basis for holding that a
resulting trust arises in cases where money has been paid under a contract
which is ultra vires and therefore void ab initio. This conclusion has the effect
that all the practical problems which would flow from the imposition of a
resulting trust in a case such as the present, in particular the imposition upon
the recipient of the normal duties of trustee, do not arise. The dramatic
consequences which would occur are detailed by Professor Burrows in 'Swaps
and the Friction between Common Law and Equity' [1995] RLR 15 at 27: the
duty to account for profits accruing from the trust property; the inability of the
payee to rely upon the defence of change of position; the absence of any
limitation period; and so on. Professor Burrows even goes so far as to conclude
that the action for money had and received would be rendered otiose in such
cases, and indeed in all cases where the payer seeks restitution of mistaken
payments. However, if no resulting trust arises, it also follows that the payer in
a case such as the present cannot achieve priority over the payee's general
creditors in the event of his insolvency—a conclusion which appears to me to
be just.

For all these reasons I conclude that there is no basis for imposing a resulting
trust in the present case, and I therefore reject the bank's submission that it was
here entitled to proceed by way of an equitable proprietary claim. I need only
add that, in reaching that conclusion, I do not find it necessary to review the
decision of Goulding J in *Chase Manhattan Bank NA v Israel-British Bank (London)
Ltd* [1979] 3 All ER 1025, [1981] Ch 105.

INTEREST

It is against that background that I turn to consider the question of compound
interest. Here there are three points which fall to be considered. These are (1)
whether the court had jurisdiction to award compound interest; (2) if so,
whether it should have exercised its jurisdiction to make such an award in the
present case; and (3) from what date should such an award of compound
interest run, if made.

It is common ground that in a case such as the present there is no jurisdiction
to award compound interest at common law or by statute. The central question
in the present case is therefore whether there is jurisdiction in equity to do so.
It was held below, on the basis that the bank was entitled to succeed not only in
a personal claim at common law but also in a proprietary claim in equity, that
there was jurisdiction in equity to make an order that the council should pay
compound interest on the sum adjudged due. It was that jurisdiction which was
exercised by Hobhouse J, whose decision on the point was not challenged

a before the Court of Appeal, on the basis that *Sinclair v Brougham* provided binding authority that a proprietary claim was available to the bank in this case. However since, in my opinion, *Sinclair v Brougham* provides no such authority, and no proprietary claim is available to the bank, the question now arises whether the equitable jurisdiction to award compound interest may nevertheless be exercised on the facts of the present case.

b I wish however to record that Hobhouse J was in no doubt that, if he had jurisdiction to do so, he should award compound interest in this case. He said ([1994] 4 All ER 890 at 955):

'Anyone who lends or borrows money on a commercial basis receives or pays interest periodically and if that interest is not paid it is compounded ...

c I see no reason why I should deny the plaintiff a complete remedy or allow the defendant arbitrarily to retain part of the enrichment which it has unjustly enjoyed.'

With that reasoning I find myself to be in entire agreement. The council has had the use of the bank's money over a period of years. It is plain on the *d* evidence that, if it had not had the use of the bank's money, it would (if free to do so) have borrowed the money elsewhere at compound interest. It has to that extent profited from the use of the bank's money. Moreover, if the bank had not advanced the money to the council, it would itself have employed the money on similar terms in its business. Full restitution requires that, on the facts of the present case, compound interest should be awarded, having regard *e* to the commercial realities of the case. As the judge said, there is no reason why the bank should be denied a complete remedy.

It follows therefore that everything depends on the scope of the equitable jurisdiction. It also follows, in my opinion, that if that jurisdiction does not extend to apply in a case such as the present, English law will be revealed as *f* incapable of doing full justice.

It is right that I should record that the scope of the equitable jurisdiction was not explored in depth in the course of argument before the Appellate Committee, in which attention was concentrated on the question whether a proprietary claim was available to the bank in the circumstances of the present case. In other circumstances, it might well have been appropriate to invite *g* further argument on the point. However, since it was indicated to the Committee that the council was not prepared to spend further money on the appeal, whereupon it took no further part in the proceedings, and since the relevant authorities had been cited to the Committee, I am satisfied that it is appropriate that the point should now be decided by your Lordships' House.

h I wish also to record that I have had the opportunity of reading in draft the speech of my noble and learned friend Lord Woolf, and that I find myself to be in agreement with his reasoning and conclusion on the point. Even so, I propose to set out in my own words my reasons for reaching the same conclusion.

j I shall begin by expressing two preliminary thoughts. The first is that, where the jurisdiction of the court derives from common law or equity, and is designed to do justice in cases which come before the courts, it is startling to be faced by an argument that the jurisdiction is so restricted as to prevent the courts from doing justice. Jurisdiction of that kind should as a matter of principle be as broad as possible, to enable justice to be done wherever necessary; and the relevant limits should be found, not in the scope of the

jurisdiction, but in the manner of its exercise as the principles are worked out
from case to case. Second, I find it equally startling to find that the jurisdiction
is said to be limited to certain specific categories of case. Where jurisdiction is
founded on a principle of justice, I would expect that the categories of case
where it is exercised should be regarded not as occupying the whole field but
rather as emanations of the principle, so that the possibility of the jurisdiction
being extended to other categories of case is not foreclosed.

It is with these thoughts in mind that I turn to the equitable jurisdiction to
award interest. In *President of India v La Pintada Cia Navegacion SA* [1984] 2 All
ER 773 at 779, [1985] AC 104 at 116 Lord Brandon of Oakbrook, delivering a
speech with which the other members of the Appellate Committee agreed,
described the equitable jurisdiction in the following words:

'Chancery courts had further regularly awarded interest, including not
only simple interest but also compound interest, when they thought that
justice so demanded, that is to say in cases where money had been obtained
and retained by fraud, or where it had been withheld or misapplied by a
trustee or anyone else in a fiduciary position.'

Later, however, he said that courts of Chancery only awarded compound, as
distinct from simple, interest in two special classes of case.

With great respect I myself consider that, if the jurisdiction to award
compound interest is available where justice so demands, it cannot be so
confined as to exclude any class of case simply because that class of case has not
previously been recognised as falling within it. I prefer therefore to read the
passage quoted from Lord Brandon's speech as Mason CJ and Wilson J read it
in *Hungerfords v Walker* (1988) 171 CLR 125 at 148, as providing examples (ie not
exclusive examples) of the application of the underlying principle of justice.

Now it is true that the reported cases on the exercise of the equitable
jurisdiction, which are by no means numerous, are concerned with cases of
breach of duty by trustees and other fiduciaries. In *A-G v Alford* (1855) 4 De GM
& G 843, 43 ER 737, for example, which came before Lord Cranworth LC, the
question arose whether an executor and trustee, who had for several years
retained in his hands trust funds which he ought to have invested, should be
chargeable with interest in excess of the ordinary rate of simple interest. It was
held that he should not be chargeable at a higher rate. Lord Cranworth LC
recognised that the court might in such a case impose interest at a higher rate,
or even compound interest. But he observed that if so the court does not
impose a penalty on the trustee. He said (4 De GM & G 843 at 851, 43 ER 737
at 741):

'What the court ought to do, I think, is to charge him only with the
interest which he has received, or which it is justly entitled to say he ought
to have received, or which it is so fairly to be presumed that he did receive
that he is estopped from saying that he did not receive it.'

In cases of misconduct which benefits the executor, however, the court may
fairly infer that he used the money in speculation, and may, on the principle 'In
odium spoliatoris omnia praesumuntur' assume that he made a higher rate, if
that was a reasonable conclusion.

Likewise in *Burdick v Garrick* (1870) LR 5 Ch App 233, where a fiduciary agent
held money of his principal and simply paid it into his bank account, it was held

a that he should be charged with simple interest only. Lord Hatherley LC applied the principle laid down in *A-G v Alford*, namely that—

b 'the court does not proceed against an accounting party by way of punishing him for making use of the Plaintiff's money by directing rests, or payment of compound interest, but proceeds upon this principle, either that he has made, or has put himself into such a position as that he is to be presumed to have made, 5 per cent., or compound interest, as the case may be. If the Court finds ... that the money received has been invested in an ordinary trade, the whole course of decision has tended to this, that the Court presumes that the party against whom relief is sought has made that amount of profit which persons ordinarily do make in trade, and in those c cases the Court directs rests to be made.' (See LR 5 Ch App 233 at 241–242.)

For a more recent case in which the equitable jurisdiction was invoked, see *Wallersteiner v Moir (No 2)* [1975] 1 All ER 849, [1975] QB 373.

d From these cases it can be seen that compound interest may be awarded in cases where the defendant has wrongfully profited, or may be presumed to have so profited, from having the use of another person's money. The power to award compound interest is therefore available to achieve justice in a limited area of what is now seen as the law of restitution, viz where the defendant has acquired a benefit through his wrongful act (see Goff and Jones *Law of* e *Restitution* (4th edn, 1993) p 632ff; Birks *Law of Restitution* p 313ff; and Burrows *Law of Restitution* p 403ff). The general question arises whether the jurisdiction must be kept constrained in this way, or whether it may be permitted to expand so that it can be exercised to ensure that full justice can be done elsewhere in that rubric of the law. The particular question is whether the jurisdiction can be exercised in a case such as the present in which the council has been ordered f to repay the balance of the bank's money on the ground of unjust enrichment, in a personal claim at common law.

At this stage of the argument I wish to stress two things. The first is that it is plain that the jurisdiction may, in an appropriate case, be exercised in the case of a personal claim in equity. In both *Alford's* case and *Burdick v Garrick*, the g cases were concerned with the taking of an account, and an order for payment of the sum found due. In each case the accounting party was a fiduciary, who held the relevant funds on trust. But the jurisdiction is not limited to cases in which a proprietary claim is being made and an award of interest is sought as representing the fruits of the property so claimed. On the contrary, the jurisdiction is in personam, and moreover an award of interest may be made not h only where the trustee or fiduciary has made a profit, but also where it is held that he ought to have made a profit and has not done so. Furthermore, in my opinion the decision of the Court of Appeal in *Re Diplock's Estate, Diplock v Wintle* [1948] 2 All ER 318, [1948] Ch 465 provides no authority for the proposition that there is no *jurisdiction* to award compound interest where the j claim is a personal claim. It is true that in that case the Court of Appeal decided not to award interest against a number of charities which had been held liable, in a personal claim in equity, to repay legacies which had been paid to them in error. But in so doing the court simply followed an old decision of Lord Eldon LC in *Gittins v Steele* (1818) 1 Swan 24, 199 at 200, 36 ER 283, 356 at 357, in which his judgment was as follows:

'Where the fund out of which the legacy ought to have been paid is in the hands of the Court making interest, unquestionably interest is due. If a legacy has been erroneously paid to a legatee who has no farther property in the estate, in recalling that payment I apprehend that the rule of the Court is not to charge interest; but if the legatee is entitled to another fund making interest in the hands of the Court, justice must be done out of his share.'

The Court of Appeal in *Re Diplock's Estate* can have had no desire to make an award of interest against the charities in the personal claim against them in that case, and they must have been very content to follow uncritically this old 'rule of court'. But it does not follow that the rule of court went to the jurisdiction of the court. It is more likely that it represented an established practice which, as Lord Eldon LC's brief judgment indicates, was subject to exceptions. In any event the Court of Appeal was there concerned only with simple interest; and in cases of the kind there under consideration, it seems unlikely that any question of an award of compound interest would ever have arisen.

I must confess that I find the reasoning which would restrict the equitable jurisdiction to award compound interest to cases where the claim is proprietary in nature to be both technical and unrealistic. This is shown by the reasoning and conclusion of Hobhouse J in *Kleinwort Benson Ltd v South Tyneside Metropolitan BC* [1994] 4 All ER 972, another swap transaction case, in which the plaintiff bank had no proprietary claim. The judge upheld the submission of the defendant council that, although they were under a personal liability to make restitution both at law and in equity, nevertheless the court had no jurisdiction to award compound interest on the sum adjudged due. He said (at 994):

'If ... the plaintiff is only entitled to a personal remedy which will be the case where, although there was initially a fiduciary relationship and the payer was entitled in equity to treat the sum received by the payee as his, the payer's, money and to trace it, but because of subsequent developments he is no longer able to trace the sum in the hands of the payee, then there is no subject matter to which the rationale on which compound interest is awarded can be applied. The payee cannot be shown to have a fund belonging to the payer or to have used it to make profits for himself.'

This reasoning is logical, assuming the restricted nature of the equitable jurisdiction to award compound interest. But if, as Lord Brandon in *President of India v La Pintada Cia Navegacion SA* [1984] 2 All ER 773 at 779, [1985] AC 104 at 116 stated, the jurisdiction is founded upon the demands of justice, it is difficult to see the sense of the distinction which Hobhouse J felt compelled to draw. It seems strange indeed that, just because the power to trace property has ceased, the court's jurisdiction to award compound interest should also come to an end. For where the claim is based upon the unjust enrichment of the defendant, it may be necessary to have power to award compound interest to achieve full restitution, ie to do full justice, as much where the plaintiff's claim is personal as where his claim is proprietary in nature. Furthermore, I know of no authority which compelled Hobhouse J to hold that he had no jurisdiction to award compound interest in respect of the personal claim in equity in the case before him.

For these reasons I am satisfied that there is jurisdiction in equity to award compound interest in the case of personal claims as well as proprietary claims.

a   I turn next to the question whether the equitable jurisdiction can be exercised in aid of common law remedies such as, for example, a personal remedy in restitution, to repair the deficiencies of the common law. Here I turn at once to *Snell's Principles of Equity* (29th edn, 1990) p 28, where the first maxim of equity is stated to be that 'Equity will not suffer a wrong to be without a remedy'. The commentary on this maxim in the text reads:

b   'The idea expressed in this maxim is that no wrong should be allowed to go unredressed if it is capable of being remedied by courts of justice, and this really underlies the whole jurisdiction of equity. As already explained, the common law courts failed to remedy many undoubted wrongs, and this failure led to the establishment of the Court of Chancery. But [it] must not
c   be supposed that every *moral* wrong was redressed by the Court of Chancery. The maxim must be taken as referring to rights which are suitable for judicial enforcement, but were not enforced at common law owing to some technical defect.'

     To this maxim is attributed the auxiliary jurisdiction of equity. The
d commentary reads:

     'Again, to this maxim may be traced the origin of the auxiliary jurisdiction of the Court of Chancery, by virtue of which suitors at law were aided in the enforcement of their legal rights. Without such aid these rights would often have been "wrongs without remedies." For instance, it was often
e   necessary for a plaintiff in a common law action to obtain discovery of facts resting in the knowledge of the defendant, or of deeds, writings or other things in his possession or power. The common law courts, however, had no power to order such discovery, and recourse was therefore had to the Court of Chancery, which assumed jurisdiction to order the defendant to
f   make discovery on his oath.'

     The question which arises in the present case is whether, in the exercise of equity's auxiliary jurisdiction, the equitable jurisdiction to award compound interest may be exercised to enable a plaintiff to obtain full justice in a personal action of restitution at common law.

g   I start with the position that the common law remedy is, in a case such as the present, plainly inadequate, in that there is no power to award compound interest at common law and that without that power the common law remedy is incomplete. The situation is therefore no different from that in which, in the absence of jurisdiction at common law to order discovery, equity stepped in to enable justice to be done in common law actions by ordering the defendant to
h make discovery on oath. The only difference between the two cases is that, whereas the equitable jurisdiction to order discovery in aid of common law actions was recognised many years ago, the possibility of the equitable jurisdiction to award compound interest being exercised in aid of common law actions was not addressed until the present case. Fortunately, however, judges
j of equity have always been ready to address new problems, and to create new doctrines, where justice so requires. As Jessel MR said, in a famous passage in his judgment in *Re Hallett's Estate, Knatchbull v Hallett* (1880) 13 Ch D 696 at 710, [1874–80] All ER Rep 793 at 796:

     'I intentionally say modern rules, because it must not be forgotten that the rules of Courts of Equity are not, like the rules of the Common Law, supposed to have been established from time immemorial. It is perfectly *a* well known that they have been established from time to time—altered, improved, and refined from time to time. In many cases we know the names of the Chancellors who invented them. No doubt they were invented for the purpose of securing the better administration of justice, but still they were invented.'

b

I therefore ask myself whether there is any reason why the equitable jurisdiction to award compound interest should not be exercised in a case such as the present. I can see none. Take, for example, the case of fraud. It is well established that the equitable jurisdiction may be exercised in cases of fraud. Indeed, it is plain that, on the same facts, there may be a remedy both at law and *c* in equity to recover money obtained by fraud (see *Johnson v R* [1904] AC 817 at 822 per Lord Macnaghten). Is it to be said that, if the plaintiff decides to proceed in equity, compound interest may be awarded; but that if he chooses to proceed in an action at law, no such auxiliary relief will be available to him? I find it difficult to believe that, at the end of the twentieth century, our law should be so hidebound by forms of action as to be compelled to reach such a conclusion. *d*

For these reasons I conclude that the equitable jurisdiction to award compound interest may be exercised in the case of personal claims at common law, as it is in equity. Furthermore, I am satisfied that, in particular, the equitable jurisdiction may, where appropriate, be exercised in the case of a personal claim in restitution. In reaching that conclusion, I am of the opinion *e* that the decision of Hobhouse J in *Kleinwort Benson Ltd v South Tyneside Metropolitan BC* [1994] 4 All ER 972 that the court had no such jurisdiction should not be allowed to stand.

I recognise that, in so holding, the courts would be breaking new ground, and would be extending the equitable jurisdiction to a field where it has not hitherto *f* been exercised. But that cannot of itself be enough to prevent what I see to be a thoroughly desirable extension of the jurisdiction, consistent with its underlying basis that it exists to meet the demands of justice. An action of restitution appears to me to provide an almost classic case in which the jurisdiction should be available to enable the courts to do full justice. Claims in *g* restitution are founded upon a principle of justice, being designed to prevent the unjust enrichment of the defendant (see *Lipkin Gorman (a firm) v Karpnale Ltd* [1992] 4 All ER 512, [1991] 2 AC 548). Long ago, in *Moses v Macferlan* (1760) 2 Burr 1005 at 1012, [1558–1774] All ER Rep 581 at 585, Lord Mansfield said that the gist of the action for money had and received is that 'the defendant, upon the circumstances of the case, is obliged by the ties of natural justice and equity *h* to refund the money'. It would be strange indeed if the courts lacked jurisdiction in such a case to ensure that justice could be fully achieved by means of an award of compound interest, where it is appropriate to make such an award, despite the fact that the jurisdiction to award such interest is itself said to rest upon the demands of justice. I am glad not to be forced to hold that *j* English law is so inadequate as to be incapable of achieving such a result. In my opinion the jurisdiction should now be made available, as justice requires, in cases of restitution, to ensure that full justice can be done. The seed is there, but the growth has hitherto been confined within a small area. That growth should now be permitted to spread naturally elsewhere within this newly recognised branch of the law. No genetic engineering is required, only that the a   warm sun of judicial creativity should exercise its benign influence rather than remain hidden behind the dark clouds of legal history.

    I wish to add that I for my part do not consider that the statutory power to award interest, either under s 3 of the Law Reform (Miscellaneous Provisions) Act 1934 or under s 35A of the Supreme Court Act 1981 (which, pursuant to s 15 of the Administration of Justice Act 1982, superseded s 3 of the 1934 Act),

b   inhibits the course of action which I now propose. It is true that s 3(1) of the 1934 Act, when empowering courts of record to award interest in proceedings for the recovery of any debt or damages, did not authorise the giving of interest upon interest. But I cannot see that it would be inconsistent with the intention then expressed by Parliament later to extend the existing equitable jurisdiction to award compound interest to enable courts to ensure that full restitution is

c   achieved in personal actions of restitution at common law. It is of course common knowledge that, until the latter part of this century, the existence of a systematic law of restitution, founded upon the principle of unjust enrichment, had not been recognised in English law. The question whether there should be a power to award compound interest in such cases, in order to achieve full

d   restitution, simply did not arise in 1934 and cannot therefore have been considered by Parliament in that year. To hold that, because Parliament did not then authorise an award of compound interest in proceedings the nature of which was not then recognised, the courts should now be precluded from exercising the ordinary judicial power to develop the law by extending an existing jurisdiction to meet a newly recognised need appears to me to

e   constitute an unnecessary and undesirable fetter upon the judicial development of the law. It is not to be forgotten that there is jurisdiction in equity, as well as at common law, to order restitution on the ground of unjust enrichment; and I cannot see that s 3(1) of the 1934 Act would have precluded any extension of the existing equitable jurisdiction to award compound interest to enable full

f   restitution to be achieved in such a case. Accordingly neither would s 3(1), which applied to all courts of record, have precluded a similar extension of the jurisdiction to enable full restitution to be achieved in actions at common law. Section 35A of the 1981 Act no doubt perpetuated the position as established by s 3(1) of the 1934 Act, in that it too did not confer a power on the courts to award compound interest; but I cannot see that this affects the position. In so far as it

g   is relevant to refer to the Law Commission's report, *Law of Contract: Report on Interest* (Law Com No 88) (1978), which preceded that enactment, it appears from the report that it was generally opposed to the introduction of any general power to award compound interest; but there was no intention of interfering with the equitable jurisdiction, and the problem which has arisen in the present

h   case was not addressed. I wish to add that such an extension of the equitable jurisdiction as I propose would, in my opinion, be a case of equity acting in aid of the common law. There is in my opinion no need, and indeed no basis, for outlawing such a development as a case of equity acting in aid of the legislature simply because the legislature, in conferring upon courts the power to award

j   simple interest, did not authorise the giving of compound interest.

    It remains for me to say that I am satisfied, for the reasons given by Hobhouse J, that this is a case in which it was appropriate that compound interest should be awarded. In particular, since the council had the free use of the bank's money in circumstances in which, if it had borrowed the money from some other financial institution, it would have had to pay compound interest for it, the council can properly be said to have profited from the bank's money so as to make an award of compound interest appropriate. However, for the reasons given by Dillon LJ ([1994] 4 All ER 890 at 947–949, [1994] 1 WLR 938 at 947–949), I agree with the Court of Appeal that the interest should run from the date of receipt of the money.

CONCLUSION

For these reasons I would dismiss the appeal.

LORD BROWNE-WILKINSON. My Lords, in the last decade many local authorities entered into interest rate swap agreements with banks and other finance houses. In *Hazell v Hammersmith and Fulham London BC* [1991] 1 All ER 545, [1992] 2 AC 1 your Lordships held that such contracts were ultra vires local authorities and therefore void. Your Lordships left open the question whether payments made pursuant to such swap agreements were recoverable or not. The action which is the subject matter of this appeal is one of a number in which the court has had to consider the extent to which moneys paid under such an agreement are recoverable.

An interest rate swap agreement is an agreement between two parties by which each agrees to pay the other on a specified date or dates an amount calculated by reference to the interest which would have accrued over a given period on a notional principal sum. The rate of interest payable by each party (on the same notional sum) is different. One rate of interest is usually fixed and does not change (and the payer is called 'the fixed rate payer'); the other rate is a variable or floating rate based on a fluctuating interest rate such as the six-month London Inter-Bank Offered Rate (LIBOR) and the payer is known as 'the floating rate payer'. Normally the parties do not make the actual payments they have contracted for but the party owing the higher amount pays to the other party the difference between the two amounts.

In the present case the swap contract was concluded between the respondent bank, Westdeutsche Landesbank Girozentrale, and the appellant, the council of the London Borough of Islington, on 16 June 1987. The arrangement was to run for ten years starting on 18 June 1987. The interest sums were to be calculated on a notional principal sum of £25m and were to be payable half-yearly. The bank was to be the fixed rate payer at a rate of 7·5% per annum and the local authority was to be the floating rate payer at the domestic sterling LIBOR rate. In addition, the bank was to pay to the local authority on 18 June 1987 a sum of £2·5m (the upfront payment) which payment was made. As a result of the provision of the upfront payment the rate of interest payable by the bank as the fixed rate payer was agreed to be lower than what would have been appropriate (9·43%) if the upfront payment had not been made.

Pursuant to the terms of the agreement, the following payments were made:

Date	Payment by bank to council	Payment by council to bank
18.06.87	£2,500,000	
18.12.87		£172,345·89
20.06.88		£229,666·09
19.12.88		£259,054·56
19.06.89		£693,407·53
Total	£2,500,000	£1,354,474·07

a   Therefore the payments made by the bank to the local authority exceed those made by the local authority to the bank to the extent of £1,145,525·93.

On 1 November 1989 the Divisional Court gave judgment in *Hazell* [1990] 3 All ER 33, [1990] 2 QB 697 declaring void swap transactions entered into by local authorities. The decision applied to the contract between the parties in the present case.

b   As will appear, it is of central importance to note the way in which the local authority dealt with the upfront payment of £2·5m made to it on 18 June 1987. The money was credited to a bank account of the local authority in which there were other moneys of the local authority, ie into a mixed account. That account itself became overdrawn overnight on several dates in June and July

c   1987. There was an overall debit balance on the account on 16 November 1987. The moneys in the mixed account were used by the local authority for its general expenditure. If the upfront payment had not been received, the local authority would have had to borrow more money if it could. The local authority had been, and was likely to be in the future, rate-capped and one of the attractions to the local authority in the swap agreement was that it obtained

d   the upfront payment in a form which did not attract statutory controls.

The bank in this action sought recovery of the amounts paid by it under the void agreement together with interest. On 12 February 1993 Hobhouse J ([1994] 4 All ER 890) gave judgment in the Commercial Court for the bank ordering payment by the local authority to the bank of the balance together

e   with compound interest on the balance as from 1 April 1990 with six-monthly rests.

The council appealed to the Court of Appeal against that order and the bank cross-appealed contending that compound interest should have been ordered as from the date of receipt of the principal sum, ie 18 June 1987.

f   On 17 December 1993 the Court of Appeal (Dillon, Leggatt and Kennedy LJJ) ([1994] 4 All ER 890, [1994] 1 WLR 938) dismissed the local authority's appeal and allowed the cross-appeal by the bank. It held that the bank was entitled to recover the balance at law as money had and received (see [1994] 4 All ER 890 at 962, 969, [1994] 1 WLR 938 at 946, 953 per Dillon and Leggatt LJJ). It also held

g   that the bank was entitled to recover the balance in equity on the ground that the local authority held the upfront payment on a resulting trust and was therefore personally liable, as trustee, to repay the bank (see [1994] 4 All ER 890 at 962, 968, [1994] 1 WLR 938 at 947, 953 per Dillon and Leggatt LJJ). The Court of Appeal further held the local authority liable to pay compound interest on the balance from time to time outstanding as from the date of receipt of the upfront

h   payment. The ability of the court to award compound, as opposed to simple, interest was founded on the equitable jurisdiction to award compound interest as against a trustee or other person owing fiduciary duties who is personally accountable and who has made use of the plaintiff's money (see [1994] 4 All ER 890 at 964–967, 969–670, [1994] 1 WLR 938 at 949–951, 953–955 per Dillon and

j   Leggatt LJJ).

The local authority now accepts that it is personally liable to repay the balance to the bank. The local authority appeals to your Lordships only against the award of compound interest. But, as will appear, notwithstanding the narrow scope of the appeal it raises profound questions for decision by your Lordships.

COMPOUND INTEREST IN EQUITY

It is common ground that in the absence of agreement or custom the court has no jurisdiction to award compound interest either at law or under s 35A of the Supreme Court Act 1981. It is also common ground that in certain limited circumstances courts of equity can award compound interest. Mr Philipson QC, for the local authority, contends that compound interest can only be ordered on a claim against a trustee or other person owing fiduciary duties who, in breach of such duty, has used trust moneys in his own trade. He contends that compound interest cannot be awarded in this case since (a) the local authority never held the upfront payment as a trustee or in a fiduciary capacity and (b) in any event, the local authority did not use the upfront payment in its trade. Mr Sumption QC, for the bank, contends that compound interest can be awarded in equity whenever the defendant is liable to disgorge a benefit received whether or not he is a trustee or a fiduciary. Alternatively, Mr Sumption contends that the local authority did receive the upfront payment as a trustee and as such is in equity accountable for the benefits it has received, including the benefit of not having to borrow £2·5m on the market at compound interest.

In the absence of fraud courts of equity have never awarded compound interest except against a trustee or other person owing fiduciary duties who is accountable for profits made from his position. Equity awarded simple interest at a time when courts of law had no right under common law or statute to award any interest. The award of compound interest was restricted to cases where the award was in lieu of an account of profits improperly made by the trustee. We were not referred to any case where compound interest had been awarded in the absence of fiduciary accountability for a profit. The principle is clearly stated by Lord Hatherley LC in *Burdick v Garrick* (1870) LR 5 Ch App 233 at 241:

'... the Court does not proceed against an accounting party by way of punishing him for making use of the Plaintiff's money by directing rests, or payment of compound interest, but proceeds upon this principle, either that he has made, or has put himself into such a position as that he is to be presumed to have made, 5 per cent., or compound interest, as the case may be.'

The principle was more fully stated by Buckley LJ in *Wallersteiner v Moir (No 2)* [1975] 1 All ER 849 at 863, [1975] QB 373 at 397.

'Where a trustee has retained trust money in his own hands, he will be accountable for the profit which he has made or which he is assumed to have made from the use of the money. In *A-G v Alford* (1855) 4 De GM & G 843 at 851, 43 ER 737 at 741 Lord Cranworth LC said: "What the Court ought to do, I think, is to charge him only with the interest which he has received, or which it is justly entitled to say he ought to have received, or which it is so fairly to be presumed that he did receive that he is estopped from saying that he did not receive it." This is an application of the doctrine that the court will not allow a trustee to make any profit from his trust. The defaulting trustee is normally charged with simple interest only, but if it is established that he has used the money in trade he may be charged compound interest ... The justification for charging compound interest normally lies in the fact that profits earned in trade would be likely to be

a

used as working capital for earning further profits. Precisely similar equitable principles apply to an agent who has retained [moneys] of his principal in his hands and used them for his own purposes (*Burdick v Garrick*).'

In *President of India v La Pintada Cia Navegacion SA* [1984] 2 All ER 773, [1985]
b
AC 104 Lord Brandon of Oakbrook (with whose speech the rest of their Lordships agreed) considered the law as to the award of interest as at that date in four separate areas. His third area was equity, as to which he said ([1984] 2 All ER 773 at 779, [1985] AC 104 at 116):

c

'Third, the area of equity. The Chancery courts, again differing from the common law courts, had regularly awarded simple interest as ancillary relief in respect of equitable remedies, such as specific performance, rescission and the taking of an account. Chancery courts had further regularly awarded interest, including not only simple interest but also compound interest, when they thought that justice so demanded, that is to say in cases where money had been obtained and retained by fraud, or
d
where it had been withheld or misapplied by a trustee or anyone else in a fiduciary position ... Chancery courts only in two special classes of case, awarded compound, as distinct from simple, interest.'

These authorities establish that in the absence of fraud equity only awards compound (as opposed to simple) interest against a defendant who is a trustee
e
or otherwise in a fiduciary position by way of recouping from such a defendant an improper profit made by him. It is unnecessary to decide whether in such a case compound interest can only be paid where the defendant has used trust moneys in his own trade or (as I tend to think) extends to all cases where a fiduciary has improperly profited from his trust. Unless the local authority
f
owed fiduciary duties to the bank in relation to the upfront payment, compound interest cannot be awarded.

WAS THERE A TRUST? THE ARGUMENT FOR THE BANK IN OUTLINE

The bank submitted that, since the contract was void, title did not pass at the date of payment either at law or in equity. The legal title of the bank was
g
extinguished as soon as the money was paid into the mixed account, whereupon the legal title became vested in the local authority. But, it was argued, this did not affect the *equitable* interest, which remained vested in the bank (the retention of title point). It was submitted that whenever the legal interest in property is vested in one person and the equitable interest in another, the owner of the legal interest holds it on trust for the owner of the equitable title: 'the
h
separation of the legal from the equitable interest necessarily imports a trust.' For this latter proposition (the separation of title point) the bank, of course, relies on *Sinclair v Brougham* [1914] AC 398, [1914–15] All ER Rep 622 and *Chase Manhattan Bank NA v Israel-British Bank (London) Ltd* [1979] 3 All ER 1025, [1981] Ch 105.

j
The generality of these submissions was narrowed by submitting that the trust which arose in this case was a resulting trust 'not of an active character' (see *Sinclair v Brougham* [1914] AC 398 at 421, [1914–15] All ER Rep 622 at 632 per Viscount Haldane LC). This submission was reinforced, after completion of the oral argument, by sending to your Lordships Professor Peter Birks' paper 'Restitution and Resulting Trusts' in *Equity and Contemporary Legal Developments*,

Papers Presented at the First International Conference on Equity (ed Goldstein, 1992) p 335. Unfortunately your Lordships have not had the advantage of any submissions from the local authority on this paper, but an article by William Swadling 'A new role for resulting trusts?' (1996) 16 LS 110 puts forward counter-arguments which I have found persuasive.

It is to be noted that the bank did not found any argument on the basis that the local authority was liable to repay either as a constructive trustee or under the in personam liability of the wrongful recipient of the estate of a deceased person established by *Re Diplock's Estate, Diplock v Wintle* [1948] 2 All ER 318, [1948] Ch 465. I therefore do not further consider those points.

THE BREADTH OF THE SUBMISSION

Although the actual question in issue on the appeal is a narrow one, on the arguments presented it is necessary to consider fundamental principles of trust law. Does the recipient of money under a contract subsequently found to be void for mistake or as being ultra vires hold the moneys received on trust even where he had no knowledge at any relevant time that the contract was void? If he does hold on trust, such trust must arise at the date of receipt or, at the latest, at the date the legal title of the payer is extinguished by mixing moneys in a bank account: in the present case it does not matter at which of those dates the legal title was extinguished. If there is a trust two consequences follow: (a) the recipient will be personally liable, regardless of fault, for any subsequent payment away of the moneys to third parties even though, at the date of such payment, the 'trustee' was still ignorant of the existence of any trust (see Burrows 'Swaps and the Friction between Common Law and Equity' [1995] RLR 15); (b) as from the date of the establishment of the trust (ie receipt or mixing of the moneys by the 'trustee') the original payer will have an equitable proprietary interest in the moneys so long as they are traceable into whomsoever's hands they come other than a purchaser for value of the legal interest without notice. Therefore, although in the present case the only question directly in issue is the personal liability of the local authority as a trustee, it is not possible to hold the local authority liable without imposing a trust which, in other cases, will create property rights affecting third parties because moneys received under a void contract are 'trust property'.

THE PRACTICAL CONSEQUENCES OF THE BANK'S ARGUMENT

Before considering the legal merits of the submission, it is important to appreciate the practical consequences which ensue if the bank's arguments are correct. Those who suggest that a resulting trust should arise in these circumstances accept that the creation of an equitable proprietary interest under the trust can have unfortunate, and adverse, effects if the original recipient of the moneys becomes insolvent: the moneys, if traceable in the hands of the recipient, are trust moneys and not available for the creditors of the recipient. However, the creation of an equitable proprietary interest in moneys received under a void contract is capable of having adverse effects quite apart from insolvency. The proprietary interest under the unknown trust will, quite apart from insolvency, be enforceable against any recipient of the property other than the purchaser for value of a legal interest without notice.

Take the following example. T (the transferor) has entered into a commercial contract with R1 (the first recipient). Both parties believe the contract to be valid but it is in fact void. Pursuant to that contract: (i) T pays £1m to R1 a who pays it into a mixed bank account; (ii) T transfers 100 shares in X company to R1, who is registered as a shareholder. Thereafter R1 deals with the money and shares as follows: (iii) R1 pays £50,000 out of the mixed account to R2 otherwise than for value; R2 then becomes insolvent, having trade creditors who have paid for goods not delivered at the time of the insolvency. (iv) R1 charges the shares in X company to R3 by way of equitable security for a loan b from R3.

If the bank's arguments are correct, R1 holds the £1m on trust for T once the money has become mixed in R1's bank account. Similarly R1 becomes the legal owner of the shares in X company as from the date of his registration as a shareholder but holds such shares on a resulting trust for T. T therefore has an equitable proprietary interest in the moneys in the mixed account and in the c shares.

T's equitable interest will enjoy absolute priority as against the creditors in the insolvency of R2 (who was not a purchaser for value) provided that the £50,000 can be traced in the assets of R2 at the date of its insolvency. Moreover, if the separation of title argument is correct, since the equitable interest is in T d and the legal interest is vested in R2, R2 also holds as trustee for T. In tracing the £50,000 in the bank account of R2, R2 as trustee will be treated as having drawn out 'his own' moneys first, thereby benefitting T at the expense of the secured and unsecured creditors of R2. Therefore in practice one may well reach the position where the moneys in the bank account of R2 in reality reflect the price paid by creditors for goods not delivered by R2: yet, under the tracing e rules, those moneys are to be treated as belonging in equity to T.

So far as the shares in the X company are concerned, T can trace his equitable interest into the shares and will take in priority to R3, whose equitable charge to secure his loan even though granted for value will pro tanto be defeated.

All this will have occurred when no one was aware, or could have been f aware, of the supposed trust because no one knew that the contract was void.

I can see no moral or legal justification for giving such priority to the right of T to obtain restitution over third parties who have themselves not been enriched, in any real sense, at T's expense and indeed have had no dealings with T. T paid over his money and transferred the shares under a supposed valid g contract. If the contract had been valid, he would have had purely personal rights against R1. Why should he be better off because the contract is void?

My Lords, wise judges have often warned against the wholesale importation into commercial law of equitable principles inconsistent with the certainty and speed which are essential requirements for the orderly conduct of business h affairs: (see *Barnes v Addy* (1874) LR 9 Ch App 244 at 251, 255 and *Scandinavian Trading Tanker Co AB v Flota Petrolera Ecuatoriana* [1983] 2 All ER 763 at 768–769, [1983] 2 AC 694 at 703–704). If the bank's arguments are correct, a businessman who has entered into transactions relating to or dependent upon property rights could find that assets which apparently belong to one person in fact belong to another; that there are 'off balance sheet' liabilities of which he cannot be j aware; that these property rights and liabilities arise from circumstances unknown not only to himself but also to anyone else who has been involved in the transactions. A new area of unmanageable risk will be introduced into commercial dealings. If the due application of equitable principles forced a conclusion leading to these results, your Lordships would be presented with a formidable task in reconciling legal principle with commercial common sense.

But in my judgment no such conflict occurs. The resulting trust for which the
bank contends is inconsistent not only with the law as it stands but with any
principled development of it.

THE RELEVANT PRINCIPLES OF TRUST LAW

(i) Equity operates on the conscience of the owner of the legal interest. In
the case of a trust, the conscience of the legal owner requires him to carry out
the purposes for which the property was vested in him (express or implied trust)
or which the law imposes on him by reason of his unconscionable conduct
(constructive trust).

(ii) Since the equitable jurisdiction to enforce trusts depends upon the
conscience of the holder of the legal interest being affected, he cannot be a
trustee of the property if and so long as he is ignorant of the facts alleged to
affect his conscience, ie until he is aware that he is intended to hold the property
for the benefit of others in the case of an express or implied trust, or, in the case
of a constructive trust, of the factors which are alleged to affect his conscience.

(iii) In order to establish a trust there must be identifiable trust property.
The only apparent exception to this rule is a constructive trust imposed on a
person who dishonestly assists in a breach of trust who may come under
fiduciary duties even if he does not receive identifiable trust property.

(iv) Once a trust is established, as from the date of its establishment the
beneficiary has, in equity, a proprietary interest in the trust property, which
proprietary interest will be enforceable in equity against any subsequent holder
of the property (whether the original property or substituted property into
which it can be traced) other than a purchaser for value of the legal interest
without notice.

These propositions are fundamental to the law of trusts and I would have
thought uncontroversial. However, proposition (ii) may call for some
expansion. There are cases where property has been put into the name of X
without X's knowledge but in circumstances where no gift to X was intended.
It has been held that such property is recoverable under a resulting trust (see
Birch v Blagrave (1755) Amb 264, 27 ER 176, *Childers v Childers* (1857) 1 De G & J
482, 44 ER 810, *Re Vinogradoff, Allen v Jackson* [1935] WN 68 and *Re Muller, Cassin
v Mutual Cash Order Co Ltd* [1953] NZLR 879). These cases are explicable on the
ground that, by the time action was brought, X or his successors in title have
become aware of the facts which gave rise to a resulting trust; his conscience
was affected as from the time of such discovery and *thereafter* he held on a
resulting trust under which the property was recovered from him. There is, so
far as I am aware, no authority which decides that X was a trustee, and therefore
accountable for his deeds, at any time before he was aware of the circumstances
which gave rise to a resulting trust.

Those basic principles are inconsistent with the case being advanced by the
bank. The latest time at which there was any possibility of identifying the 'trust
property' was the date on which the moneys in the mixed bank account of the
local authority ceased to be traceable when the local authority's account went
into overdraft in June 1987. At that date, the local authority had no knowledge
of the invalidity of the contract but regarded the moneys as its own to spend as
it thought fit. There was therefore never a time at which both (a) there was
defined trust property and (b) the conscience of the local authority in relation to

a such defined trust property was affected. The basic requirements of a trust were never satisfied.

I turn then to consider the bank's arguments in detail. They were based primarily on principle rather than on authority. I will deal first with the bank's argument from principle and then turn to the main authorities relied upon by the bank, *Sinclair v Brougham* [1914] AC 398, [1914–15] All ER Rep 622 and *Chase*

b *Manhattan Bank NA v Israel-British Bank (London) Ltd* [1979] 3 All ER 1025, [1981] Ch 105.

THE RETENTION OF TITLE POINT

It is said that, since the bank only intended to part with its beneficial ownership of the moneys in performance of a *valid* contract, neither the legal

c nor the equitable title passed to the local authority at the date of payment. The legal title vested in the local authority by operation of law when the moneys became mixed in the bank account but, it is said, the bank 'retained' its equitable title.

I think this argument is fallacious. A person solely entitled to the full

d beneficial ownership of money or property, both at law and in equity, does not enjoy an equitable interest in that property. The legal title carries with it all rights. Unless and until there is a separation of the legal and equitable estates, there is no separate equitable title. Therefore to talk about the bank 'retaining' its equitable interest is meaningless. The only question is whether the circumstances under which the money was paid were such as, in equity, to

e impose a trust on the local authority. If so, an equitable interest arose for the first time under that trust.

This proposition is supported by *Re Cook (decd), Beck v Grant* [1948] 1 All ER 231, [1948] Ch 212, *Vandervell v IRC* [1967] 1 All ER 1 at 7, 11, [1967] 2 AC 291 at 311, 317 per Lord Upjohn and Lord Donovan, *Comr of Stamp Duties v Livingston* [1964] 3 All ER 692 at 699, [1965] AC 694 at 712 and Underhill and Hayton *Law*

f *of Trusts and Trustees* (15th edn, 1995) p 866.

THE SEPARATION OF TITLE POINT

The bank's submission, at its widest, is that if the legal title is in A but the equitable interest in B, A holds as trustee for B.

g Again I think this argument is fallacious. There are many cases where B enjoys rights which, in equity, are enforceable against the legal owner, A, without A being a trustee, for example an equitable right to redeem a mortgage, equitable easements, restrictive covenants, the right to rectification and an insurer's right by subrogation to receive damages subsequently recovered by

h the assured: *Lord Napier and Ettrick v Hunter, Lord Napier and Ettrick v R F Kershaw Ltd* [1993] 1 All ER 385, [1993] AC 713. Even in cases where the whole beneficial interest is vested in B and the bare legal interest is in A, A is not necessarily a trustee, for example where title to land is acquired by estoppel as against the legal owner; a mortgagee who has fully discharged his indebtedness enforces his right to recover the mortgaged property in a redemption action, not an action

j for breach of trust.

The bank contended that where, *under a pre-existing trust*, B is entitled to an equitable interest in trust property, if the trust property comes into the hands of a third party, X (not being a purchaser for value of the legal interest without notice), B is entitled to enforce his equitable interest against the property in the hands of X because X is a trustee for B. In my view the third party, X, is not necessarily a trustee for B: B's equitable right is enforceable against the property *a* in just the same way as any other specifically enforceable equitable right can be enforced against a third party. Even if the third party, X, is not aware that what he has received is trust property B is entitled to assert his title in that property. If X has the necessary degree of knowledge, X may himself become a constructive trustee for B on the basis of knowing receipt. But unless he has the requisite degree of knowledge he is not personally liable to account as trustee: *b* *Re Diplock's Estate* and *Re Montagu's Settlement Trusts* (1985) [1992] 4 All ER 308, [1987] Ch 264. Therefore, innocent receipt of property by X subject to an existing equitable interest does not by itself make X a trustee despite the severance of the legal and equitable titles. Underhill and Hayton *Law of Trusts and Trustees* pp 369–370, whilst accepting that X is under no personal liability to account unless and until be becomes aware of B's rights, does describe X as *c* being a constructive trustee. This may only be a question of semantics: on either footing, in the present case the local authority could not have become accountable for profits until it knew that the contract was void.

RESULTING TRUST   *d*

   This is not a case where the bank had any equitable interest which predated receipt by the local authority of the upfront payment. Therefore, in order to show that the local authority became a trustee, the bank must demonstrate circumstances which raised a trust for the first time either at the date on which the local authority received the money or at the date on which payment into the *e* mixed account was made. Counsel for the bank specifically disavowed any claim based on a constructive trust. This was plainly right because the local authority had no relevant knowledge sufficient to raise a constructive trust at any time before the moneys, upon the bank account going into overdraft, became untraceable. Once there ceased to be an identifiable trust fund, the local authority could not become a trustee: *Re Goldcorp Exchange Ltd (in* *f* *receivership)* [1994] 2 All ER 806, [1995] 1 AC 74. Therefore, as the argument for the bank recognised, the only possible trust which could be established was a resulting trust arising from the circumstances in which the local authority received the upfront payment.

   Under existing law a resulting trust arises in two sets of circumstances: (A) *g* where A makes a voluntary payment to B or pays (wholly or in part) for the purchase of property which is vested either in B alone or in the joint names of A and B, there is a presumption that A did not intend to make a gift to B: the money or property is held on trust for A (if he is the sole provider of the money) or in the case of a joint purchase by A and B in shares proportionate to their *h* contributions. It is important to stress that this is only a *presumption*, which presumption is easily rebutted either by the counter-presumption of advancement or by direct evidence of A's intention to make an outright transfer: see *Underhill and Hayton* pp 317ff, *Vandervell v IRC* [1967] 1 All ER 1 at 8, [1967] 2 AC 291 at 312ff and *Re Vandervell's Trusts (No 2), White v Vandervell Trustees Ltd* [1974] 1 All ER 47 at 63ff, [1974] Ch 269 at 288ff. (B) Where A transfers property to B *j* *on express trusts*, but the trusts declared do not exhaust the whole beneficial interest: ibid and *Barclays Bank Ltd v Quistclose Investments Ltd* [1968] 3 All ER 651, [1970] AC 567. Both types of resulting trust are traditionally regarded as examples of trusts giving effect to the common intention of the parties. A resulting trust is not imposed by law against the intentions of the trustee (as is

a constructive trust) but gives effect to his presumed intention. Megarry J in *Re*
a *Vandervell's Trusts (No 2)* suggests that a resulting trust of type (B) does not
depend on intention but operates automatically. I am not convinced that this is
right. If the settlor has expressly, or by necessary implication, abandoned any
beneficial interest in the trust property, there is in my view no resulting trust:
the undisposed-of equitable interest vests in the Crown as bona vacantia: see *Re*
b *West Sussex Constabulary's Widows, Children and Benevolent (1930) Fund Trusts*
[1970] 1 All ER 544, [1971] Ch 1.

Applying these conventional principles of resulting trust to the present case,
the bank's claim must fail. There was no transfer of money to the local
authority on express trusts: therefore a resulting trust of type (B) above could
not arise. As to type (A) above, any presumption of resulting trust is rebutted
c since it is demonstrated that the bank paid, and the local authority received, the
upfront payment with the intention that the moneys so paid should become the
absolute property of the local authority. It is true that the parties were under a
misapprehension that the payment was made in pursuance of a valid contract.
But that does not alter the actual intentions of the parties at the date the
d payment was made or the moneys were mixed in the bank account. As the
article by William Swaddling, 'A new role for resulting trusts?' (1996) 16 LS 110
at 133 demonstrates, the presumption of resulting trust is rebutted by evidence
of any intention inconsistent with such a trust, not only by evidence of an
intention to make a gift.

e Professor Birks 'Restitution and Resulting Trusts' in *Equity and Contemporary*
Legal Developments p 335 at 360, whilst accepting that the principles I have stated
represent 'a very conservative form' of definition of a resulting trust, argues
from restitutionary principles that the definition should be extended so as to
cover a perceived gap in the law of 'subtractive unjust enrichment' (p 368) so as
to give a plaintiff a proprietary remedy when he has transferred value under a
f mistake or under a contract the consideration for which wholly fails. He
suggests that a resulting trust should arise wherever the money is paid under a
mistake (because such mistake vitiates the actual intention) or when money is
paid on a condition which is not subsequently satisfied.

As one would expect, the argument is tightly reasoned but I am not
g persuaded. The search for a perceived need to strengthen the remedies of a
plaintiff claiming in restitution involves, to my mind, a distortion of trust
principles. First, the argument elides rights in property (which is the only
proper subject matter of a trust) into rights in 'the value transferred' (see p 361).
A trust can only arise where there is defined trust property: it is therefore not
consistent with trust principles to say that a person is a trustee of property
h which cannot be defined. Second, Professor Birks' approach appears to assume
(e g in the case of a transfer of value made under a contract the consideration for
which subsequently fails) that the recipient will be deemed to have been a
trustee from the date of his original receipt of money, i e the trust arises at a time
when the 'trustee' does not, and cannot, know that there is going to be a total
j failure of consideration. This result is incompatible with the basic premise on
which all trust law is built, viz that the conscience of the trustee is affected.
Unless and until the trustee is aware of the factors which give rise to the
supposed trust, there is nothing which can affect his conscience. Thus neither
in the case of a subsequent failure of consideration nor in the case of a payment
under a contract subsequently found to be void for mistake or failure of

condition will there be circumstances, at the date of receipt, which can impinge on the conscience of the recipient, thereby making him a trustee. Thirdly, Professor Birks has to impose on his wider view an arbitrary and admittedly unprincipled modification so as to ensure that a resulting trust does not arise when there has only been a failure to perform a contract, as opposed to total failure of consideration (see pp 356–359 and 362). Such arbitrary exclusion is designed to preserve the rights of creditors in the insolvency of the recipient. The fact that it is necessary to exclude artificially one type of case which would logically fall within the wider concept casts doubt on the validity of the concept.

If adopted, Professor Birks' wider concepts would give rise to all the practical consequences and injustices to which I have referred. I do not think it right to make an unprincipled alteration to the law of property (ie the law of trusts) so as to produce in the law of unjust enrichment the injustices to third parties which I have mentioned and the consequential commercial uncertainty which any extension of proprietary interests in personal property is bound to produce.

THE AUTHORITIES

Three cases were principally relied upon in direct support of the proposition that a resulting trust arises where a payment is made under a void contract.

(A) *Sinclair v Brougham* [1914] AC 398, [1914–15] All ER Rep 622

The case concerned the distribution of the assets of the Birkbeck Permanent Benefit Building Society, an unincorporated body which was insolvent. The society had for many years been carrying on business as a bank which, it was held, was ultra vires its objects. The bank had accepted deposits in the course of its ultra vires banking business and it was held that the debts owed to such depositors were themselves void as being ultra vires. In addition to the banking depositors, there were ordinary trade creditors. The society had two classes of members, the A shareholders who were entitled to repayment of their investment on maturity and the B shareholders whose shares were permanent. By agreement, the claims of the ordinary trade creditors and of the A shareholders had been settled. Therefore the only claimants to the assets of the society before the court were the ultra vires depositors and the B shareholders, the latter of which could take no greater interest than the society itself.

The issues for decision arose on a summons taken out by the liquidator for directions as to how he should distribute the assets in the liquidation. In the judgments, it is not always clear whether this House was laying down general propositions of law or merely giving directions as to the proper mode in which the assets in that liquidation should be distributed. The depositors claimed, first, in quasi-contract for money had and received. They claimed secondly, as the result of an argument suggested for the first time in the course of argument in the House of Lords ([1914] AC 398 at 404, [1914–15] All ER Rep 622), to trace their deposits into the assets of the society.

Money had and received

The House of Lords was unanimous in rejecting the claim by the ultra vires depositors to recover in quasi-contract on the basis of moneys had and received. In their view, the claim in quasi-contract was based on an implied contract. To imply a contract to repay would be to imply a contract to exactly the same effect as the express ultra vires contract of loan. Any such implied contract would itself be void as being ultra vires.

a   Subsequent developments in the law of restitution demonstrate that this reasoning is no longer sound. The common law restitutionary claim is based not on implied contract but on unjust enrichment: in the circumstances the law imposes an obligation to repay rather than implying an entirely fictitious agreement to repay: see *Fibrosa Spolka Akcyjna v Fairbairn Lawson Combe Barbour Ltd* [1942] 2 All ER 122 at 136–137, [1943] AC 32 at 63–64 per Lord Wright, *Pavey*
b   *& Matthews Pty Ltd v Paul* (1987) 69 ALR 577 at 579, 583, 603, *Lipkin Gorman (a firm) v Karpnale Ltd* [1992] 4 All ER 512 at 532, [1991] 2 AC 548 at 578 and *Woolwich Building Society v IRC (No 2)* [1992] 3 All ER 737, [1993] AC 70. In my judgment, your Lordships should now unequivocally and finally reject the concept that the claim for moneys had and received is based on an implied contract. I would overrule *Sinclair v Brougham* on this point.

c   It follows that in *Sinclair v Brougham* the depositors should have had a personal claim to recover the moneys at law based on a total failure of consideration. The failure of consideration was *not* partial: the depositors had paid over their money in consideration of a promise to repay. That promise was ultra vires and void; therefore the consideration for the payment of the money
d   wholly failed. So in the present swaps case (though the point is not one under appeal) I think the Court of Appeal were right to hold that the swap moneys were paid on a consideration that wholly failed. The essence of the swap agreement is that, over the whole term of the agreement, each party thinks he will come out best: the consideration for one party making a payment is an obligation on the other party to make counter-payments over the whole term
e   of the agreement.

If in *Sinclair v Brougham* the depositors had been held entitled to recover at law, their personal claim would have ranked pari passu with other ordinary unsecured creditors, in priority to the members of the society who could take nothing in the liquidation until all creditors had been paid.

f
The claim in rem

The House of Lords held that, the ordinary trade creditors having been paid in full by agreement, the assets remaining were to be divided between the ultra vires depositors and the members of the society pro rata according to their
g   respective payments to the society. The difficulty is to identify any single ratio decidendi for that decision. Lord Haldane LC (with whom Lord Atkinson agreed) and Lord Parker of Waddington gave fully reasoned judgments (considered below). Lord Dunedin apparently based himself on some 'super-eminent' equity (not a technical equity) in accordance with which the court could distribute the remaining assets of the society (see [1914] AC 398 at
h   434, 436, [1914–15] All ER Rep 622 at 639, 640). The members (by which presumably he means the society) were not in a fiduciary relationship with the depositors: it was the directors, not the society which had mixed the moneys (see [1914] AC 398 at 439, [1914–15] All ER Rep 622 at 641). This indicates that he was adopting the approach of Lord Parker: yet he concurred in the judgment
j   of Lord Haldane LC (see [1914] AC 398 at 439, [1914–15] All ER Rep 622 at 641). I can only understand his judgment as being based on some super-eminent jurisdiction in the court to do justice as between the remaining claimants in the course of a liquidation.

Lord Sumner ([1914] AC 398 at 459, [1914–15] All ER Rep 622 at 652) plainly regarded the case as a matter of doing justice in administering the remaining assets in the liquidation, all other claims having been eliminated. He said *a* ([1914] AC 398 at 458, [1914–15] All ER Rep 622 at 651):

'The question is one of administration. The liquidator, an officer of the court, who has to discharge himself of the assets that have come to his hands, asks for directions, and, after hearing all parties concerned, the court has the right and the duty to direct him how to distribute all the assets ... In my opinion, if precedent fails, the most just distribution of the whole *b* must be directed, so only that no recognised rule of law or equity be disregarded.'

Lord Haldane LC ([1914] AC 398 at 418, [1914–15] All ER Rep 622 at 630) treated the case as a tracing claim: could the depositors follow and recover property with which, in equity, they had 'never really parted'. After holding *c* that the parties could not trace at law, he said that the moneys could be traced in equity 'based upon trust' (see [1914] AC 398 at 420, [1914–15] All ER Rep 622 at 632). The only passage in which he identifies the trust is:

'The property was never converted into a debt, in equity at all events, and *d* there has been throughout a resulting trust, not of an active character, but sufficient, in my opinion, to bring the transaction within the general principle.'

He treats the society itself (as opposed to its directors) as having mixed the depositors' money with its own money, but says that such mixing was not a *e* breach of fiduciary duty by the society but authorised by the depositors: it was intended that 'the society should be entitled to deal with [the depositors' money] freely as its own' (see [1914] AC 398 at 422–423, [1914–15] All ER Rep 622 at 632–633). On that ground, he distinguished *Re Hallett's Estate, Knatchbull v Hallett* (1880) 13 Ch D 696, [1874–80] All ER Rep 793 (a trustee is taken to have drawn his own money first) and held that the mixed moneys therefore belonged *f* to the depositors and members pro rata.

Like others before me, I find Lord Haldane LC's reasoning difficult, if not impossible, to follow. The only equitable right which he identifies arises under 'a resulting trust, not of an active character' which, as I understand it, existed from the moment when the society received the money. Applying the *g* conventional approach, the resulting trust could only have arisen because either the depositors were treated as contributors to a fund (a resulting trust of type (A) above) or because the 'trust' on which the moneys were paid to the society had failed (a resulting trust of type (B)). Yet the finding that the society was not in breach of fiduciary duty because it was the intention of the parties that the *h* society should be free to deal with the money as its own is inconsistent with either type of resulting trust (see [1914] AC 398 at 423, [191415] All ER Rep 622 at 633). Such an intention would rebut the *presumption* of resulting trust of type (A) and is inconsistent with a payment on express trusts which fail, ie with a type (B) resulting trust. Therefore the inactive resulting trust which Lord Haldane was referring to was, as Professor Birks points out, not a conventional *j* one: indeed there is no trace of any such trust in earlier or later authority. The question is whether the recognition of such a trust accords with principle and the demands of certainty in commercial dealings.

As to the latter, Lord Haldane LC's theory, if correct, gives rise to all the difficulties which I have noted above. Nor does the theory accord with a principle. First, it postulates that the society became a trustee at a time when it was wholly ignorant of the circumstances giving rise to the trust. Second, since the depositors' money was *intended* to be mixed with that of the society, there was never any intention that there should be a separate identifiable trust fund, an essential feature of any trust. Third, and most important, if Lord Haldane LC's approach were to be applicable in an ordinary liquidation it is quite

b incapable of accommodating the rights of ordinary creditors. Lord Haldane LC's inactive resulting trust, if generally applicable, would give the depositors (and possibly the members) rights having priority not only to those of ordinary trade creditors but also to those of some secured creditors, for example the common form security for bank lending, a floating charge on the company's assets. The moneys of both depositors and members are, apparently, trust

c moneys and therefore form no part of the company's assets available to pay creditors, whether secured or unsecured. This seems to be an impossible conclusion. Lord Haldane LC appreciated the difficulty, but did not express any view as to what the position would be if there had been trade creditors in competition (see [1914] AC 398 at 421–422, [1914–15] All ER Rep 622 at 631–

d 632).

Lord Parker analysed the matter differently. He held that the depositors had paid their money not to the society itself but to the directors, who apparently held the moneys on some form of *Quistclose* trust (see *Barclays Bank Ltd v Quistclose Investments Ltd* [1968] 3 All ER 651, [1970] AC 567): the money had been paid by the depositors to the directors to be applied by them in making

e valid deposits with the society and, since such deposit was impossible, the directors held the moneys on a trust for the depositors (see [1914] AC 398 at 441–442, 444, [1914–15] All ER Rep 622 at 642–643, 644). It is to be noted that Lord Parker does not at any time spell out the nature of the trust. However, he held that the directors owed fiduciary duties both to the depositors and to the

f members of the society. Therefore it was not a case in which a trustee had mixed trust moneys with his own moneys (to which *Re Hallett's Estate* would apply) but of trustees (the directors) mixing the moneys of two innocent parties to both of whom they owed fiduciary duties: the depositors and members therefore ranked pari passu.

g I find the approach of Lord Parker much more intelligible than that of Lord Haldane LC: it avoids finding that the society held the money on a resulting trust at the same time as being authorised to mix the depositors' money with its own. In *Re Diplock's Estate, Diplock v Wintle* [1948] 2 All ER 318, [1948] Ch 465 the Court of Appeal found the ratio of *Sinclair v Brougham* to lie in Lord Parker's

h analysis. But, quite apart from the fact that no other member of the House founded himself on Lord Parker's analysis, it is in some respects very unsatisfactory. First, the finding that the depositors' moneys were received by the directors, as opposed to the society itself, is artificial. Although it was ultra vires the society to enter into a contract to repay the moneys, it was not ultra vires the society to receive moneys. Second, Lord Parker's approach gives

j depositors and members alike the same priority over trade creditors as does that of Lord Haldane LC. The fact is that any analysis which confers an equitable proprietary interest as a result of a payment under a void contract necessarily gives priority in an insolvency to the recovery of the ultra vires payment. Lord Parker too was aware of this problem: but he left the problem to be solved in a case where the claims of trade creditors were still outstanding. Indeed he went

further than Lord Haldane LC. He appears to have thought that the court had
power in some cases to postpone trade creditors to ultra vires depositors and in
other cases to give the trade creditors priority: which course was appropriate,
he held, depended on the facts of each individual case (see [1914] AC 398 at 444–
445, [1914–15] All ER Rep 622 at 644–645). There is much to be said for the view
that Lord Parker, like Lord Haldane LC and Lord Sumner, was dealing only
with the question of the due administration of assets of a company in
liquidation. Thus he says:

> '… nor, indeed, am I satisfied that the equity to which effect is being given
> in this case is necessarily confined to a liquidation. It is, however,
> unnecessary for your Lordships to decide these points.' (See [1914] AC 398
> at 449, [1914–15] All ER Rep 622 at 647.)

This makes it clear that he was not purporting to do more than decide how the
assets of that society in that liquidation were to be dealt with.

As has been pointed out frequently over the 80 years since it was decided,
Sinclair v Brougham is a bewildering authority: no single ratio decidendi can be
detected; all the reasoning is open to serious objection; it was only intended to
deal with cases where there were no trade creditors in competition and the
reasoning is incapable of application where there are such creditors. In my view
the decision as to rights in rem in *Sinclair v Brougham* should also be overruled.
Although the case is one where property rights are involved, such overruling
should not in practice disturb long-settled titles. However, your Lordships
should not be taken to be casting any doubt on the principles of tracing as
established in *Re Diplock's Estate*.

If *Sinclair v Brougham*, in both its aspects, is overruled the law can be
established in accordance with principle and commercial common sense: a
claimant for restitution of moneys paid under an ultra vires, and therefore void,
contract has a personal action at law to recover the moneys paid as on a total
failure of consideration; he will not have an equitable proprietary claim which
gives him either rights against third parties or priority in an insolvency; nor will
he have a personal claim in equity, since the recipient is not a trustee.

(B)   *Chase Manhattan Bank NA v Israel-British Bank (London) Ltd [1979] 3 All
ER 1025, [1981] Ch 105*

In that case Chase Manhattan, a New York bank, had by mistake paid the
same sum twice to the credit of the defendant, a London bank. Shortly
thereafter, the defendant bank went into insolvent liquidation. The question
was whether Chase Manhattan had a claim in rem against the assets of the
defendant bank to recover the second payment.

Goulding J was asked to assume that the moneys paid under a mistake were
capable of being traced in the assets of the recipient bank: he was only
concerned with the question whether there was a proprietary base on which the
tracing remedy could be founded (see [1979] 3 All ER 1025 at 1029, [1981] Ch
105 at 116). He held that, where money was paid under a mistake, the receipt
of such money *without more* constituted the recipient a trustee: he said that the
payer 'retains an equitable property in it and the conscience of [the recipient] is
subjected to a fiduciary duty to respect his proprietary right' (see [1979] 3 All ER
1025 at 1032, [1981] Ch 105 at 119).

a   It will be apparent from what I have already said that I cannot agree with this reasoning. First, it is based on a concept of retaining an equitable property in money where, prior to the payment to the recipient bank, there was no existing equitable interest. Further, I cannot understand how the recipient's 'conscience' can be affected at a time when he is not aware of any mistake. Finally, the judge found that the law of England and that of New York were in

b   substance the same. I find this a surprising conclusion since the New York law of constructive trusts has for a long time been influenced by the concept of a *remedial* constructive trust, whereas hitherto English law has for the most part only recognised an institutional constructive trust: see *Metall und Rohstoff AG v Donaldson Lufkin & Jenrette Inc* [1989] 3 All ER 14 at 56–58, [1990] 1 QB 391 at 478–480. In the present context, that distinction is of fundamental importance.

c   Under an institutional constructive trust, the trust arises by operation of law as from the date of the circumstances which give rise to it: the function of the court is merely to declare that such trust has arisen in the past. The consequences that flow from such trust having arisen (including the possibly unfair consequences to third parties who in the interim have received the trust property) are also

d   determined by rules of law, not under a discretion. A remedial constructive trust, as I understand it, is different. It is a judicial remedy giving rise to an enforceable equitable obligation: the extent to which it operates retrospectively to the prejudice of third parties lies in the discretion of the court. Thus for the law of New York to hold that there is a remedial constructive trust where a payment has been made under a void contract gives rise to different con-

e   sequences from holding that an institutional constructive trust arises in English law.

    However, although I do not accept the reasoning of Goulding J, *Chase Manhattan* may well have been rightly decided. The defendant bank knew of the mistake made by the paying bank within two days of the receipt of the

f   moneys (see [1979] 3 All ER 1025 at 1028–1029, [1981] Ch 105 at 115). The judge treated this fact as irrelevant (see [1979] 3 All ER 1025 at 1028, [1981] Ch 105 at 114), but in my judgment it may well provide a proper foundation for the decision. Although the mere receipt of the moneys, in ignorance of the mistake, gives rise to no trust, the retention of the moneys after the recipient bank learned of the mistake may well have given rise to a constructive trust: see

g   *Snell's Equity* (29th edn, 1991) p 193, Pettit *Equity and the Law of Trusts* (7th edn, 1993) p 168 and *Metall und Rohstoff AG v Donaldson Lufkin & Jenrette Inc* [1989] 3 All ER 14 at 52–53, [1990] 1 QB 391 at 473–474.

    (C) *Re Ames' Settlement, Dinwiddy v Ames [1946] 1 All ER 689, [1946] Ch 217*

h   In this case the father of the intended husband, in consideration of the son's intended marriage with Miss H, made a marriage settlement under which the income was payable to the husband for life and after his death to the wife for life or until her remarriage, with remainder to the issue of the intended marriage. There was an ultimate trust, introduced by the words 'If there should not be any

j   child of the said intended marriage who attains a vested interest ...' for an artificial class of the husband's next of kin. The marriage took place. Many years later a decree of nullity on the grounds of non-consummation had the effect of rendering the marriage void ab initio. The income was paid to the husband until his death which occurred 19 years after the decree of nullity. The question was whether the trust capital was held under the ultimate trust for the

husband's next-of-kin or was payable to the settlor's estate. It was held that the
settlor's estate was entitled.   a

The judgment is very confused. It is not clear whether the judge was holding
(as I think correctly) that in any event the ultimate trust failed because it was
only expressed to take effect in the event of the failure of the issue of a
non-existent marriage (an impossible condition precedent) or whether he held
that all the trusts of the settlement failed because the beneficial interests were   b
conferred in consideration of the intended marriage and that there had been a
total failure of consideration. In either event, the decision has no bearing on the
present case. On either view, the fund was vested in trustees on trusts which
had failed. Therefore the moneys were held on a resulting trust of type (B)
above. The decision casts no light on the question whether, there being no
express trust, moneys paid on a consideration which wholly fails are held on a   c
resulting trust.

The stolen bag of coins

The argument for a resulting trust was said to be supported by the case of a
thief who steals a bag of coins. At law those coins remain traceable only so long   d
as they are kept separate: as soon as they are mixed with other coins or paid into
a mixed bank account they cease to be traceable at law. Can it really be the case,
it is asked, that in such circumstances the thief cannot be required to disgorge
the property which, in equity, represents the stolen coins? Moneys can only be
traced in equity if there has been at some stage a breach of fiduciary duty, ie if
either before the theft there was an equitable proprietary interest (eg the coins   e
were stolen trust moneys) or such interest arises under a resulting trust at the
time of the theft or the mixing of the moneys. Therefore, it is said, a resulting
trust must arise either at the time of the theft or when the moneys are
subsequently mixed. Unless this is the law, there will be no right to recover the
assets representing the stolen moneys once the moneys have become mixed.   f

I agree that the stolen moneys are traceable in equity. But the proprietary
interest which equity is enforcing in such circumstances arises under a
constructive, not a resulting, trust. Although it is difficult to find clear authority
for the proposition, when property is obtained by fraud equity imposes a
constructive trust on the fraudulent recipient: the property is recoverable and
traceable in equity. Thus, an infant who has obtained property by fraud is   g
bound in equity to restore it: *Stocks v Wilson* [1913] 2 KB 235 at 244 and *R Leslie
Ltd v Sheill* [1914] 3 KB 607, [1914–15] All ER Rep 511. Moneys stolen from a
bank account can be traced in equity: *Bankers Trust Co v Shapira* [1980] 3 All ER
353 at 358, [1980] 1 WLR 1274 at 1282. See also *McCormick v Grogan* (1869) LR
4 HL 82 at 97.   h

Restitution and equitable rights

Those concerned with developing the law of restitution are anxious to ensure
that, in certain circumstances, the plaintiff should have the right to recover
property which he has unjustly lost. For that purpose they have sought to   j
develop the law of resulting trusts so as to give the plaintiff a proprietary
interest. For the reasons that I have given in my view such development is not
based on sound principle and in the name of unjust enrichment is capable of
producing most unjust results. The law of resulting trusts would confer on the
plaintiff a right to recover property from, or at the expense of, those who have

a not been unjustly enriched at his expense at all, for example the lender whose debt is secured by a floating charge and all other third parties who have purchased an equitable interest only, albeit in all innocence and for value.

Although the resulting trust is an unsuitable basis for developing proprietary restitutionary remedies, the remedial constructive trust, if introduced into English law, may provide a more satisfactory road forward. The court by way
b of remedy might impose a constructive trust on a defendant who knowingly retains property of which the plaintiff has been unjustly deprived. Since the remedy can be tailored to the circumstances of the particular case, innocent third parties would not be prejudiced and restitutionary defences, such as change of position, are capable of being given effect. However, whether English law should follow the United States and Canada by adopting the
c remedial constructive trust will have to be decided in some future case when the point is directly in issue.

The date from which interest is payable

The Court of Appeal held that compound interest was payable by the local
d authority on the balance for the time being outstanding, such interest to start from the date of the receipt by the local authority of the upfront payment of £2·5m on 18 June 1987. Although, for the reasons I have given, I do not think the court should award compound interest in this case, I can see no reason why interest should not start to run as from the date of payment of the upfront payment. I agree with the judgment of Leggatt LJ in the Court of Appeal ([1994]
e 4 All ER 890 at 970, [1994] 1 WLR 938 at 955) that there is no good ground for departing from the general rule that interest is payable as from the date of the accrual of the cause of action.

Equity acting in aid of the common law

Since drafting this speech I have seen, in draft, the speeches of my noble and
f learned friends Lord Goff of Chieveley and Lord Woolf. Both consider that compound interest should be awarded in this case on the grounds that equity can act in aid of the common law and should exercise its jurisdiction to order compound interest in aid of the common law right to recover moneys paid under an ultra vires contract.

g I fully appreciate the strength of the moral claim of the bank in this case to receive full restitution, including compound interest. But I am unable to accept that it would be right in the circumstances of this case for your Lordships to develop the law in the manner proposed. I take this view for two reasons.

First, Parliament has twice since 1934 considered what interest should be
h awarded on claims at common law. Both s 3(1) of the 1934 Act and its successor, s 35A of the 1981 Act, make it clear that the Act does not authorise the award of compound interest. However, both Acts equally make it clear that they do not impinge on the award of interest in equity. At the time those Acts were passed, and indeed at all times down to the present day, equity has only awarded compound interest in the limited circumstances which I have
j mentioned. In my judgment, your Lordships would be usurping the function of Parliament if, by expanding the equitable rules for the award of compound interest, this House were now to hold that the court exercising its equitable jurisdiction in aid of the common law can award compound interest which the statutes have expressly not authorised the court to award in exercise of its common law jurisdiction.

Secondly, the arguments relied upon by my noble and learned friends were not advanced by the bank at the hearing. The local authority would have a legitimate ground to feel aggrieved if the case were decided against them on a point which they had had no opportunity to address. Moreover, in my view it would be imprudent to introduce such an important change in the law without this House first having heard full argument upon it. Although I express no concluded view on the points raised, the proposed development of the law bristles with unresolved questions. For example, given that the right to interest is not a right which existed at common law but is solely the creation of statute, would equity in fact be acting in aid of the common law or would it be acting in aid of the legislature? Does the principle that equity acts in aid of the common law apply where there is no concurrent right of action in equity? If not, in the absence of any trust or fiduciary relationship what is the equitable cause of action in this case? What were the policy reasons which led Parliament to provide expressly that only the award of simple interest was authorised? In what circumstances should compound interest be awarded under the proposed expansion of the equitable rules? In the absence of argument on these points it would in my view be imprudent to change the law. Rather, the whole question of the award of compound interest should be looked at again by Parliament so that it can make such changes, if any, as are appropriate.

For these reasons, which are in substance the same as those advanced by my noble and learned friend Lord Lloyd of Berwick, I am unable to agree with the views of Lord Goff of Chieveley and Lord Woolf.

CONCLUSION

I would allow the appeal and vary the judgment of the Court of Appeal so as to order the payment of simple interest only as from 18 June 1987 on the balance from time to time between the sums paid by the bank to the local authority and the sums paid by the local authority to the bank.

LORD SLYNN OF HADLEY. My Lords, for the reasons given by my noble and learned friend Lord Browne-Wilkinson I agree that *Sinclair v Brougham* [1914] AC 398, [1914–15] All ER Rep 622 should be departed from and that it should be held that in this case the local authority was neither a trustee of, nor in a fiduciary position in relation to, the moneys which it had received from the bank, nor had it improperly profited from the use of those moneys. For the reasons which he gives no resulting trust could arise on the present facts.

It follows that if, as I think, Lord Brandon of Oakbrook in *President of India v La Pintada Cia Navegacion SA* [1984] 2 All ER 773 at 779, [1985] AC 104 at 116, was right to say that in the Court of Chancery the award of compound interest was limited to situations 'where money had been obtained and retained by fraud, or where it had been withheld or misapplied by a trustee or anyone else in a fiduciary position,' Courts of Chancery would not have awarded compound interest in a case like the present.

It is common ground that compound interest could not have been awarded at common law as presently formulated nor under the statutory provisions in s 3 of the Law Reform (Miscellaneous Provisions) Act 1934 nor under s 35A of the Supreme Court Act 1981 as inserted by the Administration of Justice Act 1982.

a But for the legislation I would have accepted that it was open to your lordships to hold that, in the light of the development of the law of restitution, the courts could award compound interest, either by modifying the common law rule or by resorting to equity to act in aid of the common law right to recover moneys paid under a void transaction. As to whether it would have been right to do so in general terms, or whether it would have been right to

b limit the cases in which compound interest should be awarded, or whether compound interest should be awarded at all I am not, on the restricted arguments advanced in this case, prepared to comment.

I do not, however, consider that it would be right on this appeal to enlarge the cases in which compound interest can be awarded when Parliament has twice in relatively recent times limited statutory interest to simple interest.

c This is a matter which should be considered by Parliament when the merits or disadvantages of giving the courts power to award compound interest could be examined in a context wider than the present case.

Accordingly, in agreement with my noble and learned friends Lord Browne-Wilkinson and Lord Lloyd of Berwick, and despite the forceful reasoning of my

d noble and learned friends Lord Goff of Chieveley and Lord Woolf, I would allow the appeal and vary the judgment of the Court of Appeal so as to award simple interest from 18 June 1987.

LORD WOOLF. My Lords, this appeal raises directly only one issue of law. It is whether the courts have jurisdiction to make an order for the payment of

e compound interest ancillary to an order for restitution when a contract is ultra vires. All the judges in the courts below concluded that there was jurisdiction to do so.

In this case an order was made in favour of the respondent bank as against the appellant local authority which was the recipient of the ultra vires payment.

f There is no dispute that there was jurisdiction to make an order for the payment of *simple* interest. The dispute is limited to the order for compound interest.

It is accepted that if there is jurisdiction to make the order this is a case in which this achieves a just result. There is only one other issue raised by the appeal and that is as to the date from which the interest should be paid.

The transaction was a commercial transaction. The local authority in

g calculating the balance which it had to repay the bank was given credit for the sums which it had paid by way of notional interest under the contract prior to it being appreciated that the contract might be ultra vires. If the transaction had not taken place the local authority would have had to borrow (if it could find a way of lawfully doing so) the sum paid to it by the bank on terms which would

h be likely to involve compound interest being recoverable in proceedings for default. (Here see *National Bank of Greece SA v Pinios Shipping Co No 1, The Maira* [1990] 1 All ER 78, [1990] 1 AC 637 as to commercial transactions with banks.) The bank could have lent that sum on the same basis.

Hobhouse J, the judge at first instance, reflected the commercial justice of the

j situation in the passage in his judgment in which he set out succinctly why he considered compound interest was payable ([1994] 4 All ER 890 at 955):

'[The local authority] has kept that sum and has not made any restitution. In this situation I see no reason why I should not exercise my equitable jurisdiction to award compound interest. Simple interest does not reflect the actual value of money. Anyone who lends or borrows money on a

commercial basis receives or pays interest periodically and if that interest is
not paid it is compounded (e g *Wallersteiner v Moir (No 2)* [1975] 1 All ER 849,
[1975] QB 373 and *National Bank of Greece SA v Pinios Shipping Co No 1, The
Maira* [1990] 1 All ER 78, [1990] 1 AC 637). I see no reason why I should
deny the plaintiff a complete remedy or allow the defendant arbitrarily to
retain part of the enrichment which it has unjustly enjoyed. There are no
special factors which have to be taken into account. No question of
insolvency is involved nor is there any basis for any persuasive argument to
the contrary.'

This being the situation I am relieved that I am of the opinion that the judges
in the courts below were correct in concluding that in the circumstances of this
case they were entitled to award compound interest. Any other decision would
be inconsistent with the court's ability to grant full restitution. It would be a
further unhappy aspect, from a commercial standpoint, of the history of this
case in particular and the swaps litigation as a whole. This commenced with the
decision, to which I was a party at first instance, of *Hazell v Hammersmith and
Fulham London BC* [1991] 1 All ER 545, [1992] 2 AC 1. It is no secret that the
decision at first instance ([1990] 3 All ER 33, [1990] 2 QB 697) in that case, which
was approved by this House, caused dismay among some of those concerned
with the standing abroad of the commercial law of this country. That concern
is likely to be increased if the outcome of this litigation is that this appeal has to
be allowed by this House because the courts have no jurisdiction to grant
compound interest.

The position is not improved by the fact that such is the confused state of
English law as to the extent of its jurisdiction to award interest that the hearing
before their Lordships involved four days of argument. Argument that could
have lasted even longer but for counsel for the local authority courteously
informing their Lordships that because of the costs which the local authority
was incurring on the appeal he was required by his clients to curtail his
argument.

The argument had been extended by their Lordships themselves raising the
issue as to the correctness of a decision of this House of some 80 years' standing,
Sinclair v Brougham [1914] AC 398, [1914–15] All ER Rep 622. That case does not
directly involve the courts' equitable jurisdiction to award interest. Yet the
issue as to whether the case was correctly decided still needed to be raised
because the reasoning in that case was inconsistent with the submissions of the
local authority. The fact that counsel was required to take the course of seeking
to limit his argument does put in question whether the way appeals are
managed before the House and the resources available to their Lordships are
ideal for meeting both the contemporary needs of litigants and their Lordships'
responsibilities for the proper development of the law.

I have had the considerable advantage of being able to read in draft the
admirably reasoned speeches of Lord Goff of Chieveley and Lord Browne-
Wilkinson. That reasoning convinces me that the bank is not entitled to
proceed by way of an equitable proprietary claim and that the recipient of a sum
of money paid under an ultra vires contract should not be regarded as owing
either the duties of a trustee or fiduciary to the payer of that sum. Further than
that it is not necessary for me to go. This avoids the dangers which Lord
Browne-Wilkinson *identifies could flow* from the wholesale importation into
commercial law of equitable principles. I am also in agreement with Lord

a Goff's reasoning as to compound interest being able to be awarded where one party is under a duty to make restitution to another, this being a consequence of the development of the law of restitution.

THE SIGNIFICANCE OF THE DIFFERENCE BETWEEN EQUITABLE PRINCIPLES AND REMEDIES

b Such a wholesale importation is not necessarily the consequence of a finding that the courts have the equitable jurisdiction to make an order for the payment of compound interest in conjunction with the grant of a remedy of restitution. We are concerned here primarily not with equitable principles of substantive law but with the possible existence of an equitable remedy. Compound interest, if it is recoverable, will be recoverable in the circumstances of this case in c equity because of the absence of any statutory or common law remedy which will prevent the local authority being unjustly enriched at the expense of the bank if compound interest is not payable.

The situation is one in which compound interest would be awarded because it would be unconscionable to allow the local authority to make a profit out of a contract which was void because it had exceeded its own powers. This is very d much an analogous situation to those where equity has traditionally provided remedies. Perhaps the best example is provided by specific performance. It is unnecessary to inquire whether the right which is being enforced by an order of specific performance is one recognised by the common law or equity. What does matter is whether it is equitable to grant the remedy and whether an award e of damages in lieu would be an adequate remedy.

In addition, if the contract had not been void and the local authority had failed to make the payments required the bank might well, as I will seek to show, have been fully protected by its remedy in damages at common law. Because there is no contract damages are not available. Here the situation is very much in keeping with those where equity traditionally mitigates the f inadequacy of a common law remedy without having to invoke the substantive equitable law principles. This situation is described in *Snell's Equity* (29th edn, 1991) p 26:

g 'Between them, equitable interests, mere equities, floating equities and the great doctrines of equity cover most of the field of equity; and they are all concerned to a greater or lesser degree with the rights of property. Yet although the existence of such rights has long been an important factor in deciding whether equity will intervene, it is not essential. Equitable remedies, though often used in aid of property rights, are also often used in other cases. The underlying principle is the inadequacy of the common law h remedy of damages. Thus the equitable remedies of rescission and injunction may be employed in relation to contracts for personal services; and injunctions are sometimes granted in cases of tort which involve no rights of property. In this sense there may be equities unrelated to property.'

j In the same sense it can be said there may be equities unrelated to a breach of trust or fiduciary duty. I would add that equity does not only come to the aid of a claimant where damages are an inadequate remedy. It can also do so when one of the other common law remedies is inadequate. I would take as an example the remedy of an account. The advantages of the equitable remedy over the common law remedy have resulted in the latter remedy being

supplanted by the former. It may well be that the editors of *Snell's Equity* did not
have in mind the power to award interest when writing the paragraph I have set
out. The paragraph is none the less of general application and there is no reason
why it should not apply to the equitable remedy of awarding interest in the
same way as it applies to other equitable remedies. The award of interest is only
distinct from other remedies in that it is usually awarded as an ancillary to some
other remedy.

I therefore accept Mr Sumption QC's submission on behalf of the bank that
where there is a duty to make restitution equity can achieve full restitution by
granting, when it is appropriate to do so, simple or compound interest in
addition to requiring repayment of the principal sum. For this to be the
position, the defendant must have made an actual or presumed profit or a profit
which he is presumed to have derived from his having been the recipient of a
principal sum which he has not repaid. The compound interest will not be
payable as of right. The remedy of awarding interest, like other equitable
remedies, will be discretionary. Interest will only be awarded when it accords
with equitable principles to make the award.

I appreciate that Mr Sumption did not advance the argument in favour of the
grant of compound interest on the basis that I have put forward. However, he
came before your Lordships' House not expecting *Sinclair v Brougham* to be
challenged. He had no reason in his printed case to do other than base his
argument on the fact that the local authority was a fiduciary. Before your
Lordships he made clear that while he was arguing that the local authority was
a fiduciary he was also contending that, if there was power to order restitution,
equity could, as I have already indicated, achieve full restitution. This is also
clear from the statements in the bank's case to which I will refer shortly.

THE ABSENCE OF PREVIOUS AUTHORITY

There may be no clear previous authority to support this conclusion but this
is not surprising where the relatively new jurisdiction of ordering restitution is
involved. What is more important than the absence of clear support in the
authorities for the grant of compound interest is the absence from the existing
authorities of any statement of principle preventing the natural development of
a salutary equitable jurisdiction enabling compound interest to be awarded.
The jurisdiction is clearly desirable if full restitution in some cases is to be
achieved. It is relevant here to repeat what is stated at the outset in the bank's
case under the heading 'The Position in Principle':

'1. "Any civilised system of law is bound to provide remedies for cases of
what has been called unjust enrichment or unjust benefit, that is to prevent
a man from retaining the money of or some benefit derived from another
which it is against conscience that he should keep": *Fibrosa Spolka Akcyjna v
Fairbairn Lawson Combe Barbour Limited* ([1942] 2 All ER 122 at 135, [1943]
AC 32 at 61) (Lord Wright), approved in *Woolwich Equitable Building Society
v Inland Revenue Commissioners* ([1992] 3 All ER 737 at 780, 785, [1993] AC 70
at 197, 202).'

Restitution is an area of the law which is still in the process of being evolved
by the courts. In relation to restitution there are still questions remaining to be
authoritatively decided. One question, which was still undecided until the
decision on this appeal, is whether its legitimacy is derived from the common

a law or equity or both. In order to decide whether compound interest is payable in this case I do not consider it is necessary to decide which is the correct answer to that question, but I am content to assume that the cause of action is one at common law. If the principal sum is repayable as money had and received rather than under some trust or because of the existence of a fiduciary duty it is still unconscionable for the local authority to retain the benefit it made from

b having received payment under a contract it purported to make which was outside its powers. The fact that, until the law was clarified by the decision in this case, the local authority may reasonably not have appreciated that it should make restitution is not critical. What is critical is that the payment of compound interest is required to achieve restitution. A defendant may perfectly reasonably not regard himself as having been a trustee until the court so decides

c but this does not effect the remedies which the court has *jurisdiction* to grant. The jurisdiction of the court to grant remedies has to be judged in the light of what the court decides.

As to the date from which the interest should run I am in agreement with Lord Browne-Wilkinson that the decision of the Court of Appeal should not be

d disturbed.

UNJUST ENRICHMENT CREATES THE REQUIRED RELATIONSHIP

There are a great many situations where interest as an equitable remedy has been awarded. Examples are conveniently set out in 32 *Halsbury's Laws* (4th edn) para 109. The principle which connects those examples is stated in the first

e sentence of the paragraph. It is the existence of a 'particular relationship ... between the creditor and debtor'. The 'particular relationship' in this case arises out of the right of the bank to restitution and the fact that the local authority would be unjustly enriched if it retained what it had received. That made the local authority an accounting party. The bank had to give credit for the sums it had received and the local authority had to pay the balance which was still due

f of what it had received. What it had received included the use of the money. The approach is precisely that indicated in the passage of the judgment of Lord Hatherley LC in *Burdick v Garrick* (1870) LR 5 Ch App 233 at 241 already cited by Lord Browne-Wilkinson. It is the making of the award not as a punishment but to disgorge a profit made or presumed to have been made out of the

g payment of a sum of money which should not have been made. Here this was because the contract was void as being ultra vires. There would be no difference of principle if the contract was void for mistake.

NO DISTINCTION OF PRINCIPLE BETWEEN SIMPLE AND COMPOUND INTEREST

If the case is one where there is jurisdiction to award equitable interest then

h whether compound or simple interest is recoverable depends on the facts of the particular case. If it is not a situation where the defendant would have earned compound interest then as in *Burdick v Garrick* there would be no profit of compound interest so it will not be awarded. Simple interest will be awarded instead.

j

THE LAW COMMISSION'S APPROACH

In *Law of Contract: Report on Interest* (Law Com No 88) (1978), the Law Commission decided not to make any recommendations for change as to the equitable jurisdiction. It is, however, interesting to note the following paragraphs of the report:

'10. Thirdly, there is the equitable jurisdiction. Interest may be awarded
as ancillary relief in respect of equitable remedies such as specific
performance, rescission or the taking of an account. Furthermore, the
payment of interest may be ordered where money has been obtained and
retained by fraud, or where it has been withheld or misapplied by an
executor or a trustee or anyone else in a fiduciary position ...

(a) The equitable jurisdiction

21. The equitable jurisdiction to award interest and to fix the rate at
which it should be paid is extensive. It includes, for example, the power to
order the payment of interest where money has been obtained or withheld
by fraud or where it has been misapplied by someone in a fiduciary
position. In such cases the court has an inherent power to order the
payment of interest at whatever rate is equitable in the circumstances and
may direct that such interest be compounded at appropriate intervals. Our
view is that it would not be appropriate to impose statutory controls upon
the exercise of the equitable jurisdiction to award interest, beyond those
controls that are already in existence. We invited criticisms of this view in
our working paper but no one disagreed with us. Accordingly, we make no
recommendations for change in relation to the equitable jurisdiction.'

From what I have said already it is clear that I agree with the statements in
those paragraphs in so far as the equitable jurisdiction to award interest is
regarded as 'ancillary relief' but not in so far as they suggest that it is only
equitable remedies in relation to which there can be the ancillary jurisdiction to
award interest. The paragraphs are perfectly satisfactory as long as they are not
regarded as exhaustive. It has to be remembered that the Law Commission
were not intending to make any recommendations as to the equitable interest.

The fact that the paragraphs accept that compound interest is payable in the
case of fraud perhaps suggests that it is not intended to limit the relief to
situations which only give an entitlement to an equitable remedy. In many
cases of fraud the appropriate remedy will be common law damages. It is true
in the first of the only two cases referred to by the Law Commission, *Johnson v
R* [1904] AC 817 at 821. The Privy Council appeared to think that interest was
not payable in the case of an overpayment by mistake. However the authority
relied on for this conclusion was *London, Chatham and Dover Rly Co v South
Eastern Rly Co* [1893] AC 429. Lord Macnaghten ([1904] AC 817 at 821) regarded
'the law as settled by the judgment' of this House in that case. It is a case to
which I will refer later but it was not concerned with the equitable jurisdiction
to grant interest, only the common law jurisdiction. What is of interest is what
Lord Macnaghten said as to the power to award interest if there had been fraud.
He said (at 822):

'In order to guard against any possible misapprehension of their
Lordships' views, they desire to say that, in their opinion, there is no doubt
whatever that money obtained by fraud and retained by fraud can be
recovered with interest, whether *the proceedings be taken in a court of equity
or in a court of law*, or in a court which has a jurisdiction both equitable and
legal, as the Supreme Court of Sierra Leone possesses under the Ordinance
of November 10, 1881.' (My emphasis.)

Lord Macnaghten did not consider that it mattered whether the proceedings
were based on a common law or equitable cause of action.

a   The other case referred to in the report is *Wallersteiner v Moir (No 2)* [1975] 1 All ER 849, [1975] QB 373. That case is a clear authority for the existence of an equitable jurisdiction and that it can be exercised where there is breach of a fiduciary duty but the court was not concerned with extent of that jurisdiction. It was accepted by all the members of the Court of Appeal that the jurisdiction was frequently exercised in the case of breach of trust and of a fiduciary duty but

b   there is nothing in the judgments to suggest that the jurisdiction is limited to those situations. Indeed Lord Denning MR clearly did not regard it as being so limited. He said ([1975] 1 All ER 849 at 856, [1975] QB 373 at 388):

'The reason is because a person in a fiduciary position is not allowed to make a profit out of his trust: and, if he does, he is liable to account for that

c   profit or interest in lieu thereof. In addition, in equity interest is awarded whenever a wrongdoer deprives a company of money which it needs for use in its business. It is plain that the company should be compensated for the loss thereby occasioned to it. Mere replacement of the money—years later—is by no means adequate compensation, especially in days of inflation. The company should be compensated by the award of interest.

d   That was done by Sir William Page Wood V-C (afterwards Lord Hatherley) in one of the leading cases on the subject, *Atwool v Merryweather* (1867) LR 5 Eq 464n at 468–469. But the question arises: should it be simple interest or compound interest? On general principles I think it should be presumed that the company (had it not been deprived of the money) would have

e   made the most beneficial use open to it: cf *Armory v Delamirie* (1722) 1 Stra 505, [1558–1774] All ER Rep 121. It may be that the company would have used it in its own trading operations; or that it would have used it to help its subsidiaries. Alternatively, it should be presumed that the wrongdoer made the most beneficial use of it. But, whichever it is, in order to give adequate compensation, the money should be replaced at interest with

f   yearly rests, ie compound interest.'

This was a broader approach than that adopted by Buckley or Scarman LJJ.

There remains a further case to which I should make reference before leaving the authorities as to the equitable jurisdiction. It is *President of India v La Pintada Cia Navegacion SA* [1984] 2 All ER 773, [1985] AC 104. This is the leading case as

g   to the common law and statutory jurisdictions to which I will return later. I refer to it for the leading speech of Lord Brandon of Oakbrook with which the other members of the House agreed. Lord Brandon reviewed the different jurisdictions to award interest. While doing so he made the following dicta about the equitable jurisdiction (see [1984] 2 All ER 773 at 779, [1985] AC 104 at

h   116). (Lord Brandon also referred to the equitable jurisdiction ([1984] 2 All ER 773 at 780–783, [1985] AC 104 at 118–121) but he was then dealing with the position as to interest in the Admiralty Court and I do not consider those references are of any help here):

'Third, the area of equity. The Chancery courts, again differing from the

j   common law courts, had regularly awarded simple interest as ancillary relief in respect of equitable remedies, such as specific performance, rescission and the taking of an account. Chancery courts had further regularly awarded interest, including not only simple interest but also compound interest, when they thought that justice so demanded, that is to say in cases where money had been obtained and retained by fraud, or

where it had been withheld or misapplied by a trustee or anyone else in a
fiduciary position ... The first point is that neither the Admiralty Court, nor
Chancery courts, awarded interest, except in respect of moneys for which
they were giving judgment. The second point is that the Admiralty Court
never, and Chancery courts only in two special classes of case, awarded
compound, as distinct from simple, interest.'

The House had been referred in the course of argument to the report of the Law
Commission and I suspect that Lord Brandon restricted the jurisdiction of the
courts to award interest to equitable remedies following what was stated in that
report. Likewise as to the distinction which he drew between the jurisdictions
to award simple and compound interest. According to the report of argument,
counsel did not address the House on the limits of the equitable jurisdiction.
Therefore, although any statement of Lord Brandon is entitled to the greatest
respect, I do not regard these two dicta as indicating that Lord Brandon held a
considered opinion inconsistent with my views, which I have set out above. It
may well be that he was doing no more than describing the situations where in
the past the equitable jurisdiction had been exercised.

THE POSITION WHERE THE CLAIM IS BASED ON A PERSONAL EQUITY

Lord Browne-Wilkinson, in his speech, points out that two arguments were
not advanced on behalf of the bank. The first is that the local authority should
be liable to make the repayments as a constructive trustee. There is no need for
me to make any comment about this argument. The second argument which
was not advanced is that the bank was entitled to repayment because of the
existence of a personal equity based on the decision in *Re Diplock's Estate, Diplock
v Wintle* [1948] 2 All ER 318, [1948] Ch 465. This is a point which it is necessary
for me to consider because of the decision of Hobhouse J in *Kleinwort Benson Ltd
v South Tyneside Metropolitan BC* [1994] 4 All ER 972, although the decision in *Re
Diplock's Estate* dealt with very different circumstances from those which exist
here. The court in *Re Diplock's Estate* was concerned with the personal equitable
liability of a legatee to repay the executors of an estate of a deceased person a
sum which was wrongly paid to them out of the estate. In the *Kleinwort Benson*
case Hobhouse J decided that the existence of a personal equitable cause of
action did not create a power to award compound interest. This conclusion is
inconsistent with the view which I have expressed that there is a power to
award compound interest in the circumstances of this case.

Personal equitable rights are not confined to the situation considered in *Re
Diplock's Estate*. For example, a personal equitable right to contribution can
exist between co-sureties. This is regarded as being an application of an
equitable approach to restitution to a situation where the remedy at law is not
normally satisfactory. It exists without there having to be any proprietary right
which could give rise to the difficulties to which Lord Browne-Wilkinson has
referred.

The *Kleinwort Benson* case also involved a local authority which had entered
into a swap transaction which was void. Hobhouse J distinguished the *Kleinwort
Benson* case from the present case because in that case there was no reliance on
an equitable proprietary claim for repayment of the sum which had been paid
under the void swap contract. In the *Kleinwort Benson* case, the local authority
accepted that prima facie they were under a personal liability to make
restitution in law and in equity to the bank but argued it was not open to a court

a to award compound interest where only remedies in personam were established.

Hobhouse J decided that the local authority's submissions were correct. He said ([1994] 4 All ER 972 at 994–995):

b 'The position is therefore that if a plaintiff is entitled to a proprietary remedy against a defendant who has been unjustly enriched, the court may but is not bound to order the repayment of the sum with compound interest. If on the other hand the plaintiff is only entitled to a personal remedy which will be the case where, although there was initially a fiduciary relationship and the payer was entitled in equity to treat the sum received by the payee as his, the payer's, money and to trace it, but because *c* of subsequent developments he is no longer able to trace the sum in the hands of the payee, then there is no subject matter to which the rationale on which compound interest is awarded can be applied. The payee cannot be shown to have a fund belonging to the payer or to have used it to make profits for himself. The legal analysis which is the basis of the award of compound interest is not applicable. (It is possible that in some cases there *d* might be an intermediate position where it could be demonstrated that the fiduciary had, over part of the period, profited from holding a fund as a fiduciary even though he no longer held the fund at the date of trial and that in such a case the court might make some order equivalent to requiring him to account for those profits; but that is not the situation which I am asked *e* to consider in the present case.) Although the original equitable right in both situations is the same at the outset, that is to say at the time when the payment was made and received, the two situations do not continue to be the same and are not the same at the time of trial when the remedy comes to be given. The payee no longer has property of the payer. The payer is confined to personal rights and remedies analogous to those recognised by *f* the common law in the action for money had and received. In such a situation only simple interest can be awarded even though the plaintiff is relying upon a restitutionary remedy. Simple interest was awarded in *Woolwich Building Society v IRC (No 2)* [1992] 3 All ER 737, [1993] AC 70 and in *BP Exploration Co (Libya) Ltd v Hunt (No 2)* [1982] 1 All ER 925, [1979] 1 *g* WLR 783 and both those cases involved an application of restitutionary principles which carried with them remedies in personam (see also *O'Sullivan v Management Agency and Music Ltd* [1985] 3 All ER 351, [1985] QB 428.)'

h The three cases cited by the judge to support his proposition that simple interest only could be awarded do not in fact assist to determine the question of principle which is at stake here. In both the *Woolwich* and the *BP Exploration* cases, the claim which was advanced was limited to statutory interest. The position as to compound interest was not considered. In *O'Sullivan's* case, it was conceded that in relation to part of the claim compound interest was payable *j* and, in fact, it was awarded. Only simple interest was paid in relation to the balance of the claim, but this was not because of any lack of jurisdiction; it was because it was only appropriate to award simple interest in the circumstances of that case.

If Hobhouse J's reasoning is correct, then even if there had been an equitable claim in rem which would justify the award of compound interest, that would

cease to be the situation if the right to trace were lost. That this would create
an unsatisfactory state of affairs is demonstrated by the contrasting decisions to
which the judge came in this case and in the *Kleinwort Benson* case. The power
of the court to award compound interest would depend upon circumstances
over which the claimant would have no control. This is inconsistent with the
commercial realities to which the judge referred in the passage which I have
cited from his judgment in this case.

Contrary to the view expressed by Hobhouse J, the rationale on which
compound interest is awarded is independent of whether or not there is any
property capable of being traced still in the payee's hands. The critical issue is
whether, as has happened in this case, the authority was able to make a profit
(which would include making a saving in the interest which it had to pay) from
the fact it had received a sum of money to which it was not entitled. Even in
the case of a claim in rem, the profit is distinct from the traceable property. If
this were not the position the payee by returning the property to the payer prior
to the proceedings could defeat the right which a claimant would otherwise
have to compound interest.

Hobhouse J ([1994] 4 All ER 972 at 994) refers to *Re Diplock's Estate* in order
to identify the distinction between personal and proprietary equitable remedies.
He cites a passage from the very long judgment of the Court of Appeal ([1948]
2 All ER 318 at 347, [1948] Ch 465 at 521) in that case. However, although this
is not clear, I would regard that passage as dealing only with equitable
proprietary remedies. He also refers to a further passage in the judgment in *Re
Diplock's Estate*, which he does not cite. He presumably refers to the sentence
in the judgment which indicates the view of the Court of Appeal that—

'on their personal claims the plaintiffs are not entitled to any interest.
The same may not, however, be true as regards the claims *in rem*, at least
where the plaintiffs are able to "trace" their proprietary interest into some
specific investment.' (See [1948] 2 All ER 318 at 345, [1948] Ch 465 at 517.)

It is therefore probable that Hobhouse J was influenced in coming to his
decision by the judgment of the Court of Appeal in *Re Diplock's Estate*.
However, that judgment provides a shaky foundation for Hobhouse J's
decision. The passage to which he refers can, and should, in my judgment, be
regarded as doing no more than indicating the decision on the merits of the
situation which the Court of Appeal was considering in *Re Diplock's Estate*. A
situation which is very different from that which exists here. There was no
commercial relationship between the parties. The overpaid legatees' liability
was secondary and they were charities. In those circumstances, if they had
actually made a profit from the overpayment which could be traced, it would
have been reasonable to award interest but if they had not it would not have
been reasonable to do so. I would draw attention here to the following passage
of the judgment of the Court of Appeal in *Re Diplock's Estate* [1948] 2 All ER 318
at 337, [1948] Ch 465 at 503, which indicates that court's general approach:

'Since the original wrong payment was attributable to the blunder of the
personal representatives, the right of the unpaid beneficiary is in the first
instance against the wrongdoing executor or administrator, and the
beneficiary's direct claim in equity against those overpaid or wrongly paid
should be limited to the amount which he cannot recover from the party

a responsible. In some cases the amount will be the whole amount of the payment wrongly made ...'

I would also draw attention to the only passage of the Court of Appeal's judgment which gives any reason for their conclusion as to interest, which is in these terms ([1948] 2 All ER 318 at 339, [1948] Ch 465 at 506–507):

b 'We should add that ... in our judgment, the defendants are liable under this head of their claim for the principal claimed only and not for any interest. This last result appears to follow from *Gittins* v. *Steele* ((1818) 1 Swan 199 at 200, 36 ER 356 at 357), cited in ROPER ON LEGACIES (4th edn, 1847, p 461), where the language of LORD ELDON, L.C., in the case, is cited:
"If a legacy has been erroneously paid to a legatee who has no farther
c property in the estate, in recalling that payment I apprehend that the rule of the court is not to charge interest; but if the legatee is entitled to another fund making interest in the hands of the court, justice must be done out of his share."'

d The judgment of Lord Eldon LC in *Gittins v Steele* is extremely short. The Court of Appeal has cited the whole of the judgment except the opening sentence, which reads: 'Where the fund out of which the legacy ought to have been paid is in the hands of the court making interest, unquestionably interest is due.'

In fact, interest was therefore ordered to be paid in that case at 4%. The short
e judgment of Lord Eldon LC was in proceedings which followed an earlier judgment ((1818) 1 Swan 25, 36 ER 24). Having examined the case in both reports, I find they provide no support for a general proposition that equity could not in an appropriate case award interest in support of a personal equitable claim. The case supports the contrary view. In the circumstances which Lord Eldon LC is considering, the legatee had, as far as one can tell,
f benefited financially from the early payment and, that being so, the decision is merely an example of the fact that if a payee has benefited financially from his being unjustly enriched, an order for interest will be made. It is relevant that as interest had been earned (in the hands of the court), interest was payable.

Before leaving *Re Diplock's Estate* it is important to note that the case was not
g concerned with whether compound interest was payable; it was concerned with whether any interest, simple or compound, was payable. The view that no interest, not even simple, was payable was understandable on the facts but not otherwise.

While, therefore, it is not necessary on my approach to decide whether the
h sums paid by the bank are recoverable from the local authority in equity or in common law, it is necessary for me to indicate that Hobhouse J was wrong in his judgment in *Kleinwort Benson* in deciding that he would have no power to award compound interest if, as he thought was the case, the bank was entitled to a personal equitable remedy which would enable it to obtain judgment for the sums which had been paid.

j There is one more aspect of Hobhouse J's judgment to which I should refer. In his review of the authorities, Hobhouse J drew attention to two lines of authority, one where simple interest is being awarded, and the second where compound interest is being awarded. In the former situation, the court, according to Hobhouse J, is concerned to compensate the party for what he has lost in consequence of not receiving the money to which he was entitled. In the

latter situation the court is concerned with the benefit which the payee has
derived as a result of the payment having been made. The distinction is a valid
one if what is being considered is the right to interest on the one hand under the
statute or common law and on the other in equity. The distinction is not valid
if a different position is being considered, namely, whether simple or compound
interest should be awarded in equity. Equity, in the case of both simple and
compound interest, will look at the benefit which the payee has derived. If it is
equitable so to do, the payee will be ordered to pay simple or compound
interest depending upon the benefit which has resulted from the payment.

THE POSITION AT COMMON LAW AND BY STATUTE

I should now deal shortly with the situation as to interest at common law and
by statute. At common law the power to award interest was linked to the
power to award damages. While the equitable jurisdiction was concerned to
prevent profit by the recipient of funds to which he was not entitled, the
common law was concerned with the loss suffered by the payer of the funds.
The statutory jurisdiction differed from the common law because initially there
had to be a judgment for the payment of a debt or damages before interest could
be awarded and the legislator was dealing with the generality of those
situations.

As to the common law position a convenient starting-point is provided by the
decision of this House in *London, Chatham and Dover Rly Co v South Eastern Rly
Co* [1893] AC 429, which I have already cited. In that case Lord Herschell LC
and the other members of this House came to the conclusion with considerable
reluctance that *at common law* where there was no agreement or statutory
provision which permitted the payment of interest a court had no power to
award interest, whether simple or compound, by way of damages for the late
payment of a debt. The view of the House was rather surprising because the
members reluctantly followed a decision of Lord Tenterden CJ in *Page v
Newman* (1829) 9 B & C 378, 109 ER 140, based on convenience, in preference
to an earlier and more 'liberal' line of authorities, including a decision of Lord
Mansfield in *Eddowes v Hopkins* (1780) 1 Doug KB 376, 99 ER 242, and Lord
Ellenborough in *De Havilland v Bowerbank* (1807) 1 Camp 50, 170 ER 872. Lord
Mansfield stated the position in these terms—

'that though by the common law, book debts do not of course carry
interest, it may be payable in consequence of the usage of particular
branches of trade; or of a special agreement [which of course is beyond
question]; or, in cases of long delay under vexatious and oppressive
circumstances, if a jury in their discretion shall think fit to allow it.' (See
(1780) 1 Doug KB 376, 99 ER 242.)

Lord Ellenborough included among four categories of situations where interest
was payable, that where the money had been actually used and interest made on
it (see (1807) 1 Camp 50 at 51, 170 ER 872 at 873).

After the decision in the *London, Chatham and Dover Rly Co* case it was
generally accepted that at common law, apart from statute and some limited
exceptions, there was no power to award simple or compound interest for the
late payment of a sum of money.

This situation which was regarded as unsatisfactory by this House in 1893
was ameliorated in 1934 by the intervention of the legislature. Section 3(1) of

a the Law Reform (Miscellaneous Provisions) Act 1934 considerably extended the power which was contained in the Civil Procedure Act 1833 (Lord Tenterden's Act). The 1934 Act, so far as relevant, provided:

b '**3.**—(1) In any proceedings tried in any court of record for the recovery of any debt or damages, the court may, if it thinks fit, order that there shall be included in the sum for which judgment is given interest at such rate as it thinks fit on the whole or any part of the debt or damages for the whole or any part of the period between the date when the cause of action arose and the date of the judgment: Provided that nothing in this Section—(a) shall authorise the giving of interest upon interest; or (b) shall apply in relation to any debt upon which interest is payable as of right whether by *c* virtue of any agreement or otherwise ...'

It is to be noted that s 3 of the 1934 Act makes it abundantly clear that it does not authorise the giving of compound interest and that it confines the power to award interest to situations where there is a 'sum for which judgment is given.' The latter point was a cause of considerable injustice. It enabled a debtor to *d* prevent a court exercising the power under s 3 of the 1934 Act by making a late payment but a payment prior to any judgment being given. To remedy that situation, the Supreme Court Act 1981 was amended by the Administration of Justice Act 1982 by adding a new section, s 35A. Section 35A is still the current relevant statutory provision. It makes clear: (a) that it is still only simple interest *e* which is payable.; that it only applies to the recovery of a debt or damages and that interest is to be paid at 'such rate as the court thinks fit or as rules of court may provide' (sub-s (1)); (b) that the section does not apply when for whatever reason interest on a debt already runs (sub-s (4)); (c) that the section applies to payments made up to the date of the judgment (sub-s (1)(a)).

f The 1982 Act followed the *Report on Interest* by the Law Commission, to which I have already referred. Parliament did not implement by the 1982 Act all the recommendations of the Law Commission as to changes which should be made. In particular, it did not accede to the suggestion of the Law Commission that there should be a statutory standard rate of interest for reasons of administrative convenience. Instead, it retained the court's existing *g* wide statutory discretion.

There are two more cases to which I need to refer. The first is *Wadsworth v Lydall* [1981] 2 All ER 401, [1981] 1 WLR 598, and the second is *President of India v La Pintada Cia Navegacion SA* [1984] 2 All ER 773, [1985] AC 104, to which I have already referred. The decision in *Wadsworth v Lydall* received express *h* approval in *La Pintada*. I refer to *Wadsworth v Lydall* for three reasons. The first is that it brings out clearly that despite the decision of this House in *London, Chatham and Dover Rly Co v South Eastern Rly Co*, there is no inherent common law bias against the award of compound interest at common law. What is required for compound interest to be payable is that the contract either expressly or impliedly provides for the payment of compound interest or there *j* is a breach of the contract and the breach is such that compound interest will be regarded as flowing from the breach in accordance with the second limb of the principle laid down in *Hadley v Baxendale* (1854) 9 Exch 341, [1843–60] All ER Rep 461. The second reason is that while prior to the decision in *Wadsworth v Lydall* it could legitimately be thought that the situations where compound interest would be awarded at common law were necessarily of a commercial nature, this is not an essential requirement. The situations where it was clearly established that compound interest was recoverable (as, for example, in the case of bills of exchange or banking transactions) should be regarded not so much as independent exceptions to a general rule but as examples of the application of a general rule where in accordance with ordinary contractual principles compound interest should be recoverable. The third reason why I refer to *Wadsworth v Lydall* is that it clearly demonstrates that, notwithstanding the period which has elapsed since the decision in the *London, Chatham and Dover Rly Co* case in 1893, the courts will be prepared to limit the application of that decision where this can be done in accordance with principle and it is appropriate to do so.

Wadsworth v Lydall was a decision of the Court of Appeal. The facts were straightforward. The defendant and the plaintiff had an informal partnership agreement under which the partnership held an agricultural tenancy of a farm and the plaintiff lived in the farmhouse. When the partnership was dissolved the plaintiff and the defendant agreed that the plaintiff would give up possession of the farm by a specified date when he would receive £10,000 from the defendant. On the strength of that agreement the plaintiff entered into a further agreement with a third party to purchase another property on terms which required him to pay the £10,000, which by then he should have received from the defendant, to the third party. Only part of the £10,000 was paid by the defendant to the plaintiff prior to his completing his transaction with the third party. The plaintiff therefore had to take out a mortgage from the third party for the balance. In an action which he brought against the defendant the plaintiff claimed as special damages the interest and costs he incurred due to his having to obtain the mortgage.

The trial judge disallowed those two items of special damage but the plaintiff succeeded in recovering them as a result of the decision of the Court of Appeal. In relation to the argument that the Court of Appeal were bound to conclude that the appeal failed because of the combined effect of the decision in the *London, Chatham and Dover Rly Co* case and because of the provisions of the 1934 Act, Brightman LJ said:

> 'In my view the court is not so constrained by the decision of the House of Lords. In *London, Chatham and Dover Railway Co v South Eastern Rly Co* [1893] AC 429 the House of Lords was not concerned with a claim for special damages. The action was an action for an account. The House was concerned only with a claim for interest by way of general damages. If a plaintiff pleads and can prove that he has suffered special damage as a result of the defendant's failure to perform his obligation under a contract, and such damage is not too remote on the principle of *Hadley v Baxendale* (1854) 9 Exch 341, [1843–60] All ER Rep 461, I can see no logical reason why such special damages should be irrecoverable merely because the obligation on which the defendant defaulted was an obligation to pay money and not some other type of obligation.' (See [1981] 2 All ER 401 at 405–406, [1981] 1 WLR 598 at 603.)

The facts of the *President of India* case are not important. Its significance is that the approach of this House was that Parliament had chosen to remedy some of the injustices caused by the common law rule as laid down in the decision in the *London, Chatham and Dover Rly Co* case, and the restrictive *a* language of s 3(1) of the 1934 Act. Due deference to the intention of Parliament therefore prevented any further departure from the House's earlier decision in relation to interest. So the earlier decision would still apply to general damages.

In his speech, Lord Brandon of Oakbrook identified 'three cases in which the absence of any common law remedy for damage or loss caused by the late payment of a debt may arise' (see [1984] 2 All ER 773 at 783, [1985] AC 104 at
b 122). For convenience he described these cases as case 1, case 2 and case 3. Case 1 is where a debt is paid late, before any proceedings for its recovery have been begun. Case 2 is where a debt is paid late, after proceedings for its recovery have begun, but before they have been concluded. Case 3 is where a debt remains unpaid until, as a result of proceedings for its recovery being brought and prosecuted to a conclusion, a money judgment is given in which the original
c debt becomes merged.

Having examined the history and origins of the common law rule and the interventions by the legislature, Lord Brandon described qualification of the common law rule made in *Wadsworth v Lydall* as being important, and set out his conclusions as follows ([1984] 2 All ER 773 at 789, [1985] AC 104 at 129):

d
> 'First, an ideal system of justice would ensure that a creditor should be able to recover interest both on unpaid debts in case 1, and also in respect of debts paid late or remaining unpaid in cases 2 and 3. Secondly, if the legislature had not intervened twice in this field since the *London, Chatham and Dover Rly Co* case, first by the 1934 Act and more recently by the 1982
> *e* Act, and if the Court of Appeal had not limited the scope of that case by its decision in *Wadsworth v Lydall* [1981] 2 All ER 401, [1981] 1 WLR 598, I should have thought that a strong, if not an overwhelming, case would have been made out for your Lordships' House, in order to do justice to creditors in all three cases 1, 2 and 3, to depart from the decision in the
> *London, Chatham and Dover Rly* case [1893] AC 429. But, third, since the
> *f* legislature has made the two interventions in this field to which I have referred, and since the scope of the *London, Chatham and Dover Railway* case has been qualified to a significant extent by *Wadsworth v Lydall*, I am of the opinion, for three main reasons, that the departure sought by the respondents would not now be justified.'

g
The first of the reasons Lord Brandon gave for his conclusion was that the greater part of the injustice has already been remedied by the intervention of the legislature and judicial qualification of the scope of the decision in *London, Chatham and Dover Rly Co v South Eastern Rly Co.* The second was that Parliament had given effect in legislation to some of the recommendations of
h the Law Commission, but had not given effect to further recommendations which meant that for the House to intervene would be to intervene in a manner which would conflict with the policy indicated by Parliament. The third reason was that the intervention would create for creditors a remedy as of right rather than a discretionary remedy which would be again contrary to the policy of
j Parliament as indicated in the 1934 and 1982 Acts. The reasoning in *President of India* does not apply to equitable interest.

In relation to that reasoning it is important to note that none of the three reasons directly apply to the issue at present before their Lordships. The first reason does not directly apply to the present case because neither the legislation nor the decision in *Wadsworth v Lydall* addresses the injustice demonstrated by the facts of this case. The injustice arises because, contrary to the intention of the parties, there is no contract. The inroads which have been made on the decision in the *London, Chatham and Dover Rly Co* case by *Wadsworth v Lydall* can only apply where there is a contract under which either interest is expressly payable or the situation is one where the second limb of the rule in *Hadley v Baxendale* applies to a breach of contract. The second reason given by Lord Brandon ([1984] 2 All ER 773 at 789, [1985] AC 104 at 129) does not apply because the Law Commission made no recommendation as to the equitable remedy of interest. The third reason does not apply because if the court has jurisdiction to award interest in equity, like other equitable remedies, the remedy will be discretionary.

I therefore do not find anything in Lord Brandon's reasoning which makes it inappropriate to extend the right in equity so that it extends to the recovery of compound interest ancillary to a restitutionary remedy. In this case this is particularly true because if there had been a contract and non payment of the sums due under the contract by the local authority the bank may well, if proceedings resulted, have received compound interest as special damages.

THE DESIRABILITY OF THE EQUITABLE JURISDICTION BEING EXTENDED

A decision in favour of the bank in this case will mark a further improvement in the powers of the English courts. An improvement, the need for which has so frequently been recognised. While the improvement is consistent with the decision of this House in *President of India*, it should be noted that that decision has not been free from criticism. In a typically closely reasoned article 'On Interest, Compound Interest and Damages' (1985) 101 LQR 30 the late Dr F A Mann was not impressed by the reasoning of the House. Dr Mann (at 34) found it difficult to understand, if interest, including compound interest, was recoverable under the second limb under the rule in *Hadley v Baxendale*—

'why it should not also be recoverable under the first limb, where damages are such "as may fairly and reasonably be considered arising naturally, ie according to the usual course of things" from the breach?'

As Dr Mann (at 34–35) pointed out, to say that interest considered as damages is too remote is an argument which at the present time is no longer realistic or persuasive and which can only be described as an 'empty phrase'. The modern test should be whether the debtor could reasonably foresee that in the ordinary course of things the loss was likely to occur or was on the cards. Who would refuse to impute such knowledge to a debtor? Who would venture to suggest that a defaulting debtor could not reasonably foresee interest as the creditor's loss flowing from the failure to pay?

Dr Mann did not distinguish between simple and compound interest. However, if what he said with regard to simple interest is true, then adopting the same approach it must equally apply to compound interest. Dr Mann's final comment was (at 47):

'The history of interest, particularly in the field of Admiralty, displays a lack of legal analysis and a degree of positivism and inflexibility which show the common law of England at its worst.'

In my judgment, their Lordships should avoid leaving the equitable jurisdiction of the English courts open to the same criticism.

a Lord Browne-Wilkinson and Lord Lloyd of Berwick (whose speech I have also had the advantage of reading in draft) do not regard this as a case in which it would be appropriate to extend the law in the way I would wish. Their arguments, which are based on the legislative history as to interest and, in the case of Lord Lloyd, also based on *President of India,* I have dealt with already. However, as to the suggestion of usurpation of the role of Parliament, I do

b remind myself of the approach of Lord Brandon of Oakbrook in the passage of his speech in *President of India* [1984] 2 All ER 773 at 789, [1985] AC 104 at 129, which I have previously cited. Both Lord Browne-Wilkinson and Lord Lloyd also make the additional point that the local authority could feel aggrieved if this appeal were to be decided on the approach which Lord Goff and I would adopt. Here I take a different view. If their Lordships had not raised the issue

c of the correctness and scope of the decision in *Sinclair v Brougham* [1914] AC 398, [1914–15] All ER Rep 622, the bank would have succeeded. The local authority were only prepared to argue this point with reluctance. As I have indicated, the local authority also wanted the argument curtailed. In these circumstances they can hardly complain if they lacked the opportunity of dealing with the detail of

d your Lordships' reasoning.

In my recollection of his argument, Mr Sumption made it clear that his argument was not totally dependent on establishing that the local authority was a fiduciary. I have already set out how his case described the position in principle. I would also refer to para 13 of his case and the footnote thereto, where he said:

e
> '13. Quite apart from the proprietary claim, the Bank also has a *personal* claim in equity to require Islington to account for its property: Snell's *Equity* (29th edn, 1991), pp 284–287).
>
> [Footnote] In *Sinclair v Brougham* it was held that there was no personal claim in equity or at law, because to allow such a claim would be indirectly
f to enforced an invalid borrowing contract: see ([1914] AC 398 esp at 414, 418, [1914–15] All ER Rep 622 esp at 628, 630) (Lord Haldane). This part of the decision has been subjected to powerful and justified criticism by Lord Wright ((1938) 6 CLJ 805). But even if correct *it has no application to a restitutionary claim, whether at law or in equity,* arising out of a void swap
g contract since such restitution would not be legally or financially equivalent to enforcement of the contract itself.' (My emphasis.)

The passage in *Snell* refers to a personal claim in equity where there is a breach of trust. However, the footnote makes reasonably clear that Mr Sumption was applying the same approach as I would to a restitutionary claim
h 'whether at law or in equity'.

For these reasons I would dismiss the appeal.

LORD LLOYD OF BERWICK. My Lords, it was common ground before your Lordships that the bank is entitled to recover the principal sum of £1,145,526 in
j a common law action for money had and received. Judgment for that sum would carry simple interest at the appropriate rate under s 35A of the Supreme Court Act 1981. Hobhouse J ([1994] 4 All ER 890) and the Court of Appeal ([1994] 4 All ER 890, [1994] 1 WLR 938) have held (albeit for different reasons) that the bank has an alternative claim to recover the principal sum in equity, and that the equitable cause of action entitles the bank to claim a discretionary

award of compound interest, depending on the facts of the particular case. The
issue in the appeal as it came before your Lordships was whether the courts   *a*
below were right in this respect. Thus the bank's argument is stated succinctly
in para 11 of its printed case as follows:

> 'The bank's submission in summary is that where money is paid either (i)
> pursuant to a contract which is void, or (ii) under a fundamental mistake of
> fact or law, the money is impressed in the hands of the payee with a trust   *b*
> in favour of the payer. The payee is then accountable to the payer not only
> for the principal but for the entire benefit which he has obtained from his
> possession of the principal in the intervening period.'

A little later it is said, in para 12(5): 'The separation of the legal from the
equitable interest necessarily imports a trust.' In support of his argument Mr   *c*
Sumption QC relied, as he had in the courts below, on *Sinclair v Brougham* [1914]
AC 398, [1914–15] All ER Rep 622. He also relied on the speech of Lord Brandon
of Oakbrook in *President of India v La Pintada Cia Navegacion SA* [1984] 2 All ER
773 at 779, [1985] AC 104 at 116. It was not suggested in the bank's printed case
that Lord Brandon's formulation of the equitable jurisdiction to award   *d*
compound interest was incomplete, or insufficient for the bank's purposes. Nor
was it suggested that the decision of Hobhouse J in the parallel decision of
Kleinwort Benson Ltd v South Tyneside Metropolitan BC [1994] 4 All ER 972 (in
which he declined to make an award of compound interest in favour of the
bank, on the ground that the bank was in that case confined to its common law
action for money had and received) was wrongly decided.   *e*

The local authority, in para 5.1 of the its case, stated the issue for decision in
similar terms:

> 'Both parties accept that compound, as opposed to simple interest, is
> payable only if Islington received the money under the void interest rate   *f*
> swaps agreement as fiduciary: *President of India v La Pintada Compania*
> *Navigacion S.A.* ([1984] 2 All ER 773 at 779, [1985] AC 104 at 116).'

The whole thrust of the local authority's case was directed to showing that was
not a fiduciary when it received the money and did not become a fiduciary
thereafter. *Sinclair v Brougham* could be distinguished. It had never been   *g*
suggested that the mere failure to pay back the principal sum rendered the local
authority a fiduciary, otherwise 'every overdue debtor would be a fiduciary
liable to compound interest' (para 6.12).

Both parties, therefore, came before your Lordships on the basis that *Sinclair*
v Brougham was correctly decided, for whatever it did decide. But in the course
of the argument your Lordships indicated that the House would be willing to   *h*
reconsider the correctness of that decision. For the reasons given by my noble
and learned friend Lord Browne-Wilkinson, I agree that *Sinclair v Brougham* was
wrongly decided on both the points discussed in his speech, and should be
overruled. I understand that all your Lordships are agreed that the bank has
failed to make good its claim that it has an equitable cause of action against the   *j*
local authority for breach of duty as trustee or fiduciary. It follows that the
ground on which the courts below awarded compound interest cannot be
supported. The local authority has succeeded on the only issue on which the
parties came before your Lordships. Accordingly, I would be content to allow
the appeal, and leave it at that.

But my noble and learned friend Lord Woolf is of the view that, even though
a the bank has failed to prove any breach of trust or fiduciary duty, it may
nevertheless be entitled to claim compound interest by way of a general
equitable remedy ancillary to its common law claim for money had and
received; and his views receive the powerful support of my noble and learned
friend Lord Goff of Chieveley.

b   I have naturally considered these views with the greatest care; for there is
much force in the argument that the local authority ought, in justice, to pay
compound interest, if it would have had to pay compound interest (as no doubt
it would) on sums borrowed by way of more orthodox bank lending. But I
regret that in my opinion the House cannot, or at any rate should not, hold that
there is any such power in equity to make good the supposed defects of the
c common law remedy. I have come to that conclusion for three main reasons.

In the first place the point in question, which is one of great general
importance, was scarcely argued. This was not the fault of counsel. The point
only emerged from the background once it became apparent that *Sinclair v
Brougham* might fall to be reconsidered. By then there was no time to develop
d the argument. Thus the decision of Hobhouse J in the *Kleinwort Benson* case,
which would have to be overruled if the point is good, was only mentioned by
Mr Philipson QC at the very end of his argument, and then only in connection
with the date from which interest should run. The decision was never
mentioned by Mr Sumption at all.

e   Nor did Mr Sumption seek to question the reasoning or conclusion of the
House in *President of India v La Pintada Cia Navegacion SA*. On the contrary, he
relied on Lord Brandon's speech as an accurate summary of the equitable
jurisdiction to award compound interest in the two special classes of case to
which Lord Brandon referred. I may be wrong, but I do not recall any reference
to the comments expressed by Mason CJ and Wilson J in *Hungerfords v Walker*
f (1988) 171 CLR 125. It is accepted that to decide the compound interest point
in favour of the bank would mean breaking new ground, and would be
extending the equitable jurisdiction to a field where it has never before been
exercised. I do not think it right to take so momentous a course, involving such
widespread ramifications, on the back of such inadequate argument. Above all
I cannot regard it as fair to decide the case against the local authority on the
g alternative argument when through no fault of their own, they have not had a
proper opportunity to deal with the argument.

Secondly, I have difficulty in reconciling an award of compound interest as an
equitable remedy available in support of the common law claim for money had
and received with the ratio decidendi of the House in *President of India*. The
h facts of that case were that the charterers were between two and six years late
in paying sums due to the owners by way of freight and demurrage. The
owners claimed interest in respect of the late payment. The question was
referred to arbitration, and the umpire awarded compound interest in favour of
the owners for the whole period of the delay. One of the questions of law for
j the court was whether the umpire had jurisdiction to award interest in respect
of the late payment. Mr Saville QC launched a frontal attack on *London,
Chatham and Dover Rly Co v South Eastern Rly Co* [1893] AC 429, in which it was
held that a claim for interest by way of general damages will not lie at common
law for late payment of a debt, in the absence of some custom binding on the
parties, or some express or implied agreement. In giving the leading speech,

Lord Brandon said that other things being equal there was 'a strong, if not an overwhelming, case' for departing from the decision in the *London, Chatham and* *a* *Dover Rly Co* case in order to do justice to creditors (see [1984] 2 All ER 773 at 789, [1985] AC 104 at 129). But with regret he felt unable to take that course. I return to his reasons later. All the other noble Lords shared Lord Brandon's regret. Lord Roskill said ([1984] 2 All ER 773 at 775–776, [1985] AC 104 at 111):

> 'It has long been recognised that *London, Chatham and Dover Rly Co v South* *b* *Eastern Rly Co* left creditors with a legitimate sense of grievance and an obvious injustice without remedy. I think the House in 1893 recognised those consequences of the decision, but then felt compelled for historical reasons to leave that injustice uncorrected.'

Like Lord Brandon, he felt unable to depart from the *London, Chatham and Dover* *c* *Rly* case, and called for the injustice to be remedied by further legislation.

I quote these passages in order to make the point that if Mr Saville, for the owners, could have detected some way of supporting the umpire's award of compound interest, he would have found a ready ear. He pointed out in the course of his argument that the equitable jurisdiction to award compound *d* interest had survived the passing of the 1934 Act, as had the Admiralty jurisdiction, and he argued that these 'exceptional' jurisdictions should be regarded as the rule, and not vice versa. But this argument did not prevail. When Lord Brandon ([1984] 2 All ER 773 at 779, [1985] AC 104 at 116) said that 'the Admiralty Court *never*, and Courts of Chancery *only in two special classes of case*' awarded compound, as distinct from simple, interest (my emphasis); he *e* meant, I think, exactly what he said. Moreover, he regarded it as a point of importance. I cannot, therefore, agree that he was only giving examples of the application of a more general equitable jurisdiction to grant ancillary relief by way of compound interest. To my mind the immediate context, and the shape of the case as a whole, make quite clear that that was not his meaning. *f*

It may be said that in *President of India* the claim was for payment of a debt due under a contract, whereas in the present case the claim is for money had and received. But why should that make any difference? It is true that the common law action for money had and received can be given a restitutionary label; and that 'restitution' may be said to be incomplete unless compound interest is included in the award. But the label cannot change the underlying reality. The *g* cause of action remains a common law action for the return of money paid in pursuance of an ineffective contract. If compound interest cannot be recovered in a claim for debt due under a contract (in the absence of custom, or some express or implied agreement to that effect) I cannot see any reason in principle, or logic, why it should be recoverable in the case of money paid under a *h* contract which turns out to be ineffective.

It is said, nevertheless, that the reasoning which led Lord Brandon to reject the owners' claim for compound interest does not apply to the different facts of the present case. Lord Brandon identified three main reasons for his conclusion. It is to the second reason that I would draw attention. I will quote the reason *j* in full:

> 'My second main reason is that, when Parliament has given effect by legislation to some recommendations of the Law Commission in a particular field, but has taken what appears to be a policy decision not to give effect to a further such recommendation, any decision of your

that even an award of simple interest lies in the discretion of the
es the rate of interest.   But in the great majority of cases it is not   *a*
redict the amount of simple interest which is likely to be awarded.
interest, on the other hand, is not so predictable.   It presents wider
sagreement.   Disputes would be likely to end up in court, and this
e words of Lord Tenterden, 'be productive of great inconvenience'.
 weight which must attach to the views of my noble and learned   *b*
 Goff of Chieveley and Lord Woolf, I would allow the appeal.

ed.

Celia Fox   Barrister.

a   Lordships' House which would have the
     route, to the very recommendation wl
     taken that policy decision to reject,
     unjustifiable usurpation by your Lordshij
     belong properly to Parliament, rather
     departing from an earlier decision on t
b   obsolete and could still, in a limited class (
     degree of injustice.' (See [1984] 2 All ER 7!

It is true that the Law Commission in its report, .
(Law Com No 88) (1978) made no recommenda
jurisdiction to award interest, and so Parliament
c   policy decision to reject any such recommer
     objection remains. Parliament has on two occas
     1981, remedied injustices which had long been aj
     interest at common law. On the latter occasion it
     expressed by the Law Commission that the eq
     interest was working satisfactorily and called foi
d   equitable jurisdiction for the first time to cover a i
     law, which Parliament chose not to remedy, w(
     usurpation of the role of the legislature, and as (
     law-making, as it would have been in *President of Ini*
     that the courts should have a power to award com
e   law claims for money had and received, then sucl
     brought about by Parliament.

     My third reason for rejecting the bank's claim for
     am by no means certain that the policy considerati
     change. It is presumably in commercial transactic
     power to award compound interest would most fr(
f   ground that the money received by the payee would
     borrowed at compound interest. But it is in just such i
     for certainty is paramount. Disputes which would otl
     basis of simple interest would be fought in the hope of j
     an award of compound interest was appropriate. It is i
g   was on this very ground that Lord Tenterden CJ rejecte
     by Best CJ in *Arnott v Redfern* (1826) 3 Bing 353, 130 ER
     (1829) 9 B & C 378 at 380–381, 109 ER 140 at 141 Lord '

          'If we were to adopt as a general rule that which s
          attributed to the Lord Chief Justice of the Comr
h   *Redfern* would seem to warrant, viz. that interest is
          has been wrongfully withheld after the plaintiff has (
          payment of it, it might frequently be made a question
          the proper means had been used to obtain payment o
          the party ought to have used. That would be
j   inconvenience.'

As one who has in the past attempted to keep open the av;
remedies in commercial disputes, I am now conscious oi
arguments the other way: see *Scandinavian Trading Tanker (*
Ecuatoriana [1983] 2 All ER 763, [1983] 2 AC 694, disappro\
in *Afovos Shipping Co SA v Pagnan, The Afovos* [1980] 2 Lloyd

course, true
court, as do
difficult to |
Compound
room for di
would, in tl
Despite the
friends Lor

Appeal allo

R v Thornton (No 2)

a

COURT OF APPEAL, CRIMINAL DIVISION
LORD TAYLOR OF GOSFORTH CJ, HIDDEN AND EBSWORTH JJ
4, 5, 13 DECEMBER 1995

b

Criminal law – Murder – Provocation – Self-control of reasonable man – Characteristics of accused – Battered wife syndrome – Appellant with personality disorder stabbing husband – Direction to jury on provocation although not relied on by defence – Appellant convicted – Subsequent fresh medical evidence of personality disorder and battered wife syndrome – Whether appellant's abnormal characteristics eligible for consideration by jury in determining whether reasonable person having characteristics of appellant would have lost self-control.

c

In 1988 the appellant, who suffered from a personality disorder, married T, her second husband. T had a serious drink problem and as a result the marriage was stormy; T assaulted the appellant on a number of occasions. On 13 June 1989 T and the appellant argued violently, during which T called the appellant a whore and told her to leave the house. The appellant subsequently armed herself with a kitchen knife because she feared that T would attack her; however T again threatened to kill her and she used the knife to stab and kill him. At the scene of the crime the appellant told police that she had wanted to kill T and had sharpened the knife for that purpose. At her trial for T's murder the appellant relied on diminished responsibility to found a verdict of manslaughter and called psychiatric evidence that she suffered from a personality disorder which could be regarded as an abnormality of mind. The defence did not rely on provocation, but in view of the appellant's background of abuse by T, the trial judge considered that he had a duty to leave that issue to the jury. He directed them that, for the defence to succeed, the provocative words or conduct had to have caused in the appellant 'a sudden and temporary loss of self-control' and would have caused a reasonable person sharing the appellant's characteristics 'as you have been able to discover them' to lose her self-control and behave as the appellant had behaved. The appellant was convicted of murder. Her appeal in 1991 was dismissed, but in 1995 the Home Secretary referred her case to the Court of Appeal pursuant to the Criminal Appeal Act 1968 on the basis of further medical evidence to the effect that the appellant possessed two particular characteristics at the time of the killing, namely (i) her personality disorder and (ii) the effect of T's abuse over a period of time on her mental state, which would have required the judge to direct the jury to consider whether a reasonable woman with those characteristics might have lost her self-control and murdered T.

d

e

f

g

h

Held – The battered woman syndrome was a relevant characteristic which could be considered by the jury in a murder trial, although a defendant could not succeed in relying on provocation unless the jury considered she had suffered or might have suffered a sudden and temporary loss of self-control at the time of the killing. If the trial judge had had the fresh medical evidence raising the appellant's personality disorder and the battered woman syndrome as relevant characteristics before him, he should and would have given the jury directions as to the two characteristics now relied on in relation to the defence of provocation.

j

It followed that that fresh evidence cast doubt upon the basis of the jury's verdict
on the specific question whether a hypothetical reasonable woman possessing
the appellant's characteristics would have reacted to the provocative conduct so
as to do what she had done. The question whether the appellant did or might
have lost her self-control at the time of the killing was essentially a matter for the
jury to decide and was an issue which the public interest required to be
determined. The appellant's conviction would accordingly be quashed and a
retrial ordered (see p 1030 *b* to *d*, p 1031 *e* to *h* and p 1032 *b* to *d*, post).

    R v Morhall [1995] 3 All ER 659 and *R v Humphreys* [1995] 4 All ER 1008 applied.

Notes
For provocation as a defence to a charge of murder, see 11(1) *Halsbury's Laws* (4th
edn reissue) paras 438–439, and for cases on the subject, see 14(2) *Digest* (2nd
reissue) 33–48, 5260–5409.

Cases referred to in judgment
Bullard v R [1961] 3 All ER 470n, [1957] AC 635, [1957] 3 WLR 656, PC.
R v Ahluwalia [1992] 4 All ER 889, CA.
R v Duffy [1949] 1 All ER 932, CCA.
R v Hayward (1833) 6 C & P 157, 172 ER 1188.
R v Hopper [1915] 2 KB 431, [1914–15] All ER Rep 914, CCA.
R v Humphreys [1995] 4 All ER 1008, CA.
R v Morhall [1995] 3 All ER 659, [1996] 1 AC 90, [1995] 3 WLR 330, HL.
R v Rossiter [1994] 2 All ER 752, CA.
R v Thornton [1992] 1 All ER 306, CA.

Cases also cited or referred to in skeleton arguments
Bedder v DPP [1954] 2 All ER 801, [1954] 1 WLR 1119, HL.
R v Cambridge [1994] 2 All ER 760, [1994] 1 WLR 971, CA.
R v McCarthy [1992] 2 NZLR 550, NZ CA.
R v McGregor [1962] NZLR 1069, NZ CA.
R v Newell (1980) 71 Cr App R 331, CA.
R v Taaka [1982] 2 NZLR 198, NZ CA.

Appeal against conviction
Sara Elizabeth Thornton appealed against her conviction in the Crown Court at
Birmingham before Judge J and a jury on 23 February 1990 for the murder of her
husband on 13 June 1989 for which she was sentenced to imprisonment for life.
That appeal was dismissed by the Court of Appeal, Criminal Division (Beldam LJ,
Saville and Buckley JJ) ([1992] 1 All ER 306) on 29 July 1991. On 12 May 1995 the
Secretary of State for the Home Department referred her case to the Court of
Appeal pursuant to s 17 of the Criminal Appeal Act 1968 on the basis of further
medical evidence and its impact on the defence of provocation. The facts are set
out in the judgment of the court.

Michael Mansfield QC and *Edward Fitzgerald QC* (instructed by *B M Birnberg & Co*)
    for the appellant.
B R Escott Cox QC (instructed by the *Crown Prosecution Service*, Warwick) for the
    Crown.

Cur adv vult

13 December 1995. The following judgment of the court was delivered.

a

LORD TAYLOR OF GOSFORTH CJ. Sara Thornton appeals against her conviction of murdering her husband, Malcolm Thornton. The case has been referred to the court by the Secretary of State pursuant to s 17 of the Criminal Appeal Act 1968. The appellant was convicted on 23 February 1990 in the Crown Court at Birmingham after a nine-day trial. There was an appeal, which was dismissed by a different constitution of this court on 29 July 1991 (see [1992] 1 All ER 306). Subsequently, representations were made to the Secretary of State on the appellant's behalf. They were based primarily upon further medical evidence and its impact on the defence of provocation, a defence which was not relied upon by the appellant at her trial, although it was left to the jury by the judge.

c   In August 1993 the Secretary of State decided not to refer the case back to this court. Further representations followed and on 12 May 1995 the present reference was made.

The appellant comes from a comfortable background, but from childhood onwards her life was punctuated by problems and unhappy incidents. She was asked to leave her boarding school. She twice had pregnancies which were terminated before meeting her first husband by whom she had her one child, Luisa. She went abroad with that husband but left him in Venezuela because of his drinking and there was a divorce. She made a number of attempts at suicide by cutting her wrists, by cutting her throat and by overdose of drugs. In March 1981 she was admitted to a hospital for a period under the Mental Health Act 1959. She had a third abortion in 1983. It was common ground that this history was attributable to the fact that the appellant suffered and continues to suffer from a personality disorder, although after 1981 there appeared generally to be some improvement in her mental state.

She met the deceased, her second husband, in May 1987. Like her, he had been married before and he had a son, Martin, aged 18. The appellant and the deceased began living together in the autumn of 1987 and were married in August 1988. Even before the marriage, it was clear that the deceased had a serious drink problem. He underwent treatment for alcoholism but his condition and behaviour deteriorated in 1989. As a result the marriage was stormy. There were angry arguments when the deceased was drunk and he used violence to the appellant. In her evidence she described a number of assaults. It is unnecessary to specify all the incidents prior to the final weekend, but on about 20 May the appellant left the house (which was in their joint names) after the deceased had punched her in the face and knocked her out. She reported that incident to the police and the deceased was charged with assault. The case was pending at the time of his death. After the appellant left, the deceased's son, Martin, came to stay at the house. On 26 May the appellant and her daughter returned.

Matters came to a head between Saturday, 10 and Tuesday, 13 June. On the Saturday, the appellant was attending a conference in Coventry in connection with her work. According to her, she learnt by telephone that the deceased had either assaulted Luisa or otherwise driven her from the home, so that she was in night-clothes at a taxi rank. Mrs Thomas, a friend and fellow employee of the appellant, gave evidence that the appellant said after the phone call 'I am going to kill him', adding that she was not prepared to lose everything. The appellant, in evidence, denied saying these things.

On 11 June she returned home accompanied by Mrs Thomas. The deceased had been drinking and there was an angry altercation. It continued after Mrs

Thomas left. The deceased picked up a guitar and threatened to hit the appellant with it. She had a kitchen knife in her hand. According to Martin, she said 'You touch my daughter, you bastard, and I'll kill you', pointing the knife at the deceased and holding it in both hands. Martin claimed he had to take the knife from her. The appellant's account was that she had the knife in the normal course of preparing lunch, that she made no threat to kill the deceased and was not disarmed by Martin. On the same day, when the deceased was in the bath, the appellant gave him Mogadon tablets. Martin saw her administer two, but she crushed four more and concealed them amongst pieces of chicken she fed to the deceased. She then telephoned the doctor saying he had taken an overdose and was suicidal, which, as she admitted in evidence, was a deliberate lie. An ambulance and the police were called but the deceased refused to go to hospital. After they left there was an angry scene. The deceased threw a chair, which broke the glass in the kitchen door. The police were called again.

Still later on that day, the appellant spoke to Mrs Thomas on the telephone. According to the latter, the appellant talked of divorce, said she was not prepared to give everything up for the deceased and that she would set about forging some cheques. In evidence the appellant denied that account of the conversation.

Next day, 12 June, according to the appellant, the deceased said he wanted her and her daughter out of the house. He then went drinking. On his return, he was sick in the kitchen, he later burnt a hole in the armchair and he spent the night on the couch.

Tuesday, 13 June brought the fatal dénouement. The deceased was again drunk. When he arrived home he noticed the appellant was not wearing her wedding ring. She said they did not have much of a marriage. He then threw his wedding ring into the garden. He abused the appellant, telling her to get out and take Luisa. Clothes were thrown out of the window. Luisa left. The appellant spoke to Mrs Thomas on the telephone, saying: 'I'm going to have to do what I said I'd do.' The appellant said in evidence that meant merely that she going to leave. She wrote in lipstick on her bedroom mirror: 'Bastard Thornton, I hate you.' Later, she and Martin went out leaving the deceased dozing on the couch. Martin returned home first and went upstairs. The appellant got a taxi home. The taxi driver said she was arrogant and quarrelsome, which she denies.

Her account in evidence of what happened after that was that she found the deceased still lying inert on the couch. She went upstairs, changed into her night-clothes and came down again to persuade the deceased to come to bed. He insulted her, calling her a whore and alleging she had been selling her body. He wanted her out of the house and threatened to kill her. She went to the kitchen to calm down. She decided to try again to persuade him to come to bed, but looked for a truncheon retained from when he had been a policeman so as to protect herself if he became violent. Not finding the truncheon, she picked up a large kitchen knife. She returned to the deceased, who again threatened to kill her and called her a whore. She stood beside him, lifted the knife and then brought it down slowly. A post-mortem examination showed the single stab had entered just below the ribs and penetrated deeply through to the back of the ribcage. In evidence the appellant said she did not stab the deceased deliberately. She denied she did it because she was provoked or because she was mentally upset. Asked in cross-examination if it was an accident, she repeatedly said Yes.

Martin, who was upstairs when the appellant came home, had heard no quarrel or raised voices. What he did hear was the rattling of cutlery in the drawer, followed by a scream from his father. He went downstairs. The *a*   appellant said in a cold matter-of-fact tone: 'I've killed your father.' She telephoned for an ambulance and said: 'I've just killed my husband. I've stuck a six-inch carving knife in his belly on the left-hand side.' The ambulance and police came. To a police officer the appellant said: 'I've stabbed him with this carving knife.' Asked 'Have you tried to kill him?' she said: 'I wanted to kill him.' When the emergency service were making efforts to save him the appellant said:

b   'I don't know why you are bothering, let him die.' Martin heard her say: 'Let the bastard die.' The police officer asked: 'Do you understand what you are saying?' She replied: 'Yes, I know exactly what I am saying. I sharpened up the knife so I could kill him. Do you know what he has done to me in the past?' Asked 'When did you sharpen the bread-knife?' she replied:

c   'After I went to see him in there. I said are you coming to bed love and he told me to fuck off out and fuck some blokes to get some money, so I just walked into the kitchen, got the knife, sharpened it up and stuck it in his belly.

      Q. Did he beat you up tonight? A. No.

d   Q. Did he threaten to? A. He would have.'

Later, the appellant said to the police: 'I nearly did it on Sunday you know.' Whilst the police were at the house, the appellant behaved in a surprising, Mr Mansfield QC says bizarre, manner. She began to use the floor-mop, she talked about the washing, a meal, and wanting to tune the guitar. She wanted to take

e   photographs of her husband and telephone the taxi for her handbag and cigarettes. She pinched a police officer's bottom, telling him he had 'a lovely bum'.

In her interviews with the police she said repeatedly she only intended to frighten her husband.

f   At her trial the appellant did not seek a verdict of not guilty, but relied upon diminished responsibility to found a verdict of manslaughter. Three psychiatrists were called: Dr Bullard and Professor Brandon for the defence and Dr Brockman for the Crown. All of them agreed that the appellant's personality disorder could be regarded as an abnormality of mind. The issue between them was as to whether that abnormality substantially impaired the appellant's mental

g   responsibility.

The defence did not rely on provocation. Criticism of that decision was strongly argued as a ground of appeal at the first appeal hearing but the court rejected it. Before us, that criticism was more muted but still figured in the argument. Like the trial judge and the court which dismissed the first appeal, we

h   can well understand why those defending the appellant did not contend she was provoked, having regard both to the remarks she made in the immediate aftermath and to her evidence at trial. On the evidence presented to the jury, whether for the prosecution or by the appellant, we do not consider that the decision to concentrate the defence on diminished responsibility can be faulted.

j   Nevertheless, there is no doubt that the appellant had been subjected over a period to violence and abuse by her alcoholic husband and, on her evidence, abuse and threats were levelled at her shortly before the stabbing. In those circumstances the trial judge considered he had a duty to leave provocation as an issue for the jury's consideration. He was clearly right to do so. (See *R v Hopper* [1915] 2 KB 431, [1914–15] All ER Rep 914, *Bullard v R* [1961] 3 All ER 470n, [1957] AC 635 and, most recently, *R v Rossiter* [1994] 2 All ER 752.)

The duty to leave provocation to the jury even when the defence has not relied *a*
on it and even when in some cases they may regard it as an embarrassment or
distraction, creates problems for the judge. In the present case the judge's
direction was as follows:

> 'I come now to the question of loss of control and provocation. It is my
> duty to mention this to you, members of the jury, [because] you will notice *b*
> that [counsel] did not address you on the basis of provocation and it will I
> think be obvious to you why in a moment, when you have heard what I have
> to say to you about it. Members of the jury, the word "provocation" in
> ordinary language is used pretty freely and not always very appropriately.'

The judge then gave an example of colloquial use of the word 'provocative'. He *c*
continued:

> 'You are not being asked to consider "Did he lead her a miserable life?",
> whether you think he did or not on the evidence, nor are you asking yourself
> "Does she deserve sympathy?", because that is not the issue in the case. For *d*
> the purposes of the charge of murder, provocation consists of some act or
> series of acts done or words spoken or a continuation of words and acts
> which causes in the particular defendant a sudden and temporary loss of
> self-control and which would have caused a reasonable, sober person to lose
> her self-control and to behave as the defendant behaved. So there are two
> questions. The first question is whether the provocative conduct, such as it *e*
> was, if there was any, caused the defendant to lose her self-control. There
> has to be a sudden loss of self-control. The defendant herself asserts that
> there was no sudden loss of self-control. Members of the jury, that no doubt
> is why [counsel] did not address you and invite you to consider provocation.
> But, even if that were the case, there would still be the second part. The *f*
> second question is whether the provocative act would have caused a
> reasonable, sober person to lose her self-control and behave as the defendant
> behaved and on this, of course, you would take into account the whole
> picture, the whole story, everything that was said, possibly anything that was
> done, if there was anything done, on this night, according to the effect it
> would have on a reasonable, sober woman in the position in which the *g*
> defendant believed herself to be and, of course, a reasonable, sober woman,
> like a reasonable, sober man, is expected to have ordinary powers of
> self-control, normal powers expected of a person of the sex and age of the
> particular defendant and sharing her characteristics as you have been able to
> discover them. Members of the jury, so far as this aspect is concerned, even *h*
> if Mrs Thornton had lost her self-control, you would still have to ask whether
> a reasonable women in her position would have done what she did and, if
> you think (and this is for you to say) that she went out and found a knife and
> went back into the room and as a result of something said to her, stabbed her
> husband as he lay defenceless on that settee deep into his stomach, it may be .
> very difficult to come to the conclusion that that was, and I use the *j*
> shorthand, a reasonable reaction. There are ... many unhappy, indeed
> miserable, husbands and wives. It is a fact of life. It has to be faced, members
> of the jury. But on the whole it is hardly reasonable, you may think, to stab
> them fatally when there are other alternatives available, like walking out or
> going upstairs.'

a The judge then correctly told the jury that the burden was on the prosecution to prove that the appellant was not provoked or acting under provocation.

A number of criticisms of that passage were made on the first appeal. Principally it was submitted the trial judge was wrong to direct the jury that, for the defence to succeed, the provocative words or conduct have to have caused in the defendant 'a sudden and temporary loss of self-control'. That concept was
b said to be too rigid. In rejecting the submission this court traced the concept from a dictum of Tindal CJ in *R v Hayward* (1833) 6 C & P 157 at 159, 172 ER 1188 at 1189 through the well-known direction of Devlin J approved by this court in *R v Duffy* [1949] 1 All ER 932 at 932–933 up to the present day (see *R v Thornton* [1992] 1 All ER 306 at 313–314).

c In *R v Ahluwalia* [1992] 4 All ER 889 at 894–896 there was again a challenge to a summing-up which was in accordance with the *Duffy* direction. It was argued that a woman subjected over a period to verbal and physical abuse may kill her abuser because of a 'slow burn' reaction to the cumulative maltreatment rather than because of a sudden and temporary loss of self-control and the concept of provocation should accommodate such a case. In rejecting that argument, this
d court said (at 895–896):

'The phrase "sudden and temporary loss of self-control" encapsulates an essential ingredient of the defence of provocation in a clear and readily understandable phrase. It serves to underline that the defence is concerned
e with the actions of an individual who is not, at the moment when he or she acts violently, master of his or her own mind. [Counsel] suggested that the phrase might lead the jury to think provocation could not arise for consideration unless the defendant's act followed immediately upon the acts or words which constituted the alleged provocation ... Nevertheless, it is open to the judge, when deciding whether there is any evidence of
f provocation to be left to the jury and open to the jury when considering such evidence, to take account of the interval between the provocative conduct and the reaction of the defendant to it. Time for reflection may show that after the provocative conduct made its impact on the mind of the defendant, he or she kept or regained self-control. The passage of time following the provocation may also show that the subsequent attack was planned or based
g on motives, such as revenge or punishment, inconsistent with the loss of self-control and therefore with the defence of provocation. In some cases, such an interval may wholly undermine the defence of provocation; that, however, depends entirely on the facts of the individual case and is not a principle of law ... We accept that the subjective element in the defence of
h provocation would not as a matter of law be negatived simply because of the delayed reaction in such cases, provided that there was at the time of the killing a "sudden and temporary loss of self-control" caused by the alleged provocation. However, the longer the delay and the stronger the evidence of deliberation on the part of the defendant, the more likely it will be that the
j prosecution will negative provocation ... [Counsel's] argument in support of this ground of appeal amounted in reality to an invitation to this court to change the law. We are bound by the previous decisions of this court to which reference has been made, unless we are convinced that they were wholly wrong. Where a particular principle of law has been reaffirmed so many times and applied so generally over such a long period, it must be a matter for Parliament to consider any change. There are important

considerations of public policy which would be involved should provocation a
be redefined so as possibly to blur the distinction between sudden loss of
self-control and deliberate retribution.'

In the present appeal the established principle of law has quite rightly not been
challenged again. However, since reliance *is* placed upon the appellant's
suffering from a 'battered woman syndrome', we think it right to reaffirm the b
principle. A defendant, even if suffering from that syndrome, cannot succeed in
relying on provocation unless the jury consider she suffered or may have suffered
a sudden and temporary loss of self-control at the time of the killing.

That is not to say that a battered woman syndrome has no relevance to the
defence of provocation. The severity of such a syndrome and the extent to which
it may have affected a particular defendant will no doubt vary and is for the jury c
to consider. But it may be relevant in two ways. First, it may form an important
background to whatever triggered the actus reus. A jury may more readily find
there was a sudden loss of control triggered by even a minor incident, if the
defendant has endured abuse over a period, on the 'last straw' basis. Secondly,
depending on the medical evidence, the syndrome may have affected the d
defendant's personality so as to constitute a significant characteristic relevant (as
we shall indicate) to the second question the jury has to consider in regard to
provocation.

As to the background relevance, the trial judge told the jury in the present case
to 'take into account the whole picture, the whole story' and he reviewed the
evidence of abuse, both verbal and physical, which the appellant had endured e
from the deceased over the whole period of their brief marriage. Criticism that
the judge had confined the jury to considering what occurred on the fatal night
was rejected by this court, as were all other criticisms of the summing up made
on the first appeal.

What then is new on this appeal? Mr Mansfield sought leave to adduce further f
medical evidence. No objection was made by Mr Escott Cox QC for the Crown
and he agreed to the further evidence being put before the court in written form.
It consisted of further statements from Dr Bullard and Professor Brandon, who
gave evidence at the trial, a statement from Dr Glatt which was available at the
first appeal, but not put in the forefront of the appellant's case, and reports from
Dr McKeith and Dr Gudjonsson made more than two years after the trial. g
Clearly some of that evidence would have been available at the trial but we
agreed to admit it all pursuant to s 23(1) of the Criminal Appeal Act 1968.

In view of the conclusion we have reached it is unnecessary and undesirable to
lengthen this judgment by quoting from these statements and reports. Their
effect is to raise for consideration in relation to the defence of provocation two h
characteristics which it is suggested the appellant possessed at the relevant time.
The first is her personality disorder. The second is the effect of the deceased's
abuse over a period upon her mental make-up. It is submitted that these
characteristics bear upon her reaction to the stress of events at the time of the
killing. Mr Mansfield argues that had the further evidence been led at the trial, j
the jury would have had to be directed to consider whether a reasonable woman
with these two characteristics might have lost her self-control and done as the
appellant did. As it was, the judge, when defining a 'reasonable woman' in the
passage we have quoted, referred only to a person 'sharing her characteristics as
you have been able to discover them'. He did not explain what characteristics
they might find proved and relevant.

a Two points should be made in regard to this omission. First, although at the trial there was medical evidence that the appellant's personality disorder was relevant to the defence of diminished responsibility (which is why it was led) there was none to suggest the disorder was a characteristic relevant to provocation. Indeed Beldam LJ, giving judgment on the first appeal, said ([1992] 1 All ER 306 at 315–316):

b 'We cannot help feeling that, if after the very detailed study which they had made of the case [the psychiatrists] had held the opinion that her mental disorder made it more likely that in the case of verbal insult she would have given way to impulsive tendencies or aggression, they would have said so, and would have stressed this characteristic as significant in her loss of
c self-control; but, as with her legal advisers, her medical consultants were also constrained by the account which she herself gave of the events leading up to the fatal stabbing.'

The absence of such evidence may well have been due to the state at that time of medical knowledge, which we are told has since then progressed considerably.
d The further medical evidence does raise the appellant's personality disorder for consideration as a relevant characteristic. It also raises the element of 'battered woman syndrome' as a further relevant characteristic.

Secondly, what characteristics of a defendant should be attributed by the jury to the notional reasonable person and how far the judge should go in assisting the jury to identify such characteristics, are issues which have been clarified in a
e number of decisions subsequent to this appellant's trial and indeed to her first appeal. R v Ahluwalia [1992] 4 All ER 889, R v Humphreys [1995] 4 All ER 1008 and R v Morhall [1995] 3 All ER 659, [1996] 1 AC 90 make clear that mental as well as physical characteristics should be taken into account. Moreover, there is authority, especially from the judgment of the House of Lords in R v Morhall that
f a judge should give the jury directions as to what, on the evidence, is capable of amounting to a relevant characteristic (see [1995] 3 All ER 659 esp at 668, [1996] 1 AC 90 esp at 100). We consider that if the trial judge had had the assistance of those authorities and of the further evidence we have before us, he should and would have given the jury directions as to the two characteristics now relied upon. We conclude that the fresh evidence and the clarification of the law to
g which we have referred cast doubt upon the basis of the jury's verdict in this case. We cannot therefore be sure that the verdict is safe and satisfactory.

However, the evidence and arguments which have persuaded us to that view relate principally to the second of the two questions the jury had to consider regarding provocation, ie whether the hypothetical reasonable woman
h possessing the appellant's characteristics would have reacted to the provocative conduct so as to do what the appellant did. The crucial first question was whether in fact the appellant herself was caused suddenly to lose her self-control by that conduct.

Mr Escott Cox submits the prosecution had a powerful case negating loss of
j self-control, whether on the evidence of the prosecution witnesses, or on what the appellant said in the aftermath of the killing, or on what she said in evidence. Mr Mansfield sought to discount what the appellant said as being unreliable because the two characteristics we have identified caused her to be mentally in a dissociated state. He went so far as to submit that the appellant's observations and answers should not have been admitted in evidence. We have not been persuaded by any of the medical evidence that what she said should have been

excluded. Mr Escott Cox submits that if we quash this conviction, as we have concluded we must, there should be a retrial.

We are conscious and have taken full account of the matters urged by Mr Mansfield, who opposes a retrial. He stressed the ordeal it would be for the appellant, who has already served a substantial period of imprisonment and has been on bail for six months. He further suggests the press coverage would make a fair retrial impracticable. However, we are firmly of the view that the question whether the appellant did lose or may have lost her self-control at the time of this killing is essentially a matter for a jury to decide. It is not for us. Despite the points made by Mr Mansfield, we consider the public interest requires that issue to be determined. We are confident that a fresh jury will be able fairly to try the case solely on the evidence they hear. Accordingly, we quash the conviction. We order a retrial. The appellant must be arraigned on a fresh indictment within two months. The retrial will take place at Birmingham. Legal aid will be granted on the same terms as for the previous trial. We shall extend bail pending the retrial on the same terms. We order that the retrial be held as soon in the New Year as possible.

Conviction quashed. Retrial ordered.

The appellant was retried in the Crown Court at Oxford (Scott Baker J) and was convicted on 23 May of manslaughter and sentenced to five years' imprisonment.

N P Metcalfe Esq   Barrister.

Luc Thiet Thuan v R

a

PRIVY COUNCIL

LORD GOFF OF CHIEVELEY, LORD STEYN, SIR BRIAN HUTTON AND SIR MICHAEL HARDIE
BOYS

b   1 NOVEMBER 1995, 26 MARCH 1996

Criminal law – Murder – Provocation – Self-control of reasonable man – Reasonable man – Ordinary person of same sex and age as accused and sharing such of accused's characteristics as would affect gravity of provocation to him – Unusual characteristics of accused – Defendant suffering from brain damage – Defendant killing former girlfriend after she taunted him about her new boyfriend and his own sexual inadequacy – Whether defendant's brain damage relevant factor to be attributed to ordinary person for purpose of determining whether reasonable person having defendant's characteristics would have reacted to provocation as he did – Homicide Act 1957, s 3 – Homicide Ordinance (Hong Kong), s 4.

c

d

Criminal law – Murder – Provocation – Self-control of reasonable man – Characteristics of accused – Mental infirmity – Defendant suffering from brain damage – Defendant killing former girlfriend after she taunted him about her new boyfriend and his own sexual inadequacy – Provocative words or conduct not directed at specific brain damage or mental deficiency – Whether defendant required to show provocation directed at relevant characteristic.

e

Criminal law – Murder – Provocation – Self-control of reasonable man – Series of acts provoking loss of self-control by defendant – Last in series of acts by deceased unprovocative in isolation – Whether defence of provocation available.

f

The appellant and two other men were arrested in Hong Kong and charged with the murder of, and robbery from, the appellant's former girlfriend. In a statement to the police, the appellant stated that he and his co-accused had intended to rob the deceased and that one of his co-accused had killed her to prevent her informing the police that she had recognised the appellant; but at his trial he stated that he and his co-accused had gone to the deceased's flat to collect money which she owed him, that she had taunted him about her new boyfriend and his own sexual inadequacy, causing him to lose control of himself and stab her repeatedly. Two medical experts called by the defence testified that the appellant suffered from brain damage which could make it difficult for him to control his impulses. That evidence was corroborated to some extent by the Crown's medical expert. The appellant relied on diminished responsibility and provocation. The judge, when directing the jury on provocation, did not refer to the medical evidence of brain damage. The appellant was convicted. He appealed to the Hong Kong Court of Appeal on the grounds that s 4 of the Hong Kong Homicide Ordinance, which was identical to s 3[a] of the English Homicide Act 1957, required the judge, when directing the jury on the effect of the alleged provocation on a reasonable person having the characteristics of the accused, to direct them to have regard to the appellant's brain damage when considering whether a reasonable man having the characteristics of the accused would have

g

h

j

_____

a   Section 3 is set out at p 1039 *a*, post

reacted to the provocation as he did. The Court of Appeal dismissed the appeal and the appellant appealed to the Privy Council.

Held – (Lord Steyn dissenting) On the true construction of s 4 of the Hong Kong Homicide Ordinance and s 3 of the English Homicide Act 1957, and having regard to the fact that s 3 of the Ordinance and s 2 of the 1957 Act provided for the defence of diminished responsibility for persons suffering from mental abnormality which impaired their mental responsibility, a defendant's mental infirmity which impaired or reduced his powers of self-control below that to be expected of an ordinary person was not a factor to be attributed to the ordinary person for the purpose of determining whether an ordinary person having the defendant's characteristics would have acted as the defendant did. The test of provocation was an objective test, namely whether the provocation was enough to make a reasonable man do as the defendant did, and individual peculiarities of the defendant affecting his power of self-control should not, as such, be taken into account for the purposes of that test. It followed that there had been no misdirection by the judge on provocation. The appeal would therefore be dismissed (see p 1044 h, p 1046 b to p 1047 a and p 1048 a to c e, post).

DPP v Camplin [1978] 2 All ER 168 applied.

R v Newell (1980) 71 Cr App R 331, *R v Ahluwalia* [1992] 4 All ER 889, *R v Dryden* [1995] 4 All ER 987 and *R v Humphreys* [1995] 4 All ER 1008 doubted.

R v McGregor [1962] NZLR 1069 and *R v McCarthy* [1992] 2 NZLR 550 considered.

Per curiam. It is not necessary in order to establish the defence of provocation for the provocation to have been directed at the relevant characteristic of the defendant. Although in the great majority of cases in which a characteristic of the defendant is relevant to the gravity of the provocation to him, the provocation will in fact have been directed at that characteristic, as where it is the subject of taunts by the deceased, this need not always be so, for there may be cases in which, for example, previous events mislead the defendant into believing that an innocent remark by the deceased was so directed when in fact it was not (see p 1047 a, post).

Per Lord Goff, Sir Brian Hutton and Sir Michael Hardie Boys. It may be open to a defendant to establish provocation in circumstances in which the act of the deceased, though relatively unprovocative if taken in isolation, was the last of a series of acts which finally provoked the loss of self-control by the defendant and so precipitated his extreme reaction which led to the death of the deceased (see p 1048 c d g, post).

Notes

For provocation as a defence to a charge of murder and the criterion of the reasonable man, see 11(1) *Halsbury's Laws* (4th edn reissue) paras 438–439, and for cases on the subject, see 14(2) *Digest* (2nd reissue) 33–48, 5260–5409.

For the Homicide Act 1957, s 3, see 12 *Halsbury's Statutes* (4th edn) (1994 reissue) 280.

Cases referred to in judgments

Bedder v DPP [1954] 2 All ER 801, [1954] 1 WLR 1119, HL.
DPP v Camplin [1978] 2 All ER 168, [1978] AC 705, [1978] 2 WLR 679, HL.
Masciantonio v R (1995) 129 ALR 575, Aust HC.
Moffa v R (1977) 138 CLR 601, Aust HC.

a *R v Ahluwalia* [1992] 4 All ER 889, CA.
R v Baillie [1995] 2 Cr App R 31, CA.
R v Byrne [1960] 3 All ER 1, [1960] 2 QB 396, [1960] 3 WLR 440, CCA.
R v Dryden [1995] 4 All ER 987, CA.
R v Hayward (1833) 6 C & P 157, 172 ER 1188.
R v Humphreys [1995] 4 All ER 1008, CA.
b *R v Leilua* [1986] NZ Recent Law 118, NZ CA.
R v McCarthy [1992] 2 NZLR 550, NZ CA.
R v McGregor [1962] NZLR 1069, NZ CA.
R v Morhall [1995] 3 All ER 659, [1996] 1 AC 90, [1995] 3 WLR 330, HL.
R v Newell (1980) 71 Cr App R 331, CA.
R v Raven [1982] Crim LR 51, CCC.
c *R v Taaka* [1982] 2 NZLR 198, NZ CA.
R v Thornton [1992] 1 All ER 306, CA.
R v Thornton (No 2) [1996] 2 All ER 1023, CA.
Stingel v R (1990) 171 CLR 312, Aust HC.

d **Appeal**

By petition dated 10 March 1994 Luc Thiet Thuan appealed with special leave of the Privy Council, granted on 18 May 1994, from the decision of the Court of Appeal of Hong Kong (Power V-P, Macdougall V-P and Mortimer JA) dated 26 August 1993, dismissing his appeal against his conviction of murder before Ryan J and a jury in the High Court of Hong Kong on 13 January 1992. The ground of
e appeal was that the jury had been misdirected as to the availability of the defence of provocation, and the question at issue was whether brain damage or mental deficiency was a 'characteristic' which a jury should have ascribed to the hypothetical reasonable person, in considering whether the provocation was enough to make that reasonable man do as the defendant did, when the
f provocative words or conduct were not 'directed at' the specific brain damage or mental deficiency. The facts are set out in the majority judgment of the Board.

Martin Thomas QC and *Charlotte Draycott* (both of the English and Hong Kong Bars) (instructed by *Edwin Coe*) for the appellant.
Andrew Bruce QC (senior assistant Crown Prosecutor, Hong Kong) and *Mary Sin*
g (of the Hong Kong Bar) (instructed by *Macfarlanes*) for the Crown.

The Board took time for consideration.

26 March 1996. The following judgment of the Board was delivered.
h

LORD GOFF OF CHIEVELEY (delivering the majority judgment of the Board). There is before their Lordships an appeal by the appellant, Luc Thiet Thuan, from a judgment of the Court of Appeal of Hong Kong (Power V-P, Macdougall V-P and Mortimer JA) dated 26 August 1993 dismissing the appellant's appeal
j against his conviction of murder before Ryan J and a jury on 13 January 1992.

The appellant, together with Cheung Hoi Man and Lo Siu Kuen (whom their Lordships will refer to as 'the second defendant' and 'the third defendant' respectively), were charged with the murder of Candy Leung Shuk Man on 16 February 1988, and with robbery from the deceased woman on the same occasion of a necklace, a gold ring and about $HK2,000. All three were convicted of the robbery, and were sentenced to imprisonment for eight years, seven years and four years respectively. The appellant was convicted of murder and was sentenced to death. The other two defendants were convicted of manslaughter, and were each sentenced to two years' imprisonment concurrent.

The body of the deceased was found on 22 February 1988 in certain premises in Yuen Long in the New Territories. The autopsy revealed that she had suffered multiple stab and cut wounds. The doctor who conducted the autopsy was of the opinion that the cause of death was multiple stab wounds to the body, causing injury to the heart, lungs, liver and kidney. The cut wounds were consistent with defensive wounds suffered during a struggle. The condition of the face and eyes was consistent with asphyxiation.

The appellant was arrested in May 1990, over two years after the killing. He made a statement to the police to the following effect. He and the second defendant agreed to rob the deceased, with whom the appellant had previously had an intimate relationship. The third defendant provided money with which the appellant and the second defendant procured knives for the purpose of the robbery. Since the appellant feared that he would be recognised by the victim, the second defendant agreed that he would 'fix her up', ie kill her, and that was what in fact occurred. The appellant and the second defendant then left with the proceeds of the robbery, part of which was given to the third defendant to dispose of. The appellant participated in a video reconstruction of the crime, which in essence confirmed the account given by him in his statement.

At his trial, however, the appellant gave an entirely different account of the crime, repudiating his earlier statement as having been procured by inducements from the police. His new account was to the effect that he went to the premises with the second defendant to collect money which was owed to him by the deceased. Knives were taken to defend themselves with in the event of trouble. After an argument between the appellant and the deceased, a struggle ensued following which the appellant succeeded in tying her up. He then took money from her and an electronic teller card, forcing her to reveal the relevant code. A further argument developed, in the course of which the deceased compared the appellant unfavourably with her new husband/boyfriend, and the appellant then slapped the deceased. His evidence-in-chief continued as follows:

'A. Then after I had slapped her, I said to her: "Tell me what is so good about him." And while I was asking her, then I kept on pushing her and I repeated this question, that is, I asked her several times. Then after I had hit her, then at that time she became mad. She blew her head off and she said that her boyfriend could make her very happy while in bed. Then she said that that was better than me. And she said that I was so quick that I was just like a newspaper selling boy.

Q. How was your response to that? A. Then I hit her again, that is I further slapped her. I said: "You can even utter such cheap things." She said that she liked to say so, and she said that I had no right to control her, and she said that at that moment I had no relationship with her at all. After she had said so then at that moment I was very angry. What she had said made me feel despair, no hope at all, for her. I had stayed with her for so many years; and even in 1986 after we had separated and she started to treat me not so good, yet I managed to maintain relationship with her because I still had some fancy about her, that is I still imagined that one day she would change back into what she had been before, that is, she would become the girl whom I had come to know initially. That is why even later when she treated me a not so good at all, it only made me disappointed but still I had a hope on her. But then, at this moment after she had said all those words then I felt that everything had gone. All these years I was simply deceiving myself; actually she was just playing me all the time. I had wasted so much time on her and it was only at this moment that I realised that she had only played me. At that moment everything just popped up to me inside and I did not want to

b hear her any more; so I told her to shut up. Then I picked up that knife and pointed the knife at her. At that time what she had said to me made my very angry and desperate, I felt that some heat had popped up into my head, so I pointed the knife at her and I told her not to say any more. I said: "If you have the guts, then go ahead to say something." Then she said: "Really, I don't believe you dare to; and if you have the guts, then touch me", and she

c said that her husband would chop me into nine pieces and to play with me. Those words of hers were the last words I ever heard from her, for later whether she really said anything then I don't know.

Q. Why not? A. After she had said so then I could no longer control myself; I just went mad and used the knife to stab her. At that time I was

d really mad and I just kept on stabbing her. I did not know how long it lasted. I sat on the bed feeling numb.'

Following the stabbing the appellant regained his composure only to find that he had his hands round the neck of the deceased. He left, taking with him jewellery stolen from the deceased. After leaving the premises the appellant and

e the second defendant used the electronic teller card and obtained $6,000. The appellant met the second defendant and the third defendant for dinner that night, went to a movie and again used the electronic teller card, withdrawing a further $6,000.

Two defences were relied on by the appellant at the trial, viz diminished

f responsibility and provocation. Two medical witnesses were called on behalf of the defence, Dr Lee, a chartered clinical psychologist, and Dr Chan, a member of the Royal College of Psychiatrists in London. Dr Lee stated that, after conducting tests to assess the appellant's intellectual function, he found evidence which was indicative of 'some form of organic brain problem'. He concluded that the appellant's ability 'was noted to be impaired, especially in the left side of his brain

g and towards the frontal areas'. Dr Chan carried out an electroencephalogram test on the appellant, which revealed a persistent slow wave in the left frontal central area of the brain, which he concluded to be indicative of a cerebral lesion and to correlate well with Dr Lee's test. At the trial the appellant gave evidence that, following a fall in which he was rendered unconscious, he had experienced

h several episodes of responding irritably to minor provocation in which he felt 'the sense of hot flush rising from the abdomen', following which he became unable to keep control and acted explosively. His evidence was that this sensation occurred at the time of the attack by him on the deceased which resulted in her death. Dr Chan considered this experience to be a typical expression of an aura

j preceding an epileptic attack; and stated that, though the appellant showed no other manifestations of epilepsy: 'These findings are often found in patients with an organic brain damage who found difficulty in controlling an impulse.' A witness called by the prosecution, Dr Tsang, also a member of the Royal College of Psychiatrists in London, provided some confirmation of the evidence of Dr Chan to the extent that he, perhaps reluctantly, accepted that the appellant had the kind of brain damage described by the other medical witnesses, but

nevertheless noted the absence of another symptom, viz headaches, and
considered it unlikely that the appellant suffered from episodic dyscontrol   *a*
because he had exhibited no aggressive tendencies while in prison on remand.

Counsel for the appellant submitted at the trial that this evidence was relevant
not only to diminished responsibility but also to provocation. The judge,
however, rejected that submission, and so did not refer to the evidence when
directing the jury on provocation. In the result the jury convicted the appellant   *b*
of murder, rejecting both pleas. The appellant applied for leave to appeal to the
Court of Appeal against his conviction of murder, on the ground that the judge
had misdirected the jury on provocation by failing to direct them to have regard
to the medical condition of the appellant; but the Court of Appeal, having granted
leave, dismissed the appeal, holding that the judge was right to disregard this
evidence for that purpose. The court, in a judgment delivered by Power V-P,   *c*
conducted a careful review of the authorities on the subject. Their conclusion
was expressed in a passage in which they referred both to s 3 of the Hong Kong
Homicide Ordinance (which, in terms identical to those of s 2 of the English
Homicide Act 1957, introduced the defence of diminished responsibility in the
law of murder in Hong Kong) and s 4 (which, identical to s 3 of the 1957 Act,   *d*
amended the law of provocation), and said:

> 'Section 3 provides for the defence of diminished responsibility, which is
> concerned with abnormalities of the mind which substantially impair mental
> responsibility. That section provides a defence to persons suffering from an
> abnormality of the mind. There is no reasonable man test applicable thereto.   *e*
> Section 4, on the other hand, is not, as it stands, concerned with the mental
> abnormalities but, recognising that a person may be driven to kill after
> having been provoked, applies the test of the reasonable man to the
> assessment of the loss of self-control. Great difficulty, it is true, can arise
> when applying that test, particularly when it is necessary to determine the   *f*
> effect of a mental condition. Such a condition is properly the central issue
> when considering diminished responsibility but is, we are satisfied, rightly,
> when the central issue is provocation, not to be considered unless it can be
> shown that the provocation was directed at the condition.'

It is against that decision that the appellant now appeals to their Lordships' Board.   *g*

For the appellant, Mr Thomas QC submitted that an analysis of the relevant
authorities, and in particular the New Zealand authorities on the definition of
provocation contained in s 169 of the New Zealand Crimes Act 1961 (including
the analysis of North J in *R v McGregor* [1962] NZLR 1069, adopted by the English
Court of Appeal in *R v Newell* (1980) 71 Cr App R 331) revealed a development of   *h*
the law which permitted the mental condition of the defendant to be taken into
account for the purposes of the objective test in the law of provocation. For the
respondent, Mr Bruce QC submitted that to allow juries to take account of the
appellant's brain damage and episodic dyscontrol condition would be to
undermine the objective test, viz whether the provocation is enough to make a
reasonable man do as the defendant did, as interpreted by Lord Diplock in *DPP v*   *j*
Camplin [1978] 2 All ER 168, [1978] AC 705.

In considering the question in the present case, their Lordships turn first to the
words of the 1957 Act, s 3 of which (identical to s 4 of the Ordinance) provides as
follows:

a
'Where on a charge of murder there is evidence on which the jury can find that the person charged was provoked (whether by things done or by things said or by both together) to lose his self-control, the question whether the provocation was enough to make a reasonable man do as he did shall be left to be determined by the jury; and in determining that question the jury shall take into account everything both done and said according to the effect

b
which, in their opinion, it would have on a reasonable man.'

It has, of course, been pointed out many times that the 1957 Act does not codify the common law, but amends it. Even so, it is clear that the statute has not only retained the objective test, but has recognised the test to be whether the provocation was enough to make a reasonable man do as the defendant did, and

c
that 'in determining that question the jury shall take into account everything both done and said according to the effect which, in [the jury's] opinion, it would have on a reasonable man'. It is not therefore open to the courts either to discard the objective test, or to interpret it in a manner inconsistent with the statute.

The leading case on the law of provocation following the enactment of the statutory amendment, and therefore on the interpretation of the section, is *DPP*

d
v Camplin [1978] 2 All ER 168, [1978] AC 705. The question directly in issue in that case was whether, at a trial of a young man of 15 years of age for murder, the trial judge had erred in directing the jury that, with regard to provocation, they must consider the objective test in relation to a reasonable man and not to a reasonable boy of the age of the defendant. The House, affirming the decision of the Court

e
of Appeal, held that this constituted a misdirection.

The leading judgment was delivered by Lord Diplock. Lord Fraser of Tullybelton and Lord Scarman both agreed with his judgment. Moreover, at the conclusion of his judgment he encapsulated his understanding of the law in a proposed direction for juries, with which all members of the Appellate

f
Committee agreed.

The essential features of Lord Diplock's analysis were as follows. First, having traced the development of the doctrine of provocation at common law, he identified the intention of s 3, which recognised and retained the dual test, to be to mitigate in some degree the harshness of the common law of provocation as developed in recent decisions of the House of Lords (see [1978] 2 All ER 168 at

g
173, [1978] AC 705 at 716). Second, he stated that the public policy underlying the adoption of the 'reasonable man' test in the common law doctrine of provocation was 'to reduce the incidence of fatal violence by preventing a person relying on his own exceptional pugnacity or excitability as an excuse for loss of self-control' (see [1978] 2 All ER 168 at 173, [1978] AC 705 at 716). Nevertheless, the test now

h
fell to be applied in the context of a law of provocation that was 'significantly different from what it was before the Act was passed'. He continued ([1978] 2 All ER 168 at 173–174, [1978] AC 705 at 716–717):

'... for the purposes of the law of provocation the "reasonable man" has never been confined to the adult male. It means an ordinary person of either

j
sex, not exceptionally excitable or pugnacious, but possessed of such powers of self-control as everyone is entitled to expect that his fellow citizens will exercise in society as it is today. A crucial factor in the defence of provocation from earliest times has been the relationship between the gravity of provocation and the way in which the accused retaliated, both being judged by the social standards of the day ... But now that the law has

been changed so as to permit of words being treated as provocation, even
though unaccompanied by any other acts, the gravity of verbal provocation *a*
may well depend on the particular characteristics or circumstances of the
person to whom a taunt or insult is addressed. To taunt a person because of
his race, his physical infirmities or some shameful incident in his past may
well be considered by the jury to be more offensive to the person addressed,
however equable his temperament, if the facts on which the taunt is founded *b*
are true than it would be if they were not. It would stultify much of the
mitigation of the previous harshness of the common law in ruling out verbal
provocation as capable of reducing murder to manslaughter if the jury could
not take into consideration all those factors which in their opinion would
affect the gravity of taunts and insults when applied to the person to whom
they are addressed.'   *c*

This reasoning led to the conclusion that the decision of the House of Lords in
Bedder v DPP [1954] 2 All ER 801, [1954] 1 WLR 1119 (in which the House had
rejected as irrelevant the impotence of the defendant, who had been taunted with
that very failing) was inconsistent with the 1957 Act and so was no longer good
law.   *d*

Next, Lord Diplock concluded that age may be taken into account when
'determining what is the degree of self-control to be expected of the ordinary
person with whom the accused's conduct is to be compared' (see [1978] 2 All ER
168 at 174, [1978] AC 705 at 717). Finally, he epitomised his understanding of the
law in a proposed direction to juries along the following lines ([1978] 2 All ER 168 *e*
at 175, [1978] AC 705 at 718):

'The judge should state what the question is, using the very terms of the
section. He should then explain to [the jury] that the reasonable man
referred to in the question is a person having the power of self-control to be
expected of an ordinary person of the sex and age of the accused, but in other *f*
respects sharing such of the accused's characteristics as they think would
affect the gravity of the provocation to him, and that the question is not
merely whether such a person would in like circumstances be provoked to
lose his self-control but also would react to the provocation as the accused
did.'

g
As already recorded, Lord Fraser and Lord Scarman agreed with Lord Diplock.
Lord Morris of Borth-y-Gest and Lord Simon of Glaisdale delivered separate
judgments; but, as is evidenced by their agreement with Lord Diplock's proposed
direction to juries, they too agreed with him in all essential respects. In particular,
Lord Simon stated that 'the standard of self-control which the law requires before
provocation is held to reduce murder to manslaughter is still that of the *h*
reasonable person', and that the reference in s 3 to 'a reasonable man' means 'a
man of ordinary self-control' (see [1978] 2 All ER 168 at 182, [1978] AC 705 at 726,
. 727).

Their Lordships have taken the exceptional course of quoting a substantial part
of Lord Diplock's judgment to emphasise that, on the basis that a 'reasonable *j*
man' in the section means a 'person having the power of self-control to be
expected of an ordinary person', everything that Lord Diplock said was entirely
consistent with the words of the section. In particular, to take into account the
gravity of taunts or insults when applied to the person to whom they are
addressed is consistent with the hypothetical person having such power of

self-control, as is the fact that the sex and age of the defendant may be taken into
account, so that the hypothetical person is treated as having the power of
self-control to be expected, where appropriate, of an ordinary man or woman or
an ordinary young person. The same view was expressed in the unanimous
judgment of the High Court of Australia in *Stingel v R* (1990) 171 CLR 312 at 330,
with reference to age in the sense of immaturity, when it was said that 'the
approach may be justified on grounds other than compassion, since the process
of development from childhood to maturity is something which, being common
to us all, is an aspect of ordinariness'. But it is an entirely different question
whether the mental infirmity of the defendant which impairs his power of
self-control should be taken into account; and indeed it is difficult to see how it
can be consistent with a person having the power of self-control of an ordinary
person.

It is of some interest to refer at this stage to Professor A J Ashworth's article
'The Doctrine of Provocation' [1976] CLJ 292, to which their Lordships wish to
express their indebtedness. In his article Professor Ashworth observed of the
common law that 'the law's paramount concern is to ascertain whether the
accused showed a reasonable amount of self-restraint' (see [1976] CLJ 292 at 299).
He went on to observe that provocation can rarely be described as 'grave' per se;
in general, this can only be so in relation to persons of a particular class. From
this he concluded (at 300):

'The proper distinction ... is that individual peculiarities which bear on the
gravity of the provocation should be taken into account, whereas individual
peculiarities bearing on the accused's level of self-control should not.'

This conclusion, of course, also involved the rejection of the decision of the
House of Lords in *Bedder v DPP* [1954] 2 All ER 801, [1954] 1 WLR 1119.

Professor Ashworth's article was published in 1976, and *Camplin* was decided
by the House of Lords only two years later. The similarity between the approach
recommended by Professor Ashworth, and that adopted by the House of Lords
in *Camplin*, is so great that it is difficult to believe that his article did not, at least
indirectly, influence the reasoning and the conclusion in that case.

Their Lordships wish to add that the recent decision of the House of Lords in
R v Morhall [1995] 3 All ER 659, [1996] 1 AC 90 is in no way inconsistent with the
reasoning in *Camplin*. That case was concerned with the question whether a
defendant who was taunted with his addiction to glue sniffing, or solvent abuse,
was precluded from saying that that characteristic could be taken into account
when considering the objective test, because such a characteristic was
inconsistent with the concept of the reasonable man. The House of Lords
rejected that approach, holding that a characteristic such as this should not be
excluded merely because it was discreditable. In so holding, the House invoked
Lord Diplock's statement that the 'reasonable man' in the section should be
understood to be a person with the *ordinary* person's power of self-control, but in
other respects sharing such of the defendant's characteristics as the jury might
think would affect the gravity of the provocation to him.

However, it was only two years after the decision of the House of Lords in
Camplin when, in *R v Newell* (1980) 71 Cr App R 331, the English Court of Appeal
took the step of looking for sole guidance, on the interpretation placed by *Camplin*
on s 3 of the English Homicide Act 1957, to a prolonged obiter dictum of North J
when delivering the judgment of the New Zealand Court of Appeal in *R v*

McGregor [1962] NZLR 1069, on the interpretation of s 169 of the New Zealand Crimes Act 1961, which contained a new statutory definition of provocation in the crime of murder in that country. The most relevant part of the section was sub-s (2), which provided:

> 'Anything done or said may be provocation if—(a) in the circumstances of the case it was sufficient to deprive a person having the power of self-control of an ordinary person, but otherwise having the characteristics of the offender, of the power of self-control; and (b) it did in fact deprive the offender of the power of self-control and thereby induced him to commit the act of homicide.'

The 1961 New Zealand Act had been mentioned briefly in argument in *Camplin*, when Lord Scarman suggested to counsel for the Crown that s 169(2)(a) of the Act might be the same as s 3 of the Homicide Act 1957 (see [1978] AC 705 at 710). This suggestion was rejected by counsel on the basis that the wording of the two statutes was different. In the result, though it is legitimate to infer that the New Zealand Act exercised some influence on the judgment of Lord Diplock in so far as it referred to 'the power of self-control of an ordinary person', neither the Act nor *McGregor* received any mention in the judgment of Lord Diplock (with which both Lord Fraser and Lord Scarman agreed), or indeed in the judgment of Lord Morris. Only Lord Simon expressed the opinion that English law was 'substantially the same' as s 169(2) of the New Zealand Act, as explained in *McGregor* (see [1978] 2 All ER 168 at 182, [1978] AC 705 at 727). This imprecise statement cannot, in their Lordships' opinion, have been intended to suggest that precise guidance as to the interpretation of the English statute could be derived from *McGregor*. Nevertheless, it appears to have provided the genesis of the judgment of the English Court of Appeal in *R v Newell* (1980) 71 Cr App R 331.

In that case, the Court of Appeal were concerned to ascertain the meaning of the word 'characteristics' as used in Lord Diplock's judgment in *Camplin*. For that purpose, they turned immediately to *McGregor*, which had been referred to by Lord Simon in *Camplin*. The court then quoted a long passage from the obiter dictum of North J (though omitting an early part of it which shows North J relying on the particular words of the New Zealand Act); and then, without embarking on any analysis, the Court of Appeal (at 340) stated that the part quoted 'seems to us to be impeccable' and 'represents also, we think, the law of this country as well as that of New Zealand'. From it they drew the conclusion that a 'characteristic' for the purposes of provocation should be a more than transitory phenomenon—a conclusion upon which some doubt was later to be cast by the House of Lords in *R v Morhall* [1995] 3 All ER 659 at 667, [1996] 1 AC 90 at 99. The actual decision in *Newell*, which was to the effect that the judge was right to direct the jury to leave out of account the drunkenness of the defendant when considering the objective test in provocation, was doubtless correct, possibly on the basis that as a matter of policy 'intoxication does not of itself excuse a man from committing a criminal offence' (see *Morhall* [1995] 3 All ER 659 at 667, [1996] 1 AC 90 at 99 per Lord Goff of Chieveley). But in the respectful opinion of their Lordships, it must be unwise to impose uncritically upon an English statute an interpretation placed upon a statute from another jurisdiction, which is not expressed in the same words. Of course, there is a strong affinity between English and New Zealand law on this subject, reflecting their common origin; and anything which has fallen from North J is regarded with great respect *a* in this country, as it is in New Zealand. But their Lordships feel compelled to say that the wholesale adoption, without analysis, of a substantial part of this obiter dictum, which covers a wide range of points on a notoriously difficult subject with particular reference to the New Zealand statute, is not a satisfactory approach to the interpretation of the objective test in provocation as recognised in the English statute. Each point must, in Hong Kong as in England, fall to be *b* considered by reference to the words of the statute, their historical derivation from the common law, and the legislative setting (where relevant) at the time of enactment.

The passage from North J's judgment which is of most relevance for present purposes is concerned with his treatment of what he called 'purely mental peculiarities' of the defendant. He considered that these might qualify as *c* 'characteristics' to be taken into account for the purposes of the objective test, but that to do so 'there must be something more, such as provocative words or acts directed to a particular phobia from which the offender suffers' (see [1962] NZLR 1069 at 1082). For otherwise the objective test would be denied any real operation, and a substantial step would be taken towards the admission of a *d* defence of diminished responsibility in New Zealand without the statutory authority to sanction it, the defence not being recognised in New Zealand law. Their Lordships observe in passing that this approach to mental infirmity of the defendant is inconsistent with the submission advanced to them on behalf of the appellant in the present case.

The danger inherent in adopting a test laid down with reference to a different *e* statute in another jurisdiction can be seen in the fate which subsequently befell North J's dictum in New Zealand. First, it was subjected to trenchant criticism in Adams *Criminal Law and Practice in New Zealand* (2nd edn, 1972) paras 1264–1269. Next, it was found to create difficulties when applied in practice, which finally resulted in its being disapproved by the New Zealand Court of Appeal in *R v* *f* *McCarthy* [1992] 2 NZLR 550. In his judgment in that case Cooke P listed five cases in which, among others, difficulty had been caused. A particular problem appears to have arisen from North J's requirement that 'mental peculiarities' cannot be taken into account unless, in particular, the provocation was directed towards them. Judging from *R v Taaka* [1982] 1 NZLR 198 and *R v Leilua* [1986] NZ Recent Law 118, to which their Lordships were referred in the course of *g* argument, it appears that there had developed a tendency for New Zealand courts to take into account the mental infirmity of the defendant as such for the purpose of the objective test. There is every reason to believe that the spur for this development lay in the absence of any defence of diminished responsibility in the law of murder in New Zealand. At all events, in *R v McCarthy* [1992] 2 *h* NZLR 550 at 558 Cooke P considered that North J's 'added observations' may have 'unduly restricted the ambit of the provocation'. There followed a significant passage in Cooke P's judgment:

> 'The added observations appear to have been influenced by the view that diminished responsibility had not been accepted by the New Zealand *j* Parliament; yet, within a limited field, this may be seen as the inevitable and deliberate effect of the statutory changes embodied in s 169 of the Crimes Act 1961.'

In other words, Cooke P now considers that s 169 of the New Zealand Act may have had the legislative purpose of introducing diminished responsibility into the limited field of provocation. Their Lordships comment that no such purpose can have been intended by the legislature in s 3 of the Homicide Act 1957 or in s 4 of the Hong Kong Ordinance, when by a neighbouring section in the same statute the defence of diminished responsibility had been introduced by the legislature as a matter of general application in the law of murder. This is a point to which their Lordships will return. It must, however, follow from Cooke P's judgment in *McCarthy* that decisions of the New Zealand Court of Appeal in cases such as *Taaka* and *Leilua*, in which the mental infirmity of the defendant was as such taken into account for the purposes of the objective test in provocation, cannot provide any safe guidance on the construction of the English or Hong Kong legislation on the subject.

The history of the New Zealand cases on this subject reveals that the approach adopted by the Court of Appeal in *Newell* has exercised an unhappy influence upon the reasoning in subsequent decisions of the Court of Appeal in which reliance was placed on *Newell*. This applies in particular to *R v Ahluwalia* [1992] 4 All ER 889, in which *Newell* was relied on, as were *Taaka* and *Leilua*, and led the Court of Appeal to suggest that certain characteristics of the defendant relating to his or her mental state or personality may *as such* be taken into account by the jury for the purposes of the objective test (see [1992] 4 All ER 889 at 890). It is unfortunate that the attention of the Court of Appeal was not drawn to *McCarthy*, decided five months earlier, in which the obiter dictum of North J in *McGregor* had been rejected and Cooke P had expressed the view that mental characteristics of the defendant could be taken into account because of the deliberate intention of the New Zealand Parliament to achieve a partial recognition of the defence of diminished responsibility. Their Lordships feel confident that, if Cooke P's judgment in *McCarthy* had been drawn to the court's attention, they would have appreciated that the New Zealand case law on the interpretation of s 169 of the New Zealand statute no longer provided safe guidance on the interpretation of the English statute, for which it was necessary to return to the authoritative statement in Lord Diplock's judgment in *Camplin*. The same comment may be made of judgments of the Court of Appeal in other cases, such as *R v Dryden* [1995] 4 All ER 987 and *R v Humphreys* [1995] 4 All ER 1008. Their Lordships wish to add that they do not find it possible to segregate certain psychological illnesses or disorders as being 'in no way repugnant to or wholly inconsistent with the concept of the reasonable person' (see *R v Humphreys* [1995] 4 All ER 1008 at 1022), and so attributable to the reasonable person for the purposes of the objective test in provocation, notwithstanding that the effect of such an illness or disorder is to deprive the person so afflicted of the ordinary person's power of self-control.

In these circumstances, their Lordships return to the interpretation placed on the English statute in *Camplin* for guidance in answering the question posed for their consideration in the present case. Their conclusion is that, on the principles there stated, there is no basis upon which mental infirmity on the part of the defendant which has the effect of reducing his powers of self-control below that to be expected of an ordinary person can, as such, be attributed to the ordinary person for the purposes of the objective test in provocation.

First of all, for mental infirmity of the defendant so to be taken into account would be inconsistent with the statute as interpreted in *Camplin*, in which it was held that the reasonable man referred to in the statute means a person having the power of self-control to be expected of an ordinary person. But their Lordships a wish to state that, in so holding, they are not simply treating the matter as one of literal application of the principle stated in *Camplin*. That principle is, in their respectful opinion, well-founded in law. It is widely accepted that s 3 of the 1957 Act is not a codifying Act, but an amending Act which expressly recognised and retained the objective test as established in the common law, subject to the amendments provided for in the section. Having regard to the principles of

b common law then applicable, the intention must, as Professor Ashworth has convincingly demonstrated in his article ([1976] CLJ 292 at 299–300), have been that individual peculiarities of the defendant affecting his power of self-control should not, as such, be taken into account for the purposes of the objective test. Moreover, an indication of the problems involved in so taking mental infirmity into account is provided by *R v Raven* [1982] Crim LR 51, which was concerned

c with the trial for murder of a man whose physical age was 22 years, but whose mental age was only 9 years. The Recorder of London directed the jury that, in considering the objective test in provocation, they should attribute to the reasonable man the retarded development and mental age of the defendant. It is scarcely surprising that Professor Birch, in her commentary on the report, should

d have expressed the opinion that 'putting oneself in the position of a reasonable 22-year-old with a mental age of nine is a tremendously difficult feat' (see [1982] Crim LR 51 at 52). Even greater problems would arise if the appellant's argument was to be accepted in the present case, in which event the jury should have been directed to attribute to the reasonable man, ie a man having the ordinary man's power of self-control, the appellant's brain damage, with the consequent

e impairment of that power.

Their Lordships' conclusion on the effect of s 3 of the English Act is, moreover, consistent with that formed by the High Court of Australia in *Stingel v R* (1990) 171 CLR 312 with reference to s 160(2) of the Tasmanian Criminal Code, which provided:

f
'Any wrongful act or insult of such a nature as to be sufficient to deprive an ordinary person of the power of self-control and which, in fact, deprives the offender of the power of self-control, is provocation, if the offender acts upon it on the sudden, and before there has been time for his passion to cool.'

g   The court said (at 327):

'The function of the ordinary person of s. 160 is the same as that of the ordinary person of the common law of provocation. It is to provide an objective and uniform standard of the minimum powers of self-control

h which must be observed before one enters the area in which provocation can reduce what would otherwise be murder to manslaughter. While personal characteristics or attributes of the particular accused may be taken into account for the purpose of understanding the implications and assessing the gravity of the wrongful act or insult, the ultimate question posed by the threshold objective test of s. 160(2) relates to the possible effect of the

j wrongful act or insult, so understood and assessed, upon the power of self-control of a truly hypothetical "ordinary person". Subject to a qualification in relation to age … the extent of the power of self-control of that hypothetical ordinary person is unaffected by the personal characteristics or attributes of the particular accused.'

Their Lordships also refer to the similar statement of the law by Brennan, Deane, Dawson and Gaudron JJ in *Masciantonio v R* (1995) 129 ALR 575 at 581, with reference to the common law of provocation applicable in the State of Victoria.

It is, of course, consistent with Lord Diplock's analysis in *Camplin*, and indeed with the decision of the House of Lords in *Morhall*, that mental infirmity of the defendant, if itself the subject of taunts by the deceased, may be taken into account as going to the gravity of the provocation as applied to the defendant. Such a conclusion was also consistent with the opinion expressed obiter by North J in *McGregor*. But this is a far cry from the appellant's submission that the mental infirmity of the defendant, impairing his power of self-control, should as such be attributed to the reasonable man for the purposes of the objective test.

Their Lordships have reached the foregoing conclusion as a matter of construction of the 1957 English Act (and therefore of the Hong Kong Ordinance). But they are, like the Hong Kong Court of Appeal, fortified in that view by reference to the defence of diminished responsibility introduced into English law by s 2 of the same Act, and into Hong Kong law by s 3 of the same Ordinance. To accept the appellant's submission would, in their Lordships' opinion, be to incorporate the concept of diminished responsibility indirectly into the law of provocation. Such a conclusion is most unlikely to have been intended by the legislature, which, in a neighbouring section in the same statute, introduced diminished responsibility as a defence of general application in the law of murder, and moreover did so subject to the imposition of a special rule relating to the burden of proof, viz that the burden of establishing diminished responsibility should rest upon the defendant, though it should be the civil burden. If diminished responsibility was held to form part of the law of provocation, the extraordinary result would follow that a defendant who failed to establish diminished responsibility on the burden of proof placed upon him by s 2 of the 1957 Act might nevertheless be able to succeed on the defence of provocation (as recognised in s 3) on the basis that, on precisely the same evidence, the prosecution had failed to negative, on the criminal burden, that he was suffering from a mental infirmity affecting his self-control which must be attributed to the reasonable man for the purposes of the objective test. This was precisely the result for which the appellant was contending before their Lordships. They do not consider that this could have been the intention of the legislature. But their Lordships wish to add that the recognition by the legislature of the defence of diminished responsibility gives a defendant suffering from abnormality of mind the opportunity to establish a defence upon which a very wide interpretation has been placed by the courts and which, if proved, has, like provocation, the effect of reducing to manslaughter what would otherwise be murder. For the courts, in interpreting s 2 of the Act, have given to the words 'abnormality of mind' a very broad meaning, wide enough to embrace not only cases of 'irresistible impulse', but also those cases in which the difficulty of the defendant in controlling (or rather failing to control) his behaviour was 'substantially greater than would be experienced in like circumstances by an ordinary man, not suffering from mental abnormality' (see Smith and Hogan *Criminal Law* (7th edn, 1992) p 2132, referring in particular to *R v Byrne* [1960] 3 All ER 1 at 4, [1960] 2 QB 396 at 403 per Lord Parker CJ). It follows that the spur which has occasioned the developments in New Zealand law culminating in the judgment of Cooke P in *McCarthy*, to which their Lordships have referred, does not exist, at least to the same extent, in the law of England or the law of Hong Kong.

Their Lordships wish to add, as a footnote, that it may be open to a defendant to establish provocation in circumstances in which the act of the deceased, though relatively unprovocative if taken in isolation, was the last of a series of acts which finally provoked the loss of self-control by the defendant and so precipitated his extreme reaction which led to the death of the deceased. That such a series of events might cumulatively constitute provocation was the opinion expressed by Gibbs J in *Moffa v R* (1977) 138 CLR 601 at 616, cited with approval by the High Court of Australia in *Stingel v R* (1990) 171 CLR 312 at 326. Whether such a principle could be successfully invoked in cases such as, for example, the 'battered wife syndrome' is a matter upon which their Lordships can in the present case express no opinion, having heard no argument upon it, but must await a case in which the point arises for decision.

In conclusion their Lordships observe, though in no spirit of criticism, that they were not provided with any theoretical analysis of the concept of provocation, or of the various forms which it might take in the criminal law; and since the present case is ultimately concerned with a question of statutory construction, they have not thought it necessary themselves to indulge in any such exercise. Even so, it is plain that there must be a number of models from which a legislator might choose. He might, for example, adopt a purely objective approach, though doubtless this could take various forms. Such a model appears to have been adopted in those states of Australia in which the defence of diminished responsibility is not available. He might adopt an objective approach, but seek to mitigate its rigours by recognising the concept of diminished responsibility within the limited field of provocation, as Cooke P appears to have understood the New Zealand Parliament to have intended. Then again, he might adopt an objective approach, but combine the defence of provocation so formulated with a defence of diminished responsibility in the crime of murder. This appears to have been done in England and Hong Kong, and in those states of Australia in which the defence of diminished responsibility is recognised (which their Lordships understand to be New South Wales, Queensland and the Australian Capital Territory). Alternatively, he might adopt a subjective approach, which their Lordships understand some jurists find attractive. This too could no doubt take various forms; but it would probably have to be so formulated, or to be subject to exceptions, so as to exclude socially undesirable cases such as intoxication or sheer bad temper. Again he might abolish the mandatory sentence for murder (a course of action which is understood to be widely supported in the United Kingdom), or even abolish the crimes of murder and manslaughter, replacing them with a crime of culpable homicide, in which event provocation could, where appropriate, be taken into account in mitigation of sentence. It is not, however, for their Lordships to decide what model would be most appropriate as a matter of justice. They have to apply the law; and since the intervention of the legislature, it has no longer been open to them to develop the law inconsistently with the statute, even if they thought it desirable to do so. If the statute is now perceived to lead to unacceptable results, steps should be taken as soon as possible to persuade the Hong Kong legislature, and the United Kingdom Parliament, to amend it. But what appears to have been happening in the English courts in recent years is an attempt, inspired by certain New Zealand cases, to transform the objective approach, recognised by the United Kingdom

Parliament in 1957, into a subjective approach, though doubtless having the effect of excluding cases of intoxication and bad temper. This judicial modification of the statutory test has inevitably led to strains and stresses, notably in doubts about the scope of provocation in English law, but also in having to impose on juries an almost impossible task of having to adopt a subjective approach through the medium of the objective 'reasonable man' test recognised in the statute. Their Lordships are driven to say that this is not a satisfactory situation, and in their opinion the solution is to be found in returning to the objective approach recognised in the statute as interpreted by Lord Diplock in *Camplin*.

For all these reasons their Lordships, in agreement with the Court of Appeal of Hong Kong, are satisfied that there was no misdirection by the judge on provocation. There is, however, one point in the reasoning of the Court of Appeal to which they wish to refer, viz that it is necessary for the provocation to have been *directed at* the relevant characteristic of the defendant. Their Lordships accept that in the great majority of cases in which a characteristic of the defendant is relevant to the gravity of the provocation to him, the provocation will in fact have been directed at that characteristic, as where it is the subject of taunts by the deceased. But they wish to observe that this need not always be so, for there may be cases in which, for example, previous events mislead the defendant into believing that an innocent remark by the deceased was so directed when in fact it was not. For this reason, the requirement may be misleading.

Their Lordships will humbly advise Her Majesty that the appeal ought to be dismissed.

The following dissenting opinion was delivered.

LORD STEYN. I regret I am unable to agree that, on the central point in this case, the law of provocation of England and Hong Kong is as stated in the judgment of the majority.

The difference of opinion

It will be convenient to explain at the outset my understanding of the difference of opinion in this case. I agree with the conclusion of the majority that the Court of Appeal of Hong Kong erred in holding that it is a necessary precondition to the availability of the defence of provocation that the provocation must have been directed at the personal characteristic on which the defendant seeks to rely. There is no such artificial and restrictive rule. In view of the unanimity on this point I say no more about it.

The nature of the difference of opinion can be illustrated by a few simple examples. Let me imagine the case where a woman shortly after giving birth to a child stabs and kills her husband during an argument. She wishes to put to the jury as part of her defence of provocation that she was suffering from post-natal depression, which rendered her more prone to loss of self-control. A second example is the case where there is evidence that a woman, as a result of ill-treatment by her husband, suffers from 'battered woman syndrome'. When taunted by her lover she stabs and kills him. She wants to rely on evidence of battered woman syndrome as part of her defence of provocation. The third example is a woman who suffers from a personality disorder which makes her more prone to loss of self-control. During a quarrel she stabs and kills her

husband. She wants to rely on the personality disorder as part of her defence of
provocation. A common feature of the three examples is that in none of them
can the woman in any way be said to be at fault in inducing her condition. None
of these cases can be explained away on a broad view of the provocative conduct
of the husband or lover, ie the 'last straw' argument. In all three cases, the merits
or demerits of the woman's argument cannot be determined on a priori grounds:
in the context of provocation it is a matter of fact for exploration in evidence. But
in all three cases the particular characteristic of the defendant is potentially
relevant only in as much as it affects the degree of self-control of the defendant.

It is trite law that in all three cases relevant evidence of the woman's condition
may be placed before the jury. To the extent that the particular condition falls
beyond the experience of ordinary men and women, such evidence may include
opinion evidence by experts (see R D Mackay and Andrew M Colman 'Equivocal
Rulings on Expert Psychological and Psychiatric Evidence: Turning a Muddle
into Nonsense' [1996] Crim LR 88). Such evidence by witnesses of fact or experts
may be relevant and admissible on the subjective issue whether the woman had
in fact lost her self-control. Moreover, the trial judge would as a matter of fairness
be bound to direct the jury that in regard to the subjective inquiry they ought to
take into account the evidence as to the woman's condition at the time of the
killing. But in my view the logic of the position of the majority is that in all three
cases, whatever the strength of the evidence, the judge is as a matter of settled
legal principle entitled, and indeed obliged, to direct the jury to ignore the
evidence of post-natal depression, battered woman syndrome, and personality
disorder when they consider the objective issue. On this basis a trial judge would
have to direct a jury along the following lines:

> 'Members of the jury, you have heard evidence regarding the defendant's
> post-natal depression. When you deal with the first and subjective inquiry
> you must carefully consider the effect of that evidence. But when you come
> to consider the second and objective inquiry, please put that evidence out of
> your mind. It is irrelevant.'

In my view a jury would be rather puzzled by such artificially
compartmentalised directions. Faced with such examples, counsel for the
prosecution expressly and freely acknowledged the unfairness of the potential
results. His answer was: 'That is the law.' The view of the law contended for by
the prosecution will inevitably lead to injustice. It will result in convictions of
murder and mandatory life sentences in cases where that is wholly inappropriate.
In my view our law does not compel such crude and unfair results. The
principled solution is, however, not to be found in legal history or in New
Zealand and Australian statutes and case law. It is to be found in the contextual
scene of the reforming measure contained in s 3 of the English Homicide Act
1957. I shall try to explain.

The genesis of s 3 of the Homicide Act 1957

By the end of the 1940s there was considerable dissatisfaction with the law of
homicide, and notably the death sentence for murder. The Royal Commission
on Capital Punishment 1949–1953 was appointed. The Report of the Royal
Commission was presented to Parliament in September 1953 (Cmd 8932). For
present purposes it is the Royal Commission's examination of the law of
provocation and recommendations regarding that branch of the law which are of

importance. The Royal Commission first sketched the current law of provocation. They observed (para 134):

> 'Two conflicting tendencies may be traced in the evolution of the law of England with regard to provocation. On the one hand the courts have steadily limited the scope of provocation recognised as adequate to reduce murder to manslaughter, and have subjected it to increasingly strict and narrow tests. On the other hand the greater severity of the law has been tempered by leniency in its application. Judges have instructed juries in terms more favourable than the letter of the law would allow.'

The Royal Commission explained (para 135):

> 'But the advance of society has also led to an increased concern for the individual prisoner and to a desire, so far as possible, to take account of the characteristics and mental reactions of the individual in applying the law. This has shown itself in the readiness of the courts and of the Executive to give weight to provocation insufficient in law to extenuate murder.'

The Royal Commission then examined arguments for and against the retention of the objective or reasonable man test. It recommended that the objective test be retained. But it is important to note on what basis the recommendation was made. The Royal Commission concluded (para 145):

> 'We have indeed no doubt that if the criterion of the "reasonable man" was strictly applied by the courts and the sentence of death was carried out in cases where it was so applied, it would be too harsh in its operation. *In practice, however, the courts not infrequently give weight to factors personal to the prisoner in considering a plea of provocation*, and where there is a conviction of murder such factors are taken into account by the Home Secretary and may often lead to commutation of the sentence. *The application of this test does not therefore lead to any eventual miscarriage of justice.* At the same time, as we have seen, there are serious objections of principle to its abrogation. In these circumstances we do not feel justified in recommending any change in the existing law.' (My emphasis.)

The Report of the Royal Commission was the genesis of s 3 of the Homicide Act 1957. Indeed s 3 was intended to implement the recommendations on provocation of the Royal Commission. Section 3 reads as follows:

> 'Where on a charge of murder there is evidence on which the jury can find that *the person charged was provoked* (whether by things done or by things said or by both together) to lose his self-control, the question *whether the provocation was enough to make a reasonable man do as he did* shall be left to be determined by the jury; and in determining that question the jury shall take into account everything both done and said according to the effect which, in their opinion, it would have on a reasonable man.' (My emphasis.)

Parliament had before it the Royal Commission's view that if the objective test was 'strictly applied by the courts' the law would be 'too harsh in its operation'. But Parliament had the reassurance of the Royal Commission 'that the courts not infrequently give weight to factors personal to the prisoner' and that 'the application of this test does not *therefore* lead to any eventual miscarriage of justice' (my emphasis). In other words, Parliament was quite reasonably entitled

relevant characteristic of a defendant relying on provocation. The
omitted that *Dryden* had been decided per incuriam. In *Humphreys* the
cted this submission. The court (at 1022) then observed that the
was 'unduly young for her comparatively young age and thus brings the
his ground, into close comparison with *Camplin* ([1978] 2 All ER 168,
705).'

rt of the reasoning of the court is an echo of the ground of decision in
he last of the four cases is *R v Thornton*. A wife had stabbed her husband.
She was charged with murder. At the trial the defendant relied only on
d responsibility. Given that there was evidence that the husband had
tly ill-treated the defendant, the judge left provocation as an issue to the
e jury convicted the defendant of murder. Her appeal to the Court of
was dismissed (see *R v Thornton* [1992] 1 All ER 306). Further medical
e as to the mental condition of the defendant was placed before the
y of State. He referred the matter back to the Court of Appeal (see *R v*
(*No 2*) [1996] 2 All ER 1023). The new medical evidence tended to prove
appellant suffered from an obsessive personality disorder and 'battered
syndrome'. Lord Taylor CJ held that the medical evidence as to the
lity disorder of the defendant and the evidence of 'battered woman
me' revealed potentially relevant characteristics of the appellant. He
led (at 1031):

'... what characteristics of a defendant should be attributed by the jury to
e notional reasonable person and how far the judge should go in assisting
e jury to identify such characteristics, are issues which have been clarified
a number of decisions subsequent to this appellant's trial and indeed to her
st appeal. *R v Ahluwalia* [1992] 4 All ER 889, *R v Humphreys* [1995] 4 All ER
08 and *R v Morhall* [1995] 3 All ER 659, [1996] 1 AC 90 make clear that
ental as well as physical characteristics should be taken into account.
loreover, there is authority, especially from the judgment of the House of
ords in *R v Morhall* that a judge should give the jury directions as to what,
n the evidence, is capable of amounting to a relevant characteristic (see
1995] 3 All ER 659 esp at 668, [1996] 1 AC 90 esp at 100). We consider that
f the trial judge had had the assistance of those authorities and of the further
vidence we have before us, he should and would have given the jury
directions as to the two characteristics now relied upon. We conclude that
he fresh evidence and the clarification of the law to which we have referred
cast doubt upon the basis of the jury's verdict in this case. We cannot
therefore be sure that the verdict is safe and satisfactory.'

e result the Court of Appeal ordered a retrial.

inished responsibility

have not lost sight of the existence of the defence of diminished responsibility.
tion 2(1) of the 1957 Act, and s 3(1) of the Hong Kong Homicide Ordinance
vide:

'Where a person kills or is a party to the killing of another, he shall not be
convicted of murder if he was suffering from such abnormality of mind
(whether arising from a condition of arrested or retarded development of
mind or any inherent causes or induced by disease or injury) as substantially

---

to enact s 3 on the assumption that the courts in applying the reasonable man test
would seek to avoid the injustices which would follow from a rigid and
doctrinaire application of the test. It is a safe assumption that Parliament would
not have wished to entrench potential injustices which had already been exposed.
For example, Parliament could not possibly have intended that an immature
youth should be judged by the standards of self-control of a reasonable man.
Parliament adopted the not unusual course of not trying to solve an intractable
problem but leaving it to the courts in the application of the Act to work out
sensible and just solutions.

DPP v Camplin

The expectation that, in applying the reasonable man test in s 3 of the 1957 Act,
the judges would work out sensible and just solutions was falsified at first instance
in *DPP v Camplin* [1978] 2 All ER 168, [1978] AC 705. A boy, aged 15, had killed a
man. He alleged that the man had buggered him. Boreham J directed the jury
that they must consider whether the provocation relied on had been sufficient to
make a reasonable man, not a reasonable boy of the accused's age, in like
circumstances act as the accused acted. A strong Court of Appeal presided over
by Bridge LJ (later Lord Bridge of Harwich) set aside the conviction on the
ground of misdirection. On appeal, the Crown argued for a literal interpretation
of s 3: counsel said that 'if there is to be a standard it must be one which is
universally applicable and in all ages'. The Crown's argument was a classic
example of Begriffsjurisprudenz, or conceptualistic reasoning. The House of
Lords would have none of it.

Lord Diplock observed that 'to require old heads on young shoulders is
inconsistent with the law's compassion of human infirmity' (see [1978] 2 All ER
168 at 174, [1978] AC 705 at 717). I would add three observations. First, the
relevance of youthfulness was obviously not dependent upon the provocation
being directed to it. Secondly, the only relevance of youthfulness as a condition
attributed to the reasonable man is the lesser degree of self-control usually
associated with it. Thirdly, counsel for the Crown challengingly put to their
Lordships these rhetorical questions: 'If there were a different standard for a
15-year-old boy, why not for an immature 21-year-old person? Why should he
not have the benefit?' Yet there is nothing in the speeches to indicate that only
youthfulness could qualify as 'human infirmity' under the objective requirement.
If their Lordships had in mind such a rigid and artificial numerus clausus it would
have been quite easy to say so. They did not. Indeed Lord Simon of Glaisdale
expressly posed the question: 'If youth is to be considered (and, presumably,
advanced years too), what about immaturity in a person of full years or
premature senility?' He then observed:

'The original reasons in this branch of the law were largely reasons of the
heart and of common sense, not the reasons of pure juristic logic. The
potentiality of provocation to reduce murder to manslaughter was, as Tindal
CJ said in *R v Hayward* (1833) 6 C & P 157 at 159, 172 ER 1188 at 1189, "in
compassion to human infirmity". But justice and common sense then
demanded some limitation: it would be unjust that the drunk man or one
exceptionally pugnacious or bad-tempered or over-sensitive should be able
to claim that these matters rendered him peculiarly susceptible to the
provocation offered, where the sober and even-tempered man would hang
for his homicide. Hence, I think, the development of the concept of the

reaction of a reasonable man to the provocation offered, even though it may
have originally come into this branch of the law by way of testing the
credibility of the claim of the accused (who could not at that time himself
give evidence) that he had been so deprived of his self-control as to be
incapable of forming the relevant intent. *But it is one thing to invoke the
reasonable man for the standard of self-control which the law requires; it is quite
another to substitute some hypothetical being from whom all mental and physical
attributes (except perhaps sex) have been abstracted.'* (See [1978] 2 All ER 168 at
180–181, [1978] AC 705 at 724–725; my emphasis.)

The emphasised final sentence is inconsistent with any intention to treat youthful
immaturity as the only mental characteristic relevant to the objective
requirement. Indeed, later in his judgment Lord Simon made clear that 'the
entire factual situation, which includes the characteristics of the accused, must be
considered' (see [1978] 2 All ER 168 at 182, [1978] AC 705 at 727). In context, that
did not exclude mental abnormality. And on this point no relevant difference of
opinion was exposed by the speeches in *Camplin*. Indeed, all their Lordships
agreed on the terms of the model direction contained in Lord Diplock's
judgment. For my part the actual decision in *Camplin* is perfectly consistent with
a sensible interpretation of s 3 in its contextual scene.

The subsequent English cases

   The next significant step in the evolution of this branch of the law came three
years after *Camplin*. In *R v Raven* [1982] Crim LR 51 the Recorder of London,
following the rationale of *Camplin* as he understood it, ruled in a case of alleged
provocation that the fact that a defendant aged 22 years had a mental age of about
nine years was a relevant factor in the objective inquiry. It was a ruling by a judge
with great experience of this branch of the law. That ruling was reported some
13 years ago. It has not been suggested in any subsequent decision or academic
writing that *Raven* was wrongly decided. Indeed, learned authors consistently
treated it as correctly decided (see Smith and Hogan *Criminal Law* (7th edn, 1992)
361). In a contemporary comment Professor Diane Birch, while clearly taking
the view that the ruling of the judge, under existing law, was sensible and correct,
commented that 'putting oneself in the position of a reasonable 22 year old with
a mental age of nine is a tremendously difficult feat' (see [1982] Crim LR 51 at 52).
There is force in this lament about the state of the law but such practical
difficulties are inherent in employing the device of the reasonable man. It is not
significantly more difficult than asking jurors to imagine that they are one-legged,
impotent or of a different racial or cultural background. In any event, the *reason*
for the decision in *Camplin* was the lesser degree of self-control of a youth. There
is good sense in the maxim that the rule ought to follow where reason leads, and
where reason stops there ought to stop the rule. And qualitatively there is no
relevant distinction (as counsel for the prosecution put to their Lordships in
Camplin) between youthfulness and immaturity due to impaired intellectual
development. For these reasons I reject the invitation of the prosecution to hold
that *Raven* was wrongly decided.

   But there have been further developments. In *R v Ahluwalia* [1992] 4 All ER 889
a woman killed her husband. The deceased had allegedly abused and beaten the
defendant over many years. The jury rejected her defence of provocation and
convicted her of murder. On appeal, counsel for the appellant argued that the
judge had misdirected the jury by not asking them to consider in relation to the

---

objective inquiry that her ill-treatment had affe
produce a state of 'learnt helplessness', a phras
identified this condition (see at 897). That con
'battered woman syndrome'. Delivering the judgm
CJ observed (at 898):

   'In the present case, there was no medical o
   judge and jury, and none even from the app
   suffered from a post-traumatic stress disor
   syndrome" or any other specific condition v
   "characteristic" as defined in *R v McGregor* [1962
   was much evidence that the appellant had suffe
   but nothing to suggest that the effect of it was to m
   from the ordinary run of [women]", or to show th
   distinguished from the ordinary [woman] of th
   evidence which has now been put before this cour
   trial judge, different considerations may have appl
   that there was no basis for the judge to refer to a ch
   an altered personality or mental state in this appell
   that, on the evidence before them, the jury would
   finding such a characteristic.'

The court apparently considered that the alleged condit
supported by medical evidence, is relevant to the objectiv
the prosecution on the present appeal argued that the Co
wrong view of the law.

   Since *Ahluwalia* there have been four decisions in the C
need to be considered. Three of these decisions predated t
present case and the fourth was decided after the oral hear
the Board has not had the benefit of counsel's observation.
impossible to do justice to the issue in this case without ref
first case is *R v Dryden* [1995] 4 All ER 987. In that case it was
ground that the defendant, who shot and killed a planning of
property, was suffering from an abnormality of mind and clin
raised the defence of diminished responsibility and provo
convicted him of murder. He appealed on the ground t
misdirected the jury. In dealing with the judge's directions or
in particular on the reasonable man test, Lord Taylor CJ said (

   'We have come to the conclusion that this was a c
   obsessiveness on the part of the appellant and his eccentric c
   ought to have been left to the jury for their consideration.
   they were features of his character or personality which fell i
   of mental characteristics and which ought to have been speci
   jury.'

   But the Court of Appeal concluded that there was no miscarriag
dismissed the appeal. The significance of this case is that what ma
obiter dictum in *Ahluwalia* certainly ripened into ratio decidendi ii
v Baillie [1995] 2 Cr App R 31 the Court of Appeal described
authoritatively establishing the effect of s 3 of the 1957 Act. In *R*
[1995] 4 All ER 1008 the Court of Appeal had to consider whethe

a impaired his mental responsibility for his acts and omissions in doing or being a party to the killing.'

The burden of establishing this defence is on the defendant who raises it. It is an optional defence. Only if it is relied on by the defendant may the trial judge leave it to the jury. It is often a matter of tactical judgment whether a defendant, who suffers from an abnormality of mind, will be advised to rely on both defences, or
b should simply rely on provocation where he shoulders no burden of proof. In any event, it is restricted to an 'abnormality of mind' which 'substantially impaired [the defendant's] mental responsibility for his acts'. It does not cover the whole field of significant mental attributes which may affect provocation. It is no answer to the reasoning in R v Thornton (No 2) [1996] 2 All ER 1023.

c
Taking stock of the arguments.

If *Raven* was correctly decided, as I believe it was, it follows that the present appeal must succeed. Moreover, that view is supported by the decisions of the Court of Appeal, starting with *Ahluwalia* and culminating in *Thornton* (No 2). The
d judges involved were Lord Taylor CJ, Hirst and Henry LJJ and eight Queen's Bench judges experienced in criminal law. They would not have overlooked the relevance of the defence of diminished responsibility. Nor did they principally rely on New Zealand cases. Those decisions in the Court of Appeal are a logical extension of the decisions in *Camplin* and *Raven*. But even more important than the promptings of legal logic is the dictates of justice. Justice underpinned these
e decisions. And nothing in *Camplin* or *R v Morhall* precluded this development. It is simply an extension of the ratio of *Camplin*, and *Morhall* was concerned with a different problem altogether, ie a characteristic supplying the sting of provocative conduct.

The law remains that a defendant may not call in aid his own irascibility or
f pugnacity. The Royal Commission was confident that 'minor abnormalities of character' must be ignored (see para 143). That does not mean that it was right to ask the jury to ignore the defendant's brain damage.

Counsel for the prosecution argued that it may prove difficult to say where the line should be drawn. We ought not to shrink for this reason from recognising a rational and just development. The traditional common law answer is apposite:
g any difficult borderline cases will be considered if and when they occur. In the meantime nobody should underestimate the capacity of our law to move forward where necessary, putting an end to demonstrable unfairness exposed by experience.

For these reasons I conclude that the trial judge misdirected the jury by failing
h to direct them that the evidence of the appellant's brain damage, and its impact on the appellant's response to provocation, depending on what the jury made of it, was relevant to the objective requirement of provocation.

The effect of the misdirection
j The prosecution invited the Board to apply the proviso. The fact that the appellant failed to discharge the burden resting on him of proving diminished responsibility does not demonstrate how the jury reasoned in respect of provocation. It was for the jury to decide whether the prosecution had disproved the defence of provocation to a satisfactory standard. And the misdirection on provocation deprived the appellant of his best card, viz the relevance of brain

damage tending to cause the appellant to overreact to minor provocation. In
these circumstances it is impossible to apply the proviso.   *a*

Conclusion

I am accordingly of the opinion that the conviction of murder and resultant
sentence ought to be quashed; that a verdict of manslaughter ought to be
substituted; and that the matter ought to be remitted to the Court of Appeal of   *b*
Hong Kong to impose the appropriate sentence.

Appeal dismissed.

Celia Fox   Barrister.

End of volume 2